A Generation Awakes

A Generation Awakes

Young Americans for Freedom and the Creation of the Conservative Movement

by Wayne Thorburn

Jameson Books, Inc.
Ottawa, Illinois

Book and cover design by Charles King: www.ckmm.com

For information, special discounts on bulk orders and other requests please contact:

Jameson Books, Inc.
722 Columbus Street
Ottawa, Illinois 61350
815-434-7906

Phone Orders: 800-426-1357
Mail Orders: P.O. Box 738, Ottawa, IL 61350

Printed in the United States of America.

Jameson Books are distributed to the book trade by
Midpoint Trade Books, 27 West 20th Street, Suite 1102, New York, NY 10011
Bookstores please call 212-727-0190 to place orders.

Individuals please call 1-800-426-1357 to place orders.

Bookstore returns should be addressed to Midpoint Trade Books,
1263 Southwest Boulevard, Kansas City, KS 66103.

ISBN-13: 978-0-89803-168-3

6 5 4 3 2 1 \ 13 12 11 10

Library of Congress Cataloging-in-Publication Data

Thorburn, Wayne J. (Wayne Jacob), 1944–
    A generation awakes : Young Americans for Freedom and the creation
of the conservative movement / Wayne Thorburn.
        p. cm.
    Includes index.
    ISBN 978-0-89803-168-3 (alk. paper)
    1. Young Americans for Freedom—History. 2. Conservatism—United
States—History—20th century. 3. United States—Politics and
government—1945–1989. I. Title.
    JC573.2.U6 T47 2010
    320.520973—dc22
                                                    2010024233

Contents

Acknowledgments

For more than thirty years, Young Americans for Freedom was the conservative youth organization in America. On the following pages I have attempted to relate the history of the organization by focusing not merely on the decisions and actions of the national leadership but rather including the efforts of thousands of YAF members on campuses and communities across the nation. While indicating the effect this organization had on contemporary events in its history, the story of Young Americans for Freedom must also include a discussion of the influence it had on developing a conservative movement in the United States and the role played by its alumni in American society today.

So many people contributed to the content of this work that it would be impossible to thank them all. I am grateful to Barry Goldwater, Jr., whose letter accompanying the 2008 alumni survey produced a wealth of responses that provided examples of the positive effect of Young Americans for Freedom. Many others granted me the opportunity to visit with them by email, phone, and in person. Still others produced valuable documents from YAF's history that they had carefully preserved for many years. I would have confronted an even more substantial challenge in finding primary source material without the assistance of staff at the various libraries where documents and personal papers were found. The note on sources lists these various collections that together serve as a depository of historical documentation on Young Americans for Freedom.

A number of individuals were kind enough to read and critique sections of the present work. They include the Honorable James Buckley, Carol Dawson, Richard Derham, Ron Docksai, Harold Herring, Bob McDonald, Roger Ream, Ron Robinson, Bill Saracino, Arnold Steinberg, Herb Stupp, Randal C. Teague, and Michael Thompson. The errors and omissions in the text, however, are solely my responsibility. I would welcome comments and corrections from readers. As always, Judith and Pamela were ever-present aides in this effort.

This work would not have been possible, however, without the generous support of Young America's Foundation, making possible the extensive research required and the writing of this history. I am deeply indebted to the Foundation for this assistance and especially to its President, Ron Robinson, for his encouragement, advice, and support.

1. Something New Is Stirring

"Thirty years ago the innovators called themselves radicals.
Now mostly they call themselves conservatives"[1]

WITH THE END of World War II, American society was entering a period of significant change and reorientation. The transition to a peacetime economy, the return of hundreds of thousands of veterans, and the development of a more substantial threat to Western values from a wartime ally—all confronted Americans as the decade of the 1940s approached its closing. While there was no longer a President Roosevelt in the White House, his economic policies had become institutionalized and accepted by the majority of Americans. As Lionel Trilling observed, liberalism had become the dominant, if not the only, ideological viewpoint accepted by those Americans who considered broader philosophical questions.[2]

Post-war Opposition to the New Deal

Prior to the 1950s, the opposition to liberalism centered mainly around a defense of free enterprise, with Ludwig Von Mises and Frederick Hayek the leading defenders.[3] Hayek's book, *The Road to Serfdom*, not only provided a comprehensive rejection of socialism but also clearly tied together all forms of collectivism—socialism, communism, and fascism—and challenged the view that Nazism and fascism were "right-wing" movements.[4] Hayek represented the European classical liberal tradition whose emphasis on economics and individualism contributed much to late 20th century American conservatism.[5] To a large extent, however, von Mises and Hayek were perceived as crying in the wilderness while majority opinion was dominated by those who accepted the New Deal and a progressively growing involvement of the state in the economy.[6] Change would slowly begin

---

1. John Dos Passos in Foreword to William F. Buckley, Jr.: *Up From Liberalism* (New York: Ivan Obolensky, 1959), p. 7.
2. Lionel Trilling: *The Liberal Imagination* (New York: Doubleday, 1950). See also Arthur Schlesinger, Jr.: *The Vital Center* (Boston: Houghton Mifflin Company, 1949). Authors John Micklethwait and Adrian Wooldridge in *The Right Nation: Conservative Power in America* (New York: The Penguin Press, 2004), p. 8, maintain that over the period from 1930 to 1950, the term conservative was used only as a derogatory label by Democrats and avoided by Republicans.
3. Von Mises had emigrated to the United States in the 1930s and published two important works in the postwar period, *Bureaucracy* (New Rochelle, NY: Arlington House, 1969) and *Omnipotent Government: The Rise of the Total State and Total War* (New Haven: Yale University Press, 1944). Hayek's seminal work, *The Road to Serfdom* (Chicago: University of Chicago Press, 1976) was initially published in 1944 but became widely distributed in the postwar period. A valuable overview of the contributions of these two writers to the subsequent development of a positive conservatism can be found in George H. Nash: *The Conservative Intellectual Movement in America Since 1945* (Wilmington, DE: Intercollegiate Studies Institute, 1996), pp. 1–29.
4. This point is made by E.J. Dionne, Jr: *Why Americans Hate Politics* (New York: Simon & Schuster, 1991), p. 153.
5. See his essay "Why I Am Not a Conservative" in Frank S. Meyer, ed. *What Is Conservatism?* (New York: Holt, Rinehart and Winston, 1964), pp. 88–103.
6. See also Jeffrey Hart: *The American Dissent* (Garden City, NY: Doubleday, 1966), pp. 24–26 for a discussion of the emphasis on economics in the late 1940s opposition to the dominant liberal ideology.

1

to appear as conservative publications and publishing houses were established in the late 1940s.[7]

As the war was approaching a conclusion, a new periodical appeared to challenge both the economic as well as the foreign policy of the Truman Administration. Begun as a weekly newsletter distributed to daily newspapers, *Human Events* would subsequently change its format and distribution method in the early 1950s, becoming a fixture in what would develop into a conservative movement.[8] In 1947 there appeared a new publishing house that would make an important contribution to the distribution of conservative ideas and the popular acceptance of conservative writers. The Henry Regnery Company provided a vehicle for the exposition of many mid-century conservative writers and, now part of Eagle Publishing, continues publishing important conservative works.[9]

Nevertheless, in the late 1940s those opposed to New Deal economic policies and a foreign policy only slowly perceiving the challenge of Soviet Communism remained a rather small minority. Politically, the Republican party was still dominated by the forces that would nominate Wendell Willkie, Thomas Dewey and eventually Dwight D. Eisenhower as presidential candidates while the Democrats confronted a challenge from the left in former Vice President Henry Wallace's Progressive party and from the segregationists in Governor J. Strom Thurmond's Dixiecrat movement. While change was on the horizon, it was a time when, "*conservatism* was not a popular word in America, and its spokesmen were without much influence in their native land."[10]

There remained a conformity to the prevailing liberal outlook such that those who challenged it were viewed as outside the mainstream. As John Andrew commented: "whatever seemed to deviate from the 'consensus' position on any issue became susceptible to charges that it represented an 'extremist' view and should therefore be dismissed as dangerous and perhaps even un-American."[11] While the conservative presence grew in the 1950s and early 1960s, it would continue to be confronted by this charge of being outside the mainstream of liberal orthodoxy.

An additional writer whose works first appeared in the 1940s and more significantly in the 1950s is Ayn Rand. While Rand was mainly a novelist, her main characters portray a dedication to individualism, laissez-faire capitalism, and anti-collectivism. Her first important novel, *The Fountainhead* (Indianapolis: Bobbs-Merrill Company, 1943) appeared during World War II and was made into a movie by Warner Brothers in 1949. Her best-known work, however, was published in the mid 1950s and includes many of the themes she developed into a philosophical outlook known as Objectivism. *Atlas Shrugged* (New York: Random House, 1957) includes a thirty-page monologue by main character John Galt outlining the main points of her perspective on life. While many of Rand's followers became active in young conservative efforts in the 1960s and were supporters of the Goldwater presidential campaign, Rand never saw herself as a conservative and, indeed, her views were at odds with a number of essential conservative positions.

7. Nash, p. xv, described the situation as "at most, scattered voices of protest, profoundly pessimistic about the future of their country."

8. Lee Edwards: *The Conservative Revolution* (New York: the Free Press, 1999), p. 15 and Alfred S. Regnery: *Upstream: The Ascendance of American Conservatism* (New York: Simon & Schuster, 2008), pp. 62–63.

9. The influence of the Henry Regnery Company can be seen in the number of sources referenced here that were originally produced by this company. For an informative personal overview of this period in American history and the rise of an important publishing house see Henry Regnery: *Memoirs of a Dissident Publisher* (Chicago: Regnery Books, 1985). Henry Regnery was instrumental also in starting *Human Events* as well as the quarterly journal that became *Modern Age*.

10. Nash, p. xvii.

11. John A. Andrew: *The Other Side of the Sixties* (New Brunswick, NJ: Rutgers University Press, 1997), p. 13.

The Changing Fifties

As the decade of the 1950s began, several new developments were to challenge this prevailing orthodoxy. Despite the common perception of this decade as one of conformity and social conservatism, it was a time of significant challenge to the accepted American way of life. In 1951, J.D. Salinger's *Catcher in the Rye* was released. Salinger's use of profanity, sexual references and teenage angst both created controversy and became a regular feature of American Literature classes.[12] Six years later, Jack Kerouac would produce what would become a classic of the "beat generation" with his *On the Road*.[13] Through the characters of Dean Moriarty and Sal Paradise, mid-century youth traveled around underground America and experienced drugs, sex and jazz.

In general terms, however, Kerouac's heroes were expressing, and his readers were cherishing, a new emphasis on individualism. As Stan Evans observed, "[t]he world against which the beatnik reacts is not the world of conservatism, with its emphasis on volition and variety, but of Liberalism, with its insistence upon external uniformity."[14] Kerouac's fictional hero tells his readers that his "chief hate was Washington bureaucracy; second to that, Liberals, then cops." Rebecca Klatch sees this emphasis on independence and autonomy as producing a similar trend among young activists of the left and right in the 1960s that she calls "... an affinity for values such as individual freedom, the impulse against bureaucracy and big government, the questioning of centralized authority, and the embrace of decentralization and local control."[15] Indeed, a new student left also was emerging in the late 1950s, often led by "Red diaper babies," children of radical and Communist professionals. In 1957, a left-wing campus party opposed to capital punishment, nuclear testing, and anti-communism became active at the University of California at Berkeley, followed by similar efforts at the University of Wisconsin and the University of Michigan where its impetus came from Tom Hayden, then editor of the *Michigan Daily*.[16]

By the 1950s new cinematic heroes had appeared also in the form of Marlon Brando in "The Wild Ones," released in 1953 and resulting in increased interest in motorcycles and leather jackets. Two years later James Dean starred in "Rebel Without a Cause," a film whose popularity among young viewers was not lessened by the tragic death of its star at age 24. In the music world the merging of aspects of gospel, blues, and pop into a new genre called rock and roll created a specifically youth-oriented music. Perhaps best typifying this radical departure from the past was Elvis Presley whose first record appeared in 1954. Two years later Presley appeared on the highly popular entertainment program, "The Ed Sullivan Show," where his gyrations, while viewed by some adults as too sexually suggestive, were appreciated by many of the younger female viewers. By the end

---

12. (Boston: Little, Brown & Company, 1951).

13. (New York: The Viking Press, 1957).

14. M. Stanton Evans: *Revolt on the Campus* (Chicago: Henry Regnery, 1961), p. 34.

15. Rebecca Klatch: *A Generation Divided* (Berkeley: University of California Press, 1999), p. 9.

16. David Burner: *Making Peace With the Sixties* (Princeton: Princeton University Press, 1996). Two interesting personal histories by "Red diaper babies" active in the late 1950s and early 1960s are Ronald Radosh: *Commies* (San Francisco: Encounter Books, 2001) and David Horowitz: *Radical Son* (New York: The Free Press, 1997). Both Radosh and Horowitz later rejected their inherited Leftist perspectives.

of the decade, another music format became popular with college students. Folk music brought with it an emphasis on political messages, almost all oriented to the left and critical of the prevailing establishment.[17]

Even more dramatic changes to the social milieu developed out of the Supreme Court's historic 1954 decision in *Brown v. Board of Education.* Sweeping away years of *de jure* segregation based on a policy of supposed "separate but equal" facilities for Black children in public schools, the Court's decision would begin a long, painful and never ending path towards equal protection of the laws for all American citizens. The reaction of many conservatives who stressed states' rights in a Federal system of government would produce a lasting political impact on American society as more and more Black Americans shifted from their previous support of the Republican Party to an overwhelming commitment to the Democratic Party.

To a large degree these social changes, far different from a bland conformity too often placed on the decade, contributed to the rising interest among young people in creating their own alternative to what they perceived as a prevailing liberal establishment. This assertion of a role to play in the creation of America's future was present among what would be called conservative youth as well as those who challenged the establishment from the left. As one future leader of conservative youth observed in looking back at the 1950s and the rising involvement of right-wing youth, "[I]t was not strict obedience to political elders then but the rebellion of youth and the idealism of young people which while today is credited to the Left is seldom appreciated as also a vital ingredient of the young Right."[18] By the end of the decade, many American young people were ready to express their opposition to the establishment.

The Communist Challenge

Separate and apart from the social changes and trends occurring in mid-century America, political developments were also challenging the prevailing orthodoxy. For many Americans there was developing a growing realization that international Communism posed a serious threat to the West. America and its allies became embroiled in a defense of South Korea from the efforts of its Northern compatriots and the Chinese Communists to overrun it, a conflict that would end only with an uncomfortable stalemate. The internal threat of Communist subversion became known to more Americans with the trial of Ethel and Julius Rosenberg in 1951 and their execution two years later. It was also a time of House Committee on Un-American Activities hearings, the so-called "Hollywood Ten," the Whittaker Chambers testimony implicating Alger Hiss in espionage activities, and the efforts of Senator Joseph McCarthy to remove security risks from the Federal government.[19] The importance of Chambers's disclosures about Soviet

---

17. For a discussion of developing trends during this period, see also Dan Wakefield: *New York in the Fifties* (Boston: Houghton Mifflin Company, 1992).

18. Ronald F. Docksai, "A Study of the Organization and Beliefs of the Young Conservative Movement," Master's Thesis, New York University, 1972, pp. 26–27.

19. The most valuable work published in the early 1950s was Whittaker Chambers's autobiographical *Witness* (New York; Random House, 1952). Also published in 1952 and autobiographical was Herbert A. Philbrick: *I Led 3 Lives: Citizen, Communist. Counterspy* (Washington, DC: Capitol Hill Press, 1972). Philbrick's experiences were the basis for a popular television program of the same name shown from

penetration of the Federal government and his subsequent book cannot be over-emphasized. As J'Aime Ryskind, one of the early conservative youth leaders of the 1960s observed, "My mother really felt that there were two books in Western Civilization. One was the Bible and the other was Whittaker Chambers' *Witness*."[20] Likewise, it was admiration for Senator McCarthy's efforts that provided the first overt political act by a young high school sophomore in New Orleans. Setting up a table in Jackson Square, Doug Caddy collected signatures on a petition support-ing McCarthy and forwarded them to Washington, DC. Caddy would later serve as a prime organizer of the new conservative youth organization.[21]

While the United States followed a policy described as containment, the government also sent mixed messages to the captive nations of Eastern Europe and the Baltic, including messages on Radio Free Europe. Then came 1956—and the tragic efforts of the Hungarian people to become independent of the Soviet bloc, only to be crushed by the Russian army tanks while the United States and Western Europe stood by.[22] The events surrounding this tragic event had a lasting effect on several individuals who were to become leaders of a new conservative youth organization. Many early young conservative activists mention specific events associated with communism as motivating their political interest and involvement, especially the Hungarian uprising.[23] Carl Thormeyer, who was to organize a Young Americans for Freedom chapter at Penn State some five years later, cited the Soviet suppression of the Hungarian freedom-fighters as an event that radicalized him for conservative political action.[24]

The latter part of the 1950s also saw the launching of the first Soviet satellite, Sputnik, in 1957. The building of private bomb shelters became the latest home improvement project and elementary school students were instructed to cover their heads and duck under their desks during civil defense drills, supposedly protecting themselves from possible Soviet attacks. In 1959, Fidel Castro and

---

1953 to 1956. William F. Buckley, Jr. and L. Brent Bozell provided an early defense of Senator Joseph McCarthy in *McCarthy and His Enemies* (Chicago: Henry Regnery Company, 1954). An important critique of efforts to combat Communist subversion is Eric Bentley: *Thirty Years of Treason* (New York: Viking Press, 1971) that contains very selective edited excerpts from hearings before the House Committee on Un-American Activities. But see also William F. Buckley, Jr. (ed): *The Committee and its Critics* (Chicago: Henry Regnery Company, 1962). Written by one who began believing Alger Hiss was unjustly convicted and ends convinced of Hiss's guilt, Allen Weinstein : *Perjury: The Hiss-Chambers Case* (New York: Alfred A. Knopf, 1978) complements the Chambers work with additional documentation. Subsequent investigation of Soviet archives released after the fall of Communism in Russia has produced a number of valuable works that place the extent of Communist infiltration into American life in a broader context. Among the first was Allen Weinstein and Alexander Vassiliev: *The Haunted Wood: Soviet Espionage in America—The Stalin Era* (New York: Random House, 1999). Also valuable in understanding this period and how Americans perceived the threat from Communist subversion are John Earl Haynes and Harvey Klehr: *In Denial: Historians, Communism and Espionage* (San Francisco: Encounter Books, 2003); Ronald Radosh and Allis Radosh: *Red Star Over Hollywood: The Film Colony's Long Romance with the Left* (New York: Encounter Books, 2006); and M. Stanton Evans: *Blacklisted by History: The Untold Story of Senator Joe McCarthy and his fight against America's enemies* (New York: Crown Forum, 2007).

20. Rebecca Klatch: *A Generation Divided*, p. 67.

21. Douglas Caddy, "Birth of the Conservative Movement," unpublished paper in author's posses-sion, pp. 1–2.

22. Among the many works discussing the Hungarian uprising are the personal account by a Hungarian photographer, Andor D. Heller: *No More Comrades* (Chicago: Henry Regnery Company, 1957) and the retrospective overview by Charles Gati: *Failed Illusions: Moscow, Washington, Budapest and the 1956 Hungarian Revolt* (Palo Alto: Stanford University Press, 2006). Gati was also present in Hungary during the abortive battle for independence from Moscow.

23. See Rebecca Klatch: *A Generation Divided*, pp. 87–88.

24. Kenneth Heineman: *Campus Wars* (New York: New York University Press), p. 101.

his forces succeeded in defeating the government of Fulgencio Battista and installed a Communist regime in Cuba just miles off the Florida coast. In response to Sputnik and the need for more scientific and technical expertise, the Eisenhower Administration obtained congressional support for passage of the National Defense Education Act in 1958. As a measure passed on the basis of its contribution to national defense, the Act required recipients to swear loyalty to the United States and indicate whether they had belonged to any organizations deemed subversive. As will be seen later, the passage of a Federal program of aid to higher education tied to national security had a major impact on the development of a national conservative youth organization in 1960.

The Roots of American Conservatism

While the nation was undergoing dramatic social changes and confronting a growing challenge from the Soviet Union, the decade also saw the beginnings of a substantial conservative intellectual and political presence.[25] Although some may claim that modern conservatism became evident with the end of World War Two and the start of the Cold War, it did not begin to present a noticeable challenge to the dominant liberal ideology until the early 1950s.[26] It was then that the writings of William F. Buckley, Jr., Whittaker Chambers, Russell Kirk, and a few others introduced the intellectual world to a renewed challenge from the right and provided modern conservatism with a firm intellectual and historical foundation.

Building on the free-market opposition to socialism, the Foundation for Economic Education (FEE) was created in 1946 by Leonard Read and a group of distinguished scholars and business leaders. The Foundation published a number of studies on economic issues during its early years. In 1954 the Foundation took over publication of *The Freeman*, a journal that had been edited by Henry Hazlitt and John Chamberlain since 1950, and made it into a monthly vehicle for the promulgation of free market economics.[27] Over the subsequent years, FEE would sponsor numerous seminars on economic issues and have a significant influence on the development of young conservatives and libertarians.[28]

It was a precocious college student recently returned from World War II and enrolled at Yale University who would influence American society for more than a half-century and in the process help build a conservative movement. In 1946, William F. Buckley, Jr. entered what was widely perceived to be a conservative, if

25. Alfred S. Regnery: *Upstream: The Ascendance of American Conservatism* provides a valuable overview of this period by one who grew up literally in the middle of it all. See pp. 24–84 especially.

26. Some would maintain that Peter Viereck's *Conservatism Revisited: The Revolt Against Revolt* (New York: Scribner's, 1949) first introduced a serious discussion of conservatism to the postwar intellectual world. According to George Nash, "This was the book which, more than any other of the early postwar era, created the new conservatism as a self-conscious intellectual force ... it was this book which boldly used the word 'conservative' in its title—the first such book after 1945," *The Conservative Intellectual Movement in America*, p. 60. However, Viereck soon became a vocal critic of the movement that developed around the name conservative and wrote a blistering critical review of William F. Buckley, Jr.'s first book. For more on Viereck see Tom Reiss, "The First Conservative," *The New Yorker*, October 24, 2005.

27. Henry Hazlitt, "The Early History of FEE," *The Freeman*, March 1984.

28. It was at one of these FEE seminars that the author was privileged to learn from and meet Ludwig Von Mises. In fact, the current President of the Foundation for Economic Education, Lawrence W. Reed, was an active YAF member in high school and college.

not staid, institution of classical learning. He was part of the largest class in Yale's history, two-thirds of its members being veterans of World War II. As one of his classmates observed, "Bill was someone to be reckoned with immediately. He was taking initiatives as soon as he got to Yale. He arrived in full stride."[29] Active in the Yale Political Union, a member of the debating team and selected for "Skull and Bones," by his senior year he had become chairman of the *Yale Daily News*. What Buckley found was an institution living off its past heritage of orthodoxy while promoting collectivist economic and social theories and heterodox religious beliefs, if any at all.[30] Buckley made his commitment to economic individualism and Christian theology known throughout his years at Yale, often in somewhat confrontational situations. But it was once he had graduated that a major critique of his alma mater—and American higher education by extension—would be produced to major applause and condemnation.

One year after graduating from Yale, William F. Buckley, Jr., at the age of 25, had his first book published. *God and Man at Yale* became a best seller with the first printing of 5,000 copies selling out in a week.[31] He maintained that Yale "has produced one of the most extraordinary incongruities of our time: the institution that derives its moral and financial support from Christian individualists and then addresses itself to the task of persuading the sons of these supporters to be atheistic socialists."[32] Perhaps the most quoted passage occurs where Buckley describes his overall perspective on the conflict confronting the West: "I myself believe that the duel between Christianity and atheism is the most important in the world. I further believe that the struggle between individualism and collectivism is the same struggle reproduced on another level."[33] This summation of the philosophical and ideological conflict would continue to provide a foundation for the remainder of Buckley's career.

Criticism of his book came almost immediately, much of it located at Yale University. As Reuben Holden, assistant to Yale President Whitney Griswold, wrote to a Yale trustee, "We intend to take the offensive in this matter and not sit by waiting for complaints to roll in when the book is published in November."[34] The semi-official response was to come from McGeorge Bundy, a Yale alumnus and Harvard professor.[35] Bundy called the recent Yale graduate a "twisted and ignorant young man" and his book "dishonest in its use of facts, false in its theory."[36] Buckley was allowed to respond in an article the following month where he attacked Bundy's arrogance and "advocacy of irresponsible, irreproachable education by an academic elite." [37] But the most over-the-top criticism came from Yale trustee Frank Ashburn whose review maintained that "[T]he book is one which has the glow and appeal of a fiery cross on a hillside at night. There will undoubtedly

---

29. Sam Tanenhaus, "The founder," *Yale Alumni Magazine*, May–June 2008, p. 58. In the same issue, see also David Frum, "The loyal son," pp. 50–52 and Gaddis Smith, "The ideologue," pp. 53–57.

30. Buckley's time at Yale is covered in John Judis: *William F. Buckley, Jr.—Patron Saint of the Conservatives* (New York: Simon & Schuster, 1988), pp. 52–81.

31. Chicago: Henry Regnery Company, 1951. Sales totals, including the book's presence on the *New York Herald Tribune* best-seller list, are reported in Tanenhaus, p. 69. Judis indicates that the book reached number 16 on the *New York Times* list, p. 92.

32. *God and Man at Yale*, foreword.

33. *Ibid.*

34. As quoted in Judis, p. 93.

35. "The Attack on Yale," *Atlantic Monthly*, November 1951.

36. Quoted in Judis, p. 93.

37. William F. Buckley, Jr., "The Changes at Yale," *Atlantic Monthly*, December 1951.

be robed figures who gather to it, but the hoods will not be academic. They will cover the face."[38] If there had been any doubt, the invective from those associated with Yale reinforced the belief that what Buckley had written carried much uncomfortable truth.

Seeing the need for an entity that would attempt to establish outposts of free-market advocates on college campuses as a means of reaching students, Frank Chodorov at the age of sixty-three began the process of creating a new organization. Previously editor of an earlier version of *The Freeman*, Chodorov began his efforts in 1950 and two years later incorporated the Intercollegiate Society of Individualists (ISI) in Washington, DC. 1952 is also the year in which a short-lived conservative student organization was formed. After the 1952 Republican National Convention, Students for Taft and National Student MacArthur Clubs were merged into Students for America (SFA) under the presidency of Bob Munger. Much of its focus was on support for Senator Joseph McCarthy and the organization effectively ceased operations soon after the December 1954 censure of McCarthy and Munger's call to military service.[39]

One year later, in 1953, tax-exempt status was obtained for the Intercollegiate Society of Individualists and it is this year that ISI takes as its official founding. Unlike Students for America and its political roots, the purpose was clearly educational and expository. As Lee Edwards explains in his comprehensive history of the organization, "Chodorov argued that the only way to stop the descent into ever more statism was not by changing socialist laws through the political process but by inculcating the values which 'make such laws impossible.'"[40] The first President of the new organization was William F. Buckley, Jr., a position that was primarily honorary and from which he removed himself within one year. He was succeeded by Chodorov and later by E. Victor Milione, who remained President for over thirty years.

From its earliest years, ISI worked closely with FEE in the promotion of free-market ideas, writers, and speakers. Throughout the decade of the 1950s it provided the one coordinated effort to support conservative and individualist campus clubs, providing them with speakers, literature and organizational tools. Even as a more clearly political organization developed in 1960, ISI remained a major force among right-leaning youth, providing an intellectual and academic foundation for the development of a conservative movement. As early as 1960, Buckley had suggested to Milione that the organization change its name and this started a lively discussion as to the relevance of the terms "conservative" and "individualist."[41] In the end, no change occurred until 1966 when the acronym

---

38. Sheldon Rodman and Frank Ashburn, "'Isms' and the University: Two Reviews of 'God and Man at Yale,'" *Saturday Review of Literature*, December 15, 1951.

39. Information from email to the author from Professor Leonard P. Liggio dated January 22, 2009. Students for America was one of the co-sponsors of a tribute to Roy Cohn held at the Astor Hotel in New York City on July 28, 1954. George Reisman, in presenting the award on behalf of SFA, included a classic line: ". . . when Americans win back their government from the criminal alliance of communists, socialists, New Dealers and Eisenhower/Dewey Republicans (prolonged applause and crowd shouting 'more'). Well, there was more, but I thought I'd better shorten it!" Currently, Reisman is Professor Emeritus of Economics at Pepperdine University and author of the massive work, *Capitalism: A Treatise on Economics* (Ottawa, IL: Jameson Books, 1996). My thanks to Jameson Campaigne, Jr. and Roger Ream for pointing out the relevance of SFA and the Reisman remarks. See also Russell Porter, "2,000 Honor Cohn at a Dinner Here," *New York Times*, July 29, 1954.

40. *Educating for Liberty* (Washington, DC: Regnery Publishing, Inc., 2003), p. 4. The founding years of ISI are also covered in M. Stanton Evans: *Revolt on the Campus*, pp. 57–73.

41. Nash: *The Conservative Intellectual Movement in America* covers this discussion on pages 383–384.

was retained and the words converted to Intercollegiate Studies Institute. The organization continues today as a major component of the contemporary conservative movement.

One year after the Intercollegiate Society of Individualists began spreading its message on college campuses, a seminal work was published that would help to establish an intellectual basis for a clearly American conservative philosophical tradition. While much of the impetus for the creation of ISI centered around what is variously described as 19th century liberalism, free market economics, or individualism, this work would argue for a traditional conservatism based on Anglo-American sources and especially Edmund Burke. The author was Russell Kirk, then a young history instructor at Michigan State College (now University), and the book was titled *The Conservative Mind*.[42] As his publisher observed about the relevance of the work, coming as it did in the early 1950s,

> What was lacking was a general concept that would bring the movement together and give it coherence and identity. It was the great achievement of Russell Kirk's *The Conservative Mind*, published in 1953, to provide such a unifying concept. Kirk offered convincing evidence not only that conservatism was an honorable and intellectually respectable position, but also that it was an integral part of the American tradition.[43]

The book received a considerable number of reviews, both positive and critical, in widely circulated newspapers and magazines as well as more academic journals. Kirk had brought respectability and relevance to a tradition too often thought only continental and irrelevant to the contemporary American scene.[44]

The Conservative Mind was more than merely a recitation of the essential elements of a traditionalist conservatism, nor solely a compilation of the contributions of important writers of the past. It was a critique of the dominant liberal orthodoxy but it was even more than this. The work was also a call to action. In his concluding chapter Kirk summed up the challenge,

> In the sixth decade of the twentieth century, liberalism and socialism lie intellectually bankrupt, and for the most part fallen from public favor. If conservatively inclined men of affairs can rise to the summons of the poets, the norms of culture and politics may endure in defiance of the crimes and follies of the age.[45]

Clearly Kirk believed that there was an important tradition, an American tradition, which had been usurped but could be brought back to the fore of society. Kirk's message would be heard by young conservatives of the 1950s and beyond. There were others who contributed to this intellectual renaissance of conservative thought throughout the 1950s, and other works by Kirk as well, but the publication of *The Conservative Mind* had a profound influence on what was not yet a conservative movement.

---

42. Chicago: Henry Regnery Company, 1953.

43. Henry Regnery: *Memoirs of a Dissident Publisher*, p. 146. Regnery discusses the effect of Kirk and this book, as well as some of Kirk's other works, on pp. 146–166.

44. Kirk's background and his groundbreaking book are discussed in George H. Nash: *The Conservative Intellectual Movement in America Since 1945*, pp. 61–73 especially.

45. *The Conservative Mind: From Burke to Santayana*, p. 552.

What was missing more than anything else was a serious, broad-based journal in which to present, explain, and expound upon conservative thought and its relevance to contemporary America. As Lee Edwards observed, "In 1955, liberals had eight magazines of opinion they could read and write for, including *The New Republic*, *The New Leader*, the *Reporter*, and *The Nation*; conservatives really had none."[46] Once more it was William F. Buckley, Jr. who was to provide the answer. As early as 1953, Bill Buckley had been approached by William S. Schlamm, a former leftist originally from Austria who had worked for Henry Luce at Time-Life. Schlamm maintained there was a need for a right-wing magazine and that Buckley, then the 29 year old author of a well-known and controversial book, would be the ideal person as editor.[47]

With a cover date of November 19, 1955, the initial issue of *National Review* appeared and American political journalism has never been the same. In a publisher's note, Buckley stated that the magazine's purpose was to stand "athwart history, yelling 'Stop' at a time when no one is inclined to do so."[48] Buckley had recruited a broad coalition of anti-liberal writers comprising those who could be best described as traditional conservatives, libertarian and individualistic free market advocates, as well as those whose main focus was anti-communism. The editorial board included a number of former Communists and Trotskyites. There were former and present academics as well as professional journalists. As E.J. Dionne observed, "The intellectual coalition represented by Buckley's editors and contributors was to lay the basis for the conservative political coalition of the future."[49] Together they represented the three main components of the developing conservative movement: traditional values, free market economics, and anti-communism.

The significance of the founding of *National Review* cannot be overemphasized. George Nash concluded that, "if *National Review* (or something like it) had not been founded, there would probably have been no cohesive intellectual force on the Right in the 1960s and 1970s."[50] Another historian of the conservative movement in America, Jonathan Schoenwald, calls the founding of *National Review* perhaps the most important occurrence of the 1950s in terms of influencing the growth of conservatism in America.[51] In creating his magazine, Buckley had taken one more step towards the development of a conservative movement.

Some four years after founding his magazine, William F. Buckley, Jr. appeared again as the author of another book, *Up From Liberalism*. The introduction was provided by the junior senator from Arizona, Barry Goldwater, and had a forward by well-known novelist John Dos Passos. Perhaps the most representative section is the concluding two paragraphs of the book where Buckley provides his perspective on the relationship of man and government.

---

46. Lee Edwards, "The Other Sixties: A Flag-Waver's Memoir," *Policy Review* 46 (Fall 1988), p. 60.

47. The founding of *National Review* and its early years is covered in both Linda Bridges and John R. Coyne, Jr.: *Strictly Right: William F. Buckley, Jr. and the American Conservative Movement* (Hoboken, NJ: John Wiley & Sons, 2007), pp. 29–65 and in John Judis: *William F. Buckley, Jr.—Patron Saint of the Conservatives*, pp. 114–142. Much of the material in this section draws upon both these sources as well as the Buckley papers at Sterling Library, Yale University.

48. As quoted in Godfrey Hodgson: *The World Turned Right Side Up* (Boston: Houghton Mifflin Company, 1996), p. 78.

49. *Why Americans Hate Politics*, p. 159.

50. *The Conservative Intellectual Movement in America*, p. 140.

51. *A Time for Choosing: The Rise of Modern American Conservatism* (New York: Oxford University Press, 2001), p. 38.

I will not cede more power to the state. I will not willingly cede more power to anyone, not to the state, not to General Motors, not to the CIO. I will hoard my power like a miser, resisting every effort to drain it away from me. I will then use my power, as I see fit. I mean to live my life an obedient man, but obedient to God, subservient to the wisdom of my ancestors; never to the authority of political truths arrived at yesterday at the voting booth. That is a program of sorts, is it not? It is certainly program enough to keep conservatives busy, and liberals at bay. And the nation free.[52]

Buckley's book became a best seller, especially on college campuses, setting forth an aggressive and forward-looking conservatism that was beginning to appeal to many youth. In this respect *Up From Liberalism* served as a precursor to another forthcoming work by that same junior senator from Arizona that appeared on bookshelves one year later.

Buckley has been rightly described as "America's all-purpose conservative thinker."[53] But he was more than simply a thinker, writer or debater. Buckley's goal in all that he undertook was to see conservatism become a mass movement. In this sense he was, as Tom Reiss described him, "a reconciler and an institution builder."[54] Lee Edwards observed, "in the 1950s and 1960s Buckley by his words and his actions forced the reigning Liberal Establishment to acknowledge that a major new political force had emerged in America." Edwards, who knew him well and worked with him in the vineyards for more than fifty years, went one step further by calling him the founder of the modern conservative movement.[55] As we shall see, the fingerprints of Bill Buckley appear throughout the history of not only the young conservative organization but also nearly all significant responsible conservative groups over the last half of the twentieth century.[56]

Whether it was the journals and other publications distributed by the Intercollegiate Society of Individualists, the effect of books by Buckley, Kirk and several others, or the periodic information obtained from *National Review* and *Human Events*, conservatives now had a growing source of information and education. In her interviews with former conservative youth activists, Rebecca Klatch noted that this intellectual base was critical to their political development: "What is clear is that books and ideas played a key role in helping these youth think through issues, in confirming the direction of their beliefs, in instigating their commitment to politics."[57] Supplementing this written material were the various campus speakers sponsored by ISI as well as the numerous seminars and institutes for students provided by ISI and the Foundation for Economic Education. There now existed the beginnings of a consistent philosophical opposition to the prevailing liberal sentiment in American society. What remained was the ability to convert these beliefs into political action.

---

52. William F. Buckley, Jr.: *Up From Liberalism* (New York: Ivan Obolensky, 1959), p. 219.
53. J. David Hoeveler, Jr.: *Watch on the Right: Conservative Intellectuals in the Reagan Era* (Madison: University of Wisconsin Press, 1991), p. 23.
54. Tom Reiss, "The First Conservative," *The New Yorker*, October 24, 2005.
55. *Human Events*, February 28, 2008.
56. Buckley presents some interesting stories from this period in his chapter "Early Days at National Review" in *Flying High: Remembering Barry Goldwater* (New York: Basic Books, 2008), pp. 27–34.
57. *A Generation Divided*, p. 68.

Barry

His grandfather had started a small store in Gila City, Arizona in 1860 and twelve years later moved it to Phoenix. By the end of World War II, however, it had grown into the leading quality department store in what was becoming a major metropolitan area. With the exception of his time in the Army Air Force during the war, the grandson of the founder, Barry Morris Goldwater, had run the business since 1930. Upon returning from the service he became integrally involved in civic affairs and was known to thousands of Arizona residents by his first name.[58]

Postwar Arizona saw an influx of new residents, many of them Republicans now settling in a state that was overwhelmingly Democratic. Phoenix, its largest city, had been known as a "sin city" by the servicemen who visited it during and after the war and its local government was viewed by many as inefficient and corrupt. One who frequently expressed these views was Eugene Pulliam, publisher of the *Arizona Republic* and the *Phoenix Gazette*, who was himself a transplant from Indiana. Pulliam was determined to clean up his new hometown and sought out respected civic leaders to be part of a slate to reform city government in 1949. Barry Goldwater, scion of the department store family, veteran, and participant in numerous community causes, was a natural to join the effort.

Goldwater accepted the challenge and in 1949 began his first campaign for public office. Not only was his campaign for City Council successful, but also he topped the ticket and became Vice Chair of the council. Upon election, Goldwater wrote in his journal some observations that would give clues to his future career path. "It was a wonderful experience, that campaigning. I met more people than I ever dreamed I could get to know . . . I started with the idea that one could be in politics and remain clean, and I still hold to that with one campaign behind me."[59] Goldwater had been a candidate and now he was an office-holder with responsibilities of governance. The new reform slate reduced the size of city government, turned a $400,000 deficit into a $275,000 surplus and saw the city become a National Municipal League "All American City."

Goldwater originally considered a campaign for Governor of Arizona in 1950 but the Republican nomination went to radio personality Howard Pyle and Goldwater enlisted as the campaign manager. Pyle went on to be elected Governor and by 1951 Goldwater was already planning a Senate race. His opponent would be Ernest McFarland, then Senate Democratic Majority Leader, well known as a major sponsor of the G.I. Bill. Campaigning for the United States Senate in 1952 against such an established leader of the Democratic Party would be difficult but national trends were running in the Republican direction. As Dwight D. Eisenhower became the first Republican President in twenty years and the GOP took control of the Senate, the voters of Arizona provided City Councilman Goldwater with a 7,000-vote margin over Ernest McFarland. Goldwater's career

---

58. This section draws upon Robert Alan Goldberg: *Barry Goldwater* (New Haven: Yale University Press, 1995), pp. 78–116; Lee Edwards: *Goldwater: The Man Who Made a Revolution* (Washington, DC: Regnery Publishers, Inc., 1995), pp. 38–48; and Rick Perlstein: *Before the Storm: Barry Goldwater and the Unmaking of the American Consensus* (New York: Hill and Wang, 2001), pp. 23–42.

59. John W. Dean and Barry M. Goldwater, Jr.: *Pure Goldwater* (New York: Palgrave MacMillan, 2008), p. 69.

as a United States Senator, a position he ended up holding for a total of thirty years, was about to begin.

As a freshman member of the Senate, Goldwater had much to learn and much time to be accepted by his colleagues. He was selected to head up the National Republican Senatorial Committee, the party's political committee to help elect and re-elect Senators. In this capacity Goldwater traveled the country in 1955 and 1956 meeting party leaders and potential candidates as well as giving speeches. This position and his office as a United States Senator provided an opportunity to address not only Republican groups but also all kinds of business, civic, and religious organizations. Goldwater would be re-elected in 1958 and once again serve in 1959–60 as chairman of the committee.[60] In 1959, he would take on another assignment, as a syndicated columnist for *The Los Angeles Times*.[61]

By the end of the 1950s, the junior senator from Arizona was gaining recognition as the political spokesman for the nascent conservative movement. Barry Goldwater differed from Mr. Republican, Robert A. Taft. He was from a small Western state, not from a politically renowned family, not a powerful member of the Senate Establishment; yet, in these differences, Goldwater manifested the dominant characteristics of much of the developing movement.

Barry Goldwater was beginning to establish himself as a national political figure. Dean Clarence Manion of the Notre Dame Law School, a well-known conservative leader of the time, visited Goldwater in the spring of 1959 and announced that he was gathering together a group of one hundred prominent individuals to draft the Senator for the 1960 presidential nomination. In a letter to friend and supporter Bud Kelland in July, 1959, Goldwater demurred from any interest in such a campaign.

> Manion . . . came to see me in my office and told me they wanted to form a group that would be ready, if the opportunity presented itself, to submit my name and I told them I was not the least bit interested in it, but I recognized that I could not stop them if they want to proceed.[62]

One month later, on August 15, 1959, Goldwater wrote to Eugene Pulliam concerning Manion's efforts and portrayed them solely as an insurance policy should something happen to Vice President Nixon, the perceived presidential nominee in 1960. According to Goldwater, ". . . any serious outward effort at this time to place my name in nomination would result in destroying whatever little usefulness I have to my country and to our party." From his perspective, "the whole thing to me, if it is going to be, should be a matter of being prepared should a hole appear in the wall and through it we might run."[63] There would be no presidential campaign for Barry Goldwater in 1960 but that did not stop Republican activists from expressing their desire for such an undertaking.

Manion's interest in promoting a Goldwater candidacy would continue but he turned his attention also to getting the Senator to author a book reflecting his

---

60. *Pure Goldwater* contains a number of informative letters and journal entries by Goldwater during this period. See pp. 75–101 especially.

61. Stephen Shadegg: *What Happened to Goldwater?* (New York: Holt, Reinhart and Winston, 1965), pp. 24–26.

62. *Pure Goldwater*, p. 105.

63. *Ibid.* p. 109.

political philosophy and stands on a number of contemporary issues. Several years later in an interview upon retiring from the United States Senate, Goldwater recalled the discussion with Manion about the book.

> Dean Manion called me one day, and said, "Why don't you write a book." I said, "I don't know anything about writing books," and he said, "Well, we can get you some help." I said, "I still don't know enough about it, but let me try." He offered me $10,000, which was more money than I'd ever heard of.[64]

To this proposition Goldwater agreed and began to work with L. Brent Bozell, brother-in-law of William F. Buckley, Jr., on what would become one of the best-known political books of the last fifty years.[65]

The Conscience of a Conservative first appeared in March 1960 in a printing of 10,000 copies from the Victor Publishing Company of Shepherdsville, Kentucky, anything but a major publishing house and not even a known conservative imprint.[66] As Bozell described the assignment, "We are not writing a platform for the Republican Party but what I hope we can do is awaken the American people to a realization of how far we have moved from the old constitutional concepts toward the welfare state."[67] While some critics have attempted to downplay Goldwater's role in the construction of the book, it is clear from reading his memos and letters to Bozell that the Senator was the source for the major points in the book.[68] Stephen Shadegg, his campaign manager in both 1952 and 1958, as well as acknowledged ghostwriter for the Senator's newspaper column, points out, "the truth is, Goldwater and Bozell deserve full credit for the writing. The rest of us made only minor contributions."[69] With his role as chairman of the senatorial campaign committee, as a syndicated columnist, and now as author of a book, Barry Goldwater was becoming known as a national political figure.

There was no question but that *The Conscience of a Conservative* was a radical attack on the existing liberal orthodoxy and a call for greater emphasis on individual freedom and limited government. As Goldwater put it, ". . . for the American Conservative there is no difficulty in identifying the day's overriding political challenge: it is to preserve and extend freedom."[70] To this end, a true statesman has a commitment to divest himself of the power entrusted to him. In so doing, he proclaimed:

> I have little interest in streamlining government or in making it more efficient, for I mean to reduce its size. I do not undertake to promote welfare,

---

64. John Kolbe, "Arizona legend talks politics," *Phoenix Gazette*, December 3, 1986.

65. The fascinating story about Dean Manion's efforts to get the Goldwater book written, published and distributed is told in Nicole Hoplin and Ron Robinson: *Funding Fathers* (Washington: Regnery Publishing, 2008), pp. 87–117.

66. Barry Goldwater: *The Conscience of a Conservative* (Shepherdsville, KY: Victor Publishing Company, Inc., 1960). Later that year Hillman Books of New York produced it in a widely distributed paperback edition. It has been reprinted many times, including in a special 30th anniversary edition by Young America's Foundation (Washington, DC: Regnery Gateway, 1990).

67. Quoted in Stephen Shadegg: *What Happened to Goldwater?*, pp. 27–28.

68. Pages 106–111 of *Pure Goldwater* includes notes Goldwater made on the book project after meeting with Brent Bozell as well as an outline he submitted to Bozell and a similar note sent to Stephen Shadegg with his thoughts on how the book should be constructed.

69. *What Happened to Goldwater?*, p. 28.

70. *The Conscience of a Conservative*, p. 14.

for I propose to extend freedom. My aim is not to pass laws, but to repeal them. It is not to inaugurate new programs, but to cancel old ones that do violence to the Constitution, or that have failed in their purpose, or that impose on the people an unwarranted financial burden. I will not attempt to discover whether legislation is 'needed' before I have first determined whether it is constitutionally permissible. And if I should later be attacked for neglecting my constituents' 'interests,' I shall reply that I was informed their main interest is liberty and that in that cause I am doing the very best I can.[71]

This new book was clearly a call to arms that would be received not only by political activists of the day but also by a new audience of younger readers just reaching political maturity.

Upon its initial distribution in April 1960, the book became a best seller not only among the politically active but also especially on college campuses across the country. As William F. Buckley, Jr. later observed, "by the time the convention met in Chicago, it was selling by the tens of thousands, and being hailed as a lighthouse of libertarian thought. It was even likened, by its special fans, to Thomas Paine's *Common Sense*."[72] Carol Dawson was working for the Nixon presidential effort in 1960 and noted the importance of *Conscience* to students: "I recall as I traveled the country on behalf of the Nixon campaign that year that nearly every College YR or Nixon club member had either heard of the book, had just bought it, or had read it and was enthused about it."[73]

Historian John Andrew maintains that much of its appeal to college students was its directness and independence: "Goldwater attacked not only liberals and Democrats, but Republicans as well. This gave his message an aura of principled purity that sharply contrasted with other rhetoric of that political year."[74] As one of those future young conservative leaders viewed it, *Conscience of a Conservative* became a political calling card, ". . . written in the same rebellious, provocative spirit of Bill Buckley and the other Knights errant of the pioneer 50s."[75] Goldwater himself took pride in the influence he perceived his book had on thousands of young people.

> I think it had a tremendous impact. It was an inexpensive book, and young people bought that book as fast as they could buy it. I think the young people were influenced by it. The most delightful thing I hear when I travel around the country is, "You got me interested in politics, you and your book."[76]

Now the conservatives had not only a political leader in Goldwater but also a political tome that summarized their key philosophical and political positions.

Lee Edwards maintains that Goldwater, Russell Kirk, and William F. Buckley, Jr. were the three critical pillars of the developing movement: "First came the man of ideas, the intellectual, the philosopher; then the man of interpretation, the journalist, the popularizer; and finally the man of action, the politician, the

---

71. *The Conscience of a Conservative*, p. 23.
72. *Flying High*, p. 17.
73. E-mail to the author from Carol Dawson, January 24, 2009.
74. *The Other Side of the Sixties*, p. 19.
75. Docksai, p. 56.
76. John Kolbe, "Arizona legend talks politics," *Phoenix Gazette*, December 3, 1986.

presidential candidate."[77] With the contributions of these men and others, the stage was set for the creation of a national political movement.

Freedom, Tradition and Anti-Communism

As the decade of the 1950s approached a close, three essential pillars could be seen as contributing to the foundation of a new conservative movement. First in time and in emphasis for some of those who would lead this emerging movement was free-market economics and a steadfast opposition to collectivism. Whether called individualists or libertarians, they put primary emphasis on individual freedom and a government limited in its scope.[78] A second and quite different approach stressed the importance of traditional values, the relationship of society to the individual, and the need for preserving order.[79] An emphasis on opposition to communism served as the third ingredient of modern conservatism. Anti-communism was a clean break from the isolationism that had been dominant among conservatives from the 1930s forward. With the involvement of several former Marxists, "the issue was not the old fight over interventionism or isolationism; it was whether or not the United States would be willing to wage war against the evils of Communism."[80]

Bringing these three somewhat disparate trends together into a single movement would be a major challenge, and one which periodically rose up to create dissention and division in the movement. Leading this effort to create a synthesis of tradition and freedom was Frank Meyer, one of the editors recruited by William F. Buckley, Jr. when he started his magazine in 1955. Meyer maintained that both traditionalists and individualists should recognize that Western Civilization was based on reason operating within tradition, that freedom could not be exercised in any meaningful way outside a framework of order. This attempted marriage of the two outlooks came to be known as fusionism.[81] As Lee Edwards observed, "Frank Meyer, the intellectual father of fusionism, and Barry Goldwater, the first political apostle of fusionism, sought to unite, not divide, all conservatives. Their goal was a national movement guided by constitutional principles of ordered liberty."[82] It was, according to one of those soon-to-be conservative youth leaders, Donald Devine, an emphasis on using libertarian means in a conservative society for traditionalist ends.[83]

By molding together anti-communism, a concern for individual liberty, and a respect for order and tradition, a new conservative movement was being created. In this manner the decade ended with a working philosophy and a public following for conservatism.[84] Across America, stirrings of conservative sentiment were

77. Lee Edwards, "The Other Sixties," p. 59.

78. See Nash *The Conservative Intellectual Movement in America*, pp. 30–73 for a discussion of some of these libertarian and individualist contributors to the conservative movement.

79. The primary exponent of this position is Russell Kirk as outlined in his many published works.

80. E.J. Dionne: *Why Americans Hate Politics*, p. 162.

81. Meyer's attempted synthesis is explained in his book *In Defense of Freedom: A Conservative Credo* (Chicago: Henry Regnery Company, 1962) and also in the opening and closing chapters of his edited work *What Is Conservatism?* (New York: Holt Rinehart and Winston, 1964).

82. Lee Edwards, "The Conservative Consensus: Frank Meyer, Barry Goldwater, and the Politics of Fusionism," Heritage Foundation "First Principles" series, number 8 (January 22, 2007).

83. Quoted in Dionne: *Why Americans Hate Politics*, p. 161. See also, Donald J. Devine: *The Political Culture of the United States* (Boston: Little, Brown & Company, 1972).

84. Dionne, p. 169.

present among intellectuals and writers, political leaders and aspiring young politicians, journalists and commentators. This new purely American conservatism that molded together individual liberty and societal order with a firm opposition to communism was beginning to attract the attention of college undergraduates and graduate students. The effort that would eventually result in the establishment of a young conservative movement would begin, however, in the late 1950s in response to what was perceived as an unwillingness to express loyalty to the United States.

Caddy and Franke

The organization that in September 1960 became Young Americans for Freedom can be traced back to the efforts of two college students in December 1959. At that time, student opposition to repeal of the "loyalty oath" provisions of a new Federal education program first crystallized young conservative political action throughout the nation. The National Defense Education Act (NDEA) of 1958[85] was one of the efforts undertaken in reaction to the Soviet Union's launching of Sputnik. Initially, it provided funds to colleges and universities for science, mathematics, and foreign language studies and to finance low-interest loans to students. As the Act's title implies, the justification for this Federal involvement in education was to assist in the provision of defense of the nation.

One of the provisions of the Act required that college students who received loan money as part of the NDEA program must swear loyalty to the Constitution and affirm that they are not members of any organization that believes in or teaches the overthrow of government by force or violence.[86] In the fall of 1959, several university presidents announced that they would no longer participate in the NDEA student loan program because they believed the requirement of a loyalty oath pledge abridged academic freedom. Senator John F. Kennedy introduced a bill to remove the requirement for a loyalty oath and most observers anticipated that it would pass in 1960.[87] However, two college students, Douglas Caddy and David Franke, had a different perspective.

Douglas Caddy grew up in Louisiana and Texas at a time when conservatism was only beginning to develop as an alternative to the prevailing orthodoxy.[88] As a sophomore in high school he became active in conservative politics in New Orleans and volunteered to collect signatures supporting Senator Joseph McCarthy. Although Louisiana, like nearly all the South at that time was solidly Democratic, through his support of McCarthy and other anti-communists Caddy had begun to identify with the Republican Party. Convinced that he wanted to influence public policy, Caddy applied to and was accepted at Georgetown University, entering the freshman class in the fall of 1956. Soon thereafter he joined with a handful of other students to form a Young Republican club on campus and began writing for the student newspaper. One year later he helped organize the College Republican Federation with clubs at Georgetown, George Washington University, American University, Trinity College, and Dunbarton College.

85. The National Defense Education Act of 1958 (PL 85–864).
86. M. Stanton Evans: *Revolt on the Campus* covers the student loyalty oath campaign on pages 74–86. The oath and the affidavit can be found on p. 75.
87. Greg Schneider: *Cadres for Conservatism* (New York: New York University Press, 1999), p. 21–23.
88. This section relies especially on an interview with Caddy in Houston, Texas on December 10, 2007 as well as his "Birth of the Conservative Movement."

David Franke was raised in Texas and started expressing conservative political opinions even earlier than Caddy. He became interested in politics after reading a copy of John T. Flynn's attack on socialism, *The Road Ahead*, while still in junior high school.[89] Franke first attended Del Mar College in Corpus Christi and while there came under the influence of a rather rare breed: a conservative college professor. He later transferred to George Washington University where he would help form the College Republican Federation of the District of Columbia.[90]

Caddy and Franke first met in the summer of 1957 when they, along with William Schulz, were chosen in the first college journalism internship program sponsored by *Human Events*.[91] Here they worked with M. Stanton Evans who was then managing editor of the conservative weekly and would subsequently, at age 27, become editor of the *Indianapolis News*. They also met Carol Dawson, who was involved with the College Young Republicans at Dunbarton College. Once the summer ended, Franke returned to Corpus Christi and Caddy to Georgetown but they remained in contact with each other.

By the fall of 1959, Caddy had become State Chairman of the DC College Republican Federation and was working part-time for the Committee of One Million (Against the Admission of Red China to the United Nations) whose organizer was Marvin Liebman, an individual who will also play a critical role in the development of the new conservative youth organization. Franke had transferred to George Washington University and was editor of the ISI newsletter, *The Individualist*, as well as *The Campus Republican*, published by the Young Republican National Federation.

Concerned that most college students were being portrayed as opposed to the "loyalty oath" provision of NDEA student loans, the two students determined to organized campus opposition to repeal. According to Caddy, they decided to fight the repeal also as a means of coalescing conservative students around the country.[92] Caddy and Franke prepared articles and announcements that were published in *Human Events, National Review*, and *The Individualist*. Using contacts from ISI and YRs, they found representatives at campuses across the nation, including Harvard, Yale, Antioch, and University of Michigan. This helped them to compile the names of supportive college students on index cards, creating the initial basis for a national conservative youth organization. [93]

In January 1960, the "Student Committee for the Loyalty Oath" announced a governing board of students from thirty colleges and universities. Letters and petitions were delivered to Congress while news releases poured forth from the committee. Kennedy's repeal bill passed the Senate on an unrecorded vote but the proposal then died in the House Education and Labor Committee. Historian Rick Perlstein rightly describes the Student Loyalty Oath effort as the beginnings of a youth conservative movement in America.[94] Greg Schneider noted that those involved "gained something aside from preservation of the oath itself. They acquired experience in working the corridors of power in Congress and in

---

89. *The Road Ahead: America's Coming Revolution* (New York: Devin-Adair Company, 1949).

90. Schneider: *Cadres for Conservatism*, p. 21; Rick Perlstein: *Before the Storm*, pp. 69–70.

91. Schulz would later go on to become executive editor of *Reader's Digest*, which along with the *Saturday Evening Post*, tended to provide a vehicle for some conservative writers in the 1950s.

92. Douglas Caddy, "The Birth of the Conservative Movement," p. 5.

93. Richard A. Viguerie and David Franke: *America's Right Turn* (Chicago: Bonus Books, 2004), p. 65.

94. *Before the Storm*, p. 69.

using the press to their advantage." [95] As Doug Caddy summed it all up, "Out of this cauldron came the beginnings of the modern conservative mass movement. Franke and I were put in touch with hundreds of like-thinking students around the country."[96] With this under their belts, the young conservative activists could move on to greater tasks.

Chicago 1960

It was the person and political beliefs of Senator Barry M. Goldwater that provided the impetus for the next effort at organizing young conservatives. Northwestern University student Robert Croll took the lead in establishing a "Youth for Goldwater for Vice President" committee in the spring of 1960. Croll was a graduate student who had been active in Young Republican politics. At the Midwest Conference of College Young Republicans that April the first sentiment for Goldwater became evident as the delegates passed a resolution endorsing the Arizona Senator for Vice President. A fellow Northwestern student, John Kolbe, who would play an important role in the development of a permanent conservative youth organization, had sponsored the resolution.

On May 12, 1960, Croll announced the formation of "Youth for Goldwater for Vice President." The Steering Committee comprised Doug Caddy and David Franke, along with Robert Harley of Georgetown University, John Weicher of the University of Chicago, and Richard Noble, treasurer of the California Young Republicans.[97] Croll was convinced that Goldwater would be the perfect candidate and that he would accept such a request from Richard Nixon, the presumed 1960 Republican presidential candidate. "There is no doubt in my mind that if Senator Goldwater were offered the GOP vice-presidential nomination he would accept it," said Croll.[98]

That, however, may have been a mistaken assumption for, as Goldwater explained in a letter to General Bonner Fellers dated one day after Croll's announcement, he viewed the vice presidency as little more than what Vice President John Nance Garner had once described it.[99] For Goldwater,

> . . . one of the most effective ways to silence a man is to make him vice president, and I honestly feel that I can be of better service as a senator than as a vice president, or for that matter as president. Therefore, I have not been encouraging movements for the vice presidency, but I know they are in process and I can't tell free people what they have to do.[100]

Clearly, Goldwater's individualist and libertarian leanings extended to his outlook on the various organizations then advocating his candidacy for one or other higher office but he was not actively promoting himself for such positions.

Whether Croll was aware of Goldwater's sentiments or not, he continued to

---

95. *Cadres for Conservatism*, p. 23.
96. "The Birth of the Conservative Movement," p. 7.
97. Interview with Douglas Caddy, Houston, Texas, December 10, 2007.
98. M. Stanton Evans: *Revolt on the Campus*, p. 90.
99. Garner served as Vice President during the first eight years of Franklin D. Roosevelt's presidency and famously described the office as "not worth a bucket of warm piss."
100. *Pure Goldwater*, p. 113.

organize support among college students and other young Republicans. By early July, he could announce the existence of active Youth for Goldwater groups in thirty-two states and on sixty-four college campuses.[101] As one of the activists noted, "In Goldwater, we had a candidate who inspired the young as well as the old." [102] Croll's committee placed advertisements in *The Wall Street Journal* and *National Review* seeking both members and financial supporters. In an appeal to more senior readers, Croll emphasized the uniqueness of the effort: "For many years, conservatives have worried about the radicalism on our college campuses, and have hoped for a revival of youthful conservatism. We have arrived—but we need your support."[103]

Later that same month these young conservatives would gather in Chicago for the 1960 Republican National Convention. As historian John Andrew noted, "Youth for Goldwater for Vice President . . . gave these activists a focal point for their activism and led them to battle Republican moderates at the GOP national convention in Chicago that July."[104] Indeed, it was this effort to influence the direction of the GOP that would produce the nucleus for a national conservative youth organization that came into being only months later.

The 1960 Republican National Convention provided an important and rather unique political experience for the young conservatives who had been active in the "Youth for Goldwater for Vice President" organization. It was an opportunity for them to meet and become familiar with others of similar disposition who were toiling in the vineyards of the "Youth for Nixon" organization but shared their conservative outlook on issues and saw the need for a permanent conservative youth organization.[105] But it also brought them in contact with Marvin Liebman, former Communist, and then impresario of numerous right-leaning organizations. Liebman worked closely with Charles Edison, Chairman of the Board of the McGraw-Edison Electric Company and former Democratic Governor of New Jersey. While a former Democratic officeholder and briefly Secretary of the Navy under Franklin D. Roosevelt, Edison was a conservative who supported a number of Republicans, including Congressman Walter Judd of Minnesota.

Judd had been selected to serve as keynote speaker at the convention. A former medical missionary to China, he had made a name for himself as a stirring orator and an advocate of a strong policy of opposition to communism.[106] Liebman and Edison decided that they would form an organization to promote Judd for the vice-presidential nomination and four weeks before the convention they announced "Americans for Judd for Vice President" with former Governor Edison serving as Chairman. However, Liebman had also been working closely with Doug Caddy and David Franke from the "Youth for Goldwater for Vice President" effort. This resulted in one of the strangest semi-coordinated efforts at any political convention. When Liebman put up the funds for both operations,

101. Perlstein: *Before the Storm*, p. 75.
102. Caddy, "Birth of the Conservative Movement," p. 7.
103. Evans: *Revolt on the Campus*, p. 92.
104. *The Other Side of the Sixties*, p. 30.
105. Among those active in the Nixon effort was Robert Bauman, a recent Georgetown graduate, and Carol Dawson, a student at Dunbarton College who had been active in the Student Loyalty Oath campaign and was Executive Secretary of College Youth for Nixon. Robert E. Bauman: *The Gentleman from Maryland* (New York: Arbor House, 1986), p. 94.
106. Lee Edwards: *Missionary for Freedom: The Life and Times of Walter Judd* (New York: Paragon House, 1990).

"This was probably the only time two national vice presidential campaigns were charged to the same American Express account."[107] Neither Judd nor Goldwater were to receive the vice presidential nomination but the young conservatives were, nevertheless, to have an effect on the convention and were to set in place the plans to form a permanent organization. John Andrew concluded, more than any one political candidate, "what really shaped their activism was a conservative ideology and a determination to create a conservative alternative in national politics."[108]

On nominating night at the convention, Arizona Governor Paul Fannin placed in nomination the name of his state's favorite son, Barry M. Goldwater. The Youth for Goldwater forces had organized a major demonstration of support for their favorite candidate and a resounding demonstration took place on the floor of the convention. Stan Evans was among the journalists covering the convention and summarized the significance of the Goldwater support:

> That convention, and that demonstration, made Barry Goldwater a famous man in America. Millions of people who had heard of him only vaguely or not at all were exposed to his philosophy, saw the explosion of genuine sentiment for him, and heard him speak eloquently of conservatism and the future of the Republican Party. And, as it put Goldwater on the map, the demonstration put young conservatism on the map. From that time forward, reporters, commentators, and pundits became acutely aware of the rise of conservative sentiment among the young.[109]

But Goldwater realized that he was not to be the nominee for President or for Vice President in 1960 and so he went to the podium and asked that his name be removed from consideration. Among his comments to the delegates was a call for future action: "Let's grow up conservatives. If we want to take this party back—and I think we can someday—let's get to work."[110] The excitement was over, but the real work of organizing conservatives remained before them.

At the end of the convention, Senator Goldwater met briefly with the leadership of the Youth for Goldwater for Vice President group to thank them for their efforts. According to Doug Caddy, Goldwater told them they should "turn your group into a permanent organization of young conservatives. The man is not important. The principles you espouse are. Do this and I shall support you in any way I can."[111] And that is exactly what these young conservatives did shortly thereafter. True to his word, Goldwater remained a strong supporter of the organization created only a few weeks after the Chicago convention, even many years later when some members of the organization became critical of the Senator's stands on social issues.

Liebman and Edison were impressed with the effort put forth by the young conservatives and they decided to host a luncheon for them. As Edison stated, "let's see if we can get these kids to continue to work together in some way, some

---

107. Marvin Liebman: *Coming Out Conservative* (San Francisco: Chronicle Books, 1992), p. 147.
108. *The Other Side of the Sixties*, p. 73.
109. Evans: *Revolt on the Campus*, p. 105.
110. Shadegg/Goldwater collection, Box 3H506. Center for American History, University of Texas, Austin, TX.
111. Caddy, "Birth of the Conservative Movement," p. 14.

how. Let's see if we can keep this thing going."[112] The day after the convention the young conservatives gathered for lunch in the Columbia Room of the Pick-Congress Hotel. Just as Goldwater had previously, Edison exhorted them to continue their efforts by forming a permanent organization. Doug Caddy was designated to develop a plan for a subsequent meeting. A suggestion was made to hold the next meeting at the family home of William F. Buckley, Jr. and the Buckley family agreed.[113] As Buckley noted, "The word went out, and a month and a half after the convention, as summer lingered in New England, a hundred young people gathered at Great Elm, where, over three days, they would lay the foundation of Young Americans for Freedom."[114] Once more, William F. Buckley, Jr. was present at the creation of another important component of the burgeoning conservative movement.

---

112. Letter of Marvin Liebman to William A. Rusher dated April 22, 1983, Personal Papers of William A. Rusher, Box 174, Manuscript Division, Library of Congress, Washington, DC.

113. Liebman: *Coming Out Conservative*, pp. 149–151 and Evans: *Revolt on the Campus*, pp. 107–108.

114. *Flying High*, p. 20.

2. The Gathering at Great Elm

*"Long ignored by historians, the Sharon conference
represented the beginnings of a movement that
would help catapult conservatives into political
power within two decades."*[1]

BARRY GOLDWATER'S ADMONITION that conservatives should "grow up" and work if they expected to gain a dominant role in American politics was not lost on the young activists who had worked so hard in Chicago at the 1960 Republican National Convention. Once settled in New York City and ensconced at the offices of Marvin Liebman, Doug Caddy took on the assignment of setting up an organizational meeting to discuss the development of a permanent youth group. In early August, Caddy and Annette Courtemanche, a student at Molloy College, drove to Sharon, Connecticut to familiarize themselves with the facilities at the Buckley family home and make arrangements for hotel accommodations for those who would attend.[2] Known as "Great Elm" for the tree that shaded the side lawn, the Buckley home would provide a suitable setting for the gathering.

An Invitation to a Founding

By mid-August, plans were in place for an organizational meeting of young conservatives. Using the contacts developed through the Student Committee for the Loyalty Oath, the Youth for Goldwater for Vice President campaign, Youth for Nixon, and the interaction with other students in Chicago, Caddy created an Interim Committee to provide credence to the letter of invitation. Serving on the Interim Committee were James Abstine (then Chairman of the Indiana Young Republicans), Robert Croll (organizer of the Youth for Goldwater for Vice President effort), David Franke (co-chair of the Loyalty Oath committee), Robert Harley (Chairman of the DC College Young Republicans), Richard Noble (Treasurer of the California Young Republicans), James Kolbe (whose older brother had sponsored the first resolution to endorse Goldwater for Vice President), as well as George Gaines of Tulane, Clendenin Ryan of Georgetown, Scott Stanley of the University of Kansas, John Weicher of the University of Chicago, Brian Whelan of Loyola University, and Suzanne Regnery (daughter of the publisher).[3]

Over the heading "Interim Committee for a National Conservative Youth Organization" a letter, signed by Doug Caddy, went out to various students and other young adults who were perceived as likely to be interested in the goal of starting a permanent group. According to the letter, it was sent to 120 youth leaders who were invited to meet, at their own expense, in Sharon, Connecticut

---

1. Schneider: *Cadres for Conservatism*, p. 32.
2. Interview with Douglas Caddy, Houston, Texas, December 10, 2007.
3. Copy of letter dated August 16, 1960 and addressed to William J. Madden, Jr. in author's possession. For various reasons Noble, Stanley, and Regnery were unable to attend the eventual conference. Both Noble and Stanley subsequently served on the YAF National Board of Directors.

on September 10 and 11, 1960. Clearly stressed was the fact that this would be at the family home of William F. Buckley, Jr., already well known as a leader of American conservatives. The letter began:

> America stands at the crossroads today. Will our Nation continue to follow the path towards socialism or will we turn towards Conservatism and freedom? The final answer to this question lies with America's youth. Will our youth be more conservative or more liberal in future years? You can help determine the answer to this question.[4]

While recognition was made of the efforts of the Intercollegiate Society of Individualists in promoting a conservative intellectual revival on campus, the Interim Committee saw the need for a complementary political action movement for young conservatives. As the letter concluded, "The Sharon Conference can be of historic importance . . . You can be an integral part in setting the initial stages of this great movement." To enforce the connection with the effort in Chicago, printed at the bottom of the letterhead was a quote from Senator Barry Goldwater: "the preponderant judgment of the American people, especially of the young people, is that the radical, or Liberal, approach has not worked and is not working. They yearn for a return to Conservative principles." Those planning on attending were asked to respond so that additional details could be provided in advance of the meeting.

Two weeks later a memorandum was sent to the expected attendees along with a tentative agenda. In the preliminary materials, the gathering was labeled "Great Elm Conference" but it would soon become known as the Sharon Conference after the name of the Connecticut town where it was held. Events began with a hospitality hour on Friday night at the Buckley family home, with remarks by former Governor Charles Edison. On Saturday morning temporary committees were appointed and Brent Bozell spoke on "Why a Conservative Political Youth Organization Is Needed." Panel discussions were held throughout the day and at lunch the speaker was Victor Milione, President of the Intercollegiate Society of Individualists (ISI).[5]

The participation of Victor Milione from ISI was most significant as these young conservatives discussed the formation of another organization. As the initial letter of invitation made clear, this new venture was to be distinct yet in harmony with the purposes of ISI. Historian Niels Bjerre-Poulsen stresses this very point in outlining the founding of Young Americans for Freedom,

> YAF was not intended as a rival to the Intercollegiate Society of Individualists (ISI). Its purpose was rather complementary. While ISI's stated goal was a conservative intellectual awakening on the campus, YAF was almost solely designated for political action by implementing and coordinating the activities of conservative youth groups.[6]

For those who missed the synergy, one only had to remember that the new organization was coming into being at the family home of the initial president of ISI. Nevertheless, while YAF was to be a politically active organization, it did include a

---

4. Copy of letter addressed to Robert Croll in author's possession.

5. Memorandum from Douglas Caddy dated August 30, 1960. Personal papers of William F. Buckley, Jr., Box 12, Sterling Library, Yale University, New Haven, CT.

6. Niels Bjerre-Paulsen, "Organizing the American Right, 1945–64," doctoral dissertation, University of California—Santa Barbara, 1993, p. 284.

strong intellectual component whose members could clearly identify themselves with the various schools of thought under the conservative umbrella.[7] As historian Seth Offenbach observed, YAF's emphasis on political action, however, played a crucial role in the ". . . transformation of the conservative movement from one of intellectuals to a politically active movement. In the 1960s, YAF became the foot soldiers for Bill Buckley and Barry Goldwater's politically active philosophies."[8] No longer would conservatives view themselves as solely "the Remnant" standing outside and decrying the trends and tendencies in society and government. Now they would be taking direct action to influence and redirect American society.

Creating a New Organization

On September 9, 1960, nearly one hundred young conservatives from forty-four colleges met at the Buckley home for what would be an historic development in the creation of a conservative movement.[9] While the opening remarks on Friday night came from Charles Edison, the remainder of the weekend was under the direction of the young conservatives, with more senior conservatives present but mainly as observers. Historian Matthew Dallek stresses this point in his commentary on the meetings.

> It was the young who made the decisions and shaped the group. The meeting at Buckley's home in Sharon, Connecticut illustrates the point. Although Buckley, Liebman, and several other prominent conservatives over the age of thirty attended the conference at Buckley's estate, the ninety young conservative leaders from forty-four colleges in twenty-four states wrote the mission statement, took care of the logistics, and decided on a name for their organization.[10]

Clearly there was support from more senior conservatives, such as the then thirty-four year old Brent Bozell, thirty-five year old Buckley, thirty-six year old Vic Milione, and thirty-seven year old William A. Rusher. But it was those in their twenties and even teens who were to make the important decisions.[11]

---

7. Daniel McCarthy, "GOP and Man at Yale," *The American Conservative*, November 6, 2006, makes this point and also stresses that YAF was to be distinct from partisan youth organizations that would include supporters of liberal Republicans such as then-Governor Nelson Rockefeller.

8. Seth Offenbach, "Power of Portrayal: the Media and the Young Americans for Freedom: 1960–1968," unpublished paper presented at the Journal of Policy History Conference, Charlottesville, VA, June 4, 2006, p. 9.

9. For a first hand account of the events in Sharon, see M. Stanton Evans: *Revolt on the Campus*, pp. 108–124 and Lee and Anne Edwards: *You Can Make The Difference* (New Rochelle, NY: Arlington House, 1968), pp. 283–288. Another valuable source for this founding conference is John A. Andrew: *The Other Side of the Sixties*, pp. 53–74. There is some uncertainty as to who and how many attended the conference as the available list may be of those who agreed to attend, not necessarily those who were actually present. A list labeled "Attendees Sharon Conference, Sharon, Conn (Sept. 10–11, 1960)" contains 97 names and addresses and is found in Personal Papers of William F. Buckley, Jr., Box 12, Yale University, New Haven, CT. This printed list includes two "senior" conservatives, Milione and Rusher, and excludes Jameson Campaigne, Jr., a student at Williams College.

10. Matthew Dallek, "Young Americans for Freedom: The Rise of Modern Conservatism, 1960–1964," Columbia University, Master's Thesis, 1993, pp. 6–7.

11. While it would be a few years later when Jerry Rubin would advise young people to never trust anyone over thirty, it appears these conservatives were prematurely following his advice in the creation of their new organization.

This was a memorable occasion for many of those who attended the event. Bruce McAllister recently remembered that experience.

> In the fall of 1960, about to enter my second year at Harvard Law School, I received one of the most thrilling invitations of my life—to participate in the founding of the Young Americans for Freedom (the "YAF" of blessed memory) in Sharon, Connecticut at the home of my hero, William F. Buckley, Jr. . . . And I recall meeting my hero in the flesh as I rounded a corner in his home. When I offered that my mother was a Buckley (her father was a subway conductor from the Bronx), he said: "Oh, one of the Texas Buckleys?" and I blurted: "No, one of the Harlem Buckleys." He shot me that trademark grin, and strode on.[12]

Just who were these people making the decisions on the creation of a new conservative youth organization? Not counting those "senior" conservatives in their thirties mentioned above, seventy-eight were college students, undergraduate or graduate, and an additional eighteen listed no affiliation with an academic institution, nearly all having previously graduated from college. At a time when the vast majority of high school graduates were not yet enrolling in America's colleges, this was a relatively elite group. Nearly twenty-five percent (18) of those affiliated with a college were from the Ivy League, with Yale producing eight undergraduates and law school students. Twenty-two students attended what could be best labeled as private, selective enrollment institutions, with Northwestern University represented by five students. Twelve participants came from major state universities, led by a contingent of four from the University of Minnesota. Twenty-two students attended religiously affiliated colleges or universities, predominantly Roman Catholic, with Fordham University providing four students. Finally, four students, including two from Hunter College, attended other government colleges.

As in most political gatherings of the time, males predominated among the ninety-six young participants. However, the ratio was not quite as overwhelming as one might expect, with sixteen females and eighty males among the attendees. Of the eighteen without a college affiliation, some were recent graduates like Carol Dawson and Doug Caddy, while others, such as Lee Edwards and Stan Evans, had recently begun successful careers. The oldest of the ninety-six was Edwards, soon to turn the ripe age of twenty-eight.

While there was not unanimity on all points, there was agreement among the vast majority present on the need for creating a new organization. Yet, what it would be called, who would be eligible to join, and what would be its guiding principles remained to be decided. Bill Madden of Holy Cross College ended up presiding over the business sessions. As he recalled,

> I was not originally penciled in as the chairman—only as the parliamentarian. Carol Dawson was supposed to be the chairman but after some of our well trained YR participants raised one point of order too many during the opening session, Carol handed the gavel to me and wished me luck. Things calmed down and they let me preside for the duration of the conference.[13]

---

12. 2008 YAF Alumni Survey Responses: Bruce McAllister.
13. Letter to the author from William Madden dated November 7, 2008.

A lively discussion took place as to a name for the new organization. Some present wanted to continue use of the conservative label by clearly calling it "Young Conservatives of America." Still others, including David Franke and Lee Edwards, wanted a more inclusive name that would allow the participation of libertarians and anti-communists who did not associate themselves with the conservative label. Moreover, Franke argued that they should not cede the term "freedom" to the left.[14] The debate included considerations also as to how broadly representative of the Right the new organization would be. Douglas Caddy believed that the group should try to be inclusive and bring people in while some of the others in attendance wanted to exclude those who held somewhat differing perspectives.[15] In the end, in a close vote of 44 to 40, the name "Young Americans for Freedom" was chosen.[16]

The second dispute that required a vote of those present concerned the maximum age for membership. Some argued that no one over twenty-seven should be eligible to join, a limit that would have soon excluded a few of those participating. But the prevailing sentiment was that the organization should be more inclusive and, in another close vote the limit was set at thirty-five.[17] Now that a name was chosen and an age limit was set, Bill Rusher made note of the personal significance of these two votes.

> I remember not liking the acronym much—and liking it even less when Liebman, possessor of one of the world's most mordant wits, became the first to point out that this made the rest of us Old Americans for Freedom, or OAFs.[18]

What remained for the founders of the new organization was to adopt a statement of principles, a brief and concise document that would summarize the philosophical and ideological position of Young Americans for Freedom. Recently appointed as editor of *The Indianapolis News* yet still only twenty-six years of age, M. Stanton Evans had been given the assignment to draft a possible statement. He did so on his way to the conference and then at Sharon was assisted by Carol Dawson and David Franke in finalizing a document to be presented to those in attendance. The statement began by speaking of the current challenge facing society and the need for young people to take action: "In this time of moral and political crisis, it is the responsibility of the youth of America to affirm certain eternal truths."[19]

There was general agreement on most points in the draft statement, including that political freedom cannot long exist without economic freedom; that government's purpose is to preserve internal order, provide for defense of the nation,

14. 2008 YAF Alumni Survey Responses: Lee Edwards; Andrew: *The Other Side of the Sixties*, p. 36.
15. Interview with Douglas Caddy, Houston, Texas, December 10, 2007.
16. Lee Edwards: *You Can Make the Difference*, p. 286.
17. Rick Perlstein: *Before the Storm*, p. 106.
18. William A. Rusher: *The Rise of the Right* (New York: National Review Books, 1993), p. 63.
19. Personal papers of William F. Buckley, Jr., Box 12, Sterling Library, Yale University. The complete "Sharon Statement" is reprinted later in the present work. As testimony to the continued importance of the Sharon Statement, it has been credited with helping launch and define the conservative movement in America. Fifty years after its adoption a group of conservative leaders led by former Attorney General Edwin Meese issued an updated document labeled the Mount Vernon Statement to address 21st century concerns, modeling it after the Sharon Statement. Ralph Z. Hallow: "Conservative manifesto makes bid to reunify," *Washington Times*, February 15, 2010; Jerry Markon, "Notable conservative leaders craft manifesto to energize, coordinate supporters," *Washington Post*, February 16, 2010.

and administer justice; that the Constitution is the best document designed to ensure a balance between empowering and limiting government; that the market economy both maximizes individual freedom and most effectively produces goods. Those present agreed also on a strong assertion of national interest in foreign policy and recognition of the fundamental threat to freedom from communism:

> That we will be free only so long as the national sovereignty of the United States is secure; that history shows periods of freedom are rare, and can exist only when free citizens concertedly defend their rights against all enemies;
>
> That the forces of international Communism are, at present, the greatest single threat to these liberties;
>
> That the United States should stress victory over, rather than coexistence with, this menace; and
>
> That American foreign policy must be judged by this criterion: does it serve the just interests of the United States?[20]

Three points in the statement occasioned debate and discussion. Some objected to language strongly supporting states' rights. Still others believed the statement too effusive in its support of the free market. But the more significant division occurred over the reference to the Creator when the statement referred to "the individual's use of his God-given free will." As Bill Buckley noted later, "Would the Young Americans acknowledge God, so to speak, by name? That required a vote, and orthodoxy won out."[21] It was a close vote according to some of those who attended, testifying to the broad range of individuals participating in the conference. Religious questions or what are now referred to as "social issues" were not of major concern to the organization and Young Americans for Freedom remained through its first twenty-five years as basically a secular organization.[22]

Writing about the document some ten years later, its main author Stan Evans explained the reason behind the inclusiveness of the Sharon Statement: "In broad terms, the statement was meant to embrace both the 'traditionalist' and 'libertarian' schools within the conservative community . . . The statement assumes these emphases are inter-dependent and that it is impossible to have one without the other."[23] Clearly, the third element in the composition of modern conservatism, a strong anti-communism, was also present in the statement. As Matthew Dallek noted, "anti-statism, economic laissez-faire, and militant anti-communism—three of the ideological pillars that would support a resurgence of conservatism in American life—had been articulated by YAF on September 11, 1960."[24] Years later, William A. Rusher reflected back on the document adopted by these young conservatives and concluded that: "nowhere else, for many years, did anyone attempt so succinctly and comprehensively, let alone so successfully, to describe what modern American conservatism was all about."[25]

---

20. *Ibid.*
21. *Flying High*, p. 25.
22. Schneider: *Cadres for Conservatism*, pp. 33–34 discusses the vote on including reference to God in the Sharon Statement. According to Perlstein, the vote was 44–40; *Before the Storm*, p. 106.
23. M. Stanton Evans, "Reflections of the Sharon Statement," *New Guard*, September 1970, p. 9.
24. Dallek, "Young Americans for Freedom: The Rise of Modern Conservatism, 1960–1964," p. 8.
25. Rusher: *The Rise of the Right*, p. 63. The Sharon Statement has been reprinted in numerous works on 20th century conservatism, including both the Andrew and Schneider histories on Young Americans for Freedom as well as in Richard A. Viguerie: *Conservatism Betrayed* (Los Angeles: Bonus Books, 2006), pp. 227–228 and Gregory L. Schneider, ed.: *Conservatism in America since 1930* (New York: New York

Now it was time for organizational matters. For Bruce McAllister,

I recall as yesterday the ease with which all 90 of us reviewed a draft of our Sharon Statement, and approved its simple and conservative prescriptions for U.S. policy—and then the longer wrangling over YAF's Constitution, proving what we already knew—that designing the machinery of government is more difficult than divining a philosophy of government.[26]

Robert Schuchman of Yale Law School was selected to be the first National Chairman of the organization. Schuchman effectively represented the new organization until its first national convention two years later. Tragically, in 1966 at the age of 27, Schuchman died of a cerebral hemorrhage. He had graduated from Queens College with honors, received his law degree from Yale and, at the time of his death, held a research fellowship in law and economics at the University of Chicago Law School. Schuchman was a member of Phi Beta Kappa, the Mont Pelerin Society (an international association of libertarian and conservative intellectuals founded by F.A. Hayek) and The Philadelphia Society (an American society of conservative intellectuals). Schuchman's death was a tremendous loss to the conservative movement and was certainly felt by the organization that devoted three pages of its monthly magazine to a series of tributes by his friends and associates.[27]

Douglas Caddy was appointed National Director with responsibility for the day-to-day operations of the new entity. Six regional chairmen were named, five of whom had backgrounds in the College Young Republicans: Robert Harley from Georgetown University (Chairman of the D.C. College Young Republicans); George Gaines, Tulane University (Chairman of Louisiana Youth for Nixon); Richard Noble of Stanford University (Treasurer of the California Young Republicans); Robert Croll from Northwestern University (Illinois College Young Republicans Chairman); and James Kolbe, also of Northwestern University (Chairman of Arizona Youth for Goldwater). The sixth regional director was Walter McLaughlin, Jr. of Harvard Law School.

Thirteen others were selected for the National Board representing various areas of the country, eleven of whom were undergraduate or graduate students: James Abstine (Indiana University); Tom Colvin (Davidson College); Richard Cowan (Yale University); David Franke (New School for Social Research); Herbert Kohler (Knox College); William Madden (Holy Cross College); Carl T. McIntire (Shelton College); Diarmuid O'Scannlain (Harvard Law School); Howard Phillips (Harvard College); William Schulz (Antioch College); and Scott Stanley, Jr. (University of Kansas Law School). Rounding out the Board of Directors were Carol Dawson, a recent graduate of Dunbarton College and Executive Secretary of College Youth for Nixon, and Lee Edwards, press aide to Senator John Marshall Butler of Maryland. These twenty-one individuals were charged with the responsibility of bringing into reality the aspirations of the group that had assembled at Great Elm.[28]

University Press, 2003), pp. 229–230. Five years later, the volunteer organization California Republican Assembly adopted the Sharon Statement as its statement of principles when it came under conservative control. Lisa McGirr: *Suburban Warriors* (Princeton, NJ: Princeton University Press, 2001), pp. 129–130.

26. 2008 YAF Alumni Survey Responses: Bruce McAllister.

27. See: "Robert Schuchman—As His Friends Remember Him," *New Guard*, April 1966, pp. 7–9.

28. News Release, September 12, 1960, "National Conservative Youth Group organized, Delegates

As the weekend came to an end, the young people in attendance had put in place an organization to accomplish a number of objectives. Clearly they had formed an organization by and for young conservatives. After some discussion and disagreements, they had articulated their own positions in the Sharon Statement. By this statement and by their organizational efforts they were prepared to take a radical stand and challenge what they perceived as the liberal establishment in control of America. They were committed to training a new cadre of conservative leaders, leaders who were not content to view themselves as permanent outsiders in American society. To this end, they were dedicated to political action designed to bring about conservative victories. It was not enough to discuss and debate philosophical and ideological principles. They would put their beliefs into concrete action to produce change in America. As John Andrew summed it up: "Theirs was an ideological and philosophical radicalism. Whatever their opposition to the prevailing political system, they retained a firm conviction that the system would respond if only they could seize power."[29] Seeking and seizing political power would be one of the major objectives of the new organization.

Bill Buckley gave the closing speech on Sunday afternoon, commending the participants on what they had accomplished and the path that they had set for themselves. He was impressed with their desire to turn their beliefs into action. As he commented in the next issue of *National Review*,

> A new organization was born last week and just possibly it will influence the political future of this country, as why should it not, considering that its membership is young, intelligent, articulate and determined, its principles enduring, its aim to translate these principles into political action in a world which has lost its moorings and is looking about for them desperately? . . . But what is so striking in the students who met at Sharon is their appetite for power.
>
> Ten years ago the struggle seemed so long, so endless, even, that we did not dream of victory . . . It is quixotic to say that they or their elders have seized the reins of history. But the difference in psychological attitude is tremendous. They talk about affecting history; we have talked about educating people to want to affect history.[30]

Leaving Sharon, the young conservatives were excited to take on the new challenge and build a national organization of college students and young adults. Carol Dawson recalled, "We felt like pioneers. It was challenging . . . it was . . . a thrill to travel up there and be among those people."[31] Years later, writer Rick Perlstein attempted to describe the feelings of many who attended the founding meeting.

For young conservatives who had discovered their idiosyncratic political

---

from 44 Campuses Plan Political Action Program," Personal Papers of William F. Buckley, Jr., Box 12, Sterling Library, Yale University, New Haven, CT. McLaughlin would resign shortly after the meeting and by the time of an October 6th release to college newspapers, Cowan was Regional Chairman for the Northeast. News Release, October 6, 1960, "National Conservative Youth Organization Formed," Personal Papers of William J. Madden (copy in author's possession).

29. *The Other Side of the Sixties*, p. 6.

30. *National Review*, September 24, 1960. The editorial also is reprinted in Gregory L. Schneider, editor: *Conservatism in America Since 1930*, pp. 226–228.

31. Rebecca Klatch: *A Generation Divided*, p. 20.

faith from *National Review*, from ISI and Foundation for Economic Education pamphlets, from Human Events, who were ridiculed whenever they spoke up in class about the spiritual crisis for the West and against "peaceful coexistence" with a slave empire—for many of them, for the very first time they felt like they were not alone.[32]

They had formed a permanent structure; now the real work began to build YAF into an organization.

Going back to New York City and his work at McGraw-Edison, Doug Caddy vowed to make Young Americans for Freedom into a force for conservatism on campuses across the nation. His first task on Monday morning was to issue a news release labeled "National Conservative Youth Group Organized—Delegates from 44 Campuses Plan Political Action Program."[33] The framework had been established and the leadership selected. Now the organization needed to gain acceptance both in the media and from other conservatives. It would have to attract members and establish local chapters.

While the media might be slow to recognize the significance of the events in Sharon, other conservatives were encouraged. According to historian Matthew Dallek,

> Well before YAFers made their presence felt electorally, they gave the conservative movement a psychological boost not felt since the founding of *National Review* in 1955. The very appearance of YAF—the first conservative youth group devoted to political action—invigorated the larger movement.[34]

Writing in 1980 on the significance of Young Americans for Freedom, James Roberts commented, "the founding of YAF was, in retrospect, probably the most important organizational initiative undertaken by conservatives in the last thirty years."[35] For the first time, an activist group of young conservatives could organize across the country in a permanent framework. Furthermore, Young Americans for Freedom could provide a training ground in political action, public relations, and educational methods. Over the next thirty-some years, Young Americans for Freedom would play an important role in the development of a leadership cadre and become an essential part of the conservative movement that helped produce the election of Ronald Reagan as President in 1980.

The Founding Fathers and Daughters of YAF

As an organization committed to developing leaders, it is informative to review what became of these ninety plus individuals who created Young Americans for Freedom on that September weekend in 1960. Tragically, a few had their careers end early in life. Not only was Robert Schuchman to die in his twenties, but a fellow Yale Law School alumnus, Robert M. Hurt, would meet the same fate. Along with Schuchman, Hurt was one of the early advocates of the interaction between

32. Perlstein: *Before the Storm*, p. 105.
33. Personal Papers of William F. Buckley, Jr., Box 12, Sterling Library, Yale University, New Haven, CT.
34. Dallek, "Young Americans for Freedom: The Rise of Modern Conservatism, 1960–1964," p. 38.
35. Roberts: *The Conservative Decade* (Westport, CT: Arlington House, 1980), p. 25.

law and economics, having left Yale to undertake graduate work in economics at the University of Chicago. As Milton Friedman observed about Hurt, "His professional career had just begun, its promise foreshadowed by his early work, and reinforced for those of us who were fortunate enough to know him by his personal qualities."[36] Within one year of Hurt's death, Schuchman would also be gone as two young academic lights were removed from the emerging conservative movement.

As would be expected in a political organization, many of the original founders went on to law school and became attorneys, some joining the ranks of the nation's leading law firms while others started their own successful firms. After graduating from the University of Michigan Law School, William Madden built a career as a lead attorney at Winston & Strawn in Washington, DC. Madden remained active in YAF while in law school and later served on the Virginia Republican State Central Committee. The contacts he made in YAF led to some lasting friendships and a lifetime commitment to conservative principles.[37]

Peter Kilcullen was lead partner at Kilcullen, Wilson & Kilcullen, in Washington, DC and Clayton Thomas and George Decas established successful practices in Philadelphia while Frank Grazioso graduated from Yale, received his law degree from the University of Chicago, and then returned to New Haven where he co-founded the law firm of Grazioso & Hosen.[38] Bruce Shine co-founded the law firm of Shine & Mason in Kingsport, Tennessee while Stephen Slepin is a partner in Slepin & Slepin of Tallahassee, Florida

Robert Harley, who had been one of the original regional directors of YAF while an undergraduate at Georgetown, went on to receive his law degree from Columbia and spent most of his career as partner at Harley & Browne where baseball great Elston Howard was among his many clients. His time in YAF was viewed as "educating me in the ways of volunteer organizations and preparing me for a lifetime of activity in such organizations. I have been active in civic, professional, church and charitable organizations my entire life."[39]

Keith Simons has been an attorney in Minneapolis for forty years during which time he was active with supporting refugees, pro-life and mission work. As he recalled, "1960 was quite a year for young conservatives with supporting Barry at the Chicago Republican Convention and organizing YAF." Simons remained active in Young Americans for Freedom and was Minnesota YAF State Treasurer from 1963–64. While his involvement gave him a vehicle for expressing his conservative views, YAF provided a more personal contribution to his future life. "My wife Cynthia and I met socially through YAF in 1964. She had been Minnesota YAF State Secretary. We are both compatibly strongly opinionated!"[40] The Simons were not the first, and certainly would not be the last, couple to have met through their involvement in Young Americans for Freedom.

Richard Plechner, who had been a leader in Young Republicans during the 1960s as well as on the YAF National Board, is a former New Jersey State Judge who practices law in Metuchen, New Jersey. Walter McLaughlin, now living in Washington State, is another Sharon attendee whose career included a successful

---

36. *The American Economic Review*, volume 56, issue 1–2 (March 1966), p. 421.
37. 2008 YAF Alumni Survey Responses: William J. Madden, Jr.
38. 2008 YAF Alumni Survey Responses: Frank Grazioso.
39. 2008 YAF Alumni Survey Responses: Robert G. Harley.
40. 2008 YAF Alumni Survey Responses: Keith E. Simons.

law practice but the attorney with the most interesting list of former clients has to be Douglas Caddy. Over the past thirty-five years he has represented E. Howard Hunt (at the beginning of the Watergate matter), Billie Sol Estes (who claimed to have information on the assassination of President Kennedy), and more recently Jack Worthington (who claims to be the illegitimate son of John F. Kennedy).[41] Currently, Caddy practices law in Houston and is also the author of five books.

Still others went into government. James Kolbe returned to his native Arizona where he served in the state senate for six years and then was elected to Congress in 1984. Kolbe served for twenty-two years, the only Republican ever elected to Congress from southern Arizona, and was a member of the House Appropriations Committee for much of his time in Congress.[42] Paul Niemeyer was appointed by President Ronald Reagan and continues to serve on the 4th Circuit Court of Appeals. Niemeyer, who served briefly as Ohio YAF Chairman in the early 1960s, is one of eight former YAF members now serving on United States Circuit Courts of Appeal.[43]

Bruce McAllister was a candidate for New York City Council on the Conservative Party ticket headed by Bill Buckley in 1965 and later was New York County Conservative Party Chairman. A decade later he had become active in the presidential campaign of Jimmy Carter and served as Deputy Assistant Secretary of Commerce for Maritime Affairs. McAllister is currently an Adjunct Professor of Law at Nova Southeastern University and an attorney with the firm of Alley, Maass, Rogers & Lindsay in Palm Beach, Florida.[44]

Michael Uhlmann was Special Assistant to the President from 1981–1985 and is currently visiting professor of government at Claremont Graduate University and Claremont McKenna College. John Weicher briefly served as Illinois YAF State Chairman and on the National Board of Directors while a graduate student at the University of Chicago, from which he received a PhD in Economics. He was Assistant Secretary of the Department of Housing & Urban Development (HUD) and Federal Housing Commissioner from 2001–2005. He is currently a Senior Fellow and Director of the Center for Housing and Financial Markets at the Hudson Institute.[45]

Howard Phillips went on to serve the Nixon Administration as Director of the then Office of Economic Opportunity and subsequently founded The Conservative Caucus, an organization that he heads today. In 1992, he helped form what is now known as the Constitution Party and was its candidate for President of the United States in 1992, 1996 and 2000.

Carol Dawson served for nine years as a Commissioner of the Consumer Product Safety Commission from 1984–1993. Dawson had served as Executive Secretary of College Students for Nixon during the 1960 campaign. Dawson served on the original YAF National Board and as Managing Editor from 1961–1963 and then Editor for 1964–1965 of *New Guard*, the magazine of Young Americans for

---

41. David Friend, "The Man Who Would Be Jack," *Vanity Fair*, April 2008; Interview with Douglas Caddy, Houston, Texas, December 10, 2007.
42. Kolbe is one of twenty-six YAF alumni to have served in the United States Congress as of 2009.
43. A ninth, Peter Keisler, was named by President George W. Bush to serve on the U.S. Circuit Court for the Federal District but his nomination was not considered by the Democratic-majority Senate in 2008. Keisler was chairman of the Yale YAF chapter in the early 1980s.
44. 2008 YAF Alumni Survey Responses: Bruce McAllister, Jr.
45. 2008 YAF Alumni Survey Responses: John C. Weicher.

Freedom.[46] She was Director of Communications for the American Conservative Union in the mid-60s and subsequently on the staff of Secretary of Energy Donald Hodel during the Reagan Administration prior to her appointment to the Consumer Product Safety Commission.

Not all those who were politically active settled in the Nation's Capital. Haywood Hillyer, III had a successful legal career in New Orleans and served for several years as the Republican National Committeeman from Louisiana. Dick Jorandby later established an outstanding career as an attorney in Palm Beach County, Florida where he was elected for several terms as the Public Defender for the county. As one former associate noted, "Dick Jorandby was a bedrock conservative Republican. His office was filled with photos of Ronald Reagan and Richard Nixon, and he quoted the gospel according to Barry Goldwater."[47] At the same time, Jorandby was known nationally as one of the strongest opponents of the death penalty. Joseph Leo served for several years as a City Manager in New Jersey and also was active in Garden State politics. Jack Molesworth was a nationally known philatelist from Boston, where he served on the Republican State Committee and ran for Congress in 1964.

It is not surprising that many of the founders of a conservative organization would eventually enter the business world. George M.C. Dole had a successful career as an investment banker in New York City as did Arthur Bingham. Peter Wheeler Reiss graduated from Marquette University and undertook a successful career with a number of business ventures. At the present he is president of the Arcadia Water Company in Scottsdale, Arizona.

Thomas E. Reilly, Jr. graduated from Stanford and received an M.B.A. from Harvard Business School. He went on to become Chairman of the Board for Reilly Industries, a position from which he recently retired. Currently on the Board of Trustees of Indiana University, Reilly served on numerous corporate boards as well as two terms as a Trustee of the Philadelphia Society of conservative intellectuals and academics.[48]

After serving on the YAF National Board and on the staff, Herbert Kohler joined his family's firm, Kohler Industries, where he is currently Chairman of the Board. Bruce Whalen has been Vice President of Navistar International Truck & Engine for several years. J. Alan MacKay, who would later serve as National Chairman of YAF, was for many years General Counsel for the Cabot Corporation.

One of those invited to Sharon but not able to attend was John Greenagel of the University of Minnesota. Greenagel is one of the individuals who was active before the Sharon Conference. He recently recalled the early days of conservative youth politics.

> My involvement began with the 1960 Republican National Convention in Chicago. I had joined the Youth for Goldwater for Vice President organization launched by Bob Croll and decided to make the trip to Chicago to lend a hand wherever I could. I was 19 at the time and had only a few dollars in my pocket. A buddy and I made the trip by car from Minneapolis.

---

46. Founded in March 1961 as *The New Guard*, the magazine dropped "The" in 1970 and is referred to throughout this work simply as *New Guard*.

47. Michael Mello: *Deathwork: Defending the Condemned* (Minneapolis: University of Minnesota Press, 2002), p. 55.

48. 2008 YAF Alumni Survey Responses: Thomas E. Reilly, Jr.

At the Goldwater for VP headquarters I was fortunate to meet quite a few of early leaders of the conservative revival movement: Brent Bozell, Marvin Liebman, Doug Caddy, Bob Croll, and of course, Senator Goldwater and William F. Buckley, Jr.[49]

Greenagel went on to serve as the first Minnesota State Chairman of Young Americans for Freedom and remained active through the Goldwater campaign. After moving to California, he was involved in the Reagan gubernatorial and presidential campaigns.

For Greenagel, his participation in YAF showed him that he was not alone as a conservative on campus. "Conservatives were rather scarce at the University of Minnesota. The faculty was extremely liberal and many of our professors were openly hostile to conservative students."[50] Greenagel built a career working with several chambers of commerce before serving eighteen years with Advanced Micro Devices (AMD) where he was Director of Corporate Communications. He is now Director of Communications for the Semiconductor Industry Association.

Several of those present at Sharon went on to careers in journalism or publishing. John Kolbe was publisher of the *Phoenix Gazette* for many years while Ross MacKenzie recently retired as editorial page editor of the *Richmond Times Dispatch*. Bill Schulz had a successful career as an editor at *Reader's Digest* while Annette Courtemanche became Mrs. Russell Kirk and assisted her husband on his many published works. Ken Thompson was a member of the YAF National Board in the early 60s and subsequently had a distinguished career as editorial page editor at the *Dallas Morning News*. Antoni Gollan was on the staff at *National Review* and served briefly as acting editor of *New Guard* in 1963 before undertaking a career in journalism.

As previously noted, Stan Evans was editor of the *Indianapolis News* from 1960 to 1974 and then went on to serve as a syndicated columnist from 1973 to 1985 and later as a commentator in the 1990s for National Public Radio. Evans served as Chairman of the American Conservative Union from 1971 to 1977 and founded the National Journalism Center in Washington, DC. He is the author of numerous books, the most recent being a re-evaluation of the work of Senator Joseph McCarthy.[51] After attending the Sharon Conference, Jameson Campaigne served twelve years on the YAF Board of Directors from 1963 to 1975 and in 1976 formed his own publishing company, Jameson Books, which he continues to operate today. Campaigne has been a Director of the American Conservative Union for several years and served multiple terms as a Trustee of the Philadelphia Society.

David Franke, who with Doug Caddy had founded the Student Committee for the Loyalty Oath, has had a varied career in journalism and publishing. After serving on the staff of *Human Events* and then *National Review*, Franke was editor of *New Guard* from 1965 to 1967, a position he left to become Senior Editor at Arlington House publishers. He is the author or co-author of ten books and

---

49. 2008 YAF Alumni Survey Responses: John Philip Greenagel.
50. *Ibid.*
51. M. Stanton Evans: *Blacklisted by History: The Untold Story of Senator Joe McCarthy and His Fight Against America's Enemies* (New York: Crown Forum, 2007). Evans's extensive catalog of authored works began with *Rebels with a Cause* in 1961, a work that provides a valuable insider's view on the development of the conservative movement in the late 1950s and early 1960s. Among his other works are *The Liberal Establishment* (1965), *The Politics of Surrender* (1966), *The Future of Conservatism* (1968), *Clear and Present Dangers* (1975), and *The Theme Is Freedom* (1996).

is currently editorial director of the New Media News Corporation in Virginia. Another participant in the Sharon meeting was Allan Ryskind who has had a distinguished career with conservative publications. For many years, Ryskind and his partners, Tom Winter and Bob Kephart, owned *Human Events*, where he served as editor. After its sale to Eagle Publishing, Ryskind now holds the position as editor-at-large. In the early years, Ryskind was a contributing editor to *New Guard*, as was his wife, J'Aime Adams.

It is not always easy to describe individuals under a single category and Don Lipsett is a good example of the problem. Lipsett, who died in 1995, had a career that included publishing, business, academia and conservative activism. In the early 1960s, he worked for *National Review* and *The Freeman*, publication of the Foundation for Economic Education, and then for the Intercollegiate Society of Individualists. From the last position he moved on to assignments with Hillsdale College and the Heritage Foundation. Perhaps Lipsett's greatest contribution to the conservative movement was his establishment of The Philadelphia Society in 1964 as a forum for conservative intellectuals and public policy advocates. Lipsett served as Permanent Secretary of the society from 1964 until his death in 1995.[52]

Likewise, David Bontrager could be included among those who had a successful political life, spent a career in business, and also was an academic. A graduate of Hanover College with a master's degree from Ball State University, Bontrager served for thirty-six years as a human resources director. He served three years on the Elkhart, Indiana City Council and then was elected as a County Commissioner in the 1970s. While accomplishing all this, he has been an Adjunct Professor of Business at Goshen College, off and on, since 1972. Speaking of his time at the founding meeting in Sharon, Bontrager recalled, "I enjoyed the experience greatly. I have a memory of feeling like somebody sat on my head after each session, especially if William F. Buckley spoke . . . What a house! This kid from the sticks had never seen anything like it." He went on to note that his involvement in YAF "helped me solidify my political beliefs and provide the logic to support them."[53]

Somewhat surprisingly, nine of the founders spent their careers in academia, in addition to those cited above who, at one time or another, taught on college campuses. David Stuhr is Associate Vice President and Associate Professor of Finance at Fordham University, where he has taught since 1977. Stuhr graduated from Yale with a degree in Metallurgy but changed directions and obtained a PhD in Economics, Finance & Statistics from New York University. Many years later Stuhr still remembered "the organizational exhilaration of the Sharon Conference and the aftermath as chapters and state organizations were started . . . It was pretty heady times."[54] Like several other Sharon attendees, Stuhr has also served as a Trustee of the Philadelphia Society.

Robert Schuettinger received his PhD at Oxford University where he studied with Sir Isaiah Berlin. He is President of the Oxford Study Abroad Program and has taught at Yale, Oxford, and the Kennedy School of Government at Harvard University. Schuettinger has authored or co-authored nineteen books and also served as a Trustee of the Philadelphia Society. Until their recent deaths, Regis Courtemanche was Professor of British History at Long Island University, Robert

---

52. Remembrances of the contributions of Don Lipsett include William F. Buckley, Jr., "Don Lipsett, RIP," *National Review*, November 22, 1995 and John Von Kannon, "In Memoriam: Don Lipsett, an Unsung Midwesterner," *American Spectator*, January 1996.
53. 2008 YAF Alumni Survey Responses: David A. Bontrager.
54. 2008 YAF Alumni Survey Responses: David Stuhr.

Croll was Professor of Business at Central Michigan University and Dennis Brennen was an Economics faculty member for several years at Harper College.

Jeanette Doronzo went on to obtain a PhD in Classical Literature and has taught at a number of institutions while Paul Jankiewicz was a guidance counselor for many years and now serves as vice president of Human Resources Counseling. For several years Edward Facey was a faculty member at Hillsdale College, one of the most clearly conservative institutions in America. Now retired, Facey continues to live in Hillsdale, Michigan. Carl Thomas McIntire served on the initial YAF Board of Directors and since 1982 has had a joint appointment as Professor of Religion and History at the University of Toronto.

Daniel Harden was a Professor of Education at Washburn University who retired in 2009 and has been active in Kansas politics. Dr. Harden recently noted that "attending the Sharon Conference was a major event in my life" and his involvement in YAF "provided an outlet for my anti-communist energy. It, together with ISI, helped form a solid foundation for the conservative/libertarian position that I would retain throughout my life."[55]

Carol Sue (Nevin) Abromaitis graduated from the College of Notre Dame and went on to receive her PhD in English from the University of Maryland. She has been a Professor of English at Loyola College in Baltimore for several years and has been involved in various religious boards and conferences. For this young college graduate, "Sharon was one of the high points of my early years." Abromaitis believes that her involvement in YAF "sharpened my already-formed convictions. Being one of the signatories of the Sharon Statement and hearing Bozell, Buckley and Milione was an inspiration."[56]

Then there is Lee Edwards who, when he attended the Sharon Conference, was employed by United States Senator John Marshall Butler. Edwards was the first editor of *New Guard*, which he served in a volunteer capacity from 1961 to 1963. Still later, he opened up his own public relations firm, Lee Edwards & Associates. Most recently, since 1996 Dr. Edwards has been a Distinguished Fellow in Conservative Thought at the Heritage Foundation and an Adjunct Professor of Politics at Catholic University. Edwards was the founding director of the Institute on Political Journalism at Georgetown University and a Fellow at the Institute of Politics, John F. Kennedy School of Government, Harvard University. He is also a past President of the Philadelphia Society and the author or editor of eighteen works on conservative leaders and the growth of conservative organizations.[57]

Three of the new Board members were not present in Sharon. Richard Noble worked with other firms until he established his own firm, Noble & Campbell, in 1970 in Los Angeles. Noble remained active in California Republican politics but most of his volunteer efforts were directed towards twenty-five years of service on the Board of Governors of Thomas Aquinas College. Noble passed away in 2002. Scott Stanley graduated from University of Kansas Law School and went on to a career in journalism. After his involvement in YAF he became editor of *American Opinion*, the magazine of the John Birch Society and is now

---

55. 2008 YAF Alumni Survey Responses: G. Daniel Harden.
56. 2008 YAF Alumni Survey Responses: Carol Sue Nevin Abromaitis.
57. 2008 YAF Alumni Survey Responses: Lee Edwards. Among Edwards's many works are *Reagan: A Political Biography* (1967), *You Can Make the Difference* (1968), *Missionary for Freedom: The Life and Times of Walter Judd* (1990), *Goldwater: The Man Who Made a Revolution* (1995), *The Power of Ideas: The Heritage Foundation at 25 Years* (1997), *The Conservative Revolution* (1999), *Our Times: The Washington Times 1982–2002* (2002), *Educating for Liberty* (2003), and *The Essential Ronald Reagan* (2005).

a freelance journalist in Williamsburg, Virginia. Noble and Stanley had been part of the invitation committee for the meeting but could not attend. The third person not present for the meeting was Diarmuid O'Scannlain. A graduate of St. John's University, O'Scannlain was a law student at Harvard University when he was elected to the Board. Subsequently, he practiced law in Portland and served as Deputy Attorney General and Public Utility Commissioner for Oregon prior to being appointed by President Reagan to a seat on the U.S. Circuit Court of Appeals for the 9th Circuit where he continues to serve today.

From this rather abbreviated and condensed summary of the eventual careers of some of those who took part in the formation of Young Americans for Freedom, it is clear that this was a group of future leaders in business, academia, government, law, and the media. It reminds us also that while it is interesting and informative to trace through the accomplishments of the organization over its years of activity, the real impact of Young Americans for Freedom has been its development of new generations of conservative leaders, individuals who would help to bring about the conservative successes of the 1980s and beyond.

3. A Divided Decade

*"Historians of the sixties have focused chiefly on the Left
as an advocate for change, but in the early sixties the Right
was actually more active in challenging the status quo."*[1]

READING ABOUT THE DECADE of the 1960s in the 21st century, it would be easy
to conclude that this was a period of revolution, riots, and radicalism in both
politics and social mores. Indeed, most of the historical works about this time
concentrate on the activities of only the latter part of the decade.[2] But such an
emphasis overlooks the fact that the first half of the decade was one of transition
if not tradition.

The Early Sixties in America

The college campus of the early 1960s was quite different from that to be found
at the end of the decade. While very few still exist today, it was a time when there
were numerous all-male and all-female colleges. Major institutions had separate
administrative entities for female students even when the classroom was integrated.
Harvard had its Radcliffe, Brown had Pembroke, Tufts had Jackson College and
on and on. There were the Seven Sisters (highly selective all-women's colleges
perceived to be the equivalent of the Ivy League institutions) and several state
institutions, such as Virginia Military Institute, that were limited to male students
only. In fact, at some schools such as Texas A&M University, all students were
required to be members of the quasi-military "Corps of Cadets" or be enrolled
in the Reserve Officers Training Corps.

Tradition reigned on campus, especially at the more highly selective colleges
in the East where freshmen were required to wear certain regalia and follow the
instructions of upperclassmen while seniors wore their school blazers proudly.[3]
Of course, it was also a time of single-sex dormitories, limited visitation privileges,
and nightly curfews for all female students. College administrators followed a
policy known as "in loco parentis," meaning that they stood in the place of a
student's parents in regulating virtually all aspects of the student's behavior.

Author Dan Wakefield reminds us that as late as 1963 the term "hippie" was
unknown.[4] Likewise, the summer of love was still in the future, San Francisco
was not yet a place to put a flower in your hair, and "the Beatles" were spending

---

1. John A. Andrew: *The Other Side of the Sixties*, p. 76.
2. Most frequently cited as political histories of the 1960s are works by those who were active
participants from the Left during this era, including Tom Hayden: *Reunion: A Memoir* (New York:
Random House, 1988); Richard Flacks: *Making History* (New York: Columbia University Press, 1988);
Todd Gitlin: *The Sixties: Years of Hope, Days of Rage* (New York: Bantam Books, 1987). For critical
commentaries on the decade by two who were active leftists in the 1960s and revised their political
outlooks in the 1980s, see: Peter Collier and David Horowitz: *Destructive Generation: Second Thoughts
About the Sixties* (New York: Summit Books, 1989).
3. The author still retains his "beanie," similar to a jockey's cap or yarmulke, which had to be worn
on campus the first month of the freshman year lest he be reproached by an upperclassman.
4. Dan Wakefield: *New York in the Fifties*, p. 270.

much of their time in Hamburg, Germany and had yet to become known in most of the United States. It was an era of folk music and also a time when the top two movies of 1960 were "Oceans Eleven" and "Spartacus" and one of the leading ladies in filmdom was someone named Kim Novak.

The early Sixties was also a time when what later became known as "social issues" had not yet risen to public attention. It was not until 1962 when the U.S. Supreme Court ruled against prayer in the public schools and only in 1963 when school sponsored Bible reading was prohibited.[5] Not until the next decade would a majority of the Supreme Court discover a "right to privacy" in the Constitution that prevented states from prohibiting abortion.[6] While Billy James Hargis had his Christian Crusade and Carl McIntire led his American Council of Christian Churches, most evangelicals and fundamentalists shied away from political involvement, including a young preacher from Lynchburg, Virginia named Jerry Falwell who urged his fellow pastors to avoid mixing politics and religion.[7]

Young Americans for Freedom was coming into being as a national conservative youth organization at a time when there was no "conservative movement" as it is known today. As David Franke was about to leave George Washington University and move to New York City to start work at *National Review* in the summer of 1960, Doug Caddy organized a tribute dinner in his honor. The speakers at the event were Bill Buckley and Bill Rusher from the magazine, Reed Larson of the National Right-to-Work Committee, and James L. Wick, publisher of *Human Events* while telegrams were read from Senator Goldwater and Governor Edison. As Caddy noted, "About twenty-five persons were present. In 1960, this was the size of the Conservative Movement's leadership—25 persons who could easily fit into a small hotel dining room."[8]

Where conservative groups did exist on campus, there was a tendency to be both exclusive and to view themselves as part of a remnant holding forth against the tides of history. Charles Mills recalls the situation he found,

> When YAF was founded in 1960 there were already a few conservative political groups at Yale, but they were very much part of the Yale culture of secretive select groups that had to prove their exclusivity by not letting everyone in who wanted to join. YAF brought a breath of fresh air with its open recruiting of everyone it could get. I suspect a similar pattern may have been present elsewhere.[9]

It was not just Yale that had such traditions of exclusivity. At other East Coast colleges, Young Republican clubs were often seen as exclusive representatives of upper class society.[10]

It is interesting to note also that it was not until June 1962 when fewer than sixty students from eleven institutions formally adopted a statement of principles

---

5. *Engel v. Vitale* 370 US 421 (1962) and *Abington Township v. Schemp* 374 US 203 (1963).

6. *Roe v. Wade* 410 US 113 (1973).

7. John H. Redekop: *The American Far Right: A Case Study of Billy James Hargis and Christian Crusade* (Grand Rapids, MI: William B. Eerdmans, 1968); Gary K. Clabaugh: *Thunder on the Right: The Protestant Fundamentalists* (Chicago: Nelson-Hall Company, 1974). While a medical doctor and not a clergyman, Dr. Fred Schwarz was also prominent with his Christian Anti-Communism Crusade during the late 1950s and 1960s. See his *Beating the Unbeatable Foe* (Washington, DC: Regnery Publishing, Inc., 1996).

8. "Birth of the Conservative Movement," p. 9.

9. Charles G. Mills, e-mail dated January 14, 2009.

10. The author retains a formal invitation card from the Tufts University Young Republican Club to a "Sherry Hour" at the Theta Chi fraternity house on March 22, 1963.

and effectively created the organization called Students for a Democratic Society (SDS) at Port Huron, Michigan. When the school year of 1962–1963 began the left-wing group had eleven chapters and about 300 members. Even by 1964, SDS could show a membership of only 2,000 and seventy-five college chapters.[11] The major challenge of the New Left on campuses across America was still a few years away and the conflict in Vietnam remained a small, back-page news item in most publications.

The year 1960 also saw the first presidential election involving major party candidates born in the 20th century. In fact, both candidates were in their mid-forties with Kennedy at 43 years of age and Nixon at 47. After the close election had been decided there was a sense of proud patriotism as the new, young President called on his fellow citizens to "ask not what your country can do for you, but rather what you can do for your country."[12] While conservatives would disagree with his policies, the media soon portrayed the new administration as a time of "Camelot."

Change was in the air and by the middle of the decade a number of the policies and traditions of the early 1960s would be swept away. Much of this came simply from demographic changes as the post–World War II babies reached their late teens and early twenties. During the decade of the 1960s, the number of Americans aged 14 to 24 grew from nearly 26.5 million in 1960 to over 40 million in 1970—roughly a 50% increase.[13] At the same time, college enrollments were expanding. From a total of 3,640,000 students enrolled in post-secondary education in 1959, the number increased to 8,581,000 by 1970.[14] No longer was college regarded as solely for the academic or financial elite. Although the GI bill had brought literally thousands of veterans returned from World War II and the Korean Conflict onto the college campus, the decade of the sixties saw the pool of students expand even more, aided partly by what was becoming a trend of "grade inflation," by the creation of new state and private colleges and the expansion of existing ones, and by the social expectation of a college education being available to any and all. With all these changes occurring on American campuses, by the end of the decade the college scene in no way resembled that of the early 1960s.

Realizing the significant differences between the early and late 1960s is important when understanding the development of Young Americans for Freedom. To some degree, YAF was an early indicator of what would occur later in the decade. Those who joined the new organization were dedicated to bringing about change in society. Their enemy was what they perceived as the Establishment—and it was a liberal establishment that they saw in power on campus and in the Nation's Capital. Historian Matthew Dallek noted that,

> YAF was the first national youth movement to shatter the silent conformity that had reigned on campuses since World War II . . . before anyone had

11. E. Joseph Shoben, Jr., Philip Werdell, and Durward Long, "Radical Student Organizations," in Julian Foster and Durward Long, editors: *Protest: Student Activism in America* (New York: William Morrow & Co., 1970), pp. 207–209. For a look back at the founding of SDS and its objectives as seen by a leading participant, see Tom Hayden: *The Port Huron Statement: The Vision Call of the 1960s Revolution* (New York: Thunder's Mouth Press, 2005).

12. For a discussion of this inaugural address, see John A. Barnes: *John F. Kennedy—On Leadership* (New York: AMACOM, 2005), pp. 15–17.

13. Rebecca Klatch: *A Generation Divided*, p. 4.

14. National Center for Education Statistics: *1996 Digest of Education Statistics* (Washington, DC: U.S. Department of Education, 1996), Table 3.

ever heard of the counterculture, Students for a Democratic Society, the Free Speech Movement, and anti-war demonstrators, Young Americans for Freedom were busy tearing down the walls of the liberal establishment.[15]

National Chairman Robert Schuchman contrasted his views with those of an earlier generation when he said, "My parents thought Franklin D. Roosevelt was one of the greatest heroes who ever lived. I'm rebelling from that concept" while Roger Claus, a University of Wisconsin student, proudly noted that, "You walk around with your Goldwater button, and you feel the thrill of treason."[16]

What brought these young conservatives together was a general suspicion of big government and, indeed, any kind of concentration of power. This led to an opposition to the welfare state and the continued policies of the New Deal, programs that they viewed as challenging the work ethic and the sanctity of the individual. Yet they were not anti-government for it was seen as having legitimate functions to perform, first and foremost the preservation of national defense. As the Sharon Statement declared, this meant a commitment to victory over, rather than co-existence with, Communism.[17] Of the three pillars of modern American conservatism—tradition and order, free market economics, and vigorous opposition to Communism—Young Americans for Freedom would concentrate on the last two primarily in its early years.

The Beginnings of YAF

Doug Caddy returned to New York City after the conference in Sharon, Connecticut and began the process of establishing a permanent organization. Caddy was officially on the payroll of the McGraw-Edison Company and was working out of the offices of the company's public affairs consultant, Marvin Liebman and Associates. Thus, the initial offices of Young Americans for Freedom were established on Caddy's desk at 343 Lexington Avenue in New York City. A news release was sent out, recruitment material was assembled and requests for information started coming in. As Caddy observed, "From virtually the beginning we were besieged by students from around the country interested in joining. Clearly the time was ripe for such an organization to ignite a grassroots conservative revolt."[18]

Three weeks after being formed, the new Board of Directors of Young Americans for Freedom met at the Liebman offices in New York City. They had been invited to conduct a *National Review* Forum to be held at Hunter College on October 20th and "the program was totally in the hands of YAF." A decision was made to have a brief presentation explaining the organization and outlining its goals but the main topic of discussion would be "Should Conservatives Back Nixon?"[19] As Caddy explained to Buckley in a subsequent letter, Lee Edwards would take the affirmative on this question (with Carol Dawson, Executive

---

15. "Young Americans for Freedom: The Rise of Modern Conservatism, 1960–1964," p. 37.

16. "Campus Conservatives," *Time*, February 10, 1961, p. 37.

17. Based on her interviews with a number of YAF activists from the early 1960s, Rebecca Klatch lists these as core values that motivated the young conservatives. *A Generation Divided*, pp. 44–46.

18. "Birth of the Conservative Movement," p. 15.

19. Minutes of the Board of Directors Meeting of October 1, 1960, Personal Papers of William A. Rusher, Box 174, Manuscript Division, Library of Congress, Washington, DC.

Secretary of College Youth for Nixon taking second chair) while Richard Cowan would take the negative (backed up by Annette Courtemanche).[20] Also participating in the Forum would be David Franke, Robert Harley, Robert Schuchman, and Carl T. McIntire, each addressing various aspects of the new organization. Apparently the event went well as Buckley wrote back to Caddy later that month to thank the YAF leaders for the program and extend praise by saying "We bask in the reflected glory of YAF and its excellent spokesmen."[21]

With the November election approaching and no further Board meeting scheduled prior to election day, a decision had to be made on whether the organization would endorse the Nixon-Lodge ticket. In a close vote, the decision was to remain neutral.[22] The decision made it clear that YAF was to be a conservative, not a Republican, organization willing to work with those who shared their philosophy regardless of party affiliation. Just as important, however, it established a precedent that YAF would endorse those who agreed with the principles espoused in the Sharon Statement, and not simply the more conservative candidate. Being "less liberal" was not sufficient; one had to be clearly conservative to garner the support of the new organization.[23]

While launching an effort to establish local chapters on college campuses and in communities across the country, the Directors were aware of the need to place certain limits on the autonomy of the local units lest the name Young Americans for Freedom be unconsciously associated with actions possibly inconsistent with the overall goals. This was particularly a concern for an organization involved in political action, both electoral and governmental. Thus the Board adopted a resolution that: "Any statements of policy such as endorsement of a candidate or proposed legislation by a local chapter or a region must be first sent to national headquarters before being released."[24] Throughout its history, conflict over the relationship between the national office and various local chapters would occur sporadically. For an organization philosophically committed to individual rights and decentralization of power, difficult choices had to be made between protecting the organization's reputation and name while still allowing local chapter autonomy.

With limited funds, Young Americans for Freedom had to spread the news of its existence and its message in as many ways as possible. Formed during the heat of a close presidential election, YAF was competing with the campaign efforts but also benefiting from the interaction and involvement of some of its leaders in the College Youth for Nixon organization. Thus, while it did not endorse Nixon, several of its members held positions in the campaign and could recruit individuals for post-election involvement. Gaining media attention for a new organization at any time is difficult; it is even more difficult when the political world is focused on a presidential election. Seth Offenbach studied the relationship between the media and Young Americans for Freedom during the organization's early years and noted these difficulties.

---

20. Letter from Douglas Caddy to William F. Buckley, Jr., October 5, 1960, Personal Papers of William F. Buckley, Jr., Box 10, Sterling Library, Yale University, New Haven, CT.
21. Letter from William F. Buckley, Jr. to Douglas Caddy, October 27, 1960, Personal Papers of William F. Buckley, Jr., Box 10, Sterling Library, Yale University, New Haven, CT.
22. John A. Andrew: *The Other Side of the Sixties*, p. 77–78.
23. This point is expounded by M. Stanton Evans: *Revolt on the Campus*, pp. 111–114.
24. Minutes of the Board of Directors Meeting of October 1, 1960, Personal Papers of William A. Rusher, Box 174, Manuscript Division, Library of Congress, Washington, DC.

YAF had to overcome three major biases held by the press. The first was that the press implicitly endorsed the moderate liberalism of the 1950s ... The second bias was that the press gave undue deference to government officials, even when reporting on the activities of YAF ... The third bias ... was the press' tendency to take its preconceived notions regarding which members of society are deviants and retain these notions for long period. Initially, YAF was viewed as a deviant group that was not to be given any respect, but eventually the press began to slowly give YAF agency as a political participant.[25]

Throughout the fall of 1960 it remained difficult for Young Americans for Freedom to gain media coverage in most areas of the country. To break through this barrier, the organization determined that they would need to take some dramatic actions. When the Board met again after the November elections two such events would be planned for early 1961.

On the agenda for the November 26, 1960 meeting of the YAF Board of Directors were a number of proposed activities. Of greatest significance, a decision was made to sponsor what was then described as a fundraising dinner in New York City in March 1961 with Senator Goldwater to be invited to serve as the major speaker. This event subsequently was modified to become the first major political rally sponsored by YAF. A second topic of discussion concerned the efforts to abolish or severely de-fund the House Committee on Un-American Activities (HUAC). Congress had created the committee in 1938 to explore the need for legislation concerning subversive activities from the right and the left at a time when both fascism and communism were challenging the West and its democratic traditions. In the post-World War II period, the committee received public attention with its investigation into Communist penetration of the film industry in 1947[26] as well as in the dramatic Whittaker Chambers–Alger Hiss confrontation of 1948.[27] By the late 1950s, a serious effort was underway to eliminate the committee and its ability to investigate subversive activities in the United States. While many non-Communists, including Representative James Roosevelt, son of the former President, were active in this effort, there is no question that abolition of the committee was a major objective of the Communist Party of the United States of America (CPUSA).

In May 1960, a three-member subcommittee of HUAC traveled to California to hold hearings at the San Francisco City Hall. Over three days, CPUSA leaders disrupted events inside the hearing room while hundreds of protesters assembled in the halls outside the room as well as in front of the City Hall building. As protesters refused to cease, they were removed by police and what can only be described as a riot occurred outside City Hall. These "San Francisco riots" were interpreted differently and used by both Right and Left in the months and even years to follow. HUAC subpoenaed footage from two San Francisco stations and produced a film entitled "Operation Abolition."[28]

25. Seth Offenbach, "Power of Portrayal," p. 5.

26. For background, see Ronald Radosh and Allis Radosh: *Red Star Over Hollywood* (New York: Encounter Books, 2006).

27. The most thorough investigation of the Hiss matter remains Allen Weinstein: *Perjury: The Hiss-Chambers Case* (New York: Alfred A. Knopf, 1978).

28. For a discussion of HUAC and its work, see: William F. Buckley, Jr., editor: *The Committee and*

By late fall of 1960, leaders in Young Americans for Freedom became aware of the plans of left-wing groups opposed to HUAC to stage a major demonstration in Washington, DC on the opening day of the 87th Congress in January. The objective of these left-wing groups was to convince the House of Representatives to abolish the committee and, thus, cease any investigation into Communist activities in the United States. YAF leaders determined that this would be their first counter-demonstration and the word went out to be in Washington in January to confront those who would abolish HUAC.

Over the years, Young Americans for Freedom would conduct many demonstrations, both in favor of conservative policies as well as in opposition to left-wing efforts. According to Jonathan Schoenwald these activities were "only means, not ends ... YAF leaders understood that through these relatively insignificant activities they were building the basis of a long-lasting political movement."[29] Such demonstrations as the one planned for January 1961 would be a means of obtaining media coverage, of building a sense of camaraderie among its membership, of recruiting new supporters and members, and of advancing their policy objectives. David Franke, organizer of the Greater New York Council of YAF noted, "If our political enemies on the left were holding a rally, demonstration, march, etc., it was sure to be covered in the liberal media. A counter-protest thus gave us a better chance of getting coverage ourselves."[30]

The Board discussed creating ad hoc groups to advance specific policy objectives, stressing that while this would extend the influence of the organization there should be no overt connection between the new groups and YAF. Robert Croll and John Kolbe formed a group advocating support for the continued investigative powers of Congress called the Student Committee for Congressional Autonomy while Robert Harley headed a Student Committee Against the Admission of Red China to the United Nations.[31] Over the years, creating such groups was an approach successfully used by Marvin Liebman with his many letterhead ad hoc committees for various conservative causes. Throughout its own history, YAF would use this tactic to build not merely letterhead groups for a short-term objective but, rather, to create a number of lasting issue-oriented entities, many of which continue in existence today. YAF itself as an organization, as well as its individual members and alumni, was the impetus for the founding of literally dozens of other conservative organizations. Just as important, however, was the utility of these ad hoc groups in training new leaders in the tools of organizational development and sustenance from fundraising to public relations to business

Its Critics (Chicago: Henry Regnery Company, 1962). The San Francisco riots are covered extensively by M. Stanton Evans: *Revolt on the Campus*, pp. 176–211 and also in Jonathan Schoenwald: *A Time for Choosing*, pp. 52–61.

29. Schoenwald, "The Other Counterculture: Young Americans for Freedom, 1960–1969," unpublished paper, Towards a History of the 1960s, State Historical Society of Wisconsin, Madison, WI, April 28, 1993, p. 9.

30. Offenbach, "Power of Portrayal," p. 23. A rather humorous description by a left-wing author of YAF's methods was presented in Mike Newberry: *The Fascist Revival* (New York: New Century Publishers, 1961). In his section titled "Young Americans for Fascism," on page 36 Newberry claims: "Its members are trained not only in ringing doorbells, but in breaking up progressive and union meetings. Its hecklers, picketlines, and hoodlums—white collar hoodlums to be sure—have begun to descend like a plague of gnats on peace rallies and civil liberties gatherings." The Far Left clearly saw the emerging organization as a serious threat.

31. John Kolbe, "The Right to Know," *New Guard*, May 1961, p. 10. In this article Kolbe maintains the leftist attack on the House Committee on Un-American Activities is simply a challenge to the legislative power of investigation.

practices to organizational dynamics. These efforts were designed not merely to influence public policy but also to develop, as Gregory Schneider aptly called them, cadres for conservatism.

Young Americans for Freedom saw its mission as developing conservative groups on college campuses as well as in communities. To this end it was committed to involving itself in campus and student oriented issues. One of the major topics of discussion at the November 1960 Board meeting concerned YAF's attitude towards the National Student Association. Formed in 1947 as a federation of student body leaders, it had expanded over the years to include approximately 300 student governments on college campuses. Although it developed a reputation as following a left-liberal agenda, the Central Intelligence Agency began surreptitiously funding the organization in 1952, a fact that would not surface until some fifteen years later.[32] If YAF was to become an effective young conservative organization, then it needed to take stands on, and play a role in, student campus issues. Involvement to some extent in NSA would be a logical undertaking.

YAF's Board Members were provided with a confidential report on the 13th Annual Congress of NSA held at the University of Minnesota on August 17– September 1, 1960. It was prepared by one of their fellow Directors, Carol Dawson, who had represented Dunbarton College at the Congress. Dawson noted that the real power in the organization resided not with the campus delegates meeting in plenary session but, rather, with a National Executive Committee consisting of the various regional chairmen. No proposed resolution could be considered by the delegates unless it was first approved by the National Executive Committee, a body which had also the authority to introduce and pass resolutions between annual Congresses. This tended to ensure that the "power elite" of the organization retained control over the policy agenda of NSA.

While different organizations were represented at the Congress, ranging from Young Republicans to the Young Socialist Alliance, "literature on aid-to-education, disarmament, pacifism, and international relations was of one viewpoint only."[33] Among the resolutions passed at the Congress were those urging the United States to adopt a policy of unilateral nuclear disarmament and calling for the abolition of the loyalty oath and disclaimer provisions of the National Defense Education Act student loan program. Another resolution stated that radical changes should be made in the operations of the House Un-American Activities Committee or it should be abolished. These positions on foreign policy and anti-communist topics were totally at odds with the stands of YAF. Nevertheless, Dawson did not advocate disengagement from NSA.

> There is a move afoot among some of the students to organize effective opposition to the present leadership of NSA, and possibly take it over within a year or two. I am encouraged by this, but am inclined to feel that this is next to impossible because of the fact that when college students graduate,

32. Schneider: *Cadres for Conservatism*, pp. 60–64; Andrew: *The Other Side of the Sixties*, pp. 91–100. Conservative opposition to NSA did not begin with YAF. For earlier critiques of the organization see M. Stanton Evans, "The National Student Association: Where Is It Leading American College Students?" *Human Events*, December 29, 1958 as well as the report by J.B. Matthews inserted by Representative John Bell Williams in the *Congressional Record*, July 14, 1958, pp. 12517–19.

33. Carol Dawson, "Preliminary Report on the 13th Annual Congress of the National Student Association," p. 3, Personal Papers of William F. Buckley, Jr., Box 12, Sterling Library, Yale University, New Haven, CT.

they lose interest very fast. I do think, however, that we cannot ignore the potentialities in NSA, and we should always try to make our viewpoint well represented there.[34]

After much discussion, the Board unanimously agreed, "that for the present time YAF will encourage participation in NSA but only for the purpose of reformulation from within. After next year's convention of NSA, YAF will reevaluate its policy towards NSA to see whether total withdrawal should be advocated."[35] For the next few years YAF did involve itself in efforts to reform NSA but by the mid-1960s it concluded that such involvement was futile and it formed an ad hoc group called STOP-NSA, acronym for Students To Oppose Participation in the National Student Association.

Building an Organization

A decision was made to begin publishing a YAF magazine in 1961. It would be a vehicle for young conservatives to present their views on current issues as well as report on the various events taking place in the organization. Lee Edwards agreed to serve as the first editor with an editorial board consisting of Carol Bauman, Kenneth E. Thompson, William M. Schulz, and C. Robert Ritchie. The first issue would appear in March 1961.

And so the plans were laid for the months ahead as Young Americans for Freedom set out to establish itself as a national organization of young conservatives. To succeed, it needed to establish chapters on college campuses and communities throughout the country. David Franke set out to do that by establishing a Greater New York Council of YAF with an objective of creating chapters in various neighborhoods throughout the city. In the District of Columbia, an organizational meeting was held in October with Willard Edwards, Washington correspondent for the *Chicago Tribune* and father of YAF Board Member Lee Edwards, as the featured speaker. On December 2nd, a kickoff rally for the DC effort was held with William F. Buckley, Jr. and Professor Felix Morley as the guest speakers.[36] Similar efforts were taking place in other communities along the East Coast and in the Midwest.

Launching out on a new endeavor gave a sense of belonging to many young conservatives who had previously felt isolated and as merely part of a remnant, at odds with the prevailing culture. Writer E.J. Dionne quoted one observer as claiming "a flock of little Buckleys now torment social scientists in colleges large and small." According to Dionne,

> The "remnant" was growing and its members were finding each other. Conservatives were seen as doing especially well on the college campuses; the right-wing rebels drew notice before the New Left rebels did.[37]

---

34. *Ibid.*

35. Minutes of the Board of Directors Meeting, New York, November 26, 1960, Personal Papers of William A. Rusher, Box 174, Manuscript Division, Library of Congress, Washington, DC.

36. Letter of Mrs. Ruth Ziebarth to William F. Buckley, Jr., Personal Papers of William F. Buckley, Jr., Box 12, Sterling Library, Yale University, New Haven, CT.

37. E.J. Dionne, Jr., *Why Americans Hate Politics*, p. 176.

Now slightly more than three months old, the organization had to turn its attention to gaining recognition, building its membership, and forming local chapters to provide an avenue for activity by these new recruits.

The year 1961 arrived with a major challenge for Young Americans for Freedom. It had committed itself to rallying support for the House Committee on Un-American Activities. Would it be able to produce a respectable number of individuals for a demonstration in Washington? How would the left-wing demonstrators react? Would the media give any coverage to the YAF counter-demonstration? Was there sufficient support among young conservatives to pull off such an event? January 2nd would provide an answer to these questions.

As those opposed to the House Un-American Activities Committee assembled at Washington's All Souls Unitarian Church, several busloads of young conservatives, organized by the newly-formed Greater New York Council of YAF, were on their way from New York City to the Nation's Capital. Joined by DC area YAF members and other anti-communists, that afternoon more than four hundred YAF members gathered in Lafayette Square across from the White House to counteract a smaller group of anti-HUAC pickets. They had organized a conservative picket line and demonstration calling for continued support of HUAC and increased surveillance of the Communist Party.[38] Although the *New York Times* dispatch made no mention of the counter demonstration, it did receive notice in a lengthy article on growing conservative support among the young in *Time* magazine the following month.[39] Both *The Nation* and *The Progressive* commented on this audacious display by an upstart new group.[40] Stan Evans concluded, "Conservatives had finally grasped the key importance of such displays—their impact on the public mind."[41] From that point on, as Gregory Schneider observed, "YAF members served as shock troops for the conservative movement, seizing on tactics such as picket lines and marches that had been employed by leftist and Communist groups in the past."[42] The events of January 2nd indicated that techniques from the left could be borrowed and used effectively by young conservatives.

YAF's campaign in support of HUAC would continue over the next several months as an expression of both the members' antipathy towards the Left and their opposition to communism. The Student Committee for Congressional Autonomy distributed copies of *The Committee and Its Critics*, edited by William F. Buckley, Jr., lobbied Congressmen, and sponsored a pro-HUAC demonstration in Washington. One YAF member observed in commenting on the pro-HUAC demonstration,

> The reason we have been so successful with these pickets is that we are treading on the liberals' sacred ground. Informational picketing has long been an exclusively left-wing activity, and our friends on the left are surprised and, I think, dismayed by its "misuse" in our hands.[43]

---

38. Bjerre-Poulsen, "Organizing the American Right, 1945–1964," p. 281 and M. Stanton Evans: *Revolt on the Campus*, pp. 114–116.

39. Rick Perlstein: *Before the Storm*, p. 107; *Time*, February 19, 1961, p. 34.

40. Alan C. Elms, "The Conservative Ripple," *The Nation*, May 27, 1961, p. 458; Murray Kempton, "On Growing Up Absurd," *The Progressive*, May 1961, p. 12; See also Ed Cain: *They'd Rather Be Right* (New York: MacMillan Company, 1963) p. 171.

41. *Revolt on the Campus*, p. 115.

42. *Cadres for Conservatism*, p. 40.

43. *Insight and Outlook*, Volume III, Number VI (April 1961), pp. 10–11.

To indicate student support the committee organized chapters on sixty college campuses. On behalf of the Student Committee for Congressional Autonomy, John Kolbe sent a letter to all Members of the House of Representatives supporting the continuation of HUAC. Later that spring the anti-HUAC effort collapsed as the House reauthorized the committee and voted 412–6 on its appropriation request.[44]

One of the key organizing tools in communities and on college campuses over the remainder of 1961 would be the showing of the film "Operation Abolition" that focused on the Communist-led disruption of HUAC hearings in San Francisco in May 1960. The film, often with in-person commentary by the film's narrator, Fulton Lewis, III, would be a frequent program to highlight the domestic efforts of the Communist Party. By March, Lewis had appeared on 75 college campuses with the film, generating pickets outside and heckling disrupters inside.[45]

Sociologist Rebecca Klatch reported that in her interviews with several early YAF activists many mentioned specific events associated with communism as motivating their political interest and involvement. The Hungarian uprising of 1956 and the Castro victory of 1959 were still fresh in the memories of many YAF members.[46] Castro was the cause for another of YAF's many ad hoc committees. The Student Committee for a Free Cuba was organized in early 1961 by Chairman Robert Schuchman and National Director Richard Cowan. The committee circulated a petition addressed to President John F. Kennedy calling for American action to remove Castro from power. It urged the President to "take all necessary action to protect the independence of the Western Hemisphere and to expel Communist imperialism from its beach-head in the Americas as represented by the Communist regime of Fidel Castro in Cuba."[47] The committee would continue as an ad hoc project of YAF for the next few years, including in the aftermath of the Bay of Pigs fiasco and the Cuban Missile Crisis.[48]

By February, the Greater New York Council of YAF led by David Franke had succeeded in forming community-based chapters throughout the city. The clubs were formed to sponsor educational programs and social affairs, to engage in political action, and to participate in rallies and demonstrations such as the pro-HUAC effort in Washington, DC. The Council published and distributed to all members a bi-weekly bulletin, edited by Doris Sukup, so that members could be aware of the various local chapter activities and coordinated citywide projects.[49] Alfred DelliBovi recalled this time.

> I became involved in YAF in 1961 while I was in high school in New York City. There were more than thirty YAF chapters in the metropolitan area and their leaders met each month as the Greater New York Council where there was always a fierce and spirited debate about the future of conservatism. It

44. Ronald F. Docksai: "A Study of the Organization and Beliefs of the Young Conservative Movement," Master's Thesis, New York University, 1972, pp. 88–91.

45. "Operation Abolition," *Time*, March 17, 1961. See also M. Stanton Evans, "Just Who's Distorting What?" *National Review*, May 6, 1961 for a defense of the film.

46. *A Generation Divided*, p. 87–88.

47. Letter of May 20, 1961 from Robert Schuchman, Personal Papers of Marvin Liebman, Box 37, Hoover Institution, Stanford University, Palo Alto, CA.

48. *New Guard*, May 1961, p. 4.

49. The bulletins for September 15, 1961, January 2 and 15, 1962 were located in the White House Central Name Files, Box 3092, Folder: YAF, John F. Kennedy Presidential Library, Boston, MA. The Kennedy White House engaged in an active campaign of monitoring YAF and other right-wing organizations.

was a heady experience for a high school student to be in contact with the always articulate giants of the conservative movement: Bob Schuchman, Bob Bauman, Don Devine, and Lee Edwards.[50]

To Don Devine, who was Kings County (Brooklyn) YAF Chairman at the time, "New York was the center of YAF at the beginning and everything we did was new and exciting."[51]

Emphasizing the non-partisan conservatism of the organization, the featured speaker at an early meeting of the Greater New York Council was Connecticut Democratic Senator Thomas Dodd, an ardent anti-communist opponent of the admission of Communist China to the United Nations and father of the current Connecticut Democratic Senator Christopher Dodd. One of the first places where a chapter was organized was in the Greenwich Village neighborhood of Manhattan, "to let the Liberals and those to their left know that no bastion is safe for them anymore," according to Franke.[52] Going into the lion's den of New York liberalism, the young conservatives proudly displayed their anti-communism. As writer Marvin Kitman reported about a showing of "Operation Abolition" by the chapter, "Recently the Greenwich Village chapter of YAF rented an off-Broadway theater to bring the film to the attention of its community. The event was klieg-lighted by the press and picketed by the Young People's Socialist League."[53] If ever there were a question as to who was being bold, audacious and even radical, the young conservatives could provide the answer.

Karl Ziebarth was a recent Yale graduate working in New York City. Having been chairman of the "Party of the Right" at Yale, he joined Young Americans for Freedom and soon was President of the Eastside YAF chapter. As he recalled recently, it was "lots of fun and we enjoyed being the rebels in the left-wing world of New York City." He has remained committed to his conservative principles and volunteer involvement, having served as a trustee of the Philadelphia Society.[54]

At the February meeting of the Board of Directors, final plans were made for what would be the first major event in the history of YAF. A decision had been made to convert the planned March fundraising dinner into an awards rally at the Manhattan Center in New York City. This would require attracting a much larger attendance, for the center had a capacity of slightly over 3,000. With a commitment from Senator Goldwater to serve as keynote speaker, the young conservatives went ahead with their bold plans. The Board also decided to incorporate Young Americans for Freedom, testifying to the permanence of the organization they had created. The by-laws were amended to set the membership upper age limit at 39 but require that all national officers be less than 35 years of age.[55] While much discussion centered on forming new college chapters, David Franke emphasized the need to dispel the idea that YAF was limited to students. He believed that, as was occurring in New York City, YAF needed to establish a base among young professionals in the neighborhoods of major cities. Following Franke's lead, effective metropolitan councils were organized in Boston, Philadelphia, Washington,

50. 2008 YAF Alumni Survey Responses: Alfred A. DelliBovi.
51. 2008 YAF Alumni Survey Responses: Donald J. Devine.
52. David Franke, "Breaking The Liberal Barrier," *New Guard*, March 1961, p. 10.
53. Marvin Kitman, "The Button Down Revolution," *Nugget*, October 1961, p. 46.
54. 2008 YAF Alumni Survey Responses: Karl R. Ziebarth.
55. Minutes of the Board of Directors Meeting, February 12, 1961, Personal Papers of William A. Rusher, Box 173, Manuscript Division, Library of Congress, Washington, DC.

Indianapolis and other cities by the end of 1961. YAF was able to create many of these community-based young adult chapters because, to a very large extent, YAF was the only successful responsible conservative organization at that time.[56]

The New Guard Is Launched

March 1961 was a very active month for the new organization. The first issue of its new magazine, *New Guard*, appeared under the editorship of Lee Edwards. Starting out as a sixteen page publication it would grow in size and continue as a monthly or ten times a year magazine until 1978 when it was converted to a quarterly magazine with interim newsletters, and would be published sporadically thereafter. As the initial editorial noted,

> Ten years ago this magazine would not have been possible. Twenty years ago it would not have been dreamed of. Thirty-five years ago it would not have been necessary. Today, *The New Guard* is possible, it is a reality, and it is needed by the youth of America to proclaim loudly and clearly:
> We are sick unto death of collectivism, socialism, statism and the other utopian isms which have poisoned the minds, weakened the wills and smothered the spirits of Americans for three decades and more.[57]

For the first time, young conservatives had a vehicle for publishing their own writings and developing their own journalistic and research skills. *New Guard* would serve an important role in building a conservative movement, communicating ideas, events, and activities of relevance to YAF members as they constructed a "grassroots" base on campuses and in communities.

After the first issue there was a "letters" section that in the early months featured indications of support from various Senators and House Members, Republicans and Democrats alike. This was a time when there was little ideological consistency in the two major political parties with conservatives and liberals both adopting the Republican and Democratic party labels. The composition of the congressional letter writers to *New Guard* was a vivid commentary on mid-20th century American politics as letters of praise and congratulations came from several Democrats including Senators Frank Lausche of Ohio, Strom Thurmond of South Carolina, and Spessard Holland of Florida along with a number of Republican elected officials. This bipartisan nature of conservatism and support for YAF would continue for many years, as testified to by the presence of Senator Robert Byrd of West Virginia as a featured speaker at the 1971 YAF National Convention.

Initial distribution of this first issue took place on March 3rd at a rather auspicious occasion when Young Americans for Freedom sponsored its First National Awards Rally. The young conservatives had decided to take on the awesome responsibility of filling a major convention hall only six months after the organization's founding. They went out and rented the Manhattan Center with its capacity of more than 3,000 in the heart of liberal New York City. Awards would be given to a number of nationally known conservatives and the keynote speech would be by Senator Barry Goldwater. The question remained, however, just as it

---

56. Gregory Schneider makes this point in *Cadres for Conservatism*, p. 48.
57. *New Guard*, March 1961, p. 3.

had been in the early morning hours of January 2nd in Washington, DC, could YAF pull off such an audacious undertaking?

Rally at Manhattan Center

On the evening of March 3, 1961 more than 3,300 shouting and cheering conservatives filled every inch of sitting and standing room in the Manhattan Center while an estimated 6,000 others were turned away. Meanwhile, some 150 left-wing pickets paraded across the street.[58] As the *New York Times* reported the next day,

> The audience spilled into the aisles on the main floor and the two balconies. Some pressed close to the stage. Others crouched on the balcony stairs . . . The line of persons trying to get into the rally stretched five abreast to Ninth Avenue . . . The police ordered the doors closed at 8:15 P.M. when the hall filled, and told the waiting line that no more tickets were available.[59]

Young conservatives had flown in from Denver, bused in from Washington, Philadelphia and Boston, driven from Yale and Princeton, and taken the subway from Queens and Brooklyn. YAF had more than filled the hall in the middle of Manhattan.

As the evening's program began, awards were presented to Professor Russell Kirk, novelist Taylor Caldwell, publisher Eugene C. Pulliam, industrialist Herbert V. Kohler, Sr., Admiral Lewis L. Strauss, journalist George E. Sokolsky, Young Republican leader James Abstine, and editor William F. Buckley, Jr. Only Strauss could not attend and was represented by Archibald Roosevelt. Special awards also went to the Republic of China (accepted by Ambassador George K.C. Yeh), the House Committee on Un-American Activities (accepted by Democratic Congressman Morgan Moulder), and the McGraw-Edison Company (accepted by Paul J. Christiansen). While each made brief remarks, it was Taylor Caldwell who received the greatest applause when she observed, "Dear children, I did not know you had been born and God bless you that you are here."[60]

The awards were greatly appreciated and duly recognized by the audience. But the main event was still to come. As Senator Goldwater was introduced and approached the podium, the crowd went wild. Balloons filled the air and the chant went up over and over, "We Want Barry" as students held forth signs indicating the name of their colleges or neighborhoods: Bay Ridge YAF, Newton College, Yale, Queens, and on and on. Goldwater's speech was billed as "The Conservative Sweep on the American Campus" and focused directly on the occasion and the presence of thousands of young people in the audience.

> We are being caught up in a wave of conservatism that could easily become the political phenomenon of our time. . . . This wave of conservatism is beginning to take on the appearance of a unique American phenomena and, as such, can reach into every nook and cranny of human life with recognizable significance to all of our people.

58. "Pickets Busy as Goldwater Packs House," *New York Daily News*, March 4, 1961.
59. Robert Conley, "3,200 Here Cheer Goldwater Talk," *New York Times*, March 4, 1961.
60. Brochure, "Young Americans for Freedom First National Awards," Personal Papers of William F. Buckley, Jr., Box 17, Sterling Library, Yale University, New Haven, CT.

Now where is the impetus for this sudden, vigorous revival of interest in the fundamental principles upon which our nation was founded coming from? I believe it is coming from the youth of the nation. It has all the earmarks of youth. It is fresh. It is intelligent. It is inquisitive. And it is energetic. And, I'm not guessing when I say these things. I've been out there where it is going on and I've had many opportunities to observe it at first hand.

Now I have been aware for some time of this ferment of conservatism on our college campuses. I'm not just discovering it for the first time as are many of the newspaper and magazine people who come to my office for an explanation.

But, even so, I want you to know that what I am finding as I visit college after college and high school after high school is downright amazing. I have been literally dumbfounded at the numbers of students who turn out for the meetings, not by any means because I am the speaker, but because it is a conservative movement. And because they are searching for new answers. They know that this thing that has gone along for thirty years and has cost four hundred billion dollars under the phony name of liberalism has not worked.[61]

The Senator went on to urge his audience to think beyond the White House, to propose alternate policies consistent with the principles of limited government and individual responsibility, and to take a longer view of the challenge confronting them. He concluded by reminding his young listeners that the task involves reinforcing the spirit of freedom in Americans while emphasizing responsibility in their own lives.

At the conclusion of Goldwater's speech, the cheers began again, the signs went aloft and the audience left knowing that they had participated in an historic occasion. As Stan Evans later commented, ". . . it was the sheer audacity of the enterprise which made it so enjoyable."[62] Just as audacious, however, was the article reporting on the glowing success of the event that appeared in the initial issue of *New Guard*—since it was printed before and distributed at the rally itself![63]

The third major occurrence in March was YAF's participation in "The National Conference on Youth Service Abroad" sponsored by the National Student Association and a conglomerate called the "Young Adult Council" comprising the Young People's Socialist League, Student League for Industrial Democracy (soon to become Students for a Democratic Society) and the student arm of Americans for Democratic Action. The conference took place on March 29–31 at American University in Washington, DC and was focused on implementation of President Kennedy's recently announced Peace Corps project. YAF sent fifty delegates to the conference and had previously created its own group, "Committee for an Effective Peace Corps." This YAF committee maintained that the Peace Corps should be based on cold war realism and be operated as a weapon against the spread of Communism.[64] While presenting a humanitarian face, the real aim

---

61. *Ibid.*
62. *Revolt on the Campus*, p. 122.
63. "We'll Take Manhattan, the Bronx, and . . . (Written in February with full confidence in the outcome)" *New Guard*, March 1961, p. 4.
64. Arnold Forster and Benjamin Epstein: *Danger on the Right* (New York: Random House, 1964) p. 232.

would be the promotion of the national interest against that of the Sino-Soviet bloc, according to YAF.

The delegates heard from Kennedy's brother-in-law, Sargent Shriver, who had just been nominated to head up the new endeavor, along with other liberal stalwarts including Senator Hubert Humphrey. The attendees broke into workshops to discuss different aspects of the new program, including training, purpose, arrangements, and organization. As YAF National Chairman Robert Schuchman observed, "It soon developed that there was to be a party line on each issue."[65] Schuchman and a small delegation of YAF members set up camp near the conference with a mimeograph machine and a determination to build support for their proposals.

One of the major concerns for the YAF delegates was the preparation of those who would be sent off to serve in the new venture. Would they be trained in the basic principles of American democracy and able to respond to the challenge from our Cold War foes? Given the ideological challenge to the West posed by Communism, YAF maintained that it would be better to have a small, select group of properly prepared individuals representing the United States than a larger number of ill-prepared but sincere volunteers.[66] A *New Guard* editorial pointed out that:

> In every country that he visits, a Peace Corps volunteer will be part of the continuing protracted conflict which engages every one of us. Physical, mental and political standards must be kept high to weed out the weak, the indolent and the naïve even if the Peace Corps should dwindle to a battalion or even a company.

As the editorial concluded, "Sending hundreds and thousands of college graduates into the underdeveloped nations to do battle with trained, experienced communist agents would produce a political debacle almost beyond comprehension."[67]

Unfortunately, that perspective was not shared by most of the delegates or even the senior government officials who would be implementing the new program. Schuchman observed that communism was not perceived as a threat by many of the delegates, as witnessed in the reaction of one delegate,

> When a YAF member from Northwestern suggested that there was, after all, a Communist menace, a buxom young lass wearing sneakers jumped up and cried, "I take personal offense at that statement!" It was finally decided that we could not be sure whether there was indeed a Communist menace.[68]

The YAF delegates did succeed in modifying or changing at least half of the final resolutions adopted by the conference. According to historian Rick Perlstein, "At parliamentary sessions YAFers monopolized the microphones, then group members would move out across the room in diamond fashion, an old Communist trick to give the appearance of greater numbers to manufacture acclaim for their

---

65. Robert M. Schuchman, "NSA Round-Up: A Spree de Corps," *New Guard*, May 1961, p. 9.
66. Edward Cain: *They'd Rather Be Right*, p. 171. According to Cain, "YAF wanted to rename the Peace Corps the Anti-Communist Freedom Corps and insisted that all participants undergo a rigorous security check and be carefully indoctrinated in the principles of free enterprise."
67. Lee Edwards: "Which Way for the Peace Corps," *New Guard*, April 1961, p. 2.
68. Schuchman, "NSA Round-Up: A Spree de Corps," *New Guard*, May 1961, p. 9.

speakers."[69] Nevertheless, the end result was that, despite the best efforts of YAF, the Peace Corps was created by sending young people without any security clearance, political training, or on-the-job supervision out to battle against poverty, illiteracy, and disease in a bifurcated world where American values were challenged by dedicated and committed Communists.

Despite these policy setbacks, it is clear that the YAF efforts riled the left and let it be known that a serious conservative challenge would be put forth on student and campus issues. Tom Hayden, soon to be a leading force in Students for a Democratic Society, made the following observation on YAF's efforts in the mainstream magazine, *Mademoiselle*.

> A small band of YAF-ers arrived unannounced and spread out in diamond-formation (an old Communist trick) through the committees' discussion groups, in order to extend their influence. They also established a front group (another Party tactic), "Committee for an Effective Peace Corps" (there was no mention of YAF backing). Finally, they wound up their activity by distributing a statement attacking the conference, which they claim was packed, and the delegates, whom they described as fuzzy and leftist.[70]

YAF's efforts at this NSA-sponsored conference on the Peace Corps would serve merely as a warm-up for the organization's efforts in August at the annual National Student Association conference.

With the culmination of the 1960–61 academic year and YAF's first ten months of existence, the organization's focus turned to two contrasting areas of activity: education in areas of conservative economics and philosophy and direct involvement in Republican Party politics. In cooperation with the Tuller Foundation, YAF helped sponsor three summer schools at Princeton, Yale, and C.W. Post College. The schools were organized to support a greater understanding of the conservative philosophy.[71] Over the next decade, YAF would continue to sponsor weekend conferences, summer schools, and other educational opportunities either in conjunction with other organizations or by itself.

Since many of those who were present at the creation of YAF had brought with them a history of involvement in Young Republican politics, it is no surprise that the 1961 annual convention of the Young Republicans became an arena for YAF involvement. A majority of the delegates who met in Minneapolis on June 21–24, 1961 were clearly conservative. They passed resolutions defending state right to work laws, opposing federal aid to education in any form, rejecting any federally-administered health insurance plan, supporting a total trade embargo of Communist nations, and calling for the immediate resumption of nuclear weapons testing. Moreover, these were Goldwater fans. As one observer noted: "Delegates by the hundreds sported Goldwater buttons, Goldwater hats, Goldwater attaché cases. And, when the Arizona Senator addressed the convention, he was continually interrupted by a cheering throng of 3,000."[72] Among the most well received speakers at the conference were Senators Goldwater and Tower and

---

69. Rick Perlstein: *Before the Storm*, pp. 110.
70. Tom Hayden, "Who Are the Student Boat-Rockers?," *Mademoiselle*, August 1, 1961.
71. *New Guard*, May 1961, p. 10.
72. George O. Porter, "YR's Stay Right," *New Guard*, August 1961, p. 8. See also the comments of newly-selected Republican National Chairman William E. Miller in Donald Janson, "GOP Declared Shifting to Right," *New York Times*, June 25, 1961.

Representatives Judd and Rousselot, all of whom publicly wore YAF buttons.[73] The YAF leaders left Minneapolis with the knowledge that Barry Goldwater, and the conservative principles he represented, had gained substantial support among the young Republican activists.

Creating the Freedom Party

The summer of 1961 also brought some personnel changes on YAF's Board of Directors as Richard Noble of Stanford resigned his position as Western Regional Chairman to be replaced by Robert Richards of the University of Washington while Richard Cowan of Yale University resigned as Northeast Regional Chairman, a position to which Boston businessman Jack Molesworth was appointed. Herbert Kohler also resigned from the Board and was replaced by George McDonnell of the University of Detroit. McDonnell was the first YAF State Chairman for Michigan and Chairman of the Detroit YAF Chapter from 1962 to 1964. Active also in Young Republicans, this was a time when "Dave Jones was my mentor. We led the conservative takeover of the College YRs in 1963." In 1964, McDonnell joined the staff of the Goldwater for President Committee and later worked for the Richard A. Viguerie Committee. Commenting later on those times, McDonnell noted "The YAF background has been a base for my political and business activities over the years. I have remained an active donor to conservative causes."[74] Meanwhile, during the year William Cotter had joined the Board as Organization Director and assumed additional duties when Doug Caddy entered active military duty.

In July, Young Americans for Freedom released its Organizational Manual to assist those who wished to form a chapter on campus or in a community.[75] YAF also issued a report on its first ten months that was distributed to contributors and Advisory Board members. Over the summer, a number of YAF Directors engaged in speaking tours to civic and patriotic groups to raise the awareness of the organization among potential supporters. YAF wrote to all members of the U.S. House of Representatives to reaffirm the organization's support for the non-subversive affidavit required of all recipients of funds under the National Defense Education Act and National Director Doug Caddy also testified before the Ways and Means Committee opposing the enactment of socialized medicine.[76]

Perhaps the most significant and lasting action in July, however, was the decision of Robert Schuchman, David Franke, and William Cotter to form a New York corporation under the name "The Freedom Party, Inc." This was done literally hours before the New York City Central Labor Council could take the same action. The unions had determined to endorse Mayor Robert Wagner and create a new party that would give him an additional ballot line, beyond his already existing ballot position as the Democratic Party and Liberal Party candidate. Since state law provides that no new party could include the name or part of the name

---

73. "Young Americans for Freedom: The First Ten Months," p. 4.
74. 2008 YAF Alumni Survey Responses: George P. McDonnell.
75. Letter of William S. Cotter, Organizational Director, to the author on July 6, 1961, with enclosure.
76. Letter from Douglas Caddy to Congressman Al Ullman dated June 21, 1961, Group Research Archives, Butler Library, Columbia University, New York, NY; "Young Americans for Freedom: The First Ten Months," p. 4.

of another party, the Labor Council was forced to organize their efforts as the "Brotherhood Party."[77] While the Freedom Party did not play a role in the 1961 city elections, its incorporation would have a meaningful effect on the intended actions of other conservatives.

Later in 1961, a group of senior conservatives including Professor Charles Rice, *National Review* publisher Bill Rusher, and attorney J. Daniel Mahoney determined that there was a need for a new party that would challenge the long-established Liberal Party. By creating a conservative minor party that could grant or withhold its nomination to major party candidates, the founders hoped to move both parties, but especially the Republicans, more to the Right. Specifically, they wished to counteract the influence of Nelson Rockefeller on the New York Republican Party and hamper his efforts to obtain the Republican presidential nomination. At its founding, the new party was perceived as being a strategic lever to affect the two major parties rather than a force created to win elections on its own.[78]

Schuchman and the other YAF leaders had created their party mainly to protect the name "Freedom" and to deny its use by the Labor Council. With no continuing plans for their party, the YAF leaders were willing to turn the corporation over to those interested in forming an on-going conservative party. Gaining control of an existing corporation allowed them to file a name change with the Secretary of State. As one of the founders explained, "By changing the name of an existing corporation, rather than organizing a new one, we avoided the need for approval by the Attorney General and a Supreme Court judge, which might have meant delay and complications."[79] Thanks to the YAF leaders' action in July 1961, the Conservative Party of New York was on its way to fielding candidates in the 1962 state elections. In fact, its candidate for Governor, David Jacquith, received sufficient votes to secure a permanent ballot line for the party and it continues to play an important role in New York State.

Although YAF can be viewed as instrumental in providing the legal framework for the new party, there was not unanimity among YAF leaders on the wisdom of such action. In the March 1962 issue of *New Guard*, which was widely distributed to subscribers and members as well as attendees at a major rally in New York City, National Director Doug Caddy expressed his personal reservations about the effort to create a conservative minor party in New York. Caddy feared that the Conservative Party would end up taking votes away from conservative Republican Congressmen, thereby causing their defeat. Moreover, replacing Governor Rockefeller with a liberal Democrat such as Mayor Robert Wagner of New York City was not to Caddy's liking. His advice to the leaders of the new Conservative Party of New York was that,

> Before venturing further the new party backers should seriously question whether the conservative cause would be helped by the defeat of Rockefeller and his replacement in Albany by a Mayor Wagner who is answerable only to Herbert Lehman and Eleanor Roosevelt.[80]

---

77. "Young Conservatives Set Up Freedom Party to Rival Labor," *New York Times*, July 22, 1961.

78. George J. Marlin: *Fighting the Good Fight* (New York: St. Augustine's Press, 2002) provides a general overview of the party's history in the 20th century.

79. J. Daniel Mahoney: *Actions Speak Louder* (New Rochelle, NY: Arlington House, 1963), p. 33.

80. Douglas Caddy, "The Conservative Dilemma at the Polls," *New Guard*, March 1962, pp. 30–31. Ironically, the back cover advertisement in that same issue was for the Conservative Party, Inc.

One month later, J. Daniel Mahoney, Vice Chairman, The Conservative Party, Inc., responded in a letter to the editor, assuring the *New Guard* readers that the new party had no intention of running candidates for Congress in 1962 but that it would clearly seek to influence the efforts of Nelson Rockefeller to gain re-election as Governor.

Mahoney maintained that Caddy's view was not the dominant position among YAF members. He claimed, "The strong support which the Conservative Party, Inc. has received from YAF members across New York State convinces us that Mr. Caddy's views do not command any broad allegiance in the ranks of Young Americans for Freedom."[81] In fact, over the subsequent years many YAF members assumed important roles in the New York Conservative Party. Frank Cunningham was an early director of Suffolk County YAF who recalls "being a member of YAF helped me in my preparation to be one of the original people in the New York Conservative Party and run on the first Conservative ticket for councilman in Smithtown, NY."[82] While the early candidates were not elected, they helped establish a permanent organization. In fact, by 1966 it became the third largest party in the state (and thus received the symbolically important Row C for Conservative Party candidates). The question of the appropriate path for conservatives to take in New York continued, however, for several years as a matter of contention in Young Americans for Freedom.[83]

Campus Offensive Against the Left

From its inception, Young Americans for Freedom was committed to involvement in purely student and campus affairs, an area where it would continue to play a role through its first twenty-five years. YAF was concerned with the left-wing bias of the United States National Student Association, a concern exacerbated by the media's acceptance of NSA as the voice of American students. While NSA press releases claimed that the organization represented over one million American students, it consisted of student government members representing fewer than four hundred colleges. But, as Howard Phillips, President of the student government at Harvard and a YAF Director noted, "there are probably not a million students who have even heard of NSA, and the number of individuals who can correctly identify it at all is most likely in the thousands."[84] Delegates to the annual NSA Congress were chosen each year by student governments, not the overall student body. Moreover, no minority reports or vote tallies were presented when considering resolutions, two-thirds of which were passed in 1960 solely by the thirty-five member National Executive Committee, and not the delegates to the Congress.[85]

Building on Carol Dawson's report on the 1960 NSA Congress, YAF determined to continue its involvement with NSA but encourage reforms of the organization. To that end, the organization created the Committee for a Responsible National

---

81. *New Guard*, April 1962, p. 18.

82. 2008 YAF Alumni Survey Responses: Frank Cunningham.

83. See Donald J. Devine, "Conservative Hari-Kari," *New Guard*, April 1966, p. 12 and "Conservative Hari-Kari: A Rejoinder" by J. Daniel Mahoney, then State Chairman of the Conservative Party in *New Guard*, October 1966, p. 24.

84. Howard Phillips, "Inside NSA," *New Guard*, April 1961, p. 11.

85. M. Stanton Evans: *Revolt on the Campus*, pp. 145–163 discusses YAF activities concerning NSA through the 1961 NSA Congress. See also Carol Dawson's report on the 1960 NSA Congress cited above.

Student Organization (CRNSO) in an attempt to reform NSA and make it more reflective of the range of student opinions.[86] While this ad hoc YAF group became the focus of efforts at the 1961 NSA Congress, another broader-based group, Students Committed to Accurate National Representation (SCANR) worked closely with CRNSO.[87]

By May, Doug Caddy let it be known that YAF was going to participate in the 1961 NSA Congress. As he told one reporter, "We will attend in force. NSA has never before been challenged. They have a bureaucracy committed to an extremist liberal viewpoint. They are completely out of line with what the average American student thinks."[88] Meanwhile, Howard Phillips was actively raising funds to bring two hundred YAF delegates to Madison, Wisconsin for the NSA Congress.[89] Among the conservatives there was some hope that the NSA staff was reacting positively to the criticism from YAF since *Indianapolis News* editor M. Stanton Evans was among the speakers invited to the upcoming Congress. Additionally, articles by Russell Kirk and Bill Buckley were included in a pre-Congress NSA publication.[90]

While YAF was planning its strategy to influence the direction of NSA, the left took note of the challenge. On June 8, 1961, a mimeographed letter was sent to a small group of NSA activists by Al Haber, leader of Students for a Democratic Society (the newly adopted name for what had been the Student League for Industrial Democracy). Haber noted that conservatives had made inroads at the 1960 NSA Congress and called for efforts to restrict further conservative expressions at the 1961 Congress.[91] A report on "The Young Americans for Freedom and the New Conservatives" was prepared by SDS member Usher Ward and distributed in preparation for the Congress. The paper tried to link YAF with the John Birch Society and therefore outside the mainstream of American politics.[92]

Robert Walters of the NSA staff pleaded for help from the Americans for Democratic Action (ADA), warning that "It will be a blow to the entire liberal community if the conservatives can claim a victory at this meeting." At its June Executive Committee meeting, the National ADA voted to support its campus division in the efforts to combat YAF at the NSA Congress. The campus ADA strategy was to stress liberal unity on all issues, since they perceived that YAF would present a unified ideological attack. A major effort would be undertaken to work with friendly newspaper reporters to give YAF negative publicity and, as the SDS paper had suggested, associate it with the Birch Society as simply another extremist group. The Campus ADA urged their members to be prepared for YAF to be disruptive during the Congress but they recognized that there was some legitimate support for the YAF positions. As David Allen of Campus ADA wrote, "YAF offers a fresh new approach to college students who are seeking answers to

---

86. Schneider: *Cadres for Conservatism*, p. 61.

87. Kay Wonderlic, "It's Time NSA Takes the Stand," *New Guard*, August 1961, p. 10. Wonderlic was Vice President of the Northwestern University student body for 1960–61 and was, in fact, a YAF member. After the 1961 NSA Congress Wonderlic went on a speaking tour of college campuses that fall. The tour was sponsored by YAF. Schneider: *Cadres for Conservatism*, pp. 61–62. See also, "Reform is Urged in Student Group; National Association Called One-Sided by Girl Critic," *New York Times*, December 3, 1961.

88. *New York Post*, May 22, 1961 as quoted in Andrew: *The Other Side of the Sixties*, pp. 91–92.

89. Schneider: *Cadres for Conservatism*, p. 61.

90. Howard Phillips, "The Isolated Elite of NSA," *New Guard*, August 1961, pp. 11–12.

91. *Ibid.*

92. Andrew: *The Other Side of the Sixties*, p. 93. Much of the following relies on Andrew, pp. 91–101.

the pressing political problems of the day.... the point of view of a substantial portion of the college campuses of our country."[93] Whether it was Campus ADA or SDS, the left feared YAF would use reform of NSA as a wedge to elect YAF supporters to the NSA Executive Committee. This was seen as more dangerous than any frontal ideological assault.

Arriving in Madison, Wisconsin, the Committee for a Responsible National Student Organization attempted to reform the structure of NSA and redirect the NSA Congress to a more conservative position. Among the YAF leaders present were Bob Schuchman, David Franke, Doug Caddy, Scott Stanley, Jared Lobdell, Howard Phillips, Tim Wheeler, Richard Wheeler, Bob Bauman, James Linen, Jameson Campaigne, Bob Schuettinger, Dick Derham, Tom Charles Huston, and Fulton Lewis, III. Allied with them were Tommy Thompson (later Governor of Wisconsin and Secretary of Health and Human Services), Bill Steiger (future Congressman from Wisconsin), Ted Cormaney, and others associated with Kay Wonderlic's Students Committed to Accurate National Representation.[94]

According to one rather critical writer the YAF members in Madison came to all the NSA sessions armed with tape recorders and prepared texts duplicated in advance. They were able to promote their positions effectively and by "never getting too far from a microphone, speaking up on all occasions, and holding press conferences, YAF was able to create the impression of strength beyond its numbers."[95] For the first time the leaders of NSA confronted an organized conservative opposition.

NSA's Executive Committee had turned down YAF's request that conservative speakers such as Senator John Tower and Congressman Donald Bruce be included on the program. When the delegates in Madison refused to suspend the rules and allow William F. Buckley, Jr. to address the Congress, YAF and ISI sponsored a rally in the parking lot of their headquarters hotel. Buckley then spoke to about 400 people at the rally.[96] While YAF failed to make any significant and lasting impact on the left's domination of NSA, YAF National Chairman Bob Schuchman maintained that a beachhead had been established.[97] Moreover, the NSA leadership now had to devote considerable effort to retaining members as more campuses became aware of the left-wing orientation of the organization.

In an editorial, *New Guard* noted that liberals were still firmly in control of NSA and made note of the success of the left in obtaining negative press coverage of Young Americans for Freedom. That YAF did not gain majority support at the NSA Congress was portrayed by some of the media as a rejection of any growing conservative sentiment on campus, overlooking the nature of the NSA and its history of backing liberal causes.[98] Responding to an article in *Time* magazine, YAF pointed out that

---

93. Andrew: *The Other Side of the Sixties*, p. 95 quotes from "ADA Strategy on NSA" and David Allen, "Campus ADA and the Future," June 1961.

94. The list of participants is the recollection of Jared Lobdell in an email received by the author on June 17, 2008. Lobdell was a founding member of the Yale YAF chapter and later editor of *Insight & Outlook*, one of the first campus conservative publications.

95. Edward Cain: *They'd Rather Be Right*, p. 172. See also, Austin C. Wehrwein, "Rightists Divide Student Congress," *New York Times*, August 21, 1961.

96. Tom Huston claims that over 1,000 attended the Buckley speech. For a discussion concerning the uproar over some of Buckley's remarks, see Tom Huston, "NSA: The Turning Point," *New Guard*, August 1964, p. 10.

97. Robert M. Schuchman, "Charge of the Right Brigade," *National Review*, September 9, 1961.

98. "NSA: The Opposition," *New Guard*, October 1961, p. 3.

NSA is no more a liberal-conservative battleground than is a convention of the Americans for Democratic Action. It was our objective in Madison to persuade the far-left students who control NSA to make it a battle-ground by allowing the free expression of all non communistic opinion. This they were unwilling to do.[99]

The telegram also noted that only 390 colleges out of 2,278 in the United States were affiliated with NSA and fewer than 200 campuses sent delegates to the Madison NSA Congress.

YAF continued to present a conservative alternative at future NSA Congresses but its strategy changed to one of encouraging student governments to withdraw from membership in NSA. That fall, YAF sponsored a speaking tour by Fulton Lewis, III who presented the case against further participation in NSA and also supported a tour by Kay Wonderlic that sought to convince student councils to end their affiliation with NSA. Within a year, more than one hundred colleges and universities had withdrawn from the organization.[100] YAF also formed an on-going ad hoc group, Students to Oppose Participation in NSA (STOP-NSA) that continued for several years eventually operating out of a YAF regional office in Houston, Texas.

According to Greg Schneider, "In some small way, YAF's opposition to the leadership of NSA represented the first shot fired in the 1960s campus wars between Left and Right."[101] Since its founding NSA had used an unrepresentative structure to adopt left-wing positions and then promoted itself as representative of college student opinion in America. With YAF's strong opposition presented in Madison at the 1961 NSA Congress and the subsequent action by campuses withdrawing from NSA or, refusing to join the organization and ultimately in forming a new organization of student governments, the mainstream acceptability of NSA had been shattered.

Organizing Campus and Community

By the summer of 1961, YAF's National Director Doug Caddy had begun serving his six-month military service, causing Organizational Director Bill Cotter to spend more time on administrative matters rather than field work to recruit members and build chapters. Caddy had been an employee of Marvin Liebman Associates, operating under a contract between YAF and the firm to provide administration, public relations, and fundraising. Liebman needed to replace Caddy and placed a classified advertisement in *National Review* under the guise of seeking field men for another conservative organization. One of the applicants was a 27-year old graduate of the University of Houston who had been active in Young Republicans and was the 1960 Harris County (Houston) campaign manager for John Tower in his first U.S. Senate race. His name was Richard A. Viguerie and as he stated in his resume, "I am very interested in a career in politics. My political

99. Telegram to *Time* responding to article on NSA in September 1, 1961 issue, Personal Papers of William F. Buckley, Jr., Box 10, Sterling Library, Yale University.

100. Schneider: *Cadres for Conservatism*, p. 62.

101. Schneider: *Cadres for Conservatism*, pp. 63–64.

philosophy is that of a conservative. I am a great admirer of Barry Goldwater and naturally Texas' own John Tower."[102]

Viguerie was invited to travel to New York City in August and meet with William A. Rusher, Marvin Liebman, and a group of YAF National Directors. Viguerie recalls taking an overnight flight from Houston to New York where he first traveled to the apartment of David Franke whom he had known from Texas politics. His first interview was at the *National Review* offices with Rusher followed by a meeting with Liebman and then on to visit with the group of YAF National Directors.[103] Although officially to become an employee of Marvin Liebman Associates, it was deemed essential that he gain the support of the YAF leadership since overseeing the organization would be his main task.

The interviews and meetings went well and seven members of the YAF Board signed a memo recommending that the Board approve the selection of Viguerie. The memo went on to clarify that while Viguerie would not be an official of the organization, he should be given the title of Executive Secretary. Finally, the seven Directors stated that they had "been assured that our National Director, Douglas Caddy, will return to his former position upon the completion of his military service."[104] On September 2, 1961, the Board of Directors met and appointed Richard Viguerie as Executive Secretary. Shortly thereafter his career with YAF and in national conservative politics would begin.

Throughout 1961 YAF began to expand its presence on campuses and in communities across the nation. While the national projects, rallies and publications were most important in providing an overriding framework for the organization, it was the local chapter and council activities that had a lasting influence on thousands of young conservatives. YAF's anti-communism came to the fore in several local chapter activities that took place in the fall of 1961. In November, the Greater Washington Council organized a counter-demonstration outside the White House responding to students against nuclear testing. YAF members held signs proclaiming "I Like Nike," and "Test Si—Disarm No" while showing the media that there were students who supported continued efforts to ensure a nuclear defense.[105]

Indianapolis YAF members noticed that a local auto dealer had begun selling Skoda cars imported from Czechoslovakia where they were made by the Skoda Munitions operations of the Communist government. They confronted the dealer and told him, "As Young Americans for Freedom we are opposed to the sale of Communist-made goods in the United States and feel that you are, perhaps indirectly, assisting the Communist in his goal of world conquest." When this did not deter the sales, thirty-five YAF members picketed the dealership on Saturday, October 28th with signs including "Protest the sale of Communist cars" and "Foreign trade yes, Communist trade no." Thus was to begin what would become a major activity for the young conservatives until the fall of Communism nearly thirty years later.[106]

---

102. Memorandum to Board of Directors dated August 12, 1961 with attached resume, Personal Papers of William F. Buckley, Jr., Box 17, Sterling Library, Yale University, New Haven, CT.

103. Interview with Richard A. Viguerie, August 13, 2008, Manassas, Virginia.

104. Memorandum to Board of Directors dated August 12, 1961, Personal Papers of William F. Buckley, Jr., Box 17, Sterling Library, Yale University. The seven Directors signing the memo were Carol Dawson Bauman, Robert Croll, Lee Edwards, David Franke, James Kolbe, William Madden, and William Schulz. Also joining in the recommendation to retain Viguerie and designate him as Executive Secretary were Marvin Liebman, William Rusher, and M. Stanton Evans.

105. "We Like Nike," *New Guard*, December 1961, pp. 3–4.

106. Gordon L. Durnil, "Communist Cars and Polish Hams," *New Guard*, October 1961, p. 13.

The Greater New York Council, along with similar groupings in Boston, Washington, Philadelphia, Indianapolis and other metropolitan areas, was aggressive in promoting YAF and its conservative principles. After forming a Greenwich Village YAF chapter, the next task for these young conservatives was to invade enemy territory. Chairman of the chapter was Rosemary McGrath who was described as a sandal-shod ex-model and actress who could pass for a Village "beat" but in reality was the wife of a surgeon and mother of two small children.[107] The White Horse was a well-known gathering spot for left-wing radicals in Greenwich Village and Dan Wakefield, a White Horse regular reported,

> These card-carrying, flag-waving members of YAF were suddenly appearing with greater frequency in the press, and now they were showing up at the White Horse. Just like Bill Buckley, they turned out to be perfectly pleasant, witty, intelligent people, and we lefty liberals and right-wing conservatives found we had more common ground of conversation and interest with one another than with all those people who didn't give a hoot about politics, the great yawning masses of the middle.
>
> Most notable was Rosemary McGrath, a tall beauty who was president of the YAF chapter in Greenwich Village . . . With her long black hair, bright red lips, soulful dark eyes, and Goldwater rhetoric, Rosemary soon became known as "La Pasionaria of the Right," giving conservatives a heroine to match the legendary Communist orator of the Spanish civil war.[108]

Stressing the dual need to raise funds and create a community of conservative activists, the Greater New York Council held a "Young Conservatives Ball" at the Waldorf Astoria Hotel to commemorate the first anniversary of YAF.[109]

Similar events were occurring on college campuses with some 180 college conservative clubs listed in a directory published by YAF in the spring of 1961.[110] One young college student expressed the outlook of many early YAF members when she wrote to her parents, "Wow! Is politics ever fun, and ever time-consuming! The conservatives on campus are gradually coming out of the walls. Right now we have seven definite joiners—all really swinging top-rate kids—and we've by no means even begun to scratch the surface."[111] Working closely with the Greenwich Village chapter, students at Hunter College organized an active campus chapter in Manhattan led by Myrna D. Bain, one of a small number of African-American leaders in the conservative organization.[112] Bain's writings

---

107. Mary Perot Nichols, "Beat, and Conservative, Too," *Village Voice*, June 8, 1961. McGrath remained active in community affairs until her death in early 2010, having served as Chairperson (1988–89) and a member of New York City's Community Board 2 that includes the Greenwich Village and Washington Square neighborhoods.

108. Dan Wakefield: *New York in the Fifties*, p. 267.

109. According to a letter from Ed Nash to William F. Buckley, Jr. dated January 3, 1962, the event was a social success but a financial failure. A copy of the invitation to the ball is also in Personal Papers of William F. Buckley, Jr., Box 23—YAF Folder, Sterling Library, Yale University, New Haven, CT.

110. Directory of College Conservative Clubs, Personal Papers of Henry Regnery, Box 80, Hoover Institution, Stanford University, Palo Alto, CA. See also *New Guard*, July 1961, p. 12.

111. Letter of Cathy O'Hara (Malkovich) to her parents dated November 8, 1961 concerning YAF activities at Tufts University, in author's possession.

112. Dan Wakefield, "The Campus Conservatives: Where Are They Now?" *Mademoiselle*, August 1963, p. 330. Bain would go on to graduate work in cultural anthropology and become an expert on the cultural history and literature of the French-speaking Caribbean. Until her death in 2007, she taught in the African American Studies Department at New York City College of Technology.

appeared in *New Guard* over the years, including an overview of the late Sixties protests published in 1969.[113]

Ivy League campuses were a focus of attention for YAF. At Dartmouth, Tom Phillips formed a chapter in 1961 and then went on to help establish outposts on other campuses in New Hampshire. Meanwhile, Alan MacKay, Dick Derham, Danny Boggs, and Howard Phillips had established a presence on the Crimson campus. One of their early meetings in the fall of 1961 featured William A. Rusher, publisher of *National Review*.[114]

Frank Grazioso had attended the founding meeting at Sharon and was a member of the Yale group headed up by Bob Schuchman, YAF's National Chairman. He recently recalled his times with

> ... the brilliant Bob Schuchman who led YAF in its formative years. Wonderful years of collaboration in conservative causes. Frequent meetings with Bob and Bill Buckley at Yale, at Bill's home and the East River Club in Manhattan's East Side. Numerous National Review programs—debates, lectures. Happy Days!"[115]

For Grazioso, "In the early years, with almost no other conservative groups existing, YAF 'kept hope alive.' We had a stated set of objectives, had formed contacts throughout the country. YAF members became active in politics in a direct way with the two parties." After graduating from Yale, Grazioso went on to receive a law degree from the University of Chicago and then returned to New Haven where he has practiced law for forty-four years. During that time he has been involved in numerous civic endeavors and was Chairman for Connecticut's state celebration of the 500th anniversary of Columbus sailing to the New World.

Yale University was the home for several early leaders of YAF, producing not only its first National Chairman but also several inventive leaders. To dramatize their opposition to the calls for unilateral nuclear disarmament, a dozen YAF members undertook a fifty-five mile walk from New Haven to Groton, Connecticut in support of the submarines based there that were capable of firing Polaris missiles. The missile site previously had been the target of protests by groups of pacifists. The Yale students' efforts gained substantial media attention. As they arrived in Groton in December 1961 to show support for continued nuclear testing other YAF members and supporters greeted them.[116]

As part of the Greater New York Council, Columbia University was another campus with an early YAF presence. One who joined YAF in the early years was Liz Trotta, a graduate of Boston University and the Columbia University School of Journalism. When thinking about her days in YAF, for Trotta "my fondest memory is the delight I felt in realizing there were political opinions similar to

---

113. Myrna D. Bain, "Black Students and the American University," *New Guard*, May 1969, pp. 7–9. see also Bain, "March 31–April 4: Five Days to Remember," *New Guard*, May 1968, pp. 5, 22.

114. Flyer promoting October 27, 1961 meeting, Harvard-Radcliffe Young Americans for Freedom, Folder HUD 3890.7000, Harvard University Archives, Pusey Library, Cambridge, MA. The group later changed its name to the Harvard Conservative Club but remained affiliated with YAF. As on many campuses, YAF chapters would die out with the graduation of a group of effective leaders, then resurface later. After a few years of inactivity, the Harvard YAF chapter was reorganized in 1970 and continued for several years thereafter. For the early years see: Lawrence F. Schiff, "The Conservative Movement on American College Campuses," unpublished doctoral dissertation, Harvard University, 1964, pp. 116–119.

115. 2008 YAF Alumni Survey Responses: Frank M. Grazioso.

116. Edward Cain: *They'd Rather Be Right*, p. 174.

my own." Trotta has gone on to a distinguished career in broadcasting, earning three Emmys and two Overseas Press Club awards. Currently she is media critic for the Fox News Channel.[117]

At Boston University, Donald Lambro helped to establish a YAF chapter and was its first chairman in 1961–62. "I was very much influenced in my freshman and sophomore years by Barry Goldwater's *Conscience of a Conservative* but first read about YAF in the *New York Times* when National Chairman Bob Schuchman was leading protests against communism at the United Nations." Lambro related what happened next,

> I contacted YAF Board member Dan Carmen, a Boston stock broker, and he helped us set up our chapter along with another conservative, Jack Molesworth . . . We had about a dozen or so members and were active on campus. Brought in Bill Buckley and Russell Kirk to speak at B.U., passed out YAF literature and recruited members on the campus. I began a weekly radio program on the university FM station . . .[118]

Lambro then served in 1963–64 as managing editor of *New Guard*. As he recalled, "it was a heady time of great political ferment. Goldwater was in his ascendancy and I was part of a great group of people with fond memories of the experience I had as a young writer in the nation's capital." For over twenty years he was chief political correspondent for *The Washington Times*, the author of five books and a nationally syndicated columnist.

Ray LaJeunesse was a student at Providence College when he read about the founding of YAF in *National Review*. Already a conservative, he knew that this was an organization, along with ISI and the Young Republicans, where he could help advance his beliefs. YAF has had a lasting impact on him: "Thanks to YAF and *National Review*. I became and still am deeply involved in the conservative movement. Plus, I met my wife through YAF." LaJeunesse is now the Vice President and Legal Director of the National Right to Work Legal Defense Foundation.[119]

Campuses from New England to the Midwest to the Middle Atlantic states saw the founding of YAF chapters. Several national YAF leaders could be found on the Northwestern University campus. YAF members at the University of Michigan outlined how they had organized on their campus with plans for an "anti-communist week" to coincide with May Day and the showing of "Operation Abolition" and "Communism on the Map."[120] YAF was expanding throughout the country, including into the Southwest. Helen Jane Reddy Blackwell recalls vividly the affect YAF had on her and her subsequent husband, Morton Blackwell, the long-time Republican National Committeeman from Virginia and President of The Leadership Institute.

> Learning about YAF inspired my (now) husband Morton and me, along with 10 or 12 others, to found a conservative club, Students for Conservative

---

117. 2008 YAF Alumni Survey Responses: Elizabeth A. Trotta.
118. 2008 YAF Alumni Survey Responses: Donald J. Lambro. For a discussion of early YAF activities at Boston University see: Lawrence F. Schiff, "The Conservative Movement on American College Campuses," doctoral dissertation, Harvard University, 1964, pp. 123–124.
119. 2008 YAF Alumni Survey Responses: Raymond J. LaJeunesse, Jr.
120. *New Guard*, May 1961, p. 6.

Government, at Louisiana State University in 1961, and changed my entire life. I was an art history major, and continued in my education in that field, but I turned to conservative political activism as my mission in life. We brought nationally prominent conservatives to speak at LSU, and the club continued to function there for decades.[121]

Those experiences as a college student would pave the way for a lifetime of involvement in conservative activities and organizations. As Blackwell noted, "My original experience in helping to found and nurture the LSU YAF chapter has been the foundation for most of my subsequent political activities. The experience of founding that YAF chapter at LSU has had an enormous effect on our lives, both professionally and personally."[122] Indeed, over the next twenty years, Louisiana State University would produce a number of young conservative leaders, including several members of the YAF National Board.

While not initially strong in the South, YAF was building a formidable presence in Florida where a young high school teacher, David R. Jones, would become YAF State Chairman and build an influential state advisory board and establish a number of chapters. Terry Catchpole was one of those chapter leaders, serving as chairman of the University of Miami chapter from its founding to his graduation in 1963. He recalls those years as a "very exciting political time, given the context of the Goldwater movement. A lot of very smart, talented, principled, and motivated people involved in YAF of the day."[123] A writer and public relations specialist, Catchpole contributed a number of articles to early issues of YAF's *New Guard* magazine.

As noted previously, YAF had established a presence on the West Coast with a particularly strong chapter at Stanford University with Richard Noble serving on the YAF National Board. One of the members of that chapter was a graduate student working on his M.B.A. Fred Andre was a graduate of Calvin College and would later earn his law degree. Already a conservative from family influence, YAF reinforced his beliefs and led him to a position as Midwest Director of the Intercollegiate Society of Individualists. President Reagan nominated Andre to serve as a Commissioner on the Interstate Commerce Commission, a position he held from 1982 to 1989, becoming the first independent trucker to serve on the commission.[124]

A number of these early YAF leaders went on to careers in the military. Carl Thormeyer was the founding chairman of the chapter at Penn State University in 1961 and has fond memories of producing a campus newsletter, struggling for University acceptance, supporting Barry Goldwater for President and backing the Vietnam war efforts later in the mid-60s. Thormeyer enlisted in 1966 and spent twenty-five years in the United States Navy, retiring as a Commander, then spent fourteen more years in government before becoming a television meteorologist in California. He believes YAF "kept me focused on limited government, maximum freedom, and Goldwater libertarianism" and "helped me mature into a responsible citizen with conservative values."[125]

---

121. 2008 YAF Alumni Survey Responses: Helen Jane Reddy Blackwell.
122. *Ibid.*
123. 2008 YAF Alumni Survey Responses: Terry Catchpole.
124. 2008 YAF Alumni Survey Responses: Frederic N. Andre. Andre's experience as an independent trucker serving on the commission is discussed in *Overdrive*, October 1982, pp. 37–40.
125. 2008 YAF Alumni Survey Responses: Carl Thormeyer.

Likewise, Elwood Hopkins remembers how he admired and was inspired by the writings and philosophy of William F. Buckley, Jr. as a YAF member at Tufts University. Hopkins went on to receive a PhD from the University of New Hampshire and then graduated from Medical School at Duke University. Currently still on active duty as a physician in the United States Navy, he has also been an ethics instructor at the U.S. Naval Academy in Annapolis. According to Hopkins, his experiences in YAF "allowed me to intellectually make positions that I can defend."[126] A fellow YAF chapter member from the early 1960s, Rudy Peksens, also went on to a military career, rising to the position of Brigadier General. Peksens is now involved in military modeling and simulation for the Raytheon Company.

Many other YAF members in the 1960s joined the military and served in Vietnam but, unfortunately, not all returned. One particularly moving story is that of James Cross, Ohio YAF State Chairman in 1965, who, upon graduation from college, joined the Air Force, and was deployed to Vietnam in 1968 and 1969. He was awarded the Distinguished Flying Cross, the Air Medal, and Vietnamese Cross of Gallantry with Silver Star. In May 1970 the Pentagon announced his death when his Air Force U-17 was discovered crashed in Laos. It was only in 2008 that his remains were identified and returned to his family for burial.[127]

The various rallies, demonstrations, and meetings sponsored by local YAF chapters provided members with a valuable training ground for developing leadership skills. Beginning in the first year and continuing on for several more, these local chapter activities helped build a young conservative community with a shared group identity. This would be the beginning of a network of contacts and political allies that would last a lifetime for many of those who first became active in Young Americans for Freedom in the early 1960s. As Carol Dawson noted,

> I recall the excitement and the atmosphere of great responsibility for the future . . . Today, I read the great names of that period, Buckley, Hayek, Mises, Rusher, Liebman, and on and on, and now realize what a great privilege it was to have been a part of that historic period in American life.

Just as important were the great and lasting friendships made while engaged in the common task of building a new organization. According to Dawson, "Many of the young people I met then are still my best friends and we have established great bonds."[128]

One of those great names cited by Dawson, Marvin Liebman, commented when looking back some twenty plus years later on the early years.

> The first months, and the first years, were heady times indeed. The organization grew by leaps and bounds. Robert Schuchman was the first Chairman and the first board had the brightest kids imaginable. Ideas, plans, meetings, rallies, conferences abounded . . . These were happy times. Everything was based in a very large part on the principles of American conservatism as enunciated in the Sharon Statement. The leaders of YAF knew where they

---

126. 2008 YAF Alumni Survey Responses: Elwood W. Hopkins, III.
127. "Remains of Air Force Pilot from Valley Identified after 38 years," *Youngstown Vindicator*, September 25, 2008.
128. 2008 YAF Alumni Survey Responses: Carol G. Dawson.

were going because their philosophical outlook was based squarely on principle and not on political or economic expediency.[129]

The young leaders of this new organization benefited from the support and encouragement not only of Marvin Liebman, Bill Buckley, Bill Rusher, and Barry Goldwater but also from many others in public and private office. Responding to a letter received in his congressional office, Minnesota Representative Walter Judd showed his support for the organization when he responded, "I am happy to know that you are a member of YAF. I also have been happy to read that they have already achieved a nationwide spread on our college campuses."[130] By the end of 1961, YAF could proclaim a National Advisory Board that included nine Members of Congress, a number that would grow exponentially over the decade, topping out at 100 in 1973.

But all the experiences were not so positive. Discussing how conservative students often found themselves alienated by their liberal professors, University of Kansas Law student Scott Stanley maintained

> Our ideas were subject of ridicule and attack and viciousness on the college campus. Everyone hears endlessly about the McCarthy era, but there's no talk about the terrible harassment that went on against college students and professors who were anti-Communists and anti-collectivists . . . we felt ourselves persecuted for our ideas.[131]

YAF members, and indeed most politically active students, were the exception on American campuses at a time when administrators and faculty were still learning the implications of student activism.

1961 was also the year in which the left-wing media took note of the new conservative organization. Seth Offenbach surveyed the coverage of YAF in five national newspapers—*New York Times, Washington Post, Los Angeles Times, Chicago Tribune,* and *Wall Street Journal*—from 1960 to 1968. He found that ninety of the 283 articles published about YAF during this time frame portrayed the organization in a negative context.[132] Frequently the media would describe YAF as a conservative or right-wing group while not placing any ideological labels on left-wing groups. In this manner a mainstream and generally non-political publication, *Mademoiselle*, selected Tom Hayden, a leader in the new Students for a Democratic Society, to write an article on student activism. Hayden was described as editor of the University of Michigan student paper rather than as a leader in a left-wing organization.[133] Likewise, *Nugget*, a men's magazine of the early 1960s, featured a critical essay on the growth of campus conservatives.[134]

Not to be outdone, the professional left publications joined in the attack with articles on YAF and the young conservative movement in *The Nation, The*

---

129. Marvin Liebman letter of April 22, 1983 to William A. Rusher, Personal Papers of William A. Rusher, Box 174, Manuscript Division, Library of Congress.

130. Letter to Mrs. Sunnie Elliott of Santa Ana, California dated April 5, 1961, Personal Papers of Walter Judd, Box 256, Hoover Institution, Stanford University, Palo Alto, CA.

131. Kenneth Heineman: *Put Your Bodies upon the Wheels: Student Revolt in the 1960s* (Chicago: Ivan R. Dee, 2001), p. 79.

132. Offenbach, "Power of Portrayal," pp. 12–13.

133. Thomas Hayden, "Who Are the Student Boat-Rockers?" *Mademoiselle*, August 1961.

134. Marvin Kitman, "The Button Down Revolution," *Nugget*, October 1961.

Progressive, and *The New Leader*.[135] One writer for the leftist *National Guardian* gave faint praise before criticizing the methods of the YAF members when she said, "The meticulous grooming of the young conservatives seems to make them well-behaved in the minds of some observers. But behind the calm and reasonable exteriors of the standard-bearers is a rank-and-file of dirty in-fighters."[136] Similarly, Arnold Forster and Benjamin Epstein described YAF as a "bouncy, energetic, chesty, and somewhat ruthless outfit."[137] These comments were mild compared to the description of YAF as "racist, militaristic, imperialistic butchers" made by Al Haber of SDS in a June 1961 memo.[138]

Some of the commentators on the left more accurately perceived what was happening on the college campuses of the early 1960s and its subsequent influence on the political scene. As Forster and Epstein concluded,

> They may not be the wave of the future, but these youngsters of extreme conservatism are already a detectable ripple. Their energy, their dedication, and their talent for the written and the spoken word appear to overshadow anything that the more liberal youth on or off the campus can offer.[139]

Yet others were skeptical and did not see the lasting influence of the organization.[140] This was not the conclusion, however, of the ranking members of the Liberal Establishment who perceived the overall challenge from the conservative movement as a more serious threat.

The year ended with Young Americans for Freedom on its way to establishing a broad-based grassroots organization of young conservatives and building public acceptance of its place in the political arena. It was being taken seriously not only by conservatives but also by the liberal media and especially the White House. One of several organizations opposing the New Frontier policies, YAF was closely watched and monitored at 1600 Pennsylvania Avenue.[141] YAF had established chapters on a number of college campuses and in major metropolitan areas, it had begun publishing a magazine of news and opinion on a regular basis, and it had pulled off a successful rally in Manhattan Center with thousands attending. A structure had been established and a staff hired. But there was much more still to be done and, as the new organization entered 1962, it was making plans for the most ambitious undertaking yet.

---

135. Alan C. Elms, "The Conservative Ripple," *The Nation*, May 27, 1961; Murray Kempton, "On Growing Up Absurd," *The Progressive*, May 1961; Marvin Kitman, "New Wave from the Right," *The New Leader*, September 18, 1961.

136. Joanne Grant, "Right Wing Youth Groups Look to Elders for Advice," *National Guardian*, May 15, 1961, p. 7.

137. Arnold Forster and Benjamin Epstein: *Danger on the Right*, p. 224.

138. Quoted in Kenneth Heineman: *Put Your Bodies upon the Wheels*, p. 58.

139. *Danger on the Right*, p. 222.

140. See, for example, Frederick W. Obear, "Student Activism in the Sixties," in Julian Foster and Durward Long, eds: *Protest*, p. 16.

141. *The Other Side of the Sixties*, pp. 151–68 covers some of the Kennedy Administration's efforts to monitor Young Americans for Freedom and other conservative groups.

4. A Presence in the Room

*"YAF has become sort of a presence in the room
and with extraordinary speed."*[1]

The year 1962 proved to be a turning point in the development of Young Americans for Freedom both as a significant campus and community presence as well as a major player on the national political scene. It was during this year that YAF held the largest rally of young conservatives ever, weaned itself away from "adult supervision," conducted its first national convention, and moved its headquarters to the Nation's Capital. While nationwide projects and events coordinated out of YAF's headquarters continued to provide a focus for effective action, college and community chapters were springing up in more areas of the country. These chapters, often acting autonomously, brought with them involvement in local issues, diverse approaches to advancing the cause, and the creativity and vigor present in those launching a new undertaking.

Young Americans for Freedom also enhanced its leadership structure in late 1961 and early 1962 by expanding the size of its Board of Directors and adding several new members from various parts of the country. Included on the Board were Sharon attendees John Weicher of the University of Chicago, Antoni Gollan from the University of Miami, and Northwestern University's John Kolbe, whose brother was already a member of the Board. Newly appointed were Robert Bauman of Georgetown University Law School, Lynn Bouchey of Seattle, Charles McIlwaine of the University of Kansas, and Rosemary McGrath, chairman of the Greenwich Village YAF chapter. Also returning to the Board was Richard Noble of Stanford University. Noble's replacement, Robert Richards of the University of Washington, and Tom Colvin of Davidson both left the Board in late 1961.[2]

By the end of the year, Young Americans for Freedom had expanded its involvement to direct political action by rallying support for conservative candidates for Congress as well as state and local offices. Yet the focus of all political action remained the effort to promote the selection of Barry Goldwater as the GOP presidential nominee in 1964. Truly, as William F. Buckley, Jr. observed, Young Americans for Freedom was now recognized by much of the media simply as YAF and had become "a presence in the room."

Anti-Communism

Foreign policy and specifically opposition to communism continued to be a major focus of YAF attention as 1962 began. Although much of the activity was directed from the national office, local YAF chapters took the initiative in organizing a number of petitions, protests, speeches and demonstrations, as with the

---

1. William F. Buckley, Jr. commenting in the 1962 YAF recruitment film, "A Generation Awakes."
2. The expanded Board of Directors is listed on a news release from Young Americans for Freedom dated February 9, 1962 (in author's possession).

Indianapolis protests against the sale of Communist cars and the Yale student march in support of the Polaris submarine base.

While clearly opposed to much of the Kennedy Administration's domestic and foreign policies, YAF did support the President when they believed his policies correct. In an early application of its support for free trade among free nations an editorial in the January 1962 issue of *New Guard* commended President Kennedy for asking Congress to grant him the authority to bargain with the European Common Market for mutual across-the-board tariff reductions. As the editorial noted, "President Kennedy's move is a definite attempt to seize the diplomatic initiative; it is an act made in the light of the facts of economic life."[3] In the same issue, YAF took early note of the conflict taking place in Vietnam and its significance for the future of freedom, a conflict that would dominate American politics in the latter part of the decade and into the next. National Board Member Robert G. Harley's article reported on his 1961 trip to Southeast Asia. From his meetings with students and government officials he believed it essential to help South Vietnam defend itself from takeover by the North, a policy quietly being carried out at the time by the Kennedy Administration.[4]

When the pacifist organization "Turn Toward Peace" organized demonstrations to protest the nation's defense policies and any resumption of nuclear testing, YAF was there to show an alternative perspective. In February, some 200 Washington area YAF supporters marched with picket signs across the street from the White House. Recruited on short notice from DC and Maryland campuses, the YAF members effectively responded to the "Peaceniks" and obtained media coverage for their position.[5] When a few dozen "Turn Toward Peace" supporters marched in Austin, Texas, they were confronted with YAF members holding signs proclaiming "Pacifism Means Surrender: What Price Life?" and "Neither Red Nor Dead Nor Under the Bed."[6]

Some months later, during the Cuban Missile Crisis, when another pacifist group, Student Peace Union, organized a protest in front of the White House, YAF was there with more than 200 picketers supporting a strong response by the President to the Soviet placement of missiles in Cuba.[7] Perhaps the ultimate in chutzpah, however, was Lee Edwards's letter to the President in April 1962. Edwards, serving as Chairman of the Metro Washington Council of YAF, prepared a "Dear Friend" fundraising letter focusing on the organization's accomplishments and plans for the future. On the letter sent to the White House Edwards crossed out "Friend" in the salutation and replaced it with a hand-written "Mr. President." The letter stated there were ten chapters in the metro Washington area, a "freedom rally" was being planned for the fall, and the organization would be taking part in the 1962 campaigns in Maryland and Virginia. Edwards claimed

We have the will and the energy necessary for this far reaching program. *We need your help today to begin our program tomorrow.* Won't you use the

3. *New Guard*, January 1962, p. 5.
4. Robert G. Harley, "South Viet Nam: Asian Battleground," *New Guard*, January 1962, pp. 14–15.
5. Fredric Solomon and Jacob R. Fishman, "Youth and Peace: A Psychosocial Study of Student Peace Demonstrators in Washington, D.C.," *Journal of Social Issues*, October 1964, pp. 68.
6. Robert Martinson, "State of the Campus: 1962," *The Nation*, May 19, 1962, p. 435.
7. Cabell Phillips, "Pickets Parade at White House," *New York Times*, October 28, 1962. See also "YAF Highlights: 1960–1965" in Personal Papers of Herbert A. Philbrick, Box 218, Folder 3, Manuscript Division, Library of Congress, Washington, DC.

enclosed envelope for your contribution and put it in the mail today? I'm sure you will be as generous as possible. Together, we can and *will* bring about the stronger and freer America that we all desire [emphasis in original].

At the bottom of the letter Edwards added a handwritten note, "Won't *you* help to get America moving forward again?" There is no record of a contribution from the President but Kennedy's office maintained a file on the organization and the President was kept informed of various YAF activities.[8]

One area where YAF disagreed strongly with the Kennedy Administration concerned policy towards the breakaway province of Katanga in the newly independent nation of Congo.[9] After this colony won its independence from Belgium in 1960, businessman Moise Tshombe, founder of the CONAKAT political party that controlled the Katanga provincial legislature, declared that "we are seceding from chaos" and was elected President of Katanga in August 1960. Congolese Prime Minister Patrice Lumumba requested the assistance of United Nations forces to put down the independence move by Katanga. One month later Lumumba was forced out in a *coup d'état* and replaced by Cyrille Adoula, testifying to the chaos and disorganization present in the Congo government. The United States government supported the deployment of troops under the UN banner to defeat the Katangan forces and keep what had been the Belgian Congo a unified country.[10]

YAF clearly was on the side of Katanga and its anti-communist, pro-Western President. Writing in the October 1961 issue of *New Guard*, Carol Dawson Bauman took the United Nations to task for intervening in a domestic dispute. The UN had been a force advocating independence from colonial powers but now was opposing the efforts by the people of Katanga to seek their own independence.[11] In December 1961, YAF organized pickets in front of the White House to support Katanga and oppose the Kennedy Administration's decision to aid the UN effort.[12] Meanwhile, a group of Yale University YAF members offered to go to Katanga and fight the UN mercenaries. Yale student Ross Mackenzie claimed the "UN and the Kennedy Administration are embarked on a course that could be as tragically wrong as was the State Department support of Castro when he was seeking control of Cuba."[13] The travel to Katanga was called off when the State Department informed the students that any such direct action as a combatant might result in their loss of United States citizenship.

To further express their support for Katanga, YAF voted to present an award to Moise Tshombe at its planned March 7, 1962 rally. According to the YAF plans,

---

8. White House Central Name Files, Box 3092, Folder: YAF, John F. Kennedy Presidential Library, Boston, MA.

9. The area was previously known as Belgian Congo and upon independence took the name Republic of the Congo. However, its neighbor to the west, a former French colony, was also called Republic of the Congo resulting in some confusion. The former French colony is now often referred to as Congo-Brazzaville, after the name of its largest city. The former Belgian colony later was renamed Zaire under the dictator Joseph Mobutu and now is called Democratic Republic of the Congo. In the 1960s and again in the late 1990s and early 21st century this area was engulfed in civil war.

10. One of the few books written on the conflict is by a former United Nations official and was published before the end of the conflict. See Conor Cruise O'Brien: *To Katanga and Back: A UN Case Study* (New York: Simon & Schuster, 1962). Several articles and the cover were devoted to Moise Tshombe and Katanga in *Time*, December 22, 1961.

11. Carol Bauman, "UN Blackmail in the Congo," *New Guard*, October 1961, pp. 11–12.

12. "White House Scene of Varied Picketing," *New York Times*, December 17, 1961, p. 60; *Human Events*, December 22, 1961, p. 862.

13. Andrew: *The Other Side of the Sixties*, p. 138.

Tshombe would give a major address to the American people where he could outline the case for Katangan independence.[14] Meanwhile, YAF worked with other anti-communist organizations to garner support for the Katangan cause. YAF National Chairman Robert Schuchman was one of the sponsors of a pro-Katanga full-page advertisement that appeared in the *New York Times*. Under the name "American Committee for Aid to Katanga Freedom Fighters," the sponsors called on the U.S. to stop all support of UN military operations in Katanga, to recognize Moise Tshombe and his government, to secure the withdrawal of all UN military forces from Katanga, and to postpone action on purchasing $100 million of UN bonds. The ad quoted three Democratic Senators (Dodd of Connecticut, Lausche of Ohio and Thurmond of South Carolina) along with Barry Goldwater, each expressing their opposition to the UN action against Katanga.[15] The Kennedy Administration was concerned not only with the specific cause being advocated but also the ability of a number of groups to coalesce around one issue. As presidential assistant Lee White reported, the committee showed ". . . an impressive and frightening ability on the part of the various right-wing groups not only to agree on a common goal but to work toward it effectively on a nation-wide basis."[16]

YAF members were mailed a copy of the advertisement and urged to reprint the ad in their newspapers with the addition of local names to the list of sponsors. They were asked to write both Administration officials and Members of Congress as well as to issue news releases and to write letters to the editor of local publications.[17] Many local chapters followed up by sponsoring speakers and passing resolutions. The Tufts University chapter passed a resolution expressing "its opposition to the aggressive interference in the internal affairs of Katanga by the United Nations forces and the United States support of such policy."[18] Meanwhile, the Queens County (NY) YAF presented a member of the Katanga Information Service to speak at its January 1962 meeting. His topic: "The Truth About What's Happening in the Congo."[19]

Katanga's President accepted the YAF invitation to speak at its March rally in New York City. He applied for a US visa on January 19, 1962, and then the problems began. The State Department simply refused to grant him a visa. In a news release on February 9th, YAF accused the State Department of hypocrisy. Richard Viguerie claimed

In the past, the State Department has admitted Fidel Castro, Nikita Khrushchev and scores of representatives of Communist regimes throughout the world. Not only have these Communists been admitted; their visits have been conducted under the supervision of the State Department. What

---

14. "Tshombe Plans Trip for Address Here," *New York Times*, December 17, 1961, p. 3. See also Gregory Schneider: *Cadres for Conservatism*, pp. 64–65 for a discussion of the invitation to Tshombe.

15. "On the Evidence from Katanga: Shall We Bail the UN Out of Bankruptcy?" *New York Times*, January 12, 1962. The American Committee for Aid to Katanga Freedom Fighters had the same address as Young Americans for Freedom and was another project coordinated by Marvin Liebman.

16. "Confidential Report to the President," White House Staff Files: Lee White File, Box 12, John F. Kennedy Presidential Library, Boston, MA. White began his series of reports on conservative groups and activities on November 28, 1961 and continued filing them over the next year.

17. Memorandum to YAF members from Richard A. Viguerie, no date (in author's possession).

18. *Tufts Weekly*, January 30, 1962.

19. YAF Bulletin, Greater New York Council, January 15, 1962, White House Central Name Files, Box 3092, John F. Kennedy Presidential Library, Boston, MA.

possible excuse can there be for denying President Moise Tshombe's entrance into the United States?[20]

The news release was followed with another memo to YAF Members and Friends, calling on them to write the President and Secretary of State demanding Tshombe be allowed entry to address the March 7th rally. Viguerie maintained that "the Administration is attempting to cover up the United States supported UN military action against anti-communist Katanga. They obviously are fearful of President Tshombe speaking to the American people."[21]

This call for action resulted in a number of telegrams from local chapters directed to Congress and the White House. On February 16th Archer Wilder, Jr., chairman of the University of South Carolina chapter, sent a telegram to the President urging the Administration to grant a visa to Tschombe.[22] The following day brought similar messages such as one from the Montana State University chapter simply stating "we ask your help in bringing Moise Tshombe to our national rally on March 7th."[23] Still others wrote to the White House and State Department requesting a visa for Tshombe but it was all to no avail. Originally the State Department refused to provide a justification for its action but eventually claimed that a visit by Tshombe at this time would "interrupt and jeopardize" efforts to unify the Congo.[24]

In the Garden

The truth of the matter is that the denial of a visa to Moise Tshombe centered around his invitation to address YAF's "Rally for World Freedom" and the audience it would give him to defend his efforts for Katangan independence. Building on the previous year's success at Manhattan Center, the YAF leaders took the bold step of renting the historic Madison Square Garden with its 18,000 seats. Before the rally could be held there were other major challenges and conflicts, all of which were duly reported in the mainstream media. In addition to Tshombe, YAF had acceptances from Senators Thomas Dodd, Barry Goldwater, and John Tower as well as former President Herbert Hoover and Major General Edwin Walker. Dodd, Hoover and Walker were to receive awards along with a number of other prominent individuals while Tshombe, Tower and Goldwater were listed as featured speakers.[25]

First Tshombe was denied a visa and the State Department refused to reconsider its decision.[26] Then Senator Tower objected to the inclusion of Walker on the program. Walker had been invited on the basis of his establishment of courses on

---

20. News release, "National Conservative Youth Group Accuses State Department of Blocking Tshombe's Visit to US," February 9, 1962 (in author's possession).

21. Memorandum from Richard A. Viguerie to YAF Members and Friends titled "Tshombe's Appearance at YAF Madison Square Garden Rally on March 7th," Personal papers of Walter H. Judd, Box 256, Hoover Institution, Stanford University.

22. White House Central Name File, Box 3092: YAF, John F. Kennedy Presidential Library, Boston, MA.

23. *Ibid.*

24. David Lawrence, "Frustrations of a Mass Meeting," *Washington Evening Star*, February 16, 1962.

25. See advertisement for "Rally for World Freedom," *National Review*, February 17, 1962, p. 89.

26. YAF filed suit against the State Department appealing its refusal to grant a visa to Tshombe, but to no avail. Carol Dawson, who was secretary of YAF at the time, recalled "I made a trip to file the paperwork soon after the birth of my first child, Ted." Email to the author, January 24, 2009.

understanding and combating communism for the troops under his command in Germany. When liberal Senators and the media starting attacking his practice of distributing anti-communist materials to the military, Walker was recalled by the Army. In response, he resigned his commission, returned to Texas, became active in the John Birch Society, and only a few weeks before the rally announced that he would be a Democratic candidate for Governor of Texas.[27] Being the first and only Republican elected to statewide office in Texas since Reconstruction, Tower was actively supporting the party's candidate for Governor, Jack Cox. Senator Goldwater explained that Tower objected to Walker's inclusion "on the grounds that since Walker is now a Democratic candidate for Governor in Texas, his appearance with us on the same platform might imply our approval of his candidacy."[28] After a quick polling of its Board, YAF withdrew its invitation to Walker, informing him in a telegram, saying his appearance "would be interpreted as an indirect endorsement of your candidacy by Young Americans for Freedom."[29]

Then came the withdrawal of Senator Dodd, claiming that to many persons the rally had taken on "the appearance of a rather partisan political rally, at which the Democratic Administration will come under very heavy fire."[30] In declining to participate, Dodd noted, "I regard the anti-communist cause as one which, if it is to succeed, must function as a bipartisan movement which is neither dominated by nor identified with any political party or any political faction . . ."[31] He went on to say that "I now find that I am the only publicly identifiable Democrat in a rather large group of Republicans."[32] While no documentation has surfaced to prove the point, it appears that the Kennedy Administration having kept Tshombe from attending the rally was not pleased to see a senior Democratic Senator as part of the program especially since one of the featured speakers would be Senator Goldwater, a likely 1964 opponent. Dodd's anti-communism led him to oppose the President on some foreign policy issues but he was a loyal Democrat on domestic issues and on partisan alignments. Crossing the White House too directly, such as appearing at the YAF rally, might well endanger his influence with the Kennedy Administration and the Democratic majority in the Senate.

Former President Hoover was the next to withdraw from the program. In November, he had told YAF "I greatly appreciate the honor of your invitation" and his staff had twice confirmed his appearance. Yet, as the date for the event approached, Hoover decided to remain on vacation in Florida.[33] The final withdrawal was one not of partisanship, principle, or convenience but rather of contractual obligation. John Wayne, a proud conservative and member of the YAF National Advisory Board, was committed to screen work in England and could not travel to the rally in New York City.[34]

---

27. Walker ended up coming in sixth and last in the Democratic primary with 9.6% of the vote; the eventual nominee and general election victor was John Connally who had resigned as Secretary of the Navy in the Kennedy Administration to make the race. *Texas Almanac: Millennium Edition* (Dallas: The Dallas Morning News, 1999), p. 433.

28. "Anti-Red Rally Running Out of Stars, *Washington Post*, February 13, 1962, p. A2.

29. "Talk by Walker Is Canceled Here," *New York Times*, February 13, 1962.

30. Peter Kihss, "Dodd Cancels His Appearance at Rally of Conservatives Here," *New York Times*, February 15, 1962.

31. David Lawrence, "Frustrations of a Mass Meeting," *Washington Evening Star*, February 16, 1962.

32. Peter Kihss, "Dodd Cancels His Appearance at Rally of Conservatives Here," *New York Times*, February 15, 1962.

33. *Ibid.*

34. Mary McGrory, "Anti-Red Rally Has Speaker Problems," *Washington Evening Star*, February 14, 1962.

The major daily newspapers gave widespread coverage to the trials and tribulations of YAF in lining up and confirming speakers for its March rally. One political scientist's study of five national newspapers found twenty articles about the Madison Square Garden rally; two-thirds of them focused on the problems YAF had before the rally took place.[35] With all the negative coverage and the cancellations by major figures, it would be reasonable to expect that the rally would be a failure. The reality is that not an empty seat could be found in Madison Square Garden while hundreds stood outside trying to gain entrance. As writer Dan Wakefield noted, upon entering the rally he saw that

> Fresh-faced usherettes with good teeth and clean hair (what a refreshing respite for the press after the beatniks!) cradled copies of Goldwater's *The Conscience of a Conservative* the way my friends and I used to hold Franny and Zooey, and welcomed the faithful who carried signs that said "Better Dead Than Red," "Let's Bury Khrushchev," and "Stamp Out ADA."[36]

Chartered buses brought students from colleges throughout New England, New York, New Jersey, Pennsylvania and the Washington metropolitan area. Still others flew in from the Midwest and the South for what would be the largest conservative youth rally in history. College banners vied for space and attention with those proclaiming "Better Dead Than Red," "Down with the UN," and "Staten Island YAF."[37]

As the crowd settled in, the evening began with the presentation of awards to a number of distinguished Americans. Various members of the YAF Board of Directors were called upon to make the presentations. Lee Edwards still recalls the thrill of "presenting John Dos Passos with a YAF Award before 18,000 applauding conservatives in Madison Square Garden."[38] Those accepting awards and making brief remarks included Senator Strom Thurmond (D-SC), former Governor Charles Edison (D-NJ), New York University Professor of Economics Ludwig Von Mises, University of Chicago Professor of English Richard M. Weaver, *Indianapolis News* editor M. Stanton Evans, Deering-Milliken CEO Roger Milliken, and Marvin Liebman as well as author Dos Passos.[39]

While former President Hoover could not be present, his prepared remarks were printed in the rally issue of YAF's magazine. President Tshombe sent a message that was read to the audience and also published in *New Guard* magazine. His "Appeal to the People of the United States" made mention of the attacks on Katanga by UN forces in September and December 1961, noting that "the Katangan people cannot forget that it was American planes that brought reinforcements of arms and materiel to the United Nations forces, and made possible the bombardment of Katanga's capital, now partly destroyed and become a city in a stupor." He went on to distinguish the American people from the government policy and asked for aid, both materially and morally.[40] The import of Tshombe's plea for help was heightened by the action of the Kennedy Administration in denying him admission to the United States to plead his case in person.

---

35. Offenbach, "Power of Portrayal," p. 17.
36. Dan Wakefield: *New York in the Fifties*, p. 266.
37. "Notes from the YAF Rally," *National Review*, March 27, 1962, pp. 190–191.
38. 2008 YAF Alumni Survey Responses: Lee Edwards.
39. The remarks of most rally speakers and award recipients were printed in the March 1962 issue of *New Guard* that was distributed to all who attended the rally.
40. *Ibid.* p. 13.

Among the evening's speakers were Senator John Tower (R-TX), Congressman Donald Bruce (R-IN) and *National Review* editor L. Brent Bozell. Perhaps the most memorable of the remarks before the keynote speaker were those offered by Bozell. After a lengthy philosophical discussion of gnosticism nearly put the audience to sleep, he sounded the clarion call for conservative action. Noel Parmentel provided a rather humorous report on the rally that included his observations about Bozell's speech: "the high point for me came when he alerted me to the Gnostics. I knew all about the Red Menace, and the Yellow Peril. I have even done some alerting of my own about the Lavender Lapse. But I did not know about the threat of Gnosticism. Watch out for them Gnostics."[41] Bozell ended his speech by listing the orders that would go out in a conservative administration.

To the Joint Chiefs of Staff: Prepare for an immediate landing in Havana. To the Commander in Berlin: Tear down The Wall. To our chief of mission in the Congo: Change sides. To the Chairman of the Atomic Energy Commission: Schedule testing of every nuclear weapon that could conceivably be of service to the military purposes of the West. To the Chief of the CIA: You are to encourage liberation movements in every nation of the world under Communist domination, including the Soviet Union itself. And you may let it be known that when, in the future, men offer their lives for the ideals of the West, the West will not stand idly by.[42]

The crowd went wild with excitement and approval. Starting slowly, Bozell had reached a crescendo with his call for action.

The highlight of the evening, and the part of the program for which everyone was waiting, was the keynote address. When Senator Goldwater was introduced an eight-minute demonstration erupted. Alluding to the controversy that kept Tshombe from accepting his award and addressing the rally, Goldwater assured his audience, "My credentials are in order tonight. Dean Rusk gave me a passport for leaving Washington and Nelson Rockefeller gave me a visa for entering New York."[43] Goldwater's speech topic was "To Win the Cold War" and he made clear that the enemy was not the Soviet Union but rather the ideology of Communism. "Our enemy is not a nation but a political movement made up of ideologically possessed people who have organized themselves as an armed force and secured control over entire countries."[44] It was nothing that most in the audience had not heard before but coming from Barry Goldwater made all the difference. Goldwater's speech closed out the night on a high note as the thousands of conservatives left Madison Square Garden feeling a little less lonely and a little more secure in their beliefs.

The Madison Square Garden rally established YAF as a national political force with news coverage in most major newspapers and weekly newsmagazines. However, even here the coverage on the YAF rally included considerable space devoted to the liberal counter protests and rally that attracted fewer than 3,000 persons.[45] Just as important as the increased media attention and the recognition

---

41. Noel Parmentel, Jr., "Gnostics at the Garden," *The Commonweal*, March 30, 1962, p. 15.
42. "And Why Not?" *National Review*, March 27, 1962, p. 190.
43. *Ibid.* p. 191.
44. Barry M. Goldwater, "To Win the Cold War," *New Guard*, March 1962, p. 11.
45. Offenbach, "Power of Portrayal," p. 18. "The seven remaining articles about the rally all contained a reference to a counter-protest by several liberal organizations that occurred simultaneously in New

from the political establishment was the emotional effect of the rally on YAF members and potential members. As one historian concluded, "In the months that followed, YAF members exhibited a confidence (some might say naivete) that would help sustain their organization for the next few years."[46] After riding on a bus with fellow YAF members from the Boston area, one student wrote her parents and described her reaction to the event:

> Wow! Was it ever great!
> The speakers were excellent. My favorite was Senator Tower—what a little fireball he is. But all in all, I had the greatest time ever! It's such a thrill to get into this movement at its beginnings—I think you get a tremendous sense of accomplishment in starting things up. And there's certainly no lack of opposition, that's for sure.[47]

Alfred DelliBovi, who would go on to become President and Chief Executive Officer of the Federal Home Loan Bank of New York, recalled with pride many years later of serving as a volunteer usher at the rally while a high school student in Queens.[48] Charles G. Mills was one of a group of Yale YAF members who had attended both the Manhattan Center rally in 1961 and the Madison Square Garden event. Mills recalled "a lot of my early political involvement was influenced by fellow members of YAF." After graduating from Yale he obtained his law degree from Boston College and has published law review articles as well as currently writing a syndicated column.[49]

But even those living far away who could not attend the rally were affected by its success. Tim Hunter recalled later the influence it had on his decision to become active in Young Americans for Freedom. "Yes, it was a great moment in history. I had never heard of YAF until I read about the YAF rally in *Time* magazine in, I believe, 1962. I lived in Albuquerque and attended high school." A few years later Hunter went on to the University of New Mexico and formed a YAF chapter shortly after the "moral victory" of Goldwater in 1964.[50]

The historic nature of this one event was perhaps best summed up by Richard Viguerie, then Executive Secretary of YAF, and David Franke, chair of the Greater New York Council, when they noted many years later, "If you are looking for a birth date when the conservative movement emerged out of the womb and announced itself to the public, no other event would qualify better than YAF's Madison Square Garden rally."[51] Viguerie noted that YAF was the first major grassroots conservative organization and its success with the rally in the middle of Manhattan showed the nation that a conservative movement really existed, was a truly national effort, and would from that point on have a major influence on American politics and society for the remainder of the century.[52]

York City. These liberal organizations amassed between 1,500 and 3,000 people, depending on the media source. However, every post-rally article mentioned their presence."
   46. Dallek, "Young Americans for Freedom: The Rise of Modern Conservatism, 1960–1964," p. 42.
   47. Letter of Cathy O'Hara (Malkovich) to her parents dated March 9, 1962 (in author's possession).
   48. 2008 YAF Alumni Survey Responses: Alfred A. DelliBovi.
   49. 2008 YAF Alumni Survey Responses: Charles G. Mills.
   50. Tim Hunter email to the author, August 30, 2008.
   51. Richard A. Viguerie and David Franke: *America's Right Turn*, p. 66.
   52. Interview with Richard A. Viguerie, August 13, 2008, Manassas, VA.

A National Organization Develops

The YAF members left Madison Square Garden with excitement and enthusiasm and commitment, ready to organize new campus and community chapters. They were aided by a new "College and Community Organization Manual" released by the national office.[53] YAF now claimed 310 chapters throughout a growing number of states and a National Advisory Board that included 38 sitting Members of Congress.[54] One of those advisory board members was a movie actor who had most recently made a career as host of a television drama series and as a motivational speaker at General Electric plants across the country. To help raise badly needed contributions, Richard Viguerie wrote to Ronald Reagan and asked for his help, enclosing a fundraising letter to be signed by Reagan. In words few knew at the time to be so predictive of future events, the letter had Reagan proclaiming,

> I know of no other group in the nation which is going to be more effective in preserving and extending our cherished goals. There is no need to emphasize that these young people are the future leaders of the nation. As they grow and develop, so will our country.[55]

Weeks went by without a response until one day an envelope came in the mail with the proposed fundraising letter enclosed. All over the letter were crayon marks and attached was a note from Reagan: "I just found this in Ronnie's toy chest. I'm sorry it's late but if you think my name would help, go ahead and use it." With that, the relationship between Ronald Reagan and Young Americans for Freedom was established and the political career of the future President had begun.[56]

By the time of the April 1962 Board of Directors meeting the YAF leaders had a new confidence in their ability to build and administer their own organization. Under the leadership of Don Shafto, they had produced two successful rallies in the heart of liberal New York City.[57] Lee Edwards and Carol Dawson Bauman led a team of volunteers who had produced a quality magazine for over a year, a magazine that would continue publication on a regular basis for the next twenty plus years. The media and the political establishment recognized YAF's presence. Plans were underway for producing a thirty-minute recruitment film. New chapters were being chartered and state organizations developed. Now was the time to take off the training wheels and go pedaling on their own. In this environment, the Board voted to end its contract with Marvin Liebman Associates and placed Richard Viguerie directly on the YAF payroll as its full-time Executive Secretary.[58]

53. A copy can be found at Group Research Inc. Archives, Box 343, Columbia University, New York, NY.

54. Sara Diamond: *Roads to Dominion* (New York: The Guilford Press, 1995), p. 61.

55. A copy of the Reagan fundraising letter on his personal Pacific Palisades, CA letterhead dated June 18, 1962 can be found at Group Research Inc. Archives, Box 403, Columbia University, New York, NY.

56. Interview with Richard A. Viguerie, August 13, 2008, Manassas, VA. Viguerie tells the story also in Richard A. Viguerie & David Franke: *America's Right Turn*, pp. 96–97.

57. Shafto would go on to organize another successful rally on Long Island in October 1962 featuring Ronald Reagan and would be involved in orchestrating other events for YAF and the Goldwater campaign.

58. Interview with Richard A. Viguerie, August 13, 2008, Manassas, VA. Liebman had recommended

This was a time of developing experience for the young conservatives now responsible for the expansion and administration of their organization. As one leader explained "you grew up very quickly putting things together. You exposed yourself to risk and failure."[59] Commenting on plans for a chapter meeting, one college YAF member stated: "Good news. Fulton Lewis, III is coming! He's going to bring the film ("Operation Abolition") and speak on Wednesday night the 18th. I'm absolutely walking on air—it seems too good to be true."[60] When the event was held, 150 students and faculty were in the audience and the YAF chapter had established itself as a presence on campus.

From an early point in the organization's history, local chapters were encouraged to publish their own newsletters and eventually independent newspapers for distribution not only to members and supporters but to be used as a recruitment tool with a broader audience. By the end of the spring 1962 semester, over fifty chapters had their own publications. Not only did these publications inform members of political opinion and events but they also provided an opportunity to obtain experience in public relations and journalism, experience that would be valuable later in their political and community involvement.[61] Miami YAF directed one of its publications, "The Young American View," to high school students specifically, an audience that was just beginning to be approached for possible membership and chapter organization.[62] At Tufts University, the chapter newsletter focused on foreign policy issues with an article discussing American failures in China, Cuba and Angola by Bill Nowlin.[63] The titles of the publications ranged from "Evolve" at San Diego State University to "Campus Conservative" at Miami University (FL), to "New Liberal" at the University of Idaho and "Reveille" at the University of Louisville. All were locally written, locally published, and locally funded.[64]

A number of state organizations including Indiana, Ohio, and New Hampshire as well as the Nassau (NY) County Council and the Greater New York Council opened offices to coordinate the activities of their local chapters.[65] Arizona YAF chapters sponsored a rally with Senator Goldwater as the featured speaker with over 1500 in attendance. Florida YAF held a testimonial dinner in Orlando honoring one of YAF's Advisory Board members, Senator Spessard Holland (D-FL), with Senator Strom Thurmond (D-SC) serving as the featured speaker.[66] In addition, Florida YAF, under State Chairman and high school teacher David Jones, also took

this action in a memo to the Board of Directors dated January 17, 1962, Personal papers of William F. Buckley, Jr., Box 23, Folder: YAF, Sterling Library, Yale University, New Haven, CT.

59. *Ibid.*

60. Letter of Cathy O'Hara (Malkovich) to her parents dated March 30, 1962 (in author's possession).

61. "Report to YAF Supporters" from Richard A. Viguerie, September 1962. The report was widely distributed and can be found in Personal Papers of William F. Buckley, Jr., Box 23, Folder:YAF, Sterling Library, Yale University, New Haven, CT; Personal Papers of Herbert A. Philbrick, Folder 1:YAF, Manuscript Division, Library of Congress, Washington, DC; Hall-Hoag Archives, Box 49–13, Group HH 0429, John Hay Library, Brown University, Providence, RI.

62. Personal Papers of Herbert A. Philbrick, Folder 1:YAF, Manuscript Division, Library of Congress, Washington, DC.

63. *Tufts Rightings*, October 31, 1962 (in author's possession).

64. *New Guard*, June 1962, pp. 14–15; September 1962, p. 13.

65. "Freedom Group Opens Office for Indiana," *Indianapolis News*, April 10, 1962; "Report to YAF Supporters" from Richard A. Viguerie, July 1962, Hall-Hoag Archives, Box 49–13, Group HH 0429, John Hay Library, Brown University, Providence, RI. This earlier July 1962 report can also be found in White House Central Name Files, Box 3092, Folder: YAF, John F. Kennedy Presidential Library, Boston, MA.

66. "Report to YAF Supporters" from Richard A. Viguerie, September 1962.

the lead in developing and promoting a high school course in "Communism vs. Americanism." The state organization was successful in convincing the Florida legislature to enact the course for all public high schools in the state. Later, other state organizations would take up advocacy of the program and the YAF national office would re-package it as "Freedom vs. Communism."[67] In October, Nassau County YAF held a massive rally with Ronald Reagan making his debut as a speaker for YAF. According to reports, 13,000 people attended the event.[68]

Local chapters undertook a wide range of projects and activities to promote conservatism, express their opinions on specific issues, and build a sense of camaraderie and community. One New England chapter sponsored a debate on conservatism vs. liberalism featuring National Board Member Jack Molesworth and a professor of Sociology at the university.[69] Still others sponsored showings of "Operation Abolition" and the YAF recruitment film, "A Generation Awakes." YAF had hired a production company to capture some local chapter activities, including the Yale student march to Groton, Connecticut, and the Madison Square Garden rally. Interspersed with these clips were interviews with YAF leaders David Franke and Don Shafto, comments by William F. Buckley, Jr. and National Chairman Robert Schuchman, and testimonials by four congressional members of the National Advisory Board: John Ashbrook (R-OH), William Cramer (R-FL), Donald Bruce (R-IN) and William Jennings Bryan Dorn (D-SC).[70]

During the various spring break weeks of 1962, Miami YAF sponsored a booth on the Fort Lauderdale beach to attract the attention and interest of college students from campuses without a YAF chapter.[71] Greenwich Village YAF carried out a varied schedule of activities throughout the year starting with its annual party in January at the Champagne Gallery, a Village landmark.[72] Chapter Chair and National Board Member Rosemary McGrath ran as a candidate for New York State Assembly and garnered the volunteer efforts of many New York area YAF members in her campaign. The chapter also took an active role in a number of community issues, including opposing a city plan that would have eliminated push-cart vendors in Greenwich Village. Testifying before the City Board of Estimate, McGrath noted, "Remove the Montmartre from Paris, explode the Palatine Hill in Rome, tear down the Mark Hopkins Hotel in San Francisco: It is the same as destroying the pushcarts that serve their neighborhoods and preserve the flavor of old New York."[73] After McGrath's stirring presentation, the proposal was withdrawn without a vote and the pushcarts were saved. Following the lead of the Greater New York Council, the Westchester (NY) County Council held a Conservative Ball, an event that attracted many of the leading conservatives in the New York area. Those who attended received a 28-page program along with the dinner and dancing.[74] While regarded as a bastion of liberalism, the New York City area proved to be the strongest area of YAF support in the organization's

67. Gregory Schneider: *Cadres for Conservatism*, p. 64.

68. Rick Perlstein: *Before the Storm*, p. 499. The rally is also mentioned in *New Guard*, November 1962 and in "Report to YAF Supporters" from Richard A. Viguerie, September 1962.

69. Tufts YAF Newsletter, May 8, 1962 (in author's possession).

70. Interview with Richard A. Viguerie, August 13, 2008, Manassas, VA.

71. "Report to YAF Supporters" from Richard A. Viguerie, July 1962.

72. Greater New York Council Bulletin, January 15, 1962, White House Central Name Files, Box 3092, Folder: YAF, John F. Kennedy Presidential Library, Boston, MA.

73. Charles Grutzner, "Pushcart Cause Won at City Hall," *New York Times*, May 11, 1962. The McGrath campaign for State Assembly is discussed in *New Guard*, August 1962, p. 4.

74. "Report to YAF Supporters" from Richard A. Viguerie, September 1962.

early years. David Franke claimed that in one year the Greater New York Council had grown from 17 members to over 3,000 and from one central chapter to a council of 50 local chapters.[75]

Meanwhile, throughout 1962 YAF was expanding its presence geographically beyond its initial base in New England, the Middle Atlantic States, and the Midwest. When the national office held a membership contest, the winners were the University of Arizona (with 82 new members) and the South Florida Community Chapter (with 221 recruits). YAF was also beginning to build a strong unit in California under the leadership of State Chairman Barry Goldwater, Jr., son of the Senator.[76]

The availability of supportive material such as the Chapter Organization Manual and the recruitment film were valuable tools for the local chapters. Nevertheless, each one was virtually autonomous in developing its own programs and funding its own activities. Through building local chapters, developing programs, recruiting members, and raising funds, literally thousands of young conservatives gained the knowledge that would benefit them later as they assumed roles in American society and government.

Fighting the NSA

On campuses across the country, YAF continued its campaign against the liberal domination of the National Student Association by taking a two-pronged approach: encourage schools to disaffiliate or not join NSA while at the same time organizing conservative support at the NSA Congress. Prior to the 1962 NSA National Student Congress, YAF was involved in organizing opposition to NSA on several campuses. Among those voting not to join or remain in NSA were the universities of Iowa, Missouri, Nebraska, Oklahoma, and Virginia, as well as Kansas State, Ball State, Northwestern, Earlham College and Gettysburg College.[77] One example of this activity was the YAF campaign at the University of Oklahoma. Scott Stanley, Jr., a National Board Member, and William Cotter, YAF's Organization Director, arrived in Oklahoma City two weeks before a scheduled referendum on withdrawing from NSA and met with conservative students from the Norman campus to plan strategy. They also conducted a speaking tour of civic clubs throughout the state, impressing on the audiences the unrepresentative character of the NSA. With the largest turnout in the university's history, the students voted by a three-to-one margin to withdraw from NSA.[78]

On many campuses YAF gave special attention to fraternities and sororities in view of the expressed opposition of the NSA to the Greek letter organizations. YAF provided speakers to fraternities and sororities and in later years its STOP-NSA committee distributed a *Greek Report* outlining the NSA's resolutions and policy statements against the fraternity system.[79] But throughout the decade, Greek involvement in the campaign against NSA was sporadic.[80]

75. Letter from David Franke to YAF Members, White House Central Name Files, Box 3092, Folder: YAF, John F. Kennedy Presidential Library, Boston, MA.

76. 2008 YAF Alumni Survey Responses: Barry M. Goldwater, Jr.

77. Tom Huston, "Revolt Ahead in NSA?" *New Guard*, August 1962, p. 9.

78. Nan Robertson, "Struggle on the Campus: How a Liberal Group Lost at the University of Oklahoma," *New York Times*, May 15, 1962, p. 43.

79. Lee Edwards, Target Fraternities," *New Guard*, August 1962, pp. 6–7, 13.

80. According to a 1970 report to the YAF National Board of Directors from Albert Forrester,

YAF's second prong was to take part in the annual NSA National Student Congress and try to move the organization away from the far-left position it normally assumed. When the 1962 Congress was held at Ohio State, YAF attempted to organize an effective conservative floor leadership and had an unexpected degree of success. According to an interview with National YAF Board Member Bob Bauman, YAF helped to defeat several resolutions and for the first time elected a YAF member to the NSA National Executive Board.[81] In future years, YAF would send key volunteers to the NSA Congress and publish a detailed report of their experiences in the *NSA Report* booklet that was distributed to student leaders on various campuses. At times, YAF's influence was substantial not only in influencing resolutions and policy statements but also in the election of organization leadership. In 1966, YAF member Danny Boggs ran for President and received over one-third of the vote, the high water mark in terms of influencing elections.[82]

Boggs life history is a good example of the conservative leadership produced by Young Americans for Freedom. Active in the early years of the organization while an undergraduate at Harvard, Boggs was attending the University of Chicago Law School on a Mechem Scholarship at the time of the NSA Congress in 1966. President Reagan appointed Boggs to the United States Court of Appeals for the Sixth Circuit in 1986 and in 2003 he became Chief Judge of the Circuit. Judge Boggs recently recalled his times in YAF as involving "good friends, discussions, and arguments" and as an essential element in providing him with a conservative education.[83]

Despite their limited success at the 1962 NSA Congress, that fall YAF continued its efforts to have colleges disaffiliate or not join NSA. This became official policy when the YAF National Board of Directors at its December 1962 meeting passed a resolution condemning NSA as "anti-democratic and unrepresentative" of the majority of American students. The resolution decided "Until such time as NSA adopts democratic reforms, YAF urges all schools and colleges to oppose attempts to start NSA chapters on their campuses and YAF encourages withdrawal from NSA where chapters now exist."[84] First to turn down membership after the 1962 NSA Congress was Texas Christian University where the vote was five-to-one against joining. Then came the vote to disaffiliate at Ohio State University, site of the most recent NSA Congress when, with 8,300 students participating, the margin against continued membership was two-to-one.

Even at colleges traditionally perceived as liberal, YAF had success in its campaign against NSA. YAF National Board Members Scott Stanley, Jr. and Howard Phillips met with a small group of conservative students at Tufts University to plot strategy for a referendum on NSA membership. Through extensive use of the mimeograph machine, numerous letters to the school newspaper, and appearances

National Coordinator of the STOP-NSA Committee, "Greeks, recently, have minimized NSA effectiveness but it looks like they may be returning to the fight. The Edgewater Conference of Greeks wants to assist us financially with the publication of the *NSA Report* and they have offered to underwrite a separate booklet dealing solely with NSA and the Greek system. They are also confident that we can bring other groups of Greeks actively to our side." Personal Papers of Patrick Dowd, Box 3, Hoover Institution, Stanford University.

81. College Press Service, "Bauman Notes YAF Strength, Foothold on NSA Executive Board," *Tufts Weekly*, March 15, 1963. For YAF activity at the 1963 NSA Congress at the University of Indiana, see "Vote 'No' on NSA," *New Guard*, October 1963, pp. 7, 18.

82. Seymour Martin Lipset and Philip G. Altbach: *Students in Revolt* (Boston: Beacon Press, 1969), p. 207.

83. 2008 YAF Alumni Survey Responses: Danny J. Boggs.

84. *New Guard*, December–January 1963, p. 13.

at student meetings the YAF members presented the case against membership. Here the emphasis was placed on the unequal balance between membership costs and benefits rather than a clear-cut ideological assault on the left-wing nature of NSA. When the referendum was held, the vote was 863–329 with 72.4% voting against joining the organization. Syndicated columnist Fulton Lewis, Jr. (and father of YAF Board Member Fulton Lewis, III) reported: "The vote at Tufts University, a Massachusetts institution thought to be liberally-oriented, was decisive. Says a Tufts spokesman: 'The turnout was very heavy and the outcome a distinct surprise. The school newspaper had been lobbying hard for NSA.'"[85] Still more stunning was the vote to withdraw from NSA at Antioch College since the decision came approximately one year after the school had joined.[86]

In a letter to a staff member at Americans for Democratic Action, the then President of NSA, W. Dennis Shaul, recognized the effect that YAF was having on NSA membership when he reported "we have had a great deal of trouble with attacks from the right wing during the last few months. In fact vicious attacks have cost us affiliations at Indiana and Texas. Some of these were directed by YAF."[87] In light of these efforts by YAF, more and more of the NSA bureaucracy's time had to be devoted to retaining schools as members and encouraging others to join.

The effort to disengage campuses from the National Student Association continued throughout the next several years. YAF's Board of Directors at its September 1963 meeting reaffirmed its opposition to NSA as constituted. The resolution went on to urge colleges "to oppose attempts to affiliate their school with the National Student Association, and where schools are presently affiliated, Young Americans for Freedom, Inc., encourages their withdrawal from the National Student Association."[88] As part of this effort, in 1964 Robert Schuchman wrote an *exposé* on NSA that was published in a student magazine widely distributed on campuses across the country.[89]

While realizing the inadequacies of NSA, many campus leaders believed that there was a void to be filled with an organization dedicated to student services and not concerned with making political statements. After attending the 1963 NSA Congress, William Featheringill, Student Body President at Vanderbilt University, decided to visit with other student government leaders and explore the possibility of developing a new organization. After much discussion and planning, Featheringill gained the support of 23 sponsoring schools for an organizational conference in St. Louis in April of 1964. Sixty-two schools were represented at the St. Louis meeting and after lengthy sessions, a new organization called Associated Student Governments of the United States of America had been brought into being.[90] The new group continued to provide a non-political

---

85. Fulton Lewis, Jr., "Birds of a Feather," syndicated column reprinted in *Tufts Weekly*, March 1, 1963.

86. Fulton Lewis, Jr., "Liberal Antioch College Withdraws from NSA," *Human Events*, December 14, 1963. Lewis went on to observe "on virtually every campus where NSA is rejected the fight is led by members of the Young Americans for Freedom and the college Young Republicans." With turnover among students, the pattern of joining and then disaffiliating was not too uncommon. Up to the middle of the 1960s, the University of Southern California had joined NSA on three occasions and withdrawn from membership on another three occasions.

87. Letter of May 27, 1963 as quoted in Andrew: *The Other Side of the Sixties*, p. 171.

88. "Vote 'No' on NSA," *New Guard*, October 1963, p. 7.

89. Robert Schuchman, "NSA from the Right," *Moderator*, Summer 1964, pp. 16, 19. Three articles by Tom Charles Huston in YAF's magazine also cover the conservative response to NSA: "The Rise and Fall of NSA," *New Guard*, April 1964, pp. 8–10, "NSA: The Turning Point," *New Guard*, August 1964, pp. 9–10, 12, and "You, Too, Can STOP NSA," *New Guard*, September 1964, pp. 11–12.

90. Tom Charles Huston, "Student Leaders Form New Alliance," *New Guard*, June 1964, pp. 10–12.

avenue for communication on student government issues as well as direct student services for many years.

YAF's STOP-NSA committee continued to have success in convincing schools to withdraw or never join the organization. By 1966, an official of NSA had to admit that only about 280 of the 1700 eligible schools were members, adding "This number represents a significant drop in membership from 1961 when about 350 schools belonged to the organization."[91] Among the additional schools to disaffiliate from NSA were the University of Michigan, Wayne State University, University of Houston, George Washington University, and American University while Northwestern University, North Texas State University, and the University of Colorado voted not to join.[92]

The most significant controversy surrounding NSA developed, however, in February 1967 when a leftist magazine disclosed that since 1952 the Central Intelligence Agency had been providing substantial funding to the organization. Based on documentation provided by a disgruntled former employee, the article went on to describe the various foundations used by the CIA as conduits for the funding.[93] The reaction from YAF was swift and even more critical of the government than the recipient organization. National Chairman J. Alan MacKay declared that

> Young Americans for Freedom is deeply shocked that the Central Intelligence Agency should secretly attempt to influence student opinion. But we are absolutely astounded to discover that federal funds in huge amounts have been placed in the hands of irresponsible leftists who do not represent American students.[94]

YAF's Executive Director, David R. Jones, followed up with a tongue in cheek request for an application form for a CIA grant, claiming that the organization would be willing to increase its opposition to the Johnson Administration's policies since that seemed to be a prerequisite for government funding.[95]

In response to the NSA-CIA disclosure, Barry Goldwater took the occasion to both praise YAF and criticize the CIA. His March letter to David Jones made clear his continuing support of YAF, pointing out that it was succeeding with solely private, voluntary support.

> As one individual who always has supported your work, let me re-pledge that support now. I trust that you will be able successfully to continue in

---

91. Quoted in "NSA: Leftists Still in Control," *New Guard*, October 1966, pp. 4–5.

92. "NSA Exodus Continues," *New Guard*, December 1967, pp. 3–4.

93. Sol Stern: "A Short Account of International Student Politics and the Cold War," *Ramparts*, March 1967. David Horowitz, editor of the magazine at the time, recalls this incident in *Radical Son* (Glencoe, IL: The Free Press, 1997), pp. 159–160. See also Neil Sheehan, "A Student Group Concedes It Took Funds from CIA," *New York Times*, February 14, 1967 and "Student Unit Discloses CIA Subsidy," *Washington Post*, February 14, 1967.

94. "CIA Subsidy of NSA Revealed; Congress May Investigate," *New Guard*, March 1967, pp. 6–7. The reaction to the disclosure is also covered in Steven V. Roberts, "CIA is Criticized by Conservatives," *New York Times*, February 23, 1967.

95. News release with letter from David R. Jones to Richard Helms, Director, Central Intelligence Agency, dated February 14, 1967, Group Research Archives, Box 343, Columbia University, New York, NY. See also "CIA/NSA: The Central Issue," *New Guard*, April 1967, pp. 3–6 and Phillip Abbott Luce, "Fly Away with the CIA," *New Guard*, April 1967, pp. 11–12, 30.

your outstanding demonstration of what can be done with the contributions and help of private citizens in a cause that will someday triumph.[96]

The exposure of government financial assistance to NSA did provide a fundraising topic for Young Americans for Freedom. On August 28th, Special Assistant to the President Marvin Watson forwarded to Walt Rostow, National Security Advisor, a letter from W.B. Steel, California YAF Chairman, criticizing the CIA for funding NSA. Steel asked, "Why is CIA building Socialism behind our backs with our own tax money? A congressional investigation is long overdue. The CIA must be controlled and prompt action is urged."[97] There is no indication that either Watson or Rostow took any action to explore the situation further.

Despite the controversy, NSA survived the disclosure of government funding and went on to hold its 1967 Congress at the University of Maryland, just a few miles outside the Nation's Capital. According to one conservative who attended the Congress, "nothing really has changed since public disclosure of NSA's role as the domestic student arm of the Central Intelligence Agency. The same authoritarian organization is still in control and the resolutions somehow manage to become even nuttier than before."[98] YAF members and other conservatives came together early in the NSA Congress to try and make structural changes in the organization that would emphasize the provision of student services. They published a daily newspaper, "The Right Look," during the Congress and proselytized among the delegates.

Among those coordinating conservative efforts were Bob Feinberg, Bruce Weinrod, Alan Bock, Bill Overmoe, and David Friedman. Their efforts paid off in making many students aware of the problems inherent in the NSA structure. As Bock reported,

> The delegation from City College of New York, one of the few delegations which was actually elected, had not considered themselves conservatives until they got to College Park, where they found that the spectrum at NSA made them feel more comfortable on the Right . . .[99]

But the votes were not there once again and after ". . . it became apparent that there was little hope of viable reform, most came around to the opinion that NSA was not savable, and should be destroyed." Several of the more moderate and conservative delegates who had come to College Park with an open mind left determined to move for disaffiliation when they returned for the fall semester on campus.[100]

One year later, NSA held its Congress at Kansas State University and the radicalism of the delegates and especially the leadership continued. The major event to gain media attention in Manhattan, Kansas occurred when a delegate from Hawaii set fire to his selective service card and was lustily cheered by the NSA

---

96. March 1, 1967 letter to David R. Jones from Barry M. Goldwater, Group Research Archives, Box 343, Columbia University, New York, NY.

97. Both letters are in White House Central File, Name File: Alfreda Young, Box 26, Lyndon Baines Johnson Presidential Library, University of Texas, Austin, TX.

98. Alan W. Bock, "NSA's 20th Annual Farce," *New Guard*, October 1967, p. 6.

99. *Ibid.*

100. *Ibid.* After the 1967 Congress, YAF updated its "Issues Paper Number 6: National Student Association: a smear against students," to incorporate some of the resolutions passed in 1967 as well as the disclosures of CIA funding of the organization.

delegates.[101] Yet the number of participants and the roster of colleges represented continued to decline. The most crushing blow occurred in November when, just months after hosting the NSA Congress, students at Kansas State voted by a four-to-one margin to withdraw from NSA.[102]

In 1969, STOP-NSA published an updated version of its *NSA Report* and on March 3, 1969 Congressman Donald Lukens of Ohio inserted the entire report in the *Congressional Record*. Among the items included was a list of 206 colleges and universities that had withdrawn from NSA over the past eight years. Not listed were those many schools where affiliation had been voted down.[103] A small delegation of YAF members attended the 1969 NSA Congress at the University of Texas at El Paso and reported on their findings to YAF members and the STOP-NSA committee.[104]

When the 1970 Congress took place at Macalester College in St. Paul, Minnesota, YAF sent a "Documentation Mission" of five YAF members to take photos and collect materials that could be used in future editions of the annual *NSA Report*. Among those at the Congress were YAF National Board Members Ronald F. Docksai, Jack Gullahorn, and Harold Herring as well as John McGuinness and Albert Forrester, National Coordinator of STOP-NSA. Following that Congress more than thirty campuses undertook disaffiliation campaigns, including Tulane, where the vote was two-to-one to leave NSA.[105]

The following year NSA worked to gain student approval for a "Joint Treaty of Peace between the People of the United States and the People of South Viet-Nam and North Viet-Nam." According to one writer, "The idea of students adopting such a treaty was absurd, in YAF's view; indeed the treaty itself was phony . . . It was, YAF vehemently insisted, the same terms that the communists had advanced in Paris for the past two years."[106] In July of 1971, STOP-NSA Coordinator Albert Forrester testified on the organization before the House Internal Security Committee and Professor Jerzy Hauptmann of Park College sent a letter to supporters.[107] When the second Nixon Inauguration took place in January 1973, NSA gave its support to demonstrations and protests in the Nation's Capital. Forrester, representing STOP-NSA, and Ron Docksai, held a joint news conference on January 19th to express their opposition to the protests on a day when many Americans were celebrating the re-election of a President.[108]

YAF continued to oppose NSA throughout the decade of the 1970s but NSA

101. Anthony Ripley, "Hawaii Student Burns Draft Card: Act Gets an Ovation from 300 Leaders of NSA," *New York Times*, August 22, 1968.
102. Albert Forrester, "The NSA Establishment," *New Guard*, April 1969, pp. 5–6. See also, in the same issue, David R. Jones, "The NSA Issue: Will Congress Act?" pp. 6–7 for testimony by YAF's Executive Director before the House Ways and Means Committee regarding the tax-exempt status of the National Student Association.
103. "Efforts by the Young Americans for Freedom to delete the effect of a certain student organization on college campuses," *Congressional Record*—House, March 3, 1969, pp. H1380–1388, Group Research Archives, Box 343, Columbia University, New York, NY. A copy of the entire *NSA Report* is also included in the archives.
104. Ronald F. Docksai, "The Siege of El Paso," *New Guard*, October 1969, pp. 18–23.
105. 1970 report to the YAF National Board of Directors from Albert Forrester, National Coordinator of the STOP-NSA Committee, Personal Papers of Patrick Dowd, Box 3, Hoover Institution, Stanford University.
106. John Andrew, "Pro-war and Anti-Draft: Young Americans for Freedom and the War in Vietnam," in Marc Gilbert, ed.: *The Vietnam War on Campus: Other Voices* (Westport, CT: Praeger Publishers, 2001), p. 15. See also *New Guard*, May 1971, pp. 3–4, 31–32.
107. These documents and similar fundraising letters of January 31, 1972 and April 11, 1972 are found in Group Research Archives, Box 343, Columbia University, New York, NY.
108. *Ibid.*

took on less significance and less relevance and by the 1980s and 1990s it was totally off the radar as a concern for YAF.

Political Action

As it had in 1961, YAF co-sponsored summer institutes with the Tuller Foundation. Conferences on economics and political science were held at Princeton University. But YAF was definitely more action oriented and left the intellectual develop-ment of young conservatives to groups such as the Intercollegiate Society of Individualists and the Foundation for Economic Education. Writing in the July 1962 issue of *New Guard*, editor Lee Edwards made this division clear.

> YAF is the political arm while ISI is the philosophical arm of the New Right. YAF members, by and large, delight in rallies, parades, pickets, precinct canvassing and all the other tools of the activist organization. ISI members, by and large, prefer the academic approach, the textbook, the pamphlet, the reasoned debate. Properly balanced, they will produce a truly viable conservative movement among students and young Americans.[109]

While dedicated to educating young people on conservative principles, political action was one of the primary objectives of YAF and 1962 brought forth several efforts in that direction.

New York City was a focal point of YAF activity in 1962 and remained so for many years of the organization's existence. In addition to the campaigns of Rosemary McGrath and Ed Nash for New York Assembly, five other YAF mem-bers were candidates for public office and Greater New York YAF chapters were involved in seventeen separate campaigns. In Massachusetts, several YAF chap-ters supported Edward Brooke, the more conservative candidate for Attorney General, first against Elliott Richardson in the primary and then against a ma-chine Democrat in the general election. Brooke went on to win that race and then become the first African-American United States Senator since Reconstruction, although he moved significantly to the middle after he took office. Indiana and Texas YAF members took leadership roles in the campaigns of conservative candidates and in Washington State, YAF member Mike Odell was elected to the State House of Representatives from Spokane.[110] Commenting on these campaign efforts, historian Matthew Dallek concluded "the sophisticated political networks that conservatives would employ so effectively in later years, as well as the YAF alumni who ran for office, can be traced back to young conservatives like Mike Odell."[111] The growing acceptance of YAF as a force in the political arena can be seen also in the presence of Senator John Tower of Texas at the December Board of Directors meeting. Having previously been a speaker at several YAF events, Tower came to meet with the leadership of the organization and to thank them for their support of conservative candidates in the 1962 elections.[112]

---

109. Lee Edwards, "The New Right: Its Face and Future," *New Guard*, July 1962, p. 7.
110. *New Guard*, December–January 1963, p. 15.
111. Matthew Dallek, "Young Americans for Freedom: The Rise of Modern Conservatism, 1960–1964," p. 45.
112. Tower, himself, was not on the ballot in 1962. *New Guard*, December–January 1963, p. 12.

While most of the YAF candidates were not successful, lessons were learned, especially as to the extent to which ideology is or is not the controlling factor in the decision-making process of many voters. As Greater New York Council Chairman David Franke wrote in the YAF magazine "I am not suggesting that the conservative movement must give up its ideological identity in order to win elections, but I do believe it must learn to speak to the non-ideologues in their own terms." He went on to recommend, "it may be wise to limit the use of the word 'conservative' in itself, and simply to emphasize particular issues."[113] Franke's advice was offered at a time when the word conservative was too often associated in much of the media with "far right," "right-wing extremism," and "John Birch Society." By focusing on issues, rather than ideological labels, Franke was advocating a lesson never fully appreciated by many conservatives but one that was essential to the later success of Ronald Reagan.

Robert Welch and Ayn Rand

One of the challenges confronting YAF was to distinguish itself from organizations and individuals who perceived the domestic threat of communism as greater than its international component and those who too often labeled others as communist with little or no supporting evidence. Much of the media was all too anxious to portray YAF as part of what they called the "lunatic fringe." As Matthew Dallek noted, "Acutely conscious of its image, YAF generally understood that to create a 'responsible' conservative movement, it first had to dislodge the image, so firmly imbedded in the popular imagination, that most conservatives were paranoid crackpots."[114] By not separating themselves from those who saw every failure as a conscious action by someone who must be a communist, YAF was not only giving credence to such charges but also allowing the media to lump all conservatives under the label of far-right extremists.

At the beginning of 1962 YAF took the lead in the attempt to distinguish responsible conservatism from the far right by publishing an article, "Anti-Communism and the Radical Right," in the January issue of *New Guard*. The article was written especially for the organization's magazine by Eugene Lyons, a senior editor of *Reader's Digest* and author of *The Red Decade*, the classic study of communism in America during the 1930s.[115] Lyons began his article by denying the claim that there are "no enemies to the right" and stressed that the focus must always be on combating the international ideology of communism since "the central communist challenge to mankind is too important to be obscured and diluted by injecting an array of extraneous issues."[116]

For Lyons all genuine enemies of communism need to be enlisted in the common cause, whether there is agreement or disagreement on other issues and philosophical positions. "The notion that everything an anti-communist happens to dislike or distrust is necessarily the brilliant handiwork of the enemy is a species of myth-making guaranteed to divide the American people—and divide the

---

113. David Franke, "Will Conservatives Ever Win in NY?" *New Guard*, October 1962, pp. 2, 12.

114. Matthew Dallek, "Young Americans for Freedom: The Rise of Modern Conservatism, 1960–1964," p. 18.

115. Eugene Lyons: *The Red Decade* (Indianapolis, IN: Bobbs-Merrill Company, 1941).

116. *New Guard*, January 1962, p. 8.

anti-communists." Without mentioning any individuals or naming any organizations, Lyons concluded "those who lose themselves in a fantasy world of plots and devils are rarely fit to function efficiently in the world of realities."[117] In the same issue, National Board Member Richard Cowan, a senior at Yale, was quoted by Robert Novak as observing about the John Birch Society, "They're generally seeking the right goals, but they are naïve and limited in taking such an inward view of things. They see communism as an internal rather than an external force."[118]

One month later, more senior voices of the burgeoning conservative movement began to disassociate themselves from Robert Welch, if not from the John Birch Society as a whole. After meeting with Barry Goldwater and discussing the issue with the editorial board of his magazine, William F. Buckley, Jr. published an editorial maintaining that Welch was "damaging the cause of anti-communism."[119] Buckley maintained that the anti-communist challenge required a change in national policy and that Welch, rather than aiding in that effort, was turning potential supporters away by his broad-brushed labeling of individuals as communists.[120]

Reaction was mixed with several financial supporters of *National Review* and even some of the magazine's editorial staff critical. In a letter to Buckley, publisher William A. Rusher went into a discussion of the Welch editorial and the mostly negative responses to it. Yet he was supportive of the effort to distinguish the magazine from those to its right.[121] In the next issue of *National Review*, Senator John Tower described the editorial as "a courageous and responsible analysis."[122] Another letter writer also applauded Buckley's action:

> You have once again given a voice to the conscience of conservatism. As always the voice is clear and repudiates the easy downhill path of expediency (that path is so crowded with Liberals these days). Now we shall eagerly await a Liberal definition of Left and Far Left.

It was signed, Ronald Reagan, Pacific Palisades, California.[123]

Later that same month, Russell Kirk disassociated himself from Welch and his claims of communist loyalties by the Eisenhower brothers in an article in the Jesuit publication *America*. Kirk's famous quip in response to Welch's charges about the former President was that "Eisenhower isn't a Communist. He is a golfer."[124] Meanwhile, Senator Tower disassociated his brand of conservatism from that of Robert Welch when he spoke at a Princeton seminar focused on "the Responsible Right" and sponsored by ISI.[125]

Like its more senior mentors, Young Americans for Freedom was establishing its own identity as a responsible conservative organization. As Lee Edwards,

117. *Ibid.* p. 9.

118. Robert D. Novak, "The Contentious Campus Conservative," *New Guard*, January 1962, p. 18.

119. *National Review*, February 3, 1962.

120. Buckley's position and the developments surrounding the editorial are discussed on pp. 65–70 of *Flying High* as well as in Judis: *William F. Buckley, Jr.*, pp. 193–200.

121. Letter from William A. Rusher to William F. Buckley, Jr. dated February 20, 1962, Personal Papers of William F. Buckley, Jr., Box 20, Interoffice Memos, Sterling Library, Yale University, New Haven, CT.

122. *National Review*, February 17, 1962.

123. Quoted in Linda Bridges and John R. Coyne, Jr.: *Strictly Right*, p. 75.

124. Quoted in Judis: *William F, Buckley, Jr.*, p. 198. The Kirk article appeared in the February 17, 1962 issue of *America*.

125. Confidential Report to the President, February 19, 1962, White House Staff Files: Lee White, Box 12, John F. Kennedy Presidential Library, Boston, MA.

editor of *New Guard*, noted several years later, "We were beginning to get into the real world of national politics, dealing with people like John Tower and Barry Goldwater and others. It was just obvious that we couldn't carry around baggage from the John Birch Society."[126] One of the original members of the YAF Board of Directors, Scott Stanley, was believed to be close to Robert Welch. A law student at the University of Kansas, Stanley had been retained over the summer of 1961 to raise funds for YAF, an undertaking that appears not to have been successful. At the March 1962 Board meeting, just after the publication of the Lyons and Buckley writings, a motion was made to remove Stanley from the board but in a secret ballot the motion failed to receive the required two-thirds vote. Stanley remained on the Board until the first national convention in September and then withdrew from the organization. Subsequently, he became editor of *American Opinion*, the official publication of the John Birch Society.[127]

Beyond articles in its national magazine, YAF leaders worked at the local level to limit the influence of extremists and make their presence unwanted. As one writer noted, "that most chapters remained free of Birch ideology reveals a good deal about the membership's quest to create a responsible conservative movement."[128] Contrasted with some groups at the time, YAF members were more interested in domestic issues such as welfare reform and free-market econom-ics, and in the resumption of nuclear testing and a strong foreign policy than in conspiracy theories and labeling domestic opponents as communists. John Andrew concluded, "YAFers embraced ideology, not conspiracy, as the agent of change."[129] They were passionate in their dedication to conservatism but there was a difference between passion and extremism.

An additional ideological challenge during the early years of Young Americans for Freedom came from the followers of novelist Ayn Rand. Through her writings, Ms. Rand developed an all-encompassing philosophical outlook that became known as "Objectivism." She was an advocate of laissez-faire capitalism and individualism. According to Rand, man should always act in his own rational self-interest and reject any appeals to altruism or religious sentiment. Rand's philosophical position is most fully presented in her 1957 novel, *Atlas Shrugged*.[130] Reading *Atlas Shrugged* influenced many early YAF members. Sharon Presley recalled that she had been totally apolitical until she read it: "It was like, 'Oh, my God, what a revelation!' ... I read the book; it came along at just the right time.... What she did for me was get me thinking about ... things in those kinds of philosophical terms that I never had."[131] Presley then became active in YAF in California and also started attending Objectivist study groups.

---

126. Judis: *William F. Buckley, Jr.*, p. 197.

127. Minutes of the March 8, 1962 Board of Directors meeting in New York City, Personal Papers of William F. Buckley, Jr., Box 23, Folder: YAF, Sterling Library, Yale University, New Haven, CT. Schneider: *Cadres for Conservatism*, p. 49.

128. Matthew Dallek, "Young Americans for Freedom: The Rise of Modern Conservatism, 1960–1964," p. 22. Dallek discusses some of these local efforts on pp. 19–23.

129. Andrew: *The Other Side of the Sixties*, p. 171.

130. Ayn Rand: *Atlas Shrugged* (New York: Random House, 1957). Other works by Rand that outline her philosophy of Objectivism include *For the New Intellectual* (New York: Random House, 1961), *The Virtue of Selfishness* (New York: New American Library, 1964) and *Capitalism: The Unknown Ideal* (New York: New American Library, 1967). A good discussion of Rand and her influence on the development of libertarianism is presented in Brian Doherty: *Radicals for Capitalism* (New York: Public Affairs, 2007), especially on pp. 225–243. Two more recent works that explore Rand's views and life are Jennifer Burns: *Goddess of the Market: Ayn Rand and the American Right* (New York: Oxford University Press, 2009) and Anne C. Heller: *Ayn Rand and the World She Made* (New York: Nan A. Talese/Doubleday, 2009).

131. Quoted in Rebecca E. Klatch: *A Generation Divided*, pp. 69–70.

In a similar manner, Louise Lacey was influenced by Rand's writings and helped start a YAF chapter in 1961 in San Francisco, becoming involved in Objectivist circles.[132] As she recalled, "I was having fun, stretching my mind in very large ways, and meeting people, some of whom I still know today."[133] Three thousand miles away, pockets of Rand followers were active on various campuses in Massachusetts. One of those was Robert Poole, who later became publisher of *Reason* magazine. Poole was an engineering student at the Massachusetts Institute of Technology who joined YAF and "it helped steer me away from engineering to public policy. It was my introduction to grass-roots politics and one important source of my life-long commitment to libertarian principles."[134] As Poole recalls, "At MIT, the majority of us were libertarians, not conservatives, and mostly Objectivists. We were very involved in the Goldwater for President effort, and had the largest campus Goldwater group in New England."[135] One fellow member of the MIT YAF chapter was David Nolan. Nolan would go on to become a founder of the Libertarian Party in December 1971.

According to Jerome Tuccille, a writer who was active in Randian and libertarian activities in the early 1960s, "many Objectivist students joined YAF for the simple reason that they had no place else to go in order to engage in political activities."[136] With their support for laissez-faire capitalism, their commitment to strong limits on the size of government, and the anti-communism inherent in Rand's philosophy, it is not surprising that these followers of Rand would join Young Americans for Freedom. An additional factor in the early years was the personal appeal of Barry Goldwater, one political figure with whom many Objectivists could identify. Since YAF was closely identified with Goldwater and his likely presidential campaign, YAF was the place to be for political activity.

While YAF never took an official position on Objectivism or Ayn Rand, her writings did stir up controversy within the organization. As early as the fourth issue of the organization's magazine, one writer provided a somewhat critical review of *For the New Intellectual* and its self-centered egotism. According to the review, "revolted at the folly of man worshipping the State, she, in turn, preaches that man should worship himself."[137] The review stirred up some discussion but it was not until the following year when an article on Miss Rand's philosophy generated letters on both sides of the issue.

In the May 1962 issue, Eliza Simmons noted that in the first issue of *The Objectivist Newsletter* Rand states that "Objectivists are not conservatives." Simmons took Rand at her word and spelled out what she saw as the difference:

> Conservatism seeks to conserve our Judaeo-Christian culture. Conservatives wish to conserve the Ten Commandments as the best moral code ever known to mankind. They wish to conserve the Golden Rule as the most workable social code revealed through all history. Objectivism makes man answerable to man, to himself.[138]

---

132. *Ibid.* p. 219.
133. 2008 YAF Alumni Survey Responses: Louise Lacey.
134. 2008 YAF Alumni Survey Responses: Robert W. Poole, Jr.
135. *Ibid.*
136. Jerome Tuccille: *It Usually Begins with Ayn Rand* (New York: Stein and Day, 1971), p. 58.
137. Robert M. Thornton, "Too Intellectual," *New Guard*, June 1961, p. 17.
138. Eliza Simmons, "Who's an Objectivist?" *New Guard*, May 1962, p. 12.

Two months later, Nick Dellas of Syracuse wrote in to defend Rand, claiming that "everything our country stood for and all that conservatives, I hope, are fighting for is what Ayn Rand is all about. To me, Miss Rand has been the guiding light in my search for reasons why. She is the most outstanding human being that I have witnessed."[139] In the following issue Steve Miller of Reno maintained that conservatism and Objectivism are distinct outlooks and he wanted no further part in the organization. He claimed, "instead of being 'for freedom,' YAF is for Conservatism. The difference between the two is distinct."[140]

The controversy quieted down some with an article and a letter in the October 1962 issue of *New Guard*. Writer Charles F. Barr, Jr. attempted to dissect and analyze Rand's philosophy and came away with a more favorable interpretation, noting that "Ayn Rand's views should not be enshrined as a perfect cure-all to the ills that beset our culture, but many of her ideas have merit, and deserve serious consideration."[141] YAF member Karen Fadeley noted in her letter to the editor the belief that an alliance could be maintained in the organization and that religious conviction should not be made a condition of membership.[142] A few months later a similar sentiment was expressed by Michael A. Delizia of Dartmouth who indicated that he was both a member of the New Hampshire YAF Board of Directors and an Objectivist while Alan S. Quarterman of Emory University saw no reason to exclude Objectivists as long as the organization remained conservative.[143]

Below the surface, however, the conflict between conservatives and the followers of Miss Rand continued. Although not a national phenomenon in the organization, in certain areas of the country Objectivists had gained significant support and positions of authority in the organization. They worked closely with other YAF members through the Goldwater campaign with a common goal to elect a candidate dedicated to free enterprise and a strong anti-communist policy. Once the campaign was over, concern arose over whether Objectivists were attempting to take control and force out the traditional conservatives who had formed the organization. As Jerome Tuccille admitted, "there is no question that most of them joined with the explicit intention of transforming YAF into an Objectivist-oriented political institution."[144]

Massachusetts was one state where the followers of Ayn Rand gained a strong foothold in Young Americans for Freedom.[145] Prior to the 1964 election, several Objectivists achieved high positions within the state organization. Some local chapters consisted almost totally of Objectivists with their meetings devoted to tape recordings of Miss Rand's lectures. During the presidential campaign, YAF members of all philosophical persuasions concentrated on working for the Republican national ticket. After the Goldwater defeat, other YAF activities took priority and, with this, the underlying differences surfaced. In the spring of 1965, the Massachusetts Council of YAF voted to dismiss its then Executive Director, Gordon Nelson, on the grounds that he was allegedly devoting most of his time and efforts to expounding the virtues of Objectivism rather than expanding YAF's

---

139. Letter to the editor, *New Guard*, July 1962, p. 15.
140. Letter to the editor, *New Guard*, August 1962, p. 15.
141. Charles F. Barr, Jr., "How Objective Is Ayn Rand?" *New Guard*, October 1962, p. 10.
142. *Ibid.* p. 15.
143. Letters to the editor, *New Guard*, December–January 1963, p. 2.
144. Tuccille: *It Usually Begins with Ayn Rand*, p. 58.
145. Much of the following is from Wayne Thorburn, "Young Americans for Freedom: A Case Study of a Political Action Organization," pp. 65–67.

influence throughout the state. When State Chairman J. Alan MacKay removed Nelson from his position, an exodus of Objectivists from the organization took place, including one state vice-chairman and six local chapters.[146]

Later in 1965, an Objectivist-dominated chapter at the University of California at Berkeley posed a serious problem for the national leadership. Its chairman, Randal Grindle, was a dedicated follower of Ayn Rand who had formerly done an outstanding job as head of the Baltimore, Maryland chapter of YAF. Challenging the individualism and local autonomy supported by Young Americans for Freedom, Grindle's Berkeley chapter passed resolutions calling for the legalization of prostitution and marijuana and then released copies of the resolutions to the media. National YAF leaders moved to revoke the chapter's charter for bringing disrepute to the organization's name. Grindle attempted to appeal to the local chapters but failed to gain sufficient support.[147]

The University of Maryland was a third scene of friction directly related to the presence of Objectivists within the organization. A YAF chapter had been active on the campus since 1961, under the dominance of traditional conservatives. In the spring of 1966, however, the club elected Jarret Wollstein, an Objectivist, as its chairman. Wollstein succeeded in converting the chapter to near-total Objectivist control and in so doing alienating most non-Objectivist YAF members and supporters. Soon thereafter, Wollstein decided that a distinct Objectivist organization was needed. In the fall of 1967, he established the Society for Rational Individualism, taking with him several YAF members, the membership list and what remained of the club treasury. The YAF chapter was left as a shadow of its previous strength until reorganized one year later.[148]

Although some similar instances occurred in other locations, many Objectivists continued to be active in YAF. Even Wollstein remained a YAF member and wrote a cover article on Objectivism that appeared in the October 1967 issue of *New Guard*.[149] But this cooperative position was not to be the stance of Miss Rand herself. After a critical review of *Atlas Shrugged* by Whittaker Chambers appeared in *National Review*, Rand vowed never to be in the same room with Bill Buckley. She had extended her distaste to the organization founded at the Buckley family estate. When *New Guard* editor Arnold Steinberg wrote Rand seeking permission to reprint her article, "The Roots of War," he received back a curt response from Bee Fletcher of the Nathaniel Brandon Institute,

> In reply to your letter of August 17, Miss Rand has asked me to tell you that she is opposed to Young Americans for Freedom, an organization which is controlled by the policies of her avowed enemies, and therefore, she cannot grant you permission to reprint her article "The Roots of War."[150]

---

146. "Gordon Nelson Dismissed; Objectivists Resign in Protest," *Tufts YAF Newsletter*, April 1965. Interestingly enough, several years later Nelson became Chairman of the Massachusetts Republican Party and was a featured speaker at the 1977 New England YAF Regional Conference. *Dialogue on Liberty*, June 1977, Group Research Archives, Box 343, Columbia University, New York, NY.

147. Thorburn, "Young Americans for Freedom: A Case Study of a Political Action Organization," p. 66.

148. *Ibid.* pp. 66–67, from interview with Peter B. Brathwaite, then State Chairman of Maryland YAF, March 16, 1968, Baltimore, MD.

149. Jarret B. Wollstein, "Objectivism: A New Orthodoxy," *New Guard*, October 1967, pp. 14–17. Wollstein's article, while supporting the Objectivist philosophy, criticizes the control exerted over its teaching by the Nathaniel Brandon Institute, the authorized and official disseminator of educational material and courses on Objectivism at that time.

150. Letter from Bee Fletcher to Arnold Steinberg dated September 7, 1967, Personal Papers of

There was no further organized effort by her followers to gain influence in the organization from that point forward.[151] However, as early as 1962 it was becoming apparent to observers that the "National Review group" was a controlling force in Young Americans for Freedom and YAF was viewed by its ideological competitors as "the most rational and politically effective of all right-wing organizations."[152]

YAF's 1st National Convention—New York City

In addition to expanding its base on campuses and in communities, working to elect conservative candidates for public office, and establishing its presence as a major player in the political arena, YAF had some internal work that needed attention. With a growing membership spread across the country in local chapters, the organization needed to ensure that its leadership was representative of its membership and that its members had an opportunity to select those leaders. Thus, in September 1962 YAF held its first National Convention at the Commodore Hotel in New York City, an event that would take place every two years for the next thirty years.

The convention began with a reception on Thursday evening September 27th and concluded with an installation banquet and keynote address on Saturday night September 29th. At the convention, YAF premiered its new recruitment film, "A Generation Awakes," and held a series of seminars on American Strategy in the Cold War, The Common Market and the Free Market, The Domestic Program of the New Deal and The Methodology of Political Action.[153] Among the seminar speakers were Congressman Steven Derounian (R-NY), William A. Rusher and James Burnham from *National Review*, Professor Ernest Van den Haag, political strategist F. Clifton White, and William Casey, a New York attorney who would go on to serve as Chairman of the Securities and Exchange Commission during the Nixon Administration and Director of Central Intelligence during the Reagan Administration. The featured speaker at the opening session on Friday was Congressman William Cramer (R-FL) who urged the delegates to take a proactive role in spreading the conservative message among American youth. Also taking part in the convention were authors John Chamberlain and Lawrence Fertig, retired professor O. Glenn Saxon of Yale, and former Secretary of the Navy and New Jersey Governor Charles Edison.[154]

The business of the convention consisted of electing a National Chairman and Board of Directors as well as adopting resolutions. Some two hundred delegates from thirty states and the District of Columbia represented YAF college

William F. Buckley, Jr., Box 46, Sterling Library, Yale University, New Haven, CT.

151. Throughout its history, Young Americans for Freedom has experienced many internal political conflicts, some philosophical but many personal. These early battles are described in Andrew: *The Other Side of the Sixties*, pp. 109–125 and Schneider: *Cadres for Conservatism*, pp. 42–54, 127–141, and 160–176.

152. Confidential Report to the President, February 19, 1962, White House Staff Files: Lee White, Box 12, John F. Kennedy Presidential Library, Boston, MA.

153. Letter from Richard Viguerie to YAF Members and Memorandum from Donald B. Shafto, Chairman, Convention Arrangements Committee to YAF Members. White House Central Name File, Box 3092: YAF, John F. Kennedy Presidential Library, Boston, MA.

154. Andrew: *The Other Side of the Sixties*, pp. 123–124. "First Annual Convention of Young Americans for Freedom, Inc., America's Leading Conservative Youth Group," extension of remarks of Hon. Bruce Alger, *Congressional Record*, October 13, 1962 in Personal Papers of Herbert A. Philbrick, Folder 1, Manuscript Division, Library of Congress, Washington, DC. Personal notes of the author from the 1962 convention.

and community chapters. After regional caucuses on Friday night, the delegates assembled on Saturday morning to elect their officers. Robert E. Bauman was unanimously elected as the new National Chairman as were five regional chairmen. Then the contests began for fourteen seats on the Board of Directors, an election that would see a significant change in the leadership of the organization.

Fifteen members of the existing Board decided not to seek election, some wishing to move on while others had surveyed the situation, counted their likely votes, and decided not to run. Among those not running were Doug Caddy (former National Director), Bill Cotter (Organization Director), Scott Stanley, and Howard Phillips. Also not seeking election were Jack Molesworth, Charles McIlwaine, Robert Harley, James and John Kolbe, Lee Edwards, George Gaines, James Abstine, Richard Noble, Carol Bauman, and William Madden. It is interesting to note that twelve of the Board members not running for re-election (excluding Stanley, McIlwaine, and Noble) were participants in the Sharon Conference that established the organization two years earlier. Additionally, three sitting Board Members, Rosemary McGrath, George McDonnell, and Carl T. McIntire (a Sharon attendee) were defeated for re-election along with three other candidates who would later serve on the YAF Board: Joseph Leo of New Jersey (a Sharon attendee), Bill Boerum of New York, and Bud Wandling of Pennsylvania.

When the votes were cast and counted, only seven of the twenty elected to the National Board had attended the founding conference in 1960.[155] Serving as officers with new Chairman Bob Bauman were Robert Croll as Vice Chairman, Kay Wonderlic Kolbe as Secretary, and Lammot Copeland as Treasurer. The new regional directors were Daniel Carmen of Massachusetts (New England), David Franke (Middle Atlantic), David Jones of Florida (South), Kenneth Thompson of Dallas (Southwest) and Lynn Bouchey of the University of Washington (West).[156] Returning to the Board of Directors were Antoni Gollan of University of Miami, Bill Schulz of Washington, DC, Diarmuid O'Scannlain of Harvard Law School, John Weicher of University of Chicago, and former Chairman Robert Schuchman of New York City while the new members joining them were Donald Devine of Brooklyn, Craig Ihde of Los Angeles, Fulton "Buddy" Lewis, III of Washington, DC, Marilyn Manion of South Bend, Indiana, Donald Shafto of Ridgewood, New Jersey, and Edmund Zanini of Crestwood, New York.

The new chairman, Robert E. Bauman, was a native of Maryland who had graduated from Georgetown University and was then a Georgetown law student. The other new members of the Board represented an expansion of YAF's scope and influence. As Secretary, the YAF Board selected Kay Wonderlic Kolbe, a graduate of Northwestern University. Kathy Kolbe has gone on to a career as an entrepreneur, educator and best-selling author.[157] As Treasurer of YAF, Lammot D. Copeland, Jr. was a Harvard graduate who had been active in Young Republicans

155. The seven Sharon attendees serving on the new Board were Croll, Franke, Gollan, Schuchman, Schulz, Weicher, and Thompson.

156. Shortly after the convention, Tom Charles Huston of Indiana University was selected to fill the position of Midwest Regional Director, bringing the total number of Directors to 21. Later, the number would be increased to 25, including the National Chairman. Huston went on to serve as National Chairman of YAF, finish law school and assume a position in the Nixon White House. Returning to Indiana, he is currently Chairman of Brenwick Development Corporation, involved in land development throughout the state.

157. Kathy Kolbe: *The Conative Connection* (Boston: Addison-Wesley, 1989); *Pure Instinct* (New York: Random House, 1993); *Powered by Instinct: 5 Rules for Trusting Your Guts* (Phoenix, AZ: Monumentus Press, 2003).

and was publisher of the *San Fernando Valley Times*. Originally from Delaware and a member of the DuPont family, Copeland now is CEO of Associates Graphics Services in Wilmington.

Three new Board members hailed from the New York area. Edmund Zanini was a graduate of New York University and a real estate broker who served as New York YAF state chairman. Zanini believed that it "is not enough to have a sense of dedication to the basic American principles on which YAF was founded; we must also have a sense of responsibility toward our organization and its role in promoting those principles."[158] A native of New Jersey and a graduate of Princeton and University of Michigan Law School, Donald B. Shafto was known as "Rally Don" for his prodigious work in choreographing the 1962 Madison Square Garden rally, the 1963 YAF rally in Fort Lauderdale, and the floor demonstrations for Goldwater at the 1964 Republican National Convention. Donald J. Devine hailed from Brooklyn but soon after his election moved to Syracuse University where he obtained his PhD in political science and then worked for fourteen years as an Associate Professor of Government & Politics at the University of Maryland.[159]

Two of the new Board members carried with them well-known names. Marilyn Manion came from a distinguished conservative family. Her father, Clarence Manion, was a well-known conservative Democrat who served as Dean of the University of Notre Dame Law School. Marilyn Manion's brothers Chris and Dan were also subsequently active in YAF. Manion recalled that she "first met many future YAFers at the 1960 Republican National Convention in Chicago where we were backing Barry Goldwater." Later, while on the YAF Board she undertook a speaking tour for YAF "traveling through Montana in 1964 speaking in a different town each night."[160]

Another offspring of a famous family to join the Board in 1962 was Fulton "Buddy" Lewis, III, son of Mutual radio network news broadcaster Fulton Lewis, Jr. While a new member of the Board of Directors, Buddy Lewis was well known to YAF members. A graduate of the University of Virginia, Lewis was Research Director for the House Un-American Activities Committee when he produced and narrated "Operation Abolition," the film recounting the Communist-inspired riots when the committee held hearings in San Francisco in May 1960. Asked what impact YAF had on his life, Lewis reported, "It had a great impact! It provided outstanding public speaking and debating experience and great training in political organization. I lectured and debated on over 750 college campuses," many of which were at events sponsored by YAF.[161]

David R. Jones was Florida YAF State Chairman and went on to a long and distinguished career both in YAF and in the broader conservative movement. Daniel Carmen was active for many years in Massachusetts Republican politics. Craig Ihde graduated from UCLA and the University of Southern California before spending his career as a faculty member at the University of Redlands. As Ihde remembered his experience in YAF,

It was a very exciting, and somewhat uneasy time. YAF and college republicans were becoming more vocal, and more effective in promoting principles

158. *New Guard*, March 1963, p. 16.
159. 2008 YAF Alumni Survey Responses: Donald J. Devine.
160. 2008 YAF Alumni Survey Responses: Marilyn Manion Thies.
161. 2008 YAF Alumni Survey Responses: Fulton Lewis.

of freedom and conservatism. I think the uneasiness sprang from the nation's growing concern over Soviet threat. This, I believe, gave rise to organizations like the John Birch Society, and Dr. Fred Schwarz.

For Ihde, his involvement in YAF "gave me a grounding and unshakeable belief in principles of conservatism and freedom."[162] Lynn Bouchey was a student at the University of Washington when he served on the YAF Board and later became President of the Council for Inter-American Security.

All in all, a most impressive group of new Board members who would go on in their later careers to continue a pattern of contributing to the promotion and advancement of conservative principles. The turnover in leadership had been substantial as many of those who had been present at the beginning were now, two years later, passing the leadership to individuals who had been recruited into the organization after its founding. In many ways, this transition was testimony to the permanence of the organization as it had grown sufficiently in two years to provide a cadre of skilled new leaders dedicated to expanding Young Americans for Freedom even more.

After the elections, the delegates moved on to what motivated many of them—taking stands on the issues of the day. Resolutions were passed advocating the blockade of Cuba, opposing the Supreme Court decision banning school prayer, supporting the fraternity system, and opposing participation in the NSA unless it adopted democratic reforms.[163] Then it was time for the inauguration of the new officers and the conclusion of the convention. Nearly five hundred delegates and guests took part in the closing banquet on Saturday night where the organization's new officers were installed. The keynote speaker was William F. Buckley, Jr. and new National Chairman Bauman gave an acceptance speech wherein he maintained that YAF "must go into politics with a determination to win for conservatism."[164] Among his specific commitments were to expand the *New Guard* magazine, build more state organizations, establish a speakers' bureau, and move the national offices to the Nation's Capital. A few months later, YAF's headquarters would be located on Capitol Hill in Washington, DC.

Reaction from the Left

Two years after its founding, Young Americans for Freedom had held its first national convention, made the transition to new leadership among its officers, and established itself as a presence in the room. But many on the left refused to face this reality and believed that the organization would soon die out. Writing in *The Nation*, Robert Martinson claimed "much of YAF strength is ephemeral and will disappear."[165] Murray Kempton predicted "our children will remember Young Americans for Freedom, if at all, as part of a time sadly deficient in opportunities of self-expression for ordinary young men."[166] Steven V. Roberts, then editor of

---

162. 2008 YAF Alumni Survey Responses: Craig Ihde.
163. Gary Russell, "YAF Charts Far-Ranging Program for Victory," *New Guard*, November 1962, pp. 8–9.
164. *National Review*, October 23, 1962, pp. 297–298.
165. Robert Martinson, "State of the Campus 1962," *The Nation*, May 19, 1962, p. 436.
166. Murray Kempton, "On Growing Up Absurd," *The Progressive*, May 1961, p. 14.

the *Harvard Crimson* and later with the *New York Times*, claimed that YAF was all public relations and image with little real support among students and likely not to have any lasting impact.[167]

But not all on the left were convinced that YAF and the conservative movement would die out. Irving Howe related his experience on the West Coast which convinced him that "after living in California only a few months, one discovers that the upsurge on the political right is a more serious matter than anyone in New York or Boston is likely to suppose . . ."[168] Many years later, Harvard Professor Lisa McGurr summed up the problem, "By failing to take into account the deep-seated conservative ideological traditions on which the Right drew and by refusing to closely examine the ideological universe of conservatives, liberal intellectuals underestimated the resilience and staying power of the Right in American life."[169]

That resilience and staying power was a major concern of the *New Guard* editor as he expressed his views in an article published in the June 1962 issue. Lee Edwards cautioned his readers that short-range efforts would not rid the nation of a welfare philosophy that had become too prevalent. What YAF needed to do was construct not a five-year plan but rather a twenty-five year plan. To change the direction of the country "Conservatives must begin to place themselves not only in the United States House of Representatives, but in the television networks, in the universities, in corporations and companies and perhaps most important of all, in the Federal government."[170] What Edwards wrote as a projection into the future is, of course, exactly what Young Americans for Freedom did over the next twenty-five years. When the decade of the 1980s arrived, those young conservatives who had grown and developed their political skills and philosophical grounding in YAF were ready to join in the effort to affect American government during the Reagan Administration as well as influence the direction of American society through their involvement in so many other areas of American society. Two difficult years had brought about a permanent organization under new leadership and set the path for future success, some of which would not come until the twenty-five years that Edwards described had passed.

---

167. Steven V. Roberts, "Image on the Right," *The Nation*, May 19, 1962, p. 442.
168. Irving Howe, "Notebook: Journey to the End of the Right," *Dissent*, Winter 1962, p. 79.
169. Lisa McGirr: *Suburban Warriors*, p. 148.
170. Lee Edwards, "Needed: A Conservative Establishment," *New Guard*, June 1962, p. 2.

5. Barry's Boys

"We're the bright young men
Who want to go back to nineteen-ten
We're Barry's boys."[1]

Calendar year 1963 brought with it an increased emphasis on the upcoming presidential campaign. True, general election day was still nearly two years away and, even truer, the young conservatives did not have a declared candidate for the office. Nevertheless, they had a hero and much organizational work to do if they were to convince that hero to run and then elect that conservative candidate in 1964. While it was not quite all-Goldwater, all the time, the thrust of much activity in Young Americans for Freedom centered around promoting the candidacy of Barry Goldwater for President. When there were anti-communist demonstrations and protests against the Kennedy Administration foreign policy, the Goldwater alternative of *Why Not Victory?* was always present.[2] When they involved themselves in Young Republican contests, it was always to elect the Goldwater loyalist to office. When the campus chapters published their newsletters and newspapers, there was always some article promoting Barry and his views on national issues. They were preparing the way for the grand campaign of issues and ideologies, the great debate between Barry M. Goldwater and John F. Kennedy.[3]

Foreign Policy to the Front

Before that great debate could take place there was much work to do. As it had in previous years, foreign policy with a strong anti-communist outlook was a major focus for Young Americans for Freedom as 1962 came to a close and the new year began. They continued using many of the techniques developed over the past two years designed to gain media attention and public support for their positions. On a cold January 8th, seventy-five YAF members in the DC area picketed in favor of Katanga while Assistant Secretary of State for Africa, G. Mennen "Soapy" Williams, attended an art gathering.[4] The following month some 200 New York YAF members protested the Soviet occupation of the captive nations, walking from the Soviet Consulate some sixty blocks to the United Nations. The protest took place on Human Rights Day, commemorating the signing of the UN Declaration of Human Rights in 1948.[5] Meanwhile, in Houston, YAF members

---

1. With sincere apologies to the many Goldwater Girls. Words by June Reizner, copyright Mills Music Inc (ASCAP), recorded by The Chad Mitchell Trio on "Reflecting," Mercury SR 60891, original recording in 1964. Perhaps the best-known member of the trio was John Denver who joined them subsequently in 1965 and performed with them for two years.

2. Barry M. Goldwater: *Why Not Victory?* (New York: McGraw-Hill, 1962).

3. Indicative of the ever-present interest in the 1964 presidential contest, the cover article in the December 1962–January 1963 issue of *New Guard* was "Can Goldwater Win?" and it featured a photo of the Arizona Senator.

4. *New Guard*, February 1963, p. 14.

5. "YAF Highlights: 1960–1965," Personal Papers of Herbert A. Philbrick, Box 218, Folder 3, Manuscript Division, Library of Congress, Washington, DC.

picketed a hotel where Secretary of State Dean Rusk addressed the Texas Daily Newspapers Association. The signs read: "Tear Down the Wall," "Stop the Sellout," and "Better Brave than Slave."[6]

Captive Nations Week provided another opportunity for several YAF community chapters to express their anti-communism. Georgia YAF organized a march in Atlanta with signs proclaiming "YAF Wants Freedom for Red Slaves" and "Tear Down The Wall."[7] Closer to home, National Chairman Bob Bauman and Executive Secretary Richard Viguerie sent a letter to all YAF members in February 1963 criticizing the Kennedy Administration's settlement of the Cuban missile crisis. The letter claimed "The plain truth is that Cuba is today just where it was prior to President Kennedy's 'strong stand'—under the control of a Communist dictator armed and garrisoned by Soviet aid. Only this foreign intervention in Cuba sustains this horrible suppression of a once free people."[8] Enclosed was a petition from the Committee for the Monroe Doctrine that members were urged to circulate and return.

Meanwhile, YAF college chapters were also expressing their anti-communism through the sponsorship of various speakers on campus. Among the speakers presented by YAF chapters were James Burnham and Frank Meyer of *National Review*, Dr. Fred C. Schwarz of the Christian Anti-Communism Crusade, and Herbert Philbrick, author of *I Led Three Lives*. Ross Deachman, chapter chairman, recalled that Philbrick was the featured speaker at the first meeting of the University of New Hampshire YAF chapter in March of 1963.[9]

Although Indianapolis YAF had demonstrated against the sale of Communist cars in 1961, the issues of exporting American goods or building manufacturing plants in Communist countries were still on the horizon. Yet, in 1963, YAF's magazine published a critique on the sale of high technology equipment to Soviet bloc nations. According to the author, "While the Communists are waging a total cold war against our very way of life, we are shipping them vitally-needed electronic and industrial equipment to build up their economy, and, therefore, their war potential."[10] Two years later, YAF would launch one of its most successful campaigns against the construction of an American manufacturing plant in Romania. YAF's concern over the New Frontier foreign policy was best summed up, rather humorously, in the words on a bumper sticker sold at local chapter meetings:

CONGO . . . GOA . . . DUTCH NEW GUINEA
LAOS . . . CUBA . . . HYANNISPORT ?????[11]

During the summer of 1963, diplomats for the United States and the Soviet Union agreed to a nuclear test ban treaty. Once the text of the treaty was released, the Senate Foreign Relations Committee held hearings on its merits. Chairman

---

6. *New Guard*, April 1963, p. 15. The poster "tear down the wall" virtually mirrored one of Ronald Reagan's most memorable phrases delivered some twenty-five years later outside the Berlin wall.

7. "YAF Highlights: 1960–1965," Personal Papers of Herbert A. Philbrick, Box 218, Folder 3, Manuscript Division, Library of Congress, Washington, DC.

8. Letter of February 1963 to YAF members (in author's possession). Indicative of the continuing interest in promoting freedom in Cuba, the cover article in the May 1963 issue of *New Guard* was "Cuba: A Plan for Liberation."

9. 2008 YAF Alumni Survey Responses: Ross Deachman.

10. R.J. Bocklet, "Trading with the Enemy: An Indictment," *New Guard*, May 1963, pp. 7–8.

11. YAF bumper sticker from early 1963 (in author's possession). Hyannisport, Massachusetts was the site of the Kennedy family summer compound.

Bauman testified that the treaty was a "grave threat to the national security of the United States and a threat to freedom everywhere."[12] In response, YAF chapters across the country issued news releases and circulated petitions opposing the treaty.

Just before the Senate vote, Bauman held a news conference outside the Capitol with Senator Strom Thurmond. The YAF Chairman presented the Senator with petitions signed by some 15,000 Americans from every state. Both NBC and CBS television covered the presentation. Later, Thurmond inserted the wording of the petition in the *Congressional Record* and added

> I take this opportunity to commend the Young Americans for Freedom for their activity in this connection . . . It is most encouraging to find that thousands of young people on our campuses and elsewhere are standing so strongly for freedom and the preservation of a national defense posture to insure the maintenance of our freedoms in this country. . . . Again, I commend the Young Americans for Freedom. I congratulate them for the great service they are rendering to our country; and I especially commend them for obtaining this petition against the nuclear test ban treaty.[13]

Among the 19 who voted against approving the treaty were four Senators on the YAF National Advisory Board: Bennett of Utah, Thurmond of South Carolina, Goldwater of Arizona, and Tower of Texas with only Holland of Florida voting in favor. Although not successful in stopping the treaty, YAF had shown its ability to produce grassroots organization in every state on short notice and, in turn, impressed leaders in Congress with the strength of their organization.

With a presidential election before it, 1964 was a year of political action for YAF with less emphasis on foreign policy petitions and demonstrations. However, when three American flyers were shot down by Russian planes over East Germany, Bauman sent a telegram to then-President Johnson asking that the new wheat deal with Russia be renounced.[14] Chapter leaders released similar statements and wrote letters to their local newspapers.

In January 1964, YAF publicized and provided attendees for the Washington School of Anti-Communism. Coordinated with the Christian Anti-Communism Crusade, more than 500 college and high school students attended.[15] Later that year Richard Derham put forth the possibility that the United States should take a more pro-active role in assisting people under communism to throw off their oppressors. He argued that a cautious use of guerrilla techniques could put the Free World on the offensive against the Communist bloc. It might take a long-term perspective and was not without dangers, but such a change in policy, it was maintained, could result in freedom advancing around the world. "Any guerrilla

---

12. *New Guard*, September 1963, p. 5.

13. "How YAF Fought the Test Ban Treaty," *New Guard*, October 1963, p. 8. "YAF Highlights: 1960–1965," Personal Papers of Herbert A. Philbrick, Box 218, Folder 3, Manuscript Division, Library of Congress, Washington, DC.

14. Telegram of January 30, 1964 from Robert E. Bauman, White House Central File, Name File: Alfreda Young, Box 26, Lyndon Baines Johnson Presidential Library, Austin, TX.

15. "YAF Highlights: 1960–1965," Personal Papers of Herbert A. Philbrick, Box 218, Folder 3, Manuscript Division, Library of Congress, Washington, DC. Over the following years, many YAF members would attend similar schools conducted by the Christian Anti-Communism Crusade. See: Fred Schwarz: *Beating the Unbeatable Foe.*

war must take time, but if we have the strategic patience of the Communists, we can achieve some significant results."[16] Some twenty years later, one of YAF's National Advisory Board members, upon assuming the presidency, would follow similar policies, especially in Nicaragua, Angola, Afghanistan, and to some extent in Poland, designed to put the Soviet Union on the defensive.

At the Grass Roots

Meanwhile, YAF was continuing its efforts to expand the conservative presence on America's campuses and in communities large and small. Writers Stephen Hess and David Broder labeled YAF "the most robust group on the right" during this period of time.[17] Promote, publicize, and proselytize were the goals of the YAF chapters in the early sixties. The number of YAF college chapters publishing weekly or monthly newspapers continued to grow. In some areas, smaller colleges combined and circulated their product on several campuses. This was the case with *The Southern Conservative*, centered at Washington & Lee University but including contributors from Sweet Briar College, Randolph-Macon Women's College, Virginia Military Institute, and Randolph-Macon College.[18] Among the editors was Wyatt B. Durrette, Jr., then a law student at Washington & Lee and later State Delegate and candidate for Governor of Virginia.[19] A contributor to the paper was Ken Tomlinson, then a sophomore at Randolph Macon and later editor-in-chief at *Reader's Digest* and chairman of the Board of Governors of the Corporation for Public Broadcasting.

In addition to publishing their own material, local chapters used the new YAF film, "A Generation Awakes," as a recruitment tool. The film was valuable especially as a beginning of the school year program, sometimes including remarks by a graduate, as Boston College YAF did with its former chapter chairman, R. Emmett McLoughlin.[20] At nearby Babson Institute, Stuart Kobrovsky headed up an active group of YAF members who worked closely with those from other campuses in the Boston area. [21] Each issue of *New Guard* included three to four pages of a "YAF Roundup" that featured local chapter events and happenings. This section not only provided suggestions for local projects but also helped to create a sense of community and belonging among the YAF members. Typical of the schedules of events for a YAF chapter, all developed and organized by the local members, was the following at Tufts University during the 1963–1964 academic year.

September: Showing of the film, "A Generation Awakes" followed by remarks from Dan Carmen, National Board Member and Alan MacKay, State Chairman.

September: Speech by Dr. Fred Schwarz, President of the Christian Anti-Communism Crusade.

---

16. Richard Derham, "Should Freedom Take the Offensive?" *New Guard*, September 1964, pp. 13–14, 19.
17. *The Republican Establishment* (New York: Harper & Row, 1967), p. 76.
18. *The Southern Conservative*, Lexington, VA, October 1963 (in author's possession).
19. Durrette's political career is detailed in Frank B. Atkinson: *Virginia in the Vanguard* (Lanham, MD: Rowman & Littlefield, 2006).
20. Boston College YAF flyer, Hall-Hoag Collection, Box 49–13, Folder HH0429, John Hay Library, Brown University, Providence, RI.
21. 2008 YAF Alumni Survey Responses: Stuart Kobrovsky.

October:	Address by Reed Larson, Executive Vice President, National Right to Work Committee.
November:	Address by journalist and author, William Henry Chamberlin.
January:	Bus trip to New Hampshire to attend New England YAF conference and volunteer for the Goldwater campaign.
February:	Remarks by State Representative Al Gammel, a YAF member.
March:	Presentation on Ayn Rand and Objectivism by Gordon Nelson, Massachusetts YAF Executive Director.
March:	Address by Fulton Lewis, III on The Bankruptcy of American Liberalism.[22]

In addition to sponsoring their own meetings, the YAF members worked to influence the direction of the Young Republicans on campus towards support for a Goldwater candidacy.

Still other chapter leaders were fortunate enough to present their views in the official campus newspaper. Corydon Hammond was a student at the University of Utah and later Utah YAF State Chairman.

> There was a feeling of excitement and enthusiasm, but we were also a minority on a liberal campus. I wrote a weekly column in the university newspaper called The Right Side. It always stirred numerous letters to the editor and received a lot of attention . . . YAF was the lone voice of conservatism on the university campus and I believe that many students quietly appreciated what we were doing, but did not want to be in the middle of controversy . . . It was an exciting time.[23]

Reflecting back on his time in YAF, Hammond maintains "it grounded me in fundamental political values and I have remained conservative." He is now a Professor and Psychologist at the University of Utah School of Medicine.

Fred Eckert was a student at North Texas State University during the Goldwater campaign and a member of YAF from 1961 to 1964. According to Eckert, the involvement in YAF during his college years "reinforced my belief that conservatism had the right answers for the questions facing America. And it convinced me that if I wished to see our principles prevail I had to be willing to enter the political arena and slug it out there."[24] Slug it out is exactly what he did. Eckert served as Mayor of Greece, New York, then State Senator, and subsequently a Member of Congress from upstate New York.

YAF was also making a presence on a number of high school campuses. James and Mary Louise Lauerman were high school students in Belleville, Illinois who organized the Nathan Hale chapter in 1963. As James Lauerman recalls "They were some of the most interesting times of my life and the highlight of my high school years."[25] For his sister, YAF "gave me a sound economic, free-market education

---

22. Tufts University YAF schedule (in author's possession). Some 150 YAF members attended the New England Conference in Concord, New Hampshire prior to that year's presidential primary. *New Guard*, February 1964, p. 18.
23. 2008 YAF Alumni Survey Responses: D. Corydon Hammond.
24. 2008 YAF Alumni Survey Responses: Fred J. Eckert.
25. 2008 YAF Alumni Survey Responses: James A. Lauerman.

which has helped me understand and analyze current events over the years. My belief in freedom, in our Constitution, in the Founding Fathers is deep and abiding and YAF was a part of my education in freedom."[26] Mary Louise Lauerman went on to graduate from Washington University and Middlebury College before becoming a college French teacher.

George Dunlop was a high school student in Pennsylvania who had joined YAF in 1961 "at the suggestion of an English teacher who shared his *National Review* subscription with me from time to time. We engaged in Goldwater for President activity—struggling against the Scranton/Rockefeller wing of the Pennsylvania GOP." Dunlop attended the 1963 Draft Goldwater rally in Washington, DC and volunteered at the Philadelphia Goldwater headquarters in the summer of 1964 before heading off to Catawba College. While at Catawba, he served as chapter chairman and then as Vice Chairman of North Carolina YAF. Dunlop noted that his involvement in YAF was

> Fundamental. Seminal. Not only professionally, intellectually, but also in every other aspect. My life would have been totally different if I had not had a gateway into freedom and principle-based political action. It is not likely that I would have become interested in politics without the YAF gateway.[27]

At the same time, community chapters remained active on local issues as well as on anti-Communist causes and on projects involving direct political action. One example was the Bay Ridge YAF chapter, under the leadership of Jerry LeVan and Dan Calabria, which circulated petitions to oppose tax-supported construction of high-rise apartments in their community in Brooklyn, NY.[28]

As YAF continued to seek financial support, more and more it relied on letters signed by prominent conservatives who served on the organization's National Advisory Board. One such letter came from Herbert Philbrick, who had been a counterspy for the FBI and whose experiences were the bases of a popular television series some ten years earlier.[29] This continual need for funds led Richard Viguerie to recommend that he be allowed to concentrate on fundraising and be relieved of his other administrative duties.[30] Thus, when the Board met in Indianapolis on April 27–28, 1963, it made Viguerie Financial Secretary and selected Florida YAF Chairman Dave Jones as Executive Director. At the time, Bauman called Viguerie, "the person who more than anyone else sustained and energized national YAF during the past year."[31] Viguerie continued in this capacity until the end of 1964 when he launched what became the most successful direct mail fundraising career in history.

The new Executive Director was an individual who had worked his way up the organizational ladder. A high school civics and history teacher in St. Petersburg,

---

26. 2008 YAF Alumni Survey Responses: Mary Louise Lauerman.
27. 2008 YAF Alumni Survey Responses: George S. Dunlop.
28. *New Guard*, March 1963, p. 15. Calabria was one of many who went on to be successful businessmen later in their careers. For several years, Dan Calabria served as President of Templeton Funds prior to its merger with Franklin Resources.
29. Letter of March 14, 1963, Personal Papers of Herbert A. Philbrick, Box 218, Folder 3, Manuscript Division, Library of Congress, Washington, DC. Enclosed with the letter was a list of National Advisory Board members, including 45 current Members of Congress. One member was John B. Anderson of Illinois who in 1980 would run as an Independent candidate for president against President Carter and Ronald Reagan.
30. Interview with Richard A. Viguerie, August 13, 2008, Manassas, VA.
31. *New Guard*, June 1963, p. 13.

Florida, Jones was a graduate of West Liberty State College in West Virginia. He became involved in Young Americans for Freedom in 1961 and soon was appointed Florida State Chairman. At the 1962 National Convention, Jones was elected Southern Regional Chairman. Jones would go on to be the longest-serving executive director of the organization, retaining that position until 1969. This was a period that, without question, saw the greatest growth in membership and chapters in a time that began with the Goldwater effort, went through the early years of the Vietnam war, and concluded with the challenge from the New Left on college campuses.

Jones was instrumental in the founding of the American Conservative Union in 1964 and the Charles Edison Youth Fund (now The Fund for American Studies) in 1967. He served as campaign manager for the successful Jim Buckley for Senate campaign in 1970 and went on to serve as Buckley's Chief of Staff until 1975 when he left to become Executive Director of the Tennessee Republican Party. After leaving the state GOP, he became director and then Vice Chancellor for Development at Vanderbilt University before becoming President of the National Federation of Independent Business Foundation. Prior to his death in 1998 at the age of 60, Jones had been devoting his time to further expanding the work of The Fund for American Studies. Next to Bill Buckley, no single individual contributed more to the development of Young Americans for Freedom than David R. Jones.[32]

With Jones appointment as Executive Director, his seat on the Board went to Randal C. Teague, a protégé of Jones who would also go on to become Executive Director of YAF from 1969 to 1971 and currently is an attorney with Vorys Sater Seymour and Pease LLP in Washington, DC. Teague held nearly every position in YAF from chapter chairman up to head of the national office staff. When asked about the impact of YAF on his career, Teague reported, "The impact YAF had on me is enormous, then and now, and I will especially always be thankful for the network of friends and acquaintances that it gave me for the rest of my life."[33] Throughout his career, Teague has held numerous leadership positions in conservative organizations and has been Chairman of the Board of Trustees of the Fund for American Studies since 1998.

Convincing Goldwater

Throughout 1963, YAF chapters attempted to rally support behind Barry Goldwater in anticipation of a campaign that would focus on the philosophical contrast between liberalism and conservatism. None of the various events sponsored by local YAF chapters was as dramatic and successful as the Goldwater speech before 3,000 fans at Indiana University in March. The Senator was introduced by Bill Jenner, Jr., president of the Indiana University YAF chapter.[34] Now Senior Partner in the law firm of Jenner, Auxier & Jacobs in Madison, Indiana, he recalls his days in YAF fondly noting "we brought Bill Buckley, George

---

32. Several conservative leaders pay homage to Jones in *Human Events*, April 17, 1998. See also Lee Edwards: *David R. Jones—A Passion for Freedom*, monograph prepared for The Fund for American Studies, 1998.
33. 2008 YAF Alumni Survey Responses: Randal Cornell Teague.
34. Jenner was the son of the former United States Senator from Indiana and would later serve as Indiana YAF State Chairman.

Wallace and Barry Goldwater to Indiana University for speeches." Jenner has re-mained active in politics, including service as Chairman of the Jefferson County Republican Party.[35]

In speaking of the President, Goldwater declared that, "up to the first of the year I had grave doubts that he could be beaten. But now I think he can be beaten and beaten heavily." One school official described the event as the most enthusiastic rally on campus in years.[36] The next month, Peter O'Donnell, Texas Republican State Chairman, officially announced the formation of the National Draft Goldwater committee. While the Senator still refrained from making a formal decision, the unofficial campaign was underway.[37]

Two months later, YAF's magazine featured a cover proclaiming what the editors projected as the outcome of the 1964 presidential election reflecting the anticipated Electoral College votes and number of states carried:

	Electoral Votes	*States*
GOLDWATER	287	33
KENNEDY	251	18

Inside the magazine an article by T. Anthony Quinn handicapped the various United States Senate contests and the effect Goldwater was predicted to have on them. As expected, the prediction was that Goldwater's coattails would be of inestimable assistance to any number of conservative candidates running for re-election or attempting to replace sitting Democratic Senators.[38] June also brought a major victory for the Goldwater forces as they reclaimed control of the national Young Republican organization.[39]

Independence Day in the Nation's Capital was to produce the next impor-tant event in YAF's involvement towards the development of the Goldwater candidacy. Officially sponsored by the Draft Goldwater Committee and held at the DC National Guard Armory, it was coordinated by YAF National Board Member Don Shafto, impresario of the 1962 Madison Square Garden rally.[40] YAF groups chartered buses and came from Boston, New York, New Jersey, Alabama, Florida, and the Midwest. It was labeled "the most impressive display of growing conservative influence." Estimates of the crowd ranged from 8,000 to 10,000 cheering fans, a huge turnout for any event in sweltering July in the Nation's Capital and a time when Congress was not in session.[41] Perhaps what was most impressive about the event, however, was that it took place without Senator Goldwater being present. The major political leaders making remarks were Governor Paul Fannin of Arizona, Senator Carl Curtis of Nebraska, and Senator John Tower of Texas who had the crowd chanting "We want Barry!" The

35. 2008 YAF Alumni Survey Responses: William Edward Jenner.

36. "3,000 Cheer Goldwater," *New Guard*, May 1963, p. 12.

37. F. Clifton White: *Suite 3505: The Story of the Draft Goldwater Movement* (New Rochelle, NY: Arlington House, 1967), pp. 127–135.

38. T. Anthony Quinn, "He can do MORE for Conservatism," *New Guard*, June 1963, pp. 7–9.

39. The Young Republican convention is covered in Rick Perlstein: *Before the Storm*, pp. 215–221; F. Clifton White: *Suite 3505*, pp. 166–174; J. William Middendorf II: *A Glorious Disaster* (New York: Basic Books, 2006), pp. 43–44.

40. F. Clifton White: *Suite 3505*, p. 182.

41. "Over 9,000 attend Draft Goldwater Rally," *Human Events*, July 20, 1963; Gregory Schneider: *Cadres for Conservatism*, p. 75 indicates that 10,000 attended; "Thousands of YAF Members Cheer Goldwater at Washington Rally," *New Guard*, August 1963, p. 13.

demonstration started after Tower's closing speech and did not end for several minutes thereafter.[42]

One week later, Young Americans for Freedom co-sponsored a Political Action Conference with *Human Events*. Labeled "Operation Young America," the workshop was held at the Statler Hilton Hotel in downtown Washington and brought over 500 young conservatives to a three-day training session on effective campaign activities. This time their hero was present and gave the keynote speech.[43]

When the fall semester began, YAF members on campuses and in communities across the nation were geared up to promote a Goldwater candidacy. As the organization's magazine summarized the situation, "Name a place Goldwater has been in the last two months and YAF was there—New Jersey, Oregon, Boston, Massachusetts, Texas, California, and Pennsylvania." According to the *Newark Star-Ledger*, when he arrived at Newark airport in September, Goldwater was greeted by "an astonishing turnout of young supporters who chanted the now-familiar 'We Want Barry!'" Meanwhile, the Greater Grand Rapids Chapter of YAF staged a "Goldwater in '64" motorcade with more than forty cars over a sixteen mile route. When the North-South football game was played at the University of Alabama, the local YAF chapter entered a Goldwater car in the pre-game parade. Iowa State University YAF had its own float with the theme "Drown the Hoosiers in Goldwater" in its annual Homecoming parade.[44]

At the Republican Issues Conference held at Mackinac Island, Michigan YAF members met every boatload of attendees with Goldwater paraphernalia and promoted his candidacy among the Republican activists. Two hundred cheering Oregon YAF members met Goldwater's arrival at the Western States Republican Conference in Portland. Julius Duscha, reporter for the *Washington Post*, remarked it was one of the most enthusiastic airport greetings he had seen for Goldwater. So impressed was he that he called YAF National Chairman Bob Bauman to tell him about it. In Boston, on October 16th, the Arizona Senator was greeted by "twenty young ladies in white cowboy hats, red Goldwater sashes and blue shirts," representing the Greater Boston YAF Chapter. As one Republican official noted, "We were trying to keep this from becoming a Goldwater rally, but the Young Americans for Freedom seem to be running away with it."[45]

These events all took place before Barry Goldwater had made a commitment to seek the Republican presidential nomination. But, as he indicated in his remarks at Indiana University, the Arizona Senator was becoming convinced that a serious effort could defeat President Kennedy in 1964. Just as important to him, he believed that it could be a campaign of ideas and political philosophy, emphasizing those basic principles that separated him from Kennedy. It would be a choice for the American people between liberalism and conservatism, not simply between two candidates or two political parties. The month of November 1963 was to change all those plans. But first, YAF would have its second National Convention and its third awards rally.

---

42. F. Clifton White: *Suite 3505*, pp. 181–189.

43. *New Guard*, May 1963, p. 20; *New Guard*, August 1963, p. 12; "YAF Highlights: 1960–1965," Personal Papers of Herbert A. Philbrick, Box 218, Folder 3, Manuscript Division, Library of Congress, Washington, DC.

44. The quotes and the reports on activity are from *New Guard*, October 1963, pp. 16–19. Similar reports of Goldwater activity were printed in other issues of the organization's magazine.

45. *Ibid.*

2nd National Convention—Fort Lauderdale

YAF never did hold the national conservative student conference that had originally been planned for March of 1963. What YAF did have, however, was a combined 1963 National Convention and their third national rally and awards presentation held in Fort Lauderdale, Florida in November 1963. The convention began on Friday, November 8th, with a keynote address by Buckley, followed by panels and banquets on Saturday and Sunday featuring Congressmen John Ashbrook, Bill Brock, Donald Bruce, and Ed Gurney. Some 400 delegates and guests attended the convention sessions at the Galt Ocean Mile Hotel. On Sunday morning, the delegates gathered to elect officers and, once again, there was significant turnover in the YAF leadership.

Bob Bauman was elected to a second term as National Chairman but of the twenty other members of the Board, only six were returning members who had been elected at the 1962 convention in New York City: Lammot Copeland, Dan Carmen, Don Devine, Don Shafto, Fulton "Buddy" Lewis, and Marilyn Manion. Three other members were replacements who had been named to vacancies after the last convention: Tom Huston of Indiana, Alan MacKay of Massachusetts, and Randal Teague of Florida. The remaining 11 of the 21 were new members never having served before on the organization's Board. The new Directors included one who had attended the original Sharon Conference, Jameson Campaigne, Jr., a recent graduate of Williams College who would go on to be one of the longest serving Board members in the organization's history, serving continuously until 1975. Two other new members had been unsuccessful candidates at the New York convention: Bill Boerum of New York and Bud Wandling of Pennsylvania. Boerum, chairman of Staten Island YAF, graduated from Manhattan College and received an MBA from Cornell University.[46] Wandling served for six years on the YAF Board and received appointments in the Reagan Administration. He died in 1992.

Another new member was Richard Derham, a graduate of Harvard and, at the time of his election to the YAF Board, a student at Harvard Law School. Derham served a total of eight years on the YAF Board capped by his service as Treasurer from 1971–1973.[47] Californian Jack Cox joined the YAF Board at the 1963 convention, was one of the key organizers of the YAF presence at the 1964 Republican National Convention and joined Congressman Barry M. Goldwater, Jr. as his Chief of Staff from 1969 to 1976. He is currently President of The Communications Institute in Los Angeles, California and still closely associated with former Congressman Goldwater.[48]

Jim Dullenty was one of the most productive YAF state chairmen during the organization's early years, generating much activity and building several chapters in the sparsely populated state of Montana. Elected to the Board in 1963 he continued through the Goldwater election in that capacity. Dullenty was author of a book on Western history and for a time served as editor of *True West* magazine.[49]

---

46. Email to the author from William Boerum, December 27, 2008.
47. Interview with Richard Derham, Seattle, WA, March 27, 2009.
48. 2008 YAF Alumni Survey Responses: Jack Cox, Jr.
49. Jim Dullenty: *Harry Tracy: The Last Desperado* (Dubuque, IA: Kendall-Hunt Publishing, 1989). Dullenty also penned the introduction to an updated edition of James D. Horan's *Desperate Men:*

Charles Leftwich served for many years as Executive Director of Youth for the Voluntary Prayer Amendment, an ad hoc YAF group operating out of Houston, Texas. Richard Wilson served as Georgia YAF state chairman and later was active in various political campaigns in his home state.

Roger Steggerda joined the Board while a student at Michigan State University and resigned a few months later as he moved on to law school. He is currently a successful attorney with his own firm in Las Vegas, Nevada. Robert Gaston, who had recently been California Young Republican chairman and was at the time a senior partner in the Los Angeles law firm of Gaston, Keltner and Adair, filled Steggerda's seat on the Board.[50]

J. Fred Coldren served as Kansas YAF state chairman following a tradition set by his brother David who had previously been Ohio YAF state chairman while a student at Antioch College. In 1964, Fred served in the position of Organizational Director for YAF and went on a national speaking tour for YAF. Reflecting on his experiences in YAF, Coldren maintains "the sound basis of patriotic and conservative principles from my participation in YAF has been the foundation of all of my career and volunteer efforts ever since. I've adapted to some changing realities, but always remain true to our basic philosophy."[51] He went on to a career of thirty years in city management in Cape May, New Jersey where he continues to reside.

One of the most successful businessmen to serve on the YAF Board of Directors is Tom Phillips. A graduate of Dartmouth College, Phillips was New Hampshire YAF state chairman when he was elected to the Board in 1963. After working in the public relations and publishing business for several years, in 1974 he founded Phillips Publishing International, a firm that went on to become the largest newsletter publishing company in the world. Phillips currently owns Eagle Publishing and its three bulwarks of the contemporary conservative movement: *Human Events* weekly, the Conservative Book Club, and Regnery Publishing. Tom Phillips serves as a board member for Young America's Foundation, Claremont Institute, Institute of World Politics, National Journalism Center and is a trustee emeritus of The Fund for American Studies. He has earned a reputation as one of the movement's leading philanthropists, especially through his chairmanship of the Phillips Foundation. Reflecting back on his involvement in YAF, Phillips noted that it was a great experience where he learned "great lessons for life, business, and leadership."[52]

Those leaving the Board at the 1963 National Convention included Bob Croll, vice chairman and one of the founders at Sharon, and Kay Wonderlic Kolbe, as well as regional chairmen Kenneth Thompson, Lynn Bouchey, and David Franke. Also gone were former National Chairman Bob Schuchman, Bill Schulz, John Weicher, and Antoni Gollan—all of whom had attended the founding conference—along with Craig Ihde, Diarmuid O'Scannlain, and Edmund Zanini.

Nothing could more clearly reflect the growth and institutionalization of Young Americans for Freedom than this turnover in leadership. While remaining consistently loyal to the purposes first set forth in 1960 and the principles laid out in the Sharon Statement, YAF was now being led by officers and a Board of Directors basically comprised of individuals recruited into the organization since

The James Gang and the Wild Bunch (Lincoln: University of Nebraska Press/Bison Books, 1997) and authored numerous articles in *Old West* and *True West* magazines.

50. "National Board Meets in NYC; Gaston Elected," *New Guard*, February 1964, p. 17.
51. 2008 YAF Alumni Survey Responses: J. Fred Coldren.
52. 2008 YAF Alumni Survey Responses: Thomas L. Phillips.

its founding. Three years into its existence, only two of twenty-one members of the National Board of Directors (MacKay and Campaigne) had attended the Sharon Conference and neither one of them had served on the YAF Board before 1963. The torch had been passed to a new group of young conservative leaders.[53]

Dawne Cina Winter remembered the 1963 YAF National Convention not so much for the speakers or the election of officers but, rather, for the principled stand which members took when confronted with the realities of segregation. A student at Fordham University and Vice Chairman of Kings County (Brooklyn) YAF, the then Ms. Cina and her fellow delegates made known their personal commitment to equal rights.

> I remember attending a YAF convention in Ft. Lauderdale where the Galt (Ocean Mile) Hotel refused to allow Don Parker, a Kings County YAF leader and a Black to register. The Brooklyn delegation and then Bob Schuchman, the (former) National YAF Chairman, threatened to walk out and cancel the event. The hotel withdrew their objection and Don Parker integrated the hotel.[54]

Testifying to the influence this event had on the young conservatives from the north, Dr. Donald J. Devine, also then of Brooklyn and Kings County YAF leader, made mention of this incident and his involvement in challenging the hotel in remarks at a YAF alumni reunion dinner held in Newport Beach, CA in 2008, as did future Kings County YAF chairman Don Pemberton in his response to the 2008 YAF Alumni Survey.[55]

After college, Dawne Cina moved to Washington, DC where she worked at *Human Events* and later on the staffs of Senators Orrin Hatch and James L. Buckley. Her involvement in Young Americans for Freedom "inspired me to work for those candidates and individuals who shared my conservative philosophy. YAF brought me to *Human Events* where I met my husband. It provided the background which enabled me to pursue an exciting and interesting career."[56]

---

53. *New Guard*, November–December 1963, pp. 15–16.

54. 2008 YAF Alumni Survey Responses: Dawne C. Winter. It should be noted that YAF had a small African-American membership from its inception to the 1990s. Among those holding leadership positions in the 1960s were Myrna Bain and Don Parker of New York, Jay Parker of Pennsylvania, Frank Johnson of Washington, DC, Donald Warden and Eleanor Evans of California and Donovan Lewis of Ohio. Later leaders included Alexander Wells of New York, Ken Johnson and Deroy Murdock of Washington, DC, Stan Salter, Curtis Helms and Ursula Williams of California. Jay Parker, Murdock and Salter were elected and served on the YAF National Board of Directors. Jay Parker is President of the Lincoln Institute in Washington, DC while Deroy Murdock is a syndicated columnist. Donovan Lewis is currently Parliamentarian for the National Federation of Republican Assemblies, a volunteer organization of conservatives. Ken Johnson joined the Marines after graduating from George Washington University and succumbed to cancer at the age of 23. Not all early YAF members continued as members of the conservative movement; Donald Warden is an interesting case in point. In the mid-60s Warden was a talk radio host and attorney who headed up the Afro-American Association in the San Francisco Bay area. A California YAF member, Warden was a featured speaker at a Western YAF Conference in 1965 ("YAF Around the Nation," *New Guard*, June 1965, p. 23). Subsequently he changed his name to Khalid Abdullah Tariq al-Mansour and became an orthodox Muslim. According to the Social Activism project at the University of California—Berkeley, he was a mentor to Huey Newton and Bobby Seale, founders of the Black Panther party (Hugh Pearson: *The Shadow of the Panther* (Cambridge, MA: De Capo Press, 1995), p. 45. He currently lives in San Antonio, Texas.

55. Devine's remarks were at a reunion dinner attended by the author; 2008 YAF Alumni Survey Responses: Donald G. Pemberton.

56. 2008 YAF Alumni Survey Responses: Dawne C. Winter. Dawne Cina Winter is the wife of Thomas Winter, President and Editor-in-Chief of *Human Events* and First Vice Chairman of the American Conservative Union.

Likewise, George Burgess, who was then Oregon YAF State Chairman, viewed his participation in the Fort Lauderdale convention as among the highlights of his time in YAF, along with campaigning for Goldwater, meeting and talking with Bill Buckley, and counter-protesting anti-Vietnam war protesters in downtown Portland. For Burgess, a graduate of Lewis & Clark College, his time in YAF "reinforced my ability to speak out when conservative values were being challenged or trampled on by government, businessmen or radical groups. It gave me the ability to feel comfortable speaking or debating a wide range of topics before live groups or on TV."[57]

The high point of the weekend for most attendees, however, was the Third National Awards Rally held at Yankee Stadium in Fort Lauderdale on Saturday evening. While the keynote address was given by Congressman William C. Cramer of Florida, the major speeches were by former Senator William Knowland of California and Senators Strom Thurmond and John Tower. More than six thousand attended the event and, while he was not physically present, it was obvious that Barry Goldwater was on most attendees' minds. YAF had pulled off another major rally, this time far from its base in New York and Washington.[58]

As a young Boston University graduate, Don Lambro had been hired as managing editor of *New Guard* and shortly thereafter,

> I found myself on a plane flying to Ft. Lauderdale to help set up a huge rally as part of YAF's national convention. That's where I met a flamboyant young man, Donald Shafto, who was coordinating the rally. I was one of his assistants the following year at the GOP national convention that nominated Goldwater and was with him when he gave the order over a walkie talkie to drop millions of gold glitter from the rafters the moment delegates put Barry over the top. I mean, it was like, wow![59]

Just as he had done in Madison Square Garden in 1962, and would do again in the Cow Palace in 1964, Donald Shafto had produced another extravaganza for the conservative movement.

The President Is Assassinated

Shortly after the euphoria of another successful event and a convention that ushered in new blood for the organization, YAF and the entire nation were not prepared for a tragedy that no one then living had ever experienced. And then it happened. On that fateful 22nd day of November, Lee Harvey Oswald gunned down the President of the United States, the one nationally elected officeholder in our political system, the symbol of the nation. With the rest of the country, the young conservatives grieved. How could this happen to our country, to our President? No longer would there be the great philosophical contest between two men who held differing positions but greatly respected each other. The world had changed.

---

57. 2008 YAF Alumni Survey Responses: George Burgess.
58. Senator Goldwater had been promoted as the featured speaker in pre-event publicity but cancelled out and was replaced by Tower. See flyer promoting the rally, Hall-Hoag Collection, Box 49–13, Folder HH0429, John Hay Library, Brown University, Providence, RI.
59. 2008 YAF Alumni Survey Responses: Donald J. Lambro.

In its editorial published a few days after the event, *New Guard* reprinted the words of Senator Goldwater: "The tragedy that struck down our President has struck at the heart of our nation. It was a vile act. It embodied everything that America is against and against which all Americans should be united."[60] A quick transition occurred and there was a new President, a man quite different from his predecessor. Immediately Lyndon Johnson called for thirty days of mourning and a moratorium on politics while he consolidated his position and power.

The political climate heading into 1964 was not the one that everyone anticipated. There would be no Goldwater-Kennedy debates across the nation modeled after the Lincoln–Douglas debates of a century earlier. America and the free world would need to become acclimated to a new President from Texas who talked and acted quite differently from the one they had elected in 1960. The New Frontier was over and, with it, perhaps the presidential campaign of Barry Goldwater. It would take much thought and reflection now before the Arizona Senator would be convinced to run against Lyndon Johnson.

To help convince him that he should become a candidate for the presidency, Chairman Bauman wrote to all YAF members in December, noting that after the assassination, "Senator Goldwater has received a large amount of leftist hate mail somehow blaming him for the death of the President. The warped, fanatical hatred which these letters have shown has amazed and sickened many who have seen them and it has disturbed the Senator." Bauman asked YAF members to write Goldwater and urge him to run for President.[61] All across the country, YAF members responded by the thousands with messages to their political hero. Meanwhile, YAF was taking note of its place in the changed political environment. As Antoni Gollan claimed,

> America needs Young Americans for Freedom now just as surely as it did three years ago, and will just as surely twenty years from today. We are young, and we enjoy, all of us, the exultation of youth, but in our marrows we are fiercely dedicated to the principles of freedom. YAF represents part of what every political movement requires: an ideological vanguard."[62]

After the tragedy that affected all Americans, the task ahead for Young Americans for Freedom was to remain dedicated to the principles that had brought them together in 1960.

Motivating the Troops and Corralling Votes

As 1964 began, YAF members were hoping for a Goldwater presidential campaign but also becoming involved in a number of other activities and projects to advance their conservative philosophy. Many chapters sponsored speeches by conservative elected officials. Still others brought to campus conservative writers and professors to discuss the philosophy of conservatism or the principles of free market economics.[63] Astoria YAF in Queens, New York City, not only sponsored

60. "JFK: RIP," *New Guard*, November–December 1963, p. 4.

61. December 1963 letter of Robert E. Bauman to YAF Members, Group Research, Inc. Archives, Box 342, Columbia University, New York, NY.

62. Antoni E. Gollan, "YAF: '64 and After," *New Guard*, November–December 1963, p. 6.

63. *New Guard*, May 1964, p. 16; June 1964, p. 16; July 1964, p. 20.

speakers and raised funds for the Goldwater campaign but also became involved in a number of local campaigns under the leadership of Alfred DelliBovi.[64] Reflecting on that experience, he noted,

> YAF was a training ground where skills were developed, networks established and the dynamics of groups and organizations were learned. Those skills were useful in many ways in my career, civic and political involvement. YAF was an experience which helped me pick and choose the next experiences in life. The Sharon Statement was a major influence. I often make contact with people whom I knew in YAF or who were members of YAF. We are not defined by YAF although each of us carries some part of the YAF experience with us.[65]

DelliBovi went on to a distinguished career after his years in YAF, serving eight years as a member of the New York State Assembly, as Administrator of the Urban Mass Transportation Administration, then as Deputy Secretary of the Department of Housing and Urban Development, and since 1992 as President and Chief Executive Officer of the Federal Home Loan Bank of New York.

YAF chapters also attempted to publicize their organization before audiences of likely supporters. In this fashion, Texas YAF sponsored a booth at the National Junior Chamber of Commerce convention in Dallas to spread the conservative message and recruit new members. It was reported, "models from Neiman Marcus Dept. store and 'Miss Dallas' were among those who helped staff the YAF booth."[66] In Fairfield County, Connecticut, the YAF chapter carried out its "project gutter" in various towns each Saturday. Volunteers would occupy a parking space, fill the meter with the appropriate coins, and then pass out literature to pedestrians. As one YAF leader noted, "this way they don't block sidewalks, and merchants and on-beat policemen are kept happy while YAF members continue their work." The chairman of Fairfield County YAF was Louise M. Sciubba, a graduate of Regis College who would go on to serve on the National Board of Directors one year later.[67] YAF also continued its campaign against involvement in the National Student Association and saw several more colleges turn down membership, including Dartmouth College, Iowa State University, Hollins College, University of Wisconsin, and Quinnipiac College.[68]

As had been the case during its first year, YAF continued to pick up chapters when independent local groups affiliated with the national organization. Ron Docksai and Dan Levinson were among a group of high school students in Queens, New York who organized themselves under the name "Young American Conservatives" before the 1964 presidential election. The following year, the group received considerable media coverage of their demonstrations against proposals for a revised police civilian review board, a city-wide Liberal Party ballot initiative that subsequently went down to defeat. When a local YAF leader, Steven Rich, saw the media coverage he contacted Docksai and invited him and his members to join YAF. Then Docksai received a letter from Tom Charles Huston from Washington, DC and this impressed the group and they decided to affiliate with Young Americans for Freedom. Docksai became a student at St. John's

64. *New Guard*, January 1964, p. 17.
65. 2008 YAF Alumni Survey Responses: Alfred A. DelliBovi.
66. *New Guard*, September 1964, p. 23.
67. *Ibid.*
68. *New Guard*, January 1964, pp. 18–19.

University and was defeated in a campaign for the YAF National Board in 1967, only to bounce back and eventually become National Chairman in the 1970s. In a recent meeting Docksai noted,

> Many YAFers went on to later careers in academic and public service. Ken Pearlman became an award-winning physics professor at MIT and Phil Tymon became a chemistry professor at Syracuse. Donna McDonald became a clinical healthcare leader in upstate New York. Young American Conservatives Paul Knag graduated from Harvard Law School and became a prominent attorney. YAC's original treasurer, Dan Levinson, became a Federal judge and currently serves as Inspector General of the U.S. Department of Health and Human Services.[69]

Docksai and his associates from Young American Conservatives joined a growing body of YAF members who would make New York one of the strongest state organizations in YAF's history, a group that played a major role in rallying youth support for Bill Buckley in his 1965 campaign for Mayor of New York City and for his brother Jim in all three of his campaigns for United States Senator from New York.

In the neighboring state of Connecticut, David Gessert heard about YAF while in high school and founded the Douglas MacArthur Chapter where "YAF helped form my political opinions and allowed me to document why I believed what I did." Like many others, Gessert has fond memories of his time in YAF and the activities that they undertook.

> We debated liberals, campaigned for Barry Goldwater in the 1964 New Hampshire primary and later in Connecticut. [Former Governor John Davis] Lodge was the United States Senate candidate but wouldn't support Barry. We had 100 bumper stickers printed saying "Goldwater-Dodd," Lodge's Democratic opponent. We drove the Republicans crazy for a $13 investment.[70]

His experiences in YAF "gave me the confidence to fight for my beliefs the last 45 years." After graduating from Quinnipiac College, Gessert settled in Wallingford, Connecticut where he served for fourteen years on the Town Council and has now served more than 18 years on the Wallingford Public Utilities Commission.

Across the continent in Glendale, California, high school student Allen Brandstater picked up his grandfather's copy of *National Review* and saw an ad for an organization of young conservatives. "I responded and joined YAF in 1963 when Goldwater had not yet announced for president. When I was a junior in high school I joined Youth for Goldwater. After the election I formed Foothill YAF comprising mainly fellow students from Glendale Union Academy, a Seventh-day Adventist prep school."[71] He would go on to serve as State Executive Director for YAF and as a member of the National Board of Directors. Arnold Steinberg became involved in the Goldwater campaign and then enrolled at the University of California at Los Angeles where he began writing for YAF publications and in 1967 transferred to George Washington University and became editor of *New Guard*.[72]

---

69. Interview with Ronald F. Docksai, August 14, 2008, Washington, DC.
70. 2008 YAF Alumni Survey Responses: David A. Gessert.
71. Interview with Allen Brandstater, October 12, 2008, Newport Beach, CA.
72. 2008 YAF Alumni Survey Responses: Arnold Steinberg.

Karen Setterfield was another Californian who joined YAF in high school, became a "Goldwater Girl" and later a "Reagan Girl" and a regular volunteer in the YAF office. According to Setterfield, YAF had a big impact on her. "It mostly helped me to figure out my own beliefs and values. It helped me socially to 'come out of my shell' and have more self-confidence."[73] From her time in YAF, "I learned about working in a team with people of all ages, how to convert beliefs into action, respect for ideals and ideas." Now living in Aspen, Colorado, she is partner in the real estate firm of Setterfield & Bright.

Another Californian activated by the Goldwater campaign was Ralph McMullen who started the YAF chapter at San Jose City College in 1963 and was elected student body president. In addition to volunteering in the Goldwater effort, Ralph's chapter sponsored anti-communist speakers on campus, protested left-wing student organizations in the Bay area, and organized opposition when Communist Party USA Chairman Gus Hall spoke on his campus. Looking back on those years, YAF "taught me the philosophy of freedom. I have used it all my life in all my actions from my personal life to voting, etc. YAF gave me a purpose for life in a great way."[74]

Maurice Franks decided that while campaigning for Goldwater was fine, he would go all the way and become a candidate himself. The 22-year-old student at Harding College filed for the office of Justice of the Peace as an independent in a totally Democratic county. His campaign was successful and he became the youngest judge in the State of Arkansas and the first independent elected to the position. Franks went on to obtain a law degree from the University of Memphis and now is a Professor of Law at Southern University Law Center in Baton Rouge, Louisiana.[75]

Robert Gilkie was a successful businessman in a suburb of Boston when he became involved in the early Goldwater effort and then served as President of the Greater Boston YAF Chapter in 1964. What he remembers about YAF is "the level of excitement and intense knowledge of government and the direction we were heading." Among the skills he picked up in YAF was a "respect for other opinions since there were sharp adversarial views among YAF members." Gilkie continued his career in business, becoming Controller of the Puritan Clothing Company, but also remained active in politics. In 1976, he was one of a handful of YAF members from traditionally liberal Massachusetts who were elected delegates to the Republican National Convention, all of whom were pledged to Ronald Reagan.[76]

Anthony Conte is another Massachusetts YAF member who was a Reagan delegate to the 1976 Republican National Convention. Like many others, he joined YAF in high school and was involved in the organization before the Goldwater campaign. Conte was active in the Boston University YAF chapter that also produced a number of conservative leaders, including syndicated columnist Don Lambro, author Don Feder, and Tucson City Councilman Emmett McLoughlin. He recalled that YAF "helped to encourage me to become and stay politically active. My introduction to Ayn Rand/Objectivism was the most important ideological development of my life." Conte was elected as City Councilor at Large in Revere, serving as the only Republican on the Council from 1978 to 1987.[77]

---

73. 2008 YAF Alumni Survey Responses: Karen Setterfield.
74. 2008 YAF Alumni Survey Responses: Ralph E. McMullen.
75. 2008 YAF Alumni Survey Responses: Maurice Franks.
76. 2008 YAF Alumni Survey Responses: Robert J. Gilkie.
77. 2008 YAF Alumni Survey Responses: Anthony J. Conte.

Debates and Satire

Vietnam and the New Left were only beginning to surface on a few campuses in 1964. At Penn State, Berkeley, and other campuses in 1964 there was a high degree of debate and discussion involving YAF members and leftist advocates since both groups consisted of political activists who distinguished themselves from the larger body of apathetic and apolitical students.[78] As Louise Lacey, a YAF member in Berkeley, recalled,

> right and left radicals got along ... The views of the two (YAF and what were most often SDS) were not changed, but they agreed with one another that hypocrisy, greed, dishonesty, war, narrow-mindedness, violation of personal rights and freedom, and many others things that the government represented and expressed should be highlighted and verbally fought against strongly.[79]

Penn State YAF's Carl Thormeyer also recalled lively debates with various peace organizations on campus, especially as the two groups set up their weekly recruitment tables in the university student union.[80] These were the times before the Left took to violence and closing down colleges when rational debate could occur on ideological differences.

While YAF strongly backed the war in Vietnam they also defended the right of anti-war activists to speak out against the war. They drew the line, however, at outright propaganda from the enemy. When the Penn State Socialist Club sponsored a Viet Cong propaganda film, the YAF chapter objected. They declared "we didn't hear anybody yell for 'academic freedom' for the Nazis during World War II."

Another young conservative who joined YAF in 1964 was Harvey Hukari but his motivation at the time was more campus oriented. He recalled

> ... in 1964 I became involved with the YAF at San Francisco State, organizing counter-protests to antiwar demonstrations. I felt another voice needed to be heard, and students should learn about what was really going on in Vietnam, rather than just blindly accepting that it was completely wrong.[81]

Hukari later transferred to Stanford and went on to play a central role in opposition to New Left violence on that campus over the remainder of the decade. In 1969 his Stanford YAF chapter received the award as outstanding college chapter in the country.

YAF's anti-communism was reflected in more than the early conflicts over Vietnam; Cuba and Castro remained a major concern also. At the Massachusetts Institute of Technology, YAF leaders David Nolan and Mike Leavitt had one of the more active chapters in the state. One spring 1964 program featured a lecture

---

78. Kenneth Heineman: *Campus Wars*, p. 148.
79. 2008 YAF Alumni Survey Responses: Louise Lacey.
80. 2008 YAF Alumni Survey Responses: Carl Thormeyer.
81. Quoted in Sandra Gurvis: *Where Have all the Flower Children Gone?* (Jackson: University Press of Mississippi, 2006), pp. 79–80.

by Professor Ernesto Blanco of the MIT Mechanical Engineering Department. A former Director of Research in Castro's first cabinet, Blanco had fled the island in the early Sixties. His topic was "The Truth About Cuba and Our Foreign Policy."[82] Chapter Chairman David Nolan, after graduating from MIT, became the major force behind the creation of the Libertarian Party, which ran its first candidate for President, Dr. John Hospers, in 1972 and remains a consistent third party in American politics.[83]

All across the nation, activists they were, and activists dedicated to proselytizing and organizing and influencing the direction of campus and community policy. Matthew Dallek concluded that "From the outset, YAFers did not defend the status quo; they attacked it. On campus they decried the liberal economic theories of their professors. At rallies, they inveighed against the *New York Times* and other establishment media for one-sided reporting. And in letters to financial backers, they denounced thirty years of liberal rule."[84]

Serious and committed though they were, the YAF members could also have fun. It was not just the left that could produce songs like "Barry's Boys." Not to be outdone in musical creativity, in April 1963 the Boston College and Boston University YAF chapters combined to sponsor a New Frontier spoof called "The Mikado of Bravado." Dan Carmen, New England Regional Chairman wrote the three-act musical satire in the best tradition of Gilbert & Sullivan. National Board Member Alan MacKay played President Kennedy. As Castro invades Florida, negotiations are undertaken by the Kennedy State Department and then freedom is finally saved with the rebirth of a nation under Barry Goldwater in 1964. Some 250 attended and cheered as the good guys won out in the last act.[85]

Drawing on some of the left-wing songs of the thirties and the songbooks of the "Party of the Right" at Yale University, the tradition of satirizing the left as well as themselves is one that would continue throughout the organization's history. At some point in every YAF national convention, small groups of delegates could be found imbibing and carrying on the tradition of oral story-telling. The year 1964 produced two contributions to the tradition. First came a little booklet titled "Folk Songs for Conservatives by Noel X and his Unbleached Muslims."[86] Among the collection were "Cool Goldwater," "Won't You Come Home, Bill Buckley," "Let's Test Again," and the ever-popular "Orally"

> Don't put fluoride in our streams
> Don't spray our willow tree
> It's a Commy plot it seems
> To get us orally
> Orally
> Orally
> Please don't poison me
> Cast aside your pesticide
> And down with DDT."

---

82. *New Guard*, September 1964, p. 23.
83. Brian Doherty: *Radicals for Capitalism* (New York: Public Affairs, 2007), pp. 389–392.
84. Matthew Dallek, "Young Americans for Freedom: The Rise of Modern Conservatism, 1960–1964," p. 32.
85. *New Guard*, June 1963, p. 12.
86. Noel E. Parmentel, Jr. and Marshall J. Dodge, III: *Folk Songs for Conservatives by Noel X and his Unbleached Muslims* (New York: Unicorn Press, 1964).

The authors continue on to warn us "eternal vigilance is the price of a good set of choppers."[87] Little did they know that their efforts at writing, collecting, and publishing satirical political songs would be repeated many times over. The tradition of song books and satirical songs would continue with a YAF songbook compiled by Vince Rigdon and Connie Marshner for the 1971 YAF National Convention,[88] and an updated one distributed at the 1975 YAF Convention with new songs, including one dedicated to the 1976 campaign of Ronald Reagan.[89]

In a somewhat more serious vein, four Nashville YAF members bonded together to create a group called "The Goldwaters." They were brought together by the head of the Nashville office of *Billboard* magazine, a Goldwater supporter who needed a group to perform at rallies and record an album of political songs.[90] The recording was "The Goldwaters Sing Folk Songs to Bug the Liberals" and the group appeared at events across the country. According to Lee Edwards, "they were our Peter, Paul and Mary—plus Bob Dylan and Pete Seeger—all in one. They were especially active at the convention in San Francisco, playing at YAF parties and all over the place."[91] The lead singer of the group, Ken Crook, noted, "our songs are funny, but they have a serious message. Our efforts will be directed toward engendering excitement and enthusiasm at Goldwater rallies." The four vocalists were students at various colleges in the Nashville area and three of them took off two semesters to campaign, promising to return to school "after Barry gets in the White House."[92]

As 1964 began there was still some uncertainty as to whether there would be a Goldwater candidacy to sing about that year. Barry Goldwater confronted a new and unique political environment with a new President attempting to bring the nation out of the psychological loss they had just experienced. The political calendar did not allow for much indecision for the primaries and caucuses would begin before spring. If Goldwater were to seek the nomination, campaign organizations had to be built, strategy developed, and advertisements secured.

Some 22 years later, in his last days as a United States Senator, Goldwater sat down for an extended interview with John Kolbe. Kolbe was one of the founders of YAF and at that time in 1986 was a political columnist for the *Phoenix Gazette*. Kolbe asked the Senator about his decision to run.

> ... when Jack was shot, I just thought I don't want to run against Lyndon Johnson. I had looked forward to running against Jack Kennedy. I think it would have been a real change in campaigning in this country.... Well, we would have debated. We had talked together about just going across

87. *Ibid.*

88. Rigdon is now singing a different tune as pastor of Our Lady of the Presentation Roman Catholic Church in Poolesville, MD. Connie Coyne Marshner is Director of Recruitment for the American Family Business Institute, a group that promotes efforts to end the estate tax.

89. "We'll Win in 76—A Special Collection of Songs of the Right," published in commemoration of Young Americans for Freedom Fifteenth Anniversary Celebration in Chicago, August 13–17, 1975. Copy provided to the author by Eric Rohrbach, former YAF National Board Member and former State Senator in Washington State. Updated versions of the songbook were distributed by YAF Board candidates at the 1977 and 1979 national conventions and other versions continued to be distributed as late as the 1991 national convention, the final one in the organization's history.

90. Michael Long and John J. Miller, "Same Song, Different Verse," *National Review Online*, June 7, 2007. Another folk singer who appeared at several conservative events in the mid-60s and then disappeared was Janet Greene. Greene released only eight songs but they included "Comrade's Lament" about the difficulties of being a Communist.

91. *Ibid.*

92. Richard Taylor, "And Now, Presenting ... The Goldwaters," *New Guard*, March 1964, p. 14.

the country—maybe using the same airplane—but stopping at a town and standing up in the old Stephen Douglas way and debate. But I just decided not to run when he was killed. And then, right here in this room, I think it was around Dec. 15 or 16 of that year, they put the pressure on me. They said there were hundreds of thousands of young people that were looking forward to my running.

Kolbe went on to ask "And they told you there were all these young people out there waiting for you?" Goldwater responded "And on the strength of that responsibility I felt for young people, I said, 'OK, we'll go.'"[93] On January 3, 1964 in Phoenix he formally announced his candidacy for President of the United States.[94]

Finally, this was what the YAF legions had been working for, hoping for, organizing for. Now they had an official candidate for President who reflected their conservative philosophy. One can accurately say that while Bill Buckley was the impetus and mentor for the organization, the person and political philosophy of Barry Goldwater were the major uniting factors in Young Americans for Freedom. It was Goldwater who epitomized the anti-communism, traditionalism, and free market economics that were the pillars of YAF as expressed in the Sharon Statement. There were few members who did not support the Arizona Senator. Wherever the Senator spoke during 1961 to 1964, he would be greeted by YAF members bearing the ever-present "YAF Backs Barry" signs. Lee Edwards summarized this serendipitous relationship when be noted some years later, "Barry Goldwater made YAF but YAF also made Barry Goldwater—made him a national political figure and then the Republican nominee for President in 1964."[95]

The cover story for the March 1964 issue of *New Guard* was an exclusive article from Barry Goldwater titled "Why I'm Running" and its presence was an indication of the significance of Young Americans for Freedom to the entire Goldwater effort.[96] But the campaign effort by YAF had already begun as in late January New England YAF held a regional conference in Concord, New Hampshire, bringing more than 150 YAF members into the site of the nation's first primary. In addition

---

93. John Kolbe, "Arizona legend talks politics," *Phoenix Gazette*, December 3, 1986.
94. Theodore H. White: *The Making of the President, 1964* (New York: Atheneum Publishers, 1965), p. 111, 120–122. The Goldwater campaign has been the subject of numerous studies and it is not the purpose of the present work to cover it in any detail. Among the many analyses published, the following were found to be most valuable. There are a number of insider reports with rather myopic recollections of the campaign as well as more academic studies of the campaign and the conservative movement during the 1960s. In the first category would be a report on the draft efforts by F. Clifton White: *Suite 3505*; a recollection of the entire effort from draft to nomination to general election in J. William Middendorf, II: *A Glorious Disaster*; the ideological aspects of the campaign in Karl Hess: *In a Cause That Will Triumph* (Garden City, NY: Doubleday, 1967); and the defense of the campaign manager and long-time associate in Stephen Shadegg: *What Happened to Goldwater?* Two rather contemporaneous studies by political scientists, both published in 1968, are John H. Kessel: *The Goldwater Coalition* (Indianapolis: The Bobbs-Merrill Company, 1968) and Bernard Cosman and Robert J. Huckshorn, editors: *Republican Politics: The 1964 Campaign and Its Aftermath for the Party* (New York: Frederick A. Praeger, 1968). The most comprehensive recent historical study, written by an avowed liberal, is Rick Perlstein: *Before the Storm*, while from a different ideological perspective is Lee Edwards: *The Conservative Revolution* (New York: The Free Press, 1999), especially pages 101–141. The draft movement and the 1964 campaign are covered in Jonathan Schoenwald: *A Time for Choosing*, pp. 124–161 and Mary Brennan: *Turning Right in the 60s* (Chapel Hill: University of North Carolina Press, 1995), pp. 82–103. For a fascinating study of grassroots conservative activity in Orange County, California during the 1960s, see McGirr: *Suburban Warriors*, especially pages 111–146 that focus on the Goldwater campaign.
95. Quoted in Roberts: *The Conservative Decade*, p. 26.
96. *New Guard*, March 1964, pp. 7–8.

to hearing speeches and attending workshops, those present received an orientation into campaign work for the Arizona Senator. Over the following weeks until the primary on March 10th cars and buses filled with YAF volunteers from the Northeast would descend on the Granite State to campaign for their candidate. They contributed to the crowd that produced the largest political rally in New Hampshire history, an event organized by New Hampshire YAF under the leadership of National Board Member Tom Phillips.[97]

To make sure that local YAF chapters and members were using every technique available to advance the conservative cause, National Secretary Marilyn Manion authored an article on tips for effective political action.[98] All across the country YAF chapters accepted the challenge. Reporting on the efforts of YAF during the campaign, writers Stephen Hess and David S. Broder noted "their presence at countless demonstrations confirming that right-wing girls are prettier than their left-wing counterparts."[99] When the Senator arrived at O'Hare Airport, Illinois YAF turned out thousands to greet him and the following month helped garner crowds for a Goldwater campaign rally in Chicago. Whether it was New Hampshire, Illinois, Indiana, Oregon or California, the YAF troops were present. As one historian later wrote, "At every stop photographers and cameramen were taxed trying to keep the ubiquitous "YAF Backs Barry!" banners out of their shots."[100] Through victory and setback and ultimate success in the nominating battle, YAF produced an essential element of the grassroots support for Goldwater.[101]

How important was YAF's support to Goldwater's obtaining the Republican nomination? Perhaps Bill Buckley best put it in perspective years later when he observed,

> There is absolutely no doubt that the intensity factor of the Goldwater campaign was vividly affected by YAF. If YAF had not existed, with the huge amount of money spent by the Rockefeller people, plus also the feeling that the Republican party's moderates had to rescue it from decrepitness, it might very well have tipped California to Rockefeller. . . . I don't think he [Goldwater] could have won that nomination without the youth enthusiasm.[102]

It was YAF members who directed the Goldwater campaign at numerous college mock conventions and elections throughout late 1963 and early 1964; it was YAF members who worked to convince college Republican clubs and conventions to endorse Goldwater; it was YAF members who trudged through the snows of New Hampshire and continued on to the California primary, ringing doorbells, addressing envelopes, making phone calls, and attending campaign rallies; and then it was YAF members who organized the youth support and the rallies and the demonstrations that summer in San Francisco.

---

97. "YAF Highlights: 1960–1965," Personal Papers of Herbert A. Philbrick, Box 218, Folder 3, Manuscript Division, Library of Congress, Washington, DC.

98. Marilyn Manion, "What You Can Do in '64," *New Guard*, February 1964, pp. 13–15.

99. Stephen Hess and David S. Broder: *The Republican Establishment* (New York: Harper & Row, 1967), p. 77.

100. Rick Perlstein: *Before the Storm*, p. 455.

101. For a more detailed discussion of YAF's role in the nominating campaign, see Andrew: *The Other Side of the Sixties*, pp. 187–204.

102. Buckley interview with Matthew Dallek, May 12, 1993, quoted in "Young Americans for Freedom: The Rise of Modern Conservatism: 1960–1964," p. 52.

San Francisco and the 1964 Election

The Republican National Convention in San Francisco would end up being the ultimate high point of YAF's campaign to elect Barry Goldwater. Culminating years of work, YAF members came from all parts of the country to help nominate their chosen candidate.[103] The Youth for Goldwater chartered train arrived Monday under the leadership of National Board Member Tom Phillips. Then came busloads from Montana under the direction of Board Member Jim Dullenty and from Arizona coordinated by State Chairman Norman Wycoff. Next, a chartered plane touched down bringing 116 New York YAFers ready to do battle.[104] Hundreds more from all over California took part as active foot soldiers with many coming from Bay area campuses such as Stanford, UC Berkeley, San Jose State, Foothill College and others.[105]

Even before these volunteers arrived, YAF members from the West Coast were already at work led by National Board Member Jack Cox. Cox, a student at San Jose State about 50 miles from San Francisco, had established a Western YAF office that would serve as the mobilization center for YAF operations until YAF moved into a hotel suite in the Hilton Hotel in downtown San Francisco. Cox, working with Dave Jones, YAF Executive Director, began stockpiling literally thousands of signs with wood handles along with buttons and literature. Cox also rented every available station wagon to transport teams of YAFers around the Bay area to appear at rallies and events. When Nelson Rockefeller arrived at the San Francisco Airport, crews of YAF members were there and when the New York Governor stepped off his plane, "YAF Backs Barry" signs greeted him. YAF even had a Dixieland band on a pickup truck, plastered with Goldwater signs, which included many YAFers from northern California as band members. With Bob Bauman and Jack Cox on the back of the truck, it was driven right into the middle of a televised Rockefeller Rally in the courtyard of the Mark Hopkins Hotel to the consternation of the Rockefeller campaign.[106]

A YAF led crowd of 4,000 waving "YAF Backs Barry" signs met Goldwater's arrival at San Francisco on Saturday. It was Dave Jones's idea weeks before that this should be the YAF slogan consistently used in San Francisco and before the week was over it would become a household phrase. Still other YAF members were organized into a major distribution network to reach every delegate. Sunday saw teams of YAF members visit the 28 hotels where the delegates and alternates were staying. Each delegate received a personally addressed letter from Senator Tower with a copy of the special convention edition of *New Guard*. In the letter, Tower commended the organization and testified that YAF has "provided the muscle that is vitally needed in political organizations for sound, conservative politics."[107]

Inside that July issue of *New Guard* was a letter from the YAF National Board

---

103. An overview of YAF activities in San Francisco can be found in "A Generation Arrives," *New Guard*, August 1964, pp. 13–18 from which much of this section is drawn.
104. *New Guard*, September 1964, p. 25.
105. Email from John Cox, Jr. to the author, February 25, 2009.
106. *Ibid.*
107. *New Guard*, August 1964, p. 13.

of Directors addressed "To the Delegates to the 1964 Republican National Convention from Young Americans for Freedom." In addition to promoting recognition of their organization, the fundamental message was that these delegates had a critical decision to make that would affect the future of the GOP and the nation.[108] The message was clear. YAF wanted these delegates to nominate Barry Goldwater and give the nation "a choice, not an echo."[109]

Also on Sunday, Bill Buckley arrived to be greeted by 200 YAF members shouting "We Want Buckley" as a band played "Won't you come home, Bill Buckley?" One sign held by a YAF member testified to his critical role in the effort when it said, "You Made It Possible, Bill!"

It is not surprising that at a time when most states set a minimum voting age of 21, few members of a relatively new youth organization had been elected as delegates to a national nominating convention. Moreover, in 1964 the size of the national convention was much smaller than those in the 21st century, with only 1,308 delegates seated. Nevertheless, five YAF members had been successful and were there as delegates: National Chairman Bauman from Maryland; Richard Plechner of New Jersey, a Sharon attendee who was later to serve on YAF's National Board; Fred Ackel from Florida, who would become a successful dentist in Fort Lauderdale; Ted Humes of Pennsylvania; and Morton Blackwell of Louisiana, the youngest delegate, who would go on to found the Leadership Institute and serve for more than twenty years as National Committeeman from Virginia. Also on the floor as an alternate from North Carolina was A. Morehead Stack of Fayetteville.

On the second night of the convention, YAF held a rally for Goldwater at the Herbst Theater with Ronald Reagan as the master of ceremonies.[110] Bill Buckley recalled the event as one of the highlights of the entire week. "Five thousand persons were turned away. The auditorium was jammed with excited people, mostly under thirty years of age. The press was there in force. The professionalism of the physical arrangements was impressive."[111] The following day's *New York Times* gave front-page coverage to the rally. Referring to his closing speech at the theater, the paper reported, "Senator Goldwater told a cheering stomping audience last night that the country was caught up in a wave of conservatism that could easily become the political phenomenon of our time."[112] While Goldwater was correct, it would take another sixteen years before his prediction would come true.

Prior to Goldwater's nomination on Wednesday YAF sponsored another rally, this time outside the Cow Palace. While almost a thousand YAF members shouted for Barry, they also heard from Bob Bauman and Ronald Reagan. Cox, who had been working with Ronald Reagan as a YAF advisor since 1962, recruited Reagan to address the crowd. Speaking from a flatbed truck, Reagan told the crowd, "You were at this long before many, and God bless you for it."[113] The YAF members were pumped and ready to demonstrate for their candidate on Wednesday night

108. *New Guard*, July 1964, p. 4.

109. The phrase was the title of a widely distributed book in 1964 by Phyllis Schlafly (Alton, IL: Pere Marquette Press, 1964). Schlafly would go on to form a women's organization called the Eagle Forum that would take the lead in successfully organizing opposition to state adoption of the Equal Rights Amendment to the U.S. Constitution.

110. Judis: *William F. Buckley, Jr: Patron Saint of the Conservatives*, p. 229.

111. Buckley: *Flying High*, p. 141. The rally is discussed in more detail on pages 139–142.

112. Charles Mohr, "Goldwater Sees a Trend to Right," *New York Times*, July 15, 1964.

113. Schneider: *Cadres for Conservatism*, p. 82; *New Guard*, August 1964, p. 17.

and hear him give his acceptance speech on Thursday night. As Carol Dawson recalled, "I was there at the Mark Hopkins [Hotel] when the famous Goldwater acceptance speech was being mimeographed, printed and collated. The famous quotation about 'extremism' was in that speech. Little did we know it would cause such a furor!"[114]

Once again, Don Shafto was called upon to give general advice on the YAF rallies but his main responsibility was to coordinate the entire Goldwater floor demonstration on the night of the Senator's nomination. Meanwhile, a cadre of YAF members led by Richard Viguerie, Lammot Copeland, David Franke, and Jameson Campaigne set up a "Bill Miller for Vice President" committee. On Thursday, nearly every demonstrator who came onto the floor to cheer for Miller was a YAF member. With Goldwater and Miller both selected, the YAF members left San Francisco with what many of them viewed as their dream ticket. It was their greatest moment. They had captured the nomination; now they had to convince the American people and capture the White House.

Immediately after the convention and as the general election campaign began, YAF's initial National Chairman, Robert Schuchman, tried to put into perspective why so many young people were attracted to the Goldwater candidacy.

> The great appeal of Barry Goldwater to our generation is that he represents the America of the future in which we want to live. He symbolizes a nation and a world in which the individual is free, free to make his own way without the government punishing him for his successes and rewarding him for his failures . . . Thus, it is not merely dedication to an individual, but also dedication to principle which motivates the young conservative movement.[115]

Part of his appeal was personal and part of it was what he typified in terms of the ongoing regional and class divisions in America. As another young conservative later claimed, Goldwater "represented a rebel. He represented a challenge to the Eastern Establishment. He represented West versus East. He represented a new approach toward international communism. He represented freedom from the growth of the Federal bureaucracy. And he represented my personal freedom."[116] The commitment and excitement of the YAF members as they went forth from San Francisco to wage a war for the minds and hearts of the American people was hard to measure.

Writing many years later, Rick Perlstein summarized the outlook of these young conservatives who had climbed the mountain and could see the valley of victory before them.

> They were now a force to be reckoned with. They marched at the head of a presidential crusade . . . It was indescribable, the exhilaration they felt those long days, exhausting themselves for the highest cause they could imagine. It remade you; it made everything else seem small. They had no words to describe it . . . They were young, idealistic; triumph was inevitable, for they were battling for the Lord.[117]

---

114. Carol Dawson e-mail to the author, January 24, 2009.
115. *New Guard*, August 1964, p. 6.
116. Quoted in Klatch: *A Generation Divided*, p. 83.
117. Perlstein: *Before the Storm*, p. 471.

Sociology professor Rebecca Klatch conducted a series of in-depth interviews with a number of YAF members some thirty years after the 1964 campaign. In attempting to analyze and identify the significance of various events on their political development she concluded that the Goldwater campaign had the greatest effect, acting "as a beacon for young conservatives much in the way the civil rights movement did for young leftists . . . For both traditionalists and libertarians, the Goldwater campaign was a primary route to activism and to YAF."[118] Whether one was mainly an anti-communist, traditionalist, libertarian or Objectivist—all could agree that the election of Barry Goldwater would turn the country around and make America a better place.

Working on the presidential campaign staff were Lee Edwards, Carol Bauman, George McDonnell and Mary Ann Ford while National Board Members Lammot Copeland, Jr. and Fulton Lewis, III worked at the Miller for Vice President campaign. Among the volunteer leaders on the steering committee of Youth for Goldwater were: Barry Goldwater, Jr., Bob Bauman, Morton Blackwell, and James Harff, along with Sharon-attendee Brian Whalen, former YAF Vice Chairman Bob Croll, former YAF Secretary Kay Wonderlic Kolbe, and National Board Members Fred Coldren and Don Shafto. YAF members who served as Youth for Goldwater state chairmen included Larry Callaghan (California), Ken Tobin (Delaware), Barry Bowen (Maryland), Raymond Friesecke (Massachusetts), Steve Winchell (Michigan), John Greenagel (Minnesota), Tom Phillips (New Hampshire), Anthony Rapolla (New Jersey), Bill Boerum (New York), Bob Sherman (Ohio), Dick Bishirjian (Pennsylvania), Dan Joy (Rhode Island), Ken Tomlinson (Virginia), and John Patton (North Carolina).[119]

One of the highlights of the Youth for Goldwater-Miller effort was a rally at the University of Pittsburgh where Bob Bauman spoke to more than 5,000 attendees.[120] Neil Dentzer recalled bringing two chartered busloads of Greater Cleveland YAFers to what he described as a "YAF Backs Barry" rally since most of those involved in orchestrating the rally and rounding up the attendees were YAF members.[121] It was an exciting time for the young conservatives just days before the reality of election day would set in.

Unfortunately, not all would go as wished. So much attention had been focused on gaining the Republican nomination that little planning took place for winning the general election. Political scientist John Kessel described the situation at the campaign office after the San Francisco convention as one where all the attention had been directed towards obtaining the nomination and no master plan existed for the fall campaign.[122] Nevertheless, at the grassroots level YAF members were dedicated to bringing about a Goldwater victory. They rang doorbells, stuffed envelopes, distributed flyers, organized and attended rallies for the ticket. Optimism and enthusiasm were outweighing reality. But for some YAF members, the cold truth would soon confront them.

---

118. *A Generation Divided*, p. 81.
119. Youth for Goldwater Files, Group Research Archives, Box 345, Columbia University, New York, NY; *New Guard*, July 1964, p. 18.
120. *New Guard*, November 1964, p. 22.
121. 2008 YAF Alumni Survey Responses: Neil J. Dentzer.
122. Kessel: *The Goldwater Coalition*, pp. 130–131.

The Aftermath of the Campaign

On September 11, some two hundred YAF members gathered at the Commodore Hotel in New York City for the annual meeting of the organization. They approved a series of resolutions that included commending Senator Goldwater for his support of human rights, supporting the House Un-American Activities committee, and opposing participation in the National Student Association. The next day a pilgrimage was made to Great Elm to commemorate the fourth anniversary of YAF's founding. The events at Sharon, coordinated by Louise Sciubba of Fairfield County YAF, provided a glorious occasion reflecting on the accomplishments of the past and the plans for the future. It was good to be young and to be in YAF.[123]

Without question, however, the most memorable event of the conference was not the trip to Sharon but the address by Bill Buckley. Buckley spoke of the obstacles confronting Goldwater, not the least of which was that sufficient groundwork had not been completed to prepare the public to receive the Senator's message. He then spoke the words that stilled the audience: "I speak of course about the impending defeat of Barry Goldwater."[124] Much of the audience was in shock. They had expected to hear a speech calling them to increased campaign work and they were being told that their efforts would not result in victory. As Bob Bauman noted, "There were kids who came and expected to be told, 'You are going to win, here we are going to win the battle for the Lord,' and here they were told that it wasn't the case, and that we weren't going to win the battle for the Lord."[125] But Buckley went on to put the situation in perspective,

> If it were not for the presence of Goldwater as a candidate for the Republican party our opportunity to proselytize on a truly national scale would not exist . . . The point of the present occasion is to win recruits whose attention we might never have attracted but for Barry Goldwater; to win them, not only for November the third, but for future Novembers; to infuse the conservative spirit in enough people to entitle us to look about us, on November 4th, not at the ashes of defeat, but at the well-planted seeds of hope, which will flower on a great November day in the future, if there is a future.[126]

While depressing the immediate enthusiasm of some in attendance, it refocused the attention of many YAF leaders to what came next, to the continuing battle for conservatism after election day. In this context, YAF decided to delay including Buckley's speech in the organization's magazine until after the election. Taking the initiative, YAF launched a major membership recruitment drive that produced some 2,500 new members in October and a like number in November—young people who were committed to the long-term effort to advance conservatism.

One fateful development during the campaign occurred when Richard Viguerie discovered that candidates for president were required to file the names

123. *New Guard*, November 1964, pp. 19, 21–22.
124. Bridges and Coyne: *Strictly Right*, pp. 85–87.
125. Judis: *William F. Buckley, Jr.: Patron Saint of the Conservatives*, p. 231.
126. Buckley, "We, Too, Will Continue," *New Guard*, December 1964, pp. 11–12, 14.

and addresses of every donor who gave more than $50 to their campaigns. This information had to be provided to the Clerk of the House of Representatives and was available for public review. Viguerie went to the Clerk's office and began copying names and addresses on index cards. Quickly he realized that this was a monumental task and hired six women to copy names for the next five months. When the election ended, Viguerie had 12,500 names of Goldwater donors. The information was then transferred to computer tape and the direct mail fundraising business had its beginning.[127]

When the votes were counted some 27 million Americans had voted for Barry Goldwater, far less than those who voted for Lyndon Johnson. The Republican candidate had carried only six states. There will long be debate over the 1964 campaign. Several factors were involved in the outcome: the effects of the assassination of President Kennedy, the appeal for consensus and adherence to the supposed mainstream of American thought, the theory of the hidden conservative vote, the Southern strategy, and the failure of certain leading Republican office-holders to support the national ticket. What effect did the Goldwater bluntness and misstatements and direct challenges to the prevailing and accepted views have on the outcome? How does one assess the impact of the infighting and lack of planning within the campaign leadership? Could any GOP candidate have won in 1964?

Some years later Goldwater reflected back on the 1964 campaign and was asked if he were simply ahead of his time: "No, I think the basic reason was that the country wasn't ready, and I don't think they'd ever be ready, to have three presidents in two years. I've come to that conclusion a long time ago. I think that was the main reason."[128] But some observers maintained that did not fully explain the outcome. In the December issue of *New Guard*, Carol Bauman penned an editorial that minced no words in analyzing the failures of the campaign. It was expensive yet changed few votes and failed to provide a responsible alternative to Lyndon Johnson. "We would have to agree, reluctantly . . . that the conduct of the campaign in many ways failed to prove Senator Goldwater's qualifications to be President. What it most emphatically did not prove, was that conservatism is dead as a political philosophy."[129] The candidate, not the philosophy, had lost the election. Yet, on further reflection, it was the campaign that had failed the candidate as much as the candidate had failed the campaign.

Whatever the reasons, the Goldwater campaign had failed and the effect of that failure would have consequences for Young Americans for Freedom. The optimism of youth had to be tempered by the reality of defeat. To some, the defeat was demoralizing and their political involvement came to an end.[130] According to Board Member Alan MacKay, that was not the common reaction however.

> With the benefit of hindsight in history we realize that the presidential campaign, like nothing else, involves people, gets them started in the movement . . . There were very few people, despite their disappointment, who said "That's it for politics." The almost universal reaction was "By God, we're not

127. Interview with Richard A. Viguerie, August 13, 2008, Manassas, VA.
128. John Kolbe, "Arizona legend talks politics," *Phoenix Gazette*, December 3, 1986.
129. "What Went Wrong?," *New Guard*, December 1964, p. 5.
130. Gillion Peele: *Revival and Reaction: The Right in Contemporary America* (London: Clarendon Press, 1984), p. 131.

going to let that happen again. We're going to go out and take control of the Republican Party." . . . And it happened exactly that way. So the contribution of the '64 campaign can't be overestimated.[131]

Just as MacKay recalled, the campaign itself brought a significant increase in YAF's membership, many of whom were high school students attracted to the Goldwater campaign and determined to continue their involvement.

Shawn Steel, now the Republican National Committeeman and former GOP State Chairman in California, provides an example of the influence the campaign and YAF had on many young people,

> After Goldwater's defeat, we had this huge (Youth for Goldwater) organiza-
> tion, we had chapters in nearly every high school in the San Fernando Valley
> (Los Angeles). Since then, I don't know of a single right of center movement
> that's been able to achieve that. Goldwater attracted the largest percentage of
> idealists, hard-core activists of any election, including Ronald Reagan's, in
> my view. And out of that, geez, we had all this energy, and we weren't really
> expecting to win by a landslide and so we had energy and we had a focus
> and YAF conveniently was there and they immediately enveloped us and
> gave us an organizational structure and we converted Youth for Goldwater
> into Young Americans for Freedom in the fall of 1964.[132]

As Steel recalled much later, "Goldwater 1964 was the most exciting campaign I was ever involved in—there was a real passion among the young people active in that campaign." YAF provided a melding together of the philosophical and the political. Moreover, principles were most important for "no one wanted to be viewed as a squish."[133] More than merely the temporary, there was a lasting effect that would be felt throughout his career.

> YAF had an important influence on me. I realized that I could lead people
> and accomplish agreed-upon goals. The tools I learned that help me in life
> today I learned while in YAF—how to organize meetings, set up conferences,
> conduct business, persuade people, and accomplish goals.[134]

In addition to his leadership positions in the California Republican Party, Steel is a successful attorney whose wife, Michelle, was recently elected to the powerful California State Board of Equalization.

The long-term effect of the campaign was positive in other ways also. As Lee Edwards later noted, "Thousands of young conservatives entered politics because of Barry Goldwater's run for the presidency. Today they sit in Congress or head think tanks or manage government agencies or edit magazines. They form a national network committed to conservatism."[135] Ed Treick, Wisconsin YAF State Chairman before the 1964 election, recalls it being "an exciting time.

---

131. Klatch: *A Generation Divided*, pp. 83–84.
132. January 1993 interview with Shawn Steel in Dallek, "Young Americans for Freedom: The Rise of Modern Conservatism: 1960–1964," p. 32.
133. Interview with Shawn Steel, October 13, 2008, Palos Verdes, CA.
134. *Ibid.*
135. Lee Edwards, "The Other Sixties: A Flag-Waver's Memoir," *Policy Review*, Fall 1988, p 61.

We were the nucleus of a growing group of movement conservatives. Bill Buckley and Barry Goldwater were our heroes. Young people were flocking to our cause and we were giving the GOP establishment fits."[136] While that excitement may have been temporary, thousands of young people now had the "political bug" and were committed to advancing their conservative principles. Robert Roggeveen had been co-chairman of the YAF chapter at the Hotchkiss School and was permanently affected by the 1964 campaign: "At base, I have remained a 60s conservative—with roots as a Goldwaterite—a "YAF Backs Barry" bumper strip and three buttons from the '64 campaign are displayed with pride in my library. My can of AuH$_2$O finally sprang a leak!"[137] For Roggeveen and many others there would always be that emotional attachment to Goldwater, but also a commitment to involvement in civic, community and religious organizations as well as political efforts. As a student at the University of Wisconsin in 1964, Richard Wright maintained "recruiting and educating conservatives started, for me, with the Goldwater campaign, and afterwards continued through YAF." Wright went on to serve two years as Wisconsin YAF State Chairman and was part of a World Youth Crusade for Freedom "Freedom Corps" delegation to Vietnam in 1966.[138]

One who joined YAF in the aftermath of the Goldwater defeat was Bill Saracino, an individual who would hold numerous positions in the organization, assume a leadership role in the various Reagan campaigns, play an important part in the election of Jesse Helms to the Senate from North Carolina, and spend a career as a political consultant in California. As he recently recalled,

> As a freshman in high school in 1964, my sister's boyfriend had an AuH$_2$O sticker in the back window of his car. That got me interested in finding out who Goldwater was. So I volunteered at GOP headquarters and precinct walked. I was absolutely stunned when he lost. The following month, December, I was reading National Review and YAF had an ad that said "Are you mad Goldwater lost?" That was how I felt so I mailed in the coupon. YAF sent me material and I started a high school chapter in 1965.[139]

Looking back on his career, Saracino concluded,

> To the extent that I have been an effective conservative, it is due to YAF. It was a perfect blend of philosophical grounding and practical political action. I might have learned that myself, but I would not have been as effective without YAF. When YAF sent out the books, it taught me why we were conservatives—beyond the personalities that we supported. The political training we gained in YAF allowed us to advance the conservative philosophy. What YAF provided was the melding together of the philosophy and how to advance that philosophy by obtaining political power.[140]

---

136. 2008 YAF Alumni Survey Responses: Edward F. Treick.
137. 2008 YAF Alumni Survey Responses: Robert H. Roggeveen.
138. 2008 YAF Alumni Survey Responses: Richard O. Wright. As he noted in his survey, "It wasn't always just serious business. When I retired as Wisconsin State Chairman in 1971, I self published a booklet: *Unfortunately My Most Profound Quotes (sic) Are Unprintable.*"
139. Interview with William Saracino, October 11, 2008, Newport Beach, CA.
140. *Ibid.*

Saracino's experience was not alone, as literally thousands of young people originally motivated by the Goldwater campaign would continue their involvement.
Another example was Henry Durkin, a recent Fordham graduate who joined
YAF during the Goldwater campaign, became active in the New York YAF state
organization and authored numerous articles that appeared in *New Guard*.[141]

The campaign had been a baptism by fire, the first important effort to leave the
notion of the "remnant" behind and build a mass movement for conservatism.
It had shown that, properly approached, there were millions of Americans who
could be rallied behind the banner of conservatism, not merely a small band of
ideologues and true believers.[142] Young Americans for Freedom had established
itself as a national organization comprising dedicated members who were rebelling
against the status quo and attacking entrenched elites—an approach that would
continue for the remainder of the decade on college campuses. YAF had made
conservatism exciting and produced a generation of activists who would go on
to lead numerous conservative organizations and fight for an endless number of
causes.

Bob Tyrrell, who had been a YAF leader at Indiana University and is currently
editor of *The American Spectator*, noted that Goldwater revived the Republican
Party with libertarianism and anti-communism and, in so doing, gave hope to
conservatives. His campaign was "the catalytic moment for the conservative
movement. Many who in subsequent years became the most effective conservative
activists were roused to political awareness in 1964's uncommonly ideological
campaign."[143] Dana Rohrabacher was one of the young people attracted by the
Goldwater campaign who went on to be a leader in Young Americans for Freedom,
served as a speech-writer in the Reagan White House, and eventually was elected
to Congress where he continues to serve. "When I first ran for Congress, my secret weapon was the high-quality support I received from friends who had been
politically active with me since the late 1960s. As far as the media was concerned,
we didn't exist, but in the long run we won."[144]

Writing prior to the 1980 presidential election, political columnist David
Broder claimed that

> YAF has unquestionably been the primary breeding ground and training
> ground for the new generation of conservative leaders. . . . What struck me
> is that the YAF alumni have profited from the losing battles they have been
> engaged in. I'm sure some got discouraged and dropped out along the way
> but those who survived have been toughened by the experience and have
> put the lessons they learned to good use.[145]

Many of those YAF alumni of the Goldwater campaign went on to assume leadership positions in the Reagan Administration and continue even today at the
forefront of conservative organizations, in state and local government, and as a
conservative presence in Congress and the Federal government.

---

141. 2008 YAF Alumni Survey Responses: Henry Durkin.
142. This point is made especially by Niels Bjerre-Poulsen, "Organizing the American Right:
1945–1964," p. 323.
143. R. Emmett Tyrrell, Jr.: *The Conservative Crackup* (New York: Simon & Schuster, 1992), p. 145.
144. Dana Rohrabacher, "Us Young Americans for Freedom," *The American Enterprise*, May–June
1997, p. 38.
145. Quoted in Roberts: *The Conservative Decade*, p. 34.

Still others assumed leadership positions in non-profit organizations, such as Fredric M. Rohm, YAF's Delaware State Chairman in 1964, who headed up various chambers of commerce for over 35 years.[146] Donald Boyd helped found the conservative club at Montana State University, went on to obtain his PhD, and spent the next 38 years teaching Industrial Engineering courses at the same university. His involvement in YAF showed him that "by enlisting youth and supporting their natural conservatism via informed training (one) can provide America with a powerful influence for its survival."[147] Boyd is one of literally hundreds of YAF alumni who have gone on to teach on America's college campuses, helping to educate young people not only in the subjects they teach but also in the importance of defending freedom and protecting those values which have made America great.

The roots of the late 20th century conservative success, of course, ran back even further than the 1964 Goldwater campaign. As George Nash observed, "it is likely that without the patient spadework of the intellectual Right, the conservative political movement of the 1960s would have remained disorganized and defeated. Without *The Conscience of a Conservative* ... Goldwater would probably not have attained national stature. Ideas did have consequences, as Richard Weaver had long before observed."[148] One could also add that without Bill Buckley, there would be no conservative youth organization to rally support for a candidate such as Barry Goldwater and to build the network of political activists who continue today to provide leadership.

The Goldwater campaign also brought to the forefront a new spokesman for conservatism and hero for the YAF members. Throughout the entire fall campaign, the one successful element appeared to be a thirty-minute television appeal by a Hollywood actor, Ronald Reagan. Although some in the Goldwater campaign tried to stop it from ever being aired, "A Time for Choosing" raised nearly $600,000 for the national campaign through a brief plea for funds.[149] Reagan was on his way to becoming the leading political personality for the conservative movement, the Governor of California, and eventually the President of the United States. As Reagan noted in his autobiography, "Of course, I didn't know it then, but that speech was one of the most important milestones in my life—another one of those unexpected turns in the road that led me onto a path I never expected to take."[150]

Watching the speech with his father, an 18 year-old college student in Kentucky was motivated to join YAF, eventually become Kentucky YAF State Chairman, and stay active. As he told his father, "that man is going to be President. And I'm gonna work for him in the White House." True to his prediction, Reagan did become President and Gary Bauer went on to serve as Undersecretary of Education from 1982–87 and then in the White House as Advisor to the President for Domestic Affairs from 1987–88.[151]

---

146. 2008 YAF Alumni Survey Responses: Fredric M. Rohm.
147. 2008 YAF Alumni Survey Responses: Donald W. Boyd.
148. Nash: *The Conservative Intellectual Movement in America*, 1996 edition, pp. 272–273.
149. Lee Edwards: *Reagan—A Political Biography* (San Diego: Viewpoint Books, 1967), p. 79. For the story of the three contributors who funded the national television broadcast of Reagan's speech, see: Nicole Hoplin and Ron Robinson: *Funding Fathers* (Washington, DC: Regnery Publishing, 2008), pp. 131–138. The controversy within the Goldwater campaign over whether to broadcast the Reagan speech is also related in Matthew Dallek: *The Right Moment* (New York: The Free Press, 2000), pp. 66–69.
150. Ronald Reagan: *An American Life* (New York: Pocket Books, 1990), p. 143.
151. Quoted in Perlstein: *Before the Storm*, p. 509.

It was in this framework that YAF took the Goldwater campaign not as a defeat but, rather, as an organizing tool and a framework on which to build for future efforts. It worked at promoting a conservative alternative for American society as well as developing new leadership and in so doing would help to transform American politics. Historian Jonathan Schoenwald noted,

> Only YAF successfully bucked the trend of declining grassroots activism among conservative groups, and in the wake of the John Birch Society's demise, YAF filled in as the one group through which young people could meet, work together to achieve results, and then move on to another project, staying busy in their fight against the Left.[152]

In the post-Goldwater period, YAF continued to recruit young people, training them in activist tactics and responsible conservatism, providing them with a means to work towards the victories that would come some fifteen to thirty years later, first with the election of Ronald Reagan to the presidency and the eventual Republican majority in Congress in 1994.

After YAF: the ACU Is Formed

The first word in the organization's name indicated an age limit to active involvement and it had developed an image as a predominantly student organization. Thus, YAF's older members and the now developing alumni core needed an outlet for continued activity reflecting the responsible conservative position they had worked hard to develop and maintain. Such an outlet would provide a means for them to work as equals with other more senior political activists. To accomplish this, Bob Bauman contacted Marvin Liebman during the fall of 1964 and proposed an organization for YAF graduates and others. Liebman suggested that they meet with Bill Buckley and when they did Buckley enthusiastically supported the idea.[153] Buckley agreed to host a planning meeting at his office on the Saturday after Goldwater's defeat. Agreement was reached among those present and the new effort was underway.[154]

On December 18th, the initial Board of Directors met at the Statler-Hilton Hotel in Washington. Members included Buckley, Bauman, and Liebman along with several other conservative leaders. Congressman Donald Bruce was designated to serve as Chairman and for the next twenty years a Member of Congress would hold this position. The following day forty-seven leading conservatives joined together with the new Board for the founding conference of the American Conservative Union. As Liebman recalls, "the efforts to create a conservative organization to counter the powerful influence of the Americans for Democratic Action were finally bearing fruit. We aimed to be the ADA of the Right. The American Conservative Union was well on its way."[155] The name was chosen because it had "the ring of permanence" and would be representative of an inclusive responsible conservatism. Its mission was to consolidate conservative support, mold public opinion, and encourage political action.

---

152. Schoenwald: *A Time for Choosing*, p. 249.
153. Marvin Liebman: *Coming Out Conservative* (San Francisco: Chronicle Books, 1992), pp. 159–160.
154. Judis: *William F. Buckley, Jr: Patron Saint of the Conservatives*, p. 233.
155. Liebman: *Coming Out Conservative*, p. 160.

ACU gave conservatives a home separate and apart from the regular Republican Party organization.[156] Throughout its history, YAF alumni have been at the forefront of the American Conservative Union's leadership from Carol Dawson as its only staff member at its inception to David Keene, its present-day Chairman. Among the individuals who have served ACU as executive director include YAFers David Jones, John Jones and Ronald Dear. As of 2010, fourteen members of the ACU Board of Directors are former YAF members.[157] Just as YAF had helped create the ACU, the new organization in turn went on to become the source for the creation of the Conservative Victory Fund, the National Journalism Center, and the American Legislative Exchange Council—all of which continue to contribute to the conservative movement in the 21st century.

When 1964 came to a close YAF could look back with pride on its role in the Goldwater campaign and its contribution to the development of the conservative movement. By the mid-60s some of the original leaders would move on to new challenges, including helping to build the American Conservative Union. Still others would assume positions in government, law, business and the academy. But the impact and influence of Young Americans for Freedom on their lives would be felt for many years. As Carol Dawson summarized its effect on her,

> My involvement in YAF did many things for me. First . . . .it provided associations and relationships which produced lifelong contacts. Certainly it helped me advance in the Reagan Administration. Secondly, it trained me in the techniques and strategies for successful political efforts. Most importantly, it introduced me to a way of thinking and a desire for the practical application of my strongly held conservative beliefs. Those beliefs continue to inform all that I do and motivate me in expending my energy in volunteer activities.[158]

That effect mentioned by Dawson was also felt by countless other young conservatives as they devoted a considerable amount of their time and energies during their formative years to Young Americans for Freedom. As writer Niels Bjerre-Poulsen noted, "student politics provided a field of practice for a new generation of political activists who would in time take their place in the emerging conservative counter-establishment."[159] Some would fade away from YAF or from direct political involvement but the influence of those years of involvement would remain with them throughout their careers.

While the left could take satisfaction in their defeat of Barry Goldwater, it would be a short time satisfaction as the more radical left began its destructive efforts on campus and in community. The so-called New Left obtained significant media attention and even support, yet it would flame out as the years passed. Looking back some years later historian Kenneth Heineman noted the effect of the young right and left.

> For every radical student who admired North Vietnam's Ho Chi Minh, many more conservative youths became politically active as a result of Arizona

---

156. Schoenwald: *A Time for Choosing*, p. 250; Rusher: *The Rise of the Right*, pp. 132–134.

157. David Keene, Thomas S. Winter, Donald J. Devine, Jameson Campaigne, Jr., Morton C. Blackwell, Floyd Brown, Tom DeLay, Becky Norton Dunlop, Alan M. Gottlieb, James V. Lacy, Michael R. Long, Joseph Morris, Ron Robinson, and Kirby Wilbur.

158. 2008 YAF Alumni Survey Responses: Carol G. Dawson.

159. Bjerre-Poulsen, "Organizing the American Right: 1945–1964," pp. 269–270.

Senator Barry Goldwater's 1964 presidential campaign. Goldwater may have lost the election to Johnson, but the young conservatives he inspired became the architects of Ronald Reagan's triumph in the 1980 presidential election.[160]

Indeed, the lasting influence of the Goldwater campaign would be felt in American politics for the next forty years as conservatives began the takeover of the Republican Party structure, gained the nomination and election of Ronald Reagan and thirty years after the Goldwater campaign took control of both chambers of the United States Congress for the first time in more than forty years.

For the future, YAF had recruited thousands of new members and expanded its operations to more campuses and communities. Working with others, it had created an organization to keep its alumni active and involved. It had gained the respect of the Republican Party organization and the recognition of the national media as a major player in the political arena. Now it was prepared to move on to newer and much different challenges involving both foreign policy and campus issues. There was much yet to be done for conservatism.

---

160. Heineman: *Put Your Bodies upon the Wheels*, p. 28.

6. The Cause Must Go On

*". . . to infuse the conservative spirit in enough people to entitle
us to look about us . . . at the well-planted seeds of hope, which
will flower on a great November day in the future . . ."*[1]

The defeat of Barry Goldwater did not deter the YAF leadership from its commitment to advance the principles outlined in the organization's Sharon Statement.
There were thousands of additional young people now committed to the cause
who were seeking ways to continue their involvement. Young Americans for
Freedom would be the vehicle for their efforts in high schools, on college campuses, and in communities across the nation.

At the same time, YAF continued to emphasize political activities, not only
building towards the midterm elections of 1966 but also concentrating on key
races in 1965. Indeed, while it was a purely local election, the attention of young
conservatives nationwide focused on the campaign for Mayor of New York City.
The emphasis on conservative principle remained important to YAF and to its
members. Wick Allison, later publisher of *National Review* and of *D Magazine*
made this point in a letter to the organization's magazine, *New Guard*:

> I joined the Young Americans for Freedom because it was a dynamic youth
> organization fighting for conservatism. I joined the Young Republicans
> because I believe very deeply in the principles of the Republican Party . . .
> No matter how alike (YAF and the GOP) were six months ago, no matter
> how alike their memberships are, or how common their interests—their
> goals are different. One is concerned with elected Republicans, the other
> with elected conservatives. Please don't forget it.[2]

It was a message received by the leaders of the organization that was committed
to undertaking a broad range of activities to advance conservative principles.
Whether dealing with campus issues or national defense, holding educational
seminars and distributing books and articles on philosophical points or training members in political and organizational techniques, YAF would continue to
expand its programs and its membership. Remembering the mid-sixties, Mike
Thompson recalled that time as involving great activity and organizational growth.

> The YAF campaign to STOP IBM from selling computers to the Soviet bloc,
> MACK trucks from selling to the Soviets, advocating victory in Vietnam,
> fighting the National Student Association on our campuses, etc.—all were
> campaigns and activities that forged us into a national organization on
> hundreds of campuses.[3]

---

1. From an address by William F. Buckley, Jr. at the 1964 annual meeting of Young Americans for
Freedom, excerpted in *New Guard*, December 1964, p. 11.
2. Letter to the Editor, *New Guard*, April 1965, p. 2.
3. 2008 YAF Alumni Survey Responses: Michael W. Thompson.

Then a chapter member at Indiana University, Thompson would go on to be elected to the National Board of Directors in 1965 and serve as National Vice Chairman in the late 1960s.

Before these activities could begin, an overall plan had to be adopted. Thus, in a post-election meeting at the end of 1964, the Board of Directors agreed upon an ambitious program of political action and anti-communist education. The Board set forth ten goals for 1965, including increasing the number of members, local chapters, and state organizations. Separate programs were to be established for high school, college, and community groups. High school chapters were encouraged to adopt a study course called "Communism: Challenge to Freedom," with members competing for scholarships to that summer's Washington School of Anti-Communism. Community chapters were provided with a political action course titled "Mission '66." To expand YAF's influence on more campuses, a College Conservative Council was created with a goal of recruiting representatives from 1,000 campuses, including those where no chapter had yet been organized.

YAF continued to encourage schools to disaffiliate from the National Student Association and set a goal of decreasing representation from 15% of the nation's colleges to 10%. Under the leadership of Tom Charles Huston, new STOP-NSA material was made available, including a detailed booklet titled *NSA Report* that would be distributed to student government officers as well as fraternity and sorority leaders.[4] YAF distributed its Issues Paper Number 6 titled "National Student Association: a smear against students" and it was updated in 1967 to include references to the CIA funding of NSA and the outcome of the 1967 NSA Congress.

Organizationally, a series of seven regional conferences were to be held in 1965, a process that would continue every two years up to the 1990s.[5] Along with the biennial national convention, the regional conferences served as a major method of selecting the organization's national leadership with one member of the Board of Directors chosen at each regional conference. To help expand its membership base, YAF convinced Bill Buckley to sign a recruitment letter that was mailed to various lists of potential members, including Youth for Goldwater-Miller, Young Republicans, College Young Republicans, and participants in programs such as Boys' Nation and Girls' Nation. The letter, which appeared prepared on the author's own typewriter, included the following:

> The officers of Young Americans for Freedom have asked me to endorse their organization and to suggest to you that you might be glad if you join. This I am happy to do ... They have a light in their eyes, and I suspect it is the same light that shone at great moments in American history, in the eyes of the men and women who made these moments great. It shines in your eyes, perhaps. I hope so.
> Yours faithfully,
> William F. Buckley, Jr.
> Editor, *National Review*[6]

The responses to this letter produced new members in areas of the country where little YAF activity had previously taken place. One who joined around this time

4. *New Guard*, January 1965, p. 25.
5. Beginning in 1978, the regional conferences were moved from odd-numbered years to even-numbered years but continued every two years until 1990.
6. Group Research Archives, Box 342, Columbia University, New York, NY.

was Roger Candelaria, a student at Colorado State University. Already a conservative, Candelaria eventually became a chapter chairman and then Colorado YAF State Chairman. From his perspective, "YAF provided the practical organizational foundation and inspiration for political work and ISI the intellectual base to counter the leftish political and social philosophy I got as a Philosophy major." Through his involvement in YAF, Candelaria was exposed to philosophical writings and writers that helped ground him in values he has carried throughout his life.

> It helped expose me to Frank Meyer, Bill Buckley, Russell Kirk and superficially to Weaver and Voegelin and others. Understanding markets and, eventually, coming to appreciate a deeper appreciation of the religious or metaphysical truths about the human person on which a free society depends made all the difference in who I am.[7]

Candelaria went on to law school, became a judge, and now works in higher education, still reflecting the values inculcated in him as a college student many years ago.

Despite his defeat, Barry Goldwater remained committed to Young Americans for Freedom and the conservative movement he had led into battle in 1964. In what was one of his first speeches after the election, Goldwater spoke at an event sponsored by the YAF chapter at Northern Arizona University with more than one thousand in attendance.[8] As Michael Sanera, then the chapter chairman, recently recalled, "Needless to say it was a standing room only crowd and one of his greatest speeches."[9] Goldwater would continue to support YAF in many ways over the next several years, signing letters of support, speaking on campuses and appearing at many YAF national conventions. Ten years later, in 1974, it would be Young Americans for Freedom that would sponsor, with Goldwater as the honored guest, a ten-year reunion in San Francisco, commemorating his presidential nomination victory.

3rd National Convention—Washington

The third national convention of Young Americans for Freedom was held in Washington, DC on August 27–29, 1965 at the Shoreham Hotel. More than one thousand attended from 42 states to elect new officers, pass resolutions, take part in workshops and hear the featured speakers. Resolutions reflected YAF's opposition to "all trade of a strategic nature with any Communist nation" and support for the U.S. commitment to South Vietnam. The resolution on Vietnam also called for a commitment of both the needed level of ground troops as well as air strikes against missile sites around Hanoi and Haiphong and destruction of the "industrial capacity of North Vietnam." YAF also called for "a naval and air blockade of North Vietnam" and informing Communist China that any overt involvement would result in retaliation from the United States.[10]

Noting the continuing vitality of the organization, David S. Broder said, "Five years after it was founded at the Sharon, Connecticut home of William F. Buckley,

---

7. 2008 YAF Alumni Survey Responses: Roger Candelaria.
8. *New Guard*, April 1967, p. 31.
9. 2008 YAF Alumni Survey Responses: Michael Sanera.
10. "Therefore, Be It Resolved . . . ," *New Guard*, October 1965, p. 20.

the organization has 40,000 members, with an average age of 22, and an operating budget of $25,000 a month."[11] Clearly YAF had more than survived the election of 1964 and was on its way to many years of involvement in the conservative movement for the remainder of the 20th century.

One outgrowth of the convention was a decision to form a number of ad hoc groups, including the Student Committee for Victory in Vietnam, Committee for a Free China, and Youth for the Voluntary Prayer Amendment. These would join the already active STOP-NSA committee and continue as important outreach, leadership training, and fundraising entities for YAF over many years. Several of these ad hoc committees—to be joined later by the Student Committee for the Right to Keep and Bear Arms and Students for Free Enterprise—would be operated out of newly established YAF regional offices and provide assistance in funding those regional operations.[12]

The 1965 national convention once again resulted in a major turnover in YAF leadership. Twelve of the 21 member Board of Directors would be new to the Board and they would be working with a new Chairman. When the convention was over, Bob Bauman had completed his second term as National Chairman and was replaced by Tom Charles Huston of Indiana University. Huston had started in YAF as an undergraduate at Indiana University and then went on to Law School where he remained active and was elected to the Board to fill a vacancy in 1963, shortly thereafter becoming National Vice Chairman.[13] In some ways, his election was another indication of the development of a permanent and lasting organization. As he noted several years later, he was the "first national chairman to come up through the ranks, so I had a different perspective on the organization."[14] Huston would enter the Army before the completion of his two-year term as Chairman, serving as an officer assigned to the Defense Intelligence Agency from 1967 to 1969.[15]

Following his years as National Chairman, Bauman remained on the Board along with Richard Derham, Don Devine, Charles Leftwich, Randal Teague, Bud Wandling, Jameson Campaigne, and Alan MacKay. Newly elected to the Board were Richard Allen (Indiana),[16] Maureen Butler (New Jersey), Neil Dentzer (Ohio), Daniel F. Joy (Rhode Island), David Keene (Wisconsin), James Linen, IV (Illinois), Jay Parker (Pennsylvania),[17] Don Pemberton (New York), Richard Plechner (New Jersey), Louise Sciubba (Connecticut), Michael Thompson (Missouri), and David Wood (California). With Plechner's election there would be three of the 21 National Board members who had taken part in the founding meeting at Sharon, the other two being Campaigne and MacKay.[18]

David Keene was an undergraduate at the University of Wisconsin in 1965 and subsequently was elected National Chairman in 1969. Like many of the early

11. David S. Broder, "Young Rightists Plan Expansion," *New York Times*, August 28, 1965.

12. Judith Abramov, "Young Americans for Freedom—the New Guard of the 1960s," State University of New York at Stony Brook, July 1969, p. 5, in author's possession.

13. "Huston Is Elected New National Chairman," *New Guard*, October 1965, p. 21.

14. Quoted in Margaret and Richard Braungart, "The Life Course Development of Left- and Right-Wing Youth Activist Leaders from the 1960s," *Political Psychology* 11 (1990).

15. 2008 YAF Alumni Survey Responses: Tom Charles Huston.

16. Not to be confused with another YAF member, Dr. Richard V. Allen, who would subsequently serve as National Security Advisor to President Ronald Reagan.

17. Parker would be the first of three African-Americans to serve on YAF's National Board and later briefly was a member of the YAF National staff.

18. Contemporaneous biographies of these Board members, including both the new and returning ones, can be found in "Introducing the New Board of Directors," *New Guard*, October 1965, pp. 21, 24.

members, Keene was an active campus conservative who was recruited into YAF. As he recently explained,

> During the Sixties, the University of Wisconsin was developing into a national center for left-wing activism and I was contacted in the early sixties by Al Regnery who was then serving as YAF State Chairman to form a YAF chapter at Madison. I was at the time editor of *Insight and Outlook* which was a publication of the old Wisconsin Conservative Club and reputedly the first regularly published conservative student journal in the country as it had been founded in the mid-fifties. The campus YAF chapter became the core of the Collegians for Goldwater in 1963 and provided dozens of volunteers in that campaign.[19]

An associate of the Carmen Group in Washington, DC, he has been Chairman of the American Conservative Union since 1984 and is also Vice President of the National Rifle Association.

Michael Thompson began his college career as a student at Indiana University where he met and worked with Tom Huston and then transferred to the University of Missouri. For Thompson,

> YAF, to me, was/is like a national political fraternity. Being a member/leader in YAF gives you an automatic connection with others who were members of YAF, whether they are older or younger ... My involvement in YAF forged my political outlook, whatever leadership skills I have today, my involvement in local and state politics, my activities on the local level in my community, etc. The organizational ability, the public speaking and debate capabilities, and the creative juices that continue to flow were all "hatched" during those YAF days.

It was not all serious politics, however. As he added, "I met my wife at a Vietnam teach-in that our local campus YAF chapter sponsored with the campus SDS group—so YAF introduced me to the love of my life!"[20]

James Linen, IV, served two terms on the YAF Board, including as Treasurer of the organization. Linen was a Director of the American Conservative Union and, along with his business partner and fellow YAF Board member, Jameson Campaigne, was co-owner of Calumet Publishing that produced a series of suburban newspapers in the Chicago area. Later, Linen became Executive Vice President of Media General. He died in a tragic accident in London at the age of fifty-one.

Jay Parker became active in Young Americans for Freedom as an outgrowth of his support for Barry Goldwater and eventually became Philadelphia YAF chapter chairman by 1964. Parker explained his commitment to the Arizona Senator's candidacy in an article published in the November 1964 issue of *New Guard*.[21] As he noted years later,

> Did you know he was a lifetime member of the NAACP when the NAACP was a real organization ... When he was a member of the City Council, he was

---

19. 2008 YAF Alumni Survey Responses: David A. Keene.
20. 2008 YAF Alumni Survey Responses: Michael W. Thompson.
21. James A. Parker, "Why I'm Backing Barry Goldwater," *New Guard*, November 1964, pp. 11–12.

the guy who led the effort to desegregate downtown Phoenix. When he took over his family's department store, Goldwater's, he was the first to hire black junior executives and start a training program for them. All this had nothing to do with the law. There were no laws about that back then, which just reaffirmed to me that you can do things without these clowns on Capitol Hill.[22]

Parker recently indicated that YAF had a major influence on his life, helping establish life-long friendships and career opportunities.[23]

Richard Plechner was an active leader in the national Young Republicans organization, including serving as National Vice Chairman, before being elected to the YAF National Board. Louise Sciubba Young, graduated from Regis College and was the organizer of an active YAF community chapter in Fairfield County, Connecticut. After a career in public relations in New York City, she has been active in a number of community and civic affairs, as has Maureen Butler whose brother, Dr. Peter Butler, served as New Jersey YAF State Chairman in the mid-1960s. Richard Wood and Richard Allen both left the Board prior to the conclusion of their two-year terms.

Daniel F. Joy, III was a student at the University of Rhode Island when elected to the Board and subsequently received his law degree from Stetson University. After his time on the YAF Board he was editor of *New Guard* magazine and then worked on Capitol Hill before returning to Florida where he practiced law in Sarasota for over thirty years. Neil Dentzer was Ohio YAF State Chairman and subsequently became a professional fundraiser, working for the Richard A. Viguerie Company and more recently as a capital campaign consultant in central Florida. Among his accomplishments was coordinating the capital campaign for the Ashbrook Center at Ashland University.[24]

A business owner in New York City, Don Pemberton became a Kings County (Brooklyn) Republican leader for several years and was instrumental in lining up Brooklyn's delegates for Ronald Reagan at the 1976 and 1980 Republican National Conventions. Four years later, in 1984, his then eighteen-year-old daughter, Lisa, was the youngest elected Delegate to the convention. As Pemberton recalled, "YAF was my training grounds for becoming involved in politics and being involved in politics led to my career as Deputy County Clerk of Kings County from which I retired in 1996 after serving 25 years."[25] In all his efforts, in YAF and beyond, Don was supported by his wife of more than fifty years, Gladys.

Leaving the Board after the 1965 convention were Bill Boerum, Jack Cox, Fred Coldren, Jim Dullenty, Dan Carmen, Lammot Copeland, Robert Gaston, Fulton Lewis, III, Marilyn Manion, Tom Phillips, and Don Shafto. Richard Wilson had resigned earlier in the year.

For the committed YAF member the national convention was a time to meet others from around the country who shared similar views and interests and to be motivated for campus chapter work just prior to the start of the fall semester. It was an opportunity to learn the basics of convention politics and campaigning. As one writer summarized the importance of the conventions,

22. Stephen Goode, "The Conscience of a Black Conservative—Jay Parker," *Insight on the News*, February 19, 2001.

23. 2008 YAF Alumni Survey Responses: J.A. (Jay) Parker. See also David W. Tyson: *Courage to put country above color—the J.A. Parker story* (Washington, DC: Tyson Publications, 2009).

24. 2008 YAF Alumni Survey Responses: Neil J. Dentzer.

25. 2008 YAF Alumni Survey Responses: Donald G. Pemberton.

Candidates for the national board campaigned months in advance, produced pamphlets and posters, and garnered endorsements from better-known YAFers. Like so many YAF activities, what mattered most was the impression such pageantry made on the participants, not the actual outcome itself. With a thousand or more YAFers in attendance, listening in rapt attention to conservative heroes ... caucusing sessions that often lasted late into the night, and plenty of social occasions to mingle with the conservative elite, a national convention was a young conservative's utopia.[26]

Having survived the electoral defeat of 1964, the dedicated young conservatives were reinvigorated to promote their conservative views and oppose the dominant liberalism on their high school and college campuses and in communities across the nation.

Perhaps the most lasting single aspect of the 1965 convention, however, was the inaugural address of the new Chairman. Tom Huston's speech, "Building the Free Society," was later reprinted in a booklet distributed by YAF, and outlined a philosophy of constructive, positive conservatism that would be reflected in the philosophy and policy of Ronald Reagan as Governor and President. Additionally, it was another clear effort by the YAF leadership to distinguish the organization from the John Birch Society and other more extreme organizations and outlooks. Huston's speech would clearly set YAF apart from those on what could be called the "far right" of American politics.[27] Huston emphasized that while there were thousands of young people looking for answers and a political home, the Republican Party was not welcoming. What it needed is what YAF could offer: new faces, articulate spokesmen and a winning philosophy.

At the same time, unfortunately, according to Huston, "Conservatives too often believe that it is better to be right than to be President. They seem not even to consider it is possible to be both right and President." What YAF should be seeking is political power that provides the opportunity to enact positive conservative policies in government. YAF's task should be to build "a political coalition which can gain support of a majority of the people and invest us with governmental authority. All the theories, all the visions, are worth nothing to us if they cannot be converted into programs." The new YAF National Chairman claimed that conservatives frequently put second things first, create a litmus test for purity, and make it even more difficult to achieve first things—that is creating the Free Society and defeating its enemies. As Huston explained, "Of course, there is a Communist conspiracy which threatens our national existence. Of course, this conspiracy is at work at home as well as abroad. Yet, not everyone who happens to agree with the party line on one particular issue is a Communist."

It was time to oppose those who are "parasites on the conservative movement, to expel them from our circles and to render them impotent." This was true not only of those who see a Communist under every bed but also those who would discriminate against others. "I am proud that our national by-laws explicitly declare that all Americans, without regard to race, creed, color or religion are welcome to join with us in building the Free Society." As partial testimony to this, YAF had

26. Schoenwald: *A Time for Choosing*, pp. 244–245.
27. Tom Charles Huston, "Building the Free Society," address to the 1965 YAF National Convention reprinted as a brochure distributed by Young Americans for Freedom (in author's possession). Quotes in the following section are from the printed brochure.

just elected its first African-American to the National Board of Directors. Huston concluded his remarks by pointing out that YAF had to present viable solutions and not merely point out the problems with the solutions proposed by liberals. "Let others be the talkers. Let us be the builders. What greater epitaph could we etch for Young Americans for Freedom in the hearts of future generations than the simple words . . . They were the toilers for liberty, who built the Free Society."[28]

According to historian Matthew Dallek, the early 1960s were a critical turning point for conservatism as it dealt with the growth of more radical right organizations, the Goldwater campaign and its aftermath, and the challenge posed by an Administration attempting to build what it labeled a "Great Society." Playing a key role in this process was Young Americans for Freedom.

> YAF dissociated conservatism from its more radical elements, constructed a more positive political platform, organized the largest conservative rallies of the period, played an instrumental role in nominating Barry Goldwater, and helped create a new political style based not on a defense of the status quo but on a populist rebellion against the liberal establishment. At a time when the liberal consensus that had reigned since the 1930s was being shattered, YAF helped transform conservatism into a viable political contestant.[29]

Huston's remarks went a long way towards establishing YAF as a responsible conservative organization with a positive program of ideas and action to confront the liberal challenge domestically and the Communist challenge internationally. With this call to action, a new phase had begun for Young Americans for Freedom, one that would focus on another conservative standard-bearer who would soon become a candidate for public office in California. But first, for many YAF members there was another candidate for another office that involved a campaign and election in 1965.

Buckley for Mayor

No single individual reflected the conservative movement in America more than William F. Buckley, Jr., always ready to launch a new publication, organization, media program or campaign to advance the conservative philosophy he so deeply held and effectively advocated. With the defeat of Barry Goldwater there was a need to rally conservatives and expand the base, not so much around a candidacy as around a set of policies and programs that applied the conservative philosophy. Once again, Bill Buckley would be the central figure in another critical time for conservatism.

By early June of 1965, rumors began to surface that Buckley might run for Mayor of New York City, viewing the campaign as both a vehicle for spreading his conservative philosophy as well as standing in opposition to the liberal dominance of the New York Republican Party.[30] While the party primary elections would not be held until September, it became apparent by June that the Republican Party would nominate Congressman John V. Lindsay as its candidate for mayor. Lindsay

---

28. *Ibid.*
29. Dallek, "Young Americans for Freedom: The Rise of Modern Conservatism, 1960–1964," pp. 56–57.
30. Richard Witkin, "William Buckley Jr. Is Reported Considering Running for Mayor," *New York Times*, June 4, 1965.

had developed the reputation as perhaps the single most liberal Republican in the House of Representatives and, along with several other New York Republicans, had refused to support Barry Goldwater's candidacy for President the previous year. In addition to the Republican nomination, Lindsay received the Liberal Party's support for Mayor.[31]

On June 24th, Buckley made it official as he announced his candidacy for Mayor on the Conservative Party ticket.[32] In so doing, he laid out a number of general principles upon which his later policy positions would be based.[33] The candidacy would be a campaign of ideas as the author and editor spelled out his specific proposals to deal with the many problems confronting the city, issuing numerous position papers covering topics as diverse as crime, drugs, pollution, water, education, welfare, taxation, housing, and on and on.[34]

The Buckley campaign became a crusade for young conservatives throughout the Greater New York City area. One week after Buckley announced his candidacy, a group of YAF members and supporters displayed "Buckley for Mayor" signs and chanted "We Want Buckley!" as John Lindsay opened his Richmond Hills, Queens campaign headquarters.[35] Heading up the "Youth for Buckley" effort was Don Pemberton, New York YAF State Chairman, while another YAF member, Neal Freeman, served as a personal aide to the candidate. It was Staten Island YAF that opened the first Buckley for Mayor storefront. From all parts of the City as well as from neighboring areas of New Jersey, Connecticut, and Long Island, YAF members worked to promote the campaign. According to Noel Busby, who coordinated volunteer activity for the campaign, "I just have such a tremendous array of volunteers—they're just like locusts."[36]

The impact of the campaign was substantial. As James Farley, Jr. of Staten Island YAF noted,

> We have experienced such an upsurge of membership due to Buckley's candidacy that our membership now exceeds the combined membership of the Young Republicans and Young Democrats on Staten Island. We distributed over one thousand bumper stickers and over fifteen thousand pieces of literature.[37]

Pemberton, the YAF State Chairman, explained that the campaign provided an avenue for the organization into more liberal campuses in the City, surfacing the conservative students who were present and interested in an on-going political involvement.[38] John J. Sainsbury, a student at Marist College, recalled getting

---

31. New York State has a rather unique election law whereby a candidate can receive the nomination of more than one political party and the votes for each party are counted separately before being added together. Thus, Lindsay's vote on the Republican line would be counted and then added to Lindsay's vote on the Liberal line for his total vote in the election. This allows a minor party to clearly determine the number of votes it contributed to a winning major party candidate.

32. Richard L. Madden, "William Buckley in Race for Mayor," *New York Times*, June 25, 1965.

33. Announcement speech of June 24, 1965, reprinted and distributed by the Conservative Party of New York as part of a fundraising appeal signed by James L. Buckley, Campaign Manager.

34. William F. Buckley, Jr.: *The Unmaking of a Mayor* (New York: The Viking Press, 1966), pp. 169–238. There is no better history of the campaign than this first-hand recollection by Buckley.

35. "Lindsay Is Greeted with Buckley Signs," *New York Times*, July 2, 1965.

36. McCandlish Phillips, "Bright, Young Aides of Buckley Are Spirited, Stylish and Witty," *New York Times*, October 16, 1965.

37. "New York YAF: 'All the Way with WFB,'" *New Guard*, December 1965, p. 20.

38. *Ibid.*

pro-Buckley students into a candidate debate at Queens College, at the time regarded as a liberal stronghold campus, to the point of outnumbering the Lindsay contingent that had organized the event. When the candidates were introduced, Lindsay was booed while Buckley was "wildly cheered to the reward of his huge grin that lit up the auditorium."[39]

As it developed, the Buckley campaign reflected an acknowledgement of the changing dynamics of American conservatism. By the mid-1960s, YAF's membership, much as the support for conservatism in general, became more middle-class and ethnic than Ivy League. Thus, while the WASP Lindsay retained the support of his Silk Stocking district voters in Manhattan and most Protestant Republicans, Buckley's appeal was to the outer boroughs of the City, especially Queens and Staten Island. John Judis, biographer of the candidate, noted that, "Buckley's greatest base of support, they found, was among just those New Yorkers whom he knew least: the middle-class Irish, Italians, Poles and Germans from Queens, the Bronx, Brooklyn, and Staten Island."[40] This was not what the campaign planners anticipated at the beginning.

A classic example of this shifting base of support was the experience of two YAF volunteers for the campaign when confronted with the embarrassing situation of being locked out of their car in a strange neighborhood.

> While campaign walking door-to-door with Vice Chairman Kevin Cullen, we were using a wire hanger to get into our car which had the campaign literature and keys. An NYPD patrol car happened upon us and the officers inquired where we were from and what we were doing. Now a significant part of Buckley's campaign (support your local police) was against the Civilian Review Board proposition on the ballot (Liberal-Republican candidate Lindsay and Democrat Abe Beame were for it). Listening to us explain how though this was not our neighborhood, this *was* our car that had our door-to-door campaign literature, the officers inquired: "Who are you campaigning for?" Our answer brought bright smiles and instant cooperation as New York's Finest produced a ring of auto pass-keys which they then used to assist us.[41]

Throughout the campaign, Buckley was able to draw sizeable crowds, as when 4,000 attended a rally in Manhattan Center—site of the original YAF awards rally in 1961.[42] For his last major rally of the campaign, 3,000 cheering fans turned out at Sunnyside Garden Arena in Queens, the borough that ended up providing him with the most raw votes.[43]

When Election Day came and the votes were counted, Buckley received 341,226 votes on the Conservative Party line in a city with only 15,535 registered Conservative Party members. His total represented 13.4% of the vote, ranging from a high of 25.2% of the vote in Staten Island down to only 7.2% in Manhattan, home to the Silk Stocking Republicans to whom his appeal had originally been directed.[44] Although one of the objectives was to prevent a liberal Republican from being elected, in the end, Lindsay received the most votes and became Mayor.

---

39. 2008 YAF Alumni Survey Responses: John J. Sainsbury.
40. Judis: *William F. Buckley, Jr.: Patron Saint of the Conservatives*, p. 242.
41. 2008 YAF Alumni Survey Responses: John J. Sainsbury.
42. Edward C. Burks, "Buckley Assails Vietnam Protest," *New York Times*, October 22, 1965.
43. Richard L. Madden, "Buckley Cheered by 3,000 in Queens," *New York Times*, October 31, 1965.
44. *The Unmaking of a Mayor*, pp. 326–328.

No one had expected Buckley to win. His famous response to the question of what would he do first upon election was that he would demand a recount. But this campaign of ideas, issues and philosophy had caught national attention and rallied his young supporters for future battles. Across the continent, a similar campaign was taking shape; this time it would be with a candidate and in a political environment where victory was indeed possible.[45]

Reagan for Governor

Clearly, California mid-century was not New York City. The Republican Party had been successful in the state during the Eisenhower years and while Johnson had easily defeated Goldwater in California, that same year saw the election of a conservative Republican former actor to the United States Senate. The victory of George Murphy showed that it was possible to run on a conservative platform and win.

Only a few months after the Goldwater defeat, YAF was already promoting the possibility of a Reagan candidacy for Governor.[46] Meanwhile, the same Los Angeles businessmen who had been the advocates for the Reagan television speech in the 1964 campaign—Holmes Tuttle, Henry Salvatori and Cy Rubel—were now plotting to convince Reagan to run for Governor.[47] Longtime associates of Reagan, they approached him numerous times to consider becoming a candidate. As Reagan related, "The pressure didn't let up. I kept saying no and Holmes Tuttle and his group kept coming back and saying they wouldn't take no for an answer."[48] Finally, Reagan made them an offer: provide the support for him to accept speaking engagements around the state and he'd come back in six months with a decision on whether he was the right one to run for Governor.

Typical of the events was Reagan's speech before the 1,200 people attending a meeting of the Santa Ana Young Republicans where he called on conservatives to "rise from defeat" and begin "the second round to defend the Republic."[49] The response he received as he spoke to Rotary clubs, chambers of commerce, and other organizations tended to be the same: ". . . after I'd give a speech, people would be waiting and they'd come up to me and say, 'Why don't you run for governor?'"[50] After months of hearing the same request from hundreds of Californians, Reagan went back to his original supporters and agreed to run. On January 4, 1966, he formally announced his candidacy for Governor in a statewide television special followed by a news conference.[51]

YAF members were ecstatic. The February 1966 cover article in the organization's

---

45. An informative overview of the campaign was printed in two issues of *New Guard* after the election. See: David Franke, "The New York Campaign," December 1965, pp. 8–9 and January 1966, pp. 11–14.

46. The cover of the June 1965 issue of *New Guard* featured pictures of Reagan and California Assembly Speaker Jesse Unruh and the title of a cover article: "California: Whose Year is '66?" At that time, Unruh was rumored to be a Democratic candidate for Governor if incumbent Edmund G. Brown did not seek a third term.

47. Hoplin and Robinson: *Funding Fathers*, pp. 138–141. Perhaps the most valuable works on the 1966 gubernatorial election in California are Lou Cannon: *Governor Reagan: His Rise to Power* (New York: Public Affairs Press, 2003) and Matthew Dallek: *The Right Moment*. Cannon is the pre-eminent biographer of Reagan and author of several books dealing with Reagan and his political career. Dallek's work is the most comprehensive on the 1966 campaign.

48. Ronald Reagan: *An American Life* (New York: Simon & Schuster, 1990), p. 146.

49. McGirr: *Suburban Warriors*, p. 189.

50. Reagan: *An American Life*, p. 147.

51. Peter Bart, "Reagan Enters Gubernatorial Race in California," *New York Times*, January 5, 1966.

national magazine was titled "The Republican More Like JFK Than Any Other," a characterization that would be viewed as prescient several years later when Reagan entered the White House.[52] After Reagan won the Republican primary, the magazine included a soft plastic 33-rpm record of Reagan's classic speech, "The Challenge for America" with its September 1966 issue. Even before he had been elected Governor, a number of YAF activists were focusing on Reagan as a future presidential candidate. In a poll of 175 YAF members at a summer 1966 leadership conference, the preference for 1968 was Reagan 53%, Goldwater 30%, Nixon 15% and Romney 1%.[53] The torch had already been passed.

California YAF was to play a major role in Reagan's campaign for the Republican nomination against George Christopher, former Mayor of San Francisco, and in the general election against incumbent Governor Edmund "Pat" Brown. It was a reciprocal relationship with several young Reagan workers being brought into the YAF organization just as YAF members assumed leadership roles in the campaign. Once again, Shawn Steel was involved in the leadership of a campaign, this time as High School State Chairman of Youth for Reagan, both in the primary and the general election. Recalling those days, Steel noted, "I was invited to serve as state chairman of Youth for Reagan, High Schools, in the 1966 primary against the moderate Republican Mayor of San Francisco. We converted our YAF chapters into Youth for Reagan chapters."[54] In addition to Steel, a host of other YAF members had leadership roles in the campaign, including John K. Peterson as Southern California Chair, Robert O'Donnell as Northern California Chair, Bill Saracino as Los Angeles County Chair, Jeff Segal, Pat Schwerdtfeger, John Huether, Dennis dePietro, and Arnold Steinberg.[55]

The dedication of the young volunteers was substantial. Allen Brandstater recalled one in particular, "In the early years I remember Peter Sheridan from Culver City, who now teaches at Los Angeles City College. Pete would take the bus to volunteer at the CAL YAF office since he did not drive. Pete was a faithful YAF volunteer over decades and took the bus for the next 20 years (until he finally bought a car)."[56] His membership in YAF introduced Sheridan to a whole new world.

> I remember my first YAF meeting was in a park behind my house . . . YAF opened up a whole new focus on political activity and political education that was year round. By age 21, I felt (justifiably or not) that I had participated in more campaigns, issues, debates, rallies, than the average citizen does in a lifetime. Even today, when I get a few hours off from educational employment, I am thinking about the conservative movement and, if there is some way I can assist it.[57]

Today he is an Associate Professor of History sharing his knowledge and understanding to a new generation of Americans.

Once the primary was over, YAF and the Reagan campaign picked up Grover McKean, who had supported Mayor Sam Yorty in the Democratic primary and

52. Lee Edwards, "The Republican More Like JFK Than Any Other," *New Guard*, February 1966, pp. 8–9.

53. Hess and Broder: *The Republican Establishment*, p. 78.

54. Interview with Shawn Steel, October 13, 2008, Palos Verdes, CA.

55. "The California Story," *New Guard*, December 1966, pp. 10–11.

56. Interview with Allen Brandstater, October 12, 2008, Newport Beach, CA.

57. 2008 YAF Alumni Survey Responses: Peter D. Sheridan.

was President of the Mayor's Youth Advisory Council, and Steve Frank, who had been state chairman of Youth for Christopher. Frank has remained active in California politics, serving as President of the California Republican Assembly and the National Federation of Republican Assemblies. Brandstater was a student at the University of Southern California and recalls "we had a really active group, including Saracino and [Pat] Nolan. We gained lots of members out of the Reagan 1966 campaign."[58]

By the end of 1966, YAF clearly had a new hero who had become the Governor of the largest state. Bill Saracino noted, "After he became Governor, Reagan was a shorthand way of describing what YAF stood for."[59] While especially true in California, this was becoming ever more accurate all across the nation. After all, Reagan had joined the YAF National Advisory Board in 1962, had signed a fundraising letter for the organization that same year, and had appeared at various YAF rallies, especially during the Goldwater campaign. While Bill Buckley remained the intellectual and organizational godfather, and Goldwater was the candidate of the past around whom they had united, Reagan now represented the political future for those in Young Americans for Freedom.

The Sharon Foundation

While California YAF was focusing on the election of Ronald Reagan, nationally YAF was engaging in other activities and considering other possible undertakings, including the formation of a tax-exempt educational organization. On February 18, 1966, a group of YAF leaders met in Washington, DC to discuss the creation of "The Sharon Foundation" as a charitable, educational and scientific foundation to provide scholarships for college students and young journalists, underwrite seminars and discussion groups on college campuses, sponsor a national conference for college students, and conduct a summer camp, much if not all in nominal tribute to the role of the Sharon Statement. The plan would be to seek an Internal Revenue Service determination as a 501(c)(3) tax-exempt, non-profit organization. One month later, David Jones sent a memo to Bill Buckley, outlining the plans and inviting him to serve as Chairman of the foundation. While still in Switzerland, Buckley responded with a transcribed letter on March 23rd saying,

> I am very much in favor of what you project but my difficulty is purely and simply this, that I do not participate in any fund appeal ventures except in behalf of *National Review* . . . If, consistent with your understanding of my plight, you want to talk to me about the Sharon Foundation, I would be delighted to meet with you—under any pretext at all. Will be back by the end of March.[60]

Jones responded immediately and proposed a meeting in New York during the week of April 12th-15th; although there is no indication that such a meeting took place. Three months later, Jones wrote to Buckley and reported that the project

---

58. Interview with Allen Brandstater, October 12, 2008, Newport Beach, CA.
59. Interview with William Saracino, October 11, 2008, Newport Beach, CA.
60. Letter from Wm. F. Buckley, Jr. to David R. Jones, March 23, 1966. This and other correspondence referenced above concerning The Sharon Foundation are in Personal Papers of William F. Buckley, Jr., Box 41, Folder: YAF, Sterling Library, Yale University, New Haven, CT.

had been postponed but not forgotten. He gave as a reason that Tom Huston, then YAF National Chairman, was preparing for the bar examinations and, once completed, Huston would devote his time to administering the foundation.[61]

The idea for "The Sharon Foundation" soon thereafter led to a meeting on February 6, 1967 where Buckley, Jones, Dr. Walter H. Judd, Marvin Liebman and former Governor Charles Edison incorporated the "Charles Edison Youth Fund." Two years later, upon Governor Edison's passing, the organization was renamed the Charles Edison Memorial Youth Fund and in the summer of 1970 initiated the first Institute on Comparative Political and Economic Systems at Georgetown University. Subsequently renamed The Fund for American Studies, the foundation has expanded its summer programs both in terms of subject emphases and geographical spread. It now sponsors a variety of summer programs with college credit not only at Georgetown University but also in Prague, Greece, Hong Kong, and at its most recent addition in Santiago, Chile. It also sponsors a Fall and Spring Capital Semester program and in June of each year a Professors Seminar.

Many of those who have played critical roles in the success of the Fund are YAF alumni, including Jones, his successor as its chairman Randal Teague, Mike Thompson, Tom Phillips, Robert Schadler, Bruce Weinrod, Arnold Steinberg, Kathy King Rothschild, and its current President, Roger Ream. And, of course, once again Bill Buckley was present at the creation of another element of the conservative movement.

Meanwhile, at Vanderbilt University a group of students, mainly YAF members, under the leadership of Chuck Stowe, created an organization called University Information Services, Inc. as a tax-exempt educational foundation. Formed in reaction to the radicals who dominated campus, this new entity attempted to provide conservative speakers and literature to students at Vanderbilt. When Stowe graduated and entered the Navy, he approached the national office of Young Americans for Freedom to see if they would be interested in taking over the foundation and broadening its scope of activity.[62] The initial Board of Directors when YAF took effective control of the foundation consisted of Jerry Norton, Ron Pearson, and Wayne Thorburn, all of whom had served on the YAF National Board or staff. By 1973, the name was changed to what is now known as Young America's Foundation with a board comprising Pearson, Thorburn, and Frank Donatelli, at the time national treasurer of YAF.[63] Since then Young America's Foundation, under the leadership of President Ron Robinson, has grown into the premiere entry point for high school and college students into the conservative movement. Its current Board of Directors includes a number of former YAF members.[64]

The goal of sponsoring conservative speakers on campus was now broadened to a national scope and over the years has included a wide range of speakers representing all facets of the conservative movement from Margaret Thatcher,

61. However, shortly thereafter Huston went on active duty in the United States Army forcing his resignation as YAF National Chairman and effectively ending his involvement in the organization.

62. Stowe subsequently spent nearly 30 years in the U.S. Navy Reserve, taught business administration for 25 years at Sam Houston State University, and is now Dean of the College of Business and Public Affairs at Lander University.

63. Letter of August 27, 1973 to William A. Rusher from Wayne J. Thorburn announcing the formation of Young America's Foundation. Personal Papers of William A. Rusher, Box 173, File 7, Library of Congress, Washington, DC.

64. As of 2010, the Board of Directors of Young America's Foundation included two former Executive Directors of Young Americans for Freedom (Ron Robinson and Frank Donatelli), three former National Board Members (Ron Pearson, Tom Phillips and Peter Schweizer), along with former YAF members Ken Cribb, James Taylor, and Kirby Wilbur.

Colin Powell, Pat Buchanan, Dan Quayle, Newt Gingrich, Michelle Malkin, John Stossel, and yes, Bill Buckley. In 1974 the Foundation expanded its activities by initiating and financing a nationally syndicated radio program with messages from then-Governor Ronald Reagan. Young America's Foundation has sponsored annual summer institutes for high school students and for college students in Washington, DC for many years as well as regional weekend conferences in the Midwest and West Coast. In 1998, the foundation purchased the Reagan Ranch outside of Santa Barbara to preserve it for history and shortly thereafter opened the Reagan Ranch Center in downtown Santa Barbara as a focal point for West Coast conservative meetings and programs.

While many other organizations have been created by YAF alumni and play essential roles within the conservative movement, these two organizations, The Fund for American Studies and Young America's Foundation, are both integrally entwined with the history of Young Americans for Freedom and, to a large degree, developed out of the desire of YAF leaders in the mid-1960s to create a non-profit, tax-exempt charitable organization to advance conservative ideals and values.

Although it was several months after the original founding date of September 11, Young Americans for Freedom took note of its 5th anniversary with a "Salute to YAF" banquet at the Shoreham Hotel in Washington, DC on May 9, 1966.[65] Some 1,300 people, including YAF leaders, alumni, and National Advisory Board members were in a celebratory mood. It was a night for honoring the young conservative organization, but also for stressing the bipartisan nature of mid-century conservatism in America. Appropriately enough, it was the senior Democratic Senator from Florida, speaking before Goldwater, who reminded the audience that there were conservatives in both political parties who deserve the support of YAF members. Spessard Holland told those present that "not all who love the Constitution and conservatism are in one party. You must pick out the people you believe in and the causes you believe in and fight for those people and causes. Pick your shots."[66]

Then it was time for the 1964 Republican presidential candidate. As writer James Jackson Kilpatrick observed, "When Barry's time came at last, they brought down the roof. For a couple of minutes, we were back in San Francisco."[67] Goldwater told them that his dedication was not to elective office or to party politics but rather to the cause he shared with those present. As he said, "I wouldn't be here tonight if not for the fact that I'm worried for our country. I could sit on my hill in Arizona, but I'm concerned about freedom."[68] He went on to remind those present that their task was to advance a philosophy, a task that involved much more than political action. "You are not a political party, not even a second cousin to a political party. You are conservative and there's nothing wrong about being conservative."[69] To Goldwater the need was essential and the reason obvious: "Conservatism remains today the only successful political philosophy ever known by man. Let's make progress on the proven values of the past. Freedom

65. "Salute to YAF Banquet Scenes," *New Guard*, June 1966, pp. 10–11.

66. Paul Hope, "Back Conservative of Either Party, Goldwater Urges," *Washington Evening Star*, May 10, 1966. Personal Papers of Henry Regnery, Box 80, Hoover Institution, Stanford University, Palo Alto, CA.

67. James J. Kilpatrick, "Goldwater at His Best Before Young Americans," *Washington Evening Star*, May 17, 1966. Personal Papers of Henry Regnery, Box 80, Hoover Institution, Stanford University, Palo Alto, CA.

68. Hope, "Back Conservative of Either Party, Goldwater Urges."

69. Hess and Broder: *The Republican Establishment*, p. 74.

is our only cause."[70]

One of the main organizers of the event was Lee Edwards, himself a founder of the organization who had attended that initial meeting in Sharon, Connecticut. When it was over, he looked back at the event and concluded, "Young Americans for Freedom emerged once again as an organization that gets things done."[71] It had taken two months of planning and dedication to detail but had re-established YAF as a major force in the Nation's Capital.

Developing New Leadership

As summer 1966 approached, YAF's attention turned to developing new leadership and building a presence in more communities and on more college and high school campuses. To accomplish this, the organization undertook a number of programs including an extensive training, fundraising, and chapter development program called the "YAF Corps" and a summer Leadership Conference held at Franklin & Marshall College in Lancaster, Pennsylvania.

In December 1965, the organization announced "the YAF Corps" as a program to recruit summer YAF representatives with each one receiving a salary and expenses. Each YAF Corps member was said to have four basic responsibilities: (1) form new chapters, (2) visit and revitalize existing chapters, (3) address civic and conservative groups, and (4) help college students plan fall recruitment booths on campus. What was not mentioned in the early promotional literature was the 5th, and most critical, responsibility: each YAF Corps member was required to raise $1,700 from contributions and then also sell the "Two Worlds" filmstrip series to at least four YAF chapters.[72] The $1,700 was to be obtained through pledges of $12 each from 144 conservatives.[73]

Brainchild of Richard Allen, former YAF Midwest Director who had been brought to Washington as Organization Director, the YAF Corps was designed to send sixty full-time organizers throughout the country. These sixty were selected from some 350 applicants and were made responsible for specific regions. To salesman Allen, the idea seemed simple and effective. Unfortunately, the YAF leaders selected were not known for their sales ability, being more interested in political activities than retail sales or fundraising. Several spent all summer attempting to secure the $1,700 that would go towards paying their "salary" and expenses. Others had to be subsidized by the national office. Some quit in frustration. Then Vice Chairman Alan MacKay described it as "the most costly and least successful project YAF ever undertook."[74] With few exceptions, the YAF Corps proved to be a failure.

---

70. Hope, "Back Conservative of Either Party, Goldwater Urges."

71. Lee and Anne Edwards: *You Can Make the Difference*, pp. 253–257 recalls the planning required for a successful event such as the "Salute to YAF" dinner.

72. The "Two Worlds" filmstrip series was developed by the Flick-Reedy Company to show the differences between an unregimented society and a Communist society.

73. Using the Consumer Price Index as a measure over time, in 2010 dollars this would be the equivalent of approximately $11,300 to be raised in a three month period by each YAF Corps member.

74. MacKay's quote is from a letter of January 15, 1969 to the Editor of *American Mercury* magazine. MacKay was responding to an article by Richard Allen, "What Has Happened to YAF?" that appeared in the Winter 1968 issue of the publication. The article is an attack on the leadership of YAF but does not mention that Allen was let go from the YAF staff for incompetence and later made restitution in an out-of-court settlement for allegedly siphoning funds from the Southwest YAF Regional Office.

Despite its ineffectiveness as a program, the YAF Corps did have some interesting side benefits in terms of the organization's image and its effect on some individuals. In a Fall 1966 issue of *Moderator*, a free circulation magazine distributed on hundreds of campuses, an article on Tom Charles Huston makes reference to the growth in membership and cites "YAF's sixty full-time recruiters in the field last summer."[75] Meanwhile, one Democratic activist noted the promotional ad for the YAF Corps in the February 1966 issue of *New Guard*, tore it out, and sent it to the White House with the handwritten notation, "Please give this to one of those loafers on the National Committee!"[76] Apparently some Democrats believed their party was not doing enough to appeal to youth and saw the YAF Corps as a direct threat to the Johnson Administration.

For a few participants, the YAF Corps experience was life-changing. It was his experience with the YAF Corps that turned Michael Sanera's career choices in a totally different direction.

> I started my undergraduate education as a forestry major . . . This was the year that YAF created the YAF Corps program of summer jobs for YAF members. This was the critical decision in my career. I decided on the YAF Corps summer job, although it did not pay much. Ultimately, it also influenced me to change my major and begin an education program leading to a PhD in political science and becoming a college professor.[77]

Sanera went on to become Arizona YAF State Chairman, received a masters in International Relations from Boston University and his PhD in Political Science from the University of Colorado.

One of the more successful projects of the period was the YAF Summer Leadership Training School held at Franklin & Marshall College in Lancaster, Pennsylvania during the week of July 23–30, 1966. YAF College Director, Philip Wayne Cramer, was in charge of this program to produce more articulate spokesmen, better coordinated efforts, and more effective conservative activity on the college campuses. More than 175 YAF campus leaders from 32 states arrived, during a major airline strike across the country, representing a large cross-section of the 192 college chapters of Young Americans for Freedom at that time. Because of the strike, it required dedication and determination to show up in Lancaster. It took the Oregon students four days by bus, many Californians drove the long distance, and Barry Fitzgerald of the University of Oklahoma made it in two days on his motorcycle.[78]

Among those attending the summer school were a number of students who would later assume leadership roles in the organization, including Mark Watson (Indiana University), Fred Roberts (Bradley), Mike Thompson (University of Missouri), David Walter (Drexel), Stan Dyer (Louisiana Tech), Bill Williams (Georgetown), Albert Forrester (Amarillo College), James Casper (University of Wisconsin), Ron Pearson (Valparaiso), John Sainsbury (St. John's), John Whitehead

The article and MacKay's response are in Personal Papers of William A. Rusher, Box 173, Manuscript Division, Library of Congress, Washington, DC.

75. Philip Roberts, "Houston (sic) of Y.A.F.," *Moderator*, October 1966, pp. 42, 44.

76. Copy of ad and note, April 19, 1966, White House Central Name Files, Alfreda Young, Box 26, Lyndon Baines Johnson Presidential Library, University of Texas, Austin, TX.

77. 2008 YAF Alumni Survey Responses: Michael Sanera.

78. "Summer School—for Leaders," *New Guard*, September 1966, pp. 6–11.

(Duke), Michael Sanera (Northern Arizona University), David Wood (Cal State-Long Beach) and Shawn Steel (San Fernando Valley State)—most of whom were relatively new members and all of whom would serve as a YAF State Chairman in the 1960s or early 1970s with several becoming members of the National Board or national YAF staff.[79]

One of the youngest members to attend was Dana Huntley, a high school student from New Hampshire who had also participated in the YAF Corps program that summer. As he recalled the conference, "it certainly gave me good early experience in organizational leadership, the opportunity to meet and listen to many of the important voices of modern conservatism." After taking part in the Franklin & Marshall conference, Huntley was named New Hampshire YAF State Chairman in 1967, the only high school student to hold such a position at that time. That experience had a lasting effect on him. "The traveling and the speaking I did in those years gave me a great deal of confidence. The exposure to the cauldron of conservative ideas contributed significantly to my developed world view." Huntley went on to attend Kings College and then obtained an M.A. from Fordham University and his PhD from Drew University. For several years he taught at the collegiate level and is now editor of *British Heritage* magazine.[80]

Each morning during the eight days of the summer school the students heard lectures on conservative philosophy from such men as Professor Gordon Tullock (University of Virginia), Dr. Richard V. Allen (Georgetown University), author and attorney L. Brent Bozell, and Frank S. Meyer of *National Review*. Workshops on chapter activities and programs were held in the afternoon while evenings were devoted to speakers on Communist ideology and practice followed by lengthy "bull sessions" with speakers and other participants. While Bill Buckley was scheduled to participate, travel difficulties forced him to cancel.[81]

The summer school was highly successful in producing a new cadre of trained leaders for the organization, individuals who were only in elementary or middle school when YAF was founded in 1960. Many of these younger members were introduced to their first direct education on the techniques of public relations, the tools of debating, and the directing of issues to serve one's overall philosophical objectives. Out of this experience would come the leaders that would carry Young Americans for Freedom not only through the remainder of the 1960s but also into the next decade of its history. Still others, including Steel of California and Dick Foley of Connecticut, would go on to become Republican State Chairmen many years later.[82]

---

79. A partial list of participants, from which the above names were derived, is found on a telegram addressed to the President and dated July 30, 1966, stating: "The following members of the Young Americans for Freedom attending the YAF Student Leadership Conference at Franklin and Marshall College, Lancaster, Pennsylvania urge you to take immediate action which will win the war in Vietnam and bring our boys home." White House Central Files, Alfreda Young, Box 26, Lyndon Baines Johnson Presidential Library, University of Texas, Austin, TX.

80. 2008 YAF Alumni Survey Responses: Dana L. Huntley.

81. Buckley was originally scheduled to speak on the topic "Conservatism and the Academy." July 20, 1966 letter from Philip Wayne Cramer to William F. Buckley, Jr. with enclosed conference agenda, Personal Papers of William F. Buckley, Jr., Box 41, Folder: YAF, Sterling Library, Yale University, New Haven, CT.

82. 2008 YAF Alumni Survey Responses: Dick Foley and Shawn Steel. Foley was Connecticut GOP Chairman from 1989–93 and a State Representative from 1982–1992. Steel was elected California GOP Chairman in 2001 and National Committeeman in 2008.

4th National Convention—Pittsburgh

When Labor Day weekend arrived in 1967, approximately one thousand young conservatives traveled to Pittsburgh for another biennial YAF National Convention. Among the featured speakers were William F. Buckley, Jr., Barry Goldwater, Senators John Tower and Strom Thurmond, and Congressmen John Ashbrook and Donald E. "Buz" Lukens. Pittsburgh was selected as the site in recognition of the organizational efforts of the Western Pennsylvania Council YAF that had developed a strong base of chapters and sponsored weekly events of one sort or another. Dennis Gannon was instrumental in promoting and pulling the convention together.[83] The end result of this effort was that the convention was the largest to that date in terms of both delegates and overall attendance, indicating that YAF was indeed alive and well.

The first day of the convention began with a breakfast address by Buckley and ended with a banquet featuring Goldwater. Buckley reminded the delegates of their role in restoring order on campus. "So few years after it was generally assumed that you were extremists—you were the problem children of society—there is an obvious and more assertive dependence upon you to restore tranquility."[84] When Goldwater spoke he was greeted with a large banner proclaiming: "BARRY, You Will Always Be Our HERO." The recent presidential candidate reiterated his long-standing support for the organization and its continuing role in promoting conservatism among the young. In between the Buckley and Goldwater addresses, platform hearings were held with guest presenters Dr. Richard V. Allen (Foreign Affairs), Rep. Buz Lukens (Domestic Affairs) and Dr. Philip M. Crane (Student Affairs).[85]

Beyond the number of attendees and the list of heavyweight conservative speakers, Pittsburgh was important as the first convention where a heated and closely contested election for National Chairman took place, along with two competing slates for positions on the National Board of Directors. Additionally, extensive time was devoted to the discussion of resolutions on domestic, foreign, and student issues, resolutions that would ultimately be referred to the local chapters and then incorporated into a comprehensive document of YAF position statements. Perhaps even more important as lasting outgrowths of the 1967 convention were two other developments: the beginnings of a clear-cut division between libertarians and other conservatives and the formation of a youth organization designed to promote Ronald Reagan as a national political figure and possible presidential contender.

The national conventions, regional conferences and state meetings had lasting effects on many who participated. For Mike Thompson, the meetings . . .

83. According to Gannon, "Dave Jones visited often and saw what we had going. As a result the 1967 YAF National Convention was held here over the Labor Day weekend. I served as the Convention Chairman, handling the publicity and promotion. My late wife, Phyllis, ran the in-hotel social activities. We sold out breakfasts, lunches, and dinners, and sold out every other event." Dennis Gannon letter to the author, January 15, 2008.

84. Lyle Denniston, "New Right Cites a New Maturity," *Washington Sunday Star*, September 3, 1967, Group Research Archives, Box 342, Columbia University, New York, NY.

85. "YAF Meets in Pittsburgh," *New Guard*, October 1967, pp. 3–5.

...brought young people who shared our views together in a way that is still part of our "discussions" when we get together. Our internal battles steeled us for the real world and those of us who have fought business board battle and local/state political battles realize that our abilities to do well in these efforts goes back to what we learned during those early years being active in YAF. What we learned in those years has served us well in our "adult lives" whether in business, politics, or even local community work.[86]

With hundreds of high school and college students coming together to share experiences, these events helped to build networks of committed young conservatives.

On the second day of the convention, delegates turned their attention to the elections for National Chairman and nine members of the National Board of Directors. Seven other directors had been chosen at the regional conferences organized in the spring of 1967 while the remaining seven members were selected by the Board itself as Senior Directors. Leaving the Board by the spring of 1967 were Charles Leftwich, Richard Allen, Maureen Butler Moore, Richard Derham and Tom Charles Huston. Those elected at the regional conferences, all of whom were new to the Board, were William Dobson (University of Bridgeport) for New England, John J. Sainsbury (St. John's University) for the Mid-Atlantic, Mark Watson (Indiana University) from the Midwest, Bruce Eberle (Port Arthur, TX) for the Southwest, Don Walker (St. Petersburg, FL) from the Southern region, Jerry Norton (University of Oregon) for the Northwest, and William "Shawn" Steel (San Fernando Valley State) for the Western region.[87]

Bruce Eberle joined YAF in 1963 and was integrally involved in Young Americans for Freedom for the next several years, first as a National Director and then as a direct mail fundraising consultant for the organization. According to Eberle, "Without YAF I would never have started my company. In my view, it is the single most important activity I have participated in outside of my church activities. It opened my eyes to the importance of leadership and without YAF I don't really know what I would have done with my life."[88] One of his greatest thrills was serving as Reagan's fundraiser some years later when he ran for President in 1976.

Shawn Steel was both a National Director and California YAF State Chairman in the late 1960s before entering the military and subsequently graduating from law school. William Dobson had been chairman of the University of Bridgeport chapter and Connecticut YAF State Chairman at the time of his election. After graduating from college, Dobson served for 22 years in the military, almost all of the time as a commissioned officer in the Army Corps of Engineers. Most recently he has been a high school mathematics teacher and advisor to the Teenage Republicans club on campus.[89]

Mark Watson and Don Walker both served briefly on the National Board of Directors and were not subsequently active in the organization. That was not the case, however, with Jerry Norton who was first elected to the Board from the Northwest region while an undergraduate at the University of Oregon. A Phi Beta Kappa graduate in journalism, Norton went on to join the Army, including a one-year tour in Vietnam. Upon his return to civilian life he became YAF College

---

86. 2008 YAF Alumni Survey Responses: Michael W. Thompson.
87. *New Guard*, Summer 1967, p. 33.
88. 2008 YAF Alumni Survey Responses: Bruce W. Eberle.
89. 2008 YAF Alumni Survey Responses: William Dobson.

Director and then editor of *New Guard* magazine. He subsequently attended Columbia University Graduate School of Journalism from which he received his master's degree in 1974. Norton remained active on the Board and in the organization while at Columbia, holding the position of downstate vice chairman for New York YAF. Looking back on his years in YAF, Norton saw its influence as affecting

> ... the honing of my journalism skills at the New Guard, via the Free Campus News Service and in occasional PR duties for YAF nationally and various state and local organizations—all helped make me a better journalist, just as the management skills I gained there and my speaking and debating experiences ... Those were very formative years and much of what I did at and in relation to YAF was incredibly exciting, and doubtless had much to do with shaping me.[90]

After being associated with various publications and news services, Norton has had a most successful career as a journalist working overseas.

John "J.J." Sainsbury was a 24-year-old graduate student from New York City working towards his master's degree in political science at St. John's University. He was also New York YAF State Chairman at a time when that was the largest state in terms of both chapters and members. Seeking to move YAF towards a greater student focus, Sainsbury would soon decide to become a candidate for National Chairman.

Having completed a series of National Director elections at regional conferences, the delegates to the 1967 National Convention would now elect a National Chairman and nine additional Directors. For the first time in YAF's history, delegates were being asked to choose between two strong candidates for National Chairman and among two competing slates of candidates for the National Board positions as well as two independent candidates. The campaigning was long and intense as then National Chairman J. Alan MacKay faced off against National Director John J. Sainsbury. MacKay was a 31-year old attorney who had attended Sharon and became Chairman only six months earlier when Tom Huston entered military service. Sainsbury had only that spring been elected to the National Board at the Mid-Atlantic regional conference. As one writer described the difference between the two candidates,

> MacKay is intent on keeping the YAF as a political action group open to "young adults" as well as to students, while Sainsbury hopes to make YAF a political activity "training ground" for student-age youths. Their contest is the first in the top ranks of the YAF since it was formed seven years ago by conservative editor William F. Buckley, Jr. and a group of youths sharing his views. MacKay and Sainsbury do not appear to differ in their basic political outlook. Thus, the delegates will not be choosing between a "left-right" split in national leadership.[91]

When all the votes were counted, MacKay had received 330 votes to Sainsbury's 181, after which the losing candidate moved to make the election of MacKay unanimous. The Sainsbury slate of nine National Board candidates, almost all of whom

---

90. 2008 YAF Alumni Survey Responses: Jerry Norton.
91. Lyle Denniston, "Students for Reagan Move Launched at YAF Meeting," *Washington Evening Star*, September 1, 1967, Group Research Archives, Box 342, Columbia University, New York, NY.

were from the Midwest and Mid-Atlantic states, also went down to defeat, including Neil Dentzer, the only incumbent Board Member on the slate. Heading the victorious MacKay slate were three incumbents: Mike Thompson, Gerald Plas, and Jay Parker, along with six new Directors: Dan Manion of Indiana, Steve Mayerhofer of Ohio, Dave Walter from Pennsylvania, Joseph Leo of New Jersey, Ron Dear of Texas, and Allen Brandstater of California.[92]

Of the six new Directors, Dan Manion was without a doubt the most well-known in the conservative movement, but known primarily as the son of Dean Clarence Manion of the Notre Dame Law School. Son Dan had graduated from the University of Notre Dame in 1964 and then was in the Army for the following two years, serving in Vietnam. Upon returning to civilian life, he became more active in YAF. After working in Indiana state government, Manion enrolled at Indiana University School of Law, where he studied in a group that included Dan Quayle, receiving his J.D. degree in 1973. In 1978 he was elected as an Indiana State Senator and in 1986 was nominated by President Reagan and confirmed as Judge, U.S. Court of Appeals for the Seventh Circuit. By then, judicial candidate Dan Manion was sponsored by United States Senator Dan Quayle.

To Manion, his involvement in Young Americans for Freedom was a key experience at a pivotal point in his life. "It was my associations in YAF that had more political impact on me than anything . . . when I was in Indianapolis I hung around with a lot of other activists; I was a little older; we did a lot of fun things and it solidified a lot of beliefs I still hold."[93] Manion maintains that his political views have not changed dramatically but "the mainstream came to where we were, led by Reagan. Before I was on the outside, now I am in the middle of the mainstream and it's nice to be in that water rather than in some backwater struggling away."[94]

Steve Mayerhofer was a leader in the Cleveland YAF chapter and then later at Ohio State University. He became Ohio YAF State Chairman and after college, Mayerhofer moved to the Washington area and worked for various agencies but in the 1980s he "decided to start my own business instead, using what was then a new technology in data entry. The business has grown and I've been at it ever since."[95]

Allen Brandstater joined YAF as a high school student in 1963 and became active in the Goldwater campaign and then the 1966 Reagan gubernatorial campaign. Brandstater went on to a career in public relations and the media. As he recently noted,

> YAF provided an opportunity at a young age to develop leadership skills, to learn by doing as a young person. How to prepare a news release, how to organize a debate, how to attract people to a meeting, and how to raise the funds needed to carry out these projects. It was, really, management by walking around. Developing my communications skills in YAF certainly helped me as I became an afternoon radio talk show host on KRLA for ten years and in writing a regular newspaper column each week on local politics for the *Glendale News-Press*.[96]

---

92. *New Guard*, October 1967, pp. 3–5.
93. Quoted in Margaret Braungart and Richard Braungart, "Life-Course Development of 1960s Youth Activist Leaders," p. 265–266.
94. *Ibid.* p. 273.
95. Quoted in Gurvis, p. 81.
96. Interview with Allen Brandstater, October 12, 2008, Newport Beach, CA.

After being elected at the 1967 convention, Brandstater subsequently became Executive Director of California YAF during its time of substantial growth in the late 1960s.[97]

Ronald Dear was a law school student when elected to the YAF Board, having been active in Texas YAF for several years. He went on to join the National YAF staff in 1969 and subsequently became Administrative Assistant for Congressman Bill Archer (R-Texas), then Executive Director of the American Conservative Union, before returning to Texas to head up the 1976 Reagan campaign in that state. According to Dear, "those years in YAF were wonderful experiences, including our efforts against IBM trading with the Soviets and the Tell It to Hanoi campaign. I think we made a difference at the time and YAF prepared so many people for later contributions to the conservative movement."[98]

David Walter was a leader of the Philadelphia YAF Chapter and subsequently became Pennsylvania YAF State Chairman. An active and vocal libertarian, he would serve on the YAF National Board for two years before losing his re-election effort at the 1969 National Convention. Walter became a leader in the burgeoning independent libertarian movement. He donated his collection of libertarian publications from the later 1960s to the early 1980s to the Hoover Institution where it constitutes an important historical record of this movement.[99]

The final new member of the YAF Board elected in Pittsburgh was Joseph Leo of New Jersey. In effect, Leo took the seat until then held by Richard Plechner, also of New Jersey. Both Leo and Plechner had attended the founding meeting in Sharon and have remained lifelong friends and allies in New Jersey political battles. With Campaigne and MacKay remaining on the Board, there were three Directors who had been present at the creation of the organization. Also remaining on the Board were the seven Senior Board members: Bud Wandling, James Linen, IV, Don Pemberton, Dan Joy, Randal Teague, David Keene, and Campaigne. Those retiring from the Board after the 1967 convention were Bob Bauman, Don Devine, Louise Sciubba, David Wood, and Plechner.

Once the elections were over the delegates turned their attention back to the work of crafting and debating various resolutions. Attempting to design a platform that would express the views of YAF on domestic issues, conflict appeared within the Domestic Affairs Committee and compromise became almost impossible. On the one side were the traditional and "moderate" conservatives who realized that certain domestic problems existed in the United States and wanted to present constructive conservative alternatives to the liberal programs of the Great Society. One candidate for the Board even released a series of position papers advocating various ways for YAF to deal with domestic issues.[100] The emphasis on solving problems was noted by one reporter,

> A symbol of this change was plastered all over the walls and pillars of the Pittsburgh Hilton yesterday—a simple sign saying "CON-CON." That meant "constructive conservatism" to the more than 800 delegates who had come here for the national convention of the Young Americans for Freedom.[101]

---

97. Email to the author from Allen Brandstater, January 19, 2010.
98. Interview with Ronald B. Dear, July 5, 2008, Houston, TX.
99. These various libertarian publications can be found in Personal Papers of David Walter, Boxes 1–20, Hoover Institution, Stanford University, Palo Alto, CA.
100. That candidate was the author, whose campaign, alas, was unsuccessful.
101. Lyle Denniston, "New Right Cites A New Maturity," *Washington Sunday Star*, September 3, 1967, Group Research Archives, Box 342, Columbia University, New York, NY.

On the other side were the extreme libertarians and Objectivists expressing blindness to any societal problems that could not be cured by pure laissez-faire capitalism. From their perspective, all one needed to do was abolish government interference with the free market and the system would function properly.

The committee attempted to build a compromise between those who recognized that action must be taken to alleviate certain ills in society and those who did not admit that any such ills existed. This effort ended up in pandemonium on the convention floor when the committee's "compromise upon a compromise" resolutions met severe opposition from a significant minority of the delegates. Basic philosophical disagreement led to chaos when YAF attempted to define its conservatism in distinct, practical terms. Unfortunately, after all the procedural motions on Sunday morning there was insufficient time for meaningful debate and discussion, let alone agreement. The end result, after some maneuvering back and forth as to how best to deal with this problem, was the referral of all resolutions to the local chapters for their acceptance or rejection of each resolution.[102] When the votes from the chapters were tallied some months later, all sixteen resolutions presented at the 1967 convention were approved. Only three resolutions received less than a two-thirds affirmative vote: Educational reform (60.8% yes), the Draft (62.2% yes), and the United Nations (63.3.% yes), indicating a good deal of ideological unity within the organization.[103] In August 1968, prior to the national nominating conventions, YAF collected all its resolutions from 1962 to that time into a fifty page booklet titled "Young People's Platform" and distributed it at both the Democratic and Republican conventions as well as to media and YAF chapter leaders.[104]

Nevertheless, despite the strong agreement of the local chapters with most of the sixteen policy statements, one aspect of the resolutions process was the overt appearance of some important ideological differences among the delegates, differences that would be exacerbated two years later at the convention in St. Louis. According to one observer,

> Generally speaking the major split within YAF comes under the rubric of what YAFers themselves call, "the traditionalist–libertarian debate . . ." Issue after issue in the Foreign, Domestic, and Student committees the traditionalist–libertarian split arose sharply, if not explicitly, in the muted debate over what constituted "practical politics."[105]

The divisions within YAF, while summarized and simplified as libertarian and traditionalist, were much more multi-faceted in reality.

Mid-century American conservatism comprised several divergent philosophical orientations united in opposition to the liberal orthodoxy that had been prevalent

102. The debate over resolutions and how to handle them is discussed in Werdell, "Can YAF Do It Again?," *Moderator*, February 1968, pp. 11–17.

103. "YAF and the Issues," *New Guard*, Summer 1968, pp. 3–5. The education reform resolution advocated a "long range goal of replacing public university level educational institutions by voluntarily supported private institutions." The draft statement said "YAF reaffirms its support of a voluntary army as the most economically efficient and socially productive way to supplant conscription, and the most consistent with YAF's value of freedom." The United Nations resolution urged restoring the primary role of the Security Council and curtailing the decision-making powers of the Secretary General and the General Assembly.

104. "Young People's Platform," Young Americans for Freedom, August 1, 1968.

105. Werdell, p. 13.

in the United States for at least the past thirty years. American conservatives agreed on opposition to the growth of the welfare state and tendencies toward egalitarianism and the redistribution of income while supporting a policy of firm resistance to Communism. Within this broad consensus, divergence arose over the stress on freedom or on authority and tradition. This division between libertarians or classical liberals and traditional conservatives was evident in both senior and young conservative circles.[106] An additional element was introduced by the emergence of a political philosophy based on the writings of Ayn Rand. The Objectivists, as the Randians called themselves, emphasized "rational self-interest" as the correct principle on which all action should be based.[107] Advocates of all these perspectives were present in Young Americans for Freedom in the mid 1960s.

At the 1966 Leadership Conference, participants were asked to classify themselves in one of five categories identified by both a descriptive term and an individual broadly associated with that perspective. The results were:

Radical Traditionalist (Brent Bozell)	8 %
Traditionalist (Russell Kirk)	32
Fusionist (Frank Meyer)	34
Libertarian (Ludwig Von Mises)	11
Objectivist (Ayn Rand)	15 [108]

It is informative to note that each position is a philosophical, and not a purely political, identification and that the individuals associated with the terms are writers and academics rather than political personalities such as Goldwater or Reagan. While they were all well known to young conservatives, these writers were seldom discussed elsewhere in the intellectual world of that time.

Brent Bozell, Jr. was a brother-in-law of William F. Buckley, Jr. whose outlook on society had moved to a strong emphasis on Catholic traditionalism. At the time editor of the Catholic magazine *Triumph*, Bozell was moving more and more away from direct political action as the appropriate path to reforming society.[109] Russell Kirk represented a classical conservatism that emphasized tradition, order, and stability as elements of the good society.[110] Frank Meyer maintained that reason must operate within tradition while freedom is viable only in a framework of order.[111] Ludwig Von Mises was perhaps the most prominent advocate of the Austrian school of economics then living in the United States.[112] As mentioned above, Ayn Rand maintained that government should perform only the limited

---

106. For a presentation of these diverse elements in American conservatism, see: Frank S. Meyer, editor: *What Is Conservatism?* (New York: Prentice-Hall, 1964).

107. Ayn Rand: *For the New Intellectual* (New York: Random House, 1961) and *The Virtue of Selfishness* (New York: New American Library, 1967).

108. "Summer School—For Leaders," *New Guard*, September 1966, p. 6, 11.

109. Some of Bozell's writings that originally appeared in *Triumph* during the 1960s and 1970s can be found in *Mustard Seeds: A Conservative Becomes a Catholic* (Front Royal VA: Christendom Books, 1986).

110. While *The Conservative Mind* was his groundbreaking work published in 1953, the later *The Roots of American Order* (Lasalle, IL: Open Court, 1974) places his conservatism clearly within the American tradition.

111. For a good overview of his melding together the need for both freedom and order, see: *In Defense of Freedom: A Conservative Credo* (Chicago: Henry Regnery Company, 1962).

112. Author of numerous works, his philosophy is perhaps best presented in *Human Action* (San Francisco: Fox & Wilkes, 1996) and *Theory and History* (New Haven, CT.: Yale University Press, 1963).

functions of preserving internal order and protection from external threats to society's existence.

One observer at the 1967 YAF National Convention who asked various delegates about the survey and the accuracy of the results informally measured the relevance of these classifications and their relative strengths in YAF.

> Significantly, every one of the dozens to whom I showed the poll quickly identified themselves as being in one of the five categories, and, since each commented that these percentages were a fairly accurate sampling of the thousand or so at the convention, except that there were "probably just a few more" percentage-wise from their faction, it is obviously a quite accurate indication of the distribution of the factions within the Young Americans for Freedom as a whole. Which means that roughly two-fifths are traditionalist, one-quarter libertarian, and the rest fusionists who are trying to hold everything together.[113]

While temporarily muted through the remainder of 1967 and 1968, this division would become more apparent when YAF would meet again at its next national convention in 1969. However, two subsequent surveys of the YAF leadership—one in 1969 before the YAF National Convention and the other in 1970—indicate that this philosophical distribution remained relatively stable. Due to changes in category choices, especially with the 1969 survey, it is necessary to combine some of the categories originally used in the 1966 Leadership Conference survey. The number of participants in the surveys ranged from 175 in 1966 to 833 in 1969 and 230 in 1970, most of whom held leadership positions from chapter chairman to State Chairman to National Board of Directors.

Philosophical Position	*1966*	*1969*	*1970*
Radical Traditionalist or Traditionalist	40 %	21 %	35 %
Fusionist	34	9	30
Buckley—Conservative	—	48	—
Libertarian or Objectivist	26	22	29

Obviously, the inclusion of the "Buckley—Conservative" option in 1969 skewed the results, most likely drawing away many from the Fusionist choice, less so from the two traditionalist positions, and even less from the libertarian or Objectivist choices. Nevertheless, the similarities from 1966 to 1970 are striking, with a slight decline in traditionalists and a smaller increase among libertarians in the year following the divisive 1969 convention.[114]

---

113. Werdell, p. 13.
114. The 1966 results were printed in "Summer School—For Leaders," *New Guard*, September 1966, p. 6, 11. The 1969 "Summer Servicing Survey" results are at Personal Papers of Patrick Dowd, Box 2, Hoover Institution, Stanford University, Palo Alto, CA. The "Results of the Spring 1970 Leadership Questionnaire" are in the Dowd papers, Box 3.

Promoting a Voluntary Military

A clear example of an issue where the more libertarian members of YAF departed from others concerned the intensity of opposition to the draft and the appropriate tactics to be employed to end conscription.[115] By the mid-1960s, more and more YAF members were expressing their support for a voluntary military. One of the key leaders in this movement was David Franke, a YAF founder who had replaced Carol Dawson as editor of *New Guard* in 1965. Franke was instrumental in leading the National Board of Directors to adopt a resolution on conscription at its March 17, 1967 meeting. Cautiously worded, the resolution began by reaffirming YAF's support for a policy of total victory over communism, said that a voluntary military should be a goal of the United States, admitted that acute national emergency might justify temporary conscription, and opposed any form of compulsory national service.[116] After much debate and discussion, YAF had taken a stand on conscription, a stand that would be hardened over time.

The following month, on April 18th, Franke testified before the Senate Armed Services Committee. After reading the YAF Board's resolution, Franke outlined the reasons for a voluntary military, a system that would remove the element of compulsion as well as the inequities of the selection process then in effect, provide the military with individuals properly motivated and trained to serve, and force changes in military pay and procedures. Franke's testimony was reprinted in the May 1967 issue of *New Guard*, an issue almost totally devoted to the case for a voluntary military. Included in the magazine were supportive quotes from a number of political leaders, academics, business and military leaders as well as feature articles by Barry Goldwater ("End the Draft!"), Russell Kirk ("Our Archaic Draft"), and Milton Friedman ("The Case for a Voluntary Army"). An opening editorial proclaimed, "with this issue begins a long-range educational and action program by YAF promoting voluntarism not only in the military, but in other areas of society as well."[117] The demand for the issue was so great that YAF reprinted it many times and included the relevant sections in a "Voluntary Military Legislative Action Kit" distributed to YAF chapters and members over the next several years.

YAF's stand in opposition to the draft was viewed by most members as consistent with the organization's emphasis on individual freedom and the free market. Moreover, at a time when many young men were concerned about the individual application of the draft process, it placed YAF in a more favorable light. Finally, the advocacy of voluntarism contrasted with a growing liberal push for compulsory national service that would go beyond the military and include both the Peace Corps and domestic service programs.

By the time of the 1967 YAF National Convention, the organization's stand had been hardened with a more libertarian tone. Gone were the introductory words on opposition to communism, replaced by a philosophical opposition to conscription.

---

115. Andrew, "Pro-War and Anti-Draft," pp. 8–11 provides a good overview of YAF activities on this issue.

116. This resolution and the subsequent statement approved by YAF chapters after the 1967 national convention are in *Young People's Platform*, pp. 14–15.

117. *New Guard*, May 1967, p. 14.

Conscription violates man's unalienable right to his own life by compelling or threatening to compel men to serve in the armed forces. Conscription contributes to a wide-spread discontent among American youth. The totalitarian aspects of conscription encourage additional totalitarian programs and proposals, in particular the proposed National Service Program. The only system of procuring military personnel consistent with the goals of freedom and justice, and with the spirit of the Constitution, is a voluntary system.

The resolution went on to argue that conscription "facilitated the adoption of a no-win strategy in Vietnam" and that a professional, well-paid army would be more efficient and effective than one comprised of "poorly-trained inductees."[118]

Donald Ernsberger of Penn State University YAF was one of many advocates for adopting a strong voluntary military position. The extent and scope of that opposition tended to separate libertarians such as Ernsberger from other YAFers. As he explained several years later,

The conservatives always insisted if you're drafted you serve. It would be nice to have an all-volunteer army. We'd like to push for it. But when push comes to shove, you serve your country. Whereas our view was when push comes to shove, you go to Canada, you go underground, you resist.[119]

While Ernsberger is correct that the vast majority of YAF members would serve when required to do so, it remains true that YAF did make the Voluntary Military issue a major component of its overall program up until the end of conscription in 1973.

A number of chapters latched on to the voluntary military effort and sponsored educational forums, distributed YAF's new position paper opposing conscription, and wrote articles for college and independent newspapers. That fall, Washington area college chapters organized a forum on the draft at American University. Among the speakers was Dr. Donald J. Devine, former YAF National Director and then an Assistant Professor of Government & Politics at the University of Maryland. Devine "attacked the draft as involuntary servitude."[120] In a cover article titled "Coercion: The Threat to Individualism," YAF's *New Guard* linked support of a voluntary military to a more general stand against compulsion in society.[121]

California YAF sponsored a series of events during what they called "draft week" in December 1968. YAF speakers made appearances at University of Southern California, University of Redlands, University of California–Davis, Sacramento State College, Sacramento City College, Occidental College, Cal State-Fullerton, and Moorpark College. On each campus the speakers explained how a volunteer army was both more efficient and the pro-freedom position, tying in the concepts of free choice, the free market and voluntarism.[122]

As 1969 began, it was clear that opposition to the draft had become an essential element of YAF's program, included as one of the major components of what was called Young America's Freedom Offensive.[123] When the YAF National

118. *Young People's Platform*, pp. 14–15.
119. Quoted in Klatch: *A Generation Divided*, p. 121.
120. "D.C. Chapters Sponsor Draft Forum," *New Guard*, November 1968, p. 24.
121. *New Guard*, December 1968, p. 2.
122. "Freedom Forum," *New Guard*, March 1969, p. 8.
123. Andrew, "Pro-War and Anti-Draft," p. 10.

Board met in February, they adopted a resolution calling for "developing and maintaining a system of military manpower procurement based on the free choice of the individual."[124] The national office then prepared and distributed a "Volunteer Military Legislative Action Kit" to assist individuals and local chapters in advancing the anti-draft position. Taking the initiative, Arkansas YAF, under the leadership of State Chairman Ted Parkhurst, ran ads in college newspapers across the state urging that the draft be abolished.[125]

The delegates to the 1969 YAF National Convention in St. Louis adopted a similar resolution. On September 29th, YAF's Executive Director Randal Cornell Teague presented the organization's position in testifying before the President's Commission on an All-Volunteer Armed Forces and outlined the various projects taken to promote a voluntary military. In concluding, he reminded the commission "the young people of America are looking to the President to fulfill his campaign promise for an all-volunteer military, not to opt out with inadequate proposals such as the lottery or reduced draft calls."[126]

YAF continued its efforts to rally support for a voluntary military throughout the following year. The April 12, 1970 issue of *Parade*, the Sunday newspaper magazine, carried an article titled "Abolish the Draft" which began "Young Americans for Freedom (YAF) a society of collegiate conservatives rapidly expanding on many campuses, wants the draft abolished and replaced by a voluntary military." The article then went on to provide quotes from individuals cited by YAF for supporting the voluntary military.[127] The *Parade* article was followed by the insertion of the YAF position paper on the draft in the *Congressional Record* of May 19, 1970 by Congressman William A. Steiger of Wisconsin.[128] Then, in August 1970, YAF sponsored a symposium on Capitol Hill with speeches by Milton Friedman, retired General Thomas Lane, and Senators Goldwater and Mark Hatfield. Speaking for YAF, David Adcock explained that YAF had sent its voluntary military kit to all congressional offices along with personal letters from Friedman and Frank Meyer of *National Review* endorsing the concept of a voluntary military.[129] The symposium was held two weeks prior to a vote on an amendment sponsored by Goldwater and Hatfield to raise military pay as the first step toward ensuring sufficient volunteers to end conscription. The amendment failed by a vote of 52 to 35. Among those speaking against the concept of a volunteer army was Senator Edward Kennedy who claimed it "would discriminate against the poor, who would be the only ones who could be induced to volunteer by the higher pay."[130] Unfortunately, it would not be until nearly four years later when conscription would be ended.[131]

---

124. Alan MacKay, "Young America's Freedom Offensive," *New Guard*, April 1969, pp. 24–25.

125. "YAF Working for Draft End, Volunteer Use," *YAF in the News*, April 1969, p. 4. Beginning in 1969 and continuing for five years, the national YAF office reprinted a number of newspaper and magazine articles mentioning YAF or covering YAF activities in *YAF in the News*, a compilation distributed to chapter and state leadership. Most often, the exact date of original publication of these articles is not included. Thus, the reference here is to the date for *YAF in the News*.

126. "Statement on the Draft," *New Guard*, November 1969, pp. 6–7.

127. *YAF in the News*, April 1970, p. 10.

128. *YAF in the News*, May 1970, p. 2.

129. A transcript of the symposium was printed along with an extension of remarks by Senator Goldwater in the *Congressional Record*, August 19, 1970. Group Research Archives, Box 340, Columbia University, New York, NY.

130. David E. Rosenbaum, "Senate Bars Plan Designed to Bring Volunteer Army," *New York Times*, August 26, 1970.

131. For the transition see Beth Bailey: *America's Army—Making the All-Volunteer Force* (Cambridge, MA: Belknap Press, 2009).

Reagan and Miami Beach—1968

Although the hotly contested elections for National Chairman and National Board of Directors and the philosophical debates over resolutions were enough to capture the attention of most delegates to YAF's 1967 national convention, another significant development was taking place. Shortly before the convention began, several YAF members led by Mike Thompson announced the formation of Students for Reagan with the objective of promoting the California Governor and his ideas on American campuses. Although denying that it was a draft movement for a presidential candidacy, clearly the organization was building a foundation to be employed in any possible campaign that might develop. Representatives were out in force at the convention, signing up members from a hospitality suite at the Pittsburgh Hilton.

The media picked up on the Reagan surge, one story describing MacKay's victory as that of a "Reagan man" and noting, "By and large the Reagan forces were predominant at the convention. Reagan buttons and bumper stickers sold like Goldwater buttons and bumper stickers four years ago."[132] Several other newspapers in stories on the convention carried the same message. As the *New York Times* reported,

> Gov. Ronald Reagan of California appeared today to have supplanted Barry Goldwater as the national hero of the Young Americans for Freedom, a conservative, 30,000 member organization that played an important role in the successful Goldwater nomination drive of 1964. Reagan posters and pins dominated the organization's convention here and a group calling itself Students for Reagan began a national campaign to drum up campus support for the Governor's expected bid for the Republican nomination next year.[133]

In a similar vein, *Group Research Reports*, a publication of the same named organization funded by labor unions to track "right wing" organizations, commented that, "virtually all news reports noted that YAF, which grew out of a pro-Goldwater organization, seems to have shifted its allegiance from the Arizonan (who spoke at the meeting) to California's Ronald Reagan."[134] The article went on to note that the New York contact for Students for Reagan was Columbia student John C. Meyer, a YAF member and son of "Fusionist" advocate Frank Meyer. At a news conference after his election, National Chairman MacKay was asked about YAF's support for Reagan and concluded, "I think most of the delegates here would accept Nixon as the candidate but they would certainly prefer Reagan."[135]

Meanwhile, Reagan was not the only possible candidate to have representatives at the YAF convention. Also present to mingle with the delegates and measure the relative commitment of YAF leaders was Nixon staffer Patrick Buchanan and one

---

132. Sherley Uhl, "Young Americans Elect Reagan Man," *Pittsburgh Press*, September 3, 1967, Group Research Archives, Box 342, Columbia University, New York, NY.

133. Homer Bigart, "Youth Unit Shifts Fealty to Reagan; Goldwater Seems Replaced as Hero of Conservatives," *New York Times*, September 2, 1967.

134. *Group Research Reports*, September 15, 1967, p. 64, Group Research Archives, Box 428, Columbia University, New York, NY.

135. Werdell, p. 12.

of the Nixon staff's youth directors, Jeff Schechtman.[136] The degree of respect for the political action work of YAF was evident in the presence of Buchanan. One year earlier Nixon had also sewn up the support of former National Chairman Tom Charles Huston, recently returned from military service and now working on Nixon's personal staff.[137] As *National Review* publisher William A. Rusher noted, "Between Buchanan and Huston, Nixon managed to stay in touch with just about all the major personalities and institutions on the American right."[138] There were rumors that an attempt would be made to have the convention endorse Reagan, but the move never developed. Nevertheless, a few Nixon signs could be seen throughout the hotel, in contrast with the large Students for Reagan suite and the numerous delegates proudly displaying Reagan buttons.

In October 1967, Lee Edwards, former editor of YAF's *New Guard*, released what he called a "political biography" of Ronald Reagan. Published by Viewpoint Books in paperback format, it carried a cover price of one dollar but, as the back page promotion indicated, one hundred copies could be obtained for thirty dollars.[139] On campuses across the country, Students for Reagan members distributed the Edwards book along with other promotional literature describing Reagan's "Creative Society" approach to government. One of their more popular recruiting tools was a film of the 1967 debate on Vietnam policy that Reagan had with then United States Senator Robert F. Kennedy.[140] In early 1968, Students for Reagan opened a Washington office staffed by Bruce Weinrod, executive director.[141] Other officers of the group, nearly all of whom were YAF members, included Mike Thompson of University of Missouri and Charles Williams of University of North Carolina as Co-Chairmen, Kathy Forte of Dunbarton College as Secretary, and Randal Teague of American University as Treasurer.

Back home, thousands of Californians attempted to convince the Governor to move from being merely a favorite son to a serious candidate for the presidency, encouraging him to use the large bloc of delegates from the Golden State as leverage.[142] California YAF members were in the forefront of this effort. As Congressman Dana Rohrabacher recalled, "We served as the advance guard for Ronald Reagan's gubernatorial campaign and again in 1968 during his first faint-hearted try at the Presidency."[143] It was a symbiotic relationship for, in California, Young Americans for Freedom was perceived as Reagan's youth arm and the policies of the Reagan Administration were viewed as YAF's policies also.

---

136. Lyle Denniston, "Students for Reagan Move Launched at YAF Meeting," *Washington Evening Star*, September 1, 1967, Group Research Archives, Box 342, Columbia University, New York, NY. Buchanan was never a YAF member and he retells his early experience with YAF, when he feels he received a cold shoulder, in *Right from the Beginning* (Washington, DC: Regnery Publishing, Inc., 1988), p. 246.

137. According to one report, Patrick Buchanan was responsible for lining up a meeting in 1966 between Nixon and Huston who was at the time YAF National Chairman. "At dinner, the Old Man won Huston over. Huston played hardball, shutting down the Young Americans for Freedom leaders who wanted nothing to do with Nixon. Then he got himself quoted in *Esquire* saying 'only Nixon is generally acceptable to all kinds of Republicans.' For Nixon, that was quite a coup." Rick Perlstein: *Nixonland* (New York: Scribner, 2008), p. 130.

138. Rusher: *The Rise of the Right*, p. 144.

139. Edwards: *Reagan: A Political Biography*. An updated version was published in late 1981 to include subsequent events up through the assassination attempt on President Reagan.

140. 2008 YAF Alumni Survey Responses: Michael W. Thompson.

141. *New Guard*, March 1968, p. 4.

142. Schoenwald: *A Time for Choosing*, p. 217.

143. Dana Rohrabacher, "Us Young Americans for Freedom," *The American Enterprise*, May–June 1997, pp. 37–39.

When the YAF National Board of Directors was polled on their presidential preference, only two (David Keene and Gerald Plas) of the 21 members at the meeting supported Nixon, with the other nineteen all backing Reagan.[144] While the leadership of YAF was clearly behind the California Governor, the membership was more evenly split. In the spring of 1968, Young Americans for Freedom conducted a membership survey covering a number of issues. When asked their presidential choice, the results were:

Ronald Reagan	48 %
Richard M. Nixon	46
George C. Wallace	4
Other	2 [145]

Reflecting that closer division among the membership at large, the Summer 1968 issue of *New Guard* featured two competing articles advocating the candidacies of Reagan and Nixon.[146] This level of support for Nixon among YAF members, however, was transitory. By the time of the summer 1969 membership survey one year later, after Nixon's election as President, when asked with which political figure they most closely identified, the results were:

Goldwater	39 %
Reagan	37
Nixon	9
Wallace	6
Thurmond	5
Other	4 [147]

As the 1968 Republican National Convention approached, most YAF members would have felt comfortable with the California Governor as the Republican nominee and were proud of the fact that he was a member of their National Advisory Board. Still others felt that Nixon not only had the better chance of being elected but also was more experienced and would be a more effective, albeit somewhat less conservative, President.

One fact was clear from both surveys, however. There was little support among YAF members for Alabama Governor George Wallace. As early as 1966, Robert Schuettinger, one of the founders of YAF, concluded, "Wallace's supporters are united only in a common pursuit of power, jobs, and favors. There is absolutely no cohesion of principle or ideology in his ranks."[148] YAF National Chairman Alan MacKay, while recognizing that Wallace could be an appealing speaker, called him a "Pied Piper of pseudo-conservatism." MacKay maintained that "based upon his record as Governor, he simply does not qualify as a conservative but rather as a populist-segregationist who wants massive government spending but wants the control to be in his hands rather than in the hands of a Washington bureaucrat."[149]

---

144. Rusher: *The Rise of the Right*, pp. 158–159.

145. *New Guard*, October 1968, p. 3.

146. Bruce Weinrod, "The Conservative Case for Ronald Reagan," pp. 8–9 and David A. Keene, "The Conservative Case for Richard Nixon," pp. 10–11, *New Guard*, Summer 1968.

147. *New Guard*, June 1970, pp. 21–22.

148. Robert M. Schuettinger, "Wallace and Grenier: The Old and New South," *New Guard*, September 1966, pp. 24–25.

149. Alan MacKay, "Prospects for '68," *New Guard*, January 1968, p. 6.

As the survey indicated, there were a few Wallace supporters among the membership at large, one of whom was Dennis C. McMahan, a New York YAFer who became involved in a youth effort for Wallace in 1968.[150] Most YAF members, however, shared the view of another New York YAF chapter chairman who observed "Wallace supporters were few and many YAFers looked upon them as odd-balls rather than as conservatives . . . YAFers viewed Wallace as anything but a conservative and as a threat to the Republican nominee's chances for election."[151] National Director Ronald F. Docksai also prepared and distributed "A Conservative's Guide to George Corley Wallace" in the fall of 1968 with comments highly critical of the Alabama Governor.[152] Once the election was over, some of the Wallace supporters formed an organization they called the National Youth Alliance. In response, YAF sent out a news release making clear that it had no connection with that organization.[153]

Moreover, the editor of *New Guard* made evident the position of the organization's leadership when he commented on the results of the 1969 membership survey.

> The small percentage of Wallace supporters—which is 100 percent too large—is an official embarrassment to YAF leaders. The former Alabama Governor is typically referred to in the national office as a "populist demagogue" who exacerbates racial prejudice for personal gain, and who would destroy conservative politics.[154]

Clearly, the leadership of Young Americans for Freedom was not disposed to support Wallace, especially when contrasted with a conservative such as Reagan or, in the 1968 presidential election, a less-than-conservative Nixon.

While YAF had played a central role at the 1964 Republican National Convention as essential supporters of the Goldwater campaign, the organization's involvement in Miami Beach in 1968 would be substantially different. Once again, hundreds of YAF members gathered in the convention city and were treated to a series of meetings and speeches directed to them but this time most of those politically involved were supporting an outsider candidate who would fail to win the party's nomination.

As soon as spring semester was over, national YAF formed an "On to Miami Committee" to coordinate activities at the Republican National Convention. Local YAF leaders received a memo from Michael W. Thompson, Students for Reagan Co-Chairman, John Whitehead, Youth for Nixon Steering Committee member, and David R. Jones, YAF Executive Director. Thompson was a National Director of YAF while Whitehead was the District of Columbia YAF chairman. YAF members were informed of the convention activities, parties, and housing in Miami Beach.[155] A bloc of rooms was set aside for those YAF members who

---

150. In a letter to YAF leaders dated August 23, 1968 McMahan claimed to "know many state chairmen in this great organization of ours who support George Wallace. I know many chapter chairmen and members who support this great man." Personal Papers of Jameson Campaigne, Jr., Ottawa, IL.

151. Abramov, "Young Americans for Freedom—The New Guard of the 1960s," p. 24.

152. Personal Papers of William F. Buckley, Jr., Box 57, Sterling Library, Yale University, New Haven, CT.

153. News release. Young Americans for Freedom, January 16, 1969, Personal Papers of Jameson G. Campaigne, Jr., Ottawa, IL.

154. *New Guard*, January 1970, p. 22.

155. "On to Miami" memo, Personal Papers of Randal C. Teague, Washington, DC.

could travel to Miami Beach and arrangements made for those who wished to volunteer for either the Reagan or Nixon campaign operations at the convention. Regardless of their preferred candidate, YAF members helped distribute copies of "Young People's Platform."

While YAF made sure that there was an opportunity for Nixon supporters to work for their chosen candidate, much of the organized YAF activity centered on showing youth support for Governor Reagan.[156] As Marvin Liebman, himself a master organizer, observed, "I have never witnessed such rapid organization in such a short time. Wherever Reagan went there was a crowd of cheering young people waving Reagan signs."[157] Liebman was being too kind in overlooking the important role he played in helping get that "organization" going in Miami Beach. According to Mike Thompson, Students for Reagan chairman, it was Liebman who helped bring together the essential elements for carrying out that effort.[158]

Once the Youth for Reagan headquarters was set up, Thompson had volunteers pass out flyers with the hotel and time of Reagan's appearance at each delegation meeting and "hundreds of folks would show up. It was truly like something out of a movie—folks streaming across streets, out of stores and restaurants to get a glimpse of the Governor."[159] YAF members held "Students for Reagan" signs and handed out promotional literature at each Reagan appearance. One of the most unforgettable experiences took place when a group of some thirty Youth for Reagan students welcomed Reagan to his headquarters hotel. Thompson recalled, "Reagan came in, sat with us in the lobby, talked to us for about twenty minutes, thanked us. Quite a guy!"[160]

In addition to all the campaign activity, there was time for hearing conservative speakers and having fun. Starting on Monday morning, YAF members met for a breakfast where the featured speaker was California Superintendent of Public Instruction Dr. Max Rafferty who was the Republican nominee for United States Senate. Tuesday morning started with a brunch where Jim Buckley, New York Conservative Party candidate for United States Senate, introduced his younger brother, Bill Buckley. According to reporter Joe McGinnis, more than five hundred people turned out for the brunch.[161] That evening, YAF hosted a poolside party at the Monte Carlo for YAF members.[162]

While Reagan maintained that he never wanted to be an actual candidate and "never believed that a former actor who had only been a governor a matter of months could suddenly say he wanted to be president," his name was placed in nomination and he received 182 votes.[163] Nixon barely won a majority on the first and only ballot, escaping a second ballot by 25 votes. As one writer noted, "Reagan

156. A good collection of 1968 convention material, including literature distributed by Citizens for Reagan and YAF can be found in Group Research Archives, Box 403, Columbia University, New York, NY.

157. Liebman: *Coming Out Conservative*, p. 180.

158. Email to the author from Michael Thompson, April 20, 2009.

159. *Ibid.*

160. *Ibid.*

161. Joe McGinniss, "Well Scrubbed YAFs Hear Middle-Aged Idol of Right," *Philadelphia Inquirer*, August 7, 1968.

162. "YAF in Miami," *New Guard*, September 1968, p. 3.

163. Kiron K. Skinner, Annelise Anderson and Martin Anderson: *Reagan: A Life in Letters* (New York; Free Press, 2003), pp. 173–174. The Reagan comments are from a letter written in the fall of 1975, some seven years later. See also Reagan: *An American Life*, p. 177 for Reagan's surprise that delegates from other states had pledged to support him.

had the support of the grass roots, but Nixon had the backing of conservative political leaders, which was enough in 1968."[164] Still others postulated that had emotion ruled, nearly ninety percent of the delegates from the South would have gone to Reagan.[165]

Despite the disappointment of not seeing their candidate win the nomination, there were meaningful experiences for many of the young Reagan supporters, experiences that testified to the character of Ronald Reagan. Mike Thompson recently recalled two post-nomination incidents involving the candidate and his young supporters.

> When Reagan lost the nomination, out of the arena came groups of YAF kids with Reagan signs, disheartened for the loss but excited nonetheless. Up to one group of these young Reagan supporters came a black limousine and stopped. Down came the back window and there was the Governor and Mrs. Reagan. They chatted with these kids, thanked them, etc.
>
> The next day, a group of students with Reagan bumper stickers all over their car are parked at a traffic light and they hear a car honking next to them. There was Reagan, window down in his limousine, and he thanks the kids.[166]

It was experiences such as these that endeared Ronald Reagan to these YAF members, many of whom would go on to play critical roles in future presidential campaigns, including those of Reagan himself in 1976, 1980 and 1984.

For many, if not most, of the YAF members, the 1968 convention was their first experience at such an event but would not be their last. Moreover, the contacts they made in Miami Beach would be valuable to them in future efforts. Harold Herring recalled one such incident that impacted the future of Ronald Reagan, "Because of my YAF involvement, I had attended the 1968 convention where I met and worked with Tom Ellick, who was on Governor Reagan's staff in Sacramento and we became good friends and remained so for several years." Some five years later, Herring was administrative assistant to Senator Jesse Helms of North Carolina and "the Senator and I were going to California for him to speak at an association meeting. I called Tom and he arranged for the Senator to have a private meeting with then Governor Reagan at the Governor's home." This was the first time Helms and Reagan had met and they became fast friends. Only a few years later, "Governor Reagan was about to pull out of the presidential race when Senator Helms turned North Carolina for him. History tells the rest of that story."[167]

As the YAF members left Miami Beach and eventually headed back to campus for the fall semester, many were disappointed that their favored candidate had not won the nomination but nearly all were now committed to the election of Richard Nixon. Some would volunteer to help in his election; still others would focus on campus issues or defending the American effort in South Vietnam. They remained optimistic about the future of their organization and their country. One critical writer had to admit that these young conservatives were upbeat and positive as they went into battle for principle.

---

164. Brennan: *Turning Right in the Sixties*, p. 128.

165. Lewis Chester, Godfrey Hodgson and Bruce Page: *An American Melodrama* (New York: The Viking Press, Inc., 1969), p. 489.

166. Email to the author from Michael Thompson, April 20, 2009.

167. Email to the author from Harold Herring, April 21, 2009.

... YAFers see hope for the future. They believe that YAF has proved that there is a legitimate place for the conservative viewpoint in America (which they say was not so prior to 1960). They see YAF as the instrument to keep the conservative dialogue alive and growing and as a body that continually offers new ideas for evaluation. Lastly, they view YAF as a positive benefit to the two-party system, giving hope to the conservatives within, thus keeping them from breaking away into third-party splinters out of sheer frustration.[168]

Nixon would go on and win the election in November 1968. YAF's relationship with the new administration started on a positive note but would soon develop into a problematic relationship as the new decade began.

Campaigning for Conservatives

Beyond its involvement in the Reagan effort at the Republican National Convention and the subsequent general election, much of YAF's activity during 1968 was focused on supporting the effort in Vietnam, combating New Left violence and disruption on campus, and engaging in political action. As might be expected, with its Governor a prominent member of the YAF National Advisory Board, California was a hotbed of YAF political activity. During this period of time, California YAF State Chairman Dana Rohrabacher could turn out 75 or 100 YAF members in Los Angeles County to walk precincts and distribute brochures for conservative Republican primary candidates. The organization's 1968 state convention was attended by over 250 students and featured speeches by Governor Reagan, United States Senator George Murphy, and Superintendent of Instruction Dr. Max Rafferty who had just obtained the Republican nomination for the United States Senate.[169]

The national YAF organization had taken the lead earlier in the year by encouraging its local chapters to form "Youth For" groups on behalf of conservative candidates. At the beginning of the spring semester, all YAF State and Chapter Chairmen received a memo from Randal C. Teague and Charles Hooks of the national staff making suggestions on how to form such groups.[170] The memo listed fifteen different activities that could be undertaken by "Youth For" groups as outgrowths of the local YAF chapters. Unstated but obvious to all was the benefit of such groups in expanding the organization's outreach efforts towards obtaining additional members as well as financial and political supporters.

One of the interesting examples of YAF's leadership in the field of political action developed from an idea floated by Bill Saracino in January 1969. A new law had created the Los Angeles Community College Board of Trustees, a body with the responsibility of overseeing all the district's two-year colleges. The new board would have seven members elected county-wide and Saracino was convinced this was an opportunity to elect some conservative candidates. Allen Brandstater was one of the few YAF leaders meeting the minimum age requirement of 21 and

---

168. George Thayer: *The Farther Shores of Politics* (New York: Clarion Books, 1968), p. 173.

169. E-mail from Allen Brandstater, January 18, 2009. Brandstater was executive director of California YAF during much of this time.

170. Memorandum: "Youth For" Groups, January 31, 1968. Personal Papers of Randal C. Teague, Washington, DC.

he filed for office. Brandstater and Saracino then put together with their county YAF leaders a slate of seven candidates including Bill Orozco (later Los Angeles County Republican Chairman), Mike Antonovich (later state assemblyman and since 1980 Los Angeles County Supervisor), Bob Cline (subsequently state assemblyman), and Marian LaFollette (later member of the California assembly). As Brandstater recalled,

> Our conservative slate ultimately won 5 of the 7 college board seats, taking control of eight campuses and its $125 million [1969 dollars] budget. I lost in the general but won 249,000 votes, more than any 21 year old seeking any public office in the United States has ever gained, to the best of my knowledge. How and why? Largely because of Young Americans for Freedom ... And we took control of a college district—and really ticked off the liberal teachers' unions.[171]

Through this effort, an organization of conservative students—most of whom were not yet old enough to vote at a time before enactment of the 26th amendment—had not only elected a majority to an important educational board but had also helped launch the political careers of at least three members of the California Assembly and a now 28-year incumbent county supervisor. Moreover, they had trained a multitude of new young political organizers who would go on to become essential elements in the election of countless other conservatives to public office, not only in California but throughout the United States. Brandstater concluded, "all of this came about because of YAF and because a 19-year-old kid (Bill Saracino) said let's do something."[172]

Of course, YAF's political activities were not limited to California and they were not all geared to momentary victories and defeats. YAF was all about preparing young people for the future, a future that for many included a career in politics and government. Shannon Cave was a chapter chairman at the University of Missouri where his experience in YAF meant that he "learned politics and infighting, developed a philosophy, learned to influence events, and made some lifelong friends." Cave went on to serve as executive director and then State Chairman of the Missouri Republican Party before accepting a career position with the state Department of Conservation. As Cave concluded, "I'd have been teaching mathematics if not involved early in politics through YAF."[173]

But YAF was more than an organization committed to electoral politics. It was committed to opposing communism in all forms, to advancing the principles of limited government and free market economics, and to ensuring the opportunity for all students to receive an education in a campus environment conducive to learning. These three concerns: the communist challenge, the proper role for government, and the threat of New Left violence were to consume much of YAF's attention over the next few years as the decade of the 1960s was ending and a new decade was about to begin.

---

171. E-mail from Allen Brandstater, January 18, 2009.
172. Interview with Allen Brandstater, Newport Beach, CA, October 12, 2008.
173. 2008 YAF Alumni Survey Responses: Shannon D. Cave.

7. The Communist Challenge

"That the forces of international Communism are,
at present, the greatest threat to these liberties;
That the United States should stress victory over,
rather than co-existence with this menace . . ."[1]

As the year 1965 progressed and over the remaining years of the decade, anti-communist activity became even more important to Young Americans for Freedom. Two actions by the Johnson Administration were the cause for this increased focus: the determination to "build bridges" to Eastern European Communist countries and the decision to escalate American involvement in the Vietnam conflict.

East–West Trade

The anti-communism of YAF was clearly dominant in the organization's views on world trade. While the conservative movement included many who adhered to the totally free trade views of 19th century liberalism, YAF was in the forefront of those groups that would restrict the free flow of trade between the United States and the Communist nations of the world. YAF's prevailing position on East–West trade was reflected in a cover article in the February 1965 issue of *New Guard*, published before news of the Firestone Tire and Rubber Company's deal with Romania had become public.[2] YAF's overall stand on East–West trade was also reflected in a reprint from *Barron's* January 1964 issue that was distributed widely by the organization. Titled "Dangerous Bridges," it maintained that such efforts were not helping the people of Eastern Europe but simply fortifying despotic regimes and indirectly assisting the Soviet Union.[3]

One of the major political and public relations successes for YAF, not simply in 1965 but historically as to the lasting contribution of the organization, was its efforts against East–West trade and, specifically, the Firestone Tire and Rubber Company's plans to build a synthetic rubber plant in Romania. During what would be the last year of his presidency, John F. Kennedy promoted increased trade with Eastern Europe as part of an overall policy of "peaceful coexistence." Upon assuming the office of President, Lyndon Johnson continued this policy but added "differentiation" by which the United States enhanced its relations with Communist states that sought greater autonomy from the Soviet Union.[4] In early

---

1. From "The Sharon Statement," adopted in conference at Sharon, Connecticut, September 9–11, 1960.

2. R.J. Bocklet, "East–West Trade: Coup for the East, Danger for the West," pp. 12–14, 22. During the mid-Sixties, YAF distributed a series of Issues Papers on topics of general interest. These were 8½ by 11 inch three-folds that summarized the key points on an issue. Issues Paper Number 4 was titled "East–West Trade: committing national suicide." Bocklet served as an unofficial overseas correspondent for *New Guard*, authoring numerous articles on international relations. 2008 YAF Alumni Survey Responses: Richard J. Bocklet.

3. Ronald F. Docksai, "A Study of the Organization and Beliefs of the Young Conservative Movement," p. 95.

4. For much of the background to the YAF actions on the Firestone matter I relied extensively on Ryan Floyd, "For Want of Rubber; Romania's Affair with Firestone in 1965," an unpublished paper

1964, Secretary of State Dean Rusk outlined this policy in a speech, "Why we treat different Communist countries differently," in which he put forth specific measures to enhance trade relations with Eastern Europe. This was followed by President Johnson's May 1964 address at Virginia Military Institute outlining his "bridge building" policy. The President declared "We will continue to build bridges across the gulf which has divided us from Eastern Europe. They will be bridges of increased trade, of ideas, of visitors, and of humanitarian aid."[5]

Romania was one such country ready to take advantage of this outreach from the United States. Rich in oil reserves, it was attempting to follow a policy of heavy industrial development starting in the late 1950s.[6] With Romania wanting to build up its industrial capacity and needing access to advanced technology and the Johnson Administration wanting to increase relations with Eastern European Communist nations, the essential elements of a trade deal were present. Discussions began for Romania to purchase American synthetic rubber technology.

In late May 1964, immediately after the President's "bridge building" address, formal talks began between the United States and Romania. Communist officials submitted a list of fifteen manufacturing plants they wanted to buy, topped by two synthetic rubber manufacturing plants. The Defense Department expressed concern due to the possible military applications and export to the USSR which then had a shortage of synthetic rubber used for aircraft tires. Nevertheless, the State Department saw this as an opening for American business to Eastern Europe and the United States government agreed to license the sale of eleven of the fifteen plants requested, including the two synthetic rubber plants and a nuclear electric power station.[7]

Shortly after general approval was granted, Romanian officials visited several firms that expressed interest in building the rubber plants, including Firestone, B.F. Goodrich, and Goodyear. The Romanians toured a Goodyear plant in Beaumont, Texas and a delegation from Goodyear went to Romania to negotiate a sale, but the Romanians turned them down believing that Goodyear proposed an inefficient process. Rebuffed, Goodyear switched directions and started expressing its newfound opposition to trading with the Romanians. In October, Goodyear's Board Chairman, Russell De Young, wrote Secretary of State Rusk outlining his company's new concern over Romania providing the technology to the Soviet Union.

As it became clearer that Firestone was the only provider of the technology sought by the Romanians, Goodyear's public relations agents spread the word of the company's "patriotic opposition" to selling the synthetic rubber technology to Romania. In December, both Associated Press and United Press International distributed articles to newspapers outlining Goodyear's position against trade with Eastern European countries. An editorial in the *New York Daily News* praised the company for refusing "point-blank to sell a synthetic rubber plant to Red Romania, despite a Commerce Department OK on such sales and the Administration's desire to cozy up to Romania."[8]

provided to me by Jameson Campaigne, Jr. A revised version was published in two parts in the *Eastern European Quarterly*, volume 38 (December 22, 2004) and volume 39 (March 22, 2005).

5. "Johnson's Address at VMI," *New York Times*, May 24, 1964.
6. The conflicting relations involving Romania, the Soviet Union, and China are discussed in Floyd, pp. 6–13.
7. *Ibid.* pp. 17–19.
8. *Ibid.* p. 25.

Goodyear's "patriotic" opposition to the Romanian deal confronted some embarrassing facts two months later when the television program "CBS Reports" focused on Romania's trade policies, including the purchase of tires from Goodyear that were then sold to China.[9] Subsequent U.S. government investigation found some 600 tractors in Romania had Goodyear tires with 100 carrying the USA designation and the others sold by the company's Canadian subsidiary. Some ten percent of the tractors with Goodyear tires were shipped to Communist China. The duplicity of Goodyear, however, did not stop them from seeking to win away customers from Firestone on the claim of patriotism.

By the first week of January 1965, Firestone had come to an agreement with Romania to sell two synthetic rubber manufacturing plants. That same week, President Johnson used his State of the Union address to promote increased trade with both Eastern Europe and the Soviet Union. The deal was cut and it had the clear backing of the Johnson Administration. As the media became aware of the Firestone deal, *Human Events* published an article on the topic.[10] Among those who read the article was David Walter, treasurer of Philadelphia YAF, who contacted his fellow members and prepared a plan of action. As Walter explained,

> After reading in *Human Events* about the Firestone Tire and Rubber Company's plan to build a synthetic rubber plant in Communist Rumania, the Philadelphia chapter of the Young Americans for Freedom launched a drive to force Firestone to reconsider and withdraw these plans.[11]

Walter and Philadelphia YAF Chairman Jay Parker began to draw up their plans for local action and consider how best to involve others in their efforts. As Parker recalls the incident, Philadelphia YAF member Kenneth Whitlock proposed that the chapter demonstrate against Firestone.[12]

By March, the United States escalation in Vietnam had begun and with American troops battling Communist forces in Southeast Asia, the reasons for opposing East–West trade had increased. That same month, Philadelphia YAF started demonstrations outside Firestone dealerships. The picketers' signs proclaimed: "Firestone Sells the USA Down the Red River," "Scrap Iron for Japan, II World War, Now Synthetic Rubber for Soviets" and other similar messages. Their handouts claimed that Romania supplied China with heavy-duty trucks that were then provided to North Vietnam with whom the United States was at war.

To squash the picketing, Firestone sent its public relations agent to meet with YAF's regional representative, John LaMothe, explaining that Firestone was merely carrying out the President's "bridge building" policy. But the YAF members were not to be deterred and, in fact, committed to elevating the protest to a national campaign. On April 14th, LaMothe sent a memo to all YAF chapter chairmen explaining the reasons for opposing Firestone's sale of two synthetic rubber manufacturing plants to Romania and calling upon them to join a national protest against the company. That launched a nationwide campaign of picket lines, demonstrations, letter writing campaigns, and news releases against Firestone and its local dealers. Pickets started appearing before Firestone stores

9. *Ibid.* p. 27.
10. "Red Trade Opposition Grows," *Human Events*, January 30, 1965.
11. "Big Conservative Win," *Human Events*, May 8, 1965.
12. Tyson: *Courage to Put Country Above Color*, pp. 43–44.

in Brooklyn, Cleveland, Atlanta, Los Angeles, Providence, Indianapolis, Miami, and other smaller communities.[13]

While the picketing received significant local media coverage and resulted in complaints by several local dealers to Firestone claiming lost business, the corporate officials were not deterred. It would take more drastic action by the national organization to squash the deal. That came when National YAF told Firestone that it was considering handing out 500,000 pamphlets at the "Indianapolis 500" race on Memorial Day. The pamphlets would explain Firestone's plans to build a plant in Romania at a time when Americans were fighting Communist forces in Vietnam. The kicker came when YAF officials said they might hire an airplane to fly back and forth over the race site with a banner opposing the Firestone deal.[14] YAF also made plans to set up a "Committee Against Slave Labor" booth outside the Indianapolis 500 to expose labor practices in Communist countries.[15]

On April 20th, one month after Philadelphia YAF had begun its picketing at area Firestone dealerships, the corporate office in Akron, Ohio sent out a brief but historic news release: "The Firestone Tire and Rubber Company has terminated negotiations for a contract to design and equip a synthetic rubber plant in Rumania."[16] While Firestone took the heat for attempting to implement Johnson's "bridge building" policies, the Administration was reluctant to criticize YAF because it did not want to alienate YAF as a supporter in the Vietnam War.[17] Meanwhile, Goodyear, whose tires were actually installed on tractors in Communist China, continued to portray itself as the patriotic opponent of East–West trade as contrasted with Firestone, its main competitor.

Although some in the Administration wished the entire issue would simply go away, that would not be the case. The media picked up the story and then various members of Congress on both sides got involved. Young Americans for Freedom was seen as the responsible (or irresponsible) party in ending the deal with Communist Romania. Bernard Gwertzman reported in the *Washington Evening Star*, "the conservative Young Americans for Freedom almost single-handedly caused giant Firestone, the nation's second largest rubber manufacturer, to drop the deal." It was, he claimed, "a severe embarrassment to the State Department."[18]

Newspapers on both sides of the ideological spectrum took note of YAF's success. The *Washington Post* editorialized against what they called a "slashed tires" campaign by YAF. Calling Romania "Westward moving" they were conveniently overlooking the fact that it was then headed by Nicolae Ceausescu, who would become the most brutal of all East European dictators.[19] From the other side came praise for YAF's actions. As the *Richmond News Leader* editorialized, "The YAFers were right to show Firestone the fallacy of strengthening the dedicated enemies of our system."[20] This media coverage heightened the interest of left-wing

13. Schneider: *Cadres for Conservatism*, p. 101; "Big Conservative Win," *Human Events*, May 8, 1965; A report on the picketing against Firestone by the Bay Ridge (Brooklyn) YAF led by Chairman Tom Harrison and the Philadelphia YAF protests is found in *New Guard*, May 1965, p. 21.

14. "YAF Highlights: 1960–1965," Personal Papers of Herbert A. Philbrick, Box 218, Folder 3, Manuscript Division, Library of Congress, Washington, DC.

15. Bernard Gwertzman, "United States Embarrassed: Firm, Facing Boycott, Drops Rumanian Deal," *Washington Evening Star*, May 8, 1965; Lee and Anne Edwards: *You Can Make the Difference*, p. 294.

16. "Firestone Calls Off Deal with Reds," *New Guard*, June 1965.

17. Floyd, "For Want of Rubber," p. 41.

18. Gwertzman, May 8, 1965.

19. *Washington Post*, May 12, 1965.

20. As quoted in "Firestone Calls Off Deal with Reds," *New Guard*, June 1965.

members of the Senate whose vitriolic comments would keep the issue alive for the next two months.

On May 17th, Senator Stephen Young of Ohio, where the headquarters of both Firestone and Goodyear were located, inserted his remarks on the issue in the *Congressional Record*, blasting the "vigilantes of the extreme radical right." Describing YAF's efforts in stopping the Firestone deal, he declared,

> Here is a dastardly wrong perpetrated by narrow-minded, bigoted, self-appointed vigilantes who consider themselves super-duper patriots . . . America comes last with these right-wing radical leaders of Young Americans for Freedom, so-called, who, by this sort of action, undermine our national policy and help deny employment to worthy and industrious working men and women and diminish the prosperity of an entire community.[21]

Young was an advocate of the "why can't we all just get along?" approach to foreign policy and saw this backtracking by Firestone as a major setback for world peace. According to the Senator, "It is for us to seek coexistence or we will likely meet co-annihilation . . . If we are ever to achieve lasting peace in our modern world it is likely to be achieved through experiments in cooperation or specific joint ventures between the nations of the free world and those of the Communist bloc."[22]

Two months later, Senator J. William Fulbright, Chairman of the Senate Foreign Relations Committee, released a statement in which he attacked YAF, Goodyear, and the State Department for the failure of Firestone to proceed with the sale to Romania. Believing that his pre-eminence in helping to shape American foreign policy was being challenged, the Senator from Arkansas denounced "private groups or businesses or individuals [who] take it on themselves to alter, or dictate, or defeat official policies of the United States Government." He claimed that YAF literature consisted of "the familiar fulminations of the radical right along with dark hints of immorality and worse on the part of Firestone." In addition to criticizing Goodyear and YAF, Senator Fulbright contended that "the role of the State Department is, to say the least, equivocal" and had "failed to support the company as it certainly should have."[23]

President Johnson viewed Fulbright's remarks as an attack on his commitment to "bridge building" and his willingness to oppose YAF, an ally on the Vietnam War that Johnson promoted and Fulbright opposed. The President ordered his staff to launch an investigation of YAF and determine whether they had received assistance from Goodyear. The investigation failed to find any link between the company and YAF, since it depended on thousands of small donations and had little corporate financial support of any kind.[24]

The following day, on July 26th, Fulbright delivered his remarks on the Senate floor, occasioning a response from Senator Strom Thurmond of South Carolina, defending the reputation of Young Americans for Freedom. As viewed by Thurmond,

21. *Congressional Record*, May 17, 1965, Group Research Archives, Box 340, Columbia University, New York, NY.
22. *Ibid.*
23. "Fulbright Says Pressure Blocked Rumanian Deal," *New York Times*, July 26, 1965.
24. Floyd, "For Want of Rubber," pp. 49–50.

The Senator from Arkansas described Young Americans for Freedom, this country's largest and most responsible conservative youth group as "extremist" and "a vigilante group." Mr. President, if anyone who is connected with Young Americans for Freedom is an extremist, then there are 39 Members of this Congress who should be so classified because we serve as members of the National Advisory Board of Young Americans for Freedom.[25]

One week later, Congressman Ross Adair came to YAF's defense in the House of Representatives. He asked "What terrible crime did Young Americans for Freedom commit? They picketed a rubber company in a successful effort to stop this company from building a synthetic rubber plant in Rumania, and thus giving much-needed industrial production and know-how to that country."[26] Finally, on August 10th, Senator John Tower of Texas challenged his neighboring Senator from Arkansas and said "I am proud to support the remarks made in the Senate on July 26 by the distinguished Senator from South Carolina." Tower then inserted in the *Congressional Record* a number of news articles supportive of YAF's position on Firestone.[27]

The Firestone effort was only one of many campaigns undertaken by YAF in opposition to trade with Communist countries, although clearly the most successful. YAF denied that it had engaged in any boycott of the tire company, describing the efforts as an informational campaign.[28] YAF pledged to focus on contracts "which plainly give aid and comfort to the Communist enemy by building up their military power" and the National Board appointed a working group on strategic trade to provide advice on future efforts.[29] The statement made it clear that YAF's opposition to such trade would continue and realized that this would put them in opposition to the President with whom they agreed on Vietnam. "We applauded the President for his firmness in Vietnam. But we find it sheer absurdity to undermine this stand by trading with the enemy through the back door of Rumania or any other Red nation."[30]

The following year YAF was confronted with another major United States corporation attempting to trade with a Communist nation. This time, it was the Soviet Union and the company was American Motors whose former head, Governor George Romney of Michigan, was rumored to be considering a candidacy for President of the United States in 1968. On November 26, 1966, William S. Pickett, Vice President for International Automotive Operations for American Motors Corporation, announced plans to sell automobiles to the Soviet Union. Pickett told a reporter for the *Detroit News*, "I'm going to Russia, and I am going to sell some cars there. These are the kinds of deals we are looking for. I think the Communist bloc will more than pay its way."[31] A.M.C. sought to become

25. *Congressional Record*, July 26, 1965, Group Research Archives, Box 340, Columbia University, New York, NY.

26. *Congressional Record*, August 5, 1965, Group Research Archives, Box 340, Columbia University, New York, NY.

27. *Congressional Record*, August 10, 1965, Group Research Archives, Box 340, Columbia University, New York, NY.

28. David S. Broder, "Young Rightists Plan Expansion," *New York Times*, August 28, 1965.

29. "A Statement of Policy: Trading with the Enemy," *New Guard*, August 1965.

30. *Ibid.*

31. "American Motors Hopes to Sell Cars to Reds," *Chicago Tribune*, November 27, 1966.

the first United States auto firm to sell cars directly in the Soviet Union or other Communist nations in Eastern Europe.

Once again, direct action developed from the local chapter level. Ted G. Carpenter, chairman of the University of Wisconsin–Milwaukee YAF, sent a letter to National YAF announcing the chapter's plans to protest American Motors decision and urging other chapters to join them.[32] By mid-December, YAF pickets appeared at A.M.C.'s Rambler agencies in Indiana as well as at the American Motors plant in Milwaukee. Ron Pearson, chairman of Valparaiso YAF, called the A.M.C. office in Detroit to get a confirmation or denial of the plans. When no clear response was forthcoming, the picketing began. Pearson then contacted other Indiana chapter chairmen and the effort spread.[33]

On January 3, 1967, YAF's Executive Director, David R. Jones, sent a detailed memo with attachments to the National Advisory Board, National Board of Directors, State Chairmen, and Chapter Chairmen titled "National YAF Opposition to American Motors Communist Trade Deal."[34] Jones pointed out that YAF's longstanding opposition to trade of strategic goods with Communist countries was even stronger now because of the war in Vietnam. Selling autos to the Soviet Union was viewed as allowing them to divert metals, rubber, and other materials into military industrial aid to the North Vietnamese and the Viet Cong. YAF chapters were asked to establish picket lines outside American Motors dealerships beginning Monday, January 9, 1967. The purpose would be to inform the public about the negotiations to sell cars to the Soviet Union—not to encourage a boycott.[35]

In addition to applying pressure at the local level, YAF's National Chairman, Tom Charles Huston, sent a telegram to Governor George Romney asking him, as a former head of American Motors Corporation, to intervene and encourage the corporation to end any negotiations with the Soviets. Huston claimed that Romney was in "a unique position to help the United States war effort in Vietnam by opposing this trade deal which would indirectly give aid to the Communists in North Vietnam."[36] No response or reaction was ever received from Romney however.

On January 9th, pickets appeared before A.M.C. dealerships in several cities from New York to Indiana to Wisconsin and Michigan and on to Oregon.[37] One week later, less than two months after his original statement to the media, Vice President Pickett wired Jones that, "American Motors has no plans, programs, or intentions to trade with Communist bloc nations . . . The story of November 26 was a misinterpretation."[38] YAF National Chairman Huston congratulated A.M.C. for reversing its previously announced intentions and called the change in direction "a victory for the millions of loyal Americans who oppose trade with the Communists."[39] A second major American corporation had backed down under pressure from Young Americans for Freedom.

---

32. Letter to the Editor, *New Guard*, December 1966, p. 23.

33. "YAF Exposes, Halts Company's Plans to Trade with the Enemy," *New Guard*, January 1967, pp. 4–5.

34. "National YAF Opposition to American Motors Communist Trade Deal." Personal papers of Henry Regnery, Box 80, Hoover Institution, Stanford University, Palo Alto, CA.

35. *Ibid.* p. 2.

36. "Group Seeks to Block Car Sales to Reds," *Washington Evening Star*, January 5, 1967.

37. Mark W. Hopkins, "AM Aide's Musing Ignited Furor on Sales to Reds," *Milwaukee Journal*, January 22, 1967, inserted by Representative John Ashbrook in *Congressional Record*, February 1, 1967, pp. H878–880. Group Research Archives, Box 340, Columbia University, New York, NY.

38. YAF Press Release of January 24, 1967, inserted by Representative James Utt in *Congressional Record*, January 26, 1967, pp. H699–700. Group Research Archives, Box 340, Columbia University, New York, NY.

39. *Ibid.* p. 699.

As an outgrowth of this campaign, YAF was once again the recipient of editorial attacks in liberal newspapers and praise from those with a more conservative editorial policy. Among the latter, the *Richmond News Leader* commended the organization by saying, "YAF has acted as the people's stand-in in teaching AMC a painful lesson."[40] This time, neither Senator Young nor Senator Fulbright made major attacks on the organization for its efforts in thwarting trade with a Communist nation.

YAF organized a similar campaign in opposition to the sale of computer technology but in this instance the company, International Business Machines, had little direct competition and dealt mainly with corporations rather than consumers. During the mid-1960s IBM began selling its 1400 series data processing systems to Czechoslovakia, Poland, Hungary and Bulgaria, maintaining that it was doing so in accordance with the Johnson Administration's policy of encouraging East–West trade. In July 1967, California YAF began a series of demonstrations outside the Los Angeles offices of IBM Corporation, coordinated by Bill Saracino, Los Angeles County director of YAF. Allen Brandstater, California YAF's State Executive Director explained the organization's reasoning, "It seems rather illogical that we should have over half a million young men fighting communism in Viet Nam while large business firms at home are bent on helping the communists through the trading between East and West."[41] More than two-dozen protesters picketed the IBM office carrying signs that read "IBM Selling Reds Rope to Hang Us?" and "Red Trade is Bad Business." Meanwhile, across the continent Bill Williams led a group of DC YAFers who passed out flyers explaining the organization's objections to East–West trade.[42] For the next few months the campaign continued to grow slowly.

By November, the campaign against IBM began to spread to other areas of the country. Texas YAF launched pickets outside IBM offices in Austin, Amarillo, Houston, Lubbock, Dallas, Beaumont, Fort Worth, Waco, San Antonio, and Tyler—all cities where colleges or universities with YAF chapters were located. State Chairman Albert Forrester explained the group's position by saying "YAF believes that the way to effectively oppose communism is to enforce sanctions against trade with Communist countries."[43] That same month New York YAF conducted a demonstration outside IBM's Manhattan offices.[44] State Chairman John J. Sainsbury recently recalled an interesting meeting that occurred as a result of the YAF protest.

> While we were walking a picket line at IBM corporate headquarters to protest mainframe computer sales to Communist nations, an IBM person asked who was in charge and said that Tom Watson wanted to see me. (I guess it did not hurt that a number of us were in white shirt, suit and tie). Sure enough, I was led in to icon executive Tom Watson's office to discuss why we were picketing. (IBM'ers of the day were stunned at such access). We had a cordial conversation. In fact, Tom Watson said he respected our example

40. Editorial of February 9, 1967, reprinted in *New Guard*, April 1967, p. 26.

41. "YAF Launches Campaign to Halt IBM's Trade Policies," *Montrose Ledger*, July 13, 1967, as reprinted in Arnold Steinberg, "Information on STOP-IBM Project," in Personal Papers of Herbert A. Philbrick, Box 218, Folder 4, Manuscript Division, Library of Congress, Washington, DC.

42. *New Guard*, September 1967, pp. 20–21.

43. "Students Set to Picket IBM Offices," *Corpus Christi Times*, November 14, 1967.

44. *New Guard*, January 1968, p. 25.

of responsible citizenship. He produced a letter to him from Secretary of State Dean Rusk "encouraging" IBM to sell computers to the Soviet Bloc. He graciously agreed to provide me with a copy of the letter, which I forwarded to the YAF National Office.[45]

Clearly, the Johnson Administration was still committed to its policy of "building bridges" to the Communist world.

In December, pickets appeared at IBM's Pittsburgh and Philadelphia offices. As John Sokol of North Versailles Township YAF observed, "Anything we do to help the Communists is unwise and fallacious in view of the Red threat to conquer the world. Such trade must be stopped or we have sacrificed our young men in Vietnam for nothing."[46] Meanwhile, YAF members Stanley Shlegel and Jim Henderson of the University of Wisconsin YAF hung a replica of an IBM computer in effigy in front of IBM's Madison office. The protesters also carried signs reading "Trade with Communists Does Not Compute . . ." and "Bend, Fold, Spindle, Mutilate East–West Trade."[47] Tennessee YAF joined the effort as Bill Melton, state field representative, announced plans "to mount a massive protest campaign against IBM." He called on the Company to "explain the deplorable and un-American policy of trading with Communist satellites."[48] Under the leadership of Frank Bubb, Missouri YAF picketed IBM's St. Louis offices with signs saying "Keep IBM Out of Communist ICBMs."[49]

YAF ratcheted up its opposition when it launched a full-fledged public relations campaign at an IBM SHARE meeting in Houston from February 26 to March 1, 1968. The SHARE conference was a week-long event for IBM's major clients to make them aware of new products and services available from the company.[50] On Friday February 23rd, David Jones arrived in Houston to direct the STOP-IBM activities and began a series of media interviews, press conferences, and receptions with YAF members. Texas YAF leaders Ron Dear, Albert Forrester, Doug Black, Don Starns, Mike Hancock, and David Hancock coordinated local efforts.

On Monday, fifty pickets appeared outside the Shamrock Hilton Hotel, site of the meeting, while 500 copies of YAF's *IBM World Trade Report* were distributed to attendees. At midnight on both Monday and Thursday, an overnight vigil was held outside the hotel until dawn. The demonstrators displayed flaming torches and a banner reading: "IBM—Stop Trade with Red Nations." As Forrester and Dear reported,

> On Friday, the final day of the demonstration, 100 picketers assembled at the hotel, demonstrated for an hour and then marched en masse down the street to the IBM building where the protest resumed. Due to the strategic location of the IBM building at peak traffic hours, the picket was seen by

45. 2008 YAF Alumni Survey Responses: John J. Sainsbury.

46. "Group Protests Sales to Red Nations," *Pittsburgh Press*, December 27, 1967; "YAF Unit Joins in Anti-Red Move," *McKeesport, PA News*, n.d., in Personal Papers of Herbert A. Philbrick, Box 218, Folder 4, Manuscript Division, Library of Congress, Washington, DC.

47. "6 Students Protest IBM's Red Trade, *Milwaukee Journal*, February 8, 1968.

48. "YAF to Protest IBM Plan to Sell to Red Satellites," *Chattanooga Times*, n.d. in Personal Papers of Herbert A. Philbrick, Box 218, Folder 4, Manuscript Division, Library of Congress, Washington, DC.

49. *New Guard*, April 1968, p. 27.

50. This section relies heavily on Albert Forrester and Ron Dear, Memo to the National Board of Directors, "Special Report: STOP-IBM Campaign at IBM SHARE Meeting, Houston, Texas, February 26–March 1, 1968," in author's possession.

several thousand more people. The output of literature on Friday doubled the amount of any previous day.[51]

While the Houston media gave ample coverage to the protests, the demonstrations received national attention with coverage in *Human Events*. As the conservative weekly reported, "the Lone Star State YAFers threw up picket lines, distributed literature, and maintained all-night vigils protesting trade with the Reds."[52] YAF's presence at the Houston event served as a warm-up for what was planned to be major demonstrations at the upcoming IBM annual stockholder meeting.

Under the heading of "National Campaign Against East–West Trade," YAF sent an informational and fundraising letter to tens of thousands of Americans in March and April. The letter noted that IBM's annual stockholder meeting would be held on April 29 in Boston and asked recipients to send a "STOP IBM" ballot back to YAF before the meeting. David Jones explained, "Our ultimate goal is to cause the Johnson Administration to abandon its entire policy of "building bridges" and instead, to adopt a realistic one of opposition to Communist *aid* in the form of trade."[53]

One recipient of the letter was Arthur C. Nielsen, Chairman of the A.C. Nielsen Company and a long-time YAF supporter. In response, Nielsen wrote to Dick Watson, Chairman of IBM on April 11, 1968 claiming "I'm being bombarded with literature alleging that IBM is supplying computer equipment vital to the military systems of Communist countries such as Hungary, Poland and Bulgaria." He went on to point out that these were countries that with the Soviet Union were supplying over 80% of the war materiel to North Vietnam. Nielsen had a simple solution and urged IBM to eschew business relations with communist countries because "such a change would set a fine example which would undoubtedly be followed by other producers in the free world."[54] There is no record of a response by Watson to Nielsen's letter and suggestion.

The April issue of *New Guard* devoted several pages to a discussion of East–West trade.[55] In that same issue YAF chapters were encouraged to picket IBM offices, especially on the weekend of April 26–29 to show moral support for YAF's STOP-IBM activities at the annual stockholder meeting. Richmond area YAFers, led by Dick Cheatham, picketed in the Virginia state capital while North Carolina YAF did the same at the company's Raleigh offices and Pittsburgh area chapters carried signs outside the IBM offices. At the University of California–Davis, YAF members had a symbolic burning of IBM punch cards. Meanwhile, Arizona YAF chairman Emmett McLoughlin convinced the GOP State Convention to unanimously adopt a resolution opposing East–West trade.[56]

Prior to the IBM stockholder meeting, YAF and IBM worked out an arrangement whereby National Chairman Alan MacKay would be allowed ten minutes to address the meeting and YAF would refrain from picketing the hotel where the

---

51. *Ibid.*
52. "IBM Red Trade," *Human Events*, March 23, 1968 in Hall-Hoag Collection, Box 49–13, Subject HH429, John Hay Library, Brown University, Providence, RI.
53. Personal Papers of Marvin Liebman, Box 37, Hoover Institution, Stanford University, Palo Alto, CA.
54. Copy of letter of April 11, 1968 from Art Nielsen, Sr. to Dick Watson, Personal Papers of William F. Buckley, Jr., Box 57, Sterling Library, Yale University, New Haven, CT.
55. *New Guard*, April 1968, p. 26.
56. *New Guard*, Summer 1968, p. 27.

meeting was being held. He told the 2,000 stockholders attending the meeting, "by trading with the Communist nations we save them from their own economic failures, thus perpetuating regimes that are repressive and form part of a system which, taken as a whole, poses the greatest threat to human freedom in our time."[57] He went on to maintain,

> At a time when our country is at war, North Viet Nam is receiving economic aid from countries with whom IBM is trading. Surely when we are fighting a Communist enemy in Southeast Asia, serious questions can be raised about trading with Communist countries that are aiding our enemy.[58]

MacKay reported that some 50,000 individuals had sent YAF ballots protesting IBM's trade and he had brought them with him to the meeting.

Outside the meeting, YAF distributed "Stockholders' Information Kits" detailing the campaign against East–West trade. Once again, the kits were so official looking that shareholders, and even some IBM employees, carried them into the meeting not realizing that they were prepared by YAF. Don Feder of Boston University YAF was asked by a shareholder how much IBM was paying him to distribute the kits. "I'm being well rewarded," Feder replied.[59] Unfortunately, unlike the Firestone and American Motors campaigns, this one did not succeed as well for YAF. IBM continued to sell its various computers to Eastern European nations, maintaining they were of low capacity and not of significant military value. Nevertheless, YAF did receive ample publicity for its position opposing East–West trade.[60]

The setback with IBM only convinced YAF that a more concerted and focused educational and public relations campaign was needed. To help achieve this, National YAF prepared and distributed an "East–West Trade Information and Action Kit."[61] Moreover, there remained a broad consensus in the organization on this issue. In a spring 1968 poll of YAF members, almost 75% opposed all East–West trade. Among the 25% who favored some trade, nearly all believed it should be in non-strategic goods and with satellite nations, not the Soviet Union.[62]

Two years later in 1970 Ford Motor Company announced that it planned to build a truck factory in the Soviet Union. In a visit to Moscow, Henry Ford, II had indicated that his company was interested in a Soviet proposal to build a truck manufacturing plant near the city of Kazan in eastern Russia.[63] In a memo to YAF leaders, Randal Teague, now the Executive Director of YAF, urged chapters not to commence picketing of Ford dealerships until all preparations for an effective campaign had been made.[64] The proposed plant would produce 150,000 heavy-duty trucks a year, compared to total U.S. production of only 125,000 heavy-duty

---

57. Quoted in letter of April 29, 1968 from Arnold Steinberg, editor, *New Guard*, to William F. Buckley, Jr. in Personal Papers of William F. Buckley, Jr., Box 57, Sterling Library, Yale University, New Haven, CT.

58. "IBM Firm on Trade with Reds," *Human Events*, May 11, 1968, Hall-Hoag Collection, Box 49–13, Subject HH429, John Hay Library, Brown University, Providence, RI.

59. Steinberg to Buckley, *op cit.*

60. In 1970, Watson had talks in Moscow with Soviet officials on possibly establishing some relationship, but told a news conference that such an arrangement was not feasible at that time. He reported that IBM did no business with the Soviet Union and only about $15 million a year with all Eastern European countries, less than one percent of IBM's world market. "Watson Doubtful of Soviet Computer Deal," *New York Times*, October 8, 1970.

61. *New Guard*, Summer 1968, p. 31.

62. *New Guard*, October 1968, p. 3.

63. "Soviet Union: Leadership at the Crossroads," *Time*, May 4, 1970.

64. "The Fords in Russia Deal," memo to YAF Leaders from Randal Teague, April 30, 1970.

trucks in 1969. According to an article in *Human Events,* "If Ford concludes a deal with the Soviets, YAF will almost certainly engage in a massive campaign against the company, though the activist youth organization is holding fire pending an inquiry into the entire matter."[65]

This time YAF had a powerful ally in Defense Secretary Melvin Laird who made known his opposition to Ford assisting in the construction of a Soviet truck plant. Shortly thereafter, Henry Ford, II announced that the company had rejected the Soviet proposal and a letter to that effect was delivered to the Soviet Embassy in Washington, DC.[66] This time, YAF's pickets, petitions, and demonstrations had been kept in reserve and were not needed to achieve their objective.

The Mack Truck Corporation was the next object of YAF's concern when it announced plans in 1971 to build what would be the world's largest truck manu- facturing plant in the Soviet Union, basically a proposal that Ford had turned down the previous year.[67] The organization's protests started in July when Texas YAF learned that the company intended to negotiate with the Soviets for con- structing a heavy-duty diesel truck plant in the Kama River area east of Moscow. State Chairman Jack Gullahorn noted that the vast majority of trucks supplying the North Vietnamese and Viet Cong were Russian built. When approached by Texas YAF, Mack Truck officials said that the organization should devote its time to "more constructive efforts."[68]

Houston YAF began picketing a local Mack Truck dealer on July 8 after local officials refused to meet with YAF. Following up on the local efforts, the national YAF office called on local chapters to become involved in the project and issued a news release announcing the campaign against Mack Truck on July 26th.[69] Soon thereafter, pickets appeared in California, Maryland, Washington, Pennsylvania, and other states. California YAF Executive Director Dick Shirley led picket- ers outside Mack Truck's Los Angeles office while Joseph Gonzales organized Pennsylvania YAF's demonstration at Mack Truck's national headquarters. While Pennsylvania YAF leaders Bob Moffit and Tom Walsh had a lengthy conversation with Zenon C.R. Hansen, the Mack Truck President, he refused to back away from the proposed deal.[70]

On September 15th, President Hansen announced that Mack Truck's letter of intent to build the plant had expired. The three month long campaign had suc- ceeded.[71] Pennsylvania YAF State Chairman Frank Donatelli noted "YAF played the major role in this campaign and pledges to take on any other American company in the future that wishes to trade with the Reds." Hansen was anything but conciliatory in reflecting on the outcome. Speaking to a business group in Portland, Oregon, he declared: "When this started I thought these groups were well-meaning but misinformed and very patriotic. Now I think they like to take patriotic names and work for the detriment of the country."[72] Apparently it was dif- ficult to accept defeat on a billion dollar deal at the hands of a youth organization.

---

65. "YAF Has a Better Idea," *Human Events,* May 2, 1970.
66. Jerry M. Flint, "Soviet Truck Bid Rejected by Ford," *New York Times,* May 15, 1970.
67. Richard Witkin, "Accord Is Signed for Soviet Plant by Mack Trucks," *New York Times,* June 18, 1971.
68. "YAF Combats Mack Truck," *Texas YAF Notes,* July–August 1971.
69. "YAF Attacks Mack Truck Deal to Build Soviet Plant," news release from Dan Joy, YAF Communications Director, Group Research Archives, Box 341, Columbia University, New York, NY.
70. "YAF Moves Against Mack Truck," *New Guard,* September 1971, p. 30.
71. "Mack Truck Drops Plans to Build a Russian Plant, *New York Times,* September 16, 1971.
72. "YAF Helps Stop Construction of Plant in Russia" and "Superpatriots Draw Fire," reprinted news articles in *YAF in the News,* January 1972.

Throughout the 1970s YAF continued its opposition to East–West trade and in 1972 stood against an agreement to sell $750 million worth of U.S. grain to the Soviet Union. This time the opposition centered more on the favorable trade terms proposed for the Russians than on the substance of the goods being shipped. As Steve Mayerhofer, State Chairman of Ohio YAF pointed out,

> There is no reason why the taxpayers of this country should finance this deal . . . If the Soviet Union has enough money to send billions of dollars in military equipment to Vietnam and the Mideast, and to build a military superiority to the U.S. in strategic weapons, then it has enough money to pay cash for this grain.[73]

YAF's position on trade remained consistent from the presidency of John F. Kennedy forward, while both Democrats and Republicans occupied the White House. During the mid-60s to the mid-70s, an essential part of that argument concerned the conflict in Vietnam where the Soviets and their surrogates were supplying the force arrayed against American troops and our allies. It was this linkage between East–West trade and the Vietnam conflict that together reflected the strong anti-communism of YAF as originally expressed in the Sharon Statement. But even after the Vietnam war, the organization maintained its opposition to East–West trade until the demise of the Soviet Union in 1991.

Vietnam: the Early Years

Long before the American public became aware of the scope of the conflict in Southeast Asia, Young Americans for Freedom was taking note of the Communist challenge to the independence of South Vietnam.[74] In late 1961, one writer for *New Guard* favorably reviewed Bernard Fall's *Street Without Joy* and cited his critique of France for failing to invade guerilla sanctuaries in China during the 1954 war. For Allan Ryskind, later an editor at *Human Events*,

> . . . the privileged sanctuary has become the primary factor in the success of revolutionaries around the globe. The rebels in Algeria, for example, have their Tunisia and Morocco; the Angolans have their Congo; and the red guerrillas in Laos and South Viet-Nam their Red China. The Free World will have to learn how to cope with this problem if it hopes to halt guerrilla actions against it by the Communists.[75]

---

73. "YAF Raps Grain Deal with Reds," reprinted news article in *YAF in the News*, Summer 1972.

74. A valuable perspective on YAF's early involvement with the Vietnam issue can be found in John A. Andrew, "Pro-War and Anti-Draft" in Marc Gilbert, editor: *The Vietnam War on Campus: Other Voices* (Westport, CT: Praeger, 2001), pp. 1–19. There are a number of works on domestic opposition to the war, fewer on efforts to support the American position. One very comprehensive source, written from an anti-war perspective, is Tom Wells: *The War Within: America's Battle over Vietnam* (Berkeley: University of California Press, 1994). More limited in its scope and including pro-war efforts is Heineman: *Campus Wars: The Peace Movement at American State Universities in the Vietnam Era*. An interesting set of interviews with both pro- and anti-war activists some thirty years after the fall of South Vietnam can be found in Gurvis: *Where Have All the Flower Children Gone?*

75. Allan Ryskind, "Review of Street Without Joy," *New Guard*, October 1961, p. 18. Bernard Fall: *Street Without Joy—The French Debacle in Indochina* (Harrisburg, PA: Stackpole Books, 1961).

A few months later, Robert Harley, recently returned from a tour of Southeast Asia, stressed the need for continued American involvement in assisting the South Vietnamese defeat the Communist attempt to dominate Indochina.[76] By 1964, one YAF National Director was advocating the United States undertake a coordinated effort to sponsor guerrillas and guerrilla warfare around the globe in opposition to Communist regimes. By seeking out and supporting counter-revolutionaries, the United States could launch a positive freedom offensive against world communism.[77]

The conflict in Vietnam became a major focus of activity for Young Americans for Freedom soon after the Goldwater defeat. On Lincoln's Birthday in 1965, seventy-five members of New York City and Nassau County YAF chapters demonstrated at the United Nations building in support of the United States' involvement in Vietnam. Thomas Fitzgibbon of Jamaica and Alfred Delli Bovi of Astoria YAF organized the demonstration.[78] Howard Whidden, chairman of the Nassau Community College Chapter in 1965, recently remembered marching in support of the Vietnam war and how "YAF helped me develop the political/civic foundation of my life. To this day, Barry Goldwater is still my personal hero." Whidden served as a Vietnamese translator for the Marine Corps from 1967 to 1970 and then spent 31 years in education as history teacher, department head, principal, and university professor while serving for twenty years on his local Board of Education.[79]

Later that month, Washington, DC, Maryland and Virginia area YAF chapters marched in front of the White House "in support of President Johnson's firm policy against North Vietnamese aggression."[80] Similar demonstrations took place in Connecticut, New York, Pennsylvania, and Ohio. Poughkeepsie YAF, Marist College YAF and Vassar YAF joined to form a counter picket to a group of peace marchers in Poughkeepsie while Greater Cleveland YAF members did the same in their city.[81] Meanwhile, Valley State College YAF constructed a "Berlin Wall" at a busy intersection in Encino, California during that city's "freedom week" observance. Cooperating on the project were Mike McCubbins, Chairman of Valley State YAF, John Wurtz of the Pacific Council of YAF, and John Balentine of Panorama City YAF.[82]

During the months of March and April, New York Young Americans for Freedom sponsored a tour of the state by foreign correspondent Charles Wiley.[83] In April, Wiley also debated Professor Howard Zinn at Duke University at a gathering sponsored by the Duke YAF chapter.[84] He would be a frequent speaker on Vietnam and Communism over the next several years before various YAF audiences. Soon thereafter he formed the National Committee for Responsible Patriotism (NCRP), a group that organized a number of pro-Vietnam demonstrations and worked closely with YAF in support of a policy of victory in Vietnam.

---

76. Robert G. Harley, "South Viet Nam: Asian Battleground," *New Guard*, January 1962, pp. 14–15.
77. Richard Derham, "Should Freedom Take the Offensive?" *New Guard*, June 1964, pp. 13–14.
78. "Marchers at U.N. Urge U.S. to Spur Effort in Vietnam," *New York Times*, February 13, 1965.
79. 2008 YAF Alumni Survey Responses: Howard J. Whidden, Jr.
80. Notice of February 27, 1965 rally at Lafayette Park, sponsored by Joel T. Broyhill Chapter of YAF, Group Research Archives, Box 341, Columbia University, New York, NY.
81. "YAF Pickets Support LBJ on Vietnam," *New Guard*, April 1965, p. 22.
82. "Valley State YAF Erects 'Berlin Wall' in California," *New Guard*, April 1965, p. 22.
83. "Foreign Correspondent Wiley Tours New York State YAF Chapters," *New Guard*, April 1965, p. 23.
84. "Duke YAF Polls Campus," *New Guard*, Summer 1967, p. 33.

Even today, in his early 80s, Wiley continues to have an active speaking schedule before civic, veterans, and political groups and remains chairman of the NCRP.[85] As he recently observed, "I have worked with hundreds of YAFers and watched them launch careers and contribute to our country's greatness."[86]

March 1965 was also the time when the Johnson Administration began its escalation of troops in Vietnam. On April 7th, President Johnson delivered a major speech on Vietnam at Johns Hopkins University. He outlined the reasons for a commitment to Vietnam and said the United States would enter unconditional discussions at any time but would continue bombing while the discussions continued. Johnson committed the United States to providing one billion dollars in economic aid to Southeast Asia once the conflict was ended.[87]

The following month, *New Guard* editorialized that "it was a masterful stroke of foreign policy." Despite their differences on trade and domestic issues, YAF was willing to credit Johnson for his policy on Vietnam.

> Conservatives should be more than willing to throw the liberals some words and phrases, such as "negotiations" and "economic aid," as long as we get the action we want. And the fear that the President may change his course tomorrow doesn't change the fact that, as of today, his policy has been exemplary—one that hard anti-communists have been urging for years.[88]

To back up their support, National Chairman Bob Bauman called on the "overwhelming majority of the young people in America who support President Johnson's policy" on Vietnam to "make their support known . . . we must not let it seem for one minute that the small cliques of pacifists, left-wing extremists and beatniks calling for retreat speak for our generation."[89]

Responding to Bauman's call for action, across the country YAF chapters circulated petitions in support of the President's policy and forwarded them to the White House. On May 24, 1965, Carl E. Jaske, chairman of the University of Illinois YAF, wrote the President and enclosed petitions signed by 1,522 persons who supported the Vietnam war. At Michigan State University, YAF worked with others to collect signatures from 15,872 student, faculty, and community members on a petition of support.[90] From the State University of New York at Buffalo came petitions signed by 3,200 students and faculty in support of the war effort.[91] Then in November, the White House received a telegram from Charles Hanson, YAF chairman at the University of Minnesota, with a petition signed by 9,000 students and faculty supporting the war effort.[92] Likewise, on December 16th, Bruce C. Michener, Chairman of Purdue YAF, forwarded a petition with signatures from 2,000 students and faculty at that university. The signatories on the Purdue petition not only backed the Administration's policy but also went on

---

85. Interview with Charles Wiley, November 10, 2008, San Antonio, TX.
86. 2008 YAF Alumni Survey Responses: Charles Wiley.
87. Charles Mohr, "Fight Will Go On; President Says Saigon Must Be Enabled to Shape Own Future," *New York Times*, April 8, 1965. The same issue includes the text of the President's address.
88. "Vietnam: The President's Speech," *New Guard*, May 1965, p. 4.
89. Quoted in Andrew, "Pro-War and Anti-Draft," p. 6.
90. Heineman: *Campus Wars*, p. 133.
91. *Ibid.* p. 163.
92. Several other similar letters and petitions are also on file in White House Central Files, Name File: Alfreda Young, Box 26, Lyndon B. Johnson Presidential Library, University of Texas, Austin, TX.

to support American aid to "any nation endangered by Communist infiltration, subversion or aggression."[93]

At the University of Colorado more than 1,500 students signed a petition to "urge the Administration to stand firm in the face of irresponsible threats of the Communist Chinese." St. Vincent College YAF, led by Chairman William Zeitz, polled students at their small Catholic college and found nearly 80% supporting the President's policies in Vietnam. Meanwhile, on April 24th, some 150 Chicago area YAFers countered a peace march by carrying replicas of black coffins, each representing a captive nation.[94] Even more dramatic statements were made at some schools. Tim Hunter recalls his demonstration at the University of New Mexico where "I burned a Vietcong flag in front of the student union building in 1965 at the request of a U.S. Army Captain serving in combat in Vietnam." Hunter and his YAF chapter also collected thousands of signatures on a petition and he became a columnist for the student newspaper.[95]

On October 16th, Young Americans for Freedom sponsored a "Symposium for Freedom in Vietnam" at the International Inn in Washington, DC. Organized by Alfred Regnery, who had recently become National College Director for YAF, the symposium attracted 1,000 students and ended with a march to the Vietnamese Embassy where American and Vietnamese flags were exchanged. Students came from campuses throughout the East, Midwest and South.[96] As Congresswoman Charlotte Reid of Illinois noted,

> This project was YAF-created, YAF-directed, YAF-sponsored, YAF-financed, and YAF-attended. Its national coordinator was the able Alfred Regnery, a recent graduate of Beloit College in Wisconsin and a recent enlistee for duty in the armed services, who is the College Director of Young Americans for Freedom, Inc.[97]

As he recently commented on his experiences in YAF, "Although I came from conservative roots, it introduced me to politics and how to get things done, how to manage events, people, activities, etc. and helped formulate my life-long political philosophy. One of the most meaningful aspects of my youth."[98] After returning from military duty, Regnery would go on to a career advancing the conservative cause.

Later that same month, YAF's new National Chairman, Tom Charles Huston, appeared on ABC-TV's "Issues and Answers" with Carl Oglesby, President of Students for a Democratic Society. Huston challenged the prevalent assumption that the majority of students were critical of the Administration's efforts at fighting communism.[99] When General Maxwell Taylor spoke at Penn State on November 7th, the local YAF chapter, under the leadership of chairman Dennis

93. Andrew, "Pro-War and Anti-Draft," p. 6.

94. "President Receives Strong YAF Support on Vietnam, Dominican Republic Intervention," *New Guard*, June 1965, p. 20.

95. 2008 YAF Alumni Survey Responses: Tim Hunter.

96. "Youth Support U.S. Effort in Vietnam," *New Guard*, November 1965, p. 20.

97. Reid's comments, along with copies of the speeches presented at the symposium were inserted in the *Congressional Record*, November 2, 1965, Group Research Archives, Box 340, Columbia University, New York, NY.

98. 2008 YAF Alumni Survey Responses: Alfred Regnery.

99. "Youth Support U.S. Effort in Vietnam," *New Guard*, November 1965, p. 20.

Tanner, organized a standing ovation for the General as he came on stage. Penn State YAFers Malcolm Clark, Al Nicolo, Ed Lickley, Tom Bennett and Susan Healy disbursed themselves in a triangle fashion to lead the audience in giving Taylor a positive welcome. Nearly all of the 5,000 in attendance stood and recognized him for his efforts in Vietnam.[100]

The reception for Taylor at Penn State was not atypical at this point in the war. This was a time when YAF could work in support of what they thought was a Johnson Administration policy of seeking victory in Vietnam. One of those Penn State YAF members, Al Nicolo recalled those days recently and their effect on him. "My involvement in YAF gave me a good education in political issues and philosophy." In addition to providing an avenue for his determined anti-communism, the YAF experience "gave me a strong appreciation of capitalism, which led me to read Ayn Rand. I am more of a libertarian conservative or conservative libertarian than a conservative."[101]

Working with College Republicans and some local College Democratic chapters, YAF helped form a National Student Committee for the Defense of Vietnam that circulated and collected petitions on more than three hundred campuses. With nearly 500,000 signatures on the petitions, representatives of the committee met with Vice President Hubert Humphrey in January 1966. While Humphrey was gracious and supportive, it was the reaction of the media that surprised one of the student leaders who made the presentation.

> What took me aback was the hostility from many of the journalists in the room. A few reporters tried to poke holes in the results of our petition campaign, while the *New York Times* reporter implied that we had made up our figures . . . A few made it very clear that they just didn't believe that half a million American college students still supported our soldiers in Vietnam.[102]

In an effort to downplay the scope of the students' accomplishment, one reporter went to the extent of verifying the number of full- and part-time students at American colleges and universities to establish that the number of names on petitions constituted slightly more than ten percent of the total. This calculation included all institutions of higher learning and not solely the three hundred plus campuses where petitions were circulated. Moreover it did not take into consideration the reluctance of many Americans to sign any petition or the difficulty of reaching part-time students. Such efforts only reinforced the image of a left-wing media, attempting to downplay support for a foreign policy initiative undertaken by a Democratic President.[103]

Circulating petitions was not the only project undertaken by YAF members during the fall of 1965. Local chapters also sponsored clothing and food drives for South Vietnamese citizens, mailed Christmas cards to American troops, "adopted" Vietnamese orphans, and undertook other similar projects to show support. Al Zimmerman and Dolores Kuznicki of Queens College YAF collected

---

100. *The Student Conservative*, PSU YAF, November 22, 1965.
101. 2008 YAF Alumni Survey Responses: Alex Nicolo.
102. Thomas W. Pauken: *The Thirty Years War: The Politics of the Sixties Generation* (Ottawa, IL: Jameson Books, 1995), p. 55.
103. E.W. Kenworthy, "477,000 Students Listed as Favoring Policy on Vietnam," *New York Times*, January 7, 1966.

Christmas gifts for G.I.'s in Vietnam while in Chesterton, Indiana YAF members Mrs. Lawrence Magnuson and Mrs. James Chapin heard of the need for soap in South Vietnam and collected 435 bars of soap. Cleveland YAF members James Minarik, Neil Dentzer, and Steve Mayerhofer collected and wrote letters to servicemen in Vietnam.[104] These and other projects developed at the local level were designed not only to show support for the war effort at home but also to provide some meaningful assistance to those engaged in the battle against communism in South Vietnam.

As one young activist not involved in YAF noted, "By this point in the war, conservatives were providing the only real leadership on the campuses for the proposition that we should defend South Vietnam against Communist aggression."[105] After reviewing material from the time, historian Greg Schneider concluded that YAF had become "the most capable and the most vocal of conservative organizations in its denunciation of communism and its support for the U.S. war effort in Southeast Asia."[106] This analysis was supported by other scholars of the period who analyzed both support and opposition to the war by American students.[107]

In early 1965, Tom Charles Huston of Indiana University and David Keene of the University of Wisconsin had created a World Youth Crusade for Freedom to engage anti-communist students from other countries.[108] Once again, Marvin Liebman was called upon to help establish contacts abroad and to help raise the needed funds for its programs. Former Congressman Walter Judd of Minnesota signed a fundraising letter for the new entity and the effort was underway.[109] As its first major activity the group decided to sponsor a series of rallies for freedom in Vietnam during the period from November 1965 to January 1966. Rallies were held in many cities around the world, including Paris, Brussels, Copenhagen, Tokyo, and Seoul.[110] The major events took place in New York City, Philadelphia, and Washington with Ron McCoy, 18-year-old President of Boys' Nation, carrying a "torch of liberty" from the Statue of Liberty to Independence Hall and finally to Constitution Hall. Coordinator for the New York rally was Don Pemberton while John LaMothe orchestrated events in Philadelphia and Al Regnery was responsible for the DC rally.[111]

Other cities holding rallies included Boston, St. Louis, Los Angeles, Cleveland, Houston, and Salt Lake City.[112] At the St. Louis rally more than five thousand people heard from actor James Drury and baseball star Lou Brock as well as local political leaders.[113] The Boston rally, coordinated by Boston College YAF leader Lawrence

104. "More YAF Activities Supporting U.S., Vietnam," *New Guard*, January 1966, p. 23.

105. Pauken: *The Thirty Years War*, p. 55.

106. Schneider: *Cadres for Conservatism*, p. 109.

107. See: Richard E. Peterson, "The Student Left in American Higher Education," *Daedalus*, Winter 1968, pp. 293–294 as well as the Andrew and Heineman works cited in this chapter.

108. An informational brochure on the World Youth Crusade for Freedom can be found in the Personal Papers of Marvin Liebman, Box 108, Hoover Institution, Washington, DC.

109. The letter from Judd can be found in Group Research Archives, Box 343, Columbia University, New York, NY. For the founding of the World Youth Crusade for Freedom and its early activities, see Liebman: *Coming Out Conservative*, pp. 185–187.

110. Kenworthy, "477,000 Students," *New York Times*, January 7, 1966.

111. Lee and Anne Edwards: *You Can Make the Difference*, pp. 124–141 discusses these rallies and the planning involved in detail.

112. Kenworthy, "477,000 Students," *New York Times*, January 7, 1966.

113. Schneider: *Cadres for Conservatism*, p. 97.

Straw, was held in the Massachusetts State Capitol building and was sponsored by the Young Democrats and Young Republicans as well as YAF.[114] January also saw a pro-Vietnam war "teach in" at Princeton University. More than one thousand attended and heard speeches by Charles Wiley and Fr. Daniel Lyons of *Our Sunday Visitor*, a weekly Catholic publication.[115] Meanwhile, National Director and Philadelphia YAF chapter chairman Jay Parker was the speaker at a YAF rally supporting American policy in Vietnam at the University of Maryland.[116]

The following month, the Greater New York Council of YAF organized a demonstration in Union Square Park, Manhattan to show support for the war in Vietnam. Even the Left took notice of the demonstration and the anti-establishment nature of YAF's calls for the defense of freedom. Writer Jack Newfield observed this in an article for the *Village Voice*.

> There was a sharp irony to the event. The rally drew not only the familiar Old Right, but a New Right—a sociological phenomenon not very different from the New Left. Of the some 300 people who attended the rally, about 250 seemed to be either high school or college students. And they also seemed to be sensitive kids rebelling against many of the same things that drive the young activists of the left to rebellion. They are for freedom and against bureaucracy. They believe in the same Jeffersonian ideals as the students who went to Mississippi. They talk about decentralization as if they had read Paul Goodman. They recoil from what they see as the hypocrisy of liberal politicians just as the militant Students for a Democratic Society do.[117]

Indeed, it was this commitment to freedom, not only in the United States but throughout the world, that led many YAFers to rally behind the cause of South Vietnam. But it was also that skepticism about liberal politicians, those who were developing and executing the American strategy for dealing with the Communist aggression in Vietnam, that was leading more and more in YAF to question the Johnson Administration's determination and direction.

Although they had been generally supportive of the President's policy, many in YAF were becoming skeptical of the commitment of the United States to defeating the Communist forces in Vietnam. In a *New Guard* editorial titled "No More Koreas!" YAF called for more intensive bombing of missile sites in North Vietnam and industrial complexes around Hanoi and Haiphong as well as the mining of Haiphong harbor. The editors wrote that there should be no sanctuaries along the Ho Chi Minh trail. Many in YAF were convinced that the Johnson Administration's objective was not victory but negotiations with the North Vietnamese.[118]

YAF activities in support of the American presence in Vietnam, if not the strategy and tactics being employed by the government, continued through the spring semester on college campuses and communities. In the summer of 1966, YAF held

---

114. News article along with December 15, 1965 release from Young Americans for Freedom on the series of rallies can be found in Personal Papers of Herbert A. Philbrick, Box 218, Manuscript Division, Library of Congress, Washington, DC.

115. *New Guard*, February 1966, p. 26.

116. "YAF sponsors Parker Viet talk," *Diamondback*, January 6, 1966, p. 1, reprinted in Tyson: *Courage to put country above color*, p. 47.

117. Jack Newfield, "The Idealistic Charge of the Right Brigade," *Village Voice*, February 10, 1966, reprinted in *New Guard*, March 1966, p. 7.

118. "No More Koreas!" *New Guard*, January 1966, pp. 4–5.

its Student Leadership Conference, during which many of those attending sent a telegram on July 30th to the President reflecting a more critical approach to the situation. The telegram said "The following members of the Young Americans for Freedom attending the YAF Student Leadership Conference at Franklin and Marshall College, Lancaster, Pennsylvania urge you to take immediate action which will win the war in Vietnam and bring our boys home." Attached was a list of ninety-eight names of students with the colleges where they were enrolled.[119] For the first time YAF was linking the issues of success in Vietnam with a recognition of the growing desire to return American soldiers to the United States.

By that fall, YAF had launched a new ad hoc committee, Student Committee for Victory in Vietnam, under the leadership of Michael Thompson. He made clear the outcome sought by the members of his committee.

> By victory we mean the pacification of the Viet Cong, an end to communist terror, the withdrawal of the North Vietnamese invaders from South Vietnam, and the creation of a climate of law and order in which a South Vietnamese government can function.[120]

The creation of the "Victory" committee reflected a shift in the campus environment regarding the war as well as a move by YAF to slowly disassociate itself from the Johnson Administration.

Confronting the Left on Vietnam

Through the early 1960s and up through 1966, on most campuses it was possible for the right and left to maintain cordial relations. On certain issues such as support for free speech on campus or in opposition to the prevailing college policy of "in loco parentis," YAF and left-wing organizations often worked in concert.[121] To a degree, it was the commonality of political activists versus the uninvolved and often uninterested apolitical majority of students. Where the left and right disagreed, serious debate could be pursued without conservative students being called "fascist" or otherwise having their opinions denigrated. For the first part of this divided decade, political debate and discussion on campus normally occurred in a civilized manner. Unfortunately, by the latter part of the decade, all this was to change on most campuses as debate was replaced by confrontation and violence became a tool of the left on campus.[122]

Author and media consultant Don Feder noted his experience as a freshman in the fall of 1966 and the challenges faced by a teenager from a small New York community.

119. White House Central Files, Name File: Alfreda Young, Box 26, Lyndon B. Johnson Presidential Library, University of Texas, Austin, TX.

120. *New Guard*, October 1966, p. 7. See also: "Victory in Vietnam Students Escalate Campus Activities," *New Guard*, February 1967, p. 4.

121. This perspective was shared by Louise Lacey (University of California–Berkeley), Carl Thormeyer (Penn State), and David Keene (University of Wisconsin) in various published recollections as well as the 2008 YAF Alumni Survey Responses.

122. There were exceptions. Raymond Bertrand recalled that in the early 1970s at the State University of New York at Albany "our organization served as an intellectual counterbalance to various left-wing groups with whom we got along rather well surprisingly." 2008 YAF Alumni Survey Responses: Raymond Bertrand.

When I arrived at Boston University in 1966, the Left dominated the campus. The administration was wimpy, letting them have sit-ins and riots during military parades or whenever Dow Chemical came to recruit. So I started a YAF chapter there . . . the YAF took the high road—we were interested in debate and not suppression . . . Being a conservative on campus proved to be a good training ground. I developed a thick hide because I'd gotten used to being an embattled minority.[123]

Feder recently recalled his time in YAF as "Good Times, Hard Work. Great Cause . . . YAF taught me the fundamentals of political organizing. It also honed my writing skills, and gave me combat experience."[124] A graduate of both Boston University and its law school, from 1983 to 2002 he was an editorial writer for the *Boston Herald* and a syndicated columnist. Feder's writings have appeared in numerous publications and he is the author of two books on culture, religion and conservatism.[125]

As the left became more violent, YAF served for some as an oasis of sanity. Mel Davey of the University of Rhode Island recalled, "I was a Vietnam Vet so it was nice to associate with people having acceptance and respect."[126] Another returned Vietnam veteran was Robert Turner. Beginning in March 1968, Turner authored a regular column in *New Guard* called "Vietnam Myths" in an effort to better educate young conservatives on the situation in that country.[127] Committed as he was to education, Turner went on to receive a PhD in history and is currently a Professor of Law at the University of Virginia.

Meanwhile, as the Vietnam protests gained in support and intensity, YAF began attracting more high school and college students on the appeal of patriotism as well as conservative philosophy, a pattern that would intensify as the so-called New Left began to broaden its areas of concern to the takeover of college campuses. Now a County Supervisor in northern Virginia, Eugene Delgaudio grew up in New York City in a political family, describing himself as a "red, white and blue diaper baby." As he recalled, "During the Vietnam protests in the mid-60s, when my brother and I were teenagers, we caused all kinds of mischief, from raising an American flag in Central Park during an anti-war demonstration to hanging an effigy of Ho Chi Minh at a New Mobe gathering of five thousand."[128] The Delgaudio family would produce a number of leaders for YAF during the 1960s, 70s, and even into the 80s. Both Eugene Delgaudio and his brother Richard would serve on the YAF National Board of Directors.

At the beginning of 1967, the YAF chapter chairman at Cornell informed State Chairman John J. Sainsbury that a so-called "National Student Conference on Vietnam" was to be held at Cornell in February. According to Sainsbury, "it was a well underway SDS front operation that had already lined up its own student representatives from colleges around the country; and was working with *Time* to produce a cover story on the overwhelming student opposition to the Vietnam

---

123. Quoted in Gurvis: *Where Have All the Flower Children Gone?*, pp. 72–73.
124. 2008 YAF Alumni Survey Responses: Donald A. Feder.
125. *A Jewish Conservative Looks at Pagan America* (Lafayette, LA: Huntington House Publishers, 1993) and *Who's Afraid of the Religious Right?* (Washington, DC: Regnery Publishing, Inc., 1996).
126. 2008 YAF Alumni Survey Responses: Mel Davey.
127. Quoted in Gurvis, p. 91.
128. Quoted in Gurvis, pp. 76–77.

War."[129] To appear more legitimate, the conference organizers allowed additional student representatives if they were approved by their student council and paid a registration fee. Learning this, Sainsbury contacted YAF members from East Coast campuses and a small group from St. John's, Fordham, Rutgers, and M.I.T. were approved to participate. In the end, only a total of 116 delegates were present, representing a much smaller number of campuses.

The conference began with speeches and panel presentations, almost all made by those opposed to the American presence in Vietnam. Then the conference turned to debate on three proposed resolutions: one for immediate withdrawal, one for withdrawal after negotiations with the Viet Cong, and one supporting military victory. Sainsbury recalled,

> After one of the anti-war proposals was defeated, it became evident this was to be a Student Symposium with a unanimous resolution against the Vietnam War. That would be *Time* cover news! We made a number of parliamentary attempts to get the resolution supporting military victory accepted into the record as the Symposium's "minority report."[130]

When the request for a minority report was voted down, nine delegates walked out with Howard A. Cohen, Rutgers YAF Chairman, calling out "This conference is not representative of American students." Joining Cohen were Sainsbury, Peter Sansosti, Joseph Salvati, and Emil Lugo of St. John's University, Roy Latham of M.I.T. (future Massachusetts YAF State Chairman), James T. Farley (future New York YAF State Chairman and National Director), Kevin Reilly (YAF Chapter Chairman), and Tom Frederick of Fordham.[131] As Cohen explained, "We feel that to rejoin the conference at this time would give de facto recognition to the farce that this conference is in any way representative of the views of the majority of the students of the United States."[132]

The final resolution adopted at the conference accused the United States of using "abhorrent weapons" in following a policy that "has been evil from the outset." As Sainsbury explained at the time, "We have voted with our feet as a last resort to present an opinion in favor of a policy which accepts our commitment to self-determination for South Vietnam."[133] The end result was a failure for the SDS organizers, as *Time* spiked its story since a minority opinion ruined the desired effect. Once again, a few dedicated YAF members had made a difference that affected the way in which the American media portrayed student sentiment on the war in Vietnam.

"1967: The Crucial Year in Vietnam" was the theme of ten seminars sponsored by YAF in April of that year. The day-long gatherings were all held on Catholic campuses but open to all students. The schools ranged from Holy Cross and Boston College in the East to Loyola University and Seattle University on the West Coast.[134]

Although there were many tragedies involved with the war in Vietnam, one

---

129. 2008 YAF Alumni Survey Responses: John J. Sainsbury.
130. *Ibid.*
131. Homer Bigart, "Vietnam Parley Spurs Walkout," *New York Times*, February 19, 1967.
132. Homer Bigart, "Students' Parley Denounces U.S. as 'Aggressor,' But 9 Who Bolt Conference Call It Rigged by Extreme Leftists," *New York Times*, February 20, 1967.
133. *Ibid.*
134. "YAF Sponsors Ten Seminars on Vietnam in April," *New Guard*, April 1967, p. 23.

came dramatically home to YAF in May 1967. Philippa Schuyler, concert pianist and author who was Vietnam correspondent for *New Guard* and other publications, died in a helicopter crash. The helicopter was carrying Schuyler and nine orphans from Hue to Saigon when it crashed. Schuyler, daughter of conservative columnist and editor George Schuyler, was a child prodigy who made her debut with the New York Philharmonic at 14 and died at only 35.[135] Years later, the New York City Board of Education created the Philippa Schuyler Middle School for the Gifted and Talented (I.S. #383) which is one of the very few public middle schools requiring admission by competitive examination.

During the spring semester, local YAF chapters kept up an active program of calling for victory in Vietnam while criticizing the Johnson Administration for not taking the conflict more aggressively to the North.[136] That fall, over five hundred students and faculty attended a YAF rally on Vietnam at the University of Oklahoma. Chapter chairman Barry Fitzgerald said, "considering that we had just five days to organize, the rally was tremendous."[137] Among the high school chapters rallying support for the war by circulating petitions and forwarding them to President Johnson was Aurora Hi-YAF in Illinois, led by chapter chairman Randy Shilts.[138]

While YAF was becoming increasingly critical of the Administration's Vietnam policy, its members were even more critical of left-wing protesters, many of whom wanted the communists to succeed militarily. Thus, Tom Stokes of New York University YAF led one hundred students from NYU, Fordham, and Suffolk Community College to counter a demonstration by left-wing protesters outside a speech by Secretary of State Dean Rusk. YAF might have serious concerns over the policies being implemented by Rusk, but those concerns reflected tactical differences towards a common objective and not a desire to see the United States defeated.[139]

On January 29, 1968, the YAF chapters at Boston University and M.I.T. combined to hold a Victory in Vietnam demonstration outside the Federal Building in Boston while Dr. Benjamin Spock and others were being arraigned for counseling young men to evade the draft.[140] Tom Lamont was chairman of the University of Pennsylvania YAF chapter and then active while in graduate school at Boston University. He remembers, "we were a tiny minority. Philadelphia and Boston were hardly hotbeds of conservatism. But I met some terrific people, some of whom I still see. And I think we made a difference simply by making it known that not everyone opposed the war, or standing up to Communism."[141] Lamont would go on to a career in financial journalism, the last 27 years as editor of the newsletter division of Institutional Investor, Inc.

Meanwhile, YAFers maintained that a little humor never hurt a good protest. When leftist students protested the presence of Dow Chemical recruiters on the Marquette University campus, YAF members took a sheepish approach. According

135. *New Guard*, Summer 1967, p. 32. See also, "Philippa Schuyler—YAF's Correspondent in Vietnam," *New Guard*, January 1967, p. 19. Her only article for the magazine appeared in its February 1967 issue, "Marines Face Ingenious Viet Cong Weapons," pp. 18–19, 24.

136. *Ibid.* pp. 34–35 provides a detailed description of pro-Vietnam activities on these campuses.

137. *New Guard*, January 1968, p. 22.

138. *New Guard*, September 1967, p. 21.

139. *Ibid.* p. 24.

140. *New Guard*, March 1968, p. 22.

141. 2008 YAF Alumni Survey Responses: Tom Lamont.

to Donald Manzullo of Marquette YAF, "a local stockyard provided a gentle lamb whom we named the Lamb of Peace . . . if the leftists insisted on picketing Dow because Dow makes napalm for Vietnam, we set out to picket sheep, since after all sheep provide the wool to make GI's uniforms." Among the signs carried by the YAF demonstrators were "Ban the Bah," and "Sheer Victory Not Sheep."[142] One of several YAF members to be elected to the United States Congress, Manzullo currently represents the 16th congressional district of Illinois. At the University of Oregon, YAF sold hot dogs and hamburgers at a "feast-in" held to counter a "fast" by left-wing groups. Funds raised from the event were donated to a Vietnamese orphans' fund. According to Randy Gragg, YAF chairman, the event was designed to "demonstrate to the public that not all Oregon students share the views of the student-faculty committee against the Vietnam war."[143]

Neil Wallace recalled his introduction to YAF when he entered college.

> I arrived at the Syracuse campus in 1968 and immediately heard only one viewpoint. America was evil, America was imperialistic, America was killing babies on purpose in Vietnam. I went to the student paper and asked to write a column on the war. In the first article I explained that if the U.S. withdrew the killing would continue. If the NVA withdrew the killing would stop. So what did the Left really want—an end to the killing or a Communist regime in Saigon?
>
> As more students told me they liked the article, I decided to form a YAF chapter . . . I led YAF for three years and then turned it over to Ray Meier, who later became a state senator from the Utica area.[144]

Wallace went on to complete law school, had a career as President and Corporate Counsel of Wallace Industries and now holds the same positions with CPM Virginia, a company that develops beneficial uses for coal ash.

On the west coast, Steve Wiley was having similar experiences as a student at the University of Southern California. Unlike the situation at Syracuse, however, there was already a strong YAF presence on the USC campus that facilitated Wiley's involvement in pro-Vietnam activities.

> They were great times—USC during the Vietnam years where we battled the left and the university administration, setting up tables supporting the war (dangerous at times), putting out an underground conservative newspaper (the award winning Free Trojan), our heavy involvement in student politics (I was elected Junior Class President), the debates with Jane Fonda (I debated her twice), the speakers we brought to campus that ticked off the left, and the sense of a shared purpose and friendship among those of us who belonged.[145]

Wiley believes "one of the most important decisions I made was getting involved in YAF and realizing that we need to actually do something if we are to keep the freedoms we have had." That commitment led Wiley to first join the California

---

142. *New Guard*, February 1968, p. 24.
143. *New Guard*, September 1967, p. 21.
144. 2008 YAF Alumni Survey Responses: Neil T. Wallace.
145. 2008 YAF Alumni Survey Responses: Steve Wiley.

military reserve and then transfer to the National Guard where he is now Commander of the small arms training unit at Camp Roberts.[146]

Why Not Victory?

By 1968 it was becoming more apparent to YAF members that the Johnson Administration policies were not viable paths to success in Vietnam. As Bruce Kesler wrote in an article for *New Guard*, it was clear to many in YAF that there was only victory or defeat, a determination to win or withdraw from the conflict. According to Kesler, "the so-called middle path or Johnson policy of gradualism . . . has proven itself to be a failure, both on the battlefield and on the homefront."[147] YAF members were still committed to victory but becoming increasingly critical of the viability of the government's policy. In a spring 1968 survey of YAF members, nearly 90% favored a policy of victory in Vietnam, 5% wanted de-escalation and negotiation, 3% advocated withdrawal, and only 2% supported the present policy. Most significant, however, was the division among those who favored victory. When asked, "if you favor victory but the present policy is continued, would you favor withdrawal?" the response was 50.9% yes and 49.1% no.[148]

1968 was also a year dominated by many other issues and concerns, including the murders of Martin Luther King, Jr. and then Robert F. Kennedy, the various urban riots that engulfed cities across the country, the intensification of New Left protests on campus, the announcement by President Johnson that he would not seek re-election, and the Republican presidential nomination battle that involved California Governor Reagan and New York Governor Rockefeller as well as the eventual nominee and successful candidate, Richard Nixon. Although many YAF members had originally backed Reagan, as the fall campaign proceeded the choice among Nixon, Vice President Hubert Humphrey, and Alabama Governor George Wallace appeared clear. There was hope that Nixon, with a strong record of anti-communism and a pledge that he had a "secret plan" to successfully end the war, might actually produce victory not only for the American troops but for the South Vietnamese who cherished their freedom from Communist domination.

Most YAF members had supported Nixon's election reluctantly, regarding him as the least of three evils. As he assumed office and named individuals to his Administration, the criticism of the new President surfaced. In an editorial in the April 1969 *New Guard*, YAF asked "Is there still hope for Nixon?" and focused mainly on appointments made by the White House rather than specific policy positions. "The conservative movement is now telling President Nixon that the stakes are very high, and if only by joining the President's critics can we secure a greater voice in the Administration, then criticize we shall."[149] While the Paris Peace Talks continued their indefinite effort to gain an agreement between the warring parties, the issue of Vietnam receded somewhat from the focus of YAF's attention. During 1969 there were few mentions of Vietnam in *New Guard* as the organization became more focused on campus unrest and the activities of Students for a Democratic Society and other New Left groups. This focus would shift to Vietnam again, however, as the year came to a close.

---

146. Interview with Steve Wiley, Redondo Beach, CA, October 12, 2008.
147. Bruce Kesler, "Vietnam: What Went Wrong?" *New Guard*, Summer 1968, p. 19.
148. *New Guard*, October 1968, p. 3.
149. "Is There Still Hope for Nixon?" *New Guard*, April 1969, pp. 3–4.

In June, President Nixon met with President Thieu of South Vietnam and announced the first phase of a withdrawal of American troops with 25,000 to be repatriated by August. Thus began the policy shift towards "Vietnamization" of the war. Nevertheless, this change in strategy did not deter the left from its efforts at pushing for total American withdrawal. The Student Mobilization Committee to End the War in Vietnam announced in July that they were planning a nationwide student strike on November 14th.[150] Meanwhile, another organization led by Sam Brown, the Vietnam Moratorium Committee, was organizing protest events on campuses to be held on October 15th.[151]

While the left conducted anti-Vietnam teach-ins and boycotted classes, YAF chapters made their pro-Vietnam positions known. At the University of Minnesota, YAF members held a pro-victory rally and burned a North Vietnamese flag.[152] When students arrived to attend the Moratorium rally outside the University of Maryland library, they were greeted by a YAF banner quoting President Kennedy's support for the battle against aggression in South Vietnam. The YAF chapter also distributed one thousand position papers calling for victory in Vietnam. Meanwhile, at Mount St. Mary's College, students saw "The NLF Wants You" posters appear on campus to reinforce the words of support given to the Moratorium by Hanoi's representative at the Paris Peace Talks.[153] YAF members at Towson State College decided to conduct their own silent protest during the October 15th Moratorium. Eight students, led by John Malagrin and Bob Gutermuth, paraded silently through the anti-war rally at Johns Hopkins University carrying signs supporting the war.[154]

While opposing what they viewed as a "sell out," by the fall of 1969 YAF was becoming more uncertain as to President Nixon's objectives in Vietnam. An editorial in the November 1969 issue of *New Guard* advocated using only volunteer American troops in Vietnam, using the Navy and Air Force to bomb and blockade North Vietnam and to set the American objective as one designed to "end the war—win it—now."[155] Picking up on the editorial's recommendation, Wayne State University YAF, under the leadership of Pete McAlpine, began circulating a petition urging Nixon to replace the soldiers in Vietnam as their tours ended with volunteers while urging the President to work for an end to conscription entirely. As McAlpine explained, "these policies could enable the Nixon Administration to unite America for the duration of the Vietnam War and make possible a victory for freedom in threatened Southeast Asia."[156] The linkage between support for a volunteer military and for victory over communism in Vietnam could not have been made more apparent. For many in YAF, student support for "bringing the troops home" was based largely on the concern that they or their friends might be drafted and required to fight in Vietnam. Take away conscription and much of the opposition to the war would fade away.

A short time later YAF National Advisor and United States Senator John G. Tower released a statement calling for a renewal of a strong military stand and

150. Andrew H. Malcolm, "Nationwide Strike Planned by Students to Protest the War," *New York Times*, July 10, 1969.

151. Robert M. Smith, "Leaders of Moratorium Now Look to November," *New York Times*, October 17, 1969.

152. Heineman: *Put Your Bodies upon the Wheels*, p. 160.

153. Maryland YAF letter of October 17, 1969 addressed to concerned citizens, in author's possession.

154. Valerie Bouge, "And Then, Some Came to Support the Viet War," *Baltimore Sun*, October 16, 1969.

155. *New Guard*, November 1969, pp. 3–4.

156. "Wayne YAF Petitions Seek Volunteer Army," *YAF in the News*, March 1970, p. 1.

emphasizing the need to convince Hanoi of the American resolve for an honorable settlement of the war.[157] Tower's statement received major coverage in YAF's publication as representative of the organization's position on Vietnam. Military victory was not only possible, but necessary, if peace was to be achieved.

November brought about a joint effort by the two leading anti-war forces as the Vietnam Moratorium committee launched protests, teach-ins, and class boycotts on November 13 and 14 while the New Mobilization Committee to end The War in Vietnam held a rally at the Washington Monument on Saturday November 15th. When the rally took place, some 250,000 listened as various speakers called for a rapid withdrawal of all U.S. troops from Vietnam.[158]

Realizing that they could not match the crowd gathered in Washington by the New Mobe, the national office of YAF determined that they would sponsor a series of rallies, "teach-ins" and demonstrations across the country in December. The thrust of the YAF campaign was a simple message: "Tell It to Hanoi," emphasizing that those who wanted peace in Vietnam needed to direct their efforts at the aggressors who had started the war and continued to stymie efforts at a lasting peace agreement.[159] A number of local YAF chapters launched efforts to speak "against a sell-out," such as at Washington State University where the YAF chapter distributed red, white and blue armbands to counter the black armbands distributed by the Moratorium.[160] YAF members also assisted on a "Freedom Rally" held on Veterans' Day at the Washington Monument organized by a committee chaired by entertainer Bob Hope and coordinated by Lee Edwards.[161]

Boston was the site of one of the first and also more successful "Tell It to Hanoi" rallies as the YAF organizers decided to hold it on Sunday December 7th, Pearl Harbor day. The centerpiece of the activities was a rally on Boston Common that was preceded by a candlelight march from the State House and ended with the burning of a Viet Cong flag.[162] David Brudnoy titled his column in *National Review*, "This Time, *Our* Side in Boston Common," in describing the events of December 7th where "four or five thousand were in the field, to stand freezing for two and a half hours." The evening began as "candle-carrying students trooped behind a hundred-piece band and circumambulated the Commons, singing Woody Guthrie's 'This Land is Your Land' and shouting 'To Hell with Ho.'" According to Brudnoy, "Harvard YAFer Doug Cooper gave the evening's most thoughtful speech: 'The war is not hurting us as much as are its critics, who clamor only for material things; we need more than just a higher standard of living; we need a higher standard of character in America.'"[163]

Most YAF activities to counter the New Mobe took place, however on December 13–15. Ron Dear, YAF's Director of State and Regional Services organized "Vietnam Alternative Weekend." According to Dear,

157. "Statement on Vietnam," *New Guard*, November 1969, pp. 8–9.

158. John Herbers, "250,000 War Protesters Stage Peaceful Rally in Washington," *New York Times*, November 16, 1969.

159. "Campus Communique," *Time*, December 19, 1969.

160. Heineman: *Put Your Bodies upon the Wheels*, p. 160.

161. "Nixon Supporters Planning War Rallies," *New York Times*, November 9, 1969.

162. "2,500 back Nixon's Vietnam policy at 'Tell It to Hanoi' rally in Boston," *Boston Globe*, December 8, 1969.

163. David Brudnoy, "This Time, *Our* Side in Boston Common," *National Review*, December 30, 1969, p. 1315. For a critical review of the rally see "Burning for Freedom," *The Nation*, December 22, 1969, p. 686.

On campus after campus, the "sell-out kids" were bombarding their fellow students with speakers, films, demonstrations and literature calling for the immediate pullout from Vietnam. Students were being challenged: aren't you for peace or are you a war-monger? We needed to present the other side and convince students that a sellout in Vietnam would only bring more death and destruction.[164]

Dear assembled a "Tell It to Hanoi" tabloid that was shipped to YAF chapters across the country and distributed on hundreds of campuses.

As YAF National Chairman David Keene explained, Vietnam Alternative Weekend had two purposes, "to promote on college and high school campuses an understanding of the realities of the conflict in Vietnam and to demonstrate to the American people and to Hanoi that the majority of American students do not favor U.S. defeat."[165] The Maryland YAF State Chairman described the organization's position as "we believe that all who desire peace should 'Tell it to Hanoi' since it is the North Vietnamese, and not the United States, who are to blame for this war of aggression against the people of South Vietnam."[166] On more than six hundred campuses across the nation, YAF presented speakers, conducted pro-Vietnam teach-ins, distributed one million copies of the tabloid, and circulated a petition. More than sixty student body presidents signed YAF's petition to "Tell It to Hanoi."[167]

Unfortunately, for some on the left, the right to protest was available only to those who agreed with them. Towson State College YAF decided to hold its Vietnam Alternative Weekend demonstration outside the Baltimore Peace Action Center headquarters. Led by John Malagrin and chapter chairman Cyril Miller, the group marched for an hour while being encircled by "peace center" supporters carrying Viet Cong flags. As the YAF members chanted "Tell It to Hanoi," a leader of the peace center shouted over a bullhorn, "Yes, we want to tell Hanoi, we mourn the passing of their great leader, Ho Chi Minh." When the YAF members attempted to burn a cardboard replica of a Viet Cong flag, it was torn from the hands of Michael Davis. One police officer was pushed to the ground and others grabbed when they went to rescue Davis from the peace supporters. Davis later observed, "You can burn the American flag in this country but you can't burn the National Liberation (Vietcong) flag."[168] Meanwhile, at Purdue University leftists smashed a window and scrawled, "Die fascist pigs!" in the student center offices of Purdue YAF after the chapter distributed copies of the "Tell It to Hanoi" tabloid. As YAF chairman Wayne Johnson noted, "All we are doing is offering an alternative to the surrender in Vietnam which the Vietnam War Moratorium forces are offering. Apparently some people don't want our alternative . . . so the vandalism was plainly an effort to intimidate us, to discourage us."[169]

164. Interview with Ronald B. Dear, July 5, 2008, Houston, TX.
165. "Peace Group to Face Foe," *Hagerstown Morning Herald*, December 8, 1969, p. 1.
166. "Students Plan 'Vietnam Alternative' Activities Here This Weekend," *Prince George's Post*, December 11, 1969, p. 7.
167. Schneider: *Cadres for Conservatism*, p. 122; "YAF Counters December Moratorium," *New Guard*, January 1970, pp. 4–5.
168. "Three Arrested in Scuffle," *Baltimore News American*, December 14, 1969.
169. "YAF 'Tell It to Hanoi' Project Brings Retort: 'Fascist Pigs,'" *Lafayette Journal & Courier* in *YAF in the News*, March 1970.

Other pro-Vietnam efforts also met with violence as YAF attempted to counter the various "peace rallies" conducted in cities and on various campuses. Many, if not most, of these were in reality pro-Communist and pro-North Vietnam rallies rather than simply efforts to end war. When New York YAFers attempted to counter a peace rally in Central Park, they were met by leftists intent on physically silencing them. Richard Delgaudio recalled the situation,

> We came under immediate and very violent attack. We were chased out of the park as the leftist demo ended with 5,000 people chasing our little band of 10—enraged by the sight of our American and South Vietnamese flags, and especially reaching the breaking point when in full view of the entire crowd we announced that we were going to hang Ho Chi Minh in effigy for crimes against the people of Vietnam.
>
> That was the breaking point—that and the fact that all of the TV cameras had switched from aiming and recording their speakers to instead recording our announcement of the pending execution of Ho Chi Minh. Ho was saved that day as 5,000 violent leftist demonstrators attacked to silence us—with "Peace Rally Turns Violent" headline in the New York Daily News the next day.[170]

One more time, the point had been made that the so-called peace activists were intolerant of dissent.

One historian summarized the weekend activities and compared them to previous anti-communist efforts organized by Marvin Liebman.

> Using tactics reminiscent of the Committee of One Million, YAF published newspaper advertisements in college newspapers, opened eight full-time regional campaign offices, and claimed to have collected more than a half-million pro-war signatures on petitions YAF delivered to the North Vietnamese embassy in Paris.[171]

With 1969 coming to a close, Young Americans for Freedom had shown that while they questioned the commitment of the Nixon Administration to victory in Vietnam, much as they had questioned the tactics of the Johnson Administration, they still believed in defeating communist aggression in Southeast Asia and helping to ensure the independence of South Vietnam. Once again, it was a difficult balancing act between support of the goal of defeating Communism in Vietnam and opposition to the administration in Washington on its policies in many other areas. Historian John Andrew noted this conflict: "Founded as an organization determined to launch a conservative crusade against the Establishment, . . . the war had led YAF to defend the Establishment, even when it opposed some of its policies.[172] As the end of the decade approached, YAF would be challenged further on its policy towards Vietnam as well as its approach to the Nixon Administration in general.

---

170. Email to the author from Richard Delgaudio, July 24, 2009.
171. Diamond: *Roads to Dominion*, p. 119.
172. Andrew, "Pro-War and Anti-Draft," p. 16.

Other Anti-Communist Efforts

In addition to its efforts against East–West trade and in favor of the battle against communism in Southeast Asia, Young Americans for Freedom launched a number of other anti-communist efforts throughout the latter half of the decade. YAF chapters sponsored appearances by a number of anti-communist speakers. A number of local chapters also entered anti-communist themed floats in community parades and distributed literature at civic gatherings.[173] The plight of the Cuban people under Castro's communist regime was a recurring concern of many YAF chapters with programs and speakers featuring individuals who had escaped from Cuba.

YAF formed various ad hoc groups during the 1960s, one of which was the Student Committee for a Free China. Its initial chairman, David Keene, explained its purpose "to counteract the pro Red China appeasement drive on American campuses with factual information on the nature and dangers of the Peiping regime."[174] In addition to the Student Committee for Victory in Vietnam and the World Youth Crusade for Freedom discussed previously, by 1968 YAF members had formed the Student Committee for Freedom in Czechoslovakia. The Student Committee on Cold War Education, headed by Randal Teague of American University, was formed in 1966 to encourage state legislatures to enact high school instruction on the nature of communism.[175]

One of the more humorous projects that YAF undertook in 1966 and 1967 was the publication and distribution of two fake issues of *The Worker*, the official publication of the Communist Party of the United States of America (CPUSA). The first issue was distributed outside a national convention of the party in New York City in the spring of 1966 while the second one was released in conjunction with the 50th anniversary of the Russian revolution on November 7, 1967. The first issue went to delegates as they entered the convention and had a front-page welcoming article from Gus Hall telling the delegates, "we have already decided a number of issues for you prior to the convention. We have done this in order to leave your time free for socializing and sleeping during the speeches and reports." Inside a story headlined "New Nazi Threat" turned out to be about former Nazis in high positions in the East German government.[176] The November 1967 issue featured a lead article, "50 Years of Communism," by Gus Hall wherein he proclaimed, "Fifty years of continued suppression of the counterrevolutionaries in the Soviet Union have shown us the way that we will govern as soon as we have gained power in this country." Inside, the editorial was titled "On Phony Issues" and warned its readers that Young Americans for Freedom was distributing this issue and "We, as real Communists, are not at all amused with this new attempt to poke fun at us and our glorious heritage . . . it is regrettable that the forgeries of *The Worker* are actually more readable and appealing than the real newspaper."[177]

---

173. For one example see: "An Anti-Red Float Barred by Parade," *New York Times*, May 31, 1965.
174. News release, "American Student Group to demonstrate at UN in Opposition to Admission of Red China," November 22, 1965, Personal Papers of Marvin Liebman, Box 108, Hoover Institution, Stanford University, Palo Alto, CA. See also: "Students for Free China Report Progress on Campuses," *New Guard*, February 1967, pp. 3–4.
175. "Students Ask Cold War Education," *New Guard*, Summer 1967, p. 4.
176. *New Guard*, July–August 1966, p. 4.
177. A copy of the November issue of *The Worker* distributed by Stanford University YAF on November 7, 1967 is found in Group Research Archives, Box 343, Columbia University, New York, NY.

Some 100,000 copies were distributed on campuses.

Two weeks later, the real Communist Party publication ran an article headlined, "Ultra Right YAF Litters Campuses with Forged Issue of 'Worker.'" At St. John's University in New York, the YAF chapter delayed distribution until November 22nd when a Soviet official was to speak on campus. According to Teresa M. Jordan, "Upon receiving a copy from our chairman, Ambassador Kuzmin was delighted. His reaction turned to one of rage when he realized what it actually was. Distribution of *The Worker* was accompanied by a mass walkout in which members of YAF and the St. John's University Conservative Club participated."[178] An appreciation of satire was never a strong suit of those who adhered to the Communist ideology.

In 1967, a group of prominent anti-communist leaders met with Dave Jones to formulate plans for an innovative way to educate Americans on the human cost of communism. They agreed that a moot trial was an appropriate format to publicize the costs of communism in such areas as freedom of speech, freedom of religion, and national self-determination.[179] The indictment charged Communism with fomenting subversion, promoting slave labor and suppressing free speech and religion. The mock trial began on February 19, 1968 with judge Dr. Richard H. Slemmer presiding in Georgetown University's Hall of Nations.[180] New York lawyer C. Dickerman Williams, a former member of the American Civil Liberties Union Board of Directors, presented the case for the prosecution. Neither the Soviet Embassy nor the Communist Party sent representatives to the trial.[181]

To no one's surprise, when the trial was concluded Communism was found guilty of crimes against humanity. The trial received publicity in several newspapers via news services and YAF purchased a two page advertisement in the March 9, 1968 issue of *Human Events,* featuring photos from the trial and promoting a 24-page booklet, "Highlights of International Communism on Trial."[182] The Soviet news agency Tass described the trial as "an anti-communist farce . . . a ludicrous anti-communist ploy . . . [by] a pro-fascist organization with a notorious reputation."[183] A 30-minute film called "Tyranny," focusing on the trial appeared on a few television stations, was featured at the 1969 YAF National Convention, and was shown at numerous YAF chapter meetings over the next several years.[184]

Czechoslovakia

The Eastern European nation of Czechoslovakia experienced serious change during the latter part of 1967 that resulted in the selection of Alexander Dubcek as the First Secretary of the Communist Party in January 1968. To the surprise of some, Dubcek turned out to be a reformer who thought he could produce

178. *New Guard,* January 1968, pp. 22–25.

179. Background Memorandum, Young Americans for Freedom, Personal Papers of Henry Regnery, Box 80, Hoover Institution, Stanford University, Palo Alto, CA.

180. "Communism to Go on 'Trial,'" *New York Times,* February 19, 1968.

181. "Seoul Aide Says Vietnam Peace Would Set Off War in Thailand," *New York Times,* February 20, 1968.

182. Hall-Hoag Collection, Box 49–12, John Hay Library, Brown University, Providence, RI.

183. Young Americans for Freedom pamphlet on trial, Personal Papers of Walter H. Judd, Box 256, Hoover Institution, Stanford University, Palo Alto, CA.

184. Group Research Archives, Box 342, Columbia University, New York, NY. E-mail to the author from Lee Edwards dated January 16, 2009.

"socialism with a human face" and began a process of liberalization known as the Prague Spring. For the first time since Communist occupation, Western publications were circulated and ideas could be expressed freely.

Two YAF leaders, Dana Rohrabacher and David Keene traveled to Eastern Europe during the late spring and summer of 1968, spending three weeks in Czechoslovakia. As Rohrabacher described the situation he found, "Everyone had great hopes for the future. More freedom was present than in thirty years. I even participated in a student demonstration to recognize Israel."[185] Rohrabacher was able to combine political discussions and entertainment as he brought along his banjo and joined in student gatherings.

> One of the most moving experiences I've ever had was one night on the Wencelas Bridge in Prague, after an evening of singing in the Vltava Student Club. A bunch of us went out to the bridge and we all sang Bob Dylan's "Blowin' in the Wind." I played banjo and sang in English while the Czechs sang in Czech. But we all understood what the song and the night were all about, and we were really together. Some of those kids are in jail now for taking Dylan seriously.[186]

Keene had similar experiences in his meetings while in the country. It was a time when the word freedom was taking on a new meaning as hope overcame despair. As he related on his return to the United States,

> The Czechoslovakian people were demanding things that we Americans take for granted. They were demanding freedom of speech, freedom of the press and the right to travel. They were demanding the right to live as free men; to control their own destiny and to govern their own country. For a short time it appeared that they would win recognition of these basic rights.[187]

But the thaw came to an end as Soviet tanks and troops and those of four other Warsaw Pact countries invaded Czechoslovakia and once again the country was under the thumb of the Soviets.

The Czech crisis spurred nationwide protests by YAF chapters but, of course, the Left in the United States saw this as another opportunity to "blame America first." Two days after the invasion Senator George McGovern of South Dakota charged that the Johnson Administration must bear "a considerable part of the blame" for the Soviet takeover of Czechoslovakia.[188] If only the U.S. government had taken a more positive attitude towards the Soviets they would not have felt threatened by the Prague Spring actions in Czechoslovakia. In support of the Czechs, YAF chapters picketed Federal buildings in Detroit, Atlanta, Honolulu, and Pittsburgh as well as in the Nation's Capital.

---

185. Dana Rohrabacher, "Young Czechoslovakians for Freedom," *New Guard*, October 1968, pp. 9–10. Also of interest in the same issue is Paul A. Mapes, "Youth Under Soviet Communism," pp. 11–15. Mapes, a student at Eastern New Mexico State University, traveled through Czechoslovakia, Poland and the Soviet Union in 1968 while studying abroad and was an officer in the New Mexico YAF state organization.

186. Quoted in Alan W. Bock, "Tripping on Freedom," *Rap*, 1970, Personal Papers of Patrick Dowd, Box 3, Hoover Institution, Stanford University, Palo Alto, CA.

187. David A. Keene, "What Happened to the Bridges We Built?" *New Guard*, October 1968, pp. 6–7.

188. John Herbers, "McGovern Charges U.S. Is Partly to Blame for the Crisis in Czechoslovakia," *New York Times*, August 24, 1968.

Lawrence Reed was a 14-year-old high school student in a small community outside Pittsburgh who was affected by the events in Eastern Europe.

The news of the stirrings of liberty in communist Czechoslovakia dominated the newspapers and television. I cheered as the Czechs boldly rattled their Soviet cage. When Moscow crushed Czech liberties with troops and tanks, I was outraged and eager to say so. Within days, a blurb in the local newspaper mentioned that an organization called Young Americans for Freedom would be holding a rally in Mellon Square in downtown Pittsburgh to protest the invasion. I bought my first bus ticket. We burned a Soviet flag and carried pickets reading "Liberate Czecho-slovakia."[189]

Reed went home from that rally, formed the Beaver Falls High School chapter of YAF and, after his graduation, became Chairman of the Grove City College YAF chapter. After graduate school Reed became an Economics Professor at Northwood University and then for more than twenty years was President of the Mackinac Center for Public Policy. Currently he is President of the Foundation for Economic Education, Irvington-on-Hudson, New York.

Donald Harte had been chairman of his high school YAF chapter in the Bronx for three years and was about to enroll at Adelphi University when the Soviet invasion took place. He was one of several YAF members who demonstrated in front of the Soviet embassy in New York City. As he recently noted, his efforts in YAF "demonstrated that standing for principle, especially in an organized fashion, can do great things, even against the tide."[190] Since 1981, Harte has been a Doctor of Chiropractic in Marin County, California.

After the Soviet invasion, Rohrabacher and Keene formed the Student Committee for Freedom in Czechoslovakia. Soon thereafter Keene stepped aside and James Farley, New York YAF State Chairman, became Co-Chairman. Farley and Rohrabacher traveled to Czechoslovakia in December 1968, spending eighteen days in the country and establishing contact with freedom-seeking students in that Eastern bloc nation now once again totally within the Soviet orbit. Along the way, they contacted Czech refugee groups in Western Europe.[191]

Arriving in Prague just a few months after the invasion by Soviet and Warsaw Pact troops, the results of the action were apparent throughout the city. As Farley recalled recently, "there were still bullet holes in buildings and Russian troops on the streets. One night partying with a group of Czechoslovak students, one of them threw rocks at a Russian jeep. We had to run like hell through some back alleys to get away from them!" Along with some of their Czech student friends, Rohrabacher and Farley laid a wreath in St. Wencelaus Square for those killed in the invasion.[192] While success was a long time coming, nevertheless Farley could look back with some satisfaction on what they had planted in 1968. "When we were in Czechoslovakia, we brought two students back to the United States with us, and a few years later I worked hard to get Ronald Reagan elected. When the Berlin Wall came down in 1989, it made all our efforts worthwhile."[193] Farley continued to

189. 2008 YAF Alumni Survey Responses: Lawrence W. Reed.
190. 2008 YAF Alumni Survey Responses: Donald E. Harte.
191. "American Students Return From 18 Day Rendezvous with Czech Students, Blast Soviet Invasion," news release from California Young Americans for Freedom, January 2, 1969.
192. Email from James Farley to the author, February 6, 2009.
193. Quoted in Gurvis: *Where Have All the Flower Children Gone?*, pp. 78–79.

speak out on the issue of freedom in Eastern Europe and was elected to the YAF National Board at the 1969 YAF National Convention. As he recently recalled those days, he concluded, "I have many fond memories of my years with YAF."[194] Farley was one of many who met a spouse through involvement in the organization.

> I married Johanna Rutan. Been married 39 years this coming December. We met on a picket line at Fordham. In fall of 1966, there was a picket against ROTC presence on the campus. Fordham YAF was all of 3 members strong. We formed a spontaneous counter-picket saying ROTC had a free speech right to be on campus. She joined the line, and Fordham YAF, and was my partner in crime ever since. Often she'd go to class and take notes for me since I was off organizing chapters on new campuses.[195]

After completing his collegiate studies, Farley went on to a career in broadcasting, first with a major network station in New York City and currently as news director for the leading all-news radio station in Washington, DC.

YAF would continue to view Communism as the greatest threat to individual liberty and believe that the United States should stress victory over its ideological and political foe. Over the next few years, however, other challenges would confront the organization both internally and externally. On college campuses across the nation, New Left organizations began to resort to violence and destruction. In many cases, only YAF would stand against this nihilism and represent those students who were attending college to attain an education. While some of this leftist agitation used the Vietnam war as an issue around which to rally student opposition, it was clearly an organizing tactic for these radical organizations whose leadership was promoting not peace, but revolution on campus and in society at large. The story of YAF's struggle against the New Left on campus is one of survival and one that is too seldom told in the histories of the 1960s.

---

194. 2008 YAF Alumni Survey Responses: James Farley, Jr.
195. Email to the author, March 3, 2009.

8. The New Left and Campus Conflict

"It was in the early 1960s that two new student groups, of a type not known since the Depression, made themselves prominent . . . The first of the new groups to enter national politics may be dismissed easily—it was the Young Americans for Freedom, a far-right group that soared swiftly to attention in the Goldwater campaign of 1964, then quickly, unexplainedly, became dormant; it lacked apparently the skill to engage the conscience of the larger masses of fellow students in its goals. More important was the Students for a Democratic Society."[1]

Not the least of the many changes underway during the 1960s was the choice of strategy and tactics by left-wing organizations, especially on America's college campuses.[2] What started as political and philosophical debates on issues of domestic and foreign policy, as well as on overriding ideology and economic systems, degenerated into violence, destruction of property, and denial of individual rights by the end of the decade. Left-wing student activity focused initially on promoting a foreign policy supposedly emphasizing peace and the advocacy of various schools of Marxism, moved on to assisting in the struggle for equal rights by Blacks in the southern United States, shifted to efforts to abolish university policies of "in loco parentis," and then moved to an all-out assault on American society and government. Throughout these developments, Young Americans for Freedom became the major campus organization opposing the excesses of the New Left and defending the rights of students to an education free from disruption and violence.

While the leftists were organizing, the number of activists remained a very small proportion of the total population of students and the left had yet to establish a presence on most campuses.[3] In fact, it was the Goldwater movement, especially in the form of YAF, which attracted more student activists in the early 1960s. On those occasions when SDS and other left-wing groups demonstrated, YAF members were present to counter them and debate them on the issues. This

---

1. Theodore White: *The Making of the President: 1968* (New York: Atheneum Publishers, 1969), pp. 214–215. It is interesting to look back on the observations of prominent journalists concerning campus activities in the 1960s. Earlier writers had made similar claims as to the viability of YAF. White's comments in 1969, the year of the demise of SDS, are especially ironic. This chapter records the efforts of a "dormant" organization in its battles with the supposedly more important SDS, an entity that would effectively die out by the end of the decade while Young Americans for Freedom continued on.

2. While the focus of this chapter is on the response by Young Americans for Freedom to the New Left on campus, it is important to provide some background and context. Nevertheless, the coverage of SDS and other left-wing organizations must be brief. I have relied especially on Heineman: *Put Your Bodies upon the Wheels—Student Revolt in the 1960s*, as well as his *Campus Wars* and Foster and Long, editors: *Protest!—Student Activism in America* for much of the background on campus protests. Also valuable for the early years is Phillip Abbott Luce: *The New Left* (New York: David McKay Co, 1966) from the perspective of one who broke with the left and Kirkpatrick Sale: *SDS* (New York: Random House, 1973), which presents a favorable portrayal of the organization. As mentioned earlier, a number of SDS participants have written works on the 1960s, including Gitlin, Hayden, and Flacks. Few who were active on the right have done so.

3. Many of the early 1960s campus leftists were children of American Marxists of one variety or other. Heineman: *Put Your Bodies upon the Wheels*, pp. 68–72 discusses and lists some of these individuals with their backgrounds. See also, "The Red Diaper Babies Grow Up," *New Guard*, September 1965, pp. 11–12 for further discussion of the leftist involvement of these individuals and their parents.

was still a time when differing views could be expressed and divergent opinions confronted.[4] Moreover, the thrust of the early demonstrations was a focus on a general desire for "peace" or more specific and localized claims of inequality and injustice. As one observer of the times writing in the late 1960s noted, "there was little of the violent criticism of established institutions or the hostility towards the federal government which later came to characterize many protest movements."[5] What protests there were of government action were directed towards state and local governments in the South and their continued segregationist policies or for support of the promotion of peace as a national policy.

Begun in many instances as a protest to seek remedies for perceived grievances—often as mundane as dormitory regulations and the quality of food services—a shift in emphasis was occurring. By the mid-60s, "an increasing number of confrontations were based on the principle that students should govern their own affairs and should participate in making the policies of the institution."[6] This shift to a demand that students determine the rules on campus would lead to many subsequent confrontations and violent incidents.

Those active in Young Americans for Freedom were also concerned about the ability of students to make decisions for themselves and to experience the freedom implicit with becoming adults. As one college administrator commented about YAF's involvement on student issues, "they tend to be quiet in their style, and they have a disposition to work through regular channels." He went on to say, "they share with their peers on the Left an interest in student power, and they have worked hard on some campuses for a higher degree of involvement by students in the decision-making processes of the institution."[7] YAF chapters, in fact, often spoke out against many of the "in loco parentis" policies that restricted the freedom of individual students while defending their right to voluntarily enroll in Reserve Officer Training Corps courses and meet with recruiters from the military and private industries.

Beginning at Berkeley

At the University of California at Berkeley, the issue attracting the attention of students during the 1964–65 academic year was not curfews or dress codes but free speech and the dissemination of political literature. While never vigorously enforced, University administrators had long prohibited the distribution of political literature on campus, believing that allowing such would violate the state's constitutional ban on political activity on government property. This required activists to set up recruitment and literature distribution tables off campus. One popular location was outside the Sather Gate campus entrance. When a graduate student who had been part of the Mississippi Freedom Summer project set up a table one month before the presidential election, campus police attempted to remove him in the belief that he had strayed onto university property. As the officer placed the student in a police car, students gathered, surrounded the car,

---

4. Richard G. Braungart and Margaret M. Braungart, "The Effects of the 1960s Political Generation on Former Left- and Right-Wing Youth Activist Leaders," *Social Problems*, August 1991, p. 300.
5. Frederick Obear, "Student Activism in the Sixties," in Foster and Long, editors, *Protest!*, p. 17.
6. Obear, p. 19.
7. E. Joseph Shoben, Jr., "The Climate of Protest," in *Protest!*, p. 576.

and held them inside for 32 hours, using the roof of the car as a podium to rally support. Thus began the Berkeley Free Speech Movement.

While early support of the principle of free speech spanned the political spectrum, including the Berkeley YAF chapter and its more libertarian members, the consensus soon broke down as the Free Speech Movement became more radical. As two observers noted at the time,

> It was only after the movement had been captured by extreme leftists that all the talk about education factories, student alienation and power structures began to appear. Up until then it hadn't dawned on most of the participants that they were alienated.[8]

Along with Mario Savio and Bettina Aptheker, the leadership of the new group comprised several who had gone to Mississippi that previous summer as well as a coterie of red diaper babies from the Bay area. As one historian noted, "Many Berkeley militants came from affluent, upper-middle class, secular Jewish households. Their fathers were lawyers and academics whose own politics ranged from Democratic to Communist."[9] Richard Wheeler and M.M. Morton maintained that,

> Bay area radicals saw in the FSM a rare chance to establish a South American type enclave at UC by demolishing university authority and minimizing civil authority. Toward these ends they had the tacit support of some influential faculty members, and they were prepared to move just as far as their audacity would carry them—even unto the realm of revolution.[10]

The demonstrations of October were only the beginning and would lead to even more serious disruption as the fall semester approached its Christmas break.

In December 1964, 814 Free Speech Movement activists occupied Sproul Hall on the UC Berkeley campus to protest what they perceived as a repression of their movement. Those involved were not solely the dedicated activists of the left, as the emerging counterculture appeared to attract many to the protest. Some who witnessed the sit-in at Sproul Hall reported that many of the students hardly knew why they were there. As one writer observed, "it seemed as if the pursuit of sex and drugs took precedence over the struggle for free speech."[11] Soon after occupying the building, campus and city police removed the protesters. However, a new tactic had emerged, applying the civil disobedience first learned as volunteers in Mississippi to the demands for change on the American college campus.[12] One university administrator on another campus noted, "By the end of 1964, the students at Berkeley had proved that they had the power to initiate change, and that their direct action techniques would work outside the South. To some the possibilities seemed limitless."[13] Berkeley was the beginning of a major change in tactics that would result in a shift to confrontation and violence.

---

8. Richard S. Wheeler and M.M. Morton, "Rebellion at Berkeley," *New Guard*, September 1965, p. 10. At the time of the Berkeley incidents Wheeler, a YAF member, was the chief editorial writer for the *Oakland Tribune*.

9. Heineman: *Put Your Bodies*, p. 108.

10. Wheeler and Morton, p. 8.

11. Heineman: *Put Your Bodies*, p. 110.

12. A.H. Raskin, "Berkeley, 5 Years Later, Is Radicalized, Reaganized, Mesmerized," *New York Times Magazine*, January 11, 1970.

13. Obear, p. 18.

Up to the mid-1960s, YAF members could debate with SDS and other leftist groups, and even maintain friendships across the political divide, a brotherhood of the politically informed and active among a sea of apolitical students. But the tone of cordiality and intellectual competition began to disintegrate and the opposition from the left became more dogmatic and all encompassing. The New Right and the New Left, while both expressing concern over the quality of education and the rights of students, were moving in quite different directions. YAF National Chairman Tom Charles Huston defined academic freedom as a privilege granted to ensure the exploration of diverse ideas and fields of knowledge, and not a right inherent in the faculty. According to Huston, "academic freedom implies the presence of conflicting points of view, the presence on the faculty of men who disagree and who are likely to open new and different vistas to students. This goes far beyond politics."[14] For Huston, there is a clear distinction to be made between education and indoctrination. The reason for granting academic freedom is to ensure the former and not the latter.

Meanwhile, the left was moving its focus to a new target, one brought to the fore by the Johnson Administration's decision to expand the American involvement in Vietnam. In March 1965, anti-war faculty and SDS leaders at the University of Michigan organized the first "teach-in." Thirty-five other universities soon followed suit. When two speakers attempted to speak in favor of the war at the Berkeley teach-in, the same students who months earlier were protesting as part of the Free Speech Movement booed and harassed them.[15]

Although started as an independent movement on the Berkeley campus, the protests were soon to be coordinated by one major national organization. Begun as the Student League for Industrial Democracy, the organization changed its official name in 1960 to Students for a Democratic Society and was reformulated at its Port Huron conference in 1962. By 1965, SDS had cut all its ties with the League for Industrial Democracy, its original parent organization. The League's mid-60s leadership included Michael Harrington, author of the then popular and controversial book on poverty, *The Other America*. Leaving its anti-communist socialist roots behind, SDS increased its ties with the various Communist and Marxist groups then active, removing bars to Communist Party members.[16] As one former leftist noted, by 1965 "it is now fashionable in Communist circles to belong to both SDS and a Communist organization."[17]

David Keene was a student at the University of Wisconsin at Madison during the mid-1960s and recently noted the change in attitudes among the left. "This was a time of growing foment on campus, but it didn't begin to turn violent until late 1965 and continued as the anti-war movement grew at Wisconsin over the next few years, culminating in a series of student strikes, the bombing of the 'Army Math Research Center' and the killing of a student."[18] Madison became a focus for leftist activity over the next several years. Wisconsin SDS captured the university administration building, heckled Ted Kennedy and tried to prevent him

14. Tom Charles Huston, "Life in the Multiversity," *New Guard*, November 1966, p. 12.

15. Heineman: *Put Your Bodies*, p. 111. For a review of the development of the anti-war movement beginning with the peace advocates of the 1950s up to the fall of Saigon in 1975, see Charles DeBenedetti with Charles Chatfield: *An American Ordeal: The Anti-War Movement of the Vietnam Era* (Syracuse, NY: Syracuse University Press, 1990).

16. "Anatomy of a Revolutionary Movement: Students for a Democratic Society," Report by the Committee on Internal Security, House of Representatives, Washington, DC, October 6, 1970, p. v.

17. Phillip Abbott Luce, "Yes, S.C., There Really Is an SDS," *New Guard*, December 1967, p. 12.

18. 2008 YAF Alumni Survey Responses: David A. Keene.

from speaking on campus. When Lady Bird Johnson planned a visit to Madison, university officials, fearing what SDS might do, would not permit her on campus. The message to one observer was clear: "the Madison left had successfully given notice in 1966 that the right to free speech did not extend to anyone who took Lyndon Johnson's side."[19] What had begun two years earlier as a movement for free speech had degenerated into a campaign to prohibit speech by those with whom they disagreed.

No longer were demonstrations regarded by the left as a means to bring about specific changes on campus or in society. Rather, they were designed to create violent responses by the authorities that, in turn, would serve to radicalize even more students. Carl Oglesby, expressed this outlook when he said,

> The policeman's riot club functions like a magic wand under whose hard caress the banal soul grows vivid and the nameless recover their authenticity—a bestower, this wand of the lost charisma of the modern self—I bleed, therefore I am.[20]

To the leadership of SDS, violence did not beget more violence; it produced more recruits for the cause of overthrowing the dominant, repressive forces in society. It was at that point in time when more and more students, on both the left and the right, realized "the important struggle was not between Moscow and Washington but Orange County and Berkeley."[21] As SDS and other New Left groups became more violent, YAF's appeal as a rallying point for the anti-protester began to take hold. According to Keene, "YAF's growth beyond the hard-core intellectual/activists that made up its membership from 1960–64 began as students reacted to the growth of the activist left as many saw YAF as the main opponent on campus of the SDS and similar groups."[22]

By 1966, YAF began a regular feature in its magazine called "Report on the Left" that informed the organization's members of a wide range of activities undertaken by student and off-campus leftist groups. Quickly dying out among most young conservatives was the view that there could be common cause with the New Left on a shared belief in decentralization and participatory democracy, perspectives that had been presented in the SDS Port Huron Statement. For all the talk about democracy and freedom, SDS had deteriorated in their minds into even more control over individual lives.[23] Any relationship between YAF and SDS had clearly become antagonistic. Barbara Fiala Hollingsworth was a YAF chapter chairman at the University of Illinois—Chicago Circle, the campus where former SDS Weatherman Bill Ayers currently teaches. As she recalled the situation, "There was no one particular event as much as the whole mood of the left at that time was so—shrill is the word. You couldn't talk with a lot of them on any level . . . this really sealed my beliefs even further."[24] According to Hollingsworth, "The SDS and other radical groups were very active in Chicago at the time, so starting a campus YAF chapter was extremely counter cultural. I was also writing for the student newspaper and was the only conservative . . ."[25] That experience led

19. Heineman: *Put Your Bodies*, p. 118–119.
20. *Ibid.* p. 14.
21. Schoenwald, "The Other Counterculture," p. 5.
22. 2008 YAF Alumni Survey Responses: David A. Keene.
23. Luce, "Yes S.C., There Really Is an SDS," *New Guard*, pp. 10, 13.
24. Quoted in Klatch: *A Generation Divided*, p. 108.
25. 2008 YAF Alumni Survey Responses: Barbara Fiala Hollingsworth.

to a career in journalism and Hollingsworth is now local opinion editor for the *Washington Examiner* newspaper.

By the beginning of 1967, it was becoming evident that Students for a Democratic Society had supplanted some of the other leftist youth organizations such as the Student Peace Union, the Communist Party USA's DuBois Clubs, the Young Socialist Alliance, and the Young People's Socialist League. As one participant-observer, Kirkpatrick Sale, noted,

> Though there were radical groups on various isolated campuses, and any number of ad hoc student organizations for single-issue politics, SDS was the only organization with a national presence. Its chapters instigated or participated in most of the campus protests, its strategies and tactics guided virtually every university action.[26]

For the next two years, until its split in 1969, SDS symbolized leftist protest on American college campuses and became, in many ways, synonymous with the New Left.

The Left began to turn its attention to preventing Dow Chemical Company, maker of napalm and many consumer products, from recruiting on college campuses. In the spring of 1967, University of Wisconsin SDS conducted the first sit-in to disrupt Dow recruiting efforts on the Madison campus. On other campuses, protests developed against research projects funded by the U.S. Department of Defense and in opposition to the Reserve Officer Training Corps programs.

1967 saw a long, hot summer of urban riots starting in Newark, spreading to Detroit, and then on to a hundred other cities. SNCC Chairman H. Rap Brown called it a "dress rehearsal for revolution" while SDS President Greg Calvert boasted that, "We are working to build a guerrilla force in an urban environment. We are actively organizing sedition."[27] Although the cities were aflame with destructive actions, mainly by Blacks encouraged by leftist groups, most campuses remained quiet as the majority of students were on summer break.

That fall, the opposition to Dow's recruiting on campus became even more violent. On October 17, 1967, SDS launched its campaign on the University of Wisconsin Madison campus to prevent the company from meeting with students.[28] According to one historian,

> Three hundred SDSers grabbed and choked the students who were trying to get to the interviewers. Campus police officers attempted to rescue them but were beaten back by SDS. At that point the city police arrived. They were immediately hit with bricks and stomped on ... Enraged, the Madison police fought back, injuring 175 SDSers and arresting anyone they could catch ... After the Dow protest, SDS vowed to "destroy" the University of Wisconsin.[29]

David Keene was both a student at the University of Wisconsin and National Vice Chairman of Young Americans for Freedom at the time of the anti-Dow confrontations. From his perspective, "the basic issue, put simply, was whether one group

---

26. Sale: *SDS*, pp. 353–354.
27. Heineman: *Put Your Bodies*, pp. 120, 123.
28. For a detailed retelling of the incidents taking place in Madison as well as a contemporaneous battle in South Vietnam, see David Maraniss: *They Marched into Sunlight—War and Peace, Vietnam and America, October 1967* (New York: Simon & Schuster, 2003).
29. Heineman: *Put Your Bodies*, p. 125.

would be allowed to impose its values and desires on another by force."[30] YAF's magazine claimed that the issue was not Dow Chemical since defense contracts were only a small portion of its sales. If the issue were the war, SDS would be picketing large defense contractors. Rather Dow was only the start to a larger attack on American industry.[31]

Most students did not support the SDS effort to banish Dow from meeting with potential employees. When polled in a campus referendum, nearly 70% of Columbia University students favored open recruiting on campus. At the Massachusetts Institute of Technology, YAF counter-picketed SDS and supported the school's policy of inviting Dow and other firms to interview job applicants. The University of California at Los Angeles YAF chapter printed up posters satirizing SDS with the claim "Join the CAUSE—Committee Against University Student Employment."[32] At Penn State, YAF members Linda Cahill and Laura Wertheimer became reporters for the campus newspaper, *The Daily Collegian*, and started presenting a more balanced view on the campus situation. Under the leadership of Harold Wexler, "YAF also benefited from the influx of hawkish students from Philadelphia and New York City. Many of these students were culturally conservative Jews who viewed SDSers, doves, and Black Power advocates as anti-Semitic fascists."[33]

By the spring of 1968, most YAF leaders were convinced that the organization needed to take a firm stand against SDS. Keene explained YAF's position, making the analogy with Communist speakers,

> If free speech is rejected as a right for all except those approved by the left, we must reject it for them. To put it more plainly, if the left doesn't allow Dow on the campus, why should we allow Herbert Aptheker, and if force may bring about the removal of Dow, why may it not also be used to remove Aptheker and his friends.[34]

Meanwhile, the assassination of Martin Luther King, Jr. on April 4th set off riots in more than 120 cities across the nation and demonstrations on over one hundred college campuses. As these events died down, the focus of attention shifted to New York City and Columbia University.

Columbia and SDS

The first protest actions by SDS at Columbia began in 1965 when the organization obstructed the annual Navy ROTC review. By the spring of 1967, SDS organized a sit-in to protest CIA recruiting and the efforts of the Marine Corps to recruit on campus. These initial moves were viewed as leading to the leftist group's control of the university. John Meyer, soon to be a graduate student at Columbia, maintained that if SDS could succeed, "abolish military recruiting and you take the first step to make the campus a closed society."[35]

---

30. David A. Keene, "Freedom, Force and the University," *New Guard*, March 1968, p. 10.
31. Editorial, *New Guard*, January 1968, p. 3.
32. *Ibid*. p. 4.
33. Heineman: *Campus Wars*, p. 158. Cahill later became editor of *The Daily Collegian*.
34. Keene, "Freedom, Force and the University," *New Guard*, March 1968, p. 12.
35. Sophy Burnham, "Twelve Rebels of the Student Right," *New York Times Magazine*, March 9, 1969.

During the fall of 1967, those in favor of allowing recruiters of all kinds on campus formed the Students for a Free Campus (SFC) and distributed information in advance of an undergraduate referendum on the issue. When the votes were counted, open recruiting was endorsed by 67.6% of the vote. The Columbia SDS chapter continued to oppose recruiting by Dow and the military but began to shift its focus to the university's affiliation with the Institute for Defense Analysis (IDA) and the university's decision to build a new gymnasium in Morningside Park between the Columbia campus and the Harlem neighborhood of Manhattan. These two issues allowed SDS to rally additional support and attack the Columbia University administration as an evil instrument of the "white, racist, capitalist, imperialist, warmongering, power structure of the United States."[36]

It was the spring of 1968 that brought the most dramatic confrontations. On March 27th, SDS launched a demonstration against the IDA by briefly occupying Low Library, in reality not a library but the administration building that included the office of the President. This resulted in six SDS leaders, including chairman Mark Rudd, being placed on probation. Much to the chagrin of the SDS, the incident received little publicity with nary a mention in the *New York Times*. However, it served as a warm-up for a much more serious challenge one month later.

SDS distributed a leaflet on Monday morning April 22nd calling students to a mass rally on the following day at the Sundial outside Low Library. Reading the leaflet, Roger Crossland notified his allies in SFC and printed up a counter-leaflet calling on those opposed to SDS to meet and protect the building from being occupied.[37] Tuesday afternoon, SDS marched toward Low Library where the SFC supporters were seated four deep on the steps, blocking their path. Meyer recalled what happened,

> After a long, tense, but nonviolent confrontation SDS withdrew and moved onto the site of the controversial gym, where SDS enthusiasts tore down an iron fence and had a brush with the police. Frustrated there, SDS returned to the campus and seized Hamilton Hall, a classroom building, and held the Dean of the College, Dean Coleman, a prisoner in his own office.[38]

The number of protesters grew in Hamilton Hall while the administration did nothing. Soon that afternoon, the SDS demonstrators were joined by members of the Student Afro-American Society who, by the next morning, decided to evict SDS from the building. Meyer watched "the bedraggled mass flow out of Hamilton Hall, ooze across the campus, break into Low Library, and disappear therein, all without a single sign of administration awareness, let alone opposition."[39] By Thursday, three more buildings were "liberated" by SDS. At the same time, the Student Afro-American Society members remained in control of Hamilton Hall. Meanwhile, three students crept through the tunnels that link university buildings and found the master fuse box for Hamilton Hall, broke the lock, and turned

36. John C. Meyer, "What Happened at Columbia (and Why)," *New Guard*, September 1968, p. 14. The classic recollection of the Columbia incidents from the perspective of a radical participant is James Simon Kunen: *The Strawberry Statement* (New York: Random House, 1968).

37. SFC flyer, Box 14, folder 8, series 8: Students for a Free Campus, Columbia University Archives, Columbia University, New York, NY.

38. Meyer, p. 15.

39. *Ibid.*

off the power. As one writer later described them, "They were guerrillas of the right, engaged in the war against the radical left."[40] Shortly thereafter, his captors released Dean Coleman.

Meanwhile, opposition to the SDS and Afro-American Society actions was building with the formation of a Majority Coalition comprising Students for a Free Campus, Students for Columbia University, Young Democrats, Young Republicans, Conservative Union and the Committee Against Student Terrorism. In a joint statement, the participating groups made clear, "Despite our differences we stand united on one principle: There shall be no use of coercion, disruption, or blackmail to influence the future of this great academic institution."[41] The new Majority Coalition called for a meeting to discuss their future actions. As the coalition stated in its flyer, "Events are moving fast—don't get left out in the cold. Find out what is happening. Influence what is happening. Are you excluded? You are if you let SDS and SRU speak for you."[42] The Majority Coalition advocated a simple program of no amnesty for those who took over the buildings and support for any positive steps to end the occupation. The group circulated a petition condemning the SDS tactics and obtained 2,600 signatures from concerned students and faculty.

Still other student groups were forming and making demands. Believing that President Grayson Kirk had followed a policy of appeasement and had acquiesced to radical student demands, the Committee for Defense of Property Rights called for Kirk's resignation. In a letter to Kirk, the Committee claimed, "Even more shocking than the guerrilla tactics of the protestors was the fact that you made no effort to protect the property rights of the University." Amidst the smokescreen of the IDA and the Morningside Park site, Kirk had overlooked the fundamental issues at hand. "You have acted as if the issues at Columbia were actually defense projects and gymnasiums. But the hoodlums know, if you do not, that the real choice is force vs. individual rights."[43] Mark Rudd would admit what the committee was noting as to the nature of the conflict only a few months later in a speech that fall before activists at Harvard.

> We manufactured the issues. The Institute for Defense Analysis (I.D.A.) is nothing at Columbia, just three professors. And the gym issue is bull. It doesn't mean anything to anybody. I had never been to the gym site before the demonstrations began. I didn't even know how to get there.[44]

To Rudd and his followers, the issues were immaterial, the radicalization of the student body and the demand for political power were the real motivations for the SDS takeovers of the buildings.

Over the next few days, SDS rejected all attempts at compromise and remained in possession of the campus buildings. By Sunday afternoon the Majority Coalition agreed on a plan to blockade the west side of Low Library where SDS was located,

---

40. Burnham, p. 32.

41. Flyer from Majority Coalition, Box 14, Folder 8, Series 8: Students for a Free Campus, Columbia University Archives, Columbia University, New York, NY.

42. *Ibid.*

43. Box 10, Folder 15, Series 8: Committee for the Defense of Property Rights, Columbia University Archives, Columbia University, New York, NY. Also in the folder is a copy of the letter to President Grayson Kirk dated April 26, 1968 and signed by seven Columbia students.

44. Quoted in Burnham, p. 119 from an article in the *Boston Globe*, October 1, 1968.

given that the administration was totally incapable of removing the SDS protesters and restoring order to the campus. At 5 P.M. that Sunday, the Majority Coalition began its blockade of Low Library. In its flyer, the Majority Coalition called for a silent vigil with non-violent action to cordon off Low Library. Participants were asked to wear coats and ties to show the seriousness of their determination.[45]

The Majority Coalition established a successful blockade that continued overnight and into Monday. At peak moments, seven hundred students could be counted on the line outside Low Library organized by the Coalition.[46] Kurt Rogerson recently retold the story, "We formed a barricade to prevent supplies from being brought in to sustain the occupation, and the NYPD Tactical Patrol Force and motorcycle officers formed a line in front of us to protect us from the occupation sympathizers."[47] Despite various attempts by SDS members to break through and aid their fellow leftists in the building, the blockade remained firm. The next morning, SDS attempted to talk their way in or slip through the lines, sometimes using supportive faculty or clergy as intermediaries, but the Coalition forces remained dominant. The SDS leaders were becoming frustrated and then came the violence. Meyer recalled the incident, "After marching three times around the line, about fifty of them, mostly non-students penetrated the lines by throwing ammonia in the faces of those opposing them. A struggle ensued and the invaders were repulsed before they could enter Low."[48] Monday night the police were called in, the SDS supporters were removed from Low, and the Majority Coalition's 33-hour vigil ended. Rogerson remembered that, "when the bust came, I contacted the police command post and University officials to set up the password of "Freedom" to let advancing police know that we were "friendlies."[49]

Mark Rudd and the other SDS leaders immediately claimed police brutality as they were removed from the administration building they had been occupying. An SDS-called student strike was held and lasted for some four weeks. During the strike the various groups leafleted students almost on a daily basis. On May 6th, the Majority Coalition distributed a lengthy flyer under the heading: "Defend Peace: Defeat SDS!"[50] Around the same time, the Students for a Free Campus asked "Politics or Your Education?" and then on May 11th simply demanded "Abolish SDS."[51] Meanwhile, the Committee for the Defense of Property Rights proclaimed "SDS: Today's Version of Nazi Thugs" in its flyer of May 13th. According to the group, made up primarily of Objectivists, "The announced long-range purpose of the rebels is a collectivist society indistinguishable in principle from the Fascist regimes of the 20th century." Addressing the issue of how to deal with those who had occupied buildings and effectively shut down the university, the committee was adamantly opposed to any amnesty: "If amnesty is granted in any form, society will have given the rebels an engraved invitation to escalate their demands ceaselessly. Amnesty will serve as an explicit sanction for future acts of force and

45. Box 11, Folder 13, Series 8: Majority Coalition, Columbia University Archives, Columbia University, New York, NY.
46. Burnham, p. 32.
47. 2008 YAF Alumni Survey Responses: Kurt Rogerson.
48. Meyer, p. 16.
49. 2008 YAF Alumni Survey Responses: Kurt Rogerson.
50. Box 11, Folder 13, Series 8: Majority Coalition, Columbia University Archives, Columbia University, New York, NY.
51. Box 14, Folder 8, Series 8: Students for a Free Campus, Columbia University Archives, Columbia University, New York, NY.

violence."[52] This position was shared not only by the Majority Coalition and the Students for a Free Campus but also by a majority of the students participating in a student referendum where amnesty was rejected 3,166 to 2,054.[53]

Not willing to allow SDS the victory of shutting down the university, the Majority Coalition pleaded with students, "Do Not Support the SDS Strike— Attend Classes." Students were asked to wear a blue armband to indicate opposition to the SDS and its strike.[54] When the strike began to fade out, SDS decided to take more extreme action. First they occupied a Columbia building, were arrested, but gained little support or attention. On May 21st, SDS again occupied Hamilton Hall and were peaceably removed by the police with 148 students arrested. Then fires broke out in the building and also in Fayerweather Hall, bringing the police back on campus and the resumption of violence. John Meyer recalled, "Numerous attacks on police, both organized and unorganized occurred. I personally saw a mass of hundreds of students charge across the campus and break a police line in front of my dormitory, John Jay Hall."[55] This led the administration to decide to clear the campus entirely, effectively ending the spring semester.

There were several lessons to be learned from the experience at Columbia University, lessons that would be important for YAF over the next few years as it continued to battle SDS and other New Left organizations on campuses across the nation. Meyer believed a successful resistance could be developed when it is broad-based, inclusive, and focused on the specific objective of keeping the campus open and free debate and discussion allowed. What was needed is "the presence of an organized opposition, which could serve as a focus and rallying point for latent anti-SDS feeling." To Meyer "even on a campus as far left as Columbia, the majority of the students are neither ideological liberals nor radicals. They are non-political, usually with vague Liberal leanings."[56] Historian Kenneth Heineman echoed this analysis of the situation when he claimed, "two thirds of Columbia's undergraduates opposed the SDS and Afro-American Society sit-ins and supported the efforts of the Young Americans for Freedom to oust the radicals."[57]

The efforts at Columbia convinced YAF to launch a nationwide program to encourage the creation of Majority Coalitions on campuses. As Meyer had shown, YAF members could work with others on campus to rally opposition to the SDS efforts to close down the university, take over buildings, and deny free speech to those with whom they disagreed. Through effective training and guidance, YAF members could take the lead in such efforts, although the organization itself would not always gain credit for stopping SDS. An additional outgrowth of the Columbia resistance was the decision to use blue armbands, or what soon became blue buttons, as a symbol of peace on campus and opposition to SDS demands. Finally, YAF members learned that they would need to assume leadership in keeping their campus open since unfortunately, in most instances, they could not rely on the university administration and especially not the faculty to do so.

---

52. Box 10, Folder 15, Series 8: Committee for the Defense of Property Rights, Columbia University Archives, Columbia University, New York, NY.
53. Meyer, p. 16.
54. Box 11, Folder 13, Series 8: Majority Coalition, Columbia University Archives, Columbia University, New York, NY.
55. Meyer, p. 17.
56. *Ibid.*
57. Heineman: *Put Your Bodies*, p. 141.

The battle against the Left at Columbia certainly did not end with the spring semester of 1968. Students for a Free Campus continued to leaflet during the fall and expressed its opposition to SDS by declaring "We've Had Enough!" and opposed a Vietnam Moratorium called for October 10th with "No Moratoriums! We Want Classes."[58] Richard Macksoud entered Columbia as a freshman in the fall of 1968 and became involved in YAF. From then on, "I joined the Columbia chapter and found myself meeting with YAFers from all over New York. YAF provided support and confirmation that I was not alone in the world, that others across the country shared my views and in fact disagreed over various kinds of conservatism . . ." Meanwhile, back on the Columbia campus, "we were all moderate non-radicals who saw the university as a producer of problem solvers and not itself the problem solver. Sounds trite now but it was not trite in the early 70s. Fights were fought, lives threatened, and lives changed because of those words." As the semester progressed, "we took turns waving the flag, ignoring the death threats and carrying on."[59] After practicing law in New York City and New Jersey, Macksoud is now an attorney in the quieter confines of another Columbia, a small city in Tennessee.

Then, on January 9, 1969, twelve Columbia students filed suit in New York Supreme Court to remove the Columbia Board of Trustees for breach of contract, contributing to the riots by not taking a firm stand, and depriving the students of the education for which they had paid. Moreover, they sought an injunction "against political discrimination in the hiring of faculty members." Most of the twelve students were YAF members, including Meyer, Vincent Rigdon, Kurt Rogerson, Louis Rossetto, and David Carpenter. Rogerson recalled those times recently,

> I remember how we personally served the legal papers on the University Trustees. Dave Carpenter and I personally served the CEO of Manufacturers Hanover Bank and Frank Hogan, the long serving District Attorney of Manhattan . . . He met with us very graciously at the very same time that the University Trustees were holding a meeting that he was too busy to attend.[60]

While the students realized they had no hope of winning, their goal was to bring pressure on the administration, to better ensure the protection of all students' rights.[61] Just as with the coalitional approach and the use of blue armbands, legal action would become a method employed by YAF members on other campuses in responding to what they viewed as the insensitivity of university administrations to ensuring free access to classes and an education.

The left continued its demonstrations and sit-ins over the next two academic years but a firm base of opposition among the student body had been developed. When a group of radicals calling themselves the December 4 Movement threatened to disrupt classes, their efforts "broke up after a couple of hours with the admission of speakers that they were too weak at the moment to carry out tactics of disturbance."[62] The leftists were demanding that the Trustees of Columbia University put up the more than one million dollars bail for 13 Black Panthers

58. Box 14, Folder 8, Series 8: Students for a Free Campus, Columbia University Archives, Columbia University, New York, NY.
59. 2008 YAF Alumni Survey Responses: Richard M. Macksoud.
60. 2008 YAF Alumni Survey Responses: Kurt Rogerson.
61. Burnham, p. 32.
62. Murray Schumach, "Columbia Rebels Fail in Protest," *New York Times*, March 20, 1970.

accused of conspiracy to blow up public buildings in New York City. Scores of demonstrators prepared to break into the office of Professor Harold Barger, chairman of the Economics department, who had served on the grand jury that indicted the Black Panthers.

> As the radicals gathered outside the door, a Columbia student put himself between them and the door and refused to move. There was some shoving back and forth. A couple of other students joined him. The radicals then walked away. The student later identified himself as Vincent Rigdon, a 19-year-old junior and chairman of the Young Americans for Freedom, a conservative group on the campus.[63]

Rigdon had been one of the twelve students to sue the University one year earlier.

After disruptions caused the cancellation of classes in the spring of 1970, David Carpenter penned his response to those whom he held responsible, the university trustees. From his experiences over the preceding four years Carpenter maintained he had "seen a once-great university become a third-rate political tool for a mob of Viet Cong flag waving animals who trample the rights of anyone who dares to disagree with them." Carpenter had come to Columbia in search of an education and left without any respect for the institution.

> During the last three years I have had my life repeatedly threatened because I chose to stand against the mob and now I'm finished. Gentlemen, I've had enough. I'm throwing in the towel. I have fought for Columbia for the last four years and now I believe that there is nothing left worth fighting for . . . I am leaving Columbia this week to return to my native land, the United States of America, and I only hope its people will take me back.[64]

Carpenter was not alone in feeling as a stranger in a strange land abandoned by those who held responsibility for ensuring that an education was available on campus. As a new decade was about to begin, YAF would place more emphasis on meaningful reform of the university environment with a program called the Movement for Quality Education. But before that could receive their attention, YAF members had to battle the left on other campuses.

Other Campuses, More Conflict

While Columbia was gaining much national attention it was by far not the only campus where SDS and other New Left groups were causing disruptions. At Arizona State University, SDS students occupied the administration building. Michael Sanera was leader of the YAF chapter and noted that they were able to rally opposition forces: "YAF members picketed the building with signs such as 'The Hitler Youth is alive and well in the SDS.' We got a lot of press coverage because the TV cameras were rolling when the state Highway Patrol arrived to arrest the SDS students."[65] For Sanera, "YAF reinforced my views, provided the

---

63. *Ibid.*
64. David B. Carpenter, "To the Trustees of Columbia: Gentlemen, I'm going home," *New Guard*, Summer 1970, p. 10–11.
65. 2008 YAF Alumni Survey Responses: Michael Sanera.

intellectual grounding to support my views and was an avenue for training in political organizing."[66]

At the University of California at Los Angeles, Purdue, and the University of Wisconsin leftist organizations attempted to use the issue of Vietnam as a rallying point. This failed when YAF leaders on the three campuses were instrumental in defeating anti-Vietnam referendums.[67] During the fall of 1968, the Student Peace Union at Purdue University organized a sit-in to disrupt the CIA and other agencies from recruiting on campus. Purdue YAF, under the leadership of Larry Dorsch and Jim Kulas, took the initiative in condemning their action and, on the day before a trustees meeting where the school's policy on recruiters was to be discussed, held an anti-anarchism rally attended by 400 students.[68]

The national YAF office prepared and distributed a new issues paper titled "Student Subversion: The Majority Replies," which was geared specifically to attracting moderate and apolitical students who were finally being activated by their opposition to the leftists' actions.[69] Although there had been internal debates as to the most effective means of opposing the left on campus, with some arguing that only an intellectual and philosophical challenge to left-wing ideology was the appropriate response, YAF was now committed to rallying those students who opposed SDS violence and making direct action against the left a weapon in the organization's arsenal. One writer on the campus scene noted the growing role of YAF in rallying such students.

> By far the most permanent and widespread of the anti-activist groups has been Young Americans for Freedom (YAF), which has chapters on hundreds of college campuses ... YAF is actually the most effective and consistent of the various student groups opposing the New Left on campus.[70]

Indeed, on a growing number of campuses throughout 1968 and beyond, campus chapters of YAF would take the lead in opposing the leftists, sometimes by themselves and at other times in concert with a few other organizations or operating in a Majority Coalition of concerned students.

On many campuses, the presence of reserve officers training programs was the target for SDS and other leftist demonstrators, demanding that ROTC programs be removed from the college program and no credits be allowed for completing ROTC courses. YAF chapters, maintaining that a well-educated military was in the best interest of the nation, vigorously defended these programs. It was YAF that led the campaign for the continued presence of ROTC on the Rutgers–New Brunswick campus when the left tried to shut it down in the spring of 1969.[71] At Northwestern, Robert Ritholz and John Jensen led YAF's efforts in support of Naval ROTC on campus and later rallied students against the student strike.[72] Looking back on those times, Ritholz noted, "I very much enjoyed fighting the

66. *Ibid.*
67. Letter from David R. Jones, Executive Director, YAF. Personal Papers of Jameson Campaigne, Jr., Ottawa, IL.
68. "Purdue YAF Counters Left," *New Guard*, December 1968, p. 24.
69. Young Americans for Freedom, Issues Paper Number 7, Personal Papers of Walter Judd, Box 256, Hoover Institution, Stanford University, Palo Alto, CA.
70. Jacquelyn Estrada, "Putting Out the Fire" in Estrada, editor: *The University Under Siege* (Los Angeles: Nash Publishing Company, 1971).
71. *YAF in the News*, Mid-June 1969.
72. Jack Nusan Porter: *Student Protest and the Technocratic Society—The Case of ROTC* (Chicago: Adams Press, 1973), pp. 65–78.

left by bringing in speakers, distributing literature, getting elected to student government."[73]

Penn State YAF leaders became enraged by the increased militancy of the Left and its threats to close the campus down. They warned University President Eric Walker that they would file suit against the University if disruptions prevented classes from taking place.[74] Under the leadership of Chapter Chairman Doug Cooper, YAF's Student Committee for a Responsible University (SCRU) sent a telegram to Walker in the fall of 1968, "By accepting our tuition, this university has entered into a contract with us ... If the actions of a belligerent minority deny us our rights by interrupting classes, we will bring suit, if necessary to have the university live up to its contractual obligations."[75] The wording was to be used over and over again by other YAF chapters and was incorporated in YAF's Majority Coalition Campus Action Kit.

Indeed, at Penn State it was not an idle threat as in the spring semester of the following year, Penn State YAF decided to take direct legal action. YAF's Laura Wertheimer and two other members, Jack Swisher and Charles Betzko, obtained a court injunction to stop radicals from demonstrating against recruiters on campus. This was the first time one student group had obtained an injunction against another and resulted in President Nixon sending a letter of commendation to Doug Cooper, Penn State YAF's Chairman.[76]

As the Vietnam Moratorium committee attempted to shut down colleges and halt classes, YAF chapters at more and more campuses sought injunctions or issued threats to sue their administrations. Their argument was that the suspension of classes was a breach of contract resulting in the YAF members and others losing the option of attending classes. At Monmouth College, YAF chairman C. William George also sent a similar telegram to college president William G. Van Note, informing him that the YAF members would instigate lawsuits if classes were disrupted.[77] As Sheldon Richman of Temple YAF put it, "We pay our tuition, which entitles us to an education. If Temple should close down as a result of campus disorders, then YAF will not hesitate to bring suit against a negligent administration." The University of Houston YAF issued a similar statement.[78] YAF leaders at Adelphi University, Wayne State, Ohio State, and Wisconsin used this technique effectively to publicize their opposition to the New Left tactics.[79]

Indiana University was one campus where SDS had gained considerable success by playing campus politics. In the mid-60s, the President of the SDS chapter was elected first to the Student Senate and then in 1967 as Student Body President. YAF members were committed to seeing an end to SDS control of student government and brought together a coalition of conservatives and moderates to elect a new, responsible candidate in 1968. Not only did they defeat the SDS candidate for President but also they swept into office their candidates for all campus elected positions. Chief strategist for the winning party was YAF leader R. Emmett Tyrrell, Jr.[80] According to historian Gregory Schneider, "if there was one person who represented YAF's shift to direct action against the Left, it was

73. 2008 YAF Alumni Survey Responses: Robert E.A.P. Ritholz.
74. Heineman: *Campus Wars*, pp. 198, 201.
75. "Disorder at PSU? YAF Will Sue," *New Guard*, December 1968, p. 26.
76. Heineman: *Campus Wars*, pp. 204–205.
77. *New Guard*, February 1969, p. 25.
78. *New Guard*, May 1969, p. 19, 24.
79. Klatch: *A Generation Divided*, p. 222.
80. R. Emmett Tyrrell, Jr., "The Demise of the Politics of Emptiness," *New Guard*, September 1968, pp. 18–19.

Tyrrell. . . . Along with other like-minded conservatives (many of whom were members of YAF), he founded *The Alternative* in the spring of 1968."[81] Tyrrell's independent campus publication shortly thereafter would grow to become a respected national publication, move its offices to suburban Washington, and be renamed *The American Spectator*.[82]

Indiana University YAF, under the leadership of Jim Bopp, was a major force on campus through the 1960s and into the following decade. As Tyrrell noted, however, "You hear a lot about leftists on campus and hardly anything about campus conservatives and yet we are doing a lot of things. It's just that we are working within the system and not trying to tear it down."[83] One of the many successful young conservatives to be part of the YAF effort at Indiana University was John A. "Baron" Von Kannon. Soon after arriving on campus, Von Kannon started working for *The Alternative*, became involved in student politics, and took on more tasks in Young Americans for Freedom.

> By the time I got to college, I was heavily into the YAF . . . It's tough to leave home with a set of beliefs at age eighteen or nineteen and go to a college where people oppose your thinking . . . That's where the community of fellow conservatives came in—we shared common values and the belief that Communism needed to be stopped. I also learned a lot about strategy and communications, how to raise money, how to sell our ideas and institutions.[84]

Von Kannon would serve on the YAF National Board of Directors in the mid 1970s. For Von Kannon, his involvement in YAF "helped nurture a life-long interest in and commitment to conservative principles."[85]

YAF's organized efforts against the Left were not limited to the continental United States. At the University of Hawaii, YAF Chairman Dennis Clarke charged Acting President Robert Hiatt with appeasement of the SDS. When a Marine recruiter was on campus, leftists set a fire with a pile of Marine Corps literature. Rather than taking action against SDS, Hiatt asked the recruiters to leave campus.[86] The following year Clarke's picture would be in newspapers across the country as, with the support of Hawaii conservatives, he and a fellow UH YAF member, Bill Steele, flew to San Francisco to pin a blue button on, and give a Hawaii lei to, Dr. S.I. Hayakawa, the courageous President of San Francisco State College.[87] Under the leadership of Sam Slom, Hawaii YAF was one of the most active and outstanding small state organizations for several years, with high school, community and campus chapters. Slom, who has been a Hawaii State Senator since 1996, recalls those days as "exciting times and lifelong friendships made. Gained experience from YAF meetings, forums, and contact with National leaders and spokesmen." His time in YAF "reaffirmed and expanded conservative knowledge and leadership skills."[88]

---

81. Schneider: *Cadres for Conservatism*, p. 115.
82. Tyrrell discusses his time at Indiana University in *The Conservative Crack-Up*, pp. 43–68. He is one of the individuals featured in Hoeveler.: *Watch on the Right—Conservative Intellectuals in the Reagan Era*, pp. 207–232.
83. *New Guard*, February 1969, p. 25.
84. Quoted in Gurvis: *Where Have All the Flower Children Gone?*, pp. 102–103.
85. 2008 YAF Alumni Survey Responses: John A. Von Kannon.
86. *New Guard*, February 1969, p. 24.
87. "Flower Shower for Hayakawa," *Oakland Tribune* in *YAF in the News*, March 1969.
88. 2008 YAF Alumni Survey Responses: Sam Slom.

When SDS members at UCLA ripped up and stepped on photos from a display on Viet Cong atrocities, the Bruin YAF chapter under chairman Barry Hunt insisted that the school take action. In response, the Board of Review suspended SDS from activity on campus for 15 months.[89] Alan Bock was one of the YAF leaders at UCLA who was convinced that the threat posed by SDS and other leftists was so great that it demanded an alliance of conservatives, moderates and liberals. In a *New Guard* article, Bock appealed to his fellow YAF members to be inclusive in their efforts to battle the leftists on campus. "There are many liberals who are getting genuinely concerned about the violence, division and impending revolution in our country. When they make noises like this, we should welcome them with open arms."[90] What Bock was proposing in 1968 turned out to be the Majority Coalition first instituted by YAF members at Columbia and subsequently adopted as a national strategy for campus action. Bock recalled his time in YAF as what "made me decide (or helped in the process) to devote my life to promoting liberty. Also gave me contacts that led to internship at *Human Events*." That paid off for Bock as he has been editorial writer for the *Orange County Register* since 1980.[91]

YAF was present with counter demonstrators on various occasions when the left tried to rally their supporters and gain media attention. New York YAF was particularly active in countering the left, despite the fear of physical retribution. Richard Delgaudio recently told of one such occasion where only New York's finest prevented leftist attacks on the YAF counter demonstrators.

> I very much recall our YAF state chairman Jim Farley leading us in a counter-demonstration at a leftist rally circa 1968. The left reacted with violence and rage, demanding that we shut up. Only the presence of police in between our lines prevented them from physically attacking us to shut us up. I'd never experienced or even contemplated such a thing—naively thinking that we simply had differences of opinion . . . We didn't seek to silence our opposition. The left did and still does.[92]

Delgaudio recalled another similar incident when the YAFers attempted to counter a "peace rally" in New York's Central Park. For many on the left, peaceful protest was their right, but not the right of others who wished to disagree with their political stands.

By the end of 1968, Young Americans for Freedom had prepared and distributed a Majority Coalition Campus Action Kit designed to help its local campus chapters organize a coordinated campaign against leftist violence and disruptions. As National Chairman Alan MacKay explained, most students wanted their campuses open, "but the revolutionaries exploit the apathy and unawareness of most students. This year, more than ever before, the role of YAF is to mobilize the majority of students to thwart revolutionary plans." According to MacKay, the goal for college YAF leaders was to see the majority of students "organized into non-political Majority Coalition organizations, which have already appeared around the nation under YAF leadership."[93]

89. *New Guard*, October 1968, p. 22.
90. Alan W. Bock, "Conservatives in Crisis," *New Guard*, September 1968, pp. 4–5.
91. 2008 YAF Alumni Survey Responses: Alan W. Bock.
92. Email to the author from Richard A. Delgaudio, July 24, 2009.
93. Alan MacKay, "Majority Coalitions," *New Guard*, March 1969, pp. 24–25.

Satire and Sit-Ins

While YAF members clearly understood the seriousness of the situation on campus, this did not deter them from having a little fun at the expense of SDS. At George Washington University, the Majority Coalition headed by YAF member Mark Rhoads put out a flyer titled "Up Against the Wall—Mother Nature!" and alleged it came from the GWU chapter of the Sandbox Dictatorship Society. This "SDS" complained that their rally on November 7th was thwarted by rain. As the flyer explained, "Inclement weather is a favorite weapon of the military-industrial complex and they do not hesitate to use it when it suits their purposes. What more proof do you need? It is clear that Mother Nature has joined the conspiracy against us!"[94] Rhoads later was elected to the Illinois State Senate, during which time he was one of the founders of the American Legislative Exchange Council.

At the University of California at Berkeley, the YAF chapter decided to make its own demands and in their independent newspaper invited students to join the "right world" liberation front. Led by chapter chairman Dave Van Sciver, Harley Thronson, Michael Grupp, and Frank Morris, they called for the implementation of a College of Conservative Studies "to meet the needs of the intellectually disadvantaged liberal and radical community," and that Right World students be placed on academic senate committees and be given "voting rights, veto rights, and Thursdays off."[95]

Neil Wallace recently recalled some of his experiences as YAF chairman at Syracuse University, using both satire and some of the Left's own tactics to combat them on campus. "We published a spoof of the student paper that had headlines all students would be required to take ROTC next fall semester. I got a huge chuckle out of hearing kids that day claim they weren't coming back to school." On another occasion at Syracuse, "when the protesters took over the administration building and held a fast for peace, we had a counter-demonstration outside—pizza for freedom rally."[96] Similar incidents took place on other campuses. Columbia SDS leader Mark Rudd made a visit to the Rutgers–Newark campus and was greeted by a YAF delegation headed by Ken Brown and Paul Hanke. The YAF members held posters claiming "Rudd Eats Grapes," "Rudd Borrows from Low Library," and "Rid Rutgers of Rudds."[97] When SDS leader Tom Hayden spoke at Villanova University, YAF set up a booth to distribute anti-SDS literature and gave away free grapes so that his audience could chew on something healthy.[98] Needless to say, this was a time when all good leftists were supporting Cesar Chavez and the United Farm Workers boycott of grapes.

More dramatic action was undertaken by New York YAF when it entered the Manhattan offices of the "National Mobilization Committee to End the War in Vietnam" on August 21st and began a "sit-in." Twenty-one members of YAF, led by State Chairman Jim Farley spent the night in the offices. The "Mobe" was the group that planned and coordinated the "massive confrontation" under the direction of Tom Hayden and Rennie Davis during the 1968 Democratic National

---

94. "Up Against the Wall—Mother Nature!," *New Guard*, December 1968, p. 25.
95. "UC-Berkeley YAF's 'Non-Negotiable' Demands," *New Guard*, Summer 1969, p. 32.
96. 2008 YAF Alumni Survey Responses: Neil Wallace.
97. *New Guard*, February 1969, p. 21.
98. *New Guard*, May 1969, p. 24.

Convention in Chicago. Callers to the Mobe office were told "this headquarters is now under the control of the National Committee for Freedom in Vietnam."[99] The YAF occupiers left peacefully the next morning after raising a South Vietnamese flag from the committee's offices.

Less than three months later, ten members of YAF seized the "SDS communiqué center" in Greenwich Village. At 9:00 A.M. on Election Day, Jim Farley, Ron Docksai, and Greg Bradley entered the SDS offices and informed the lone staff person present "YAF is hereby liberating this office." The three YAFers were then joined by seven more, including John Meyer of Columbia's Students for a Free Campus. That morning other YAF members hand-delivered news releases to five daily newspapers and seven other major media outlets in New York City. Farley, Bradley, and Docksai all gave interviews to radio stations and by 11:00 A.M. four television crews, six radio news broadcasters and several newspaper reporters showed up at the offices.[100] Farley told the media that the date and location had been chosen because YAF had learned that anti-election protests were to be coordinated out of the center.[101]

Bradley, who was a student at St. Francis College and Executive Director of New York YAF at the time, reported he "received two threatening phone calls from the Black Panthers," resulting in a call to the police who soon arrived. Although he went on to obtain a M.B.A. degree, Bradley recently commented, "I've always felt that I learned more from my involvement with YAF and conservative politics than I learned in college."[102]

It was not until 11:15 when the pastor of the Washington Square Methodist Church, whose space was being used by the SDS to organize anti-election activities, finally asked the police to remove the YAF members. As Docksai indicated, "Jim Farley and I made it clear to reporters that we consider demonstrations against private or public property wrong; and once we were asked to leave by the police (which took nearly three hours) we did so."[103] Once again, the YAFers had made their point in a dramatic and newsworthy fashion.

Ten days later, not to be left out of the fun, twenty-two members of YAF from Boston College, Boston University and Boston State College occupied the Resistance headquarters in Boston. YAF State Chairman Don Feder proclaimed that YAF was liberating the office in the name of the free peoples of South Vietnam and had no intention of staying long because they respected property rights.[104] Eight Resistance members still in the office protested the occupation and tried to contact the Black Panthers for backup support. One hour after first arriving, the YAF members marched out carrying the flags of South Vietnam and the United States while calling for victory in Vietnam.

Three months later, a dozen students from the Student Coalition at Queens College occupied the campus newspaper office in protest of the paper's condoning violence by a group of student protesters. On five occasions in January, leftist protesters ransacked various college offices without police intervention or disciplinary action. Joseph Paladino, leader of the Student Coalition, said, "the

99. *New Guard*, October 1968, p. 22.

100. "New York YAF Liberates SDS Office," *New Guard*, December 1968, p. 25.

101. Sylvan Fox, "Scores of Youths Seized in Anti-Election Protests Across the Nation," *New York Times*, November 6, 1968.

102. 2008 YAF Alumni Survey Responses: Gregory R. Bradley.

103. Docksai letter to Arnold Steinberg dated November 6, 1968. Personal Papers of William F. Buckley, Jr., Box 57, Folder: YAF, Sterling Library, Yale University, New Haven, CT.

104. "Massachusetts YAF Liberates Resistance Office," *New Guard*, January 1969, p. 22.

disruptions will continue until the administration decides to do something to stop the violence." Paladino charged College President Joseph McMurray with having "constantly groveled at the feet of a small group of radical students, rather than assert leadership or responsibility."[105] Meanwhile, at Syracuse University, the YAF chapter under the leadership of Neil Wallace, found a way to stop further leftist disruptions. "After several building takeovers by the Left, I got a few kids together and we took over their student government building. David Ifshin was the president at the time. We held a building all day and made national news. There were no more takeovers."[106] Such radical actions as the takeover and disruption of buildings were rare and dramatic moves by YAF members at a time of prevalent violence on American campuses and proved to be the exception to the rule of more orderly protests.

Building on its success with the phony issues of *The Worker*, in the spring of 1969, YAF distributed 100,000 copies of "New Left News" on one hundred college campuses. The four page tabloid was a satire of the SDS "New Left Notes" and featured a report by Mark Crudd and spoke of SDS efforts against Girl Scout recruiters. However, by the time the fake issues were distributed, Students for a Democratic Society was already in the throws of disintegration.[107]

Violence and Threats of Violence

Spring semester 1969 saw an intensification of the violence and destruction on and off American campuses. During the first six months there were protests on 232 campuses with 20% of them involving bombings, arson, and property destruction. Perhaps one of the most dramatic and tragic of all was the burning of the Bank of America branch, viewed as "a symbol of imperialist finance capitalism," and the bombing of the faculty club at the University of California at Santa Barbara, resulting in the death of the club's janitor.[108]

San Francisco State College was the site of the longest student strike, lasting 134 days from November 1968 to March 1969. Each day, protesting students would gather at noon and march to the administration building where they protested outside the offices of President S.I. Hayakawa who became a national symbol of resistance to the student left. When Mark Seidenberg, YAF chairman, attempted to attend a meeting of the Third World Liberation Front, main supporters of the strike, he was attacked and kicked repeatedly in the head. Seidenberg was rushed to a nearby hospital where he was treated for body bruises and had a cast placed on his injured arm.[109] Seidenberg was not alone. At the University of Wisconsin, YAF chairman Charles Yanke was threatened with being beaten up if he continued to take part in counterdemonstrations on that campus. According to Yanke, "We take these things to the police and they send us to Protection and Security on the campus. Protection and Security sends us to the police. We just go back and forth."[110]

---

105. "Conservative Students Ransack Office of Queens College Paper," *New York Times*, February 19, 1969.

106. 2008 YAF Alumni Survey Responses: Neil Wallace.

107. "YAF Publishes 'New Left News,'" *New Guard*, Summer 1969, p. 23.

108. Heineman: *Put Your Bodies*, pp. 153–154.

109. "Campus Rebel Beats SF State Student Leader," *Fresno Bee* in *YAF in the News*, Mid-June, 1969.

110. "Moderate Students Tell Their Side of the Campus Uproar," *U.S. News & World Report*, March 10, 1969, p. 74.

Arnold Steinberg, who at the time was a student at George Washington University, dramatically describes the intensity of the feelings of radical leftists.

> I debated one of the people blown up in that townhouse—Cathy Wilkerson, SDS/Weatherman faction, daughter of a wealthy Republican ad executive. When I debated her—at the University of Maryland, I think—one of her fellow leftists offered me a ride back into D.C. (I was editor of *The New Guard* then, age 19). She was so upset that she took me aside and said something like, "I hate you. I hate what you stand for. I don't want to be in the same car with you. If I had the opportunity, I would KILL you.[111]

Dan Arico, a student at Duquesne University in Pittsburgh, had some chilling experiences himself as he recalled several years later, "I remember the death threats from the SDS crowd."[112] Richard Delgaudio remembered seeing a message, "Kill the Pigs!" scrawled in red letters across from the New York YAF office and assumed it was from the Weather Underground active in Manhattan.[113]

Perhaps not quite as dangerous but still very frightening was the experience of Roy Nirschel of Southern Connecticut State College when he found an effigy of himself being burned outside his dormitory. Nevertheless, Nirschel recalled his involvement in YAF as providing him with communication and leadership skills, independence and intellectual development, as "an important marker in my life and made me 'stand out.'"[114] Nirschel is one of several YAF alumni who devoted themselves to a career educating young people. He went on to obtain a PhD in Higher Education Administration and is currently President of Roger Williams University in Rhode Island.[115]

When the SDS attempted to disrupt the annual ROTC awards ceremony at Ohio State University, YAF members physically blocked several attempts by SDS to storm the front door of the auditorium. As one article noted, "SDS chants of 'Ho, Ho. Ho Chi Minh, the NLF is going to win' and 'Fuck ROTC,' were drowned out by YAF-led chants of 'Go Home, SDS,' 'Up with America,' and 'Neo-Nazi SDS.' . . . The confrontation with the police that SDS had hoped for was avoided as fellow students had the situation in hand."[116] Tom DeWeese was a student at Ohio State University and was one of the YAF members to thwart the SDS attempt to disrupt ROTC graduation exercises on campus. Recently he recalled those experiences.

> In the spring of 1969, I found myself standing in front of the ROTC building on the Ohio State University campus. Inside, graduation exercises were taking place. Also, just inside the front door, was a group of grim-looking police officers, dressed in full riot gear.

111. Email from Arnold Steinberg, January 16, 2009. Wilkerson, whose father owned the townhouse, was not killed in the blast when SDS members were making bombs. She and Kathy Boudin escaped from the rubble and went underground until 1980. Three Weather Underground members were not as lucky and died in the explosion: Diana Oughton, Terry Robbins, and Theodore Gold. Just before the blast, Robbins had successfully bombed the home of the judge presiding over the murder trial of 21 Black Panthers in New Haven. Mel Gussow, "The House on West 11th Street," *New York Times*, March 5, 2000; Heineman: *Put Your Bodies*, p. 173.

112. 2008 YAF Alumni Survey Responses: Dan Arico.

113. Email from Richard Delgaudio, January 16, 2009.

114. Roy Nirschel, "A Summer in Free Asia," *New Guard*, March 1973, pp. 12–13.

115. 2008 YAF Alumni Survey Responses: Roy J. Nirschel.

116. *Congressional Record* insert of June 4, 1969 by Representative Sam Devine, Group Research Archives, Box 340, Columbia University, New York, NY.

Outside with me, wearing no such equipment, was a rag-tag band of about one hundred students. Most, like me, were members of Young Americans for Freedom (YAF) ... We were there because the violent Students for a Democratic Society (SDS) had vowed to disrupt and stop the ROTC graduation exercises. My colleagues and I had vowed they would never get inside.

And so there we stood, barehanded, as the SDS, led by the soon-to-be Weatherman terrorist, Bernadine Dohrn, came over the hill, several hundred strong, Viet Cong flag flying. They charged, throwing rocks, bottles and eggs. Hand-to-hand combat ensued. We drove them back. The cops never had to get into the battle.

That's how I spent my early days in the political arena; locked in a titanic battle against those who sought to destroy the very core of the nation I loved.[117]

As DeWeese added, "I remember my heart pounding as they came over the hill with their Viet Cong flags flying. But we felt so cool after we survived it." Forty years after that incident at Ohio State University, DeWeese observed, "YAF set the course for my life and changed it forever. To this day I think of myself first and foremost a YAFer."[118]

On other campuses YAF leaders also stood against the senseless violence and destruction that was being brought about and also preventing students from receiving their education. At the University of Maryland, YAF joined a group of veterans in blocking the entrance to the computer science building so that leftists, who were protesting government contracts and alleged war research, could not enter. The YAF members found a more supportive administration on the College Park campus as Warren Parker, YAF chairman, reported "two or three deans have expressed support for YAF confidentially while maintaining impartiality in their public roles." As one dean at the university told a reporter, "I'm very glad to see the other side being presented. These boys helped us get through the spring in peace, despite all the dire projections."[119] The YAF chapter also established its own newspaper, *The Alternative*, which was distributed on the College Park campus and eventually on a number of Baltimore area campuses.[120]

At Towson State University in the Baltimore suburbs, not only was *The Alternative* distributed but also the YAF chapter started its own campus newsletter, "Freedom Press." Tom Bodrogi was editor of the YAF publication and maintains his involvement in YAF made him a "lifelong conservative—influenced my son and daughter to hold conservative views and not be influenced by liberal ideology in college."[121] Another Towson YAF chapter chairman, Wes McDonald, went on to an academic career and is Professor of Political Science at Elizabethtown College.

An additional campus where YAF found a receptive administration was at the University of Notre Dame. The YAF chapter commended the Reverend Theodore Hesburgh, president, for his hard line stand against demonstrations that disrupt school activities. As the YAF members said, "We hope that university presidents

---

117. E-mail from Tom DeWeese to the author, February 18, 2009.
118. 2008 YAF Alumni Survey Responses: Tom DeWeese.
119. Robert Pear, "Campus Conservatives Launch 'Offensive' Aimed at New Left," *Montgomery County Sentinel*, July 19, 1969.
120. Cissy Finley, "YAF Members Compete," *Washington Star*, March 30, 1969; "New Newspaper on U. of M. Scene," *Baltimore Sun*, July 27, 1969.
121. 2008 YAF Alumni Survey Responses: Thomas I. Bodrogi.

throughout the nation will follow this example by likewise condemning those who are inconsistent with the concepts of our free society."[122] Queensborough Community College saw a three-week long sit-in turn into an occupation of administrative offices for three hours and when the students refused to leave, President Kurt Schmeller called the police and said he would sign a complaint against the occupiers. As the media reported the events,

> While students sympathetic to the take-over were congregating outside a barred door on the third-floor level, other students—members of the Young Americans for Freedom, which opposed the seizure—gathered nearby. "The students who have taken over the building don't represent the feeling of the majority of the students on the campus," said one student wearing a blue button to identify him with the Young Americans for Freedom.[123]

When the police arrived, they lined up between the protesters and the YAFers to avoid any confrontation between the two groups of students.

The incidents at Queensborough brought home to the YAFers that they could be more effective if they coordinated their efforts in the New York metropolitan area. To this end, Jim Farley, NY YAF Chairman, brought together a coalition of YAF chapters from Columbia and St. John's universities and Marist, Pace, Brooklyn, Kings, Adelphi and Queens colleges to support their fellow YAF members whenever a problem developed. When leftists attempted to hold an anti-ROTC rally at St. John's, YAF members from the various campuses gathered, distributed blue armbands and formed a brigade to defend the gym from a takeover.[124] Meanwhile in Iowa, Iowa State University YAF under Dick Bjornseth and the University of Iowa led by Clete Uhlenhopp coordinated efforts to protest the sponsorship of radical speakers on campus using state funds. At the University of Arkansas, Steven Beck and Marc Knott led the YAF chapter in a petition drive calling for "reason, rather than disruption, as a means for change."[125] At Michigan State University, YAF and others opposed to campus disorders collected over 10,000 signatures on a petition against the "atmosphere of intimidation, violence and disruption" they perceived on campus.[126]

Perhaps the most publicized example of YAF resistance to SDS actions in 1969 took place at Stanford University. Led by Harvey Hukari, the YAF chapter already was publishing its own weekly newspaper, *The Arena*, as an alternative to the official leftist-leaning campus paper.[127] The Stanford YAF chairman did not appear to be your stereotypical conservative student. As writer George Fox described him in an article in *Playboy* magazine, "Physically, he looks farther left than Mark Rudd—shoulder-length hair, Mao jacket, cord bell-bottoms, etc. According to Hukari, 'It makes me a little more difficult for the SDS to attack.'"[128] When SDS held a rally and tried to take over the Applied Electronics Laboratory,

122. *Indianapolis Star* in *YAF in the News*, Mid-May 1969.

123. Roy R. Silver, "Queensborough Sit-In Ends as Police Arrive," *New York Times*, May 8, 1969.

124. "Farley Says 'No' to Left," *New Guard*, Summer 1969, p. 26.

125. *YAF in the News*, Mid-May, 1969.

126. Kenneth Reich, "Conservatives Strike Back on U.S. Campuses," *Los Angeles Times*, March 2, 1969.

127. Mary Madison, "A Hip Rightist at Stanford," *San Francisco Chronicle* in *YAF in the News*, Mid-May, 1969.

128. George Fox, "Counter Revolution," *Playboy*, March 1970, p. 178. Personal Papers of Patrick Dowd, Box 3, Hoover Institution, Stanford University, Palo Alto, CA.

YAF was there with signs reading, "SDS Is Revolting" while Hukari, armed with a bullhorn, led cheers of "Pigs Off Campus" against the leftist demonstrators. Reflecting its left-wing bias, the *Stanford Daily* described the situation as follows, "The right-wing militants continued to hound the SDS students for the rest of the afternoon, blocking doorways at the Applied Electronics Laboratory (AEL) as SDS members tried to get in."[129] The YAF effort was successful in preventing the takeover. As Hukari noted, however, "In the future one can expect to see more militancy develop (on our part) in various areas of the campus, as long as the Administration fails to act firmly with campus disorders."[130] The Stanford YAF chapter would continue to put pressure on the left and also on the administration as thirty YAF members met with university officials to call for continued ROTC courses on campus. Later that year, at the 1969 YAF National Convention, Stanford University YAF would receive recognition as the "Best Large Campus Chapter."

In addition to opposing SDS, YAF also took a stand against Black radicals who used sit-ins and building takeovers to push their demands for race-based programs and policies. At Rutgers University's Newark campus, militants seized a campus building in their campaign for open enrollments and the establishment of a Black Studies program. Ralph Fucetola, chapter chairman in Newark, maintained that YAF was ready to clear them out. "YAF rounded up enough moderate students to take the building back ... We were all set to go when the administration heard about it and gave in to the militants. They were hunting for an excuse, anyway. They really don't have any guts."[131] Although YAF was not successful in defeating the radicals' demands, they did make evident their strength on campus. Randal Teague, YAF's Executive Director at the time, noted, "Every time the left takes over a building, we pick up more members. The moderate student—the guy who just wants to get an education—has nowhere to turn but to us. We're the only legitimate group that's able to challenge the SDS and the black militants."[132]

Majority Coalitions and Blue Buttons

Throughout the spring semester of 1969, YAF continued to distribute its "Majority Coalition Campus Action Kit" stressing that only a few dedicated leaders were needed, a small band of activists who could rally the silent masses of moderate and apolitical students.[133] On more and more campuses, YAF leaders took the advice of the national organization and helped form coalitions.

At the University of Tennessee, YAF activists Jim Hager and Jim Duncan formed a Majority Coalition that captured over 4,000 signatures on a petition in support of the school's stand against the left.[134] Hager ran a close race for student government president, helped elect a number of other conservatives to

---

129. "Conservatives Disrupt SDS Old Union Rally," *YAF in the News*, March 1969. See also Alexander W. Astin, Helen S. Astin, Alan E. Bayer and Ann S. Bisconti: *The Power of Protest* (San Francisco: Jossey-Bass Publishers, 1975), p. 126.

130. Reich, "Conservatives Strike Back."

131. George Fox, "Counter Revolution," *Playboy*, March 1970, p. 138.

132. *Ibid.*

133. No copy of the manual has been located but it is described in David Jeffery, "Good Grief, Here Comes the New Right," *George Washington University Alumni Magazine*, 1969, pp. 29–33. Personal Papers of Patrick Dowd, Box 1, Hoover Institution, Stanford University, Palo Alto, CA.

134. *New Guard*, May 1969, p. 23.

student government and was in many ways an atypical YAF leader. A Vietnam veteran, married with two children, Hager returned to school to obtain a degree in Electrical Engineering with high honors while also running for student government, serving as Tennessee YAF State Chairman, and subsequently being elected to the Board of Directors at the 1969 YAF National Convention. After a career as an engineer and owner of a sales and marketing company, Hager "tried retirement—did not work—now working as a marketing analyst."[135] Duncan went on to obtain a law degree, work as an attorney and then State Trial Judge until he was elected to Congress in 1988. He continues to represent the 2nd district of Tennessee, an area that includes the campus of the University of Tennessee.

The University of Georgia YAF chapter was responsible for forming a Majority Coalition on the Athens campus, starting with a petition drive as the spring quarter was beginning. They presented University President Fred Davison with 3,368 signatures of students calling on the administration to expel or take legal action against any who engage in disruptive acts on campus. As Antony Weaver, chapter chairman, and James Baldwin observed, "What we accomplished on our campus in eight days proves the relevance of the Majority Coalition concept."[136] A similar situation occurred at Colorado State University where YAF chairman Linda Panepinto and Rick Barth organized Students for CSU and collected 6,000 signatures on a petition opposing the SDS boycott of classes.[137]

At American University, YAF members, athletes, and fraternity members removed the SDS from the President's House, "liberated it" and cleaned up the mess before returning it to its proper residents. Harvard YAF formed the Committee to Keep Harvard Open and distributed "Keep Harvard Open" ribbons on campus. Boston University YAF, under the leadership of Steve Zierak, threatened to sue the administration for breach of contract if SDS were permitted to seize and retain a classroom, preventing students from attending classes. As Tom Lamont noted, "When SDS announced plans to seize a building, we wanted to make sure that the university did something. It has a history of doing nothing in such cases. We were convinced that if we did not put pressure on the administration they would continue to do nothing."[138]

While YAF continued to advocate the use of majority coalitions, some were concerned that the organization was not getting appropriate credit for its leadership. New York YAF State Chairman Jim Farley felt that "YAF members working in such a situation do most of the actual work, organizing and financing and end up with none of the credit."[139] But the national organization was aware of the problem and in a spring 1969 memo from its Chapter Director pointed out to the local leaders, "the importance of keeping YAF's name before the public . . . work through a Majority Coalition to organize the responsible majority but ensure that your YAF chapter does not disintegrate in the eyes of the mass media.[140]

By the end of 1969, YAF had re-evaluated its position and Ronald B. Dear, YAF director of state and regional activities, was telling members to put the name of

---

135. 2008 YAF Alumni Survey Responses: James C. Hager, Jr.
136. "University of Georgia YAF Forms Majority Coalition," *New Guard*, Summer 1969, p. 25.
137. *New Guard*, Summer 1969, p. 24.
138. Tom Henshaw, "The Right," *Boston Herald Traveler*, April 20, 1969, p. 44.
139. Memo from James Farley to Randal Teague, May 1, 1969. Personal Papers of Patrick Dowd, Box 1, Hoover Institution, Stanford University, Palo Alto, CA.
140. Memo from Wayne Thorburn to Chapter Chairmen. Personal Papers of Patrick Dowd, Box 1, Hoover Institution, Stanford University, Pal Alto, CA.

YAF first when opposing the left. As he noted, "in some few cases the 'majority coalition' concept worked, but in most cases it was not a complete success. The objective conditions dictate that local chapters of Young Americans for Freedom take the offensive on their individual campuses."[141] Realizing the importance of keeping the YAF name front and center, the organization began to place more emphasis on other projects, including the threat of legal action either against those who disrupted the campus or the college administration that failed to keep classes open. These would be clearly YAF projects carried out in the name of the campus YAF chapter.

While the SDS and other leftist groups seemed to be dominating the media coverage, some in YAF were determined to increase coverage for YAF and for those opposed to violence and destruction on campus. Phillip Abbott Luce determined that YAF should come up with its own means of launching an offensive strike against the left and obtaining coverage from the media. That project would be the blue button campaign. As Allen Brandstater, then executive director of California Young Americans for Freedom recalled,

> Phil Luce came up with the idea, saying we need a symbol, something to identify with peace on campus. As we distributed these on campus, we were able to raise lots of money and got lots of publicity for YAF. Perhaps the best-known picture is of a YAF leader pinning a blue button on S.I. Hayakawa, who was then president of San Francisco State College.[142]

The picture, which gained national coverage when it was placed on the Associated Press newswire, showed Dennis Clarke of the University of Hawaii YAF pinning a button on Hayakawa in the midst of the 134-day student strike at his college.[143]

On February 17th, California YAF launched a statewide blue button campaign with news conferences in San Francisco, Sacramento, Los Angeles, and San Diego. Patrick Dowd, a graduate student at Sacramento State College, explained the program.[144] With the buttons, California YAF distributed a two-page flyer that explained its purpose was to support peace on campus. It claimed 100,000 buttons were being distributed by students in California colleges. As the flyer stated, "We want the people of California to know that the student majority is with them, that we are not a lost generation, that there is an alternative to the militant leftists inhabiting the campus community." It maintained that terror is wrong, whether by a mugger or a student leftist on campus.

In an appeal beyond the campus and to the citizens at large, the flyer claimed that, in reality, what the radicals are demanding is control of the educational process.

> What they are demanding is that YOU pay all the bills while they determine all the programs. They believe THEY have the right to use your hard earned money as they see fit. The radical left wants to oppress the taxpayer! It is your rights and the rights of the student majority that are being denied.

---

141. Ronald B. Dear, "Young America's Freedom Offensive, a 1969 report," *New Guard*, January 1970, p. 12.

142. Interview with Allen Brandstater, October 12, 2008, Newport Beach, CA.

143. A number of articles and photos of Clarke and Hayakawa reprinted from various newspapers can be found in *YAF in the News*, March 1969.

144. Michael Fallon, "Blue Buttons Rebut Campus Terrorism," *Sacramento Union*, February 18, 1969.

Most student radicals come from well to do homes: most taxpayers do not. Yet, the rich student militants act as if they have a claim on the hard earned money of the poor.[145]

The flyer concluded by expressing YAF's concern that radical leftist actions would lead to a lessening of support for the state's college and university system and noted that university bonds were defeated in the last election in California. While many in the organization were opposed to the concept of publicly supported university education, that did not stop them from using this argument in seeking support.

Later that spring, California YAF distributed a three-fold brochure titled "Who's Behind the Blue?" which noted some of the recent California YAF projects, reprinted the Sharon Statement, and explained the reasons for wearing the blue button. It ended with the claim that "YAF is where it's at."[146] As Luce pointed out in his "Against The Wall" column in YAF's national magazine, YAF was openly challenging SDS and the other leftist radicals by showing that more and more students were willing to wear a sign of their opposition to violence and disruption.[147] Patrick Nolan, leader of the YAF forces at USC, noted that the blue button project had become the major YAF activity on his campus. "This is a big project now. It symbolizes opposition to terrorism. There's been tremendous support for it."[148]

A few days after the YAF news conferences, the *Los Angeles Herald Examiner* printed an editorial calling YAF the "unsung heroes." As the editorial explained,

> Last week 30 members appeared at the State College Board of Trustees meeting in Los Angeles, wearing buttons and carrying signs proclaiming their support for Gov. Ronald Reagan and Dr. S.I. Hayakawa. Governor Reagan gratefully accepted a blue button, signifying YAF's peace on campus campaign. A trustee remarked he'd never before seen a group of students appear at any trustees' meetings carrying placards saying they were FOR anything.[149]

YAF was finally getting the recognition and positive publicity that Luce had desired when he advocated the blue button campaign.

It was impossible to keep such an effective idea limited to the Golden State. Soon thereafter it had spread to New York, New Jersey and a host of other states. Jim Farley of New York YAF stated, "we are hoping to make this a mass demonstration of support for 'open campus.' Basically, by open campus we mean the right of any group to legally demonstrate on campuses, but not to violate the rights of others."[150]

One year later at the beginning of the fall semester in 1970, national YAF called on its chapters to hold a series of news conferences and to distribute blue buttons on campus.[151] Fifty news conferences were held across the country. At

145. "The Blue Button: Support Peace on Campus" flyer. Personal Papers of Patrick Dowd, Box 1, Hoover Institution, Stanford University, Palo Alto, CA.

146. "Who's Behind the Blue?" brochure. Personal Papers of Jameson Campaigne, Jr., Ottawa, IL.

147. Phillip Abbot Luce, "Against The Wall," *New Guard*, April 1969, pp. 8–9.

148. M. Stanton Evans and Walter W. Meek, "Campus Conservatives Challenge Radical Forces, *Syracuse Herald Journal* in *YAF in the News*, June 1969.

149. Quoted in Luce, *New Guard*, April 1969, p. 9.

150. Memo to YAF Leadership from Wayne J. Thorburn, Chapter Director, March 1969. Personal Papers of Patrick Dowd, Box 1, Hoover Institution, Stanford University, Palo Alto, CA.

151. Memo to YAF Leadership from Jerry Norton, Director of College Services, and Wayne J. Thorburn, Director of State & Regional Activities dated September 8, 1970. In author's possession.

the Washington, DC conference, new National Chairman Ron Docksai said, "We hope by the end of this term there will be enough buttons in sight on campus to convince administrators that most students are fed up with those who come to school to fight, not study."[152] In Denver, YAF State Chairman Tom Prater said the buttons will "make it clear that a majority of Colorado students oppose campus violence and want firm action against it." [153] Ed Grebow of George Washington University joined Mike Pikosky and Ken Tobin of American University for a news conference outlining the District of Columbia YAF plans for the fall semester. As Pikosky explained, "the blue button is a symbol of opposition to these new Nazis—the radical, left-wing militants who believe in no one's rights but their own."[154] Similar news conferences were held in Los Angeles, New York and other cities as YAF launched the second phase of its blue button campaign.

The Legal Offensive

YAF's national convention in 1969 would witness the most significant challenge to the prevailing leadership of the organization, a challenge discussed in more detail in the following chapter. Nevertheless, YAF members left their August 1969 convention committed to a more aggressive approach to combating the left on campus. While the rather corny convention slogan, "Sock it to the Left," seemed to imply a lighthearted approach, the reality of the YAF position was quite different. At the convention, one YAF member, New Orleans attorney Maurice B. Franks, said that the time had come for "massive law suits against the pusillanimous leadership of the large universities." Franks went on to argue that, "Whenever the class schedule listed in the catalog is altered, as for example by leftist campus disorders, any one student has a right to sue to compel refund to all students of the tuition for the days on which classes are interrupted."[155]

Newly elected National Chairman David Keene echoed this sentiment in an interview with a California newspaper at the convention. Speaking of the anticipated disruptions on campus during the fall semester as well as the anti-Vietnam war activists' desire to have classes cancelled during the Moratorium, Keene indicated YAF's plans for 1969. "This year what we expect to do is bring legal action against groups that are involved in this sort of activity as well as bring legal action against college administrators who don't do anything about it which is as great a problem as those who involve themselves in the first place."[156] The September issue of *New Guard* told it all on its cover with the message "Back to the Barricades" and a theme of beginning a new semester involving continued challenges from the campus left. Inside was a chapter report stressing the types of activities in which chapters should engage to be effective on campus. Its concluding message was "No longer will YAF chapters consist of five or six conservatives who meet

---

152. William Greider, "YAF Moves to Curb Campus Violence," *Washington Post*, September 28, 1970. Group Research Archives, Box 342, Columbia University, New York, NY.

153. Joan White, "YAF Plans Antiradical Campus Fight," *Denver Post*, September 28, 1970 in *YAF in the News*, December 1970.

154. Peter Lennon, "YAF vows hard line against campus violence," undated and unlabeled news clip. Group Research Archives, Box 486, Columbia University, New York, NY.

155. Doug Thompson, "YAF Watches SIU," *Alton Telegraph* in *YAF in the News*, September 1969.

156. "YAF Plans Legal Action Against Disrupters," *Santa Ana Register* in *YAF in the News*, September 1969.

monthly to bemoan their plight in a liberal and leftist controlled area. We must move out and fight the battles for our principles, and we will."[157]

Later in September, Congressman M.G. "Gene" Snyder of Kentucky introduced a statement in the *Congressional Record* about the 1969 national convention and praising YAF for the work it was doing.

> YAF does not stand for the status quo. They do not let somebody else fight their battles for them. For instance, citing the failure of campus authorities and community leaders to take effective action against the storm-trooper tactics of the New Left, YAF developed in St. Louis last month a comprehensive legal blueprint for frustrating the militants through hard-hitting tests in court. They had, in the past, mobilized campus majorities to oppose the left wherever it appears.[158]

A few of the more libertarian YAFers who had challenged the fusionist majority in St. Louis were uncomfortable with using the courts to stifle SDS. This contributed to the division that occurred on some campuses, such as at Penn State, where some radical libertarians left to form their own organization, Students for Individual Liberty. Meanwhile, other conservatives led by Harold Wexler and Laura Wertheimer, "re-affiliated with the national YAF and intensified the struggle against those on the campus who supported Communists."[159]

To assist local YAF chapters and state organizations, national YAF prepared and distributed a 54-page document, "Legal Responses to Campus Disorder," that was to be used in preparation of court cases. As the preface explained, while school administrators and civil authorities have been relied on to maintain order and protect student rights to an education, too often these officials have not provided that protection. The document described various legal arguments that could be employed by students with citations of relevant court cases. It outlined the relationship between student and university, possible causes of action by students against the university, actions against disruptive students, and other possible legal actions.[160]

On October 3, 1969, YAF leaders held news conferences in 57 cities to announce a campus legal offensive against leftist radicals while reaffirming their support of legitimate free speech for all individuals and groups. *New Guard* editor Ken Grubbs, Allan Brownfeld, and YAF National Secretary Ron Docksai conducted the news conference at the National Press Club in Washington. As Docksai noted, "YAF will force the New Left onto the defensive. YAF will no longer sit back and allow administration buildings to be burned, students to be blackmailed and beaten, buildings to be burned down, or fear and intimidation to replace academic freedom."[161] The targets of the legal offensive "would be both university administrations that failed to act against 'disruptive students' and the students themselves."[162]

In commenting on the possible use of physical force, Brownfeld noted, "In general terms that approach is not our approach."[163] At the time a graduate student in political science at the University of Maryland, Brownfeld recently looked back

---

157. "Chapter Report," *New Guard*, September 1969, p. 26.
158. *Congressional Record*, September 11, 1969. Group Research Archives, Box 340, Columbia University, New York, NY.
159. Heineman: *Campus Wars*, pp. 206–207.
160. "Legal Responses to Campus Disorder," Young Americans for Freedom, September 1969.
161. "YAF Declares Legal War on Campus Disrupters," *New Guard*, November 1969, pp. 4–5.
162. "Suits Threatened in Campus Rioting," *New York Times*, October 4, 1969.
163. *Ibid.*

on those times. "YAF was in every way a positive influence and enabled me to advance my ideas in the political arena." From his experience, "YAF introduced me to many idealistic young men and women throughout the country who shared my values, many of whom I have remained in contact with through the years."[164]

All across the country, YAF leaders explained the new program. Illinois YAF Chairman Bill Mencarow and state treasurer Loren Smith declared in Chicago, "We have been a silent majority. We are going to be silent no longer. While we have been waiting our campuses have been burning."[165] Robert Faulkingham, New Hampshire Chairman, and Miles Drake, UNH chapter chairman, stressed that, "We believe in progressive change, as opposed to revolutionary change, an alternative to radicalism."[166] Faulkingham became active in YAF while a high school student and was named State Chairman while attending the University of New Hampshire. For him, the period was "an exciting time to be in school and to be involved politically" and his experience in organizing YAF in the state "helped me to become a people person."[167] That experience led him to a career in retail management.

Among the many others holding news conferences to announce YAF's legal offensive were Jere Lamb (Grand Rapids) and Ray Semmons (Northwood Institute) in Michigan; Benny Wynn (University of South Carolina); Edward Grebow (George Washington University); James Newman (St. Paul, Minnesota); John Rawls (University of the South); Jim Farley (Columbia University); Al Zeller (University of Washington); David Adcock (University of North Carolina), George Dunlop (Charlotte), and Harold Herring (Raleigh) throughout North Carolina; Steve Mayerhofer (Ohio State University); Frank Donatelli (University of Pittsburgh) and Dan Arico (Duquesne University) in Pittsburgh; John Kwapisz (University of Virginia) and Bob Hawthorne (Virginia Military Institute) in Virginia; Greg Brown (University of Denver); Gary Young (Fort Wayne); Bill Kanninen (Drew); and Douglas Black (Houston).[168]

Fall 1969 was also a time when YAF was exposed to some of the national media outlets, which provided coverage on its activities, beliefs, and programs. First came the participation of Phillip Abbott Luce, recently named College Director for the organization, as a member of the panel on student revolt in *Playboy* magazine. When asked why YAF was opposing New Left groups on campus, Luce explained to the magazine's millions of young readers, "We're fighting them because we oppose violence and collectivism and totalitarianism and the Nazi storm-trooper tactics they use against anybody who opposes them."[169] Unlike past years, YAF was now going to take the offensive. Luce pleaded with students "to stand up to those who would try to take over their classrooms and disrupt the functioning of the university. I think we can show the world, if it pays any attention to what we're doing, that this tactic works."[170]

---

164. 2008 YAF Alumni Survey Responses: Allan C. Brownfeld. Brownfeld was also the author of one of the early articles on the emerging young conservative movement, "America's Angry Young Men," *Modern Age*, Spring 1962, pp. 197–201.

165. "Group Vows Suits to Bar Campus War," *Chicago Tribune*, October 4, 1969.

166. Pat Broderick, "YAF Chairmen Favor Change, Not Revolution," *The New Hampshire* in *YAF in the News*, November 1969.

167. 2008 YAF Alumni Survey Responses: Robert A. Faulkingham.

168. Newspaper coverage of the press conferences held by these YAF leaders can be found in *YAF in the News* issues for October 1969 and November 1969. Listed are the locations of the news conferences and not necessarily the colleges attended by the participants.

169. "The Playboy Panel: Student Revolt," *Playboy*, September 1969, p. 91.

170. *Ibid.* p. 108.

For Luce, the former revolutionary leftist, the distinction between the right and left was more than one of tactics and strategy, of means to bring about change in society. It was to him a difference between individual rights and collective enforcement.

> The New Right is arguing for the freedom of the individual against the collectivist nature of the present Government and the totalitarian proposals of the left wing. No matter how you cut it, the New Left is philosophically socialistic. We on the right want an end to government control over the actions of the individual, not simply a usurpation of that control by New Left totalitarians.[171]

Luce's media presence was bringing more attention to Young Americans for Freedom and its efforts to oppose the left. In a full-page feature article, YAF's aggressive efforts received major coverage in a national newspaper Sunday supplement magazine. The article included interviews with Luce and New York YAF Chairman Jim Farley and noted

> The word is out: "Get SDS." And the plan of action is well mapped. YAF will no longer wait out each SDS move before it acts. It will use the same harassment techniques, though just short of breaking the law, that SDS used against the college administrations.[172]

As Farley outlined some of the possible tactics, "Most people don't realize that you're not trespassing until somebody calls the police and asks that the intruders be removed. We will occupy SDS headquarters this year, and would like to see them call the police. Then it would be the pot calling the kettle black."[173] Farley had personal knowledge of the subject since he and his fellow New York YAF members had twice occupied leftist organization offices in the previous year.

Activating the Silent Students

Apart from the news conferences and the public relations push, something significant was occurring on campuses across America. New YAF chapters were being formed and existing ones were being reinvigorated. When the once-inactive chapter at the University of Michigan held a rally in support of ROTC classes and in opposition to leftist disruptions, 200 students took part.[174] At the University of Texas at Austin, 19-year old Mary Kay Davis resuscitated a dormant YAF chapter in her freshman year and made it into a major force on her campus. As a campus magazine noted, "On this campus she is a determined leader, an articulate opponent of liberal doctrine."[175] Davis was named to fill a vacancy on

---

171. *Ibid.* p. 249.
173. Linda Gutstein, "Students on the Right Get Ready for Battle," *Parade*, October 5, 1969.
173. *Ibid.*
174. Bernard Weinraub, "Unrest Spurs Growth of Conservative Student Groups, *New York Times*, October 12, 1969.
175. "SDS vs. YAF," *Texas Ranger*, December 1969, pp. 12–20 features a debate between Davis and Larry Waterhouse, graduate student and SDS leader on the UT campus. Personal Papers of William F. Buckley, Jr., Box 284, Folder 2487, Sterling Library, Yale University, New Haven, CT.

the YAF National Board of Directors in June 1969 and then re-elected at the 1969 National Convention.

Freshman Laszlo Pasztor was determined to reorganize a YAF chapter at Harvard when he reached campus in the fall of 1969. The chapter's goal was "to promote the principles of capitalism and the free market economy, combat SDS and educate people to provide a vocal stance for conservatism at Harvard." Pasztor had some significant help in the form of Doug Cooper, a new graduate student from Penn State where he had been YAF chairman, and in two outstanding faculty advisors, Professors Gottfried Haberler and Edward C. Banfield.[176]

At the Massachusetts Institute of Technology, freshman David Horan stepped before 35 students to call to order the first chapter meeting in over a year.[177] One month later, the chapter voted to peacefully oppose and counter-picket a demonstration by the anti-Vietnam "November Action Coalition" on the M.I.T. campus. YAF member Richard Kline said the chapter would attend the NAC rally "to make our voices heard. Both officially and unofficially the YAF is not planning to initiate violence. But if someone hits me, I'll hit back."[178] Fortunately, the counter-picket went off without any violence.

Pat Nolan had reorganized a YAF presence at the University of Southern California in the fall of 1968, starting with a small group of members and expanding to become a major force on the Trojan campus. As YAF member Bob McDonald described the chapter's founder, "He was a dynamic visionary who was politically astute enough to realize that in order to make a real difference one had to be committed for the long run."[179] Nolan would become a well-known campus leader, including serving as Tommy Trojan, the mounted mascot of the university. By the spring of 1970, the chapter chairman was John McGuinness, a campus political leader who was dedicated to activism. McDonald recalled, "John focused initially on the "barricades" and on campus media. North Vietnamese flags would be burned, literature tables would be staffed, "Tell it to Hanoi" buttons would be distributed, communism and the war would be debated, and American prisoners of war (POWs) would be honored and remembered."[180] USC YAF was one of the most active and effective chapters, continuing to produce leaders over the next twenty years, including a National Chairman and several members of the National Board of Directors.

At the University of North Carolina at Chapel Hill, during the October 15th Moratorium, leftist students lowered the American flag at the center of the campus. Then members of the YAF chapter "took over control of the pole, keeping the flag flying at the top of the pole. There were no major incidents." YAF had warned professors to hold classes and, according to the *Raleigh News & Observer* only one part-time instructor failed to hold scheduled classes during the Moratorium.[181]

---

176. Michael E. Kinsley, "Conservatives Open Harvard Unit of Young Americans for Freedom," *The Harvard Crimson*, October 3, 1969.

177. Weinraub, "Unrest," *New York Times*, October 12, 1969.

178. "YAF Votes to Fight NAC Non-Violently," *The Harvard Crimson*, November 3, 1969.

179. Bob McDonald: *YAF in the Arena*, p. 18 (unpublished paper in author's possession). I am grateful to Bill Saracino for introducing me to this most informative history of the USC YAF chapter in the late 1960s and early 1970s as well as to Bob McDonald for allowing me access to this valuable review of one chapter's activities.

180. *Ibid.* p. 39.

181. News clips from *North Carolina YAF in the News*, January 1970.

More dramatic action took place at Fordham University in New York City. When 35 SDS members took over the executive offices of the administration building and barricaded themselves for seven hours, six campus security guards were injured with one being hospitalized after he was struck with an iron pipe. Fordham officials finally called in city police, but many of the demonstrators, who were protesting the ROTC program on campus, escaped. In response, YAF members organized a rally the following day. "Several hundred Fordham students led by two conservative groups marched on the university's administration building . . . and demanded that the leftist Students for a Democratic Society be banished from campus" was the lead paragraph in the *New York Times* along with a picture of hundreds of students protesting SDS outside the administration building.[182]

Meanwhile, more and more YAF chapters began to go beyond the official campus newspapers and started their own publications. As the *New York Times* observed,

> Dozens of conservative newspapers have begun competing with traditionally liberal dailies on such campuses as Stanford, the University of Wisconsin and the University of California at Berkeley. Last month, a student conservative weekly began distribution at Duke University, North Carolina State and the University of North Carolina.[183]

Bob Tyrrell continued editing his *The Alternative: An American Spectator* at Indiana University, *The Arena* kept publishing at Stanford, and the University of Maryland YAF started its second year of distributing its own *The Alternative* on the College Park campus and at Baltimore area colleges with Paul Skocz as editor. At UC–Santa Barbara, Mike Engler became editor of what was facetiously called *The Daily Planet* and at USC the YAF chapter published the *Free Trojan* while Massachusetts YAF distributed *Counterpoint* to a number of campuses in the Boston area. Later that fall, for those chapters unable to publish their own independent newspaper, national YAF created the "Free Campus News" edited by Phillip Abbott Luce and shipped a total of 200,000 copies to various campuses for free distribution.[184]

Perhaps the most successful of all the campus-based publications first appeared on September 10, 1969 as *The Badger Herald* showed up on the University of Wisconsin campus in Madison. It all started with discussions over a beer for Patrick S. Korten, Mike Kelly, Wade Smith and Nick Loniello and ended with the decision to launch an alternative weekly newspaper. For these visionaries, it was more than fighting off the SDS. As editor-in-chief Korten analyzed the situation, "Let's be realistic. We'll never have the campus think Barry Goldwater is a wonderful man. But that isn't really our goal. We want to create a training ground now, on campuses, for articulate and effective conservative leaders." For Korten, "no matter what S.D.S. says, it's not the kids who rule the world, it's the adults. And this is foremost in our minds."[185] Nearly forty years later, *The Badger*

---

182. John Sibley, "Fordham Groups Demand SDS Ban," *New York Times*, November 15, 1969.
183. Weinraub, "Unrest", *New York Times*, October 12, 1969.
184. Philip Manger, "Conservative Youths Are Alive on Campus," *Baltimore News American*, May 27, 1970.
185. Weinraub, "Unrest", *New York Times*, October 12, 1969.

Herald is still an independent newspaper on the Madison campus but since 1980 it has become a daily with a circulation of 16,000. It has had a lasting influence not only on the University campus but also throughout the Capital city.

Later that academic year, the national organization assembled a handbook for local YAF chapters called "Do It! Or Publishing A Conservative Underground Newspaper." The 48-page manual covered all the basics of publishing from finances to staff to content to distribution. Soon thereafter national YAF started the "Free Campus News Service" under the direction of Jerry Norton. Twice a month the service mailed news releases, pictures, features, cartoons, columns and editorials to any campus newspaper requesting the material. FCNS continued as a regular distribution tool by the national organization for the next five years. By the 1970–1971 academic year, seventy-one YAF chapters were publishing independent alternative newspapers.[186]

The Left Resorts to Violence

As 1970 began and students were starting spring semester, the violence on campus did not let up. From the perspective of forty years later, it is hard to realize the extent to which the United States was engulfed in serious societal breakdown and destructive behavior. According to one report, during the sixteen months from January 1969 to April 1970, there were approximately five thousand terrorist bombings in the United States, most of which took place on or near college campuses.[187] Several of these acts of violence ended in death for participants or innocent bystanders. After the conviction of the Chicago 7 in February, Ann Arbor witnessed destruction at the hands of the University of Michigan SDS led by Robert Meeropol, son of convicted Soviet spies Ethel and Julius Rosenberg. Meeropol was a graduate student at the University of Michigan supported with a Ford Foundation grant. Under SDS direction, "five thousand Michigan students and campus hangers-on marched to the Ann Arbor city hall, breaking the windows of downtown businesses and wrecking a police car along the way."[188] One month later, in New York City, a bomb factory in the townhouse owned by Cathy Wilkerson's father blew up killing three members of the Weatherman Underground faction of SDS.[189]

Then on April 18th, radical leftists set fire to the temporary Bank of America building in Isla Vista, next to the University of California at Santa Barbara campus. This was the same bank that had been bombed by SDS one year earlier. As firemen arrived to put out the fire they were fired upon by snipers and these attacks continued as the police arrived. Three students opposed to the terrorists left their apartment and went in the bank to put out the fire. As they emerged, 22-year old Kevin Moran was shot dead. It was later determined that Moran

---

186. Randal C. Teague, "YAF: A Presence in the Room," *New Guard*, January–February 1971, p. 19.

187. This count is reported in Heineman: *Put Your Bodies*, p. 170. See also Peter Collier and David Horowitz: *Destructive Generation* (New York: The Free Press, 1996) for a discussion of the Weather Underground activities in this period.

188. *Ibid.* p. 171. These are only a few of the radical events during spring 1970 covered in Heineman on pp. 170–180.

189. Douglas Robinson, "Townhouse Razed by Blast & Fire," *New York Times*, May 7, 1970. It was only days later when the bodies found in the destruction could be identified. Wilkerson and Kathy Boudin fled the scene with minor injuries and were underground for the next ten years.

was accidentally shot by a policeman who thought he was one of the individuals responsible for the fire. Responding to the tragedy, Harvard YAF released a statement in which they said, "Kevin Moran's story doesn't fit, so it won't be discussed, no vigils held, no money collected, no outrage expressed. Kevin was on the wrong side."[190] Meanwhile, at Berkeley, SDS was ordered off campus and its rallies banned from university property after there had been a wave of fire bombings and window smashings that resulted in more than eighty arrests. The Berkeley YAF chapter expressed its support for the administration's decision given the violence spawned by SDS.[191]

Dramatic as these events were, they were soon to be surpassed by what occurred in early May. On April 30th, President Nixon announced that American troops would be going into Cambodia to halt the continued infiltration into South Vietnam of North Vietnamese regular forces.[192] This action, viewed by the left as a widening of the war, set off major opposition on campuses and in the Democratic-controlled Congress. As the lead sentence in a *New York Times* article explained, "The national anti-war movement, drained of vigor in recent months, seemed yesterday to have found a new rallying point and an impetus to renewed protest in President Nixon's announcement of direct intervention in Cambodia by United States troops."[193]

On May 1st, ROTC buildings were firebombed at the University of Wisconsin and at Michigan State University. At Kent State, home to a radical wing of the SDS, students marched to the downtown area where a riot broke out and much property was damaged. One day later, the ROTC building was set afire and when the firefighters arrived, leftist students assaulted them. Soon thereafter, Governor James Rhodes called out the National Guard and ordered them onto campus. On May 4th, students called for a "peace rally" on the commons but then began attacking the National Guard with bottles, rocks, blocks of wood with nails and spent tear gas canisters. After much provocation, some of the Guardsmen began firing back. The end result was four students killed and nine wounded. From that point on, the Kent State disaster would move from impetus to action to myth to history.[194]

Over the next few days, anti-war protests occurred at more than one thousand campuses as students reacted to the deaths at Kent State. Leaders of the Student Mobilization Committee called for a student strike to oppose the Nixon Administration's move into Cambodia. As the national executive secretary of Student Mobe declared, "If there is still a campus in this country which has not yet struck against these crimes of the Nixon Administration we call on them to join us immediately." Meanwhile, the violence continued. The National Guard had to be called out at the University of Maryland. One hundred SDS members took over the president's office at Boston College while others broke into and destroyed the ROTC offices. At the University of Wisconsin, hundreds of students set fires and smashed windows on campus. At Boston University, administrators cancelled exams and commencement and urged all students to go home.[195]

190. Flyer, "Leftist 'Young Idealists' Cause Student Death," Harvard-Radcliffe Young Americans for Freedom, HUD 3890–7000, Harvard University Archives, Pusey Library, Harvard University, Cambridge, MA.

191. "News Briefs, California Violence," *The Harvard Crimson*, April 20, 1970.

192. Robert B. Semple, Jr., "Nixon Sends Combat Forces to Cambodia," *New York Times*, May 1, 1970.

193. Linda Charlton, "Big Rallies Are Planned, Students Protest Nixon Troop Move," *New York Times*, May 2, 1970.

194. Heineman: *Put Your Bodies*, p. 176.

195. Frank J. Prial, "Students Step Up Protests on War," *New York Times*, May 6, 1970. J.W. Stillman, "Strike Hits 166 Colleges, Administrators Close B.U.," *The Harvard Crimson*, May 6, 1970.

Two days later, the number of colleges on strike had increased to 350.[196] At the University of Kentucky, students burned the Air Force ROTC building and at American University students blocked traffic in the northwest section of Washington, DC. Meanwhile, Black radicals were using the situation to make their own demands. Students at New York University occupied three buildings and demanded a ransom of $100,000 to be paid to the Black Panther Defense Fund.[197] On Saturday, May 9th, the New Mobilization Committee attracted nearly one hundred thousand to an anti-war rally in the Ellipse. While an impressive number, the attendance was considerably less than what anti-war forces had attracted on past occasions, even though a familiar list of speakers was present, including Jane Fonda, Benjamin Spock, Judy Collins, Coretta King, Allen Ginsburg, and Chicago Seven defendants John Froines and David Dellinger.[198] When it was all tallied, some nine hundred colleges shut down, many not opening again until the fall semester. More than 160 bombs were reported to have exploded on campuses in reaction to the Cambodia and Kent State actions.[199]

The events of early May led YAF to take a number of stands against the violence on campus as well as in favor of ensuring that students continue to receive the education for which they had paid tuition. Ohio State University YAF won a temporary injunction against nine radicals designed to ensure the rights of the eleven student plaintiffs.[200] At Wayne State University, eight YAF members led by Peter McAlpine convinced a Circuit Judge to order classes be reopened, a decision that was unfortunately overturned on appeal. Meanwhile, at George Washington University Randal Teague and 14 co-plaintiffs filed suit to get reimbursement for tuition spent for cancelled classes.[201] As one historian noted, "YAF's arguments were compelling and offered a contrary opinion to the growing tendency of universities to be arms of radical and social change."[202]

The New York area saw a number of threatened lawsuits by YAF members and chapters. At Adelphi University the YAF chapter, led by chairman Donald Harte, obtained an injunction to force college administrators to open the campus. The school was reopened and classes were held as usual. YAF members formed a group called "Strike Back" at Hofstra University, threatened a lawsuit, and negotiated with the administration to have the school opened again on May 10th. Classes also resumed at Nassau Community College after YAF instituted a lawsuit to force the reopening. The New York Institute of Technology reopened after YAF met with school officials and threatened to sue for $37,000, the tuition lost by students who could not attend classes because of the protests. Following a YAF threat to sue, Suffolk Community College resumed classes. As Patrick Tracey, executive director of New York YAF, concluded, "Right now we're very pleased.

---

196. Robert D. McFadden, "College Strife Spreads, Over 100 Schools Closed and Up to 350 Struck," *New York Times*, May 8, 1970.

197. Marion E. McCollom, "324 Universities Strike Nationally; Protests Expand," *The Harvard Crimson*, May 7, 1970.

198. John Herbers, "Big Capital Rally Asks U.S. Pullout in Southeast Asia," *New York Times*, May 10, 1970.

199. Heineman: *Put Your Bodies*, p. 176.

200. Ron Dear, "YAF's Legal Attack," *Texas Challenge*, July–August 1970. Personal Papers of Jameson Campaigne, Jr., Ottawa, IL.

201. Andrew H. Malcolm, "Some Colleges in Area to Reopen Today; Lawsuits Threatened," *New York Times*, May 11, 1970. Teague, now an attorney in Washington, DC, reported that among the co-plaintiffs were a future Assistant Secretary of the Interior Department, Secretary of the Senate, senior managing partner for a major New York investment firm, and an elder in the Church of Jesus Christ of Latter Day Saints. E-mail to the author, June 6, 2009.

202. Schneider: *Cadres for Conservatism*, p. 124.

We may have other legal actions to announce later."[203]

The New York City Board of Education ordered all seventeen city colleges to hold regular classes while three other area colleges "reopened when the Young Americans for Freedom threatened to file suits for tuition losses."[204] At Marymount College in Tarrytown, New York, an all-female Catholic institution, six students charged the college administration with breach of contract for canceling classes in support of the student strike. After the school agreed to resume classes for the remainder of the semester, it was dropped. However, the attorney for the female students announced that he "intends to use the suit as a precedent for suits against strikes at campuses throughout the country and that volunteer attorneys for the Young Americans for Freedom would prepare free legal briefs for students anywhere."[205]

YAF activity during the aftermath of the Cambodian incursion and Kent State was not limited to lawsuits and injunctions, however. At Towson State College in Maryland, fifteen YAF members surrounded a flagpole on campus to prevent leftist students from lowering the American flag. A short while later, when a group of radicals decided to change the name of Agnew Drive to Kent State Avenue, several YAF members used cans of spray paint to paint over the new lettering. YAF was attracting formerly apolitical students for, as Towson YAF leader John Malagrin noted, "We've got a lot of moderates in YAF now. Many of them are disillusioned students who were part of the silent campus majority before the tactics of the left opened their eyes."[206]

Towson State was one campus where college administrators were openly supportive of YAF's efforts to resist the radical takeovers of the left. Writing to YAF chairman Charles Schorr, Towson State College President James L. Fisher had this to say,

> In the press of the activities of the aftermath, I cannot neglect to write you. I want to tell you that to my knowledge you and your associates conducted yourselves admirably through the activities of the past week on the Towson State College campus.
> I am grateful.[207]

Meanwhile an end-of-semester article in the University of Maryland campus paper noted YAF's effect on campus by saying, "Well known and probably admired by the University's central administration and Board of Regents, YAF chairman Joe Spelta is one of the students most readily received and consulted by University decision makers."[208]

As colleges closed for the summer, the demonstrations and destruction died down but did not totally disappear. That August, one of the most destructive attacks took place on the University of Wisconsin campus. The "New Year's Gang" was formed by Karl Armstrong and his brother, and between December 1969 and August 1970 this group of radicals firebombed the campus ROTC building, the

203. Malcolm, "Some Colleges in Area to Reopen Today; Lawsuits Threatened."
204. "Colleges Reopen; Protests Continue All over Nation," *The Harvard Crimson*, May 12, 1970.
205. Linda Greenhouse, "Suit Still Stirs Marymount Girls," *New York Times*, May 26, 1970.
206. Manger, "Conservative Youths Are Alive on Campus."
207. Letter of James L. Fisher to Charles Schorr, May 15, 1970. Copy in author's possession.
208. Chad Neighbor, "YAF Still Working Within System," *Diamondback*, reprinted in *Maryland YAF in the News*, June 1970.

Selective Service offices, and even unsuccessfully tried an aerial bombing of a munitions plant. Then in August, the Gang attempted to bomb the Army Math building on campus with the equivalent blast of 3,400 sticks of dynamite. Instead of hitting their intended target, the bomb destroyed the Physics department, killing a graduate student and blinding a night watchman. Subsidiary damage was done to twenty-six campus buildings and a major cancer research project inside the Old Chemistry Building was destroyed. Despite the death and destruction, the New Year's Gang and the bombing was supported by Madison's alternative leftist newspaper and local SDS members. The left in Madison refused to cooperate with the FBI investigation and all four attackers escaped, eventually making their way to Canada.[209]

To prepare students for the fall 1970 semester, YAF held a leadership conference for forty students at Fordham University in August. It was designed to bring together veterans of confrontations, including Vince Rigdon and Doug Cooper, along with incoming freshmen and sophomores to discuss the most effective tools for keeping colleges open. As Alan Gottlieb, then a senior at University of Tennessee, declared, "Anybody has a right to demonstrate but there should be no infringement on students' rights." Injunctions against student radicals were seen as an effective means to prevent disruptions and violent confrontations. According to James Kelly of St. John's University, "they are the most effective method without turning off the majority of silent or apathetic students and their parents who are watching but not saying anything."[210] Herb Stupp of YAF's College Conservative Council reported that the YAF chapter at the University of New Hampshire had stopped the student government from paying radical speakers out of mandatory student fees. Cooper made clear YAF's overall objective when he said, "We want to change people's minds. We want to get more legislation enacted—or repealed. But we never make or engage in the use of threats or violence."[211]

But, of course, the violence on campus did not cease, nor did YAF's commitment to standing up for student rights and opposing the radical leftists in their actions. On October 14th, a bomb was set off and seriously damaged the Center for International Affairs on the Harvard campus.[212] Two days later, Harvard-Radcliffe YAF held a rally condemning the bombing and urging the University to prosecute those responsible. YAF chairman Laszlo Pasztor indicated that a telegram would be sent to President Nathan Pusey and YAF leader Doug Cooper said, "Unless we preserve a peaceful legal and rational framework to work in, we will not be able to produce meaningful change."[213]

Unfortunately, spring semester 1971 saw a continuation of violent confrontations with the left on the Harvard campus. On March 26th, Harvard-Radcliffe YAF planned to hold a Vietnam Teach-In at Sanders Theater with speakers including the Royal Thai Ambassador to Canada, the Counselor for Political Affairs of the Embassy of South Vietnam, Professor I. Milton Sacks of Brandeis University, Dolph Droge of the White House, and Dan Teodoru of the National Student Coordinating Committee. Three radical leftist organizations on the Harvard

209. Heineman: *Put Your Bodies*, pp. 178–179.
210. C. Gerald Fraser, "Conservatives Plan to Thwart Campus Disruptions," *New York Times*, August 9, 1970.
211. *Ibid.*
212. Robert Reinhold, "Harvard Bomb Blast Damages Center for International Affairs," *New York Times*, October 15, 1970.
213. Joyce Heard, "200 Attend Rally Against Bombing," *The Harvard Crimson*, October 16, 1970.

campus vowed to prevent the speakers from being heard and they packed the meeting, attended by approximately one thousand students. When the meeting was called to order, militant demonstrators began 45 minutes of ceaseless chanting, clapping and booing. Archibald Cox, as a representative of Harvard's President, pleaded with the crowd for ten minutes "on behalf of the President and Fellows" to no avail.[214] At 8:45 P.M., the university police chief informed Cox that a rowdy crowd outside was attempting to break in. Cox then met with moderator Lawrence McCarty and YAF chairman Laszlo Pasztor, and said, "In view of the crowds of people massing outside the building, I ask you to call off the meeting," and the program ended before it began.[215]

The three leftist groups who organized the suppression of free speech were Harvard SDS, the Radcliffe-Harvard Liberation Alliance, and University Action Group (UAG), an organization of radical graduate students and faculty members. For them, the disruption was a resounding success. As one SDS member commented, "This was the largest mass action I've seen on this campus in my four years here. We should use this to build up a tremendous momentum to fight the war." A spokesman for the UAG agreed that the demonstration had been a "tremendous success."[216] Two weeks later, a Harvard Professor of Philosophy was the speaker at a Progressive Labor Party "Forum on Free Speech" where he called the disruption a "genuine act of internationalism" and "advocated more militant actions in the future, suggesting a picket line around University Hall to force a confrontation with University officials on the issue of discipline in the wake of disruption."[217] Still other students interviewed by the *New York Times* approved of the disruption and maintained that the principle of free speech was not involved since those attempting to speak were not students but government officials.[218]

Not all agreed with this distorted view of free speech. Three days after the event, President Nathan Pusey issued a release saying

> the disruption last Friday evening of the open meeting in Sanders Theater was an abhorrent affront to the basic right of freedom of expression. The very fact that the speakers were individuals representing an unpopular view made it all the more important that they be allowed to speak and be heard. We must not lose sight of this central issue ... Last Friday's reprehensible occurrence in Sanders Theater puts the whole community on trial.[219]

One student in a letter to the campus newspaper said that Friday night "a determined and ultimately successful effort was made forcefully to eliminate free speech at Harvard." He went on to reflect on the meaning of the events.

> "Immorality" is a term used loosely these days. But surely to sit quietly by while gangs of stomping and screaming extremist thugs destroy free speech at

214. Roger Rosenblatt: *Coming Apart: A Memoir of the Harvard Wars of 1969* (Boston: Little, Brown & Co, 1997), p. 173.

215. "Pro-War Teach-In Dissolves in Turmoil; Administration Warns of Full Discipline," *The Harvard Crimson*, March 27, 1971.

216. "Rads Rate Teach-In Socko; Cite SRO House: Tremendous," *The Harvard Crimson*, April 1, 1971.

217. "Putnam Cheered at Free Speech Forum," *The Harvard Crimson*, April 15, 1971.

218. "Clash at Teach-In Upsets Harvard," *New York Times*, April 4, 1971.

219. News release from the Office of the President, March 29, 1971. Harvard-Radcliffe Young Americans for Freedom, HUD 3890–7000, Harvard University Archives, Pusey Library, Harvard University, Cambridge, MA.

Harvard is a moral crime. Those who engaged in this attack on the liberties of their fellow students have no place in our community, for they subvert our one basic tenet: that freedom to think and speak the truth as we each see it is inviolate. We must demand their expulsion from our University."

That student, who had attended the Counter Teach-In, was Elliott Abrams who would subsequently serve in the Reagan Administration as Assistant Secretary of State and in the George W. Bush Administration as Deputy National Security Advisor.[220]

Meanwhile, Harvard-Radcliffe YAF met and reviewed pictures to identify students who disrupted the counter teach-in. Stephen Rosen, program director for YAF, said "We poked through the photos we had and identified 12 to 15 people. We are decided to hold off any action . . . We'd like to wait and see what the University does. If the University lives up to its implied promises, we may decide not to do anything."[221] Two weeks later, Students for a Just Peace, the YAF ad hoc group, filed charges against 16 disrupters and called on the Dean of Harvard College to bar the three groups who organized the disruption from campus.[222] Interestingly enough, Rosen, the YAF chapter's program director, was a roommate of Bill Kristol and Alan Keyes, went on to receive a PhD from Harvard and is currently Professor of National Security and Military Affairs at Harvard.[223]

At another Ivy League school, Rob Natelson recalled a Communist-led group of students took over a building in the spring of 1971. Natelson, who is now a Professor of Law at the University of Montana, and another student formed a "majority coalition" to oppose it. One of his fellow Cornell YAF members at the time was Michael Nozzolio, now a New York State Senator.[224]

Two YAF members from Queens College filed suits against college officials contending that the "administration has remained intransigent and is afraid to preserve the standards of the school because of a small but militant group of students." One of the major issues involved the ability of personnel recruiters, private and military, to come on campus. In March 1969, two hundred SDS protesters forced a recruiter for General Electric off the campus and the administration called for a suspension of recruiting pending a student vote. When a referendum went in favor of open recruitment, the administration announced it would not be bound by the vote. YAF then invited a speaker from the Naval Officers Candidate School to address a chapter meeting and the dean of students at Queens College requested that the Navy not send a recruiter. The two YAF members were suing to reverse the college's ban on recruiters.[225]

By the end of spring semester in 1971, campuses were once again beginning to quiet down. But the left was still most active, even with the breakup of Students for a Democratic Society. Especially active in the early 1970s were the Trotskyite

220. "The Mail: Extremist Thugs" by Elliott Abrams, *The Harvard Crimson*, March 31, 1971.

221. Samuel Z. Goldhaber and J. Ryan O'Connell, "YAF Studies Photographs, Claims 12 Identifications," *The Harvard Crimson*, March 31, 1971.

222. Jeff Magalif, "Students for Just Peace Press Charges Against 16 for Disruption," *The Harvard Crimson*, April 16, 1971.

223. Nina J. Easton: *Gang of Five* (New York: Simon & Schuster, 2000), p. 27. Easton relates Kristol's experiences as a student at Harvard during the 1970s on pp. 23–47.

224. Email from Rob Natelson to the author, February 8, 2009. Natelson relates how leftists pushed Cornell to support a Cesar Chavez–backed lettuce boycott in 1971 in "The Boycott at Cornell," *New Guard*, June 1972, pp. 4–7.

225. "Campus Policies Fought in Court," *New York Times*, May 16, 1971.

"Young Socialist Alliance" and the ultra-leftist Progressive Labor Party, the group that basically picked up the pieces of the dying SDS. As Phillip Abbott Luce observed, "I am convinced that this may very well be the lull period. The left-wing is obviously struggling to 'get itself together' and we should not view the present as a time of leftist impotence."[226]

While the organized campus left was in disarray, Young Americans for Freedom remained a strong presence on many campuses with a second generation of leaders ready to take on the decade of the 1970s. As historian Greg Schneider commented ". . . YAF survived the Sixties, even thriving during times when emotions ran the highest on campus. YAF made it through the decade intact as an organization—a testimony to the idealism and work of the hard-core membership who believed the time for conservative principles had come."[227] Steve Wiley was one who had a long career of involvement in YAF but it all began in the late 1960s as a student at the University of Southern California. As he recalled, "They were great times—USC during the Vietnam years where we battled the left and the university administration . . . and the sense of a shared purpose and friendship among those of us who belonged.[228] Through the involvement of Wiley, Bill Saracino, Allen Brandstater, Pat Nolan, John McGuinness, Jim Lacy, Randy Goodwin, John Lewis and many others, USC was a training ground for young conservative leaders of subsequent decades as well as an example of a campus where YAF overcame the efforts of SDS and other leftist groups to re-orient the campus.

At Indiana University, another major campus where YAF had great success and which produced many leaders for the conservative movement, Louisa Porter recalls, "YAF taught great organizational skills, teamwork and goal orientation. YAF educated on the intrigues of politics (both good and bad). It provided perspectives which have allowed a balanced view as I have matured."[229] After graduating from Indiana, Porter worked in the Indiana state government and established a very active YAF community chapter in Indianapolis. But she was determined to attend law school, enrolled at the University of San Diego and received her degree in 1977. After private practice for several years, since 1991 she has been United States Magistrate Judge in San Diego.

Michael Connelly was YAF chapter chairman at Louisiana State University during the turbulent late 1960s and early 1970s, later serving as State Chairman and on the National Board. Surviving the battles with SDS taught him important lessons; "I don't believe I would have been as successful in my law practice or my current activities as a teacher and writer if I had not had the valuable training I received from my fellow members of YAF."[230]

Many others were on campuses where leftist violence was not as critical a challenge but their experiences in YAF, nevertheless, prepared them for future debates on issues, provided organizational skills, and in several instances influenced their career decisions. Dianne Gordon was a member of the YAF chapter at Carthage College, a small, not very politically active campus, and her involvement strengthened her political beliefs. "I believed strongly in personal responsibility

226. Phillip Abbott Luce, "Whatever Happened to the New Left?," *New Guard*, May 1972, pp. 5–7.
227. Gregory Schneider, "The Other Sixties: The Young Americans for Freedom and the Politics of Conservatism," doctoral dissertation, University of Illinois–Chicago, 1996, p. 7.
228. 2008 YAF Alumni Survey Responses: Steve Wiley.
229. 2008 YAF Alumni Survey Responses: Louisa S. Porter.
230. 2008 YAF Alumni Survey Responses: Michael R. Connelly.

and small government and in YAF I found others who shared those values. I'm still conservative. My husband reads *National Review* cover to cover." Gordon was another YAF alumnus who pursued an academic career. She currently teaches English composition on the faculty of the University of Wisconsin at Green Bay.[231]

Richard Cheatham organized the YAF chapter at Virginia Military Institute in the mid-1960s and then became Virginia YAF State Chairman. While SDS did not infect his campus, where participation in the Reserve Officers Training Corps was still mandatory in the 1960s, the effect of his involvement in YAF was lasting. "YAF inspired and encouraged me to continue to learn and teach about fundamental human nature through American history."[232] Cheatham did just that and now is Director of Living History Associates, an organization based in Richmond that creates presentations based on historical characters.

Diane Kozub started a high school YAF chapter in 1967 at Benedictine Academy in Elizabeth, New Jersey and remained active through her four years at American University and then at Seton Hall University School of Law. There were many fond memories, including organizing two busloads of people to travel from New Jersey to the Honor America rally in Washington, DC and becoming active at American University during the anti-war protests as well as participating in many rallies in support of the troops in Vietnam. As Kozub recalls, "Through my participation in YAF, I made contacts that enabled me to obtain the intern positions with Senator Buckley and the White House, and positions with the California Assembly Republicans and the Reagan Administration." Since 1985 she has been an Assistant United States Attorney for the Northern District of Texas.[233]

The high school and college students who helped build YAF during those turbulent years, whether on campuses with active SDS chapters or not, did succeed and meet head on the challenge of the left. As Greg Schneider noted, "During a time when radicalism swept society and the very order of the nation was being challenged, YAF held its own against the tide. In so doing, YAF helped make possible for conservatives what only appeared to be a dream at the dawn of the 1960s—political power."[234] Other historians of 20th century conservatism made a similar conclusion.[235]

Patrick Korten, one of those YAF members who started the *Badger Herald* newspaper at the University of Wisconsin, might have had his years off slightly but he was prescient when he boasted, "We're thinking of the future and what we're doing now won't be felt for another five years. But we're going to be felt and we're going to be felt strong."[236] Looking back on that time several years later, historian Jonathan Schoenwald concluded, "the leaders always knew that demonstrations, press conferences, and the like were only means, not ends . . . understood that through these relatively insignificant activities they were building the basis of a long-lasting political movement."[237] As YAF approached its second decade, its presence was being felt not only as an organization but as the birthing ground for political and community leaders who would begin assuming positions of

---

231. 2008 YAF Alumni Survey Responses: Dianne Gordon.
232. 2008 YAF Alumni Survey Responses: Richard A. Cheatham.
233. 2008 YAF Alumni Survey Responses: Diane M. Kozub.
234. Schneider, *The Other Sixties*, p. 8.
235. See also, Ronald Story and Bruce Laurie: *The Rise of Conservatism in America: 1945–2000* (New York: Bedford/St. Martin's, 2007), pp. 10–11.
236. Weinraub, "Unrest," *New York Times*, October 12, 1969.
237. Schoenwald: *The Other Counterculture*, p. 9.

leadership in American society. They had more than survived; they had grown, matured, and thrived.

Meanwhile, within YAF itself, serious fissures were developing in the coalition that had constituted the young conservative movement, a movement previously united behind Barry Goldwater's candidacy and opposition to the radical leftists on campus. As YAF's leaders headed to St. Louis for the organization's fifth national convention, those fissures would grow into a lasting split that would cause a sizeable segment of the organization to depart. Facing these challenges, the organization would be tested but survive and go on to achieve further success in the decade of the 1970s.

9. Division in the Ranks

"[T]he preservation of internal order, the provision of national defense, and the administration of justice . . . When government ventures beyond these rightful functions, it accumulates power which tends to diminish order and freedom"[1]

Ever since its founding in 1960, Young Americans for Freedom had been a broad coalition of individuals on the political right. Although encompassing a diverse group of individuals and political outlooks opposed to liberalism, the dominant thrust of the organization was associated with *National Review* and the "fusionist" approach to conservatism first articulated by *NR*'s Frank S. Meyer. True, there had been challenges to this approach by those more closely attuned to moderate Republicanism or Ayn Rand's philosophy of Objectivism or the John Birch Society. These attempts to redirect the focus of the organization had been rebuffed, even as they resurfaced from time to time. As the divided decade came to a close, the organization faced two new challenges to its place as a representative of what its leaders believed to be responsible conservatism.

The first challenge was the least serious and has been discussed previously. It came from those enamored of Governor George Wallace of Alabama and supportive of his candidacy for President in 1968. As the membership surveys cited earlier clearly demonstrated, Wallace support among YAF members was minimal, never above five percent among the members and even less among the organization's leadership. After the 1968 presidential election, a few former YAF members were involved in converting the Youth for Wallace group into the National Youth Alliance (NYA).[2] In its early period, much of the NYA's efforts were directed towards attacking Young Americans for Freedom. The NYA became a clearly racist organization committed to posturing as a violent organization willing to battle the Left by any means.[3] As Dennis McMahan, NYA Vice President claimed, "The NYA will meet violence with violence . . . the left will be forced to cower in the sewers underground as they hear the marching steps of the NYA above them."[4] Despite these strong words, NYA never became a viable force on any campus, even in the South, and did not pose a credible threat to SDS and other leftist groups.[5] By 1974, the organization changed its name to National Alliance, came under the total control of William Pierce until his death in 2002, and still exists as a far-right racist and anti-Semitic element in American society.[6]

---

1. From "The Sharon Statement," adopted in conference at Sharon, Connecticut, September 9–11, 1960.
2. "Racist Groups Exploit Campus Unrest," *New Guard*, Summer 1969, p. 3.
3. Leslie H. Whitten, "Militant Rightists Have Woes," *San Antonio Light*, March 30, 1969. Among the early leaders were John Acord, Daniel Paulsen, and Dennis McMahon, each of whom had either been expelled from YAF or had left the organization and involved themselves in attacking it from the outside.
4. Quoted in Jacquelyn Estrada, "Putting Out the Fire" in Estrada, editor: *The University Under Siege*, p. 200.
5. "Racist Groups Exploit Campus Unrest," *New Guard*, Summer 1969, p. 3.
6. David Cay Johnston, "William Pierce, 69, Neo–Nazi Leader, Dies," *New York Times*, July 24, 2002.

The Libertarian Push

A more serious and lasting challenge came from those who believed in limited or even no government—radical libertarians and anarchists. Several had joined YAF as conservatives and over time moved further to the libertarian position from which they attacked many of the YAF programs as being statist. Still others joined YAF as the only viable group for young people on the right, bringing with them their strongly held libertarian or anarchist beliefs, hoping to influence the organization ideologically. From its beginning, YAF had a significant element of its membership that described itself as libertarian.[7] Prior to and after the Goldwater campaign, some YAF members were strongly influenced by Ayn Rand's Objectivism while others advocated a classical liberal position associated with Friedman, Hayek, von Mises, and those associated with the Foundation for Economic Education (FEE). Some YAF members worked for support of the Liberty Amendment to the Constitution that would repeal the 16th amendment and abolish the Federal income tax.[8] Yet, up until 1969 there was a willingness on the part of these individuals to work together in a coalition on the right with Young Americans for Freedom as the appropriate vehicle.

Indeed, as the threat of the SDS and other left-wing organizations mounted on college campuses there was a natural desire of YAF members to seek allies. This meant to some that a peace treaty needed to be signed with aspects of the counterculture then gaining followers among the nation's youth. Bill Rusher noted some years later,

> From the standpoint of YAF, confronting the onslaught of the New Left on American campuses in the 1960s, the beauty of libertarianism was that it seemed congruent with many of the things that students of that generation were beginning to say and feel: Big Is Bad. Do Not Fold, Spindle or Mutilate Me. Let Me Do My Own Thing. Stop The World—I Want to Get Off. It's My Life—Let Me Live It. Big Brother Will Get You. And so on.[9]

What appealed to many of the non-political were the elements of conservatism that stressed individual freedom, namely its libertarian component. This tact could be used as an entre to those who were opposed to the radicalism of the left and open to a more developed political outlook.

At the summer 1966 YAF leadership conference, slightly more than one in four members chose either Libertarian or Objectivist to describe their philosophical position. This division among YAF members continued with roughly the same proportion at least through the beginning of the next decade, with the highest percentage found in a survey some months after the 1969 YAF National

---

7. For an excellent historical perspective on this philosophical position by a former editor of *New Guard*, see David Boaz: *Libertarianism—A Primer* (New York: The Free Press, 1997). A collection of writings on the major themes of this philosophy can be found in David Boaz, editor: *The Libertarian Reader* (New York: The Free Press, 1997). Brian Doherty: *Radicals for Capitalism* (New York: Public Affairs, 2007) is described by the author as "a freewheeling history of the American libertarian movement."

8. The opposing sides of this question were presented in the November 1965 issue of *New Guard*: David F. Nolan, "Why We Need The Liberty Amendment," pp. 5–6, 25; Richard S. Wheeler, "Forget The Liberty Amendment," pp. 7–12.

9. William A. Rusher: *The Rise of the Right*, p. 134.

Convention. It could be seen in the debates before the various platform subcommittees at the 1967 YAF National Convention.[10] Much of this division in 1967, however, might well have represented an anti-establishment mood within the organization rather than a clear-cut ideological divide. However, David F. Nolan, former Massachusetts Institute of Technology YAF Chairman, was a libertarian who quickly found some allies in Pittsburgh.

> ... it soon became evident that I was not the only one who had some ideas about "radicalizing" YAF; in particular, I found that there were strong pockets of libertarian or crypto-libertarian YAFers in New York, Pennsylvania, and Ohio as well as in my then native Massachusetts.[11]

When the convention ended, Nolan and a few others attempted to form a Libertarian Caucus and held a meeting attended by some eighty individuals. For David Walter, newly elected to the YAF National Board of Directors, this convention and its outcomes were the start of increased libertarian influence and communication in YAF. Walter recalled that,

> 1967 was the year that Libertarianism made breakthroughs in YAF. We became aware of each other ... we became aware of the other pockets of libertarianism in YAF and of other libertarian leaders such as Jarret Wollstein in Maryland, Dave Friedman in Illinois, Frank Bubb and Ted Frech in Missouri, Dave Nolan in Massachusetts, and many Californians.[12]

The list of the attendees at that convention meeting became the beginnings of a libertarian network at a time when there were few libertarian organizations or publications outside of YAF.

YAF had always advocated free market economics and from 1967 forward its magazine began featuring even more articles by a number of libertarian writers. Arnold "Arnie" Steinberg followed David Franke as editor of *New Guard* in the fall of 1967 and soon thereafter he introduced a regular column titled "The Radical," written by David Friedman, son of economist Milton Friedman, as well as another by Philip Abbott Luce called "Against the Wall." Friedman's column reflected a clear libertarian perspective on economic issues while Luce was more representative of a social libertarian outlook. Jarret B. Wollstein, until a few months earlier the YAF chairman at the University of Maryland, had articles published in 1967 and 1968 while the writings of Rod Manis and Jerome Tuccille appeared three times each during this period. Other articles by libertarians Dana Rohrabacher, Alan Bock, Joseph M. Cobb, Tibor Machan, and Ron Kimberling also appeared. Kimberling described himself in the magazine as "one of California's new crop of super-libertarians."[13] Each of these individuals described themselves as libertarians and was known among YAF members as representative of that philosophical outlook.

---

10. Philip Werdell, "Can YAF Do It Again?," *Moderator*, February 1968, pp. 11–17.

11. David F. Nolan, "Present at the Creation," *New Libertarian Notes*, November 1974, p. 7. Personal Papers of David Walter, Box 1, Hoover Institution, Stanford University, Palo Alto, CA.

12. David Walter, "The Activist Origins of the New Libertarian Movement," *New Libertarian Notes*, November 1974, p. 21. Personal Papers of David Walter, Box 1, Hoover Institution, Stanford University, Palo Alto, CA.

13. Friedman's first article appears in the Summer 1967 issue. Wollstein had a cover article in the October 1967 issue and was featured again in April 1968. Rod Manis was published in the November 1967, February 1968, and Summer 1969 issues while Jerome Tuccille's contributions appeared in the

While YAF was featuring more libertarian articles in its magazine, senior libertarians Dr. Murray Rothbard, an economics professor at Brooklyn Polytechnic Institute, and Karl Hess, former speechwriter for Barry Goldwater, established a radical libertarian journal eventually called *The Libertarian Forum*.[14] Although not directed specifically to students, nor especially to members of Young Americans for Freedom, the semi-monthly newsletter became a source of information and issue development for libertarians within YAF. Meanwhile, the National YAF Board established a Student Committee for Economic Education in the spring of 1968 and named libertarian Dave Walter of Pennsylvania as committee chairman. As Walter explained the committee's purpose, it would seek to locate representatives on as many college campuses as possible, creating "a nationwide network of campus and chapter representatives who will aid us in distributing the books, pamphlets and papers that we will obtain from other free enterprise groups."[15] The libertarians now had an internal organizational vehicle that would allow them to communicate with YAF members. The basis for the formation of a libertarian caucus within YAF was now established.

Although support for a voluntary military had been promoted by YAF for some time and the national office had provided chapters with a "Voluntary Military Action Kit," some libertarian chapters wanted more drastic action. It was not enough to write articles and letters, sponsor speakers and debates, lobby Congress and circulate petitions. Picketing draft boards, promising to defy the selective service system, and supporting those who left the country when called to report became acceptable positions for some in the libertarian camp.

Beyond the issue of the draft, some local YAF chapters began undertaking more clearly libertarian projects, indicating support for the decriminalization of marijuana and for abolishing social security. In the spring of 1969, Orange County, California YAF members conducted a demonstration where they burned social security cards. Ken Grubbs, chairman of Cal State–Fullerton YAF and later editor of *New Guard* was quoted as saying, "the Social Security system is a fraud and not a proper function of government. If it is here to stay, it should be voluntary." YAF State Chairman Dana Rohrabacher and John Schureman were shown lighting a social security card while other YAF members looked on.[16] Meanwhile, the San Fernando Valley State College and Cal State–Long Beach chapters co-sponsored a Libertarian Action Conference in April that included Ludwig von Mises as the featured speaker.[17]

Three interlocking developments were contributing to a rise in libertarian sentiment among existing YAF members while the increased focus on libertarian writers and projects was attracting those not previously involved in the organization. Foremost was a more positive attitude by some YAF members towards the counterculture that was becoming more dominant among mid-decade American youth. YAF had developed as a radical challenge to what was perceived as the liberal establishment dominant in 1960. College professors and administrators were seen as reflecting this liberal outlook. As the decade progressed and the left began to attack those in power on campus, some in YAF were not philosophically

---

April, May and Summer 1969 issues. Rohrabacher was published in October 1968, Bock in September 1968 and Kimberling in April 1969.

14. Gregory Schneider: *Cadres for Conservatism*, p. 131.
15. "SCEE Formed," *New Guard*, April 1968, p. 24.
16. *New Guard*, Summer 1969, p. 27.
17. *Ibid*. p. 24.

attuned to defending that liberal campus establishment. What began as opposition to liberals in control became broadened into a general anti-establishment posture. This led to a supportive view of the counterculture and its supposed opposition to the establishment.

One specific aspect of the counterculture affected many students in the late 1960s and that was the use of marijuana and other hallucinogenic drugs. While the use of marijuana certainly was not limited to libertarians in YAF, for libertarians the laws against marijuana possession were seen as an example of government intervention prohibiting the exercise of individual rights. Some in YAF from the beginning had advocated the decriminalization of marijuana, a position subsequently advocated by William F. Buckley, Jr. In fact, one of those who attended the initial Sharon conference and served on the YAF National Board of Directors in its early days, Yale graduate Richard Cowan, has devoted his life to the issue of the legalization of marijuana.[18] But others saw the issue as one that could be used to attack those who supported the dominant fusionist position. As Professor Murray Rothbard declared in an article directed to libertarians in YAF, "Every time some kid is busted for pot-smoking you can pin much of the responsibility on the Conservative Movement and its fusionist-Buckleyite misleaders." He went on to ask, "what kind of a free market position is one that favors the outlawry of marijuana? Where is the private property right to grow, purchase, exchange, and use?"[19] To Rothbard and his followers the question was not whether marijuana should be legalized but rather whether there should be any laws at all.

In addition to marijuana legalization there was a whole range of other questions such as the extent to which demonstrators should be restrained, the use of personal property could be restricted, and the government could make demands on its citizens.[20] After interviewing a number of former YAF members, sociologist Rebecca Klatch concluded that there were significant differences in attitudes between libertarians and other YAF members.

> While traditionalists viewed libertarians as flag-burning, dope-smoking leftist sympathizers, libertarians viewed traditionalists as law-and-order, drug-suppressing authoritarians who were obsessed with communism at the expense of civil liberties.[21]

Beyond specific issues was an overriding identification with the music, clothes and lifestyle of what was known as the counter-culture that was appealing to many libertarians. Supporting the concept of individual liberty led to a practical belief that one should be free to "do your own thing." This difference in attitude, values, and outlook would surface in practical political terms as the YAF members gathered for another biennial national convention in St. Louis over Labor Day weekend.

David Friedman saw the difference also as one caused by a fundamental disagreement on strategy and target audiences. He maintained that when you are selling an idea, how you sell it and what you label it is affected by the values and outlooks of those whom you are trying to reach. From his perspective, he saw the fusionists and traditionalists in YAF as seeking

---

18. Cowan writes a regular blog on http://marijuananews.com.
19. Murray Rothbard, "Listen, YAF," *The Libertarian Forum*, August 15, 1969.
20. Sara Diamond: *Roads to Dominion*, p. 123–124.
21. Rebecca Klatch: *A Generation Divided*, p. 213.

to convert and to organize people who wear ties, people who live in suburbia, people who live in the South—people who, however much they object to certain elements of present-day America, basically identify with it, and see their objective as the preservation of existing freedom.

Libertarians, on the other hand, were attempting to reach a different audience, "those dissatisfied with our existing society, especially the young, that what is wrong is not too much capitalism but too little. It is directed at those who seek, not to preserve freedom, but to gain it."[22]

Thus, according to Friedman, the approach taken towards the counterculture depended not so much on the inherent value of that or any other cultural outlook but whether or not those in the counterculture were the audience one was trying to reach. This is where and why libertarians and traditionalists reacted differently to changing attitudes among students and emphasized different issues when appealing to them. From Friedman's perspective, "For the 'traditionalist,' anti-communism and support of the war are useful issues. For the 'libertarians' they are liabilities. The people we are trying to persuade are already strongly anti-war."[23] It seemed to him that the positions emphasized by the libertarians antagonize the people the traditionalists want to attract and the positions of the traditionalists offend those the libertarians want to convert. For Friedman, one's stand on the counterculture becomes a marketing decision: what is the product you want to sell and who is your target audience.

For some in YAF, the logical extension from libertarianism and its opposition to the state's involvement in the lives of its citizens was the move to anarchism or, as sometimes formulated, anarcho-capitalism.[24] The question centered on whether there should be limited government or no government at all. This debate was joined in companion articles that appeared in the April 1969 issue of *New Guard*, just months before the upcoming YAF National Convention. Leading off was Jerome Tuccille who criticized Karl Hess for advocating anarchy and for a wrongheaded view of the New Left as in any way libertarian. Tuccille maintained that any system that moved to anarchism would quickly be supplanted by a dictatorial order. In effect, Tuccille claimed that on practical terms an anarchistic society could not long survive. As to Hess's fascination with an alliance with Students for a Democratic Society (SDS) and other elements of the New Left, Tuccille could not see any strains of libertarianism in these organizations.[25]

Karl Hess had made his name as a speechwriter for Barry Goldwater and as the individual who penned the famous phrase on extremism that Goldwater uttered in his acceptance speech at the 1964 Republican National Convention.[26] After the election, Hess went through a major reconsideration of his political views and ended up with a position sometimes referred to as anarcho-capitalism combining

---

22. David Friedman, "What Are We Fighting Over?," undated, Personal Papers of Jameson Campaigne, Jr., Ottawa, IL.

23. *Ibid.*

24. This is not the place to discuss the technical differences among various schools of anarchism and the terms "anarchism" and "anarcho-capitalism" should be taken in the broadest context. My apologies to those whose distinctive philosophical position may best be described by a more specific term.

25. Jerome Tuccille, "The False Libertarians," *New Guard*, April 1969, pp. 14–15.

26. Hess: *In a Cause That Will Triumph* recounts the campaign from the Hess perspective at a time prior to his conversion to anarcho-capitalism. Uncertainty remains whether it was Hess or Harry Jaffa or Cicero who first used the phrase.

support for a radically free market system with the absence of any government institutions. He adopted the counter-culture lifestyle, became a welder, and determined that he would no longer pay obeisance to government and refused to file any federal income tax returns. Hess had gained broad public attention to his newly adopted perspective on society with an article in the March 1969 issue of *Playboy* magazine.[27]

In his *New Guard* article, Hess maintained that those he labeled conservative libertarians or "reform statists" are pessimistic about Man (with the word capitalized by Hess) and optimistic about the state.[28] For Hess, this is a reversal of reality and that those who believe in individual liberty must have a positive view of mankind. According to Hess, this proper understanding of the individual leads to a distrust of government and the need to see it abolished. "Anarchy is the social 'yes' of every man who believes in Man and believes him fit to be fully free." From his discussions with those active in New Left organizations such as SDS, he believed that common cause could be made with those who, while on the left, shared his belief in individual liberty. He concluded his article by declaring, "I stand with those who stand with Man and against the state. If this means anarchy, I hope we all make the most of it, left and right."[29] Hess became a regular feature of debates and discussions in YAF.

In April, Hess participated in a panel discussion with Tuccille, Frank Meyer and Professor Henry Paolucci of St. John's University during YAF's Mid-Atlantic regional conference in New York City. This panel became a significant turning point in the division between the traditionalists and fusionists on one side and the libertarians and anarchists on the other. During the panel discussion, Paolucci vigorously attacked anarchism and the views of both Hess and Tuccille. When Paolucci said that anarchists shot one of his relatives in the street, some of Hess's supporters stood up and cheered. As one observer noted, "It was either provocateurish on their part or it aligns them directly with the crazy element within the left."[30] Yet, from another perspective, Tuccille maintains he became radicalized by the reaction of what he claims was a predominantly anti-libertarian audience of YAF members, an audience that apparently included a number of rather vocal anarchists.[31]

Tuccille's recollection of a traditionalist-dominated gathering was not shared by a number of libertarians also present at the conference. According to Donald Meinshausen,

> The debate made an impression on me and many others who later became libertarians. It was here that I first met Karl, and Murray Rothbard, the Karl Marx of Libertarianism. It was here that the East and West Coast leaders of YAF first met to plan to organize a libertarian caucus.[32]

Writing a few years after the conference, David Walter remembers that meeting as one where "libertarian ideas carried that conference—laissez-faire and TANSTAAFL

---

27. Karl Hess, "The Death of Politics," *Playboy*, March 1969.
28. Karl Hess, "In Defense of Hess," *New Guard*, April 1969, pp. 15–16.
29. *Ibid.* p. 16.
30. Phillip Abbott Luce quoted in "The Phillip Luce–Karl Hess Debate," monograph distributed by Young Americans for Freedom, 1970, p. 20.
31. Jerome Tuccille: *It Usually Begins with Ayn Rand*, pp. 84–91.
32. Don Meinshausen, "Memoir: Present at the Creation," *Liberty*, June 2004.

banners hung on the walls, speeches were libertarian in tone, and the trads came off looking like a mob of slightly dimwitted high schoolers." Finally, this was a conference where libertarian candidate Ernsberger received close to 40% of the vote running against an incumbent in the election for National Board, an election where many libertarians supported the incumbent.[33]

In August, just prior to the YAF National Convention, Hess debated Phillip Abbott Luce on the topic of anarchism at the *New Guard* offices and the transcript was subsequently published and distributed by YAF. While the vast majority of YAF members did not support anarchism, Hess had become a new political personality on the youthful right. Being featured in *New Guard* and taking part in YAF debates made Hess a draw to some YAF members while also bringing to the organization some libertarians who were enamored of the Hess persona and philosophical position. Reflecting the libertarian concern over the growth in state power, two members of the YAF National Board of Directors, Shawn Steel of California and David Walter of Pennsylvania, proposed amending the Sharon Statement to read "That international communism *and domestic statism are* the greatest threats to these liberties." As they argued in support of the change,

> We believe that this change in the Sharon Statement is in keeping with YAF's direction against domestic statism—our increasing emphasis on combating the New Left's activities for instance.
>
> The more sophisticated college students to which YAF must appeal, are slightly put off, we believe, by the current emphasis on "international communism" as "the greatest single menace to our liberties." It sounds too Birchy and unbalanced by a recognition of domestic menaces.
>
> YAF has already recognized such menaces—publication of "The Fascist Threat to America" as an example—it is now time to incorporate a specific denunciation of this evil in the Sharon Statement.[34]

The amendment was not approved, partially because some Directors maintained that the founding document should not be amended, a position that prevailed in the organization even after the fall of the Berlin Wall and the disintegration of the Soviet Union.

Still others were concluding that their libertarian position was in no way encompassed by the term conservatism. Howard Calloway, Chairman of the Philadelphia YAF chapter and a candidate for the National Board at the upcoming convention, published a flyer titled "An Introduction to Radicalism" wherein he defined libertarianism as radical and not in any fashion conservative. "Conservatism never was nor never could be a concept which could represent the ideals of the right to life. . . . We do not seek to conserve any great portion of America's political institutions or principles."[35] Clearly, to some libertarians, the idea of a unified right under the term conservative was no longer valid. This would have

---

33. David Walter, "The Activist Origins of the New Libertarian Movement," *New Libertarian Notes*, November 1974, p. 21, Personal Papers of David Walter, Box 1, Hoover Institution, Stanford University, Palo Alto, CA. "TANSTAAFL" is the acronym for a favored libertarian statement that "there ain't no such thing as a free lunch," a saying that was made popular by Robert Heinlein in his 1966 book, *The Moon is a Harsh Mistress.*

34. Resolution proposed by David Walter and William (Shawn) Steel to the National Board of Directors, 1969. Personal Papers of Jameson Campaigne, Jr., Ottawa, IL.

35. Howard Calloway, "An Introduction to Radicalism," no date. Personal Papers of Jameson Campaigne, Jr., Ottawa, IL.

serious implications for their perceived ability to work together within Young Americans for Freedom and would lead to a proposed change in the language of the organization's founding document to eliminate the opening phrase, "We, as young conservatives."

Building from a positive view of the counter-culture and adding in a serious opposition to the state, many libertarians began challenging the American effort in Vietnam. While YAF had expressed support of the Johnson Administration's efforts in the mid-60s, at the same time the organization had consistently advocated victory as the overriding goal. As the war continued with what appeared to be limited objectives, YAF began to shift away from outright support and increased criticism of the Administration's conduct of the war. By 1969, a new Administration was led by a President who had claimed in his election campaign to have a "secret plan" for the war in Vietnam. Yet the war continued with never-ending peace talks and ever-mounting violence and the loss of lives.

Convinced that the South Vietnamese were not willing to fight for their independence, by 1968 David Walter had decided that the United States should withdraw from Vietnam. Walter's position, while certainly not the prevailing view, is less surprising when one recalls the spring 1968 YAF membership survey. Although nearly nine in ten favored victory, when asked what they would support should the present policy continue, roughly half said withdraw. When one concluded that the government's policy was a failure, withdrawal became the preferred policy for some YAF members. According to Walter, "At some point before the purge there were actually YAF chapters that were out joining antiwar marches. So there was a real . . . personality crisis in YAF. Some chapters were this and some chapters were that."[36] Local chapters in New York, New Jersey, Pennsylvania and California included the highest percentage of libertarians and also the greatest number of those opposed to continued American participation in the Vietnam war.

For some, it was not merely an anti-war position but a determination that the United States was conducting an evil war against the Vietnamese people. Ron Kimberling was chairman of Cal State–Long Beach YAF and a libertarian who represented this perspective. He was,

> . . . opposed to the U.S. imperialist venture in Vietnam, which is being con-
> ducted in a manner that seriously undermines freedom for the Vietnamese
> and for citizens in our own country, who are being subjected to fascism in
> the name of freedom.[37]

While few were as convinced that the American support of the South Vietnamese was immoral, many more viewed what they perceived as a "no win" policy in Vietnam as immoral. This determination to end the war, either as not winnable or even as immoral, led some in YAF to form alliances with the left. After working together with the left on the war issue, the idea of a right-left alliance advocated by Karl Hess became less of an alien concept.

From the perspective of most fusionist and traditionalist members of YAF, the positions of some radical libertarians posed a direct threat to the nature of the organization. While they continued to believe that the effort in Vietnam was designed to stop communist aggression, even if it were not being conducted in

---

36. Klatch: *A Generation Divided*, p. 123.
37. From an article in the college newspaper quoted in Heineman: *Put Your Bodies upon the Wheels*, p. 161.

the manner they wanted, the fusionists and traditionalists saw their fellow YAF members participating in antiwar demonstrations and expressing support for resistance to the draft. Although they saw the New Left and SDS as threats to peace on campus and the ability to obtain an education, the more radical libertarians spoke of the need to form alliances with what they perceived as "anti-statist" elements in the leftist organizations. Where the traditionalists saw licentiousness in the counterculture, the libertarians saw expressions of individual freedom. When the fusionists and traditionalists pledged allegiance to the American flag, the anarchists in their organization waved the black flag and supported the right of individuals to burn the flag on the grounds of private property rights. Young Americans for Freedom had been created as a conservative organization; now some of their members maintained that the term conservative did not encompass their ideological positions. Clearly, a serious division was surfacing in YAF.

While these philosophical debates and changes in positions were occurring, YAF held its regional conferences during the spring of 1969, conferences at which delegates would elect eight members of the National Board of Directors. As previously discussed, the Mid-Atlantic region saw a contested battle between incumbent Ron Docksai of New York and libertarian leader Don Ernsberger of Pennsylvania with Docksai prevailing. Two other libertarian candidates, however, were elected—Don Feder from New England and Patrick Dowd from the Western region. The other regional conferences chose candidates more attuned to the traditionalist or fusionist positions. Albert Forrester was re-elected to the Southwest regional position and Richard Derham returned to the Board from the Northwest region. New Directors were J. Harold Herring of North Carolina from the Southern region, Bill Overmoe from Minnesota in the Plains region, and Gary Brown of Illinois representing the Midwest. Brown would resign a few months later to accept a position on the YAF national office staff while Overmoe would serve one term on the Board before undertaking graduate work in England. Herring would remain actively involved for several years and became a key player in the election of Jesse Helms to the United States Senate from North Carolina in 1972, subsequently joining the new legislator's Capitol staff.

Meanwhile, two political movements were developing that would challenge the prevailing order in Young Americans for Freedom, one calling itself the Libertarian Caucus and the other the Anarchist Caucus.

The Libertarian Caucus

In the spring of 1969, Don Ernsberger contacted some of the YAF members he had known over the past two years and announced the formation of a Libertarian Caucus with an objective of influencing the direction of YAF at the upcoming national convention. The reaction from several in the leadership of the organization was swift. David Keene was the current Vice Chairman and the leading, eventually only, candidate for National Chairman to succeed Alan MacKay. Keene had been forwarded a copy of Ernsberger's announcement and responded to him on June 26th saying "I was rather disappointed by your decision to engage in activities which I see as potentially divisive at a time when we are facing a threat on our campuses that should force us to overlook petty sectionalism." Keene maintained that few libertarians saw him as an enemy and said that he was committed to including "any legitimate point of view consistent with the basic tenets of the Sharon Statement."[38]

Keene then sent a copy of his letter to Ernsberger along with a memo to YAF leaders from the "Vote for YAF Committee" supporting a slate of Keene for National Chairman, Michael Thompson for Vice Chairman, Ron Docksai for Secretary, and Daniel Manion for Treasurer. In his memo Keene claimed,

> The crux of the charges being circulated seems to be that YAF is strictly controlled by a "traditionalist" clique that is woefully out of touch with the membership. I have been a member of the national board since 1965, and I still don't think I could definitely categorize my colleagues as either "traditionalist" or "libertarian" ... Most YAF directors, like most YAF members, are libertarian on some issues, traditionalist on others, and unclassifiable on still others.[39]

Ernsberger followed with additional mailings to the Libertarian Caucus outlining their goals for the organization. They were committed to (1) electing libertarians to the Board, (2) changing the by-laws so that all Board members would be elected by delegates to the regional and national conventions (thus abolishing the seven Board-selected senior director slots), (3) proposing two modifications to the Sharon Statement that would remove the word conservative and add along with international communism, "domestic statism" as an equal threat to liberty, (4) adopting a resolution clarifying the direction YAF would take in the 1970s, (5) promoting a program to educate all YAF members in libertarianism and laissez-faire capitalism, and (6) establishing a permanent communications system among libertarian members in YAF. Clearly, the libertarians were undertaking a full-force challenge to the existing leadership and programmatic emphasis of the organization.

Don Feder was a new Board member, having been elected at the 1969 New England regional conference. Feder had been chairman of Boston University YAF, was State YAF Chairman for Massachusetts, and regarded himself at that time as a libertarian. However, he was not pleased by what he saw as an exclusionary Libertarian Caucus. After receiving Ernsberger's mailings he wrote to Shawn Steel, Ernsberger and Ralph Fucetola of New Jersey YAF critiquing their efforts. He sent a copy also to fellow new Board member Patrick Dowd of California.

> Among other things you call for abolition of morality laws, striking God from the Sharon Statement, complete support of the "social and economic principles of laissez-faire capitalism." But what concessions are you willing to make to the Traditionalists in YAF? A coalition implies compromise, give and take. Yet it seems all you're willing to do is take. Are you saying to Traditionalists in YAF "either become Objectivists or leave the organization?" This seems to be the case.

Feder went on to maintain that the Caucus was "perpetrating a monstrous fraud by constantly implying that there is a nationwide purge of libertarians occurring

---

38. A copy of Keene's letter to Ernsberger was attached to a memo from Keene to YAF leaders under the letterhead of the "Vote for YAF Committee."

39. *Ibid.*

in YAF." Feder noted that he was a libertarian, that the chairman of his chapter at Boston University was an Objectivist, and that he had asked Alan MacKay to appoint Fucetola, a Caucus leader from New Jersey, to the convention's student affairs committee.[40]

One week later, Patrick Dowd responded to Feder by denying any involvement with the Libertarian Caucus. "I do not consider myself a member of the Libertarian Caucus . . . If the charges you make in the letter about the attitudes and statements of the Libertarian Caucus are true, I do not ever want to have anything to do with them."[41] At the same time, Phillip Abbott Luce wrote to Shawn Steel in an effort to convince him that the national leadership was willing to work with and appoint libertarians to positions of responsibility. He noted that both he and Kenneth Grubbs were then working at the national office while fellow libertarians Rod Manis and David Friedman had been featured speakers at the Leadership Training Conferences held through the summer of 1969.

It is safe to say that while today there is no real serious philosophical cleavage among most YAFers, illfounded charges will help to create a division. Indeed, at a time when we are faced with a serious battle on the campuses it is incredible (if not outright provocateurish) for some ultra-libertarians to take on the mantles of martyrdom and to holler whether they are being hit or not. God knows that few people worry more about the role of libertarians in the movement than I do and this is what bothers me so much about the recent outpouring of spleen from various sources in the past weeks.

Luce concluded, "When all is said and done, few will remember us, but they may just remember what we contributed to the movement in the form of a concerted program for change in the nation and just perhaps the world."[42]

Ernsberger responded to the mounting criticism by modifying the scope of the Caucus objectives. In a late July newsletter, the Caucus stated that the goals of amending the Sharon Statement and changing the by-laws to allow electing all National Directors were long-range goals that they did not expect to achieve immediately. Moreover, the Caucus denied that it wished to eliminate all traditionalists. "We are not exclusionary; we are not a 'rule or ruin' group; we do not advocate anything more than that YAF maintain a consistent pro-freedom policy." As to whether they were attempting to change the direction of YAF entirely, the Caucus claimed "we wish only to have a greater say in the direction of YAF in the 1970s." The memo claimed a membership of 213 YAF members.[43] Ernsberger was also reacting to concern from some of his potential backers. When Patrick Dowd, California YAF Chairman, indicated that one of his organization's financial supporters was upset with what she was hearing, Ernsberger wrote to her to say that any claim the Libertarian Caucus was "planning to walk out of YAF after the

40. Letter of July 17, 1969 from Don Feder to Don Ernsberger, Ralph Fucetola and Shawn Steel. Personal Papers of Patrick Dowd, Box 1, Hoover Institution, Stanford University, Palo Alto, CA.

41. Letter of July 25, 1969 from Patrick Dowd to Don Feder. Personal Papers of Patrick Dowd, Box 1, Hoover Institution, Stanford Unversity, Palo Alto, CA.

42. Letter of Phillip Abbott Luce to William (Shawn) Steel, July 25, 1969. Personal Papers of Patrick Dowd, Box 1, Hoover Institution, Stanford University, Palo Alto, CA. At the time Luce was Director of College Services at the YAF National office.

43. Libertarian Caucus Memo #6, July 24, 1969. Personal Papers of Patrick Dowd, Box 1, Hoover Institution, Stanford University, Palo Alto, CA.

convention" is "unfounded and irresponsible."[44]

By late summer, the Libertarian Caucus had determined that it would run a slate of candidates for the nine positions on the National Board to be elected at the 1969 Convention but not contest the National Chairman office where David Keene was expected to win. The slate would be headed by William (Shawn) Steel, a former California State Chairman whose term on the National Board had ended that spring; David Walter of Pennsylvania, an incumbent Board Member seeking re-election; Dana Rohrabacher, a former California State Chairman; William Chaisson, New Jersey YAF State Chairman; Howard Callaway, chairman of the Philadelphia YAF chapter; Jerry Biggers, chairman of Northern Illinois University YAF; and Mike Ingallinera, former Treasurer of Virginia YAF.[45] The other two positions were left vacant after Ray Semmens, a libertarian who was Michigan YAF State Chairman, defected and joined the fusionist slate of candidates.[46]

Meanwhile, the majority on the National Board was taking action to preserve the fusionist nature of the organization.[47] Believing that David Walter would not ensure fair representation of all elements in the convention delegation, National Chairman Alan MacKay removed him as Pennsylvania YAF State Chairman and replaced him with Jay Parker, a National Director. That allowed Parker, rather than Walter, to name the state's eight at-large delegates to the convention. As Walter described it, "When it became obvious that I was backing the libertarian slate at the '69 convention, they just removed me and put Jay Parker in charge."[48]

---

44. Letter of Don Ernsberger to Marquita Maytag, August 1, 1969. Personal Papers of Patrick Dowd, Box 1, Hoover Institution, Stanford University, Palo Alto, CA.

45. "Libertarian Caucus Slate," flyer distributed at 1969 YAF National Convention. After listing the above names, the flyer noted: "We, of the Libertarian Caucus, also highly recommend the independent candidacy of Harvey Hukari, chairman of YAF at Stanford Univ." Personal Papers of Jameson Campaigne, Jr., Ottawa, IL.

46. David Walter, "The Activist Origins of the New Libertarian Movement," *New Libertarian Notes*, November 1974, p. 23, Personal Papers of David Walter, Box 1, Hoover Institution, Stanford University, Palo Alto, CA.

47. Much has been written about the 1969 YAF National Convention, almost all of it from the libertarian or anarchist position, especially since some maintain that the contemporary libertarian movement developed in the aftermath of that convention. Three relatively fair presentations on the events are Klatch: *A Generation Divided*, pp. 225–234; Schneider: *Cadres for Conservatism*, pp. 127–141; and Jared C. Lodbell, "Meet Them in St. Louis," *National Review*, September 23, 1969, p. 949. Two critical articles from the far right are Conservatus, "A Disillusioning Convention," *The American Mercury*, winter 1969, pp. 12–15 and Brad Evans, "The Young Conservatives: Coming Unglued?," *Triumph*, November 1970, pp. 11–15. Also interesting is the perspective from the left provided in "Special Report: The 'Libertarian' split—a 'New Right,'" *Group Research Report*, March 3, 1971, pp. 9–11. Portrayals of the convention and the events leading up to it can be found in the articles by David F. Nolan, Samuel Edward Konkin, III, Eric Scott Royce, David Walter, Kathy Greene, and Ralph Fucetola, III in *New Libertarian Notes*, November 1974. Also interesting but biased is Samuel Konkin (a.k.a. SEK3), "History of the Libertarian Movement" at www.bradspangler.com/blog/archives/288. More contemporaneous are John K. Everson, "The Freedom Scene," *The Rational Individualist*, September 1969, p. 10 and Frank Mintz, "Libertarians and YAF: A Personal Editorial," *The Rational Individualist*, September 1969, pp. 2–3. Jerome Tuccille: *Radical Libertarianism*, pp. 96–109 recounts his personal experience but Konkin labeled it "a piece of puerile propaganda, highly self-serving to the 'Anarchist Caucus.'" Joseph M. Cobb, "Young Authoritarians for 'Freedom,'" *The Libertarian Connection*, February 1970, is full of inaccuracies as to when the convention occurred and what happened in St. Louis. It can be found in the Personal Papers of Patrick Dowd, Box 2, Hoover Institution, Stanford University, Palo Alto, CA. Finally, a detailed but very subjective history of libertarian activities involving the 1969 convention is provided in Doherty: *Radicals for Capitalism*, pp. 353–359. Compared to all these writings from the libertarian and anarchist perspectives there is virtually nothing in writing from the fusionist and traditionalist point of view.

48. Klatch: *A Generation Divided*, p. 223. Walter provides the same explanation for his removal in his "The Activist Origins of the New Libertarian Movement," *New Libertarian Notes*, November 1974, p. 21. Personal Papers of David Walter, Box 1, Hoover Institution, Stanford University, Palo Alto, CA.

California YAF precipitated the second crisis involving a state organization when, on August 17th, its board voted to discharge the California YAF executive director, Allen Brandstater. Brandstater and California YAF state chairman Patrick Dowd were both members of the National Board of Directors and had worked in an uneasy truce since April. Dowd was close to the more libertarian members of YAF while Brandstater's support rested with the more traditionalist members. In response to the action, National Chairman Alan MacKay removed Dowd as state chairman and suspended the functioning of the California YAF board of directors with further remedial action to take place only after the national convention.[49] The action of California YAF's board and then National YAF's response added fuel to the fire for the libertarian challenge. Dowd fired off a letter to a number of individuals active in YAF nationwide asking them to demand that Chairman MacKay reinstate him. He claimed that National YAF removed him because removing Brandstater as state executive director just before the convention was inappropriate. "If the Board had acted after the Convention there supposedly would have been no problem. In a word, it was 'inconvenient' for the National Office."[50] "Inconvenient" may not be the most appropriate word to describe the situation. California was a state organization closely divided between libertarians and fusionists. YAF was two weeks away from a national convention where a libertarian caucus was lodging a major challenge to the existing leadership. Removing a traditionalist executive director before the convention was bound to look like a power move by the libertarians and the state chairman they supported. Given this situation, it is little surprise that the National Chairman made the move that he did and left the state chairman situation in limbo until the convention was over.

However, the result in California was to push some members to the libertarian position in protest of the national organization's involvement in what they regarded as purely state matters.[51] Harvey Hukari, chairman of the Stanford YAF chapter that would receive the award for "best college chapter" at the St. Louis convention, had been slated to run for the National Board of Directors on the Conservative Caucus slate. After Dowd was removed as state chairman, Hukari dropped off the slate and determined to run for the National Board as an independent candidate. Other chapter leaders in California were now motivated to go to St. Louis and vote against any candidates perceived as supporting the actions of the national organization in removing Dowd. Caught in the crossfire was David Keene, whose candidacy for National Chairman had to that point been unopposed. In responding to those upset with the national organization's move, Keene promised to travel to the state and meet with all elements after the national convention and only then to appoint a new state chairman. This promise temporarily quelled some of the discontent.[52]

For a different view of the reasons for his removal see the letter of Phillip Abbott Luce to Bill Steel dated July 25, 1969 and cited above.

49. Memo to California and National YAF Leaders from Randal Cornell Teague, August 20, 1969. Copy in author's possession provided by Michael Sanera.

50. "A Nation-wide Mailing to Leaders of Young Americans for Freedom," Personal Papers of Patrick Dowd, Box 1, Hoover Institution, Stanford University, Palo Alto, CA.

51. At least 22 California YAF chapter chairmen sent letters to MacKay protesting the removal of Dowd and in support of the dismissal of Brandstater. Copies are in Personal Papers of Patrick Dowd, Box 1, Hoover Institution, Stanford University, Palo Alto. CA.

52. Keene appointed a committee consisting of Phillip Abbott Luce, Dick Derham of Washington State, and himself. The group arranged to travel to California for meetings in Los Angeles and San Francisco. When Derham arrived he was notified that Luce's wife had just given birth to their child

The Anarchist Caucus

The Libertarian Caucus came to St. Louis with the objective of electing their slate to the National Board of Directors. Some believed that libertarians were underrepresented in the leadership of YAF and they wished to correct this by seeing some or all of their candidates join the National Board. Still others maintained that the nature of the organization had to change, from being a coalitional conservative group to a clearly libertarian organization. Nevertheless, virtually all members of the Libertarian Caucus approached the convention with a determination to fight for their beliefs and to continue to work within Young Americans for Freedom. That was not the case, however, with the other major group challenging the prevailing consensus in YAF for their goal was to defect and take as many members with them as possible. That other group was the Anarchist Caucus.

The Anarchist Caucus was headed by Karl Hess, IV, a student at the University of Virginia who had been the YAF chapter chairman but had not been previously active in organizational matters. The caucus never had more than fifty members but they were determined to make a visible presence at the convention. Unlike the Libertarian Caucus, however, this group was committed to splitting off from YAF and forming alliances with the New Left.[53] Prior to the convention, Murray Rothbard, who served as editor of *The Libertarian Forum* with Karl Hess, III as the Washington editor, issued a blistering editorial directed to libertarians in Young Americans for Freedom. Rothbard urged all libertarians to leave the organization and use the national convention as an opportunity to urge others to leave also. In the August 15, 1969 issue of his newsletter he attacked the leaders of YAF as false friends.

> This letter is a plea that you use the occasion of the public forum of the YAF convention to go, to split, to leave the conservative movement where it belongs: in the hands of the St. Something-or-others, and where it is going to stay regardless of what action you take. Leave the house of your false friends, for they are your enemies.

Rothbard's main attack was against the fusionists who he claimed were "apologists for the State using libertarian rhetoric as their cloak." They were deceivers on the political make, attempting to curry favor with those in power. He concluded by urging libertarians to break away from any alliance with the fusionists who controlled the organization.

> I plead with you to leave YAF now, for you should know by now that there is no hope of your ever capturing it. It is as dictatorial, as oligarchic, as close

---

and he would not be traveling from DC. Then came a call from Keene that his plane was grounded by snow at O'Hare Airport in Chicago. What was to have been a three-person delegation ended up with Derham, an attorney from Seattle, spending a weekend meeting with various YAF leaders from the libertarian and fusionist camps. After Derham filed his report with Keene, the National Chairman appointed William Saracino, a student at the University of Southern California who had been selected by the Board to fill a vacancy after the convention, and he became the California YAF State Chairman in late 1969. Interview with Richard Derham, Seattle, WA, March 27, 2009.

53. Tuccille: *Radical Libertarianism*, p. 104.

to fascism in structure as is so much of the content of YAF's program . . .

Why don't you leave now, and let the "F" in YAF stand then for what it has secretly stood for all along—"fascism"? Why don't you get out, form your own organization, breathe the clean air of freedom, and then take your stand, proudly and squarely, not with the despotism of the power elite and the government of the United States, but with the rising movement in opposition to that government? Then you will be libertarians indeed, in act as well as in theory.[54]

Rothbard had thrown down the gauntlet and his managing editor Hess, Hess's son, and the few other members of the Anarchist Caucus would pick it up.

One who was directly influenced by Hess was Donald Meinshausen, a 19 year old from New Jersey who had agreed to become involved in SDS and provide information to the House Committee on Internal Security. Meinshausen attended the YAF Mid-Atlantic Regional Conference where he heard Hess debate with Tuccille, Meyer and Paolucci. Intrigued by the Hess fear of the state, Meinshausen began meeting with him and fell under his influence. He joined with Hess and his son in the Anarchist Caucus. Like Hess, he became convinced that the New Right and the New Left could join together in opposing what he viewed as domestic fascism. This is the message he wanted to promote.

I intend to go to the national YAF convention and try to convince them not to fight the SDS but to join it in fighting the government. The goals of the Libertarian Right and the New Left are morally and politically common. It is the only way to defeat laws you don't want. And a lot of people in YAF agree with me.[55]

With a few other, mainly East Coast, radical libertarians and anarchists, Meinshausen viewed the American government as a greater threat to individual liberty than international communism and maintained that an alliance with the so-called libertarians of the New Left could be forged to fight off the domestic threat posed by the state.

On August 17th, before going to the YAF convention, the Anarchist Caucus met on the houseboat of Karl Hess, III, which was piered in Washington's Anacostia River, and drew up what they called the Tranquil Statement, a document to be presented to the national convention in St. Louis.[56] Designed to be a replacement for the organization's Sharon Statement, this substitute labeled the United States as the greatest threat to peace and freedom in the world. It called on YAF to fight against what they called American Imperialism and support the principle of universal freedom. YAF should reaffirm its commitment to free expression and

54. "Listen YAF," *The Libertarian Forum*, August 15, 1969, pp. 1–2. This view of the organization was also reflected in Cobb, "Young Authoritarians for 'Freedom,'" *The Libertarian Connection*, February 1970, Personal Papers of Patrick Dowd, Box 2, Hoover Institution, Stanford University, Palo Alto, CA. Cobb was a YAF member prior to the convention and former editor of the *New Individualist Review* whose article on draft avoidance had appeared in *New Guard*.

55. "Informer on S.D.S. Vexes House Unit," *New York Times*, August 17, 1969. See also: David R. Schweitzer and James M. Elden, "New Left as Right," *Journal of Social Issues*, volume 27, number 1 (1971), p. 156–158.

56. The references to the Hess family can be confusing. Karl Hess, father, was referred to as Karl Hess, III while his son used the moniker Karl Hess, IV at the time. Currently, the son of the former Goldwater speechwriter goes by the name of Karl Hess, Jr.

support the student right to revolution against the bureaucratic forces controlling education in America.[57]

When the Anarchist Caucus arrived in St. Louis, they attempted to have Karl Hess, III added to the Convention program although, at that late date, the agenda and the events for the next few days had long been finalized. Bill Buckley was scheduled to give the opening address that very evening. Upon being told this, Hess's son announced to the media that his father would speak later that night at the Gateway Arch. Hess IV and two other radical libertarians, Walter Block and Jerome Tuccille, made a point of interrupting William F. Buckley, Jr.'s news conference to challenge him to debate Hess at the Arch, an offer that was declined. There are differing reports on the number who turned out to hear Hess speak and where it actually occurred. One participant claims some two hundred plus were there and Hess made his call for an alliance among libertarians, anarchists, and the New Left under the Gateway Arch.[58] However, a less involved reporter from the media claimed only fifty followers of Hess showed up and "they were turned away by two guards who told them that meetings on the Arch grounds required a special permit." Apparently, as the reporter commented, "the anarchists were given one more reason to oppose government regulation."[59] Using the terminology adopted by some libertarians, another writer for a libertarian journal also reported that, "a peaceful meeting of the Anarchist Caucus under the arch was broken up by the local Gestapo."[60]

The Anarchist Caucus did have one candidate for the National Board who was part of the Libertarian Caucus slate: Michael Ingallinera, a student at the University of Virginia. He was described in his nominating speech as "an enemy of the state" and received a total of 53 votes from the 723 delegates voting at the convention, coming in last among nineteen candidates. But their objective was not to remake YAF but, rather, to encourage as many as possible to leave the organization. This objective could be reached more effectively through a dramatic action rather than a traditional election campaign. That action would come during the resolutions debate on abolishing the draft and replacing it with a voluntary military.

5th National Convention—Libs versus Trads

While the Libertarian Caucus was attempting to line up delegate votes for their slate so they could influence the direction of YAF, the Anarchist Caucus was attempting to recruit defectors from the organization. Meanwhile, the fusionist and traditionalist elements had put together their own slate of candidates operating as the Conservative Caucus. The name was chosen not only to accurately reflect their position but also to emphasize their commitment to retain the phrase "we, as young conservatives" in the Sharon Statement. The slate of nine candidates was headed up by two incumbents seeking re-election, Dan Manion of Indiana, and Mary Kay Davis, Chapter Chairman at University of Texas, along with seven

---

57. Schneider: *Cadres for Conservatism*, pp. 133–134. The Tranquil Statement, Personal Papers of Jameson Campaigne, Jr., Ottawa, IL.

58. Tuccille: *Radical Libertarianism*, p. 103.

59. "Arch No Place for Anarchists," *St. Louis Post Dispatch*, August 28, 1969. Group Research Archives, Box 340, Columbia University, New York, NY.

60. John K. Everson, "The Apple Pie Nightmare," *The Rational Individualist*, September 1969, p. 10. Personal Papers of David Walter, Box 1, Hoover Institution, Stanford University, Palo Alto, CA.

new candidates: James Farley, State Chairman of New York; Jack Gullahorn, Texas YAF State Chairman; Bradley Warren Evans, State Chairman of Kentucky; Wayne Thorburn, Maryland YAF State Chairman; Bob Moffit, a chapter chairman in Philadelphia; Jim Hager, Tennessee YAF State Chairman; and Ray Semmons, State Chairman of Michigan.[61] Semmons had been on the Libertarian Caucus slate, withdrew from it, and was subsequently slated by the Conservative Caucus. He and Farley were regarded as the most libertarian of the nine candidates on the Conservative Caucus slate.

The process of selecting individuals for the Conservative Caucus slate was more competitive as two other candidates, Jim Minarik of Ohio and Michael Ritchey of Florida sought the designation and while saluted as "outstanding candidates" did not receive the endorsement. Both withdrew from the election before the roll call of delegates took place and Minarik was subsequently, some months later, appointed to a vacant position on the Board.[62]

The official theme for the 1969 National Convention was "A Return to Freedom" and as the preface to the convention program stated, "the purpose is to involve dedicated young men and women in the Freedom Offensive of Young Americans for Freedom." It concluded by informing the delegates, "The need for 'A Return to Freedom' has never been greater. Your hard work and concerted effort will insure that Young Americans for Freedom continues to pose the only viable alternative to both the Liberals and the New Left."[63] Convention Director Michael Thompson in his welcoming letter claimed that, "the people of the United States are looking to YAF for responsible leadership. In these times of turmoil, we are in a position to bring sanity back to our campuses and responsibility into the political arena."[64] The message was clear: this was a time for responsible policies and thoughtful action.

Nevertheless, the actual rallying cry promoted to the delegates via banners, posters, and slogans, was a more catchy and direct message: "Sock it to the Left." Presented in the language of a then popular television program, the message was a determination to counter the efforts of Students for a Democratic Society, the Black Panthers, and other groups who were attempting to take over campus buildings, impose ideological standards on curricula, and otherwise disrupt the ability of students to obtain an education. The slogan was emblazoned on a banner outside the convention hotel and in the main ballroom where general sessions were held. Yet, its simplicity did not fully describe the views of many members on how best to combat their campus opponents. As Jim Wallis, a delegate from Southern Illinois University, observed,

> We have to find an answer to the new left, and that's what this convention is all about. Some of our members have talked about counteracting demonstrations on campuses this fall but that won't stop how these people feel. We have to solve the problem rather than just react to it.[65]

---

61. The author needs to acknowledge his role as a participant-observer here, having served as Chapter Director at the YAF National Office from December 1968 to July 1969 and then being a candidate for the National Board of Directors at the 1969 convention on the Conservative Caucus slate.

62. "Memo from Conservative Caucus." Personal Papers of Jameson Campaigne, Jr., Ottawa, IL.

63. *1969 National Convention—Young Americans for Freedom*, program, p. 3.

64. *Ibid*. p. 5.

65. "'Sock it to the Left' YAF Parley Theme," *Indianapolis Star*, August 29, 1969, Personal Papers of Jameson Campaigne, Jr., Ottawa, IL.

As the delegates began to assemble in St. Louis, the question of how best to respond to the New Left challenges on college campuses was forefront in their minds, at least for those not totally engrossed in the internal politics of YAF.

The convention began on Thursday afternoon, August 28th, with organizational meetings of the three subcommittees of the Platform Committee dealing with Student Affairs, Domestic Affairs, and Foreign Affairs. Each subcommittee received testimony and debated various proposals that had been submitted from the local chapters. Student Affairs Subcommittee Chairman Donald Feder outlined the challenge from SDS and its allies,

> Across the country they have burned, they have intimidated, they have killed, they have destroyed, they have taken the same course of action as the storm troopers of the Third Reich. A concentration camp society—that is their goal. If we don't oppose them, then we have lost the reason for our existence.[66]

Meanwhile, at the Subcommittee on Foreign Affairs delegates were debating the appropriate position for the organization regarding the continuing conflict in Vietnam while the Domestic Affairs subcommittee took up controversial issues such as the legalization of marijuana and the extent to which government should be limited or, as the anarchists proclaimed, totally abolished. For those who would now be called "policy wonks," this was the reason for attending a national convention. The debates and discussions, formal and informal, went on long into the night and the following day.

That evening William F. Buckley, Jr. was the featured speaker at the Opening Session. Controversy surfaced even before his address as Patrick Dowd, recently removed as California State Chairman, attempted to take a seat with other state chairmen on the platform behind the podium where Buckley would speak. When he was denied a place on the platform, several libertarian delegates from California protested. As the delay in the program continued, other delegates started chanting "We Want Buckley." This led the Anarchist Caucus and some of their allies to respond with "We Want Hess." In turn, these calls were followed by the respective chants of "Sock it to the Left" and "Sock it to the State." After several minutes of chanting, convention officials agreed to allow Dowd to sit with the other state chairmen and the formal program began.[67]

In his address, Buckley called for a reaffirmation of traditional conservative values and outlined the fusionist position that freedom and order were complementary elements. Freedom must be guaranteed, Buckley maintained, within the traditions of Western civilization. Some libertarians and anarchists subsequently claimed that Buckley's presentation was modified to become a direct attack on, and response to, Murray Rothbard and Karl Hess. According to Brian Doherty, "Buckley's speech, as Hess Jr. recalls, was obsessed with nothing so much as debunking his little anarchist caucus declaration," the Tranquil Statement.[68] Likewise, Tuccille claimed that "the first fifteen minutes was devoted to a ringing denunciation of Rothbard's open letter to the convention and criticism of some remarks

---

66. Anthony Ripley, "Young Conservatives Vow Militancy Against Left," *New York Times*, August 31, 1969.

67. Tuccille: *Radical Libertarianism*, pp. 101–102. See also, Tuccille, "The Revolution Comes to YAF," *The Libertarian Forum*, September 15, 1969, pp. 1–4.

68. Doherty: *Radicals for Capitalism*, p. 356.

made by Karl Hess in the same issue of their *Libertarian Forum*."[69] However, a review of the copy of Buckley's speech indicates that his comments on freedom and order and the perceived fallacies of anarchism were in the original text written days before the distribution of the *Libertarian Forum* issue in question.[70]

Acknowledging the fact that this was a convention attended primarily by high school and college students, the first session on Friday morning was a brunch at the reasonable hour of 10 A.M. The featured speakers were Dr. Harold Demsetz, an economics professor from the University of Chicago, and Stephen Shadegg, campaign manager for Barry Goldwater's 1964 presidential campaign. This was followed by a panel on "Conservatism—1969" involving Frank Meyer, William A. Rusher, Dr. Philip M. Crane, and Professor William Oliver Martin. The remainder of the afternoon was devoted to subcommittee meetings of the Platform Committee. Friday night was "Candidates' Night" with addresses by Congressman Donald "Buz" Lukens and former YAF National Director Fulton "Buddy" Lewis, III. Their remarks were followed by the nomination of candidates for National Chairman and National Board of Directors, with delegates engaging in demonstrations for their favored candidates after the nominating speeches. Later that night, candidates made the rounds of the various state delegations in a last minute effort to round up votes.

Saturday morning began with the unopposed election of David Keene as the new National Chairman and then the round of delegations voting for nine candidates for the National Board of Directors. To the surprise of few, all nine candidates on the Conservative Caucus slate were elected, followed by the independent candidacy of Harvey Hukari, and then the candidates on the Libertarian Caucus slate and two other independent candidates. An analysis of the votes cast by the 723 delegates is informative of the distribution of the members participating. James Farley received the most votes, 559, meaning that 77.3% of all delegates cast one of their nine votes for him while the lowest vote-getter on the Conservative Caucus slate, Ray Semmons, obtained a vote from 59.3% of the delegates. Interestingly, Farley the top vote getter and Semmons the ninth and final candidate elected were both regarded as the most libertarian candidates on the Conservative Caucus slate.

For the libertarians and anarchists, it was apparent that they were indeed a minority segment of the organization. Running as an independent candidate, Harvey Hukari obtained votes from 32.6% of the delegates while the leading candidate on the Libertarian Caucus slate, Shawn Steel was supported by 25.4% of all the delegates in St. Louis. Coming in last of the nineteen candidates was Michael Ingallinera, the self-described "philosophic anarchist" whose 53 votes meant that 7.3% of all delegates supported his candidacy.[71]

Saturday afternoon was devoted to debate, discussion and voting on the YAF Platform with each of the three subcommittees presenting proposed resolutions with majority and minority reports.[72] This presented another opportunity for

---

69. Tuccille: *Radical Libertarianism*, p. 102.

70. "Address to the 1969 YAF National Convention," Personal Papers of William F. Buckley, Jr., Box 65, Yale University, New Haven, CT.

71. The classification of Ingallinera is in Samuel E. Konkin, III, "History of the Libertarian Movement," www.bradspangler.com/blog/archives/288. Konkin was a student at the University of Wisconsin who attended the convention as a delegate to support fellow UW student David Keene but became enamored of the Libertarian Caucus and subsequently became a major player in the nascent libertarian movement.

72. I am grateful to Michael Sanera for providing me with a copy of the resolutions voted out of the platform committee and presented to the convention for final approval.

the libertarians and anarchists to make their views known. It was also a time for plotting and planning strategy. As one delegate explained later,

> I went to the California room and had my first "hit." I cussed out those damn anarchists who were going to screw it up for the rest of us by turning off everyone we might reach. I plotted on the vote for legalization of marijuana, and even waffled on whether I supported an abolition of the draft or the minority report in favor of support of evaders.[73]

Then came the votes on the controversial issues separating the libertarians from all others in the organization. A minority report was proposed calling for the immediate withdrawal of American troops from Vietnam; after it was defeated the delegates approved a resolution calling for victory in Vietnam. When a resolution denouncing domestic fascism was presented, it was defeated. And there was no end to the efforts to amend the platform. One of the most closely contested resolutions called for the legalization of marijuana. After much debate and parliamentary maneuvering, the resolution was tabled. Then the delegates resolved to oppose campus radicals and ensure campuses would remain open.[74]

From the foreign affairs subcommittee the majority had reported a resolution basically supporting the position of Barry Goldwater advocating an all-volunteer military with the gradual abolition of the draft. This had been YAF's stance for some time and had been the focus of much of the organization's publicity, including a special issue of *New Guard* and the distribution of a Volunteer Military Action Kit.[75] As one writer on the history of the organization has noted, "Far from reflecting a pro-draft stance, YAF for two years had been fighting to eliminate the draft and install a voluntary military system. This reflected the fact that defensible libertarian arguments, rather than being rejected by members of the board, were supported by most."[76] Before the majority resolution could be approved, the delegates had to vote on a minority resolution supported by the libertarians that called for active resistance to the military draft and support for those who evade it, legally or illegally.

After the minority report was voted down and the majority report was approved, the convention witnessed what has been called "a symbolic, flamboyant gesture . . . that many who were energized by it mark as the beginning of the libertarian movement."[77] Dave Schumacher of Princeton, a member of the Anarchist Caucus, with the encouragement of another anarchist, Donald Meinhausen of New Jersey, obtained a photocopy of a draft card from a California libertarian going by the name of Skye D'Aureous (now known as Durk Pearson), and a lighter from Maryland libertarian Jarret Wollstein. In the middle of the convention floor, Schumacher lit the make-believe draft card and held it high like the YAF torch

73. Konkin, "Where I Was in '69," *New Libertarian Notes*, November 1974, p. 11. Personal Papers of David Walter, Box 1, Hoover Institution, Stanford University, Palo Alto, CA.

74. Interview with Richard Derham, Seattle, WA, March 27, 2009. Klatch: *A Generation Divided*, p. 228.

75. Andrew, "Pro-War and Anti-Draft," pp. 8–11 discusses these efforts starting in 1966.

76. Schneider: *Cadres for Conservatism*, p. 136. See also: "Conservatives Back Abolition of Draft," *New York Times*, April 13, 1969 that reports on the Mid-Atlantic Regional YAF Conference.

77. Doherty: *Radicals for Capitalism*, pp. 356–357. Konkin, in his "History of the Libertarian Movement," begins by saying "Prior to 1969, there was no 'organized' Libertarian Movement" and cites the YAF National Convention as the starting point. Sara Diamond: *Roads to Dominion* makes a similar claim when she says, "The pivotal event in the formation of the 1970s libertarian movement was the 1969 convention of Young Americans for Freedom," p. 124.

of liberty. At that point, according to some recollections, all hell broke loose as several delegates attempted to put out the flaming photocopy and some attacked Schumacher.[78] Surrounded by members of the Anarchist Caucus, Schumacher was whisked from the convention floor. Once the platform debate was over, a motion was made that his membership be revoked and a brief recess was called.[79]

The effect of this one symbolic event would serve to radicalize several of the libertarian delegates. One delegate described its impact:

> The draft card burning and the violent reaction to it was the most significant event of the convention because it proved to every libertarian that he could not make common cause with the traditionalist conservatives except on libertarian grounds and libertarian issues. YAF cared more about obeying the laws than about ending the draft.[80]

For many of the more traditionalist delegates that sentiment was shared, although most in the organization still believed that a fusionist approach uniting both libertarians and traditionalists could be maintained in YAF. After all the excitement of the afternoon, the convention continued on with speeches, a workshop and an inaugural ball followed by a full day of sessions on Sunday and a closing awards banquet that evening where cartoonist Al Capp spoke.[81]

The Aftermath of St. Louis

Once the convention was over, those who had been unsuccessful in their efforts to transform the organization had to decide whether to continue and work for change or move on and create one or more new groups. Clearly, those who followed Hess and Rothbard and the Anarchist Caucus were convinced that there was no future in YAF. Frank Mintz, a YAF member who had been active also in the Society for Rational Individualism, made evident his opinion when he recommended "the best thing for libertarians in YAF to do would be to leave that organization as quickly as possible. Why put any money, however minimal, into YAF coffers, thereby sending more bills to Buckley and his *National Review* crowd of mystic authoritarians?"[82] Mintz's view was shared by some of the other

---

78. One of the participants, Don Meinshausen recalls the events in his "Memoir: Present at the Creation," *Liberty*, June 2004. Dick Derham has a different recollection of the events. Presiding at the time as Chairman of the Platform Committee, he recalls that Schumacher's actions occurred at a microphone toward the rear of the convention. When Schumacher and those associated with him left, the convention continued with its business without disruption. Derham states that he doubts delegates in the forward half of the convention were even aware of what the "rowdiness" involved. Interview with Richard Derham, Seattle, WA, March 27, 2009.

79. As then National Chairman Alan MacKay recalled, "I was presiding. I called for immediate revocation of his membership . . . The convention overwhelmingly voted in favor of doing that." Klatch: *A Generation Divided*, pp. 230–231.

80. Cobb, "Young Authoritarians for 'Freedom,'" *The Libertarian Connection*, February 1970.

81. *1969 National Convention—Young Americans for Freedom*, program, pp. 18–20. An interesting side note to the lasting influence of that one convention: The official script of the 2003 Oregon Shakespeare Festival was a play by David Edgar titled "Mothers Against," one of two plays about an election for Governor in a western state. In the play, the Republican gubernatorial candidate talks about having returned from the 1969 YAF convention and having been purged for nihilism. My thanks to Richard Derham for bringing this play to my attention.

82. Frank Mintz, "Libertarians and YAF: A Personal Editorial," *The Rational Individualist*, September 1969, p. 4, Personal Papers of David Walter, Box 1, Hoover Institution, Stanford University, Palo Alto, CA.

East Coast libertarians who joined together that fall to create a new organization, Society for Individual Liberty. Its leadership included David Walter and Don Ernsberger, both of whom were from Pennsylvania and had been candidates on the Libertarian Caucus slate, as well as Jarret Wollstein from Maryland and Ralph Fucetola of New Jersey. Although the organization would remain active for several years, it retained its northeastern base and never truly became a national entity.[83]

On the West Coast, the decision as to whether to remain in YAF or separate from it took a slower pace and was finally precipitated by the membership revocation of two California libertarians, John Schureman and Rod Manis, at the National Board of Directors meeting on October 3, 1969. Schureman had been executive director of the Los Angeles County YAF council while Manis, an economist, had authored several articles in *New Guard*. A few weeks later, National Director Patrick Dowd reported that the defection was about to occur: "Steel called me this morning at 1 A.M. to tell me that he, Schureman, Manis, Rohrabacher and several other YAF activists were holding a press conference this morning at 10 A.M. to pull out of YAF. They took 27 of California YAF's 65 chapters with them."[84] After the news conference had been held, Dowd wrote to David Jones and claimed that 27 chapters had left YAF.[85] Unfortunately no list of the defecting chapters was provided.

Following the Steel and Rohrabacher move in the Los Angeles area, Harvey Hukari of Stanford University led 13 members of his chapter in a demonstration where they dramatically burned their YAF membership cards and dropped them into a white coffin. Hukari claimed that the split occurred because traditionalists who are "too authoritarian" and "advocate placing the force of the law behind their moral beliefs and perpetuating the status quo" controlled the national organization. According to a report in the *San Jose News*, "the impetus for the membership card burning came after William Saracino, a traditionalist from the University of Southern California, was named state YAF chairman."[86] There had been rumors that Hukari would be named as the new state chairman and the failure of this to occur might have factored into the dramatic exit from the organization.[87] Another media report claimed that the Stanford chapter withdrawal brought to 15 the number of California chapters to quit, substantially below the previously claimed 27, along with some ten Pennsylvania chapters. According to this report, the motivation for leaving centered more specifically on YAF's support of victory in Vietnam, since "the dissidents charge YAF advisory board members seek to perpetuate an 'interventionist foreign policy.'"[88]

---

83. As of January 1971, the Society for Individual Liberty had a total membership of 1,268 and claimed 103 affiliated clubs. *SIL News*, January 1971. Personal Papers of David Walter, Box 1, Hoover Institution, Stanford University, Palo Alto, CA. Walter's collection of 20 boxes at the Hoover Institution archives includes a wide assortment of libertarian publications from the 1960s to the early 1980s, including most newsletters from the Society for Individual Liberty. Walter served as co-editor of the *SIL News* along with Donald Ernsberger.

84. Patrick Dowd letter to Wayne Thorburn dated October 23, 1969, Personal Papers of Patrick Dowd, Box 1, Hoover Institution, Stanford University, Palo Alto, CA.

85. Patrick Dowd letter to David R. Jones dated October 27, 1969, Personal Papers of Patrick Dowd, Box 1, Hoover Institution, Stanford University, Palo Alto, CA.

86. "Student Group Drops National Affiliation," *San Jose News*, November 7, 1969, Personal Papers of Jameson Campaigne, Jr., Ottawa, IL.

87. Patrick Dowd letter to Wayne Thorburn dated October 23, 1969, Personal Papers of Patrick Dowd, Box 1, Hoover Institution, Stanford University, Palo Alto, CA.

88. "YAF Revolt," *Fort Worth Press*, November 9, 1969, Personal Papers of Jameson Campaigne, Jr., Ottawa, IL.

Two weeks later, Patrick Dowd decided to send out his own news release and claimed that the YAF staff and National Board had engaged in "vicious character-defaming ideological purges and organizational power plays." His four-page release then went into a long philosophical discussion attempting to define and differentiate libertarianism and traditionalism. The release closed by calling on the national leadership to "end its vicious ideological purges, to end its interference in local YAF affairs, and to end its unfair procedures and practices."[89] While Dowd remained on the National Board for the remainder of his two-year term, with this public attack on his fellow Board members he had greatly lessened the ability to form constructive coalitions and influence the direction of the organization. As one of his fellow Board members wrote to Dowd, "what really aggravates most Board members in the current matter is that some people in YAF, handing themselves the libertarian label and then going off on an ego trip, decide that their differences are what the whole world is breathlessly waiting to hear about."[90] According to Jim Minarik, "these people have become so infatuated with seeing their names in print that they'll do anything to keep on doing so, yes even burn their YAF cards."

Dowd's support in the organization was also affected by his failure to cooperate with the new California YAF State Chairman who had invited him to serve ex-officio on the California YAF Board of Directors. One of the libertarians who remained active in the state organization wrote to Dowd and urged him to take part in state YAF affairs.

> As far as YAF goes, I sure wish you would be willing to participate in Cal YAF state board meetings. Your knowledge is really needed. As you have seen, Saracino has put on many libertarians. We are trying to have a few more put on including Scot Harris. We need you Pat . . . Hope to see you soon, and please really consider coming back to the board. YAF can be used for our goals![91]

While Dowd continued to serve on the National Board he was not willing to assist the state organization of which he had previously been chairman.

Two of the most prominent backers of Young Americans for Freedom were rightly concerned about occurrences in the organization and the aftermath of the 1969 convention. California Governor Ronald Reagan questioned Bill Buckley about his opinion of what was occurring in YAF and told him what he saw happening in his own state. Buckley suggested that Reagan contact David Keene, the new National Chairman and express his concerns to him. He added his view that "I tend to believe that we should stand by YAF at this moment of difficulty, and if ever I think that the organization is unsalvageable I'll certainly let you know."[92] Reagan responded a few days later, telling Buckley, "I have written a milder letter than I had first anticipated to David Keene after receiving your letter."[93] It was in this context that Reagan wrote Keene:

89. News release from Patrick Dowd dated November 21, 1969, Personal Papers of Jameson Campaigne, Jr., Ottawa, IL.

90. James Minarik letter to Patrick Dowd, January 21, 1970, Personal Papers of Patrick Dowd, Box 1, Hoover Institution, Stanford University, Palo Alto, CA.

91. Craig Huey letter to Patrick Dowd, February 4, 1970, Personal Papers of Patrick Dowd, Box 1, Hoover Institution, Stanford University, Palo Alto, CA.

92. William F. Buckley, Jr. letter to Ronald Reagan, September 30, 1969, Personal Papers of William F. Buckley, Jr., Box 64, Sterling Library, Yale University, New Haven, CT.

93. Ronald Reagan letter to William F. Buckley, Jr., October 7, 1969, Personal Papers of William F. Buckley, Jr., Box 64, Sterling Library, Yale University, New Haven, CT.

Young Americans for Freedom was formed because enough young people wanted to preserve the principles of our free society. From recent reports, I have been concerned that a faction within YAF would seek to thwart those goals under the guise of "libertarianism." From newspaper and other sources, it is obvious that there are those who would try to destroy YAF as an effective and powerful force among our young people, united against the onslaught of liberalism on our campuses today. As Honorary Chairman of YAF, I would sincerely appreciate your comments on these recent events and the measures being taken to keep YAF single in purpose, dedicated to those goals we hold in common.[94]

At that time, Keene was campaigning as a candidate in a special election to the Wisconsin Senate and did not immediately respond to the Governor's letter.

Nine days later Buckley wrote to Reagan, apparently after receiving some discouraging news about Harvey Hukari of Stanford University from the Governor. It appears that Reagan was calling for a reorganization of YAF, at least in California. In discussing the issues that seem to have surfaced, Buckley let it be known that he was skeptical of the arguments used for the continued enforcement of criminal laws dealing with marijuana.

Thanks for your letter and the enclosure. I have passed along the word to David Keene and others and I don't doubt that there will be such reorganization as is necessary. I would be deeply disappointed if it became necessary to expel such people as young Hukari, who is a vigorous young conservative temporarily seduced by a touch of anarchy. I do very much regret that the battleground seems to be over marihuana. I happen to believe that the marihuana laws are preposterous in their severity, and that the difference between the apparent dangers of marihuana and the empirically tested dangers of marihuana threaten the credibility of our generation.[95]

A few days later, Keene's response to Reagan maintained that the Sharon Statement, as the guiding document for the organization, served as an umbrella under which most conservatives could work together for common goals. "In an organization which allows some diversity, there is always the possibility that some will join who do *not* share the consensus, and we recently have found that there is a very small group of pseudo-anarchists in YAF who are not in accord with our organization's beliefs." Because of this, a small group of YAF members from California had been expelled for "taking stands in the name of YAF, or apparently representing the opinions of YAF members, which are contrary to our beliefs." Keene concluded by informing the Governor that he would be appointing a new state chairman and board for California YAF. "I believe that their positive leadership will emphasize the conservative ideals for which YAF stands and will be the most effective answer to your inquiry."[96]

Reagan also received a report from the new state chairman, Bill Saracino,

94. Ronald Reagan letter to David A. Keene, October 8, 1969, Personal Papers of Jameson Campaigne, Jr., Ottawa, IL.

95. William F. Buckley, Jr. letter to Ronald Reagan, October 16, 1969, Personal Papers of William F. Buckley, Jr., Box 64, Sterling Library, Yale University, New Haven, CT.

96. Letter of David A. Keene to Ronald Reagan, October 30, 1969, Personal Papers of Jameson Campaigne, Jr., Ottawa, IL.

outlining the progress that was being made in rebuilding the state organization. The Governor seemed pleased to hear of his efforts.

> Just a quick line to thank you for your good letter and to tell you my faith has never been shaken, but I'm delighted at what you've accomplished and proud of my association with YAF. It was inevitable that YAF would be infiltrated and an attempt made from the inside. But you've handled it quickly and correctly, and don't worry about any faltering on the part of us. We're with you.[97]

The letter came to Saracino at a time when Reagan was clearly the most prominent political figure on the YAF National Advisory Board, epitomized the kind of political leadership that YAF promoted, and provided the most visible entry into state government for the organization. At the same time, Reagan could now feel more secure backing an organization less likely to embarrass him as he launched his campaign for re-election as Governor of California.

In January, Bill Rusher served as an emissary from *National Review* and met with some of the YAF National Board in Washington. In a memo to Bill Buckley he reported that the Board was basically sound and aware of its problem. As YAF had broadened its program focus to the voluntary military and general opposition to campus violence, "it has brought into YAF a number of people who are not, in the broader perspective, really very conservative at all." Added to this is the extent to which young conservatives accommodate themselves to the prevailing social mores on campus. Moreover, as an ideological organization committed to upholding certain beliefs,

> It can never, however, be simply a question of making YAF more "democratic" for much the same reason that the Catholic Church cannot solve its own problems by becoming more "democratic." Both organizations have a *depositum fidei* which is guarded by a central authority. In such cases, total democracy obviously might be counter-productive.

Rusher then concluded, "On the whole, I think we (and YAF) are on the right course."[98] It was a course on which YAF would continue for the next decade.

Continuing Libertarian Influence and Involvement

Although the word "purge" was thrown around extensively at the time and has become part of the folklore of the organization, it is not truly reflective of what had occurred in 1969.[99] Several chapters, especially a number of those in California,

---

97. Letter from Ronald Reagan to William Saracino, December 19, 1969, Personal Papers of William F. Buckley, Jr., Box 284, Folder 2488, Sterling Library, Yale University, New Haven, CT.

98. William A. Rusher memo to William F. Buckley, Jr., January 7, 1970, Personal Papers of William F. Buckley, Jr., Box 284, Folder 2488, Sterling Library, Yale University, New Haven, CT.

99. Many libertarians regarded it as a "badge of honor" to have been "purged" from YAF but, in truth, very few were ever awarded that badge. On the other side, the belief that a "purge" took place also became part of the oral history of YAF. The following is from one edition of the unofficial "YAF Songbook" that was distributed at YAF gatherings as late as the 1990s. The words were sung to the tune of "I Want a Girl." "I want a purge, just like the purge, that California had. It was a splurge, and

Pennsylvania, and New Jersey did leave the organization of their own accord.[100] A very small number of individuals, most of whom described themselves as anarchists and some of whom proudly claimed to be members of Students for a Democratic Society, were removed from the membership rolls. In St. Louis, the individual who created the disturbance on the convention floor by torching a purported draft card, David Schumacher, was expelled and the Board passed a resolution declaring that membership in SDS was inconsistent with the Sharon Statement and grounds for expulsion from YAF.[101] At the October 3–5, 1969 Board meeting, Michael Ingallinera and Karl Hess, IV, leaders of the Anarchist Caucus and self-proclaimed members of SDS were expelled from YAF. The memberships of Donald Meinhausen, Schumacher's aide de camp in the draft card burning and an SDS member, and those of California libertarians Rod Manis and John Schureman were cancelled.[102] A small number of other individuals chose to demonstrate their disagreements with YAF by publicly renouncing their membership in the organization but such voluntary actions could not be labeled "purges." Several months later, at the February 1970 Board meeting, the membership of William (Shawn) Steel was suspended after he had claimed on several public occasions to have left the organization.[103]

Despite all the dispute and dissension that occurred at the 1969 National Convention, there continued to be a very important libertarian segment in the organization. David Friedman continued to have his column, "The Radical," appear in *New Guard* into 1970. Contemporaneous to the events in St. Louis, Friedman had written Frank Meyer, an editor at *National Review* and most prominent advocate of the fusionist position, of the value of interaction among the various components of the conservative movement.

> The libertarian–traditionalist alliance was useful to libertarians, if only as a restraint keeping them from the excesses of people like my friend Karl Hess. It was also useful in other ways . . . I feel that there is much of value in the traditionalist view of man and society. The decision to be in favor of freedom does not answer all questions. If I and those who agree with me are entirely cut off from contact with the traditionalist view, we will be the poorer.[104]

Most recently he recalled that his time in YAF "provided me an opportunity to improve my writing. Helped encourage me to write on political, economic, and philosophical issues. Some of what I wrote for the *New Guard* ended up in my first book."[105]

---

the only purge that Randy ever had. A good old fashioned purge with lots of blood. That covered the libertarians with lots of mud. Oh, I want a purge, just like the purge, that California had."

100. The decrease in chapters was most dramatic in California. At the time of the National Convention there were 66 California chapters and by January 1970 the total had declined to 42. However, in Pennsylvania the number of chapters increased from 23 to 25 and in New Jersey from 11 to 22 during that same four-month period. David A. Keene, "Confidential Report to National YAF Leadership," January 16, 1970, Personal Papers of Patrick Dowd, Box 3, Hoover Institution, Stanford University, Palo Alto, CA.

101. "Minutes of the August 31, 1969 Board Meeting," Personal Papers of Patrick Dowd, Box 2, Hoover Institution, Stanford University, Palo Alto, CA.

102. "Minutes of the October 3–5 Board Meeting," Dowd Papers, Box 2.

103. "Minutes of February 6–8, 1970 Board Meeting," Personal Papers of Jameson Campaigne, Jr., Ottawa, IL.

104. David Friedman letter to Frank Meyer, December 1, 1969, p. 3. Personal Papers of William F. Buckley, Jr., Box 284, Folder 2487, Sterling Library, Yale University, New Haven, CT.

105. 2008 YAF Alumni Survey Responses: David Friedman.

Phillip Abbott Luce continued to write his column, "Against the Wall," for *New Guard* well into the next year and he remained on the national staff as Chapter Director and featured speaker at YAF chapter events and numerous YAF conferences. Nevertheless, to those who had abandoned YAF such as Jerome Tuccille, "Phillip Abbott Luce is not a libertarian. Nor is he a radical. With his long hair and hippie demeanor he is an effective weapon for the New Right in its attempts to co-opt the libertarian Right and, in its desire to cloak its authoritarian nature with a façade of superficial libertarianism."[106] To the dismay of critics such as Tuccille and his fellow radical libertarians and anarchists associated with *The Libertarian Forum*, not all libertarians were leaving YAF and, thus, those who stayed had to be declared outside the movement. As Murray Rothbard had declared of those who chose to work from within to advance their libertarian goals, "As long as they continue to do so, they will continue to provide a libertarian cover for fascism."[107]

In addition to the Friedman and Luce columns, YAF continued to publish the works of libertarian writers in its monthly magazine and shortly after the national convention, California libertarian Ken Grubbs became editor of *New Guard*. Two years later, Jerry Norton became editor of the magazine.[108] An associate editor during much of the 1970s was David Brudnoy whose libertarian positions generated much discussion, including his cover article of 1973 on "Victimless Crimes."[109] Other libertarian writers such as Gaines Smith, Juliana Geran Pilon, and Tibor Machan appeared in the pages of *New Guard*.

Several of those who had campaigned for the libertarian slate in St. Louis remained active in YAF, including Friedman, onetime chairman of the University of Chicago YAF chapter, and Jerry Biggers, chairman of the Northern Ilinois University chapter and one of the candidates for National Board on the libertarian slate.[110] Libertarians Patrick Dowd, Ray Semmons, James Farley, Steve Mayerhofer and Don Feder were on the National Board of Directors after the 1969 National Convention while others on the Board supported various specific libertarian positions. On the reconstituted California YAF Board of Directors, four of the seventeen members had been promoters of the libertarian slate in St. Louis: San Diego County Chairman Jim Kenshalo, Director of Campus Action John Murphy, El Camino College Chairman Craig Huey, and Bill Sauk of Ventura County.[111]

New York continued to have a significant libertarian segment among its campus members. At Baruch College, City University of New York, the YAF chapter proposed an alternative libertarian program in place of the National office's "Young America's Freedom Offensive." Basically, they proposed dropping a coalitional

---

106. Jerome Tuccille, "Phony Libertarianism," *The Libertarian Forum*, February 15, 1970, p. 2. Personal Papers of David Walter, Box 2, Hoover Institution, Stanford University, Palo Alto, CA.

107. "Note on Libertarians," *The Libertarian Forum*, September 15, 1969, p. 3. Personal Papers of David Walter, Box 2, Hoover Institution, Stanford University, Palo Alto, CA.

108. The position of editor seemed to rotate between libertarians and traditionalists in the period. Libertarian Arnie Steinberg was succeeded briefly in 1969 by traditionalist Allan Brownfeld who edited only a few issues before libertarian Ken Grubbs assumed the position. Grubbs's replacement was traditionalist Daniel Joy who was followed in 1971 by libertarian Jerry Norton. Norton was succeeded by traditionalist Mary Fisk with the November 1973 issue and returned as interim editor for four issues in 1976. Alan Crawford was editor for four issues in 1976 before being replaced by libertarian David Boaz with the December 1976 issue. Boaz remained until the magazine became a quarterly in the fall of 1978.

109. "Decriminalizing Crimes Without Victims: The Time Is Now," *New Guard*, April 1973, pp. 4–8.

110. Basil Talbott, Jr., "Split of student rightists parallels the New Left's," *Chicago Sun-Times*, November 2, 1969, Personal Papers of Jameson Campaigne, Jr., Ottawa, IL.

111. "Memo to National Board of Directors from Bill Saracino," no date, Personal Papers of Jameson Campaigne, Jr., Ottawa, IL.

approach to opposing the New Left on campus, an emphasis on the differences between freedom and communism, and the opposition to East–West trade. In their place the chapter advocated a "Taxation Is Theft" program, an emphasis on "Community Affairs and Community Control" as an alternative to focusing on Federal and state government issues, and the legalization of abortion. The last objective was being promoted at a time when abortion remained an illegal procedure in New York State and the Supreme Court had not yet issued its landmark decision of *Roe* v. *Wade*.[112] It was also a time when a significant portion of the YAF membership supported a woman's right to choose whether to terminate a pregnancy. In 1971, Gary Potter and John Wisner began a publication titled *Rough Beast*. Strongly Catholic and fervently pro-life, the back cover of the magazine featured a photo of an aborted fetus in a hospital disposal can. After mailing a copy to YAF leaders, "the editors received in return mail nothing but two used condoms."[113]

Despite their differences with the national organization as to the appropriate projects to be emphasized, the Baruch chapter wanted to become "the model for Young Americans for Freedom chapters throughout the country." Baruch YAF and its allies were committed to working within Young Americans for Freedom. As they noted,

> In order for the pro-freedom movement to be successful in America, an intellectual base of thinkers, innovators and, yes, radicals must first develop. Young Americans for Freedom is the one group today that has the "seed" needed to begin this new modern repeat of history. YAF has the cadre of youth who must form the vanguard of the movement for freedom. YAF has the talent and the minds needed for the movement to grow. However, YAF must become more than a conservative Young Republicans; it must reverse certain patterns of its past; it must proclaim to all America that it is now the vanguard of the pro-freedom movement—the intellectual radical movement.[114]

Although the national organization never did adopt the proposed new projects, the autonomy of local chapters in YAF allowed them to choose, adopt, or adapt whatever was being emphasized nationally as well as undertake other projects developed locally.

YAF's libertarian influence continued into the 1970s and well beyond. Eric Scott Royce, who became active in YAF at the University of Virginia after the

---

112. Legalization of abortion was a prominent topic in New York at this time. Later in 1970, a Republican Assemblywoman sponsored a bill to repeal the state's anti-abortion laws for the first 24 weeks of pregnancy and the proposal passed into law. "Constance E. Cook, 89, Who Wrote Abortion Law, Is Dead," *New York Times*, January 24, 2009.

113. Patrick Allitt: *Catholic Intellectuals and Conservative Politics in America: 1950–1985* (Ithaca, NY: Cornell University Press, 1993), p. 157. There was no unanimity on the abortion question among YAF's financial supporters either. DeWitt Wallace, publisher of *Reader's Digest*, wrote former Congressman Walter Judd shortly after the *Roe* v. *Wade* decision wondering why YAF would take a position opposing abortion. Judd visited with National Chairman Ron Docksai on the matter. Docksai maintained the difficulty arose from a slip-up in a letter he wrote which meant to attack the radicals' demand for "legalized abortion on demand" but left off the last two words. Judd reassured Wallace that "YAF has greater balance, strength, and influence today than at any time in its history." Letter from Walter H. Judd to DeWitt Wallace, March 12, 1973. Personal Papers of Walter H. Judd, Hoover Institution, Stanford University, Palo Alto, CA.

114. "Libertarians Gain Strength in YAF," *The Reporter* (Baruch College), February 16, 1970, pp. 6, 8, Personal Papers of Jameson Campaigne, Jr., Ottawa, IL.

1969 convention, attended the 1973 convention and noted the presence of many fellow libertarians. Royce reported he was, "amazed at the proceedings. There was a brand new libertarian caucus, small to be sure, but remarkably vocal and a definite thorn in the side of the National crowd." Four years after the St. Louis convention, "Libertarians and their allies made themselves felt both in the voting for officers and in floor discussion on platform planks such as amnesty and pot."[115] In later years, several libertarians served on the national board or staff. David Boaz was both a national director and later editor of *New Guard* in the 1970s, John Buckley was elected National Chairman in 1977, and Roger Ream served on the national board. Boaz is now Executive Vice President of the Cato Institute while Ream is president of The Fund for American Studies. In the 1980s, Tom Lizardo of New York served on the National Board including a term as Vice Chairman, and later as Executive Director. Until recently, Lizardo served as Chief of Staff to Congressman Ron Paul (R-Texas). In the early 90s, Jim Bieber of California was one of several libertarians on the YAF National Board.

A number of those who were involved in the libertarian caucus campaign at the 1969 YAF National Convention went on to careers in politics or to serve in Republican administrations. William (Shawn) Steel became involved in the state leadership of the California Republican party in the 1990s, served as State GOP Chairman, and is currently the Republican National Committeeman from California. Dana Rohrabacher subsequently became a speechwriter in the Reagan White House and was then elected to Congress in 1988, where he continues to represent a California district. Looking back on forty years ago, Rohrabacher reflected on the changes in his life.

> . . . we did what young people always do: carried our ideals out to the very farthest logical extension. Once you push abstract theory out too far in reality it becomes unworkable. So right now I've drawn back a whole lot to what I think is practical, but still pushing to maximize human liberty and justice.[116]

Joseph Michael Cobb served during the Reagan Administration as Deputy Director of the White House Office of Policy Formation, staff director of the Congressional Joint Economic Committee and then as Chief Economist for the Senate Republican Policy Committee. Don Ernsberger formed Students for Individual Liberty after the 1969 convention and then went on to be a teacher in public education for thirty years before serving for seven years as Deputy Chief of Staff to Congressman Rohrabacher.[117] C. Ron Kimberling was a member of the California libertarian faction that challenged the fusionist leadership of the organization in St. Louis but looks back with a belief that "time and the common enemy of collectivism have healed most" of the wounds from that convention. Retrospectively it was YAF that provided him with a base of life-long friends and sharpened his political beliefs.

> I owe my seven years of service in the 1980s Reagan Administration to those formative experiences, and I feel I know exactly where to turn for

---

115. Eric Scott Royce, "Memoirs of a Post-'69 YAF Grad," *New Libertarian Notes*, November 1974, p. 27, Personal Papers of David Walter, Box 1, Hoover Institution, Stanford University, Palo Alto, CA.
116. Quoted in Doherty: *Radicals for Capitalism*, p. 536.
117. 2008 YAF Alumni Survey Responses: Don Ernsberger.

information and opportunities for political engagement as a result of those formative years. Most people I have met have episodic experiences with politics and political philosophy that leaves them largely uncertain about most issues. YAF in its heyday truly attracted the "best and the brightest," and many of its young leaders have made a major imprint on America and the world.[118]

After his involvement in YAF, Kimberling graduated from California State University—Northridge, went on to earn three master's degrees, and a PhD in English from the University of Southern California. Kimberling was a presidential appointee in the U.S. Department of Education from 1981 to 1988, ending as Assistant Secretary for Postsecondary Education. He left that position to become the first executive director of the Ronald Reagan Presidential Foundation and then held a number of positions at various colleges and now is President of the Chicago campus of Argosy University.

1969 was also the year in which Students for a Democratic Society disintegrated, separating into a Maoist Progressive Labor faction on one hand and a violent terroristic Weatherman faction on the other. Its role as a force among students on campus was quickly dying out. YAF had its divisions also in 1969, but it lived on to survive and thrive, overcoming the dissensions and the conflicts of St. Louis to move on to other battles in the 1970s. As Bill Rusher, long a mentor and an observer of YAF, pointed out,

> ... by and large YAF came through the trauma of the sixties in remarkably good shape. Fate dealt it, in that decade, a singularly poor hand, but it survived with its principles intact, to stand proudly beside all the other (and mostly newer) organizations when victory came at last to American conservatism.[119]

True, some had left to form their own organizations and still others dropped out of involvement in anything dealing with politics. But Young Americans for Freedom continued as it had started some nine years earlier, the national conservative youth organization.

---

118. 2008 YAF Alumni Survey Responses: C. Ronald Kimberling.
119. William A. Rusher: *The Rise of the Right*, p. 135.

The Great Elm at the Buckley estate in Sharon, CT where Young
Americans for Freedom was formed. All photos are from *New Guard*
magazine unless other credits are indicated.

The mentors and early leaders of Young Americans for Freedom. L–R, Bill
Rusher, Bob Bauman, Bill Buckley, Robert Schuchman, and Doug Caddy.

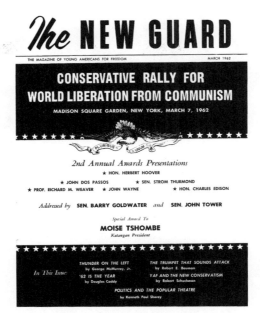

The NEW GUARD

THE MAGAZINE OF YOUNG AMERICANS FOR FREEDOM   MARCH 1962

CONSERVATIVE RALLY FOR
WORLD LIBERATION FROM COMMUNISM

MADISON SQUARE GARDEN, NEW YORK, MARCH 7, 1962

★ ★ ★ ★ ★ ★ ★ ★   ★ ★ ★ ★ ★ ★ ★ ★

2nd Annual Awards Presentations

★ HON. HERBERT HOOVER

★ JOHN DOS PASSOS   ★ SEN. STROM THURMOND
★ PROF. RICHARD M. WEAVER   ★ JOHN WAYNE   ★ HON. CHARLES EDISON

Addressed by **SEN. BARRY GOLDWATER** *and* **SEN. JOHN TOWER**

Special Award To

MOISE TSHOMBE

Katangan President

★ ★

	THUNDER ON THE LEFT	THE TRUMPET THAT SOUNDS ATTACK
	by George McMurray, Jr.	by Robert E. Bauman
In This Issue:	'62 IS THE YEAR	YAF AND THE NEW CONSERVATISM
	by Douglas Caddy	by Robert Schuchman
	POLITICS AND THE POPULAR THEATRE	
	by Kenneth Paul Shorey	

The March 1962 issue of *The New Guard* served as the program for the rally at Madison Square Garden where an overflowing crowd showed the media that the young conservative movement had arrived.

The rafters were full and thousands were turned away as YAF held its second awards rally in New York City less than eighteen months after the organization's founding.

YAF had a major presence at the Republican National Convention in San Francisco as shown by the signs on the Cow Palace convention floor.

In September 1964 the YAF Board of Directors met in New York City. L–R Dan Carmen, Jameson Campaigne, Jr., Bill Boerum, Jack Cox, Marilyn Manion, Bob Bauman, Tom Huston, Randal Teague, Dick Derham, Bud Wandling, Don Devine and J. Fred Coldren. Missing from the picture are Tom Phillips, Lammot Copeland, Buddy Lewis, Charles Leftwich, Alan MacKay, Jim Dullenty, Don Shafto, and Robert Gaston.

David R. Jones and Bill Buckley at the 1964 annual meeting.
Jones served from 1963 to 1969 as executive director and built
YAF into a permanent organization with an essential role
in creating a conservative movement.

In the Fall of 1964 YAF members campaigned across the nation for
Barry Goldwater. One of the more successful YAF rallies for their
presidential candidate, with more than 3,500 attending, was held at
O'Hare Field in Chicago. Photo from Jameson Campaigne, Jr.

One of YAF's early victories was the campaign against Firestone and its agreement to build a rubber plant in Communist Romania. It all started in 1965 with pickets outside a dealership in Philadelphia.

In 1967 YAF took on the IBM Corporation for selling data processing systems to Eastern European countries. One protestor's sign indicates his choice for a Nixon-Reagan ticket in 1968. YAF members were divided in their support for these two possible presidential candidates.

New York YAF Chairman Don Pemberton headed up
Youth for Buckley in the 1965 campaign.

Throughout the 1960s, YAF chapters held rallies and marches like this
one in Philadelphia to support American involvement and call for a
policy of victory in Vietnam.

YAF chapters did more than march and demand support for the war. Cleveland YAF members collected and wrote letters of encouragement to servicemen in Vietnam. Neil Dentzer, Steve Mayerhofer, and Jim Minarik led the effort.

THERE IS
NO PRICE
ON FREEDOM
WIN IN
VIET NAM

In 1966, Downtown Manhattan YAF concluded a three-month Vietnam Relief Drive, sending off ten large cartons of clothing, blankets, soap and shoes for South Vietnamese war orphans and refugees.

For many years, Yale YAF was one of the organization's most active chapters. The chapter's new officers for 1966 included L–R David Joralemon, Sylvia Sanders (chairman), Phil McCombs, May Cheng, and Michael Bouscaren.

Senator George Murphy was a featured speaker at the 1968 California YAF state convention banquet. With the Senator are Randy Goodwin, Bill Saracino, and Dick Shirley.

In 1969, YAF was featured in an article on student resistance to the New Left that appeared in the Sunday supplement *Parade*. Here New York YAF State Chairman Jim Farley is shown in the organization's headquarters at 25 Jane Street, Manhattan. Photo, *Parade* magazine.

YAF high school leader John W. Tower of Rockville, MD reads an issue of *The Alternative* published by the YAF chapter at the University of Maryland. From the mid-60s onward, many YAF chapters started their own independent campus newspapers. Photo, *Montgomery Sentinel.*

California YAFers burned their social security cards at a protest in Orange County. Ken Grubbs, Cal State–Fullerton YAF chairman called the system "a fraud and not a proper function of government." Shown here torching a card are John Schureman, Mike Johnson, and Dana Rohrabacher.

YAF chapter spokesman Tom Lamont and chairman Steve Zierak confront an SDS leader at a Boston University demonstration. As SDS and other leftist groups threatened peace on campus, YAF chapters called on college administrators to protect the rights of those who wished to learn. Photo, *Boston Herald.*

A Gathering of libertarian YAF members prior to the 1969
YAF National Convention. Seated are Phillip Abbott Luce and
Harvey Hukari. Standing L–R are Pat Dowd, Rod Manis, Kathy Forte,
Bill "Shawn" Steel and Dana Rohrabacher.

"Sock It to the Left" was the theme for the 1969 YAF National
Convention. Here David Keene addresses the delegates while
Michael Connelly and Randy Goodwin are shown on the right.
Photo by Tom Dey.

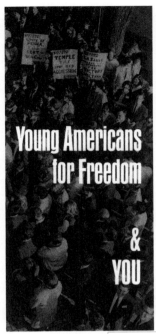

YAF's membership recruitment brochures reflect the changes in
American campus life from the early 1960s to the late 1960s
to the mid 1970s.

291

10. Moving Beyond Vietnam: YAF's Campus Initiatives

"YAF has never been afraid to stick its neck out when it thought principle was at stake. It has never feared to champion unpopular causes; and it has never had occasion to consult with George Gallup or the New York Times *before acting."*[1]

As Young Americans for Freedom entered its second decade, it faced a number of new challenges and opportunities. Just as the campus scene of 1960 was quite different from that of the late 1960s, change was to occur in the 1970s. While leftist organizations continued to be active on many campuses, Students for a Democratic Society and, to a large degree, the Black Panthers were no longer the forces they had been in the previous decade. The National Student Association retained affiliation on a small number of American campuses and YAF still had its STOP-NSA committee but, as the decade progressed, NSA lost most of its luster as a viable representative of American college students. Campus takeovers, moratoriums, and class shutdowns became a less frequent method of protest for radical students. The draft became modified first by a lottery system and then abolished entirely.

YAF continued to battle efforts by American corporations to engage in trade with the Soviet Union and its satellite nations but not to the extent of the 1960s campaigns against Firestone and American Motors. With a Republican in the White House for the first six years of the decade, the organization confronted a changed political situation in which on many occasions it staked out a position of opposition to the administration, causing some fissures with a few members and a few more contributors.

New issues would surface in the 1970s and older ones would come to the fore. Most of these were college issues as YAF turned more of its attention to the campus. Mandatory student activity fees, Public Interest Research Groups, the election of conservatives to student government, the publication of independent campus newspapers, unbalanced speakers programs, student government support for leftist demonstrations, and YAF's own "Movement for Quality Education" took precedence for many chapters. For the more active college chapters, the focus turned inward towards influencing the direction of thought on their own college campuses. Mary Fisk, later to serve on the YAF National Board and as editor of *New Guard*, appreciated the effect YAF had in helping her deal with a liberal campus environment. It was from YAF that she recalled,

> ... benefiting from guidance in starting my own college newspaper, Disrespect, in opposition to official campus newspaper; having support to oppose antiwar and other left-wing activities on campus, including a lawyer to keep the campus open when the moratorium was proposed; finding other young conservatives at the campus, state, and national levels; general

1. James L. Buckley, quoted in "What They're Saying About Young Americans for Freedom," April 1973.

political companionship in the unwelcoming climate of the campuses—others with whom to share ideas, explore new approaches, discuss tactics, and so much more.[2]

Fisk's efforts in creating her own independent newspaper were duplicated on numerous other campuses by YAF members, assisted by the Free Campus News Service sent out from the YAF national office.

YAF was also willing to take on controversial topics where there were differences among conservatives. Under the general topic of "Privacy, the Rights of the Individual, and the Role of Government," the organization's magazine featured debates and discussions on what are now referred to as social issues. The decade of the 1970s also saw a renewed involvement of YAF in direct political action with a number of candidates rallying the support of young conservatives from New York to North Carolina to California and beyond. By mid-decade, YAF was once again involved in the heart of a presidential nomination campaign, one that, while unsuccessful in the moment, led to eventual victory in 1980.

YAF's influence continued to grow, as did its involvement in youth affairs outside the campus. When writer Alan Rinzler put together a compendium of views from the youth of America, six of the twenty-nine authors featured in his book—Jameson Campaigne, Jr., Terry Catchpole, David Friedman, Rod Manis, Arnie Steinberg, and Bob Tyrrell—were members of YAF.[3] At the 1971 White House Conference on Youth held in Estes Park, Colorado, the few conservatives present were YAF members, including John Von Kannon, Steve Frank, Bob Schadler, and Mark Souder. For Nixon and conservatives, the conference was a "White House Woodstock" as "the Nixon Administration, in another of its seemingly masochistic moves, had assured a radical and leftist orientation" to the conference. Steve Frank observed, "we came here to unite as youth and all this conference has done is divide."[4]

Meanwhile, some areas of involvement continued into the early years of the decade. Vietnam was an issue that would not go away, but it was one whose focus and involvement would change as the 1970s began. For the first few years of the decade, YAF could not get beyond Vietnam, although downplaying the issue was a position which some in the organization's leadership wanted to see occur. While others in the organization continued to push for victory over communism, the policies of the administration and the conditions on the ground were moving more towards a hoped-for peace treaty, a treaty that would never be enforced as the forces of North Vietnam and the Viet Cong eventually overran South Vietnam after the pullout of American troops.

Vietnamization and the POWs

In March 1970, YAF sent a delegation of eleven members led by National Chairman David Keene on a fact-finding mission to South Vietnam. The group included executive director Randal C. Teague, "Tell it to Hanoi" coordinator Ron Dear and

---

2. 2008 YAF Alumni Survey Responses: Mary Fisk.

3. Alan Rinzler, editor: *Manifesto—Addressed to the President of the United States from the Youth of America* (New York: Collier Books, 1970).

4. Wayne Thorburn, "Unrepresentative Youth," *New Guard*, Summer 1971, pp. 18–20.

other national officials including Harold Herring, Ron Docksai, Albert Forrester, Richard Wright and Mike Thompson.[5] The youngest member in the group was William D. Clarke of Oregon State University. The trip was designed to check on the progress of the war in view of the Vietnamization process underway and the upcoming national student referendum calling for a unilateral withdrawal of all American troops from Vietnam. During their visit, the delegation met with college students, military officers, private citizens and government officials as well as United States diplomatic representatives, including Ambassador Ellsworth Bunker.

Upon their return, Keene spoke at a news conference in Honolulu and reported that the delegation was convinced that Vietnamization was working. Criticizing the previous policies, he maintained that fewer American troops would have been required "if we had gone in there with the attitude the Vietnamese could help us. We took the attitude that these guys don't have it, they are not up to snuff and pushed them aside."[6] The trip had such an effect on Clarke, the student from Oregon State, that upon his graduation he volunteered to join the United States Army.[7]

YAF continued to use rallies and demonstrations to show support for the American commitment to Vietnam. YAF was a co-sponsor of a "Wake Up America" rally held in late April on Boston Common and City Hall Plaza. As Massachusetts YAF state chairman Dan Rea noted, "we are trying to use rallies, such as the one to wake up America to radicalize people to the Right, just as the Student Mobilization groups are trying to radicalize people to the Left." Rea added, however, that YAF was totally against violence and this distinction "will spell the difference in our attracting people to the conservative side."[8]

As the student strikes took place on campuses in early May after the incursion into Cambodia and the unfortunate student deaths at Kent State University, YAF ran advertisements declaring its support for American troops in Southeast Asia and "for a continued American presence in South Vietnam, for gradual Vietnamization of the war, and for victory over Communist aggression in Asia."[9] YAF pledged its support to the cause of freedom and peace in South Vietnam and urged Americans to "Tell it to Hanoi." Local YAF chapters used a number of different techniques to show support for the war and opposition to the student strike. The University of Tennessee at Knoxville hired a small plane to fly over campus pulling a banner calling on Americans to "Give Nixon a Chance."[10] Meanwhile, at Mount St. Mary's College in Maryland, Michael O'Malley, sophomore and Vietnam veteran, held his own 72-hour vigil. As the *Baltimore Sun* reported, "A bearded sleepy and hungry Vietnam war veteran continued his watch over a butane flame at Mount St. Mary's College in a symbolic support of America's role in the Indo-China war." O'Malley, who had just been elected president of the junior class, explained "the purpose of my vigil is to draw interest to those students like myself who are supporting the President's commitment in Vietnam.

---

5. Richard Wright was Wisconsin YAF state chairman at the time. Upon the end of his term in 1971, he self-published a booklet, *Unfortunately My Most Profound Quotes Are Unprintable* (Milwaukee, WI: Heritage Publishing Company, 1971) which included his observations on Vietnam on pp. 6–8.

6. *Honolulu Advertiser* as quoted in *YAF in the News*, April 1970.

7. Telephone interview with Ron Dear, February 27, 2009. Dear was the YAF coordinator for the trip.

8. Stephen Kurkjian, "YAF: Wake Up America," *Boston Globe*, April 26, 1970.

9. Similar ads appeared in *Washington Star* on May 4, 1970 and in the *Washington Post* on May 10, 1970 as well as other newspapers across the country.

10. *Knoxville Journal* as reprinted in *YAF in the News*, May 1970.

There has been a disproportionate amount of attention already focused on the anti-war."[11] Outside the Washington headquarters of the Student Mobilization Committee, twenty-five YAF members from two Virginia high schools and Notre Dame Academy in DC marched and demonstrated their support for the war.

On the campus of the University of Southern California, the administration ordered the American flag to be lowered to half-mast in honor of the four students killed at Kent State, without setting any end date. After a few days of the lowered flag, YAF activist Pat Nolan attempted to raise it and a tug of war developed with a student striker. As Marty Morfeld, USC YAF chair, indicated, "The incident wasn't planned. Some members became emotional. We just couldn't see the reasoning behind lowering the flag for four students at that time. They've never done it for the men killed in Southeast Asia, and we've had over 50 thousand killed there."[12] A short time later, YAF held a pro-Vietnam rally on the USC campus where Mark Johnson burned a Viet Cong flag.[13]

Two YAF chapters in Arkansas co-sponsored a "Victory in Vietnam" rally with Mike Thompson as the featured speaker. Thompson, National Vice Chairman of YAF, praised Nixon's decision to go into Cambodia. The rally was co-sponsored by the *Jacksonville Daily News* whose city editor, Steve Collins, was also chairman of Jacksonville YAF.[14] Thompson also spoke at a candlelight procession of one hundred YAF supporters that began at St. Louis University, an event that Thompson said was designed "not only to show that we are against the Moratorium but that we support our troops."[15]

The culmination of this approach was an event that was billed as non-partisan and not designed specifically to indicate support for the Vietnam war. "Honor America Day" was a huge rally in the Nation's Capital led by entertainer Bob Hope and evangelist Billy Graham. YAF was one of the major sponsors of the day's festivities, which brought somewhere between 250,000 and 500,000 Americans to the Mall on July 4, 1970. Local YAF chapters joined in promoting the event and bringing their members and supporters to Washington. In New York, Great Neck YAF under the leadership of 16-year old Larry Penner, chartered two buses that left Long Island at 1:45 A.M. on Saturday morning and returned back some twenty-four hours later with tired but proud rally participants.[16]

By the end of the summer in 1970, differences were beginning to surface among the leadership of YAF over the appropriate approach to the issue of Vietnam. A memo from Jerry Norton, YAF's chapter director at the time, to Randal C. Teague, executive director, generated the internal discussion when it was circulated to the National Board of Directors. Titled "A Quiet YAF Withdrawal from Vietnam" and authored by one of the few Vietnam veterans in the organization's leadership, it maintained that "Vietnam is seriously damaging our national defense, the security of other allies, and our economy, is alienating students and G.I.'s from the right, and continues to kill Americans." Norton maintained that over the past five years YAF had moved from a position calling for victory to support of Nixon's policy of gradual withdrawal.

---

11. *Baltimore Sun*, May 10, 1970 as reprinted in *YAF in the News*, May 1970.

12. Michael Coates, "All's quiet on the right wing," *Daily Trojan*, February 22, 1971, p. 15.

13. The Morfeld quote appears in *YAF in the News*, May 1970. A detailed retelling of this period in USC YAF history is provided in Bob McDonald: *YAF in the Arena*, unpublished paper, in author's possession.

14. *North Little Rock Times* as appeared in *YAF in the News*, July 1970.

15. *St. Louis Post-Dispatch* in *YAF in the News*, July 1970.

16. "The Fourth: Showing the Flag," *Newsweek*, July 13, 1970. Martin Flusser, Jr., "Rally Round Trip: Anticipation to Anger," *Newsday*, July 6, 1970.

From his perspective, the Johnson-Nixon policy on Vietnam was a disaster that diverted billions from ensuring an adequate nuclear shield and the development of modern weaponry, had enabled liberals to cut military aid to friendly nations, provided the main impetus for the growth of the New Left, led to a suffering economy because of the amount of war spending, and resulted in more than 40,000 (at that time) American lives lost.[17] His recommendation was that YAF "back quietly away from Vietnam. No official reversal or withdrawal from the field but no new national projects either . . . leaving Vietnam up to local chapters while concentrating on worthier things nationally."[18]

In response, Mike Thompson partially agreed with Norton but came to a totally different conclusion. Chairman of the Student Committee for Victory in Vietnam, Thompson concurred that "we have seemed to quietly step away from our policy of victory to one of saying 'Yes, Mr. President.'" His conclusion, however, was that YAF should once again actively push for victory.[19] Perhaps the strongest disagreement with the Norton position came, however, from Ron Docksai. In his memo he maintained that any retreat by YAF would result in justifying the claim by the Left that students favored withdrawal and leave the anti-communist position to extremists on the right.[20] Docksai advocated a policy supporting the supplying of Vietnam and Cambodia with all the equipment they needed to ensure national autonomy. Abandon Vietnam and YAF would have retreated from an important area of conflict with the radical leftists on American campuses.[21]

After much debate and discussion, in February 1971 the Board supported action to cut off supply routes and deny to the Communists the privileged sanctuaries of Laos and Cambodia. The Board also gave qualified support to the strategy of Vietnamization, the qualification being that the strategy be one based upon the policy that the Communist aggression in Southeast Asia must be stopped.[22] While it sounded strong, the reality of the situation was that there would no longer be any highly coordinated drives such as "Tell it to Hanoi" coming out of the national office. The focus would shift to rallying support for American prisoners of war, providing assistance to wounded Vietnam veterans, and opposing amnesty for those who fled the country to avoid being drafted.

True, there were times when YAF would speak out on Vietnam from that point forward. When President Nixon stepped up the bombing of North Vietnam in late 1972, YAF state organizations did hold a series of news conferences in support of the action. As Kirby Wilbur stated at the University of Washington, "President Nixon had no alternative but resume heavy bombing. The way to achieve a lasting peace is to convince aggressors that aggression does not pay."[23] California YAF State Chairman Patrick Geary maintained, "the North Vietnamese Communists have shown that they respect only force and consider any conciliatory moves by the United States as a sign of weakness."[24] Despite these statements, however, a shift in emphasis was already underway and YAF was focusing on other related

---

17. Memo from Jerry Norton to Randal Teague, no date. Personal Papers of Patrick Dowd, Box 3, Hoover Institution, Stanford University, Palo, Alto, CA.

18. *Ibid.*

19. Memo from Michael Thompson to Jerry Norton, no date. Personal Papers of Patrick Dowd, Box 3, Hoover Institution, Stanford University, Palo, Alto, CA.

20. Ron Docksai memo to National Board of Directors, October 22, 1970. Personal Papers of Patrick Dowd, Box 3, Hoover Institution, Stanford University, Palo, Alto, CA.

21. This position is drawn out also in John Andrew, "Pro-War and Anti-Draft," pp. 13–15.

22. "YAF and Vietnam," *New Guard*, April 1971, p. 20.

23. *Seattle Times* reprinted in *YAF in the News*, January 1973.

24. *Santa Ana Register* in *YAF in the News*, January 1973.

but distinct issues. As historian John Andrew noted, "this shift was subtle but unmistakable. Although YAF still gave lip service to the concept of victory in Vietnam, it really longed for an honorable withdrawal as quickly as possible."[25]

One aspect of the war on which all YAF members could agree was concern over the treatment and return of American prisoners of war. In the spring of 1970, Wichita State University YAF sponsored a rally in support of American POWs/MIAs. According to Gary Leffel, the rally was designed "to demonstrate to the wives and other relatives of American prisoners that Americans do care and to show the North Vietnamese and the Viet Cong that their conduct is not condoned by the American public." Speakers at the May 2nd rally included local Congressman Garner Shriver and Professor Dwight D. Murphey, faculty advisor to the YAF chapter.[26]

Later that spring, the YAF national office prepared and distributed to local chapters and state organizations a Prisoner of War Action Kit with information on possible projects by chapters as well as by individual members.[27] National Director Mary Kay Davis of the University of Texas prepared most of the material in the kit and Texas YAF, under State Chairman Jack Gullahorn, carried out an active campaign on the POW issue.

By the fall of 1970, the prisoner of war issue had become a major focus of activity for many YAF chapters, involving high school and community chapters as well as those on college campuses. Greater Richmond Hi-YAF circulated petitions throughout the Virginia capital and presented them to Governor Linwood Holton, who added his signature to the sizeable list.[28] University of Florida YAF members picketed outside Gainesville Mall when the management firm would not allow the Arnold Air Society to collect petition signatures calling for fair treatment of prisoners of war. However, after YAF's action and much negative public relations in the community, the Mall officials backed off and allowed the ROTC members to circulate their petitions.[29]

In October, a number of Boston area YAF chapters joined together for a fast and vigil in downtown Boston, gaining the attention of shoppers and office workers as well as the media. At the University of Texas as well as at Boston College, YAF members built POW cells to dramatize the conditions under which the North Vietnamese were holding Americans. LSU YAF made their major fall semester activities an effort to inform students of the plight of American POWs. To this end they carried out a "Free the Hanoi 1600" publicity campaign.[30] Herb Stupp, New York YAF State Chairman, launched a campaign to inform the public of "these Americans who have received so little attention, especially among their own countrymen."[31] He urged the state's YAF chapters to take up the issue of American prisoners.

One of the major efforts to garner public support for the cause took place on December 6th as Massachusetts YAF, led by State Chairman Dan Rea, held a rally on Boston Common. David Brudnoy described the scene.

25. Andrew, "Pro-War and Anti-Draft," p. 12.

26. "YAF Plans Rally to Support POWs," *Topeka Capital*, April 30, 1970, and also *Wichita Beacon* in *YAF in the News*, May 1970.

27. "Prisoner of War Action Kit," Young Americans for Freedom, June 1970.

28. "Unit to seek money for POW paper," *Richmond News-Leader* in *YAF in the News*, December 1970.

29. "Mall Picketing Slated After 'Help POW' Booth Denied," *Gainesville Sun* in *YAF in the News*, December 1970.

30. *New Guard*, January–February 1971, p. 40.

31. Joseph Modzelewski, "Group Drives to Publicize Plight of PWs," *New York Daily News* in *YAF in the News*, December, 1970.

Young Americans for Freedom is one of the few groups at home which is sufficiently concerned about the plight of American prisoners in North Vietnam to do anything about it. Last night, in subfreezing temperatures augmented by a 35-mph wind, Massachusetts YAF staged a rally on Boston Common to dramatize the situation. Coming a year to the day after Mass YAF's first rally in support of America's role in Vietnam, this gathering on behalf of the prisoners was more moving, although the impossible weather kept the crowd small.[32]

Among the speakers in that bitter cold were cartoonist Al Capp, YAF National Director Don Feder, and Commander Lloyd Bucher, who with his crew on the USS Pueblo had only recently been released from a North Korean prison. Bucher and Capp both urged those in attendance to send post cards to Hanoi to show that Americans wanted decent treatment of those held prisoner.

During the spring semester, a number of other YAF chapters used the technique of showing the conditions in which POWs survived as a means of dramatizing the need for pressure on Hanoi. Creighton University YAF built a replica of a POW cell in the State Capitol building in Lincoln, Nebraska and Governor J.J. Exon dedicated the exhibit. The project was coordinated by YAF member Bob Passavanti and Creighton YAF chairman John Scully.[33] Scully was one of many young conservatives who had first become active in YAF while a high school student. He recalled his experiences at a St. Louis area high school, "confronting the left wing students and teachers during Vietnam war protests by burning North Vietnamese flags, demanding time to speak in favor of victory." According to Scully, "although as a conservative we seemingly marched to the beat of a different drummer from most students, YAF gave me comrades in arms in the battle of freedom to march with and provided opportunities for my education as a conservative and to act on my principles." He is now a staff attorney with the National Right to Work Legal Defense Foundation.[34]

Daniel Webster Hi-YAF erected a POW cage in downtown Astoria, New York. YAF member Jerry Gavin was "locked" in the cage while other members collected signatures on a petition calling for humane treatment. Shiloh Hi-YAF, headed by James O'Neill, demonstrated in front of the United Nations building with an all-night candlelight vigil in support of the prisoners of war and calling on North Vietnam to live up to its commitments under the Geneva Agreement. Meanwhile, in Hawaii the Honolulu Hi-YAF chapter was successful in having Mayor Frank Fasi proclaim "POW Day."[35]

During the late 1960s and early 1970s, YAF recruited a number of high school activists. Among those active in the Washington suburbs were John Tower of Rockville High, Hal Schuster of Silver Spring, James Stevens of Potomac, and Kevin O'Bryon, chairman of Bethesda-Chevy Chase Hi-YAF. Stevens served as Maryland YAF state chairman before entering Gordon College in the fall of 1973 while O'Bryon graduated from Tulane University and then its law school. O'Bryon remained in New Orleans where he practices law and has been in-

32. David Brudnoy, "Free Them Now!," *National Review*, December 29, 1970, p. 1404.
33. *New Guard*, Summer 1971, p. 29.
34. 2008 YAF Alumni Survey Responses: John Connor Scully.
35. *New Guard*, November 1971, p. 30.

volved in Republican activities. Looking back on his YAF involvement, including organization conventions, he noted that it "helped reinforce my political beliefs" and brought him into contact with other young conservatives.[36]

At Lutheran High School South in Afton, Missouri, Walt Busch headed up the General "Blackjack" Pershing Memorial Chapter that helped out often at the Missouri YAF state headquarters in Kirkwood. YAF reinforced his conservatism and influenced him in other ways also. "I am the only public servant in the family and spent 32 years in law enforcement at least in part because of YAF . . . I teach history and state/local government at a junior college part time and some of my views definitely come across to students."[37] In Ridgefield, Connecticut, James Farfaglia formed a chapter that obtained excellent coverage of its activities in the local media. As he recently noted, "YAF gave me an opportunity to defend the values that have made America great and gave me the opportunity to fight against communism, to grow as a leader and stand firm in my convictions."[38] After high school, Farfaglia attended Magdalen College and upon graduation entered the Legionaires of Christ, a new Roman Catholic order in the United States. Following mission work in Mexico, he founded new parishes in Lufkin and Corpus Christi, Texas where he now serves as pastor of St. Helena of the True Cross of Jesus Catholic Church.[39]

Hollis Vasquez Rutledge was the founder and chairman of Mission Hi-YAF near the Texas border with Mexico. Encouraged by teachers who served as sponsors, it was his first political activity. Rutledge went on to become state chairman of his church denomination's high school group and then student government president at Pan American University. In the 1980s, he held positions in the Reagan and Bush Administrations and served eight years as president of the Texas Republican County Chairman's Association. He is now a political consultant.[40]

Local YAF chapter efforts to provide support to American troops in Vietnam and those wounded and living in Veterans Administration hospitals began as early as 1965 with the escalation of troop assignments and American ground troop involvement in the war. YAF chapters took a variety of approaches to showing support for American troops. During the fall semester of 1968, the University of Colorado chapter led by John Carr collected paperback books to be sent to servicemen in Vietnam while the University of Dayton chapter collected gift items and Christmas cards to be delivered to wounded veterans in VA hospitals. Likewise, Southern Illinois University YAF solicited donations for "Operation Buddy" to send Christmas gifts and cards to servicemen in Vietnam.[41] The Indianapolis Community YAF chapter, led by Louisa Porter, sponsored a program to send messages to Vietnam. Anyone having a relative or friend serving in Vietnam was invited to send a taped Christmas message. The YAF chapter enclosed an American flag lapel pin and a blue button and then forwarded the recording on to the serviceman.[42]

The national organization launched a major, coordinated effort to provide

---

36. 2008 YAF Alumni Survey Responses: Kevin C. O'Bryon.
37. 2008 YAF Alumni Survey Responses: Walter E. Busch.
38. 2008 YAF Alumni Survey Responses: Salvatore James Farfaglia.
39. *Ibid.*
40. Interview with Hollis Vasquez Rutledge, Harlingen, TX, December 1, 1999.
41. *New Guard*, February 1969, pp. 24, 26.
42. "Group to Tape Messages to G.I.'s in Vietnam," *Indianapolis Star* in *YAF in the News*, December 1970.

assistance to wounded veterans in the fall of 1971 when it announced "Project Appreciation." Local chapters were sent Project Appreciation kits that included personal items such as toothbrushes and paste, aftershave lotion, playing cards and dominoes, as well as copies of conservative periodicals such as *Human Events*, *New Guard*, and *National Review* and paperback editions of *Conscience of a Conservative*. Once they received their shipment, the YAF chapters would assemble the kits, organize a visit to a nearby Veterans Administration hospital, and present the kits to wounded servicemen. The program was described as "a united effort by patriotic citizens to demonstrate how we care."[43]

Kings County YAF took on this project throughout the spring of 1972, delivering Project Appreciation kits to those in the Brooklyn Veterans Administration hospital.[44] The District of Columbia YAF community chapter assembled kits and helped DC college chapters deliver them at Walter Reed Army Medical Center. Canisius College YAF, led by Carole Allwein, paid Easter visits to patients at the Buffalo VA hospital and presented them with Project Appreciation kits. The University of Akron and Kent State University YAF chapters joined together to work on the project. According to Brad Ellis, Kent State chairman, the YAF members wanted "to show in some small but meaningful way, that we appreciate these veterans and to make a public statement in opposition to those persons who want to write off our veterans as 'war criminals.'"[45]

Amnesty and China

YAF's final involvement in the Vietnam war controversy was on the question of whether or not to grant amnesty to those who either avoided military service illegally or deserted from the military after induction. An early indication of the organization's position came when its executive director testified before the Democratic National Convention Platform Committee in June 1972. According to his statement, "to permit amnesty is, in effect, to say 'If you think a law is immoral, break it, because you may very well find that society changes its mind, forgives you and does not punish you.' More simply it says, 'You were completely right to disobey the law.'"[46] He summed up the prevailing position in the organization by maintaining, "primarily because for a democratic government to be viable its citizens cannot pick and choose what laws they will obey and what laws they will ignore, most of us in Young Americans for Freedom oppose amnesty."[47]

During the 1972 campaign, President Nixon took a firm stand against amnesty and continued to express that throughout 1973 but the public cries for amnesty continued, especially after the withdrawal of the last American troops from Vietnam in the spring of the year.[48] National Director William Bell of New York made the case for opposing the granting of blanket amnesty to the thousands

---

43. Copies of the solicitation letters are in Group Research Archives, Box 341, Columbia University, New York, NY. The letter signed by Martha Mitchell was also printed as a "Letter From a Friend" in the *Harvard Crimson*, October 8, 1971.

44. "YAF Visits Veterans," *Brooklyn Home Reporter*, April 21, 1972.

45. *YAF in the News*, Summer 1972.

46. Statement by Wayne J. Thorburn, Executive Director of Young Americans for Freedom, before the Democratic National Convention Platform Committee, June 23, 1972, on Amnesty.

47. *Ibid.*

48. "No Aid to Hanoi," *New Guard*, May 1973, p. 2.

who "chose to cut out rather than face their responsibilities to their country." Acknowledging that certain situations might indeed justify the granting of an exception, Bell was opposed to any unconditional amnesty for all those who fled the country or went underground.[49] The national office also released a new "No Amnesty" issues paper for recruitment and distribution purposes.

In New York, State Legislative Director Chris Braunlich lobbied state and national lawmakers on the issue and devised a petition for chapters and members to circulate. Ralph Munroe, State Vice Chairman of Virginia, held a news conference in Richmond to outline his state organization's opposition to blanket amnesty and called on the Old Dominion state's congressional delegation to stand against any unconditional and all-encompassing amnesty for deserters and draft evaders. State Chairman Pat Geary and National Director Pat Nolan led a similar effort in California.[50]

The most prominent YAF spokesman on the amnesty issue was Jerry Norton, YAF's publications director and a Vietnam veteran. Norton was the author of the brief YAF Issues Paper on amnesty where he summarized the organization's position by saying "For a democratic government to be viable, its citizens cannot pick and choose with impunity what laws they will obey and what laws they will ignore; that is why we oppose amnesty."[51] Norton made a tour of Maryland, including a talk on the issue at Towson State College and an appearance on Baltimore television. At the University of North Carolina–Greensboro, he debated the issue with UNC–G professor James Reston, Jr., son of the *New York Times* columnist. Meanwhile, National Director Bill Bell debated the amnesty question before the Stamford, CT Forum for World Affairs and Illinois YAF leader Fran Griffin debated Joseph Buta of the American Friends Service Committee at a gathering in Chicago.[52]

YAF continued to oppose amnesty, as did Richard Nixon while he remained in the White House. However, shortly after assuming the office of President, Gerald Ford issued a conditional amnesty offer in exchange for two years of public service work. Few of those eligible took advantage of the program and a report one year later showed that of those few who accepted, sixty percent evaded or deserted from their public service commitment.[53] Then, in the face of a failing program of conditional amnesty, one day after becoming President, James Earl Carter pardoned all who had illegally evaded military service. As of early 1977, the United States had removed all military personnel from Vietnam, the war against Communism in Southeast Asia had been lost, and those who had violated the draft laws of the United States had now been exonerated. It was the end of a long and contentious period in American history but one whose consequences would be felt for many years thereafter. Just as for the nation as a whole, the issue of Vietnam had ended for Young Americans for Freedom.

Some believe that YAF suffered from its involvement in anti-New Left and pro-Vietnam activities. As Richard Derham observed, "we were casualties of the Vietnam War. We moved from training a cadre of conservatives more to the activist mentality." According to Derham,

---

49. William Bell, "No Amnesty," *New Guard*, May 1973, pp. 11–12.
50. *New Guard*, June 1972, p. 20.
51. Jerry Norton, "No Amnesty, YAF Issues Paper, 1973.
52. *YAF in the News*, June 1973.
53. Don Nordheimer, "60% of Deserters Leave Amnesty Service," *New York Times*, September 15, 1975.

Students were attracted to YAF on what we did against the Left and in favor of the Vietnam War rather than for the philosophical ideas of conservatism as reflected in the Sharon Statement. In a way, this was great for membership, but it undercut our concept of training a generation of future conservative leaders. In the early years, we had focused on ideas and philosophy, and "action items" were useful mainly for recruitment of people to give them a place to deepen their philosophy.

During the early years, YAF was a place you invested for a 40-year return. It was designed to be about long-term development of leaders for the future.[54]

Derham's position was shared by another Board member in the early 1970s, Jameson Campaigne, Jr., who maintained that turning activists concerned about the New Left into conservative cadres was a tricky proposition at best.[55] Campaigne was one of the prime movers for what he considered more intellectual efforts, such as YAF's programmatic emphasis on what was called the "Movement for Quality Education."

Yet others would maintain that there was a place for activist "bomb throwers" within YAF and that not everyone could be a philosopher-king. While it is true that many who were first motivated by anti-New Left and pro-Vietnam activities faded from involvement as the campuses quieted down, nevertheless YAF continued to produce effective future conservative leaders throughout the 1970s and 1980s.

In the early 1970s, Randal Teague disputed the claim that there had been too much emphasis on action and not enough on thought. Viewing the organization's members at the start of the decade he saw,

> . . . the emergence of a new breed of well-grounded philosophical-activists. For years the problem has been how to organize YAF to meet the demands both of the political activist and of the young intellectual. In 1970 we have seen the emergence of leadership which, in the same embodiments, is both the political activist and the young thinker, activist and thinker in one.[56]

YAF was integrally involved in the political process but its objective was to advance conservative principles more than to promote individual personalities. Its standard was the Sharon Statement and its campaign efforts were directed towards assisting those who would advance conservative principles. Action, in other words, had a definite purpose grounded in philosophical roots.

Moreover, the leftist challenge to the American university system had to be opposed and only YAF was there to provide student opposition to their radical goals. Just as importantly, YAF provided an oasis of support for conservatives in a sea of liberalism. Jeff Kane remembers the influence this had on him and other young conservatives. "Everything was politicized on campus and I remember the ostracizing the left tried to do to all of those in our YAF chapter. The thought that anyone supported the war was so out there that we were branded as something less than human."[57] Kane was not alone in feeling that isolation and YAF

---

54. Interview with Richard A. Derham, Seattle, WA, March 27, 2009.
55. Schneider: *Cadres for Conservatism*, p. 151.
56. Randal C. Teague, "YAF: A Presence in the Room," *New Guard*, January–February 1971, p. 19.
57. 2008 YAF Alumni Survey Responses: Jeffrey Kane.

provided the needed moral and philosophical support to continue standing for principle. As John Krilla, chapter chairman at Rutgers University in the early 1970s recalled recently, his involvement in YAF "helped keep my focus during some very turbulent times (Vietnam war, riots, etc.)."[58]

This essential role of Young Americans for Freedom in standing up to the radicals who wished to destroy the entire system was noted by others also. Reporting on YAF's Tenth Anniversary celebration in 1970, C.S. Horn noted,

> Again and again, the note was sounded: radicalism is fragmented, discredited, disordered, dying, and in its death struggle it will pull our universities and our political system over with it if it can; it is up to YAF—because YAF is the only organization available willing to do it—to make sure the universities survive.[59]

Looking back on the conflicts and confrontations occurring on American campuses in the 1960s and the overwhelming campaign of the Left to defeat American efforts in Vietnam, one can surely ask, if YAF had not rallied those forces opposed to the Left on campus and garnered support for the Vietnam War among the youth of America, then who would have done it?

A related foreign policy issue during 1971 concerned the growing sentiment for a change in the United States relations with the Republic of China and Communist China. In view of these developments, YAF determined to put more emphasis on its long-standing support for the Republic of China government on Taiwan. The Summer 1971 issue of *New Guard* featured a cover article, "Mao's Experiment: A Chinese Misfortune," by retired General B.H. Krulak.[60] With the support of other conservative and anti-communist groups, YAF sponsored "Free China Week" consisting actually of three days of events on July 12–15. Coordinating the events were Ron Pearson, chairman of the Student Committee for a Free China, and Frank Donatelli of Duquesne University. While the project included a series of events sponsored by local YAF chapters across the country the main focus was placed on activities in the Nation's Capital.[61]

Surprisingly, in the midst of YAF's Free China Week ceremonies, President Nixon announced that he had been invited to visit Communist China and had accepted the invitation. After Nixon's announced trip, Jeff Burslem and Wayne Johnson organized a vigil in front of the Chinese Embassy that continued for several days.[62] That fall, prior to the United Nations vote on admitting Communist China, YAF sponsored more than one hundred demonstrations, dinners, and declarations of support across the country, showing continued support for the Republic of China. Unfortunately, the vote at the UN was lost, Nixon went to Peking in 1972, a liaison office was established in Communist China in 1973, and U.S. recognition of the Red regime took place in 1979.

Despite these setbacks, YAF continued to maintain a close relationship with,

---

58. 2008 YAF Alumni Survey Responses: John Krilla.

59. C.S. Horn, "Reunion in Sharon," *National Review*, October 6, 1970, p. 1057.

60. *New Guard*, Summer 1971, pp. 5–9.

61. YAF's "Free China Week" activities are reported in "Free China Week Torpedoed by Nixon," *New Guard*, September 1971, pp. 29–31.

62. YAF's position was reinforced in an editorial, "Nixon to Peking: The Unleashing of Mao," *New Guard*, September 1971, pp. 5–6. See also, David Nelson Rowe, "US Policy and the China Question in the UN," *Ibid.* pp. 10–13.

and support for, the people of the Republic of China. Working with the World Youth Crusade for Freedom, many YAF members visited Taiwan in the 1970s as part of a sponsored summer study tour. One who did so was Alice Anderson, Purdue chapter chairman who studied at the National Chengchi University in Taipei. Anderson remains active in and a financial supporter of several conservative groups today.[63]

Young America's Freedom Offensive

When Young Americans for Freedom was formed in 1960, the original members saw themselves in a philosophical and ideological battle against "the Establishment"—an establishment of Eastern liberal politicians in control of both national political parties, an establishment of liberal media forces, and an establishment of liberal administrators and professors on most American campuses. As the decade progressed, the expansion of the Vietnam war and the rise of radical leftist organizations occasioned a shift in focus for YAF. In national politics, their candidate had won the Republican presidential nomination and more young conservatives were assuming positions within the party structure. In defense of the effort to defeat communism in Southeast Asia, it became necessary to support many of the Johnson and Nixon Administration policies. On campus, when the radical leftists took over buildings, closed down campuses, and resorted to other forms of violence, YAF chapters were sometimes viewed as supporting the established order on campus.

By the 1970s, YAF was once again on the offensive against what they perceived as the establishment, a liberal establishment on most American college campuses. To battle this liberal establishment, consisting of administrators, faculty and fellow students, YAF chapters used a number of different approaches. While the latter part of the 1960s saw much of YAF activity focused on combating the New Left and rallying support for the war in Vietnam, the organization always promoted a broad range of issues. Early on, YAF determined that an effective means of spreading the conservative message and recruiting new members was through the use of brief 8½ by 11 inch three-fold issues papers. The initial seven covered topics ranging from social security to student subversion.[64] Periodically these issues papers were updated with more current information and supplemented with additional topics.

Beginning in 1969, national YAF packaged six programs under the title "Young America's Freedom Offensive" designed to allow individual chapters to select from the list and focus on those they believed more applicable to their situation. Initially, the six were (1) the Freedom versus Communism high school study course which YAF lobbied state legislatures for inclusion in the high school curriculum; (2) majority coalitions to combat the left on campus; (3) support for a voluntary military; (4) opposition to East–West trade in strategic goods; (5) youth

---

63. 2008 YAF Alumni Survey Responses: Alice R. Anderson.

64. Although revised and updated over time, the initial seven papers were (1) Social Security: fraud on young people; (2) The Minimum Wage: crime against the Negro; (3) The Draft: there is an alternative; (4) East–West Trade: committing national suicide; (5) Victory in Viet Nam: the American imperative; (6) National Student Association: a smear against students; (7) Student Subversion: the majority replies. Subsequent papers dealt with a range of subjects such as Sell the Post Office, Firearms Control, The Right to Leave, and the Open University.

in politics; and (6) member involvement in independent sector solutions to societal problems. Soon thereafter, YAF re-thought its emphasis on the coalitional approach to combating SDS and modified it to a more encompassing Campus Freedom Offensive that included possible legal action, campaigns against mandatory student fees, involvement in student government elections, a push for free market economics courses, and a commitment to open recruitment on campus.[65] The overall slogan for Young America's Freedom Offensive was "political action through philosophical motivation."

In the spring of 1969, YAF's College Director sent a letter to college chapter chairmen in which he noted that "too many chapters do not devote enough effort to local programming and fail to effectively take an active role in campus affairs." This was a call for more active involvement in activities that would influence the direction of the college campus, including recruiting and supporting conservative candidates for student government positions.[66] To assist the chapter leaders, during the late 1960s and through the 1970s, the national office prepared and distributed a number of "how to" manuals. There were separate high school, college and community chapter organizational manuals that had initially been prepared in the early 1960s. These were updated and supplemented by a 112 page book, *The Complete Chapter Chairman*, written by Jerry Norton and distributed beginning in 1970. That same year saw the publication of Jim Hager's *Politics: Campus Style* and Bruce Eberle's *Direct Mail Fundraising for State Organizations* along with updated versions of *Film Programs for YAF Chapters*, *Speakers Program for YAF Chapters*, and *A Capsule Course in Communications*. The previous year, a rather comprehensive *State Organizational Manual* was made available and then revised and updated in 1972. Around the same time, Don Feder of Boston University and David Havelka and Paul Skocz of the University of Maryland co-authored *Do It! or publishing a conservative underground newspaper*, a 44 page manual. All of these publications were designed to assist the YAF member and chapter in their efforts at becoming more effective agents for conservatism.

YAF also placed a major emphasis on training and equipping its members for ideological battle by encouraging participation in seminars and workshops sponsored by other organizations such as the Intercollegiate Studies Institute, the Christian Anti-Communism Crusade, and the Foundation for Economic Education. The national office supported a series of fourteen state leadership conferences during July and August, 1970 with an additional five as the fall semester began.[67] Among the conferences was one at Fordham University that obtained coverage in the *New York Times*.[68] Building on the success of the state leadership conferences, the national office sponsored "Freedom Offensive Conferences" during the 1970–71 academic year. These were designed to be one-day conferences focusing on one aspect of Young America's Freedom Offensive, conducted by YAF state organizations but with speakers provided by the national office.[69]

---

65. Ronald B. Dear, "Young America's Freedom Offensive, a 1969 report," *New Guard*, January 1970, pp. 12–15.

66. Letter to Teona Tone Sidney from Wayne Thorburn, College Director, March 12, 1969. Personal Papers of Patrick Dowd, Box 3, Hoover Institution, Stanford University, Palo Alto, CA.

67. *New Guard*, October 1970, pp. 32–33.

68. C. Gerald Fraser, "Conservatives Plan to Thwart Campus Disruptions," *New York Times*, August 9, 1970.

69. Memo to State Chairmen, National Board of Directors from Wayne Thorburn, September 23, 1970.

Ever since its founding, YAF had established and employed ad hoc organizations to advance one particular issue or cause. Over time, some of these groups became located in YAF regional offices and were a source of funding for YAF regional programs. This continued in the group's second decade with the STOP-NSA Committee headed by Albert Forrester and later, Patrick Perry, as well as the Youth for Voluntary Prayer committee headed by Mary Kay Davis, both operating out of YAF's Southwest regional office in Houston. In the Northwest, Jim Casterline headed the Student Committee for the Right to Bear Arms and served as YAF regional representative.[70] With his replacement by Alan Gottlieb in 1972, the group's name was changed to Citizens Committee for the Right to Keep and Bear Arms, a very active and more broad-based organization still in existence today. David Walter was the initial chairman of the Student Committee for Economic Education and Donald Feder, National Director from Massachusetts, succeeded him. Michael Thompson served as Chairman of the Student Committee for Victory in Vietnam.[71] In addition, David Keene headed up the Student Committee for a Free China, followed later by Ron Pearson. Each of these ad hoc committees provided support to local YAF chapters and other young conservatives with literature, reports, speakers, and organized projects. National YAF was aware of the fact that not all members were involved in a local chapter and, thus, always emphasized a number of "Committee of One Projects" that individuals could undertake to advance the conservative cause, many of which encouraged involvement in projects carried out by the ad hoc committees.[72]

Mandatory Student Fees

While many YAF members had long expressed concern over the funding of leftist projects and speakers out of mandatory fees collected by student governments, no real organized effort to resist payment or simply abolish such fees took place until 1969 when separate efforts launched the campaign on both coasts. In May of 1969, the University of Southern California YAF chapter initiated a campaign to abolish the mandatory fee.[73] Two months later, on July 14, 1969, Judith Abramov, chairman of the YAF chapter at the State University of New York at Stony Brook, wrote to the student government executive committee, with a copy to the Chancellor and University President. She declared, "It is with great sadness and anger that I inform you of my intent not to pay the Student Activities Fee for the 1969–70 academic year. I have urged all those with whom I have come in contact to do the same in the hope of crippling—even if ever so slightly—student government."[74] Abramov went on to cite the use of mandatory student fees for funding a trip to Africa by leaders of a Black students organization and funds for bail money for students indicted after a drug bust. The letter was reprinted in *New Guard* and became the impetus for other chapters launching similar campaigns against mandatory fees.

---

70. 2008 YAF Alumni Survey Responses: James Casterline.
71. "YAF Student Committees," October 1970. Personal Papers of Patrick Dowd, Box 3, Hoover Institution, Stanford University, Palo Alto, CA.
72. "Committee of One Projects," *YAF Action Line*, June 1969. Personal Papers of Herbert Philbrick, Box 218, Library of Congress, Washington, DC.
73. Mark Deardorff and Pat Nolan, "The Siege of USC," *New Guard*, July–August 1975, pp. 10–11.
74. "Resistance at State University of New York," *New Guard*, September 1969, p. 7.

YAF chapters attacked mandatory fees by using a number of specific arguments, depending on the situation at that campus. A major concern was the use of the fees by student governments, with chapters citing examples similar to those at SUNY–Stony Brook as well as the more common complaint about the leftist and liberal bias in speaker programs. On some campuses, student newspapers and radio stations were charged with using government funds to endorse political candidates or causes, including use of student fee money to support leftist rallies and demonstrations. Conservative, moderate, and apolitical students were being taxed to support positions contrary to their own beliefs and desires.

Beyond raising public concern over the issue through news releases, independent publications, and appearances before student government, YAF chapters frequently used petitions and forced referenda on campus to measure student opposition to the continued imposition of mandatory fees. On several campuses, the fee issue was a spur to YAF involvement in campus politics, resulting in the election of YAF members to student government positions.

For several YAF chapters, one avenue to increased influence and a possible remedy to the situation was to encourage state legislative action, ideally designed to abolish the mandatory nature of the student activity fee. While not ultimately successful in ending the fees, these efforts resulted in enhanced recognition within the political arena and valuable experience for those YAF members who lobbied legislators, testified before legislative committees, and held news conferences outlining their position on the issue. This brought both attention to the organization and recognition of the presence of conservative students on college campuses in that state. Finally, YAF chapters increasingly used the court system in an attempt to provide relief from the mandatory student activity fees. Having used petitions, injunctions, and lawsuits against college administrators and leftist student demonstrators over the previous few years, this was a familiar approach to some YAF chapters, especially those with law school student members.

In the fall of 1969 at the University of Tennessee at Knoxville, the YAF chapter under the leadership of Alan Gottlieb, Ron Leadbetter and Jim Duncan and with the support of National Director Jim Hager, launched an investigation into the use of student fees. Of particular concern was the speakers funded by such fees. As Hager explained, "These fees are mandatory and often require the moderate and conservative students on campus to support programs run for and by liberals and leftists."[75] UT YAF would continue its attack on fees and use it as a major issue in rallying support for conservative candidates for student government. Hager ran a close campaign for student government president while several other YAF members were elected. One of those elected was Ron Leadbetter. He recalled, "I openly campaigned for a seat in the Student Government Association at UT as a YAF member and came in third out of several dozen candidates despite a decidedly liberal student bias in 1968–69."[76]

Looking back on his college years, Leadbetter concluded, "YAF helped shape and fine-tune my conservative views and also provided an excellent framework for expressing those views through political action."[77] Leadbetter continued at the University of Tennessee to receive his law degree and then worked for 36 years as an attorney in the Office of the General Counsel at the University.

75. Michael J. Bonafield, "YAF Officers Probing UT Student Fees," *Nashville Banner* as printed in *YAF in the News*, October 1969.
76. 2008 YAF Alumni Survey Responses: Ronald C. Leadbetter.
77. *Ibid.*

Also during the fall 1969 semester, the University of Maryland YAF chapter launched its own campaign to abolish mandatory activity fees. YAF Chairman Joe Spelta cited several examples of what he called "improper use of SGA funds," including the payment of $1,600 in fees to Abbie Hoffman and Rennie Davis, $1,000 to the Black Student Union and $1,400 "that was appropriated by rather suspect means to the Vietnam moratorium committee."[78] In a letter to members of the House Ways and Means Committee, Spelta urged support for two bills filed in the Maryland House of Delegates, one that would make student fees voluntary and one that would eliminate them completely.[79] The bills were not passed but that did not deter the YAF chapter from continuing its campaign. The following year, new chapter chairman David Havelka requested an opinion of the Maryland Attorney General on the use of mandatory student fees for political and social causes. As he noted, "students on the College Park campus are being forced to financially contribute to political and social causes which many do not support." Havelka went on to stress that students should be free to voluntarily support whatever cause they wanted.

> If these organizations and causes have the support of as many students as their leaders claim, then there is no reason why all students should be forced, under penalty of expulsion from school, to pay for them. They should have no trouble in financing themselves by voluntary means. Our chapter of Young Americans for Freedom has done so for our projects, including the "Alternative" newspaper and our speakers' series.[80]

YAF members at Maryland and at other universities were no longer willing to sit back and see their money used to support leftist causes.

Later that academic year, Ohio State University YAF issued a "list of ten requests," among which was "Student Services fees be made completely voluntary and that students pay for any incidental services they may need."[81] Meanwhile, at Mississippi State University, YAF chairman John Hightower attacked the use of mandatory fees for a "preponderance of liberal speakers" and maintained that the program should be balanced.[82] The University of Missouri chapter, led by David Weir, held a news conference to expose their findings that student fees had been used to finance participation in the Vietnam Moratorium, the Cambodian and Kent State demonstrations, lobbying at the State Capital, and the payment of a salary to the student body president.[83]

At the University of Tennessee at Chattanooga, Todd Gardenhire organized a drive that obtained signatures from 1,600 students on a petition to eliminate mandatory fees. While that effort was not successful, the following semester, YAF was able to get signatures from 51% of the student body on their petition to end fees. As Gardenhire pointed out, "Students who work, students who commute from nearby towns, must pay a $25 activity fee each semester, knowing very well that they will not be able to attend any activities." The UT-C chapter joined

78. "YAF Protesting SGA's Fees Use," *Diamondback* in *Maryland YAF in the News,* 1969.

79. "State YAF chapter attacks student fee," *Diamondback* in *Maryland YAF in the News,* 1969.

80. "YAF Chapter Head Questions Use of Student Fees for Political Causes," *Prince George's Post* as appearing in *YAF in the News,* December 1970.

81. Ohio State University YAF release dated May 26, 1970 appearing at http://www.history.ohio-state.edu/osuhist/1970riot/yaf.htm.

82. "Want More Conservative Speakers," *Laurel Leader-Call* in *YAF in the News,* December 1970.

83. *New Guard,* January–February 1971, p. 40.

with YAF groups at UT–Knoxville and UT–Martin in filing suit in Federal court contesting the legality of the mandatory participation requirement.[84] Gardenhire and seventeen other YAF members then sought an injunction to stop the collection of fees.[85] Just as at the Knoxville campus, the UT–Chattanooga YAF chapter used the issue to help elect several members to student government while one member was elected to the area Chancery Court.

At the same time, Brown University YAF, led by chairman Alan Jolis along with Ernest Evans, Gary Westmoreland, and Terence Carle, filed suit to prohibit tuition money being used for political purposes.[86] YAF members Bonnie Good, Galen Tyler and Chuck Scantleberry at the University of Washington filed a similar suit while YAFers Ralph Larsen and Bruce Wimmer filed suit against the University of Nebraska at Lincoln. Following a similar path, the University of New Hampshire chapter launched a suit to enjoin the use of mandatory fees for political activities.[87] At Queens College, Joe DiVierniero and Eugene Flynn filed suit to prevent funding to a student newscaster who had made a political endorsement. In April of 1973, the University of Texas chapter filed a petition for a temporary injunction against the *Daily Texan* newspaper for endorsing candidates. This was denied but the issue of state funds being used for political purposes had been brought to the public's attention.

On the campus of the University of Arkansas, State Chairman Alan Leveritt began a campaign against mandatory fees as did the chapter at Adelphi University in New York.[88] Likewise, Iowa State University YAF, led by Rhonda Hurlbutt, launched its campaign for voluntary student fees in the fall of 1970, a campaign carried on later by new chapter chairman Mike Mulford.[89] At the traditionally radical leftist campus of San Francisco State College, Pat Colglazier led YAF in collecting 1,885 signatures against mandatory fees.

The University of Arizona's Paul Lenkowsky criticized the use of fees to bring only liberal and leftist speakers to campus. On one occasion, those fees paid to bring Communist leader Angela Davis to campus. When she refused to debate Phillip Abbott Luce, YAF made an issue of it, pointing out the clear bias in the speakers program. A similar situation existed at Adelphi University where mandatory fees were used to pay for a speech by Black Panther leader Bobby Seale.[90] At the University of South Carolina and Louisiana State University, YAF members took a different tack and made sure some of their members were appointed to the universities' speakers' committees.[91] Youngstown University YAF and its chairman, Bill Boni, used the fee issue to elect several YAF members to the Student Senate.[92] Also in 1972, *New Guard* presented an article on the philosophical opposition to mandatory fees by Gary Leffel of Wichita State University in which he paraphrased Lincoln's famous speech and applied it to the issue of student fees.[93]

84. Dick Kopper, "Group at University to Contest Programs Fee in a Federal Suit," *Chattanooga Times* in *YAF in the News*, January 1972.

85. *New Guard*, June 1972, p. 21.

86. "Four at Brown Seek Curb on Use of Tuition," *Providence Journal* in *YAF in the News*, January 1972.

87. *New Guard*, July–August 1972, p. 23.

88. *New Guard*, January–February 1972, p. 31; *New Guard*, May 1972, p. 23.

89. *Ibid.* p. 25.

90. "YAF Attacks Activity Fees," *Long Island Press*, quoted in *New York YAF in the News*, April 1972.

91. *New Guard*, March 1973, p. 22.

92. *New Guard*, October 1974, p. 33.

93. Gary Leffel, "Gettysburg Address: Mandatory Student Activity Fees Version," *New Guard*, June 1972, p. 13.

State organizations also took on the issue in a concerted effort to abolish fees at all state colleges and universities. Ed Martin of New York YAF called on the New York Senate and Assembly to ban the mandatory participation in such programs. In a statement released in Albany he maintained, "These mandatory activities fees are being misused by universities in as much as they are being used to present one-sided left-wing programs which include speakers such as Abbie Hoffman from the SDS and radical attorney William Kuntsler."[94] New Hampshire YAF Chairman John B. Tarrant testified in Concord in favor of a bill to ban mandatory fees at state universities while Nebraska YAF had a similar bill introduced in the Senate to abolish fees.[95] Similar efforts were undertaken in Indiana, where a legislative resolution calling for an end to fees passed, and Texas, where the Speaker of the House of Representatives agreed to support the effort.

One of the campuses where YAF was successful was at the University of California at San Diego. YAF chairman Jim Sills led a referendum campaign in March 1972 that saw fees defeated in a vote of 1,387 to 516.[96] YAF leaders went one step further and attempted to "work out a complete alternative package of voluntaristic action . . . showing how our system might function in practice."[97] Grit and determination finally paid off at the University of Southern California where YAF overcame the opposition of university bureaucrats and student government "wannabees" when they won the final vote against fees. As two of those active in the effort concluded, "In February of 1975, six months after that vote and five and a half years after we had begun our campaign, the fee was collected on a voluntary basis."[98]

The University of Alaska, led by YAF chairman Charles Hutchins, was able to obtain 72% of the vote in a student referendum against mandatory fees in 1974 but through some machinations the Student Body President was able to call a second vote where the YAF victory was overturned.[99] At Towson State College, the YAF chapter under Rich Firestone narrowly lost the vote to abolish student fees but, not giving up, they came back the following year and held a rally against fees featuring Ron Docksai, Maryland YAF Executive Director Bruce Hoffman, and national staff member Albert Forester.[100] Over the next several years, both local YAF chapters and the national organization continued the campaign against mandatory fees. YAF also began distributing a light-hearted flyer in the 1970s titled "Are you old enough to make your own decisions?" with a drawing of a Linus-like character sucking his thumb and holding a blanket. The message at the bottom was "End Mandatory Fees."

While most of YAF's campaigns were not successful in banning mandatory fees, either through state legislative action or by vote of the students on campus, they did open up the system on some campuses by either requiring a vote of all students before fees could become mandatory or allowing some form of rebate or waiver to those who wished not to pay student activity fees. YAF's involvement

94. "YAF Criticizes Use of Activities Fees," *Valley Stream Maileader* in *YAF in the News*, January 1973.
95. *New Guard*, April 1973, p. 23.
96. *New Guard*, June 1972, p. 21.
97. Stephen Karganovic, "Is There an Alternative to Mandatory Fees?" *New Guard*, July–August 1975, pp. 14–16.
98. Mark Deardorff and Pat Nolan, "The Siege of USC," *New Guard*, July–August 1975, p. 10.
99. *New Guard*, July–August 1974, p. 34. See also: Jeff Kane, "The Northwest Campaign," *New Guard*, July–August 1975, pp. 12–13, for a discussion of anti-fee activity at the University of Alaska, University of Washington, and Washington State University.
100. *New Guard*, December 1972, p. 25; *YAF in the News*, June 1973.

on this issue did point out the use and misuse of funds by student governments, brought such funding under closer public scrutiny, and showed YAF's commitment to individual choice and free association as opposed to compulsory actions, whether by government or by student entities.

At least one aspect of the mandatory fees issue—the composition of the speakers paid with mandatory fees—is now addressed on a regular basis by Young America's Foundation. While encouraging pressure on college administrations and student governments to provide more balance in their speakers' programs, the Foundation has taken positive action by assisting students in sponsoring prominent conservative spokesmen. The Foundation has distributed a "Campus Conservative Battle Plan" to assist students determined to bring about change and it provides financial assistance or outright sponsorship of conservative speakers. William F. Buckley, Jr. was a frequent speaker on campuses at lectures sponsored by Young America's Foundation and believed that they were "experiences of infinite importance."[101] In addition to Buckley, some of the prominent political leaders sponsored by Young America's Foundation on American college campuses have included Margaret Thatcher, Lech Wałęsa, Colin Powell, Edwin Meese, and John Ashcroft. Others presented by the Foundation include William Bennett, Ward Connerly, Ann Coulter, Dinesh D'Souza, Michael Reagan, John Stossel, and Walter Williams.[102]

Fighting the PIRGs

A closely related effort by YAF college chapters throughout the decade of the 1970s was its campaign against the Ralph Nader–created "Public Interest Research Groups" (PIRGs). The first student PIRG was incorporated in 1971 on Minnesota college campuses and the effort soon spread to Oregon and Massachusetts. Over the following years, a number of campus-based and statewide PIRGs were established.[103] However, due to opposition from YAF and other groups, as of 2009, only twenty states had functioning Student PIRGs and they were in existence at less than one hundred college campuses.[104]

According to a report by YAF activist Jeff Kane, PIRGs were initially established as a means of redirecting the "peace movement" of the 1960s to issues of environmental preservation, consumer protection, and greater government involvement in controlling corporations. Eschewing violence in favor of other forms of intimidation and creating a permanent bureaucracy of "public interest advocates," the PIRG approach was seen as more effective in bringing about change in American society.[105] While conservatives would disagree with much of what Ralph Nader and the PIRG's view as the "public interest," one of the most controversial aspects of the entire program is the funding mechanism they attempt

---

101. Letter from William F. Buckley, Jr. to Ron Robinson, President, Young America's Foundation, May 13, 1996.

102. http://yaf.org/students/speakers/speaker_master.cfm.

103. www.usprig.org/about-us/pirg-campus-chapters accessed on March 5, 2009.

104. www.studentpirgs.org accessed on March 5, 2009.

105. Jeffrey Kane: *A Comprehensive Report on Public Interest Research Groups* (Washington, DC: Young Americans for Freedom, 1972), p. 3. Kane's report was subsequently reprinted in brochure form titled "Nader's Campus PIRG Groups" by the Southern States Industrial Council Educational Foundation, Nashville, TN.

to establish. To ensure a continuous funding source for a permanent organization, PIRG has employed two methods: mandatory student fees and door-to-door solicitation by young people.

Initially, the main activity of PIRG volunteers on campus was to obtain signatures on a petition whereby the students agreed to "tax themselves x dollars" through an additional amount paid as part of the mandatory student activity fee. Once a sizeable number of signatures were obtained, the PIRG advocates would present them to the college authorities and request that the student fee be increased to include payments to PIRG.[106] Throughout the 1970s and for many years thereafter, this was the major source of funding for PIRGs and one that YAF attacked on campus after campus.

Many years later, the organization adopted the method of hiring young people they called canvassers but more accurately could be described as "solicitors" or even "panhandlers" who would be dropped into a community to seek funds door-to-door or on busy street corners. This approach became a secondary source of funding for PIRGs in recent years by "outsourcing" the solicitors to other left-wing organizations and then taking a cut of the proceeds for PIRG. The PIRG solicitation program and its use of young people not tied to the community is, in many respects, similar to the efforts of some who "hire" high school students for the summer, ship them to a community far from their homes, drop them off in residential neighborhoods, and require them to sell magazine subscriptions or candy to earn their room, board, and expenses. Not surprisingly, the use of such canvassers, and their outsourcing to other organizations, has come under serious question and criticism, including from some on the left.[107]

Since Nader's group first appeared in Minnesota and Oregon, it was logical that YAF's efforts started locally in those states. Minnesota YAF chairman James Newman was one of those who first brought the issue to the attention of the YAF national leadership. Soon the concern spread to the Northwest where, in March 1972, four state chairmen from Washington, Oregon, Utah and Idaho held a joint news conference. They announced a campaign designed, as Jeff Kane, at the time Washington YAF state chairman, stated to "expose PIRG for what we regard it to be." Oregon YAF chairman Randy Shaw, a student at Lewis & Clark College, declared that Oregon Student PIRG "under the guise of corporate responsibility" would "undermine our free market system."[108]

Throughout the spring semester, more YAF organizations became involved in the fight as efforts were made to spread the PIRGs to additional areas of the country. In Rhode Island, YAF undertook a statewide campaign, led by State Chairman Ron Pearson, focusing especially on the University of Rhode Island, Roger Williams University and Brown University.[109] The University of South Carolina began a major literature distribution effort to ensure that students knew the full story about public interest research groups before being coaxed into signing a petition to allow the collection of student fees. George Washington University YAF lobbied student government against authorizing mandatory fee

106. *Ibid.* p. 6.
107. Dana Fisher: *Activism, Inc.: How the Outsourcing of Grass Roots Campaigns Is Strangling Progressive Politics in America* (Palo Alto, CA: Stanford University Press, 2006).
108. "YAF Fights Consumer Programs," *Walla Walla Union-Bulletin* in *YAF in the News*, Summer 1972.
109. 2008 YAF Alumni Survey Responses: Ronald Pearson.

collection for PIRG and mailed out a survey to parents designed to show opposition to PIRG at that campus.[110]

Knowing that Nader's Raiders would be expanding their reach to more campuses, national YAF began intensifying coverage of the anti-PIRG efforts. In the summer of 1972, Richard Andrews, YAF state chairman for Utah, wrote a critique of the so-called refund program that PIRGs maintained protected the rights of students. He pointed out the difficulty of collecting refunds "after the fact" and the inequity of mandating fee payment in the first place.[111] National YAF prepared, published and distributed Jeff Kane's report, making it available to all college chapters. YAF's executive director held a news conference in front of PIRG's Washington, DC office, announcing a drive to oppose the establishment of PIRGs. He explained that YAF was opposed to their formation due to both the anti-market philosophy of the PIRGs and the imposition of financial support for them on all students.

During the fall, Florida YAF was typical of a number of state organizations that, while in the middle of a presidential campaign, shifted emphasis to campus issues and the effort to form PIRGs on campuses. YAF state chairman Tim Baer held a news conference to announce YAF's opposition and coordinated the effort throughout the state, including at the University of Florida where chapter chairman Peter Gioia claimed that, "PIRG is a tapeworm on the fee system. Students have no initial choice, and they won't have time to get their refund during the first two weeks of class, as PIRG proposes."[112] Northwestern University YAF, under chapter chairman Jeanette Dewyze, formed a coalition of groups opposed to PIRG, distributed anti-PIRG literature to students on the Evanston campus, and helped to direct activity on the issue throughout Illinois.[113]

To provide guidance to other chapters, Charles Floto prepared an article on Brown University YAF's efforts where they were successful in halting the PIRG campaign for support from mandatory fees.[114] The YAF chapter made sure two of its members attended the first organizational meeting for PIRG and then formed a front group called Students for Voluntary Action that responded to every PIRG claim. The crowning blow came when the campus paper came out against the mandatory fee structure. The Rhode Island PIRG scrapped its petition drive and began work on a complete revision of its proposal to be presented at some undetermined date in the future. As Floto observed,

> Our sources indicated that the revisions proposed led to a split with national PIRG organizers and that the latter became somewhat paranoid about YAF, having already experienced difficulty from that direction in the Northwest. Rhode Island PIRG has not been heard of or from since as a result of YAF involvement in non-elective politics on one campus.[115]

Floto's recitation of the YAF experience at Brown University encouraged other campuses to fight off the creation of PIRG units.

---

110. *New Guard*, May 1972, p. 23.
111. Richard Andrews, "PIRG," *New Guard*, July–August 1972, pp. 14–15.
112. *New Guard*, April 1973, p. 25. "YAF Maintains FPIRG Funding Farce," *YAF in the News*, January 1973.
113. *New Guard*, May 1973, p. 29.
114. Charles Floto, "Negating Nader's PIRGs, *New Guard*, July–August 1973, pp. 12–13.
115. *Ibid.* p. 13. As of March 2009, there is no Student Rhode Island PIRG organization.

At Western Michigan University, students defeated PIRG in a referendum where YAF leader Blaine Prior led the opposition forces. At SUNY–Buffalo students voted four to one against an increase in student fees to cover funding for PIRG. YAF chairwoman Jackie Davies organized the "Vote No" campaign, covering the campus with flyers and posters. Davies pointed out to students, "The involuntary student fees approach is the road to a lock-step bureaucracy, the antithesis of the goal set forth by PIRG leaders. If there is wide support for PIRG activities, surely students would be willing to give money voluntarily."[116] At the University of Texas at Austin, Terry Quist, Coby Pieper and James Meadows used all the resources of the YAF chapter, including its independent newspaper and its contacts with prominent state legislators, to ward off the drive to fund PIRG with student mandatory fees. A similar effort was underway at the University of Connecticut.[117]

Even where PIRG had been able to establish its mandatory funding mechanism, YAF chapters were determined to make it difficult for them. At Queens College, YAF chairman Joyce Marks indicated that while YAF was basically against the whole method of funding, they were committed to publicizing the availability of the refund process. Meanwhile, YAF member Joe DiVerniero, editor-in-chief of the campus newspaper, printed the refund form in the paper.[118] For the remainder of the decade and into the 1980s, YAF continued to rally opposition to PIRGs on college campuses and the limited number of functioning units as of 2009 is partial testimony to the dogged determination of YAF members to oppose the mandatory funding and the anti-free enterprise orientation of the programs.

Campus Politics

Ever since its founding, some YAF leaders had been actively involved in student government.[119] During the battles against SDS and other leftist groups in the late 1960s, several YAF chapters successfully ran candidates for student government. By the early 1970s, more YAF chapters and members were becoming involved in campus elections. Jim Hager's booklet, *Politics—Campus Style*, had been published and distributed by the YAF national office and influencing student government became a priority for many chapters.

The YAF national College Director put forth this message in an article in *New Guard* where he claimed, "at campus after campus across the country, YAF members and other conservatives have been and continue to be successful in gaining influence in the student power structure." His advice to local chapter leaders: (1) analyze your campus, (2) get your members involved in non-YAF activities and organizations, (3) run people for student senate and campaign on campus issues, and (4) run a candidate for student body president.[120] Shortly thereafter in early 1972, YAF formed a Student Election Committee with co-chairmen Todd Gardenhire, a student senator at the University of Tennessee at Chattanooga

---

116. "Ind. PIRG Funding Defeated at U.B.," in *YAF in the News*, December 1973.

117. *New Guard*, January–February 1974, p. 33.

118. Joseph Bigman and Paul Zeizel, "YAF Publicizes PIRG Refunds," *Newsbeat* in *YAF in the News*, December 1973.

119. While several could be cited, the best example is Howard Phillips, a Sharon attendee who was on YAF's initial Board of Directors while serving as president of the student government at Harvard University.

120. Jerry Norton, "YAF and Student Government Politics," *New Guard*, March 1971, pp. 13–14.

and Mike Pikosky, Secretary of the Student Association at American University. Serving as Committee members were Richard Firestone (Student Senate, Towson State), Randy Goodwin (Student Senate, University of Southern California), John R. Hightower (Student Senate, Mississippi State University), Jeff Hollingsworth (Student Senate, University of Maine), Steve Sobotta (Student Government, Vice Chairman, Stanislaus State College), Ken Tobin (Student Senate, American University), Mark Souder (Student Government President, Indiana Purdue at Ft. Wayne), and Bob Ulmer (Student Government President, University of Houston).[121] Firestone, Goodwin, Hightower, Hollingsworth and Souder all would become YAF state chairmen.[122]

Jeff Hollingsworth remembers his time in YAF and in student government at the University of Maine as leading to "some prejudice in classes, a degree of 'notoriety.' One event in particular was debating novelist Stephen King's wife on the campus radio station." Now serving as Vice President of Eagle Publishing in Washington, DC, Hollingsworth noted, "it was the primary gateway to my subsequent career. I met my spouse through YAF."[123] Many of the YAF members who served in student government went on to future careers in politics, including Mark Souder, who served in Congress from Indiana for fifteen years from 1995 to 2010. For several years YAF activists at the University of Southern California held leadership positions in student government. Among them were Pat Nolan, who became California Assembly Minority Leader, John Lewis, who served in both the California Assembly and State Senate, and Jim Lacy, who served as Mayor Pro-Tem of Dana Point, California. YAF's success on the USC campus led Nolan to conclude in 1971 that, "YAF isn't so much concerned with the Left anymore. They're a thing of the past. The revolution is over. We're not out to make headlines anymore. We're putting people into areas of effectiveness rather than publicity."[124]

When the YAF Board of Directors met in February 1971, they elected three new members who would play significant roles in the organization throughout the decade of the 70s and beyond. In late 1970, David Keene had resigned as National Chairman to become a Special Assistant to Vice President Spiro T. Agnew. The Board elected Ron Docksai of St. John's University, then serving as the Mid-Atlantic regional member of the National Board, to become National Chairman. His Board position went to Ron Robinson of Canisius College, New York YAF's Western regional coordinator. With Jay Parker joining the national staff, Frank Donatelli, then Pennsylvania YAF State Chairman and a student at Duquesne University, filled his seat on the board. Finally, Herb Stupp, who had headed up the successful Youth for Buckley campaign in New York, filled a vacant Board position. Both Donatelli and Robinson would later become executive director of Young Americans for Freedom while Stupp would serve as Mid-Atlantic regional representative, a staff position operating out of New York City.

Looking back on his campus experiences in YAF, Frank Donatelli saw them as providing training and practical experience that have been critical in all of his subsequent activities and jobs.

---

121. "YAF Student Election Committee—Student Election Fund," Personal Papers of Jameson Campaigne, Jr., Ottawa, IL.
122. "Student Government Advisory Council Launched," *New Guard*, November 1972, p. 20.
123. 2008 YAF Alumni Survey Responses: Jeff Hollingsworth.
124. Rich Wiseman, "Left Throttled on Campus—Nolan," *Daily Trojan*, February 23, 1971, p. 3.

During the sixties and early seventies, YAF was the main voice of reason on the college campuses. I participated in demonstrations for the war in Vietnam, against Mack Truck building a plant in the Soviet Union, against college disruptions, and against the Cesar Chavez inspired grape boycott. With virtually all of the faculty and many members of the Administration against you, you had to sink or swim on your own. It was invaluable training for the rest of my life.[125]

In 1973, Donatelli would become executive director of the organization and then go on to play increasingly important roles in national politics, including as Special Assistant to the President for Political Affairs during the Reagan Administration. As he recently noted, "the training and practical experience YAF provided has been critical in all of my subsequent activities and jobs."[126] Among other activities, he is currently Chairman of the Board of Governors of the Reagan Ranch, a director of Young America's Foundation, and chairman of GOPAC, a political action committee formerly headed by Newt Gingrich.

At that same meeting, the Board voted to revise Young America's Freedom Offensive and added a new program labeled *Movement for Quality Education* that advocated an Honors College program and the adoption of a Conservative Studies program on college campuses.[127] This programmatic emphasis was perhaps the one area most out of character for Young Americans for Freedom, an organization devoted to political and campus action that was now beginning to delve into a realm normally the province of its sister organization, the Intercollegiate Studies Institute. YAF's involvement in formulating alternatives to the current educational environment, of course, can be traced back over the past decade with any number of articles in its magazine, *New Guard*.[128] As the Movement for Quality Education drive began, YAF included an article on the current university by Professor Stephen J. Tonsor in a Fall issue of *New Guard*.[129] In 1970, YAF had also started issuing periodic reprints of articles on educational issues under the title *Creative Politics*.[130] With educational vouchers being adopted as the topic for high school debates in 1972–73, YAF prepared and distributed "A Debate Handbook on the Voucher System of Financing Education." It also reprinted Russell Kirk's essay, "Reforming the American College: Relevance to the Human Condition" and distributed it in booklet form.

What concerned YAF leaders was best expressed by two chapter members at the University of Maine. As Philip Diming noted about his experiences in college, "In my freshman year I used to speak up quite a bit but I found that professors of a liberal strain never took up my ideas . . . There's only so many times you will speak up before realizing that the professor thinks you're imposing on him."[131] The overall problem, of course, was not just keeping quiet to avoid antagonizing

---

125. 2008 YAF Alumni Survey Responses: Frank J. Donatelli.
126. *Ibid.*
127. *New Guard*, April 1971, p. 19.
128. While several examples could be cited, typical would be Tom Charles Huston, "Life in the Multiversity," *New Guard*, November 1966, p. 10–14.
129. Stephen J. Tonsor, "Authority, Power and the University," *New Guard*, September 1971, pp. 5–10.
130. For example, see Robert W. Fox, "Problems in Education," *Creative Politics*, February 1971.
131. Lloyd Feriss, "Campus Critics Take Aim at Liberal Teachers," *Maine Sunday Telegram* as reprinted in *Human Events*, November 11, 1972.

a liberal professor and ending up with a poor grade on one's transcript. The real concern was that apolitical and even conservative students would be ideologically influenced. Another University of Maine YAF member observed, "the average student comes here naive and open to some extent to what they hear from the rostrum. They come here basically without any politics and leave in four years pretty much infected with liberal or way-out leftist philosophies."[132] It was the presence, and even dominance, of liberal professors in the social sciences and humanities that concerned the YAF leaders who formulated and pursued a "Movement for Quality Education."

Some local chapter leaders did work for change in the educational environment. At the University of Texas, chairman David Dillard pointed out in the official campus newspaper, "There is no greater indignity that anyone can pay to a student than to offer him but one point of view; the assumption is the student is not intelligent enough to make up his own mind."[133] While most YAF students shared Dillard's sentiment, it was hard to convert that concern into an action project for a local YAF chapter. Still, the effort continued. As the fall 1972 semester began, New Guard published an article by one of its high school members calling for reform at that level.[134] Of course, liberal influences were present in many high schools also. Kim Cooney was active in the Bellevue (Washington) High School YAF chapter in the late 1960s and remembers that he "took a sometimes lonely but impassioned stand against far leftist teachers and extreme fellow students." YAF gave him a sense of not being alone and "the Sharon Statement was a foundational component of my core political philosophy."[135]

In 1973, YAF made a push to promote the Movement for Quality Education as a major project. The cover and a special section of the organization's magazine were devoted to three articles, including "An Introduction to MQE."[136] Unfortunately, short of sponsoring addresses by individuals on the topic and distributing articles and monographs, there was little for YAF chapters to do. National YAF made one more push on the topic, dedicating the summer 1974 issue of New Guard to a series of articles, including one by Milton Friedman, under the overall theme, "A Solution for Big Education."[137] Yet, for the organization's annual report, all that could be said was "the Movement for Quality Education, a committee of YAF, now has an explanatory brochure by Robert Moffit to add to the essay by Russell Kirk on the problems of the university."[138] With that, national YAF moved on to other projects and concerns while still publishing articles and reprinting monographs on the overall topic.

There were a number of other campus issues that arose in the early 1970s and attracted the involvement of YAF at the state and local level. With the autonomy of each local chapter and the flexibility to adopt different approaches and projects, each YAF chapter provided an opportunity for leadership development, consensus

132. *Ibid.*

133. David Dillard, "University No. 2," *Daily Texan* in *YAF in the News*, January 1972.

134. Hal Schuster, "High School Reform: A Plea for a Viable Program," *New Guard*, September 1972, pp. 7–9. Interestingly, Schuster went on to a career as a writer and author of a large number of unauthorized Star Trek, X-Files and other science fiction books and commentaries.

135. 2008 YAF Alumni Survey Responses: Kim P. Cooney.

136. Robert Moffit, "Introduction to MQE," pp. 13–14; Mary Fisk, "The Case for Radical Reform in School Financing," pp. 15–16; Frank Donatelli, "The Constitutionality of Federal and State Tax Credits for Financing Education," pp. 17–20; all in *New Guard*, May 1973.

137. *New Guard*, July–August 1974, pp. 8–22.

138. Mary Fisk, "From the Publications Director," *New Guard*, January 1975, p. 20.

building, and effective organizational work. Out of all these diverse efforts, new leadership for the conservative movement was developing. Joe Morris was chairman from 1970 to 1973 of Students for Capitalism and Freedom, the group that held the YAF charter at the University of Chicago. The club was also affiliated with ISI, College Republicans, and the Radical Libertarian Alliance, what Morris called "one-stop shopping for right-wing kids."

> SCAF visibly lived out the model of Frank Meyer fusion. Our ranks included a full complement of partisans, ranging from national security hawks and national security skeptics to anarcho-capitalists to Randians to social traditionalists. We were Jews observant and secular, Catholics orthodox and lapsed, several Hindus, many agnostics and atheists, and at least one fellow who went on to the Lutheran pastorate. Our heroes included Friedman, Buckley, and Reagan.[139]

Each week the group met for debate and discussion on issues political and philosophical. Out of this group came Dr. Warren Coats, for many years at the International Monetary Fund; Dr. David Friedman, now a professor at Santa Clara College of Law; Juliana Geran Pilon, Research Professor at the Institute of World Politics; Dr. Roger Pilon, Vice President for Legal Affairs at the Cato Institute; and Morris himself who is partner in the Chicago law firm of Morris & De La Rosa as well as president of the Lincoln Legal Foundation.

Still other chapters and YAF leaders were involved in direct confrontation with the leftists on campus. Dominick Caravella, was a student at the University of Houston and recalled debating the Young Socialist Alliance and how YAF made a difference on campus. That experience, "made me appreciate conservative thinking and people and in many ways I am still a big conservative."[140] Jeffrey Bothen was editor of "Bullsheet" published by the YAF chapter at Washington and Lee University. To him, the early seventies was a time of crisis in our nation and "the world would have been a very lonely place without a group of like-minded conservatives who gave me the hope that there were more like me in numbers greater than I could imagine."[141]

Another YAF leader was Dwight L. Borgstrand of Drake University. Borgstrand, whose brother Dwayne and sister Becky were also YAF activists, claimed "YAF activities formulated my foundational political worldview and enhanced my leadership ability. YAF's impact makes me wonder where the nation would be today had it not been for the work done in dormitory room meetings prior to the Reagan Revolution."[142] Jeff Swiatek was active in YAF at Lehigh University in the late 70s and is now a reporter for the *Indianapolis Star*. As he remembered his times as a college student, "I recall YAF as a breath of fresh air intellectually. YAF was one of several organizations and magazines that helped inform, inspire, and shape me intellectually."[143]

Steven Brakey and Stephanie Stearns Frederick both became involved as teenagers and ended up in the YAF chapter at the University of Maine in the early 1970s.

---

139. Email from Joseph Morris, June 8, 2009.
140. 2008 YAF Alumni Survey Responses: Dominick Caravella, II.
141. 2008 YAF Alumni Survey Responses: Jeffrey Herbert Bothen.
142. 2008 YAF Alumni Survey Responses: Dwight L. Borgstrand.
143. 2008 YAF Alumni Survey Response: Jeff Swiatek.

Frederick first joined YAF as an offshoot of the Teenage Republicans and works today as an international wine consultant in New York City and looks back on YAF having "a big impact. There were many intelligent people in YAF who truly believed. This intensity has stayed with me. I am still involved in politics on a local level. My viewpoints are almost the same as then . . ."[144] Steven Brakey first formed a high school chapter in Vero Beach, Florida and then became YAF chairman at the University of Maine. Looking back, he maintains that his experience in YAF "gave me an opportunity for leadership. It made me feel that I was a part of the political process of our country. It helped focus my political philosophy which has not changed much."[145]

James Taylor led the YAF forces at Swarthmore College during the early 1970s and that involvement "focused my innate conservatism into action and my whole career has been inside the movement. Over the years I would say that the most committed conservatives came up through YAF." Taylor went on to work for the Intercollegiate Studies Institute and the National Right to Work Legal Defense Foundation before becoming founder and chairman of America's Political Action Committee. In addition, for several years he has been on the Board of Directors of Young America's Foundation.[146]

Emerging Social Issues

While YAF remained true to the core principles laid out in the Sharon Statement, the 1970s brought to the forefront a number of what would subsequently be called "social issues" that showed division within the conservative ranks. Many YAF members welcomed the changing attitudes in American society as enhancing individual freedom and for them social change did not require acceptance of left-wing ideologies. As Kathy Forte, YAF chairman at University of Southern California in 1969, explained her position,

> It seems clear that the cultural revolution which is now taking place in America will indeed succeed in changing America for the better; however, doubts emerge at the point where I am urged to take part in a more devastating political revolution.
>
> I will not join a violent revolution, I will not swallow Marxist ideology any more than I will follow the rantings of George Wallace . . . If a war is to be waged, it must be a war of the minds, in which a free interplay of ideas are interchanged and assimilated in the making of a better, more beautiful society.[147]

Forte's differentiation between political revolution and social change was one shared by many in YAF, not merely those of a more libertarian persuasion. What began as a debate over the changing attitudes towards women, soon extended into a discussion of individual rights and the role of government.

First up in the period before the Supreme Court's decision on abortion was the

---

144. 2008 YAF Alumni Survey Responses: Stephanie Stearns Frederick.
145. 2008 YAF Alumni Survey Responses: Steven Brakey.
146. 2008 YAF Alumni Survey Responses: James Taylor.
147. Quoted in McDonald: *YAF in the Arena*, p. 24.

question of women's liberation and what should be the appropriate conservative response to the movement. In April 1972, Carol Dawson Bauman, former National Director and editor of *New Guard*, presented what she called "A Conservative View of Women's Liberation." She came to the discussion as a life-long conservative who had been active in politics since her undergraduate days, as a Roman Catholic who had been educated at a Catholic college, and as a married mother of three at the time pregnant with her fourth child.[148] Apart from the drive to achieve equal treatment, Bauman saw the women's liberation movement as awakening women to the possibility and the delight of interacting with other women on an equal and non-competitive basis. While disagreeing with some of the tactics employed by leaders of the women's liberation movement, Bauman saw its overall development as positive for all women.

It did not take long for an opposing view to surface. Two months later, the magazine presented a rebuttal by Kathy King Teague, a long-time YAF activist from Missouri and then Executive Secretary of the Charles Edison Youth Fund. Teague's response basically centered on defending the positive attributes of the traditional American female as wife and mother. She viewed the women's liberation movement as placing too much emphasis on equal work opportunities with goals that are short sighted and materialistic. Viewing women's liberation as an attack on the traditional family, Teague noted, "as if Gloria Steinem and her contingent of braless spinsters aren't enough, we have one of our own conservatives, Carol Bauman, who has been taken in by their sharp-tongued assaults on marriage and the family."[149] The advice Mrs. Teague had for Mrs. Bauman and others who looked positively on women's liberation was clear: "What women's liberation should be fostering is more good mothers, who believe that their role as a mother is indeed a unique one."[150]

Then came the letters. Judith Abramov Thorburn, a former college chairman, maintained that the women's liberation movement was not against marriage, but for individual choice. Acknowledging the leftist influence and use of the movement, Thorburn maintained that conservatives had a responsibility to separate out the positive aspects from the radical demands of some.

> Among the women's liberation advocates there are individuals who are of the socialist-Marxist school of thought and regard women's rights as another theater of the war. We must, therefore, separate these individuals and their views out and place them in perspective.

To her, it was essential that conservatives distinguish between the desire for equality and the radical leftist collectivist approach that would lead to a destruction of individual rights.[151]

The following month, Anne Edwards, one of the original members of YAF, defended the women's liberation movement as focusing on real problems, much like the civil rights movement had done.[152] In the same issue were two more let-

---

148. Carol Dawson Bauman, "A Conservative View of Women's Liberation," *New Guard*, April 1972, pp. 4–8.

149. Kathy Teague, "The Most Admired Woman," *New Guard*, June 1972, pp. 12–13.

150. *Ibid.* p. 12.

151. Letter to the editor from Judith Abramov Thorburn, *New Guard*, July–August 1972, pp. 2, 25.

152. Letter to the editor from Anne Edwards, *New Guard*, September 1972, p. 23.

ters on the topic. Susan St. John Orvis of Brooklyn reported, "Carol Bauman is not the only conservative who upholds the basic ideas of Women's Liberation . . ." However, Teague was not alone in her sentiments as a letter from author and commentator, Phyllis Schlafly, told her, "I agree with you 100%—and you stated the case very well."[153]

Schlafly was the focal point for the next controversial topic to appear in the magazine. One year later, the cover of YAF's magazine asked the question, "ERA: are women more equal?" What concerned her, more than anything else, were the rights and benefits attributed to women under the present law. According to Schlafly, "the effect of the Equal Rights Amendment would be precisely to deprive wives of the right to be supported by their husband, of the benefits that working women had under protective labor legislation and Social Security, and of the exemption that draft-age girls have from the military."[154] Schlafly's campaign as leader of the Stop-ERA forces was successful as the amendment died from failure to obtain positive adoption in a sufficient number of state legislatures.

But there were opposing views within the organization on this issue. For the next few months there were letters back and forth on whether the Equal Rights Amendment was needed. Yale YAF member Verna Harrison maintained that laws should judge people as individuals and not according to some group characteristic. Reminding YAF members of their commitment to individual freedom, Harrison maintained "Conservatives in general and YAF in particular can oppose it only at a risk to their principles. And if any theme dominated the convention in Washington, it was that we must either stick to principles or jeopardize our cause."[155] The most prominent defender was Alice Lillie, chairman of the UCLA YAF chapter who argued in a feature article in *New Guard*, that the amendment was needed from an individualist perspective.

> The Equal Rights Amendment will not automatically restore a free society. It is one of the many requirements however, that must be met to do so. Unless and until we are equal under the civil law, freedom is impossible. Responsible and informed advocates of freedom must support ERA.[156]

The position taken by Harrison and Lillie was a minority one in the organization, however, as most YAF activists worked with other conservatives to stop ratification of the proposed amendment.

YAF's willingness to bring up and debate controversial issues, especially those on which there was no unanimity of opinion in the organization, was evident throughout the early 1970s. In addition to the differences on women's liberation and the equal rights amendment, YAF's magazine launched a series of articles on the overall topic "Privacy, the Role of Government, and the Rights of the Individual." The series focused on six issues involving individual rights that were topics of popular discussion at the time: population control, childhood training, military conscription, religion and social values, privacy and surveillance, and victimless crimes.

---

153. Letters to the editor from Susan St. John Orvis and Phyllis Schlafly, *New Guard*, September 1972, p. 23.
154. Phyllis Schlafly, "Let's Stop ERA," *New Guard*, September 1973, pp. 4–6.
155. Verna Harrison, letter to the editor, *New Guard*, November 1973, p. 2.
156. Alice Lillie, "ERA: The Individualist Case," *New Guard*, March 1974, pp. 19–21.

The series began in March 1973 by focusing on population control. The movement for zero population growth had begun to receive more attention and support at that time with some individuals predicting a near-Malthusian future for the world if drastic measures were not taken. As the author warned,

> With the population controllers, we may be dealing with not merely an effort to control the size of the population but also an effort to control its character. Not merely an effort to control the quality of life for those living but to control the quality of the human stock itself.[157]

Just a few years later, in 1979, the People's Republic of China introduced its family planning policy, commonly referred to as the one-child policy, to forcibly restrict population growth.

This presentation was followed the next month with an article on victimless crimes by conservative author and radio host David Brudnoy. He maintained, "What is needed is a general, wide-reaching 'decriminalization' of social acts committed by individuals and between consenting mature persons."[158] From a conservative and libertarian perspective, Brudnoy gave the reasons for decriminalizing marijuana and removing the prohibitions on consensual sex, whether between individuals of the same gender or for payment of sexual services. The following month, a graduate of the Air Force Academy defended the volunteer army, followed by an article on the right to life, and finally on child development and day care.[159]

While each of these topics generated a good deal of discussion among YAF members, both in terms of letters to the magazine as well as programmatic discussions for local chapter meetings, it was the "victimless crimes" article that generated the most debate. That fall, Randy Goodwin and Jim Sills of California YAF responded to Brudnoy's argument for decriminalization of marijuana by pointing out what they regarded as the dangerous aspects associated with its use. To them, marijuana was a harmful and addictive drug that, if made legal, would do irreparable harm to all of American society.[160] The letters, pro and con, came in to the magazine, over the next few months. Then came Richard Cowan's article in defense of decriminalization a few months later. Cowan, one of YAF's founders and a former National Director, had become a noted proponent of marijuana legalization and was active with the National Organization for the Reform of Marijuana Laws. In his article he stressed the medical uses for marijuana and disputed the claims of its harm and addiction.[161] The flow of letters began once again.

Although some libertarians had left the organization after the 1969 national convention, throughout the decade of the Seventies there remained a significant libertarian element within YAF that emphasized laissez-faire economics and less government involvement in what were regarded as social issues. The University of Virginia and the University of Chicago YAF chapters both reflected this per-

---

157. Wayne Thorburn, "Population Control: Who Lives and Dies?," *New Guard*, March 1973, p. 7–8.
158. David Brudnoy, "Decriminalizing Crimes Without Victims: The Time Is Now," *New Guard*, April 1973, pp. 4–8.
159. Ronald K. Wishart, "In Defense of the Volunteer Army," May 1973, pp. 10–11; Mike Connelly, "The Right to Life," June 1973, pp. 14–15; Mary Fisk, "Child Development and Day Care," July–August 1973, pp. 11–12.
160. "You'd Better Get Straight," *New Guard*, October 1973, pp. 7–9.
161. "Marijuana—the Continuing Debate," *New Guard*, March 1974, pp. 12–13, 25.

spective but there were many others across the country. Patrick Peterson was a student at St. Lawrence University who related that his time in YAF "helped me become a more thoughtful libertarian." After graduating he became a development director for The Heartland Institute and the founding president of the Free Market Society of Chicago.[162] Mark Coleman was chapter chairman at Florida State University and then obtained a master's degree at the University of Hawaii where he became State Chairman of the Libertarian Party and chapter president of the Society of Professional Journalists.[163] Charles Borum maintained his experience in YAF "made me realize later that I was a libertarian. Didn't really know that term when I belonged to YAF but it has made me a lifelong libertarian." For more than twenty years, Borum has been a physician in private solo practice and remains committed to the same principles that led him to become a member of YAF.[164]

For others, their time in YAF led to increased involvement in the Republican party at the local level. Phillip Bayston was active in YAF in Chattanooga and today is a member of the GOP Pachyderm Club and various gun owners' organizations.[165] Ted Coulter was involved in YAF through the late 1970s while a student at Capital University and Case Western Reserve Law School. Since that time he has served as chairman of his county Republican party in Ohio and president of a local GOP club.[166] For Neil Deininger, his experience in YAF at the University of Delaware "let me know I wasn't crazy, that other rational, intelligent people thought as I did." Now a tax attorney in Little Rock, Deininger was an alternate delegate to the 1984 Republican National Convention and has been treasurer of the Pulaski County, Arkansas Republican Committee.[167]

One point was clear. While there were differences and disagreements on important issues and concerns, the young conservative movement was alive and well in the 1970s. It had moved beyond Vietnam, had taken a more active role in campus affairs, and was willing to address controversial social issues even when no consensus was present on how best to deal with those issues. But the organization was also involving itself in a number of political battles as it entered the decade of the 1970s. These would test its strength as well as provide an opportunity for the development of new leaders, a second generation whose members would go on to assume leading roles in American politics into the 21st century. There would be victories in unexpected places, trials and tribulations with the downfall of a presidency, and excruciatingly close defeats that, over time, would turn into a historic victory. It was a new decade and a new era for politics and YAF was ready to assume a leadership role on the American scene.

---

162. 2008 YAF Alumni Survey Responses: Patrick T. Peterson.
163. 2008 YAF Alumni Survey Responses: Mark Coleman.
164. 2008 YAF Alumni Survey Responses: Charles D. Borum, M.D.
165. 2008 YAF Alumni Survey Responses: Phillip E. Bayston.
166. 2008 YAF Alumni Survey Responses: Ted Coulter.
167. 2008 YAF Alumni Survey Responses: Neil Deininger.

11. We Are the New Politics!

"I grew up in a conservative, politically active family, so it was
natural that my sister and I would become involved. We started
working on Jim Buckley's campaign for Senate in 1970 and have
been at it in one way or another ever since . . ."[1]

While 1970 was not a presidential election year, it was a significant one for
conservatives and Young Americans for Freedom. That year marked the tenth
anniversary of the organization's founding, an occasion that was recognized with
a return to YAF's birthplace in Sharon, Connecticut. Later that fall, two political
victories showed the increased influence of the young conservatives who played
major roles in the re-election of Governor Reagan and the election of James
Buckley to the United States Senate. Soon thereafter, YAF and the conservative
movement began a separation and eventual divorce from a Republican President,
considered the possibilities of encouraging the formation of a third party, and led
the challenge to a sitting President's nomination. Throughout the decade, YAF
played an important role in the political process and was viewed as an essential
element of the growing conservative movement. As executive director Randal
Teague observed at the time, "YAF is the only organization to combine a complete
campus program with a political program . . . to educate its members and others
and also provide the means for implementing conservative principles."[2] With stops
and starts, YAF's efforts during those ten years led to the eventual presidential
victory of Ronald Reagan as another new decade was about to begin.

As the 1970s started, Young Americans for Freedom made a major commitment to expanding its members' involvement in political campaigns. While the
right to vote for 18 year olds would not be extended to all elections until 1971,
high school and college students could and did play essential roles in many
campaigns. During the summer of 1970, national YAF sponsored twenty-two
"Youth in Politics" conferences across the country, training young conservatives
in the various techniques that could be employed to increase support for their
candidate.[3] To increase their effectiveness, YAF published a booklet titled *You &*
Politics, showing members how to organize "youth for" campaigns, to maximize
involvement of young people by combining practical projects with fun activities
that would attract more participants, and to obtain media coverage for the youth
projects and the candidate.[4]

Election year 1970 brought about YAF involvement in several campaigns
across the country from Ronald Reagan and George Murphy in California to Bill
Brock in Tennessee and Harry Byrd in Virginia, to Jim Buckley and Jack Kemp
in New York. YAF members were involved in each of these campaigns and many

---

1. Eileen Schmidt Braunlich, quoted in Gurvis: *Where Have All the Flower Children Gone?*, pp. 70–71.
2. Randal C. Teague, "YAF: A Presence in the Room," *New Guard*, January–February 1971, p. 20.
3. Paul Healy, "Kid Power and the New Politics," *New York Daily News*, September 11, 1970 in *YAF in the News*, September 1970.
4. *You & Politics* (Washington, DC: Young Americans for Freedom, 1970). Personal Papers of Walter H. Judd, Box 256, Hoover Institution, Stanford University, Palo Alto, CA.

others. In a key Senate race in Tennessee, Bill Brock's youth campaign included YAF leaders Jim Duncan, Alan Gottlieb, Todd and Mary Gardenhire and many others while YAFers from throughout Virginia provided a base of youth support for Independent candidate Harry Byrd, Jr. It was the YAF members from Canisius College, led by Ron Robinson, and from SUNY–Buffalo, under Rick Gorsky and Jackie Davies, that provided youth support for Jack Kemp in his first campaign for Congress, a race won only due to the votes he received on the Conservative Party's ballot line.[5]

YAF members from the University of South Carolina took the lead in providing support for Floyd Spence in his first election to Congress while Ron Dear left the YAF national staff to join the successful campaign of Bill Archer in Texas's 7th congressional district. Meanwhile, in suburban Chicago, Phil Crane won his first re-election after being victorious in a 1969 special election. 1970 was also the year that a former YAF National Chairman was elected to the Maryland State Senate. Bob Bauman's campaign was assisted by the efforts of Harold Herring, North Carolina YAF leader, as well as volunteers from Maryland YAF led by State Chairman Joe Baldacchino.[6]

Of particular interest to conservatives was the re-election effort of Governor Reagan who was already being viewed as a future GOP presidential candidate. This was also the year in which Senator George Murphy was a candidate for re-election and YAF members were involved in both campaigns. Led by State Chairman Bill Saracino, YAF members volunteered for Reagan and Murphy and put in long hours stuffing envelopes, knocking on doors, and providing enthusiasm at campaign rallies. Saracino had been chairman of Youth for Rafferty in the 1968 contest for Senate and gained valuable statewide campaign experience.[7]

Patrick Geary was a student at UC–Irvine who had joined YAF just before the Reagan re-election campaign, an experience he remembers fondly: "YAF enabled me to meet great Americans like Ronald Reagan and William F. Buckley. YAF helped me formulate and articulate the political beliefs which I still hold today."[8] The Reagan re-election campaign was also the entry point into YAF for John Lewis while he was still a high school student. As he recently noted, "my entire life was shaped and changed by my involvement in YAF. Joining the YAF in the early 70s shaped my philosophy, led to lasting friendships and was a primary influence on my elected success."[9] First elected to the California State Assembly in 1980, Lewis served there until 1991 and then for the next ten years was a California State Senator before term limits ended his career in the legislature. While Reagan would go on to a re-election victory by a margin exceeding 500,000 votes, liberal Congressman John Tunney defeated Murphy and captured the Senate seat.[10]

---

5. Kemp obtained 82,939 votes on the Republican line while his opponent had 86,142 votes on the Democratic line. It was only with the additional 14,050 votes Kemp received on the Conservative Party line that he became the winner.

6. 2008 YAF Alumni Survey Responses: Joseph Baldacchino.

7. Interview with William E. Saracino, October 11, 2008, Newport Beach, CA.

8. 2008 YAF Alumni Survey Responses: Patrick S. Geary.

9. 2008 YAF Alumni Survey Responses: John Lewis.

10. The Reagan 1970 re-election campaign is discussed in Lou Cannon: *Governor Reagan—His Rise to Power* (New York: Public Affairs, 2003), pp. 336–347.

Isn't It Time We Had a Senator?

Perhaps the most significant victory for conservatives in 1970 took place in New York state as James Buckley became the junior United States Senator, elected on the Conservative Party line. The story begins, however, a few years earlier. The Buckleys were a unique family of ten children whose home became the birthplace of Young Americans for Freedom. Of the ten, Jim was the second oldest son, followed by Bill whose own campaign for Mayor of New York City some five years earlier had been the first family political campaign.[11] In fact, the senatorial election of 1970 was not the first venture in politics for Jim, who had been his brother's campaign manager in that mayoralty race and also the Conservative candidate for United States Senator in 1968.

While the Conservative Party leadership had attempted in the fall of 1967 to draft Bill Buckley as the party's candidate against liberal Republican Senator Jacob Javits, he believed that he had already fulfilled his duty and turned them down. The leaders then focused on Jim and asked him to be the candidate. When asked for advice, younger brother Bill urged him to run, noting that from his experience in 1965, "nothing is quite the same again. There is a certain exhilaration in making one's points well, in feeling the response of a crowd in reaction to one's own rhetorical arguments."[12] Jim Buckley succumbed and his first campaign for the United States Senate was underway.

Just as YAF had been integrally involved in the 1965 campaign for Mayor, chapters and members throughout the state and ultimately nationally played important roles in the 1968 Jim Buckley campaign for U.S. Senate against the Republican incumbent, Jacob Javits, who also obtained the Liberal Party nomination, and Democratic candidate Paul O'Dwyer. New York YAF state chairman Jim Farley held the additional position as chairman of Youth for Buckley and involved as many YAF members as possible in the campaign.[13] Throughout the summer and into the fall, YAF leaders Paul Nicola, Ron Docksai, Greg Bradley, Judith Abramov, Johanna Rutan and John Pawson assisted Farley as they traveled the state, forming Youth for Buckley units and recruiting YAF members. On several campuses, Youth for Buckley worked with College Republicans and the Youth for Nixon effort. At St. John's, the YAF chapter set up tables on campus for the "Nixon-Buckley" ticket.[14]

When the votes were all tallied, combining those he received on both the Republican and Liberal Party lines, Jacob Javits was re-elected, but with only 49.7% of the vote while Jim Buckley on the Conservative Party line received 17.3% of the total vote and pulled in 1,139,402 votes. Buckley's vote total was the most

---

11. The victory of Jim Buckley was viewed by the media as significant enough to warrant a cover photo and story in what was then perhaps the most popular mass magazine. For an interesting overview written and photographed just after the 1970 election, see Betty Dunn and Alfred Eisenstadt, "The Buckleys of Great Elm," *Life*, December 18, 1970, pp. 34–44. Also valuable is Reid Buckley: *An American Family: The Buckleys* (New York: Threshold Editions, 2008).

12. Letter from William F. Buckley, Jr. to James L. Buckley, quoted in Judis: *William F. Buckley, Jr.: Patron Saint of the Conservatives*, p. 311.

13. *New Guard*, Summer 1968, p. 28.

14. *New Guard*, October 1968, p. 22. Nixon had both the Republican and Conservative Party endorsements in 1968 so technically it was a "Nixon-Buckley" ticket on the Conservative Party row on the ballot.

to that point for a Conservative Party candidate, more than twice the previous high of Paul Adams in his 1966 gubernatorial campaign.[15] As Arnold Steinberg indicated, "the 1968 campaign was a campaign of impact but not one designed to win."[16] Yet, in many ways, the 1968 campaign helped make possible the victory two years later. To the media and conservatives nationwide, what it did was give a certain level of credibility to the 1970 campaign before it even began. Having campaigned statewide and having polled more than one million votes against a Republican incumbent, Jim Buckley could be viewed as a serious candidate when the 1970 contest started, if he could be convinced to run again.

Moreover, the 1968 campaign was, in many ways, a dry run for the young conservative activists who would be trained in the first campaign and go on to assume leadership positions in the 1970 effort. Farley and Docksai were already YAF leaders in 1968 and would play key roles in the subsequent campaign. But others were learning and gaining campaign experience. As Herb Stupp recently noted, "I was 18 and just getting involved in YAF. I was a basic volunteer in Jim Buckley's campaign, going door to door with literature in Queens neighborhoods like Rego Park and Middle Village."[17] Richard Macksoud started his freshman year at Columbia in the fall of 1968 and decided that he was going to become involved.

> I found no one who agreed with me in my class and saw no sign of conser-
> vatives on campus. So I went down to the Conservative Party headquarters
> and received signs and flyers. I found an old table and out on the plaza I
> went. A conservative for Nixon-Buckley. A lonely place but then a funny
> thing happened—fellow students who would become lifelong friends started
> coming to the table. Who the hell was I? Where the hell did I come from?
> Etc. I had found some fellow travelers in a sea of left wing mush.[18]

Donald Harte had just graduated from high school in Nassau County, where he had been a YAF high school chapter chairman, and became involved in the 1968 Jim Buckley campaign. When the next senatorial election rolled around, Harte was beginning his freshman year at Adelphi University and ready to put in more hours for the Buckley campaign. He went on to become chairman of the Adelphi YAF chapter and played an important role in the 1970 Buckley campaign.[19] And there were many others.

It was the tragic murder of Robert F. Kennedy in June 1968 that produced the forces leading to a second Jim Buckley campaign for the United States Senate in 1970. When Governor Rockefeller appointed upstate Republican Congressman Charles Goodell in September 1968, he was perceived as a moderate conservative who had represented the Jamestown area for ten years. Upon becoming a member of the United States Senate, Goodell veered sharply to the left on a wide range of issues, including opposition to continued American involvement in the Vietnam war. With the election of Richard Nixon to the White House in November 1968,

---

15. Six years later, Javits would be re-elected again as the Republican-Liberal nominee besting Ramsey Clark and the Conservative candidate, Barbara Keating. Keating polled 822,584 votes or nearly 16% of the total votes cast.

16. E-mail to the author, February 29, 2008. Steinberg was editor of *New Guard* at the time and would become press secretary to Buckley in the 1970 campaign.

17. E-mail to the author, February 6, 2009.

18. 2008 YAF Alumni Survey Responses: Richard M. Macksoud.

19. 2008 YAF Alumni Survey Responses: Donald Harte.

Goodell became a leading Republican critic of the Administration when he joined liberal Democrats in sponsoring legislation to cut off money for the war effort and in 1969 introduced a sense of the Senate resolution calling on the House to impeach Nixon for expanding the war into Cambodia. By 1970, when Goodell was in line to become the GOP nominee for a full term in the Senate, Vice President Spiro T. Agnew labeled Goodell a "radical liberal."[20] In fact, Goodell's ideological shift was sufficient to earn him the Liberal Party nomination in addition to the Republican nod.

The Democratic nominee was Richard Ottinger, a three-term Congressman. Ottinger had first been elected in 1964, ousting a conservative Republican after spending personal and family fortunes to finance it. Six years later, he was opposed in the Democratic primary by Congressman Richard "Max" McCarthy, Theodore Sorensen, a former speechwriter for President Kennedy, and Paul O'Dwyer, attorney and anti-war activist who had been the Democratic nominee two years earlier.[21] In the primary, Ottinger outspent his opponents seven to one to receive the party's nomination. In the pre-Watergate era without limits on contributions, Ottinger would go on to spend some five million dollars in the November race, most of it from his mother, whose wealth came from the U.S. Plywood Corporation. While his official campaign slogan was "Ottinger Delivers," Buckley staffer Arnie Steinberg changed it to "Ottinger's Mother Delivers." Denied the Liberal Party endorsement, Ottinger did gain the backing of Americans for Democratic Action and the New Democratic Coalition. During the fall, Goodell and Ottinger both battled for the desired label of liberal while criticizing each other's records in Congress.[22]

While Goodell was solidifying his Republican support and picking up the Liberal Party endorsement and Ottinger was fending off the challenge from his Democratic primary opponents, James L. Buckley was slowly starting to build a campaign team to seek victory on the Conservative Party line. As Arnie Steinberg recalled, "I flew into NYC on June 3, precisely 5 months before the election; there was no campaign; we arranged to borrow $50,000 in seed money; I operated out of Catawba (Buckley family company), and we slowly started to hire."[23] Having completed a "dry run" less than two years earlier, this time the Buckley team was determined to mount a serious effort to win in 1970.

But Jim Buckley had come to the decision to enter the race only after much thought. In the spring of 1970, *National Review* publisher Bill Rusher had arranged a meeting with Buckley and F. Clifton White to encourage him to become a candidate once again.[24] Buckley wanted to be assured that the race was winnable and White agreed to arrange for a survey to be taken. In early April, Jim Buckley called Bill Rusher to ask him whether he believed there was a serious chance of winning, and Rusher told Buckley that he believed there was.[25] Having done his

---

20. Frank Lynn, "Charles E. Goodell, Former Senator, Is Dead at 60," *New York Times*, January 22, 1987.

21. Maurice Carroll, "O'Dwyer Finishes Second on Strong City Showing; Ottinger Beats Three Senate Rivals," *New York Times*, June 24, 1970. The seat that McCarthy gave up to run for the United States Senate would fall in the 1970 election to former Buffalo Bills quarterback Jack Kemp. Kemp would hold that seat for eighteen years before making a run for the presidential nomination in 1988.

22. Samuel G. Freedman: *The Inheritance: How Three Families and America Moved from Roosevelt to Reagan and Beyond* (New York: Simon & Schuster, 1996) presents an interesting overview of the 1970 Senate campaign.

23. Email to the author, March 18, 2009.

24. Email from James L. Buckley to Herb Stupp, March 21, 2009 (in author's possession).

25. William A. Rusher: *The Rise of the Right*, p. 173.

duty to the movement and run once, as had his younger brother Bill, Jim Buckley did not want to spend his time on another quixotic third party effort. The survey results came back and showed that he would start with a base support level of 25% with a like number of voters definitely in opposition. On the basis of those results, Clif White concurred with Bill Rusher—it was doable.[26] Buckley decided to enter the campaign and became the Conservative Party nominee.[27]

What started with only two staffers in June, soon expanded into a team worthy of carrying a campaign to all areas of the geographically large and politically diverse state. The overall campaign strategist was F. Clifton White while the campaign director handling all day-to-day aspects of the effort was David Jones, who had recently left his post as Executive Director of Young Americans for Freedom. The first person hired by Jones was Arnie Steinberg, former *New Guard* editor, as press secretary and second in command for the day-to-day operations of the campaign. Steinberg had managed Dave Keene's state senatorial race in Wisconsin and then handled press for Phil Crane's successful special election for Congress in Illinois. As he recalled, "White said he would only do it if Jones would manage the race; Jones said he would only manage the race if I were involved and also if I did the press operation."[28]

With White, Jones and Steinberg on board, the staff began to come together and the campaign took shape. Steinberg's assistant was Tony Dolan, later a speechwriter in the Reagan White House. Dolan, in turn, brought on as his assistant Kate Walsh, who took a leave from studies at Good Counsel College. A few years later she married and is now known as Kate O'Beirne, Washington editor of *National Review*. Steinberg, Dolan, and Walsh were among a number of young campaign staffers working for Buckley's election. As Steinberg observed,

> It was a challenging campaign, and a fun campaign, and certainly a testament to, among other things, the influence of Young Americans for Freedom. Clif White entrusted the day-to-day administration of the campaign to YAF's former executive director, Dave Jones. Certainly my own experience, most of it gained in YAF, helped me in directing the campaign's news and press operation. It was a young staff and the youth division in particular, headed by New York YAF state chairman Herb Stupp, was particularly effective.[29]

Another key early hire for the campaign was its research director, Daniel Oliver, who provided essential briefing materials for the candidate and served on the Senator's staff after the election.

On June 23rd, Democratic primary voters brought the November election contest into focus as they selected Richard Ottinger over his three opponents. Immediately, Ottinger began attacking Goodell as if it were a two-man contest. This perception of the almost irrelevancy of the Buckley campaign existed in the

---

26. F. Clifton White with Jerome Tuccille: *Politics as a Noble Calling*, p. 192.

27. Not all movement conservatives, especially those based in Washington, were as optimistic about Buckley's chances for success. According to Steinberg, it was not until a column by Richard Reeves appeared that sentiment began to change. Reeves discussed the efforts of the "Silent Majority Mobilization Committee" to distribute "Rockefeller-Buckley" buttons and literature. Richard Reeves, "Rockefeller and Buckley; Governor's Staff Studies the Handling of Efforts to Present Them as Ticket," *New York Times*, July 20, 1970.

28. Email to the author, March 18, 2009.

29. Arnold Steinberg, "It Happened in New York," *New Guard*, December 1970, pp. 7–9.

media for the early months of summer 1970. It was a misperception that shrewd political observers would have avoided. As one former reporter for the *New York Times* later noted, "Any sensible politician or thoughtful journalist should have remembered that in another three-way Senate race, just two years earlier, Buckley had polled 1.1 million votes while spending only $115,000."[30]

Once Ottinger became the Democratic nominee, the Buckley campaign strategy became evident. As Clif White recalled later, it was to "portray Goodell and Ottinger as birds of the same feather despite their party allegiances, and have them split the liberal vote evenly so that Jim could squeak in with a bare plurality."[31] The Buckley campaign was able to have their candidate participate in three debates including both Ottinger and Goodell. According to White, Buckley's standing in the polls went up after each debate as more New Yorkers became aware of him. On October 25th, the *New York Daily News* released its final poll: Buckley 37%, Ottinger 30%, Goodell 24%. Goodell considered dropping out of the race but then purchased a 30-minute spot on television to make his last appeal to the voters, vowing to stay in the race and win. On October 30th, the *New York Times* endorsed Goodell, a move that many believe prevented any significant seepage of liberals to Ottinger but also may have kept a number of upstate New Yorkers behind the candidate.[32]

As the campaign progressed, it became clear that other Republicans were beginning to vacillate in their support for Goodell. Rockefeller was running for his fourth term as Governor and did not want to be dragged down by the lagging support for the Republican Senate candidate. While remaining officially committed to Goodell, the existence of "Rockefeller-Buckley" bumper stickers and signs reflected the intentions of many New York voters. With Agnew criticizing the liberal voting record of Goodell, the White House appeared ambivalent also. In fact, Nixon advance personnel tipped off the Buckley campaign that the President would make a stop outside New York City on his way back to Washington. As YAF's magazine reported the events, "When President Nixon stopped at Westchester Airport, Youth for Buckley organized hundreds of youths with Buckley signs to greet him . . . The great bulk of the delegation were YAFers."[33] It was a "carefully advanced maneuver" with a "wordless endorsement worth a thousand words."[34] Clearly, at least some at the White House were not adverse to a Buckley victory.

When the votes were tallied, New York had a new United States Senator and the conservative movement had a new hero. Buckley received 2,288,190 votes running on the Conservative Party line while Ottinger as the Democratic candidate had 2,171,232 votes, a margin of slightly more than 100,000 votes. Combining his votes on both the Republican and Liberal lines, Senator Goodell had obtained support from 1,434,472 New Yorkers. The only counties carried by Goodell were rock-ribbed GOP counties upstate, especially in his congressional district. At his celebration, Buckley made the now famous declaration: "I am the voice of the new politics." New York had elected not only a conservative, but a Conservative.

Beginning in the summer and throughout the fall, the youth campaign was the essential secret ingredient of the Buckley effort. As Dave Jones observed,

---

30. Freedman: *The Inheritance*, p. 253.
31. White: *Politics*, p. 193.
32. Freedman: *The Inheritance*, p. 258.
33. "Youth for Buckley: A Success," *New Guard*, December 1970, p. 30.
34. Rick Perlstein: *Nixonland*, p. 530.

"They were our blitz squad. They distributed leaflets and performed tasks on a moment's notice, providing a solid base we could always depend on."[35] The Youth for Buckley effort came up with innovative ways of drawing attention to their candidate, using techniques that would make the voter smile with satisfaction. A most effective technique was to organize a group to head for shopping center parking lots armed with windex and paper towels.

> They washed more than 100,000 windshields, placing a circular under each windshield wiper reading: Your windshield has been washed courtesy of James L. Buckley. Now that you can see your way clearly, we hope you'll vote for Jim Buckley on November 3rd.[36]

In the New York City metropolitan area, most young Buckley volunteers were students at commuter colleges who lived at home with their parents, many holding part-time jobs. Others were high school students from the City and its suburbs.[37]

The official campaign student organization, Youth for Buckley, was headed by Herb Stupp of St. John's University as Chairman with Rich Macksoud of Columbia as Vice Chairman, Lynn Courter of Fordham as Secretary and Dave Gronsbell of Pace as Treasurer. Jim Minarik came in from Ohio to work as a fulltime organizer of Youth for Buckley groups on college and high school campuses.[38] Among those who were back again for their second Buckley campaign as volunteers were Jim Farley, who had headed up the 1968 effort, Ron Docksai and Don Harte, as well as Stupp and Macksoud. The number of future leaders who got their start in the Buckley campaign is impressive. Many went on to leadership positions in YAF and then outstanding careers in government, the media, academia and the business world.[39] The enthusiasm of youth was critical to the success of the campaign. As Steinberg noted, "Basically, I was too idealistic and work-centered to believe that hard work would not pay off, and so were the YAFers. Had they been around politics for a longer period, they would have been jaundiced and skeptical. Not knowing they could not win, they did win."[40]

In fact, several of the Youth for Buckley organizers were high school students in the fall of 1970. Ed Martin was a 16 year old student in Lynbrook, New York when he opened a storefront campaign operation for "Youth for Buckley and Lent," supporting both the senatorial candidate and a victorious Conservative-Republican candidate for Congress. Subsequently he became press spokesman for Senator Al D'Amato and also served as an appointee in the Reagan Administration. Chris Braunlich was a Nassau County high school student and later became YAF leader at Hofstra University. Lillian Fisher was a high school YAF leader in Westchester County who was active in the campaign. She recently recalled her efforts on behalf of the Buckley campaign.

---

35. Steven R. Weisman, "Buckley's Drive Mobilized the Youth of the New Right," *New York Times*, November 7, 1970.
36. Steinberg, "It Happened in New York," p. 29.
37. Weisman, "Buckley's Drive," *New York Times*, November 7, 1970.
38. "Youth for Buckley: A Success," *New Guard*, December 1970, pp. 29–30.
39. Much of the following information on those active in Youth for Buckley and their subsequent careers is from emails to the author from Herb Stupp, February 6, 2009 and March 19, 2009 as well as an interview with Stupp in New York City on July 24, 2008.
40. Email to the author, March 18, 2009.

I was very involved in 1970. I was in 11th grade and ran the Mock Election for the 10th grade Republicans because the liberal history teachers wouldn't mentor/sponsor them. We did a fabulous job, won the Mock Election, had an article run in the local newspaper about the Mock Election, my part in it. During the student debates where we read the talking points that Youth for Buckley provided, I overheard the teacher in charge say to another student, "I HATE that girl!" I thought, "YES!! He hates me! We're winning!"[41]

Fisher went on to serve as YAF chairman at SUNY–Delhi. Dana Blankenhorn was a student at Massapequa High School and active in YAF and Youth for Buckley. Looking back on his involvement in YAF, Blankenhorn said "it gave me experience in the world and treated me seriously. It helped me get internships with James L. Buckley and Human Events in 1974, giving me a front-row seat for the Nixon impeachment."[42] Under the leadership of Queens County YAF director Rich Delgaudio and his brother, Eugene, a Youth for Buckley storefront was opened, entirely directed and financed by students. It became the base for extensive canvassing and literature distribution projects.[43]

The leadership of Youth for Buckley comprised almost exclusively members of Young Americans for Freedom. As Herb Stupp, Youth for Buckley chairman, summed up the situation, "Most YAF chapter chairmen formed their own clubs, most of the campaign county chairmen were YAF members, and a large proportion of the youth campaign's manpower was supplied by tireless YAFers performing thankless tasks."[44] Many of those YAF members involved in the campaign would go on to be candidates themselves. Three of the Youth for Buckley leaders later served in the New York State Senate. Ray Meier was a Youth for Buckley leader as chairman of Rome High YAF before heading to Syracuse University where he eventually became YAF chairman. Meier subsequently served as Oneida County Executive and ten years as a State Senator. Vincent Leibell ran the Queens County operation for Buckley and is now a Senator from the suburbs to the north of New York City. Mike Nozzolio was a YAF member from the Finger Lakes area and is also currently a New York State Senator.

Interestingly enough, two of the New York YAFers who were active in the Buckley campaign became state representatives, but not in the Empire State. Both Gary Giordano and John Kavanagh were elected to the Arizona House of Representatives at different times. After receiving his associate degree from Nassau Community College, Giordano was starting at the State University of New York at Cortland in the fall of 1970 and became a key upstate leader in Youth for Buckley. When he graduated from college, Giordano moved to Arizona, joined the YAF national staff and served as Western YAF Director. Giordano was an Arizona State Representative from 1985–89. He believes that "YAF provided the foundation and springboard for my political positions held, service as an Arizona state legislator and my political philosophy." Looking back on those experiences in YAF, "It was a tumultuous time with campus unrest, Vietnam war, Nixon and Watergate. I received my political baptism of fire and training and my philosophical foundations

---

41. Email to the author, March 31, 2009.
42. 2008 YAF Alumni Survey Responses: Dana Frederick Blankenhorn.
43. "Youth for Buckley: A Success," *New Guard*, December 1970, p. 30.
44. Herbert Stupp, "We Have a Senator!" *New Guard*, September 1975, pp. 15–16.

through YAF . . . All my political involvement, positions, philosophy, et al, come out of my involvement in YAF."[45]

John Kavanagh was a YAF leader at New York University and involved with a number of Columbia University students in the Manhattan campaign for Buckley. Kavanagh retired after 20 years as a detective with the Port Authority of New York and New Jersey Police Department. From his time in YAF, "I made good lifelong friends, learned public speaking and leadership skills and had a lot of fun fighting for conservatism and against campus radicals . . . YAF gave me the speaking and organization skills that helped me succeed in life." And succeed in life he has. Kavanagh served on two town councils in New Jersey and Arizona and is the head of the criminal justice department at Scottsdale Community College. Currently he is in only his second term as an Arizona State Representative but is the chairman of the powerful House Appropriations Committee.[46]

Also among the Manhattan Youth for Buckley leaders was George Sierant, YAF chapter chairman at New York University. Sierant started out as chairman of Xavier High School YAF before enrolling at NYU. Columbia University produced a number of active YAF members to work in the Buckley campaign including Ralph Coti, Vince Rigdon, Lou Rossetto, J. Michael Marion, Stan Lehr, Howard Lim and Rich Macksoud. For Coti, just a freshman during the campaign, it was the beginning of a lifetime of support for conservative candidates and causes.[47] Lim's volunteer efforts for the Buckley campaign led to a commitment to the New York Conservative Party, reflected in his present service as State Secretary of the party and previous role as New York County Chairman. After graduating from Columbia, Rigdon began his studies for the Roman Catholic priesthood. Father Rigdon is now pastor of Our Lady of the Presentation church in suburban Washington, DC. By the fall of 1970, Macksoud was a junior at Columbia and involved in his second Buckley U.S. Senate campaign. As he noted, "most if not all of the active leaders in Youth for Buckley were YAF members or officers. That election victory was one of the most joyful nights I had in college."[48]

Charles Ferrigno of Fordham University YAF was one of the campaign leaders in the Bronx and is now director of the Criminal Alien Branch of the New York office of the Immigration and Naturalization Service. Bill Bell later became New York YAF State Chairman and a YAF National Director. For many years he was the chief executive officer of various non-profit organizations in New York State. Tom Bivona, Adrienne Flipse (Hausch), and Marguerite Donnelly were also involved in the campaign and are now successful attorneys as is John Roselle who headed up Staten Island YAF and organized Richmond County for Youth for Buckley. Donnelly practices law in Maryland while Roselle is now an attorney in Oklahoma for the Army Corps of Engineers. Jim Quinn was chapter chairman of Daniel Webster YAF in Queens and Youth for Buckley volunteer before becoming an attorney. He was chief of the homicide division of the Queens County District Attorney's office for more than a decade and is now Senior Executive Assistant District Attorney.

Adrienne Flipse has fond memories of her time in YAF and the Buckley campaign. As she recalled, "It gave me the guts to speak up for what I believed, no matter how unpopular. It convinced me to go to law school; it gave me the tools

45. 2008 YAF Alumni Survey Responses: Gary S. Giordano.
46. 2008 YAF Alumni Survey Responses: John Kavanagh.
47. 2008 YAF Alumni Survey Responses: Ralph Coti.
48. 2008 YAF Alumni Survey Responses: Richard M. Macksoud.

to run for office. It gave me the skill to debate without rancor . . . It made attending a liberal institution bearable. It gave me friends for life."[49] After graduating from Hofstra University, she received her law degree from St. John's University and, some twenty years later, a Master's of Divinity degree. She is now a partner in the law firm of Carway and Flipse as well as Pastor for Congregational Care at the Community Church of Douglaston.

A number of other female students, in addition to Flipse-Hausch and Donnelly, were actively involved in the Youth for Buckley campaign. Michelle Easton was a student at Briarcliff College and Youth for Buckley volunteer. She completed her law degree at American University, served as Deputy Undersecretary for the Department of Education during the administration of President George H.W. Bush, and is now President of the Clare Booth Luce Policy Institute.

In Queens, there were the Schmidt sisters: Delores, Eileen, and Mary. It was, as Eileen recounted, a family affair.[50] Cyndi Reilly was a YAF chapter chairman in Nassau County and is now involved in health care at Sarah Lawrence College. Donna McDonald-Donato was YAF State Secretary while attending Adelphi University, putting in long hours at the state headquarters at 25 Jane Street in Manhattan. She believes that due to her involvement in YAF, "I became more of a leader and was able to stand and voice my opinions and try to get a movement going."[51] Mary McCartan led the Youth for Buckley contingent at Manhattanville College while Dorothy McCartney was active in the northwest Nassau County Youth for Buckley organization. McCartney went on to be the primary researcher for the "Firing Line" television program and veteran staff member at *National Review*.

One of the leaders in Nassau County was Christian Braunlich, a student at Adelphi University. Of all his experiences, the Buckley campaign stands out.

> Without any real resources, it was perhaps the most grass-roots oriented operation we'll ever witness. Across New York, bands of Republicans, Conservatives, Independents, and what we would later call Reagan Democrats banded together—scraping together funds for storefronts, taking up collections, selling bumper stickers, printing our own literature, silk-screening our own T-shirts . . . whatever we needed to do. It was citizen involvement at its best . . . Whatever the headquarters couldn't supply (and there was a lot they couldn't), we went out and raised the funds for ourselves or did it ourselves . . . The result was a mobilization we'd never seen before.[52]

After graduating from Adelphi, Braunlich helped lead the conservative takeover of the New York Young Republicans and then became Chief of Staff to another YAF member, Congressman John LeBoutillier.

Since this was a statewide contest, not all the Youth for Buckley volunteers came from New York City and Long Island. Ron Robinson of Canisius College was the key upstate leader for the effort and later served as Upstate Vice Chairman for New York YAF. Also involved in the Buffalo area were Patricia Doro of Canisius and Jackie Davies of the University at Buffalo. Doro is now a dentist practicing on the east side of Manhattan while Robinson later joined the YAF staff, served as executive director, and is president of Young America's Foundation.

---

49. 2008 YAF Alumni Survey Responses: Adrienne Flipse Hausch.
50. Gurvis: *Where Have All the Flower Children Gone?*, pp. 70–71.
51. 2008 YAF Alumni Survey Responses: Donna McDonald-Donato.
52. 2008 YAF Alumni Survey Responses: Christian N. Braunlich.

At Syracuse, where Ray Meier became active, Neil Wallace led the Youth for Buckley effort. Lisa Warnecke was the founder of Kingston High School YAF and a key upstate Youth for Buckley activist. David Williams was the main Youth for Buckley organizer on the Kings College campus where he headed up the YAF chapter. Williams went on to serve in the Reagan Administration and teach political science. Bill Schmidt was chairman of Northern Westchester-Putnam YAF while in high school and active in the Buckley campaign. He later graduated from St. John's University where he was active in the 1976 Buckley effort. Schmidt served on the Peekskill City Council from 1997–2006 and narrowly lost a race for Mayor in 2007. For him,

> YAF was an early training ground for the rough and tumble of political life. It honed my intellectual and debating skills and taught me when (and under what circumstances) to consider compromise, as well as when to hold my ground. Learning "people skills" at an early age was crucial to my future activities. The exposure, as a teenager, to prominent elected officials from around the country as well as the intellectual leaders of the movement provided motivation and incentive to pursue my political career.[53]

Pat Reilly was an Albany YAF activist and became a staff member for Senator Buckley after the election. He is now a vice president of the New York Association of Realtors, one of the largest realtor groups in the country. Clif White's daughter, Carole, was a Youth for Buckley leader at Ithaca College while Rob Natelson led the efforts at Cornell University along with undergraduates Nick Cooper and Simone Sieman.

Fred Eckert was a 29-year old Town Supervisor of a large suburban town bordering Rochester who supported the Youth for Buckley effort in Monroe County. He was a YAF member while at the University of North Texas and a *New Guard* contributor for many years. Fred later defeated an incumbent Democratic state senator and served ten years in the New York Senate, one of the few elected officials in the state to openly support Ronald Reagan in 1976. In 1983, Reagan appointed Eckert Ambassador to Fiji, from which position he returned to be elected to Congress in 1984.[54] Still further north, Dan Dickinson was YAF chairman and YFB leader at SUNY–Plattsburgh. After college, Dickinson worked in the New York Senate and is now an official with the New York State Department of Health.

Out of state volunteers came from Rhode Island, New Jersey, and Pennsylvania; even a busload from Virginia traveled north to help out in the campaign. They stuffed envelopes, provided support at rallies, washed car windows, and rang doorbells. Mark David Goret was a student at Rider College and among those from New Jersey who crossed the river to help elect a conservative senator. His time in YAF is where he "met people who shared my views and I became active in New York City conservative politics."[55]

Another who might be classified as an "out of state" activist was Alan Gottlieb, a New York City resident who was attending the University of Tennessee. Over the summer, with little funding, Gottlieb determined that the Youth for Buckley volunteers would set up tables on the streets of Manhattan, hand out flyers and bumper strips, and solicit donations. From these efforts, the YFB forces were able

---

53. 2008 YAF Alumni Survey Responses: William K. Schmidt.
54. 2008 YAF Alumni Survey Responses: Fred J. Eckert.
55. 2008 YAF Alumni Survey Responses: Mark David Goret.

to undertake other activities on behalf of their candidate. Interestingly enough, Gottlieb's first venture in politics was as a high school senior when he headed the Youth for Lindsay for Mayor efforts against Jim's younger brother Bill. Some months thereafter, a friend gave him a copy of *The Unmaking of a Mayor*, which introduced him to Barry Goldwater's *Conscience of a Conservative* and after reading these books, Gottlieb had found a philosophy that truly reflected his values.[56]

Gottlieb volunteered throughout the summer until he returned to Knoxville for the fall semester. After that campaign he held nearly every office in YAF from chapter chairman to regional staff director. As he recently observed, "it was a great networking experience that made lasting business and personal friendships. The internal politics was great training for the real world." According to Gottlieb,

> It served as the foundation to my whole career in politics. It was a training ground where I was allowed to not just be active but be able to formulate policy and implement projects as a leader in the conservative movement. I owe much to my YAF experience. I would not be who I am or where I am today without YAF. I learned organizational skills, fundraising, as well as political philosophy.[57]

Gottlieb converted what was a student group into the Citizens Committee for the Right to Keep and Bear Arms, a group that some have regarded as the major activist gun rights organization, of which he remains chairman.[58]

Without a doubt, the key individual in the entire Youth for Buckley operation was Herb Stupp, a 20-year-old student at St. John's University who had been a foot soldier in the first Buckley senatorial campaign. Within YAF, Stupp served as State Chairman, National Board member, and Mid Atlantic regional representative, as well as chapter chairman. Stupp was press secretary to the 1974 Conservative Party candidate for Senate, Barbara Keating, and then Legislative Assistant to State Senator Fred Eckert, a YAF alumnus. From 1975–81, Stupp was editorial director of WOR-TV in New York City. During the Reagan Administration he was Regional Director of ACTION and then deputy and acting Regional Director for the Department of Education during the George H.W. Bush Administration. For eight years he was Commissioner of the New York City Department of Aging, serving in the cabinet of Mayor Rudy Giuliani. Looking back, Stupp concluded that

> I was privileged to be given leadership training and then increasing leadership in YAF during an exciting and challenging time in US history. Being able to meet and work with the likes of Bill Buckley, Jim Buckley, Jack Kemp and conservative intellectuals like Henry Paolucci, Frank Meyer et al was an honor for someone from an immigrant family.
>
> The leadership training, formal and mostly informal, I received in YAF enabled me to deal with many different personalities to accomplish goals throughout my career and civic involvement. Each successive responsibility and achievement gave me additional confidence to tackle new challenges. Further, I find that I am still drawing on my network of colleagues, comrades,

---

56. Interview with Alan Gottlieb, Bellevue, WA, March 26, 2009.

57. 2008 YAF Alumni Survey Responses: Alan M. Gottlieb. Among his most recent books, co-authored with Dave Workman, is *America Fights Back: Armed Self-Defense in a Violent Age* (Bellevue, WA: Merril Press, 2007).

58. Gottlieb's entrepreneurial success is described in Micklethwait and Wooldridge: *The Right Nation—Conservative Power in America*, pp. 179–182.

and friends made in YAF as assets . . . YAF was one of the most important formative experiences in my life, enabling me to become a "conscious" conservative more rapidly and giving me critical analytical skills—a gift for life. I would not be the person I am today without my experiences in YAF.[59]

Stupp is a classic example of the lasting contribution of Young Americans for Freedom in the development of leadership—leadership exemplified in his efforts in public service and non-profit community organizations. One could say that it all began with the challenge of the Buckley campaign and his performance in organizing and leading the Youth for Buckley effort. Nearly forty years later, reflecting on that historic campaign, Buckley commended Stupp for "the heroic work performed by the troops under your command . . . and thanks yet again for ensuring my 1970 victory!"[60]

Asked about the appeal of Jim Buckley to young voters, one volunteer, Vincent Apicella of St. John's University, said the reason was "he's not a hack, he has personality, he has convictions."[61] The character of the campaign and the candidate is perhaps best summed up by Arnie Steinberg.

> Of the many, many campaigns I've been involved in—there has never been anything like the spirit of the Buckley campaign—and no real hassles, divisiveness, power trips—everyone just sort of pitched in. Syracuse University conducted a study after the election and found the media coverage favored Buckley. One reason was the candidate—he was impressive and nice and genuine . . . He was a class act, and the campaign, as a whole, reflected him.[62]

The character of the candidate can be seen also in a recollection by Alan Gottlieb. Volunteering for the Buckley campaign over the summer of 1970 he was leaning towards taking a semester off and continuing his campaign efforts. At a campaign reception, Gottlieb's mother spoke with the candidate and told him her son was planning on dropping out to help him. Hearing this, Buckley quickly informed Gottlieb that he should return to the University of Tennessee and he would contact his friend, Bill Brock, to make sure he would be involved in Brock's Senate campaign.[63] The sincerity of the candidate and the quality of the campaign could be seen by thousands of young people who gave of their time and energy to help elect Jim Buckley against what were seen by some as overwhelming odds.[64]

How important was the Youth for Buckley effort? Liz Doyle, who was intimately involved in the Buckley campaign and later served on his senatorial staff noted that they were blessed to have so many YAF members who volunteered in the Youth for Buckley campaign.[65] Shortly after the campaign ended, Arnie Steinberg put it all in perspective: "if there had been no state organization of Young Americans for Freedom, if YAF leadership past and present had not been building over the last years, it would have been impossible to create and carry out an undertaking

---

59. 2008 YAF Alumni Survey Responses: Herbert W. Stupp.
60. Email from James L. Buckley to Herb Stupp, March 21, 2009 (in author's possession).
61. "Youth played Key Role in Buckley's N.Y. Race," *Houston Chronicle*, in *YAF in the News*, December 1970.
62. Arnold Steinberg e-mail to the author, March 10, 2009.
63. Interview with Alan Gottlieb, Bellevue, WA, March 26, 2009.
64. Buckley authored two books that reflect his character. As a United States Senator he wrote *If Men Were Angels* (New York: G.P. Putnam's Sons, 1975). Years later, his observations for an oral history project were recorded and published as *Gleanings from an Unplanned Life* (Wilmington, DE: ISI Books, 2006).
65. Email to the author, December 17, 2008.

of the magnitude of the Youth for Buckley effort."[66]

The benefits were mutual. As Herb Stupp noted, there were 59 YAF chapters in New York before the election; by spring of 1971 there were 121. Stupp, Ron Robinson, Richard Delgaudio and others led the effort to organize new chapters, but especially valuable was Jim Minarik, a YAF leader from Ohio who worked in the Buckley campaign and then remained in upstate New York converting Youth for Buckley groups into YAF chapters. According to Stupp, "Jim made a big difference in those areas where full time students like Ron Robinson and I could not visit easily."[67] New chapters had been formed but, just as importantly, new leadership had been identified that would carry New York YAF forward as one of the strongest state organizations throughout all the remaining years of YAF's active life. And, of course, the Buckley victory was a tremendous shot in the arm for the morale of young conservatives. If it could be done in New York State, well then, it could be done anywhere!

Immediately after the 1970 elections, with the success of Buckley, Reagan, Kemp, and so many other candidates strongly backed by YAF members, optimism was reigning. As Randal Teague concluded, "There is a sense of 'we're winning' out there among these young conservatives, on the high school and college campuses and in the communities. There is a tremendous spirit which must be captured and, once captured, must be nurtured, recognized, rewarded."[68] Unfortunately, it was an enthusiasm that would not last very long as the attention turned from elective politics to the continuing battles against the left on campus, to the drawn-out conflict against communism in Southeast Asia, and to the leftward movement of a Republican administration in the White House.

The Manhattan Twelve

A few weeks after his brother's election to the United States Senate, Bill Buckley invited a number of YAF members to participate in a taping session for his television program, "Firing Line." On December 8, 1970, the YAFers served as an audience for the taping of a Buckley interview program with Vice President Spiro T. Agnew. The second program taped consisted of Buckley being questioned on a wide range of topics by the YAF members. Perhaps the most significant exchange centered on the question of why Buckley had not been as critical of President Nixon and his departures from conservative policies as he would have been with the same programs advocated by a President Hubert Humphrey. Buckley's response was that "conservatism, as I understand it, is always about two things—it's about the paradigm, how things ought to be, and it's about what can you wrest out of the current situation." While working with Nixon was viewed as better than nothing at all, Buckley went on to add, "I think that the conservative movement ought always to make clear what it is that is ideal."[69]

In the response to this one question, Bill Buckley had summarized the dilemma facing young conservatives, and the entire conservative movement, as they considered the Nixon Administration. Nixon was, indeed, on a wide range of issues

66. Steinberg, "It Happened in New York," *New Guard*, December 1970, p. 30.
67. Email to the author, February 6, 2009.
68. Randal Teague, "Youth in Politics–For *Our* Guys," *Human Events*, December 12, 1970.
69. "Firing Line," Box 59 (218), Folder 228, Hoover Institution Archives, Stanford University, Palo Alto, CA.

better than any likely Democratic President. Yet there were so many issues on which he departed from the conservative position. Moreover, to many on campus, Nixon was perceived as a conservative and his policies as those supposedly supported by an organization such as YAF. Should they continue to wrest what they could out of the situation or stand boldly for the ideal?

By the start of the decade YAF was playing a more crucial role in the developing conservative movement in America. As early as January 1969, David Jones had proposed that YAF, the American Conservative Union, *Human Events*, and *National Review* co-sponsor a conservative conference in the spring of 1969.[70] This memo was followed by a letter to Bill Buckley the following month.[71] While it would be five years before the first such conference was held, in 1970 YAF joined with the other three entities to sponsor an annual conservative awards dinner in Washington, DC, an event that was continued in 1971. During the fall campaign of 1970, YAF proposed that representatives from the four entities who co-sponsored the awards dinner meet periodically to coordinate policy positions on major issues. The first meeting was held in January and those present expressed concern over the direction of the Nixon Administration but did not agree on any specific path to follow.[72]

By spring, YAF leaders were searching for alternatives. National Chairman Ron Docksai launched a short-lived "Draft Reagan" movement. On May 21st, the California Governor wrote to Docksai and politely asked that he cease and desist in his efforts. "While I am naturally proud that you hold me in such high regards, I still must ask with all the urgency I can express that you desist. To publicly repudiate any activity of YAF is not something I'm eager to do but, in this instance, I'll have no alternative if this effort continues."[73] Docksai and YAF backed off, not wanting to lose the support of one of their most important advisors. A few days later, on May 25th, representatives of the four groups met and considered expanding their numbers. They would review their options and meet again in two months.

May 1971 also saw the appearance of a critical article on Nixon in YAF's magazine by Jeffrey Bell of the American Conservative Union. Bell's article predicted electoral defeat for the President unless he changed policies that were alienating his 1968 constituency. In words that some would say rang true again forty years later, Bell proclaimed, "Gone are the days when Republicans could excoriate big Government, high taxes, unbalanced budgets, welfare abuses, and Great Society scandal and profligacy. If Republican candidates tried to revert to these successful past themes now, they would be laughed out of the house."[74] It was a plea for the President to change direction and return to the conservative beliefs and policies that Bell saw as having brought about his victory in the election against Humphrey and Wallace.

With frequent state and regional conferences, YAF was an organization that provided opportunities for feedback from its members. Those members were more and more expressing their opposition to Administration policies and

---

70. David R. Jones memo to William A. Rusher, January 7, 1969. Personal Papers of William A Rusher, Box 46, Manuscript Division, Library of Congress, Washington, DC.

71. David R. Jones to William F. Buckley, Jr., February 17, 1969. Personal Papers of William F. Buckley, Jr., Box 67, Sterling Library, Yale University, New Haven, CT.

72. The Ripon Society and Clifford W. Brown, Jr.: *Jaws of Victory*, p. 302.

73. Kiron K. Skinner, Annelise Anderson, and Martin Anderson, editors: *Reagan: A Life in Letters* (New York: Free Press, 2003), pp. 174–175.

74. Jeffrey Bell, "The Ordeal of the President," *New Guard*, May 1971, pp. 5–9.

increasingly the President himself. Reporting on the seven YAF regional conferences of spring 1971, a YAF publication noted, "the delegates' hearts were not behind any massive effort to re-elect the Richard Nixon of March and April 1971. Their indecision as to the viable alternatives for conservatives in 1972 was a reflection of the dilemma facing all conservatives today."[75] The time for indecision had passed and it was not only the young conservatives of YAF who were seeking a way to separate themselves from the Nixon Administration. As Jerry Norton, editor of *New Guard*, observed, over the remaining months of spring 1971, "it became clear to leaders of other Movement elements that YAF's feelings were not unique. Conservatives in general were frustrated by the tendency of the media and public to classify them as supporters of an Administration that they were in fact dissatisfied with."[76] A growing number of conservatives became convinced that Nixon could be influenced more by direct, public criticism than by private pleas for a more conservative direction. It was time for a dramatic step and one that included more than the initial four groups.

On July 26th, a gathering of conservative leaders that became known as the "Manhattan Twelve" released a statement in New York and Washington announcing that they were suspending support of President Nixon. Among those signing the document was YAF executive director Randal C. Teague. National Chairman Ronald F. Docksai, who joined the group in later statements, was out of the country at the time. While critical of several of the administration's domestic policies, the statement focused more on the overtures to Red China, the failure to respond to Soviet advances in the Mediterranean, and the perceived deterioration of the nation's military position. The statement proclaimed, "in consideration of this record, the undersigned, who have heretofore generally supported the Nixon Administration, have resolved to suspend our support of the administration." They would not be encouraging formal opposition to Nixon in the primaries but were keeping all options open at the time. The statement concluded by saying, "We consider that our defection is an act of loyalty to the Nixon we supported in 1968." The signers included individuals representing the original four entities as well as Anthony Harrigan of the Southern States Industrial Council, Neil McCaffrey of the Conservative Book Club, and J. Daniel Mahoney from the Conservative Party of New York.[77]

The most significant name among the signers was Bill Buckley, not only because of his public recognition but also due to the efforts of those in the administration, especially Henry Kissinger, to appeal for his continued support of Nixon. As one Washington newspaper noted,

> The anti-Nixon movement has been building for several months in conservative publications. It took a great leap forward yesterday with the announcement that William F. Buckley, Jr., editor-in-chief of the *National Review*, had joined with 10 other conservative editors, authors and organizers to announce they planned to "suspend" their support for Nixon.[78]

75. "YAF Regionals Attract 1000," *yaf letter*, June 1971, p. 4. Newsletter published by Young Americans for Freedom.

76. Jerry Norton, "The Ashbrook Campaign: The Making of a Conservative Candidate," *New Guard*, March 1972, p. 7.

77. Memo from Randal Teague to Board of Directors and State Chairmen, July 29, 1971. Personal Papers of Jameson Campaigne, Jr., Ottawa, IL. See also Lee Edwards: *The Conservative Revolution*, pp. 169–172.

78. James Doyle, "President Facing Growing Rebellion in GOP Right Wing," *Washington Star*, July 29, 1971.

The following month Nixon added to the conservatives' consternation by taking the United States off the gold standard and imposing wage and price controls. By August, the young conservatives were even more convinced that a divorce from Nixon was needed. It was in such a frame of mind that they were to gather in Houston for their bi-ennial national convention. With Nixon having moved too far to the left, Reagan having disavowed and disowned any effort to draft him, and no elected officials likely candidates, what would they do?

While those attending the YAF regional conferences in the spring of 1971 expressed much dissatisfaction with the Nixon Administration, the delegates also took part in the election of eight National Directors and heard speeches from Governor Reagan, Senator John Tower, and Congressmen Bill Archer, Jack Kemp and Phil Crane. Delegates unanimously elected Dan Rea, Massachusetts state chairman to the New England regional seat; Pat Nolan of the University of Southern California to the Western regional board position; Steve Loewy of Washington University to represent the Plains region, and Charles Black, Florida state chairman, to represent the Southern region. In contested races, Bruce Eberle of Texas defeated Chris Till of Texas and Maurice Franks of Louisiana for the Southwest regional board seat; Ron Robinson of Canisius College in upstate New York was re-elected from the Mid-Atlantic after defeating fellow Board member Joe Leo of New Jersey; James Minarik of the University of Dayton was re-elected in a close contest with Illinois YAF state chairman Bill Mencarow; and Roger Koopman of the University of Idaho took the Northwest seat after Jeff Kane, Washington state chairman, withdrew. Many of those elected at the 1971 regional conferences would go on to further leadership positions in YAF as well as later positions in American society.

Rea recently concluded that his "involvement in YAF opened the door to a wider world of philosophy, politics and civic commitment. I have wonderful memories of YAF and many of my life long friends were people I met through YAF."[79] For Eberle, "ever since I joined YAF in 1962, it was an important part of my life and brought me into a lifetime commitment to the conservative movement."[80]

6th National Convention—Houston

Labor Day weekend 1971 saw some fifteen hundred YAF members and supporters converge on the Shamrock Hilton Hotel in Houston, Texas for YAF's sixth national convention.[81] The organization had, for the first time in its history, surpassed 800 local chapters and had a record number of state organizations in place. Despite all the divisiveness resulting from the 1969 convention, the 1971 convention had the largest turnout in history with the number of voting delegates in Houston surpassing the number voting in St. Louis.[82] An article in the convention pro-

79. 2008 YAF Alumni Survey Responses: Dan Rea.

80. Interview with Bruce Eberle, Austin, TX, March 9, 2009.

81. The estimate of 1,500 attendees is from Diamond: *Roads to Dominion*, p. 116. David S. Broder, "Conservative Youth Meet on '72 Strategy," *Washington Post*, September 3, 1971, estimated 1,200 were in attendance.

82. According to J.C. Lobdell, "Meet Them in St. Louis," *National Review*, September 23, 1969, there were 723 voting delegates at the 1969 convention. While the top vote getter in St. Louis had 559 votes, the top two vote getters among the 13 candidates for 9 Board positions at the 1971 convention received 701 (Jack Gullahorn) and 699 (Bob Moffit) votes. Since not every delegate voted for these two candidates it is highly likely that there were more voting delegates in Houston than in St. Louis.

gram saw the delegates confronting a "choice between principle and expediency, between the real and the ideal, between a commitment to conservatism or to normalcy . . . Conservatives—and the nation at large—are watching and waiting to discover in which direction the 'New Politics' of young conservatism will turn."[83] Perceiving such a challenge before them, it was no surprise that the theme of the convention was "We Are the New Politics!" and the organizers had added a mock presidential nominating convention to the overall agenda. This time, in Houston, young conservatives would not only elect the leaders of their organization but would be asked to express their preference for President ahead of the 1972 election.

As in past years, the convention included a number of recognized conservative leaders as speakers and panelists, walked the delegates through a series of platform committee meetings ending with the adoption of an updated platform, and allowed the YAF members present to elect the organization's leadership for the next two years. The evening's program began with a welcome from the district's congressman, Bill Archer, and the traditional keynote address by Bill Buckley. Regional and state caucuses took place into the early morning.

Friday's program included addresses by Senator James Buckley and several conservative luminaries. In an effort to reflect its non-partisan nature, the evening's featured speaker was Democratic Senator Robert Byrd of West Virginia, who had earlier in the year defeated Ted Kennedy for the position of Senate Majority Whip. Byrd, who at that time was considered more conservative than his later voting record reflected, accepted the invitation "to demonstrate that the Democratic party is broad-based enough to include both liberals and conservatives."[84] Both Senators Buckley and Byrd criticized the Supreme Court's school busing decisions. One report described Byrd's remarks,

> In a strongly worded speech to the national convention of the conservative youth group, Young Americans for Freedom, Byrd said the busing rulings were "preposterous, authoritarian, nonsense, pure folly." The speech by the Senate's majority whip was the strongest condemnation of the court rulings that has been delivered by a congressional leader of either party.[85]

The delegates warmly received Byrd's speech and beyond its content saw his presence as reinforcing the organization's independence from the Republican party. His remarks were followed by nominations and demonstrations for National Board candidates and National Chairman.

Saturday brought YAF elections, the adoption of a platform, and in the evening, the "Young America's Presidential Nominating Convention." It was a propitious time for YAF to be sponsoring such an event. Not only was there general dissatisfaction with the Nixon Administration as expressed in the statement of the "Manhattan Twelve," but also the mock nominating convention came two months after the enactment of the 26th Amendment to the Constitution establishing the voting age qualification at 18. The coming contest would be the first time that most individuals aged 18–21 could vote in a national election.[86]

83. Wayne Thorburn, "Agenda for the New Politics," *New Guard*, October 1971, p. 13.

84. Comments from a spokesman for Byrd quoted in Broder, "Conservative Youth Meet on '72 Strategy," *Washington Post*, September 3, 1971. A few months later an article by Byrd, "In Defense of Conservatism," was published in *New Guard*, March 1972, pp. 11, 14–15.

85. David S. Broder, "Democrat Byrd Attacks Court's Busing Rulings," *Washington Post*, September 4, 1971.

86. R.W. Apple, Jr., "The States Ratify Full Vote at 18," *New York Times*, July 1, 1971.

National Chairman Ron Docksai was opposed for election by Mike Carr, chairman of the University of Florida chapter, who campaigned from a more libertarian position and as a supporter of President Nixon, but when the votes were counted it was no contest.[87] However, there were a number of lively contests for the nine National Director positions to be filled in Houston. Once again, there was an "establishment" slate called the YAF Caucus, co-chaired by Ron Pearson, Rhode Island YAF state chairman, and Linda Zimmerman, a YAF member and College Young Republican chairman for Florida. As in the past, some candidates sought support and then dropped out of the race before the votes were counted, including Richard Delgaudio and Rich Macksoud of New York as well as John Hightower, Mississippi YAF state chairman. By the time of the convention, the YAF Caucus endorsed eight candidates, including five incumbents seeking a second term on the Board. Bob Moffit and Jack Gullahorn had been first elected by the delegates in 1969 and would end up being the high vote getters. Bill Saracino had filled a vacancy in 1969 while Herb Stupp and Frank Donatelli were selected for vacancies earlier in 1971.

The YAF Caucus endorsed three new candidates: Alan Gottlieb of the University of Tennessee, Mary Fisk of Monmouth University in New Jersey, and Louisa Porter of Indianapolis. Fisk later became editor of *New Guard*. Looking back on her involvement, she remembers, "YAF provided a 'place' in which I learned to develop my political views, engage in activities to further them, develop friends who shared those views, and enter young adulthood as a much stronger person."[88] At the time of her election Louisa Porter was chairman of the Indianapolis YAF community chapter.[89]

The contest for the final spot up for election to the National Board attracted five candidates, including three YAF state chairmen. The victorious candidate was Michael Connelly, Louisiana YAF chairman, who continued to serve on the YAF National Board until 1978. An attorney, writer and teacher, he now lives in the Dallas area.[90] The four unsuccessful candidates were James Altham, Connecticut YAF chairman; James Newman, Minnesota YAF chairman; John Roselle, chairman of Staten Island YAF; and Mark Souder of Indiana Purdue University at Ft. Wayne.[91]

Once the Board elections were over, Senator John Tower was a surprise guest and spoke on the need for greater military preparedness. Along with both Bill and Jim Buckley and Barry Goldwater, Tower urged that the convention not make an open break with the Nixon Administration. Goldwater's position was made known in a letter to all delegates as well as in the remarks of his former campaign manager, Stephen Shadegg, who spoke to the convention on Friday. A small coterie of YAF members supportive of the President opened a Nixon suite during the convention and attempted to quiet down the dissatisfaction with the administration. Also present, "doing missionary work for the administration" as one reporter described their activities, were two past National Chairmen: Tom Huston and David Keene.[92]

After Tower's address to the delegates it was time to debate and approve a platform. National Director Richard Derham was back as Platform Chairman

---

87. Molly Ivins, "The Observer Goes to a YAF convention," *Texas Observer*, September 24, 1971, p. 3, 4.
88. 2008 YAF Alumni Survey Responses: Mary Fisk.
89. 2008 YAF Alumni Survey Responses: Louisa Porter.
90. 2008 YAF Alumni Survey Responses: Michael R. Connelly.
91. David Brooks, "Portrait of a Republican," *New York Times*, August 28, 2004, provides a profile of Congressman Mark Souder.
92. Broder, "Conservative Youth Meet on '72 Strategy," *Washington Post*, September 3, 1971.

but, unlike two years earlier, the debates were not as contentious and there was no dramatic display of opposition to a prevailing position. One commentator described it as "the largest convention ever and the most peaceful, intelligent debate on resolutions, a veritable era of good feelings."[93]

During the platform discussions, the sentiment against several policies of the Nixon Administration became evident. The platform condemned the President's welfare reform plan as a step towards "a guaranteed annual income to a swollen welfare constituency" while another called on the President "to promptly terminate" wage and price controls and "restore freedom to the economy."[94] The most divided vote of the day came on opposition to the Strategic Arms Limitation (SALT) Talks. The Platform Committee proposed indefinitely postponing the talks but some delegates wanted those words removed. The eight words in contention were "and we urge that they be indefinitely postponed." As Molly Ivins reported,

> The last eight words of that resolution were approved by a vote of 160 to 130, the closest of the day. The debate over their approval centered not on how the delegates actually felt but on how the resolution would look to "outsiders." All the delegates seemed to agree that more weapons are preferable to disarmament, but some of them worry about their image.[95]

The platform also called on the President to take prompt steps to "return the United States to superiority in strategic weapons."[96] Another resolution called his scheduled trip to Communist China "morally offensive" and a threat to American alliances with free Asian nations.

The observations of newly elected National Director Mike Connelly of Louisiana were reflective of the sentiments of many delegates towards the President when he noted,

> I heard him make all those promises to the South and to conservatives and I saw him begin to break them almost as soon as he was elected. I became more and more disenchanted with his Vietnam policy and I am very wary of any government interference in the economy. But the final breaking point was the visit to Red China. Nixon specifically promised in the 1968 campaign that he would do the opposite. I think it was even part of the Republican platform. He said we would not recognize Red China. And now look.[97]

Connelly led the fight on the convention floor to strengthen YAF's stand against the Nixon Administration. After the Platform Committee produced a resolution disavowing Nixon but concluding with two conciliatory paragraphs, the delegates eliminated them. Stripped out of the committee recommendation were the words "we do not plan at the moment to encourage formal political opposition to President Nixon in the forthcoming primary."[98] The final resolution as passed condemned the administration for "inflation and unemployment, excessive

---

93. Jared C. Lobdell, "Scenes from Houston," *National Review*, October 8, 1971, p. 1131.

94. David S. Broder, "YAF Condemns Nixon, Backs Agnew for '72," *Washington Post*, September 5, 1971. Warren Weaver, Jr., "YAF Suspends Support of Nixon," *New York Times*, September 5, 1971.

95. Ivins, "The Observer Goes to a YAF Convention," p. 3.

96. Broder, "YAF Condemns Nixon, Backs Agnew for '72."

97. Ivins, "The Observer Goes to a YAF Convention," p. 3.

98. Broder, "YAF Condemns Nixon, Backs Agnew for '72," Nicholas C. Chriss, "Young Conservatives Drop Nixon Support," *Los Angeles Times*, September 5, 1971.

taxation and inordinate welfarism" at home as well as the deterioration of the American military and the overtures to Communist China "done in the absence of any public concession by Red China."[99]

In speaking with the media after the platform debates, executive director Randal Teague expressed surprise at the delegates' fervent opposition to the President. As the convention began on Thursday, he predicted "They just won't work for Nixon next year unless they are convinced he's a conservative."[100] But after the platform debates on Saturday afternoon, Teague maintained, "I'm a little shocked by it. What YAF has done is to say that maybe there should be a conservative candidate in New Hampshire. This shows that the anti-Nixon feeling is stronger than I thought it was."[101]

Once the platform debate was concluded the delegates and guests moved into the mock presidential nominating convention. Kicked off by a stirring keynote speech from Maryland State Senator Bob Bauman, the YAF members had a grand and entertaining time in putting forth the names of some twenty candidates for consideration. Among those nominated were the late Senator Joseph McCarthy (who truly believes "Better Dead than Red"), Senator Strom Thurmond, who, at the age of 66, had recently married a 23 year old (he's not too old for anything), and Congressman H.R. Gross of Iowa, with a reputation for voting against nearly all spending bills ("in your heart, you know he's cheap!"). Most humorous of all was the nomination of Chicago Mayor Richard Daley by Loren Smith of Illinois. Molly Ivins reported that,

> The finest nomination of the evening was made by a fellow in a yellow hardhat wearing a "Darwin is a Fairy!" sweatshirt. In finest hardhatese, the delegate from Illinois nominated the state's favorite son—RICHARD J. DALEY: "The Mayor will go through those reformers like crap through a goose . . . He knows the biggest problem we face today—commie pinkos! . . . He's seen his opportunities and he's took 'em . . . Where he stands on military surveillance: if you ain't got nothin' to fear you should be for it . . . Daley's a man who believes God gave the right for every man to vote, living or dead."[102]

After almost every nominating speech, there would be a rousing demonstration from the delegates on the convention floor.

Mixed in with the humorous nominations were the real candidates: President Nixon, Vice President Spiro Agnew, Governor Ronald Reagan, Senator Henry Jackson, Senator James Buckley, and Congressman Phil Crane. Tom Lamont of New Jersey had the difficult task of making a nominating speech for the President and stressed his appointment of two conservatives to the Supreme Court (Warren Burger and Harry Blackmun) as well as withdrawing U.S. troops from Vietnam "without losing an inch of territory to the Communists."[103] Meanwhile, the Maryland delegation sponsored a hospitality suite where they distributed Agnew bumper stickers, buttons and literature. They called on the delegates to be both "pragmatic and principled" by choosing Agnew.

99. "Houston: Making It Perfectly Clear," *New Guard*, November 1971, p. 2.
100. Broder, "Conservative Youth Meet on '72 Strategy."
101. Ivins, "The Observer Goes to a YAF Convention," p. 3.
102. *Ibid*. p. 4.
103. Broder, "YAF Votes Fund to Oppose Nixon," *Washington Post*, September 6, 1971.

Assuming the President is renominated, our nomination of Spiro Agnew for President will be a clarion call to the Administration that they cannot expect conservative campaign workers unless the Vice President remains on the ticket, which will guarantee that there is a conservative voice in the Administration and that at the 1976 GOP convention the Vice President will be a serious contender for the nomination. Our nomination of Agnew will tell the press and the public that, contrary to the line the media is selling, there are young people willing to support a principled conservative.[104]

While many of the delegates preferred Ronald Reagan, the candidate they had supported for the nomination in 1968, he had made it clear that he was supporting the President and would disown any effort to nominate him. Thus, he was introduced as his state's favorite son.

At the end of the first ballot, with all the serious and frivolous candidates receiving votes, Reagan led the pack with 258 votes, followed closely by Senator Buckley with 210 and Agnew with 206. Prior to the second ballot, Senator Buckley's name was withdrawn and the frivolous candidates were eliminated. A massive shift to Agnew began appearing and he ended up receiving 976 votes, followed far behind by Reagan with 204, Phil Crane with 105, Senator Henry Jackson with 66 and President Nixon with 46. Maryland YAF, which had nominated Agnew, then moved that Senator Buckley be nominated by acclamation for Vice President. As YAF's magazine noted,

> Pragmatically, the effect of nominating Agnew should be to demonstrate that this man, whose role the President had been downgrading of late, is considered a genuine leader by conservatives, and that if the President removes Mr. Agnew from the ticket, his hopes, slight enough now, of having conservative campaign workers, would be lost entirely.[105]

One writer noted that "amid chants of 'Dump Nixon,' YAF members denounced administration policies on China, strategic nuclear weapons, welfare and wage-price controls and pledged to raise $750,000 to finance primary challenges to Nixon."[106] As Ron Docksai said in remarks the following day, it was evident to him that the young conservatives in YAF "feel disenfranchised. The man they helped elect President on a conservative platform seems instead to be carrying out the program of Hubert Humphrey. Young conservatives are not kids who can be satisfied with an occasional lollipop from the Administration."[107]

Some days later, the Vice President wrote Docksai and acknowledged YAF's actions while still calling on the organization's members to support Nixon's re-election. Senator Buckley also responded with a letter supportive of the organization and its efforts on behalf of conservative principles.[108] National political reporter David Broder noted, "The YAF delegates, who consider themselves the vanguard of the conservative movement, are realistic enough to know Agnew is not

---

104. Agnew flyer prepared by Maryland YAF, in author's possession.
105. "Houston: Making It Perfectly Clear," *New Guard*, November 1971, p. 2. Warren Weaver, Jr., "Young Conservatives Back Agnew Over Nixon in '72." *New York Times*, September 6, 1971.
106. Diamond: *Roads to Dominion*, p. 116.
107. "Houston: Making It Perfectly Clear," p. 3.
108. *Ibid.*

going to challenge Mr. Nixon for the nomination." The signal they were sending was that they want Agnew on the ticket and "to tell any possible conservative challengers for the presidency that they are willing to back a contest against Mr. Nixon in the presidential primaries, if anyone can be found to make it."[109] In what was a purely symbolic action, but one that reinforced their determination to back a serious effort for the nomination, the delegates also voted to raise $750,000 to support a conservative challenge to Nixon's re-election in 1972.

Sunday brought addresses by Dean Clarence Manion and Herbert Philbrick as well as workshops on campus action, moderated by Doug Cooper of Harvard University; organizational development, led by Mike McIver of Oklahoma YAF; and high school programming conducted by Tom Dahlberg of Anoka Hi-YAF in Minnesota. The 1971 convention saw a record number of high school students in attendance, many of whom would go on to lead college YAF chapters in the next few years. The influence of the event on many of these younger attendees was lasting. As Lillian Fisher recently noted, "I went to the Houston '71 convention in Texas. That was my first time in a plane and my first time on a trip all alone." After high school, Fisher would go on to serve as YAF chapter chairman at SUNY–Delhi and has been an active conservative her entire adult life. Her YAF involvement influenced others, as Fisher found out years later. "Funny, at my 30th HS reunion, a guy ran up to me and said, 'Oh my God! Lillian, I can't believe it. YOU changed my life . . . after HS, I decided to become a history teacher so that I could influence students and teach them the truth about politics and history!'"[110]

Sunday evening was devoted to the Inaugural Banquet for the newly elected YAF officers and featured an address to the delegates by telephone from Governor Reagan. He commended the young conservatives for holding to their beliefs in the midst of great challenge: "When I think of the philosophy prevalent in so much of the intellectual community, I marvel at the way you have obtained an education yet remained steadfast in your beliefs, resisting the zeitgeist—the wind of our times." Reagan recited a brief overview of 20th century political history and then spoke to their concerns about the administration, "Be critical, be vocal and forceful in urging your views on the President. He needs that input to counter the constant pressure from the opposite side; he needs the arguments you can provide.[111] While acknowledging that Republicans would be horrified if Hubert Humphrey had announced a presidential visit to China, he nevertheless defended Nixon doing so on the basis of his long-standing support for the Republic of China and his actions as Vice President in standing up to Khruschev. Nixon would remain strong in his meetings with the Chinese Communist leaders, according to Reagan. Reiterating his support for the organization, he concluded by advising the delegates to "consider very carefully the long hard struggle that lies ahead, and how far we've traveled together to reach this moment of hope for all the things we believe in. Weigh the alternatives, and use your strength wisely and well."[112]

The leaders of the young conservative organization would take Reagan's words seriously but their resolve to make evident their programmatic disagreements with the Nixon Administration would not go away. As the YAF members left Houston, they were emboldened and encouraged. The largest convention in the organization's

109. Broder, "YAF Votes Fund to Oppose Nixon."
110. Email to the author from Lillian Fisher D'Allaird, March 31, 2009.
111. Kiron K. Skinner, Annelise Anderson, and Martin Anderson, editors: *Reagan, In His Own Hand* (New York: Simon & Schuster, 2001), pp. 449–453.
112. *Ibid.*

history, and one which displayed a commonality of purpose and direction, would lead them on to new challenges in the months ahead. YAF's role as an essential element in the growing conservative movement would become apparent as they weighed the possibilities of a direct challenge to the re-nomination of the President.

Ashbrook for America—No Left Turn

As the fall semester began, the YAF members went back to their campuses determined to battle the latest in left-wing challenges, whether it be the use of student fees to pay radical speakers, the efforts by Ralph Nader and his supporters to organize and fund PIRGs, or the more positive activities such as publishing their own campus newspapers and electing YAF members to student government. Despite all the concern and involvement over presidential politics, YAF retained a strong campus focus that would guide it through the decade of the Seventies.

Nevertheless, it was also clear that YAF had now become a serious player in national politics. The media could not ignore the impact of YAF's divorce from Nixon as expressed at the national convention in Houston. YAF community chapters were becoming even more involved in political action, including efforts to move the Republican party in a more conservative direction. Over the next few weeks, YAF leaders and those from other conservative entities weighed their alternatives and considered the unthinkable—a direct primary challenge to a sitting Republican President. Throughout the fall, discussions were held among the Manhattan Twelve as to the next step to take after suspending their support of the President. YAF's selection of Agnew at its nominating convention under-lined the young conservatives disillusionment with Nixon but clearly Agnew was not a viable alternative candidate. Months earlier, Reagan had disavowed YAF's effort to start a draft movement and indicated his support for Nixon's re-election. Goldwater and Tower had both endorsed a second term for the President, conveying their decisions by letter and convention speech to the YAF members. Jim Buckley was a freshman Senator and both Phil Crane and Jack Kemp were serving their first full terms in the House.

On October 21st, the Manhattan Twelve hired campaign consultant Jerry Harkins to explore the possibility of primary opposition to Nixon. Five weeks later, on November 30th, he reported back on his initial soundings and concluded that a campaign in New Hampshire could achieve significant success.[113] After receiving Harkins's report, Bill Rusher, Ron Docksai, and Tom Winter met with Congressman John Ashbrook to discuss the possibility of a challenge to Nixon. Ashbrook was a former national chairman of the Young Republicans who had first been elected to Congress in 1960 and served as chairman of the American Conservative Union from 1965 to 1971. The Congressman listened to their appeals and promised a decision by late December. Quickly, the media picked up on his potential candidacy and heightened the interest in a possible challenge to the President.[114]

Before the announcement of any possible Ashbrook candidacy, David Brudnoy had posited three alternatives for conservatives as they approached the 1972

---

113. Jerry Norton, "The Right Wing Heals," *New Guard*, March 1972, p. 8.

114. "Ashbrook Weighs Race in Primary," *New York Times*, December 8, 1971. Ken Clawson, "News of Ashbrook Challenge Perils Nixon Bid to Pacify Conservatives," *Washington Post*, December 8, 1971.

election: they could suspend support for Nixon and sit out the presidential election or support George Wallace or build up a rival candidacy. To Brudnoy, and to most thinking conservatives, the idea of supporting Wallace was an untenable proposition. His recommendation was to draft a known conservative such as Reagan, Agnew or Goldwater. "One of these three men must be boosted for the presidency, starting now," he proclaimed while overlooking their protestations to the contrary. "Let us not forget 1968. Lyndon Johnson, said the wags, would run and win. But Mr. Allard Lowenstein thought otherwise, then Senator Eugene McCarthy thought otherwise, and suddenly the field was open."[115] Brudnoy concluded by maintaining that the movement needed a conservative Lowenstein to think such a challenge possible and then to build a grassroots effort to replace Nixon.

Meanwhile, after the session with Ashbrook, Docksai and executive director Wayne Thorburn met with New England YAF leaders to discuss building a campaign organization. Docksai was especially concerned that "all hang together" in any effort to oppose Nixon. As he wrote Bill Rusher on December 4th,

> Wayne and I, representing YAF, believe very strongly that a challenge in New Hampshire must be made, as you know. However, we also believe that damage to YAF and the three other participating concerns (i.e., damage in the form of our losing pro-Nixon contributors, Advisory Board members) can *only* be prevented if the cooperation and support for the project is shared equally by YAF, NR, HE, and ACU. Any weak link in this four piece chain works to the detriment of the others.[116]

YAF's support of any Ashbrook campaign, said Docksai, would be "proportionate to the overt aiding and abetting of the other parties." The veiled reference was to Bill Buckley, who had left the November 30th meeting without committing himself to support a primary challenge. A few days later, Buckley made his personal commitment to the campaign and YAF, in a major sigh of relief, communicated their thanks to him in a telegram: "Glad to hear you support the challenge of John Ashbrook. Our members ready to go to New Hampshire. Victory will be ours."[117]

While Ashbrook was weighing his options, the Conservative Party of New York added fuel to the fire when it announced that it would be officially suspending support of Nixon, a serious and practical action that directly challenged the ability of the President to retain a second ballot line in New York State that he had claimed in 1968.[118] Although not yet ready to commit himself to a primary challenge, Ashbrook spoke out strongly on December 15th, criticizing the President on a wide range of issues. Nixon's planned trip to Red China and the abandonment of Free China was a prime concern of Ashbrook who had served on the Steering Committee of the Committee of One Million Against the Admission of Communist China to the United Nations.[119] But China was only one of a large number of issues bothering Ashbrook and other conservatives. As Steven Hayward has observed, "It has long been fashionable to say, 'Only Nixon could go

115. David Brudnoy, "Conservatives and 1972," *New Guard*, December 1971, pp. 14–16.

116. Emphasis in original; letter to William A. Rusher from Ronald Docksai, December 4, 1971. Personal Papers of Jameson Campaigne, Jr., Ottawa, IL.

117. Telegram from Wayne Thorburn, executive director, to William F. Buckley, Jr., December 8, 1971. Personal Papers of William F. Buckley, Jr., Box 284, Folder 2494, Sterling Library, Yale University, New Haven, CT.

118. Frank Lynn, "Nixon Scored by State Conservatives," *New York Times*, December 11, 1971.

119. Diamond: *Roads to Dominion*, p. 120.

to China,' but it has never made sense to say, 'Only Nixon could have expanded the Great Society.' Yet he did, and therein lies the other half of the reason why John Ashbrook's challenge to Nixon was a significant public act.'"[120]

After pointing out what he viewed as liberal policies pursued and enacted by the Nixon Administration, Ashbrook lamented the unwillingness of others to speak out on principle, especially his colleagues in the Senate. "I have spoken out often but, unfortunately, I have been joined very few times, particularly on the other side of the Capitol."[121] Concurrent with his speech on the floor of the House of Representatives, Ashbrook also authored a guest column in the *New York Times* that brought additional attention to his concerns over the leftward movement of the Nixon Administration.[122]

By the middle of the month YAF leaders had met with Ashbrook to discuss the ways in which they could help any Ashbrook campaign. Even before an official announcement YAF members were instrumental in lining up the needed signatures to place his name on the New Hampshire ballot. On December 29th, John Ashbrook announced that he would run in the New Hampshire and Florida primaries and the challenge had begun. As Hayward noted, "it was vital in 1972 that someone step forward to say that Nixon's course was unacceptable to conservatives. John Ashbrook was the only man with the courage to make the challenge."[123] A decision had been reached and a candidate had been recruited. Clearly, 1972 would be a volatile political year for conservatives and YAF would be in the midst of it all.

The effort would be known as "Ashbrook for America" and the slogan for the campaign would be "No Left Turn" with the international traffic signal identifying that prohibition as the campaign logo.[124] Immediately upon the announcement of an Ashbrook campaign, YAF swung into action. Connecticut YAF chairman Jim Altham and National Director Dan Rea of Massachusetts moved into New Hampshire to organize youth activity. They were followed by literally hundreds of volunteers. As Lee Edwards recalled, "Ronald Pearson helped coordinate volunteer workers in New Hampshire, especially members of Young Americans for Freedom, which bused in hundreds of students from New England, New York, New Jersey and Pennsylvania."[125]

Essential to the Ashbrook youth efforts was Young America's Campaign Committee (YACC) which funded Youth for Ashbrook operations and provided travel, rooms and meal money for volunteers from Michigan, Ohio, Indiana, Virginia, Maryland, New York, New Jersey, Pennsylvania and the New England states, allowing those YAF members to spend weekends campaigning in New Hampshire. YACC paid the salary and expenses for Altham and for Charles Floto

---

120. Steven Hayward, "Why the Ashbrook Challenge Was Necessary," *On Principle*, special addition on the 15th anniversary of the Ashbrook Center for Public Affairs, 1998, p. 9. Hayward notes the growth of new Federal bureaucracies continued apace throughout the first three years of the administration, contrary to campaign statements and expectations of many who had supported Nixon in the 1968 election.

121. Quoted in Norton, "The Right Wing Heals," *New Guard*, March 1972, p. 7.

122. John M. Ashbrook, "Those Rumblings on Mr. Nixon's Right," *New York Times*, December 16, 1971.

123. Hayward, "Why the Ashbrook Challenge Was Necessary," p. 10.

124. One of the few studies on the Ashbrook for America campaign is Charles A. Moser: *Promise and Hope: The Ashbrook Presidential Campaign of 1972*, published in 1985 as a monograph by Free Congress Foundation, Washington, DC. A copy of the Moser study can be found on the website of the John M. Ashbrook Center for Public Affairs, Ashland University (www.ashbrook.org). For an interesting perspective on the Ashbrook campaign from a liberal Republican viewpoint, see The Ripon Society and Clifford W. Brown, Jr.: *Jaws of Victory* (Boston: Little, Brown & Company, 1973), pp. 300–304.

125. Edwards: *The Conservative Revolution*, p. 173.

of Rhode Island, who served as youth coordinator in the campaign. The committee also provided seed money for the Florida operation where YAF's national chapter director, Charles Black, assisted Florida YAF state chairman Richard Green in organizing volunteers. Seed money was provided also for youth campaigns for Ashbrook in Rhode Island and Louisiana. Nationwide, YACC printed and distributed thousands of Ashbrook for President bumper stickers, having them ready before the official campaign committee or anyone else.[126] As YACC explained in a letter seeking funds for its efforts, "John Ashbrook stands for principle, for the campaign pledges of 1968 and for the common-sense conservatism which is needed to get our nation back on the right track."[127]

While technically a separate political committee, the ties to Young Americans for Freedom were obvious to the politically involved and aware. The address for both YACC and Youth for Ashbrook was the same as that for the national YAF office. Through the efforts of YAF and its political action committee hundreds of young conservatives stood for principle in 1972 and promoted a conservative alternative to Richard Nixon.[128] Unfortunately, it was a lonely battle and, in the end, a losing campaign. Ashbrook obtained 9.6% of the vote in New Hampshire, less than 9% in Florida and 10% in California with limited efforts in Rhode Island, Louisiana and a few other states. As one of those YAF volunteers, Dr. Josiah Strandberg recalled the effort, "A number of us participated in the John Ashbrook campaign. We got him on the ballot in Rhode Island. I was the treasurer of the campaign. We got less than 200 votes. We worked hard but were not effective."[129]

Despite these electoral setbacks, the Ashbrook campaign was an essential element in both the maturation of the conservative movement as distinct from the Republican party as well as the role of YAF within that movement. One of his colleagues in the House and later leading conservative spokesman, Jack Kemp, noted Ashbrook's consistent stand for principle.

> John had enormous courage. He was willing to risk everything for an idea, even undertaking what he surely knew was a hapless presidential campaign against Richard Nixon in 1972 . . . He ran knowing he risked losing his national base in the House. He was, characteristically, the first House Republican to call for President Nixon's resignation.[130]

Summing up the campaign, Lee Edwards concluded, "His campaign preserved the conscience of the conservative movement. It demonstrated that conservatives within the Republican party couldn't be taken for granted."[131] On June 7, 1972, John Ashbrook withdrew from the campaign for president but vowed to continue to work for the "principles that made our party great" and so carried forth his efforts in the platform committee deliberations in Miami Beach that August.[132]

---

126. Letter of Wayne Thorburn to Kieran O'Doherty, August 2, 1972. Personal Papers of William A. Rusher, Box 173, File 7, Library of Congress, Washington, DC.

127. Young America's Campaign Committee fundraising letter, February 1972, in author's possession.

128. Schneider: *Cadres for Conservatism*, p. 153. Interestingly enough, confusing matters somewhat in New Hampshire was a totally unauthorized write-in campaign for Spiro Agnew coordinated by Anthony Campaigne, a YAF member from New Hampshire.

129. 2008 YAF Alumni Survey Responses: Josiah Strandberg.

130. Jack Kemp, introduction to the posthumous publication of John M. Ashbrook: *No Left Turns: A Handbook for Conservatives Based on the Writings of John M. Ashbrook* (Ashland, OH: Hamilton Hobby Press, 1986).

131. Edwards: *The Conservative Revolution*, p. 174.

132. Charles Moser: *Promise and Hope*, p. 21.

Youth Against McGovern

Not everyone in YAF, and certainly not in the conservative movement, was interested in supporting a candidate against the President. There were those YAF members such as former National Chairman David Keene and former University of Maryland chapter chairman Warren Parker who worked in the White House or held positions in other departments of the executive branch. There were those not directly involved with the administration who feared that a conservative challenge would harm the movement and the country. Larry Mongillo had published several articles in *New Guard* and responded to David Brudnoy's call for a conservative Lowenstein. He claimed an unsuccessful challenge—as he predicted it would be—would be disastrous for conservatives, as a "Democratic administration would be virtually assured, and the conservative element within the Republican Party would suffer a severe loss of power and authority."[133] Mongillo maintained that conservative voices were being heard in the Nixon Administration, a situation that would not exist with a Democrat in the White House. He reminded the magazine's readers that while not viewed as a conservative by those active in the movement, Nixon was thought of as a conservative by others. Finally, he pointed out that while the Left succeeded in bringing down Johnson, their effort resulted in Nixon as President, certainly not the left-wing Democrat that they desired.

Mongillo's advice became even more relevant as the Ashbrook campaign faded and Nixon was renominated in Miami Beach. YAF and other conservatives were present and played a role at the convention but their main focus was on the platform and on the rules committee.[134] In the battles over rules for future conventions, historian Theodore White claimed that "Young liberal Republicans, led by the ivory-tower men of the Ripon Society, matched wits with young conservative Republicans of the Young Americans for Freedom in an effort to sway the votes and opinions of their elders."[135] In the end, the conservatives prevailed by a margin of 910 votes to 434. However, as it turned out, Nixon ended up carrying every state except Massachusetts and the District of Columbia, thus negating any delegate strength advantage for traditionally Republican states at the 1976 nominating convention.

As the presidential contest shaped up between Richard Nixon and George McGovern, YAF took two complementary approaches to the election. One was to form a youth group geared to opposing McGovern's election and the other was to emphasize youth involvement in the campaigns of conservative candidates for Congress. To aid those who were concerned over McGovern inroads among young voters in the first presidential election that included 18 year olds in all states, YAF—through its Young America's Campaign Committee—formed "Youth Against McGovern" (YAM) with Ken Tobin of American University as executive director and John Buckley of the University of Virginia as Chairman. YAM's Board of Directors consisted almost entirely of YAF members, although their titles for identification often indicated other groups in which they were active.[136]

---

133. Larry Mongillo, "Conservatives and 1972: A Rebuttal," *New Guard*, March 1972, p. 9.
134. Jerry Norton, "The Meaning of Miami," *New Guard*, November 1972, pp. 9–11.
135. Theodore H. White: *The Making of the President 1972* (New York: Atheneum Publishers, 1973), p. 320. This is the same author who in 1969 wrote that YAF had faded from the scene.
136. The Executive Board is listed in "Memo to Board Members" from Ken Tobin, Executive Director, November 14, 1972. Personal Papers of Jameson Campaigne, Jr., Ottawa, IL.

Rather than dedicated to the re-election of Nixon, Youth Against McGovern could be seen as ideologically partisan, with a goal to speak out on the issues. YAM was attempting to reach young people turned off by McGovern and his radical stands, hoping to move their gut reaction against McGovern into a conscious belief in conservatism.[137] Across the nation during the fall campaign, Youth Against McGovern formed "truth squads" to follow McGovern supporters and show what they perceived as the likely results of the Senator's policies were he to be elected.[138] They attacked McGovern on a wide range of issues from national security to Vietnam to economic policies.

Youth Against McGovern distributed nearly 500,000 buttons, bumper strips and pieces of literature during the campaign. National Director Pat Nolan and Pat Geary led California YAM where among their activities was "A Frightening Halloween Night with George McGovern" held in Orange County. In South Carolina, Vietnam veteran Wayne Ives headed YAM efforts while Ron Robinson headed the efforts in New York State and Bob Love did the same in Texas.[139] YAF Chairman Ron Docksai denied McGovern's claim that a majority of young people would support him, noting "there is no discernible majority among young people."[140] Docksai's analysis was proven correct as exit polls on Election Day indicated that voters under age 25 were almost equally divided in their support of presidential candidates.

YAM members were encouraged to show up at McGovern appearances waving white flags. They distributed on campuses and at political rallies a biting tabloid that attacked the South Dakota Senator's far-left proposals. They printed and distributed "Misgovern with McGovern" buttons. Wherever possible, their goal was to show that not all young people were enamored with George McGovern and his liberal agenda. As Ken Tobin reported after the election, "Our efforts were directed at cutting down McGovern's support among young voters, and in many areas it appears that YAM was the only youth group working to achieve this result. Most of the hecklers and demonstrators that Senator McGovern encountered were part of YAM's activities."[141] The cover of YAF's November 1972 magazine featured an Alfred E. Neuman-like drawing of McGovern on the cover with a caption of "What, Me Govern?" and the character wearing an "Eagleton for VP" button.[142] Whatever hopes the South Dakota Senator had for defeating President Nixon faded rapidly and on election day he was swamped in both popular votes and the Electoral College.

137. Letter of Wayne Thorburn to Kieran O'Doherty, August 2, 1972. Personal Papers of William A. Rusher, Box 173, File 7, Library of Congress, Washington, DC.

138. "YAF Blasts McGovern, Plans Truth Squads," *YAF in the News*, Summer 1972.

139. "YAF and the Right Scene," *New Guard*, January–February 1973, pp. 31–33.

140. The quotes are from articles appearing in the *Massapequa Park (NY) Observer, Queens Illustrated News, Peekskill Star*, and *Rochester Times-Union* reprinted in *YAF in the News*, Summer 1972.

141. "Memo to Board Members" from Ken Tobin, Executive Director, November 14, 1972. Personal Papers of Jameson Campaigne, Jr., Ottawa, IL.

142. Alfred E. Neuman was a dunce-like character popularized by *MAD* magazine. McGovern had selected Senator Tom Eagleton of Missouri as his vice presidential candidate and then dropped him after it became known he had received electro-shock treatment for mental illness. He was replaced on the ticket by R. Sargent Shriver, brother-in-law of the late President John F. Kennedy and father of Maria Shriver Schwarzenegger. White: *The Making of the President 1972*, pp. 256–289.

Beyond Presidential Politics

YAF was not focused entirely on the presidential election as it involved itself in the political arena. As one YAF leader pointed out after the 1971 YAF convention, the members

> . . . are calling for, and participating in, a new politics of conservative principle based on ending big government bureaucracy, protecting individual rights, and preserving the national security . . . The new politics exemplified by YAF concerns itself with the course of our nation not only for the next two, but also the next twenty to forty years.[143]

Two months later, this approach was echoed in a *New Guard* editorial written by Jerry Norton. "As conservatives, then, we contradict our philosophy when we act as though one massive showing at the polls will somehow bring utopia. We must push on all fronts, from the Presidency on down, and not be disappointed if the world is not immediately dazzled by our wisdom."[144] For young conservatives, this meant that there needed to be a long-term dedication to the cause and a realization that no single event or victory would bring about the changes they desired.

It was a message well learned by most of the YAF members as they continued to pursue the promotion of principle over politics. This same message was reinforced in an article by Charles Black, YAF's chapter director, in the following issue of *New Guard*.

> If we are to end the rule of liberalism in America, it will take a dedicated, comprehensive campaign, sustained over many years. Though we can right many injustices and start many trends in the next couple of years, it will take much longer to produce the emergence of the large number of American leaders that we need; leaders who will take the initiative and momentum away from the liberals in every important field; leaders who, having heard liberalism's siren song, have rejected its beckoning melody for the more rigorous strains of common sense and the discipline that produces human freedom.[145]

It was in this context that YAF members played important roles in electing new conservative leaders to Congress in 1972, individuals who would continue to affect American politics through the end of the 20th century and into the 21st. While YAF Advisors Strom Thurmond and John Tower were being re-elected, they were joined in the Senate by James McClure of Idaho, Bill Scott of Virginia and Robert Taft, Jr. of Ohio, each of whom received campaign support from many YAF members. Four new House members would eventually move up to the United States Senate: Bill Armstrong of Colorado, Steve Symms of Idaho, and Thad Cochran and Trent Lott of Mississippi. YAF members played important roles in each of those contests as they did also in the elections of Robert Huber of Michigan and Jack Conlan of Arizona.

---

143. Wayne Thorburn, "Agenda for the New Politics," *New Guard*, October 1971, pp. 12–13.
144. Editorial, *New Guard*, December 1971, p. 3.
145. Charles Black, "A Presence in History," *New Guard*, January–February 1972, p. 20.

No single congressional contest of 1972 had a more lasting effect on American politics than the campaign of broadcast editorialist Jesse Helms for the United States Senate seat from North Carolina. Jesse Helms had gained a statewide reputation as a conservative commentator for twelve years on WRAL-TV in central and eastern North Carolina. Helms became a proud advisor and supporter of Young Americans for Freedom. As he said in a broadcast editorial,

> Young Americans for Freedom reject the idea of campus takeover by students. They'll fight any guy who tries to desecrate the American Flag. They are disgusted with draft-card burners. They are concerned at the rise of communist domination around the world. They are alarmed about the apathy and indifference of so many Americans at this critical juncture in the history of the republic. These are clean, moral, intelligent young people—the kind of young people most adults wish all young people would be.[146]

It was these same YAF members, led by former North Carolina YAF state chairman Harold Herring, who would be essential to Helms's campaign for the United States Senate.

Jesse Helms had served on the Raleigh City Council for several years and had a vehicle for expressing his views on public policy through the wide-ranging coverage of WRAL-TV. In 1972, however, he was convinced to seek election statewide and attempt to become the first Republican elected to the United States Senate from North Carolina. Helms defeated two other candidates for that Republican nomination before going on to face Congressman Nick Galifianakis, who represented a congressional district in central North Carolina. Galifianakis had defeated the ailing incumbent Senator, B. Everett Jordan, in that year's Democratic primary.[147]

In that critical first Senate campaign for Jesse Helms, it was YAF members who provided key campaign staff support. Harold Herring, who had first met Helms in 1969 while promoting North Carolina YAF to the television commentator, recalls how he came to serve as campaign director for the senate nomination and general election campaigns.

> I had offered to take a leave of absence from my position as Southern Regional Representative for YAF to run Helms' youth campaign. When we met to discuss the campaign, the Senator had something larger in mind; he told me to go to Raleigh and just begin doing whatever was necessary.... Of course, Mr. [Tom] Ellis, who got the Senator to run in the first place, was named the overall Campaign Manager but he still maintained his legal office. I handled the day-to-day grunt work of the campaign. Within a week, they sent out a release announcing me as the Campaign Director.[148]

Prior to joining YAF as a regional representative, Herring had served as campaign manager for Bob Bauman's successful 1970 effort in Maryland. As Herring remembered the time, "As the campaign grew, I just began calling folks whom I'd met through YAF inviting them to work in the campaign. My first call was to Charlie

146. Reprinted in *YAF in the News*, Mid-May 1969.
147. William A. Link: *Righteous Warrior* (New York: St. Martin's Press, 2008), pp. 118–120.
148. Email to the author from Harold Herring, April 21, 2009.

Black who had been the best man in our wedding on March 4, 1972."[149] Black, who had left his position as Chapter Director for national YAF and had coordinated John Ashbrook's primary efforts in Florida, became Director of Organization.

With Herring as campaign director and Black building a grassroots structure, it was only a matter of time before other YAF members were involved in the Helms campaign. Youth coordinator was David Adcock, North Carolina YAF chairman who had been appointed to a position on the YAF National Board in the fall of 1971. Tim Baer (Florida YAF chairman) was a field representative, Jim Minarik (YAF National Director) served as director of scheduling, while Fil Aldridge (later to become a YAF regional representative and National Director) was an advance man. Bill Saracino (former California YAF chairman and then National Director) and Pat Reilly (New York YAF Western Regional Director) both served as special assistants to the candidate. Rick Miller (later North Carolina YAF chairman) and Norman Stewart (Lenoir Rhyne College YAF chairman) did research while Bev Classon Herring (a YAF leader at Rollins College) provided support to her husband and David Nolan (Duke University chairman) helped out in various areas.[150]

YAF members were also the backbone of the young volunteers in that 1972 campaign. A core group consisted of five YAF members who, according to Helms, "slept on the floor of our offices. They got up early in the morning and took their showers and dressed for the day before anyone else arrived."[151] Reflecting back on the motivation of those YAF members, Helms noted,

> For them the challenge was not about getting an individual elected, it was about adding one more conservative vote in the Senate ... These young people did not have "clout" and they certainly did not have funds, but they were more than willing to invest what they did have in energy and dedication. Their enthusiasm for conservatism was a real encouragement.[152]

One North Carolina reporter described Helms's headquarters as resembling "a Young Americans for Freedom convention."[153] Clearly, the Helms campaign was a YAF family affair.

While Herring worked with Helms's associate, Tom Ellis, on overall organization of the campaign, Black organized "Citizens for Helms" committees in all one hundred counties. With Helms's support from his broadcasting recognition in eastern North Carolina, a long-standing Republican base in the western mountain counties, and a Republican President supported by seventy percent of North Carolina voters, this was the candidate and the time for a breakthrough in the state's politics. If ever there were to be a Republican Senator from North Carolina, 1972 was the year in which it would occur.

Helms went on to win that campaign and a Republican, James Holshouser, became the party's first Governor since 1896. Without the leadership and dedication of YAF members it is possible that these victories would not have occurred. As Herring has noted,

---

149. *Ibid.*
150. 2008 YAF Alumni Survey Responses: David Brian Nolan, Sr.
151. Helms: *Here's Where I Stand* (New York: Random House, 2005), p. 54.
152. *Ibid.* p. 94.
153. Link: *Righteous Warrior*, p. 122.

On election day in November 1972, there were 21 people on our staff and the average age was 23 and a half ... At a defining moment in American political history YAF provided the foot soldiers, field commanders and headquarters' leadership for what we saw as a holy crusade. The campaign was the ultimate opportunity for us to implement everything we'd taught and been taught through the years. We elected the first Republican Senator from North Carolina since the turn of the century.[154]

The YAF connection with Jesse Helms would not end on that day in November but would continue for years. As he made his plans to go to Washington, Helms once again relied on his young supporters in YAF to help him establish his place in the United States Senate.

Among those joining the Helms Senate staff were Harold Herring as administrative assistant, at 25 reportedly the youngest in Senate history to hold that critical staff position, Charlie Black as legislative assistant, and George Dunlop (NC YAF state vice chairman) as field representative for Eastern North Carolina.[155] The Senator commented on the extent of this involvement in a 1973 address to the George Washington University YAF chapter, "So, as you can see, our campaign last year and our Senate staff this year have been delightfully infiltrated by YAF people."[156] Helms continued to be re-elected for the next thirty years, retiring in 2002 at the end of his fifth term in the United States Senate.[157] YAF had helped elect another conservative to the United States Senate and in so doing had gained an important and influential supporter for many years to come.

The emphasis on promoting new spokesmen who would go on to represent the conservative movement for many years was an important objective for Young Americans for Freedom. Moreover, the campaigns provided an opportunity to train a new cadre of campaign professionals that would influence American elections throughout the remainder of the 20th century and into the next. As one historian noted, "YAF focused on the future, using actions to attain the more important goal of capturing political power. As adults, YAF alumni and alumna were all conscious that in retrospect their time in YAF was for learning and that their actions had less important consequences than the decisions they made as adults."[158] Training young people and electing new conservative leaders to Congress ensured a continuing expansion of the conservative movement. In this way, YAF "has made its influence known in ways that proponents of other causes could only dream about."[159]

---

154. Email to the author from Harold Herring, April 21, 2009.
155. Link: *Righteous Warrior*, p. 133.
156. Jesse Helms, "YAF and the Troubled Nation," *New Guard*, July–August 1973, pp. 4–7.
157. Unfortunately, there is no comprehensive, impartial work on Helms career. His recollections were published as *Here's Where I Stand: A Memoir*. One of the few works to appear on Helms is by a liberal historian who admitted voting against him in each of his elections. See William A. Link: *Righteous Warrior*, cited above.
158. Schoenwald, "The Other Counterculture," p. 10.
159. *Ibid.* p. 11.

Which Way for Conservatives?

From the end of the 1972 election to the summer of 1974, the American people went through another calamitous time. First, Vice President Spiro Agnew was forced to resign in October 1973 under a cloud of corruption charges and a plea of no contest to failure to report income on his tax returns. Meanwhile, the nation was absorbed in the continuing unraveling of the Watergate affair and its attempted cover-up by the Nixon Administration. Finally, in August 1974 Richard Nixon boarded Marine One for his last helicopter ride from the White House and Gerald Ford, less than one year since being elevated to the vice presidency, was now the President of the United States.

Like most Americans in the days of 1973 and into the early months of 1974, YAF members were divided on their response to the charges against the President. Long opposed to what they viewed as his departure from conservative orthodoxy in both foreign and domestic policies, Nixon was not one of them and had been merely the lesser of two evils in the 1972 election. At the same time, his most vocal enemies were also their enemies. This led some in YAF to challenge what they saw as an attack on the presidency more than an attack on Nixon. YAF, through its front group Citizens Opposed to Impeachment, collected petition signatures and sponsored a series of newspaper ads under the theme, "Millions Say No to Impeachment."[160]

As Nixon departed and Ford assumed the presidency, there was some hope for change in a more conservative direction. After all, Ford had a relatively conservative voting record as a Congressman from Grand Rapids, Michigan and, while never a YAF Advisor, had supported a number of conservative positions. The honeymoon was brief. Some in the conservative movement, especially William A. Rusher, were already wondering whether there was any future for the Republican party, especially a party led by Gerald Ford. As Rusher recalled the situation, "the Republican party under Ford seemed to be going nowhere that we wanted to go, even though its relatively liberal eastern wing no longer controlled it."[161] A similar perspective was taken by YAF when the *New Guard* said of Ford, "Since his inauguration he has zealously followed the pattern of catering to the schemes of liberal-left proponents established by its predecessor."[162]

In fact, that December issue of *New Guard* had as its dramatic cover in bold letters the words: "A New Third Party: Has Its Time Come?" while inside were articles on the topic by Senator Jesse Helms, Lee Edwards, and Ron Docksai. Earlier that fall Docksai had sent an advance copy of his article to Rusher who responded by saying, "I read it with interest, and of course share your fascination with the possibility. So stimulated was I by our discussion on the subject that I wrote the enclosed column about it. I also intend to have a crack at outlining a book on the subject, though that will be a pretty large order."[163] Rusher enclosed a column discussing the possibility of a third party and soon was on his way to

160. Copies of the advertisement, fund-raising appeal, and October 1974 report on expenditures by Young America's Campaign Committee, in author's possession.

161. Rusher: *The Rise of the Right*, p. 196.

162. *New Guard*, December 1974, p. 4.

163. Letter from William A. Rusher to Ronald F. Docksai, October 15, 1974. Personal Papers of William A. Rusher, Box 26, Folder 5, Library of Congress, Washington, DC.

writing that book he described as a possible project. In early 1975, *The Making of the New Majority Party* appeared in bookstores.[164] Rusher sent a copy to Docksai with the note, "I wrote the first draft in two and a half months, between October 15th and the end of last year . . ."[165] Apparently Docksai's article, which reviewed the history of third parties in American politics, had encouraged Rusher to pursue the possibilities further.[166] The book called for the development of a new party to eventually replace what he saw as a dying GOP. Over the next several months Rusher would pursue both the development of a new party as well as the attempted takeover of an existing third party.[167]

Jesse Helms was concerned not with creating a new political party but, rather, with the realignment of the two major parties on ideological lines. As he maintained in his article in YAF's magazine, "If we are going to have honesty in government today, we must have honesty in the basic philosophies of our political parties." The challenge for Helms was "the task of realigning our existing political parties, so that the people when they go to the polls, will know what they are voting for—instead of merely whom."[168] Cautioning against the likelihood of campaign success for any new party, Lee Edwards maintained that a party seeking philosophical impact was possible but one that sought electoral impact was unlikely.[169]

With so much discussion centering on the political future of the conservative movement and whether it should attempt to pursue its goals through the existing parties or through the development of a new party, YAF brought together a group of young conservative leaders for a weekend seminar and discussion on "options for conservative political action." Thirteen YAF members met in Chicago on January 10–12, 1975 under the sponsorship of Young America's Campaign Committee. While no conclusions were sought or arrived at, the various possibilities for future political action were discussed, debated, and considered. Taking part were future YAF chairmen Jeff Kane and John Buckley, future Judge Dan Manion, political consultants Bill Saracino and Ron Pearson, and future GOP leaders Charles Black and Frank Donatelli.

Six other YAF leaders made formal presentations at the seminar that were revised and published in a book issued later in 1975.[170] Ron Docksai discussed "Building a Second Major Party," and concluded that the Republican party had failed to represent its former constituency resulting in the need for a new broad-based center-right coalition to avoid one-party government. Wayne Thorburn reviewed the decline of the Republican party over the past thirty years and pointed out the "perils, pitfalls and potentialities" in forming a new party. Robert Moffit covered "Conservatism and the New Politics of Realignment," stressing that what was needed was a more cohesive vehicle than the Republican party but certainly not a purely doctrinal party. Former National YAF Vice Chairman Daniel Rea

---

164. *The Making of the New Majority Party* (New York: Shedd & Ward, 1975).

165. Letter from William A. Rusher to Ronald F. Docksai, February 10, 1975. Personal Papers of William A. Rusher, Box 26, Folder 5, Library of Congress, Washington, DC.

166. Ronald Docksai, "Lessons from History," *New Guard*, December 1974, pp. 12–14.

167. For a discussion of these efforts see Rusher: *The Rise of the Right*, pp. 195–215.

168. Jesse Helms, "American Parties: A Time for Choosing," *New Guard*, December 1974, pp. 6–9. Interestingly enough, this same call was made some twenty-five years earlier by the Committee on Political Parties of the American Political Science Association in its *Toward a More Responsible Two-Party System* (New York: Rinehart, 1950). The trend towards responsible parties was strengthened by both the McGovern nomination of 1972 and the Reagan victories of 1980 and 1984.

169. Lee Edwards, "A Conservative Party: Has Its Time Come?" *New Guard*, December 1974, pp. 9–12.

170. Wayne Thorburn, editor: *Which Way for Conservatives?* (Baltimore: Publications Press, 1975).

addressed the issue of "Democratic Support for a New Party" and cited a number of issues on which appeals to disaffected Democrats might be made. Jerry Norton posed some doubts as to the possibilities of a new party winning in 1976 while Ron Robinson focused on elections "Beyond Presidential Politics," emphasizing that whatever path was taken in 1976, conservatives needed to continue to work in the two existing parties to have input into congressional and state politics.[171]

Following the seminar in Chicago, YAF, ACU, *Human Events* and *National Review* co-sponsored their second political action conference on February 13–15, 1975 in Washington, DC and the entire focus was on the correct path for conservatives to take as the presidential election approached. Some five hundred conservatives from across the country attended. Stan Evans, at the time Chairman of ACU, made evident his belief that a new party was needed at the presidential level but his position was rebutted by Karl Rove, then described as "a brilliant young orator," who emphasized the futility of a third party effort in presidential elections while Senator Helms spoke of the need for philosophical realignment of the two existing parties. As Daniel Oliver noted, "Certainly they were divided on how best to proceed, but not about their own dissatisfaction with the present Administration. There was very little outright support for President Ford.[172] Bill Rusher was there to drum up support for his idea of forming a new political party while Thomas Anderson of the American Party, an offshoot of the 1968 Wallace presidential campaign, attempted to recruit supporters for his third party effort. While Rusher received a welcome audience from many in attendance, Anderson's reception was less favorable and his group ended up holding a separate meeting.[173]

The closing speaker on Saturday night, introduced by Senator James Buckley, was former California Governor Ronald Reagan. If there was unanimity on any one point among those attending the conference, it was that Ronald Reagan would be their ideal candidate for President. But Reagan was not predisposed to lead a third party challenge to the existing party system. As he asked the assembled conservatives, "is it a third party we need, or is it a new and revitalized second party, raising a banner of no pale pastels, but bold colors which make it unmistakably clear where we stand on all the issues troubling the people?"[174] Despite Reagan's remarks, those attending the conference voted the next day to establish a Committee on Conservative Alternatives (COCA). Initial members included Senator Helms, Congressmen Ashbrook and Bauman, YAF Chairman Docksai, ACU Chairman Evans, Bill Rusher and Tom Winter of *Human Events*.[175]

The committee began researching ballot access laws in all the states to determine the viability of establishing a new party that could be competitive in the upcoming presidential election. While this continued, Bill Rusher's book on *The Making of the New Majority Party* appeared and, as an outgrowth of the COCA research efforts, Rusher headed up a committee dedicated to helping put the American Independent Party on the ballot in as many states as possible. Rusher

171. *Ibid.*

172. Daniel Oliver, "Taking the Initiative," *National Review*, March 14, 1975, pp. 276–278.

173. Diamond: *Road to Dominion*, p. 146.

174. Steven Hayward: *The Age of Reagan: The Fall of the Old Liberal Order—1964–1980* (Roseville, CA: Prima Publishing, 2001), p. 449.

175. R.W. Apple, Jr., "Study of 3d Party for '76 Approved by Conservatives," *New York Times*, February 17, 1975. The conference speeches of Congressmen Bauman and Ashbrook, Senators Helms and Buckley, Governor Reagan, M. Stanton Evans, Kevin Phillips, and Ron Docksai are reprinted in *New Guard*, April 1975 along with all the resolutions passed at CPAC. Also included is the motion creating the Committee on Conservative Alternatives with a list of committee members.

was supported in these efforts by a number of other conservatives, including Stan Evans, Richard Viguerie, and Howard Phillips but while Docksai remained a member of COCA, YAF's focus and energy was elsewhere.[176]

With Reagan out of office, Young America's Foundation initiated the "Reagan Radio Project" directed by Frank Donatelli, YAF's executive director, and Ron Docksai. As Craig Shirley, noted, "A long, warm relationship existed between the old actor and the young YAFers."[177] The Foundation raised contributions through the mail, in a campaign coordinated by Bruce Eberle, to sponsor a five-minute daily broadcast of political commentary by Reagan. Among the other sponsors was *Human Events*. These radio broadcasts helped to gain greater name recognition and support for the former California Governor prior to his announcement of candidacy in November 1975. After the 1976 effort, Reagan resumed his broadcasts and they continued until 1979.[178]

Reagan and the 1976 Campaign

While an exploratory committee, Citizens for Reagan, was formed in the summer of 1975, it was not until November that Reagan officially became a candidate for the Republican presidential nomination. The members of the Reagan campaign team composed a virtual "who's who" in YAF annals. In fact, "of the 40 national staff members of Citizens for Reagan, almost half of the executive staff are now or were once active YAF members."[179] Charles Black was Midwest coordinator while David Keene held the same position in the South. Loren Smith was legal counsel for the campaign and Roger Stone, a former Hi-YAF chairman in Connecticut, served as youth director. The Youth for Reagan operations in the various states were headed in most instances by YAF members, among which were National Chairman Jeff Kane as well as future YAF national chairmen John Buckley and James Lacy and future YAF executive director Robert Heckman. Former YAF Director Bruce Eberle was in charge of raising funds for the campaign.

Literally thousands of YAF members volunteered for the effort to gain the Republican presidential nomination. As Frank Donatelli noted,

> From the early days of New Hampshire and Florida, YAF members were knee deep in the Reagan campaign. They canvassed neighborhoods and universities, manned telephone banks, leafleted shopping centers, and performed a myriad of other campaign tasks. With the strict new Federal

---

176. See Rusher: *The Rise of the Right*, pp. 195–213 for their efforts to gain control of the American Independent Party, an effort that ultimately failed as the party nominated former Georgia Governor Lester Maddox, an avowed segregationist, as its presidential candidate. See also Edwards: *The Conservative Revolution*, pp. 188–191 for a discussion of this effort. YAF's opposition to Mattox and segregation was long-standing. Massachusetts YAF boycotted the 1970 New England Rally for God, Family and Country because the keynote speaker was Lester Maddox. "We have no intention whatsoever of associating with racists or racism," said Don Feder, YAF's State Chairman at the time. Samuel Brenner, "Shouting at the Rain: The Voices and Ideas of Right-Wing Anti-Communist Americanists in the Era of Modern American Conservatism, 1950–1974", doctoral dissertation, Brown University, 2009, p. 550.

177. Craig Shirley: *Reagan's Revolution* (Nashville: Nelson Current, 2005), p. 67.

178. Reagan taped more than one thousand radio addresses; each address was three minutes in length. He composed his own commentaries and some 670 handwritten drafts by Reagan have been located and catalogued. Their titles, dates, and catalog numbers can be found in Skinner, Anderson, and Anderson, editors: *Reagan, In His Own Hand*, pp. 503–525.

179. Pam Dutton, "The YAF Voice in the Reagan Campaign," *New Guard*, April 1976, pp. 16–17.

spending limitations, these volunteer efforts by YAF members were more important than ever.[180]

They performed the tedious but critical chores that define a successful campaign and these YAF members were vital elements in several states, including that first losing effort in New Hampshire as well as the first victorious primary in North Carolina.[181]

But the young conservatives were undertaking more than simply these tasks; they were using their experience in previous campaigns and conservative projects to get elected to the 1976 Republican National Convention in Kansas City. In the end, a total of ninety-three YAF members and alumni were represented on the convention floor with 45 as Delegates and 48 as Alternate Delegates. Reflective of its strength in all areas of the country, these YAF members could be found in twenty-seven different state delegations. It was no surprise that California sent 13 YAF members and Virginia 9 but the next largest groups of YAF delegates and alternates were from Massachusetts and Louisiana with 8 each and New York with 6 YAF members serving as Reagan delegates. The Pennsylvania, Washington and Minnesota delegations each had five YAF members committed to Ronald Reagan.

YAF was instrumental in leading many young conservatives to the Reagan campaign. Gary Kreep is now the president of the United States Justice Foundation and was a chapter chairman at the University of California at San Diego in the early 1970s, rising to become state chairman and National Director. For him, "YAF changed my life from one of observer to one of action in the political and social stages. It directly led me into involvement in the 1972 Ashbrook for President, and the 1976 and 1980 Reagan for President campaigns through which I met a number of now long-term friends and allies."[182] It was a similar experience for James Foster, now president of his own fundraising firm.

> I got involved with YAF on campus at the University of Texas in 1975–76. Our YAF chapter took over the Young Republicans in support of Ronald Reagan for President. As a result, I became Chairman of the College Republicans. Our YAF chapter also brought William F. Buckley to campus to speak and I vividly remember having a beer with him afterward. For such a well-known intellectual he was a very engaging personality and related well to college students.
>
> YAF introduced me to the conservative movement and broadened my perspective in my younger years. Thanks to YAF I have met and worked with many leaders of the conservative movement of the past 30 years. After working for the Republican Party of Texas (led by Wayne Thorburn), I went to work for Bruce Eberle (another YAFer) in DC, then opened my own political direct mail firm in 1983.[183]

Gary Hoitsma worked with Foster at the Republican Party of Texas in the late 70s, having moved to the state after being chapter chairman at Montclair State College in his native New Jersey. For him, the YAF experience "Provided the contacts that

---

180. Frank Donatelli, "Developing the Cadre," *New Guard*, January–February 1977, p. 15.

181. Jeffrey Kane, "The Liberation of the Conservative Movement," *New Guard*, January–February 1977, p. 14.

182. 2008 YAF Alumni Survey Responses: Gary G. Kreep.

183. 2008 YAF Alumni Survey Responses: James Foster.

led to my staff work on the 1976 and 1980 Reagan campaigns, which in turn led to my work with the Republican Party of Texas and my subsequent work in the Reagan Administration, in eight consecutive Republican National Conventions, at the NRSC, on Capitol Hill, in campaigns, in the conservative movement and beyond."[184] For seven years, Hoitsma served as press secretary and senior advisor to Senator James M. Imhofe and is now Managing Associate at the Carmen Group, Inc. in Washington, DC where one of his fellow associates is former YAF National Chairman David Keene.

Another who was activated during the Reagan campaign was Kurt Ament of the University of Minnesota. Ament believes

> YAF gave me a good introduction into the political process and the way to bring the conservative political philosophy to bear on real-life political activities. Overall, it helped me develop a coherent logical political and economic philosophy that helps to bring some order and understanding to daily news events. Now that I have two small children, I feel better prepared to help them understand the world around them and maintain standards of achievement in education.

As he recently recalled, "our group primarily directed its efforts to influence the Republican Party by attending caucuses and becoming delegates to congressional district and state conventions."[185] Their efforts paid off as Minnesota sent five YAF members to Kansas City as delegates for Reagan. David Bufkin was chairman of Vanderbilt University YAF in 1975–76 and was actively involved in the Reagan campaign at the campaign headquarters in DC. He described the volunteers for Reagan as ranging from "Ivy Leaguers to hippies to cowboys, all types."[186] Looking back on his days in YAF, Bufkin claimed, "YAF shaped my career and my entire adult life. Contacts I made there are still my friends and associates. Because of YAF I am more than just a conservative, I am a conservative who has devoted his life to building and sustaining our movement."[187] Among the other conservative and libertarian leaders who were part of that Vanderbilt YAF chapter in the mid-70s are David Boaz of the Cato Institute, Roger Ream of The Fund for American Studies, Bill Lacy of the Dole Institute of Politics, and John Lott, now Senior Research Scientist at the University of Maryland.

YAF's efforts, through its Young America's Campaign Committee, were more substantial and direct in one crucial state as, under the leadership of Ron Robinson, it established a "Reagan California Fund" to sponsor independent expenditure radio commercials featuring Effrem Zimbalist, Jr. before the important, winner-take-all, California primary where 167 delegates were at stake.[188]

As the date for the convention in Kansas City approached, it became clear that while the two candidates each were close to obtaining a majority, neither one had been able to lock up the requisite number of votes to obtain the nomination. It was in such a situation that Reagan announced his selection of Senator Richard Schweiker of Pennsylvania as his choice for Vice President. The Reagan camp hoped to swing Schweiker-supporting delegates from Pennsylvania to their cause

---

184. 2008 YAF Alumni Survey Responses: Gary Hoitsma.
185. 2008 YAF Alumni Survey Responses: Kurt R. Ament.
186. Quoted in Shirley: *Reagan's Revolution*, p. 194.
187. 2008 YAF Alumni Survey Responses: David Bufkin.
188. Shirley: *Reagan's Revolution*, p. 229.

and perhaps influence some delegates from other Northeast states. As Frank Donatelli described it, "It was the last attempt to break free the desperately needed Northeast delegates that remained elusive to the end."[189] Moreover, since Ford had been dangling the possibility of the vice presidential nomination before more than a dozen Republicans, the announcement of Schweiker would be coupled with a demand that Ford declare his own choice before the convention convened.

At first, the Schweiker selection created havoc among a number of conservatives, some of whom felt betrayed. Many YAF members were confused and uncertain. As one member told Molly Ivins at the New York YAF state convention, "First we hear no, it was a terrible thing for him to do, then we hear yes, he had to do it. I'll probably end up maybe. If it gets him the nomination, we'll live with it, but if it backfires on him, we'll know it was wrong."[190] While concerned over Schweiker's record, YAF's support for and long-term ties to Reagan overcame their initial uncertainty and the National Board issued a press release "reluctantly" praising the selection of Schweiker. As Craig Shirley noted, YAF "had been close to Reagan since the 1960s but it was one of the few conservative groups or individuals to praise Reagan's decision."[191]

It was in such a situation that more than two hundred YAF members descended on Kansas City to undertake a last minute blitz to help nominate their favored candidate for President. The YAF effort in Kansas City was coordinated by Frank Donatelli, Jeff Kane, and Ron Robinson. Before most of the volunteers arrived, YAF national vice chairman John Buckley was in Kansas City to testify before the Platform Committee. As he reminded the delegates, "Americans everywhere want most of all to be left alone. They are satisfied with, and accept the fairness of, keeping the fruits of their own labor."[192] Meanwhile, other YAF members and alumni were promoting the Reagan position before the Rules Committee, the critical arena for what would become the test procedural vote. YAF members Roy Brun of Louisiana, Dick Derham of Washington, and Wayne Thorburn of Arkansas represented their state delegations on this committee and Derham made the closing speech in favor of the Reagan position on the convention floor.

YAF had arranged for housing of its volunteers at Park College and "when housing wasn't available anywhere else, Suzanne Scholte would find one more room for a bewildered young Reaganite."[193] As expected, the largest delegations of volunteers came from New York, led by state chairman Robert Heckman, and California. They met Reagan as he arrived at the Kansas City airport and both Reagan and Schweiker at a reception held at the Alameda Hotel. Volunteers distributed literature to all the various delegation hotels spread throughout both the Missouri and Kansas suburbs. On Monday morning, New York YAFers, organized by Michelle Easton, handed out copies of the special convention issue *New Guard* to those arriving for the first convention session. That afternoon, other YAFers handed out literature and held "YAF Supports Reagan" signs at the reception sponsored by the ACU.

Monday night was the time allotted for the official YAF reception for delegates and alternatives. More than two thousand attended the event at the Hilton

---

189. Frank Donatelli, "Why Reagan Lost," *New Guard*, September–October 1976, pp. 11–13.
190. Molly Ivins, "Young Conservatives Convention Abuzz with Talk of Schweiker," *New York Times*, July 31, 1976.
191. Shirley: *Reagan's Revolution*, p. 278.
192. Robinson, "YAFers Storm Kansas City," *New Guard*, September–October 1976, p. 16.
193. Ron Robinson, "The Cause and YAF's Crescendo," *New Guard*, January–February 1977, p. 16.

Plaza Inn, including both Reagan and Schweicker as well as California delegates Efrem Zimbalist, Jr. and Pat Boone. "YAF Supports Reagan" signs could be seen everywhere. Meanwhile, New York YAF chairman Robert Heckman organized another literature distribution at convention hotels while Frances Owens, whose husband later served two terms as Governor of Colorado, and D. Richard Cobb were responsible for supervising a reception for YAF supporters in Overland Park, Kansas.[194]

Wednesday night was nominating night and the time for demonstrating support for their candidate. Ron Robinson recalled, "Countless YAFers participated in the official Reagan floor demonstration on Wednesday night. National Director Cobb had worked for weeks in advance on the plans for this demonstration. Most observers agree that it was the most spirited demonstration of the convention and political year."[195] Without a doubt, these YAF members "were witnessing the climax of the most effective challenge to an incumbent president in an intra-party struggle during this century."[196]

It would be impossible to describe the 1976 nomination effort here and others have done so already.[197] Suffice it to say that while Ronald Reagan was not successful in obtaining the nomination, falling sixty votes short in the final roll call, he had established himself as a national conservative spokesman who would be the leading candidate in a future presidential contest. As Reagan said in his bittersweet remarks to his dedicated volunteers after the convention had closed,

> The Cause goes on. Nancy and I aren't going back, to sit in a rocking chair and say that's all there is for us. We're going to stay in there and you stay in there with me—the Cause is still there. Don't give up on your ideals. Don't compromise.[198]

They did not give up. In truth, literally thousands of supporters, young and older, had been identified in every state, providing a base of support for the next campaign. YAF had been there for Reagan in 1976 and it would be there for him in 1980 also.

---

194. Cobb recalled that experience and its aftermath: "That was a tough convention where a lot of Republicans left telling me 'My heart was with Reagan but my vote went to Ford.' That year, when I voted, I wrote in the name of Ronald Reagan, and then went over to the Republican Poll Watchers and told them 'My heart was with Ford, but my vote went to Reagan!'" 2008 YAF Alumni Survey Responses: D. Richard Cobb.

195. Robinson, "YAFers Storm Kansas City," p. 17.

196. *Ibid.* p. 14. It is interesting to note that only four years later, Senator Edward Kennedy would attempt a similar challenge to a sitting President, Jimmy Carter. Kennedy's efforts, however, came nowhere near as close to success as the challenge of Ronald Reagan to Gerald Ford.

197. The most comprehensive and insightful study of the 1976 Reagan campaign is Shirley: *Reagan's Revolution: The Untold Story of the Campaign that Started It All.* Also valuable is Hayward: *The Age of Reagan*, pp. 451–484; Jules Witcover: *Marathon—The Pursuit of the Presidency 1972-1976* (New York: The Viking Press, 1977); and Elizabeth Drew: *American Journal: The Events of 1976* (New York: Vintage Books, 1976). From YAF's perspective, see Frank Donatelli, "Why Reagan Lost," *New Guard*, September–October 1976, pp. 11–13.

198. Robinson, "The Cause and YAF's Crescendo," p. 14.

12. YAF in the Seventies

"Today's YAF leaders are tomorrow's national leaders. You can't possibly understand the impact your organization has had and is having in the politics of the nation. I know this because I see it happening all over the nation . . . It proves that what began at Sharon, Connecticut in September of 1960 is having an increasingly important impact on American politics and the battle for sound Constitutional government in a system of ordered justice."[1]

While the 1970s saw Young Americans for Freedom involve itself in a wide range of campus issues and undertake even greater involvement in the political process, it was also a time of reflection, recognition, and acknowledgement of what had been achieved by the organization. After all, 1970 marked the tenth anniversary of a youth organization that had survived the traumatic prior decade and grown into a major element of the conservative movement. As testimony to its place in the movement, YAF co-sponsored a conservative awards dinner and was one of the four founding organizations responsible for the creation of the Conservative Political Action Conference in 1974, a year that also saw the young conservatives recognize the 10th anniversary of Barry Goldwater's nomination, as well as the dedication of a permanent office building.

YAF continued to hold its biennial national conventions to educate its members, obtain additional news coverage, and elect its national officers. During the latter part of the seventies, Young Americans for Freedom launched several new projects that reflected its role in the overall conservative movement, including Zero Government Growth, opposition to the Panama Canal Treaty, and the Carter Watch as it once again transitioned to operating within the environment of a Democratic administration and Congress. To accurately tell the story of Young Americans for Freedom in this transitional decade, one must begin with the YAF10 celebration and move forward to the eve of the conservative victory that would take place as the decade ended in 1980.

A Return to Sharon

Ten years after the historic meeting in Sharon, Connecticut nearly six hundred members of Young Americans for Freedom gathered at the University of Hartford to celebrate their organization's anniversary. The events were designed to not only reflect on the past and project into the future, but also to educate YAF members and train them for effective political and campus action. At the opening session on Wednesday evening, September 9th, Waggoner Carr, former Attorney General of Texas gave the keynote address. Carr "welcomed the delegates with a

---

1. From an address by Barry M. Goldwater to the YAF conference commemorating the 10th anniversary of his nomination for President, July 18, 1974, San Francisco, CA, reprinted in *New Guard*, September 1974, pp. 6–7.

ringing plea for faith in the American ideal and action in accordance with that faith."[2] He urged the young conservatives to take the offensive against campus radicals and to tell those who attempted to disrupt classes to "hit the books or hit the road."[3] Following the keynote address was a panel on "Historical Perspectives on the Conservative Movement." Later that night, and each of the three nights in Hartford, YAF members could attend workshops continuing well past midnight. Each one was led by a YAF leader or outside expert.

The second day began with an address by Dr. Donald J. Devine on the topic "Conservatism: Theory and Principles." Dr. Russell Kirk was scheduled also but could not attend and Wayne Valis, editor of the *Intercollegiate Review*, delivered his speech. Next followed four afternoon panel discussions focusing on the Constitution, the News Media, the Academy, and Political Action. Thursday evening's program featured an address by Senator Barry Goldwater. The Arizona Senator received a raucous welcome as he was greeted with cheers of "Barry in '72" and "Barry in '76," many from students who were not even teenagers when he ran for President in 1964.[4]. One who remembered that evening years later was Dick Foley: "One of my fondest memories was of the 10th reunion at Sharon ... By chance I escorted Goldwater for about an hour and had the pleasure of driving John Ashbrook back to New York City."[5] After a rousing speech from Goldwater, most of the YAFers went off to late night workshops.

Friday's program included a luncheon featuring Senator Strom Thurmond, whose speech centered on his fear that the United States was falling behind the Soviet Union in its strategic military preparedness.[6] F. Clifton White and political strategist Jerry Harkins discussed the question, "Is the Republican Party the Answer?" without reaching any definitive conclusions. The afternoon ended with David Keene moderating a panel on "YAF: This Fall and Beyond."

Dr. Philip Crane, the first YAF member to be elected to Congress, spoke on Friday night. His remarks were rather prescient, foretelling both the Reagan presidency and the Republican resurgence in Congress that was to occur in the last decade of the 20th century.

> If YAF has not been at the center of every philosophically partisan battle in the past decade, it has been very close to all of them ... It may well be that when another group of Young Americans for Freedom gathers again in 1980, they will look back upon us and upon our predecessors as the founding fathers of the new wave of conservative pre-eminence in the closing decades of this century.[7]

That evening the YAF members had the opportunity to attend more late night workshops. Clearly, with all the speakers, panelists, and other sessions there was something for every YAF member in attendance.

One of the presenters for the workshop on the conservative tradition was Dr. James B. Whisker, at the time West Virginia YAF state chairman and a young professor in the political science department at West Virginia University. Nearly forty years later, Whisker retired with a reputation for fairness and excellence. As one of

---

2. C.S. Horn, "Reunion in Sharon," *National Review*, October 6, 1970, p. 1056.
3. William Keifer, "YAF Urged to Ask Demands on SDS," *Hartford Courant*, September 10, 1970.
4. "YAF Celebrates 10th Anniversary," *Human Events*, September 26, 1970.
5. Email to the author from Dick Foley, December 15, 2008.
6. Strom Thurmond, "An Emerging Soviet Superiority," *New Guard*, September 1970, pp. 19–22.
7. Philip M. Crane, "In Ten Short Years," *New Guard*, September 1970, pp. 11–13.

his former students said, "He was one of the great ones. The man changed my life. I will be forever grateful for what he taught me, both in class and about myself. Happy retirement, sir!"[8] No better example can be found of the lasting influence of Young Americans for Freedom and the leaders it produced, individuals who contributed to the training of future generations who would assume important roles in American society firmly grounded in the traditions and principles on which our nation was founded.

Early Saturday morning, the YAF members boarded buses to Sharon for a special luncheon at the Buckley family estate, Great Elm. It was a well-behaved group of young conservatives who were in awe and proceeded with respect as they toured the estate. As one reporter observed, "the Buckleys threw their entire house open to 600 strangers. No security guards. No credentials. No rooms closed off. No one went into the huge swimming pool, naked or otherwise."[9] Once the luncheon was concluded, the delegates heard "reflections, recollections, and prognostications," by Stan Evans, John Ashbrook, James Buckley, Al Capp, and William F. Buckley, Jr. The response when Buckley rose to make his remarks was overwhelmingly one of gratitude and respect. According to one recollection, "Earlier sessions of the gathering had gone wild for Barry Goldwater, Strom Thurmond, and Philip Crane, the rugged and articulate young Illinois congressman who broke into politics through YAF, but Buckley . . . was what they had really been waiting for."[10] He reminded those young conservatives present that "the responsibility of the conservative is altogether clear: it is to defend what is best in America. At all costs. Against any enemy, foreign or domestic."[11]

Once all the speeches were concluded, it was time to commemorate the place and the occasion. YAF executive director Randal Teague had drafted language for a plaque to be installed at Great Elm and sent the proposed wording to Buckley. Buckley revised it, submitted it to Teague, and his version became engraved on the plaque that was installed in Sharon.

> On this site, on September 9–11, 1960, young Americans gathered to found an organization through which they might more effectively show their devotion to the ideals that brought forth this country. They called themselves Young Americans for Freedom, they enumerated their common beliefs in the Sharon Statement, and they returned to the communities from whence they came, to work in behalf of the principles they understood it to be the great historical mission of America to serve. This memorial is to their faith. It is mounted here prayerfully, it being our common hope that when time will have reduced these letters to dust, the freedom these young Americans strove for, will flourish in a peaceful world.[12]

The words would be engraved in 1970 but the work and efforts of these young conservatives would go on for many years more. For those who attended the Sharon 10 celebration, it was an event that would leave lasting impressions and help to motivate them to further efforts.

---

8. http://www.ratemyprofessors.com/ShowRatings.jsp?tid=88136&page=1.

9. Barbara Long, "A Day at the Buckleys: Big Blight at Great Elm," *Village Voice*, September 17, 1970.

10. Michael Kenney, "Buckley and YAF Wind Up a Decade," *Boston Globe*, September 13, 1970.

11. William F. Buckley, Jr., "Conservatism Revisted," *New Guard*, September 1970, pp. 14–18.

12. *New Guard*, September 1970, p. 35. The correspondence involving Randal Teague and Buckley is found in Personal Papers of William F. Buckley, Jr., Box 284, Folder 2490, Sterling Library, Yale University, New Haven, CT.

Ronald Docksai, soon to become YAF National Chairman, was well aware of the many sacrifices made by high school and college students to attend this ceremony and the workshops at the University of Hartford. He related in particular the story of one YAF member.

> One student, a young English history major of the University of Hawaii, informed me that he had worked at a restaurant as a waiter all summer in order to shell out the $700 needed to trade for a plane ticket with American Airlines. However, he was all smiles and offered no regrets during the four-day ceremony where he joined hundreds of other future grownups at the largest "think in" American educators could have witnessed in many moons.[13]

Another YAF member, still in high school at the time, viewed the conference as "an overwhelming success. The stimulating atmosphere provided the incentive for many Young Americans for Freedom to become outstanding conservatives in the political world."[14] As one of the senior conservatives reported, "it was unquestionably a success—testifying both to the ability and hard work of Randy Teague's national office and Jim Altham's Connecticut state YAF, and to the fact that just now, on the Tenth Anniversary, YAF is a healthy organization."[15]

Teague and Altham both viewed the celebration as more than an acknowledgement of the past. Altham, himself in his early twenties, looked at all the younger members and said, "I hope the kids learned from this that conservatism isn't only a bunch of guys sitting in a room planning strategy; there's a tradition to it and its something you can enjoy."[16] For Teague, the events in Hartford and Sharon were testimony to the central role played by Young Americans for Freedom in the growth of conservatism in America. "Let there now be no question about whether or not YAF is an integral part of the uniquely American Conservative Movement of this century, for we are."[17] The YAF members also knew they were going back to campuses where they remained a minority, but a minority now reinvigorated for the challenge of confronting the campus left. Sometimes that challenge required one to conform to the tenor of the times in order to gain more influence and impact for one's lasting and essential beliefs. Mike Yeager, a Vietnam veteran and student at the University of Connecticut, was one who was ready for the battle on campus. "In a couple of days I'll start growing a beard, letting my hair go and dig out my torn dungarees. I'll look like a radical but talk like a conservative."[18] YAF had begun its second decade looking back and now was ready to move on to new challenges.

As the 1970s proceeded, YAF continued to hold a number of major events, including the biennial regional conferences and national conventions held in odd-numbered years. The 1971 YAF National Convention in Houston was perhaps the largest in the organization's history and featured the mock presidential nominating convention where YAF clearly divorced itself from Richard Nixon. It was only one of the five national conventions held in the 1970s, however, and each one occurred following eight regional conferences earlier in the spring.

---

13. Ronald F. Docksai, "A Quiet Weekend in Connecticut," *New York Column*, September 18, 1970 in *YAF in the News*, September 1970.

14. John Cabaniss, letter to the editor, *Washington Post*, September 21, 1970 in *YAF in the News*, September 1970.

15. C.S. Horn, "Reunion in Sharon," *National Review*, October 6, 1970, p. 1056.

16. *Ibid.* p. 1057.

17. Randal C. Teague, "YAF: A Presence in the Room," *New Guard*, January–February 1971, p. 19.

18. Joseph B. Treaster, "500 Youths Plan Antiradical Crusade," *New York Times*, September 14, 1970.

For the 1973 regional conferences, YAF lined up a number of outstanding conservative speakers to be featured at each of them. First off was the New England regional conference held in Boston and coordinated by Regional Conference Chairman John Walker of Rhode Island. National Director Dan Rea of Boston University Law School was re-elected in a contest with Jim Altham. The Mid-Atlantic conference in New York City was organized by Regional Representative Herb Stupp as New York YAF state chairman Bill Bell defeated Ed Martin, also of New York, and Chuck McLenon of George Washington University. Heading farther south, YAFers met in Columbia, South Carolina while unanimously electing John Buckley of the University of Virginia to the National Board. Meeting in New Orleans, delegates to the Southwest conference re-elected Mike Connelly.

Chicago was the site for the 1973 Midwest regional conference featuring Senator John Tower and Stan Evans as speakers. In a unanimous vote, John (Baron) Von Kannon of Indiana University was elected to the National Board. Meanwhile, delegates to the Plains regional conference met in Omaha where Terry Cannon of Nebraska was elected to the Board after Mike Mulford, Iowa YAF state chairman, withdrew from the contest. Seattle was the only regional where an incumbent was defeated as Jeff Kane, Washington YAF chairman, received more votes than Roger Koopman of the University of Idaho.

The final 1973 regional conference was a major production in Pasadena, California as Western states delegates met to re-elect Pat Nolan of USC over Mike Silva of San Francisco State. Among the lineup of speakers were Los Angeles Mayor Sam Yorty and Governor Ronald Reagan at a dinner recognizing the efforts of long-time YAF supporter Mrs. Frank Seaver.[19] Delegates were treated to a second conference banquet featuring William F. Buckley, Jr. as well as remarks from YAF alumnus and California State Assemblyman Mike Antonovich.[20]

7th National Convention—Washington

The eight regional conferences were a prelude to the 1973 YAF national convention held for the first time since 1965 in the Nation's Capital. This convention came at a time of significant turmoil as the Watergate affair continued to unfold and the American military presence in Southeast Asia was winding down. In this context, YAF determined that it would put forth an expression of its faith in the country and the future. Its theme for the convention was "We Believe in America." Bill Rusher commented on the appropriateness of this declaration.

> I particularly congratulate you on your theme: "We Believe in America." There is every reason for you to do so—indeed, more reason than ever at a time when men who placed their faith in individuals or factions or parties have been so sharply disillusioned. In this as in so much else, YAF proves again that it knows how to keep its eye on the ball.[21]

---

19. Carol Thornton, "Governor Honors Mrs. Seaver," *Van Nuys Valley News* in *YAF in the News*, June 1973.

20. An interesting side note regarding the 1973 regional conferences is that three of the eight individuals elected to the National Board would go on to serve as YAF National Chairmen: Jeff Kane from the Northwest, John Buckley from the Southern region, and Terry Cannon of the Plains region.

21. Letter from William A. Rusher to Wayne Thorburn, July 26, 1973. Personal Papers of William A. Rusher, Box 173, Library of Congress, Washington, DC.

To increase local support YAF formed a Host Committee headed by Herbert Philbrick of the District of Columbia, Congressman Joel Broyhill of Virginia, and State Senator Bob Bauman of Maryland.[22] YAF also took the occasion to start "Operation Recommitment" as a program to reactivate YAF alumni. In a letter signed by all living former National Chairmen and the current one, the organization admitted that it had allowed its former members to fade away and now wished to reconnect with them.[23] A reception in honor of YAF alumni was held on Friday night at the convention followed by a private event on Saturday and an alumni luncheon meeting on Sunday.

On Wednesday, August 15th, more than nine hundred young conservatives gathered at the Sheraton-Park Hotel in Washington, DC for the opening of the 1973 YAF National Convention.[24] The first session included addresses by Congressmen Stanford Parris of Virginia and John Ashbrook of Ohio, followed by workshops on State Politics, Student Government, and High School Activities. In his speech, Ashbrook reminded the delegates that the conservative principles they espouse are the right ones and decried "loyalty to individuals rather than principles" in referring to the troubles then confronting President Nixon.[25]

Then came the workshops. Five state legislators from New York, Maryland, Virginia, South Carolina, and Louisiana who had been YAF members served as panelists to discuss involvement in state politics.[26] Mike Pikosky of American University and Todd Gardenhire of the University of Tennessee at Chattanooga chaired the student government session. Among the panelists discussing high school YAF activities was Kirby Wilbur, who maintained,

> I want to help mentor other young people, just the way I was mentored by YAF when I was in high school. That is why I love speaking at Young America's Foundation high school and college conferences. It's my small way of giving back a little bit of what I gained from my years in Young Americans for Freedom.[27]

Today, Wilbur is a frequent speaker at student conferences sponsored by Young America's Foundation, on whose Board of Directors he currently serves.

Later that afternoon, YAF members could attend various workshops and panel discussions. Christopher Manion attended the workshop on abortion and reported, "about thirty people agreed that abortion should be illegal, all for different reasons, while one girl spoke in favor and then disappeared from our midst."[28] This seemed to have been the general sentiment present in YAF; most members were pro-life but a significant minority was pro-choice. As Joe Morris recalled his time at the University of Chicago, "There were certainly 'pro-choice'

22. Letter from Broyhill, Philbrick and Bauman soliciting membership on the Host Committee, no date. Group Research Archives, Box 343, Columbia University, New York, NY.

23. Letter to YAF alumnus signed by Bob Bauman, Tom Charles Huston, Alan MacKay, David Keene, and Ron Docksai to YAF alumni, no date. Group Research Archives, Box 343, Columbia University, New York, NY.

24. The hotel is now known as the Marriott Wardman Park.

25. Linda Charlton, "Conservative Unit Seems in Doubt on Nixon's Role," *New York Times*, August 16, 1973.

26. They were Senator Owen Johnson, Delegate C.A. Porter Hopkins, Delegate George Mason Green, Representative Sherry Shealy, and Representative Woody Jenkins.

27. Kirby Wilbur telephone interview with the author, March 24, 2009.

28. Christopher Manion, "Remember," *National Review*, September 14, 1973, p. 998.

members who argued passionately for 'keeping government out of the bedroom' (and pretty much every other room). But I do believe—alas, I have retained no supporting documents—that pro-lifers were in the majority."[29]

Wednesday night began with a reception for Young Political Leaders, reached its peak with a keynote address by Bill Buckley and then concluded with delegates watching President Nixon's speech on Watergate on a special television hookup. There were mixed reactions regarding the President's involvement in the Watergate case at a time when the evidence remained murky. Gene Flynn of Brooklyn claimed Nixon should "come forward and release the tapes" of his Oval Office conversations but doubted the President was involved in the cover-up. Believing it was done by others on his staff, John Lynch of Louisiana said, "I think he should have known, should have been in touch more with his people but I don't fault him, I fault the people" on his staff. Joan Kehlhof, then a high school student who would later serve on the YAF National Board, was prescient in telling a reporter "I feel that if he did do anything that broke the law, he should be impeached." Meanwhile, Elliott Graham of Los Angeles said, "I'm in a position of being an 'I told you so' Republican. I was right and they were wrong. I know Nixon was very dishonest." But Marianna Decker of New Jersey said she and a few other delegates were taking "a gift of confidence for the President and a gift of love for Mrs. Nixon" to the White House to show their support. Clearly, while most were critical of the President on policies the verdict was still out on his involvement in the cover-up one year before his resignation.[30]

The featured speaker at Thursday's brunch was Senator Jesse Helms who had gained election the previous year with much support from members of Young Americans for Freedom. Helms told the delegates, "My loyalty, like your loyalty, is to the principles of American conservatism, not to any particular regime."[31] Thursday afternoon began with delegates choosing to attend one of three concurrent panels and presentations. "The Conservative Coalition in the Nation's Capital," "Bias in the Media," or "The Campus Left Today." Following these presentations, the foreign, domestic, and student affairs subcommittees took general testimony on the proposed platform. The hours of intense discussion and consideration of the issues resulted in a comprehensive YAF Freedom Offensive for the fall and an agenda for action well into the Seventies.[32]

Thursday night began with a reception for the National Advisory Board, followed by an address by Senator Barry Goldwater. As Christopher Manion recalled the event, "Barry was great. We were raised on him, in our hearts he was always right. An American eagle forty feet high behind him . . . And what a great speech—the big issues, the recurring message—conservative principles would have kept us out of all this."[33] When he concluded his remarks, Goldwater

29. Email from Joe Morris, June 8, 2009. Among the public policy issues discussed as part of the YAF platform, opposition to legalized abortion received the lowest level of support from the delegates and local chapters in a subsequent ratification vote. *New Guard*, March 1974, p. 7.

30. Charlton, "Conservative Unit Seems in Doubt on Nixon's Role," *New York Times*, August 16, 1973.

31. *Ibid.* p. 999.

32. "We Believe in America," *Dialogue on Liberty*, Fall 1973, published by Young Americans for Freedom. Personal Papers of Jameson Campaigne, Jr., Ottawa, IL. As it had in the past, YAF sent all convention resolutions to its chapters for ratification. All received over 90% support except for the resolutions on the Equal Rights Amendment (90% favorable), Amnesty (90%), Watergate (86%), Right to Life (70%), and the decentralization of the organization (46% favorable), the last being the only resolution to not pass. *New Guard*, March 1974, p. 7.

33. Christopher Manion, "Remember," *National Review*, September 14, 1973, p. 999.

received a resounding applause from those in attendance and then it was on to internal YAF politicking and the regional caucuses.

Friday morning's brunch session featured one who had become a fixture at YAF conventions of the day, cartoonist Al Capp, whose humorous remarks and attacks on the Left always received a positive response from YAF audiences. Then came a much more serious presentation by noted futurist Herman Kahn of the Hudson Institute. Kahn's speech was one of several academic presentations interspersed with the conservative political leaders and the internal YAF business.

It was a jam-packed schedule and Friday afternoon began with three workshops on China, the Right to Bear Arms, and YAF: Past, Present and Future. Among those taking part in the workshop on gun control was John Snyder, then a young editor of *The American Rifleman*. As he recently recalled, "YAF played a most significant part in my civic and political involvements. It was through YAF that I, as an NRA editor, met the people who became lifelong friends and associates in my professional endeavors and in many of my social ones as well."[34] These three workshops were competing with YAF's Legal Action Committee reception honoring Clarence Manion, former Dean of the Notre Dame Law School. It was out of those who were involved in the Legal Action Committee that the first stirrings in the creation of The Federalist Society took hold some years later.

That afternoon's general session was the time for presenting awards recognizing outstanding YAF state organizations as well as high school, college and community chapters and publications.[35] Next came three more workshops on community chapter issues, political action, or "The Conservative Tradition in America." This last panel had an outstanding collection of conservative academics moderated by Professor John P. East, later to serve as a United States Senator from North Carolina. He had lined up the participation of Dr. Russell Kirk and Professors James McClellan, George Carey and Donald J. Devine to discuss the roots of the American conservative movement. The day was far from over as Friday evening began with two receptions, one honoring Russell Kirk sponsored by YAF's Movement for Quality Education and the other honoring YAF alumni. At Candidate's Night they began a series of nominating speeches and demonstrations on behalf of nineteen candidates for the National Board of Directors and the unopposed Chairman Ron Docksai. After the speechmaking, another round of caucuses went on into the early morning hours.

Saturday was the time for casting votes, electing officers, and adopting a 1973 platform. A total of 678 delegates were present, slightly less than the roughly seven hundred voting in St. Louis and Houston. The contests for seats on the National Board were always lively and sometimes divisive aspects of YAF, but they did serve an important function in preparing members for later involvement in state and national politics. Kirby Wilbur reflected back on those activities and noted that, "YAF provided experiences that were most helpful in practical politics later in life. When it came to conventions, counting votes, and making deals, those of us who came up through YAF already had our training."[36]

Unlike past conventions, only four incumbent Board members—Bill Saracino of California, David Dillard of Texas, Rich Delgaudio of New York, and Todd Gardenhire of Tennessee—were slated by the YAF leadership while fifteen

---

34. 2008 YAF Alumni Survey Responses: John M. Snyder.
35. "YAF Achievements Cited," *Dialogue on Liberty*, Fall, 1973, p. 12.
36. Telephone interview with Kirby Wilbur, March 24, 2009.

candidates competed, in effect, for the other five spots to be filled on the Board. The successful candidates were John Meyer, who had previously served on the Board; Fil Aldridge, former Southern Regional Representative who had been a key player in the Helms victory of 1972; Jeff Burslem of George Washington University and DC YAF chairman; Connie Coyne of Maryland; and Fran Griffin, Illinois YAF state chairman. The 25-member board thus continued to have two female members as Coyne and Griffin replaced Louisa Porter and Mary Fisk, whose terms ended in 1973.

The most dramatic, emotional, and patriotic event at the convention was Saturday night's "Salute to American Prisoners of War," an event that also commemorated those missing in action. It was a major extravaganza put together by Dan Rea, who would soon become YAF National Vice Chairman. Hollywood star Pat O'Brien, who had made the famous comment "Win just one for the Gipper," in the film *Knute Rockne, All American,* served as master of ceremonies for a program that included thirteen returned prisoners, Colonel Joseph Cataldo, who participated in the Son Tay raid to free American POWs, and *USS Pueblo* Commander Lloyd Bucher. As reported in a YAF publication, "Pat O'Brien's emotional tribute to the POWs and his musical presentation in their honor brought the convention to its feet repeatedly, tears in every eye. O'Brien presented a huge birthday cake to 6 year old Jimmy Plowman. Jimmy's dad is one of several hundred Americans still listed as Missing in Action."[37] Following this moving recognition of American military heroes, the young delegates held a Victory Night Celebration honoring those elected as YAF's officers.

Before heading home, delegates attended a Sunday general session featuring Congressman John Rousselot and Howard Phillips. The convention ended with a State Chairman's meeting and a gathering of YAF alumni on Sunday afternoon. Two days later, YAFers learned that Bob Bauman had been elected to Congress from the 1st congressional district of Maryland. Bauman became the 99th congressional member of YAF's Advisory Board and shortly thereafter Democratic Senator James Eastland of Mississippi joined as the Board topped the 100 mark, another indication of YAF's growing stature within the conservative movement.

In reporting on the convention, one writer maintained, "YAF embodies an able, very dedicated group of young Americans. The time and the effort that the conservative community invested in YAF in its young years are paying off in its maturity."[38] Such a glowing picture might well be expected from an article in *National Review,* where indeed it did appear. What is more surprising was the following favorable comments that appeared in the *Washington Post* where its reporter saw the significance of the event as "the resilience of the organization, and the fact that 900 young people came to Washington to take part in an intensely political meeting during a non-election year—and at a time when public regard for the political process is at an ebb."[39] Despite the deteriorating situation in Vietnam and the depressing news from the White House, YAF members remained involved and dedicated to the principles on which their organization was founded. It was now thirteen years after that meeting in Sharon and few who participated in that original event remained active. By 1973, the torch clearly had passed to a new generation of young conservatives who would take the organization through the decade of the Seventies and into the Reagan Revolution.

37. "We Believe in America," *Dialogue on Liberty,* Fall 1973.
38. Christopher Manion, "Remember," p. 999.
39. Ted Frederickson, "YAF: Resilient and Resolute," *Washington Post,* August 20, 1973.

Young America's Foundation

Soon after the 1973 convention, the leadership of YAF converted an existing non-profit and tax-exempt foundation into Young America's Foundation. Throughout its history, Young Americans for Freedom had been hampered by its tax status— unable to directly endorse candidates due to its corporate organization while at the same time having to solicit contributions that provided no tax advantage to its donors. While the media attempted to portray conservative organizations such as YAF being funded by wealthy industrialists, the truth was quite different. YAF had relied on the support of thousands of individuals contributing small amounts, with an average contribution of less than $25. At various points in the organization's history, this lack of any substantial donors would result in serious financial difficulties for YAF. To overcome one of these limitations, YAF had formed a political action committee, Young America's Campaign Committee, which was able to endorse candidates as well as provide cash contributions and volunteer assistance. Now, with the formation of Young America's Foundation, the third essential element had been established.

Beginning in the fall of 1973 the new entity sponsored a series of student conferences on national defense, Southeast Asia, and the rights of the individual and the role of government.[40] From these humble beginnings, Young America's Foundation became a major player in the conservative movement. In 1975, the Foundation was a sponsor of Ronald Reagan's five times a week, five-minute radio commentary. A fundraising campaign was undertaken to put Reagan on the radio. After one year of mailings, there were 20,000 donors on the Young America's Foundation contributor list.[41] When Reagan announced for President in late 1975, that Foundation list was the first one used by the campaign. The mailing brought in a record-breaking amount for a simple single appeal and that money was used to pay postage on mailings to larger lists producing an eventual total of $7,000,000 in just seven months. As Richard Delgaudio observed, "there is just no way that all of this could have happened, except for the role of YAF through its foundation. . . . At the end the Reagan house list was 170,000 donors which built and funded the conservative cause for the next 10 years."[42]

The Foundation remained a side-note to the overall activity of Young Americans for Freedom throughout the remainder of the 1970s, undertaking projects such as the Reagan radio program, sponsoring conferences and speakers, and providing scholarships to young conservative leaders. The critical development in the Foundation's history came in late 1979 when Ron Robinson stepped down as executive director of Young Americans for Freedom and became the full-time President of Young America's Foundation. It was a tremendous leap of faith on Robinson's part that a separate organization could be established and funded. Thus began the Foundation's phenomenal growth, including its historic purchase in 1998 of "Rancho del Cielo," the western White House, from Ronald and Nancy Reagan and the subsequent establishment of the Reagan Ranch Center in down-

---

40. Letter of Wayne Thorburn to William A. Rusher, August 27, 1973. Personal Papers of William A. Rusher, Box 173, Library of Congress, Washington, DC.
41. Email to the author from Richard Delgaudio, July 22, 2008.
42. *Ibid.*

town Santa Barbara, California. Today, under the continued strong leadership of Robinson, Young America's Foundation sponsors a wide range of conferences, seminars, campus speakers, and a book distribution program to help spread a better understanding of conservative principles among America's youth. In light of its emphasis on young people, the Foundation proudly proclaims, "the conservative movement starts here."

CPAC Begins

The year 1974 was to be an important one for Young Americans for Freedom as it became a co-sponsor of the first Conservative Political Action Conference, held a major event in San Francisco commemorating the 10th anniversary of Barry Goldwater's nomination for president, and dedicated a new national headquarters in the Virginia suburbs of the Nation's Capital. It was a year of events, of YAF playing an essential role in the conservative movement, and of a shift to a greater emphasis on direct political action and involvement.

For many years the conservative publication *Human Events* had sponsored political action conferences in Washington but by the middle of the 1960s these were no longer being held. In early 1969, YAF's executive director wrote a number of conservative leaders and proposed a spring conference. In February, he wrote to Bill Buckley urging that there be a "National Conference of Conservatives."[43] While the conference was not held, in 1970 YAF joined with ACU, *National Review*, and *Human Events* to co-sponsor a Conservative Awards Dinner. The awards dinner was repeated in 1971 when Senator James Buckley was the main speaker shortly after his election.[44] Once the 1972 elections were over, YAF's executive director wrote Bill Rusher conveying the Board's interest in co-sponsoring a conservative conference.[45] Rusher met with YAF's Board at its February 1973 meeting in New York City and endorsed the idea of a jointly sponsored conference. One year later, in January 1974, the four entities co-sponsored the first Conservative Political Action Conference (CPAC).[46]

That first CPAC was held at a time when President Nixon was struggling to hold onto office and Vice President Agnew had resigned in disgrace to be replaced by Gerald Ford. Nixon did not have much support among those in attendance however. The closing banquet speaker was the one individual most in attendance wished would be running for president, Governor Ronald Reagan of California who pleaded, "Let those guilty of wrongdoing accept the consequences. But for America's sake, let's get on with the business of government."[47]

As the year proceeded, some YAF members rallied in opposition to the president's impeachment on the basis of "the enemy of my enemy is my friend" and a

---

43. Letter of David R. Jones dated January 7, 1969 to several conservative leaders; letter of Jones to William F. Buckley, Jr., dated February 17, 1969. Personal Papers of William A. Rusher, Box 46, Manuscript Division, Library of Congress, Washington, DC.

44. "New Mood in U.S. Seen by Buckley," *New York Times*, February 5, 1971.

45. Letter of Wayne Thorburn to William Rusher, January 18, 1973. Personal Papers of William A. Rusher, Box 173, Manuscript Division, Library of Congress, Washington, DC.

46. "Conservative Political Action Conference Held," *YAF in the News*, April 1974. CPAC has grown in recent years to the point where its attendance is now in the thousands, many of them high school and college students.

47. R.W. Apple, Jr., "Dismay and Outrage Over Nixon Erupt at Conservatives' Parlay," *New York Times*, January 27, 1974.

fear of the lasting effect of impeachment and removal on the nation. Still others, feeling betrayed by the president on policy as well as legal grounds, wanted him removed and hoped for the best in Vice President Gerald Ford. It would remain a long, drawn-out process until August when an impeached Nixon finally resigned.

YAF continued its emphasis on national political issues in 1974 with its ad hoc group, Youth for the Energy Solution (YES), attempting to show the role of the government in creating the energy shortage and opposing any policy of gasoline rationing. Also in 1974, YAF created Students Taking Action Against Monopoly Postal Services (STAAMPS) in support of Congressman Phil Crane's proposal to eliminate the postal service's monopoly on first class mail. University of Virginia YAF leader Mary Gingell prepared a new issues paper on the post office that was used in conjunction with the STAAMPS project. YAF also opposed the United Farm Workers boycott with counter-boycotts, debates, and speakers telling the workers' side of the story. A delegation of YAF leaders including Gary Giordano, Mary Fisk and Jeff Kane made a fact-finding trip to the San Joaquin Valley in California.[48]

Goldwater 10th Anniversary in San Francisco

It was July of 1974 and Richard Nixon's hold on the White House was quickly crumbling. Amidst the gloom of Watergate, YAF brought together a phalanx of conservatives to celebrate a happier time when their efforts had contributed to the nomination of Barry Goldwater as the Republican presidential candidate of 1964. Ten years after that momentous nomination which redirected the ideological focus of the Republican party for years to come, they met at San Francisco's Sheraton Palace Hotel—ironically the site of the Rockefeller campaign headquarters during the 1964 Republican National Convention. Many of those present were only in elementary school in 1964, but there were others who had played important roles in the nomination of Barry Goldwater or the founding of YAF, including Stan Evans, author of the Sharon Statement, and Doug Caddy, the organizer of that original meeting in September 1960.

On July 18, 1974, exactly ten years after he gave his historic acceptance speech, five hundred YAF members and supporters honored Senator Barry Goldwater at a reunion conference. They were there to recognize the individual who was responsible for changing the direction and focus of American politics because, "For them, his nomination was the high point in the lives of most living American conservatives. And they have not forgotten Y.A.F.'s role in that triumph."[49] As Arnold Steinberg, former editor of *New Guard* and political aide to Senator James Buckley recalled, "For many young conservatives like me, the Goldwater campaign was the unique blend of philosophical motivation and novice political activism we craved."[50]

Before the Senator arrived, Stan Evans read a telegram from his son, Congressman Barry M. Goldwater, Jr., that summarized the views of those present when he wrote, "Is there any question in anyone's mind tonight that my dad was right and

48. "Chavez Charges Investigated," *Dialogue on Liberty*, September 1974, pp. 6–7.

49. Douglas E. Kneeland, "Young Americans for Freedom Pay Tribute to Sen. Goldwater at Conference," *New York Times*, July 20, 1974. A copy of the conference program is found in Group Research Archives, Box 342, Columbia University, New York, NY.

50. Arnold Steinberg, "Where Were You in '64?" *National Review*, August 16, 1974, p. 917.

everyone who supported him was right? Keep up the good work and continue to stand up for America."[51] Many others sent letters and telegrams that were read to those commemorating Goldwater in person. Almost on cue after his son's letter was read, Senator Goldwater arrived with Congressman Sam Steiger of Arizona, who was to introduce him. Echoing Barry Jr.'s remarks, Steiger maintained, "In the hearts of this country they damned sure knew he was right. He's never changed. Twenty years ago he stood for conservative principles and he's still doing it."[52] Then came the five-minute ovation as their hero moved to the podium. Goldwater made due recognition of the role YAF played in both his nomination and the future of conservatism in America. He then discussed the threat inflation and excessive Federal spending posed to the nation's economy.[53]

After fondly looking back ten years, the next two days saw those in attendance focus on the future at a time when everything was uncertain. The following month would bring Gerald Ford to the presidency. Soon thereafter Nelson Rockefeller, bête noire of all conservatives, would be named Vice President and the Republicans would lose a substantial portion of their House and Senate delegations. Truly, it was a time for analysis and evaluation as to the proper path for conservatives to follow in electoral politics.[54]

Fittingly, the final event of the conference was a banquet featuring Governor Ronald Reagan who had come to national political attention in the Goldwater campaign with his televised speech, "A Time for Choosing." Reagan's welcome was "reminiscent of the Goldwater rallies of the 1960s," according to Arnie Steinberg.[55] Beginning with a retrospective on the conservative takeover of the Republican party, reviewing the various options for conservatives as the party of Richard Nixon seemed to implode, the conference ended with a message from the one who would lead them out of opposition and into the White House at the end of the decade. The symmetry was fitting.

Despite all the good feelings displayed in San Francisco towards the hero of '64, young conservatives could sometimes be unforgiving. After Gerald Ford became president, Goldwater was one of several conservatives who pledged their support to his election at a time when Reagan was still an unannounced candidate. YAF criticized the actions of Goldwater and Senator John Tower of Texas in news releases and a *New Guard* article that resulted in Tower resigning from the National Advisory Board where he had served for fifteen years.[56] In a rather bitter article, *New Guard* claimed it was time for Goldwater, Tower and Senator Carl Curtis of Nebraska—all of whom had endorsed Ford—to bow out of leadership in the conservative movement. It claimed Goldwater was supporting the Ford Administration because he "enjoys a position of stature within it and does not want to jeopardize that situation." Its conclusion was that Goldwater was no longer a leader of conservatives: "the facts about Barry Goldwater are clear: whatever his motivations, he has let conservatives down. And he leaves young conservatives no alternative but to look elsewhere for leadership, inspiration,

---

51. Kneeland, "Young Americans for Freedom Pay Tribute to Sen. Goldwater at Conference."
52. *Ibid.*
53. Barry Goldwater, "The Enemy Is Inflation," *New Guard*, September 1974, pp. 6–7. Goldwater's speech at the San Francisco conference was the featured cover article in this issue of YAF's magazine.
54. "YAF Honors Barry," *Dialogue on Liberty*, September 1974, p. 1, 4–5.
55. Steinberg, "Where Were You in '64?"
56. Tower's relationship with YAF would improve shortly after the 1976 convention and he was a speaker at both the 1977 and 1978 Southwest regional conferences.

and guidance."[57] Somewhat ironically, Alan Crawford, who was editor of *New Guard* for only four issues in 1976 and subsequently wrote a scathing attack on American conservatives, was the author of the article.[58]

YAF's attack on Goldwater and others for supporting Ford was viewed as "over the top" by some of those who had been leaders of the organization, even those who were actively supporting Reagan for the presidential nomination. Ron Docksai, a strong Reagan supporter in both 1968 and 1976, wrote to Goldwater to say he thought the Senator was getting a raw deal from conservatives and noting "Everything I read about the conservatives' newfound disenchantment with Senator Goldwater reduces to a disagreement with him for supporting President Ford." Goldwater responded with his observations on the situation a few days later,

> I made one major discovery this year and that is if you disagree with a Reagan conservative on one single point, you disagree across the board . . . Since that time I have been read out of YAF. I have been accused of every left-wing situation known to man from supporting women's lib on through the whole gamut . . . Thank you very much, Ron, for your letter and I appreciate it more than I can tell you for after having given one-third of my life to the promotion of conservative politics, I have felt somewhat let down by the attitudes of some of those who never have to stick their necks out, just their tongues and feeble minds.[59]

The following month, Docksai wrote Bill Rusher saying, "Removing Barry Goldwater from the YAF Advisory Board, speaking ill of him to newspapers, and other demonstrations of ill manners sincerely sadden me . . . The way Barry Goldwater is being treated by some people down here is spectacularly wrong."[60] When the 1976 contest ended, relations between Barry and YAF would improve, but would never be the same as the sentiments reflected at that celebration in San Francisco in 1974.

YAF's Freedom Center

On October 20, 1974, YAF took a major organizational step forward that could have led to its becoming a permanent fixture of the conservative movement. On that day, YAF dedicated its new national headquarters in Sterling, Virginia, thirty miles outside the Nation's Capital and near Dulles International Airport. After an extensive search effort led by Albert Forrester and Frank Donatelli, YAF had purchased the property in late 1973 and converted the existing ranch-style house into offices, a storeroom, and a large conference room. Called the "YAF Freedom Center," the property had the potential for future expansion to conference halls, library, and possibly a dormitory to house students attending events at the site.

---

57. "The Sunshine Boys Bow Out: Goldwater and Tower—Stage Left," *New Guard*, June 1976, pp. 7–9.
58. Alan Crawford: *Thunder on the Right* (New York: Pantheon, 1980). On page 116 of his book, Crawford discusses and attacks the position advocated in his own article for *New Guard*.
59. Letter from Ronald F. Docksai to Barry M. Goldwater dated June 14, 1976; letter from Barry M. Goldwater to Ronald F. Docksai dated June 30, 1976. Personal Papers of William A. Rusher, Box 26, Manuscript Division, Library of Congress, Washington, DC.
60. Letter from Ronald F. Docksai to William A. Rusher dated July 16, 1976. Personal Papers of William A. Rusher, Box 26, Manuscript Division, Library of Congress, Washington, DC.

Just as important, it provided a level of permanence and stability badly needed by any youth organization.[61]

It was appropriate that the featured speaker at the dedication ceremony was M. Stanton Evans, given his essential role in the founding of the organization some fourteen years earlier. Evans reminisced about the formative years of YAF and noted that while left-wing student groups had either withered or died, YAF had endured and was assuming an even more significant role in the conservative movement.[62] For the next twelve years, the YAF Freedom Center would serve as an anchor for the organization, both symbolically and practically providing a solid base for YAF operations. As Frank Donatelli reported, YAF would be spending "substantially less than our former rent payments. And what is most important, we are building equity in a long-term investment that is hard to match in today's tight money market."[63] Unfortunately, a series of decisions affecting the organization's finances resulted in the sale of this property in 1986, leaving the organization with no permanent headquarters and starting it down the road to demise as a national organization coordinating the efforts of young conservatives.

Throughout 1975, local YAF chapters continued to carry out campus and community projects, including the addition of a new program, "Zero Government Growth," a coordinated effort of advertising, pamphlets and speakers to emphasize the need to rein in government spending. The most memorable aspect of the program was a series of advertisements run in college newspapers with a picture of a hefty government employee and the slogan, "Help Starve a Feeding Bureaucrat!"[64] At the same time, it was a year of uncertainty and transition as the organization approached the upcoming presidential election. This was also the year when the freedom of the people of South Vietnam was finally lost and television viewers watched the ignominy of Americans and Vietnamese attempting to frantically latch on to helicopters as they left Saigon.

In April, District of Columbia YAF sponsored the first in a series of "roasts" of prominent conservatives, this time with M. Stanton Evans as the recipient. DC YAF chairman Steve Some and Mary Jo Werle coordinated the event that was held at the Mayflower Hotel and included Senator Strom Thurmond, Congressmen Trent Lott and Bob Bauman, and Roger Stone among those roasting Evans.[65] To assist others interested in holding such events, national YAF published a booklet, "On Planning a Dinner" by D. Richard Cobb, YAF National Director and Chairman of Rochester Community YAF.

During the spring, once again YAF held its series of eight regional conferences with an estimated fifteen hundred in attendance. Serving as speaker at one of these events was Senator Harry Byrd, Jr., who received a freedom award at the Southern regional conference in Charlottesville. In his acceptance remarks Byrd praised the work of Southern YAFers and urged them to continue to work for a strong

---

61. "Building for the Future: YAF's New Home," *1973 Annual Report: Young Americans for Freedom.* Personal Papers of Jameson Campaigne, Jr., Ottawa, IL.

62. "Evans Speaks at YAF Dedication," *Dialogue on Liberty*, December 1974, pp. 1–3.

63. Frank Donatelli, "From the Executive Director," *New Guard*, January–February 1975, p. 16.

64. Zero Government Growth was the cover topic discussed in a series of articles in *New Guard*, June 1975.

65. *New Guard*, July–August 1975, p. 32. The program for the dinner can be found in Group Research Archives, Box 341, Columbia University, New York, NY. Future DC YAF events would roast Secretary of the Treasury William Simon (1976), Senator Richard Schweiker (1977), Bob Bauman (1978) and Lyn Nofziger (1981). For the 1976 event see Patrick S. Korten, "Roasting Bill Simon," *New Guard*, June 1976, pp. 20–22.

free enterprise system.[66] It was a year for the re-election of incumbent Board members at six of these regional conferences. Elected to another term were Mike Connelly (Southwest), John Buckley (Southern), Terry Cannon (Plains), John Von Kannon (Midwest), Pat Nolan (Western) and Eric Rohrbach (Northwest) while the new members were New York state chairman Bob Heckman and Boston College chairman Peter Flaherty.

8th National Convention—Chicago

Near the end of summer 1975, just prior to the beginning of another academic year, YAF held its national convention at the McCormick Inn in downtown Chicago. The delegates were meeting at a time of transition, with Ron Docksai completing his fifth year in office and stepping aside for a new member to assume leadership. Two candidates announced for the position: Fran Griffin, an incumbent Board member and former Illinois YAF state chairman and Jeff Kane, who was Oregon YAF state chairman and a Board member. Kane ended up victorious and became the first YAF National Chairman from west of the Mississippi River.[67]

Before the delegates could elect a new chairman and nine members of the Board of Directors, there was much debate, discussion, and learning to take place. They attended workshops on building membership, influencing the campus in an era of apathy, YAF's fall offensive, and youth involvement in the 1976 elections. Thursday night brought the traditional address by Bill Buckley and a special filmed message from Ronald Reagan.[68] Friday morning's brunch saw Senator Jesse Helms speak to the efforts of the Committee on Conservative Alternatives that he headed. Saturday morning's election produced a significant change in the national leadership of the organization, with only one incumbent Board member seeking re-election. Director Jerry Norton came in first among the nine successful candidates. He was followed by Ken Boehm, Pennsylvania YAF chairman; D. Richard Cobb, chairman of Monroe County (Rochester, NY) YAF; DC YAF Chairman Steven Some; James Meadows, Texas YAF chairman; David Boaz, chairman of Kentucky YAF; Larry Penner, downstate Vice Chairman of New York YAF; Don Carpenter, chairman of University of Virginia YAF; and Terry Quist of University of Texas YAF. Quist actually tied for the ninth slot with Sam Slom, chairman of Hawaii YAF, who stepped aside for Quist and was later elected to the National Board.

It was another group of future leaders of the conservative movement that joined the YAF Board in 1975. Richard Cobb recently recalled, "I remember some wonderful political efforts, back when the Reagan Revolution was underway. There were some great success stories as well as defeats that only made us stronger."[69] For Steve Some, his time in YAF "was critical to everything I do professionally. It prepared me to undertake a career in public affairs and government relations and enabled me to fully understand the formulation of public policy and governance."[70]

---

66. "YAF Regionals Draw 1500," *Dialogue on Liberty*, Summer 1975, p. 4.
67. "YAF Convention Held in Chicago," *Dialogue on Liberty*, Fall 1975, p. 3.
68. "The Eighth Biennial Convention-Young Americans for Freedom Program," August 13–17, 1975, in author's possession.
69. 2008 YAF Alumni Survey Responses: D. Richard Cobb.
70. 2008 YAF Alumni Survey Responses: Steven E. Some.

James Meadows maintains his YAF experience "introduced me to business and political leaders I would not otherwise have met, mentors who helped me with my first job in the legislature and a scholarship to the Institute on Comparative Political and Economic Systems by the Fund for American Studies."[71] That time in YAF "caused me to see the big picture in politics and the importance of continued education and dissemination of information on the philosophical and moral basis of limited government and free markets."[72]

For Terry Quist, involvement in YAF meant "the excitement of making philosophical war on the campus left through speakers, rallies, and the independent press. The bracing fellowship with kindred souls who believed in America, believed in freedom—and had a great and sympathetic sense of humor."[73] David Boaz later became editor of *New Guard* magazine and is the author or editor of several books, including his latest book, *The Politics of Freedom*.[74] Sam Slom is now president of Smart Business Hawaii and since 1996 a member of the Hawaii State Senate.[75] At a Board meeting at the conclusion of the convention, Roy Brun of Louisiana State University and James Lacy of the University of Southern California were chosen to fill two vacancies on the Board.

Saturday afternoon included YAF's second Presidential Nominating Convention. Amidst much demonstration of excitement and support, James Lacy of the California delegation nominated Ronald Reagan with all three of the television networks filming the event. While a multitude of individuals' names were put in nomination, over two-thirds of the vote went to Reagan and by acclamation Senator James Buckley was selected as the preferred candidate for Vice President. In a resolution concerning the political tactics to be employed, they left open the door to various approaches: "If the conservative majority is unable to be represented through one or both of the present political parties, Young Americans for Freedom will support the creation of a new major political party aimed at embodying the conservative principles of the majority of the American people."[76]

Sunday was the closing day of the convention when attention was directed to debating and voting on resolutions. The delegates rejected détente, advocated a stronger defense, condemned what they perceived as a "giveaway" of the Panama Canal, supported the Republic of China and called for the continued independence of South Korea, while welcoming Vietnam refugees to the United States and supporting statehood for Puerto Rico. They also called for the abolition of mandatory student fees and the implementation of state voucher systems to ensure education choice for all students.[77] It was then time to pack up, get ready for the fall semester, and a few months later become actively involved in an attempt to nominate a conservative presidential candidate.

71. 2008 YAF Alumni Survey Responses: James Meadows.
72. Interview with James Meadows, Austin, TX, January 24, 2009.
73. 2008 YAF Alumni Survey Responses: Terry Charles Quist.
74. *The Politics of Freedom* (Washington, DC: Cato Institute, 2008).
75. Interview with Sam Slom, Honolulu, HI, May 27, 2009.
76. M. Stanton Evans, "YAF's Dilemma: Contradictions in Chicago," *National Review*, September 26, 1975, p. 1044.
77. "The 1975 Platform—Young Americans for Freedom," *Dialogue on Liberty*, Fall 1975, p. 5.

Firing Line

YAF gained some additional national publicity from the Chicago convention as eleven members of its Board of Directors, executive director Frank Donatelli and outgoing Chairman Ron Docksai were the guests on Bill Buckley's "Firing Line" television program. The subject was "The Concerns of Young Conservatives" and the discussion focused mainly on changes affecting the American campus.[78] That appearance on "Firing Line" would be the first of three such opportunities for Young Americans for Freedom throughout the decade. Each would help attract additional members, many in areas where little local YAF activity was taking place. Just as importantly, the exposure on "Firing Line" introduced the organization to more senior conservatives whose financial support made possible much of YAF's programs and publications. After his appearances in 1975 and 1977 as part of the YAF contingent, Frank Donatelli was asked to serve as a commentator on a number of "Firing Line" programs, directing questions to that week's guest.

Fall 1975 saw the National Board launch a project called the "Struggle for Human Rights" that new National Chairman Jeff Kane described as an effort to "alert the American people to the continued dangers Communism poses to the rights of all men."[79] As part of the overall effort, the November 1975 issue of *New Guard* included a number of articles on Soviet repression and featured a cover drawing of Aleksandr Solzhenitsyn as well as a reprint of the Soviet dissident's address to the AFL-CIO in New York City on July 9, 1975.[80]

The year 1976 saw Young Americans for Freedom integrally involved in a presidential campaign once again. Ronald Reagan's challenge to Gerald Ford for the Republican nomination became the focus of much attention for the first seven months of the year as has been discussed previously. But YAF continued to encourage its college chapters to take up campus issues. Community and high school chapters promoted the Zero Government Growth campaign that included a number of YAF advertisements in campus and local newspapers.

YAF also took an active role in supporting efforts to recognize the American Bicentennial. One of the more impressive projects was undertaken by Hawaii Young Americans for Freedom under the direction of state chairman and National Director Sam Slom. During the summer of 1976, they organized and sponsored a "Proud to Be an American Day" that was held in Honolulu and attracted more than 2,000 participants. The Mayor of Honolulu, Frank Fasi, issued a proclamation naming the day "I Am Proud to Be an American Day" and spoke at the celebration along with YAF National Chairman Jeff Kane. The Royal Hawaiian Band provided entertainment for the event. Hawaii YAF also sponsored a float that took part in the city's Independence Day parade.[81]

---

78. Program Number SO196, "The Concerns of Young Conservatives," taped at WTTW in Chicago on August 15, 1975. Transcript available from Hoover Institution, Stanford University, Palo Alto, CA. Those participating in the discussion were Docksai, Donatelli and the following National Directors: John Buckley (University of Virginia), Jeff Burslem (George Washington University), Terrell Cannon (University of Nebraska), Michael Connelly (Baton Rouge, LA), Robert Heckman (Adelphi University), Jeff Kane (Lewis & Clark Law), Dan Manion (South Bend, IN), Robert Moffit (University of Arizona), Jerry Norton (Washington, DC), Ronald Pearson (Washington, DC) and Eric Rohrbach (Washington State University).

79. *New Guard*, November 1975, p. 33.

80. Alexander Solzhenitsyn, "From Under the Dragon's Belly," *New Guard*, November 1975, pp. 6–13.

81. *Dialogue on Liberty*, Fall 1976, p. 3.

After the Reagan defeat in Kansas City, YAF members turned their efforts to the election contests of a number of conservative congressional candidates. They participated in the successful senatorial campaigns of Orrin Hatch in Utah, S.I. Hayakawa in California, Malcolm Wallop in Wyoming, and Harrison Schmidt in New Mexico as well as supporting a number of candidates for the House of Representatives.[82] But the major focus of much YAF activity was on the re-election effort of James Buckley in New York State.[83]

As had been the case in 1968 and 1970, the leadership of Youth for Buckley came from the ranks of YAF. Heading up the campaign was Larry Penner of Long Island University with Jay Young serving as Upstate Vice Chairman and Eugene Delgaudio as Downstate Vice Chairman.[84] Other youth leaders for the Senator included Connie Campanella and Leo Carey in Nassau County, Tony Marshall for Suffolk County, Geraldine Voelkel for Bronx, Sheldon Fosberg (Brooklyn), Duhamel Alexander Puig (Manhattan), Carol Santafede Masiello (Queens), and Kitty Higgins (Erie). Also playing key roles in the effort were Gail Marciano (Columbia University), Paul Kalka (New York University), Susan Migliaccio (Queens College), Richard Seufert, and Stuart Feigel. Many of these YAF members had been active two years earlier in the senatorial campaign of Conservative nominee Barbara Keating who had mounted a serious but unsuccessful campaign.

Just as the previous Buckley campaigns had produced many new YAF members and chapters, the same positive result came out of the 1976 effort. Stephen Didovich was a student at Long Island University and as he recently recalled, "I had a double YAF experience through Larry Penner, Bruce Kogan and Joe Gentili at L.I.U. YAF and Douglas MacArthur Republican Club with Penner, Kogan, Gentili, Sheldon Fosburg and George L. Clark, Jr." which made him "once a conservative, always a conservative." Didovich maintains "if not for YAF you would think the mainstream liberal way of solving problems was the only way to solve problems of government. The answer to our problems is not more government but less government. I'll always believe that."[85]

Nationwide, YAF undertook a coordinated fieldwork program to rebuild the chapter base and convert Youth for Reagan members into YAF activists. It was described as the "most intensive chapter development drive in their 16 year history." Field workers were sent to various campuses and communities where individual members existed but no formal YAF chapter was currently functioning. "Chapters have been formed for the first time at over 60 priority campuses and in communities previously without the young conservative alternative."[86]

The election of November 1976 not only saw Buckley's loss but also the election of Jimmy Carter as President of the United States. No longer did YAF confront a GOP President who, while popularly perceived as a conservative, had been undertaking policies contrary to YAF's views. Once again there would be a Democratic occupant of the White House, one who was elected with significant religious right support and came from the South. Despite this background, YAF anticipated that he would be moving to the Left once in office and facing a large Democratic majority in both the House and Senate. It was in this context that YAF announced its "Carter Watch" program in late November, vowing to closely

---

82. John T. Dolan, "Rising Stars in the West," *New Guard*, December 1976, pp. 8–9.
83. "New York YAFers and the Buckley Campaign, *New Guard*, November 1976, p. 23.
84. For a report on the 1976 Youth for Buckley see Larry Penner and Eugene Delgaudio, Jr., "New York Loses a Senator," *New Guard*, January–February 1977, pp. 22–24.
85. 2008 YAF Alumni Survey Responses: Stephen Didovich.
86. "YAF Chapter Development on Upsurge," *Dialogue on Liberty*, Fall 1976, pp. 1, 10.

monitor the actions of the new President and committed to speaking out when his proposals, appointments and policies were perceived as counter to conservative principles. Over the next four years, the Carter White House would provide ample opportunities for YAF to take an oppositional stand.[87]

Under the editorship of David Boaz, who had taken the helm of *New Guard* with the December 1976 issue, the magazine took on a new, clean graphics appearance and a number of lively new components. Over the spring semester, the magazine featured exclusive interviews with several important names in the news. National Director Sam Slom interviewed Karl Hess while Greg McDonald, Northwest Regional Representative, interviewed Dr. Milton Friedman and Cliff White, chairman of George Washington University YAF, asked questions of Senator Richard Schweiker.[88]

Also appearing in 1977 were two cover feature satirical articles by Brad Linaweaver, part of a trilogy that would be completed in the Winter 1978 issue of *New Guard*. He would subsequently become a well-known science fiction author of novels including *Moon of Ice, Sliders*, and *The Land Beyond Summer* and collaborator on several others. Linaweaver's stories in *New Guard* introduced his work to both Bill Buckley and Ronald Reagan. As he recalled, "the most amazing result of my YAF years is that Ronald Reagan did an entire radio commentary on an article of mine that appeared in *New Guard*. That piece ended up in the book *Stories in His Own Hand: The Everyday Wisdom of Ronald Reagan*."[89] Linaweaver was involved with YAF at Florida State, Penn State and Rollins College throughout the 1970s and, as he recently said, "in other words, YAF was a very important part of my life."[90] Another YAF member whose reviews appeared frequently was Haven Bradford Gow, a freelance writer who was active in the Boston College YAF chapter.[91]

An emphasis on leadership development was continuing throughout the 1970s. Jim Marshall was a student at Boise State University and recently summarized his experience when he said "YAF provided me with a structure and network to advance conservatism." Marshall went on to be a field representative for the National Right-to-Work Committee, chief of staff for the Oklahoma Department of Labor, and now Deputy County Commissioner in Oklahoma City.[92] It was a similar experience for John Uible of Denison University that "made me more conservative and certainly reinforced my principles, gave me a greater appreciation for those serving in public office and a sensitivity to the conservative point of view on public issues." Now a bank vice president, Uible has served on his city council and the central committee for his political party.[93]

From its earliest days, while the organization had promoted the development of local chapters it had also emphasized the range of "Committee of One" projects

---

87. "YAF Begins Carter Watch," *Dialogue on Liberty*, December 1976, p. 1.

88. The Hess interview is on pp. 6–9 of the March 1977 issue; Friedman's discussion is on pp. 6–10 of the April issue; Schweiker's interview appears on pp. 6–9 of the June issue.

89. Brad Linaweaver email to the author, November 6, 2008. Linaweaver's *New Guard* articles are "A Scandal in Transylvania," May 1977, pp. 6–8; "The Adventure of the Dancing YAFers," September 1977, pp. 10–11; and "Détente Is Forever," Winter 1978, pp. 37–39. Reagan's reference to the Linaweaver article is on p. 89–92 of Kirin K. Skinner, Annelise Anderson, and Martin Anderson, editors: *Stories in His Own Hand: The Everyday Wisdom of Ronald Reagan* (New York: Free Press, 2001).

90. *Ibid.*

91. 2008 YAF Alumni Survey Responses: Haven Bradford Gow.

92. 2008 YAF Alumni Survey Responses: Jim Marshall.

93. 2008 YAF Alumni Survey Responses: John B. Uible.

that individual members could undertake. As Ron Robinson noted, "No YAF project has ever had sustained success until it was picked up by YAF members and carried on in their local papers, on talk shows, through film showings, and by the numerous other committee-of-one activities."[94] With fewer chapters than at earlier times, it was important to remind the membership of the opportunities for individual action. However, as the fall semester started, YAF called upon three of its college chairmen to discuss the need and the opportunity for forming chapters. Karol Lamos from the University of Virginia explained her chapter's role in responding to the leftist domination of the official campus newspaper. Ken Reis, chairman at Washington State University, discussed his chapter's program of distributing issues papers to liberal arts faculty in an effort to present the conservative alternative to liberal bias in political science classes. Vanderbilt's Robert Proctor stressed what he viewed as the philosophical arguments that YAF should make on campus. To him, conservatism is idealistic in its belief that individuals can make their own decisions and are responsible for their own destiny.[95]

The push for forming new chapters even appealed to some who had previously held leadership positions in the organization. In May 1977, former National Chairman Ron Docksai started the Capitol Hill Community Chapter, described as "the newest oldest chapter in the nation." Docksai was at the time on the staff of Congressman Bob Bauman. The chapter's members included Christopher Buckley, son of Bill Buckley and now a noted novelist; T. Coleman Andrews, III, who became one of the founders of Bain Capital with Mitt Romney; Linda Love, former California YAF activist who was executive secretary to Congressman Robert Dornan; Timothy Wheeler, an active conservative journalist and founder of *Rally* magazine who passed away in 2007; and Douglas Bulcao, a government relations specialist.[96]

Spring 1977 saw the last regional conferences to be held in odd-numbered years as the National Board voted to move these conferences to even-numbered years beginning in 1978. Once again, YAF had arranged for a stellar lineup of speakers. Among those on the program at this round of regional conferences were Senators John Tower, Paul Laxalt, Richard Schweiker and Harrison Schmidt, Governor Meldrim Thompson, Congressmen Dan Marriott, John Duncan, Steve Symms, Robert K. Dornan, Del Clawson, and Phil Crane, along with a long list of journalists and academics. Highlight of the Mid-Atlantic conference was another roast coordinated by the District of Columbia YAF. This time the subject was Schweiker and before all the fun began there was a gracious amplified telephone call from Governor and Mrs. Reagan to the Senator who had been his choice for vice president one year earlier. Among the roasters were former Senator Jim Buckley and speechwriter Vic Gold as well as Reagan campaign leaders John Sears, Lyn Nofziger, and Ray Barnhart. Jointly serving as masters of ceremonies were YAF executive director Frank Donatelli and Young Republican National Chairman Roger Stone.[97]

---

94. Ron Robinson, "A Program for the Individual," *New Guard*, May 1977, pp. 18–20.

95. "Why YAF? Conservatism and Young People," *New Guard*, September 1977, pp. 18–19.

96. The list of members is found in an undated note from Docksai to Buckley. Personal Papers of William F. Buckley, Jr., Box 127, Sterling Library, Yale University, New Haven, CT.

97. News release from District of Columbia YAF, no date. Group Research Archives, Box 342, Columbia University, New York, NY.

When the delegates met to decide who would represent the various regions on the National Board, five incumbents were re-elected: Peter Flaherty, Larry Penner, Roy Brun, Terry Cannon, and Eric Rohrbach. Only Rohrbach was opposed as he defeated Steve Jeske of Pacific Lutheran University in Seattle. For the open seats, Southern region YAFers unanimously chose William B. Lacy, a law student at the University of Tennessee, while in the Western region Pat Geary of UC–Irvine defeated Leon Waszak of Cal State–Los Angeles and, in the closest contest, Ohio YAF chairman Dennis Bechtel edged out Illinois YAF chairman Fred Dempsey to represent the Midwest region.[98]

9th National Convention—New York City

New York City had been the site of YAF's first national convention and now, fifteen years later, the organization returned to Gotham for its ninth biennial convention. This year the convention theme was "Freedom—Not Socialism" and a large banner proclaiming it was placed immediately behind the podium to maximize press coverage of its message. The 1977 event was a rebound for the organization with an increase of nearly 25% in voting delegates over the previous convention. Almost 500 delegates participated in the YAF elections while a total of nearly 850 attended various convention activities.[99] Holding a convention in New York City had multiple benefits as all the news services, the major daily newspapers, and even *Time* magazine covered parts of the week's events.[100]

Wednesday, August 24th provided the attendees with a choice among a series of workshops focusing on organizational and leadership development, a Conservative Film Festival, and addresses by former Senator James Buckley and Congressman Jack Kemp. Frederick Dempsey, Illinois YAF chairman, reported

> Jim Buckley's speech was personal and reflective, and he spoke to YAF as a father who is proud of his sons. He reminisced about YAF's founding in Sharon, urged the organization to greater activity, and restated his own devotion to the principles of the Sharon Statement—which Statement, he said, cast in bronze, is permanently embedded in an old well at Great Elm.[101]

As Dempsey concluded, among YAFers there was agreement that if men were angels, they would all be like Jim Buckley. Jack Kemp was once again the quarterback, "leading the team against creeping socialism in America—not, he warned, nationalization of the means of production (though that too may occur), but socialization of the ends of production."[102]

For Dempsey, Thursday "may well be remembered as one of YAF's finest."[103] It started with a breakfast address by former Treasury Secretary William Simon who maintained President Carter was more interested in his image than the substance of running the country. According to Simon, "this is not leadership, it's followship."[104] A series of panels and platform testimony occupied the delegates

98. Frances Owens, "Two Thousand Participate in Regionals," *Dialogue on Liberty*, June 1977, p. 4.
99. Memo from Executive Director to National Directors, September 12, 1977, in author's possession.
100. See especially "Carter's Dog-Day Afternoons, *Time*, September 5, 1977, p. 12.
101. Frederick R. Dempsey, "Wisdom in New York," *National Review*, September 16, 1977, p. 1052.
102. *Ibid.*
103. *Ibid.*
104. "Simon Takes Slap at Carter," *Oklahoma City Times*, August 25, 1977.

throughout the remainder of the day. One of the highlights of the convention took place that night as Congressman Robert Dorman served as emcee, Illinois Representative Phil Crane was the introductory speaker and former Governor Reagan addressed those in attendance. Ambassadors Sol Linowitz and Ellsworth Bunker had earlier in the day briefed Reagan on the proposed Panama Canal treaties and his position on the treaties would be the most significant part of his remarks to the delegates.[105]

When Ronald and Nancy Reagan arrived at the dais, those in the audience broke out into ten minutes of applause, cheers and stomping. As Dempsey reported, "Where else but at a YAF convention is there so concentrated a group of loyal, admiring Reagan disciples? Nowhere; and Reagan repaid YAF's devotion by delivering a speech that put their convention on the front page of the *New York Times.*"[106] In his speech, widely covered by the media, Reagan declared that the Senate should refuse to approve the treaties designed to turn over control of the canal to Panama. A report from one news wire service noted, "Reagan told several hundred cheering people at the Young Americans for Freedom convention Thursday night at the Statler Hilton Hotel, 'I do not believe we should ratify this treaty.' The young conservatives jumped to their feet and chanted, 'Keep our canal!'"[107] To no one's surprise, the delegates later passed a resolution strongly opposing the treaties as part of their platform.

Friday started with remarks by Congressman John Ashbrook at a breakfast session. The delegates gave him a standing ovation. Saturday morning brought forth the unanimous election of John Buckley as the new National Chairman. A first cousin of Bill and Jim Buckley, he was a graduate of the University of Virginia and had held nearly every position in the organization, starting as a high school member in his home state of Louisiana.[108] Six of the current Board members were re-elected at the convention while three new members joined them. Those returned for another term were D. Richard Cobb, Terry Quist, Coby Pieper, James Meadows, Sam Slom, and Steve Some. The three new members were Cliff White, Eugene Delgaudio, and Roger Ream, a recent graduate of Vanderbilt University.[109]

After the elections, the delegates debated and approved various platform planks. Perhaps the most controversial was one favoring the decriminalization of marijuana. Avoiding what might have been a divisive stance, the resolution was tabled. The organization received significant positive media attention, however, from its stands regarding Israel. Former National Director Steve Loewy, now an attorney in the Maryland suburbs of the Nation's Capital, prepared a detailed report on the convention that appeared in a number of Jewish weekly publications across the country. He cited resolutions affirming YAF's "fundamental support for a militarily strong Israel capable of preserving peace by resisting attack" and claiming that "the forced return of Israel to its pre-1967 borders would only encourage Arab and Communist aggression."[110] In another, more detailed discussion of conservative support for Israel, Loewy interviewed Ron Robinson, who would become executive director of YAF after the 1977 convention. According to Robinson, who had visited Egypt and Israel recently, "Conservatives have a basic support for the position of Israel in the Middle East. This is in part because Israel is treated as

105. "Reagan Fears Canal Treaty," *Chattanooga News-Free Press*, August 26, 1977.
106. Dempsey, "Wisdom in New York," p. 1052.
107. "Reagan Inspires 'Keep Our Canal' Cheer," *Chicago Daily News*, August 26, 1977.
108. Jean Korten, "Buckley Elected President of YAF," *Vienna Connection*, September 16, 1977.
109. "New YAF Leaders Chosen," *New Guard*, December 1977, p. 23.
110. "Young Conservatives Back Israel," *Jewish Herald Voice* (Houston, TX), September 15, 1977.

an ally in a consistent two-way relationship and because it represents many of the American ideals."[111]

The delegates also passed resolutions criticizing UN Ambassador Andrew Young and calling for a stronger defense posture. Consistent with the convention theme of "Freedom—Not Socialism," they called for the abolition of tariffs, subsidies, licenses, zoning regulations and agricultural acreage allotments, and the elimination of Federal regulatory bodies. In his closing speech, Kane observed, "the lunacies of the planned society are becoming apparent to many of our peers."[112]

After electing their leaders and debating the serious issues of the day, it was time to let down their hair and attend a roast of YAF's godfather.[113] Taking part in the satirical salute to Bill Buckley was a disparate group of individuals. From the right came Congressman Henry Hyde, Bill Rusher, Stan Evans and David Keene. From the left was Allard Lowenstein. Representing the media was CBS News broadcaster Mike Wallace. And somewhere in the universe was Dr. Henry Kissinger. While most of the comments were directed at Buckley, several were focused on the other participants.[114]

As had been the case two years earlier, a group of YAF leaders were invited to participate as guests on "Firing Line" which was taped in New York on August 29th. Taking part were new national chairman John Buckley, and directors Dennis Bechtel, Robert Heckman, and James Lacy along with outgoing executive director Frank Donatelli and his replacement, Ron Robinson, and national staff member Michelle Easton. The program was broadcast in early September and provided additional national media coverage for YAF, resulting in several inquiries for membership information and new contributors.

With the year 1977 coming to a close, new executive director Ron Robinson looked back on the history of YAF and its continuing mission. Building new leaders for the future took precedence even over the temporary impact on present-day issues. According to Robinson, "YAF has succeeded in its primary function. We have developed an excellent cadre of conservative leaders who recognized that through hard work and continued dedication they could have a profound impact on the future of their country."[115] None of this could happen without the involvement of individual members throughout the country, as well as the "financial mentors" whose contributions made possible the efforts of the national organization and its local chapters. While it was a loose confederation of young conservatives, in the end it was the efforts of individuals that produced new leaders. As Robinson noted, "YAF's challenge is ultimately a personal one. Each of us must rededicate ourselves to making our maximum contribution to continuing the "loose confederation," in building the crucial conservative cadre."[116] Clearly, as YAF entered another challenging year its leadership was aware of the need to focus on the future and the development of those leadership traits that would help produce conservative activists for many years into the future.

---

111. Steve Loewy, "U.S. Right Warms Up To Israel," *Jewish Herald* (Providence, RI), September 8, 1977.

112. Eric Pace, "Young Conservatives Elect a Buckley as Leader," *New York Times*, August 28, 1977.

113. "Buckley, Kissinger Are 'Roasted' at Convention," *Houston Chronicle*, August 29, 1977.

114. Marc Rosenwasser, "Conservative Cohorts Liberally 'Roast' Buckley," *Portland Oregonian*, August 29, 1977.

115. Ron Robinson, "YAF and the Movement," *New Guard*, February 1978, p. 14.

116. *Ibid.* p. 15.

Affirmative Action and Other Issues

During the fall of 1977 and all of 1978, YAF emphasized a number of campus issues. Many chapters called for the abolition of mandatory student fees, or at least limits on the use of those fees for political purposes. At the University of Nebraska, YAF was able to convince the Board of Regents to restrict the use of such fees to non-political purposes while at the University of Texas the YAF chapter backed a student referendum that voted to eliminate student government.

Somewhat indicative of the aging of many YAF leaders, more efforts were directed towards retaining and activating law school students. YAF's legal affairs committee continued distribution of its newsletter, *Amicus Curiae*, and involved its law student members in projects to take legal action on various issues. John Kwapisz, a YAF activist at the University of Wisconsin Law School, was instrumental in forming a conservative law students association and led the effort to expand it nationwide. This drive eventually culminated in the formation of The Federalist Society.

Perhaps the major campus-oriented campaign during late 1977 and throughout 1978, however, was YAF's project in support of Alan Bakke's effort to strike down affirmative action and gain admission to medical school. The University of California at Davis Medical School had established an admissions policy where 16 of a total of 100 spots were set aside for disadvantaged minority applicants. Bakke, a Caucasian, applied in both 1973 and 1974 and was denied admission even though his scores on the Medical College Admission Test were higher than some admitted under the special admissions program. Bakke filed suit against the Regents of the University of California and, while the trial court declared the special program violated the Federal and State constitutions, it did not order the admission of Bakke to the medical school. On appeal, the California Supreme Court commented only on what it viewed as a violation of the equal protection clause of the 14th amendment and declared that since UC–Davis could not prove that absent the special program Bakke would not be admitted, the Court ordered his admission. This decision was appealed to the United States Supreme Court, which granted certiorari.[117]

As the controversy developed and before the Supreme Court had issued its opinion, YAF strongly supported Bakke. YAF rounded up support for the potential medical student's position on campuses across the country.[118] Local chapters made use of an issues paper, "Bakke: The Case Against Discrimination," and the organization's magazine featured a review of the main issues at hand prepared by a YAF member from the University of Kentucky Law School.[119] Meanwhile, YAF retained attorney Marco DeFunis, who had brought the first significant case challenging affirmative action against the University of Washington Law School in 1971, to prepare its amicus curiae brief for submission to the Supreme Court.[120] The brief maintained that the practice of establishing quotas and giving

---

117. *Regents of the University of California* v. *Bakke*, 438 U.S. 265 (1978).
118. "Students Back Bakke," *Dialogue on Liberty*, Winter 1977, p. 6.
119. John F. Zink, "The Legal Issues of Reverse Discrimination," *New Guard*, November–December 1977, pp. 6–8.
120. For the relationship between the two cases see: Allan P. Sindler: *Bakke, DeFunis and Minority*

preference to minority groups violated the equal protection clause and that the Constitution requires neutral equality rather than race-conscious equality.[121] As Frank Donatelli, YAF's executive director and a law student, explained, "in our judgment, affirmative action attempts to guarantee equality of result, not equality of opportunity."[122]

While national YAF had filed its amicus curiae brief with the Supreme Court, distributed an issues paper on the topic, and created an Affirmative Action Task Force, local chapters were carrying out their own complementary activities.[123] The University of Toledo YAF, led by Cliff Kincaid, sponsored a symposium on the Bakke case that resulted in YAF members appearing on television talk shows while YAF leader Gary Kreep debated an attorney for the National Association for the Advancement of Colored People (NAACP) at California State University–Long Beach and YAF chapter chairman Neil Nahser took part in a similar debate at Georgia State University.[124] Meanwhile, the Columbia YAF chapter participated in a symposium on affirmative action, including YAF members Frank Connolly, Lou Antonelli, Kevin Kennedy, David Hecht, and Frank Mann. At the University of Hartford, YAF chairman Barry Miller brought in Bob Heckman of the national YAF staff to speak on the Bakke case and received considerable media coverage.[125]

When the Supreme Court issued its opinion ordering the admission of Alan Bakke to the Medical School but upholding the use of race as a consideration in admissions decisions, YAF swung into action once again. As *New Guard* reported, "Minutes after the decision was announced, YAF was on the scene at the Supreme Court building telling the press that we applauded the decision to admit Bakke to medical school but were disappointed that race may still be allowed as a criteria in admissions practices."[126] Two days later, John Buckley held a news conference that received wide coverage. Across the country, other YAF leaders held similar conferences and issued press releases, including Jim Lacy and Gary Kreep in California; Tom Waters in Georgia; Robert Dolan, Ken Grasso and Gordon DeLetto in New York; Tim Rader in Ohio; Steve Antosh in Oklahoma; Les Bloom in South Carolina; Mark Agee in Tennessee; and Steve Munisteri in Texas. This media outreach was followed by a Capitol Hill seminar on affirmative action in July that was coordinated by Ken Boehm and Cliff White and attended by 150 congressional interns and staff.

YAF's task force issued a lengthy report outlining the organization's reasons for opposing affirmative action and restating its belief in individual rights. Congressman James Collins of Texas chaired an advisory board consisting of faculty, attorneys, legislators, and public policy specialists.[127] As Cliff White described the ongoing project, "The YAF Task Force will seek ways of preventing

---

Admissions: The Quest for Equal Opportunity (Old Tappan, NJ: MacMillan Publishing Co., 1978).

121. "Bakke Reverse Bias Case Backed by Young Americans for Freedom," *New York Times*, August 28, 1977.

122. Steven V. Roberts, "Longtime Allies on Rights Split by Bakke Case," *New York Times*, September 25, 1977.

123. The issues paper, "Bakke: The Case Against Discrimination," was prepared by Robert Heckman of the national YAF staff and reprinted in *Dialogue on Liberty*, Spring 1978, p. 6. See also, John Parker, "Affirmative Action and the American Dream," *New Guard Bulletin*, October 1978, p. 7.

124. *New Guard*, May 1978, p. 25.

125. *New Guard*, June 1978, pp. 23–24.

126. "YAF Begins Post-Bakke Effort," *New Guard*, September 1978, p. 22.

127. The 102-page report can be found in *Task Force Report on Affirmative Action* (Sterling, VA: Young Americans for Freedom, 1978).

the federal government from continuing to require quotas as a condition for receipt of federal grants and contracts." He emphasized that "YAF is committed to guaranteeing the right of every citizen to be judged without regard to race."[128] The report discussed the question of what could be done to assist minorities in attaining more equitable participation in society and possible legislation to eliminate other forms of group classification and discrimination. YAF would continue to stress the importance of the individual and oppose efforts to classify people as members of specific groups in society.

A second major concern of YAF during 1978 was the efforts of the Carter Administration to obtain Senate approval of a series of new treaties that would cede control of the Panama Canal and the Panama Canal Zone to the nation of Panama. YAF's position had been made official at the 1977 national convention. That fall, YAF held a rally outside the Pan American Union building; Georgetown University YAF sponsored a debate on the treaty between Congressmen Philip Crane and Paul Simon, both of Illinois; and national YAF projects director Ken Boehm testified against the treaty before the Senate Foreign Relations Committee.[129]

Across the country local chapters put pressure on their senators to oppose the treaty. The University of Tennessee chapter hired a plane to fly over the UT–Memphis State football game with the banner: "Keep Our Canal—Write Sen. Baker;" and then later in the spring, led by chairman William Hawkins, a group of UT YAFers picketed outside the hall where Ellsworth Bunker was giving a speech favoring the Canal treaties. Meanwhile, Indianapolis YAF, led by Rich Loy, collected petitions opposing the treaty and delivered them to Senator Birch Bayh while Texas A&M University YAFers Mark Elam and John Weaver flew to DC to present 10,000 signatures opposing the treaty to Senator Lloyd Bentsen. Other YAF leaders took the anti-treaty position in campus debates, including Robert E.A.P. Ritholz at the University of Wisconsin, Jeff McKinney and Joe Curren at Ohio University, and Bob Rybka at Wittenberg College. Hawaii YAF made a strong push against the treaties as State Chairman Sam Slom and Honolulu YAF leader Steve Rohrmayr arranged for Congressman Phil Crane to give a major speech opposing the treaty.[130]

Phill Linderman, Georgia YAF state chairman, led twenty YAFers in a demonstration outside a dinner attended by Georgia's United States Senators Sam Nunn and Herman Talmadge, and worked with Newt Gingrich against ratification of the treaty. Linderman recalled campaigning also against the SALT II treaty with Congressman Larry McDonald, protesting Communist Chinese vice premier Deng's visit to Atlanta, the Jane Fonda lecture tour, and the drive to free the hostages in Iran as well as issuing a ratings report on the Georgia Legislature. As he summarized his experience, "Without YAF I could not have been part of the organized conservative movement. I am profoundly grateful for what YAF did for me. I gave YAF much—it was in many ways the center of my life in the late 1970s—but I was immensely rewarded."[131] Another who was involved in

---

128. Cliff White, "Affirmative Action Task Force Undertakes Additional Projects," *Dialogue on Liberty*, Fall 1978, p. 5. See also, "YAF Task Force Fights to End Racial Quotas," *New Guard Bulletin*, October 1978, p. 1.
129. *New Guard*, January 1978, p. 20.
130. *New Guard*, March–April 1978, p. 24; May 1978, p. 25; June 1978, p. 23.
131. 2008 YAF Alumni Survey Responses: Phillip Linderman.

YAF during this time period was Daria Novak, chairman of the YAF chapter at Mary Washington College. Novak was a Reagan delegate to the 1976 Republican National Convention and is now completing her work on a PhD. Novak saw her experiences in YAF as "developing critical thinking skills, leadership mentoring, and finding others who shared my beliefs on the correct path for the country."[132]

In a related foreign policy project, YAF continued an effort against East–West trade that had brought them success and much national publicity in the 1960s. As more and more American companies began selling computers, missile guidance parts and advanced technology to the Soviet Union—all with the support of the Carter Administration—YAF once again pointed out the folly of trading with the enemy. One focal point was N.L. Industries, a company that had signed a contract for engineering and technology used in the offshore production of gas and oil. When the company held its 1978 stockholders' meeting, Kelly Kehrer, vice chairman of Texas YAF, spoke against the company's policy while other YAFers handed out flyers explaining the reasons for opposing the deal.[133] YAF followed this in 1979 by working with Phillips Publishing and introducing resolutions at the stockholders' meetings of General Electric, Control Data, and IBM—all of which were selling or negotiating to sell highly technical equipment to the Soviet Union and Communist China.[134] When IBM held its stockholders' meeting in San Diego, California YAF distributed a flyer to all attendees calling for passage of a resolution to halt the company's sales to Communist nations. Though unsuccessful, the efforts informed stockholders of the IBM policy of trading with the Communists.[135]

Throughout the year, YAF continued to emphasize national policy issues. When the United States Postal Service raised first class rates to 15 cents, YAF launched a national protest on what they called "Postal Competition Day." Among the YAF leaders organizing protests outside post offices and issuing news releases were Charles Orndorff in Charlottesville, Virginia; Greg McDonald in Seattle; Sally Cromwell and Vickie Bezanilla in the District of Columbia; David Graham in Kansas City; Larry Penner and Eugene Delgaudio in New York City; Paul Novelanko in Great Falls, Montana; Mark Travis in Denver; Doug Kagan in Omaha, Bill Butterly in Hartford; and Gayle Dean in Savannah.[136] YAF was more successful in advocating deregulation of the commercial airline industry. National directors Roger Ream and Cliff White, along with DC chairman Sally Cromwell, led the effort to contact members of Congress and push for deregulation, an effort that finally brought about greater competition and increased service in airline travel.

YAF's first series of regional conferences held in even-numbered years took place in the spring of 1978. First off was the Mid-Atlantic regional where Ken Grasso defeated incumbent Board member Eugene Delgaudio. Next came the Southern conference where Democratic Congressman Larry McDonald, and YAF alumni Peter Braithwaite and Dr. Roger Pilon were featured speakers. Georgia state chairman Mitch Skandalakis was elected to the National Board. The New England regional featured some non-traditional program highlights

132. 2008 YAF Alumni Survey Responses: Daria I. Novak.

133. Ken Boehm, "YAF Launches Project to Halt Technology Sales to the Soviet Union," *Dialogue on Liberty*, June 1978, pp. 1, 8.

134. Memo to YAF Leadership from Bob Heckman, Director of State and Chapter Services and Rick LaMountain, Publications Director, March 19, 1979 (in author's possession).

135. "California YAF Fights Red Trade," *New Guard Bulletin*, volume XIX, number 4 (1979), p. 6.

136. Douglas Farquhar, "Picketing for Private Post Office," *Fairfax (VA) Journal* in *YAF in the News*, Summer 1978; *New Guard*, July–August 1978, p. 22.

as Democratic state representative Raymond Flynn was named "Man of the Year" and the featured speaker was Gordon Hall, a self-described expert on extremist organizations, who spoke on the topic "Where Have All the Radicals Gone?" Flynn would later serve as Mayor of Boston before being appointed Ambassador to the Holy See by President Clinton. Hall's collection of political documents, including much on Young Americans for Freedom, is now available at the John Hay Library at Brown University and was a valuable source of material for the present work. National Director Peter Flaherty was re-elected after Barry Miller withdrew from the race.[137]

Among the speakers at the Southwest conference in Austin were Senator John Tower, former Congressman Ron Paul, James Baker, III, and Republican state chairman Ray Barnhart. John Parker, chairman of the University of Texas YAF, was elected to the Board. The Midwest conference in Dayton, Ohio saw YAF alumni Professor William Stanmeyer and Buz Lukens as the featured speakers. Re-elected unopposed was Dennis Bechtel.[138]

When the delegates to the Northwest regional convened in Seattle, they heard from an outstanding list of speakers that included Senator James McClure of Idaho, Congressmen Jack Cunningham of Washington and Mickey Edwards of Oklahoma and Marco DeFunis. Washington YAF state chairman Brad Peterson was elected to the National Board replacing Eric Rohrbach who was then serving in the Washington state legislature. The new Washington YAF state chairman was Kurt Witzel, a graduate of the U.S. Naval Academy, who recalled the impact and influence of meeting Bill Buckley, Ronald Reagan, Stan Evans, Bob Novak and Ron Robinson and how "these folks helped form my early conservative views." Now living in Missouri, Witzel has been involved in Republican politics and was elected a delegate to Republican National Conventions.[139] At the Western regional, Howard Jarvis, author of Proposition 13, was given the Guardian of Freedom award from California YAF while Pat Geary was re-elected to the National Board. Meanwhile, in St. Paul, Minnesota, former YAF chapter director Phillip Abbott Luce addressed the delegates and Terry Cannon, Nebraska YAF state chairman, was re-elected to the Board.[140]

At the state level, YAF organizations took on projects that were traditionally associated with adult public policy organizations, filling a void in the conservative movement of the time. Thus, a number of YAF state organizations, including those in California, Georgia, Hawaii, New York, North Carolina, Tennessee, Texas, and Virginia, analyzed state legislative voting records and rated all legislators on their support for conservative positions. These legislative ratings provided needed publicity for YAF, obtained recognition for the organization among political leaders in the state, and established a means and a method for recognizing outstanding conservative legislators. In this way, YAF's role as an important political player became more recognized while it performed an essential function for the movement.[141]

---

137. "Regionals Off to Fast Start," *New Guard*, June 1978, p. 22. 1978 New England Regional Conference Flyer, Hall/Hoag Collection, Box 49–13, Subject HH429, John Hay Library, Brown University, Providence, RI.

138. Robert C. Heckman, "YAF Holds Regional Conferences," *Dialogue on Liberty*, June 1978, pp. 4, 6.

139. 2008 YAF Alumni Survey Responses: Kurt Witzel.

140. "West Hears Jarvis Talk," *New Guard*, July–August 1978, p. 23.

141. Examples can be seen in the following articles reprinted in the Summer 1978 issue of *YAF in the News*: "Legislators Given Low Ratings by YAF Group," *Nashville Banner*; "YAF Names Sebo Worst N.C. Senator," *Greensboro News*; "Sen. McFarland Gets Top Rating of Youth Group," *Buffalo News*.

The year also brought about some internal changes as the organization's Board of Directors voted in July to make *New Guard* a quarterly publication starting in December 1978 with an eight-to-twelve page "New Guard Bulletin" distributed in intervening months beginning in October. Meanwhile, at its December Board meeting, John Buckley resigned as national chairman and was replaced by James Lacy of California.[142] Lacy had served as California YAF chairman, was a graduate of the University of Southern California, and at the time of his election was a law student at Pepperdine University. He would be re-elected at both the 1979 and 1981 national conventions and continue to serve nearly five years in the top volunteer position until the 1983 convention. With a new chairman in place, YAF was ready to enter the last year of the 1970s in solid condition.

Campus Concerns

While national domestic and foreign issues and political campaigns consumed a great deal of YAF's attention in the late 1970s, there remained a strong YAF presence on several college campuses with chapters that stressed student issues, sponsored conservative speakers, trained new leaders, and published independent right-wing newspapers. Some of these YAF chapters were able to establish a continuing presence on campus, with leadership transferring from one class to another, resulting a consistent and active YAF chapter.

In Madison, the University of Wisconsin chapter was one such continuing presence, having started in the early 1960s with leaders such as Richard Wheeler, through the late Sixties time of David Keene, and the early Seventies of Mike Kelly and Pat Korten, among others. By the latter part of the 1970s, Robert E.A.P. Ritholz was chapter chairman and John Kwapisz served as Wisconsin state chairman while the independent conservative newspaper, *Badger Herald*, was still being published with six of seven members of the Board of Directors being YAF members.[143] At Purdue, a strong YAF presence continued through two decades and by the late 1970s, under the direction of chairman David Stanton and Alice Anderson, the chapter was regularly sponsoring conservative speakers. In New York, Adelphi University YAF held a dinner to celebrate its 10th anniversary of continuing activity, including a regular campus newspaper column put together by John Abernethy and Doug Brusa under the leadership of chairman Gordon DeLetto.[144]

Georgetown University, led at the time by Steve Collier, continued into the 1980s as a strong YAF chapter, as was the YAF unit at George Washington University. Just outside DC, Robert Frisby kept the YAF flame alive at the University of Maryland, following the earlier leadership of Warren Parker, Joe Spelta, David Havelka and Kristin Kazyak. At the University of Virginia, Karol Lamos built

---

142. Interview with James Meadows, Austin, TX, January 24, 2009.

143. As of 2009, forty years after its founding, the *Badger Herald* is the largest fully independent daily campus newspaper distributing copies five days a week on the Madison campus. Many other campuses have continuing independent papers published less frequently. Among them are the *Dartmouth Review*, published since 1980, whose alumni include Dinesh D'Sousa and Laura Ingraham and the *Harvard Salient*, founded in 1981 by YAF National Director Terry Quist and others, still being published as a bi-weekly.

144. Among the previous chairmen were Bob Heckman, soon to become YAF executive director, and Connie Campanella, now president of Stateside Associates government relations firm in DC. "The Right Scene," *New Guard*, Spring 1979, pp. 46–47.

upon the foundation established by Dennis Stull and Boyd Marcus, Joe Bishop, Jay Buckley, Don Carpenter and Mary Gingell. Elwyn Darden was active in both College Republicans and YAF at UVA and saw a clear difference.

> YAF was always interesting: speakers, projects, literature and conferences. While in college I spent most of my time and energy with the College Republicans but I never ceased to remain active with YAF and went out of my way to promote both organizations to promising conservatives.
>
> YAF encouraged engagement on philosophical issues whereas College Republicans suppressed full examination to the extent that you weren't seeking to correct error but rather to stuff envelopes and marshal votes. Having YAF to draw the distinction so clearly taught me to never lose my hold on principle.[145]

Lewis Doherty, Tami Day and Chris Hammon continued the tradition at Louisiana State University, a tradition that went back to the early 1960s when Helen Blackwell was an active member and later through the involvement of Mike Connelly and Roy Brun.

Both the University of Texas, with John Parker, Greg Gegenheimer and Steve Munisteri, and the University of Tennessee at Knoxville, under the direction of Lloyd Daugherty, Bill Hawkins and Richard Beeler, continued to produce a number of YAF leaders who would go on to contribute to the growing conservative movement. Del Gustafson was involved in YAF at two campuses with a long tradition of activism. As an undergraduate at the University of Nebraska he served briefly as chapter chairman, working with long-time YAF leader and future National Chairman Terry Cannon. As he recalled those experiences, "I wanted to join YAF as soon as I arrived in Lincoln, Nebraska as a college freshman. In high school, I had drunk deeply from works such as *Up from Liberalism* and *Conscience of a Conservative* and was ready to enlist in the conservative movement. And within no time, Terry Cannon, the driving force behind YAF at the University of Nebraska, had signed me up."[146] Gustafson attended the 1975 YAF convention, "meeting kids who did want to discuss political questions and listening to the gods of the conservative movement." As a law student at Vanderbilt he was a member of the chapter led by Roger Ream and served on the platform committee at the 1981 YAF convention.[147]

On the West Coast, the University of Southern California and the University of Washington both carried on proud traditions of YAF involvement throughout the 1970s and served as recruiting and training grounds for conservative activists. Among the USC leaders were Mark Deardorff, Larry Orr and John Lewis, promoting activism at that campus.[148] Floyd Brown was a student at the University of Washington, a campus that also produced YAF leaders Kirby Wilbur, Mary Kay Whistler, David Benoit and Greg McDonald.

Two campuses where the YAF presence had faded and was resuscitated in the early 1970s were Brigham Young University and the University of Michigan. Joan Hendricks Benson brought a number of speakers and rallied students at a

---

145. 2008 YAF Alumni Survey Responses: Elwyn LaBauve Darden.
146. 2008 YAF Alumni Survey Responses: Del L. Gustafson.
147. *Ibid.*
148. For the late 60s and early 70s period, see Bob McDonald: *YAF in the Arena*. The USC chapter continued to produce YAF leaders throughout the 1980s and early 1990s.

traditionally conservative yet apolitical campus, then went on to serve as Utah YAF state chairman. Now the owner of a trucking company, Benson believes that her experience convinced her "what a few dedicated individuals can accomplish. I have the same political ideology and dreams I have always had. I believe that small businesses are the backbone of our freedoms. That is why I have never given up, even though the odds have been against me."[149] Miles Schmidt chaired the YAF chapter in the early 1970s in traditionally leftist Ann Arbor, where his involvement "helped congeal conservative values and positions and challenged me to overthrow liberal views on campus—especially abortion."[150]

Yet there were new campuses also where a YAF presence was first being established in the late 1970s. At traditionally liberal Vassar College, Abram Feurstein led the YAF chapter in defeating a referendum to fund a Public Interest Research Group (PIRG) out of mandatory student fees while at Oklahoma State University, John Bryant led a chapter that produced future journalist Pat McGuigan, Janet Slaughter, and conservative activist Steve Antosh while presenting a regular column in the school newspaper.[151] Robert Lightner formed a YAF chapter at Blue Ridge Community College in the mid-1970s and later became Virginia YAF state chairman. For Lightner, that experience "grounded and sharpened my worldview in support of free enterprise, limited government, and strong national defense. It exposed me to Republican leaders, one of whom got me started in the insurance business."[152] Roy Jones formed a YAF chapter at Liberty Baptist (now Liberty University), an institution founded by Jerry Falwell. Jones recalled his time in YAF as "critical to making the connection between public policy and the costs associated with grassroots organizing and running for public office . . . Opened my eyes to the breadth and diversity in the conservative movement."[153] Charlie Gerow was YAF chairman at Messiah College in the mid-70s and recalls "YAF was an invaluable training ground for me and helped to mold my political views and hone my leadership skills."[154]

While the end of the decade saw YAF continue as a strong force on many campuses and a major player in the conservative movement, it also brought the sad news of the tragic deaths of two outstanding young conservative leaders in separate automobile accidents. John Parker had been editor of the independent newspaper, *Texas Forum*, and then YAF chairman at the University of Texas before being elected to the YAF National Board of Directors and subsequently named editor of *New Guard*. Less than two months in his new position in suburban Virginia, Parker was killed in an automobile accident.[155] Coby Pieper graduated from the University of Texas, had a key role in the 1976 Reagan campaign in Texas and was regional service director for YAF before becoming Political Director for the Republican Party of Texas and National Secretary of YAF. His death came in

---

149. 2008 YAF Alumni Survey Responses: Joan Hendricks Benson.

150. 2008 YAF Alumni Survey Responses: Miles V. Schmidt.

151. McGuigan is a former editorial page editor for the *Daily Oklahoman*. Slaughter (Eissenstat) was director of the President's Commission on White House Fellowships during the George W. Bush Administration. Antosh has been involved in numerous campaigns and is currently executive vice president of M&H Enterprises where he manages fundraising and membership recruitment for the National Pro-Life Alliance. 2008 YAF Alumni Survey Responses: Steve M. Antosh.

152. 2008 YAF Alumni Survey Responses: Robert T. Lightner, Jr.

153. 2008 YAF Alumni Survey Responses: Roy C. Jones. Jones is now Director of Development for Liberty University.

154. 2008 YAF Alumni Survey Responses: Charles Gerow.

155. Greg Gegenheimer, "John Parker: R.I.P.," *New Guard Bulletin*, volume XIX, number 1 (1979), p. 3.

early spring in San Antonio and his absence was felt by many for some time. As fellow Texan Terry Quist commented on both Parker and Pieper,

> While John was the dynamic and articulate public advocate of conservatism, Coby was the quiet manager, the one who diligently took up all the unglamorous backstage organizational work, which makes everything else possible. Though fewer of you knew him, all of us are indebted to his tireless and selfless labor for YAF and for the movement.[156]

The conservative movement lost several of its future leaders early in life. Parker and Pieper had already contributed much in their short time and would have done so much more over the last thirty years in advancing the cause of liberty in which they both believed strongly.

As the new year began, the Carter Administration invited Red China's vice premier, Teng Hsiao-ping, to visit the United States and he made stops in Seattle, Los Angeles, Houston, Atlanta, and Washington, DC. The visit was a follow-up to Carter's announcement in late 1978 that the United States would recognize Communist China and abandon its long-standing recognition of the Republic of China.[157] At each location, YAF organized protests, including fifty YAFers led by Pat Geary who "welcomed" the Communist leader when he visited Disneyland. Texas YAF, led by Steve Munisteri, sponsored an advertisement in the *Houston Chronicle* denouncing the visit while state vice chairman Greg Robertson rounded up 150 YAFers to rally against Teng's visit to Houston. In Atlanta, R.E. Phillip Linderman, II and Ryan Murphy greeted Teng's arrival wearing Neville Chamberlain and Adolf Hitler costumes emphasizing what they viewed as Carter's capitulation to Communist China.[158] National YAF distributed a poster, "Welcome a Tyrant?" that pointed out mass killings, forced labor, and aggression by Red China.[159] Given the historical record of the Communist Chinese and Teng's role in both the party and government, YAF objected strongly to the treatment being provided him by many Americans, including the Carter Administration and various academic institutions. Temple YAF's Stephen Kranz denounced the school's granting of an honorary degree to Teng.

Even in places where Teng did not appear, YAF made evident their opposition to the regime he represented. Hawaii YAF's Sam Slom devoted a commentary on the weekly YAF radio program to US–China relations while Paul Taylor, Minnesota YAF state chairman, organized sixty pickets outside the Minnesota state capitol. YAF National Chairman Jim Lacy was part of a delegation that traveled to Taiwan to show support for its freedom. As Lacy noted, "Continued friendly relations with Taiwan are essential to our status as a dependable ally. To break with a country that's always lived up to its end of a treaty can only bring us down in the eyes of

---

156. Terry Quist, "In Memory of Coby Pieper," *New Guard Bulletin*, volume XIX, number 2 (1979), p. 6. As executive director of the Republican Party of Texas at the time, I was blessed to have had the knowledge and dedication of Coby Pieper in the position heading up our work with local candidates and conducting political training workshops. He contributed much to the early efforts in changing the partisan climate of Texas politics.

157. Hedrick Smith, "China Move Reflects Carter's Aim to Protect Arms Pact and Taiwan," *New York Times*, December 16, 1978.

158. "Carter Shanghais Taiwan," *New Guard Bulletin*, volume XIX, number 1, pp. 1, 5.

159. Poster distributed by Young Americans for Freedom China Project, included with *Leadership Bulletin* dated January 23, 1979, in author's possession.

the world."[160] YAF continued to be a strong supporter of the Chinese government on Taiwan even after the actions of the Carter Administration had redirected U.S. government relations.

Later that spring, YAF shifted its focus to preventing the ratification of the second Strategic Arms Limitation Treaty (SALT-II). YAF maintained "our analysis of SALT II shows that far from reducing arms, the treaty would allow the immense Soviet buildup to continue."[161] The campaign brought together a number of local efforts to gain media attention and collect petition signatures for presenting to various Senators. In the Spring issue of its magazine, YAF devoted fourteen pages to the SALT II issue.[162] In the end, the treaty was not ratified by the Senate and withdrawn from consideration once the 1980 presidential election was concluded.[163]

10th National Convention—Washington

YAF held its 10th national convention in Washington, DC on August 15–18, 1979. Bill Buckley was back to give his traditional keynote address, a series of panels featured leaders of the conservative movement, and there were the platform hearings and debates as well as the election of a National Chairman and nine members of the Board of Directors. Thursday night featured a roast of syndicated columnist James Jackson Kilpatrick. The event was emceed by Stan Evans and had Rick Abell (Young Republican National Chairman), Jim Lacy (YAF National Chairman), Jeffrey St. John (Mutual radio commentator), Congressman Henry Hyde and former Senator Eugene McCarthy as the roasters.[164] Not quite the roast of Bill Buckley, but still an entertaining and even informative time for all the young conservatives present.

In covering the convention the media could see YAF's success in terms of influence and the acceptability of its positions as it concluded its 19th year. As one reporter for the *New York Times* observed,

> Through most of their 19 years, the "Yaffers," as they call themselves, have made up the youth minority of the conservative minority of the Republican minority. But at their 10th national convention here this week, their actions and many of the speakers indicated that the young conservatives had somehow been shifted to a more centrist and inside role.[165]

Frank Donatelli reflected on the fact "We've outlived Woodstock, we've outlived Students for a Democratic Society. Now we find Y.A.F. has helped set the current national agenda of issues: Tax cuts, business initiatives, maintaining military strength, regulatory reform, the whole thing."[166] This change was evident when the delegates held their third mock presidential nominating convention on Saturday.

---

160. "Carter Shanghais Taiwan," *New Guard Bulletin*, volume XIX, number 1, pp. 1.
161. "YAF Launches Campaign to Stop SALT II," *New Guard Bulletin*, volume XIX, number 2, p. 1.
162. "Senator Jake Garn on SALT II," pp. 20–24 and Greg Gegenheimer, "The Soviets: Preparing for a First Strike?" pp. 28–31, *New Guard*, Spring 1979.
163. Carl Marcy, "A SALT Opportunity," *New York Times*, December 6, 1980.
164. "Tenth National Convention Stunning Success," *New Guard*, volume XIX, number 7 (1979), p. 1.
165. Warren Weaver, Jr., "Conservative Youth Group Finds Itself in a More Centrist Position," *New York Times*, August 18, 1979.
166. *Ibid.*

It was a landslide for Ronald Reagan with 78% of the vote while Phil Crane came in second with 18%, leaving only a few isolated votes for George H.W. Bush, Bob Dole, Howard Baker and John Connally. One year later, the American people would elect Reagan to the presidency.[167]

Fittingly, the major speaker on Saturday night was Reagan who, while not present, had prepared and taped a special message for the convention. Reagan praised YAF for its efforts in opposing the radical left on campus and in training leaders for the future. He criticized the Carter Administration on a wide range of issues from its energy policy to the Panama Canal treaty to the SALT II treaty. Citing Margaret Thatcher's recent victory in Great Britain, he maintained that much of the West was moving away from socialism. In closing, he rallied the YAF members for the upcoming presidential election: "America is better off with leadership that reflects the philosophy, the principles, and the aspirations of Young Americans for Freedom." Citing the longstanding relationship he had with YAF, Reagan reminded the delegates, "We still have very much to accomplish and after 19 years of activity I know that YAF will be up to the tasks before us and that together we will do what we must to realize that 'Shining City on a Hill.'"[168] Just as many of their predecessors had done in 1968 and 1976, most of these YAF members were ready and willing to devote their time and energies to another Reagan campaign for the presidency.[169]

But the delegates could not leave Washington without devoting some time to internal organizational matters. Jim Lacy was elected without opposition as National Chairman while some twenty-two candidates had filed for the nine slots to be filled on the National Board of Directors. Only one incumbent, Cliff White, was re-elected while Greg McDonald's attempt at a second term was unsuccessful. The new Directors were Frank Connolly of Columbia University, Robert Dolan of St. John's University, William Hawkins of the University of Tennessee, Barry Miller of Suffolk University, Sam Pimm of New Jersey, Paul Prince of Ohio, Suzanne Scholte of Virginia, and Steve Wiley of California.

As the fall semester began, Jane Fonda and her then husband Tom Hayden launched a five week nationwide campus speaking tour. All across the country, YAF chapters turned out to protest and show opposition to the leftist pair. Ed Bender organized one hundred demonstrators with signs and distributed literature at Albright College in Pennsylvania when Fonda and Hayden appeared. John Abernethy set up a literature distribution when she spoke at Adelphi University while demonstrators held signs saying "Fonda to boat people: drop dead." Meanwhile, Todd Zirkle and Lori Saxon led demonstrators against the pair at American University. According to Saxon, "If it were not for YAF, I never would have met Jay Parker at the 1979 convention and subsequently had the opportunity to work with him and be introduced to the many people in the Reagan Administration." As Saxon noted, "Our daughter Jayne Saxon Zirkle was born in late 2001 and named after Jay Parker ... YAF was a big part of my life—from marriage, child to work and career."[170] Saxon is now a successful real estate agent in Virginia and the District of Columbia.

167. "Reagan's Candidacy Is Endorsed by Young Americans for Freedom," *New York Times*, August 19, 1979.

168. "Reagan: 'America Better Off with YAF,'" *New Guard*, volume XIX, number 8 (1979), pp. 1, 6.

169. Not all YAF leaders were for Reagan, however. David Keene was a political director for the campaign of George H.W. Bush while Roger Ream was part of the Phil Crane presidential effort.

170. 2008 YAF Alumni Survey Responses: Lori Saxon. Email to the author from Lori Saxon Zirkle, August 8, 2009.

On other campuses, YAF made known its opposition to Fonda. YAFers leafleted the Yale campus before Fonda and Hayden made their appearance. In Boston, Ted Temple and Bill Abely organized demonstrators on four area campuses while at Temple University, YAF leader Gary Seflin made an issue of the money paid to Fonda from student fees. At Fordham, Chris Brennan and Ken Grasso arranged to have a banner saying "Go Home, Hanoi Jane" unfurled as Fonda spoke. New Hampshire YAFers Doug Bourdon, Laurie Titus, and William MacKenzie issued a challenge to Fonda to debate them, an offer she refused. At Rutgers, Joe Galda and Rick LaMountain rounded up the YAF members to greet Fonda while similar efforts were undertaken by Mark Judd at the University of Michigan, Roger Blaine at Indiana University, and Rick Loy at IU–PU Indianapolis. The most publicized protest, which made it onto national network news, took place when fifty YAF members held a mock trial outside Fonda's Santa Monica home and hanged her in effigy. Organized by Steve Wiley, Robin Bittick, and Dave Nolan, the "trial" provided a fitting end to the Fonda-Hayden national tour.[171]

November brought another situation where YAF could protest and make known their support for a strong foreign policy. As Iranian student radicals occupied the American embassy in Tehran and held Americans prisoner, the YAF Board met and passed a resolution calling for the release of all Americans and American property, advocating a freeze on Iranian assets in the United States until the crisis was ended, demanding a cessation of all American foreign aid to Iran and a blockade of the country, and the withdrawal of diplomatic recognition to the new government. On November 14th, YAF leaders attempted to meet with the Charge D'Affaires at the Iranian Embassy and present him with a copy of the resolution. While much media coverage was obtained, the embassy refused a meeting with the YAF representatives.

One week later, YAF had organized a "Youth Coalition" including the College Democrats, College Republicans, Young Republican National Federation, Young Social Democrats, and Frontlash. The coalition, led by YAF executive director Robert Heckman, met with Iran's U.S. Charge D'Affaires and press attaché at the embassy on November 23rd.[172] While YAF would continue protesting the Iranian students actions, it would not be until Inauguration Day 1981 when the American hostages would be finally released.

That November meeting of the YAF Board of Directors also saw some significant changes in the organization's staff structure. Ron Robinson resigned as executive director to become the fulltime president of Young America's Foundation. Replacing Robinson was Bob Heckman, a graduate of Adelphi University who had been chapter chairman, New York YAF state chairman, and for the previous two years on the YAF national staff as Director of State and Chapter Services. Cliff White took Heckman's former position while Peter Flaherty became the new Director of Projects and Conferences. Rich LaMountain, a YAF activist at Rutgers, was named editor of *New Guard* and remembers that experience fondly. "The organization gave me the opportunity to broaden my knowledge of conservative philosophy and its application to national issues, and to sharpen my writing and editing skills as editor of an actual magazine." He went on to conclude, "All this was a rare and heady experience for a man in his early twenties. And, to be honest,

171. Ken Boehm, "YAF Rains on Fonda/Hayden Parade," *Dialogue on Liberty*, Fall 1979, pp. 4–5.

172. Young Americans for Freedom News Release: "Youth Coalition Meets with High Iranian Officials," November 23, 1979, in author's possession.

it was an experience I did not fully appreciate until some years after it was over. I was fortunate to have been a part of YAF."[173] Today, LaMountain is a freelance writer whose work appears in publications including *Investor's Business Daily*.

Also at that National Board meeting, two new Board members were elected to fill vacancies: Richard Abell, former Pennsylvania YAF state chairman, and Lloyd Daugherty, chairman of the YAF chapter at the University of Tennessee at Knoxville. Abell had served for two years in the Peace Corps and then two years in the military in Vietnam from 1969 to 1971. For Abell, "the Peace Corps experience had a huge impact on making me conservative. I saw the bodies of peasants in the back of dump trucks who were killed by the Communist guerrillas in Colombia" while the American volunteers were helping to set up local governments and providing materials for communities to help themselves.[174]

As the decade came to an end, more and more observers appreciated YAF's contribution to the growing conservative movement in the United States. As one writer on the development of American conservatism noted, "the generation of conservative activists that came of age in the 1970s was filled with alumni of YAF and ISI."[175] Looking back many years later, Daniel McCarthy claimed, "Campus conservatives are not just the future of the movement, they are its present as well. Alumni of the major right-wing youth organizations fill the ranks, and hold the commanding heights, of the institutions that mold conservative orthodoxy today."[176]

Perhaps no better testimony to the continued influence of YAF could be found than an article in *The Chronicle of Higher Education*, the "Bible" for college faculty and administrators published weekly to report on trends and influences on university life. Not only did the reporter conclude that "politically conservative students are increasing their influence on college campuses" but she obtained substantiation from YAF's opponents. According to the legislative director for the United States Student Association (the renamed NSA), YAF "is getting stronger on campuses" and "the conservatives work against everything we are working for. We must stop them before they stop us." Wesley McCune, who made his living researching right-wing organizations for a union-funded entity called Group Research, Inc. claimed, "The new young conservatives are a smarter bunch. They are an intelligent collection of young politicians, who learned from the 60s, who have more political savvy, and who are increasingly powerful."[177] McCune admitted that a trained cadre of right-wing student leaders who once supported the Vietnam war and countered left-wing protesters was moving into legislative and executive positions of government. He maintained that former and present YAF members were in great demand as staffers on Capitol Hill.

YAF's campaign against mandatory student fees and in opposition to Ralph Nader's PIRG's were cited as YAF projects along with its support for Alan Bakke's suit against reverse discrimination. Speaking of the mandatory fees campaign, the director of the youth caucus of Americans for Democratic Action said, "This is the type of activity which is most dangerous to campus liberals. The fees are

173. 2008 YAF Alumni Survey Responses: Richard F. LaMountain.

174. Interview with Richard Abell, Washington, DC, October 5, 2008.

175. Jerome L. Himmelstein: *To the Right: The Transformation of American Conservatism* (Berkeley: University of California Press, 1990), p. 88.

176. Daniel McCarthy, "GOP and Man at Yale," *The American Conservative*, November 6, 2006.

177. Noreen McGrath, "Right-Wing Students Exert Growing Influence on Campus," *The Chronicle of Higher Education*, January 8, 1979.

the life-blood of student governments" and "conservatives are very quietly taking over and making inroads" in student governments. As Frank Connolly, chairman of the YAF chapter at Columbia University noted, "we have given students an alternative point of view. We fought the hippies, and now we are in place ready to fight the liberals on every issue they raise."[178]

As the 1970s came to a close, the new executive director, Robert Heckman, sounded an optimistic note for the future of the organization. "YAF stands ready to continue its unique mission in American politics. Organizationally, we have built the foundation necessary to launch new programs while carrying on our duties of training new leaders and expanding the conservative movement."[179] For the conservative movement as a whole, Heckman's optimism would be well founded as one year later Ronald Reagan would be elected President of the United States and the "Reagan Revolution" soon would be underway. YAF had much to do in the intervening months to help make the Reagan victory possible and its members and alumni would play critical roles in the new administration. But for YAF as an organization, the decade of the 1980s would bring greater challenges to its continued existence than any they had faced before.

---

178. McGrath, "Right-Wing Students Exert Growing Influence on Campus."
179. Robert Heckman, "YAF and the Future," *New Guard*, Winter 1979–1980, p. 23.

Do you want to **STOP** Student Radicals from

- – DISRUPTING ACADEMIC LIFE
- – PROMOTING VIOLENCE & DESTRUCTION BY STORM-TROOPER TACTICS
- – DENYING SERIOUS STUDENTS THEIR RIGHTS TO ATTEND CLASS
- – MISREPRESENTING STUDENT VIEWS ON NATIONAL & LOCAL ISSUES

all in the name of Academic Freedom?

Join with **yaf**

YOUNG AMERICANS FOR FREEDOM

In the forefront of the fight against those attempting to shut down our universities.

LEGAL ACTION PROGRAM to protect students' rights

FREE CAMPUS NEWS to bring responsible student opinion to the American campuses

CAMPUS ACTION PROGRAM to combat radical demands and tactics

YOUNG AMERICA'S FREEDOM OFFENSIVE to take the lead in involvement in the critical issues of the '70s

---

Application for Membership

Young Americans for Freedom
1221 Massachusetts Avenue, N.W.
Washington, D. C. 20005

I enclose my membership dues of: $_____

NAME_____
Please Print

MAILING ADDRESS_____

CITY_____ STATE_____ ZIP_____

AGE_____ SCHOOL OR OCCUPATION_____
*I understand that $2.50 of my dues is for a subscription to the *New Guard* for one year.

Check One

☐ Student $3.00*
☐ Student $1.00 (Does not include the *New Guard*.
☐ Non-Student $3.00 (Under 40)*
☐ Non-Student $1.00 (Does not include the *New Guard*.
☐ Joint Membership for Married Couples $4.00 (Under 40)*
☐ Associate Membership $10.00 (Over 40)*
☐ I enclose a contribution in the amount of $_____
☐ I would like more information about YAF.

Recruitment flyer from the early 1970s stressing
YAF's efforts against the New Left on campus.

405

On campuses across the country YAF sponsored "Tell It to Hanoi" rallies like this one at the University of Southern California in the spring of 1970. Randy Goodwin is in the center while John McGuiness is on the far right. Photo from Bob McDonald.

Puamohala Taroc, State Secretary, and Dennis Jung of Hawaii Hi-YAF lead a march in support of American POWs and against appeasement in Southeast Asia. Hawaii was consistently one of YAF's most active state organizations during the 1960s and 1970s.

Randal Teague and Dan Joy interviewed Vice President Spiro T. Agnew for a cover feature in the Summer 1970 issue of *New Guard*. Agnew would be chosen for President at the 1971 Mock Nominating Convention in Houston.

The YAF10 celebration included the planting of an elm tree at the Buckley family estate. Dan Manion plants the tree while Alan MacKay, Randal Teague, Bill Buckley and David Keene observe.

Outside the 1971 Western Regional Conference YAFers led by Pat Geary wait to greet Governor Reagan on his arrival.

1971 saw a continuation of YAF's opposition to trade with Communist countries as the young conservatives successfully took on the Mack Truck Corporation and its plans to build a truck factory in the Soviet Union.

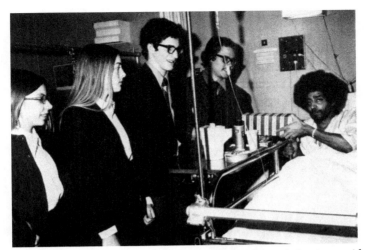

In the early 1970s YAF chapters carried out Project Appreciation to provide candies, toiletries and other personal items to wounded Vietnam veterans. Here DC YAFers led by Chuck McLenon and Richard Marschall help deliver a Project Appreciation kit at Walter Reed Army Medical Center.

Frank Donatelli hands out credentials at the 1973 YAF National Convention. Young Americans for Freedom held sixteen biennial conventions where delegates heard conservative leaders, adopted policy positions, and elected the organization's leadership. The last convention was held in 1991.

YAF was one of four original sponsors of the Conservative Political
Action Conference. Senator Jim Buckley greets Rich Delgaudio and a
group of New York YAFers at the first CPAC in 1974.

1974 saw the dedication and opening of YAF's national headquarters in
Sterling, Virginia. Ron Docksai introduced Senator Strom Thurmond
and M. Stanton Evans who were guests at the event.

410

In 1975, YAF held its 2nd mock presidential nominating convention in conjunction with the Chicago national convention. Here delegates demonstrate for their favorite and convention winner Ronald Reagan.

YAF leaders Alan Gottlieb, Jeff Kane, Bob Moffit and Dan Manion celebrate at the 1975 National Convention in Chicago. Candidate posters adorn the back wall of the convention hall.

Fifteen years after its initial national convention, Young Americans for Freedom returned to New York for the 1977 event. The roast of Bill Buckley was for many the highlight of this year's event.

Outgoing executive director Frank Donatelli and National Chairman Jeff Kane were honored by the organization at the 1977 convention while Congressman Bob Dornan looks on.

Incoming executive director Ron Robinson presents an award to Barry Miller of Canton, MA for Outstanding Hi-YAF chapter of the year at the 1977 New York City national convention.

Texas received the award for most improved large state organization. L–R James Meadows, Steve Munisteri, newly elected National Chairman John Buckley, Gary Hoitsma, Coby Pieper, and Terry Quist.

Throughout the latter half of the 1970s, YAF's zero government growth program benefited from a number of professionally designed advertisements such as the one above. These appeared in several college newspapers across the country and helped recruit those concerned with individual liberty.

In 1979, Young Americans for Freedom returned to Washington for its convention. With 22 candidates for 9 National Board seats, it was a lively campaign. Delegates cheer for their favorite candidates on nominations night before the Saturday election.

During the fall of 1979, Jane Fonda and her then-husband Tom Hayden undertook a national campus speaking tour. Nearly everywhere they stopped, the pair were greeted by YAF protesters. The tour began at Albright College where more than one hundred demonstrators made known their opinions.

YAF took an active role in the effort to prevent Senate approval of the SALT-II agreement. As part of that effort, retired General John K. Singlaub helped Oklahoma YAF kick off its Stop SALT-II drive. Meeting with Singlaub are Linda Emery, chairman of Oklahoma University YAF, and State Chairman Steve Antosh.

The national office held periodic training conferences for new state chairmen. Shown attending this one in 1979 are L–R Kevin Baadsgaard of Utah, Sam Pimm of New Jersey, Larry Hunter of South Carolina, and Chuck Cunningham of Virginia.

13. The Reagan Era

"I've enjoyed a special relationship with Young Americans for Freedom
for many years . . . America, and Young Americans for Freedom,
are entering a new decade together. It will be a decade of fearsome
challenges . . . But Americans, and especially Young Americans for
Freedom, have always had a clear understanding of the road America
was destined to travel . . . Americans, and especially Young Americans
for Freedom, are eager to undertake the journey."[1]

It was the beginning of a presidential election year and YAF had been there before, but never in quite the situation that presented itself in early 1980. While Ronald Reagan was the overwhelming favorite of YAF members and supporters, some YAF members were active in the campaigns of other candidates, including a few who were supporting the Libertarian Party and its efforts to establish itself as a third force in American politics.[2] After all, this was not YAF's first crusade for a conservative presidential candidate. Its genesis had been the Goldwater for Vice President effort at the 1960 Republican convention in Chicago and then there had been the Goldwater effort four years later, the last-minute effort for Reagan in 1968, the campaign against Gerald Ford in 1976. But this time, there was a new generation of young conservatives who were assuming leadership roles in American politics and, this time, the results would be different.

As expected, when one thought of the presidential contest it was the Reagan campaign that attracted the greatest involvement by YAF members. Some played key roles in the early development of the campaign, including former chapter director Charles Black and former executive director Frank Donatelli. California YAF state chairman Gary Kreep was picked to head Youth for Reagan in the Golden State with former Stanford YAF chairman Doug Bandow holding a key position in the California campaign operations. Meanwhile, DC YAFers John Smathers (Catholic University), Todd Zirkle (American University), Chuck Miller and Barry Morse put in many hours at the DC campaign office.

One of YAF's spinoff organizations, Fund for a Conservative Majority (FCM), launched an independent expenditure effort on Reagan's behalf. FCM came into being after the 1976 campaign as the renamed Young America's Campaign Committee and was headed by YAF executive director Robert Heckman. On its staff were Ken Boehm and John Gizzi, then a Texas YAFer and currently political editor for *Human Events*. One of FCM's first projects was to round up volunteers for the New Hampshire primary effort. Some forty YAF members were bused into the state

---

1. Ronald Reagan, "YAF: Twenty Years of Conservative Leadership," *New Guard*, Fall 1980, p. 13.
2. In a poll of donors conducted by YAF, among a field of twelve candidates Reagan received 51.6% of the 174,993 votes cast with Representative Phil Crane a distant second with 18.8% of the votes. "Reagan Wins YAF Presidential Poll," *Dialogue on Liberty*, Winter 1980. Reagan had also received 70% of the vote from participants at the 1979 CPAC and 78% from the delegates to the 1979 YAF National Convention. In both of these surveys, Crane was second with about 18% support from those participating. Among those backing other candidates, David Keene was Political Director for the George Bush campaign, Roger Ream was a regional director for the Crane for President effort while David Boaz was Director of Research for Libertarian candidate Ed Clark.

including a large contingent from Virginia headed by Mike Baroody, David Tyson, and Van Dalton. New York YAF brought a group led by Alexander Wells and Jay Young while chapter chairmen Richard Beeler (University of Tennessee–Knoxville), Robert Frisby (University of Maryland), David Sanders (William & Mary), and Roy Jones (Liberty Baptist) brought students from their campuses. Coordinating the effort were YAF's Peter Flaherty and Lloyd Daugherty of Tennessee.[3]

While the primary season was starting, YAF once again co-sponsored the annual Conservative Political Action Conference. During the CPAC events National Chairman James Lacy held a news conference to urge Congressman Phil Crane, who had received only 7% of the vote in the Iowa caucuses, to withdraw from the presidential race in favor of Reagan. A few days later, after winning the Vermont primary and coming close in Massachusetts, Reagan called Lacy to thank him for YAF's support and for encouraging Crane to withdraw. Reagan "thanked YAF for its work on his behalf throughout the country. Jim and the Governor spoke for some ten minutes about YAF and the campaign."[4] Reagan's call to Lacy was one more indication of the respect held by the former Governor for the work of the organization.

Another indication of YAF's contribution to the conservative movement could be seen at the CPAC event. Some thirty-one groups set up display tables to hand out literature and explain their purpose, a testimony to the emergence of a national movement and also to the success of YAF as most of these groups were either established or led by YAF alumni.[5] Notice of YAF's influence also came from the Left as *Rolling Stone* magazine called YAF "a movement of young conservatives that is thought by some to have generated the most influential political thinking on the right, and indeed the ideas that have framed the national political debate, in recent years."[6]

The Spring 1980 quarterly issue of *New Guard* featured a special section on "Ronald Reagan: Conservative Choice in 1980" with articles by Jim Lacy, Lee Edwards, Stuart Mollrich, and John Gizzi as well as an interview with Lyn Nofziger, longtime political advisor and confidant of Reagan.[7] Across the country, YAF chapters became an organizing base for student support for Reagan and, as they had in 1976, several YAFers were elected as delegates or alternates to the Republican National Convention in Detroit. Still others were attracted to the campaign of Ed Clark, including Robert Poole, former chapter chairman at M.I.T. and then an editor at *Reason* magazine; David Boaz, research director and traveling aide with Clark; and Tom Palmer, assistant communications director for the Clark campaign.[8]

As the spring semester proceeded YAF chapters and members continued to be active on a wide range of other issues. Gerard Kassar of Pace University remembers the time as one when YAF members from various New York City chapters would march repeatedly outside the Iranian consulate and on occasion outside

---

3. "YAFers Heavily Involved in 1980 Elections," *New Guard*, volume XX, number 1 (1980), p. 1. "YAF Members Active in FCM Reagan Effort," *Dialogue on Liberty*, Winter 1980, p. 7. The most comprehensive review of the Reagan campaign in 1980 is Craig Shirley: *Rendezvous with Destiny* (Wilmington, DE: ISI Books, 2009). Shirley discusses the FCM efforts on pages 107, 191, and especially 612–613.

4. Memo from the executive director to the Board of Directors, March 6, 1980, p. 2.

5. Memo from Cliff White, Director of State and Chapter Services to YAF Leadership, February 15, 1980. See also: Roberts: *The Conservative Decade*, p. 39.

6. "Profile on George Bush," *Rolling Stone*, March 20, 1980, p. 60.

7. *New Guard*, Spring 1980, pp. 11–26.

8. E.J. Dionne, Jr., "Libertarian Party Bids for Conservative and Liberal Votes," *New York Times*, July 10, 1980.

the United Nations building to protest the holding of American hostages in the embassy in Tehran. America was being challenged and President Carter seemed helpless.[9]

Meanwhile inflation and the cost of living continued on an upward spiral. In response to the economic failures of the Carter Administration, the Northwest YAF office launched "Project Free Enterprise" to inform high school and college students about laissez-faire economics. Advertisements were placed in campus newspapers, showings of "The Incredible Bread Machine" were scheduled, and speakers were brought to campuses and communities throughout Oregon, Idaho, and Washington. The project was headed by National Treasurer Brad Peterson and involved the leadership from the three states.[10] A small contingent of conservatives, led by Connie Coyne Marshner, served as delegates to the 1980 White House Conference on Families, a gathering dominated by liberals appointed by the Carter Administration.[11]

With so much conservative effort directed towards the presidential campaign, less attention was paid to basic organizational development and maintenance. By the beginning of 1980 YAF state organizations were fully functioning in only 24 states plus the District of Columbia and Puerto Rico, although individual chapters operated in some other areas of the country.[12] In early March, YAF received a further blow to its organizational strength when much of the Texas membership and chapters, led by then National Director Steve Munisteri, left the organization. At a conference held in Austin on March 2nd, Texas Independence Day, the dissidents broke from YAF and formed "Young Conservatives of Texas" as an independent group.[13] Munisteri had been on the losing side of a number of internal Board votes over the past year and his regional seat would be up for election again in a few weeks. He and his fellow Texans had attempted to elect three Texas candidates to the nine slots on the YAF National Board filled at the 1979 convention. When urged to focus on electing only one or two candidates, the Texans refused. All three candidates were unsuccessful.

National YAF quickly moved to rebuild a presence in Texas and assure YAF members, alumni and supporters of their continuing interest in the state. National Chairman Lacy named George Blackman, a sophomore at Southern Methodist University, as the new Texas YAF state chairman. Dallas and SMU became the focal point of YAF activity for the next few years. With support from Young America's Foundation, the new Texas YAF leadership sponsored three Free Enterprise Forums at SMU that involved the business leadership of the Dallas area. Stanley Marcus (Nieman-Marcus) and Herman Lay (Frito-Lay) were the speakers in 1980 while Donald Zale (Zale's Jewelers), Norman Brinker (Steak & Ale), and Charles Jarvie (Dr. Pepper) were among the presenters in 1981. Kip McClinchie became state chairman and coordinated the 1981 event while Rod Knoll presided over the 1982 Free Enterprise seminar.[14]

9. Telephone interview with Gerard Kassar, July 7, 2009.

10. "YAF Chapters Active Throughout Nation," *New Guard*, volume XX, number 1 (1980), p. 4.

11. William Martin: *With God on Our Side* (New York: Broadway Books, 1996) discusses Marshner's efforts on pp. 174–177.

12. Early in a critical election year, YAF had no viable state organizations in such areas as Illinois, Michigan, Georgia, and a number of smaller states while near the bottom in organizational development were Pennsylvania, Florida, and New Jersey. Memo to State Chairmen from Cliff White, Director, State and Chapter Services, February 22, 1980.

13. Fred Bonavita, "Texas YAF Membership Cutting Ties with National Group," *Houston Post*, March 5, 1980.

14. *New Guard*, Fall 1981, p. 49; *Dialogue on Liberty*, Fall 1982, p. 4.

YAF never regained the influence it had in Texas and the strength of the Young Conservatives of Texas ebbed and flowed as new leadership developed and then moved on to other activities. Nevertheless, the YCT managed to solidify itself as a permanent organization in Texas politics and continues to have active chapters on several major campuses today. Its biennial state legislative ratings obtain substantial statewide media coverage and the local chapters work with organizations such as Young America's Foundation to sponsor nationally recognized conservative speakers on campus.[15]

While the loss of many members and chapters in Texas required the attention of the organization, YAF had other internal work to be accomplished since 1980 was the year for the biennial regional conferences. Seven National Directors were re-elected: Barry Miller (New England), Ken Grasso (Mid Atlantic), Dennis Bechtel (Midwest), Terry Cannon (Plains), Lloyd Daugherty (South), Pat Geary (Western), and Brad Peterson (Northwest). The only new member was George Blackman of Texas.[16] In appreciation of the Canadian government's rescue of six Americans from Iran earlier in the year, and in recognition of its one Canadian chapter, YAF scheduled its June 13–15 Board meeting for the Royal York Hotel in Toronto.[17] The Board finalized the plans for YAF's presence in Detroit during the Republican National Convention and received a report on the upcoming 20th anniversary celebration from Lee Edwards, whose firm was coordinating the event.

YAF in Detroit

Soon it was July and time for the Republican National Convention and YAF was prepared to take part in the nomination of their candidate for President of the United States. YAF arranged to house some 120 activists at the University of Detroit where at breakfast each morning they heard from Congressman Robert Dornan, William Rusher, Charles Black, and Kathy King Teague, another YAF alumnus then serving as executive director of the American Legislative Exchange Council. Volunteers engaged in literature blitzes to the various delegations, provided bodies and noise at rallies, met conservative leaders when they arrived at the Detroit airport, and distributed six thousand copies of *New Guard*. Prominent in the magazine was a letter to the delegates from Chairman Lacy and executive director Heckman, reminding the GOP delegates of YAF's contributions to the conservative movement.

> When those young people met some 20 years ago to found YAF, they couldn't possibly have known what would result from their efforts. For the history of the conservative movement over the last two decades is really a history

---

15. For more information, see www.yct.org. The YCT chapters have been aggressive in publicizing their opposition to liberalism. In December 2007 the University of Texas chapter, led by Liz Young, constructed a mock nativity scene with a terrorist shepherd and a gay couple, Gary and Joseph; portraying the wise men as Lenin, Marx and Stalin and the angel as Nancy Pelosi. It was a parody on what they saw as the ACLU idea of the holiday season. "Nativity parody," *Austin American-Statesman*, December 4, 2007.

16. See "First 1980 Regional Held in New England," *New Guard*, volume XX, number 1 (1980), p. 5; "YAF Regional Conferences," *New Guard*, volume XX, number 2 (1980), p. 1; *New Guard*, Summer 1980, p. 44.

17. News release from Young Americans for Freedom dated March 7, 1980.

of the many YAF leaders and graduates who have moved on to build that movement, and make it grow.

Then they reminded the delegates of the responsibilities they had in bringing about a real change in the direction of the country. "The Republican Party has this golden opportunity to show, once and for all, that it stands for something, and that what it stands for means a safer, freer and more prosperous America for all of us."[18] It was a challenge that the delegates would meet that week.

The YAF troops were omnipresent throughout the convention. Kevin Dywer of Washington & Lee University explained that, "I'm here this week to help Reagan. I think it's important that we restore some fiscal sanity to this country. We need a balanced budget." As Mary Lee Horton from Auburn University YAF said, "I consider myself a feminist. But I consider myself a states-righter first, and that's why I'm opposed to the ERA—although I am in favor of abortion."[19] Gerard Kassar of Brooklyn recalled the experience fondly.

> We got there the week before the convention and we had training sessions at the University of Detroit . . . And it was so well organized. To be 21 years old and seeing Reagan at rallies or events two or more times a day where we provided YAF support. It was one of the most wonderful experiences of my life.[20]

Daniel Griswold was a YAF leader at the University of Wisconsin who recalled, "We carried Reagan-Kemp signs in the Joe Lewis Arena." For him, "The organization enabled me to be a small part of a big event—Reagan's nomination in 1980" and "it made me more politically aware and more supportive of the ideals of the 'Reagan Revolution.'"[21] Now Griswold is a trade analyst at the Cato Institute in Washington, DC.

The YAF volunteers not only took part in demonstrations around the city but also were able to attend sessions in the convention hall. Wyoming YAF chairman Dave Scholl and National Director George Blackman, both of whom were in their states' delegations, rounded up gallery passes for the YAF volunteers while Mark Judd and the Michigan YAF members provided a local orientation to the out-of-staters.[22] Special emphasis was given to rallying support for Reagan at his appearances. As *Human Events* reported,

> Wherever Reagan went in Detroit, YAFers were there too. They cheered him upon his arrival at the hotel, twice when his motorcade arrived at Joe Lewis Arena, and during his addresses at the Convention Hall itself. "YAF Backs Reagan" signs, buttons and bumper stickers were everywhere. Though YAF's "Detroit '80 Youth Operation" was a serious program with set goals to accomplish, it obviously was a celebration as well.[23]

18. James Lacy and Robert Heckman, "An Open Letter to Our Friends at the Republican National Convention in Detroit," *New Guard*, Summer 1980, p. 2.

19. Mike Barnicle, "YAF: Youth in a Time Warp," *Boston Globe*, July 18, 1980. Group Research Archives, Box 505, Columbia University, New York, NY.

20. Telephone interview with Gerald Kassar, July 7, 2009.

21. 2008 YAF Alumni Survey Responses: Daniel T. Griswold.

22. Memo from Executive Director to National Board, August 1, 1980.

23. "YAF's Detroit '80 Youth Operation," *Human Events*, August 2, 1980, p. 694.

Among the celebratory events were two receptions attended by overflow crowds. Congressman Bob Bauman was the spokesman at a news conference of YAF delegates and alternates that was followed by a reception in their honor. A total of eighty-four YAF members and alumni were elected as delegates or alternates to the convention.[24]

The most retrospective YAF reception, however, was held to honor Senator Barry Goldwater whose campaign sixteen years earlier was a preface to the events in Detroit. Unfortunately, due to recent surgery and a schedule mixup, Goldwater could not be present. Some five hundred did attend as he was recognized for "his heroic 1964 presidential campaign and essential support of Young Americans for Freedom as an Advisor and Friend." Accepting on his behalf was F. Clifton White.[25] Shortly after the event, Goldwater wrote and apologized for missing the reception and thanking YAF for their honor.

> How sorry I was to have missed being with you and all of those wonderful members of YAF the other day as you paid tribute to me at your reception at the Pontchartrain. . . . I did see Clif White Tuesday evening and he told me how wonderful it was and that he had received the award in my absence. I am truly sorry it wasn't possible for me to be there and I want you to know your honoring me in this way means more to me than you will ever know.[26]

Whatever strains existed from YAF's criticism of the Arizona Senator some four years earlier were now gone. Barry Goldwater was once again YAF's cherished advisor and friend.

While some YAF members were engaged in rallies, literature distribution and receptions, many other YAFers and alumni were involved with official convention responsibilities. Dick Derham presided as Chairman of the Rules Committee while Roy Brun was a key member of the Platform Committee. YAF alumni Frank Donatelli, Charles Black, Roger Stone, Loren Smith and others were Reagan campaign staffers involved with all the convention campaign details in Joe Lewis Arena.

YAF came out of Detroit with renewed media respect. The *Washington Post* said simply that "Reagan's triumph is YAF's triumph" while *Newsday* spoke of the "large throng of Young Americans for Freedom" who filled the convention aisles during the demonstrations for Reagan. Due to the many "YAF Backs Reagan" signs present, a major Reagan campaign rally was described as one where the candidate was "greeted by Young Americans for Freedom" as if YAF had organized the event.[27] When Reagan accepted the nomination, phase one was complete. Now the YAF members had an even more important task ahead of them during the fall—the campaign of their candidate for President of the United States. But before election day, YAF would pause to take note of another historical marker.

24. Memo to YAF Leadership from Peter T. Flaherty concerning "Detroit'80 Youth Operation" Wrap-Up, August 1980.

25. "YAF's Detroit '80 Youth Operation," *Dialogue on Liberty*, Summer 1980, p. 1.

26. Letter from Barry Goldwater to Clifford J. White, III dated July 17, 1980. Goldwater's letter was to YAF's Director of State and Regional Activities while F. Clifton White, manager of the 1964 Draft Goldwater movement, accepted the Senator's award.

27. Memo from Executive Director to National Board, August 1, 1980. Howell Raines, "Reagan Voices Optimism on Unity for Convention," *New York Times*, July 15, 1980.

YAF's 20th Anniversary

Fall 1980 was more than a presidential campaign period for Young Americans for Freedom. It also marked the 20th anniversary of the organization and this milestone was commemorated in a celebration on September 27th at the Mayflower Hotel in Washington. Five distinguished members of the YAF Advisory Board agreed to serve as co-chairmen of the 20th Anniversary Committee: Barry Goldwater, Ronald Reagan, Bill Buckley, Stan Evans, and Bob Bauman. The celebration would have three elements starting with a day-long conference on "The History of the Conservative Movement" sponsored by Young America's Foundation, a 20th anniversary dinner, and on the following day a groundbreaking ceremony for the proposed YAF conference center on the grounds of the YAF national office in Sterling, Virginia.[28]

To commemorate the anniversary YAF prepared a special issue of *New Guard* that was distributed at the dinner. In it, two of the co-chairmen who could not be present at the dinner related their experiences with YAF and its contributions to American society. Barry Goldwater recalled first hearing of the organization's formation from Bill Buckley and how he agreed to speak at its first 1961 rally in Manhattan Center with some trepidation. In the end, YAF not only filled the auditorium but left thousands standing outside disappointed. One year later, he had doubts again about YAF's ability to fill Madison Square Garden, only to be pleasantly surprised. As he noted, "With that rally at Madison Square Garden, YAF really moved into high gear. From then on, every significant conservative action throughout the country bore some trace of YAF involvement." According to Goldwater, "I feel a great measure of pride every time I encounter a leader in politics, in business, or in the newsgathering profession who cut his teeth in YAF. And their numbers are growing. I am amazed at YAF's input into the leadership ranks of this nation, and I believe this is only the beginning."[29] Goldwater concluded by saying he had a tremendous debt to the early YAF leaders who contributed much to his campaign of 1964, a campaign that laid the groundwork for future conservative success.

Reagan also praised YAF and said that it was always invigorating to be around its members. "It is when I am among young people like those in YAF that I am most forcefully reminded that what makes America different from other nations is that we're always looking forward, and never backward." He added, "a generation of young people received a priceless education in practical political action. Working in everything from campus elections to national political campaigns, YAFers have learned how to get things done in a democratic society."[30]

These themes of survival, success, resilience, and continued challenges were echoed in the various remarks as YAF gathered to review its past and project a future that they hoped would be spent as part of a Reagan Administration in the 1980s. Bob Bauman served as emcee for the evening and the program began with a toast to the organization by Senator Strom Thurmond, another of its

---

28. Letter from Congressman Robert E. Bauman to Rick Abell, June 2, 1980, in author's possession. Memo to Interested Parties from Executive Director, Young Americans for Freedom, August 26, 1980.
29. Barry Goldwater, "YAF and the Early Years," *New Guard*, Fall 1980, pp. 14–15.
30. Ronald Reagan, "YAF: Twenty Years of Conservative Leadership," *New Guard*, Fall 1980, pp. 12–13.

long-standing Advisory Board members. Then Stan Evans, its author, read the Sharon Statement to remind all of the principles on which YAF was founded and the foundation on which it continued to operate. Next came the YAF Hall of Fame presentations to Russell Kirk (by Lee Edwards), Phyllis Schlafly (presented by Carol Bauman), and H.E. "Eddie" Chiles (by George Strake). The award to Reagan, who was busy campaigning at the time, was made by Jim Lacy and accepted by actor Mike Connors, star of the television series "Mannix."[31] YAF Freedom Fighter Awards were presented to President Chiang Ching-Kuo of the Republic of China (accepted by Ambassador Konsin Shah), Simas Kudirka (the Lithuanian sailor who sought refuge in the United States), Dr. Stefan Korbanski of the Assembly of Captive European Nations, and Captain John McCain (later Senator and presidential candidate in 2008). Then came an address by Bill Buckley, the organization's godfather.[32]

Writing about the event later, Stan Evans stressed the work of YAF in producing a bevy of conservative leaders for the present and future in America. Twenty years after its founding YAF had succeeded in making many of its views mainstream, much more so than the organization's founders could have thought possible. As Evans noted, "Somehow, limited government, the market economy, and defense of America's national interests overseas don't seem so laughable today as they did in 1960."[33] Less than one month later, the American people would elect a new President dedicated to those same conservative principles enumerated by Evans in the organization's credo.

On November 4, 1980 Ronald Reagan did not merely win the presidential election against President Carter and Congressman John B. Anderson. Reagan's victory was nothing less than a landslide, carrying 44 states.[34] As YAF Chairman Jim Lacy stated in the organization's annual report for 1980, "President Reagan. Those two words express the pride and optimism which all of us feel as we enter the third decade of Young Americans for Freedom."[35] The Reagan landslide also produced the first Republican control of the United States Senate since 1955. Sixteen new GOP Senators were elected to give the party a 53–47 Senate majority. Among the new members were several backed by YAF's independent political action committee, Fund for a Conservative Majority.[36] With so many new Republican Senators and party control of all Senate committees, literally hundreds of new staff positions opened up in the Senate at the same time a new conservative administration was staffing the Executive Branch. If ever there were

---

31. Chiles was a businessman who ran five minute radio spots that were introduced with "What's got you mad today, Eddie?" followed by his critique of various government policies and decisions. Thousands of cars displayed bumper stickers proclaiming "I'm Mad Too Eddie!" Strake, a YAF member at Harvard, was Texas Secretary of State.

32. "YAF Celebrates 20th Anniversary," *New Guard*, volume XX, number 10, pp. 1, 4–6. Personal Papers of William F. Buckley, Jr., Box 189, Folder: YAF, Yale University, New Haven, CT.

33. M. Stanton Evans, "The Conservative Mainstream," *National Review*, October 31, 1980, p. 1326.

34. Much has been written on the 1980 election and especially its aftermath. The most comprehensive history is Craig Shirley: *Rendezvous with Destiny* (Wilmington, DE: ISI Books, 2009). Among those which provide a review are Lee Edwards: *The Conservative Revolution*, pp. 200–224; Steven Hayward: *The Age of Reagan*, pp. 677–717; Gerald Pomper: *The Election of 1980: Reports and Interpretations* (Chatham, NJ: Chatham House Publishers, 1981); Jack W. Germond and Jules Witcover: *Blue Smoke and Mirrors* (New York: Viking Press, 1981).

35. James Lacy, "YAF's Principles Triumph in 1980," *New Guard*, Winter, 1980–81, p. 8.

36. "Conservatives Achieve Senate Control in '80!" *FCM Report*, Fund for a Conservative Majority, Winter 1980. FCM was originally Young America's Campaign Committee and its chairman in 1980 was Robert Heckman, at the time executive director of YAF.

a time for young conservatives to move to Washington and seek employment, the early months of 1981 was the time.

On campuses, the Reagan victory was an opportunity to consolidate conservative support and build new YAF chapters. Even on unfriendly territory, YAF launched active organizational efforts. One week after the election, an organizational meeting for revitalizing a YAF chapter was held at Harvard University. James Higgins, YAF chapter chairman, admitted that, "I don't expect to convert a lot of people" but the organization would "let people know that there are conservatives on campus."[37] While the Harvard chapter had only 12 members, its chairman played an active role as leader of a statewide effort against mandatory funding for Nader's PIRGs and became chairman of the Massachusetts College Republican Union.[38]

At Columbia University, Vasos Panagiotopoulis and Henry Kriegel revitalized a chapter that had become almost dormant. With Reagan's victory, a sense of pride and hope developed among campus conservatives.[39] One year later, YAF had become such a recognized force on the Columbia campus that Kriegel's picture was featured on the cover of the *Columbia Spectator* magazine section. Kriegel noted, "the problems on campus for conservatives are fear and the effect of the "me generation." . . . We are strongest where the opposition is greatest. They're stronger in YAF because they have to be. It's not numbers—it's quality."[40] Similar efforts resulted in chapters being formed at the University of Pennsylvania, Dartmouth and Cornell as well as a revitalized effort at Yale.

YAF ended 1980 with big plans for the future. It would use the election of a conservative President in appealing to students on campus as well as to supporters who could help expand the services available from the organization. One day after the 20th anniversary dinner, Strom Thurmond had broken ground for the new YAF conference center in Sterling and the organization's leaders were optimistic that the funding for this new building could be obtained. Prior to the November election, Bob Heckman claimed, "Perhaps the most significant event of the year for YAF, then, was the launching of plans for YAF's modern new Conference Center on our grounds in Sterling."[41] Unfortunately, those plans would never come to fruition.

With Reagan in the White House and Republicans in control of the Senate, it was no wonder that YAF looked to the decade of the 1980s with renewed optimism. As Cliff White, State and Chapter Services Director, commented, "YAF has come of age. We're ready to lead."[42] But YAF's success in training young conservatives for leadership and in their maturing meant that they had less time and interest for building and maintaining a youth organization. More and more their focus turned from the high school and college campus to Washington, to positions in government or the growing number of conservative organizations expanding their presence in the Nation's Capital. Having won the battle for the White House there was simply less interest and involvement in the battle for the campus. To those who had "come of age," there were bigger battles to be waged to redirect

37. Jacob M. Schlesinger, "YAF Meeting," *The Harvard Crimson*, November 14, 1980.
38. "Purging PIRG," *The Harvard Crimson*, March 16, 1983.
39. Interview with Vasos Panagiotopoulis, New York, New York, June 22, 2009.
40. Rifka Rosenwein, "Fighting the Liberals at CU," *Broadway: Columbia Spectator's Bi-weekly Magazine of Issues and the Arts*, October 29, 1981, pp. 5–6.
41. Robert Heckman, "Annual Report," *New Guard*, Winter 1980–81, p. 10.
42. *New Guard*, Winter 1980–81, p. 14.

American government and society. This paradox would haunt Young Americans for Freedom throughout the decade as they tried to keep alive an organization, many of whose members were focused on other issues, environments, and battles.

A New Beginning for America

January 20, 1981 was a cold and windy day in the Nation's Capital but the weather did not deter the enthusiasm of the thousands of conservatives gathered for the inauguration of a new President. For them, it was truly "a new beginning" and the opportunity to put into practice the principles and policies they had been articulating and advocating for years. To bring about those changes would require more than one individual. YAF members and alumni were ready to put aside their other occupations and careers to serve Ronald Reagan as he assumed the office of President of the United States.

The list of YAFers who joined the administration was extensive. In the Office of the President were speechwriters Dana Rohrabacher and Tony Dolan. Wayne Valis was in the Office of Public Liaison while Ken Cribb served as an aide to Edwin Meese. Former Stanford YAF chairman Doug Bandow worked in the Domestic Council while Richard Beal was in Planning and Evaluation and Bill Schneider was at the Office of Management and Budget. James C. Roberts oversaw the White House Fellows Program while Willa Johnson and Becky Norton-Dunlop helped to screen applicants in the Office of Presidential Personnel.[43] As Ken Grasso, New York YAF state chairman, observed, "Practically everyone under 40 in the Administration is an alumnus of YAF."[44] By the summer of 1981 it was reported that some fifty YAF members or alumni had been appointed to the White House staff.[45]

Outside the White House complex itself, YAF members and alumni held other key positions in the administration. Don Devine was Director of the Office of Personnel Management where he was assisted by Pat Korten, Cliff White, Michael Sanera, and Bob Moffit, among others.[46] Richard Abell, a YAF Director and former Peace Corps volunteer was appointed to a key position at the Peace Corps while Connie Campanella, former Adelphi University chairman, and Mark Levin, Temple University YAF leader, joined the staff at ACTION. A number of YAF alumni were appointed to positions in the various Cabinet departments including Carol Dawson Bauman at the Department of Energy, Michelle Easton at the Treasury, James Meadows and John Schrote at Agriculture, David Williams and Steve Some at Labor and James Lacy at Commerce. Carl Olson of Los Angeles County YAF became a special assistant at Health and Human Services while Bud Wandling

---

43. Rohrabacher, a former California YAF state chairman, is currently a Congressman from California while Dolan, a Pulitzer prize-winning reporter, later served in the George W. Bush Administration. Valis is now president of Valis & Keelen, government affairs consultants in DC while Cribb is president of the Intercollegiate Studies Institute. Bandow is a Senior Fellow at The Cato Institute and Schneider, later an Undersecretary of State, is president of International Planning Services, Inc. Roberts is president of Radio America and the American Studies Center while Norton-Dunlop is Vice President of External Relations at the Heritage Foundation.

44. Rosenwein, "Fighting the Liberals at CU," p. 5.

45. Dudley Clendinen, "After 20 Years, Young Conservatives Enjoy a Long-Awaited Rise to Power," *New York Times*, August 22, 1981.

46. Devine's experiences at OPM are described in his *Reagan's Terrible Swift Sword: Reforming and Controlling the Federal Bureaucracy* (Ottawa, IL: Jameson Books, 1991).

became marketing director at the Government Printing Office. These YAFers received their appointments during the first few months of the Administration while others joined it later, either in Washington or the various regional offices of the Federal government.[47]

Still others obtained positions on Capitol Hill either with the new conservative members of the House and Senate or among the various Senate committees now controlled by the Republican majority. Joining YAF alumni Phil Crane, Barry Goldwater, Jr., and James Sensenbrenner in the House of Representatives were Jack Fields of Texas and John LeBoutellier of New York while Dan Quayle joined the Republican majority in the Senate. With so many conservatives in government, the Left was in a state of apoplexy. For Molly Ivins there was little satisfaction in the fact that many were former YAFers.

> The government has been taken over by YAFers. All you one time college students will remember YAFers—the Young Americans for Freedom—who used to bustle around on campus in those dorky suits, like Mormons on speed. Well, now they're in Congress. Some of the new representatives were just Young Republicans in college, rather than the YAFers, which is worse news, because at least YAF had that nice, goofy subset of libertarians who were a lot of fun. Young Republicans were never fun.[48]

Little did the Left know in 1981 that Reagan would be re-elected in a landslide and Republicans would continue to be in charge of the Senate for six years before relinquishing control in 1987.

As President Reagan said in his taped remarks to the 1981 YAF convention, "Many members of the White House staff had their start in Young Americans for Freedom. Individuals like Don Devine, serving as director of the Office of Personnel Management, are former YAFers and now hold sensitive and important jobs in this administration."[49] Through their contacts in YAF, any number of young conservatives were brought to Washington to help staff the new administration. Roger Pilon, a YAF member at the University of Chicago, was one of the early appointees at OPM and recommended attorney Joe Morris, a fellow University of Chicago YAF member, to Don Devine. As he retold it,

> I'll never forget Don's reaction when I urged him, after summarizing Joe's credentials, to consider Joe for the job: "What? You want some 29-year old kid to be the General Counsel of OPM?" "Just interview him," I answered. "You'll hire him." And he did! The rest is history, which we were all making back then when we were young.[50]

---

47. As is the custom, many of these YAF appointees changed positions within the Reagan Administration and several continued in Federal service during the administration of George H.W. Bush. See: Donald Devine, "YAF and the Reagan Administration," *New Guard*, Fall 1981, pp. 12–14; James C. Roberts, "YAF and the Reagan Administration," *New Guard*, Fall 1961, pp. 14–15; "YAF Alumni Join Administration," *Dialogue on Liberty*, Spring 1981, p. 3. Beal and Schrote were mentioned as YAF alumni in Group Research Archives, Box 400, Columbia University, New York, NY.

48. Molly Ivins: *You Got to Dance with Them What Brung You* (New York: Random House, 1998), p. 142.

49. Clendinen, "After 20 Years."

50. Email from Roger Pilon, January 5, 2009.

Morris later served as an Assistant Attorney General in the Reagan Administration and then returned to Chicago where he practices law and served from 1995 to 2001 as president of B'nai B'rith in the Midwest.

More and more YAF members came to the Nation's Capital and became involved in the Reagan Revolution, leaving fewer active young conservatives on the campuses and in communities across the nation. Unfortunately for the organization's well being, too few of them followed the pattern of Morris. Just as the old World War One song asked, "How you gonna keep 'em down on the farm after they've seen Paree?" the same problem was being felt by Young Americans for Freedom as a broad swath of the organization's leadership came to Washington and never left. A common comment in Washington at the time claimed "Conservatives know when they come to Washington that it's a sewer; trouble is, most of them wind up treating it like a hot tub." Apparently, for many the temperature was just right in the Nation's Capital. According to Steve Wiley, whose involvement in YAF spanned three decades, "Reagan's victory was almost the worst thing that could have happened to us. Our best guys either went home or used the Reagan connection as a stepping stone to jobs."[51]

While the new administration took much of the attention of young conservatives, YAF continued to co-sponsor the annual Conservative Political Action Conference. The 1981 event was a display of conservatism's newly won power with addresses by the President, Vice President, and numerous White House officials. CPAC played an important role in allowing YAF members to meet with conservative political leaders. As University of Pennsylvania YAF chairman Alan Ashkinaze recently recalled, "For a young conservative, CPAC was an unbelievable experience. For college and high school students, it was a special opportunity to see and meet the leaders of the conservative movement and even to have one's picture taken with people like Jack Kemp."[52] John Fifer, chairman at the University of Nebraska, was asked by the secret service to take tickets as guests were passing through the metal detector outside the room where the President would speak.

> One lady in particular started to enter without giving me a ticket. At this point I held out my arm and said to her, "excuse me, I need your ticket," at which point the gentleman behind her said to me, "son, I'm Senator Jesse Helms and we don't need a ticket." What a thrill it was.[53]

In his speech that night, the President reminded those present of the seriousness of the challenge before them. "Fellow citizens, fellow conservatives, our time is now. Our moment has arrived ... If we carry the day and turn the tide we can hope that as long as men speak of freedom and those who have protected it, they will remember us and they will say, 'Here were the brave and here their place of honor.'"[54]

YAF took up the challenge and launched "Youth for the Reagan Agenda" to rally support for the President's legislative program with literature and speakers as well as related efforts on campuses and in communities across America.

---

51. Quoted in Clancy Sigal, "Doing the Right Thing," *Los Angeles Times Magazine*, April 29, 1990, p. 28.
52. Telephone interview with Alan Ashkinaze, December 16, 2008.
53. 2008 YAF Alumni Survey Responses: John Fifer.
54. "Conservative Political Action Conference Features President, Administration Officials," *Dialogue on Liberty*, Spring 1981, p. 1.

National Chairman Jim Lacy explained, "The project is focused on generating youth support for the President's economic program which is under fire from liberals in Congress though supported by a majority of American citizens." Lacy concluded, "Only by helping ensure a stable, thriving economy now can America's young people look forward with optimism to the future."[55]

While a new conservative administration was taking hold in Washington, that did not mean the immediate end of liberal policies being carried out by businesses more interested in trade than opposing communism. To combat this practice, YAF continued its opposition to East–West trade in strategic goods by purchasing shares in several corporations. This allowed YAF to have a vote at annual stockholder meetings and introduce a resolution calling for an end to trade with Communist countries. According to Peter Flaherty, Project Director for the organization, "YAF has had a Stop Red Trade project for 16 or 17 years—almost since our inception. In the past, individual members have used their stock at annual meetings. This is the first year we're going as an organization." Flaherty maintained that the dealings of General Electric, DuPont, and Standard Oil of Ohio provided Communist nations with both capital and technological advancements that aided their expansionist military policies.[56]

The following year YAF kept alive its opposition to East–West trade with a well-publicized demonstration outside the Los Angeles headquarters of Occidental Petroleum. Its chairman was Armand Hammer, an individual who had been a friend of V.I. Lenin and in 1982 had a multi-billion dollar grain deal with the Soviet Union. Some 35 YAF protesters carried signs reading "US grain builds strong Soviet soldiers," and "Stop the (Armand) Hammer and Sickle." The demonstration was coordinated by high school YAFer Deroy Murdock and Carl Olson.[57] Olson would be the impetus for many stockholder resolutions, including those that called on corporations to cease providing funding to colleges and universities where military and CIA recruiting was prohibited.

By 1983, YAF was focusing its attention on other companies. One proposal before the Gulf Oil Corporation would require the company to cease operations in Angola, where an anti-communist force led by Jonas Savimba was attempting to overthrow a Marxist government. Resolutions presented before IBM, Exxon, and PepsiCo would require the companies to "stop dealing with countries that use prisoner or slave labor." While the various corporations spent literally hundreds of thousands of dollars attempting to keep the proposals off stockholder proxy statements, YAF remained successful in getting the issues debated and voted upon. The end result was great publicity for YAF and for the issue of dealing with Communist countries but no success in obtaining a majority of votes from the shareholders.[58]

YAF also had its continuing mission to promote conservatism to fellow students. The principles of free market economics and the Reagan program were of particular interest and comprised a number of YAF chapter programs. Boston College YAF presented economist Walter Williams to discuss the negative effect of

55. "YAF Project Mobilizes Conservative Youth," *Dialogue on Liberty*, Spring 1981, p. 6.

56. Michael F. Conlon, "YAF Buying Stock to End Trade with Communists," *Washington Post*, March 19, 1981.

57. "Rightists picket Occidental Petroleum," *Los Angeles Herald-Examiner*, February 14, 1982. The demonstration was also carried in the *Los Angeles Times* of the same day.

58. Paul Goldberg, "The New Right Plays Politics on The Proxy Circuit," *Washington Post*, April 17, 1983. Group Research Archives, Box 511, Columbia University, New York, NY.

the minimum wage on youth employment. Louisiana State University YAF, under the leadership of chairman Chris Hannon, heard a presentation on "Reaganomics" by Economics Professor David B. Johnson.[59] At Rutgers, chairman Brian Pollock lined up 1978 Senate candidate and former Reagan advisor Jeffrey Bell to address a chapter meeting. David Bustamonte of Queens College YAF debated a campus socialist at one chapter meeting while Southern Methodist University YAF sponsored its second Free Enterprise Forum on campus.[60]

Foreign policy issues and the battle against Communist expansionism around the globe drew the attention of campus YAF chapters also. At Washington & Lee University, the YAF chapter, led by David Tyson, sponsored an appearance by Dr. Cleto DiGiovanni of the Central American Working Group, who discussed insurgent efforts in El Salvador. This was also the topic for Enrique Altamirano, newspaper editor from San Salvador, when he spoke before Vassar College YAF. At Liberty University, Roy Jones and Bryan Kurtz organized Human Rights Week and circulated petitions supporting Polish freedom as well as hosted a speaker from the Committee for a Free Afghanistan.

More than economics and foreign policy caught the attention of YAF campus chapters. Washington & Lee YAF held a mock gubernatorial election that received coverage in the Richmond and Roanoke newspapers. Southern Methodist University YAF held a forum on "Judeo-Christian Roles in American Politics," while Rutgers YAF sponsored an address by Richard Freund of the American Jewish Forum. Among a number of speakers it brought to campus, Columbia University YAF hosted Dr. Mildred Jefferson of the Right to Life Crusade.[61] Phillip Buhler, chairman of the College of William & Mary YAF chapter, recalled those times on campus as a "tremendous experience, quite active particularly as this was during the Reagan Revolution."[62]

Beyond hosting speakers and rallying support for the Reagan agenda, the University of Washington chapter launched a full-scale attack on fees for PIRGs while across the country at Rutgers University Joseph P. Galda continued his fight, first with a lawsuit against the university and then with a student referendum.[63] Galda's crusade did not end the practice on his campus but it did receive editorial support from an unlikely source—the *New York Times*. In a brief editorial, the paper stated,

> It's perfectly appropriate for universities to collect mandatory student fees for nonpartisan, educational activities. But the Public Interest Research Group, one of many campus organizations inspired by consumer advocate Ralph Nader, has a political agenda that some students support and others don't. No one should have to pay such a fee.[64]

As YAF's campus chapters continued the battle, the national office distributed a new issues paper titled "Mandatory Fees: Wouldn't You Rather Have Control of Your Own Money?" YAF's argument was that college students were mature enough

---

59. *New Guard*, Fall 1981, p. 48.
60. *New Guard*, Spring 1981, p. 48.
61. *New Guard*, Fall 1981, p. 48.
62. 2008 YAF Alumni Survey Responses: Phillip A. Buhler.
63. Donald Janson, "Rutgers Senior Presses Fight to Abolish Mandatory Fees to Advocacy Group," *New York Times*, November 11, 1981.
64. Editorial, "Fee Frustration," *New York Times*, November 15, 1981.

to make decisions for themselves. The paper claimed, "Apparently the college bureaucrats feel that a 18–22 year old student is not old or wise enough to make their own decisions." YAF opposed mandatory fees on both a philosophical and practical basis. "In the end, Young Americans for Freedom asks you: 'Wouldn't you rather have control over your own money?' More importantly, 'don't you think you are old enough to make your own decisions?'"[65]

11th National Convention—Boston

August 19, 1981 was the first day of YAF's eleventh national convention, this time held in Boston. As had been traditional, William F. Buckley, Jr. gave the opening keynote address. Considering the conservative successes of 1980, one observer noted, "It was difficult not to be taken up in the swell of enthusiasm, and it became the duty of YAF leaders and convention speakers to counsel and caution the group as to the battles yet to come."[66] Buckley emphasized three points for the young conservatives to keep in mind. First, supply-side economics cannot replace traditional support for budget restraint. Second, distrust of the military draft needs to be balanced with the service young Americans owe their nation in recognizing "collective responsibility as well as individual liberty." Third, YAFers were urged to devote some of their lives to caring for the elderly, an increasing part of the population.[67]

The second day was filled with a series of panels on practical and philosophical topics and included an address by Congressman John LeBoutellier, himself a YAF member from New York and author of a scathing attack on campus liberalism at his alma mater.[68] Young America's Foundation sponsored a luncheon for the YAF delegates with Professor Jeffrey Hart as the featured speaker. One afternoon program focused on "The Conservative Youth Movement Internationally" with participants from the United Kingdom, West Germany, El Salvador, and the European Democratic Students organization.[69]

Thursday night was devoted to the Reagan Administration with addresses by Interior Secretary James Watt and Labor Secretary Raymond Donovan preceded by a taped special message from the President. Before Watt and Donovan could speak to the delegates they were greeted by some 80 demonstrators from Greenpeace and the Sierra Club marching outside the Park Plaza Hotel, protesting what they viewed as Watt's anti-environmental policies. To counter the anti-Watt picketers, "YAFers quickly abandoned a reception and charged into the streets in suits, tuxedos, and formal gowns to outshout the jeering neo-Luddites."[70] Inside, Watt and Donovan received loud ovations when they approached the dais, prompting Watt to remark, "It's great to be in front of a rowdy crowd that's with me!"[71]

65. "Mandatory Fees" issues paper, Young Americans for Freedom, 1981. Personal Papers of Jameson Campaigne, Jr., Ottawa, IL.

66. Janette Imholz, "Buckley Urges YAFers to Give More Help to Care of Nation's Senior Citizens," *Conservative Digest*, October 1981, pp. 36–37. Personal Papers of William F. Buckley, Jr., Box 189, Folder: YAF, Sterling Library, Yale University, New Haven, CT.

67. David Pietrusza, "Coming of Age," *National Review*, September 18, 1981, p. 1081.

68. *Harvard Hates America* (Chicago: Regnery Publishing, 1978).

69. "Boston '81 Convention Program," Hall-Hoag Collection, Box 49–13, John Hay Library, Brown University, Providence, RI.

70. Pietrusza, "Coming of Age."

71. Imholz, "Buckley Urges YAFers," p. 36.

In his taped message the President thanked YAF for its support over the years and urged them to continue proselytizing and training new leaders. According to Reagan, "Your dedication, your enthusiasm and your energy play an important role in shaping the American political scene. And in the years ahead, I am sure we can count on all of you, just as we have on YAF members over the years, to fight the good fight."[72] Reagan reminded them that they had a continuing responsibility on their high school and college campuses. "You must continue to provide the kind of philosophical and practical training which offers alternatives to today's youth in order to develop the next generation of leaders for America."[73] The President concluded his remarks by proclaiming, "As we chart the difficult course toward America's new beginning, our nation needs Young Americans for Freedom more than ever."[74] It was the message these young conservatives wanted to hear.

While National Chairman Jim Lacy was unopposed for another two-year term, there were lively contests for the nine slots on the National Board of Directors. Elected by the delegates were four incumbents and five new members. Re-elected were Suzanne Scholte, Patrick Geary, Sam Pimm, and Paul Prince. The new members were John Abernethy and Gerard Kassar of New York, Floyd Brown of Washington, Mark Judd of Michigan, and Larry Hunter of South Carolina.[75] Perhaps the only controversial debate during the platform deliberations involved whether opposition to the draft should be universal or limited to peacetime. After a lengthy struggle, the YAFers modified their previous position by keeping their opposition to a peacetime draft but leaving open the possibility of support for one during wartime.[76]

Saturday evening featured a banquet billed as "A Salute to America's Forgotten Heroes" with an address by ACTION Director Tom Pauken, the administration's highest ranking Vietnam veteran, and by former POW John McCain, a frequent speaker at YAF events of the time. As one writer concluded, "The most emotional part of the convention was a tribute to veterans of the Vietnam War. John McCain, now a Senator from Arizona and a former POW, gave a stirring speech about his comrades."[77] Recognized for their sacrifices were a number of disabled veterans, former POWs, and the parents of a pilot missing in Laos.[78] The 1981 convention ended on Sunday morning with an address in historic Fanueil Hall by Congressman Mickey Edwards, chairman of the ACU, who told the delegates, "We need to keep the pressure on to stop cities and local governments from running to the government for subsidies every time they want to build a park or improve a roadway."[79]

It was a heady time for the 360 delegates as they met in Boston. As Deroy Murdock, a high school student from Los Angeles observed, "President Reagan has made us proud to be Americans. He's been able to focus public attention on one issue at a time." According to Michael Cross of the University of Oregon, YAF's new influence over the nation's affairs had its members in a state of euphoria.

---

72. *Ibid.*
73. Clendinen, "After 20 Years."
74. Imholz, "Buckley Urges YAFers," p. 36.
75. "Boston '81 Charts Young Conservative Course," *New Guard*, volume XXI, number 7, p. 6. See also *Dialogue on Liberty*, Fall–Winter 1981, p. 1.
76. Pietrusza, "Coming of Age."
77. Gregory Schneider: *Cadres for Conservatism*, p. 171.
78. Imholz, "Buckley Urges YAFers," p. 36.
79. *Ibid.* p. 37.

For Sam Stafford of Portland State University, the future looked bright. "I see the conservatives in America—should we have a good year in 1982, because that's the watershed year—running this country for the next 50 years."[80] YAF's success, according to University of Wisconsin graduate student Mark Huber "is because YAF is concerned with the issues that Americans are concerned with these days, taxes and the economy." California high school student John Manly claimed, "When the government is feeding you instead of stimulating you to work, the poor are still poor and the unemployed still unemployed. You get on the dole and there's no incentive to work." As Sergio Picchio observed, "We've never changed. The mood of the country changed."[81]

Perhaps what was changing also was the perception of the media, still stuck in its stereotypical image of young conservatives as crew cut, long skirts, and button-down shirts. As Peter Flaherty summarized it, "If you look at YAF, you would see that we're not the sons and daughters of the affluent. We are middle class movers." Dressed in jeans, Geraldine Voelkel did concede however, "Even if we're wearing jeans, they're still clean jeans."[82]

One of the guests in the hotel at the time of the YAF convention was television personality Phil Donahue, whose left-wing loyalties were worn as a badge of honor. Donahue was fascinated by the presence of young people who actually supported Ronald Reagan and his conservative philosophy. He invited Chairman Lacy and executive director Heckman to appear on his show, thus giving additional national exposure to the organization.[83] Leaving Boston, the delegates were on a high note. Although the convention attendance was below that of most previous years they were united and they had their man as President of the United States. Unfortunately, personality disputes would soon raise their ugly head and YAF would be embroiled in the most serious challenge to its continued existence.

Division in the Ranks—Once More

By the fall of 1981 a clear division was apparent in Young Americans for Freedom between the National Chairman, James Lacy, and the executive director, Robert Heckman. The tension appeared to heighten after Lacy moved from California to accept a position with the Reagan Administration in Washington, DC. Soon it was involving all members of the National Board. While six of the nine Directors elected at the Boston convention were allied with Heckman, the division on the entire Board was much closer. At its August 1981 meeting, the Board voted to select a site for the 1983 National Convention. Lacy preferred Los Angeles while Heckman wanted it held in New York City. In a precursor of what was to come, Lacy prevailed by one vote.[84] By fall, the divisions on the Board were solidifying.

It was in such a context that Lacy decided to ask the Board of Directors to remove Heckman as executive director. Word spread quickly in advance of the December meeting and the letters and phone calls on both sides of the issue began. One letter sent to a number of YAF leaders and advisors, signed by eight

80. Clendinen, "After 20 Years."
81. Gloria Negri, "Young Conservatives—with Jeans," *Boston Globe*, August 20, 1981.
82. *Ibid.*
83. Schneider: *Cadres for Conservatism*, p. 172.
84. *Ibid.*

chairmen of YAF chapters recently recognized by the organization as "outstanding," called on members to "Call, write and visit your National Director and ask him to present any substantive reason why Bob Heckman should not be retained. Short of doing so, ask them to reaffirm their support."[85]

Those wanting to remove Heckman claimed that, "it is absolutely necessary that a majority of the National Board of Directors and the National Chairman have full confidence in the ability and integrity of the Executive Director." The Directors supporting Lacy declared "we no longer hold Mr. Robert C. Heckman in such confidence and that we hereby terminate his employment in Young Americans for Freedom."[86]

On December 20, 1981, the National Board of Directors met and voted to terminate Heckman's contract. The vote was 12–12 with the National Chairman breaking the tie. A few days later, YAF leaders received a memo from Peter Flaherty, who had resigned as Projects Director at the national office when Heckman was removed. Attacking the Heckman firing, he maintained that six of ten staff members had left and the only solution to the crisis was for Lacy to resign.[87] Flaherty became the point person for those opposed to Lacy's removal of Heckman.

For the next several months there was, in effect, a rival organization operating as the "Committee to Save YAF."[88] Led by Flaherty, the Heckman supporters filed suit in Delaware, where YAF was incorporated, claiming that six Board members were improperly elected or otherwise should not hold office. In addition to the time and cost eaten up on both sides of the lawsuit, according to one observer, "the most damaging and demoralizing part of the whole business was a nationally circulated paper storm of accusations and denials generated by YAFers at all levels."[89]

As the internal disputes continued, four leading conservatives who were YAF advisors—Bill Buckley, Stan Evans, Bill Rusher, and Tom Winter—called upon former executive director Frank Donatelli to propose a settlement aimed at ending the YAF dispute. Unfortunately, when Donatelli met with representatives of the two factions in September 1982, no agreement could be reached. Reporting back to the four advisors, Donatelli concluded, "the Flaherty faction apparently believes that it can obtain majority control of the Board of YAF by pursuing its suit in the courts."[90] To this end, Flaherty sent a formal letter to the advisors and Donatelli turning down the proposed settlement.[91]

---

85. The letter was signed by the chairmen of the four chapters recognized as outstanding for 1979–1981 at the Boston National Convention as well as the "Chapter of the Month" for August, September, October and November 1981. However, the decisions on recognizing these chapters would have been made by the staff headed by Heckman. Personal Papers of William F. Buckley, Jr., Box 189, Folder 1983, Sterling Library, Yale University, New Haven, CT.

86. Unsigned and undated statement from certain National Directors of Young Americans for Freedom, in author's possession.

87. Leadership Bulletin, December 22, 1981. Letter to William F. Buckley from James V. Lacy dated December 23, 1981. Letter to YAF Activists from Peter T. Flaherty. Personal Papers of William F. Buckley, Jr., Box 189, Folder YAF, Sterling Library, Yale University, New Haven, CT.

88. Personal Papers of William F. Buckley, Jr., Box 189, Folder 1982, Sterling Library, Yale University, New Haven, CT. A list of some members of the committee can be found in Schneider: *Cadres for Conservatism*, p. 234.

89. Jeff Nelligan, "All Together Again?" *National Review*, September 16, 1983, p. 1136.

90. Memo to Jim Lacy, Peter Flaherty, Vernon Procter and Wyatt Durrette from Frank J. Donatelli regarding YAF Settlement dated September 3, 1982. Memo to William F. Buckley, Jr., M. Stanton Evans, William A. Rusher, and Thomas S. Winter from Frank J. Donatelli dated September 17, 1982. Personal Papers of William F. Buckley, Jr., Box 189, Folder 1982, Sterling Library, Yale University, New Haven, CT.

91. Letter to Buckley, Rusher, Evans, Winter and Donatelli from Peter T. Flaherty, September 17, 1982. Personal Papers of William A. Rusher, Box 173, File 10, Library of Congress, Washington, DC.

Eight months later the Court of Chancery in Delaware issued its opinion, ruling in favor of the Lacy position and chastising the group for engaging in such litigation.[92] The two factions had settled two of the original six disputed seats with each side recognizing one from the other faction. A third seat was awarded to the Lacy faction in the Chancellor's decision. Both parties agreed to refer the remaining three seats to an arbitrator. Three months later the arbitrator ruled in favor of the Lacy faction on all three of the remaining disputed seats. Flaherty conceded defeat in a memo to his supporters and sadly concluded, "This sorry chapter in the annals of the conservative movement is over . . . YAF introduced us to politics. It remains to be seen whether YAF can ever recover and play the role it did so successfully for 20 years."[93] That same month YAF held its 12th biennial convention in Los Angeles. Whether due to its geographical location (it was the first time a convention had been held west of Houston) or the internal dissension (few of the Heckman-Flaherty supporters made the trip) it was attended by fewer delegates than any in the organization's previous history.

The Grass Roots Remains Alive

Despite the internal discord and legal battles that consumed much of national YAF's time and resources throughout the year of 1982, YAF continued its co-sponsorship of CPAC and held eight regional conferences over several weeks in the spring.[94] Re-elected to National Director positions were George Blackman (Southwest), Gary Kreep (Western), Doug Bourdon (New England), Bob Dolan (Mid-Atlantic), and Terry Cannon (Plains) while Nate Buff joined the Board by being elected at the Northwest regional and Lewis Doherty won election in the Southern region.[95] Conflict arose over the elections in the Plains, Mid-Atlantic, and Midwest regional conferences with supporters of both Lacy and Heckman claiming to have won. Perhaps the most hotly contested race was in the Midwest where Ted Lesley of Michigan (a Heckman supporter) won the election but Lacy, who was at the conference, declared the election "null and void" and set another date for the election, allowing incumbent Director Dennis Bechtel to retain his place on the Board. While Bechtel was seated, and later replaced by Rob Schuler of Ohio, the Chancery Court in Delaware ruled the following year that Lesley should have been declared the winner and he joined the Board for a brief period of time.[96]

Although the internal political and legal disputes continued, local chapter activity remained high. Working with Young America's Foundation, many YAF chapters sponsored a series of speakers on their campuses.[97] At Hillsdale College, the YAF chapter led by Tim Hoffman and Michelle Wing sponsored supply-side

---

92. From the Judge's order: "this has to constitute the most sophomoric exercise that I have yet been compelled to endure in the name of disposing of legal issues." Order of Grover C. Brown, Chancellor, Court of Chancery, Delaware issued on May 20, 1983. Personal Papers of William F. Buckley, Jr., Box 189, Folder 1983, Sterling Library, Yale University, New Haven, CT.

93. Memo to Friends from Peter T. Flaherty dated August 18, 1983. Group Research Archives, Box 505, Columbia University, New York, NY.

94. "Conservatives Ready for 'Sob Sisters,'" *Dialogue on Liberty*, Spring 1982, pp. 1, 3–5.

95. "Regional Conferences Smashing Success," *Dialogue on Liberty*, Spring 1982, p. 2.

96. Interview with James Lacy, Laguna Niguel, CA, October 13, 2008.

97. "YAF Sponsored Speakers Continue to Spread the Conservative Message," *Dialogue on Liberty*, Fall 1982, p. 1.

advocate Jude Wanniski while at American University chairman Jeff Michaels arranged an address by James Watt. Meanwhile, Georgetown chairman Richard Mathias, sponsored a series of lectures by White House aides Morton Blackwell, Rich Williamson, and Lyn Nofziger as well as an address by author and columnist George Will.[98] All across the country, YAF chapters were bringing to campus speakers who could describe, defend and advocate the policies of the Reagan Administration.

As an outgrowth of the speakers' tours, new chapters were formed on several campuses. By the fall semester, YAF had chartered chapters at all eight Ivy League campuses for the first time in its history. Terry Quist helped reorganize the Harvard chapter with Tom Clark as the new chairman while Rachelle Kopperman and Henry Kriegel headed up the YAF group at Columbia. The YAF chairman at Dartmouth was Brad Mont while Robert Guiffra headed YAF efforts at Princeton. Dave Goldberg led the University of Pennsylvania YAF chapter and the chairman at Yale was Rob Dial. At Cornell, Aidan Conway and Scott Fowkes were among the YAF chapter leadership.

At the same time, a number of new independent publications appeared on college campuses. Among them were Mike Waller's *Sequent* at George Washington University, Avery Lachner's *The Red & Blue* at the University of Pennsylvania and Terry Quist's *The Salient* at Harvard. Jon Brossel and Steve Sego started publishing *Washington Spectator* at the University of Washington. Among the best known of the group formed after the Reagan election is the *Dartmouth Review*, established by Ben Hart and Greg Fossedal, a publication whose later staff included Dinesh D'Souza and Laura Ingraham. Nearly thirty years later, several of these publications are still circulated.[99]

Meanwhile, YAF officially declared its publication *New Guard* was a quarterly, abandoning the 8 to 12 page newsletter editions briefly printed from 1978 to 1981. Susan Juroe became the new publications director in 1982. It was a quirk of fate that turned Juroe from an intern into an editor when Mark Huber took a job at *Conservative Digest*. "I was hired as the full time editor and enjoyed this job as one of the happiest of my career. Had I not had the experience with YAF, I would not have developed a national network of friends and political activists that have remained friends and business colleagues."[100] As had been the case in past years, a number of budding writers appeared in the quarterly *New Guard* under Juroe's editorship, including Michael Waller, Dinesh D'Souza, Martin M. Wooster, Cort Kirkwood, and Deroy Murdock.[101]

Reflecting back on that time, Murdock recently observed that, "YAF helped me get started as a libertarian political commentator and advocate. It was one of my key launch pads. I would give YAF plenty of credit for fueling the early part of my time in the free-market movement."[102] Kirkwood, who succeeded Juroe as

98. *New Guard*, Winter 1982–83, p. 56.

99. *New Guard*, Winter 1982–83, p. 56.

100. 2008 YAF Alumni Survey Responses: Susan Juroe.

101. Waller is author or editor of five books, including *Secret Empire: The KGB in Russia Today* (Boulder, CO: Westview Press, 1994). D'Souza is an author and lecturer whose most recent book is *What's So Great About Christianity* (Washington, DC: Regnery Publishing, 2007). Wooster, author of six books, was the Washington editor of *Harper's* magazine before becoming a Senior Fellow at the Capital Research Center. Kirkwood is now editor of the Harrisonburg, VA *Daily News Record*. Deroy Murdock is now a contributing editor to *National Review Online* and the Scripps Howard News Service syndicates his column to some 400 newspapers.

102. 2008 YAF Alumni Survey Responses: Deroy Murdock. Interview with Deroy Murdock, New York City, June 23, 2009.

editor of *New Guard* in late 1983, was a graduate student when he became aware of the magazine and Young Americans for Freedom. "I was in the journalism master's program at Boston University and was looking for a place to be published. I called up on the phone and asked 'Do you want an article?' When I saw the magazine, I said, 'Gee, this is great. Send me more information on YAF.'"[103] Kirkwood is also a graduate of the National Journalism Center now run by Young America's Foundation.

The magazine featured a special section on Aleksandr Solzhenitsyn in the Summer 1982 issue and one on the "Zero Option" project in the Fall 1982 issue.[104] The "Zero Option" project was YAF's answer to the nuclear freeze movement then gaining support on college campuses and in the Congress. YAF member Brett Sciaroni, a national security analyst at the Hoover Institution, coordinated the project.[105] As the national debate on nuclear arms control continued, YAF chapters distributed information on "Zero Option" and the dangers of freezing nuclear weapons at their present levels. To counter the Left's efforts Connecticut YAF state chairman Marianne Kopko organized an anti-freeze demonstration in the state capital and west coast YAFers demonstrated in Los Angeles and Seattle. At the University of Pennsylvania, Dave Goldberg led an "anti-freeze" rally as did Alan Okonski at the University of Maine.[106]

At the University of Maryland, led by chairman Norman White and John Metry, the chapter organized a protest to counter the Progressive Student Alliance's mandatory fee-funded seminar on the military while Rachelle Kopperman, Columbia YAF chairman, debated the draft registration issue with representatives from the War Resisters' League. At the University of Pennsylvania, Alan Ashkinaze sponsored a series of forums on Reagan Administration policies and helped organize a campaign for student government elections that resulted in six posts being won by YAF members.[107] When Jane Fonda appeared at the Jackson, Michigan Sheraton Hotel, 25 Hillsdale College members rallied outside and conducted "Conservative Aerobics" to respond to the radical's promotion of her aerobics program inside.[108] UCLA chairman Caleb Gluck led a pro-Reagan demonstration when the President appeared at a fundraiser in Los Angeles.

YAF members and chapters were always involved in campaigns for conservative candidates and 1982 was no exception. While it was not a banner year, YAF members worked to elect conservatives so that President Reagan could maintain a working majority in the Congress. In New Hampshire, YAF member Robert C. Smith was the GOP candidate for the House in the 1st congressional district. Smith lost that 1982 contest but came back to win in 1984 and continued in the House until joining the United States Senate where he served for 12 years. In New York, the Lewis Lehrman campaign for Governor attracted the involvement of many YAFers, including National Director John Abernethy, Charmaine Grieco,

103. Bill Kling, "*New Guard*, Founded 1961, Upgrades Image but Retains YAF's Conservative Outlook," *Washington Times*, January 24, 1985.

104. "Alexander Solzhenitsyn: From under the Dragon's Belly," *New Guard*, Summer 1982, pp. 23–33. "Zero Option: A Guide to the Debate on Nuclear Arms Control," *New Guard*, Fall 1982, pp. 33–42.

105. Susan Juroe, "YAF Meets the Freeze Challenge with 'Zero Option' Project," *New Guard*, Fall 1982, p. 42. See also Deroy Murdock, "Dress Rehearsal for a Soviet First Strike," *New Guard*, Fall 1982, p. 41.

106. Bretton G. Sciaroni, "Zero Option: A Guide to the Debate on Nuclear Arms Control," published by Young Americans for Freedom, 1982. Sciaroni was a Public Affairs Fellow at the Hoover Institution and former Special Assistant to the Director of the United States Arms Control and Disarmament Agency. See also: *New Guard*, Fall 1982, p. 64; *Dialogue on Liberty*, Fall 1982, p. 4.

107. *New Guard*, Summer 1982, pp. 48–49.

108. David M. Les Strong, "YAF-1, Fonda-0," *New Guard*, Winter 1982–83, pp. 44–45.

Abe Fuerstein, and Al Wells. Steve Shymkevich, chairman of Avon High YAF, organized volunteers from the Boston area to work in the re-election campaign of conservative Democratic Governor Ed King. Despite any differences over the direction of the national organization, all YAF members agreed on the importance of working to elect conservatives to public office.[109]

YAF organized a tribute to Labor Secretary Raymond Donovan at the Mayflower Hotel in Washington on October 13, 1982. The event was attended by some 900 individuals, including Attorney General William French Smith, Health and Human Services Secretary Richard Schweiker, Secretary of Agriculture John Block, Chief of Staff James Baker, Director of the CIA William Casey, Counselor to the President Ed Meese, and other Reagan Administration appointees.[110] The dinner was an overwhelming success and provided needed positive publicity for YAF among the political and journalistic community in the Nation's Capital.[111]

By the spring of 1983 Young Americans for Freedom had expanded to a number of campuses where the organization had not been active for several years or never had chartered a chapter. Some of the new chapters were on religiously affiliated campuses such as Brigham Young University, led by Steve Reiher; Bob Jones University, chaired by Phil Quandt; Oral Roberts University with Charles Lyon; Ohio Wesleyan University, with Kenneth Nunnenkamp; and Loyola University of New Orleans, where Tom Ruli and Leon Kellum helped establish a chapter. For Nunnenkamp, now an attorney with Patton Boggs in the Washington area, his involvement in YAF is what "solidified my conservative thought."[112] Still others were at state universities in traditionally conservative states: Bryan Daniel and Steve Bergstrom's YAF chapter at the University of Kansas; the Ole Miss chapter headed by Britt Herrin; Tom Rock's new chapter at Colorado State; and the University of Alabama chapter headed by Robert Meacham and Rusty Johnson. YAF outposts were established even on some less hospitable, smaller liberal arts campuses, including John Yetter's chapter at Swarthmore, the YAF chapter jointly organized at Haverford and Bryn Mawr colleges by Craig Stetson, and Dawn Sciarrino's new YAF chapter at Ithaca College.[113] At the University of California at Davis, Tyrone Maho formed the YAF chapter during the fall of 1982 and by the next semester, they were distributing 2,000 copies of their own paper, *The Davis Dossier*.[114] There was no question but that the appeal of Ronald Reagan and his association with YAF was helping to recruit new conservative leaders.

As one would expect, the District of Columbia was an area with active YAF campus chapters at all major schools. Being active in YAF in the Nation's Capital provided many opportunities for a college student. Georgetown's Quin Hillyer brought a special family connection to his involvement. Hillyer recently recalled helping sponsor speakers from George Will to Lee Atwater and his pride in fol-

---

109. *Dialogue on Liberty*, Fall 1982, p. 4. Memo to YAF Activists from Committee to Save YAF, July 9, 1982. Personal Papers of William F. Buckley, Jr., Box 189, Folder: YAF 1982, Sterling Library, Yale University, New Haven, CT.

110. Seth S. King, "Donovan Dinner Dais: No Reagan, No Bush," *New York Times*, October 13, 1982. Reagan was addressing the nation on television that evening and Bush was making campaign appearances only a few weeks before the mid-term elections.

111. "Donovan Honored by 1,000 Friends," *New York Times*, October 14, 1982. "YAF's Tribute Dinner for Secretary Donovan—A Smashing Success," *Dialogue on Liberty*, Fall 1982, p. 5.

112. 2008 YAF Alumni Survey Responses: Kenneth Nunnenkamp.

113. *New Guard*, Spring 1983, p. 48; *New Guard*, Summer 1983, p. 57; *New Guard*, Winter 1983–84, pp. 50–51.

114. Mike Fitch, "Conservatives Publish Paper," *Davis Enterprise*, January 12, 1983. Brent Coleman, "USD Students Begin Conservative Paper," *Daily Democrat*, January 12, 1983. Copies from Tyrone Maho.

lowing his father's footsteps. "I felt especially pleased to be active in YAF because my father, Haywood H. Hillyer, III had been there at its founding at the Buckley estate in Sharon, CT in 1960 along with Lee Edwards, Carol Dawson, and the others."[115] At George Washington University, Andrew Dudek was YAF chapter chairman and "it was the best of times. Reagan was in the White House, the communist threat was clear and obvious, and we knew who were our political friends and adversaries." For Dudek, "YAF was the most influential part of my undergraduate experience. It developed my organizational and leadership skills, as well as building my confidence and empowering me."[116] Other chapters were active at American University, where Nicholas Kocz was chairman, at Catholic University, the University of Maryland and Howard University, where DC Chairman Deroy Murdock helped organize a group prior to the 1984 presidential election.[117]

YAF also was able to establish new community chapters in a wide range of locations including Carlsbad, New Mexico where Patricia Haynes developed a strong local unit and Fairbanks, Alaska with the community chapter headed by Paul Brown. Mike Simpfenderfer organized a new Little Rock community chapter while high school student William Daroff brought life back to the Cleveland community chapter. Banastre Tarleton had graduated from Hong Kong University and was a professional musician when he formed a YAF community chapter in Missouri. For him, "The Reagan years brought renewed hope and pride in the USA and I was happy to be involved with an organization that supported his ideals."[118] Perhaps the most active of the new community chapters was the Miami-Dade County chapter headed by Manny Sanchez. Miami YAF played an essential role in the election of State Representative Ileana Ros, now Congresswoman Ileana Ros-Lehtinen, the first Hispanic woman elected to both the Florida Legislature and the United States Congress.[119]

12th National Convention—Los Angeles

With the rulings in favor of the Lacy position on nearly all issues, Jim Lacy could announce that he would not be a candidate for another term as Chairman of YAF. Looking back on those experiences recently, Lacy concluded that, "My involvement in YAF helped me in life in many ways, not the least of which was the interactions with others. We had a sense of purpose in what we were doing and could actually have an effect on politics and society."[120] Jim Lacy had joined YAF as a 17-year-old high school student in 1969 and now some 14 years later was an aide to the United States Secretary of Commerce, part of the presidential administration of YAF's best-known national advisor.

As YAF members traveled to Los Angeles for the 12th biennial national convention, the Lacy-Flaherty battle was winding down and few of the remaining National Directors or chapter leaders who had supported Flaherty's lawsuit made the trip to California. This did not prevent, however, another dispute from

115. 2008 YAF Alumni Survey Responses: Quin Hillyer.
116. 2008 YAF Alumni Survey Responses: Andrew F. Dudek.
117. Interview with Deroy Murdock, New York, New York, June 23, 2009.
118. 2008 YAF Alumni Survey Responses: Banastre Tarleton.
119. *New Guard*, Spring 1983, p. 49; *New Guard*, Summer 1983, p. 57.
120. Interview with James Lacy, Laguna Niguel, California, October 13, 2008.

briefly developing and presaging even more battles over the next several months. According to one report,

> Lacy and executive director Sam Pimm squared off, and their proxies, Bob Dolan and Floyd Brown respectively, ran neck and neck for the post of national chairman . . . As quickly as the fight began, it ended. At the Thursday night banquet, Floyd Brown suddenly announced that he was dropping out of the race for national chairman . . . Brown and his backer, Pimm, in perhaps the first gesture of accommodation seen by YAF in a year and a half, bowed out and got behind the "white ballot," an unopposed consensus ticket.[121]

Nevertheless, the various candidates already had spread a good deal of negative charges.[122] When the compromise was reached, outgoing chairman Lacy was optimistic about the organization's future. In speaking to a reporter he said, "With Bobby Dolan's election and a new, young, dynamic national board, YAF will be working as fervently as ever to help translate conservative ideas into public policy." Dolan put the best face forward in describing the commitment of those YAF members who ventured to Los Angeles to attend the convention when he claimed, "the numbers and enthusiasm of the YAFers present at this convention surely means that the conservative movement is alive and healthy with young people."[123]

None of the nine candidates elected at the 1981 convention in Boston was re-elected in 1983. Floyd Brown, who had withdrawn from the race for National Chairman with a commitment to become vice-chairman, held a senior board position by the time of the meeting in Los Angeles. The six Flaherty supporters who had been elected in 1981 did not seek re-election in Los Angeles while Lacy supporter Pat Geary was now in a senior board position and Sam Pimm was YAF's executive director. The new members constituted a mixture of both Dolan and Brown supporters elected on a compromise slate supported by nearly all present at the convention. Three new directors were from the Nation's Capital: Richard Mathias, J. Michael Waller, and Robert Hahn while David Nolan lived in suburban Virginia. The northeast was represented among the nine by Jay Young of upstate New York, Alan Ashkinaze of New Jersey, and Carolyn Malon of Connecticut. Peter Schweizer of Washington state and Sergio Picchio of California rounded out the list of new directors. The ability of this compromise slate to work with a new National Chairman and the continuing directors would seriously test the organization over the next two years.

When elected to the National Board, Peter Schweizer was a student at Pacific Lutheran University. For Schweizer, "being in YAF changed everything. It got me passionate about ideas and politics. Without it, I would have ended up being a stockbroker instead of a writer."[124] Schweizer, the author of numerous books, is currently a Research Fellow at the Hoover Institution and on the Board of Directors of Young America's Foundation.

Alan Ashkinaze joined YAF while in high school and then was YAF chairman

---

121. Jeff Nelligan, "All Together Again?" *National Review*, September 16, 1973, p. 1136.
122. These campaign flyers distributed in Los Angeles can be found in Group Research Archives, Box 305, Columbia University, New York, New York.
123. "YAF Launches Campus Offensive," *Conservative Digest*, September 1983, p. 34.
124. 2008 YAF Alumni Survey Responses: Peter Schweizer. Among his recent books are *Reagan's War* (New York: Doubleday, 2002) and *The Bushes: Portrait of a Dynasty* (New York: Doubleday, 2004).

at the University of Pennsylvania. After working on the national staff for one year he entered law school at Seton Hall and later obtained a Masters of Public Administration degree from Columbia University. For Ashkinaze, "Young Americans for Freedom was a phenomenal training ground and an opportunity to be with others who thought like you well before the Internet, Facebook, and all the other vehicles available now."[125] Carolyn Malon saw YAF as "a great training ground. Got me thinking. My first trip to Washington, D.C. was for a YAF convention at age 18—loved it."[126]

As was traditional, the program had an extensive series of workshops and a number of conservative Congressmen addressed the gathering. But HUD Secretary Samuel Pierce was the highest-ranking Reagan Administration official to take part.[127] Missing from the agenda were the names Buckley, Reagan, Evans, Goldwater, Thurmond, and Crane—fixtures at nearly all previous YAF gatherings.[128] As one senior leader summarized, "YAF is on probation," indicated by the absence from the convention of so many recognizable names in the movement.

The Dolan Controversy

Robert Dolan was a 27-year-old lawyer from New York City when he became National Chairman. He came to the office with the support of some of the senior conservatives who had been essential in the formation of the organization back in 1960. Earlier in April 1983, Marvin Liebman had written to Bill Rusher and appealed for his support of Dolan's candidacy. Liebman saw hope and a continuing need for the group, since "YAF has too many years, too many hopes and dreams to let it wither away. The youth of our country have too much to contribute . . . A reinvigorated YAF can provide them with the direction they need. Bob Dolan and his team will provide the leadership."[129] Rusher agreed to keep an open mind and also to speak at the 1983 convention in Los Angeles.

After Dolan's victory, Rusher wrote him in an effort to move beyond the conflicts of the past two years and gave the new chairman some advice: "I hope that, above and before all else, you will devote yourself to preventing future public brawls of the kind that have disfigured YAF's image in recent years."[130] Ron Docksai wrote to Bill Buckley about the convention in a cautiously optimistic tone, pointing out that with the election of several new board members, "the dead branches all seem to have been pruned, and there is a better chance than existed earlier for a new growth. In short I would not write it off."[131] However,

---

125. Telephone interview with Alan Ashkinaze, December 16, 2008.

126. 2008 YAF Alumni Survey Responses: Carolyn J. Malon.

127. According to one report, "HUD Secretary Samuel Pierce spoke Friday afternoon to scarcely more than sixty people, of whom half a dozen were media" and "there were fewer than forty YAFers and only a handful of YAF leaders at the Peace Through Strength demonstration at City Hall." Nelligan, "All Together Again?" *National Review*, September 16, 1983, p. 1137.

128. Official Convention Program, Young Americans for Freedom, 12th National Convention, LA'83, Westin Bonaventure Hotel, Los Angeles, California, August 3–7, 1983. "YAF Launches Campus Offensive," *Conservative Digest*, September 1983, p. 34.

129. Letter of Marvin Liebman to William A Rusher, April 22, 1983. Personal Papers of William A. Rusher, Box 174, Library of Congress, Washington, DC.

130. Letter of William A. Rusher to Robert Dolan, August 17, 1983. Personal Papers of William A. Rusher, Box 174, Library of Congress, Washington, DC.

131. Letter of Ron Docksai to William F. Buckley, Jr., August 16, 1983. Personal Papers of William A. Rusher, Box 174, Library of Congress, Washington, DC.

even though he had attempted to rally support for Dolan a few months before the Los Angeles convention, after attending the event Liebman was not convinced of YAF's continued viability. Liebman now felt that YAF had been in business too long and its current leaders had lost sight of why it was founded. Unlike Docksai's analysis of the new board, Liebman noted that most of those on the board were not students and were distant from the college campus scene. From the information he had gathered, the organization was some $500,000 in debt.[132]

Liebman sent his memo to twelve conservative leaders, inviting them to discuss the topic further at a meeting on September 30th at the Cosmos Club in the Nation's Capital.[133] After the group met and discussed the situation, Bill Buckley drafted a letter to Robert Dolan that was circulated to the group and then mailed on October 12th under Liebman's signature but on behalf of the twelve conservatives. The letter posed four broad questions to Dolan and requested specific answers concerning what can be accomplished by June 1, 1984.[134]

The memo noted that given what had transpired over the past two years, the individuals signing the memo could not continue to lend their good names to YAF unless they were convinced "the rehabilitation and rejuvenation of YAF are taking place."[135] While the letter was addressed to Dolan as National Chairman, it said "We would like to hear from you what you and the Board think can be done with YAF." Dolan regarded the questions as being directed at him personally and did not want to involve the Board in any response. When he declined to call any fall meeting, the requisite number of eight National Directors petitioned to call a meeting and it was held on November 6th.[136] The petition asked for a discussion of the points raised in Liebman's letter, noting that the Board must "formulate concrete and specific answers to these questions and that a written response formulated by YAF's Board of Directors be sent to Buckley et. al. by November 12, one month from the date of their letter to you."[137]

When the meeting was held, a majority voted to allow Dolan to answer each of the points without discussion and then voted to ratify his views as those of the organization. After only two and one half hours, the meeting adjourned. The eight directors reported to Buckley "the Board meeting this weekend was the

---

132. Memo from Marvin Liebman to Those Concerned, September 2, 1983. Personal Papers of William F. Buckley, Jr., Sterling Library, Yale University, New Haven, CT.
133. Those receiving the September 13, 1983 memo were Buckley, Ron Docksai, Tony Dolan, Frank Donatelli, Stan Evans, Michael Joyce, James Meadows, Dan Oliver, Ron Robinson, Bill Rusher, Tom Winter and Richard Viguerie. It appears that Joyce did not attend the meeting. Tony Dolan was a White House speechwriter at the time and is not related to the YAF Chairman Bob Dolan. The Liebman memo can be found in Personal Papers of William A. Rusher, Box 174, Library of Congress, Washington, DC.
134. The group asked Dolan (1) what corporate reforms would be brought about to avoid future legal battles, (2) would he ensure the distribution of a regular monthly journal to YAF members and activists, (3) what efforts would be undertaken to organize and assist local YAF chapters, and (4) what was YAF's true income picture and projections for the next several months? Memo from Marvin Liebman dated October 5, 1983 attaching Buckley draft letter. Letter from Marvin Liebman to Robert Dolan, October 12, 1983. Both in Personal Papers of William F. Buckley, Jr., Sterling Library, Yale University, New Haven, CT.
135. *Ibid.*
136. Those petitioning for the meeting included the two anti-Dolan leaders in Los Angeles, Floyd Brown and Sam Pimm, as well as Alan Ashkinaze, Jeffrey Michaels, Michael Waller, Peter Schweizer, Nathan Buff and Michelle Easton. While Brown had been named vice chairman as part of the compromise, he was soon replaced by Randy Goodwin. By the summer of 1984, Brown had resigned from his Board position.
137. Copy of petition listing 18 questions and 42 requested actions attached to letter to William F. Buckley, Jr. from Floyd Brown, November 7, 1983. Personal Papers of William F. Buckley, Jr., Box 189, Folder: YAF 1984, Sterling Library, Yale University, New Haven, CT.

final turning point for all of us."[138] Over the next few weeks various individuals corresponded with conservative leaders regarding the situation, an unfortunate repeat of the Lacy-Flaherty battle minus the lawsuit.[139]

On January 13, 1984 Bob Dolan responded. His letter concluded by claiming, "YAF has come out of its difficult times. Some wounds are still sore and feelings hurt, but YAF will and should survive to lead, as it once did, again."[140] Dolan's letter seemed to have temporarily satisfied most of the conservative leaders for, as Buckley wrote a few days later, "We have all received a memo from Dolan, the effect of which is to persuade the majority that June should be the day when collective judgment is passed."[141] Dolan and YAF were on probation for the next five months during which time their task was to convince those nationally known conservatives associated with YAF that their continued support was justified.

Unfortunately, dissension and disruption were to continue. Dolan had moved to Washington and basically assumed the dual roles of chairman and executive director, making day-to-day decisions as to the administration of the organization. Dolan's management style and personal behavior led to the termination of the organization's fundraising contract with Bruce W. Eberle & Associates. A dispute over finances resulted in a fissure of relations with Congressman Mickey Edwards, ACU chairman. Then on March 31st, in an annual audit report YAF's longtime certified public accountant, James Burgess, reported "management has elected to omit substantially all of the disclosures required by generally accepted accounting principles."[142]

Amy Moritz, a former YAF member at the University of Maryland and director of the National Center for Public Policy Research, was a speaker at the Southern and Northwest regional conferences in the spring of 1984. In a letter to Buckley she noted that fifteen members were at the Southern regional in Richmond. Many more were at the Northwest regional, including some thirty relatively new and young members but "the national representatives purged them in a manner so callous I can only conclude that they intentionally wished to drive out the young, committed members."[143] Douglas Green, chairman of the University of Oregon chapter, served on the credentials committee where the majority disqualified one candidate for Director and three chapters, including Green's own as well as that chaired by Peter Schweizer, an incumbent Board member. When the final vote was held, Sam Basso replaced National Director Nathan Buff. Both Schweizer

---

138. *Ibid.*

139. Two National Directors, Richard Mathias of Georgetown University and Jay Young of New York wrote in support of Dolan's efforts to revitalize YAF while former National Chairman Ron Docksai and former National Director Jeff Burslem were more skeptical. Richard J. Mathias to Marvin Liebman, September 16, 1983; Ron Docksai to William F. Buckley, Jr., October 3, 1983; William F. Buckley, Jr. to Jeffrey Burslem, January 24, 1984 in Personal Papers of William A. Rusher, Box 174, Library of Congress, Washington, DC. Jay L. Young to William F. Buckley, Jr., October 23, 1983, Personal Papers of William F. Buckley, Jr., Box 189, Folder: YAF 1983, Sterling Library, Yale University, New Haven, CT.

140. Robert E. Dolan to Marvin Liebman, January 13, 1984. Personal Papers of William F. Buckley, Jr., Box 189, Folder: YAF 1984, Sterling Library, Yale University, New Haven, CT.

141. William F. Buckley, Jr. to Jeffrey Burslem, January 24, 1984. Personal Papers of William A. Rusher, Box 174, Library of Congress, Washington, DC.

142. Email from Richard A. Delgaudio to the author, January 14, 2009 and "Compiled Financial Statements, February 28, 1985," by James Burgess Associates, Ltd. discuss the Eberle contract termination. Schneider: *Cadres for Conservatism*, pp. 175, 235 mentions the dispute with Edwards. The Burgess letter of March 31, 1984 is in Personal Papers of William A. Rusher, Box 174, Library of Congress, Washington, DC.

143. Amy Moritz to William F. Buckley, Jr., June 28, 1984. Personal Papers of William A. Rusher, Box 174, Library of Congress, Washington, DC.

and Buff had signed the petition forcing Bob Dolan to hold the November 1983 Board meeting.[144] After the regional conferences Dolan appeared to be in control of the organization. However, the internal problems did not go away.[145] With financial difficulties continuing, the YAF policy committee voted to list for sale the national headquarters and its eight acres, collateral for a $144,000 note, at a price of $250,000.[146]

One month later, Alan Crawford, a former editor of *New Guard* who had published a highly critical attack on conservatives in 1980, wrote a column for the *Wall Street Journal*. Crawford maintained that, "YAF seems increasingly interested in high-publicity projects that advance the careers of its aging Yuppie inner circle but have only a tangential connection to the lofty sentiments on which the organization was founded." Claiming there was little YAF influence on most college campuses, Crawford concluded "the days when YAF's leaders were campus counterrevolutionaries are long past."[147] In responding with a letter to the editor a few days later, YAF's Columbia chairman John Crane rebutted Crawford by saying "there exists another dimension of YAF, that of the many individual university chapters across the country" who operated on their own, ignoring the internal politics of the organization. According to Crane, "YAFers of the original mold are still out there, spreading the good word, but national YAF is going to have to descend from its ivory towers to our college campuses before we will pay it any heed whatsoever."[148]

Dolan remained in control of the organization throughout the remainder of 1984 and YAF did have a presence at the Republican National Convention in Dallas as well as in the general election campaign. Chapters such as Crane's Columbia University unit continued to sponsor speakers, distribute literature, publish independent newspapers, and engage in debates on campus. But further upheavals were still to come. On March 3, 1985, YAF's Board of Directors met in Washington and Dolan was forced to resign after being questioned about possible unauthorized use of YAF funds.[149] National Director Terry Cannon maintained the Board was not aware of Dolan's involvement in other "private political action

---

144. Report on Northwest Regional submitted by Douglas F. Green, May 25, 1984. He concluded his detailed report by noting, "Subsequently, Doug Green resigned as U.O. chapter chair. Many YAF members in Oregon and Washington have renounced membership or stopped all activities. Common sense and devotion to YAF's important goals could have prevented this." Document in author's possession.

145. First, YAF was sued by an attorney for Walter Polovchak, a Ukrainian-American youth who refused to return to Soviet Ukraine with his parents and sought asylum in the United States. YAF had raised funds on the issue but did not provide any support to the Polovchak defense fund. By the spring of 1984, an agreement was reached to provide a contribution to the defense fund in the "midrange five figures" and cease mailing on the issue. Then came a fundraising letter signed by Agriculture Secretary John Block that claimed Reagan's views were not "presented honestly by a biased news media." Once the letter hit, Block's office wrote Dolan and told him to stop distributing the letter, claiming "an overzealous staff member" had approved the letter. Robert Dolan to Marvin Liebman, July 26, 1984 with attached letter from Daniel Oliver to Robert E. Dolan, March 21, 1984 and letter from MacKenzie Canter, III to John C. Keeney, Acting Assistant Attorney General, U.S. Department of Justice, May 31, 1984. Personal Papers of William F. Buckley, Jr., Box 189, Folder: YAF 1984, Sterling Library, Yale University, New Haven, CT. See also: "Block Disavows Campaign Letter," *New York Times*, April 22, 1984. One year later YAF agreed to pay a $9,400 civil penalty to the Federal Election Commission since the Block letter urged President Reagan's re-election. "Conservatives Get Fine over Letter from Block," *New York Times*, September 17, 1985.

146. Meeting Book, YAF National Board of Directors, March 3, 1984. At the time, the assessed value of the land and building for tax purposes was $192,000.

147. Alan Pell Crawford, "YAF's Slow Suicide on Washington's Fast Track," *Wall Street Journal*, August 9, 1984.

148. "Rejuvenating a Youth Group," *Wall Street Journal*, August 22, 1984.

149. Ron Cordray, "Head of YAF Quit After Use of Funds Was Questioned," *Washington Times*,

committees."[150] According to one newspaper report, documents obtained by the Board "showed that Dolan may have diverted as much as $150,000 in YAF funds for personal expenses."[151]

After Dolan's resignation, the Board elected Terry Cannon, an attorney from Lincoln, Nebraska and longtime Board member, as the new National Chairman. To the public Cannon maintained that Dolan quit because of philosophical differences with other Board members. Unfortunately, neither the internal battles nor the financial crises would end. As the staff members appointed by Dolan left the national office, Cannon named a close ally from the Plains region, National Director Charley Ohlen, as the new executive director. Soon thereafter, YAF sold its headquarters building and land, was forced to rent office space, and engaged in some questionable financial dealings to confront a number of aging accounts payable. One year later, Cannon was forced to resign and was replaced by Sergio Picchio of California. YAF experienced a brief renaissance in the late 1980s and momentarily put aside its internal squabbles.

The experience of the 1980s seemed to indicate that the organizational structure under which Young Americans for Freedom operated was a contributing factor to its internal conflicts. Established as a corporation, Young Americans for Freedom was limited in what it could do and how it could raise needed funds, a reality that resulted in the creation of two subsidiary organizations. The Fund for a Conservative Majority took on many of the direct political efforts to support Ronald Reagan that a corporation could not engage in under recently enacted Federal election laws. Young America's Foundation assumed the responsibility of helping provide conservative speakers on college campuses, sponsoring conferences and seminars to train conservative leaders, and publishing a conservative journal of history. As these activities were undertaken by new entities, Young Americans for Freedom was left with a reduced role in the overall conservative movement and a more difficult task of obtaining financial support.[152]

In its early years, Young Americans for Freedom had confronted a number of internal political battles but they were always based on some ideological or philosophical or organizational differences. In each case, political battles had to be fought, the organization retained its clear commitment to conservative principles, and the losers departed from YAF or worked within the framework of the Sharon Statement. Unfortunately, by the 1980s the divisions centered basically on personal and power conflicts that were taken to the ultimate level of filing an expensive law suit or removing the elected National Chairman. As one reporter commented, "What differed in the more recent YAF power struggle that ended up in court was a lack of ideological content and the fact that it went public." Ron Robinson added, "When you lost a battle in the '70s, you basically left the organization. But the fights in the '80s were bad. They were more vindictive."[153]

March 15, 1985. Personal Papers of William F. Buckley, Jr., Box 190, Folder: YAF 1985, Sterling Library, Yale University, New Haven, CT.

150. David Hoffman, "Conservative Group's Leader Abruptly Quits," *Washington Post*, March 8, 1985. Personal Papers of William A. Rusher, Box 174, Library of Congress, Washington, DC.

151. Niles Lathem and Rachel Flick, "Scandal Forces Right-wing Big to Resign Top Post," *New York Post*, March 9, 1985. Personal Papers of William A. Rusher, Box 174, Library of Congress, Washington, DC. See also: "Shift at Conservative Group," *New York Times*, March 10, 1985.

152. By the 1980s, both FCM and Young America's Foundation were totally independent entities and no longer affiliated with or in any way controlled by Young Americans for Freedom.

153. Charlotte Hays, "The Right Stunts—YAF's Young Conservatives Dare to Be Outrageous," *Washington Times*, March 9, 1988.

An additional factor that contributed to the conflicts was the role of the organization in the American political arena. Alan Ashkinaze started in YAF as a high school student in the 1970s, was Director of State and Chapter Services in the early 1980s, and then served on the National Board of Directors through the mid-1980s. From his perspective, part of YAF's difficulties arose from its own success. "Conservatism had become so mainstream in the mid-1980s it was hard to find our footings. The country had pretty much moved to right of center. In a sense, we were the victims of our own success after Reagan was elected."[154] This same opinion of the change in the political environment was expressed back in 1988 by a YAF alumnus who had been an appointee in the Reagan Administration when he said, "My political views are no different than they have been, but there has been a change toward the mainstream—not that I went to the mainstream, but the mainstream came to where we were, led by Reagan. Before, I was on the outside, now I'm in the middle of the mainstream."[155] With a conservative President and a Republican majority in the United States Senate, it was harder to be a right-wing radical defending what now appeared to many to be the establishment. Rather than attacking liberal programs, YAF members were called upon to defend the policies advocated by their President.

Counterrevolutionaries

By the fall of 1983 foreign policy issues dominated the news and occasioned a number of protests by local YAF units. When the Soviets shot down a Korean Airlines plane carrying 269 passengers and crew, including Congressman Larry McDonald of Georgia, YAF organized a rally in Lafayette Park across from the White House. The crowd carried a variety of homemade signs protesting the Soviet attack. As Tim Phares, former YAF chapter chairman at Hillsdale College, told one reporter, "I think we should kick out all their diplomats and embargo them down to their last drop of Pepsi-Cola."[156] In other cities, YAF chapters organized similar protests against the Soviet regime.

Then came the crisis in Grenada where a Marxist government, aided by Cuban Communists, attempted to establish another foothold in the Caribbean. As opposition developed and order broke down, the security of American residents, including some 1,000 medical students studying there, came into question. When fellow radicals overthrew the prime minister, an appeal was made by other Caribbean nations for American assistance. In concert with other area countries, the United States sent a small contingent of troops to restore order and free the medical students.[157]

Two days later, the District of Columbia YAF organized a demonstration to

---

154. Telephone interview with Alan Ashkinaze, December 16, 2008.
155. Unnamed YAF alumni quoted in Margaret M. Braungart and Richard G. Braungart, "The Effects of the 1960s Political Generation on Former Left- and Right-Wing Youth Activist Leaders," *Social Problems*, 38:3 (August 1991), p. 307.
156. John A. Barnes and Dwight Cunningham, "More than 400 protest near Soviet Embassy," *Washington Times*, September 2, 1983. Robert D. McFadden, "U.S. Says Soviet Downed Korean Airliner; 269 Lost; Reagan Denounces 'Wanton' Act." *New York Times*, September 2, 1983.
157. Michael T. Kaufman, "1,900 US Troops, with Caribbean Allies, Invade Grenada and Fight Leftist Units; Moscow Protests; British Are Critical," *New York Times*, October 26, 1983. Hedrick Smith, "Reagan Says Cuba Aimed to Take Grenada; Bastion Reported to Fall; Battle Goes On," *New York Times*, October 28, 1983.

support Reagan's sending of the troops. As one speaker told those assembled in Lafayette Square, the invasion of Grenada was "the first time since 1917 there's been a rollback of communism. For the first time we've taken the initiative against the Soviets instead of responding to their actions after the fact."[158] The views of the YAF members were summarized by DC YAF chairman Deroy Murdock when he concluded, "it is heartening to see a Communist country freed from its totalitarian rulers for a change. It is truly an historic event. Hopefully, Grenada will be the first of many Marxist states to regain their liberty."[159] Using his talents as a professional musician, YAF Missouri state chairman Banastre Tarleton released a song called (*We Got To*) *Invade Grenada* with lyrics including "The dormitory door swings open. Is it friends or strangers? A voice rings out loud and clear, 'You're safe, we're the Rangers.'"[160] A Marxist regime had been rolled back, American students were safe, and young conservatives could be proud of their President's actions in thwarting a communist advance.

One year later, YAF chapters on a number of campuses celebrated the victory over communism with teach-ins, rallies, speeches, and debates. Some 75 of the rescued American medical students took part in various events. As Deroy Murdock said in a rally held to commemorate the one-year anniversary of the Grenada action, "When crisis strikes, a leader must not twittle his thumbs, pace across the floor, or bite his fingernails. Instead, he must act and act decisively. Thank God America has a President who knows what to do and gets it done."[161] Auburn YAF, led by George Kreel sponsored a speech by rescued medical student Steve Barry while Britt Herrrin's Ole Miss chapter hosted another. Other medical students rescued from Grenada spoke before Wichita State University YAF, led by chairman Dan Walker, and at the University of Kansas, hosted by YAF chairman Victor Goodpasture.[162]

In the fall of 1983, the ABC television network broadcast a horror film, *The Day After*, portraying a nuclear attack on Kansas City that allegedly left few people alive in Lawrence, Kansas. YAF chapters responded by advocating Peace Through Strength and pointing out the fallacies of the movie. At the University of Kansas, YAF held a seminar attended by former Congressman Jim Jeffries who proclaimed, "We need more than hope, love, and wishful thinking to keep the Soviets at bay."[163] That Saturday, YAF volunteers handed out 20,000 Peace Through Strength petitions outside the Kansas–Missouri football game.

Meanwhile, in New York City some 100 YAF members picketed outside the ABC network headquarters.[164] On the west coast, YAF pickets marched outside the ABC studio in Hollywood and chanted "Better dead than red" while National Director Sergio Picchio called the film a "powerful propaganda tool" for the nuclear freeze movement.[165] In the Nation's capital, YAF leaders met to watch the program with a reporter from the *Washington Post*. Among them were Nicholas

---

158. "Rally Supports Reagan Policy in Caribbean," *Washington Post*. October 29, 1983.
159. News release from DC Young Americans for Freedom, October 28, 1983.
160. *Dialogue on Liberty*, October/Fall 1984, p. 3.
161. News release from DC Young Americans for Freedom, October 25, 1984.
162. "Grenada Liberation Celebrated by YAF Across the Nation," *Dialogue on Liberty*, November/Fall 1984, pp. 1–2.
163. "Project America the Free, Not the Freeze, Awakens America," *Dialogue on Liberty*, January/Winter 1984, p. 1.
164. "It's 'Day' Time for Millions," *New York Post*, November 21, 1983.
165. "'Day After' Sparks New Arms Debate," *Los Angeles Daily News*, November 21, 1983.

Kocz, chairman at American University; Andrew Dudek, chairman at George Washington; and Gerard Alexander, vice chairman of Georgetown University YAF. In outlining their concerns, National Director Richard Mathias felt that, "ABC is using passion rather than reason to convey a biased message." According to Bridget Brooker of Georgetown, after the opening scenario was set, "this is where the logic ends. The rest is pure emotion. This is so annoying. It's written to play on your emotions without giving the full story."[166] YAF took the lead in showing the American people that there was a better way of defending our country from nuclear annihilation.

Peace Through Strength was supplemented over the next several years by support for Reagan's Strategic Defense Initiative and the "High Frontier" program to develop a nuclear shield to protect against Soviet attack. As Kipp Coddington, now an attorney in private practice in the District of Columbia, recalls the effort, "While I was a conservative long before I became aware of YAF, it was YAF that brought me to Washington and in that summer played no small role in influencing the rest of my life."[167] YAF chapters sponsored speakers and distributed thousands of pieces of literature supporting the project.

Once again during the spring of 1984 YAF held a series of eight regional conferences but, except for the Western regional in Culver City, they were smaller gatherings than had taken place in previous years. Re-elected to the Board were Doug Bourdon, Rob Schuler, Charles Ohlen, Dave Nolan, Jonathan Gibson and Sam Basso. New members were Jeff Michaels of New Jersey and Doug Boyd of California.

Summer 1984 was the occasion for YAF's involvement in both the Republican and Democratic National Conventions. First up was the Democratic gathering in San Francisco during July. California YAFers Tim Wikle, Jeff Wright, and Curtis Helms joined DC YAF chairman Deroy Murdock as the delegation arrived early, obtained press credentials, and began spreading the conservative message in the wilderness surrounding the Moscone Center.[168] First out was a news release proclaiming "YAF Denounces Democratic Platform." As Murdock proclaimed, "If the Democrats wish to express their support for America's defense needs, it will include a 'Peace Through Strength' plank in its platform. If the Democrats fail to endorse a policy of Peace Through Strength, America will know that the Democrats' ignorance is compounded only by their irresponsibility."[169]

Then came a flyer calling for the Democrats to support a "Human Rights and National Survival Program" aimed at stopping aid and high technology trade with communist governments and stopping the importation of slave labor goods. Under the heading "Why is our party selling us out in Central America?" YAF noted the party's traditional support of the poor and the oppressed and asked, "Why then have the leaders of our Party turned their backs on the oppressed and the poor in Central America?" The YAF flyer concluded by declaring "THE TIME HAS COME FOR AMERICA TO STOP PROPPING UP COMMUNIST DICTATORSHIPS!"[170]

---

166. Carol Krunoff, "The Right & The Wrong of It," *Washington Post*, November 21, 1983.
167. 2008 YAF Alumni Survey Responses: Kipp Coddington.
168. Deroy Murdock, "Fear and Loathing in San Francisco," *New Guard*, August 1984, pp. 20–. A condensed version of this article appears also in *Conservative Digest*, October 1984, p. 20.
169. News Release, "YAF Denounces Democratic Platform," July 17, 1984.
170. Flyer distributed by Young Americans for Freedom under the title National Coalition for America's Survival, July 1984, Democratic National Convention, San Francisco, CA.

The most direct and dramatic challenge was still to come. On the third day of the convention, the four YAF members set up a table across from the Moscone Center where the plenary convention sessions were being held. The table was decorated with signs proclaiming "Democrats for Reagan" and "Democrats Defect Here" surrounded by YAF banners showing the torch of freedom logo.[171] Also present in San Francisco was former YAF executive director Richard Viguerie, an individual who had led YAF during its days of rallies and demonstrations for Goldwater. Meeting with the four YAF leaders, Viguerie was told of their plans for manning a "Democrats for Reagan" literature table outside the convention. "That's the kind of thing YAF used to do in the sixties, not sit behind a desk in a three piece suit like so many conservatives do today," commented Viguerie.[172]

The following month, YAF members were in friendlier territory as they assembled in Dallas for the Republican National Convention. Coordinating the various activities was National Director Richard Mathias of Georgetown University. Some 300 activists gathered for daytime leadership conferences at the Dallas Marriott Hotel interspersed with attending official convention sessions at Reunion Arena.[173] On the second day of the convention, YAF held a Youth Rally at the Dallas Convention Center. When Ambassador Jeane Kirkpatrick addressed the convention, YAF volunteers distributed 2,000 copies of the *New Guard* with her picture on the cover. Likewise, on the occasion of Newt Gingrich's appearance, YAF members gave out copies of the *New Guard* that featured a cover article by the Georgia Republican. Then came the demonstrations on the convention floor as the President was re-nominated and the young conservatives proudly displayed a 15-foot banner proclaiming "YAF Backs Reagan."

Not only were the current members showing youth support for the President but dozens of YAF alumni were now delegates and alternates to the convention and still others were there as either leaders of conservative organizations or officials of the Reagan Administration. Looking ahead to the fall election, it was possible to set aside the internal disputes and personality conflicts and work in unison for the re-election of a conservative President.

In the November 1984 elections, Ronald Reagan carried every state except Walter Mondale's home state of Minnesota and the Republicans continued to hold a majority in the United States Senate. YAF could look forward to four more years of the Reagan Administration and continued to focus on national defense and foreign policy issues. Central America, South Africa, and Afghanistan all became critical areas of concern in the battle against the spread of communism while YAF continued to combat the Left's efforts to promote nuclear disarmament.

Meanwhile, national YAF was distributing posters and bumper stickers proclaiming, "Nicaragua is Spanish for Afghanistan" and "Stop the Soviet Takeover of Central America" while sending out flyers asking "Help Get the Soviets Out of Central America." The Spring 1985 issue of *New Guard* featured an article by Dr. Jack Wheeler on the various ways individuals could help those fighting communism in Nicaragua, Cambodia, Angola, and Afghanistan. According to Wheeler, in what would soon be viewed as a prophetic statement,

---

171. Murdock, "Fear and Loathing in San Francisco," p. 47.

172. *Ibid.* p. 40.

173. "YAF Dominates Dallas," *Dialogue on Liberty*, September/Summer 1984, p. 1. See also Richard Mathias, "YAF Dallas '84 Preliminary Project Report," Young Americans for Freedom, July 17, 1984.

The Soviets are on the defensive now. They don't have the money to back up their colonies. Marxism-Leninism is a spent ideological power, an aberration of history. All the Soviets have left is brute force. Once that starts to fail, the Red Empire will begin to dissolve.[174]

Former foreign correspondent Charles Wiley also spoke before several YAF audiences on the topic of "Central America: Under Fire," outlining the need for American support of those who were battling Marxist regimes and rebel forces.

California YAF was a center of activism during the 1980s and was known for its ability to organize sizeable and successful demonstrations and counter-demonstrations. In August, leftists organized a protest outside the President's Century City office in Los Angeles. Chris and Jim Bieber saw the leftist demonstration on television, and decided to drive there to show that there were supporters of Reagan. As Chris recalled, "across the street was a group of YAFers counter-demonstrating and they invited us to join them." For Chris, "YAF was my life in the late 80s to mid 90s. I chose to make it my life. I learned what freedom is and what friendship is at a time in life where that is a major factor in one's development." One lasting impact of his involvement was that "YAF changed me to care about other people and the importance of fighting for the freedom of other people as well as preserving our own."[175]

For Jim Bieber, it was a similar awakening as he became more and more active in YAF, rising to California state chairman and then the National Board of Directors. "I lived and breathed YAF and all the activities that went with it. It was real training for politics and leadership where you were only accountable to your peers, unlike other Party organizations that were controlled by 'adults.'" Looking back on those days Jim noted that, "all of my best friends in my youth and still best friends today came from my involvement with YAF."[176] Chris went on to work as an aide to the Speaker of the California Assembly and his brother is now owner of Bieber Communications, involved in numerous candidate and issue campaigns in California and other Western states.

Another foreign policy issue of concern to YAF during the mid-1980s was the situation in South Africa. Joe Robison, a YAF member at Hillsdale College, was one of the organizers of the Free Africa Coalition dedicated to opposing both apartheid and communism. As he explained in the YAF magazine, "Members of the Free Africa Coalition believe that all forms of oppression are morally unacceptable: apartheid and socialism in all their forms. It is therefore unacceptable to end apartheid by destroying the South African economy."[177] In his call for support Robison proclaimed, "Apartheid must end. Communism must also end."

One of the most effective spokesmen against both apartheid and disinvestment was Deroy Murdock. In November 1985, Murdock led a group of students who met with the South African ambassador at the embassy in Washington and presented a petition calling for an acceleration in the process of racial reform, engagement

---

174. Jack Wheeler, "Anti-Soviet Liberation Movements: What You Can Do to Help," *New Guard*, Spring 1985, pp. 27–28, 39.

175. 2008 YAF Alumni Survey Responses: Chris Bieber. Interview with Chris Bieber, Newport Beach, CA, October 11, 2008.

176. 2008 YAF Alumni Survey Responses: Jim Bieber. Interview with Jim Bieber, Santa Ana, CA, October 13, 2008.

177. Joe Robison, "Students Mobilize to Free Africa," *New Guard*, Fall–Winter 1985, p. 35.

with moderate non-white leaders, and creation of incentives to attract increased Western investment in South Africa. Labeling apartheid as "immoral," Murdock called on the government to "grant blacks national citizenship, end the repressive pass laws and influx control, and consider exempting mixed-race couples and their families from the Group Areas Act as a first step towards the complete abandonment of that harsh law." By reducing tax rates and excessive regulations, South Africa could attract more Western corporations and "The resulting economic growth will give non-whites job opportunities, incomes, and hope—three things they need and deserve and in many cases never had."[178]

In speaking at SUNY–Buffalo, where Mike Caputo was YAF chapter chairman, Murdock was clear in his belief that conservatives must continue pressuring the South African government for change, calling on them to "urge our government to pressure South Africa to dismantle apartheid with all deliberate speed and grant black South Africans the rights they deserve as men. Only this will bring justice to that land and keep the ANC out of a position to spill more blood across the continent."[179] He called for increased American support to the freedom movements fighting Marxist regimes in Angola, Mozambique, and Ethiopia.

13th National Convention—Denver

When YAF held its biennial convention in Denver in July 1985, the pro-active anti-communist sentiment remained evident. One of the most well received presenters was Robert K. Brown, the publisher of *Soldier of Fortune* magazine. In addition, the convention included a "Freedom Fighter Forum" with representatives from the anti-communist movements in Nicaragua, El Salvador, Ethiopia, and Angola and a panel on South African Investment policy.

Once again, the YAF delegates faced a contest for National Chairman with Terry Cannon running for election and being opposed by David Nolan, YAF's treasurer at the time. Nolan questioned many of the financial decisions made by YAF but before the votes were cast, Nolan withdrew and Cannon was elected unanimously. Among the new National Directors were Bryan Daniel of Kansas, Tyrone Maho of California, and Larry Sarraga of New York while Steve Wiley of California, who had previously served some six years earlier, once again joined the Board. In reporting on the meeting, YAF's publication had to admit "although this convention was small, the 'wimp ratio' was at an all-time low, as was the average age of the delegates."[180] Given the emphasis on freedom fighters and the reception provided the publisher of *Soldier of Fortune*, the hard-core nature of the participants appeared to be an accurate description.

178. Statement of Deroy Murdock, Chairman, Free Students of America, Before the South African Embassy in Washington, November 7, 1985, in author's possession.

179. Interview with Deroy Murdock, New York, New York, June 23, 2009. Speech at State University of New York–Buffalo, March 1986.

180. "Convention 1985," *New Guard*, Fall–Winter 1985, pp. 28–29. The Fall–Winter 1985 issue was the only one published under the chairmanship of Terrell Cannon. It would be the last regular publication of YAF's magazine as organizational difficulties and financial constraints led to its demise. One more issue was produced in 1989 while Sergio Picchio was National Chairman and the final one in the Fall of 1992 under National Chairman Jeffrey Wright. For nearly twenty-five years, *New Guard* had provided a vehicle for young conservative journalists as well as a source of information and inspiration to campus and community activists. Its demise was another indication of the organization's decline as a major force in the conservative movement. By 1986, YAF's only remaining national publication was the quarterly newsletter, *Dialogue on Liberty*.

YAF had planned a 25th anniversary dinner to be held on September 10th at the Sheraton Washington hotel but was forced to postpone it, mainly due to financial and logistical issues.[181] However, when the rescheduled event was held on November 15th, it "drew little more than 50 guests," and featured Representative Bob Dornan as the highest-ranking officeholder to attend. Nevertheless, National Chairman Terry Cannon was upbeat, claiming "We've gotten several hundred new members on campus just since this Fall."[182] Three months later, YAF held another 25th anniversary event, a luncheon during the 1986 CPAC. This time some 250 attended and various individuals from YAF's history spoke about the organization's role in the development of the conservative movement.[183] At last, YAF had a 25th anniversary event worthy of its history.

Later that spring, YAF held its eight regional conferences where three new members were elected to the Board—Don Derham of New York for the Mid-Atlantic, Dirk Miller of Louisiana State University for the Southwest, and Steve Fillman of York, Nebraska for the Plains region. Of the eight regionals, only the Western and Plains had more than forty delegates participating.[184] However, the Western regional once again was well attended and its Guardian of Freedom award was presented to Patrick Nolan, at the time Minority Leader in the California Assembly.

YAF Comes to Life Again

In conjunction with the Western regional, the National Board of Directors held a meeting where Terry Cannon resigned as chairman and was replaced by Sergio Picchio of California.[185] Picchio was the son of Argentine immigrants of Italian descent and had been active in YAF since the late 1970s, serving as California YAF state chairman and first being elected to the National Board at the 1983 YAF convention. By the spring of 1986 California was the strongest state organization in YAF with 36 chartered chapters, including 21 on college campuses.[186] YAF continued to emphasize foreign policy issues and published issues packs on Nicaragua and South Africa. In late fall, Steve Baldwin was hired as executive director and opened a YAF office on Capitol Hill. Baldwin, another Californian, had been involved in both the College Republican National Federation and another conservative group, Students for America. He had been a member of YAF while in California and was a delegate to the 1985 Denver convention but did not become actively involved until he moved to the Nation's Capital in 1986. With Picchio's support, Baldwin started revitalizing YAF.[187]

Placing an emphasis on areas where anti-communists were taking the offensive, Baldwin made a trip to El Salvador and met with army officials who were battling

---

181. Bill Kling, "YAF Gaffes Leave It in Disarray at 25," *Washington Times*, September 10, 1985. The invitation to the originally scheduled event is in Personal Papers of William F. Buckley, Jr., Box 190, Folder: YAF, Sterling Library, Yale University, New Haven, CT.

182. Cheryl Wetzstein, "Elite few celebrate at YAF dinner," *Washington Times*, November 19, 1985.

183. Jeffrey E. Wright, "YAF's Silver Anniversary Shines," *Dialogue on Liberty*, Spring 1986, p. 1.

184. Memo to YAF By-Laws Reform Committee from Terrell Cannon, no date. In author's possession.

185. Letter from Sergio Picchio to William A. Rusher, April 24, 1986. Personal Papers of William A. Rusher, Box 174, Library of Congress, Washington, DC.

186. Interview with Sergio Picchio, Redondo Bach, CA, October 12, 2008.

187. Interview with Steve Baldwin, Washington, DC, August 12, 2008.

FMLN guerrillas, much as Mike Waller had previously traveled to Nicaragua to meet with Contra rebels. Across the country, YAF chapters were rallying support against Communist advances in Latin America, Africa and Asia. William Daroff coordinated a pro-Contra rally in downtown Cleveland that included representatives from Polish and other Eastern European ethnic communities. In Albany, as pro-Sandinista elements marched, YAF members led by Rich Sciotis, Chris Christopher and Joann Di Tomasi led a counter-demonstration in favor of Contra aid.[188]

When a Soviet peace delegation visited Minneapolis, YAF leaders Jamey Wheeler and Randall Fuller organized a protest that included representatives from the Vietnamese, Ukrainian, Jewish and Christian communities concerned about ethnic and religious freedom in Soviet controlled countries. Meanwhile, San Diego State University YAF, led by Scott Johnston, took the initiative and erected 25 tombstones on campus to represent Communist-controlled countries. As Johnston reported, "With the media constantly focusing its attention on places such as South Africa, it was high time to pay heed to other countries in which, historically, repression has been much worse."[189] Grossmont College YAF led by Suzanne Schmidt constructed a similar "mock graveyard." In Niagara Falls, New York, National Director Tom Lizardo led a group of YAF members in demolishing a Berlin Wall replica on the 25th anniversary of the wall's construction.

During the fall of 1986, left-wing activists began a campaign to convince universities to refuse to undertake research associated with the Strategic Defense Initiative (SDI). In response, YAF contacted Congressman Dan Burton of Indiana who agreed to introduce legislation cutting off Federal funding to universities that officially ban SDI research from their campuses. As Burton claimed, "SDI will indeed work, it's the radical college professors who won't work."[190] YAF then purchased ads in a targeted number of college newspapers warning that if they banned SDI research the school would be in jeopardy of losing all federal aid.[191]

The future of South Africa was another ongoing concern of many YAF chapters, fearing the dominance of Communist elements within the African National Congress.[192] After leftists at UCLA built what they called a "Mandela Shanty" to protest the policies of the South African government, YAF build a "Sakharov Shanty" next to it. Shortly afterward, the UCLA director of student affairs had the Sakharov structure torn down while the Mandela shack remained. YAF rebuilt, only to find it torn down again. Attorney Shawn Steel reminded the UCLA administration of the words "equal access" and "lawsuit" and both shanties were allowed to remain on campus. A similar conflict had occurred at Dartmouth and on other campuses when YAF challenged the leftists.[193] At American University, YAF chairman Mike Gottert and his members set up a "Peace Through Strength" shanty on campus next to the Mandela Shanty.[194] University of Virginia YAF circulated flyers calling for the removal of Mandela shanties from "the Lawn,"

---

188. "The Right Scene," *Dialogue on Liberty*, Spring 1986, p. 4.
189. Pam Glienke and Karen Vandergrift, "YAF Graveyard Buries S.D.S.U.," *The Creative Californian*, Holiday 1986, p. 1.
190. John Elvin, "Get Them Profs," *Washington Times*, January 17, 1987.
191. Memo from Steve Baldwin to YAF National Board, no date, in author's possession.
192. Flyer distributed by Young Americans for Freedom, PO Box 847, Sierra Madre, CA. The Mandela quote first appeared in the *Washington Post*, April 14, 1986.
193. "The Protracted Conflict," *The Dartmouth Review*, January 28, 1987.
194. "The Right Scene," *Dialolue on Liberty*, January–March 1988, p. 6.

hallowed ground in UVA campus tradition. YAF then threatened to build a Berlin Wall replica and the shanties were removed.[195]

YAF was among the conservative organizations that protested when Secretary of State George Shultz agreed to meet with Oliver Tambo, a leader of the ANC. Tambo then went to Los Angeles to accept an award from Mayor Tom Bradley.[196] Following Tambo's meeting with the media, California YAF Chairman Jeff Wright and Deroy Murdock joined Jim Bieber for their own press conference where they explained the ANC policy of using a necklace of a burning tire against blacks they claimed were collaborating with the South African regime. Meanwhile, at USC, Paul Hughes, Jon Horrocks, and Wayne Bowen had an "ANC Tire Sale" outside a screening of the film "Mandela."

University of Virginia YAF, led by John Tate, organized a successful effort to stop the University's Board of Visitors from calling for divestiture in firms doing business in South Africa. They stressed that it was easy for students to support disinvestment, since those who would suffer directly are South Africans as "the evidence is overwhelming, disinvestment hurts the very people it is supposed to help . . . black South Africans."[197] When the Board met, Tate and other YAFers presented signed postcards while leftist radicals conducted a sit-in. The Board adjourned without considering any proposals to divest. University officials told Tate that the Board would have given in to the radicals had the conservatives not launched their own campaign.[198] In a less dramatic but effective protest, William & Mary YAF, led by Doug Phillips and James Lamb, defeated a move in the college's student assembly and faculty senate that called for the divestiture of any companies doing business in South Africa.[199]

14th National Convention—Washington

Under the new leadership of Sergio Picchio and Steve Baldwin, YAF appeared to be back on track. An emphasis was placed on activism and programs designed to appeal to students. Plans were made to hold the 1987 national convention on a university campus, at George Washington University, with the theme "Back to the Battle, Back to Our Roots." Baldwin wrote to Bill Buckley explaining YAF's plans and the progress to date. As he committed, "I do want to let you know that I am doing everything I can to return YAF back to greatness." He reported to Buckley that the organization was on the upswing in terms of activity and organization and added, "I won't lie to you. We still have a lot of work to do before YAF is back on top again, but I think we are making the right moves so far."[200] For the first time in over ten years, YAF had an office in Washington, DC, had settled its legal fights and was raising funds to avoid further budgetary problems.

---

195. Letter from John F. Tate to the author, August 5, 2009.

196. Larry King, "Cal–YAF Denounces Tambo Visit," *The Creative Californian*, Spring 1987, p. 1.

197. Letter from John F. Tate, Chairman, UVA YAF, to "fellow student," March 12, 1987.

198. "Inside the Beltway," *Washington Times*, April 3, 1987. "Graduates Fight Marxist ANC on Campus," *Building Leadership—The Newsletter of the Leadership Institute*, Spring 1987.

199. "William & Mary Defeats Divestment," *Dialogue on Liberty*, Winter 1986, p. 3. Phillips was an example of the second generation of YAF leaders since his father, Howard Phillips, had been present at the initial founding of the organization in Sharon, Connecticut.

200. Steve Baldwin letter to William F. Buckley, Jr., April 8, 1987. Personal Papers of William F. Buckley, Jr., Box 197, Folder: YAF, Sterling Library, Yale University, New Haven, CT.

A few weeks later, Baldwin wrote Buckley to thank him for a positive mention of YAF in *National Review*, ask him to address the 1987 convention, and plead that he would contact President Reagan and urge him to attend also. As Baldwin noted, "You used to attend our conventions faithfully for over twenty years, but we seem to have lost you in recent years. If YAF has alienated you in the past with our internal strife, I want you to know that we are genuinely united in our resolve to re-build YAF."[201] When he responded two weeks later, Buckley was skeptical saying "I hear only good things about you, and about Sergio Picchio. The trouble is of course that there is so much to be done to compensate for the awful five or six years gone by . . ." He then asked Baldwin how long he would stay and "what assurance is there that a year from now or two years from now, YAF won't have gone back to the empty futile bickering that gave so fine an organization such a bad name?"[202] Baldwin assured Buckley that Picchio was running unopposed for a two-year term as National Chairman and "Personally I intend to stay on as long as is necessary to see that YAF regains its ground."[203]

One month later, Marvin Liebman sent a letter to Buckley indicating that he believed YAF had accomplished a great deal in its heyday until self-destructing in the early 1980s. But he maintained that Baldwin, Picchio and Mike Waller, then National Secretary of YAF, were as good as any past leaders of the organization and asked Buckley to give them his support.[204] When Buckley accepted Baldwin's invitation, it was the first time in six years that he had addressed a YAF event.

The 12th national convention convened in early August with an opening address by Dr. William Allen, recently appointed to the U.S. Civil Rights Commission. That session was followed by a briefing for the delegates at the White House conducted by Secretary of Defense Caspar Weinberger and Special Assistant to the President Frank Donatelli. That evening, Bill Buckley gave the keynote address. As Larry King noted, "His return to YAF after a long hiatus symbolized more than anything at the convention that YAF is back, stronger than ever; his speech was a personal inspiration to us all."[205] King was one of eighty delegates from California to make the trip to attend the YAF convention. Many of those who attended were brand new to the organization. David Ray first joined YAF at the convention when he was 23 and working at the Legal Services Corporation. As he recalled, "When I got to the YAF convention at GWU, my first impression was 'Gee, everyone here thinks like me!'"[206] Less than two years later, Ray was elected to the National Board.

Once again, the YAFers heard from a number of conservative congressmen: Jack Kemp, Henry Hyde, Dan Burton, Bob Dornan, Newt Gingrich, and former Representative Ron Paul, then a likely Libertarian Party candidate for President in 1988. Just as important for the many new YAF members, however, was a series of workshops on political technology, group organizing, publishing newslet-

201. Steve Baldwin letter to William F. Buckley, Jr., April 25, 1987. Personal Papers of William F. Buckley, Jr., Box 197, Folder: YAF, Sterling Library, Yale University, New Haven, CT.
202. William F. Buckley, Jr. letter to Steve Baldwin, May 12, 1987. Personal Papers of William F. Buckley, Jr., Box 190, Folder: YAF, Sterling Library, Yale University, New Haven, CT.
203. Steve Baldwin letter to William F. Buckley, Jr., May 27, 1987. Personal Papers of William F. Buckley, Jr., Box 190, Folder: YAF, Sterling Library, Yale University, New Haven, CT.
204. Marvin Liebman letter to William F. Buckley, Jr., June 17, 1987. Personal Papers of William A. Rusher, Box 174, Library of Congress, Washington, DC.
205. Larry King, "California Sweeps YAF Convention '87," *The Creative Californian*, Fall 1987, pp. 4–5.
206. Interview with David Ray, Washington, DC, August 14, 2008.

ters, public relations, fundraising, organizing demonstrations, and carrying out guerrilla tactics on campus.[207]

When the elections were held, Sergio Picchio was unopposed for a two-year term as Chairman and the election of nine National Directors occurred with minimal conflict. Re-elected were Tom Lizardo and Larry Sarraga of New York, Eric Koch of Indiana, Andy Dudek of New Jersey, Mike Centanni of the District of Columbia, and Jeff Wright of California. Joining the Board for the first time were John Fifer of Nebraska, John Tate of Virginia, and Brian Darling of Massachusetts.[208] Chairman Picchio felt that the convention was a watershed.

> YAF has gone back to its roots, back to concentrating on the campus—our traditional source of support—and away from the tendency of becoming a fundraising organization. We've gone back to our original purpose: to be the training ground for the conservative movement and fight for the principles of the Sharon Statement.[209]

With some 300 delegates representing thirty different states, the convention came off as a success and a milestone on the road back for YAF. Steve Baldwin noted several years later, "This was one of the most peaceful times in YAF. I worked hard to minimize the conflicts as well . . . It was fun and intellectually stimulating. By the time the YAF members walked out of the 1987 convention they were on fire and ready to dedicate their life to conservatism."[210]

That fall, Baldwin announced that he would be leaving by the end of the year, returning to California to launch a campaign for the state assembly. He was replaced at YAF by his second in command, Christopher Long. Long had been the 1987 convention coordinator and for two years executive director of the George Washington University YAF chapter.[211] Throughout the 1987–88 academic year, there were more protests and counter-demonstrations on a wide range of foreign policy issues, perhaps more than at any previous time in YAF's history. One reporter commented on YAF by saying "It likes nothing better than to hold counter-demonstrations whenever liberal students protest U.S. policy." As Eugene Delgaudio, Southern regional director, noted, "We fight the left with humor. YAF takes the juggernaut of the left and flips it over. We find the weakest point on the left and penetrate it."[212] When leftist activists carried out a demonstration against aiding the Contras at Senator Pete Wilson's district office in Los Angeles, YAFers led by Jim Bieber and Wayne Bowen tried to block the elevators with their "Victory Over Communism" banners. Also taking part in blocking the leftists were Alex Ignatovsky and Yvette Patko, both of whom were refugees from communist countries, Craig Donofrio and Chris Bieber.[213]

Clint Feddersen is an attorney in Glendale now but was co-chairman with Matt Roberts of the San Diego State University YAF chapter in 1988. For Feddersen,

---

207. "Conservative Forum," *Human Events*, reprinted article. Personal Papers of William F. Buckley, Jr., Box 190, Folder: YAF, Sterling Library, Yale University, New Haven, CT.
208. Jeffrey E. Wright, "YAF National Convention," *Dialogue on Liberty*, January–March 1988, p. 6.
209. "Conservative Forum," *Human Events*, reprinted article. Personal Papers of William F. Buckley, Jr., Box 190, Folder: YAF, Sterling Library, Yale University, New Haven, CT.
210. Interview with Steve Baldwin, Washington, DC, August 12, 2008.
211. Memo to Board of Directors from Steve Baldwin, October 1, 1987.
212. Charlotte Hays, "The Right Stunts—YAF's Young Conservatives Dare to Be Outrageous," *Washington Times*, March 9, 1988.
213. Jim Bieber, "Contra Vote Sparks Protest," *The Creative Californian*, Spring 1988.

YAF's influence was "Immense. YAF cemented my desire to see the defeat of international, Soviet-led Communism, and helped me to play a small role in declaring the end of the Cold War and laying some groundwork for free enterprise in the former Soviet Union."[214]

Various YAF chapters generated so much publicity in only four months in spring 1988 that California YAF produced a half-inch thick book of news clippings, predominantly from college newspapers.[215] Jeff Greene joined YAF while attending Fullerton Community College and then transferred to UCLA where he chaired the YAF group on campus. As he recalled those days, "Seems like we had a protest or rally to crash nearly every other weekend while living at UCLA, as we were right around the corner from the Federal building and other regular left-wing protest spots."[216] By the late 1980s, the membership in YAF was smaller than in the first two decades of its history but it was still aggressively conservative and training future political and community leaders.

While California clearly had the most campus activity, other chapters throughout the country were also active. When leftists protested Contra aid at Indiana University, twenty-four YAFers, led by Charles Haywood, Jeff Esarey and Jenna Miller, counter protested chanting "Hey, Hey, Ho, Ho, Danny Ortega's Got to Go!" At the University of Michigan, Debbie Schlussel and Christine Zarycky led the YAF effort to support the Contras while the University of Massachusetts chapter under chairman Greg Rothman actively opposed various leftist moves. When the left demonstrated against U.S. troop movements in Honduras, twenty Penn State YAFers, led by Ted Ewing and Vince Daino, counter-demonstrated. While seven thousand leftists marched in Boston Common, Bill Spadea and the Boston University YAFers linked arms, blocking the march and making news on several TV stations.[217]

Meanwhile, at the University of Arizona, YAF leaders Manuel Figueroa, Glenn Rempe and Scott Hufault brought to campus a number of speakers, including Congressman John Kyl and Ambassador Lewis Tambs to discuss the need for a pro-active effort against communism. At Canisius College, chairman George Lodick lined up Roy Innis and Morton Downey as speakers while SUNY–Buffalo YAF had Charles Lichenstein speak at a chapter meeting. Upstate New York became one of the more active areas for YAF in the late 1980s and the University of Rochester, led by Al Mayorga, was one of the more aggressive chapters. During the spring of 1988 it held a protest for Contra aid, organized a candlelight vigil for the victims of communism, burned the Soviet flag, and created a replica of a Nicagaruan refugee camp—all of which resulted in newspaper, television and radio coverage for YAF.[218]

Under Sergio Picchio's leadership, YAF was successful in recruiting a number of new leaders to the organization. Bryan Wilkes had joined YAF while in high school but it was not until he was at the University of Delaware that he became active in a chapter. He and a few fellow conservatives started a YAF chapter in 1988 because they were "tired of all the leftists organized in groups that were each receiving funds from student fees." Unable to end the fee system, they needed a non-partisan group to advance conservative goals and thus formed a YAF

214. 2008 YAF Alumni Survey Responses: Clint William Feddersen.
215. California YAF Press Coverage, Post CPAC, Spring 1988.
216. 2008 YAF Alumni Survey Responses: Jeff Greene.
217. "The Right Scene," *Dialogue on Liberty*, June–September 1988, p. 2.
218. *Ibid.*

chapter.[219] Casey Hubble joined the YAF chapter at Wichita State University in 1988 and recently recalled that, "Young Americans for Freedom taught me courage. YAF taught me that my opinion mattered, and it taught me to stand up for conservatism on college campuses."[220]

During the spring of 1988, YAF held its series of regional conferences again. The elections brought on three new members: Marlynn Morse of Southeastern Louisiana University, Ken Royal of the University of California at Irvine, and Bill Spadea of Boston University. While Morse and Royal were unopposed, Spadea defeated long-time director Terry Quist for the New England regional seat. Spadea recently recalled the YAF protests outside the Soviet embassy in Washington, working for Jack Kemp in the New Hampshire primary, and pushing for Kemp to be picked as Vice President during the 1988 Republican National Convention. From his time in YAF Spadea "learned about convention and board meeting tactics and took many of the lessons into other political activities—helped me win election as College Republican National Committee national Secretary in 1989 and national Chairman in 1993."[221] At the other conferences, delegates re-elected Don Derham for the Mid-Atlantic, Bridget Brooker from the Midwest, Steve Fillman from the Plains, and Eugene DelGaudio from the Southern region.[222]

New Orleans '88

Throughout the 1988 primary season, YAF members had been divided in their choice of a successor to President Reagan. Many believed that Jack Kemp was the logical successor to carry on the Reagan Revolution; others backed the candidacy of television evangelist Pat Robertson or Senator Bob Dole of Kansas; to some, Reagan's Vice President, George H.W. Bush, was the best prepared to continue what Reagan had started; still others were attracted to the Libertarian party candidate Ron Paul. Regardless of their initial candidate preference, all active YAFers were committed to helping the Republican party "stay right" in terms of its rules, its platform, and its candidates for president and vice president. They were all determined to see the "Reagan Revolution" continue into the next administration.

New Orleans '88 became a major project of the organization with the theme, "The Movement at a Crossroads." According to a memo from Tom Lizardo, coordinator for the project, "We will be organizing teams of YAF members to visit other young people from all over the country. The goal of this important program is to bring new members, chapters, and leaders into YAF and the Conservative Movement."[223] Beginning on Saturday August 13th, nearly 250 YAF members took part in the program and heard from both political and organizational leaders of the conservative movement.[224] Senator Dan Quayle had accepted an invitation to address the YAF assembly but had to cancel once he had been named as

---

219. Interview with Bryan Wilkes, Washington, DC, August 14, 2008.
220. 2008 YAF Alumni Survey Responses: Casey Hubble.
221. 2008 YAF Alumni Survey Responses: William Spadea.
222. *Dialogue on Liberty*, June–September 1988, p. 1. It appears that by the late 1980s YAF no longer had a Northwest region; only seven regional conferences were held in 1988.
223. Memo to State Chairmen/Key Contacts from Tom Lizardo, July 1988.
224. Memo and schedule for New Orleans '88 from Sergio Picchio, August 12, 1988.

Bush's choice for vice president. But there were more than educational sessions, speeches, and greetings from political figures. It was a time to learn how to be an effective activist and also to have fun and fellowship with other young conservatives. On Saturday some 75 members met in Lafayette Park in New Orleans's French Quarter to demonstrate against social security. As they shouted "No way, we won't pay!" the YAF members burned their cards in a bonfire set in a trash can. While the New Orleans police quietly stood by, the media took note of this defiant action by young people who had no faith in the future of the social security program.[225]

For the organization, New Orleans '88 could be seen as a success. As one participant summarized the experience, "Most of us left New Orleans with new friends and a deeper commitment to YAF and her principles. Not to mention, new energy and information to be directed towards activism."[226] Following the convention, YAF would launch another organizational drive that resulted in the formation of new chapters in areas that had not seen YAF activity for several years.

Over the next few months, many YAF members organized "Youth Against Dukakis" activities as they felt more comfortable combating Michael Dukakis, the liberal Democratic Governor of Massachusetts who had been nominated as his party's presidential candidate. When a Dukakis rally was held at Southeastern Louisiana University, Marlynn Morse brought two dozen YAF members to show their opposition to his candidacy. YAFers led by Mike Kalon, Jeff Durbin and Scott Kjar posted anti-Dukakis flyers all over their campuses at the University of Rochester and Ithaca College while Christine Zarycky of the University of Michigan organized a YAF protest on Labor Day in Detroit. As the campaign progressed, Willie Horton became a household name thanks to the research and publicity of former YAF National Director Floyd Brown. At SUNY–Buffalo, Tom Lizardo and George Lodick organized a showing of the anti-Dukakis video, "Justice on Furlough" and Nick Tsouroullis at Wayne State University carried out a protest with signs proclaiming "Murderers for Mike." When the second Bush–Dukakis debate took place at UCLA, forty-five YAF activists demonstrated outside the hall behind Barry Jantz and Dave Knactal, who were dressed in black and white striped convict suits.[227]

Not all campaign activity was directed towards the presidential election. California YAF backed the candidacies of a number of their own members and alumni for the California Assembly and Senate as well as the congressional campaigns of YAFers Rohrabacher and Cox. Other strong conservative candidates for Congress across the country gained the time and talent of YAF members while in Connecticut, YAF leader Maeghan Brong was responsible for pulling off a major "Dump Weicker" rally at a time when many conservatives were supporting Democratic Senate candidate Joseph Lieberman in his successful effort to retire liberal Republican Senator Lowell Weicker.

225. Larry King, "The Second Battle of New Orleans, or Hunting French Elephants on the Bayou," *The Creative Californian*, Autumn 1988, p. 4.

226. Post Convention report from Tom Lizardo, Coordinator, New Orleans '88, September 1988.

227. *Dialogue on Liberty*, January–March 1989, p. 1.

Sharon III

In the midst of the 1988 presidential campaign and the fall semester on campus, YAF stepped back briefly to reconsider the legacy and continuing relevance of its statement of principles. With the strong emphasis that had taken hold in the late 1980s on confrontational politics, demonstrations, and anti-leftist literature, it was especially important for YAF to return to its philosophical roots and give consideration to the founding document that had unified young conservatives. Sponsored by the executive advisory board of YAF and under the direction of Dr. Mickey Craig of the Political Science department at Hillsdale College, "Sharon III: A Conservative Reappraisal" was held on September 22–25 on the Hillsdale campus. Thirty-five invited conservatives took part in rather weighty and highly academic discussions in a search for the conservative center. Prior to arriving at Hillsdale, each participant received an inch thick book of readings compiled by Dr. William Allen that included book chapters, journal and law review articles, op-ed columns, and even a few Supreme Court cases. Reading this was their assignment in advance of the deliberations at Sharon III.[228]

After all the discussions of the weekend there was general agreement on a statement maintaining that, "nothing defines America and Americans so well as our common expectation of mankind's capacity for self-government." Of particular concern was the perceived "bureaucratization of justice" and the substitution of the regulator for the "spontaneous and orderly enforcement efforts of citizens themselves." As the participants said, "We find that the greatest domestic threat to the God-given rights to life, liberty, and the pursuit of happiness is the rise of the bureaucratic state." Allen noted in his report on the conference, conservatives feared the "growing government pretensions to organize all life at the center, the general assault on intermediary bodies and orders, and the almost instinctive recoil from self-government."[229]

Just as dangerous to individual liberty as the centralization of all government was the view that rights came from government, and especially the officials who governed, enhancing not only a dependency on government but also the expectation of receiving benefits from that government. Dr. Allen summarized this broader concern, "This we know also, for when rulers purport to give to citizens what human beings received from God at birth, namely the right, the empowerment to rule their own lives, they lay claim to a gratitude they do not

---

228. My thanks to Dr. William B. Allen, compiler of the items, for sharing with me a copy of the reading materials sent to each participant in advance of the sessions as well as a list of the 35 participants in the conference. Three of the participants had been present at the original Sharon Conference in 1960—Marvin Liebman and Bill Rusher were already viewed as senior conservatives at that time and Stan Evans was the primary author of the statement adopted by the young conservatives. At the other end of the age and experience spectrum were six individuals active in 1988: National Chairman Sergio Picchio, executive director Chris Long, American University YAF leader Leslie Carbone, and National Directors Eric Koch, Tom Lizardo, and Steve Wiley. Among the alumni taking part were David Keene, Don Devine, Ron Robinson, Larry Straw, Alan Bock, Ken Cribb, Patrick McGuigan, and Floyd Brown. Still others were academics with no direct involvement in YAF, including Professors Peter Stanlis, Jeffrey Wallin, and Peter Schramm, Dr. George Roche, and Charles Heatherly.

229. William B. Allen, "Footsteps to the Future, A Report from the Gathering at Sharon III." Other quotes are from summary papers distributed at the conference and provided to the author by Dr. Allen.

deserve."[230] With the Reagan Administration quickly coming to an end, the conservatives young and old who gathered to reflect on the state of conservatism and the American Republic saw the need for the revitalization of a federalism which at once precludes state interference with legitimate national powers and prevents national cooptation of legitimate state power. Looking back now from the vantage point of the 21st century and the ever-growing involvement of the Federal government in more and more areas of American life, one can see that this group of conservatives could foresee concern over the future of federalism and the protection of the right to self-government among the American people.

The Reagan Era Ends

In November 1988 the American people had to decide once again who would lead them from the White House. For many, the decision centered on whether to continue the policies and programs of the past eight years, albeit with the modifications that any new President would create. Ronald Reagan left office with his popularity high and that support transferred to his vice president who rather easily defeated the Democratic candidate, Governor Michael Dukakis of Massachusetts, and the Libertarian candidate, former Congressman Ron Paul. Bush became the first vice president to immediately succeed a living predecessor since Martin Van Buren. Reagan had entered politics denigrated by much of the media and the so-called establishment as merely an actor, the "great performer" who read his lines well. He left the presidency having helped to redirect much of American political thought. Whether it is vouchers and charter schools, tax reductions and "no new taxes," privatization, strategic defense initiative, or "tear down this wall," America now had a more positive self-image, an emphasis on entrepreneurship, and a determination that it could truly be a City on a Hill. Soon after he left office, the world changed dramatically and that wall was down. While the United States faced many new challenges and more than a billion people still felt the oppression of communism every day, the cold war had ended and the West had won. Ronald Reagan had served the American people well and would always be a hero to his fellow conservatives. The Reagan Era was over.

---

230. *Ibid.*

14. The Last Convention

"What is remarkable, in the end, is not just that an organization like YAF existed, but that it existed and served the conservative political movement so long and so well."[1]

Young Americans for Freedom began 1989 on a high note. Reagan's Vice President had just been elected to continue a Republican administration in the White House. YAF had established itself as a positive force in American public opinion as a study by Peter D. Hart Research Associates found that 34% of a random sample had a favorable view of Young Americans for Freedom while only 6% had an unfavorable opinion.[2] And it had the backing, as honorary advisory board chairman, of the popular former President of the United States.

One YAF member of the time was honored to drive the Reagans' personal luggage from the airport to their home in Bel Air when the President returned to California on January 20, 1989. It was the experience of a lifetime for Jon Fleischman, now a political commentator in Southern California. After thanking him, Reagan "expressed his appreciation for everything that YAFers had done to support him throughout his time in public office and during his Presidency. It was a very short exchange, but one I will remember forever."[3]

Reagan's ongoing commitment to YAF was reinforced a few years later for Fleischman who had become California YAF state chairman and sent out a fundraising letter to send YAFers to CPAC in Washington. Back came an envelope from Reagan's office. "I opened it to find a $400 check from Reagan, along with a handwritten note to me letting me know that the enclosed check was to help send YAFers to the CPAC conference." As Fleischman concluded, "Pretty amazing—that a former leader of the free world took the time to read my note, and respond with a generous personal contribution."[4] While he was part of the final youth generation to actually interact with President Reagan, his legacy will live on as others work hard to promote the ideals that he lived and espoused, "faith, freedom, free enterprise—and above all eternal optimism for all things."[5]

Under Sergio Picchio's leadership as National Chairman and with strong staff support from Steve Baldwin and his successor Christopher Long, Young Americans for Freedom was more active, in more areas of the country, than it had been in several years. Just as important, YAF seemed to have regained the confidence and support of those senior conservatives who had always served as key advisors and emissaries to the wider conservative movement. Nothing symbolized this renewed faith in the organization any better than Bill Buckley's appearance at the 1987 YAF convention and the involvement of several senior conservatives

---

1. Schneider: *Cadres for Conservatism*, p. 176.
2. E.J. Dionne, Jr., "A.C.L.U. Studies Its Image and Finds It Intact," *New York Times*, May 14, 1989. The study found the liberal group with a 47% favorable rating and 18% negative. Hart conducted a telephone survey of 1,000 adults with a margin of error of plus or minus 3%.
3. Interview with Jon Fleischman, Newport Beach, CA, October 11, 2008.
4. From a column by Jon Fleischman on June 7, 2004, forwarded to the author by Sergio Picchio on June 7, 2009, the fifth anniversary of Reagan's passing.
5. *Ibid.*

in the 1988 Sharon III conference. In early 1989, for the first time in four years, YAF published an issue of its magazine, edited by Michael Johns and focusing on "the Movement after Reagan."[6]

Division in the Ranks—Again

At the 1989 CPAC conference in Washington, the YAF National Board of Directors also held a regularly scheduled meeting. At that time, personal and regional divisions on the Board became evident and once more YAF was engulfed in internal disputes. Part of the division centered around who should become the next national chairman and whether the convention should be moved from California to an eastern United States location.

When the Board meeting took place, four incumbent directors were not re-elected to senior board positions and an effort designed to move the 1989 national convention from San Diego to Niagara Falls failed. Christopher Long was asked to resign as executive director and replaced by Tom Lizardo. As part of the arrangement, Jeffrey Wright of California was designated as the favored candidate for National Chairman at the 1989 National Convention to succeed the retiring Sergio Picchio. As the meeting progressed, five new Directors were elected: Robert Jansen and Gerard Sorrentino of New York and David Ray, David Targonski and Leslie Carbone of the Washington, DC area. Losing out in the votes were the Board members from Nebraska, New Jersey and Massachusetts, a shift in geographical influence that would be finalized at the 1989 YAF National Convention.[7]

While there was never to be another issue of *New Guard* published in 1989, YAF did continue to distribute its newsletter, *Dialogue on Liberty* and it served as a vehicle for spreading news to YAF members on various chapter activities across the country. One major activity during this time period was to rally support for Oliver North and for the ongoing Contra effort to overthrow the Marxist Sandinista regime in Nicaragua. YAF also called for an end to the Screen Actors Guild "blacklisting" of performers who had appeared in South Africa, taking out full-page advertisements in *Daily Variety* and the *Hollywood Reporter* to express their opposition to this move by the left.[8]

Across the country a number of local YAF chapters and state organizations continued their emphasis on protests and counter demonstrations and taking stands on controversial social issues such as abortion and homosexuality. Larry King viewed the challenge as recreating what the left had supposedly accomplished

---

6. *New Guard*, Winter–Spring 1989.

7. Those not re-elected to senior board seats were Terrell Cannon, George Blackman, John Stirrup and Carolyn Malon. All but Malon were at the meeting where they were denied another term. The votes on the senior board positions were the result of an arrangement between Jeffrey Wright of California and Tom Lizardo of New York to replace those who were opposed to a Wright candidacy for National Chairman. Minutes, National Board of Directors meeting, Washington, DC, February 25, 1989. Letter from Christopher Long to Marvin Liebman, March 9, 1989. Personal Papers of Marvin Liebman, Hoover Institution, Stanford University, Palo Alto, CA. Letter from Sergio Picchio to William F. Buckley, Jr., March 21, 1989. Personal Papers of William F. Buckley, Jr., Box 190, Folder: YAF 1989, Sterling Library, Yale University, New Haven, CT. This section relies also on interviews with Michael Centanni, August 12, 2008 and October 6, 2008; Tom Lizardo, August 13, 2008 and October 7, 2008; Larry King, October 4, 2008; David C. Ray, August 14, 2008; Bryan Wilkes, August 14, 2008—all in Washington, DC. Also important sources were personal interview with Steve Wiley and Sergio Picchio, Redondo Beach, CA, October 12, 2008 and email from Eric Koch, August 29, 2008.

8. "YAF Calls for End to Blacklist," *Dialogue on Liberty*, April–June 1989, p. 1.

in the 1960s. "I had this idea that we could have a 60s like demonstration from the right. We accepted as a truism in the high school class of '82 that the Hippie movement changed the world and stopped the Vietnam War. And that in the 80s we could do the same from the right."[9] One leftist writer reporting on YAF noted this change in orientation.

> Originally shaped in the cerebral image of its wealthy, intellectual East Coast founder, YAF has increasingly emerged as a California-style populist group, hell-bent on more street action and fewer hallway debates over the theories of columnist Russell Kirk, novelist Ayn Rand, economist Ludwig von Mises and other rightist intellectuals who influenced Buckley's original cell.[10]

While California YAF was perhaps the most active proponent of the demonstration and counter protest tactic, other areas also produced similar YAF efforts.

In some areas of the country, YAF chapters worked with local units of Operation Rescue to protest outside abortion clinics. By the 1980s there was one party line on the abortion issue and it was stridently pro-life or anti-abortion. Satire was used to point out YAF's opposition to so-called establishment positions. At UCLA, YAF issued a news release from a fake group called "Students for Reproductive Rights" announcing that the anniversary of the *Roe v. Wade* decision on January 22nd would be commemorated by an abortion performed on a dog on the steps of the UCLA Medical Center. According to the release, "We think that a termination of pregnancy performed on a person, in public, would probably not be acceptable. So we thought that a dog would be." The release stirred up the expected opposition on the UCLA campus.[11]

In other areas, YAF chapters organized efforts against the presence and influence of gay rights groups on campus. In April 1990, the University of Massachusetts YAF chapter held a demonstration for "straight pride" attended by some 150 students waving American flags and holding anti-homosexual posters. The opposition to gay rights was based on both moral and fiscal grounds. As Theodore Maravelias, one of the YAF activists, explained, "I'm against homosexuality because I think it's perverse. It goes against God's law. I don't want my tax money subsidizing a gay week."[12] One year later in March 1991 UMass YAF held its second annual "straight pride" rally but the 50 conservatives were drowned out by 500 protesters.[13] Later that year when the University of Oklahoma Regents adopted measures to prohibit campus student organizations from discriminating on the basis of sexual preference, Chris Wilson, co-chairman of the YAF chapter on campus, maintained universities should not give protection to homosexual activities.[14]

The YAF national office took up the issue and declared November 1990 as "Straight Pride Month" saying "we encourage every activist to undertake some

9. Interview with Lawrence King, Washington, DC, October 4, 2008.
10. Clancy Sigal, "Doing the Right Thing," *Los Angeles Times Magazine*, April 29, 1990, p. 26.
11. Copy of news release from "Students for Reproductive Rights," January 1990, provided to the author by Lawrence King.
12. "Campus Life: UMass, Mt. Holyoke; Rallies Opposing Gay Students Disrupt Campuses," *New York Times*, May 6, 1990.
13. "Campus Life: Massachusetts; Angry Gay Groups Drown Out Rally by Conservatives," *New York Times*, March 10, 1991.
14. "Campus Life: Oklahoma; "Regents Adopt Measure to Ban Anti-Gay Bias," *New York Times*, April 14, 1991.

activity to promote heterosexuality on their campus. The national office can provide anyone interested with a detailed information packet upon request."[15] The campaign against gay rights and gay student organizations on campus would continue with several of the remaining YAF chapters throughout the early 1990s.[16]

15th National Convention—San Diego

YAF's 1989 National Convention was held on August 9–12 at the Hanalei Hotel in San Diego.[17] Former President Reagan videotaped a special message for the YAF convention that was shown at one of the evening banquets.

The one speaker who received the strongest response from the delegates and obtained the most media coverage was an individual who had not been scheduled and made a surprise appearance at the convention, former White House aide Oliver North. North had recently been convicted in the Iran-Contra matter and given a three year suspended sentence.[18] North thanked YAF for its vocal support and the delegates enthusiastically welcomed his remarks. As one YAFer noted, "North was interrupted for applause on more than two dozen occasions as the YAF members listened in awe to their hero's impassioned plea for a dedication to world freedom."[19] That fall, YAF followed up North's appearance with a drive to obtain a presidential pardon for him. Also among the speakers was Randall Terry, leader of the controversial pro-life group Operation Rescue, an organization that frequently used civil disobedience to express its opposition to legal abortion.

By the time of the 1989 convention, YAF had a total of 92 local chapters in 25 states. Unfortunately, many of these chapters did not send delegates to the West Coast convention and the number of voting delegates was the smallest to date. When the delegates cast votes to elect the YAF leadership, Jeffrey Wright of California was unopposed for National Chairman and only two members of the National Board of Directors were re-elected. Leslie Carbone and David Targonski, both of whom had been appointed to their positions at the February 1989 Board meeting, were elected to two of the nine slots filled by the delegates. In addition, eleven new members joined the Board either by election or by appointment to fill vacancies: Sara Armstrong of Arizona, Rick Harlan and Charles Haywood of

---

15. *Leadership Bulletin—Young Americans for Freedom*, October 1990, p. 3.

16. The irony of publicly opposing homosexuality escaped the later YAF members given that a number of the earlier leaders of the organization were gay. See: Robert Bauman: *The Gentleman from Maryland—The Conscience of a Gay Conservative*; Marvin Liebman: *Coming Out Conservative*; Mike Hudson, "Our Deep Throat—Gay Lawyer Douglas Caddy . . ." *The Advocate*, August 16, 2005. Among others, Randy Shilts, author of *And The Band Played On* (New York: St. Martin's Press, 1987) and *The Mayor of Castro Street: The Life and Times of Harvey Milk* (New York; St. Martin's Press, 1982), was the founder of a YAF chapter in Aurora, Illinois while a high school student. "YAF Around the Nation," *New Guard*, March 1968, p. 22; William Grimes, "Randy Shilts, Author, Dies at 42; One of First to Write About AIDS," *New York Times*, February 18, 1994.

17. Official convention program, "San Diego '89, The Fifteenth Biennial National Convention of Young Americans for Freedom."

18. One year later North's convictions were vacated and in 1991 Judge Gerhard Gesell dismissed all charges against North on the motion of the independent counsel. David Johnston, "North, Spared Prison, Gets $150,000 Fine and Probation for His Iran-Contra Crimes," *New York Times*, July 6, 1989. David Johnston, "Judge in Iran-Contra Trial Drops Case Against North After Prosecutor Gives Up," *New York Times*, September 17, 1991.

19. Jon Fleischman, "Address of Lt. Colonel Oliver North Headlines San Diego '89, YAF's 15th National Convention a Great Success," *Dialogue on Liberty*, Fall 1989, p. 1.

Indiana, Jim Bieber and Carol Royal of California, Karl Virgil Rodgers of Virginia, Casey Hubble of Kansas, Jeff Crouere of Louisiana, Al Mayorga of Florida, Bryan Wilkes of Delaware, and Michael Zummo of New York.

The turnover in leadership went beyond the election of a new National Chairman and eleven new directors, however. Of the 22 serving on the National Board of Directors at the conclusion of the 1989 convention, 14 would be gone within one year's time, including eight of those who first joined the Board in 1989. As vacancies and resignations occurred, Wright left the positions open so that one year later on the occasion of YAF's thirtieth anniversary, membership on the National Board was down to only 14 directors and the chairman.[20] The change was not limited to the board, however. Within one week of his election, new National Chairman Jeffrey Wright had dismissed Marvin Liebman from his position on the Executive Advisory Board. On the letter informing him of his termination, Liebman scribbled, "I've waited almost 30 years, but I finally made it. I've been purged!!!" on a copy he sent to Bill Buckley.[21] Additionally, by 1990 Tom Lizardo had left his position as executive director and was replaced by George Lodick who had previously served as Director of State and Chapter Services.

During the spring of 1990 YAF held another series of regional conferences. When they were concluded the National Board had five new members: Vincent Burruano, chairman of Catholic University YAF; Eric Klein of the University of Iowa; Jon Fleischman of California State University—Fullerton; Steve Holden of San Diego State University; and Michael Irving of Elmhurst, Illinois.[22] Looking back on that time Burruano believes "it was a great opportunity to learn and debate topics of personal importance and to become involved in promoting and preserving those ideals. I think it is worth reminding conservatives that we need a base of young leaders who can carry the message."[23]

Fleischman built on his YAF experience to develop a career in politics and journalism.[24] Fleischman noted that YAF in California had developed a pervasive alumni base that helped provide useful contacts for those who wished to become more involved in politics. But those contacts were based on more than friendship or simple membership. "YAF provided a way to realize that having convictions was a good thing. In YAF, the more committed you were to your ideology, the more you rose up in the organization," according to Fleischman.

YAF continued to obtain media coverage for its various demonstrations and in April of 1990 the *Los Angeles Times Magazine* published a lengthy and somewhat favorable article on the organization, its leaders, and its activities in California. The article compared the YAF of 1990 with the Communist youth organizations on the UCLA campus in which the author was involved in the late 1940s. It was the aggressiveness and radical approach to advancing ideological principles that was most evident to this writer.

> They make life miserable for liberals, whether college professors, Democrats or Republicans like Pete Wilson. They love noise, argument, debate, counter-

---

20. Interview with Lawrence King, Washington, DC, October 4, 2008.
21. Copy of letter from Jeffrey E. Wright to Marvin Liebman dated August 21, 1989 with handwritten notation by Liebman. Personal Papers of William F. Buckley, Jr., Box 190, Folder: YAF 1989, Sterling Library, Yale University, New Haven, CT.
22. "Regionals 1990," *Leadership Bulletin—Young Americans for Freedom*, April–May 1990.
23. 2008 YAF Alumni Survey Responses: Vincent D. Burruano.
24. Interview with Jon Fleischman, Newport Beach, CA, October 11, 2008.

demonstrations, media attention. Blink an eye and they're short-haired Abbie Hoffmans or Jerry Rubins standing on their heads.[25]

The article was forwarded on to Bill Buckley who, in turn, sent it to Bill Rusher, Marvin Liebman, Stan Evans, and Tom Winter with the observation, "it does suggest signs of life in YAF greater than I supposed were there."[26]

That fall, Orange County YAF organized a tea party to protest "King George" when President George H.W. Bush broke his pledge not to support any new taxes. Many in YAF had not supported Bush during the 1988 election, would oppose his efforts to remove Iraqi troops from Kuwait, and in 1992 would support the candidacy of Pat Buchanan in the Republican primaries.

Still other issues attracted the attention of YAF chapters around the nation. At the University of Iowa, YAFers led by Kurt Adams countered a leftist protest against ROTC recruitment on campus while across the state at Iowa State University, Greg Fetterman's YAF chapter counter-protested a peace march on campus, both activities gaining significant media coverage.[27] YAF also had an active presence on a number of other campuses in Indiana, Arizona, Ohio and Louisiana.

On September 13, 1990, YAF celebrated its 30th anniversary with a banquet at the Washington Marriott Hotel. Among the speakers were several YAF alumni including Congressmen Christopher Cox and Dana Rohrabacher and Howard Phillips, chairman of the Conservative Caucus. The invocation was given by Father Vincent Rigdon, former New York YAF state chairman and currently a parish priest in the Washington area. Rohrabacher discussed the role YAF played in his political development, both philosophically and tactically, while Cox maintained that events of the time showed that individual liberty and the free enterprise system best ensure human welfare.[28] Although Bill Buckley could not be present he sent a statement to be read on the occasion claiming, "the return of YAF as a force among young people seems to be assured under the present leadership, and we have no alternative than to pray that this will be so. My salute to the officers of YAF, and to its constituency . . ."[29] In retrospect, the evening turned out to be one of the last successful events put together by Young Americans for Freedom.

Foreign Policy and Dan Quayle

By the end of 1990 attention was more and more directed to the Iraqi invasion and occupation of Kuwait. The Bush Administration worked diligently to line up agreement and support from a wide range of nations for a campaign to remove Iraqi forces from Kuwait. In January 1991, operation Desert Storm began and a wave of patriotic support developed among most Americans, a situation which

25. Sigal, "Doing the Right Thing," p. 24.

26. Memorandum from William F. Buckley, Jr., July 10, 1990, Personal Papers of William F. Buckley, Jr., Box 190, Folder: YAF 1990, Sterling Library, Yale Unversity, New Haven, CT.

27. Sonja West, "Protesters Diverge on ROTC Issue," *Daily Iowan*, October 14, 1990; "2 ISU Groups Get into Fracas at Peace Rally," *Des Moines Register*, November 10, 1990.

28. Program, "Thirtieth Anniversary Reception and Dinner," The Washington Marriott Hotel, Washington DC, Thursday, September 13, 1990. "YAF Celebrates 30th Anniversary," *Leadership Bulletin—Young Americans for Freedom*, October 1990, pp. 1–2.

29. Statement for YAF 30th Anniversary Dinner, Personal Papers of William F. Buckley, Jr., Box 190, Folder: YAF 1990, Sterling Library, Yale University, New Haven, CT.

should have been ideal for recruiting students to a young conservative organization. But the Gulf War became what some described as a calamity for Young Americans for Freedom. Historically, there had always been an isolationist and non-interventionist strain in American conservatism and with the collapse of Communism it was surfacing again among some of the 1990s YAF leadership. They believed that the United States should stay out of international affairs, fearing the nation might become engulfed in a "New World Order." With such a perspective, it was impossible to recruit patriotic young people who supported the Gulf War when so many YAF leaders were opposed to it.[30] An opportunity for growth and revitalization on campus was lost.

As the dominant force in the organization, California YAF was heavily influenced by a non-interventionist foreign policy position. This continued throughout the remainder of the organization's existence as a coordinated national entity. In October 1993, some fifty YAF members demonstrated in Costa Mesa, California, calling for the withdrawal of U.S. troops from Somalia. National Director Jim Bieber, who claimed that YAF had always opposed American intervention on behalf of other countries, including in the Gulf War, organized the protest. According to Bieber, "We would also not favor sending troops to Bosnia or any other country. At least in the Gulf War we had a vested interest in oil. What are we going to get out of Somalia or Bosnia?" Matt Zandi added, "We shouldn't send our troops anywhere else—only if we have to protect our nation."[31] In just a few years the organization that had actively promoted efforts to topple the Marxist regimes in Nicaragua, Ethiopia, Afghanistan, and Angola and had celebrated the efforts of Oliver North to provide support to the Contras was now proclaiming that the United States should retreat from attempting to advance individual freedom in other areas of the world. The neo-conservative approach to foreign policy had been supplanted by a paleo-conservative and libertarian isolationism.

Ironically enough, throughout 1991 one of the major activities of national YAF was an effort to ensure that Vice President Dan Quayle was kept on the Republican presidential ticket.[32] Quayle had been the object of critical media coverage ever since he was nominated and some in the party saw an opportunity to remove Quayle and provide an opening for others to be chosen by Bush. YAF members showed up at various gatherings throughout the year and circulated petitions pledging support for Quayle. In May, Chairman Jeffrey Wright, Vice Chairman Tom Lizardo, and YAF staffer David Warrington met with Quayle to present him with more than 5,000 petitions of support. As Wright stated, "The Vice President was very pleased with YAF's show of support and wanted to convey his thanks to Young Americans for Freedom—its members and supporters."[33] Quayle observed, "You and I both know the media is not friendly to conservatives. That's

---

30. Interview with Lawrence King, Washington, DC, October 4, 2008. Richard Delgaudio remembers one National Board member at the time announcing, "it isn't the communists I'm worried about, it is our own government." Email from Richard A. Delgaudio, June 5, 2009.

31. David A. Avila, "Noisy Demonstration Calls for U.S. Withdrawal from Somalia," *Los Angeles Times*, October 10, 1993. Chris Boucly, "Youths Urge U.S. to Leave Somalia," *Orange County Register*, October 10, 1993.

32. Interview with David Ray, Washington, DC, August 14, 2008.

33. "YAF Chairman Presents over 5000 Petitions of Support to Vice President Dan Quayle," *Leadership Bulletin—Young Americans for Freedom*, June 1991, p. 1. Support for Quayle was not unanimous, as several libertarian members in the organization regarded this YAF alumnus as representative of a traditionalist conservatism, which they opposed.

why it is so important that YAF is out there."[34] The effort to support the Vice President continued throughout 1992, even though many YAFers campaigned for Pat Buchanan against George H.W. Bush in the Republican primaries.[35] The last issue of *New Guard* was published in the fall of 1992 with a cover article, "Dan Quayle and His Enemies." Also included in the magazine was a plug for the 1993 YAF National Convention scheduled for Newport Beach, California—a convention that was never to be.[36]

16th National Convention—Rosslyn

In August 1991, Young Americans for Freedom gathered at a Best Western hotel in suburban Rosslyn, Virginia for what would be the last national convention. Given the optimistic developments in the world, the convention's theme was "Victory Over Communism—Finishing the Job."[37] Although the attendance was but a fraction of the numbers at prior conventions, with some 250 in attendance, the lineup of speakers was impressive. Bill Buckley was back again to give a stirring keynote speech. Defense Secretary Dick Cheney represented the Bush Administration while former Attorney General Edwin Meese provided a connection to the Reagan presidency. There were even taped remarks by Vice President Quayle who could not attend in person. As National Chairman Jeff Wright commented, "he made a special effort on YAF's behalf. He fit time into his busy schedule for this YAF video because he thinks YAF is that special. I'm very grateful to him"[38]

When it was time for the election of YAF officers, National Director Eric Klein of Iowa attempted to run against Wright but was ruled ineligible by the credentials committee for faulty paperwork.[39] Once again a major turnover occurred on the National Board with ten new members either being elected by the delegates or chosen by the sitting board to fill vacant positions. New to the Board were Stuart Grimes, Ann Heighton-Wiseman, and David Wiseman from Ohio, Angela Orem and Shun Ravago from Indiana, Jeff Greene, Ty McCutcheon and Stan Salter of California, Michael Ortega of Washington state, and Wayne Bowen, a Californian who was attending graduate school in Illinois. Only seven of the 22 who served on the Board after the 1989 national convention were still serving three years later. By 1992, nine of the 20 members of the National Board were from California, with three each from Ohio, Indiana, and New York and one each from Illinois and Washington. This would be the last time that delegates sent from active chapters around the country to a national convention elected the leadership of Young Americans for Freedom. After 30 years as an organization under the control of, run by, and operated for young conservatives, YAF would soon end as a viable national entity.

---

34. *Ibid.*

35. According to columnist John Elvin, writing just prior to the 1992 CPAC, Buchanan "has been their hero for years now, and YAFers are among those working as volunteers in the 'Buchanan Brigade.'" John Elvin, "Inside The Beltway," *Washington Times*, February 20, 1992.

36. Richard A. Delgaudio with Jeff Wright, "Dan Quayle and His Enemies—The War on Reagan Continues," *New Guard*, Fall 1992, pp. 5–7, 11, 17. The issue also included a laudatory article titled "What Buchanan Accomplished for Conservatives."

37. "Yikes, It's YAF," *Washington Times*, August 2, 1991.

38. "YAF Quayle Campaign Continues in High Gear," *Leadership Bulletin—Young Americans for Freedom*, October 1991, p. 1.

39. Email from Tom Lizardo, August 3, 2009.

The back page advertisement of the 1992 *New Guard* featured pictures and quotes from Reagan and Quayle and offered two free conservative books to all who joined as members of Young Americans for Freedom. Unfortunately, much of the follow-up was missing and many who signed up never received an acknowledgement from YAF.[40] That year YAF also launched what they called the "Anita Hill Truth Squad" to provide background information on the University of Oklahoma law professor as she spoke on campuses across the country. As Jeff Wright observed, "many of these speaking engagements are sponsored by left-wing groups like the American Civil Liberties Union, the Communications Workers of America and others."[41] YAF made a small presence at the Republican National Convention where Jeff Wright met with the Vice President.

Attempted Reorganization—1994 CPAC

For whatever reason, by the end of 1992 National Chairman Jeffrey Wright appeared to lose all interest in the organization and the plans for a national convention in 1993 were never carried out. Tom Lizardo had stepped down as National Vice Chairman when in early 1992 he had accepted the position as city manager of Niagara Falls, New York and was replaced by Don Derham.[42] After 1993 passed without a YAF convention, alumni chairman Richard Delgaudio determined to take action and breathe new life into the organization. At the 1994 CPAC he arranged for a reception and meeting room to be used by those interested in reorganizing YAF. Delgaudio circulated a flyer declaring "If you like Oliver North . . . you'll love Young Americans for Freedom," as an appeal to young conservatives to sign up for $5 and become a voting delegate to help select a national board and chairman.[43]

At the meeting on the evening of Lincoln's birthday, former National Chairman James Lacy spoke on "YAF's Historic Role in the Conservative Movement and the Need for YAF in the Future." While Jeff Wright was not present, outgoing vice chairman Donald Derham called the formal meeting to order. Chosen to serve as the new National Chairman was Joseph Shun Ravago, an Indiana University senior who had been elected to the Board at the 1991 national convention. Those present who wished to serve on the National Board were asked to give brief speeches explaining why they should be chosen. There was no requirement of a history in the organization, no minimum number of members recruited, nor any record of conservative activism required. Looking back, this could be viewed as a major contributing factor to the failure of this effort at revitalizing an organization whose time had apparently passed.[44]

Of those selected to lead YAF at that February 1994 meeting, only six individuals in addition to the new chairman had ever served on YAF's prior National Board

---

40. The books, *Conscience of a Conservative* by Goldwater and *The Roots of American Order* by Kirk, were supplied by Young America's Foundation in an effort to further disseminate two of the classics of American conservatism. Email from Richard A. Delgaudio to the author, August 4, 2009.

41. "Young Americans for Freedom Leads Movement to Fight Radical Anita Hill," *New Guard*, Fall 1992, p. 11.

42. John Elvin, "Lizardo Makes Good," *Washington Times*, February 3, 1992.

43. "An Urgent Message for Young Conservatives at CPAC," flyer distributed by the Legal Affairs Council at the 1994 Conservative Political Action Conference.

44. Email to the author from Richard A. Delgaudio, August 4, 2009.

of Directors. Jim Bieber of California had been elected in 1989 and re-elected two years later. Both Bryan Wilkes of Delaware and David Ray of Virginia joined the National Board in 1989 but served only one term. Californians Jon Fleischman and Jeff Greene had been elected in 1990 and 1991 respectively. Angela Orem had been elected at the 1991 convention while a student at Indiana University. Clearly, there was little historical perspective among those who would be called upon to bring national YAF back to life and to a large degree California YAF was functioning almost as an independent entity by this time. The new members of the National Board selected in 1994 were Chris Carmouche of Virginia, who had been active in the Christian Coalition; Erik Johnson, a high school student from Pennsylvania who would soon attend Vanderbilt University; Jim Sheehan, chairman of the YAF chapter at Catholic University; Paul Smith of the University of Delaware; Lukasz Urban and David Pascual-Alemany of Hamilton College; Ken Wysocki of the University of Virginia; Matt Wilkinson and Leisa Mohler of Indiana University; Gavin Goschinski of New Jersey; Rachel Krausman of James Madison University; and Jon Pastore, a University of Delaware graduate who was working for the Intercollegiate Studies Institute.[45]

Charged with the task of basically creating a new organization, Ravago opened a post office box in Bloomington, Indiana, printed a generic membership brochure and three issues papers dealing with foreign policy, free enterprise, and the right to bear arms, and went about completing his last semester at Indiana University and applying to law schools. Former YAF chairman Jim Lacy, then serving on the ACU Board, was asked to prepare a status report on YAF for the ACU directors. To this end he wrote Shun Ravago on two occasions seeking basic information on the organization. Some seven weeks later Ravago responded with few specifics as to activities, plans or any concrete understanding of how to obtain the funds necessary to operate a national organization. Unwilling to accept assistance from those who had served YAF in the recent past, Ravago commented about Richard Delgaudio, the one who had taken the initiative to sponsor the reorganization meeting at the 1994 CPAC, "we understand that he has a lot of information and experience to offer YAF, but we are not interested at this time."[46]

In late 1994, Jon Pastore and Paul Smith wrote to the other National Directors and proposed holding a meeting prior to the 1995 CPAC. It appears that little activity was taking place, that Ravago had moved from Bloomington, Indiana after graduating, and there was a question as to whether anyone was picking up YAF mail from its post office box.[47] Soon thereafter, Pastore and Smith discovered that the corporate charter for Young Americans for Freedom had expired and the organization had been dissolved with $12,000 in debt. They then started a new corporation by filing the appropriate paperwork in Delaware with a registered agent and a new set of by-laws, with Pastore and Smith constituting the initial board. An additional entity, however, was formed as "YAF Foundation" and incorporated in Delaware by Jon Pastore on January 18, 1995. In conversations with James Lacy, Pastore claimed that he talked to all members of the new

45. Letter and attachments from Rachel M. Krausman to Jim Lacy, February 22, 1994. Minutes of the Meeting of the Board of Directors for YAF, February 12, 1994. The three California members, Bieber, Fleischman, and Greene were not present at the meeting in Washington but were named to the Board to provide greater geographical representation.

46. James Lacy to Shun Ravago, March 4, 1994; James Lacy to Shun Ravago, April 18, 1994; Shun Ravago to James Lacy, undated; James Lacy to Shun Ravago, April 25, 1994.

47. Memo to National Board of Directors from Paul J. Smith, Jr. and Jon C. Pastore, no date.

Board of Directors and no one was opposed to the creation of this new legal entity.[48]

By early 1995, a board meeting was held in the office of Senator Larry Craig, where Bryan Wilkes was the press secretary. Ravago participated by phone and was informed that he was no longer National Chairman, having been replaced by Jon Pastore. A few years later, Pastore resigned to become executive director of the organization, moved its location to Delaware, and Erik Johnson assumed the title of National Chairman, a title he continues to hold some ten years later.[49] Despite the titles and the incorporations, it is safe to say that the Young Americans for Freedom founded in 1960 as the national conservative youth organization ceased to function by the end of 1992 despite the efforts of many to keep alive or resurrect the organization. The 1994 creation of a new board ultimately failed to revitalize YAF. An effort to merge Young Americans for Freedom with the non-profit Young America's Foundation in 1997 and 1998 never did come to fruition. The original legal entity, created in 1960, died in 1994 and, as a viable national organization, Young Americans for Freedom no longer existed.[50]

Despite all the turmoil at the national level, there remained pockets of YAF activity throughout the country, campus chapters and statewide units that organized and operated on their own. California Young Americans for Freedom continued as a strong conservative force on campuses and in the state's political arena. In late 1994, it claimed fifteen active chapters and had adopted an aggressive plan for expansion. As Jeff Greene, California YAF chairman noted, "the rebuilding process has been done without any direct or substantial funds, and the current growth of Cal-YAF has been accomplished without any help from National YAF or any other organization."[51] In the summer of 1994, California YAF held a regional conference attended by some 120 young conservatives from throughout the state.[52]

During the late 1990s, Brian Park of Chapman University served as California YAF state chairman and recalled the organization's involvement in the Indian gaming question and defense of conservative members on the Orange County Republican Central Committee when moderate Republicans challenged them in a concerted and well-financed effort. For Park, "being able to influence public policy at a young age through an organization like YAF," is an experience he

---

48. Interview with Chris Carmouche, Washington, DC, August 12, 2008. Copy of notes from James Lacy dated January 1995. According to Pastore, YAF's corporate status was revoked for back taxes in 1989 and then reinstated in 1990. On March 1, 1994 this legal entity was dissolved as a dead corporation. The new corporation was filed on January 19, 1995. Certificate of Incorporation of Young Americans for Freedom, Inc., State of Delaware, Secretary of State, Division of Corporations. See also filings for Young Americans for Freedom, Inc. and YAF Foundation at State of Delaware, Department of State: Division of Corporations. https://sos-res.state.de.us/tin/controller. Pastore then filed a corporate charter for Young Americans for Freedom on December 11, 1998 with the DC Department of Consumer and Regulatory Affairs and this is the entity that now uses the name Young Americans for Freedom. While the legal machinations are complicated, it is apparent that the original organization died in 1994 and new entities using the name Young Americans for Freedom were subsequently created.

49. Interview with Chris Carmouche, Washington, DC, August 12, 2008. Carmouche resigned as executive director and was replaced by Pastore in early 2000, at which time Johnson was designated as National Chairman, a position he continues to hold in 2010.

50. As of early 2010, an effort to once again develop a national organization under the name "Young Americans for Freedom" is being made, with an office located in the Washington, DC area. It is unclear whether this effort will succeed and the extent to which it has campus chapters or members.

51. Letter from Matt Zandi, Cal-YAF Executive Director to James V. Lacy, November 15, 1994. "A Business Plan for Cal YAF," 1994.

52. Ted Balaker, "YAF Convention Oozes Conservatism," *The Creative Californian*, Fall 1994, pp. 4–5.

will never forget.[53] During the remainder of the decade to the present time, the California YAF state organization publicized the organization's stands on various statewide initiatives and endorsed candidates for public office. Rather than focusing its efforts on campus, California YAF functioned as an important advocate for conservative positions in statewide politics.[54]

Across the country, however, a number of campuses did have active YAF chapters. In the early 1990s, a YAF chapter was formed at Florida International University and continued to be a strong voice for conservatism on campus for several years, sponsoring addresses by a number of nationally known conservatives such as Jack Kemp and Phyllis Schlafly. Founded by Craig Herrero in 1992, its leaders included Cesar Vasquez and Manuel Prieguez, who went on to serve in the Florida House of Representatives from 1998 to 2004. That same year, the YAF chapter at Pennsylvania State University was reorganized and has continued to the present day as a voice for responsible conservatism on that campus, featuring appearances by a first-class list of speakers, including William F. Buckley, Jr., Dinesh D'Souza, Star Parker, G. Gordon Liddy, and many others. Its chairman in the mid-1990s was Patrick Coyle, now Vice President of Young America's Foundation. Also among its activists were Jennifer Narramore, senior radio meteorologist for The Weather Channel; Jason Belich, senior software development at Adicio corporation; and Sean Clark, Director of Finance and Operations for the Foundation for Individual Rights in Education.[55]

Greg Fetterman was Iowa YAF state chairman in the early 1990s and was followed by Sandi Jaques. Fetterman is now with the Department of Homeland Security while Jaques served as a state director for FreedomWorks. At the University of Massachusetts, Brian Darling and Daniel Flynn were among those who kept the chapter alive for several years, including publishing an independent conservative paper, "The Minuteman." Darling is now Director—U.S. Senate Relations for the Heritage Foundation while Flynn is a freelance writer and author of several books including *A Conservative History of the American Left* and *Why the Left Hates America*.[56]

At the University of Pennsylvania, Mark Leventhal led a small YAF chapter in the early 1990s and now practices law and runs his own executive weight-loss company. Each year the UPenn chapter would hold a "happy birthday SDI" party on March 23rd as well as sponsor speeches by conservatives on campus. As Leventhal recently recalled, the experience "taught me leadership which I use in business."[57] William C. Daroff had served as Ohio YAF state chairman while still in high school and continued his activity at Case Western Reserve University. Today, he is the Vice President of Public Policy for United Jewish Communities in Washington, DC. Dennis Fusaro was active at George Mason University and recalled the good friends he found in YAF, the conventions, and the various conservative leaders he met.[58]

53. 2008 YAF Alumni Survey Responses: Brian Park.

54. For further information on California YAF activities during the 1990s, see Hieu Tran Phan, "The Life of the Party," *Orange County Register*, October 22, 1996; Jean O. Pasco, "Young Americans for Freedom Say the Time Is Right for a Resurgence," *Los Angeles Times*, July 5, 1998; Bud Lembke, "Pulse Beats: GOP's Young Turks embrace confrontation," *Political Pulse*, August 27, 1999, accessed on September 2, 1999 at http://www.capitolalert.com/pulse/pulse2.html.

55. 2008 YAF Alumni Survey Responses: Patrick Coyle. 2008 YAF Alumni Survey Responses: Sean Clark.

56. 2008 YAF Alumni Survey Responses: Daniel J. Flynn.

57. 2008 YAF Alumni Survey Responses: Mark Leventhal.

58. 2008 YAF Alumni Survey Responses: Dennis Fusaro.

It is important to note that while division and disorganization and eventually decline was occurring in National YAF, several individuals who were active in Young Americans for Freedom during the 1990s have remained valuable participants in the conservative movement in one capacity or another. Leslie Carbone was chairman of the American University chapter at what she called "the beginning of the post-Reagan era . . . and it was great to have reliably conservative friends." Carbone went on to work as executive director of Accuracy in Academia and is now a freelance writer and author of *Slaying Leviathan: The Moral Case for Tax Reform*.[59] Ken Wysocki was briefly on the board created in 1994 while at the University of Virginia School of Law and is now an associate with the Clausen Miller law firm and a past president of the Chicago Ornithological Society. David Ray served briefly on the National Board in 1989–90 and then came back on the newly created YAF board in 1994. Ray noted from his experience "there was an amazing solidarity in being with other people who thought like me and realizing it was not just me who held these conservative beliefs. When you meet a fellow YAFer, there is an immediate bond that develops." Ray is now associate director of the Federalist Society.[60] Bryan K. Wilkes was elected at the 1989 convention and then came back on the new board created in 1994. Wilkes is now Director of Programs and Outreach for the Nuclear Threat Initiative, an organization whose CEO is former Senator Sam Nunn.[61] John Stirrup was on the board in the late 1980s, served in the Reagan Administration, and was elected to the Board of Supervisors for Prince William County, Virginia in 2003. He is in his second term of office.

Two of the YAF National Directors in the early 1990s pursued academic careers and now contribute to providing a solid educational experience for future generations. Wayne Bowen was chairman of the University of Southern California YAF chapter and then chosen to serve on the National Board while in graduate school at Northwestern. He was an alternate delegate to the 2008 Republican National Convention and is currently Professor and Chair, Department of History at Southeast Missouri State University. As he recalled, "YAF was the formative experience of my college years, especially since I spent more time on politics than my studies. It trained me to be a leader, to face overwhelming odds with a cheerful spirit, and understand how blessed we are to be Americans."[62] Casey Hubble was elected to the National Board while a student at Wichita State University. Currently he teaches government at McLennan Community College. As one of his students recently posted on the web site Rate my Professors, "Casey Hubble is the best professor I've had. He genuinely cares about his students, and is very approachable and willing to help whenever needed."[63] With positive feedback from students such as that, Hubble's academic career should be secure.

Just as it had in the 1980s, California continued to be a source of leadership for YAF and when the national organization ceased functioning, the Cal-YAF state organization kept operating, even to the present day, as a force in state politics. Barry Jantz was a Cal-YAF chairman who has continued his involvement in conservative activities. Elected to the La Mesa City Council in 1990, he

---

59. 2008 YAF Alumni Survey Responses: Leslie Carbone.
60. Interview with David Ray, Washington, DC, August 14, 2008.
61. Interview with Bryan Wilkes, Washington, DC, August 14, 2008.
62. 2008 YAF Alumni Survey Responses: Wayne H. Bowen.
63. www.ratemyprofessors.com, accessed on October 12, 2009.

was re-elected three times and served for 16 years. Presently he is CEO of the Grossmont Healthcare District in San Diego County. Another activist at San Diego State University in the early 1990s was Jodi Shelton, now executive director of the Global Semiconductor Alliance. Carol Royal Savage served on the National Board, was chairman of the University of California–Irvine chapter, and also Orange County chairman. As she recently recalled, "I have many fond memories of my time in YAF. As an undergraduate at UCI during the 1980s, I saw first hand a resurgence of conservatism versus the ideas of the campus leftists. At the time, it was very exciting. It was a huge part of my young adulthood."[64] Savage now lives in Milford, Virginia where her husband is a professor at the University of Virginia. Two other California YAF leaders of the 1990s have had distinguished legal careers. Matthew Zandi is an associate with Nixon Peabody in Los Angeles while Michael Houston is a partner with Rutan & Tucker and a member of the California Republican Party Central Committee.

Among those who tried to keep the flame of liberty alive in YAF was a young high school student in Washington state who, in the absence of any organization, was declared YAF state chairman. Hans Zeiger was typical of a new generation of young conservatives maturing and seeking to become involved in a nonpartisan conservative youth effort. His experience reflects the reality of YAF in the 21st century when he reported,

> Over time, YAF lost its influence. A few YAF chapters held on in some corners of the country, but all in all it is no more . . . It would be worth mourning, except that the conservative youth movement is stronger than ever. YAF was an organization for its time; Reagan's Children are rising for such a time as this.[65]

Zeiger graduated from Hillsdale College and lives in Tacoma, Washington where he is a 2010 candidate for State Representative. This new generation of Americans born during the presidency of Ronald Reagan will be called upon to carry forth that same dedication to individual liberty, free enterprise, and a strong national defense that previous generations advanced through Young Americans for Freedom.

The End of a National Organization

With the failure of the 1994 reorganization there may no longer be the same Young Americans for Freedom that put forth the Sharon Statement in 1960 as the overriding principles to guide them, that confronted and overcame ideological, political and financial challenges through more than thirty years of hard work and determination, that trained several generations of young Americans who helped

---

64. 2008 YAF Alumni Survey Responses: Carol A. (Beaucage) Savage.

65. Hans Zeiger: *Reagan's Children—Taking Back the City on the Hill* (Nashville: Broadman & Holman Publishers, 2006), pp. 157–158. Little can be found on a 2003 meeting of Young Americans for Freedom. John Suarez of Miami has posted on Facebook (www.facebook.com/profile.php?id=1251608002 accessed on April 7, 2009) a resolution denouncing Castro that was adopted at this convention on October 11, 2003 in Lansing, Michigan. Whatever its precise nature, it was not a national convention of the organization founded in 1960 at Sharon, Connecticut. For a lengthy review of conservative youth in the early 21st century as reflected in the independent Bucknell University Conservative Club see John Colapinto, "Armies of the Right: The Young Hipublicans," *New York Times*, May 25, 2003.

change America. In all their efforts they were determined to, as their President once said at a YAF convention, "raise up a banner of no pale pastels, but of bold and vibrant colors." The story of Young Americans for Freedom is an important element in the political history of the United States in the last half of the 20th century. Those who created the organization can look back with pride on the obstacles overcome and the successes accomplished.

Throughout its history, Young Americans for Freedom blended together an appreciation of conservative philosophy and principles with an understanding of the means to influence public opinion and public policy. Young people were exposed to a firm foundation of free market economics, strong anti-communism, and traditional American values as expressed in the organization's credo. They took this commitment into the political arena, having been trained in effective argumentation, mass communication techniques, and political organizing principles. As one historian summarized this effort, during the late 1960s and 1970s, "YAF filled in as the one group through which young people could meet, work together to achieve results, and then move on to another project, staying busy in their fight against the Left."[66]

Despite various political setbacks, those active in Young Americans for Freedom were optimistic that they could redirect American society for they believed that, down deep inside, most Americans agreed with the principles they espoused. As historian John Andrew concluded, it was YAF that provided,

> A cadre of young men and women ideologically committed to the cause of conservatism rather than to the Republican Party or to the politics of compromise and conciliation ... Unlike other grass-roots conservative or right-wing groups at the time, YAF wanted to do more than stir the masses; it wanted to create a political commonwealth grounded in conservative principles. YAFers believed their articulation of those principles could mobilize a mass of dormant voters and create a conservative majority.[67]

Imbued with this belief in the possibility of success, YAF both helped to create the shift in American institutions and took advantage of that shift. Contrasted with other youth of the time, most YAF members "became integrated into mainstream politics. Using the skills and resources they acquired through their activism in YAF, as adults they worked for conservative causes in mainstream institutions."[68] As one YAF founder summarized the situation, "the Left battled for the campus; the Right won politics."[69] Author Sandra Gurvis compared the lasting effects of Students for a Democratic Society and Young Americans for Freedom and concluded, "If you were to weigh the durability of YAF versus SDS, it is obvious who tips the scale."[70] Through YAF a community of conservative activists was created that would change the ideological orientation of the Republican Party and eventually much of the country.

Thirty years ago James Roberts wrote *The Conservative Decade* as a precursor

66. Schoenwald: *A Time for Choosing*, p. 249.
67. Andrew: *The Other Side of the Sixties*, p. 216.
68. Klatch: *A Generation Divided*, pp. 260–261.
69. Unnamed YAF alumni quoted in Margaret M. Braungart and Richard G. Braungart, "The Effects of the 1960s Political Generation on Former Left- and Right-Wing Youth Activist Leaders," *Social Problems*, 38:3 (August 1991), p. 309.
70. Gurvis: *Where Have All the Flower Children Gone?*, p. 93.

to the coming Reagan Administration and the young conservatives poised to take a leadership role in national politics. As one reads through the names and organizations cited as having developed from the 1960s forward, the importance of Young Americans for Freedom cannot be overestimated. Name after name of those mentioned can be found on the old membership rolls of YAF, an organization that played an essential role in their leadership development. Since Roberts's book was published, these alumni of YAF have become, to employ Marvin Liebman's phrase, OAFs or Old Americans for Freedom. The early members of the organization are either retired or quickly approaching that status. Like their compatriots in the "Baby Boom" generation, many who joined YAF have now reached the pinnacle of their careers. Time passes on. Now others would need to carry forth and prepare future generations of young Americans dedicated to conservative principle for the challenges ahead.

As the Young Americans for Freedom step away from the center stage of American politics and society, one must ask from whence will the new conservative leaders come? Fortunately, those who were active in YAF saw the need for producing and promoting upcoming leaders many years ago and helped to create other lasting organizations. Today, in the 21st century, there are many more groups and resources, conferences and publications, heroes and helpers, services and mentors than any new young conservative ever dreamed about way back in 1960 when Young Americans for Freedom began its effort to create a national organization of students and young people dedicated to individual freedom. There's even one essential resource for today's young conservatives that shares those original initials—Young America's Foundation. The torch must continue to be held high and, with the advice, counsel and financial support of those who were once young Americans dedicated to individual freedom, the effort to train, educate, and equip young conservatives and to nourish and expand the network must continue.

YAF chapters and individual members went all out for Ronald Reagan and
other conservative candidates in the 1980 election. Here California YAFers
Dean Campizzi, Jon Garrison, and Sergio Picchio show their support for
Reagan and Congressman Bob Dornan. Photo from Sergio Picchio.

S.I. Hayakawa was a hero to many YAFers, especially for his efforts
to oppose leftist violence while President of San Francisco State
College. Here Senator Hayakawa visits with James Lacy prior to the
Conservative Political Action Conference.

President Reagan addresses the 1982 Conservative Political Action Conference. On the dais L–R are James Lacy, Congressman Mickey Edwards, President Reagan, former YAF National Treasurer James Linen, and Mrs. Reagan.

In 1983, YAF leaders met with Secretary Ray Donovan at the Department of Labor. L–R: Alan Ashkinaze, Richard Mathias, Susan Juroe, Deroy Murdock, and Jeff Michaels. Donovan was the honoree at a YAF sponsored dinner at the Mayflower Hotel in Washington.

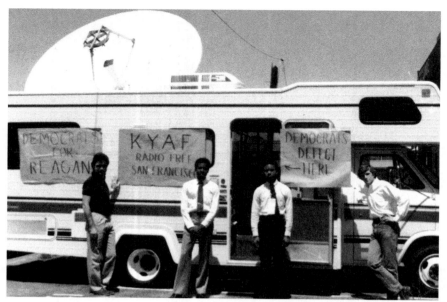

YAFers Jeffrey Wright, Deroy Murdock, Curtis Helms and Tim Wikle recruit Democrats for Reagan at the 1984 Democratic National Convention. The RV behind them was their home for the week and in this picture was parked outside the Moscone Convention Center. Photo from Deroy Murdock.

A few weeks later, YAFers were a major presence in Dallas at the Republican National Convention as their favorite President was renominated for a second term.

By the late 1980s YAF was placing more emphasis on an aggressive policy of opposing Communist advances in Latin America, Africa, and Afghanistan. The Contras effort against the Sandinistas in Nicaragua had particular appeal to many YAF activists.

YAF's 1987 convention was held on the George Washington University campus as a symbol of its commitment to campus action. It was also the first appearance in several years at a national convention for Bill Buckley. On the dais L–R are David Keene, Bill Buckley, Tom Lizardo, Jack Kemp, Frank Donatelli, and Sergio Picchio.

Throughout the late 1980s and 1990s, YAF retained a presence on a number of California campuses. In this 1989 photo, a UCLA YAF leader is shown staffing a recruiting table on Bruin Walk. The "missile" has the logos of companies trading with the Soviet Bloc. Photo from Jeff Greene.

While a United Nations official speaks inside a hall at the University of California–Irvine, YAFers protest outside. L–R: Marcus Kroenke, Vincent Puccio, Jeff Greene, Colleen Robledo, Jim Bieber, Chris Bieber, and Craig D'Onofrio. Photo from Jeff Greene.

Nearly 20 years before the current Tea Party movement, California
YAFers protested an appearance by Michael Dukakis as well as the 1990
tax hike signed by President George H.W. Bush.

New Guard ceased publication as a quarterly in 1985 but made brief
reappearances in 1989 and again in 1992. YAF came to the support of an
alumnus who was being attacked by liberals in his own party as well as
much of the media. The 1992 issue was a one-shot effort to revive the
publication and YAF on the national level.

Join the struggle to keep your freedoms!!!

PS-YAF

**Penn State
Young Americans
for Freedom**

**Meetings:
Every WEDNESDAY
7:00 PM
265 Willard Building**

By the mid-1990s, the YAF national organization ceased to coordinate or provide assistance to local chapters. Nevertheless, on a small number of campuses active YAF chapters continued to promote conservatism. Penn State YAF was one of the most active independent YAF chapters and has continuously operated under strong autonomous leaders to the present day.

Roger Ream, former YAF National Director and now President of The Fund for American Studies, reads a copy of the 2010 version of *New Guard* magazine published by the new group attempting to revitalize Young Americans for Freedom on America's campuses. Photo by Jordan Marks.

484

New YAF leaders at 2010 CPAC as another generation awakes to conservatism. L–R Chris Bedford (MA), John Stapleton (DC), Eva Moreno (Howard University), Lance Christopher (University of the District of Columbia), Jordan Marks (new YAF executive director). Photo by Carrie Devorah.

In 2009 several former California YAF State Chairmen gathered for a reunion and to honor Pete Sheridan, a long time YAF volunteer. L–R Gary Kreep, Jon Fleischman, Randy Goodwin, Jim Lacy, John Lewis, Sergio Picchio, Chad Morgan, Matt Zandi, Jim Bieber, Pete Sheridan, Dana Rohrabacher, Pat Nolan, Barry Goldwater, Jr., Jack Cox, and Bill Saracino. Photo, Randy Goodwin.

15. What Hath YAF Wrought?

*"The conservative activists who first organized themselves in the early
1960s were the force behind the rise of Barry Goldwater, the election
of Ronald Reagan as Governor of California, the takeover of the
Republican Party from the liberal wing that controlled it for decades,
the election of Ronald Reagan as president, and the reversion of
Congress to Republican control for the first time in 40 years."*[1]

From its beginning as an outgrowth of the efforts to obtain the Republican vice
presidential nomination for a conservative in 1960 up through its determined
campaign to ensure that a conservative vice president was renominated in 1992,
Young Americans for Freedom was a major player in the politics of late 20th
century America. No one can deny YAF's important role in the drive to nominate
Barry Goldwater in 1964, nor the organization's long-term commitment, beginning in 1968, to nominate and elect Ronald Reagan to the presidency. As YAF
members and as alumni, they played vital roles as candidates, campaign managers,
fundraisers, contributors, and advocates for conservative candidates beginning
with the New York City campaigns of Ed Nash and Rosemary McGrath in 1962
up through the end of the century. In election after election, wherever there was
a clear-cut conservative candidate, YAF members and alumni were involved.

While much of the academic and popular media discussion of the 1960s focused
on the various New Left organizations that attempted to destroy American society
and take control of American campuses, the previous chapters have shown that
there was a vigorous and determined alternative working for peace on campus,
traditional education, and opportunity for students to learn. Young Americans for
Freedom was a voice of reason on college and high school campuses during some
turbulent times in America's history. At the same time, it was YAF that took the
lead in defending the American military effort to aid its allies in South Vietnam
as they attempted to preserve their independence and freedom. On campuses
and in communities, YAF stood tall as an organization of young people calling
for victory over Communism in Southeast Asia and in other areas from Angola
and Nicaragua to Afghanistan and Ethiopia.

In previous chapters, the YAF story has been told chronologically, outlining
the many efforts undertaken to elect conservatives to public office, to oppose
leftist violence and propaganda on campuses, and to defend the American military and diplomatic efforts against Communism. The contributions of this one
organization of conservative young people played an essential part in the political
history of the United States during the latter half of the 20th century. Were this
the totality of YAF's contribution to America, it would be worthy of recognition.
But from its initial founding, Young Americans for Freedom had a more lasting
purpose than merely to influence the course of American history through political action, campus activities and community projects. Through its emphasis on
youth, YAF was training and preparing young Americans to be effective leaders

---

1. Karl Zinsmeister, "The Other Activists," *The American Enterprise*, May–June 1997, p. 37.

for the conservative movement and other undertakings in American society.

The conservative movement that exists in America today, and especially its beachhead in the Nation's Capital, would not have developed were it not for Young Americans for Freedom. This is a bold but verifiable and undoubtedly true statement. It is a fact that is not only true in the 21st century but was true some thirty years ago when M. Stanton Evans, one of those responsible for the development of the modern conservative movement, testified to its importance when he said,

> If you take a look at the conservative organizations and publications of the present . . . they are for the most part staffed and run by products of the conservative movement on the campus. The same is true for conservative campaigns and conservative activities on Capitol Hill.[2]

While there were other organizations appealing to conservative youth, from the time of its formation in 1960 through its demise as a national force in the mid-1990s, Young Americans for Freedom was the one entity that brought together varied elements of the right in a concerted effort to oppose communism, promote free enterprise, and advance individual freedom.

Although YAF members and chapters were engaged in many projects to influence public policy and elect conservative candidates to office, the leadership of the organization was well aware that their goals and objectives were more long-term. YAF was recruiting, training, and preparing young people to assume even more important roles later in life. They were indeed creating "cadres for conservatism," as author Gregory Schneider described YAF's contribution to contemporary America. That single youth organization spawned many of the organizational elements of the 21st century conservative movement and provided the leadership and manpower to build those publications, organizations, and foundations into the significant elements of American society that they are today.

Beyond the various elements that constitute the contemporary American conservative movement, YAF has produced a wide range of leaders for other areas of society. YAF alumni have served in public office at all levels of elective government, as appointees to numerous state and Federal positions, and as members of the American judiciary at all levels. In the varied world of media and communications, a number of YAF alumni have developed careers as radio talk show hosts, newspaper columnists, authors, and publishers. Still others have devoted their lives to educating future generations through careers in academia. As can be expected of an organization dedicated to free-market economics and the rule of law, numerous YAF alumni took up careers in business or law.

The organizational affiliations described below are the most accurate that were available as of 2010 but are in no way comprehensive of the involvement of many individuals who hold leadership positions in several conservative groups. Likewise, time has a way of modifying any discussion of organizational membership and leadership, as well as occupational affiliations. In the sections reviewing YAF alumni in public office, the communications arena, academia, the law, and business, some of the affiliations may no longer be current at time of publication. However, the associations listed are indicative of the scope of involvement

---

2. Quoted in Roberts: *The Conservative Decade*, p. 35.

by YAF alumni in the various areas of American life during the latter part of the 20th century and the beginning of the 21st.

Moreover, the later career paths of many individuals active in Young Americans for Freedom have been described as part of the chronological history of the organization in earlier chapters. In many cases, those organizational and occupational affiliations are not repeated once again in this chapter. Thus, this is not meant to be an all-inclusive listing of YAF alumni in the various organizations and occupational categories discussed here.

Finally, it is important to note that, given the absence of any central, organized depository of historical records of Young Americans for Freedom, the inclusion of individuals in this chapter is the result of reviewing scattered membership lists from various periods in the organization's history, references in correspondence, and names cited in YAF publications such as *New Guard* and *Dialogue on Liberty*. It is possible that some individuals listed here may have never formally become dues-paying members of national YAF but their names were associated with YAF projects or publications at some time. More to the point, however, is the realization that many other individuals who had been YAF members during its thirty-plus years of existence as the national conservative youth organization, may be missing from the following pages. For those omissions, apologies are in order and extended in the hope that, should another subsequent printing occur, those individuals can be added to the roster of alumni who contributed to American society and the conservative movement.

Creating a Conservative Movement

In attempting a broad overview of the contemporary American conservative movement, one first realizes the amazing organizational growth that occurred over the last thirty years of the 20th century. Whether it be organizations with a wide focus on a variety of public issues or those groups limited to one or a few major concerns, bringing together grassroots activists or providing the academic and philosophical basis for sound public policy, concentrating on state-level action or attempting to influence national policy—in all these areas of activity, the growth of conservative organizations has been phenomenal and had produced an environment quite different from that in which young conservatives operated in the 1950s and early 1960s. To a large degree, this development of a movement is one of the most significant and lasting outgrowths of the presidential campaign of Barry Goldwater. Out of that campaign came many of the leaders who saw the need for a permanent structure for conservative activity in America.[3]

Young Americans for Freedom played a critical role in the development of many, if not most, of those new conservative organizations that would be established in the 1960s, 1970s and beyond. Those who were college students and young adults active in YAF went on to form new groups or serve as important personnel in conservative organizations founded by others. To fully understand the influence of YAF on the creation of a lasting movement in America, it is helpful to view

---

3. Viguerie and Franke: *America's Right Turn*, claims the first actual reference to a conservative movement appearing in *National Review* was made in an article by Revilo Oliver, "Reflections on a Right-Wing Protest," September 29, 1956. Viguerie and Franke discuss some of the elements in the development of the conservative movement on pp. 61–73 of their book. A more detailed and scholarly review of this development can be found in Gregory L. Schneider: *The Conservative Century—From Reaction to Revolution* (Lanham, MD: Rowman & Littlefield Publishers, Inc., 2009).

those organizations formed by YAF alumni and then those in which YAFers have played important contributing roles.

Perhaps no single organization brings together the disparate elements of the modern conservative movement as effectively as the American Conservative Union. Founded after the Goldwater defeat of 1964, YAF's then executive director David R. Jones was one of the key individuals in bringing into being a senior conservative organization. ACU has always represented an inclusive responsible conservatism dedicated to influencing public opinion and encouraging political involvement. As mentioned in an earlier chapter, YAF alumni have been at the forefront of the American Conservative Union's leadership from Carol Dawson as its only staff member at its inception to David Keene, its present-day Chairman.[4] Keene has been ACU chairman since 1984. Elected as National Chairman of YAF in 1969, he recently concluded, "all of this began with YAF and I can honestly say that it was my work with YAF that launched whatever career I've enjoyed."[5] In addition to Keene, the current ACU Board includes these former YAF members: Don Devine, Jameson Campaigne, Jr., Morton C. Blackwell, Floyd Brown, Tom DeLay, Becky Norton Dunlop, Tom Winter, Alan Gottlieb, James Lacy, Michael R. Long, Joseph Morris, Ron Robinson, and Kirby Wilbur.

Out of ACU developed the Conservative Victory Fund, now led by YAF alumnus Ronald Pearson, a political action committee that continues as a significant source of campaign funds for conservative congressional candidates. Pearson, a former YAF National Director, has been a director of Young America's Foundation for many years. In a similar fashion it was ACU that served as the impetus for the founding of the American Legislative Exchange Council, a non-partisan organization formed in 1973 to bring together conservative state legislators. Its initial executive director was Kathy King Rothschild, assisted by Connie Campanella, both of whom were active YAF leaders in Missouri and New York respectively. The National Journalism Center, now sponsored by Young America's Foundation, was founded in 1977 by M. Stanton Evans, at that time outgoing chairman of ACU

Perhaps the best known project of the American Conservative Union is the annual Conservative Political Action Conference held each year in Washington since its founding as a joint project of YAF, ACU, *Human Events* and *National Review* in 1974. From its beginning as a small gathering of a few hundred, CPAC now attracts literally thousands of conservatives, including a large contingent of high school and college students, each year. Over his career, Ronald Reagan was a featured speaker at twelve conferences.

Another broad-based but strongly conservative organization formed by a YAF alumnus is The Conservative Caucus. Organized in 1974, ten years after the ACU, it attempts to mobilize local conservatives to take action on a wide range of issues. Howard Phillips, a participant at the Sharon Conference while student government president at Harvard College and an original member of the YAF National Board of Directors, created the caucus and remains as its chairman. Phillips also founded the United States Taxpayers Party (now the Constitution Party) and was its presidential candidate in 1992, 1996, and 2000.[6] One-time University of Virginia YAF leader Charles Orndorff serves as administrative vice-chairman of

---

4. See the discussion on the founding of the American Conservative Union at the end of chapter 5.

5. 2008 YAF Alumni Survey Responses: David A. Keene.

6. Michael Rust, "1996 Ad," *Insight on the News*, September 11, 1995, discusses Phillips's 1992 presidential campaign and his plans for 1996. For an interesting leftist view of Phillips see Adele M. Stan, "Howard Phillips' World," *Mother Jones*, November 3, 2008.

the Conservative Caucus and former YAF National Chairman J. Alan MacKay sits on the board of directors.

YAF alumni were responsible for the creation of a number of other conservative organizations focused on a wide range of issues. Citizens United was founded by former YAF National Director Floyd Brown in 1988. It was a party to the Supreme Court case of *Citizens United* v. *Federal Election Commission*, challenging the constitutionality of the McCain-Feingold Act and its restrictions on campaign financing.[7] Current president of Citizens United is David Bossie and its Board of Directors includes former YAFers Michael Boos, Brian Berry, Ron Robinson and Kirby Wilbur.

American Values is an organization dedicated to faith, family and freedom. Its president is Gary Bauer, former Kentucky YAF state chairman and 2000 candidate for the Republican presidential nomination. The National Center for Public Policy Research is a non-profit communications and research foundation established in 1982 by Amy Moritz Ridenour, a YAF member while a student at the University of Maryland. Kenneth Boehm and Peter Flaherty formed the National Legal & Policy Center in 1991. Both had previously served on the YAF National Board of Directors and on the national YAF staff. The center is committed to promoting ethics in government and has taken the lead in investigating and publicizing a number of ethical lapses in both Congress and the Executive Branch.

The American Policy Center is dedicated to protecting property rights and promoting back-to-basics education. Tom DeWeese, former Ohio YAF state chairman, started it in 1988. As he recently concluded, "YAF taught me the root philosophy that has carried me through my life. The skills of organizing, writing (even running a printing press) have been my greatest education and set the stage for my life-time work." DeWeese noted that "many of the people I met in YAF are still the people I deal with on a daily basis, as political allies, business associates and vendors."[8]

Another who benefited from his experience in YAF and went on to form a conservative activist organization is Chris Carmouche. Having been active in the Christian Coalition, Carmouche came to YAF involvement in the mid-1990s after his college and graduate school years, serving briefly during the effort to reorganize YAF. He maintains that his experience in YAF was "tremendously beneficial. The fact that I was involved has really helped me. A lot of the contentious fights were great learning experiences, learning how not to make mistakes, how not to go there."[9] Now he is president of Grasstops USA, an effort to use the power of the Internet to organize support for conservative causes and raise funds for conservative campaigns.

Still other organizations formed by YAF alumni are focused on a narrower range of policy interests. The Lincoln Institute for Research and Education was founded in 1978 by Jay A. Parker, former YAF National Director, to study public policy issues that affect the lives of black middle America, and to make its findings available to elected officials and the public. Those on its advisory board include former YAFers David Franke and Ross MacKenzie, both of whom were participants at the Sharon Conference in 1960. Parker recalled YAF as having

---

7. In a decision issued in January 2010, the Court sided with Citizens United and struck down restrictions on corporate sponsorship of policy advertisements prior to an election but went further to allow corporate efforts on behalf of specific candidates also.

8. 2008 YAF Alumni Survey Responses: Tom DeWeese. See also: Stephen Goode, "Conservative Activist DeWeese Keeps Fighting for Freedom," *Insight on the News*, January 5, 1988.

9. Interview with Chris Carmouche, Washington, DC, August 12, 2008.

a major influence on his life as it "established lifelong friendships and career opportunities."[10] In addition to its research efforts, the Institute publishes *The Lincoln Letter* and holds monthly breakfast gatherings in Washington where guest speakers discuss issues of concern, including those that specifically affect the African-American community.

Former YAF member Cliff Kincaid is president of America's Survival, Inc, an organization that describes itself as a United Nations watchdog group and focuses on issues concerning American sovereignty. Kincaid is also editor of the Accuracy in Media (AIM) Report. He is a graduate of the University of Toledo where he served as YAF chapter chairman. Suzanne Scholte, a former YAF National Director and national staff member, was one of the founders of the Defense Forum Foundation and since 1989 has served as its president. In recent years, the organization's forums on Capitol Hill have focused on how to win the war on terror and how to protect the United States' homeland from terror attacks as well as promoting freedom and human rights around the globe. YAF alumnus Herman Pirchner established the American Foreign Policy Council in 1982 and serves as its president. Robert Schadler, a former member of both YAF and the Intercollegiate Studies Institute, is Senior Fellow in Public Diplomacy.

Several former YAFers have organized legal action committees that have played central roles in advancing the conservative cause through both bringing civil actions and providing defense support when conservative activists have been challenged in court. The United States Justice Foundation was organized in 1979 by Gary Kreep and two other conservative activists. Kreep is a former California YAF state chairman and YAF National Director. Kreep reported that his involvement in YAF "directly led to the founding of the United States Justice Foundation, Justice PAC, Republican Majority Campaign PAC, and the Family Values Coalition."[11] Kreep serves as president of the organization and Michael Reagan, son of the former President, is chairman of the advisory board for the foundation.

Daniel Popeo, who was a YAF member while at Georgetown University School of Law, founded the Washington Legal Foundation in 1977 and has seen it grow to become a major legal force in the Nation's Capital. In Chicago, Joe Morris is chief executive officer of the Lincoln Legal Foundation, which is a public interest law office and legal research center. Morris was a YAF chapter chairman while a student at the University of Chicago. The Landmark Legal Foundation, was founded in 1976 as the Great Plains Legal Foundation and has offices in Kansas City and Washington, DC. Its president is Mark R. Levin, who was a YAF member while a student at Temple University and currently hosts a syndicated radio talk show. Levin has authored two best-selling books, *Men in Black* and *Liberty and Tyranny*.[12]

Clint Bolick was a co-founder in 1991 and vice president of the Institute for Justice, which calls itself the nation's only libertarian public interest law firm. He is now director of the Scharf-Norton Center for Constitutional Litigation at the Goldwater Institute in Scottsdale, Arizona and recently argued that only an activist court can protect individual and constitutional rights against an aggressive

---

10. 2008 YAF Alumni Survey Responses: J.A. (Jay) Parker.
11. 2008 YAF Alumni Survey Responses: Gary G. Kreep. This organization should not be confused with a "mortgage rescue company" in Las Vegas using the same name.
12. David Wagner, "When Conservatives Lay Down the Law," *Insight on the News*, August 10, 1998. Mark R. Levin: *Men in Black* (Washington, DC: Regnery Publishing, 2005) and *Liberty and Tyranny* (New York: Threshold Editions, 2009).

legislative and executive branch.[13] Bolick was a YAF member while a student at Drew University in his native New Jersey. Richard Delgaudio, former YAF National Director, was founder of the Legal Affairs Council, an organization that at various times was headed by former YAF National Directors Joan Kehlhof and Donald Derham, attorneys in Texas and New York respectively.[14]

Two important organizations in the area of gun rights—the Citizens Committee for the Right to Keep and Bear Arms (CCRKBA) and the Second Amendment Foundation—are led by former YAF National Director and Regional Representative Alan Gottlieb. CCRKBA started out as an ad hoc student group founded by YAF and was subsequently converted by Gottlieb into a broader organization with a name change. It continues as one of the most active organizations on gun rights issues in America and Gottlieb has become publisher of *Gun Week*. The Second Amendment Foundation was established in 1974 and serves as a tax-exempt educational effort to explore and publicize the right to keep and bear arms as guaranteed in the Constitution. Looking back on his time in YAF, Gottlieb recalled it as "a great networking experience that made lasting business and personal friendships. The internal politics was great training for the real world. It had a tremendous impact on my life."[15] Gottlieb's wife, the former Julie Versnel, was an active YAF member in the Nation's Capital while working for the ACU in the mid-1970s.[16]

Another former DC YAF activist and one-time editor of *The American Rifleman*, John Snyder has been Director of Publications and Public Affairs for CCRKBA and treasurer of the Second Amendment Foundation. As Snyder recently commented, "YAF has had a most significant and positive impact on my life and so many YAFers are friends and associates of mine now that it would be well nigh impossible to list them all . . . It really was my introduction to the conservative movement."[17] YAF alumni who have served on the boards of the two organizations include National Directors Sam Slom, Michael Connelly, and Herb Stupp as well as YAF members Kirby Wilbur and Snyder.

With its strong emphasis on free market economics, it is no surprise that some of the libertarian members of YAF went on to develop their own organizations. The International Society for Individual Liberty (ISIL) came about in 1989 through a merger of the Society for Individual Liberty and the Libertarian International. While the Libertarian International was founded at the University of Michigan in 1980, the Society for Individual Liberty developed after the 1969 YAF National Convention. Its founders were Jarrett Wollstein, former YAF chairman at University of Maryland; David Walter, YAF National Director and Pennsylvania YAF state chairman from 1967–1969, and Donald Ernsberger, YAF activist at Penn State. Among speakers at recent ISIL conferences have been Richard Cheatham, former Virginia YAF state chairman, and Dr. Sharon Presley, YAF activist in the early 1960s who recently retired as a professor at California State University–East Bay and is currently director of Resources for Independent Living. Today, ISIL publishes libertarian materials, holds conferences, and runs the online company Laissez-Faire Books, originally founded by Presley.

---

13. Clint Bolick: *David's Hammer—The Case for an Activist Judiciary* (Washington, DC: Cato Institute, 2007).

14. Telephone interview with Richard Delgaudio, August 4, 2009.

15. 2008 YAF Alumni Survey Responses: Alan Gottlieb.

16. Interview with Alan Gottlieb and Julie Versnel Gottlieb, Bellevue, WA, March 26, 2009.

17. 2008 YAF Alumni Survey Responses: John Michael Snyder.

A former YAF chapter chairman at the Massachusetts Institute of Technology, Robert W. Poole, Jr. started Reason Foundation and was its chief executive officer from 1978 to 2001. The foundation publishes *Reason* magazine and carries out research efforts from a libertarian perspective. Poole continues his involvement as the Searle Freedom Trust Transportation Fellow at Reason Foundation.[18] The Ludwig von Mises Institute was founded in 1982 as the research and educational center of classical liberalism, libertarian political theory, and the Austrian School of economics. Founder and chairman of the Mises Institute is Lewellyn Rockwell Jr., a YAF member while an undergraduate at Tufts University. Among the adjunct faculty are Harry Veryser, a professor at University of Detroit Mercy who was a Michigan YAF activist, and William Luckey, YAF chapter chairman at St. John's University and now Professor of Political Science at Christendom College.

Still other YAF alumni have ventured out into areas traditionally associated with the left. The Media Research Center was organized in 1987 by a small group of young conservatives who were determined to prove that liberal bias does exist in the mainstream media. With offices in Alexandria, Virginia, the center's research has been invaluable in providing evidence of that bias and countering its effects on American society. Founder and president of the Media Research Center is L. Brent Bozell, III, nephew of Bill Buckley and a YAF member while a student at the University of Dallas. Brent Baker is Vice President of Research and Publications for the center. Baker was an active YAF member at George Washington University and editor of *The Sequent*, YAF's independent newspaper on campus.

In addition to creating a large number of new organizations, YAF alumni have performed important functions for a wealth of others that are part of the conservative movement in America. They range across the entire gamut of policy interests and include most groups associated with 21st century conservatism. Among those involved in organizations concerned with a broad range of policies and issues, Kathy King Rothschild is Senior Development Officer for Freedom Alliance, an organization founded by Oliver North. Doug Bandow, former YAF chairman at Stanford University, is Vice President of Policy for Citizens Outreach, whose slogan is "putting the public back in public policy." At the Institute for Policy Innovation, founded in 1987 by former House Majority Leader Dick Armey, Peter Ferrara, a YAF member while at Harvard, is senior policy advisor.

YAF alumni can be found on the rosters of all the leading think tanks and research institutions that contribute to the policy analysis and development that is an essential element of the contemporary conservative movement. Among the scholars at the Hoover Institution are Peter Schweizer, former YAF National Director, and Dr. Tibor Machan, a frequent contributor to *New Guard* magazine during the 1960s and 1970s. Holding down a key staff position at Hoover is Mary Gingell, Director of Development Events and Services. Gingell was YAF chapter chairman while a student at the University of Virginia. At the American Enterprise Institute, Gerard Alexander, former Georgetown University YAF chairman and Associate Professor of Political Science at the University of Virginia, is a Visiting Scholar while Dr. H.E. "Ted" Frech, former Missouri YAF state chairman and Professor of Economics at the University of California at Santa Barbara, is an Adjunct Scholar.

Another think tank with a large number of former YAF leaders is the Heritage Foundation. Former National Director John Von Kannon is Vice President and

18. 2008 YAF Alumni Survey Responses: Robert W. Poole, Jr.

Treasurer while Becky Norton Dunlop, a former DC YAFer, is Vice President, External Affairs. Von Kannon believes that his experience in YAF "helped nurture a life-long interest in and commitment to conservative principles."[19] Brian Darling was a YAF National Director in the late 1980s while a student at the University of Massachusetts and is now Director, U.S. Senate Relations for Heritage while Dr. Robert Moffit, a YAF Board member first elected in 1969, is Director, Center for Health Policy Studies. Lee Edwards, one of the original founders of YAF, is Distinguished Fellow in Conservative Thought at Heritage. Edwards still looks back with pride on his role in the new organization, including "editing the first issue of the *New Guard* for the Goldwater rally at the jam-packed Manhattan Center in March 1961; presenting John Dos Passos with a YAF award before 18,000 applauding conservatives in Madison Square Garden in March 1962."[20]

At the Hudson Institute, John Fonte is Director, Center for American Common Culture, and a Senior Fellow. Fonte was a YAF member while a student at the University of Arizona. John C. Weicher attended the Sharon Conference in 1960, was a National Director, and served briefly as Illinois YAF state chairman. After serving in various Republican administrations under presidents Nixon, Ford, Reagan and both Bushes, Weicher is Director, Center for Housing and Financial Markets, at the Hudson Institute.[21] At the Claremont Institute, Dr. Angelo Codevilla, Professor of International Relations at Boston University, is a Senior Fellow. He wrote for *New Guard* in the early 1960s.

Edward Crane formed the Cato Institute in 1977 to increase the understanding of public policies based on the principles of limited government, free markets, individual liberty, and peace. Today, its executive vice president is David Boaz, former YAF Vanderbilt University chairman, Kentucky state chairman, National Director, and editor of *New Guard*. Serving as vice president for legal affairs and Director, Center for Constitutional Studies, is Dr. Roger Pilon, a YAF activist at the University of Chicago while Daniel Griswold, a YAF leader at the University of Wisconsin at Madison, is director of the Center for Trade Policy Studies. For Griswold, his time in YAF "made me more politically aware and more supportive of the ideals of the Reagan Revolution."[22] Ted Galen Carpenter, a YAF chapter chairman while an undergraduate at the University of Wisconsin at Milwaukee, is Cato's vice president for Defense and Foreign Policy Studies. Both Doug Bandow, former Stanford YAF chairman, and Daniel J. Mitchell, former University of Georgia YAF chairman, are Senior Fellows at the Cato Institute.

The Future of Freedom Foundation was established in 1989 and posts nearly 2,000 articles on its web site, one of the most comprehensive libertarian economics resource banks on a wide range of issues. Serving as Senior Fellow is Sheldon Richman, YAF chapter chairman at Temple University in the late 1960s. Richman is also editor of *The Freeman*, a free market economics periodical that has been published for nearly fifty years by the Foundation for Economic Education (FEE). FEE's president now is Lawrence Reed, an active YAF member in high school and as a student at Grove City College. He recalled his experiences in high school in the 1960s,

19. 2008 YAF Alumni Survey Responses: John Von Kannon.
20. 2008 YAF Alumni Survey Responses: Lee Edwards.
21. 2008 YAF Alumni Survey Responses: John C. Weicher.
22. 2008 YAF Alumni Survey Responses: Daniel Griswold.

In those days, YAF provided its new recruits with a wealth of books, maga-zines and articles—most notably for me, F.A. Hayek's *The Road to Serfdom*, Henry Grady Weaver's *The Mainspring of Human Progress*, Henry Hazlitt's *Economics in One Lesson*, and a subscription to The Freeman, the monthly journal of the Foundation for Economic Education. The message was simple: If you want to be an effective anti-communist, you had better know something about philosophy and economics.[23]

Reed went on to join the faculty at Northwood University and became president of the Mackinac Center for Public Policy before assuming his current position with FEE in 2008.

The interaction among the various groups influencing young conservatives can be seen in two individuals and their relationships to the Foundation for Economic Education and Young Americans for Freedom. While YAF led a young Lawrence Reed to FEE, Roger Ream was coming in the opposite direction.[24] Today, Ream is not only president of The Fund for American Studies but also a vice president of The Philadelphia Society, a distinguished invitation-only society of academ-ics, journalists, policy researchers and advocates, and clergy founded in 1964 by YAF member Don Lipsett. Over the years, some thirty YAF alumni have served as trustees for the Philadelphia Society, including Lee Edwards, Stan Evans and Ken Cribb as president.[25]

The Atlas Society, which began as the Institute of Objectivist Studies in 1990, is dedicated to advancing the philosophy of Ayn Rand. According to its literature, the goal of the Atlas Society is to help create a new culture in our society, a culture that affirms and embodies the core Objectivist values of reason, individualism, freedom, and achievement. From 2005–2008, the editor-in-chief of its publication, *The New Individualist*, was Robert James Bidinotto. While in high school in the mid-1960s, he became active in YAF. As he recently explained,

> I formed a local chapter of Young Americans for Freedom. Back then, YAF was the national organization for conservative and libertarian youth (I mean, there weren't enough of us to have even two national right-wing organizations) . . .
> I graduated from high school in June 1967 . . . That same summer, prior to starting my first year of college, I attended the national YAF convention in Pittsburgh, as an official voting member of the Pennsylvania delegation. It was a heady experience to meet hundreds of very smart kids who shared my political interests. I didn't feel quite so weird and alone anymore.[26]

---

23. 2008 YAF Alumni Survey Responses: Lawrence W. Reed.
24. Roger Ream email to the author, May 18, 2009.
25. Among the YAF alumni who have served as trustees of the Philadelphia Society are Joseph Baldacchino, Morton Blackwell, The Honorable Danny Boggs, Linda Bridges, Ronald Burr, Jameson Campaigne, Jr., Dr. Warren Coats, Kenneth Cribb, Dr. William C. Dennis, Michelle Easton, Dr. Lee Edwards, M. Stanton Evans, Jeffrey B. Gayner, Charles Heatherly, Willa Johnson, Don Lipsett, Eugene Meyer, Joseph Morris, Jay Parker, Dr. Roger Pilon, Roger Ream, Ron Robinson, Robert Schadler, Dr. Robert L. Schuettinger, Dr. David P. Stuhr, James Taylor, Wayne Valis, John Von Kannon, Tim Wheeler, and Karl Ziebarth.
26. Robert James Bidinotto, "*Atlas Shrugged* Changed My Life," *The New Individualist*, October 2007, pp. 72–74.

Bidinotto went on to be YAF chapter chairman at Grove City College, a chapter that also produced Dr. Camille Castorina, a former associate professor of business at Brewton-Parker College, Dr. Jeffrey Hummel, Assistant Professor of Economics at San Jose State University, and Lawrence Reed of FEE. Current trustees of the Atlas Society include Robert Poole and Frank Bubb, former Missouri YAF state chairman.[27]

Dr. William Hawkins, former YAF National Director and college economics professor, is Senior Fellow in National Security Studies for the United States Business and Industrial Council Education Foundation, formerly headed by Anthony Harrigan and known as the Southern States Industrial Council. Until recently, Thomas Atwood was president and chief executive officer of the National Council for Adoption. Atwood was YAF chairman at Kent State University in the late 1960s and early 1970s. Steve Antosh, YAF chairman at Oklahoma State University, is responsible for fundraising and membership recruitment for the National Pro-Life Alliance. Among his prior activities he was a professor of political science at Universidad Francisco Marroquin in Guatemala.[28] Martin Morse Wooster, a YAF member while at Georgetown, is Senior Research Fellow at the Capital Research Center.

Pat Nolan was a YAF National Director while a student at the University of Southern California. Elected to the California State Assembly in 1978, he became Minority Leader in 1984 and worked aggressively to elect a Republican majority. Nolan was caught up in an FBI sting operation for accepting what were deemed illegal campaign contributions. He pleaded guilty to one count and served 25 months in a federal prison. Nolan's goal of a Republican majority was reached a year after he left the Assembly. With a new understanding of the impact of imprisonment on families as well as prisoners, Pat joined Chuck Colson's Prison Fellowship to lead its criminal justice reform arm, Justice Fellowship. Nolan has built broad coalitions that passed the Prison Rape Elimination Act and the Second Chance Act. He is the author of *When Prisoners Return*, describing the role the Church can play in helping prisoners get back on their feet after they are released.[29]

Joseph Baldacchino has been president of the National Humanities Institute since 1984. NHI promotes research, publishing, and teaching in the humanities, with emphasis on the ethical preconditions and purposes of culture and society, the centrality of personal freedom and creativity, and the historical nature of human existence. Looking back on his days in YAF, Baldacchino noted that, "I gained a great deal of practical experience during my relatively short period with YAF. Moreover, it was through YAF that I first became acquainted with the writings of Kirk, Buckley, Burnham, Mises, Hayek, and other thinkers who have influenced me deeply."[30] While an undergraduate Baldacchino was Maryland YAF state chairman and for many years a reporter and editor for *Human Events*. Among the members of the NHI Board of Trustees are former YAFers Juliana Geran Pilon and Jameson Campaigne, Jr.

David Denholm is president of the Public Service Research Council, a non-

27. 2008 YAF Alumni Survey Responses: Robert Poole.
28. 2008 YAF Alumni Survey Responses: Steve M. Antosh.
29. Pat Nolan: *When Prisoners Return* (Longwood, FL: Xulon Press, 2004). See also Pat Nolan, "Take It from Experience: Prisons Need Reform," *Sacramento Bee*, August 30, 2009.
30. 2008 YAF Alumni Survey Responses: Joseph Baldacchino.

profit research and education organization founded in 1973 and concerned with public policy on unionism in public employment and union political influence on the size, cost and quality of government services.[31] Ray LaJeunesse is Vice President and Legal Director at the National Right to Work Legal Defense Foundation where he has worked since 1971. LaJeunesse joined YAF while a student at Providence College and "thanks to YAF and *National Review*, I became, and still am, deeply involved in the conservative movement."[32] One of his associates as a staff attorney is John C. Scully, who first joined YAF as a high school student and remained active through law school. Scully credits YAF with providing the opportunity to combine career and principles: "YAF gave me the knowledge to know who to contact to get a job serving the cause of freedom."[33]

Serving as vice president of the National Rifle Association is David A. Keene and as Director of Federal Affairs is Charles "Chuck" Cunningham, former Virginia YAF state chairman. President of Gun Owners of America is Larry Pratt, a former member of the Virginia House of Delegates.

Michael J. Caslin, a YAF member at Manhattanville College in the early 1970s, has held a number of positions with the National Foundation for Teaching Entrepreneurship, an organization dedicated to promoting entrepreneurship courses in American high schools, including most recently as chief executive officer. William E. Saracino, former California YAF state chairman and National Director, serves as executive director of the Americanism Educational League, a California-based non-profit dedicated to educating America's youth about the moral, political, social and economic values that made America free and strong, instilling in students the core principles that guided America's founders.[34] Sean Clark was chairman of Penn State YAF and is now Director, Finance and Operations, for the Foundation for Individual Rights in Education.[35]

Finally, one area that has seen a tremendous expansion in the reach of the conservative movement is the creation of state public policy research institutes. YAFers have played an important role in this arena also. The Thomas Jefferson Institute is the premiere conservative think tank in Virginia, headed by former YAF National Vice Chairman Michael Thompson with YAF activist Chris Braunlich as vice president, former YAF executive director Randal C. Teague as secretary/treasurer, and former YAFer Robert Turner as a member of the board of directors. Thompson concluded that,

> What we learned in those years has served us well in our "adult lives" whether in business, politics or even local community work. What we learned and the friendships we made during these years is truly a major part of our lives and we are grateful of this opportunity.[36]

For Braunlich, who also served for eight years as a member of the Fairfax County School Board, the value of his involvement in YAF was

---

31. 2008 YAF Alumni Survey Responses: David Denholm.
32. 2008 YAF Alumni Survey Responses: Raymond J. LaJeunesse, Jr.
33. 2008 YAF Alumni Survey Responses: John Conner Scully.
34. See www.americanism.org for further information, including the organization's current Board of Directors.
35. 2008 YAF Alumni Survey Responses: Sean Clark.
36. 2008 YAF Alumni Survey Responses: Michael W. Thompson.

Most importantly, discovering you weren't alone. It was a time when we banded together without regard to the differences among conservatives. We hadn't yet divided into libertarians, anti-taxers, pro-lifers, and anti-communists who focused only on our own issues to the exclusion of all others (and demanded 100% fealty), but instead undertook to build something that was greater than any one of us. I miss that.[37]

Teague, who served as YAF executive director is Chairman of the Board of Trustees of The Fund for American Studies while Turner is a Professor of Law at the University of Virginia.[38]

In North Carolina, the John Locke Foundation plays a similar role where Dr. Michael Sanera is Research Director and Local Government Analyst. Sanera, a former Arizona YAF state chairman, was the founding president of the Goldwater Institute. As Sanera recently concluded, "YAF reinforced my views, provided the intellectual grounding to support my views and was an avenue for training in political organizing."[39] Brandon Dutcher is Vice President for Policy at the Oklahoma Council of Public Affairs and was an active YAF member while a student at the University of Oklahoma in the late 1980s. Many more YAF alumni are involved in various state public policy educational centers.

Public Service

Developing public policy alternatives and advocating their adoption was one of the most valuable contributions of the conservative movement in the latter half of the 20th century. Those various components of the conservative movement described above took the lead in advancing policies that would put into practice the conservative philosophy they espoused. But it takes more than academic studies and public advocacy groups to influence the direction of American government and society. In the end, public policy is made and implemented by elected officials and their appointees in government at all levels. As the members of Young Americans for Freedom left college and graduate school and began their professional careers, a significant number became candidates for public office or accepted non-elective positions within government.

Perhaps the most prominent YAF alumnus to hold public office is Dan Quayle. First elected to Congress in 1976, he became a United States Senator in 1980, and then Vice President of the United States from 1989 to 1993. Quayle joined YAF as an undergraduate at DePauw University and continued while in law school at Indiana University. As he has noted, "In my college days I became a member of Young Americans for Freedom. YAF has truly made a difference."[40] On another occasion, in a 1996 fundraising letter for the organization, Quayle reminded his readers that "Years ago, as a college student, I was proud to be a member of Young Americans for Freedom. Back then we had a tough, uphill battle fighting the liberal agenda and radical teachings which were forced on college students

---

37. 2008 YAF Alumni Survey Responses: Christian N. Braunlich.
38. 2008 YAF Alumni Survey Responses: Randal C. Teague.
39. 2008 YAF Alumni Survey Responses: Michael Sanera.
40. *New Guard*, Fall 1992, p. 24.

nationwide."[41] In a letter to another YAF alumnus in 1997, Quayle concluded that, "No other conservative youth organization has played a more important role in the development of conservative leaders than Young Americans for Freedom. I should know; YAF was an important part of my college years."[42]

Two other former YAF members were also elected to the United States Senate and served in that body after Quayle. Robert C. Smith, a graduate of Lafayette College and a YAF member in New Hampshire, was elected to the United States House of Representatives in 1984 and then to the Senate in 1990, where he served slightly more than two terms. Jeff Sessions, a YAF member while at Huntington College, was elected in 1994 and continues to represent Alabama in the United States Senate.

Twenty-five YAF alumni have served in the United States House of Representatives, including Quayle and Smith. Current members include James Sensenbrenner, former Wisconsin YAF state chairman who was first elected in 1978 and is now in his 16th term representing the 5th district of Wisconsin. Both Dana Rohrabacher and John "Jimmy" Duncan, Jr. were elected to Congress in 1988 and continue to serve today. Rohrabacher is a former California YAF state chairman who was involved while a student at California State University at Long Beach. A former White House speechwriter, Rohrabacher represents the 46th congressional district of California. Duncan was an active YAF member in the outstanding University of Tennessee at Knoxville chapter in the late 1960s. Now as the congressman from Tennessee's second district, he represents Knoxville in the United States House of Representatives.

Donald Manzullo was a law student at Marquette University when he became an active member of the campus YAF chapter. After practicing law for several years he was elected to represent Illinois's sixteenth congressional district in 1992 and continues today from a district centered around Rockford, Illinois. Also first elected in 1992 was Edward Royce, a YAF member while at California State University at Fullerton. Royce served for ten years as a California State Senator prior to being elected to Congress. He currently represents the 40th congressional district located in Orange County. Peter King has represented the 3rd district of New York since the 1992 elections also. King was a YAF member at St. Francis College in the early 1960s. Jeb Hensarling, who represents the 5th congressional district of Texas was a key staff member for Senator Phil Gramm before first being elected to Congress in 2002. While a student at Texas A&M University, Hensarling was a member of a YAF chapter that also included future political operatives Mark Elam and John Weaver. The latest addition to the ranks of YAF alumni in the U.S. House is Ted Poe, also from Texas. Poe was a YAF member while at Abilene Christian University.

The list of former congressmen who were members of Young Americans for Freedom is long and impressive. Among them are 36-year Illinois Representative Philip M. Crane; former California YAF state chairman Barry M. Goldwater, Jr; Sharon Conference participant and YAF National Director James Kolbe, who represented the Tucson area for 22 years; former YAF National Chairman Robert E. Bauman; and former University of Pennsylvania YAF chapter chairman Phil English, who represented the northwest corner of Pennsylvania for 14 years. Fred

41. Fundraising letter from Dan Quayle for Young Americans for Freedom, 1996.
42. Letter from Dan Quayle to Gary Kreep, October 21, 1997.

Eckert, who was an Ambassador prior to and after his service in Congress, also served ten years as a New York State Senator before being elected to Congress. Looking back on his time in YAF, Eckert concluded that, "It reinforced my belief that conservatism had the right answers for the questions facing America. And it convinced me that if I wished to see our principles prevail I had to be willing to enter the political arena and slug it out there."[43] In 1970, while holding office as a Republican Mayor, he campaigned for the election of Jim Buckley, the Conservative party candidate for U.S. Senator. Six years later, while a State Senator, Eckert was a delegate to the 1976 Republican National Convention pledged to Reagan over Ford.

Still other YAF alumni elected to Congress are Christopher Cox, who later served as chairman of the Securities and Exchange Commission; Jack Fields, a YAF member and student government president at Baylor University who served sixteen years in Congress; John LeBoutellier, elected in 1980 and author of a critical attack on his alma mater, *Harvard Hates America*; Tom Tancredo, who served ten years from a Colorado district; Mark Souder of Indiana from 1995–2010; Bill Baker, who represented a northern California district in the 1990s; Donald E. Lukens, an Ohio Congressman first elected in 1966; Tom DeLay, a YAF member while a student at the University of Houston; John Doolittle, a sixteen year member from California; and Charles G. Douglas, III, active in YAF while a student at the University of New Hampshire. As time goes on, even more YAF members from the 1970s and beyond who have committed themselves to a career in public service are likely to join these YAF alumni as Members of Congress.

One likely source of new congressmen consists of those who have served in the various state legislatures. The list of all of the YAF alumni who have been elected to the various state legislatures would be too lengthy to include here and would inevitably be incomplete. Among those who held prominent positions in YAF, former National Director and Hawaii YAF state chairman Sam Slom has served in the Hawaii Senate since 1996 while former California YAF state chairman John Lewis was a member of the California Assembly from 1980–91 and then in the Senate from 1991 to 2000, when he was term-limited from office. Slom remembers his days in YAF as a time when he "gained experience from YAF meetings, forums, and contact with national and regional leaders and spokesmen." For him, YAF "reaffirmed and expanded conservative knowledge and leadership skills."[44] It was a similar experience for Lewis, who noted that, "My entire life was shaped and changed by my involvement in YAF. Joining the YAF in the early 70s shaped my philosophy, led to lasting friendships and was a primary influence on my elected success."[45]

National Director Eric Rohrbach was briefly a member of the Washington House of Representatives and Senate in the late 1970s. YAF's impact on Rohrbach was substantial. "YAF gave me a new way of looking at the world ... It taught me how to think strategically and how to plan things out. It provided me with a coherent political philosophy. I never had trouble finding out where I was on an

---

43. 2008 YAF Alumni Survey Responses: Fred J. Eckert. Eckert's article "More UN Peacekeeping in Katanga" appeared in the September 1962 issue of *New Guard*. He is listed as a contributing editor of the magazine in its March 1963 issue.

44. Interview with Sam Slom, Honolulu, HI, May 27, 2009. 2008 YAF Alumni Survey Responses: Sam Slom.

45. 2008 YAF Alumni Survey Responses: John Lewis.

issue when I was in the legislature because I had a firm philosophical foundation on which to make decisions."[46] Another YAF member, Mike Mattingly, served as a Washington state senator in the early 1970s and Tony Strickland, a graduate of Whittier College, is currently a California State Senator. Others who were state senators include Mark Rhoads and Robert Hatch of Illinois, Sherry Shealy Martschink of South Carolina, C.A. Porter Hopkins of Maryland, Ken Yager of Tennessee, Frank Hill of California and the late Dennis O'Grady, who had been Florida YAF chairman.

Interestingly enough, the state with perhaps the largest contingent of State Senators is New York. Currently serving in Albany are Owen Johnson, Vincent Leibell, and Michael Nozzolio. Johnson was first elected to the Senate in 1972 and was a featured speaker at the 1973 YAF National Convention in Washington. Vincent Leibell was a YAF member at St. John's University prior to serving twelve years in the State Assembly and since 1994 as a State Senator. Michael Nozzolio has been a Senator since 1992 and was a YAF member at Cornell University in the late 1960s. Among the previous legislators, H. Douglas Barclay served from 1965–1984 in the New York State Senate and was later appointed by President George W. Bush as Ambassador to El Salvador. Ray Meier was YAF chapter chairman at Syracuse University and served ten years as a New York State Senator. John Sabini served six years as a New York Senator before being named to become director of the New York State Racing & Wagering Board. While a student at New York University, he was chairman of the YAF chapter.[47] Fred Eckert, cited above as a Congressman, also served ten years as a New York State Senator from 1972–1982.[48]

State legislative lower houses have also included a number of YAF members, starting with Mike O'Dell whose election in 1962 from a district in Spokane, Washington was probably the first example of a YAF member becoming a state representative.[49] When Al Gammel of Worcester, Massachusetts joined YAF in 1961 he was already a state representative. The following year John H. Connolly and Raymond Kahoun were elected to the Illinois House of Representatives where Connolly served five sessions before being elected to the State Senate and Kahoun was in the House for four sessions. Currently there are at least seven YAF members in the lower chambers of state legislatures. William Batchelder was Ohio YAF state chairman in the early 1960s, served for 30 years as a State Representative, became a state judge, and then returned to the House in 2006. His wife Alice is a Federal judge on the 6th Circuit Court of Appeals. California Assemblyman Joel Anderson was a YAF member while at Cal Poly–Pomona and his chief of staff, Chip Englander, was a YAF activist at the University of Michigan. Also serving in the California Assembly is Van Thai Tran, a YAF member while a student at the University of California at Irvine, who was the highest-ranking Vietnamese-American when first elected in 2004.

Will Hartnett, a YAF member at Harvard and later active with the Young Conservatives of Texas, has been a Texas State Representative since 1990. Former National Director Eric Koch was first elected to the Indiana House of

---

46. Interview with Eric Rohrbach, Seattle, WA, March 25, 2009.
47. Sabini's political career began early when, as a 16-year-old member of Daniel Webster YAF, he was elected to the Elmhurst Hospital Advisory Board. *New Guard*, October 1973, p. 24.
48. In addition to Eckert, a number of the Members of Congress cited above previously served in their state legislatures but those affiliations are not repeated here.
49. *New Guard*, December–January 1963, p. 15.

Representatives in 2002, where he continues to serve as the ranking minority member of the Courts and Criminal Code Committee. Koch held a number of positions in YAF during the 1980s, as he recently recalled. "I was Chairman of the Georgetown University chapter, then DC chairman, then Indiana chairman when I returned to Indiana for law school. I went onto the National Board and served as National Vice Chairman.[50] Dr. John Kavanagh was the YAF chapter chairman at New York University in the late 1960s and early 1970s and was a police detective in the New York City area for 20 years. In describing his current situation, Kavanagh reported that he is "currently the head of the criminal justice program at Scottsdale (AZ) Community College and am starting my second term as an Arizona State Representative, where I currently chair the Appropriations Committee."[51] After 16 years as a County (Executive) Judge, C.B. Embry joined the Kentucky House of Representatives in 2003 and continues to serve in that body. In 1975, Embry had been named outstanding Young Republican in the nation.

But the one YAF alumnus who rose to the highest position in a state legislature was Ramona Barnes, who served 20 years in the Alaska House of Representatives, including two years as the first female speaker. Barnes joined YAF in Hawaii while her Air Force husband was stationed there and moved to Alaska in 1971, first being elected to the legislature in 1978. The longest serving woman legislator in Alaska, she died in 2003. Pat Nolan, a former YAF National Director, is another who rose to become Minority Leader of the California Assembly.[52]

Perhaps the most prominent of the YAF alumni who were state legislators is Alfred A. DelliBovi. He was an early recruit to YAF. "I became involved in YAF in 1961 while I was in high school in New York City. There were more than thirty YAF chapters in the metropolitan area."[53] DelliBovi was chairman of Astoria YAF and then attended Fordham University, from which he graduated in 1967. He served four terms in the New York State Assembly and was the Republican candidate against Geraldine Ferraro in her first campaign for Congress. Later he served as Administrator of the Urban Mass Transit Administration during the Reagan presidency and as Deputy Secretary for the Department of Housing and Urban Development during the administration of George H.W. Bush. Although his time as an active YAF leader was many years ago, the experience has left its mark on DelliBovi. Through all his years of government service, the Sharon Statement has remained a concise summary of his essential beliefs and a guidepost in his decision-making.[54] Today, Alfred DelliBovi is president of the Federal Home Loan Bank of New York, a position he has held since 1992.

Among the YAF National Directors who served in their state legislatures are John Buckley, who served in the Virginia House of Delegates in the 1980s; Roy Brun, for nine years a state representative from Shreveport; Roger Koopman, a former state representative from Bozeman, Montana; and Mitch Skandalakis, who served briefly in the Georgia General Assembly before defeating Martin Luther King, III to become Chairman of the Fulton County Commission. In addition, Frank DeFilippo was Colorado YAF state chairman while enrolled at the Colorado School of Mines after a brief stint with the New York City Police Department.

50. Eric Koch email to the author, August 29, 2008.
51. 2008 YAF Alumni Survey Responses: John Kavanagh.
52. Interview with Patrick Nolan, Newport Beach, CA, October 11, 2008.
53. 2008 YAF Alumni Survey Responses: Alfred A. DelliBovi.
54. *Ibid.*

From 1978–84, he served in the Colorado House of Representatives and most recently was appointed by Governor Bill Owens as a member of the Board of Trustees of his alma mater. As an aside, Owens's wife Frances was a YAF member while working in the DC area. Gary Giordano is another New Yorker who moved west and became a state representative. For Giordano, it was Arizona where he served two terms in the legislature.[55] Brad Cates was New Mexico YAF chairman in the late 1960s and later served in the New Mexico House before accepting a position in the Reagan Administration.

Dick Foley was an active leader in Connecticut YAF from 1965 to 1971, attending the YAF Leadership Conference at Franklin & Marshall College in 1966, the 1967 YAF National Convention and the YAF 10 celebration in Sharon, Connecticut. Foley served for ten years as a State Representative and from 1989–93 was GOP State Chairman.[56] Former YAF members who have served in the California Assembly include Dennis Brown, Bill Hoge, Eric Seastrand, and Don Sebastiani. Brown was Los Angeles County YAF chairman and an Assemblyman from the Long Beach area from 1978–1990.[57] Hoge was a legislator from South Pasadena in the 1990s while Sebastiani served from 1980–86. Eric Seastrand served in the Assembly from 1982 until his death in 1990. His wife, Andrea, completed his state legislative term and then was elected to Congress where she served one term.[58] Edmund E. "Sonny" Jones was elected to the Texas House of Representatives in 1967 and was part of the "Dirty Thirty" reformers who eventually forced the resignation of Speaker Gus Mutscher.[59] Bob Ware was chairman of the University of Texas YAF chapter and was elected in 1978 from a district in Fort Worth. Both are now deceased.[60]

Other YAF alumni who have served in state legislatures include Paul Dietrich in Missouri; Bob Eberle, a five-year member of the Washington House of Representatives; the late George Mason Green who represented an Arlington district in the Virginia House of Delegates; and Manuel Prieguez, a YAF activist in the early 1990s at Florida International University who was term-limited in 2004 after serving six years in the Florida House of Representatives.

When Republicans controlled the White House during the past forty years, a number of YAF alumni were appointed to important positions. Eight individuals who had been active in YAF were selected by the President and confirmed by the Senate to lifetime appointments on the United States Circuit Court of Appeals, one step below the Supreme Court of the United States. Danny Boggs was active in YAF while a student at Harvard and was the conservative candidate for president of the National Student Association in 1966. He serves on the 6th Circuit, having been appointed by President Reagan in 1986.[61] Also joining the Circuit Court in 1986 were Diarmuid O'Scannlain, one of the original members of the YAF National Board, and one who has become known as a leading conservative

55. 2008 YAF Alumni Survey Responses: Gary Giordano.
56. Dick Foley email to the author, December 15, 2008.
57. Ralph Frammolino, "Legislator Is Working Religiously on New Life," *Los Angeles Times*, April 1, 1990.
58. Daniel M. Weinstraub, "Assemblyman Eric Seastrand; Salinas Republican Was 52," *Los Angeles Times*, June 21, 1990.
59. Brian Sweeny, "Dirty Thirty," *Texas Monthly*, September 2001; John Knaggs: *Two Party Texas* (Austin: Eakin Press, 1986), pp. 116–117.
60. Knaggs: *Two Party Texas*, p. 231.
61. 2008 YAF Alumni Survey Responses: Danny J. Boggs. Seymour Martin Lipset and Philip G. Altbach: *Students in Revolt* (Boston: Beacon Press, 1969), p. 207.

on the 9th Circuit Court, and Daniel Manion, YAF National Vice Chairman, who joined the 7th Circuit in 1986 after much opposition from liberal Democratic Senators.[62] O'Scannlain is known for his dissenting opinions on the most liberal circuit court but also has written some important prevailing opinions. As he said in upholding California's Proposition 209 prohibiting affirmative action, "A system which permits one judge to block with the stroke of a pen what 4,736,180 state residents voted to enact as law tests the integrity of our constitutional democracy."[63] Manion took senior status in 2007.

The following year, Reagan nominated and the Senate confirmed Jerry Smith to the 5th Circuit and David B. Sentelle to the Federal Circuit Court. Smith was an active YAF leader while at Yale, a leader in the 1976 and 1980 Reagan campaigns, and chairman of the Harris County (Houston) Republican party. Sentelle had been chairman of the University of North Carolina YAF chapter and later a Republican county chairman in North Carolina.[64] It was George H.W. Bush who selected the three remaining former YAF members, Randall Ray Rader, Paul V. Niemeyer, and Alice Batchelder. The first two were named in 1990 with Rader joining the Federal Circuit Court in DC and Niemeyer becoming a judge on the 4th Circuit Court of Appeals. Rader had been active in YAF while at Brigham Young University while Niemeyer took part in the Sharon Conference and was an early Ohio YAF state chairman as a student at Kenyon College. Batchelder joined YAF while a student at Ohio Wesleyan University and her husband was Ohio YAF state chairman. Batchelder had previously been named a District Judge by President Reagan.

One final YAF alumnus, nominated by President George W. Bush, never made it through consideration by the Senate. Peter Keisler was a YAF member and chairman of the Party of the Right while a student at Yale. He was Acting Attorney General between the terms of Alberto Gonzales and Michael Mukasey. Keisler had been named by Bush to serve on the Court of Appeals for the District of Columbia Circuit but his nomination died after the Democratic majority took control of the United States Senate in 2007.[65]

Too many other YAF alumni have held judicial positions at the state and Federal levels to include them all here. Four former National Directors should be mentioned however. Richard Plechner was a member of the YAF National Board in the mid-1960s and after private practice for many years was Judge of the Superior Court for the State of New Jersey from 1988 to 2002.[66] Louisa Porter served on the National Board in the early 1970s and has been a United States Magistrate Judge for the Southern District of California since 1991.[67] Roy Brun, another former National Director mentioned above, is currently a State Judge in Louisiana. Richard Abell, a Director in the early 1980s, is a Special Master at the U.S. Court of Federal Claims in Washington.[68]

---

62. Philip Shenon, "Senate, Ending Judicial Fight, Gives Manion Final Approval," *New York Times*, July 24, 1986.

63. Tim Golden, "Federal Appeals Court Upholds California's Ban on Preferences," *New York Times*, April 9, 1997.

64. Peter Applebome, "Judge in Whitewater Dispute Rewards Faith of His Patron," *New York Times*, August 17, 1994.

65. Charles Savage, "Appeals Courts Pushed to Right by Bush Choices," *New York Times*, October 28, 2008.

66. 2008 YAF Alumni Survey Responses: Richard F. Plechner.

67. 2008 YAF Alumni Survey Responses: Louisa S. Porter.

68. Interview with Richard Abell, Washington, DC, October 5, 2008.

Among others holding important judicial positions, Loren Smith was Senior Judge of the U.S. Court of Federal Claims from 1985 to 2000 when he took senior status. Smith was an active YAF leader at Northwestern University in the late 1960s and early 1970s and is best remembered for his stirring nomination of Mayor Richard Daley at the 1971 YAF mock presidential nominating convention.[69] One of the more recent appointments to the Federal judiciary, S. James Otero was active in YAF while a student at California State University—Los Angeles and was appointed as a Federal District Judge by President George W. Bush in 2003. Among those serving in state court positions, Stephen Markman was chairman of the YAF chapter at Duke University in the late 1960s and now serves on the Michigan Supreme Court. First appointed by Governor John Engler, Markman was elected in 2006.

Campaign Professionals

Conservatives can only be elected to office with the assistance and advice of trained political professionals. Serving as campaign managers, fundraising consultants, and political party officials, these individuals help to operate the machinery of democracy, ensuring that voters have meaningful choices when they enter the polling place. There are simply too many former YAF members who have had careers as campaign professionals to mention them all here. Among them are Frank Donatelli, former YAF executive director, who was a key regional campaign director for the 1980 Reagan campaign, went on to serve as Special Assistant to the President for Political Affairs, was deputy director of the Republican National Committee, and is now chairman of GOPAC, a political action committee dedicated to helping elect Republican candidates to state and local offices.[70]

Since his initial involvement in the Jesse Helms senate campaign of 1972, Charles Black has been a key figure in every Republican presidential campaign to the present time. A former YAF National Director and National YAF Chapter Director, Black was a key advisor to Senator John McCain, himself a frequent speaker at YAF gatherings after his return from imprisonment in Vietnam.[71] George Gorton was a key youth coordinator for the 1970 Senate campaign of James L. Buckley and now heads a campaign consulting business in California while serving as a key political aide to Governor Arnold Schwarzenegger.[72] Former *New Guard* editor Arnie Steinberg is a political polling expert and political consultant in California while Boyd Marcus heads up Marcus-Allen political consultants in Virginia. Marcus was chief of staff to Governor Jim Gilmore from 1998 to 2002.

Other key Republican campaign operatives include former National Director and Tennessee YAF state chairman William Lacy, campaign manager for Fred Thompson in 2008 and director of the Robert J. Dole Institute of Politics, and two graduates of Texas A&M University, John Weaver and Mark Elam. Weaver was an advisor to both Senators Phil Gramm and John McCain in their presidential

---

69. For a discussion of Smith's nominating speech, see chapter 11 above.
70. 2008 YAF Alumni Survey Responses: Frank Donatelli.
71. Kate Zernike, "Steady Hand for the G.O.P. Guides McCain on a New Path," *New York Times*, April 13, 2008.
72. Todd S. Purdum, "A New Player Enters the Campaign Spending Fray," *New York Times*, April 2, 2000.

campaigns and until recently worked with Utah Governor Jon Huntsman prior to his nomination to be Ambassador to the People's Republic of China. Elam was one of the founders of Young Conservatives of Texas and is president of Campaign Resources, Inc.

One of the longest serving members of the Republican National Committee is Morton Blackwell, also president of the Leadership Institute. Blackwell, a former Louisiana YAF member who was the youngest delegate for Barry Goldwater at the 1964 national convention, was first elected as Virginia's Republican National Committeeman in 1988 and continues to serve in that capacity. Also on the committee are Shawn Steel and James Bopp. For Steel, "YAF provided a melding together of ISI and CRs, since you had both philosophical underpinnings and direct political action. Moreover, principles were most important. No one wanted to be viewed as a squish."[73] Bopp is a former Indiana University YAF chairman who now serves as Indiana's Republican National Committeeman and was the original attorney in the *Citizens United* effort to strike down portions of the McCain-Feingold law. Bopp also is general counsel for both Focus on the Family and the National Right to Life Committee and was a key advisor to the 2008 presidential effort of former Governor Mitt Romney.[74] Among those who have previously served on the RNC is Haywood Hillyer, III, one-time Louisiana Committeeman and participant in YAF's founding meeting at Sharon.

A number of YAF alumni have been state chairmen for the Republican Party including John Cozad and Shannon Cave in Missouri. Cave was YAF chairman at the University of Missouri, later became executive director and then Chairman of the Missouri Republican Party, and is now with the Missouri Department of Conservation. For Cave, his involvement was "an important formative experience. YAF was certainly a better introduction to adulthood than MTV and the media culture today."[75] Gordon Durnil was a YAF community chapter chairman in Indianapolis during the early 1960s and later became Republican state chairman. He is the author of *The Making of a Conservative Environmentalist*, which was published by Indiana University Press in 1995.[76] Dick Foley, as mentioned previously, was both a legislator and the Connecticut GOP chairman from 1989–93. Steve Minarik was a YAF activist at the University of Rochester, served 16 years as Monroe County GOP chairman and then two years from 2004–2006 as New York State Republican Chairman. At the age of 49, Minarik died of a heart attack in 2009.[77] Doug Boyd and Jon Fleischman are both vice chairmen of the California GOP.[78] Finally, former National Director Steve Munisteri won election as Texas GOP Chairman in 2010.

Not everyone involved in party politics chose to do so in the Republican party. Some such as former New York University YAF chairman John Sabini, became active in the Democratic party while others were involved in third party efforts.[79]

---

73. 2008 YAF Alumni Survey Responses: Shawn Steel.

74. James Bopp, "The Best Choice Is Also a Good Choice," *National Review*, February 21, 2007. Bopp has been a leading expert on 1st Amendment free speech as it relates to elections and campaign financing. See: David D. Kirkpatrick, "A Quest to End Spending Rules for Campaigns," *New York Times*, January 24, 2010.

75. 2008 YAF Alumni Survey Responses: Shannon D. Cave.

76. Keith Schneider, "The Green Republican," *New York Times*, August 27, 1995.

77. Elizabeth Benjamin, "RIP: Steve Minarik," *New York Daily News*, April 12, 2009.

78. Interview with Jon Fleischman, Newport Beach, CA, October 11, 2008.

79. Nicholas Confessore, "Resolution in OTB Dispute Fades Away," *New York Times*, June 14, 2008.

David F. Nolan was the YAF chapter chairman at the Massachusetts Institute of Technology and later youth coordinator for the proposed Liberty Amendment to abolish the Federal income tax. In 1971, he was a co-founder of the Libertarian Party. Meanwhile, YAF had played an important role in the formation of the New York Conservative Party, providing it with its initial ballot place prior to the 1962 election.[80] The party's current leadership includes Chairman Michael Long, a YAF activist in Kings County (Brooklyn) during the early 1960s; Secretary Howard Lim, Jr., YAF chairman at Columbia University in the early 1970s and later executive assistant to Senator Al D'Amato; and from the 1980s, former National Director Gerard Kassar of Pace University, now a Vice Chairman of the party.[81]

Still others were involved in issues campaigns on the ballot in states allowing initiative and referendum. Randy Goodwin, former California YAF chairman and National Director, was executive director of the "Yes on 13" campaign that enshrined proposition 13 in California government. Goodwin served as executive director of the American Tax Reduction Movement headed by Howard Jarvis. He is now a political consultant in the Golden State. Jim Lacy is among a number of YAF alumni involved in promoting and distributing sample ballots to voters that advocate support for both candidates and issues.

Communications and the Media

Conservatives have long bemoaned the "liberal media" and the perceived left-wing bias of Hollywood. Fortunately, a number of younger conservatives decided to make a career in communications running the gamut from newspaper and magazines, to radio-television and movies, to books and public relations. Once again, it is impossible to be inclusive when discussing former YAFers who embarked on careers in the communications industry but perhaps a few examples can show the importance that this one organization made on trying to bring balance and objectivity to the mass media.

It is not surprising that many YAF alumni who pursued a career in journalism ended up in the Nation's Capital. At the *Washington Times*, Donald Lambro was chief political correspondent. Lambro was a YAF chapter chairman at Boston University and served briefly as editor of *New Guard*. He is the author of five books and a syndicated columnist.[82] Quin Hillyer is associate editor at the paper and senior editor of *The American Spectator*. Looking back on his experience in YAF, Hillyer concluded that, "it reinforced my existing belief that standing up for conservative principles, and the right to express them in public, is a worthwhile and rewarding undertaking. In addition to helping me become exposed to a broader conservative network, YAF helped me learn what does and doesn't work in public advocacy."[83] For two decades, George Archibald was national and investigative reporter for the *Washington Times*. A graduate of Old Dominion University, Archibald was Arizona YAF state chairman in the late 1960s and is author of a recently published memoir.[84]

---

80. For a discussion of YAF's role in securing a ballot place for the new party, see chapter 3.
81. Telephone interview with Gerard Kassar, July 7, 2009.
82. 2008 YAF Alumni Survey Responses: Donald J. Lambro.
83. 2008 YAF Alumni Survey Responses: Quin Hillyer.
84. George Archibald: *Journalism Is War* (LeCompton, KS: High Way Publishers, 2009).

Across town, Phil McCombs, a YAF member at Yale in the mid-1960s, was a long-time reporter for the *Washington Post*. Newly competitive to these two existing papers, the *Washington Examiner* has as its editorial page editor Mark Tapscott, a YAF member at Oklahoma State University, and as its local opinion editor Barbara Fiala Hollingsworth. As she recently noted, "my time in YAF was foundational. All I learned about economics, and most of what I learned about history, was self-taught from various conservative writings I devoured in the little time I had between commuting, classes, and work."[85] Barb Fiala was YAF chairman at the University of Illinois–Chicago Campus during the time of New Left disruptions in the late 1960s and early 1970s.

Across the country, other YAF alumni are involved in the newspaper business at all levels. Alan Bock, vice chairman of the YAF chapter at UCLA, has been editorial writer at the *Orange County Register* since 1980. Looking back on his college years, it was YAF that "made it more fun and more purposeful."[86] Meanwhile, Jeff Swiatek, a YAF leader at Lehigh University, is a reporter for the *Indianapolis Star* and recalls YAF as "a breath of fresh air intellectually."[87] John Fund, who was a YAF member after high school and while a student at California State University–Sacramento, is a columnist for the *Wall Street Journal* while Jerry Norton, a former YAF National Director and National YAF Chapter Director, is an overseas bureau chief for a major international news service.[88] For the last 27 years, Tom Lamont has been editor of the newsletter division of *Institutional Investor News*. While at the University of Pennsylvania, Lamont was YAF chairman and continued his activism when he moved to graduate school at Boston University. Active in YAF from 1964 to 1975, his involvement "taught me to respect others' opinions and not to assume everyone thought like me (clearly most didn't!). This is useful to practice in all walks of life, but especially politics where arrogance can be off-putting. YAF didn't affect my career choice but has helped me develop as a leader."[89]

Among other working journalists, Cort Kirkwood, a former editor of *New Guard*, is editor of the *Harrisonburg* (VA) *Daily News-Record* and author of a profile of ten courageous Americans.[90] Buddy Baker, a Virginia YAF member in the 1970s, was editor of the *Danville Register Bee* while John A. Barnes, YAF member at New York University, writes for the *New York Post* and is author of the book, *John F. Kennedy on Leadership*.[91] Mike Bonafield, Tennessee YAF state chairman in the early 1970s, recently retired after a career with the *Minneapolis Star-Tribune* while Ross MacKenzie retired from the *Richmond Times-Dispatch* after 37 years as editorial page editor. Bonafield now writes for *MinnPost.com* while MacKenzie's columns are syndicated by Tribune Media Services. Bill Williams, former chairman of the District of Columbia YAF, was a long-time reporter for the *Hartford Courant* while Richard J. Bocklet, whose reports from foreign lands provided perspective in *New Guard* over many years, continues as a freelance reporter.[92] James Bencivenga was education editor and book review editor for the *Christian Science Monitor* after being active in Boston YAF while Patrick

85. 2008 YAF Alumni Survey Responses: Barbara Hollingsworth.
86. 2008 YAF Alumni Survey Responses: Alan W. Bock.
87. 2008 YAF Alumni Survey Responses: Jeff Swiatek.
88. John Fund email to the author, June 25, 2009. 2008 YAF Alumni Survey Responses: Jerry Norton.
89. 2008 YAF Alumni Survey Responses: Tom Lamont.
90. R. Cort Kirkwood: *Real Men: Ten Courageous Americans to Know and Admire* (Nashville: Cumberland House Publishers, 2006).
91. John A. Barnes: *John F. Kennedy on Leadership* (New York: AMACON, 2005).
92. 2008 YAF Alumni Survey Responses: Richard J. Bocklet.

McGuigan, chapter chairman at Oklahoma State University, is managing editor of the *City Sentinel* in Oklahoma City, having previously worked as editorial page editor at the *Daily Oklahoman*.

Several syndicated columnists have YAF backgrounds, including Deroy Murdock, Jeff Jacoby, Lowell Ponte, and Allan Brownfeld. Murdock was DC YAF state chairman and National Director and now the Scripps Howard News Service distributes his column. As he recalled his involvement, "YAF provided me and my colleagues with a deeper understanding of conservative, libertarian, and free-market principles and the methods needed to communicate those ideas to others in hopes of promoting a freer and more prosperous USA and Earth."[93] Jacoby writes for the *Boston Globe* and has his column syndicated to several papers. He was vice chairman of the YAF chapter while an undergraduate at George Washington University in the late 1970s. Ponte was a YAF member in the 1960s who went on to host a talk radio show in Los Angeles for 17 years, work for 15 years as a reporter for *Reader's Digest* and is now a contributing editor for *NewsMax*. The McNaught Syndicate and the Hoiles Freedom Newspaper chain have syndicated his column. Allan Brownfeld maintained recently that, "I have many fond memories of the time I was involved with YAF . . . All of us at that time were committed to certain principles—advancing the idea of a free society, with limited government and national strength."[94] Brownfeld is a former editor of *New Guard* and the Fitzgerald Griffin Foundation syndicates his column, "The Conservative Curmudgeon," to a number of newspapers. For nearly twenty years, Donald Feder was a regular columnist for the *Boston Herald* and had his articles syndicated to a number of papers.[95]

From the other side of the newspaper business, former Tufts University YAF member Nackey Elizabeth Scagliotti is a director of the E.W. Scripps Company and former Board Chairman of the Union Leader Corporation in New Hampshire. Tom Phillips, who was Dartmouth YAF chairman and a National Director, is president of Eagle Publishing, which among other endeavors produces the conservative weekly *Human Events*. Phillips recalled his time in YAF as a "great experience."[96] One-time Arkansas YAF chairman Alan Leveritt is publisher of *Arkansas Times* while Wick Allison, a YAF member in Texas, is now publisher of *D Magazine* after serving briefly as publisher of *National Review*.

Several former YAFers are now freelance writers, including former National Director Leslie Carbone, one-time *New Guard* editor Richard LaMountain, and Haven Bradford Gow. Carbone was executive director of Accuracy in Academia in the late 1980s at a time when ". . . it was great to have reliably conservative friends. My YAF friends were helpful when I was running Accuracy in Academia."[97] For LaMountain, his involvement in YAF gave him opportunities he would not have otherwise had. "My time at *New Guard* helped me hone my research, writing and editing skills, which serve me well today in my avocation as a freelance public-policy writer."[98] Now a freelance writer, Gow was previously associate editor of *Police Times* and his articles have appeared in a wide variety of publications.[99]

93. 2008 YAF Alumni Survey Responses: Deroy Murdock.
94. 2008 YAF Alumni Survey Responses: Allan C. Brownfeld.
95. 2008 YAF Alumni Survey Responses: Donald Feder.
96. 2008 YAF Alumni Survey Responses: Thomas Phillips.
97. 2008 YAF Alumni Survey Responses: Leslie Carbone.
98. 2008 YAF Alumni Survey Responses: Richard F. LaMountain.
99. 2008 YAF Alumni Survey Responses: Haven Bradford Gow.

YAF alumni are involved in numerous conservative magazines, starting with *Human Events*, where Tom Winter is editor in chief, Allan Ryskind is editor-at-large, John Gizzi is political editor and M. Stanton Evans is a contributing editor. Ryskind one of the original contributors to *New Guard* in the early 1960s, Gizzi was a YAF member while a student at Fairfield University and in Texas, and Evans was author of the Sharon Statement. At *National Review*, Linda Bridges was a YAF member at the University of Southern California and is now editor-at-large for the magazine and co-author of *Strictly Right*. Kate O'Beirne is Washington editor of *National Review* and was active in YAF in New York City in the early 1970s. Over at *The American Spectator*, founder and editor-in-chief R. Emmett Tyrrell, Jr. was a YAF activist while a student at Indiana University and publisher Alfred S. Regnery is a former National Director and College Director. For Regnery, author of *Upstream*, a concise history of American conservatism in the late 20th century, his time in YAF was "My introduction to politics. Goldwater campaign, early Reagan, met both Goldwater and Reagan and many other political people . . . A very exhilarating time for me."[100] Publisher of *The Weekly Standard* is Terry Eastland, a YAF member at Vanderbilt. As mentioned previously, Robert Poole was publisher of *Reason* magazine from 1978 to 2001.[101]

The range of interests for YAF alumni who went into magazine journalism is much wider than politics. Louis Rossetto was an active YAF member at Columbia University and founded *WIRED* magazine, which he subsequently sold to Conde Nast. A fellow Columbia YAF member from the late 1960s is Andrew Attaway, senior editor for *Guideposts*, a magazine and publishing company founded by Dr. Norman Vincent Peale and his wife Ruth in 1945. Bill Schulz, one of the YAF founders at Sharon and then a National Director, spent a career as editor at *Reader's Digest*. Dana Huntley, New Hampshire YAF state chairman in the late 1960s, is editor of *British Heritage* magazine.[102] Finally, one should mention Terry Catchpole, chapter chairman at the University of Miami who went on to a varied career as a contributing editor at *National Lampoon* and then at *Playboy* before becoming editor-in-chief at *Computerworld*. He remembered his experience in YAF as a "very exciting time, given the context of the Goldwater movement. A lot of very smart, talented, principled, and motivated people involved in YAF of the day."[103] For the last twenty years he has headed The Catchpole Company, which designs corporate visibility strategies and executive branding and messaging for companies.

Jeff Hollingsworth, Maine YAF state chairman, is among those involved in other aspects of publishing. He is Vice President of Eagle Publishing. For Hollingsworth, involvement in YAF "was the primary gateway to my subsequent career."[104] Prominent among book publishers is Jameson Campaigne, Jr., whose Jameson Books has been the imprint for a number of works by conservative authors.[105] Ted Parkhurst and a partner founded August House Publishers in Little

100. 2008 YAF Alumni Survey Responses: Alfred S. Regnery.
101. 2008 YAF Alumni Survey Responses: Robert W. Poole, Jr.
102. 2008 YAF Alumni Survey Responses: Dana L. Huntley.
103. 2008 YAF Alumni Survey Responses: Terry Catchpole.
104. 2008 YAF Alumni Survey Responses: Jeff Hollingsworth.
105. Among the valuable resources on the conservative movement produced by Jameson Books are W. Glenn Campbell: *The Competition of Ideas* (2000) which traces the formation of the Hoover Institution, and Lee Edwards: *The Power of Ideas*, published in 1997 to commemorate the 25th anniversary of the Heritage Foundation.

Rock in 1978 and by the late 1980s it was a national institution specializing in folklore, poetry and Arkansas history. By 2005 when it was sold to Marsh Cove Productions, August House had published more than 600 titles.[106] Parkhurst was a National Director in the late 1960s and early 1970s. Alan Gottlieb, another former National Director, is president of Merril Press, located in Bellevue, Washington.

As would be expected, several YAF alumni are the authors of books dealing with politics and public policy. Lee Edwards's work in terms of chronicling the conservative movement has been prolific and several of his books have been cited throughout this work. From biographies of key conservative personalities to institutional histories of important organizations to overviews of the development of the conservative movement, Edwards has lived up to his position as Distinguished Fellow in Conservative Thought at the Heritage Foundation and has provided an invaluable compendium of information on late 20th century conservatism in America. Another YAF founder who has written extensively is M. Stanton Evans, beginning with his first book on the growth of conservatism among young people, *Revolt on the Campus,* to his most recent detailed profile of Senator Joseph McCarthy, *Blacklisted by History.* David Franke, a YAF founder and early National Director, is the author of many books on political issues, including *America's Right Turn,* written with Richard A. Viguerie.

Peter Schweizer is author of several works, including *Victory: The Reagan Administration's Secret Strategy That Hastened the Collapse of the Soviet Union.* Looking back on his days in YAF, Schweizer concluded that, "being in YAF made me more conservative and it also made me more confident in my views."[107] Terry Eastland's *Ending Affirmative Action: The Case for Colorblind Justice* was published in 1996 and his *Freedom of Expression in the Supreme Court* appeared in 2002.[108] John Lott, a YAF activist at UCLA and Vanderbilt, is another YAF alumnus who has produced several books, including *Straight Shooting—Firearms, Economics and Public Policy* and *Freedomnomics: Why the Free Market Works and Other Half-Baked Theories Don't.*[109] Daniel Flynn, a YAF activist at the University of Massachusetts, is author of his most recent work, *A Conservative History of the American Left.*[110]

David Pietrusza, YAF chairman at SUNY–Albany in the early 1970s, has written a number of books including *1920: The Year of the Six Presidents,* which *Kirkus Reviews* selected as one of their Best Books of 2007, and his more recent *1960—LBJ vs. JFK vs. Nixon: The Epic Campaign That Forged Three Presidencies.*[111] Jerome Tuccille was a YAF member in the 1960s and the author of more than 20 books covering a wide range of topics. Two of his works, *It Usually Begins with Ayn Rand* and *Radical Libertarianism,* are highly critical of Young Americans for Freedom but he has also written biographies on Rupert Murdoch, Donald Trump, the Hunt family of Texas, and Alan Greenspan. Another writer whose political

---

106. http://www.encyclopediaofarkansas.net/encyclopedia/entry-detail.aspx?entryID=3017.

107. 2008 YAF Alumni Survey Responses: Peter Schweizer.

108. *Ending Affirmative Action* (New York: Basic Books, 1996). *Freedom of Expression in the Supreme Court* (Lanham, MD: Rowman & Littlefield Publishers, 2002).

109. *Straight Shooting* (Bellevue, WA: Merril Press, 2006). *Freedomnomics* (Washington: Regnery Publishing, 2007).

110. 2008 YAF Alumni Survey Responses: Daniel J. Flynn. *A Conservative History of the American Left* (New York: Crown Forum, 2008).

111. David Pietrusza: *1920* (New York: Carroll & Graf, 2006); *1960* (New York: Union Square Press, 2008).

outlook changed was Randy Shilts, who became a reporter for the *San Francisco Chronicle*. Shilts, who formed a YAF chapter while in high school in Aurora, Illinois, was the author of *The Mayor of Castro Street: The Life and Times of Harvey Milk* as well as *And the Band Played On: Politics, People and the AIDS Epidemic*.

Many other authors have concentrated on non-political topics. Included in this group are several whose emphasis has been on science fiction. In addition to novelist Ayn Rand, one of the major influences on young libertarians in YAF was Robert Heinlein and his many science fiction novels. Thus, it is no surprise that this genre became popular with those YAF alumni whose career involved writing. Perhaps best known is Brad Linaweaver, whose works include *Moon of Ice* and *The Land Beyond Summer*.[112] Another prolific writer of science fiction and fantasy is Nicholas Yermakov, a YAF member while at American University. After publishing a few books in the early 1980s, he began writing under the name "Simon Hawke" and later changed his legal name to Hawke. He has also written adventure novels under the pen name "J.D. Masters."[113] Hal Schuster joined YAF while a high school student in Montgomery County, Maryland in the early 1970s. Building on his love of science fiction and comic books, he progressed from owning comic book stores in the Washington area, to national distribution and eventually to writing. Schuster became an expert on pop culture and author of numerous unauthorized books on *Star Trek*, the *X-Files* and even works on Elvis Presley and the Beatles. Schuster passed away in 2000 but his work remains available in some two million copies of his books that were sold in the 20th century.[114]

Jared Lobdell was active in YAF while a student at Yale, then went on to receive a PhD in literature and has become a well-known expert on J.R.R. Tolkien, authoring several books on his writings as well as an important work on alcoholism.[115] Rich Marschall was another writer who was active in YAF while a student at American University, later becoming DC YAF state chairman. Marschall was a frequent cartoonist for *New Guard* and his love for drawing is reflected in collector's edition books on cartoons, comics, and illustrations.[116]

Another YAF alumnus who turned his pastimes into a career is Bill Nowlin, a YAF member at Tufts University. When not studying, folk music and baseball became Nowlin's passions. While working on his PhD, Nowlin and two associates formed Rounder Records in 1970, an entity that eventually became one of the largest independently owned record labels with over three thousand releases. In 2004, Rounder Books was formed and since then has released a library of books written by Nowlin dealing with another passion, the Boston Red Sox. Although he was a professor of political science at the University of Lowell for twelve years, his time now is devoted to music and publishing.[117]

Richard S. Wheeler, a graduate of the University of Wisconsin and an early

---

112. *Moon of Ice* (New York: Arbor House, 1988); *The Land Beyond Summer* (Pahrump, NV: Pulpless.com, 1999).

113. Among his recent works are *The Merchant of Vengeance* (New York: A Forge Book, 2003) and *Much Ado About Murder* (New York: A Forge Book, 2002).

114. Among his works were *The Trekkers Guide to Deep Space Nine* (Roseville, CA: Prima Lifestyles, 1997) and *The Unauthorized Guide to the X-Files* (Roseville, CA: Prima Lifestyles, 1997).

115. *The Rise of Tolkienian Fantasy* (Chicago: Open Court, 2005); *The Scientifiction Novels of C.S. Lewis* (Jefferson, NC: McFarland & Company, 2004); *This Strange Illness: Alcoholism and Bill W* (Piscataway, NJ: Aldine Transaction, 2004).

116. Perhaps Marschall's best-known work is *America's Great Comic Strip Artists* (New York: Stewart, Tabori & Chang, 1997).

117. http://www.rounderbooks.com/authors/archives/2005/02/bill_nowlin.html. Nowlin has written

contributor to *New Guard*, is the author of more than fifty novels dealing with the American West. Prior to devoting his time to novels, Wheeler was an editorial writer for the *Phoenix Gazette* and the *Oakland Tribune*.[118] Kathy Kolbe, who graduated from Northwestern and served on the YAF Board in the early 1960s as Kay Wonderlic, is a best-selling author and leading authority on human instincts. Her research that identified a distinct cluster of human behaviors has led to breakthroughs in the understanding and use of innate abilities. The results of her studies are presented in three books beginning with *The Conative Connection*, published in 1989.[119] Kolbe also serves as an adjunct professor of education at Arizona State University.

For many years, radio was a major vehicle for most Americans to receive their daily news. One of those familiar voices who brought news and commentary from a conservative perspective was Fulton Lewis, Jr. With his death in 1966, his son took over the nightly fifteen-minute newscast over some 500 Mutual Broadcasting Network stations, continuing until 1979. Fulton Lewis, III began his own radio career after five years of active involvement in Young Americans for Freedom, serving on the National Board and as National Field Director. As he recently recalled, "I lectured and debated on over 750 college campuses." YAF provided "outstanding public speaking and debating experience. Great training in political organization."[120] Lewis originally became prominent in conservative circles as the producer and narrator of *Operation Abolition*, the film which described the 1960 riots in San Francisco against the House Un-American Activities Committee.

If there is one area of the communications world where conservatives have exerted a strong presence, however, it is with talk radio. Rush Limbaugh and Sean Hannity have become household names with millions of listeners each day to their radio programs. But there are many more conservative talk radio hosts across the country, some also syndicated like Limbaugh and Hannity while others have a local listener focus. It is difficult to describe Mark Levin solely as a radio personality; in fact, he has already been mentioned as the head of the Landmark Legal Foundation in the discussion of conservative organizations. Levin, a graduate of Temple University where he was a YAF member, is the host of a daily talk show on WABC in New York City that is syndicated to other stations by the Citadel Media Networks. He is also the author of two bestselling books. Another nationally syndicated radio host is Michael Smerconish, a Lehigh graduate and former YAF chairman whose show originates in Philadelphia and is syndicated by Dial-Global. Smerconish also writes different weekly columns for both the *Philadelphia Daily News* and the *Philadelphia Inquirer*.

Hosting the popular "Night Side" talk show on WBZ radio in Boston is Dan Rea, former Massachusetts YAF chairman and National Vice Chairman from 1973–1975. As Rea noted, "I have wonderful memories of YAF and many of my life long friends were people I met through YAF."[121] Prior to taking over the popular radio program, Rea had been an on-air television reporter in Boston for 31 years. One of Rea's predecessors as host of the "Night Side" program was the late David

---

or edited more than twelve books dealing with the Boston Red Sox. Rounder Records artists include Alison Krauss, Mary Chapin Carpenter, and Irma Thomas.

118. http://www.richardswheeler.com.
119. Kolbe's other books are *Pure Instinct* (New York: Random House, 1993) and *Powered by Instinct: 5 Rules for Trusting Your Guts* (Phoenix: Monumentus Press, 2003).
120. 2008 YAF Alumni Survey Responses: Fulton Lewis.
121. 2008 YAF Alumni Survey Responses: Dan Rea.

Brudnoy, another former YAF member. At the opposite end of the lower 48, Kirby Wilbur is the host of Kirby & Company, a morning drive-time talk radio program in Seattle. Wilbur joined YAF in high school where he was chairman of his chapter and also held a leadership position at the University of Washington. As he recalled, "I started at the University in the fall of 1971 and graduated in 1975. There was a strong YAF chapter there with several YAF members in student government. Some of the leaders were older Vietnam Vets—Al Zeller and Chuck Scanterberry in particular."[122] Today, Wilbur is a director of both the American Conservative Union and Young America's Foundation.

Other YAF alumni host local talk show programs. Lloyd Daugherty, former YAF National Director and now chairman of the Tennessee Conservative Union, is co-host of "The Voice" each afternoon on Knoxville radio while Seth Grossman, chapter chairman at Duke in the early 1970s, is a talk show host on radio in northern New Jersey. Henry Kriegel, YAF chapter chairman at Columbia in the early 1980s, hosts a radio talk show in Bozeman, Montana.

Still others have played important roles in radio-television communications. Jim Farley, former New York YAF chairman and National Director, is now news director for the all-news station WTOP in the Nation's Capital. Looking back on his involvement, Farley said, "I have many fond memories of my years with YAF."[123] Although Farley's career seems like a steady progression to the top, Pat Geary had a major change in direction, as well as in geography. While attending University of California at Irvine and then Loyola Law School, Geary was California YAF state chairman and a National Director. He then worked as a prosecutor for several years before relocating to Glasgow, Scotland. But even across the pond, Geary retained his love of country music and eventually became involved in broadcasting that music to a British audience. A few years ago, he moved to Nashville where he is now Director of Programming and hosts an afternoon program on "Voice of Country," an Internet radio station focused on an audience in the United Kingdom. Even though he is no longer involved in politics, Geary maintains that, "YAF helped me formulate and articulate the political beliefs which I still hold today."[124]

Television has been the career for both Liz Trotta and Steve Dunlop. Trotta has been a network television correspondent, national and foreign, for NBC news and CBS news and is now the Fox News channel media critic. She is the recipient of three Emmy awards and two Overseas Press Club awards. Trotta joined YAF as an undergraduate at Boston University and maintains that YAF had "a major impact. It all started with *The Conscience of a Conservative*. Bill Buckley was a major force."[125] Steve Dunlop was a YAF member at Fordham in the mid 1970s and has spent several years at CBS News, as Bulletin Center correspondent, covering breaking news for the CBS Evening News program, and also working as a freelance communications trainer.

After a 25-year career in the United States Navy followed by another 14 years in the Federal government, Carl Thormeyer is a television meteorologist in northern California. Thormeyer was Penn State YAF chapter chairman in the early 1960s and maintained that his experience in YAF "kept me focused on

---

122. Telephone interview with Kirby Wilbur, March 24, 2009.
123. 2008 YAF Alumni Survey Responses: Jim Farley.
124. 2008 YAF Alumni Survey Responses: Patrick S. Geary.
125. 2008 YAF Alumni Survey Responses: Elizabeth A. Trotta.

limited government, maximum freedom, and Goldwater libertarianism. Great organization!"[126] Nearly thirty years later, Jennifer Narramore was another meteorology student at Penn State University and served as secretary of the Penn State YAF chapter in the early 1990s. Since 1997 she has been with the Weather Channel, as Senior Radio Broadcast Meteorologist, with her daily reports beamed to radio stations across the country.

An individual whose career spanned both print and broadcast journalism is Kenneth Tomlinson, an active YAF member at Randolph-Macon College and later Virginia YAF state chairman. Tomlinson started with the *Richmond Times Dispatch* and then moved to *Reader's Digest* where he rose to become editor-in-chief. During the Reagan Administration he was called upon to become director of Voice of America for two years and then appointed to the Board for International Broadcasting. President George W. Bush appointed Tomlinson to be chairman of the Corporation for Public Broadcasting board, a position he held for more than two years despite vociferous criticism from liberals. Tomlinson's objective as chairman was to ensure that ideological bias did not dominate news programs on the public broadcasting system.[127]

It would be inaccurate to discuss those involved in the communications world without mentioning some of the YAF alumni who have established their own firms or work for organizations as communications specialists. Jack Cox started his involvement in YAF at Foothill College in 1962 and then became chairman at San Jose State. He was named California YAF state chairman, elected to the National Board at the 1973 YAF National Convention, and was integrally involved in planning YAF's presence at the 1964 Republican National Convention. Cox became chief of staff to Congressman Barry Goldwater, Jr. and now is president of The Communications Institute in Los Angeles.[128] James Harff, another YAF leader and head of Youth for Goldwater in 1964, is chairman and chief executive officer of Global Communicators, a major firm in Washington, DC.[129] Among other YAF alumni involved in public relations and communications, Tom Amberg, former chapter chairman in St. Louis, is president of Cushman/Amberg in Chicago.

Charlie Gerow, YAF member at Messiah College and Villanova Law School, is president of Quantum Communications in Philadephia while former Illinois YAF state chairman and National Director Fran Griffin heads up Griffin Communications outside the Nation's Capital. As Gerow recalled his experiences, "YAF was a great place to start. I made friends through YAF and remain close today and I got involved in the political process in ways I would not otherwise."[130] Ron Burr was Indiana YAF state chairman and later publisher of both *The Alternative* and the renamed *American Spectator* before forming Burr Communications while Thomas Doherty, a YAF member in New York, became a partner at Mercury Public Affairs after serving as Deputy Secretary of Appointments for Governor George Pataki. Former Director James Bieber heads up Bieber Communications in Santa Ana, California while Kimberly Bellisimo and Michael Centanni, both George Washington University graduates, hold key positions at BMW Direct in Washington, DC.

126. 2008 YAF Alumni Survey Responses: Carl Thormeyer.
127. Paul Farhi, "Kenneth Tomlinson Quits Public Broadcasting Board," *Washington Post*, November 4, 2005.
128. John E. Cox, Jr. email to the author, March 26, 2008.
129. F. Clifton White: *Suite 3505*, p. 209.
130. 2008 YAF Alumni Survey Responses: Charlie Gerow.

Partners at The Strategy Group for Media include Brian Berry, a YAF member while attending American University, and Rex Elsass, a chapter chairman in Ohio. At Clear Word Communications, David Bufkin, YAF chairman at Vanderbilt in the mid 1970s, is founding partner and Rick Hendrix, a New York YAF member, is also a partner. As Bufkin looked back on his involvement he noted that, "YAF shaped my entire career . . . Contacts I made there are still my friends and associates."[131] Two other prominent YAF alumni should be mentioned also—John Greenagel and Patrick Korten. Greenagel was present at YAF's founding in Sharon and later became Minnesota YAF state chairman. He is now Director of Communications for the Semiconductor Industry Association.[132] While a student at the University of Wisconsin, Patrick Korten was one of the founders of the *Badger Herald.* Active in YAF in Wisconsin and the District of Columbia, he is now Vice President for Communications for the Knights of Columbus Catholic lay organization.

Academia

Although YAF is best described as an activist organization several YAF members have devoted their life to the academic world, especially as faculty on college and university campuses. It is here that they are able to balance the left-wing bias found in many, if not most, social science and humanities faculties while effectively presenting conservative values and principles in an intellectual framework and introducing those principles to more young people. From its founding, Young Americans for Freedom was committed to preparing and training young people in conservative principles and the techniques of influencing public policy. Thus, it is not surprising that several YAF alumni chose to carry on that responsibility as college and university faculty members. Once again, it would be impossible to be inclusive in this section; thus, a select number of YAF alumni in academia will be discussed here.

Several YAF alumni pursued careers in university administration. Among those who currently are, or have been, college Presidents are Roy Nirschel, C. Ron Kimberling, Peter DeLuca, Richard Bishirjian, Dennis Tanner, and John Agresto. Dr. Roy J. Nirschel has been President of Roger Williams University since 2001. His YAF involvement helped to provide "communication skills, leadership skills, independence, intellectual development."[133] One of his highlights was meeting Senator Goldwater at YAF's 10th anniversary celebration in 1970. Kimberling was a YAF chairman at Cal State–Long Beach and Assistant Secretary for Postsecondary Education during the Reagan Administration. For Kimberling, "YAF gave me a base of lifelong friends and sharpened my then-developing political philosophy."[134] Today, he is President of the Chicago campus of Argosy University. Peter DeLuca is Interim President of Thomas Aquinas College, an institution with which he has been associated since 1971, most recently as Vice President for Finance and Administration. After being a YAF member during his time at St. Mary's College in the early 1960s, DeLuca worked for the Intercollegiate Studies Institute. Richard

131. 2008 YAF Alumni Survey Responses: David Bufkin.
132. 2008 YAF Alumni Survey Responses: John Greenagel.
133. 2008 YAF Alumni Survey Responses: Roy J. Nirschel.
134. 2008 YAF Alumni Survey Responses: Charles Ronald Kimberling.

Bishirjian taught for many years at the College of New Rochelle and is now President of Yorktown University. Dennis Tanner was chairman of Penn State YAF during the mid-1960s, served from 1991–99 as President of Bacone College, and is now Vice President of Princeton Information Management Corporation. John Agresto, a YAF member while a student at Boston College in the mid-1960s, was President of St. John's College–Santa Fe from 1992 to 2002 and is now a Fellow at the James Madison Program in American Ideals and Institutions at Princeton.

Among others with key administrative positions in higher education is David Stuhr, a participant at the initial Sharon Conference. After graduating from Yale and while in graduate school Stuhr held various leadership positions in New York and New Jersey YAF. As he recently recalled, "YAF was one of many associations that informed my resolve to contribute to the maintenance of a free and civil society."[135] Today, Stuhr is Associate Vice President of Fordham University. David Adcock served on the YAF National Board from 1971 to 1973, graduated from the University of North Carolina and Duke Law School and was a partner in an Atlanta law firm before becoming General Counsel of Duke University in 1982, serving for 24 years before retiring. Ron Leadbetter was vice chairman of the University of Tennessee at Knoxville YAF chapter and then worked for 36 years as an attorney in the Office of the General Counsel for his alma mater. For him, "YAF helped shape and fine-tune my conservative views and also provided an excellent framework for expressing those views through political action."[136]

Dennis Stull was Virginia YAF state chairman in the mid-1960s and is currently Provost and Vice President for Academic Affairs at Alderson-Broaddus College. Gary Gaffield was a leader in Columbia University YAF during the early 1970s, became Assistant Provost at Wittenburg College, and is now deputy executive director of the Council for International Exchange of Scholars, the entity that coordinates the Fulbright Scholar Program in conjunction with the U.S. Department of State. Philip E. Cleary, a YAF member while at Boston College, is now Dean Emeritus and professor of law at Southern New England School of Law. Chuck Stowe, a YAF leader at Vanderbilt in the late 1960s, is Dean of the College of Business and Public Affairs at Lander University.

Still others holding important administrative positions include Roger Candelaria, James Chiavelli, and Roy Jones. Roger Candelaria was Colorado YAF state chairman during the late 1960s. YAF's effect on him included, "Understanding markets and, eventually, coming to a deeper appreciation of the religious and metaphysical truths about the human person on which a free society depends made all the difference in who I am."[137] Candelaria is now Campus Compliance Officer in the Office of Human Relations Programs at the University of Maryland. James Chiavelli was a YAF member at Harvard during the early 1980s and is now Director of Communications for Northeastern University. Roy Jones was YAF chapter chairman at Liberty University in the late 1970s and early 1980s. He recalled with great satisfaction, "Being presented the chapter chairman of the year award by Chairman Jim Lacy and Ronald Reagan in 1979 at the Conservative Political Action Conference."[138] After many years in various marketing positions, Jones returned to his alma mater in 2005 to become Director of Development.

---

135. 2008 YAF Alumni Survey Responses: David Stuhr.
136. 2008 YAF Alumni Survey Responses: Ronald C. Leadbetter.
137. 2008 YAF Alumni Survey Responses: Roger Candelaria.
138. 2008 YAF Alumni Survey Responses: Roy C. Jones.

The following former members of the National Board of Directors of Young Americans for Freedom hold faculty positions in political science or were previously on college or university faculties: Donald J. Devine (University of Maryland, 1967–80 and Director, The Federalist Leadership Center at Bellevue University, 2001–); Lee Edwards (Catholic University); Kenneth Grasso (Texas State University); Casey Hubble (McLennan Community College); William B. Lacy (Director, Robert J. Dole Institute of Politics, University of Kansas); and J. Michael Waller (Institute of World Politics). Among other political science faculty, Professor David C. Amidon at Lehigh and Angelo Codeveilla at Boston University were YAF members in the 1960s as were Peter Gubser, a faculty member at Georgetown, and Juliana Pilon, now a Research Professor at the Institute of World Politics. As undergraduates at Harvard, Stephen Rosen was an officer in the YAF chapter and Habib C. Malik a member. Rosen is now a professor at Harvard and Malik at the Lebanese American University. James Whisker spent his career in the political science department at West Virginia University and served briefly as West Virginia YAF state chairman.

A number of YAF chapter chairmen have pursued academic careers in political science. Ira Straus headed Princeton YAF and later became a Fulbright Professor at Moscow State University. Gerard Alexander was YAF chapter chairman at Georgetown and now teaches at the University of Virginia. Daria Novak was chairman at Mary Washington College and is a faculty member at Eastern Connecticut State University. Robert F. Cuervo and William Luckey were both chairmen at St. John's University. Cuervo now teaches at Pace University and Luckey at Christendom College. Archie Jones was chairman at Texas A&M University and is on the faculty at St. Leo College while former Towson State chairman W. Wesley McDonald teaches at Elizabethtown College and Robin Bittick, YAF chairman at Biola College, is on the faculty at Sam Houston State College. John Kavanagh, former NYU YAF chairman, heads the Criminal Justice department at Scottsdale Community College while Leon Waszak, YAF chairman Cal State–Los Angeles, taught at Glendale College.

Among the various faculty members in History departments, former National Director and USC YAF chairman Wayne Bowen is chairman of the department at Southeast Missouri State University. As Bowen looked back on his time in YAF he recalled that, "I was very active from 1986 to 1989 . . . Larry King and Jeff Wright recruited me to be a chapter chairman and in 1987 I won chapter of the year."[139] Carl Thomas McIntire, a participant at the original Sharon conference and National Director, has been professor of History and Religion at the University of Toronto for several years. John Pafford served as YAF state chairman in both Maryland and Nevada and for many years taught history at Northwood University. Among the former chapter chairmen are Rorin Platt, a faculty member at Campbell University, George Prokopiak at Edison State College, and Bruce Bendler at the University of Delaware. Former YAFer Richard Blanke is a faculty member at the University of Maine, Martin Claussen teaches at the University of San Francisco, and J.D. Forbes is a faculty member at the University of Virginia. William C. Dennis, one-time president of the Philadelphia Society, is retired from the history department at Denison University.[140]

---

139. 2008 YAF Alumni Survey Responses: Wayne H. Bowen.
140. 2008 YAF Alumni Survey Responses: William C. Dennis.

With its strong support for Constitutional government, it is not surprising that a number of YAF alumni now teach courses in law at various institutions. David Friedman, son of the late Nobel prize-winning economist, teaches at Santa Clara University School of Law while Daniel Hays Lowenstein, a YAF member in the early 1960s at Yale, has been on the faculty at the UCLA School of Law since 1979.[141] Stephen Markman was chapter chairman at Duke and teaches law at Hillsdale College. Bruce McAllister participated in the Sharon conference and later served in the Carter Administration. He now teaches at Nova Southeastern University. Maurice Franks, whose YAF involvement began as a student at the University of Memphis, is now a professor at Southern University Law Center.[142] Among others, Rob Natelson, former Cornell YAF activist, teaches at University of Montana School of Law; Jan Ting is a professor at Temple University Law School, and Robert Turner is on the faculty at the University of Virginia School of Law.

Free market economics and a respect for entrepreneurship were essential elements of the tenets first propounded by YAF in its Sharon Statement. This belief has led a number of YAF alumni to careers teaching business and economics courses on campus. Warren Coats, one-time Hawaii YAF state chairman, taught at the University of Virginia, the University of Hawaii, and George Mason University as well as spending 26 years as an economist with the International Monetary Fund. He is now working on the rehabilitation of the money and banking systems of Afghanistan and Iraq and is a director of the Cayman Islands Monetary Authority.[143] H.E. "Ted" Frech, III, was Missouri YAF state chairman and is now a professor of economics at UC–Santa Barbara. Another Missouri YAF member while at Washington University, Clay Singleton is Professor of Finance at Rollins University.

Two graduates of Grove City College, where the late Professor Hans Sennholz was chairman of the economics department until 1992, became economics professors themselves. Jeffrey Hummel is a faculty member at San Jose State University while Camille Castorina has taught economics at a number of colleges. Lou Gasper was an active participant in YAF affairs while a young faculty member at the University of Arizona. Since 1992 he has served on the economics faculty at the University of Dallas where Scott Kjar, a YAF member as an undergraduate at the University of Rochester, also teaches economics. Michael J. Caslin was a YAF member at Manhattanville College and now teaches entrepreneurship at Babson College while Clifford Thies, a YAF member in high school and at Boston College, is a professor of economics at Shenandoah University.

Tibor Machan, a frequent contributor to *New Guard* during the 1960s and early 1970s, is professor emeritus of philosophy at Auburn University. James Gwartney was Washington YAF state chairman while in graduate school at the University of Washington in the early 1960s and since 1968 has been on the faculty at Florida State University. He is the co-author of *Economics: Private and Public Choice*, a widely used textbook now in its 12th edition.[144] For thirty years Thomas Ireland taught economics at the University of Missouri at St. Louis after having been in YAF chapters at Miami University of Ohio and the University of Virginia. As he

---

141. 2008 YAF Alumni Survey Responses: David Friedman.
142. 2008 YAF Alumni Survey Responses: Maurice Franks.
143. 2008 YAF Alumni Survey Responses: Warren Coats.
144. James D. Gwartney, Richard L. Stroup, Russell S. Sobel, and David Macpherson: *Economics: Private and Public Choice* (Mason, OH: South-Western Cengage Learning, 2009).

recently recalled, "I was a member of YAF, but an inactive member. I remember my experiences with YAF positively, but was never a leader in YAF."[145] Rolando Pelaez was active in YAF at Louisiana State University and as a graduate student at the University of Houston where he has been a professor of Finance for nearly thirty years.

Among the English and Humanities faculty are Carol Sue Nevin Abromaitis, who was a participant at the Sharon Conference while an undergraduate at the College of Notre Dame. She recalls that meeting as "one of the high points of my early years."[146] Abromaitis went on to obtain her PhD from the University of Maryland and has taught at Loyola College for more than 45 years. By the mid-1960s, Dianne Gordon was a YAF member at Carthage College. A senior lecturer in Composition at the University of Wisconsin—Green Bay, she noted, "I read a range of news sources, mostly conservative. I encourage my students to read and think critically and to be engaged in public life."[147]

Peter Knupfer was a YAF chapter chairman at the University of Wisconsin in the 1970s and Nicholas Kocz had a similar position at American University in the 1980s. Knupfer now is a member of the Humanities faculty at Michigan State University while Kocz teaches at Virginia Tech. John Tagg was a chapter chairman at Cerritos College and has been on the English faculty at Palomar College for several years. Jared Lobdell was the founding secretary of Yale YAF in 1961 and editor of the conservative student publication, *Insight and Outlook*, in the 1960s. Lobdell, whose many books on Tolkien and C.S. Lewis were mentioned previously, teaches at Millersville University.

In other academic fields, Sharon attendee and chairman at the University of Minnesota G. Daniel Harden recently retired from the Education department at Washburn University where he taught for 23 years.[148] A fellow Sharon participant, Robert Schuettinger, is president of the Oxford Study Abroad Program, which places American students in one of the historic colleges of Oxford University for a semester. Perhaps one of the more interesting transitions was Verna Harrison who, after graduating from Yale where she was active in YAF in the early 1970s, joined a religious order of the Orthodox Church in America, and is now Sr. Nonna Verna Harrison, Assistant Professor of Church History at Saint Paul School of Theology.

Among YAF members active prior to the Goldwater campaign who became faculty members were Samuel Acerbo, Myrna Bain, Joy Bilharz, Donald Boyd, Jerry Ericksen, Corydon Hammond, and Sharon Presley. Acerbo, a YAF chairman in Westchester County, New York in the early 1960s, retired from the Chemistry department at Iona College while Bain, a YAF leader at Hunter College and the Greenwich Village YAF chapter, taught African-American Studies at the New York City College of Technology. Joy Bilharz was active in the Bucks County YAF chapter, graduated from Bryn Mawr College, and teaches anthropology at the State University of New York–Fredonia. Donald W. Boyd helped form "Students of Conservative Conscience" at Montana State after reading Barry Goldwater's classic book. Later on in life, "I discovered that being a conservative professor that I was able to influence the lives of many students." Boyd retired in 2002 and is now Professor Emeritus of Industrial Engineering at his alma mater.[149]

145. 2008 YAF Alumni Survey Responses: Thomas R. Ireland.
146. 2008 YAF Alumni Survey Responses: Carol Sue Nevin Abromaitis.
147. 2008 YAF Alumni Survey Responses: Dianne Gordon.
148. 2008 YAF Alumni Survey Responses: G. Daniel Harden.
149. 2008 YAF Alumni Survey Responses: Donald W. Boyd.

Psychology became the career path for three YAF activists from the early years. Jerry D. Ericksen was YAF chairman at the University of North Dakota in the early 1960s and is now retired from the Psychology department at Carlton College. Corydon Hammond is Professor and Psychologist in Physical Medicine and Rehabilitation at the University of Utah School of Medicine. Considering his experience in YAF, Hammond noted "I found great fulfillment in realizing that while I may not be able to influence national politics, that I could make a difference in the lives of individuals ... I switched my major from pre-law to Psychology and have had a very fulfilling career helping thousands of people to improve their lives."[150] Sharon Presley was a member of the Berkeley YAF chapter in the early 1960s, co-founded Laissez-Faire Books in the 1970s, and recently retired as a professor of psychology at Cal State–East Bay.

Tom Hazlett was chapter chairman at Cal State–Northridge in the 1970s and is a professor of Agricultural Economics at the University of California–Davis. Jeffrey Oschner was involved in YAF while a student at Rice University in the early 1970s and is now Professor of Architecture and Associate Dean for Academic Affairs at the University of Washington. Dallas Kennedy, a YAF member at the University of Maryland in the early 1980s is a former faculty member in Physics at the University of Florida. Space does not allow a discussion of either those many YAFers who went on to careers in pre-collegiate education or those who have contributed to the enhancement of knowledge through publications in journals, magazines, and books. While its focus was on activism, Young Americans for Freedom also produced an intellectual base for American society and the conservative movement.

Religion

Religion has played an important role in the lives of many, if not most, former members of Young Americans for Freedom. This commitment to the transcendent has led some YAF alumni to devote their lives to practicing and advancing their faith as a fulltime profession. Among those who became Roman Catholic priests are Bryan Adamcik, pastor of Our Lady of Victories parish outside New York City in the New Jersey suburbs;[151] James Farfaglia, pastor of St. Helena Catholic Church in Corpus Christi, Texas; C.J. McCloskey, III, a resident fellow with the Faith and Reason Institute in Washington and a contributor to *The American Spectator*; and Vincent Rigdon, pastor of Our Lady of the Presentation parish in Poolesville, Maryland.[152] Richard Cuneo is the lay leader of the Catholic Traditionalist Movement.

Several former YAF leaders became pastors of Protestant churches. Adrienne Flipse-Hausch is both a practicing attorney and pastor for congregational care of the Community Church of Douglaston in New York.[153] Ian Pacey, a YAF member in the 1990s while at UCLA, is pastor of Christ Lutheran Mission in Marana, Arizona and Campus Pastor for the Lutheran Student Fellowship at the University of Arizona. Craig Donofrio, an Orange County YAFer in the 1990s, is

---

150. 2008 YAF Alumni Survey Responses: D. Corydon Hammond.

151. Kevin Coyne, "Redux in a Parish, the Latin Mass," *New York Times*, April 20, 2008.

152. 2008 YAF Alumni Survey Responses: James Farfaglia; Email to the author from Vincent Rigdon, September 24, 2009.

153. 2008 YAF Alumni Survey Responses: Adrienne Flipse Hausch.

pastor of Mount Olive Lutheran Church in Pasadena, California while former UC–Berkeley YAF member Ray Van Buskirk is pastor of Redeemer Lutheran Church in Baytown, Texas. John R. Riley, a Rutgers YAF member, is pastor of the First Presbyterian Church in Smyrna, Delaware and former Illinois YAF state chairman William Mencarow is pastor of Reformation Church in Boerne, Texas.[154] Robert Lightner, former Virginia YAF state chairman, is pastor of a Baptist church in North Carolina while former Texas YAF state chairman William Warnky until recently was senior priest at Good Samaritan Episcopal Church in Dallas, Texas.[155] Brian Cox, a leader in the University of Southern California YAF chapter in the early 1970s, serves as rector of Christ the King Episcopal Church in Santa Barbara, California.[156]

Still others work in religious professions apart from being local pastors. Gordon Shadburne, former chairman at the University of Plano, is president of the evangelistic group, Warriors for Christ. Former National Director Harold Herring is president of the Debt Free Army, whose objective is to convince Christians to become debt free, "because you're never really free, until you are financially free."[157] Among other religious leaders, former Brooklyn YAF activist Benzion Bochner is a rabbi in New York City while, as mentioned previously, Yale YAF alumnus Nonni Verna Harrison belongs to a religious order of the Orthodox Church in America. Victor Krambo, a YAF member in high school and as a freshman at Southern Methodist University, converted to Islam, adopted the name of Abdul Kabib, and follows the mystical branch of Islam called Sufism.[158] Today, Krambo is the owner of a solar energy design company in California where he is a leader in the Islamic Center of Yuba City.

Entrepreneurs and the Business World

It should be no surprise that many YAF alumni embarked on careers in the business world, including several entrepreneurs who formed their own successful business ventures. Among the early National Directors of YAF, Herbert Kohler is chairman of the board of Kohler Industries, Kathy Kolbe is chief executive officer of the Kolbe Corporation, Tom Phillips is chairman of the board of Eagle Publishing, and Bruce Eberle is president of the Eberle Communications Group. Sharon attendee Thomas E. Reilly is now the retired chairman of Reilly Industries and was appointed by Governor Mitch Daniels to the Indiana University board of trustees in 2007.[159] Fellow YAF founder Brian Whalen has long served as vice president of Navistar International.

Four former National Chairmen have had successful careers in business. Tom Charles Huston, is chairman of Brenwick Development Corporation in Indianapolis, Indiana, a land development company which he co-founded in 1976.[160] J. Alan MacKay spent a career as general counsel to the Cabot Corporation.

154. 2008 YAF Alumni Survey Responses: William Mencarow.
155. 2008 YAF Alumni Survey Responses: Robert T. Lightner, Jr.; "New Rules for Episcopal Priests," *Austin American Statesman*, September 6, 2009.
156. McDonald: *YAF in the Arena*, Appendix, p. 2.
157. www.debtfreearmy.org.
158. Paul M. Barrett: *American Islam: The Struggle for the Soul of a Religion* (New York: Farrar, Straus & Giroux, 2006), pp. 179–182.
159. 2008 YAF Alumni Survey Responses: Tom Reilly, Jr.
160. 2008 YAF Alumni Survey Responses: Tom Charles Huston.

Ronald F. Docksai is Vice President for Federal Government Relations for the Bayer Corporation. He is also chairman of the board of directors of the German-American Business Council. Jeffrey Kane is president and chief executive officer of National Distributors, Inc. in Portland, Maine. As Kane recently noted about his experience in business, "During these years I utilized my political and legal skills to help shape policy as it affected our business. Recently I have joined the Board of Trustees of the Maine Heritage Policy Center. I have really enjoyed getting back into movement politics."[161] Kane is also a former president of the Portland Symphony Orchestra and trustee of the Portland Museum of Art.

Among others with successful careers in business, Karl Ziebarth, a YAF member and chairman of Eastside YAF in New York City in the early 1960s, is chairman of the board of the Santa Fe Southern Railroad. Ziebarth saw his time in YAF as promoting the conservative cause in a liberal environment, providing him an opportunity to advance views he already held prior to joining YAF. As he recalled, he "was a staunch free-market small government advocate before, and so I remain."[162] Brian Stanley, chapter chairman at Arizona State University in the early 1970s, is vice president and general counsel at The Hefner Company while Steven Himelstein, a New York YAF member in the 1980s, is senior director and associate general counsel at Canon. Paul Cellupica, a Harvard YAF member in the 1980s, is chief counsel for the MetLife Group and Anthony Dennis, a Tufts student in the 1980s, is legal counsel at Aetna. Tony Ellsworth, a YAF member while at Loyola Law School in the 1960s, is president and general counsel of Pacific Financial Resources. As Ellsworth commented, "I was an early member of the Young Americans for Freedom ... Only difference was that I was actually 'young' back then."[163] Jake Hansen, former Idaho YAF chairman, is vice president of government affairs for Barr Laboratories and former National Director Bill Spadea is vice president for Career Development for the national real estate company, Weichert Realtors.[164]

Several YAF alumni chose to establish careers in the investment world. One of the more successful was Dan Calabria, who spent 42 years in the mutual funds industry, rising to president and chief executive officer of Templeton Funds Management Corporation.[165] In the early 1960s, Calabria was a leader in the Bay Ridge (Brooklyn) YAF chapter. T. Coleman Andrews, a member of YAF in the mid-1970s, was one of the founders of Bain Capital. Keith Grundy, New York YAF activist in the 1970s, is senior vice president of Shattuck Hammond Partners, investment banking and financial advisory firm, in charge of the San Francisco office. Former National Director Craig England, a YAF leader both in high school and at Johns Hopkins University in the 1980s, is managing director of England & Company, investment bankers while former national YAF executive director Christopher Long is chief executive officer of the Endowment Capital Group and former National Director Todd Gardenhire is senior vice president with Morgan Stanley Smith Barney in Chattanooga.

James Lucier, whose affiliation with YAF began as a student at the University of Michigan, is Senior Washington Analyst for Prudential Securities. Charles

161. 2008 YAF Alumni Survey Responses: Jeffrey Kane.
162. 2008 YAF Alumni Survey Responses: Karl Rex Ziebarth.
163. Note from Tony Ellsworth to Ron Robinson, June 7, 2008, copy in author's possession.
164. 2008 YAF Alumni Survey Responses: William Spadea.
165. Calabria is the author of *Mutual Funds Today—Who's Watching Your Money?* (St. Petersburg, FL: Mutual Funds Bureau, 2009).

Pohl, a YAF activist at the University of Chicago, is chief investment officer for Dodge & Cox mutual funds while Jerome Tuccille is a vice president with T. Rowe Price Investments. Paul Atanasio, YAF chairman at Holy Cross College, is a partner at UBS Paine Webber and former Connecticut YAF chairman Bill Butterly is chief operations officer at Robeco Investments in New York. Among others, Joseph Galda, chairman at Rutgers, is president of Corsair Advisors; William Chettle, a Maryland YAF member in the 1980s, is Managing Director of Marketing at Loring Ward International investment advisors; Joseph Lupica, chairman at Cornell, is president of Stroudwater Capital; Wayne Wilkey, chairman at Georgetown, is hedge fund manager for Ampere Capital; Alvin Hirano, a chapter chairman in Hawaii in the early 1960s, is president of Pacific Orient Investment Company; and Lee Forlenza, a YAF leader at New York University in the 1970s, is senior vice president of Ameritrans Capital. Two other YAF alumni have had important roles with the New York Stock Exchange. George Sierant, YAF chairman at NYU in the early 1970s, was Managing Director of international listings for the NYSE while Melanie Grace, YAF chairman at the University of California–Riverside in the late 1980s, is associate general counsel at NYSE Euronext in San Francisco.

The information technology area also attracted a number of former YAF members. At Cisco, J. Atchison Frazer, a YAF member at the University of Louisville, is director of enterprise services security while Landon "Curt" Noll, a Linfield College YAF leader in the early 1980s, is the company's cryptologist and security architect. Andrew Mendelsohn, YAF chairman at Princeton in the mid-1970s, is senior vice president for server technology at Oracle while retired Brigadier General Rudolf Peksens, a YAF member at Tufts in the early 1960s, is assistant vice president for Science Applications International. Andrew Yiannakos, chairman at NYU in the early 1980s, is director of Information Technology Risk Management for Credit Suisse. John Greenagel, a founding member of YAF mentioned earlier in the discussion of the Communications industry, is director of communications for the Semiconductor Industry Association, while Jodi Shelton, a YAF leader at San Diego State University in the closing days of the national organization, is president of the Global Semiconductor Alliance.[166]

Still other YAF alumni have been involved in organizations representing various aspects of the business community, as have Greenagel and Shelton. Rob Bohannan, former Arizona YAF chairman, is manager of state government affairs for the American Academy of Dermatology; Mark Brunner, Minnesota YAF chairman in the mid-1970s, is president of the Minnesota Manufactured Housing Association; Richard Coorsh, a YAF leader at Lynchburg College, is vice president for communications at the Federation of American Hospitals; and Patrick Reilly, a New York YAFer in the 1970s, is Vice President of Member and Board Services for the New York State Association of Realtors. Eron Shosteck, a chairman at the University of Maryland in the late 1980s, is senior vice president of the American Bus Association while Jade West, former Duke chairman and national YAF staffer, is senior vice president for government relations at the National Association of Wholesalers and Distributors.

166. 2008 YAF Alumni Survey Responses: John Philip Greenagel.

Practicing Law

So many former YAFers became attorneys that it would be impossible to discuss and describe more than a small portion of them here. Several law school graduates engaged in careers where their law degree was important but not essential, including many who entered elective office or became campaign strategists. Still others entered various business enterprises, either as entrepreneurs or corporate employees. Even eliminating these individuals as well as many of those whose later careers were discussed in previous chapters, any comprehensive section on YAF alumni engaged in the practice of law would be too lengthy, detailed and cumbersome for most readers. Therefore, the following section discusses only some of those attorneys who held leadership positions in Young Americans for Freedom as members of the National Board of Directors or state chairmen.

Among those who served on the National Board during the 1960s, Richard A. Derham is now retired after working as managing partner at Davis, Wright, Tremaine in Seattle. Robert G. Harley, a Sharon attendee, retired as a partner at Harley & Browne in New York and now does mediation work. Daniel F. Joy, III, who also served as editor of *New Guard*, is an attorney in Sarasota. William J. Madden, Jr., another Sharon participant, is retired from the firm of Winston & Strawn while Mary Kay (Davis) Maxwell is an attorney in Houston. Since 1973, Donald B. Shafto has been a partner with Gilmartin, Poster & Shafto in New York City. Roger Steggerda practices law in Las Vegas while Randal C. Teague is a partner at Vorys, Sater, Seymour and Pease in their Washington office. Michael A. Connelly is now an attorney in Dallas while Steven A. Loewy practices law in Germantown, Maryland.

James Lacy is managing partner with his wife Janice in the firm of Wewer & Lacy in Laguna Niguel, California. Alan Ashkinaze practices law in Hackensack, New Jersey while George Blackman has a solo practice in Dallas. Steven B. Fillman is an attorney in York, Nebraska and Tyrone J. Maho is a partner in the Santa Barbara law firm of Maho & Prentice. Fellow National Director from California John C. Manly, IV is a partner with Manly & Stewart in Newport Beach. David B. Nolan has a solo practice in Alexandria, Virginia while Robert Dolan practices law in Winnemucca, Nevada.

Michael R. Houston is a partner with Rutan & Tucker in Costa Mesa, California while Kenneth Wysocki, is associated with the Chicago office of Clausen Miller. Matthew Zandi is an associate in the Los Angeles office of Nixon Peabody while Michael Zummo is associate court attorney at the Criminal Court of the City of New York and president of the Long Island chapter of the Federalist Society.

Among former state chairmen, Taylor W. Jones, Georgia YAF chairman in the 1960s, is managing partner of Jones, Jensen & Harris in Atlanta. Three former Illinois YAF chairmen in the late 1970s are attorneys. Nicholas J. Kaster is with the global information services and publishing company Wolters Kluwer in their Riverwoods, Illinois office. Fred Dempsey is of counsel at Mayer Brown's Chicago office while Roibin J. Ryan is an attorney with Baxter Healthcare in Deerfield, Illinois. William E. Jenner, Indiana YAF chairman in 1965, is senior partner at Jenner, Auxier & Jacobs in Madison, Indiana. David Lowrance, Mississippi YAF state chairman in 1965, practices law in Memphis while Richard Wright, Wisconsin YAF chairman in the late 1960s, is a former Circuit Judge in Wisconsin.

In addition to Steve Loewy, two other former Missouri YAF chairmen had careers in law. Frank Bubb was a corporate general counsel and is now retired in Florida while T. Nelson Mann is an accomplished attorney in Kansas City. Henry Luthin, Massachusetts YAF chairman in the late 1970s, is a Corporation Counsel with the City of Boston while Malcolm "Kip" McClinchie, Texas YAF chairman in the early 1980s, is an assistant district attorney for Bexar County (San Antonio), Texas. Former Michigan YAF chairman Christine Zarycky practices law in Birmingham, Michigan while Nathanael Pendley, North Carolina YAF chairman in 1990, is an attorney in Clemens, North Carolina.

The legacy of Young Americans for Freedom constitutes both its substantial contributions to the political history of late 20th century America as well as the development of leaders for all areas of American society well into the 21st century. Many of those who were involved in YAF as young persons now provide leadership for various conservative organizations and campaigns. Still others are less involved in direct political efforts or have modified their positions, but in each case they continue to provide leadership for American society in professional and fraternal organizations, trade associations and chambers of commerce, religious congregations and charitable groups, art museums and symphony orchestras, schools and universities. In all these various ways, those whose early years included membership in Young Americans for Freedom continue to contribute to the conservative cause and to the betterment of American society.

As a national conservative youth organization, Young Americans for Freedom had a lasting effect on America. Those who were involved in YAF are now well beyond the point of being described as young. Other generations born after the end of the Reagan presidency are now entering college and the work force. Whether they will continue to provide a dedicated and committed conservative leadership for the future of the United States depends greatly on the ability of other organizations to take up the challenge and fill the void created on campuses and communities among today's youth. Fortunately, there are such groups that exist to instill conservative values and train young people to assume positions of leadership.

16. The Continuing Challenge
of the 21st Century

"In its heyday, YAF was an intellectual beacon to the handful of
us who rejected our generation's rebellion against authority and
tradition. I actually emerged from college more conservative than
when I entered and even more convinced that my radical peers
were on the wrong side of history and morality."[1]

In the summer of 1966, a young doctoral student in sociology at Penn State interested in gaining a better understanding of the burgeoning political movements on American college campuses, contacted Young Americans for Freedom and obtained permission to administer a brief survey at the organization's leadership conference being held at Franklin & Marshall College. In addition to a questionnaire covering a wide range of background items, those responding were asked to imagine the nation's history from the present to the year 2000. Richard Braungart was surprised by what he described as the belief of YAF members that a "continued drift to the welfare state and socialism and moral decay" would be reversed by an awakening of the American people resulting in moving "the train of events back to common sense."[2]

Braungart also surveyed members of Students for a Democratic Society, Young Republicans and Young Democrats and reported on his results in an article he co-wrote. It is interesting to view some of the projections of these YAF members in 1966. One YAF member predicted a redirection of American society towards freedom and conservative principles:

> The United States led by hypocritical and unprincipled leaders becomes very bureaucratic and increasingly socialistic. The United States generally loses the battles (politically, etc.) in foreign affairs because it does not present its philosophy of free enterprise, libertarian beliefs, etc., as well as it should. Finally in the 1980s or thereabouts the American people realize that economic security is not necessarily freedom. They realize their freedoms are being abridged. They realize the economy is becoming too regimented and the government too bureaucratic. The people will then change the trend of events back to common sense, conservative principles of government.[3]

Braungart cited another YAFer as predicting the following events in the near future: 1968, Republican victory; 1972, Reagan elected President; 1976 Reagan reelected; 1978 fall of Soviet Russia; 1980, fall of Red China; 1985, end of welfare, social security and medicare; 2000, end of unions.[4] He and his co-author noted,

---

1. 2008 YAF Alumni Survey Responses: Barbara Fiala Hollingsworth.
2. "YAF Members Optimistic, Sociological Study Finds," *New Guard*, November 1967, p. 8.
3. David Westby and Richard Braungart, "Activists and the History of the Future," p. 173, in Foster and Long, editors: *Protest !—Student Activism in America.*
4. "YAF Members Optimistic, Sociological Study Finds," *New Guard*, November 1967, p. 8.

"Compared with their SDS counter-parts on the Left, YAFers seem to have a mountain of naïve faith."[5]

Looking back nearly forty-five years later, this "naïve faith" seems to have been rather prescient. Change a few of the dates and modify a few of the conclusions and these YAF members, then only high school and college students, have laid out the political history of the last third of the 20th century. Nixon's victory in 1968 brought both a realignment in American politics as well as, admittedly, the disgrace of Watergate, impeachment and resignation. Reagan's victory came eight years after the YAFer's prediction and was indeed followed by a landslide re-election. It took nine more years for the Berlin wall to fall, closely followed by the demise of the Soviet Union. Then, in his 1993 State of the Union address, a new Democratic President promised to "end welfare as we know it," and the reforms were enacted a short while later as the Republicans gained a majority in Congress in 1994.

Two years later that same President declared, "the era of big government is over" in his State of the Union message. No longer was the talk of allowing alternatives to social security participation limited to academic discussions, and the establishment of individual retirement accounts and 401(k) plans provided additional means of preparing for retirement. Educational vouchers were being used in school systems across the country, including in the District of Columbia. These ideas were not only being discussed, but being implemented in areas foreseen only as hopeful possibilities by the YAF members of the mid-sixties.

It is not merely the optimism of youth nor the ability to predict the future that is most significant in these projections. Something even more important can be seen: this "naïve faith" of these YAF leaders in 1966 became the battle cry for the young conservative activists as they moved on to involvement in American politics throughout the remainder of the century. In adulthood, they contributed to making their faith a reality in so many ways that affected American society and moved it in a more conservative direction. What is just as amazing is that this optimism, about the future of America and the conservative beliefs they held, was being expressed less than two years after the devastating defeat of their candidate for the presidency. These college and high school students could look beyond a time when a conservative candidate carried only six states to a time when a conservative President would win 49 of 50 states in his re-election campaign.

While some of these young activists of the 1960s came from conservative backgrounds—Regnery, Campaigne, Lewis, Manion, Copeland to name a few—most had mainstream families whose parents voted, occasionally discussed current events at the dinner table, but were politically inactive. Still others had modified their beliefs and moved in a conservative direction. A psychology graduate student, Lawrence F. Schiff, who interviewed conservatives from nine northeastern colleges, conducted another early academic study of YAF members. About two thirds of those studied "had made such a strong break with their previous attitudes and behavior that it would be legitimate to call them converts," he concluded.[6]

---

5. Westby and Braungart, "Activists and the History of the Future," p. 173.

6. Lawrence F. Schiff, "Dynamic Young Fogies—Rebels on the Right," *Transaction*, 4 (November 1966), p. 34. See also Schiff, "The Obedient Rebels: A Study of College Conversions to Conservatism," *Journal of Social Issues*, 20 (October 1964), pp. 74–95, and Schiff, "The Conservative Movement on American College Campuses," doctoral dissertation, Department of Psychology, Harvard University, 1964.

Students who were beginning to identify their values with conservatism in the early 1960s had few resources on which to draw. Nevertheless, this conversion to conservatism was facilitated by the appearance of a new, albeit limited, collection of works from writers such as Whittaker Chambers, Russell Kirk, William F. Buckley, Jr., Barry Goldwater, and Ayn Rand. Along with the fortnightly *National Review*, these works supported an intellectual foundation for their newly developed beliefs and provided, in the words of Schiff, "a means by and through which the young conservatives can come out in the open on campus and, more significantly, the embrace of the conservative ideology can come out in the open from within the individual."[7]

For those who became campus conservatives in the early 1960s, there was only a nascent conservative movement to support and encourage them, no litany of organizations devoted to espousing conservative policies and principles, only a limited collection of books on philosophy and current issues, and few periodicals beyond *National Review*, *The Freeman*, and *Human Events*. In essence, there was little more than a Goldwater campaign and Young Americans for Freedom. In this context, it is easy to see why, if a conservative movement were to develop as a major force in late 20th century America, it would be an outgrowth in many respects of YAF—the only responsible conservative grassroots organization dedicated to developing future leaders. Out of this one organization came the impetus for creating a wide range of entities, which together constitute the conservative movement, as well as many of the individuals who provided leadership for those various groups.

Young conservatives today confront an environment that is quite different from that of some fifty years ago. As a movement developed and established itself, the resources needed to assist college and high school students in their philosophical and political journey became much more available. According to Roger Ream, now President of The Fund for American Studies, and himself a former YAF activist from the 1970s,

> If there are unserved conservative college students, it is very likely due to their own failure to seek services. There are so many resources available through the dozens of groups in our movement that focus primarily on the student population and other groups that have campus and student outreach initiatives as part of their broader mission. Conservative college students can find intellectual and organizational resources, including seminars, speakers, books and magazines, financial assistance, training, and legal support.[8]

Today's students do not stand isolated and apart but rather can tap into an established movement covering a wide spectrum of conservative views, beliefs, approaches and interests. They can "come out in the open" knowing they will be supported by others and have access to resources never thought possible by their predecessors some forty or fifty years ago.

---

7. Schiff, "The Obedient Rebels," pp. 89–90. Schiff's phrase, "come out in the open," when discussing those professing conservative beliefs, is indicative of the prevailing intellectual conformity on many American campuses in the early 1960s.

8. Email to the author, August 28, 2009.

Intercollegiate Studies Institute

It would be impossible to list, let alone describe, all the various groups and organizations that promote conservatism among high school and college students but certain ones with connections to Young Americans for Freedom need to be mentioned. Foremost among those groups is the oldest, having preceded YAF by some seven years. Formed as the Intercollegiate Society of Individualists and now renamed the Intercollegiate Studies Institute, ISI provides a solid foundation of conservative philosophy and economics for young conservatives. Since its founding in 1953, ISI has been an intellectual oasis for both conservative students and faculty.[9]

Today, ISI has a presence on many college campuses through individual campus representatives as well as affiliated groups who help arrange and promote speakers provided by the organization. Its Collegiate Network brings together more than one hundred independent campus newspapers and supplies them with columns, news items, and feature articles. Students are also afforded the opportunity to attend ISI conferences and seminars held throughout the country, allowing them to meet with and learn from noted conservative intellectuals.

Each year ISI awards a number of undergraduate and graduate fellowships, the most prestigious of which is the Weaver Fellowship. Awarded after a highly competitive review, Weaver Fellows are for a limited number of graduate students committed to teaching at the university level and provide a stipend of $5,000 plus tuition. Along with other named fellowships, ISI has awarded more than 500 graduate fellowships over the past 40 years. No single organization or foundation is as responsible for the nurturing and advancement of conservative faculty members as ISI and its various fellowship programs.

Most recently, ISI Books has become a major publishing house for works on philosophy, culture, history, and current affairs. Among its catalog entries are books by Aleksandr Solzhenitsyn, Robert Bork, Harvey Mansfield, and George Nash as well as reprints of works by Russell Kirk, Eric Voegelin, Richard Weaver, and Wilhelm Ropke. Perhaps its best-known publication is *Choosing the Right College,* which it claims is the only source of information on colleges for those interested in a genuine liberal education. The guide focuses on nearly 140 of the nation's leading colleges, using on-campus sources to profile the best and the worst of each institution. ISI is also the publisher of a number of quarterly and annual journals and reviews, including the *Intercollegiate Review, Modern Age, Political Science Reviewer,* and *University Bookman,* each of which are popular with both students and faculty.[10]

Many of those who lead ISI, including its President, T. Kenneth Cribb, are among the long list of YAF alumni continuing to advance conservative principles with America's youth. Cribb recently noted,

I am proud to say that I organized the very first chapter of Young Americans for Freedom in South Carolina (Spartanburg) shortly after YAF's founding ...

9. For an insightful review of the founding of the Intercollegiate Society of Individualists and its evolution into today's Intercollegiate Studies Institute, see Edwards: *Educating for Liberty.*
10. Descriptions of these journals and a listing of works published by ISI Books can be found at www.isi.org.

I was a rising 10th grader when I got in touch with YAF, so I'm not even sure the chapter strictly met the guidelines in those days. I proudly wore the YAF pin, and did what I could do to further the YAF motto "to preserve and extend freedom."[11]

Doug Minson, YAF chapter chairman at Boston College, is executive director for academic affairs at ISI and among its previous key staff members are Christopher Long, a George Washington University graduate who was executive director of YAF in the late 1980s, as well as Robert Schadler and Wayne Valis.

The synergy of ISI and YAF during its more than thirty years as the national conservative youth organization produced thousands of leaders who combined a solid philosophical foundation with a knowledge of practical political action. Together they nurtured young conservatives for leadership positions in academia as well as government. Today, ISI continues to provide the intellectual base for young people committed to obtaining a firmer understanding of conservatism.

Leadership Institute

While ISI concentrates its efforts on espousing and advancing the intellectual foundation of conservatism, another long-standing organization stresses teaching young conservatives the nuts and bolts of how to succeed in the public policy process. Formed in 1979 by Morton C. Blackwell, another YAF alumnus, the Leadership Institute (LI) strives to produce a new generation of public policy activists dedicated to free enterprise, limited government, traditional values and a strong national defense. LI's mission is to increase the number and effectiveness of committed young conservatives in the public policy process through identifying, recruiting, training and placing them in government, politics, and the media.[12]

Leadership Institute efforts begin by helping to form independent conservative student groups and assisting in the publication of independent newspapers on campus. On many campuses the organization's participants have assumed leadership roles in College Republican, Young Conservative and other student groups.[13] LI also sponsors campus election workshops designed to teach young conservatives how to seek and win student government elections. Each year, LI holds a series of broadcast and print journalism workshops as well as seminars on public relations and public speaking to better equip students for an active role on campus and in public affairs.

Moving beyond the campus environment, LI focuses on developing future political leaders. Through extensive training programs and seminars, students are equipped with the skills and knowledge to manage political campaigns and to become candidates for elective office or help formulate policy for elected officials. The Leadership Institute claims that more than 500 current state legislators are graduates of LI programs and seminars as well as an uncounted number of staff

---

11. Kenneth Cribb email to the author, September 24, 2009.

12. www.leadershipinstitute.org is the organization's official web site and provides much information on the range of programs and activities it sponsors.

13. Among other campus groups that work with LI are the remnants of the reorganized Young Americans for Freedom, the new Young Americans for Liberty, and the Young Conservatives of Texas chapters.

members in Federal, state and local government positions. Over the past thirty years, the Leadership Institute has become an important element of the American conservative movement. Its emphasis on practical political skills and campaign management continues that training of young conservatives so effectively carried out in the past by Young Americans for Freedom.

Clare Boothe Luce Policy Institute

One special area of concern for conservatives is to show that all young women in America do not endorse the liberal feminist outlook dominant on many university campuses, especially in the various Women's Studies departments and programs. Most recently, several strong conservative women have assumed important roles in the media and in public office, ranging from Ann Coulter and Laura Ingraham to Michele Bachmann and Sarah Palin. They serve as mentors and role models for conservative women on campuses.

One such leader who saw a need for a permanent organization assisting such students is Michelle Easton, an attorney and mother of three, who is a YAF alumna. In 1993, after having served for twelve years in the administrations of Presidents Reagan and George H.W. Bush, Michelle Easton established the Clare Boothe Luce Policy Institute in suburban Washington, DC Named after the late playwright, Congresswoman from Connecticut, and United States Ambassador, the Clare Boothe Luce Policy Institute mentors and trains the next generation of conservative young women to become effective leaders.[14] The organization attempts to accomplish this through the role models, resources, and relationship opportunities the Luce Institute provides to college students and young professional women.

The Luce Institute sponsors a number of lectures on college campuses featuring speakers such as Christina Hoff Sommers, Nonie Darwish, Suzanne Fields, Michelle Malkin, Ann Coulter and Kate Obenshain. One of the campus groups with which the Luce Institute works is the Network of enlightened Women (NeW), an organization of conservative women founded by Karin Agness at the University of Virginia with chapters now across the nation.[15]

In addition to helping bring conservative speakers to various campuses, the Luce Institute carries on a number of other programs. Interested students are provided with brief synopses on major issues in the Luce Institute's *Policy Express* and encouraged to apply for a limited number of semester-long paid internships at the organization's headquarters in northern Virginia. Each month the "Luce Women" gather for a Conservative Women's Network Luncheon held at the Heritage Foundation building in Washington, DC, where they are addressed by various authors and speakers. Throughout the year, the Luce Institute sponsors a Women and Career Development Workshop, a Media Communications Seminar, and a Capitol Hill Training Seminar in addition to special events on the West Coast and in Washington. Under the leadership of Michelle Easton, the Clare Boothe Luce Policy Institute has carved out an important role in the contemporary

---

14. Unfortunately, there is no comprehensive contemporary biography of this fascinating personality. Written before her demise, Wilfred Sheed: *Clare Boothe Luce* (New York: E.P. Dutton, 1982) portrays her life from the perspective of a personal friend while Sylvia J. Morris: *Rage for Fame* (New York: Random House, 1997) is a much more critical view of her earlier years.

15. Helena Andrews, "Conservative Women Fight Culture War on Campus," *Politico*, August 12, 2008, p. 29.

conservative movement by putting forward a number of programs to prepare dedicated young women for effective leadership, carrying on a tradition formerly promoted by Young Americans for Freedom.[16]

Federalist Society for Law & Public Policy

In April 1982, a small group of law students from Harvard, Stanford, the University of Chicago, and Yale organized a symposium on federalism at Yale Law School. From this initial effort came the formation of the Federalist Society for Law & Public Policy Studies. Among that original group of founders were E. Spencer Abraham (later United States Senator from Michigan) and David M. McIntosh (later Member of Congress from Indiana).[17] Since its formation nearly thirty years ago, its mission and purpose has been to provide "a forum for legal experts of opposing views to interact with members of the legal profession, the judiciary, law students, academics, and the architects of public policy." In terms of legal outlook, the Society is "committed to the principles that the state exists to preserve freedom, that the separation of governmental powers is central to our Constitution, and that it is emphatically the province and duty of the judiciary to say what the law is, not what it should be."[18]

Today, the Federalist Society operates through a Student Division, a Lawyers Division, and a Faculty Division with programs coordinated from a national office located in downtown Washington, DC. The Student Division includes more than 10,000 members, with law students at every ABA-accredited law school as well as additional chapters at international and non-accredited law schools. Each spring, the Student Division sponsors a National Student Symposium patterned after that first symposium at Yale that served as the impetus for creating the Federalist Society. In addition, the organization sponsors speeches and debates at law school chapters, and distributes a number of publications to its student membership, including *The Federalist Paper*, a newsletter that covers organizational happenings.

Involvement with the Society is not limited to students, however. The Lawyers Division is comprised of over 30,000 legal professionals and others and includes active chapters in sixty cities throughout the United States.[19] Among its past members are Supreme Court Justices John G. Roberts, Antonin Scalia, and Samuel Alito. While the organization was established during the Reagan Administration, it has had a major effect on the composition of the Federal judiciary, especially through the appointments of both President George H.W. Bush and President George W. Bush.[20] In 1999, the Federalist Society created a Faculty Division to provide events and publications to encourage traditional legal scholarship and constructive academic dialogue. Among its most important publications is the *Harvard Journal of Law & Public Policy*, the society's law journal.

---

16. These programs are described more fully at www.cblpi.org, the organization's web site.
17. "The Federalist Society—Student Division Membership and Benefits," brochure distributed by the Federalist Society for Law & Public Policy Studies, Washington, DC, no date.
18. "Our Background," http://www.fed-soc.org/aboutus/id.28/default.asp, accessed on November 25, 2009.
19. *Ibid.*
20. Jason DeParle, "Debating the Subtle Swing of the Federalist Society," *New York Times*, August 1, 2005; Charlie Savage, "Appeals Courts Pushed to Right by Bush Choices," *New York Times*, October 28, 2008.

Eugene B. Meyer serves as president of the Federalist Society. Meyer is a son of the late Frank S. Meyer and was chairman of the YAF chapter at Yale in the mid-70s. A former YAF Director, David C.F. Ray, is Associate Director of the Lawyers Division for the Federalist Society.[21] Through its programs for students, faculty and the legal community at large, the Federalist Society for Law & Public Policy Studies has become a major force in the direction and composition of legal thought and trends in the United States.[22]

Campus Groups

Still other youth organizations have been formed to help educate and train conservatives, as well as promote those principles on campus. The longest functioning group is the Young Conservatives of Texas, a spinoff from Young Americans for Freedom that has been in continuous operation since 1980 on several Texas college campuses.[23] More recently organized is the Young Americans for Liberty, which is an outgrowth of the Students for Ron Paul effort in the 2008 presidential campaign, and Students for Liberty, another predominantly libertarian group that works with affiliated but independent campus clubs. Another group is the Young Conservatives Coalition, formed in the Washington area after the 2008 presidential election. It describes itself as a DC-based young professional conservative advocacy and networking organization. There is also a handful of campus clubs still operating under the name of Young Americans for Freedom, including a most active one at Penn State University that was formed in 1993.[24] Of these, the one with the largest national reach is the clearly libertarian Young Americans for Liberty that, as of February 2010, claimed a presence on 153 high school and college campuses.[25]

In addition, several conservative organizations and foundations have programs directed towards students and other young people as part of their overall outreach efforts. YAF alumni have played key roles in creating these opportunities for young people. Unlike the young conservatives of the early 1960s, those young people who wish to learn more about conservative philosophy, principles and policies today, as well as how to become effective public policy advocates, have many resources available to them.

---

21. Interview with David Ray, Washington, DC, August 14, 2008.
22. Steven M. Teles: *The Rise of the Conservative Legal Movement: The Battle for Control of the Law* (Princeton, NJ: Princeton University Press, 2008). See especially chapter 5, pp. 135–180 where Teles discusses the influence of the Federalist Society on the contemporary Federal court system.
23. Recent efforts to organize Young Conservatives of California and Young Conservatives of Pennsylvania appear to have been unsuccessful.
24. As of early 2010 an effort was underway to reorganize Young Americans for Freedom as a national organization with a fulltime executive director. In February, the new YAF published a magazine under the title *The New Guard* and announced plans to digitize all past issues of the publication. News release, "YAF Launches 34th edition of The New Guard Magazine at CPAC," February 19, 2010.
25. www.yaliberty.org/note/2 accessed on February 5, 2010.

The Fund and the Foundation

Perhaps the most important organizational legacy of Young Americans for Freedom in terms of educating and training youth, however, was the formation of The Fund for American Studies and Young America's Foundation. These two groups, whose founders and current leadership came out of Young Americans for Freedom, promote slightly different but basically complementary approaches to reaching young people and educating them in conservative principles. In many ways it is "the Fund" and "the Foundation" which together carry on the work first begun by those young conservatives who met in Sharon, Connecticut in September of 1960.

The Fund for American Studies

It was 1966 when David R. Jones, then executive director of Young Americans for Freedom, put forth the idea of creating the Sharon Foundation as a non-profit educational body designed to promote conservative principles in an academic setting. One year later his idea took birth as the Charles Edison Youth Fund. The original incorporators included Jones, Edison, Dr. Walter Judd, Marvin Liebman, and of course the undisputed midwife of the conservative movement, Bill Buckley.[26] When Governor Edison died in 1969, the organization was renamed the Charles Edison Memorial Youth Fund. In 1987, its name was changed to The Fund for American Studies (TFAS) to respect Edison's request that his name be used for only its initial twenty years.[27]

Born in the midst of the 1960s campus turmoil, the Fund was committed to providing a balanced perspective on political and economic institutions. It would attempt to influence the lives of its students by passing on the principles of freedom, individual responsibility, and free markets, the essence of the American political tradition. The Fund would attempt to reach beyond those students already active in conservative organizations and include those whose involvement in and knowledge of conservative philosophy and principles might be limited. It was seeking students willing to learn and expand their horizons, students who would become future leaders in society. Application for Fund programs would be open to all college students but participation necessarily limited. Thanks to generous financial supporters, some scholarship assistance would be available to help students cover a portion of the various program costs.

Three years after its founding, the Edison Fund held the first Institute on Comparative Political and Economic Systems (ICPES) at Georgetown University, where it has remained ever since. Students spent the summer in the Nation's Capital attending two college credit classes, serving as interns in government and public policy organizations, and attending evening lectures. More than four thousand college students have completed this Institute's program over the past

---

26. The discussions surrounding the formation of a Sharon Foundation and the birth of the Charles Edison Youth Fund are presented in chapter 6.
27. The Fund for American Studies: *2007 Annual Report*, p. 4.

forty years.[28] From its initial program in 1970 to the present day, the Fund's success is rooted in a solid academic foundation and a commitment to both learning and doing through a combination of classes for academic credit, guest lectures, and internships at some of Washington's most important institutions.

Realizing the need for more specialized programs, TFAS expanded its offerings of summer programs at Georgetown University by establishing the Institute on Political Journalism in 1985 with a program designed to "develop young journalists with high ethical standards and a solid understanding of free market economic principles."[29] Some twelve hundred students have completed the summer journalism program taking six hours of course work along with participating in a media internship and hearing from leaders in the media at seminars and lectures. Added to the lineup of summer seminars were the Institute on Business and Governmental Affairs in 1990 and the Institute on Philanthropy and Voluntary Service in 1999. By 2010, these two programs alone had a roster of some 1,400 graduates. In 2007, TFAS launched a Legal Studies Institute for pre-law and law school students.

While summer institutes at Georgetown were reaching an ever-increasing number of students, TFAS determined to provide a more in-depth program and began its Capital Semester fifteen-week fall- and spring-semester program in 2003. More than two hundred and fifty students have taken part in this program alone. In 2007, a Capital Semester in Political Journalism was added as a separate track for both fall and spring semesters.

By the early 1990s, The Fund for American Studies began expanding its program to other areas of the world. In 1993, the American Institute of Political and Economic Systems was launched in the Czech Republic with a program patterned after the initial institute at Georgetown University. More than 1,400 students from twenty-seven countries have participated as of 2010. Three years later, a second program was begun in Greece and in 2002 the Asia Institute was formed in Hong Kong. The most recent effort is the Institute for Leadership in the Americas, begun in 2009 in Chile.

Originating with the executive director of Young Americans for Freedom more than forty years ago, The Fund for American Studies still retains a close relationship with its roots. Serving as chairman today is Randal C. Teague with Roger Ream as President of TFAS. Among its trustees are Michael Thompson, Charles Black, and Frank Donatelli along with former trustees Tom Phillips, Philip M. Crane, Neal B. Freeman, Bruce Weinrod and Arnold Steinberg. Jay Parker, Michael Caslin, and Kathy King Rothschild are YAF alumni on the TFAS Board of Regents.[30] Since its first summer institute in 1970, literally hundreds of YAF members have benefited from the Fund's programs. Its outreach, however, is much broader in scope, reaching a wide range of students, some of whom are first introduced to conservative philosophy and principles through their attendance at TFAS institutes and programs.

The Fund for American Studies has been teaching freedom since 1967, in the

---

28. The program is now officially called the Engalitcheff Institute on Comparative Political and Economic Systems in recognition of a major bequest in 1990 from the estate of John and Virginia Engalitcheff. The Fund for American Studies: *2007 Annual Report*, p. 34. The estate provided substantial funding to Young America's Foundation also. For information on John Engalitcheff and his legacy see Hoplin and Robinson: *Funding Fathers: The Unsung Heroes of the Conservative Movement*, pp. 211–232.

29. The Fund for American Studies: *2006 Annual Report*, p. 11.

30. The Fund for American Studies: *2009 Annual Report*, pp. 32–35.

United States and throughout the world, to college students who will become the leaders in their communities and countries. In 2008, TFAS launched its "Building Future Leaders" campaign and opened a Center for Teaching Freedom near their headquarters building in the Nation's Capital. As it reaches out to more and more young leaders, The Fund for American Studies will continue to play an essential role in teaching freedom. Its existence, and the individuals who have helped develop it into the major institution TFAS is today, are testimony also to the lasting influence of Young Americans for Freedom and its role in the development of the conservative movement in America.

Young America's Foundation

Chartered as University Information Systems, Inc. in the late 1960s, the non-profit educational entity that became Young America's Foundation shares not only the same initials as Young Americans for Freedom but calls itself YAF in its literature and on its web site.[31] Just as the idea for The Fund for American Studies emanated with YAF's executive director, so too the creation of what became the Foundation started with one YAF member while an undergraduate at Vanderbilt University. Although the Foundation provided scholarships and sponsored the Reagan Radio Project in the mid-1970s, it was not until 1979, when Ron Robinson became its full-time president that Young America's Foundation began to expand in both projects and financial support.[32] Today, the Foundation is led by a Board of Directors comprised mainly of those who in their youth had been active in Young Americans for Freedom.[33]

With a motto, "The Conservative Movement Starts Here!" today's list of programs and projects sponsored by Young America's Foundation is impressive. From its start, the Foundation has provided assistance to college and high school students by helping sponsor campus lectures. These programs are based on a belief that,

> For campus conservatives, inviting alternative speakers to their college is one of the best ways they can gain visibility, galvanize fellow conservatives, and introduce traditional and free market ideas to other students. This is the service that Young America's Foundation was first established to perform and it is how many students are introduced to the organization.[34]

The list of speakers sponsored by Young America's Foundation over its history is impressive, ranging from statesmen including Margaret Thatcher, Lech Wałęsa, Colin Powell and former President George W. Bush to public policy leaders such as John Ashcroft, Ed Meese, Zell Miller, and Steve Forbes, to commentators Fred

---

31. The web site for Young America's Foundation is www.yaf.org while the address for the reorganized Young Americans for Freedom is www.yaf.com. There is no official connection between the two organizations. For the founding and early years of Young America's Foundation, see chapters 6 and 12.

32. A limited collection of material from the earlier years of Young America's Foundation can be found in the Hall-Hoag Collection, Box HH2214, John Hay Library, Brown University, Providence, RI.

33. As of 2010, the YAF alumni on the Board of Young America's Foundation are Ron Robinson, Ronald Pearson, Frank Donatelli, Tom Phillips, Kenneth Cribb, James Taylor, Peter Schweizer, and Kirby Wilbur.

34. Young America's Foundation, 25th Anniversary Report 1969–1984, pp. 13–14.

Barnes, Michael Medved, Ann Coulter, John Fund, and George Will to media personalities Chuck Norris, Ben Stein, Ted Nugent, and John Stossel.

Even more impressive is the reach of the campus speakers program. In 2008 alone, more than 500,000 individuals attended 631 lectures sponsored by Young America's Foundation. After giving one such lecture a few years ago, William F. Buckley, Jr., observed,

> On the matter of your lecture series, these are experiences of infinite impor-tance. As recently as last night, a 42-year old affluent influential conservative told an audience of 400 people that his orientation came from hearing such a talk (yes, by me) at Cornell when he was a sophomore. So I do hope that your important Foundation will be able to continue to support such appearances in the years ahead.[35]

With support from the Foundation, the number of students who have been in-fluenced by these campus lectures is uncountable.

More than thirty years ago, the Foundation established the National Conservative Student Conference, an intensive one-week program held in the Washington, DC area. Those attending the conference hear from many of the same speakers who participate in the campus lecture program as well as Members of Congress, political commentators and consultants, professors and authors. Each year, C-SPAN broadcasts a number of the conference sessions to more than 93 million cable and satellite television households across the nation. More than 400 college students attended the 2009 conference from 38 states. As one student from Cornell noted after attending the 2008 conference,

> Living in the Northeast and attending an Ivy League school has often left me feeling alienated, isolated, and alone in my beliefs. This conference changed all that. In essence, this conference has transformed me into an informed, convicted, and powerful warrior of the right.[36]

Since the first conference in 1979, countless college students have benefited from hearing from conservative leaders and participating in lively discussions on philosophy, history and contemporary political issues. Several of the student conference attendees have gone on to become published authors with works on the *New York Times* bestseller lists, including Malcolm Gladwell, Todd Buchholz, Peter Schweizer, Marc Thiessen, and Wynton Hall.[37]

Over the past twelve years, the Foundation has conducted a similar summer weeklong program in Washington for high school students. Some 130 students from 28 states took part in the 2009 Gratia Houghton Rinehart National High School Leadership Conference. An additional West Coast high school conference

---

35. Quoted in Young America's Foundation: *Libertas*, Spring 2008, p. 6.
36. Young America's Foundation 2008 Annual Report, p. 2.
37. Young America's Foundation 1980–81 Annual Report, p. 5. Among their published works are Malcolm Gladwell: *The Tipping Point* (Boston: Little, Brown & Company, 2000) and *Blink!* (Boston: Little, Brown & Company, 2005); Todd Buchholz: *New Ideas from Dead CEOs* (New York: Harper Collins, 2007); Peter Schweizer: *Friendly Spies* (New York: The Atlantic Monthly Press, 1993) and *Makers and Takers* (New York: Doubleday, 2008); Marc Thiessen: *Courting Disaster* (Washington, DC: Regnery Press, 2010); and Wynton Hall: *The Right Words* (Hoboken, NJ: John Wiley & Sons, 2007). Hall and Schweizer currently serve on the Foundation's Board of Directors.

is now held in Santa Barbara, California, during the spring of each year, with 75 students taking part in the 2009 weekend conference.

The National Journalism Center is another program in Washington, DC, sponsored by Young America's Foundation. Founded in 1977 by M. Stanton Evans, in 2001 it became a project of the Foundation. Since its origin, more than 1,700 alumni have graduated from NJC's twelve week training sessions. The 2009 summer session included 41 interns while another 36 took part in the fall and spring semester programs. Among the well-known authors who were NJC interns are John Barnes, Ann Coulter, John Fund, Maggie Gallagher, Malcolm Gladwell, Steven Hayward, and Richard Miniter.

Perhaps the most critical decision ever made by Young America's Foundation was to purchase Rancho del Cielo, from Nancy and Ronald Reagan in 1998. Preserving for future generations the 688-acre ranch outside of Santa Barbara ensured that what was "the Western White House" during Reagan's term of office would be a national treasure that personalized the accomplishments of the 40th President of the United States. No place reflects the principles and values of Ronald Reagan more than this simple, yet impressive, retreat where the President spent roughly one year of his Presidency.

Carol Dawson described her experiences in seeing the ranch as "a true inspiration to be there. It brought tears to my eyes to be in a place that I can only agree is 'sacred' at least to those of us who fought the battles in the 60s and 70s."[38] Allen Brandstater noted that "Reagan's living room bookshelves are still stocked with many of the same books which brought tens of thousands of young men and women into the conservative movement in the 1960s. I was one of them."[39] For Bill Saracino, visiting the ranch was

> . . . a moving experience that manages (at least it did for me) to combine the best of nostalgia and remembering a true giant with constant reminders of the IDEAS that fueled that great man. The table where the '81 tax cut was signed can be looked at as a piece of furniture—or as a reminder of what happened on that table, the reasons for it and the economic growth consequences. The library shelves full of 60s era Conservative Book Club books—all showing obvious signs that they were read many times—shout IDEAS . . . Other than the few western bios that I remember (perhaps a couple of Zane Grey as well), the books are all about IDEAS . . . our ideas.[40]

Over the past twelve years, Rancho del Cielo has been lovingly preserved and the grounds maintained and upgraded by the Foundation. It has become a site where conservatives come to be reminded of the contributions of Ronald Reagan to America and the principles on which he based his personal and political life.

Shortly after acquiring Rancho del Cielo, Young America's Foundation purchased a 22,000 square foot downtown Santa Barbara building located on State Street across from the busy railroad station. After extensive gutting, earthquake protection, and reconstruction, the Reagan Ranch Center opened in 2006 as a center for the Foundation's West Coast programs, offices for the Reagan Ranch staff, and an education center featuring interactive Reagan Ranch-related exhibits

---

38. Email to the author, August 25, 2009.
39. Email to the author, August 25, 2009.
40. Email to the author, August 25, 2009.

and artifacts. On display are paintings and memorabilia associated with President Reagan as well as the ranch table where Reagan signed the 1981 tax cut, the blue Jeep in which Reagan drove Mikhail Gorbachev around the ranch, and a large segment of the Berlin Wall donated by the citizens of Berlin, Germany. The Reagan Ranch Center is open to the public and has hosted elementary, secondary and college student groups as well as various conservative organizations. Prominent visitors to the Center include Mitt Romney, John Boehner, Jack Kemp, Robert Novak, Newt Gingrich and other leading conservatives.

Each month, a Reagan Ranch Roundtable luncheon is held at the center as an opportunity to introduce local area residents to the principles reflected in the career of Ronald Reagan. Many of these luncheon programs have been covered by C-SPAN. The center is also the site of a number of activism training seminars for college students, an annual weekend-long West Coast Leadership Conference in November, and the annual high school conference in the spring. A number of conservative organizations have also held leadership sessions at the Reagan Ranch Center, as it has become a focal point for conservative activity on the West Coast.

Several other projects are carried out by Young America's Foundation as they provide resources and training to college and high school students. Each year, the Foundation provides supportive materials to campus groups wishing to participate in Freedom Week activities to celebrate the fall of the Berlin Wall, the "9/11: Never Forget" project, "No More Che Day" and a reminder of the millions of victims of Communism. In 2009, 215 campuses took part in the "9/11: Never Forget" project while 115 commemorated the destruction of the Berlin Wall. Throughout the year, Young America's Foundation brings in various speakers for intern events on Capitol Hill, and hosts a student luncheon and other programs as a co-sponsor of the annual Conservative Political Action Conference. The Foundation also holds regional student conferences and seminars around the country; recent programs have been held in Chicago and Minneapolis.

Over the past thirty plus years, Young America's Foundation has grown and expanded into one of the major institutions of the contemporary conservative movement in America. With leadership that developed out of Young Americans for Freedom, the organization has continued to provide the resources, information, and training for high school and college students in the 21st century. Truly, as the Foundation proclaims, the conservative movement starts here.

The Legacy of Young Americans for Freedom

During the latter half of the 20th century, Young Americans for Freedom was a major contributor to the development of a conservative movement in the United States. The efforts of those who met in Sharon, Connecticut in September of 1960 resulted in the creation of grassroots cadres of dedicated supporters on campuses and in communities across the nation. Over the following years, these YAF chapters and members carried out numerous projects and programs to advance the principles elaborated in the organization's statement of principles. Just as importantly, their efforts helped to train, educate, and develop leaders for the emerging conservative movement. As time passed, it was these same individuals who helped to create many of the components of today's conservative community.

Still others went on to become public officials in appointed and elected positions, journalists and authors, teachers and professors, entrepreneurs and business leaders who have contributed to the making of modern America.

Young Americans for Freedom was born at a time when few identified with the term "conservative" and many associated it with unsavory opinions. To overcome this unpopularity and negative connotations, it took the power of both ideas and individuals. Through their efforts to boldly proclaim conservatism in hostile campus environments, the members of Young Americans for Freedom helped to advance the philosophy of conservatism. That philosophy took hold and became personified in William F. Buckley, Jr., Barry M. Goldwater, and Ronald Reagan, without whom conservatism would not have become the dominant philosophical and political identification it is today.[41] Despite the fact that the Democratic party controls the White House and both chambers of Congress in 2010, the American people identify more with the term conservative than any other. This is a drastic change from the early 1960s, when liberal was the more acceptable label. It is in this framework that the history of Young Americans for Freedom is in so many ways the history of the development of the conservative movement and of the growth in support for conservatism among the American people.

Despite the situation in which they found themselves, those young conservatives of the mid-1960s could retain their optimism for the future and turn that optimism into reality through dedication, preparation, hard work, and a continuing commitment to conservative principles. It is a different political environment that confronts young people today from that which faced the young men and women who created Young Americans for Freedom in 1960. Today, there is no single writer or popularizer of conservative philosophy to match the impact and influence of William F. Buckley, Jr. Of course, Buckley was much more than this, becoming a major influence in popular culture, as host of one of the longest-running television programs, as candidate for public office, and as motivator and instigator for many organizational components of today's conservative movement.

There is no single political figure who can compare with Barry Goldwater or, later in the century, Ronald Reagan. While others have attempted to pick up the mantle of leadership and commitment to principle, there was only one Barry Goldwater and definitely only one Ronald Reagan.[42] The American conservative movement in the 21st century continues to look for that leader who can approximate the broad appeal and the dedication to conservatism exemplified by Reagan.

Rather than one or two major publications, which served to focus and unify the conservative cause, there is a multitude of magazines and newspapers with ideological perspectives spanning across the many facets of conservatism and competing with Internet blogs and news sources as well as talk radio and cable television. Where the youth of 1960 created one umbrella organization for all who called themselves young conservatives, today there is a wide spectrum of

41. A summary of 16 surveys conducted by the Gallup organization during 2009 showed 40% of respondents choosing the label conservative, 36% selecting moderate, and 21% identifying with the term liberal. Almost exactly the same percentages were found in surveys conducted by the Pew Center during June–October 2009. For these numbers and a critical analysis of them, see E.J. Dionne, "Is America really becoming more conservative?," *Washington Post*, October 28, 2009.

42. For some, in the beginning years of this century, George W. Bush was viewed in these lights. As his administration proceeded to expand domestic programs, increase the Federal deficits, and face further difficulties in Iraq and Afghanistan, that hope died. See Lou Cannon and Carl M. Cannon: *Reagan's Disciple—George W. Bush's Troubled Quest for a Presidential Legacy* (New York: Public Affairs, 2008).

youth organizations and support groups to help promote values and perspectives from the Right.

Freedom, tradition, and anti-communism: these were the three pillars on which Young Americans for Freedom and the conservative movement of the 20th century was constructed. When young conservatives of the 1960s spoke of individual freedom, they saw the growth of the Federal government as perhaps the most serious domestic challenge to that freedom. After decades of expansion in size, scope and costs, the Federal government of today cannot be compared to that confronted by the earlier young conservatives. Moreover, there are now those who believe in a "big government conservatism" that would harness the power of the Federal government for what they perceive as conservative purposes.

The tradition advocated by those conservatives of mid-20th century America would not be recognizable to many young conservatives today. Since that time, our country has experienced an upheaval in personal relationships, societal mores, and patterns of acceptable behavior. Those who emphasized individual freedom may have seen it blossom in contemporary America but those changes brought with them a new populism, a reaction quite different from that promoted by the advocates of tradition.

While there remain repressive regimes still claiming an adherence to Marxism-Leninism, the international Communist conspiracy is no longer a serious threat to the Free World. There is no longer an Iron Curtain separating "us" from "them." Today, our freedom and security are challenged by an ideological fanaticism cloaked in religion and spread across ethnic and geographic boundaries.

It is now the 21st century and new challenges and opportunities confront the youth of America. Conservatism, however defined, is much more accepted and valued by Americans today. Thanks to the efforts of Young Americans for Freedom and those who were nurtured by it, there are ample resources available to assist today's young conservatives. It is their turn and their time to assume leadership in the conservative movement and in American society. They, too, like their predecessors, are concerned about the future of America and are committed to bringing about positive change. The story of Young Americans for Freedom is one that shows a dedication to principle can indeed bring about change. Today's young conservatives have a responsibility and an opportunity to do the same.

The torch of freedom has been passed. For those who benefited from their involvement in Young Americans for Freedom during the last century, they have a continuing responsibility to nurture and mentor the young conservatives of today and contribute the needed financial support for those organizations that provide the support mechanism they received when they were young Americans for freedom.

The Sharon Statement

Adopted in conference at Sharon, Connecticut
September 9–11, 1960.

In This Time of moral and political crisis, it is the responsibility of the youth of America to affirm certain eternal truths.

We, as young conservatives, believe:

That foremost among the transcendent values is the individual's use of his God-given free will, whence derives his right to be free from the restrictions of arbitrary force;

That liberty is indivisible, and that political freedom cannot long exist without economic freedom;

That the purposes of government are to protect these freedoms through the preservation of internal order, the provision of national defense, and the administration of justice;

That when government ventures beyond these rightful functions, it accumulates power which tends to diminish order and liberty;

That the Constitution of the United States is the best arrangement yet devised for empowering government to fulfill its proper role, while restraining it from the concentration and abuse of power;

That the genius of the Constitution—the division of powers—is summed up in the clause which reserves primacy to the several states, or to the people, in those spheres not specifically delegated to the Federal Government;

That the market economy, allocating resources by the free play of supply and demand, is the single economic system compatible with the requirements of personal freedom and constitutional government, and that it is at the same time the most productive supplier of human needs;

That when government interferes with the work of the market economy, it tends to reduce the moral and physical strength of the nation; that when it takes from one man to bestow on another, it diminishes the incentive of the first, the integrity of the second, and the moral autonomy of both;

That we will be free only so long as the national sovereignty of the United States is secure; that history shows periods of freedom are rare, and can exist only when free citizens concertedly defend their rights against all enemies;

That the forces of international Communism are, at present, the greatest single threat to these liberties;

That the United States should stress victory over, rather than coexistence with, this menace; and

That American foreign policy must be judged by this criterion: does it serve the just interests of the United States?

A Note on Sources

One major obstacle in attempting to tell the story of Young Americans for Freedom is the lack of any central depository or archives containing documents, memoranda, correspondence, and publications from the organization's history. This is particularly important when attempting to verify facts, as opposed to opinions, surrounding events in the now-distant past. Fortunately, some of those who were involved in YAF's founding and early years did retain a wealth of documents and these have been essential in assembling *A Generation Awakes*.

I am grateful especially to William A. Rusher for access to his papers at the Library of Congress. Equally important was the permission of Christopher Buckley, who allowed access to his father's papers at Sterling Library, Yale University and encouraged me in this endeavor. The one individual active in the organization who has retained the most documentation from YAF's history is Jameson Campaigne, Jr. I am indebted to him for allowing me to spend several days going through nine large containers of material. Once catalogued and archived, Campaigne's collection will constitute the closest there is to a documentary history of Young Americans for Freedom. There are too many former YAF members who provided documentation to list them all here and most are cited in the notes for each chapter. My thanks go to Michael Centanni, J. Fred Coldren, Richard Delgaudio, Tom DeWeese, Lawrence King, James Lacy, Tom Lizardo, Cathy O'Hara Malkovich, Deroy Murdock, Sergio Picchio, Roger Ream, Eric Rohrbach, Michael Sanera, Herb Stupp, Randal C. Teague, and Michael Thompson for providing me with documentary material of particular value in covering events and projects not otherwise known to me.

The search for documents concerning Young Americans for Freedom went beyond the sources listed above to a number of archives across the country. At the Library of Congress I was able to access the papers of Herbert A. Philbrick in addition to those of Bill Rusher. The Hoover Institution at Stanford University contained the most collections related to YAF, including the papers of Marvin Liebman, Henry Regnery, Walter Judd, Patrick Dowd, and David Walter. At the Center for American History at the University of Texas I was able to review Stephen Shadegg's material concerning his relationship with Barry Goldwater. The John F. Kennedy Presidential Library and the Lyndon Baines Johnson Presidential Library contained documentation of YAF efforts during the 1960s, showing also how closely the two administrations followed the activities of these young conservatives. There were also some surprising sources of much YAF material, including among the Group Research, Inc. Archives at Columbia University and the Hall-Hoag Collection at John Hay Library, Brown University. The Columbia University Archives provided valuable materials surrounding various student efforts against the leftist disruptions on that campus in the late 1960s. The Pusey Library of Harvard University provided archived materials on YAF campus efforts in the 1960s and 1970s.

I was fortunate to have access to several unpublished papers, theses, and dissertations, all of which are cited at the appropriate sections in the text. For providing copies of their works or otherwise assisting in locating them, my sincere thanks to Douglas Caddy, Jameson Campaigne, Matthew Dallek, Ronald Docksai, Bob McDonald, Lisa McGurr, Seth Offenbach, and Jonathan Schoenwald. Without these sources of information, the current work would be even more incomplete. Still other unpublished works, while not specifically noted in the text, provided valuable background and context. Among published sources, Young Americans for Freedom has been the subject, directly or indirectly, of numerous magazine and journal articles as well as books. Rather than list them all here, the reader can find such source material in the notes at the appropriate section of the text. I am most grateful to those who completed the YAF alumni survey as well as Barry M. Goldwater, Jr., whose letter of encouragement accompanied the request for completion of the survey.

No work such as this is ever complete. Due to space limitations, much has had to be cut, overlooked, or only briefly discussed. Eliminated were some fascinating personal recollections from YAF's history. Important source material may have been missed or only surface after publication. It is my hope that those who possess additional documentation relating to Young Americans for Freedom will make it available and that sometime in the near future, a suitable depository of material will be found. Such an effort would facilitate the process for future historians of the American conservative movement in the 20th century and the critical role played in it by Young Americans for Freedom.

Additional Information and Resources

It was impossible to include here much of the information that may be of interest to YAF alumni and others researching the conservative movement in the latter half of the 20th century. For those interested in more historial information on Young Americans for Freedom, the following lists are available on the web site of Young America's Foundation— http://yaf50.yaf.org :

1. Attendees—Sharon Conference, Sharon, Connecticut, September 10–11, 1960
2. National Directors of Young Americans for Freedom with Years on Board of Directors: 1960–1994
3. State Chairmen of Young Americans for Freedom: 1960–1994
4. *In Memoriam*
5. Respondees to 2008 YAF Alumni Survey
6. Individuals interviewed for *A Generation Awakes*
7. Bibliographical Sources on Young Americans for Freedom

Index

Key:
IM = *In Memoriam*
SH = Attendees at the Sharon Conference, September 1960
ND = National Directors of Young Americans for Freedom
SC = State Chairmen

Aaron, Thomas J.[SC]
Abell, Richard[ND, SC] 400, 403, 423, 426, 504
Abely, William[SC] 402
Abernethy, John[ND] 396, 401, 432, 437
Abraham, E. Spencer 533
Abramov (Thorburn), Judith 138, 167, 307, 321, 327
Abrams, Elliott 245
Abstine, James[ND, SH] 23, 29, 52, 96
Accuracy in Academia 474, 509
Accuracy in Media 491
Acerbo, Samuel 520
Ackel, Fred 123
Adair, Ross 177
Adamcik, Bryan 521
Adams (Ryskind), J'Aime 5, 36
Adams, Kurt 467
Adams, Paul 328
Adams, Robert Caruthers[SH]
Adcock, David[ND, SC] 163, 235, 357, 517
Adoula, Cyrille 72
Agee, Mark[SC] 392
Agness, Karin 532
Agnew, Spiro T. 242, 316, 329, 331, 339, 345–350, 352, 359, 377, 407
Agresto, John 516–517
Alden, John T.[SC]
Aldridge, Filmore[SC, ND, IM] 357, 375
Alexander, Gerard 448, 493, 518
Alito, Samuel 533
Allen, David 59, 60
Allen, Richard[ND, SC] 138, 140, 150, 154
Allen, Richard V. 138, 152–153
Allen, Steven J.[SC]
Allen, William 455, 460
Aller, Douglas[SC]
Allison, Wick 135, 509
Allwein, Carole 301
Altham, James[SC] 344, 351, 370–371
Althouse, David[SC]
Amberg, Tom 515
Ament, Kurt 364
America's Political Action Committee 320
America's Survival, Inc. 491
American Conservative Union 34–35, 106, 111, 132–133, 139, 157, 340, 349, 489, 514
American Enterprise Institute 493
American Foreign Policy Council 491
American Independent Party 361–362
American Legislative Exchange Council 133, 223, 420, 489
American Party 361
American Policy Center 490
American Tax Reduction Movement 507
American Values 490
Americanism Educational League 497
Americans for Democratic Action 53, 59, 61, 84, 132, 329, 403

Americans for Judd for Vice President 20
Amidon, David 518
Amshoff, Ted[IM]
Anarchist Caucus 258, 261, 263–265, 267, 269–270, 275
Anderson, Alice 305, 396
Anderson, Annelise 168, 340, 348, 362, 386
Anderson, Joel 501
Anderson, John 105, 424
Anderson, Mark[SC]
Anderson, Martin 168, 340, 348, 362, 386
Anderson, Thomas 361
Anderson, William[SC]
Andre, Fred 66
Andrew, John 2, 15, 20–21, 25, 27–28, 30, 39, 43, 46, 59–60, 72, 84, 87, 91, 95, 121, 161–162, 184, 186–187, 189, 200, 269, 297–298, 476
Andrews, Helena 532
Andrews, Richard[SC] 314
Andrews, T. Coleman, III 387, 523
Antonelli, Lou 392
Antonovich, Mike 171, 371
Antonsanti, Luis[SC]
Antosh, Steve[SC] 392, 398, 416, 496
Aptheker, Bettina 208, 212
Archer, Bill 157, 326, 342–343
Archibald, George[SC] 507
Arico, Dan 226, 235
Armey, Dick 493
Armstrong, Bill 355
Armstrong, Craig[SC]
Armstrong, Karl 242
Armstrong, Sara[ND, SC] 465
Ashbrook, John 81, 109, 140, 153, 178, 341, 349–353, 357, 361, 363, 368–369, 372, 389
Ashburn, Frank 7, 8
Ashcroft, John 312, 537
Ashkinaze, Alan[ND] 428, 437, 440–442, 446, 479, 525
Associated Student Governments of the USA 84
Atanasio, Paul 524
Atlas Society 495–496
Attaway, Andrew 510
Atwood, Thomas 496
Ayers, Bill 210
Baadsgaard, Kevin[SC]
Babler, Scott[SC]
Baer, Timothy[SC] 314, 357
Bain, Myrna[IM] 63–64, 111, 520, 523
Baker, Bill 500
Baker, Brent 493
Baker, Buddy 508
Baker, Howard 401
Baker, James, III 395, 438
Bakke, Alan 391–392, 403
Baldacchino, Joseph[SC] 326, 495–496
Baldassarre, Robert D.[SC]
Baldwin, James 230

NATIONAL INSTITUTE SOCIAL SERVICES LIBRARY
NO. 35

ENDS AND MEANS IN SOCIAL WORK

National Institute Social Services Library

Ends and Means in
Social Work

The Development and Outcome of a
Case Review System for Social Workers

E. MATILDA GOLDBERG

and

R. WILLIAM WARBURTON

London
GEORGE ALLEN & UNWIN
Boston   Sydney

First published in 1979

GEORGE ALLEN & UNWIN LTD
40 Museum Street, London WC1A 1LU

© E. Matilda Goldberg and R. William Warburton, 1979

British Library Cataloguing in Publication Data

Goldberg, Elsa Matilda
   Ends and means in social work. – (National
Institute for Social Work Training. Social services
library; no. 35).
   1. Social service – England
   I. Title II. Warburton, R William III. Series
   361'.942   HV245

ISBN 0–04–360053–0
ISBN 0–04–360054–9 Pbk

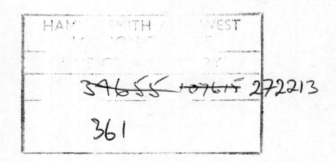
Phototypeset in V.I.P. Times by Western Printing Services Ltd, Bristol and
printed in Great Britain by Billing & Sons Ltd, Guildford, London and Worcester

CONTENTS

ACKNOWLEDGEMENTS

————◆————

Many people have contributed to the research discussed in this book, as the references to previous publications indicate. David Fruin was mainly responsible for the design of the case review form and developed the computer programme for the system. Ann Glampson carried out the consumer studies and June Neill the social worker studies. Brendan McGuinness made an imaginative contribution to the area analysis by using the statistical method of cluster analysis. Rosemary Lewin, Hemlatta Shah and Ann McKenzie exhibited exemplary patience in typing and retyping the manuscript, and they made many helpful suggestions.

The research was financially supported by the DHSS, and we want to express our special thanks for his helpfulness and support throughout to our liaison officer, Robin Guthrie, now director elect of the Joseph Rowntree Memorial Trust. We also gratefully acknowledge the permission given by the *British Journal of Social Work* to incorporate in this book much of the material which appeared in that journal as a sequence of three articles on 'Accountability in social work'.

Last but not least we want to offer our thanks to the director of social services, area officer, team leaders and field workers concerned, without whose active collaboration and lively criticism this work could never have been accomplished.

EMG
RWW

April 1979

INTRODUCTION

This book has arisen from a series of surveys and action studies carried out in a social services department of a town in southern England during the early and mid-seventies shortly after the reorganisation of the local authority personal social services. This reorganisation integrated into one department the hitherto separate services responsible for the social care of the disabled and elderly, children and the mentally disordered. Throughout the book we will call this town Seatown.

Our aims were first to find out what the clients thought of, and expected from, the newly reorganised social services, and how the social workers saw the changes and their new responsibilities. These views were to be fed back to those delivering the services and those responsible for their direction and management. Secondly, we wanted to discover how social work skills and other resources were used to meet different client needs. Thirdly, we wanted to enable social workers to become more explicit about both the means and ends of their activities.

In the following chapters, after considering social work in the 1970s, we give an account of the clients' and social workers' attitudes and expectations shortly after the reorganisation of the personal social services and three years later. The task of establishing who the people were who passed the threshold of an area office of a social services department, and what happened to them, proved to be much more difficult than we had anticipated. The creation of instruments capable of recording these events reliably as a process which related means and ends of social work became an action project in itself. Thus the main part of the book is devoted to describing the development of a monitoring tool called the Case Review System (CRS), and to an account of what the CRS data revealed about one year's referrals to an area office and their fate during the subsequent twelve months. Similarly, we explored the problems the long-term clientele presented to the social workers during the same period, how these problems were approached, with what aims in mind, and with what results.

In our concluding discussion we use the evidence emerging from the use of the CRS to suggest tentative principles for the allocation of social work and social service tasks, and the deployment of different types of skill in the fieldwork of an area office.

Chapter 1

SOCIAL WORK IN THE 1970s –
THE NEED FOR ACCOUNTABILITY

In the 1960s most professional social work was casework directed towards the amelioration of psycho-social problems of individuals and families. Moreover, social work was a relatively small-scale enterprise, and specialised social workers were dealing with the social needs of fairly well-defined client groups. Since the reorganisation of the social services in 1971 following the Seebohm Report (1968), social work has become big business. The boundaries are ever extending. They range from psychotherapy to social planning.

Although evidence is difficult to come by, it is fairly certain that the volume of referrals in the integrated social services departments is greater than the sum of referrals to the three separate Health, Welfare, and Children's Departments before reorganisation. Evidence does exist that in many local authority social services departments the number of referrals has substantially increased since integration. With these demands goes a growing investment of resources, both absolute and proportional, in the personal social services. While public expenditure has risen in constant prices by 5 per cent between 1972 and 1977 (from £51,577 million to £54,320 million), the expenditure on the personal social services has risen by 33 per cent (from £836 million to £1,110 million) (HM Treasury, 1978). However, we need to remember that this expenditure started from a very small base constituting only 1·6 per cent of all public expenditure in 1973, rising to 2 per cent in 1977. Compared with other social services, for every £1 spent on the personal social services, £5 was spent on health, and £6·50 on education in 1975 (Central Statistical Office, 1976).

The rise in money expenditure is mirrored in an increase in provision of services. Nearly 50 per cent more people – most of them elderly – received home help services in 1976 compared with the early 1970s, and 60 per cent more received meals-on-wheels. The number of children received into care had risen by 14 per cent, and the number of those registered as physically handicapped had more than doubled. The number of places in residential homes provided by local authorities had increased by 9 per cent.

This expansion in provision has been accompanied by an increase in staff which has been most marked in those facilities which started from very low base lines, such as day care and hostels for the mentally handicapped. The social work staff, with whom we shall be mostly concerned, increased by 11 per cent, from 21,680 in 1974 to 23,971 in 1976 (DHSS, 1977).

Yet with the increasing expenditure and the widening demands made on the services, ranging from simple requests for information to the most intractable problems our society is capable of producing, there has been a growing scepticism about the effectiveness of these services. This scepticism arises from three main sources: research, scandals and socio-political ideologies.

Let us examine these three sources of scepticism in turn. There has been serious criticism of social casework, which began in Britain with the almost forgotten onslaught by Barbara Wootton in the late 1950s (Wootton, 1959). Some of her indictments – deeply resented and contested by the social work profession at the time – seem prophetic in view of very recent developments towards more modest and down-to-earth goals in social work. For example, she attacked the social worker's conviction that 'she can understand other people better than they understand themselves' (p. 293), and the social worker's duty to penetrate below what is called the presenting problem. 'So we pass out of the frying pan of charitable condescension into the no-less condescending fire – or rather cool detachment – of superior psychological insight' (p. 293). 'If she uses a request for practical help as an opportunity to intrude into other aspects of her client's life, she does so, or should do so, at her peril' (p. 295).

However, the notions which most affronted caseworkers in the late 1950s were that of the social worker as an expert 'middle man' helping to mobilise facilities within the complex network of state and voluntary services to suit the requirements of particular individuals, and that of the poor man's secretary who could provide acceptable substitutes for those services which the rich can afford to buy. In our concluding chapter we shall discuss recent developments which approximate both these roles.

Research studies carried out in the 1960s mainly in the USA (Meyer, Borgatta and Jones, 1965; Brown [ed.], 1968; Mullen, Chazin and Feldstein, 1970; Fischer, 1973) have cast much doubt on the effectiveness and appropriateness of casework as the main method of intervention, particularly in situations of basic social and economic deprivation which require practical assistance, social reform and social action for their resolution. The widely accepted conclusion is that social work with individuals and families, however good and caring, cannot hope to achieve substantial improvements in social functioning in the absence of basic social provision, such as sufficient money, housing, education, employment opportunities, and so on. A number of investigations, and especially Reid and Shyne's experimental study into brief and extended casework (1969), have called into question the belief in the invariable superiority of long-term intensive casework in dealing with problems of family relationships. In this country the melancholy results of the probation experiment in long-term intensive casework with young delinquents point in a similar direction (Folkard, Smith and Smith, 1976).

Other studies (Brown [ed.], 1968; Davies, M., 1969; National Institute for Social Work, unpublished) suggest that social workers are most successful with those clients who apparently need least help. That is to say, greatest improvement tends to occur in the low-risk groups receiving a limited amount of help, and deterioration is most likely among those clients with the severest problems despite a massive amount of social work input. The issues raised by these findings are:

(1) that social workers take on, or are forced to take on, situations which are not amenable to the social work methods employed;
(2) that there might be in operation a law of diminishing returns, and that by continuing social work over long periods of time in an open-ended, non-specific way, certain behaviour patterns may be unwittingly reinforced, dependencies induced, and a greater awareness of underlying problems encouraged for which there do not appear to be any solutions (Reid and Shyne, 1969);
(3) that, by concentrating their efforts on 'moderately severe' problems, social workers could possibly use their skills to the greater benefit of their clients.

We will return to these issues in the concluding discussion after we have considered some of the evidence arising from our consumer studies and the monitoring exercise in one area office.

A few tentative positive findings have also emerged, namely that training and resulting skills of social workers are associated with more successful outcomes in work with the elderly in both the material and non-material spheres, compared with the intervention by untrained social workers (Goldberg, Mortimer and Williams, 1970). A recent field experiment of social work in prison (Shaw, 1974; Sinclair, Shaw and Troop, 1974) indicates that clients with a high degree of introversion benefit more from counselling than extrovert types of clients. In addition, research in the field of behaviour modification suggests that personality variables such as introversion/extroversion (Eysenck, 1957) influence the response to some forms of intervention.

Finally, suggestions are arising, both from the residential and social casework field (Reid, 1967; Mullen, 1969; Sinclair, 1971) that the personality and style of the key worker, be it the warden of a hostel or the fieldworker, is a very important and relatively unchanging ingredient which is not adapted as much as had been supposed to the differing needs of different types of clients. Thus careful matching of clients and care-givers warrants more attention and systematic exploration.

All the findings quoted so far are bedevilled by the fact that much of the evaluative experimental research on the effectiveness of social work has been carried out in a specific situation; hardly any of these studies have been replicated, which is particularly important in experiments that show positive outcomes (Reid, 1974). Operational definitions of inputs and outcomes are as yet too general so that we are still very uncertain about the association – let alone any causal relationships – between type of problem situation, type of social work input and specific outcome. Fur-thermore, no generally accepted terms and categories exist to describe different problem situations and different components of the social-intervention process which social workers could adopt to provide more systematic evidence about their inputs in different problem situations and their outcomes.

The next source of growing unease about social work is the accelerating number of scandals mainly related to injury and deaths of children caused by battering parents as manifested in the Colwell Report (1974) and followed since by a number of similar inquiries. Such scandals notoriously arise in extreme situations, and although they can highlight gross deficiencies and lead to significant reforms (for example, the Curtis Report, 1946, and the Children Act of 1948), they are hardly ever representative of the wide variations in current practice. However, the recent spate of public inquiries raises questions whether current practices and their monitoring devices need a thorough overhaul, or whether the community's expectations of social workers have become unrealistic in terms of the problems they are supposed to solve having regard to the skills, knowledge and resources that are at their disposal.

The scepticism with which certain political and sociological ideologies view social work is important, if only to remind us that much social work effort is directed towards problems to which it can make at best only a marginal contribution and which may be more capable of solution by collective action on a much broader scale (Heraud, 1973; Leonard, 1975). On the other hand, even in a more compassionate society, enjoy-ing a more equitable distribution of economic resources and political power, such phenomena as severe mental and physical handicap, difficul-ties in interpersonal relationships, frailty in old age, and so on, are likely to persist for the foreseeable future and call for some kind of personalised social intervention. It is surely the height of naïvety to postulate that 'in the absence of oppression, human beings will, due to their basic nature or soul, which is preservative of themselves and their species, live in har-mony with each other' (Steiner, 1974).

The conclusion we draw from this discussion is that both trends – the growing demands on the personal social services and the lack of evidence of their differential effects – point to the need for social workers to develop more accurate and informative ways of accounting for their efforts in their ordinary day-to-day activities. In addition, the constant demands for more resources make accountability as to how the present resources are being used all the more urgent.

Chapter 2

THE VASTNESS AND VAGUENESS OF THE SOCIAL WORK TASK

A general haziness and indeterminateness surround the whole concept of social work and social services, so that even now in the late 1970s, some fifty years after the introduction of systematic training for social workers, colleagues in related professions – doctors, nurses, teachers – often ask in exasperation: 'But what do they do?' Since the span of social work activities is so broad and since many problems landing in the huge final dustbin of the social services departments are well nigh insoluble at present, this blurred image of social work is explicable. Recently the British Association of Social Workers (BASW, 1977) has made an attempt to delineate the 'social work task' by trying to distinguish those roles which require professional social work expertise from social service and administrative roles by using such criteria as client vulnerability, complexity of case situation and the weightiness of the decisions to be made. However useful such a theoretical exercise may be, it does not remove the need for operationally based descriptions of tasks to be performed and skills needed. Neill's social worker studies in Seatown and Stevenson's more extensive studies in thirty-one area offices are building up a picture of social work tasks as perceived and described by the social workers (Neill *et al.*, 1973; Neill, Warburton and McGuinness, 1976; Stevenson and Parsloe, 1978); there are also some studies (Mayer and Timms, 1970; McKay, Goldberg and Fruin, 1973; Rees, 1974; Glampson and Goldberg, 1976) of the clients' perceptions. But what we lack so far is documentation of what actually happens in different circumstances and problem situations. The monitoring exercises to be described in later chapters are small beginnings in this direction.

Meanwhile the indeterminate boundaries of social work and the social services generally do not excuse social workers from becoming more explicit about the problems they are trying to tackle with, or on behalf of, their clients, the specific goals they set themselves and the expertise and resources required to attain these objectives. Many social workers shy away from stating specific problems to be tackled and aims to be pursued, putting them on the table as it were for both client and social worker to examine, agree or argue about. Instead some social workers prefer an implicit, non-verbal understanding which they assume is shared by the client. Such an assumed understanding can easily lead to misperceptions between social workers and clients, documented vividly in several research studies (Mayer and Timms, 1970; McKay, Goldberg and Fruin, 1973; Rees, 1974). Goals are often perceived and stated in vague, rather general terms: 'improved social functioning', or in terms that beg the question of means and ends, e.g. 'support'. Recent exploratory research in what is called the task-centred approach and in the field of behaviour modification suggests that less misunderstanding and a greater sense of achievement for both client and worker ensues if aims are specific (preferably agreed between social worker and client), relatively modest and capable of achievement (Reid and Epstein, 1972; Goldberg, Walker and Robinson, 1977; Reid and Epstein [eds], 1977).

It is conceded, of course, that some situations are so complex that it is difficult to know where to begin and where to go. Nor are social work aims in the social services always associated with change in the short run. For example, the aim in the case of a child happily settled in a foster home or of an old arthritic lady well supported by domiciliary services and social contacts may be the maintenance of a reasonable equilibrium. Nor can there always be agreement about the aims of intervention between client and social worker, since in a statutory setting the social worker is often called in without the express consent of the client and has to exercise a protective or control function. But here again, greater clarity and honesty about aims and functions of the intervention may help to demystify the comings and goings of social workers whose presence is imposed on the client.

We also realise that in the present welter of problems bombarding large, general social services departments, it is becoming more, rather than less, difficult to arrive at differentiated assessments of problem situations, to plan specific intervention strategies and to determine the level of expertise required. Indeed, the intake worker has to be a super jack-of-all-trades, expected to be knowledgeable about the terrified young mother who has hit her nine-month-old baby; the boy who has run away from a tight, overprotective home; the adolescent drug user who lands on his relatives on returning from Morocco; the marital complexities in a family where one partner is mentally ill; the unpaid bills and eviction order of a problem family; the guilt and doubt of parents who are at the end of their tether coping with a severely mentally handicapped child at home; the wife who refuses to have her husband home again after a severe stroke; the lonely, old, frail lady whose only son has married and who has nothing left to live for in her large empty house. These examples represent a small sample of problem situations taken more or less at random as they were encountered in recent contacts with social workers in social services departments. We shall discuss the issues arising from the enormous heterogeneity of problems presented to social workers in later chapters.

Yet another trend in demands on social work skills is discernible. While in the recent past a large proportion of social workers could hope to be involved in direct service or counselling contact with their clients, they now have to take on new roles as managers allocating resources, as enablers to social work aides, volunteers, neighbourhood groups and as community workers thinking in terms of 'at risk' groups rather than individual clients. These new roles, as well as the issues of accountability discussed earlier, make it imperative that social workers, particularly in middle and top management, should have the tools with which to carry out these new tasks, for example adequate information and record systems or comprehensive and updated indexes of resources in their area.

Social work education and the slender body of validated social work knowledge have not been able to keep pace with these widening and changing demands made on social workers so as to equip them for these varied and enlarged functions. The basic education of social workers is mainly in the humanities and an important part of their professional training is directed towards achieving some insight into their own and other people's emotional and cultural biases. Problems of measurement or the search for objective evidence in support of the assumptions on which social work intervention is based do not occupy a central place in the social work curriculum in Britain. Putting people into categories and quantifying phenomena, which in part consist of subjective experiences, is at variance with the social worker's belief in the uniqueness of each individual experience and the need to individualise problems in order to help people in their difficulties. Some social workers feel that social work is an art based on intuition and feelings and the ever-changing dynamics of a therapeutic relationship which are not amenable to scientific analysis.

Some people suggest that the integrated or unitary approach to social work (Pincus and Minahan, 1973; Specht and Vickery, 1977) which provides a framework for the different knowledge bases and responses relevant to different kinds of problem situations, is capable of wielding into a coherent whole the values, the underlying theories, the practice wisdom and the bits of empirically tested knowledge which make up social work. Experience will tell whether we are as yet ready to erect such an edifice and make use of it. At present some of the foundations needed for this structure, for instance social epidemiology (i.e. the study of the health and social well-being of populations in relation to their environment and ways of living) and aetiology (the establishment of causal relationships) seem distinctly weak.

THE RESEARCH TASK

Where should a practice-oriented social work researcher put his emphasis when so many questions clamour for answers? At least six areas suggest themselves:

(1) The tasks to be performed by those who man the social services will have to be systematically re-examined.

(2) The skills needed to perform these tasks will have to be defined and tested.

(3) Thought and research need to be devoted to the professional's accountability to individual clients and to the community (Klein, 1973). Studies of client expectations and satisfactions will be a first step in making social work more relevant and useful to clients.

(4) Systematic record and review systems need to be developed to provide basic information about social worker activities and their effects on different client groups and in order to provide monitoring, educational and planning tools.

(5) Studies about the relative costs of various forms of social services will have to be undertaken.

(6) Lastly, carefully controlled experimental studies will have to be mounted to test the client's and the caregiver's evaluation of the outcome of social work, using criteria that are meaningful to both clients and social workers. Such studies need to be concerned with effectiveness – Is the client better off?, as well as efficiency – At what cost?

It will be noted that experimental studies are put last. This is deliberate. Until we know what it is we are evaluating and can formulate relevant descriptive categories for types of clients, problems, social work/service inputs and desired objectives there is very little point in mounting such experimental studies.

Hence, our studies concentrated first on the clients' and social workers' perspectives of the newly organised social services and their effects, and secondly, on the creation of systematic record and review systems which would enable social workers to establish who their clients are, what problems they were trying to tackle, by what means and with what objectives in mind. At the same time by feeding back the resulting information we tried to encourage a climate of critical evaluation and readiness for change in practice.

Since much of the work we intended to do was of an exploratory and developmental nature it depended for its success on close collaboration with the staff in our location. The choice of a medium-sized town on the south coast of England was determined by several factors: its demography, which resembled the national average in age distribution, social class composition, housing, and so on. It was thus neither a deprived inner-city area nor a sedate cathedral town. In 1975, Seatown's population exceeded 200,000. It is a fairly typical English town with roughly a quarter of the population aged under 15 and 13 per cent aged 65 or over. The area office in which our main study was carried out serves the largest of Seatown's social work areas with a population of approximately 73,000. The demographic structure of the population, and the housing and other environmental features of the area are in most respects representative of the town.

In addition, Seatown was within reasonable travelling distance from London where the Research Unit was located. It had an enthusiastic Director of Social Services who welcomed the kind of exploratory action-oriented research we wished to undertake. Finally, the Department was reasonably well staffed, somewhat above the staffing norms in the country, so that the demands that the research team inevitably had to make on the time of the social workers would not cause undue hardship to them or their clients.

Chapter 3

━━━◆━━━

SOCIAL WORKER AND CONSUMER PERSPECTIVES

The exploration of the consumers' and the caregivers' views is an essential preliminary when attempting to evaluate the working of the personal social services, but particularly at a time when they are being cast into a new pattern. The subjective perspectives of both social workers and consumers provided an important backcloth to the subsequent action studies in which the social workers monitored what they were actually doing with and for their clients. Ideally one would want to explore client and social worker perceptions in relation to the same case situation and such studies have recently been attempted (Goldberg, Walker and Robinson, 1977; Butler, Bow and Gibbons, 1978; Sainsbury and Nixon, 1978). But as our investigations were the first forays into consumers' and social workers' views in the newly reorganised social services, it was essential to guarantee complete anonymity and confidentiality to both clients and social workers without arousing the remotest suspicion that any client's or social worker's opinion could be divulged to the other participant in an individual case. Since we obtained the views of a representative sample of consumers of the Social Services Department and of all the area-based fieldworkers in Seatown we were able to make group comparisons on certain general topics presented to both social workers and consumers. The differences in perspective between social workers and clients revealed by these comparisons are highly instructive and show that the social workers were inclined to undervalue their contribution to the welfare of their clients.

The attitudes of a random sample of 300 consumers of the Social Services Department in Seatown, and of all the area-based social workers, were studied at two points in time – in 1972 soon after the integration of the services and the establishment of area offices, and again in 1975 to see what changes, if any, had occurred during this vital period of reshaping the personal social services (McKay, Goldberg and Fruin, 1973; Neill *et al.*, 1973; Glampson and Goldberg, 1976; Neill, Warburton and McGuinness, 1976).[1]

THE SOCIAL WORKERS

The early studies took place only three months after the integration of the hitherto separate children's welfare and mental health services. From the social workers, we wanted to discover what their perceptions were of the size and type of their caseloads, the time pressures they experienced, the areas of new knowledge they felt they needed, and the aspects of integration they found difficult or rewarding. We also wanted to learn how they perceived their clients' expectations, and their likes and dislikes about the service.

The early 1970s were generally a period of great restlessness and mobility among social workers. Many senior jobs became available to those who were professionally trained, and opportunities for promotion seemed almost limitless in the fast-expanding, reorganised social services. Thus in 1972 staff turnover was very high: half of the seventy area-based social workers intended to leave their job within two years. Over half the workers felt under considerable or severe time pressure which was only partly related to the current workload. Unsorted caseloads, unclear goals for social work intervention, lack of criteria for assessment, allocation and for closure, were mentioned as reasons for the workers' feelings of pressure as much as the amount of work to be done. The merging of three separate departments had made social workers aware of persistent gaps in services which they had previously assumed were filled by other departments. Now there was no escape from these deficiencies and this too caused a feeling of pressure. In these early days the caseloads of the social workers were still highly specialised and most thought that specialisation would continue indefinitely and considered this to be desirable. Not only was much doubt and resistance expressed towards giving up specialism but considerable confusion reigned about terms like 'generic', 'specialist', 'intensive casework'.

One of the most striking findings in the study was the social workers' marked preference for work with family problems and children. Yet the highest proportion of the Department's clientele consisted of the physically disabled and the elderly for whom the least preference was expressed. Work with the elderly was perceived as requiring practical services and surveillance. This was borne out by the consumer study in which the old respondents stated that they had mainly received practical services, while the younger clients also described receiving what might be termed 'casework'. These views were further confirmed by the case review data as we shall see later.

Nearly two-thirds of the staff thought that integration of the personal social services had, in general, been a good thing and most felt that understanding and co-operation between different types of worker had improved. The majority of the social workers considered that most other aspects of the service had deteriorated or had remained the same. One telling quote sums up these feelings:

> There has been a decline in services that we have spent years in struggling to improve. The major frustrations are the feelings that senior management staff appear to know very little about managing – this is a national feeling not just a local one. The clamouring for higher salaries and top positions has been very disillusioning. The 'better deal for the clients' is rarely spoken of these days (qualified social worker in her mid-30s).

Most of these social workers also thought that staff morale was lower and associated this with less satisfactory liaison between central administrative staff and the area social workers, and confusion in administrative procedures.

> The gap between the director, assistant directors, social services committee and social workers has grown since the social work department became integrated. We are now unable to comment on suggestions about organising and planning to top level directly. Items need to go through more levels than before. Whatever the level of communication upwards is, communication coming down is very poor, on paper, and often arrives long after the event has happened because documents take so long to be circulated. At times one feels almost non-existent. The personal contact and involvement with management which did so much to keep up morale has been lost.

When asked what they thought about their clients' satisfaction with the Department, most of the social workers were unsure, while the clients' feelings were distinctly positive: two-thirds of the clients in the consumer study expressed satisfaction and 80 per cent considered that their social workers were understanding, sympathetic and easy to talk to. Another discrepancy between social workers' perceptions and clients' perceptions was revealed when the social workers were asked what types of help they felt clients expected from the Department. Most social workers thought that clients expected, above all, advice, sympathy, information and freedom to discuss personal problems. Most clients, on the other hand, said they expected practical help and few looked specifically for help in the form of sympathy or listening, although, as we have just seen, they appreciated the social workers' understanding and capacity to listen.

When asked what they thought clients most liked and disliked about the Department, the social workers took a gloomier view than their clients. They listed far more client complaints than client likes, possibly mirroring their own current malaise. The majority thought that clients would complain about administrative delays, unclear definitions of the Department's functions and the problems of contacting social workers. In fact, nearly two-thirds of the clients had no overt complaints about the services. The social workers imagined that their clients were finding it difficult to get social workers on the phone, would complain about the long delays in the reception area and of infrequent visits. However, the clients who had called at the office did not find access to their social worker difficult. The majority said that they had seen their own social worker on their last visit to the office and achieved the purpose of their visit. Most social workers thought that clients valued a feeling of security from knowing that support was available from a beneficent department. This view was in part accurate. A third of the clients mentioned a feeling of security and relief of emotional stress and a quarter said that they had received helpful advice. About a third, however, also mentioned benefits derived from the provision of aids, practical services and material goods – such as clothes or bedding – while the social workers seldom mentioned these sources of satisfaction for their clients.

By 1975 the atmosphere seemed more settled despite another upheaval due to the reorganisation of local government which meant that Seatown had become merged with the surrounding county into one of the largest social services departments in the country. While in 1972 four-fifths of the social workers under the age of thirty intended to move within two years, less than two-fifths expressed a similar plan in 1975. Relationships between social workers in these area offices had improved between 1972 and 1975 and so had staff morale. More social workers said they enjoyed their jobs despite continuing problems over the increased size and hierarchical structure of the Social Services Department.

Although the social workers' caseloads were much smaller than in 1972 (the average size had decreased from ninety-two to fifty-seven) they still felt under considerable pressure. Again, this was only partly related to the amount of work, but also to their perception of whether work was worthwhile and appropriate. Over half the social workers described a range of clerical and administrative tasks which they considered to be a waste of their time. Whilst in 1972 one of their main complaints had been lack of information from central office, in 1975 surfeit of information was a problem! Some workers described a feeling of pressure and conflict over deciding priorities and many commented on the need for more precise definitions of social work roles and tasks. Anxiety was evident among many about the potentially infinite demands which might come through the 'one' door of an area office. The preferences for work with children and families had persisted.

There was little evidence of more enthusiasm or new ideas about work with the large group of physically disabled and elderly clients. At the same time both the consumer and the CRS data show that an enormous amount of practical service help was arranged for this client group and greatly appreciated by them.

There was continuing confusion over terms like 'generic' and 'specialisation'. Although caseloads were more mixed in 1975 than in 1972 a considerable number expressed reservations about 'the generic social worker'. A qualified social worker voiced a typical opinion: 'I have reservations about every "good" social worker being generic. Although there is some enjoyment in variety, lack of knowledge and experience inevitably leads to a feeling of impotence and less efficient service.' A less experienced untrained social worker felt even more strongly: 'I feel after nine months I am a jack-of-all-trades and a master of none. The multiplicity of problems to be dealt with by a generic social worker is very difficult and I hope I will specialise in future and thus narrow my knowledge to be effective.' On the other hand, one senior staff member liked the flexibility of using any one of a group of social workers for a given task, regardless of former rigid boundaries. The term 'specialisation' was commonly used to refer to different client groups rather than to different methods of intervention, a finding also commented on by Stevenson (1978).

The perceptions of clients and social workers still diverged on many topics. While the majority of the social workers thought that at least half the clients wanted to discuss their personal problems, only 8 per cent of the clients expected to do this. While half the social workers thought that the personal relationship with the social worker would be one of the positive aspects the clients would point to in their contact with the department, this was only mentioned by 16 per cent of the clients. Here we may have the nub of the difference in perception between social workers and clients. The clients appear to take a sympathetic receptive attitude by social workers for granted: she understands your problems (81%), is able to see things from your point of view (71%), is sympathetic (77%), easy to talk to (84%) and is a good listener (81%). But the majority of clients do not single out the relationship *per se* as an important ingredient in the help received. This is not surprising when one considers that the majority of clients have infrequent and fleeting contacts with the social workers, and receive in the main practical help and advice. The social workers also overestimated the clients' expectations for help with finance and housing, and they seemed unaware of the fact that nearly a third of their clients really had no idea what to expect. As in 1972, social workers felt far more pessimistic about their clients' satisfactions and attitudes towards the Department than the clients did themselves. Thus, practically all the social workers thought that almost all clients would have a complaint, while this applied to only 37 per cent. For instance, over two-fifths of the social workers thought that most clients would be critical of the workers, while this only applied to one-fifth of the clients.

Over half the social workers thought that most clients would complain about delays in receiving services, but only 9 per cent did so.

As we shall see presently it seems as though clients had more realistic expectations about what is possible under present staffing conditions and with the skills available among social workers, although they were by no means uncritically accepting of the services offered. The social workers were acutely aware of the skills they lacked; for example, three-quarters felt they needed to know more about the resources of other departments in their authority and over half felt the lack of legal knowledge. All grades of staff expressed the need for structured, well-thought-out in-service training – the social work assistants and unqualified social workers by way of induction, the trained personnel by way of exchange and cross-fertilisation. Many thought that professional training had not prepared them for the realities of area office social work.

THE CLIENTS

The aims of the consumer studies in 1972 and 1975 were to explore the clients' expectations, feelings of satisfaction and views on the services they had received, and to gain a picture of their general knowledge of the functions of the social services and their perceptions of social workers. A random sample of clients from all the four area offices in Seatown were first of all approached by the Director of Social Services and given an opportunity to refuse to participate, which 12 per cent did in 1972 and 15 per cent in 1975. Some 300 clients were interviewed along the lines of a structured questionnaire[2] by a team of specially trained interviewers. The majority, particularly the younger clients, had some specific expectations, but the group with the fewest expectations were those over the age of sixty-five of whom approximately half said they did not know what to expect from the Department.

The majority of the consumers in both surveys said that they had received some help and almost two-thirds felt that they got what they hoped for. The two groups who received mainly practical help were the elderly and the physically handicapped, and those who came with housing and financial difficulties. Two-thirds of the physically handicapped – young and old – in both surveys said that the help they had received had made a difference either to them personally or to their lives. About a third felt that the aids, services and practical help had made their lives easier or more comfortable. The handicapped, whatever their age, valued a feeling of security or support in the background on which they could rely: 'I think it's the very fact that they're there and you get in touch when there are difficulties. The word "security" comes to mind' (widow aged sixty-three living alone).

'Casework type' of help was most often mentioned by those whose reason for contact was mental disorder and by clients experiencing child care and family problems. The majority of these clients who had this kind of help felt that it had made a difference to them. Emotional relief was most frequently mentioned. Others said that they had become less anxious or depressed or better able to cope: 'In a period of crisis – it's a help. They've put my mind at ease, made me feel better, I don't know how we'd have survived without them' (young mother with child-care problems).

To the question as to how satisfied they had been with the services about three-quarters of the consumers replied positively. In contrast, as already mentioned, only two-fifths of the social workers in 1975 thought that clients would be satisfied with their services.

While in 1972 the degree of satisfaction was fairly evenly distributed, in 1975 satisfaction varied in different client groups. The elderly and the physically handicapped and those who approached the Department with housing and financial problems were the most satisfied. These were the two groups who received predominantly practical help. Again, in 1972 equal proportions in all client groups had complaints, while in 1975 interesting differences emerged between client groups. The elderly and physically handicapped over sixty-five made fewer complaints than the rest. When they did, it was mostly about infrequency of visiting and about delays in receiving services, both of which the social workers had also identified as a possible source for complaint. In contrast to the elderly, half of those with child-care and family problems made complaints which most frequently referred to the social workers or the service given.

Comments often mentioned the youth and inexperience of social workers dealing with children or complex family problems: 'They must have an awful lot on their hands. By putting in more mature people their work would be cut in half.' These clients did not refer so much to lack of empathy on the part of younger social workers as to immaturity and resulting lack of understanding.

Some uneasiness about lack of specialisation had permeated to the consumers: a small proportion, 6 per cent, voiced this concern, feeling that workers could not hope to deal adequately with every type of problem.

The consumers' perceptions of social workers had also changed between 1972 and 1975. In 1972 more than a third of the consumers stressed the need for practical knowledge and skills and a quarter mentioned the importance of a good basic education. In 1975 only a quarter of the consumers thought that social workers should have practical skills such as first aid or domestic work, and even fewer stressed a good basic education. Instead twice as many consumers emphasised the need for training and specialised knowledge.

The Seebohm Report (1968) emphasised the importance of the local community's participation in the running of the social services, and we explored the views of consumers on this issue in both years.

In 1972, 28 per cent of the consumers felt they would like to have some say in the running and planning of services. In 1975 considerably more – 38 per cent – said they would like to participate. The main reasons given for wanting to participate were that the experience of users seemed important for planning and organisation. Some consumers made concrete suggestions about the ways in which they would like to be involved, such as offering advice through liaison groups. Others suggested interchange of information through meetings and lectures. Some felt that they could most usefully contribute their views through surveys, and yet others expressed ideas of self-help.

Appropriate use of the social services is very much dependent on adequate knowledge about services available, hence in both surveys we tested how much knowledge clients had of the social services. We presented respondents with six fairly common problem situations and asked them what sort of help they would suggest. We were also interested to find out which problems consumers thought needed professional rather than informal help from the community and how far they themselves would be prepared to get involved. Several important points emerged. First, on the whole clients appeared to be well informed about the functions of the social services and made many useful and appropriate suggestions. Secondly, the social services department is increasingly seen as an information and advice centre which can direct clients to more specialised forms of help. Thus the boundaries between the social services department and the citizens advice bureau tend to become blurred. Thirdly, users of Seatown Social Services Department made more suggestions to each problem situation in 1975 than in 1972; this may indicate an increase in knowledge and sophistication about sources of help which in turn may reflect the increase in publicity and information the media provide about the social services. Finally, a most interesting development was the greater importance that consumers in 1975 placed on informal, rather than professional, help. Particularly striking were the growing number of consumers who would be prepared to intervene themselves, and that age did not seem to make any difference to this desire to help. If this means that more people are ready to help their neighbours, it may carry important implications for the future use of social services resources. Further studies and experiments will have to show whether what people say coincides with what they will actually do.

Thus, in 1975, this random sample of 300 consumers of the personal social services in one town emerged as more sophisticated and articulate than a similar sample in 1972. Clearly, the greater visibility of social work and social services, mainly brought about by discussions in the media, has contributed to this trend. Most clients, in particular the elderly and the disabled, appreciated the many practical services available and the reassurance that the presence of a general social services department can give them. Perhaps one can see the dim outline emerging of a social service agency being there in the background in time of need much as the general practitioner service is available when one's health breaks down. Many consumers now expect social workers to be trained professionals rather than practical universal aunts with little specialised knowledge or training. These perceptions of a professional social service do not apparently lead to greater passivity and dependence but coexist with a blossoming of interest in mutual support and in involvement in the social services. These tentative straws in the wind in one area only appear to contradict recent sociological arguments (Keller, 1968; Hirsch, 1977; Abrams, 1978a) that under 'advanced state capitalism' we should expect an increasingly negative relationship between public welfare provision and community care arising from primary group and local neighbourly involvement. The many neighbourhood and mutual-help groups springing up all over the country also seem to indicate that the tide may be beginning to turn.

The data emerging from monitoring the social work of one area office to be discussed in later chapters also impinge on this issue. In our concluding discussion we shall address ourselves to what is possibly one of the most important considerations in planning the personal social services: how to optimise both public provision and informal community care based on family and neighbourhood involvement – for one cannot exist without the other – and how to establish optimal collaboration and integration between them.

NOTES

1   The consumer studies were carried out by Ann Glampson (*née* McKay) and the social worker studies by June Neill. For fuller accounts see references to these studies.
2   The questionnaire is available at the library of the National Institute for Social Work.

Chapter 4

THE DEVELOPMENT OF THE CASE REVIEW SYSTEM

Aware of the magnitude and complexity of the tasks facing social workers in the reorganised social services and equipped with some notion of the consumers' expectations and attitudes to these services we embarked on a piece of action research in one of the four area offices in Seatown. One of us began to pay regular visits to the area office in which we were to work for some four years. The choice of this particular office was largely determined by demographic and staffing factors. The district served contained a good cross-section of Seatown's population; the area office was reasonably well staffed and the social workers were prepared to 'have a go'. In 1972 there were twenty social workers divided into two teams, and everyone took it in turn to be on duty for incoming referrals.

TOWARDS DEFINING AIMS

We began by reviewing with each of the twenty social workers some half-a-dozen cases which were chosen more or less at random. At this point our options were still wide open. We hoped to gain an idea of how these social workers saw their jobs, what skills they were using, and what aims they were pursuing in different case situations. We also thought that this type of evaluation might stimulate the social workers to review the rest of their workload in a similar manner so that they could move into their new area office and face new and possibly increasing demands with a pruned caseload. Four features stood out among the 113 case reviews:

(1) The indeterminate nature of the aims the social workers were pursuing.

(2) The difficulties the social workers experienced in formulating a plan for the future rather than a description of the present situation.

(3) The very long-term nature of the majority of cases discussed which had been known to the Department for a long time, and which were expected to remain open more or less indefinitely.

(4) The reluctance of the social workers to involve other, possibly less-trained colleagues, volunteers or other community resources in situations which appeared to be fairly stabilised and not to require the special skills of a trained social worker.

It also became clear that the social workers, some of whom had very large caseloads, would not, even with the help of their seniors, be able to review their cases without some instrument along the lines of the structured questions we had been asking in the discussions with them.

The results of our two baseline studies on consumer and social worker attitudes highlighted certain discontinuities and difficulties in service delivery: for example, as we have seen, differences emerged in what clients expected from social workers and what social workers thought their clients wanted from them. Ambiguities about closure of cases became apparent: a number of clients thought they were still in contact with the service when officially their cases had been closed; conversely, others believed that their contact with the Department had ceased while the social workers considered them current. Some elderly clients complained about lack of social contacts and loneliness and seemed to expect more contact than the social workers were able to achieve. Social workers experienced pressures which were only partly related to the size of their caseloads. All these factors pointed at the operational level towards the need for more clearly defined aims of social work, a more explicit understanding of these by client and worker, a regular system for reviewing progress and readjusting aims, a broader perspective and more use of outside resources which might provide relief to the social workers and a better service for the client. These notions were strongly reinforced by our increasing involvement in task-centred casework with its emphasis on clear problem formulation, on specificity of aims and tasks, and on a planned, time-limited approach.

At the same time, one member of the team, working in another local authority on records and information systems, had become interested in the technical aspects of setting up computerised, that is to say readily accessible, record and monitoring systems which would be capable of supplying on-going, updated information on cases. Finally, the social workers themselves, stimulated by the case discussions during the review sessions, began to question some of their practices. Thus the climate seemed ripe for the practitioners to work closely with the research team in creating a basic tool they lacked – a case review scheme which would eventually become part of an on-going system.

At this stage we defined our action-research aims as follows:

(1) To develop a model information and review system which would enable fieldworkers and management to monitor their social work and social services activities in order to discover how professional skills and other social service resources are used in relation to different problems presented and to different aims pursued.

(2) To encourage social workers to become more explicit about both means and ends of their activities.

'ACTION RESEARCH'

This kind of developmental applied research demanded an exploratory, action-oriented approach which sought to involve the practitioners closely in the creation of the instruments which they were going to use in their daily work. 'Action research' has been described as 'the introduction of planned change and the observation of its results' (Cherns, 1971). There are certain difficulties inherent in this approach.

First of all, action research often represents a solution to a specific problem in a particular context and is thus least open to generalisation of all research procedures (Town, 1964; Cherns, 1971). We therefore had to be careful not to limit the problems we were exploring and the instruments we were building to the specific needs of one area only.

Secondly, evaluation of the results of intervention is difficult since action research necessitates on-going feedback and hence continual change in the mode of intervention. This intimate involvement between researcher and practitioner contains another hazard – the pressure on the researcher to become a consultant/teacher.

Thirdly, the need to win the confidence and co-operation of practitioners and to be responsive to their needs may lead to diversions on to side tasks which can slow up progress. There is thus a tension between the systematic procedure of planned innovation on the one hand, and response to the needs of the field situation on the other. Yet much can be learned from the process of exploration/innovation/feedback leading to further research efforts/innovation/feedback.

Fourthly, there is also a tension between the necessity to work very closely with practitioners and middle management if real commitment is to be achieved at the fieldwork level, and the need to keep in touch with top management and to encourage their willingness to accept change.

While we did not avoid all the pitfalls of action research, and progress seemed at times painfully slow and circuitous, we finally emerged with an instrument capable of general application and with replicable – albeit crude – findings of social workers' assessments of problems, their activities, aims and their assessments of cases at closure.

DEVELOPING A CASE REVIEW SYSTEM

A Working Party consisting of five fieldworkers and a senior met regularly once a fortnight with two members of the research team from January 1973 onwards. Problem categories were developed from the pilot material. A simple pre-coded review form took shape which deliberately concentrated on the specification of current problems and future aims in terms of a social work plan, the type of worker required to carry it out, and estimated length and intensity of social worker involvement.

Instructions for filling in the form were carefully piloted, and finally in March 1973 the scheme was launched at an area meeting when all the social workers in the area undertook to review their current allocated cases and thereafter at intervals to be determined by them according to the needs of the particular case. The reviews were done on no-carbon-required forms. One was retained in the case file and the other went to the National Institute for Social Work Research Unit for computer analysis via an administrative assistant situated in the area office. After about three months some 90 per cent of the allocated cases in the area were incorporated in the review system. Once a month a computer print-out of reviews due reached the administrative assistant who then prepared the new review forms and passed them on to the relevant social workers for completion.

It is likely that much of the resistance of social workers to providing codified information on their cases is due to the fact that they hardly ever receive any interesting feedback which makes sense of the data they are supplying. We therefore decided early on to make the review system as relevant as possible to their needs and interests and to encourage a constant dialogue of questions and answers based on the data we were accumulating with them.

A few months after the start of the system we were able to feed back some information which raised considerable issues for practitioners and management. For example, two-thirds of the 1,500 allocated cases on the CRS were expected to be open for more than three years from the date of the review; at least a third of these cases were 'dormant' and receiving little or no service; a third were said to require the limited skills of social work assistants only, but such personnel hardly existed; the use of volunteers was only ever mentioned by one out of the twenty area social workers. Individual workers were still highly specialised, some social workers carrying caseloads consisting almost entirely of elderly and disabled clients and others having mostly family and child-care cases. The huge, almost static caseloads of elderly and disabled clients aroused much heated discussion among the workers, some claiming that persons on the disabled register could never be 'closed'.

These findings and other pressures led the team leaders to develop the concept of an 'agency caseload', of cases which only need occasional surveillance for indefinite periods, thus freeing the social workers from the stifling effects of over-large individual caseloads.

Meanwhile the Working Party continued on the second phase of the enterprise. Plans for the future are all very well, but the concept of review implies comparing plans with actual achievement. So our next task was to describe 'work done' in ways that were meaningful to social workers and at the same time amenable to statistical analysis. The practical and tangible aspects of social work presented relatively few difficulties.

Categories for 'practical services and tangible changes effected' and for 'contacts with other agencies' were evolved from the pilot material and from current cases. But we also built on our previous research into social work intervention (Goldberg, Mortimer and Williams, 1970; Goldberg and Neill, 1972).

The more intangible aspects of social work, namely the nature of the current transaction between client and social worker, proved more problematical and were described at this stage in somewhat over-simplified and dichotomised terms of 'casework' and 'review visiting'. After trial runs in which the categories were tested on current cases and continually amended, Mark II of the review form was introduced in May 1974. It now consisted of two parts called 'Work Done Since Last Review' and 'Current Problems and Plans for the Future'. Although the form had grown longer it was more satisfying to the social workers, since it enabled them to report on their actual work about which they felt more certain than about the projections into the future, which still often turned out to be descriptions of the present situation rather than an outline of specific plans.

Although we were getting nearer to our aim of encouraging social workers towards a more evaluative attitude to their work by comparing plans with achievements, there were still several hurdles to be taken. The instrument as yet lacked ready comparability between past and future activities; the practical aspects of the social work activities had been broken down into meaningful components but plans for the future still remained in a narrative form and hence often ill-defined. At this stage the area staff members of the Working Party suggested an arrangement which the researchers had not dared to mention since it seemed so dehumanised. This was the simple expedient of using the same categories for practical services and contacts with other agencies for past activities and future plans in adjacent columns. In the final version (see Figure 4.1), the social workers can tick side by side what they have done in the preceding period and what they intend to do during the next review period. This still left the type of social worker/client transaction to be described more adequately. Once more the precise thinking that the task-centred approach demands helped us to formulate more specific components of the social worker/client contact and to discard the simplistic notions of 'casework' and 'review visiting'. We conceptualised the essential ingredients of social work transactions in the following terms:

(1) Exploratory/(re-)assessment activity – exploration of current and past situations in order to gain an understanding of the present issues and to re-assess possibilities and constraints of future work.
(2) Information/advice – self-explanatory.
(3) Mobilising resources – activities mainly concerned with arranging

practical help such as aids, meals-on-wheels, holidays, clubs, grants, work possibilities, voluntary help etc.

(4) Advocacy – activities in which social workers plead their clients' cases with formal organisations such as Housing Departments, the Department of Health and Social Security (DHSS), Electricity Boards, and with other professionals of various kinds.

(5) Education in social and physical skills – e.g. helping families with budgeting, home management, practical child care; teaching the disabled how to use aids or other environmental supports to daily living.

(6) Check up/review visiting – short 'popping-in' visits to ensure that everything is OK.

(7) Facilitating problem solving/decision making – various ways of counselling or casework, e.g. helping clients to ventilate their feelings, to discuss, sort out and try to solve problems, make choices, become aware of their behaviour and its effect on others.

(8) Sustaining/nurturing – mainly friendly encouragement and 'caring' rather than activities directed towards problem solving or change.

(9) Group activities – engaging in group work with clients either as a group leader or as an active member of the group. (Very little group work was taking place in the area, hence no opportunities occurred for breaking this category down into different types of group work.)

The social workers' response to these descriptions of their activities was very positive, and trial runs on live cases achieved a high level of agreement between practitioners in allocating their activities to these nine headings. The feeling gained ground that a beginning had been made in breaking down the amalgam called 'social work with individuals and families' into some recognisable component parts, free from casework mumbo-jumbo jargon. However, some complaints have been voiced about the overlap between the categories, and it has also been pointed out that during a certain period several modes of social work may be employed. We coped with these difficulties by asking the fieldworkers to indicate 'the most important activity', but clearly there is much scope here for further development and refinement of categories.

The remaining area of dissatisfaction was still the one of 'aims'. The idea occurred to us that if one encouraged social workers first of all to describe the present situation and then asked what changes they were aiming at, one might obviate the tendency to substitute a description of the present situation for goals. Although social work aims can never be encompassed in a series of ticks, it became possible to define at least the areas of change aimed at, while still retaining a narrative description for the specific content as follows:

Figure 4.1 Case Review Form

NATIONAL INSTITUTE FOR SOCIAL WORK

Case Review Form

Case No.

Case A.

Surnames B.

Last Reviewed on

Last Reviewed by

This Review due

Office Use [4] 9

Tick as appropriate
Practical services/tangible changes

ACTIVITIES

	Since last Review: Actual	Before next Review: Planned 10
01 None		
02 Home Help		
03 Meals-on-Wheels		
04 Day Centres/Clubs/Outings		
05 Holidays		
06 Aids/Adaptations		
07 Material improvements		
08 Financial		
09 Volunteer referral		
10 Assistance with applications		
11 Changes in living group		
12 Help with employment		
13 Temporary accommodation i.e. homelessness		
14 Permanent accommodation i.e. rehousing		
15 Admission/referral for assessment/treatment		
16 Part III: long term		
17 Part III: short-term		
18 Reception into care		
19 Discharge from Part III or care		
20 Change of legal responsibility to client		
21 Other (specify)		

Office Use .... [5] 9   This Review No. [ ] 11

Problems

PRESENT

	Tackled since last Review	Present at this Review 12
01 Physical disability/illness		
02 Elderly		
03 Mental illness		
04 Mental handicap		
05 Emotional disturbance in adults		
06 Social isolation and/or loneliness		
07 Child behaviour problems		
08 Delinquency		
09 Family relations problems		
10 Family break-up		
11 Child neglect		
12 Problems in home management		
13 Financial difficulties		
14 Housing problems		
15 Employment difficulties		
16 Problems arising from residential or foster care		
17 Transport difficulties		
18 Other (specify)		29

Code most outstanding problem

02 General Practitioner
03 Health Visitor/Nurse
04 Psychiatric Hospital/Outpatient Services
05 Other Hospital/Outpatient Services
06 Other AHA (Chiropody, Ambulance, etc.)
07 Child Guidance Clinic
08 Community Homes
09 Educational/School
10 Housing Department
11 DHSS
12 Probation
13 Police
14 Court/Solicitors
15 SSD's in other LA's
16 Voluntary Agencies (clergy, WRVS etc.)
17 Other (specify) . . . .

48

Types of workers

1 None
2 Qualified Social Worker
3 Unqualified Social Worker
4 Social Work Assistant
5 Volunteer
6 Others with specialised knowledge
7 Social Worker plus specialised knowledge

55

Social worker activities

01 None
02 Exploratory/(re-) assessment activity
03 Information/advice
04 Mobilising resources
05 Advocacy
06 Education in social skills
07 Check up/review visiting
08 Facilitating problem solving/decision making
09 Sustaining/nurturing
10 Group activities

64

Code most important activity

80

Estimate no. of contacts

Spare 1

1 2 3 4 5 6 7 8

35

Code case status to be

1 Current   3 Closed
2 Dormant   4 Transferred

FUTURE

OPEN CASES What changes are you aiming for? Specify . . . .

36

Code Major Change Area

1 No change intended   4 Social role
2 Major environmental   5 Behaviour/attitude
3 Social/personal environment   relationships

37

Code time before case likely to be closed

1 Up to 3 months   3 1 year   5 3 years
2 6 months   4 2 years   6 More than 3 years

38

CLOSED CASES Code Reason for Closure

1 Aim achieved   6 Contact not achieved
2 Change in circumstances   7 Social Worker/Dept. withdraws
3 Client died   8 Referral to other facilities
4 Client withdrew   9 Other (specify) . . . .
5 Client left area

44
Date of last social work contact

50
Today's date

56
Date of next Case Review

60
Social Worker & Team

64
Next social worker & team to review (if different)

80
Spare 2

a b c d e f g h i j k l m n o p

(1)   No change intended – this category often applies to dormant or agency review cases where no change is anticipated. In some cases where a stable equilibrium has been achieved (e.g. a stable happy foster-home placement), the aims may be to preserve the *status quo*.

(2)   Major environmental change – denotes a complete change of the physical environment, e.g. rehousing, move to a foster home, admission to a residential home etc.

(3)   Changes in the social/personal environment – denotes changes in the immediate environment brought about by a variety of services (e.g. home help, aids, grants, holidays, clubs), which are intended to enable clients to lead fuller and more satisfying lives.

(4)   Changes in social role – here the aim of social work is to help people in their transition and adjustment to role changes, e.g. adjustment to widowhood, to disablement, to giving up one's home, to starting work again, and so on.

(5)   Changes in behaviour/attitudes/relationships – the aim of intervention may be to help clients towards a better marital or parent–child relationship, to help a mentally ill person to become more active socially, or a child to become less anti-social etc. (For the full set of coding instructions see Appendix 1.)

In summary, the case review form now consists of three sections:

(1)   past activities
(2)   the present situation
(3)   the intended future activities and aims.

The final version was launched in the area office in February 1975. By this time three teams were in existence, one intake and two long-term teams, each led by a senior social worker. More resistance was encountered to this version, since the form now contained more pre-coded elements. It necessitated more precise thinking about social work activities, and thus took longer to complete. However, it seems that familiarity with the form and regular feedback of information on individual and team caseload profiles has led to greater acceptance of the review form and a decrease in criticisms.

When finalising the CRS, the Research Unit was also involved in redesigning the referral form used for incoming cases. The remodelling of this form enabled us to collect some information on all cases, including the very short-term cases which do not reach the stage of being 're-viewed'. These short-term cases had been increasing steadily throughout the years of our involvement with the area teams, and – as we learned to our astonishment from the case review data – by 1975 formed about 90 per cent of the incoming referrals. We could thus trace all clients referred to this area office throughout the remaining period of our fieldwork involvement. Hence we were finally able to monitor all the referrals coming to this area office during one calendar year, and similarly all the on-going cases dealt with during the same period.

In conclusion, the CRS if fully utilised can fulfil five functions:

(1) As a practice tool it enables social workers to evaluate and plan their work with individual clients and in this way encourages 'good' social work practice.
(2) As an educational tool it can assist the process of supervision.
(3) As a management tool it can contribute towards the planning of fieldwork services by showing what resources in terms of level of training, time, practical services and counselling activities are used for different client groups.
(4) As an information system it gives an on-going account of the size, nature and scope of social work activities with different client groups to those running the services, both locally and centrally and also to the general public.
(5) As a research tool it can explore possible associations between aims pursued in different problem situations, methods and skills used. It makes longitudinal studies of 'client careers' possible and it provides a ready sampling frame for different types of *ad hoc* studies.

Chapter 5

———◆———

THE EXERCISE OF FEEDBACK

TRIAL AND ERROR

We had succeeded in actively engaging the social workers in the development of the case review form, but at least as great a challenge was to involve them in the output side of the exercise. This meant helping them to absorb and interpret the data they had generated, viewing them not only as longitudinal comparative data on an individual case, but as patterns of social work activities in relation to similar types of cases. The next step was to encourage the social workers to make use of what they were learning from this novel inspection of their own work. Time and again we had to remind the workers that this was not just another ticking exercise to produce statistical information for 'them' (i.e. management), but a social work tool to be used by social workers in order to evaluate and plan their work – individually, as a team, and as an area office.

At first the aggregated statistical information given to individual social workers on their own long-term cases and to the team leaders on their team's activities meant little, since they were mainly interested in the evaluation and interpretation of individual cases. The researchers were repeatedly asked to supply fewer statistics and more interpretative comments. Thus one of the crucial problems emerging was how to present the data in a form that was meaningful to practising social workers and their managers and which enabled them to raise questions and to adjust their practices in the light of the information they were receiving.

While the social workers were not used to receiving statistical information about their social work input and outcomes, the researchers were equally unfamiliar with appropriate methods of presentation. But we were willing to learn by trial and error which method seemed to work best, what tables made most sense, whether individual team or area discussions were most effective, and so on.

We tried out several types of feedback report, one which was mainly narrative and interlaced with figures, a second one which combined tables with a commentary, and a third which contained tables only. To our pleasurable surprise, the majority of fieldworkers chose the second version and rejected the narrative form on the grounds that it tended to mask the figures and did not enable them to compare their own activities over time or their own cases with those of their colleagues.

FEEDBACK TO LONG-TERM TEAMS

Although we were not sure how much detail the social workers could absorb, we were certain about one point: we wanted them to be able to see their work within the context of their team's activities and those of the area office as a whole. Hence the left-hand side of the feedback report gave information on their own cases (see Figure 5.1) and on the other side we presented similar data for the teams. In our written comments we tried to make relevant observations on their activities and point to interesting configurations and also to possible inconsistencies. We soon learnt that it is better to present a small number of facts clearly set out, rather than to bombard practitioners with a set of complicated tables from which – comprehensive though they may be – it is difficult to draw general conclusions. For example, in order to highlight the differences in the types of social work 'packages' provided for different client groups we combined the physically disabled and frail elderly into one client group and children and families with disturbed relationships into another group, and only presented comparisons between these two major long-term client groups.

The next problem was how to communicate the information so as to enhance interaction between researchers and practitioners, keep interest alive and – last but not least – promote learning. We tried individual discussions first, but there was little evidence that this led to any general interchange of information with colleagues or to any common learning experience. Next we tried presenting general issues in an area meeting. Although this produced a lively discussion it did not encourage individual workers to talk about their reports or their own preoccupations, or to voice any criticisms they might have of the researchers' approaches. Finally, we discovered that team meetings were the right medium. The seniors became more involved, and the fieldworkers felt free to raise questions about their own cases as well as on team matters and area issues. It was rewarding to observe how the workers learnt to read and interpret their reports, handle statistical information, make relevant observations and raise questions on policy emerging from the trends shown up by the aggregated information. The team meetings also gave the researchers the opportunity to test how the system was working, to make occasional checks on interpretations of instructions and to encourage stragglers to complete their reviews.

Altogether we held six feedback meetings with teams at three-monthly intervals, of which the last two were the most successful. By that time the social workers had become used to aggregated information, we had

Figure 5.1. *Caseload Profile*

NATIONAL INSTITUTE FOR SOCIAL WORK CASE REVIEW SYSTEM

FEEDBACK TO AREA OFFICE

Report No. 6 31.3.76

INDIVIDUAL CASELOAD PROFILE for ....

Since the start of December you have:

ADDED ...... cases to the Case Review System
PLACED ...... cases on Agency Review
CLOSED OR TRANSFERRED ...... cases
& REVIEWED ...... cases

WORK DONE WITH CASES ON WHICH YOU AND YOUR COLLEAGUES HAVE REPORTED OVER THE PAST THREE MONTHS (N.B. CASES NOT WORKED ON FOR OVER 6 MONTHS HAVE BEEN EXCLUDED).

For the cases on which you reported the most frequently tackled main problem was ....

Most frequently mentioned Practical Services

All Your Cases n =	No. Cases	Allocated long-term cases: Ageing/ Physical disability n = 54	No. Cases	Family/child Problems n = 46	No. Cases	All allocated cases n = 173	No. Cases
		Financial	16	Ch. living group	16	Financial	40
		Applications	16	Financial	8	Applications	40
		Aids/adaptations	15	Applications	5	Ch. in living group	30
		Day centres/clubs	11	Discharge Pt 3/care	5	Day centres/clubs	15
		Home helps	7	Admission/referral for assessment/treatment	7	Aids/adaptations	15
		Admission/referral for assessment/treatment	7	Reception into care	3	Material help	13
		Part 3: short term	7	Child in legal resp.	3	Admission/referral for assessment/treatment	13
		Meals-on-wheels	4	None	15	Discharge Pt 3/care	13
		None	15			None	60

All Your Cases

All Your Cases n = _____ — No. Cases: _____

Ageing/Physical disability n = 54

	No. Cases
General practitioners	25
Hospitals (not psych.)	19
HVs/Nurses	14
Housing	6
Psych. hospitals	5
Voluntary agencies	5
None	14

Family/child Problems n = 46

	No. Cases
Educational/schools	16
Police	15
Courts/solicitors	13
Community homes	12
General practitioners	7
DHSS	7
None	7

All allocated cases n = 173

	No. Cases
General practitioners	47
HVs/Nurses	33
Educational/schools	32
Housing	32
Hospitals (not psych.)	26
Court/solicitors	26
None	43

Most Important Social Worker Activity

All Your Cases n = _____ — No. Cases: _____

Ageing/Physical disability n = 54

	No. Cases
Check up/review visits	20
Exploration/assessment	9
Mobilising resources	4
Facilitating prob. solv.	4
Sustaining/nurturing	2
None	1

Allocated long-term cases — Family/child Problems n = 46

	No. Cases
Facilitating prob. solv.	13
Check up/review visits	8
Exploration/assessment	7
Mobilising resources	7
Sustaining/nurturing	5
None	0

Allocated long-term cases — All allocated cases n = 173

	No. Cases
Check up/review visits	45
Exploration/assessment	36
Facilitating prob. solv.	26
Mobilising resources	24
Advocacy	16
None	6

Average No. Contacts per Quarter

	All Your Cases	Ageing/Physical disability	Allocated long-term cases — Family/child Problems	All allocated cases
Estimated		2.4	7.0	5.5
Actual		3.8	10.2	7.2

THE PRESENT PICTURE FOR ALLOCATED CASES OF THE LONG-TERM TEAMS

Case Status	Your Cases		Ageing Phys. disability		Family/child Problems		All allocated cases	
	No.	%	No.	%	No.	%	No.	%
Current			246	65	159	92	660	79
Dormant			131	35	13	8	180	21
Total no. of on-going cases			377	100	172	100	840	100

Main Problem Group	Your Cases		All allocated	
	No.	%	No.	%
Problems of Ageing/Physical Disability			377	45
Mental/Emotional Disorders			54	6
Family/Child Problems			172	20½
Environmental/Material Problems			39	5
Residential/Foster-Care Problems			130	15½
Other Problems/No Outstanding Problem			68	8
Totals			840	100

THE FUTURE

Major Change Area*

	Your Cases		Ageing Phys. disability		Family/child Problems		All allocated cases	
	No.	%	No.	%	No.	%	No.	%
No change intended			155	60	42	34	314	52
Major environmental			18	7	18	14	75	12
Social/personal environment			78	30	11	9	108	18
Social role			3	1	4	3	18	3
Behaviour/attitude/relationships			6	2	50	40	94	15
Totals			260	100	125	100	609	100

(* These figures refer to those cases reviewed on the Review Form introduced in February 1975.)

Time Before Closure

	Your Cases		Ageing Phys. disability		Family/child Problems		All allocated cases	
	No.	%	No.	%	No.	%	No.	%
Up to 1 year			19	5	32	18½	114	14
Up to 3 years			33	9	41	24	120	14
More than 3 years			325	86	99	57½	605	72
Totals			377	100	172	100	839	100

COMMENTS

become better at putting over the information, and the format and content of the reports which had been modified in the light of experience at long last gave a good rounded picture of what was going on.

The practice issues discussed ranged over a wide area. The social workers were beginning to detect recurring patterns of practices, to compare the activities of different teams and to become aware of different worker styles and assumptions. For instance, we observed that of two teams with a similar caseload and an equal number of social workers, team one had significantly more contacts with their clients than team two. Furthermore, whilst team one consistently underestimated the number of contacts they were going to have with their clients within the next review period, that is to say they did more than they expected, team two consistently overestimated the number of future contacts and thus achieved less than they had planned. How were these differences to be explained? On the individual level what did one make of the fact that of two workers with an essentially similar caseload, worker A estimated that all his cases were likely to be open for more than three years, while worker B expected that only a third of his cases would be open for more than three years after the current review? What was the meaning of the dearth of cases being passed on from the intake to the long-term teams? Was this related to a silting-up process of long-term static caseloads? Was it a response to staff shortages in the long-term teams? Did the intake team hang on to promising cases? Or did they close them – possibly at times prematurely? Or did they refer them to other facilities? What were the implications of the finding that just under 20 per cent of all referrals were reopened within three months of being closed? Had problems not been recognised? Did the clients have unrealistic expectations from the social services? How was it that since 1973 an unvarying 70 per cent of the cases which survived the intake stage were estimated to be open for more than three years, despite the changing climate of opinion in the area office and the very great efforts that were made to 'prune' caseloads and to engage in more focused social work? There was the eternal topic of how best to keep in touch with the chronically disabled and the frail elderly, and whether it was permissible to 'close' the cases of clients who were registered as chronically disabled.

Another question which the CRS helped to keep on the agenda was how best to deploy different types of social work staff. A very experienced worker had estimated that unqualified social workers or social work assistants could deal with ten of her cases. On her feedback report we had asked: 'Do you intend to transfer these cases?' At the same time, an unqualified social worker who sat next to her in the office had reported that six of the sixteen allocated cases he carried needed the skills of a qualified worker. In the discussion it transpired that as yet no transfers of these kinds had been effected, and it was decided that in future the team leader should be notified when workers carried cases which they felt were not appropriate to their skills.

In addition to these outputs related to individual practice and use of area resources, we also produced more general management information which was immediately recognised as useful. For example, the seniors received monthly updated lists of individual caseloads, of all cases due for review and of all six-monthly statutory reviews due for children in care. This enabled seniors to carry out spot checks on the completion of reviews, and to pick out cases for discussion which were not in a state of crisis or presenting special difficulties – these would come up in any case – but those that were drifting along without any particular problems and possibly also with no particular social work aims.

FEEDBACK TO THE INTAKE TEAM AND 'ON REQUEST'

The information provided for the intake team was of a different character, since most of their cases were closed after a short period of intervention and did not have on-going reviews. Hence we produced monthly and quarterly analyses of referrals for the intake team. This helped them to detect trends – for example, in numbers referred throughout the year, in the ratio of old to new referrals, in the sources of referral, problem types, age groups, closures, and so on. It was this kind of information which first alerted the intake senior to the sizeable proportion of certain types of cases which were re-referred within a very short period.

As the seniors became more familiar with handling statistical information they began to ask other epidemiological questions of the case review data. For example, they requested an analysis of single-parent family referrals from a prewar housing estate to use as background information for some group work they were planning to undertake with these parents (Warburton and Willmott, 1976). On another occasion they requested the numbers of new referrals and on-going cases and estimates of their duration, of clients living in an outlying district. This information was to be used to discuss the feasibility of transferring this district to a neighbouring area office.

EVALUATION OF FEEDBACK

In a questionnaire that was sent to all the social workers in the area office to assess the impact of the CRS (discussed more fully in Chapter 14), a few questions were also asked about the usefulness of the feedback information. Four-fifths of the workers said that the reports and discussions had proved useful. A further half also felt that the feedback had facilitated discussion and supervision. Some typical comments were as follows: 'It certainly helped give me an overall picture of area functioning and brought home the need to revise methods of working'; 'It has heightened the need for discussion on area policies and where our resources should and do lie'; 'Feedback helps in understanding the role of other agencies involved with clients and the patterns which review takes.'

It seems from these and other comments that the feedback exercise achieved one of its purposes – to help social workers to see their work in a broader team and area context. One of the seniors put these points in a somewhat different way: he thought that the overall effect of feedback had been to bring the intake and long-term teams closer together and had led to the long-term workers seeing themselves more as a 'task force' than a collection of individuals.

To a question whether they wished the CRS to be extended to other areas, most replied in the affirmative. Some, whilst recommending extension, stipulated certain conditions; for example, one worker said: 'Yes, it should be extended, but only if the CRS became an integral part of office work and the staff had actual involvement in the analysis and evaluation of reviews.' This last point is of crucial importance if a case review system is to be an educative tool for the individual practitioner and his team as well as a monitoring device to assist management decisions.

Whether the CRS had an impact on individual casework practices remains an open question. It is our impression that some of the workers continued working as they had always done. Others told us that the case review experience had led them to look more critically at their practices. One worker informed us several years later that the experience had 'turned them upside down'!

It needs to be remembered that the detailed analysis of a whole year's flow of cases and its implications for practice as set out in the following chapters were not yet available during our close involvement with the area teams. These more comprehensive results were discussed with the teams as they became available, and the three seniors participated actively in the interpretation of the massive data which were published in journal articles (Goldberg and Fruin, 1976; Goldberg, Warburton, McGuinness and Rowlands, 1977; Goldberg et al., 1978).

Chapter 6

———◆———

'NEEDS' AND DEMANDS ON SOCIAL SERVICES IN THE AREA
by Brendan McGuinness, E. Matilda Goldberg and R. William Warburton

Before presenting the case review data, we want to describe the area in which the exercise took place in more detail and most importantly to see whether the social work activities bore any relationship to the 'needs' of the area. The Seebohm Report (1968) stressed that the social services for individuals and families should be firmly rooted in the needs of local areas. Yet, like many of their predecessors, the Seebohm Committee did not succeed in defining these needs, and ever since arguments have been raging as to whether the much extended personal social services are reaching those most in need of them. While basic material needs for food, warmth and shelter can be identified and measured fairly objectively, the more subjective needs for security, affection and recognition are less easily identified and measured. As Bradshaw (1972) pointed out in his suggested taxonomy of needs, it also matters from whose point of view needs are defined – those in need, experts, or according to an agreed standard, and so on.

Many studies have shown that certain 'social indicators' largely derived from census information, such as housing, income, social class, family structure and size, are separately or in combination highly correlated with survival and physical disease (Morris, 1975). These indicators are also associated with many forms of social pathology, ranging from educational backwardness (Wedge and Prosser, 1973) through delinquency and child abuse (Smith, Hanson and Noble, 1974) to depression (Brown and Harris, 1978). The well-known study of social malaise in Liverpool related areal characteristics to certain features of social pathology (Amos, 1971). Webber (1975) extended the methodology of areal description using cluster analysis, a method which allowed him to represent more fully the different social structures found in urban environments. His work provides a general base from which areal typologies can be developed and used for different analytic and planning purposes. Central government is also interested in developing areal typologies in order to arrive at a measure of territorial justice in allocating resources for social services (Imber, 1977).

Thus one, albeit crude, measure of social need in an area is its relative position on a social indicator, or a combination of indicators, in comparison with other areas. One would expect that areas with a concentration of high-need indicators would make more demands on the social services than those ranking low on need indicators. Hence we wanted to find out:

(1) whether, using some of these social indicators, we could distinguish neighbourhoods with differing 'social-need' profiles within the social work area, and

(2) whether the geographical distribution of high and low indicators of need bore any relationship to the distribution of clients in touch with the area office in the year beginning 1 February 1975.

The CRS enabled us to allocate clients and their demographic characteristics to enumeration districts, which were coded on to the case review forms. An enumeration district is the smallest urban unit for which census data are available, and consists typically of between 200 and 250 households. The next biggest census unit is a ward, an electoral district made up of a number of enumeration districts. There were eighteen wards in Seatown, and the social work area contained four whole wards and parts of three others.

The task facing us was to develop an areal classification that would reflect the different types of social environment prevailing in the area, and to relate these neighbourhoods in terms of social indicators of need to clients' demands on the social services. While an enumeration district was too small for a meaningful description of neighbourhoods and a comparison between them of demands for social services, wards were too large and too few, and contained considerable variety within them. Moreover, the boundary of the social work area in which we carried out our action studies cuts across the boundaries of the wards.

The exercise we undertook had two parts. The first phase involved the establishment of a provisional zoning of the area through discussion with the senior social workers. The second phase was based on census information, and involved using the statistical technique of cluster analysis (Webber, 1975) to produce groupings of enumeration districts into larger units which would be internally homogeneous and as distinct from one another as possible.[1] The two phases, although distinct, were not separate. The subjective mapping served throughout the analysis as a reference point against which clustering solutions could be compared. In addition, the observations the social workers made concerning access to community facilities, the location of special housing for the vulnerable elderly and handicapped, and other features of the area, supplemented the picture derived from these census data.

THE SOCIAL WORKERS' VIEW OF THE AREA

The senior social workers identified twenty-three neighbourhoods which they characterised in thumbnail sketches. These neighbourhoods originated at different times and reflected different patterns of housing development and utilisation. They described a bedsitter and lodging-house district near the city centre and within reach of the docks; neighbourhoods of old terraced housing occupied by working-class and middle-class communities; areas of prewar and postwar council housing, including large estates and scattered high-rise blocks; and the high-status areas of home-owning households.

In addition, they characterised areas of low-standard prewar council housing by the apparent 'resilience of their population', and pointed out those districts which had suffered badly from vandalism and those whose population had earned a reputation for delinquency. As well as providing some insight into characteristics of the areas which would not be reflected in the census data, they also drew attention to those areas in which significant housing developments had taken place since 1971. As a result, two of the enumeration districts on the northern periphery of the social work area had to be omitted from further analysis. Here some 2,300 dwellings had been completed and occupied since the census and the population had trebled to approximately 7,000 people, being a mix of families with young children and special housing for the elderly. Although this area was making considerable demands for social services, it could not be included in the analysis since census data were not available.

A STATISTICAL VIEW OF THE AREA

The technique of cluster analysis used in the statistical exercise works by combining units (in this case enumeration districts) into clusters, so that a cluster contains units which are more alike than those allocated to other clusters. As the units are combined, so the distinctions between them are submerged and individual differences sacrificed for the sake of common characteristics. In general, the larger the clusters and the fewer of them, the more variety is lost, and the risk that important distinctions are blurred is increased. The art of clustering depends on applying this technique so as to achieve a balance between the loss of variety and the simplicity of the final solution. A further consideration influenced the final choice of clusters; namely, that wherever possible they should consist of adjacent enumeration districts or groups of identifiable neighbourhoods.

We selected thirty-four census variables covering a range of social and environmental factors including age structure, household composition and tenure, housing conditions, educational attainment, and economic activities. These variables were given equal importance within the clustering procedure. When we applied the cluster analysis to the census data, the final solution grouped 136 enumeration districts into nine clusters, which accounted for 55 per cent of the original variance between enumeration districts.

Cluster 1: old terraced housing, poor amenities

This cluster contains approximately 16 per cent of the area's population, and comprises twenty-five adjacent enumeration districts concentrated to the south of the area near the city centre and docks.

As Table 6.1 shows, the cluster contains one of the highest proportions of elderly people, and had been picked out by the seniors as a neighbourhood with high referral rates for elderly and physically handicapped clients. The cluster consists mainly of owner-occupied and privately rented accommodation. It comprises much old terraced housing with poor amenities. For example, 20 per cent of households lack an inside WC – the figure for the area as a whole is 9 per cent; and again proportionately twice as many households share or lack hot water compared to the area as a whole (20% as against 11%). There is a high degree of under-occupancy related to the preponderance of the elderly and a comparately low proportion of large families.

Cluster 2: modernised terraced housing

This cluster is similar in size to cluster 1, and shares a number of common features with it. For example, it contains many elderly people, has a high degree of under-occupancy and proportionately fewer pre-school and school-age children compared with the area. Unlike its neighbouring cluster, this neighbourhood contains a relatively high proportion of professionals, managers and non-manual workers, and low proportions of semi-skilled and unskilled heads of households. This is congruent with the fact that 76 per cent of the households are owner-occupied – the second-highest percentage amongst the nine clusters. Although much of the accommodation is again old terraced housing, amenities are much better than in the neighbouring cluster 1, e.g. only 3 per cent of households lack an inside WC.

Cluster 3: bedsitter land

This cluster is small and contains 4 per cent of the area's population. comprising seven adjacent enumeration districts all very close to the city centre. The social workers had picked out this area as the bedsitter, lodging-house district of the town. In accordance with this observation, this cluster contains the highest proportions of single-adult households, of New Commonwealth-born people, and of unemployed males (Table

6.1). Nearly half of the population are aged between 15 and 44 years, and there is also a fairly large elderly population. Recent research has shown that this cluster of transients has a high rate of deliberate self-poisoning for both men and women in comparison with the town as a whole (Gibbons *et al.*, 1973).

As one would expect in a bedsitter area, two-fifths of all households are in privately rented furnished accommodation, and a fifth in privately rented unfurnished dwellings. Thirteen per cent are in shared dwellings, and there is the highest rate of overcrowding – 5 per cent compared with 1 per cent for the area as a whole.

Cluster 4: intermediate-status area
Cluster 4 comprises 7 per cent of the area's population, and its enumeration districts tend to lie on the boundaries of cluster 3. In many respects it resembles cluster 3, though the typical features described above are less pronounced. It contains a relatively high proportion of young adults and of single-person households, many of them in shared dwellings. Two-fifths of the households are privately rented compared with three-fifths in cluster 3. However in contrast to cluster 3 the majority of households are owner-occupied and there is a somewhat higher proportion of white-collar workers.

Cluster 5: high-status area
This area is unique. It contains 7 per cent of the area's population, and is made up of eight enumeration districts in the north-east of the district. It consists mainly of the high-status areas bordering the Common on the outskirts of the social work area. The senior social workers had pointed out this neighbourhood as an affluent one noted for its low referral rates. It has the greatest concentration of professional and managerial heads of households (52 per cent as against 13 per cent for the area as a whole) and the highest proportion of qualified people – 53 per cent have HNC or degrees, compared with 12 per cent for the area as a whole. Nearly nine out of ten heads of households own their homes, and four out of five own a car. Housing amenities are the best for the area, and nearly two-fifths of all households have seven or more rooms at their disposal (as against 9 per cent of the area's households).

The cluster contains the average number of elderly people, but few of them live alone. Although there are above-average proportions of large families, the proportion of school-age to pre-school children suggests that more of the families in this cluster are completed.

Cluster 6: postwar council housing – barrack style
This is the first of three clusters (6, 7 and 8) which comprise the majority of council housing in the area, and consists mainly of a peripheral estate

Table 6.1 Social indicators and Clusters

Social indicator	Cluster									
	1 Old terraced housing, poor amenities	2 Modernised terraced housing	3 Bedsitter land	4 Intermediate-status area	5 High-status area	6 Postwar council housing – barrack style	7 Postwar council housing – young and old people	8 Prewar council housing – poor amenities	9 Mixture of public and private housing	Are..
	%	%	%	%	%	%	%	%	%	%
Age structure (Base = A)										
0–4 years	6	5	4	5	5	7	11	9	6	7
5–14 years	12	13	9	12	18	21	15	22	19	16
15–24 years	14	13	22	20	13	20	15	14	17	16
25–44 years	21	21	25	20	22	22	26	22	23	22
45–64 years	29	29	24	26	29	24	21	21	24	25
65 years and over	18	19	15	17	13	6	12	12	11	14
Socio-economic status (Base = B)										
Professional/ managerial	9	18	14	16	52	4	6	6	15	13
Non-manual	18	25	31	39	30	10	14	7	18	19
Skilled manual	35	31	22	21	5	49	41	47	36	36
Semi-skilled	19	19	17	15	2	21	20	22	16	17
Unskilled	8	5	6	3	1	13	9	10	5	8
Education Students (Base = A)	3	5	5	6	8	3	2	2	3	4
HNC or degree (Base = C)	6	21	28	19	53	1	3	1	12	12

Housing tenure (Base = D)										
Owner-occupied	53	76	39	61	89	16	13	11	58	43
Council tenants	4	5	4	1	—	82	83	86	30	39
Rented privately unfurnished	37	15	19	23	7	2	3	3	11	13
Rented privately furnished	6	4	39	15	3	—	1	—	2	5
Housing conditions (Base = D)										
In shared dwellings	5	4	13	16	2	—	—	—	2	3
Lacking inside WC	20	3	3	6	—	1	1	44	11	9
Sharing/lacking hot water	20	6	17	15	2	2	2	41	9	11
Over 1½ persons per room	1	—	5	2	—	1	—	2	1	1
Under ½ person per room	43	45	28	41	44	12	16	25	31	31
With 7 or more rooms	7	7	23	27	38	4	1	2	2	9
With 1 to 3 rooms	18	10	44	21	5	15	31	10	9	17
Household composition (Base = D)										
Single pensioner	15	13	10	12	8	6	15	8	8	11
Single adult	9	4	26	13	5	3	5	3	5	6
Large families (5 or more dependent children)	—	1	—	2	1	1	—	1	2	1

Table 6.1 *Social indicators and Clusters (cont.)*

Social indicator										Total
Vulnerable minorities										
New Commonwealth-born (Base = A)	1	1	3	2	1	1	1	1	1	1
Males seeking work (Base = E)	4	3	6	4	2	5	3	6	4	4
Males off work sick (Base = E)	1	1	1	1	—	1	1	2	1	1
Other										
Not owning a car (Base = D)	59	40	54	49	15	53	60	64	45	50
Economically active married females (Base = F)	42	39	48	43	34	47	43	33	47	42
Total population (Base = A)	10,480	11,000	2,540	4,490	4,490	13,470	8,260	5,660	4,750	65,072
Total households (Base = D)	4,170	4,100	1,130	1,650	1,490	3,850	3,060	1,650	1,490	22,649

Note: All the figures presented in Table 6.1 are percentages. The base figures used to calculate these percentages vary with the different social indicators. The key below defines each base and shows which bases relate to which social indicators.

Base A – Population within each cluster and the area as a whole.
Social indicators – age structure, students and New Commonwealth-born

Base B – Heads of households.
Social indicators – socio-economic status.

Base C – Economically active adults.
Social indicators – HNC or degree holders.

Base D – Households.
Social indicators – housing tenure, housing conditions, household composition, and households not owning a car.

Base E – Economically active males.
Social indicators – males seeking work and males off work sick.

Base F – Married females.
Social indicator – economically active married females.

which was built in the postwar years and laid out in barrack style with few community facilities. It contains 21 per cent of the area's population, in the west of the social work district. Eighty-two per cent of all households are council tenants, and only 16 per cent are owner-occupiers. The greatest concentration of manual labour, both skilled and unskilled, and the lowest proportions of professionals and managers, are found here. The housing conditions and amenities enjoyed by the households are amongst the best in the area.

This cluster has the lowest proportion of elderly people, and a relatively high proportion of larger family units. The age structure shows a high proportion of children aged 5 to 14, and also a large proportion in the 15 to 25 age group, suggesting the presence of families in which many children had grown up but had not yet left home.

Cluster 7: postwar council housing – young and old people

This cluster is similar in many respects to cluster 6. It contains 13 per cent of the area's population, and includes widely dispersed areas of postwar council housing, partly bordering on cluster 6.

Eighty-three per cent of all households are council tenants – again enjoying the type of good conditions and amenities found in cluster 6. There are more white-collar workers compared with cluster 6 (Table 6.1).

Demographically, it contains a mixture of young families and elderly people living alone. The highest proportion of under-5s coincides with a low proportion of school-age children, a low incidence of large families and of households of all types with more than five persons.

Cluster 8: prewar council housing – poor amenities

Cluster 8 contains 9 per cent of the area's population, with the highest proportion (86%) of council tenants. The seniors described this neighbourhood as an inner estate of prewar council housing, much of it lacking in basic amenities and making high demands on social services. This turned out to be an accurate observation. Forty-four per cent of all households lack an inside WC, and 41 per cent share or lack hot water. In addition, the highest rates of overcrowding in council accommodation occur here.

As in cluster 6, manual workers, both skilled and unskilled, make up over four-fifths of the workforce, with only 13 per cent in white-collar jobs. Although this cluster has the highest rates of male unemployment and sickness-absence rates, it has the lowest rates of married women going out to work. Interestingly, this low economic activity rate for married women is only approximated in the two affluent clusters. Finally, there are high proportions of children of all ages in this cluster – 9 per cent in the under-5 age range and 22 per cent in the 5 to 14 years group – no doubt partly accounting for the low proportion of mothers going out to work. The proportion of elderly people was slightly below average for the area as a whole, and few of them lived alone.

An examination of the distribution of one-parent families confirmed an earlier observation made by the social workers of a high concentration in this neighbourhood.

This cluster, then, presents the prototype of social disadvantage as described, for example, by Wedge and Prosser (1973), and predictably produced the highest referral rates to the area office.

Cluster 9: mixture of public and private housing

This cluster, containing 7 per cent of the area's population, mainly lies in the centre of the social work area. It is very similar to the area as a whole in its demographic and social structure, as Table 6.1 indicates. It contains somewhat fewer elderly people, and appears to be slightly more affluent than average with regard to home and car ownership.

THE SOCIAL WORK CLIENTS

We now want to see whether the demographic and social characteristics of these clusters are reflected in the patterns of demands made on the social services in the area. In other words, did this mechanical analysis predict the demand for, and supply of, services? Some problems arise when trying to compare the characteristics of cases with those of the general population in the area since the CRS data are based on cases which may represent individuals or whole or parts of households. Two or more cases may be identified within a household and lead to double counting of households; clients also may have changed their demographic characteristics during the study period (for example, they may have changed their civil state and living group, they may have moved from one neighbourhood to another), but it did not prove feasible to take account of such changes.

Despite these problems the counts of referrals and on-going cases have been compared to counts of the related households in the area and approximate rates computed for selected demographic groups of clients. (In this analysis and in the following accounts of the social work in the area office we distinguish between incoming 'referrals' during one year and 'on-going cases' already open at the start of the year.)

Direct comparison of all cases referred and on-going during the study year with the population and household totals (Table 6.2) suggests the following rates. For every 1,000 households 72 cases were referred during the year and 51 were already current at the beginning of the year – a total of 123 per 1,000 households. In terms of population, 25 cases per 1,000 were referred and 18 per 1,000 already open – a total rate of 43

Table 6.2 Clusters, their Populations, and Cases in Contact in the study year (beginning 1 February 1975)

Cluster	Persons %	Households %	Referrals %	Rate*	Ratio†	On-going cases %	Rate*	Ratio†
1 Old terraced housing, poor amenities	16·1	18·4	18·5	72	1·00	18·3	51	0·99
2 Modernised terraced housing	16·9	18·1	11·7	46	0·65	16·2	46	0·90
3 Bedsitter land	3·9	5·0	5·2	75	1·04	3·0	30	0·59
4 Intermediate-status area	6·9	7·3	5·8	56	0·78	5·4	37	0·73
5 High-status area	6·9	6·6	3·2	35	0·48	3·4	26	0·51
6 Postwar council housing – barrack style	20·7	17·0	22·3	94	1·31	20·9	63	1·23
7 Postwar council housing – young and old people	12·7	13·5	14·3	76	1·06	16·9	64	1·25
8 Prewar council housing – poor amenities	8·7	7·3	12·8	126	1·75	11·2	78	1·53
9 Mixture of public and private housing	7·3	6·6	6·3	69	0·95	4·7	36	0·72
Bases (= 100%)	65,072	22,649	1,631	(72)		1,151	(51)	

* Rates are expressed as cases per 1,000 private households.
† The ratio compares the cluster rate to the overall rate.

cases per 1,000 population. These estimates, however, need adjustment. We have already mentioned factors which might inflate these rates. In addition, there are others which could deflate the estimates, in particular the exclusion from the comparison of those living in non-private house-holds and clients in touch with the area social workers who were living outside the area (for example, children in care outside the area boun-daries). These exclusions amounted to about 8 per cent of cases referred and to nearly one-fifth of on-going cases. Taking all these distorting factors into account our best estimate is that the social workers were concerned with between 3 per cent and 5 per cent of the population of the area, or between 9 per cent and 15 per cent of households during the course of the study year. This includes about one in eight of all elderly over 65 years and about one in five of the population over 75 years, and, in particular, nearly one in four of the elderly living alone. The latter is an impressive figure, especially if we take into account that those in receipt of domiciliary services only are not included in this estimate.

The overall variations in the geographic distribution of the cases in contact, on the whole reflect the differential distribution of the social and demographic indicators between the clusters. The contact rates are low-est, at about half of the overall rates, in the high-status area (cluster 5) and are approximately a third and a quarter below the overall average in the less well-off but still fairly affluent areas of clusters 2 and 4, which also have the highest proportions of white-collar workers. The contact rates are highest and up to three-quarters above the average in the most socially disadvantaged prewar estate (cluster 8). In general, the public-sector housing areas (clusters 6, 7 and 8) containing also the largest concentrations of semi- and unskilled occupations have above-average contact rates both as regards referrals and on-going cases. Those areas with a higher rate of on-going cases also tend to have a higher referral rate but there are exceptions: first, the fringe estates around the public-sector housing estates where the referral of delinquents was high and accounted for 29 per cent of all cases referred, as against 15 per cent overall. The explanation is, as we shall see in the next chapter, that referrals for delinquency were largely automatic police notifications which were usually closed after an administrative check. Similarly, in the bedsitter and lodging-house area (cluster 3) there were high rates of referrals for financial and housing problems which tended not to attract a long-term commitment from the social workers, as we shall see in later chapters.

The majority of people referred during the study year and of on-going clients were either elderly or children and families. The elderly comprised 30 per cent of all referrals and two-fifths of the on-going cases; whilst families with dependent children accounted for half of the referrals and a quarter of cases open at the beginning of the year. Given the predominance of these two groups of clients, the rest of this chapter looks at them in detail.

Elderly clients

During the year, the social workers were in contact with approximately a thousand elderly clients living alone or in two-pensioner households, of whom one-half were referrals (Tables 6.3 and 6.4).

The areas of old terraced housing, clusters 1 and 2, contain nearly half of the total of pensioner households in the area. But the rates for referrals and on-going cases differ in the two clusters and reflect their demographic characteristics. The rates are higher for referrals, about 20 per cent above average in cluster 1 where there were more dwellings rented unfurnished, fewer people owned their houses and where the standard of amenities was much lower. In the more affluent and higher socio-economic status cluster 2, the proportion of elderly households in contact with the social workers was at least 20 per cent below the overall average. These data suggest that the lower standard of accommodation and the lower socio-economic status of cluster 1 are associated with higher referral rates of the elderly. There may, however, be other factors – for instance, lack of informal sources of help because offspring may have moved to better housing areas. It is also likely that the elderly living in rented property who may have lived there for a considerable time were materially worse off than those owning their homes.

Some of the above speculations are not borne out by the service picture in cluster 8. Since cluster 8 is the most deprived area showing the highest demands for social services overall, particularly in relation to poverty, family problems, physical and mental ill health, it is remarkable that the elderly were not making greater demands on the services. As Table 6.3 shows, referrals of elderly living alone were about average although the contact rate for on-going cases was above average, but still the lowest for any of the council-housing areas. In this connection it is interesting to note that the senior social workers spoke about the 'resilience' of the population in this neighbourhood.

Regarding the other areas, mention has already been made of the high referral rates and the low rate of on-going contacts in cluster 3 – the inner area of bedsitters and lodging houses. Here requests for help were largely concerned with housing and accommodation problems. The picture is quite the opposite for cluster 7 which includes most of the sheltered housing for the elderly (except in the new post-census development which we could not include in our analysis). Understandably a relatively large proportion of the elderly here were in contact with the social workers on a long-term basis.

Cluster 6 stands out as the one cluster producing above-average numbers of referrals and on-going cases of the elderly. This at first sight is

Table 6.3   Clusters and Elderly living alone

Cluster	Population	Referrals			On-going cases		
	%	%	Rate*	Ratio†	%	Rate*	Ratio†
1 Old terraced housing, poor amenities	25·7	31·4	147	1·22	25·0	107	0·97
2 Modernised terraced housing	20·5	15·2	90	0·75	16·0	86	0·78
3 Bedsitter land	4·5	6·0	162	1·34	2·8	68	0·62
4 Intermediate-status area	7·4	7·6	124	1·03	4·2	62	0·56
5 High-status area	4·8	2·2	56	0·46	1·7	40	0·36
6 Postwar council housing – barrack style	9·3	12·1	156	1·29	16·3	193	1·75
7 Postwar council housing – young and old people	17·9	15·6	104	0·86	24·0	148	1·34
8 Prewar council housing – poor amenities	5·4	5·7	128	1·06	6·9	142	1·29
9 Mixture of public and private housing	4·6	4·1	107	0·89	3·1	74	0·67
Bases (= 100%)	2,610	315	(121)		288	(110)	

* Rates are expressed as cases per 1,000 single pensioner households.
† The ratio compares the cluster rate to the overall rate.

Table 6.4 Clusters and Two-Person Pensioner households

Cluster	Population %	Referrals			On-going cases		
		%	Rate*	Ratio†	%	Rate*	Ratio†
1 Old terraced housing, poor amenities	21·2	24·0	99	1·16	22·8	99	1·01
2 Modernised terraced housing	26·7	21·1	68	0·80	20·1	69	0·75
3 Bedsitter land	3·8	2·9	65	0·76	2·1	52	0·56
4 Intermediate-status area	8·6	9·1	91	1·06	6·3	68	0·74
5 High-status area	7·4	4·6	53	0·62	5·8	73	0·79
6 Postwar council housing – barrack style	9·1	12·6	118	1·38	16·4	167	1·80
7 Postwar council housing – young and old people	10·2	8·0	67	0·78	14·3	129	1·40
8 Prewar council housing – poor amenities	7·7	10·3	115	1·34	7·4	89	0·97
9 Mixture of public and private housing	5·3	1·7	28	0·33	4·8	83	0·90
Bases (= 100%)	2,046	175	(86)		189	(92)	

* Rates are expressed as cases per 1,000 two-person pensioner households.
† The ratio compares the cluster rate to the overall rate.

baffling as cluster 6 contains the lowest proportion of elderly and has rather good housing conditions. Explanations may be found in the preponderance of young families which may contribute to the feelings of isolation and loneliness in the elderly. Also some of the elderly may have been recently transplanted to the council estates of cluster 6, and may not yet feel settled. Another factor may be the comparatively low socioeconomic standing of the neighbourhood.

Interesting questions arise as to why a socially very disadvantaged area – cluster 8 – should produce an average number of referrals of old people living alone, whilst a demographically and socially similar area – cluster 6 – with better environmental conditions should produce above-average proportions of referrals. Since the numbers involved are very small (for example, in cluster 8 eighteen old people living alone were referred during the year and in cluster 6 thirty-eight people) the following speculations are offered with caution. Could the comparatively low referral rates for elderly people in the more disadvantaged but older prewar estates be associated with stronger extended family ties and obligations, reminiscent of the Bethnal Green studies of the late 1950s (Young and Willmott, 1962; Townsend, 1957)? Some support for this hypothesis may be found in low numbers of potential female/daughter carers going out to work in this area (33%). In the postwar housing area of cluster 6 47 per cent of married women went out to work.

Children and Families

The analysis, as for that of the elderly, encompasses on-going cases and referrals concerned with families with dependent children (defined as aged under seventeen in the CRS data) living in private households. We have not been able to include those families accommodated in hostels, or the families of children received into care (since the case record is in the name of the child) unless the families are recorded as open cases in their own right or have been referred for another reason.

Table 6.5 summarises the results of a comparison of referrals and on-going cases involving families with dependent children with the census figures for the most similar category, that is to say families with children aged under fifteen. The comparisons will be inaccurate for several reasons since, apart from the incompatibility of the definitions, the changes since the census of household composition cannot be estimated directly. However, data which are available on the age and sex distributions of the population in mid-1975 suggest that despite a migration from the area to the new peripheral estate of young families which could not be included in the analysis, the number of children under fifteen in the area has altered very little.

With some caution we estimate that contact with or concerning families occurred at a rate of 140 cases per 1,000 families in the area, excluding

Table 6.5 *Clusters and Families with dependent children**

Cluster	Population %	Referrals			On-going cases		
		%	Rate**	Ratio†	%	Rate**	Ratio†
1 Old terraced housing, poor amenities	13·4	10·5	79	0·78	13·2	38	0·98
2 Modernised terraced housing	14·9	7·6	51	0·51	9·8	26	0·66
3 Bedsitter land	2·5	3·3	132	1·31	1·7	26	0·67
4 Intermediate-status area	5·3	3·4	64	0·64	3·7	27	0·70
5 High-status area	6·7	2·1	32	0·31	2·0	12	0·30
6 Postwar council housing – barrack style	23·9	30·7	130	1·29	27·7	45	1·16
7 Postwar council housing – young and old people	16·0	16·1	102	1·01	12·8	31	0·80
8 Prewar council housing – poor amenities	9·7	17·9	179	1·77	23·0	92	2·36
9 Mixture of public and private housing	7·5	8·5	114	1·13	6·1	32	0·81
Bases (= 100%)	7,577	765	(101)		296	(39)	

* The census identified families with children under 15 years whilst the CRS identified family groups with any child under 17 years
** Rates are expressed as cases per 1,000 related population.
† The ratio compares the cluster rate to the overall rate.

the new estate. As these figures include referrals for delinquency, of which few are taken up by the social work teams, the rate can be adjusted to between 10 per cent and 11 per cent of families in contact. The referrals considered include a variety of problems ranging from welfare-rights inquiries, homelessness or threatened eviction to marital breakdown and child problems, and constitute some two-thirds of the total cases included here.

Cluster 8, the old inner housing estates, stands out clearly in Table 6.5 as a source of social services clients. These areas emerge from the analysis of census data as being particularly deprived with over 60 per cent of households lacking a basic amenity, high rates of overcrowding and unemployment, and the lowest rates of car ownership in the social work area. The proportion of one-parent families is about twice the general average, and a considerable number of these are clients of the area office, as described in a paper by Warburton and Willmott (1976). Referrals from this area include those symptomatic of instability – family break-up, and child-care problems, particularly delinquency. Similarly, on the fringe of the estates (cluster 9) there is a high incidence of delinquency and reception-into-care, but here referrals for material problems are below average.

Other major sources of cases and referrals are the council estates of cluster 6; this includes most of the large barrack-style estate mentioned by the seniors as a particular source of children taken into care. The estate, built after the war, is settled and contains many large families, and possibly many completed families. Although the estate lacks community facilities and amenities it does not emerge from the census data as an area of deprivation. However, it is possible that some poverty and stress may have been masked: for example, a roughly average level of unemployment may conceal a high rate of youth unemployment, and this may well have grown in magnitude and importance since the census; again the large families living on the estate, where the head is unskilled or semi-skilled, may be especially vulnerable at a time of recession and falling employment. The area generates above-average referrals relating to delinquency, family-relationship problems and material problems, and although the latter are much lower than the rate for cluster 8, the two clusters are comparable in the referrals for non-material problems. The data suggest a high level of instability in an area which cannot on the evidence available be described as deprived. To this we need to add the previously discussed high referral rates for the elderly.

The inner-city area of cluster 3 likewise produced many referrals relating to family problems as well as to housing problems. However, relatively few families here became long-term cases, and this may well be related to rehousing of families on the new estate, but we unfortunately have no data on this and cannot explore this line of inquiry.

CONCLUDING COMMENTS

This chapter has described a first, crude and tentative approach to the problems of relating an area's potential needs to the problems of people actually coming to the attention of the social services and receiving some social work help. This ecological approach is, of course, an indirect one which can only relate broad structural factors of an area to the chances certain groups of the population have of coming into contact with social workers of an area office. It cannot pin-point the unique circumstances of the individual case within these broad group characteristics.

The analysis has exemplified once more that high use of social work services is still very much associated with low socio-economic status, above-average unemployment, large families and poor housing conditions. The consistently high contact rates for the postwar housing areas in cluster 6 may indicate that improved housing conditions alone without appropriate community facilities do not seem to impinge a great deal on the generation of social problems. The analysis has also suggested that the differences in contacts with the social workers between the relatively well-provided and disadvantaged areas are not nearly so great when it comes to the problems of the elderly. Whilst the chances of being in touch with the social workers of the area office are six times as great for families living in the most socially disadvantaged area than for those living in the most affluent neighbourhood, they are only between two and three times higher for elderly people living in socially disadvantaged areas than for those in the affluent neighbourhood. This may tell us the old truth that old age and disability afflict rich and poor alike, but also that domiciliary services, aids and adaptations, and residential care cannot so easily and appropriately be supplied by the private sector as by the statutory one.

This analysis of the case review data within the framework of the area typology has been presented as an illustration of the potential of the method. The weaknesses of the data sources have been considered and possible improvements – for example, preservation of family-address codes for children taken into care – have been indicated. The analysis could also be taken much further by relating type and amount of help received to the social and demographic characteristics of clients and the neighbourhoods from which they come. We may then discover the strengths and weaknesses of informal sources of help in various neighbourhoods, and also the possible gaps and biases of social service coverage.

NOTE

1 The analysis presented is based on Webber's approach and makes use of his statistical programmes which he kindly made available.

Chapter 7

—◆—

A YEAR'S INTAKE TO AN AREA OFFICE

So far we have described the development of certain analytic tools designed to monitor the allocation of staff resources, practical services and counselling help to different client groups, and to relate these resources and activities to territorial indicators of 'need'. We have also discussed how we tried to help practitioners to make use of such tools in their daily work.

Apart from developing new tools to monitor and evaluate social work practice over time, we intended to use this unique data bank on a client population in one area to undertake a systematic study of the characteristics of the total client population, the problems that brought them into contact with the social services, their expressed demands and the types of help they received over the span of one year. How were social work resources deployed among the different client groups? Was it possible to assess not only the volume and types of activities, but also to arrive at a crude estimate of outcome?

We do not as yet know how typical the emerging picture is, since information based on the CRS is only just beginning to be assembled in other areas as this book goes to press.[1] Our impression from contacts with other area offices in social services departments and from a study of the literature is that neither the composition of the client population, nor the kind of help received, nor the time-span before closure, are unique to this particular office (Duncan, 1973; Jones, 1974; Lowenstein, 1974; Camden Social Services Department, 1975; O'Loughlin and Birkhead, 1975; Titcomb, 1974; Boucher, 1976; Corrie, 1976; Wetton, 1976). However, one of the reasons for reporting these findings is to encourage other social services departments to use similar monitoring devices in order to discover what they are doing.

METHOD OF DATA COLLECTION

The data on the year's referrals were collected on a referral form which contains information on the age and sex of the client, his address, his living group, the source, method and date of referral, problems presented and the nature of the request made. The 'no-carbon-required' form was adapted from the referral document already in use in the department. Subsequent reviews were coded on to the case review form, but the intake team used a shortened version for the majority of cases they closed. This procedure was adopted because at this experimental stage the case review form was *additional* to all the other obligatory paper work and we could not expect the intake workers to fill in a detailed form on every inquiry with which they dealt in a single contact, often on the telephone only. The continuous stream of information was then transferred on to punch cards and magnetic tape for computer processing.

The referral and case review forms were filled in reasonably well considering the number of clients dealt with, but inevitably the pressure of work, the scant information on some of the casual referrals and the fleeting 'one-off' contacts with many clients resulted in incomplete information. While we tried our best to retrieve missing data, we accepted some deficiencies since we wanted to learn how much systematic information can be gained in a routine manner under ordinary working conditions.

THE INTAKE TEAM

Most incoming cases were dealt with by an intake team comprising the equivalent of five and a half social workers and a part-time occupational therapist, led by a senior social worker. The senior was readily accessible for advice and consultation, and he endorsed all closures. During the study year staff shortages occurred which at one time reduced the intake team to four workers in all. The intake team as a rule only undertook short-term work, estimated to last three months or less, but this did not always work out in practice. Cases requiring longer-term care were usually passed on to the two long-term teams, each having the equivalent of six full-time social workers and two ancillary staff.

NUMBERS REFERRED – OLD AND NEW CASES

Data collection began on 1 February 1975, and during the subsequent year there were approximately 2,500 referrals, representing some 2,000 cases (Table 7.1).

The number of referrals ranged from 170 to 240 per month, averaging about 200 – roughly just under 50 referrals per week. A referral was defined as 'any incoming case requiring some social work input which is neither currently on an allocated nor on the agency review caseload'.

Comparing the number of referrals in 1975 and 1973, when a member of the research team carried out a study of referrals (Neill, 1974), there was an increase of one-fifth. A similar percentage increase has been reported in several other studies (London Borough of Hillingdon, 1976; Devon County Council Social Services Department, 1977). However,

Table 7.1   *Referrals and Cases in the study year*

Number of times referred	Number of cases	Percentage of cases	Number of episodes
1	1,747	85	1,747
2	255	12	510
3	44	2	132
4	8	—	32
5	3	—	15
Totals	2,057*	100†	2,436

* Includes 804 cases known to have been in contact with the Department before 1 February 1975.

† As percentages have been rounded off to whole figures in this and subsequent tables, the totals do not always add up to 100 per cent.

just under half of the referrals in 1975 were reapplications from clients who had previously been in contact, whereas in 1973 only one-third of the referrals were old cases. This trend is also reflected in the figures we have been able to collect from other social services departments (Kingston upon Thames Social Services Department, 1976; Wetton, 1976; Devon County Council Social Services Department, 1977). The increasing proportion of re-referrals raises a number of questions.

First, has the area office discovered most of its potential clients? This seems unlikely, although there are indications of considerable coverage among the elderly. For instance, the area teams at a conservative estimate were in touch with an eighth of the area's population aged over 65, including a fifth of the over 75s. This estimate excludes clients receiving home help or meals-on-wheels services only. Similarly the number of cases of physical disability and frailty compared favourably with those expected on the basis of the national survey of the handicapped and impaired carried out by Harris (1971): the social workers were in contact with about 30 per cent of the estimated number of very severely, severely, or appreciably handicapped among the over 65s, and with about 45 per cent in the over 75s. In contrast, contact with the younger handicapped adults, estimated on the same basis, could be as low as 5 per cent.

The second question is: had record-keeping improved so that identification of old cases was more efficient? This is the case. A better filing and central record system supported by the CRS had improved the effectiveness in tracing old client records.

Thirdly, had the area policy changed with regard to closure of cases? This is a likely hypothesis. Since the formation of the intake team in the autumn of 1974, the aim was to deal mainly with explicit requests on a short-term basis unless there were clear indications for more intensive and longer-term involvement, for example a child at risk or a vulnerable elderly person living alone. The result of this policy was that approximately 81 per cent of all incoming cases were closed within three months, as we shall show below (Table 8.1). At the same time, clients were encouraged to come back if they experienced further problems.

In describing the client population we have taken the case – whether an individual or a family – as the unit of analysis and confined ourselves to client characteristics as they presented at the first referral recorded during the study year.

AGE AND SEX

The age and sex distribution of the client population differed from that of the area, particularly in relation to the elderly. At least 20 per cent of the individual clients were aged 75 and over, compared with 5 per cent in the general population in the area.[2] On the other hand, the middle-aged were under-represented compared with the general population. This is presumably a phase when children have grown up, when financial and family problems have eased and the more serious disabilities associated with growing old have not yet begun.

The sex ratio of this client population showed two unusual features: first, boys predominated among teenagers because of their proneness to delinquency. Secondly, contrary to demographic norms, there were equal proportions of men and women in the 65 to 74 age group. Further exploration showed that a considerable number of men living in two-person pensionable households came to the area office in the winter months with financial problems, many of them related to fuel bills.

Unfortunately, it was not possible to collect reliable data on social class, family size, or housing amenities, as this would have imposed too many demands on the social workers. Hence we cannot determine whether the individual clients differed in these social characteristics from the local population, although the areal analysis showed that the clients tended to live in the less privileged neighbourhoods. We did collect data on marital status and living group, and we shall refer to these social characteristics in the appropriate contexts.

PROBLEMS PRESENTED ON REFERRAL

Nearly a third of the main problems given by the referrer or identified by the social worker were associated with physical disability, illness, or ageing (Table 7.2). Financial and material problems (17%), delinquency (15%) and other child behaviour and family relationship problems (14%) constituted the other large groups.

When we tried to compare the problem distribution with those of other referral studies, we encountered several difficulties. First, some analyses

Table 7.2   *Main Problems given at First Referral in the study year*

Main problem	No.	%
Physical disability/ageing	614	30
Financial/material	337	17
Housing/accommodation	217	11
Child behaviour/family relationships/etc.	284	14
Mental/emotional disorder	152	8
Delinquency	296	15
Other	119	6
Total	2,019*	100

* Problem not known in 38 cases.

did not distinguish between types of problems and client group. Secondly, in some studies referrals for domiciliary services only were included, while in others, like our own, only social work referrals were enumerated. These differences greatly affect the proportion of frail elderly in the total number of referrals. Thirdly, some authorities treat casual requests and automatic notifications of delinquents by the police as purely administrative matters. The only percentage of referrals which occurs with astonishing regularity is that for mental or emotional disorder – between 6 per cent and 9 per cent. Thus, until more uniform problem classifications and definitions are adopted in social services departments, it would be hazardous and misleading to compare referral information on problems in different areas. The DHSS Social Work Service Development Group encountered similar difficulties in their study *Records in Social Services Departments* (DHSS, 1977). They say (para. 31, p. 11) 'At present on all the evidence available, it would be difficult for many directors of social services to state how many people in a year have asked their departments for help, who referred them, why they came, and whether or not they were known to other agencies who have information about them'. Even where such information is available (loc. cit.) 'A director cannot compare his situation with other local authorities, since information other than national statistics is not generally assembled in comparable form either between local authorities or even sometimes within parts of the same local authority'

Since we had referral data for 1973 it was possible to study trends. In both years just under a third of all cases were referred because of problems of physical disability or ageing. In 1975 twice as many clients presented financial and material difficulties as in 1973. Many of these were referred several times during 1975 – in fact, of the substantial number coming back to the office within three months of closure, 27 per cent presented financial and material difficulties. This large increase was also noted in our study of social services consumers in Seatown, and probably reflects the consequences of rising unemployment and inflation (Glampson and Goldberg, 1976). The comments of the consumers also suggested that the Social Services Department is increasingly used as an information and advice centre and as a referral agency, particularly in relation to financial difficulties. In contrast, we observed a fall in the proportion of cases referred with housing and accommodation difficulties; this trend is associated with the transfer of responsibility for homelessness to the district housing authority in February 1975.

A slightly higher proportion of delinquents were notified by the police. The proportion of child behaviour and family relationship problems has remained the same at 14 per cent for both years, which is somewhat surprising in view of the growing concern with children at risk.

Finally, referrals concerned with mental or emotional disorders had decreased slightly. This decrease is probably related to the establishment of a specialist team operating from a different base in close association with the local psychiatric services.

PROBLEMS AND PEOPLE

We have already mentioned that the preponderance of boys was almost entirely due to their frequent referrals for delinquency. In contrast, among the 175 girls referred, only a third were notified for their delinquent behaviour; a further third came with other behaviour problems, of which a substantial proportion centred around adolescent difficulties.

Single people between the ages of 17 and 44 presented a variety of problems. This was the group with the highest proportion of mental and emotional disturbances (24%), possibly illustrating yet again that single people are more at risk of developing mental disorder than those who have ever been married.

There was a notable difference in the types of problems presented by single people living alone and those living in families. The former tended to complain of housing and financial problems, whilst the latter were often referred by their relatives for emotional troubles.

Among young families financial difficulties were the reason for referral in over a third of all cases. There were instances of unpaid electricity bills, wrangles with the DHSS over social security payments, deserted spouses who found themselves left with heavy debts, and so on. Just over a quarter of the young families presented problems related to family relationships or behaviour disturbance in their children. This category includes cases of serious family disruption and child neglect. A further 17 per cent of the families were referred on account of housing and accommodation difficulties.

Almost half of the middle-aged presented problems of physical disability which included serious illness such as terminal cancer or progressive diseases such as multiple sclerosis. A further fifth of these clients came with financial difficulties, and 14 per cent were referred because of mental illness or emotional problems.

As we move up the age range, problems related to disability increase proportionately. Three-quarters of the elderly aged 65 to 74 living with their families came into contact with the area office because of needs arising from frailty or disability. A further fifth had either housing or financial difficulties: for instance, a man in his early 70s, who had lived with his married daughter, wanted to move to a place of his own as his daughter's marriage was breaking up; subsequently he returned to the office with requests for furniture and floor-covering for his new flat. Proportionately more clients in this age bracket who lived alone experienced financial problems (26%) compared with those living with their families (10%). Correspondingly fewer had needs resulting from physical disability (57%) compared with 74 per cent of clients in family settings. These observations resemble the findings of a socio-medical study of the needs of elderly welfare clients in 1969, when those who lived alone were found to be fitter but financially worse off than those living with families or friends (Goldberg, Mortimer and Williams, 1970).

Among the very old, needs arising from infirmity and physical disability were the main reason for referral in three-quarters of the cases, whether they lived with their families or alone. We observed that financial need as a main problem occurred less often among the very old than in any other adult client group. Possibly financial entitlements have been sorted out by that time or are pushed into the background by the problems of physical disability and day-to-day living which assume increasing importance. Many of the referrals in this age group reflected the mounting burden on relatives who were themselves ageing. Not infrequently, a short stay in an old people's home was requested to enable the family to take a holiday, or during an emergency when the caring relative suddenly fell ill. Problems of bereavement and depression also occurred, which sometimes resulted in a request for a recuperative holiday. Needs for domiciliary services occasionally arose in otherwise self-sufficient situations because a small accident, such as a fall, could for a while completely incapacitate an old person living alone.

THE REFERRAL ROUTE

Nearly half the clients made contact with the area office through informal channels: almost a third came on their own initiative, and 14 per cent were referred by relatives and friends (Table 7.3). Self-referrals showed a small but significant increase compared with 1973, and may be associated with the intake team's policy to respond quickly to immediate problems, to close the case wherever possible, and to encourage clients to come back if further need arose. The next largest group, 21 per cent of referrals, came from health personnel. Police notifications of young delinquents accounted for most of the 18 per cent of referrals from legal sources.

Comparing informal sources of referral and referrals by health personnel with other studies, we found similarities. In over half of the thirteen studies we traced, clients who came on their own initiative or on the suggestion of relatives and friends comprised about 50 per cent, and the referrals by health personnel in most areas clustered around the 20 per cent mark.

Four distinct configurations stand out if we relate mode of referral to type of problem: those who experienced financial and material troubles, and to a lesser extent housing problems, came largely on their own initiative; just under half of the frail elderly and physically disabled were referred by health agencies; delinquents were practically all referred by the police; whilst those with child behaviour or family relationship problems were referred by a variety of agencies (Table 7.3).

Age trends were also observable in relation to source of referral. Self-referrals peaked among young families (61%), their troubles being mainly financial, decreased among the middle-aged (50%), fell steeply among the recently retired (27%), and were lowest among the very old (17%). There was a corresponding rise in referrals by health personnel. It is worth noting, though, that when it came to financial problems even the very old tended to make the first move.

THE REQUEST OF THE REFERRER

We distinguished between three types of request: information and advice, specific services, and investigation. Unfortunately, this categorisation is so broad and open to interpretation by the intake workers that it tells us comparatively little, although conceptually it is useful to distinguish between client characteristics, problems and requests. One finding is firm: in 40 per cent of all cases a request for specific services was made, and this rose to 76 per cent among the elderly and physically disabled. The consumer study also showed that the majority of these clients came to the department expecting some form of practical help. The category of information and advice (27%) masks a multiplicity of financial, personal and legal problems which families tend to bring, and the so-called 'request' might be very vague and hardly formulated. 'Investigation' (31%) can mean an administrative check to discover whether a client is known, as in the automatic police notification of delinquents, or a request for a thorough exploration and assessment in a case of child neglect or of an elderly person at risk.

Table 7.3   Referrer and Main Problems at First Referral in the study year

| Referrer | Main problem | | | | | | | All cases |
	Physical disability/ ageing %	Financial/ material %	Housing/ accommodation %	Child behaviour/ family relationships %	Mental/ emotional disorder %	Delinquency %	Other %	%
Informal channels								
Self	20	72	56	27	18	1	34	32
Family/friends/ neighbours	20	9	16	19	22	2	13	14
Formal channels								
Health personnel	45	4	8	19	31	—	10	21
Police/probation/ courts/solicitors	1	2	1	11	7	94	24	18
Other local authority departments – including Housing	7	7	16	15	13	2	4	9
Other – including DHSS	7	5	3	9	9	1	15	6
Base (= 100%)	607	335	216	279	149	294	119	1,999*

* Referrer or problem not known in 58 cases.

In summary: one year's intake to an area office of Seatown's Social Services Department consisted of 2,436 referrals, representing 2,057 cases of whom half were already known to the area office. Demographically the clientele fell into two very broad groups: the elderly, and young families with children. The main problem groupings consisted of those with physical disabilities or suffering from frailty in old age mainly referred by health agencies, those with financial and environmental problems coming predominantly on their own or on other informal initiatives, and families with disturbed relationships and child care problems referred by many different social, educational and medical agencies.

NOTES

1 Work on replicating the Seatown study in Cambridgeshire is in progress. Findings from pilot studies of two social work teams covering rural areas have shown similar patterns of social work help and use of resources.
2 It was not possible to identify a principal client within the 339 referrals designated as family cases; nor were we able to allocate the members of these families to their respective age and sex groups. Hence we have not produced an age and sex breakdown for the total client population. It is fairly certain, however, that had we been able to enumerate the total client population the proportion of the elderly would have been somewhat lower.

Chapter 8

———◆———

SHORT-TERM SOCIAL WORK IN AN INTAKE TEAM

INTERVENTION POLICY ON INTAKE

Before analysing the case review data, we asked the area staff, and in particular the members of the intake team, to tell us what criteria determined the type of help clients received. For incoming cases, five possible ways of disposal were identified.

First were *cases in which a minimal social work service was given.* These included police notifications of delinquent behaviour where court inquiry reports were not requested or where the case was not currently known or did not present a serious risk; persons requesting a home help service only; and physically disabled people requiring aids or adaptations whose needs were carefully assessed by the occupational therapist who would arrange for the appropriate devices to be supplied.

Secondly, *applicants who received one-off type of information and advice.* This group comprised those who needed help in sorting out their welfare benefits. In these cases, the intake workers often mediated between the client and the DHSS. There were also people with fuel debts who might be given advice on budgeting and on whose behalf the social workers sometimes got in touch with the DHSS over allowances or with the fuel boards to arrange repayment schedules. Lastly there were clients with marital problems seeking advice. (Occasionally these applicants were referred to marriage guidance counsellors or taken on for short-term casework.)

The third method of disposal was *short-term social work within the intake team.* Such work was undertaken where the supportive structure of the client was threatened; where the welfare of children was endangered by family break-up; or where elderly clients were at serious risk and immediate action was necessary.

Fourthly, some *cases were transferred to the long-term teams.* These included children coming into care; children whose family situations placed them at risk of neglect or injury or caused serious emotional disturbance; blind or partially-sighted clients; some of the very vulnerable or disabled elderly and some younger persons with serious progressive disabilities. Supervision orders were passed to the long-term teams as a matter of course.

Finally, after the intake team had arranged a service some cases were placed on *agency review* in order to assess, say in three months' time, whether the intervention had been appropriate.

In general, the staff said that the clearer the client's problem, the more likely he was to receive attention compared with people whose problems were initially hidden or ill-defined because of inadequate referral information.

CLIENT FLOW AND 'SURVIVAL'

We now want to explore what actually happened to applicants from the time when they were identified as potential clients, and how far the methods of intervention reflected the area's explicit policy. The flow diagram (Figure 8.1) traces the complex disposal channels which the CRS enabled us to disentangle successfully.

Of the 2,057 incoming cases in 1975, 149 (7%) could not be traced – an acceptable loss compared with other studies in the health field; 484 (roughly 25 per cent of the remaining cases) were closed on the day of referral. Of the remaining 1,424 cases, 1,203 had been closed by the intake team during the study year, 11 cases were still being dealt with by the intake workers, and 210 had been passed on to the long-term teams. Of these, 124 were allocated to individual social workers, 65 were placed on agency review for occasional check-up and surveillance, and 21 had yet to be reviewed. By June 1976, a further 93 cases had been closed by the long-term teams. Thus, five months after the end of the study year, of the 2,000 intakes, 128 cases, or about 6 per cent, were still receiving continuous social work help from the date of their original referral.[1] It should be remembered, however, that an unknown number of clients were still having home help or meals-on-wheels or using aids and adaptations provided by the Department and benefiting from other services to which they might have been referred.

Similar trends of containing the increasing number of referrals within the intake team and of transferring very few cases to the so-called long-term teams are described in several other studies (Titcomb, 1974; O'Loughlin and Birkhead, 1975; Corrie, 1976; Gostick, 1976). The rationale often given is to enable the long-term team to concentrate on constructive and planful long-term casework.

Client survival

An examination of the length of time cases remained open (Table 8.1 and Figure 8.2) shows that 47 per cent were closed within one week of referral, 64 per cent within a month, and 81 per cent by three months. Once more similar trends have been reported in some of the studies already quoted. By six months, only 11 per cent of the referrals were

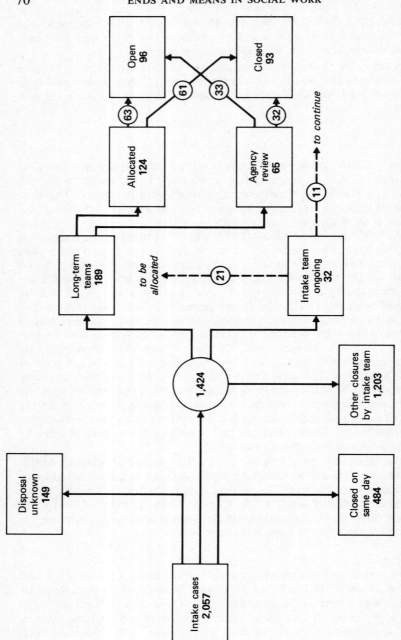

Figure 8.1 *Flow of clients referred in the study year* (First episode only: cases followed up to 30 June 1976)

Table 8.1 'Survivorship' of Clients on First Referral in the study year

Main problem	No.	One day	One week	One month	Three months	Six months	Nine months	Twelve months
					Percentage remaining open after:			
Physical disability/ageing	564	87	73	52	28	17	13	9
Financial/material	319	49	30	15	5	3	1	1
Housing/accommodation	202	52	34	22	11	4	3	3
Child behaviour/family relationships/etc.	260	79	60	48	28	17	14	12
Mental/emotional disorder	135	84	71	57	35	20	13	8
Delinquency	284	94	36	15	5	2	1	1
Other	104	72	57	46	20	9	7	7
All referrals	1,902*	75	53	36	19	11	8	6

* Includes 34 cases where problem not specified; and excludes 6 cases where closure date not given and 149 cases where disposal not known.

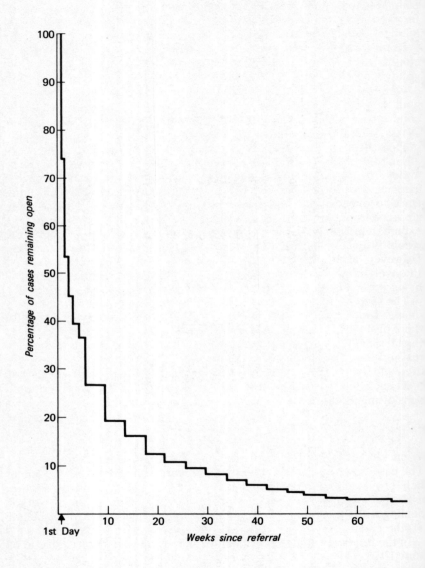

Figure 8.2 *Survival curve for all clients since first referral in the study year* (n = 1,902)

estimated to be open, but thereafter the closure rate slowed down, and by nine months 8 per cent were still open. We are now witnessing what our medical colleagues would call the build-up of a 'chronic population'. Among these long survivors were the very young and the very old. In contrast, the highest closure rates were found among the families and young single people.

One explanation for these trends is that speed of closure is correlated with the type of problems presented. Among the young survivors were children coming into care, delinquents under supervision orders, children at risk, and a few mentally or physically handicapped children.

Physical disability was clearly associated with longer client survival among the elderly. Comparing the elderly aged 75 and over with those under 75, we observed certain differences in closure rates which are associated with the domestic unit in which the clients lived. Thus, contrary to expectations, elderly people under 75 who lived alone were closed earlier, on average, than those living with their families. The explanation is that clients in this age range who lived alone were on the whole fitter and less disabled than those who lived with their families. However, after the age of 75 the degree of disability seemed to be the over-riding factor, and closure rates were almost identical for those living on their own and those living with others.

The speedy closure of young family cases mainly asking for help with financial and material difficulties reflects the area's policy to deal with these problems by advice and referral to the appropriate agencies, such as the DHSS, Housing Department, and so on. This intake team strenuously resisted the temptation to use their powers under Section 1 of the Children and Young Persons Act 1963 to prop up families in debt, and instead used such funds towards more truly preventive purposes, for example subsidising children attending playgroups and nurseries.

THE SOCIAL WORK CLIENTS RECEIVED

What kind of help did clients with different kinds of problems receive? The case review form (see Figure 4.1) records information on practical help provided and tangible changes effected, outside agencies in contact with the social worker, social worker activities, type of social worker dealing with the case, and the number of contacts made with, or on behalf of, the client.

In the following analysis we examined cases reviewed up to the end of June 1976. This cut-off point ensures that cases referred in January 1976 (almost at the end of the study year) had a chance of being reviewed up to five months after referral. The analysis includes all cases referred in the study year which were still open on their most recent review, and a one-in-twelve random sample of closures for which the intake workers completed full reviews rather than the shortened version in general use.

Looking at the general picture of help for the total client population before examining the different problem groups in detail, we note that three types of social worker activities predominate (Table 8.2). Exploration and assessment was recorded for over three-quarters of the cases – clearly an essential part of intake; information and advice was given to nearly half the clients; and a variety of resources were mobilised in over a third of the cases. The problem-solving activity most frequently associated with social work – namely, casework – was only recorded for a fifth of all clients. Over half the applicants received some form of practical service: help with applications, mostly for welfare benefits, topping the list. Social workers were in contact with a wide variety of outside agencies, most often health agencies, on behalf of four-fifths of their clients. Finally, in only a third of the cases did the social workers feel that they had achieved the aims they had set themselves. In nearly a third of all cases the Department withdrew, either because they did not have the appropriate resources to meet the client's needs or because other cases were deemed to have higher priority. A fifth were passed on to other agencies.

All in all, a clear picture emerges of much information, advice, practical help and inter-agency contact for these clients: but, as we shall see below, the 'service packages' contained different ingredients according to the specific needs of different client groups.

Old age and physical disability

We have already noted that the health services were the largest source of referral for this frail and disabled group. The service package received by these clients reflects their needs for an array of practical support in order to live reasonably independent lives in the community. Eighty-four per cent had some form of practical help, the highest percentage of any client group. These services ranged from aids and adaptations (36%), meals-on-wheels (23%) and home helps (22%), to a mere handful for whom a holiday was arranged (3%) or who were referred to a voluntary visitor (3%).

The sixty-one longer-term cases still open at the end of the study period received even more intensive help, the average number of services supplied being 2·6 per client compared with 1·2 for those elderly whose cases had been closed by the end of the study year. Practically all these sixty-one clients (93%) had received some practical service, over a half aids and adaptations, one-third home help, and nearly two-fifths had had help with applications relating to holidays, special supplementary benefit allowances, and occasionally to short- or long-term admission to a welfare home. Altogether we estimate that only about 3 per cent – 18 of the 560 old people referred – went into a welfare home for long-term care during the year.

Apart from carrying out assessments on referral, the social workers were busy mobilising resources, that is to say arranging practical help and supports to daily living, in over two-thirds of the cases. Information and advice was given to nearly half these clients. Again differences emerge between the relatively short-term cases closed during the study year and those remaining open. For the relatively short-term and less complex cases, assessment, advice, and mobilising practical services were the main social worker activities. For the more vulnerable and severely disabled longer-term cases, regular surveillance (41%), some form of counselling (39%) and emotional support (33%) were also part of the social work intervention.

Table 8.2 shows that social workers were in contact with an outside agency on behalf of over four-fifths of this client group. The three agencies most frequently involved strongly reflect the central importance of disability in the lives of those clients. Social workers were most frequently in contact with GPs in over two-fifths of the cases, hospitals follow in about a third of the cases, and health visitors and district nurses in nearly a third of the cases. For the longer-term clients these proportions were even higher, particularly the contacts with the GP which occurred in almost two-thirds of these cases. In only three of the sixty-one open cases was no contact with an outside agency recorded. The average number of agencies contacted on behalf of the continuing cases was 2·3 per case, compared with 1·4 for the shorter-term cases. It is clear that these contacts, even if they only consist of a printed notification to the GP of the type of aid supplied or a short telephone call to the health visitor, took up a sizeable part of the social workers' time.

Finally, what about outcome? So far we have only developed somewhat crude and basic categories of outcome as reflected in the reasons for closure, since the initial thrust of the CRS was directed towards the nature of the problems tackled in relation to social work input and aims to be achieved. Also, the reliability and validity of subjective assessments of outcome are questionable. We see from Table 8.2 that in over half the cases in this problem group the aims, which were mainly directed towards bringing about small changes in the personal/social environment by providing a service or practical aid, had been achieved. It will also be noted that this achievement rate is almost twice as high as in other problem categories. These assessments, made by the social workers themselves, correspond well with the findings of our independent study of a random sample of consumers of social services in the same area, in which the elderly and physically disabled emerged as the group who had received most practical help and were the most satisfied.

Financial, material and housing problems
Table 8.2 shows that clients coming to this area office with predominantly

Table 8.2 Summary of Help Given and Reasons for Closure

	All cases %	Physical disability/ ageing %	Financial/ material %	Housing/ accommodation %	Child behaviour/ family relationships/ etc. %	Mental/ emotional %
Social workers' activities*						
	Information/advice 46	Mob. resources 69	Information/advice 72	Information/advice 77	Problem solving 56	Information/advice 43
	Mob. resources 36	Information/advice 46	Problem solving 26	Mob. resources 47	Information/advice 31	Mob. resources 23
	Problem solving 21	Review visiting 29	Advocacy 25	Review visiting 16	Review visiting 26	Problem solving 23
	Review visiting 19	Problem solving 14	Mob. resources 22	Problem solving 16	Mob. resources 20	
	Sustaining 10	Sustaining 10	Review visiting 11	Sustaining 15	Educ. soc. skills 16	
					Sustaining 15	
					Advocacy 14	
	Assessment 78	Assessment 69	Assessment 82	Assessment 62	Assessment 85	Assessment 99
Practical help*						
	Applications 20	Aids/adaptations 36	Applications 43	Applications 31	Applications 17	
	Aids/adaptations 12	Meals-on-wheels 23	Home helps 11	Home helps 16	Ref. hosp./clinic 15	
	Home helps 11	Home helps 22		Ch. living group 15		
		Applications 16		Rehousing 15		
	None 47	None 16	None 39	None 45	None 59	None 95

Outside agencies*

GPs	27	GPs	44	DHSS	39	GPs	30	Educational	38	GPs	59

Outside agencies*

Box 1:
- GPs 27
- HVs/nurses 21
- Police 16
- Hospitals 15
- DHSS 15
- Housing Dept 11
- Educational 10
- None 17
- Base (100%) 1,908**

Box 2:
- GPs 44
- Hospitals 32
- HVs/nurses 30
- Housing Dept 12
- DHSS 11
- None 16
- Base (100%) 564

Box 3:
- DHSS 39
- HVs/nurses 18
- GPs 11
- Psych. hospitals 11
- None 21
- Base (100%) 321

Box 4:
- GPs 30
- Housing Dept 24
- HVs/nurses 23
- DHSS 15
- Hospitals 15
- Vol. agencies 15
- None 46
- Base (100%) 202

Box 5:
- Educational 38
- HVs/nurses 36
- Psych. hospitals 15
- Vol. agencies 15
- DHSS 13
- GPs 12
- Hospitals 12
- Housing Dept 12
- Child Guid. Cln. 10
- None 5
- Base (100%) 261

Box 6:
- GPs 59
- Psych. hospitals 23
- HVs/nurses 22
- Educational 22
- None —
- Base (100%) 137

For closed cases only

Reasons for closure

Box 1:
- Aims achieved 33
- Dept withdraws 31
- Referred on 22
- Base (100%) 1,752†

Box 2:
- Aims achieved 53
- Dept withdraws 13
- Referred on 13
- Base (100%) 497

Box 3:
- Referred on 41
- Aims achieved 30
- Dept withdraws 22
- Base (100%) 314

Box 4:
- Referred on 38
- Dept withdraws 27
- Aims achieved 20
- Base (100%) 191

Box 5:
- Aims achieved 32
- Dept withdraws 29
- Referred on 18
- Client withdraws 10
- Base (100%) 214

Box 6:
- Dept withdraws 29
- Aims achieved 25
- Referred on 22
- Client withdraws 10
- Base (100%) 124

* The percentages are estimates based on all open cases and a one in twelve sample of closures – only aspects of social work help recorded for at least 10% of cases within each group are shown.

** This total excludes the 149 cases where disposal not known (see Figure 8.1).

† Reason for closure not known in 28 cases.

Abbreviations: Mob. resources (mobilising resources), Educ. soc. skills (education in social and physical skills), Applications (help with applications), Ch. living group (changes in living group), Ref. hosp./clinic (admission/referral to a hospital or clinic for assessment/treatment), Child Guid. Cln. (child guidance clinic).

financial and material problems received a very different social services package. They were in the main young families, often beset by many other environmental and inter-personal difficulties. As already mentioned, the large majority (four-fifths) came on their own or on their relatives' or friends' initiatives. Contrary to general belief very few – less than 5 per cent – were formally referred by the DHSS, though in some instances they may have suggested that clients consult the Social Services Department. Half of these cases with mainly material needs were closed on the day of referral and 85 per cent by the end of one month (see Table 8.1). The average case was closed within one week and received two to three contacts. The main form of practical help was assistance with applications for supplementary benefits and special grants (43%). Information and advice was recorded in 72 per cent of these cases and advocacy in a quarter, almost always with the social security officers of the DHSS. Hence it comes as no surprise that the DHSS was the main outside agency with which the social workers were in contact on behalf of these clients. Observations in the area office and study of case records suggested that the initiative for contact with the DHSS came almost entirely from the social workers, who often acted as a go-between. The area staff commented that this time-consuming mediation would be unnecessary if the DHSS staff learnt to communicate in a more relaxed, patient and clear manner with claimants. These comments have been echoed by social workers in an inner London borough. On the other side, DHSS staff in that borough have suggested 'that the social workers identify too readily and too closely with their clients . . . take an uninformed and unrealistic view of the action DHSS can take' (DHSS and London Borough of Islington, 1978). The other agencies contacted most often on behalf of these clients – health visitors (in 18% of the cases), GPs (11%) and psychiatric hospitals (11%) – indicate that child care, physical health and emotional or psychiatric problems were not uncommon in this client group. These complexities probably explain why some form of casework was deemed appropriate with a quarter of this client group.

In stark contrast to the elderly and disabled, only 30 per cent of the clients who approached the area office with financial and material difficulties were closed because the social workers considered that their aims had been achieved, and over two-fifths were referred on to other agencies, mainly the DHSS. In a fifth of these cases the social workers decided to withdraw, presumably because it was not in their power to produce the financial and other social resources necessary to put these families on their feet again. Many closure notes refer to family tensions and environmental problems which were detected but not pursued. Some of these families repeatedly found themselves in financial and other crises, but the area team's policy was to respond on an *ad hoc* short-term basis rather than to get involved in long-drawn-out supportive relationships with very uncertain outcomes. However, when the CRS data revealed the frequent reappearance of certain families in a variety of crisis situations the intake team tried to undertake a more searching exploration in a small sample of these families in order to get to grips with their more basic problems. The social workers encountered great difficulties in obtaining these clients' consent to explore their problems beyond the obvious trigger events, and eventually it was decided to continue with the short-term crisis help.

The pattern of social work response was very similar for another group of environmental problems for which the Social Services Department did not command the appropriate resources – the 202 cases in which housing difficulties and problems about accommodation were the main reason for referral. Again a substantial proportion were young families, although a quarter were over retirement age. In this elderly group the difficulties centred around unsuitable living conditions, rather than homelessness. Assistance with applications was the main form of practical help (31%) and over three-quarters in this problem group received information and advice. Mobilisation of resources, mostly in relation to housing and health, were recorded in half these cases. These activities, as well as the frequent contacts with the GP (30%) and the health visitor (23%), indicate that other difficulties besides housing became evident in a substantial number of cases. The homeless young families and single people often faced family break-up and financial problems. Some old people experienced loneliness and depression, and consequently tended to neglect themselves and their homes so that other living arrangements had to be explored.

As in the client group with predominantly financial troubles, about two-fifths of those with housing problems were referred to other facilities which were either already in touch with the clients or considered to be the more appropriate agency. In only 20 per cent of cases did the social workers consider that their aims had been achieved.

If we compare this gloomy picture conveyed by the social workers – of short-term advice, some practical assistance, and referral on to other agencies resulting in little or no immediate change – with the statements made by consumers to independent interviewers, astonishing differences in perception become apparent. Clients who had approached the area office with financial and housing problems emerged along with the elderly as the most satisfied client group. Clients did not expect the Social Services Department to provide money or a house, but to act as an advice and information centre which would direct them to the appropriate resources. This the intake team was able to do, thus fulfilling their clients' modest expectations.

Child behaviour and family-relationship problems
This group consisted mainly of grossly disturbed families in which deser-

tion, separation, divorce, conflict over who was to have the care of children, marital violence, child neglect and adolescent revolt were common occurrences. Almost every referral presented a complex situation in which several other agencies might already be involved.

As Table 7.3 showed, almost half the families came on their own initiative or on that of their relatives and friends, a fifth via medical agencies, mainly health visitors and GPs who were worried about children at risk. Schools were also frequent referring agents, suspecting family problems or neglect, and the police referred absconders from community schools, children who had run away from home and cases of serious parental neglect affecting small children.

In these circumstances it is not surprising that the social workers were in contact with a great variety of outside agencies on behalf of these families (Table 8.2): schools and health visitors topped the list, followed by psychiatric hospitals and voluntary agencies. In only 5 per cent of these referrals was no contact with any outside agency recorded. The average number of agencies involved in the 34 cases still open at the end of the study period was nearly 4 whilst it was under 2 for the shorter-term cases, most of which were closed within three months.

The average number of contacts per case among these very vulnerable families was the highest for any client group, about one per week. A great deal of emphasis was put on exploration and assessment, and casework was undertaken with more than half these families. There was correspondingly less emphasis on practical services. These were concerned with applications for supplementary allowances, arrangements for temporary accommodation and holidays, and lastly with referrals to psychiatric hospitals and clinics. In the cases still open at the end of the study year and likely to be long-term, surveillance and regular support also played a considerable part in the intervention repertoire. Mobilising of a variety of resources, such as placements for children, financial help under Section 1 of the 1963 Children Act, help with clothing and furniture, arranging outings and camps, was recorded for half these long-term situations.

In only a third of the family and child-care cases did the social workers feel that they had achieved the aims they had set themselves. These aims were usually very modest – for instance, to help someone to reach a decision whether or not to embark on a certain course of action, or to clarify a complex situation by acting in a consultative capacity to another agency. In a slightly smaller proportion of these family cases (29%) the intake team decided to withdraw, mainly because they considered that they had not got the resources in personnel or community facilities to enter more closely into these precarious family situations. In accordance with area policy, once they had sorted out the immediate crisis and ensured that the family had a roof over their heads, some basic income, and their children were not neglected or otherwise at serious risk, they closed the case, often aware that many stresses and problems were still present and had remained untouched by their intervention. The intake team also considered that when other professionals, such as probation officers, health visitors or GPs, were involved on a regular basis, they could rely on them to alert the social services if and when necessary.

Mental and emotional disorders

The 137 cases of mental and emotional disorder were mainly referred at a crisis point when the mental handicap or the chronic psychiatric illness seriously upset the family equilibrium. The well-being of children might be endangered, and in a small proportion of cases the care of the chronically mentally handicapped had to be reconsidered because of an elderly parent's incapacity to carry the burden any longer. Table 8.2 shows that exploration and assessment played an important part in most interventions, and so did information and advice. Casework was mainly undertaken with the twelve cases which were still current at the end of the study period. Outside agencies were contacted on behalf of every single case in this group, in particular GPs (in 59 per cent of all cases).

Only a quarter of the cases referred with problems of mental or emotional disorder were closed because aims had been achieved. In a substantial proportion (29%) the social workers withdrew, sometimes because they considered that the situation was not amenable to social work help, or because other agencies such as psychiatric hospitals or clinics and GPs were involved. One also wonders whether lack of specialist training and of familiarity with mental illness or handicap played a part in the social workers' reluctance to become involved in these kinds of cases.[2]

Delinquency

As already indicated, the area policy regarding most of the automatic police notifications was to consider the severity of the problems referred and to check whether the case was currently known. Most of the cases were then closed after any relevant information had been passed on to the police.

SOME QUESTIONS RAISED

What accounts for the service responses to the demands of clients who came to the notice of this area office throughout the year?

The area social workers themselves suggest that their responses were largely determined by legislative mandates embodied in the Local Authority Social Services Act 1970 and the Chronically Sick and Disabled Persons Act 1970. Their first priority therefore was to provide protective services for the most vulnerable groups – the very young and helpless and the very old and disabled. These two groups also emerged as those most likely to receive long-term care.

The question then arises whether skills and resources were optimally deployed to fulfil these legislative mandates as well as the many other requests made for advice and help.

We saw that the intake team spent a great deal of their time in four ways: screening incoming demands, many of them for straightforward practical services; providing practical help of all kinds for the elderly and disabled; acting as a kind of citizens advice bureau for a great variety of material and inter-personal problems; and taking on the role of a go-between or advocate *vis à vis* the DHSS, the Housing Department, and other statutory bodies.

We also observed that in about a third of the cases the social workers withdrew mainly because resources had to be allocated to other urgent social casualties. Among this third were families with a variety of material and relationship problems. Early and containable manifestations of family stress of various kinds, and non-material problems of the elderly, were only rarely taken on.

Another feature was the area's policy to deal with specific episodes as they arose – much as a GP would treat episodes of common or serious ailments – and to encourage clients to return should the need arise. In our consumer study, clients, and especially the elderly, expressed feelings of reassurance and security that a social services department was there in the background in times of need.

If this analysis of a year's intake into an area office and the social workers' responses are at all typical, three further issues arise. Should the aims and functions of social services departments be as diverse and all-embracing as they are at present, or should they be concentrating on more clearly defined areas of human misery? Secondly, do social workers have the requisite skills for the roles which they are currently taking on? For example, are they equipped to act as information-givers and advisers on such a broad front, or are they landing themselves between several stools, being neither information experts, nor advocates, nor case-workers? Thirdly, how appropriate are the solutions attempted in response to the problems presented?

Finally, what are the advantages and disadvantages of separate intake and long-term teams? How realistic is the claim that this separation, whilst providing a flexible, rapid and efficient response to demand, gives the long-term teams the 'chance for constructive long-term casework' (Titcomb, 1974) and 'greater caseload control and the opportunity for more planned closures' (Wetton, 1976)?

We shall take up these questions in our concluding discussion after we have examined the work of the long-term teams in our area office in Seatown.

NOTES

1 A study of referrals to an area office with an intake team in Buckinghamshire shows similar patterns of client survival (J. Robinson, personal communication).
2 Since the time of the study the area team have arranged for regular consultation with a psychiatrist and a psycho-geriatrician, and practices may well have changed as a result.

Chapter 9

THE LONG-TERM TEAMS AND THEIR CLIENTS

During the study year two long-term teams were in operation in Seatown's area office, comprising two-thirds of the social work force and carrying about 1,500 on-going cases. Approximately half of these had been known to the department for more than two years, and were estimated to stay open for three or more years. In this and the next chapters we want to explore the characteristics of these long-term cases, what kind of help they received during the year, and where appropriate to compare the nature of long-term help with the kind of short-term intervention reported during the intake stage.

THE LONG-TERM TEAMS

The two long-term teams were both led by seniors qualified in social work with more than five years' experience in the field. The seniors had divided the area into two, one team taking cases from the west and the other from the east side of the district.

Overall during the study year, taking account of people leaving and arriving, and of part-time workers, the two seniors had at their disposal the equivalent of $14\frac{1}{2}$ full-time workers, ranging from $12\frac{1}{2}$ in the early part of the year to 17 by the end. Seven of these were qualified (2 by experience only), 5 were unqualified; there were 2 home teachers for the blind, and a half-time occupational therapist. In addition, 2 students – supervised by experienced and qualified social workers – were attached to the teams.

Criteria for matching social work skills to the needs of particular cases were not laid down explicitly, but the seniors suggested that they allocated cases by taking into account the social workers' special aptitudes, interests and availability. Thereafter little reallocation took place. Some skilled workers preferred to keep cases which did not need their particular expertise any longer as 'low-priority' cases. On the other hand, unqualified social workers and social work assistants occasionally struggled with immensely difficult cases which appeared to need highly skilled social work (see p. 105). No clear policy emerged about the involvement of volunteers, although they were increasingly used for the surveillance of elderly or disabled clients on agency review.

The unqualified staff and the newly qualified young workers were supervised regularly, while the more experienced workers operated fairly independently and only had occasional consultative sessions with the seniors. Both seniors operated an 'open-door system', being accessible for short consultation and advice at almost any time.

THE DATA

For the purposes of this exercise, a long-term case was defined as one which was open on 1 February 1975, either on an individual social worker's caseload or on agency review, and on which some action was taken during the following twelve-month period. The problem group to which a client has been assigned is based on the most outstanding problem tackled by the social worker as shown in the last review dealing with work done during the study year. The analysis which follows is derived from data contained in this review form. It also draws on a random sample of 160 cases which were studied more intensively by reading all the existing reviews on them and by talking to the social workers concerned.

INTAKE AND LONG-TERM POPULATIONS

The fifteen social workers and the two seniors reported on 1,424 cases within the study period, of whom 804 (56%) were allocated to individual social workers and 620 (44%) were on agency review (Table 9.1). During the year, 208 (26%) of the allocated cases and 268 (43%) of the agency review cases were closed or transferred. At the end of the study period two-thirds of all cases still remained open, while one-third had been closed or transferred to other area offices.[1]

Table 9.1   *Case Status and Caseload Type at Most Recent Review in the study year*

	Caseload type					
	Allocated to individual caseloads		Agency Review caseload		All cases	
Case status	No.	%	No.	%	No.	%
Open	596	74	352	57	948	67
Closed	208	26	268	43	476	33
Totals	804	100	620	100	1,424	100

This picture is in dramatic contrast to the lifespan of the 2,000 intake cases discussed in the previous chapter, of whom 90 per cent had been closed at the end of six months, and only 6 per cent remained open at the end of the study year. These clients were mainly the very disabled or frail elderly and children who were at serious risk or about to be taken into long-term care. Thus we would expect the characteristics and the problems presented by the long-term population to differ markedly from those of the newly referred clients.

This turned out to be the case: while people aged 65 and over comprised 30 per cent of the referrals, they constituted 51 per cent of the long-term cases. The percentage of cases where the family was regarded as the client had decreased steeply, from 27 per cent in the intake population to 6 per cent of the long-term clients. This may be partly an artefact of record-keeping, since once a child comes into care or is designated 'at risk' the record will be in the name of the child rather than the family.

The different distribution of problems tackled at intake and among the long-term clients is particularly illuminating if we divide the long-term clients into those allocated to social workers and those receiving occasional surveillance as agency review cases (Table 9.2). We see that problems of physical disability, excluding visual handicaps (which were dealt with by specialists), were tackled in 30 per cent of the intake population and in 47 per cent of the long-term cases. But these problems were mainly assigned to agency review and constituted 80 per cent of all agency review cases. In other words, of the 659 physically disabled and elderly clients looked after by the long-term teams, 495 received occasional surveillance and only 164 were allocated to individual social workers.

Cases presenting child-care, delinquency and family problems constituted 29 per cent of the intake population and 22 per cent of the long-term population. However, if we exclude automatic police referrals of delinquency (most of whom were closed after an administrative check), then child/family problems comprised only 14 per cent of the intake but 20 per cent of the long-term cases. Most of these cases – in contrast to the elderly and disabled – were on allocated caseloads.

Another feature of Table 9.2 is the steep drop in problems of finance, material resources and housing, from 27 per cent of the referrals to 4 per cent of the long-term cases. The intake analysis showed that clients who came for help with these problems received mainly information and advice, and were then referred on to other agencies. Thus very few of them were considered for long-term intervention.

As the table shows, the proportion of mentally disordered clients was similar in the intake and long-term populations.

We now want to examine in greater detail the circumstances and the kind

Table 9.2 Main problems: Long-term* and Intake†

Main problem	Long-term cases						Intake	
	Allocated to individual caseloads		Agency Review caseload		All cases		All referrals	
	No.	%	No.	%	No.	%	No.	%
Physical disability (65+ years)/ageing	124	15	384	62	508	36 ⎱	597	30
Physical disability (under 65 years)	40	5	111	18	151	11	17	1
Visual handicap	199	25	—	—	199	14		
Problems arising from long-term care	102	13	9	1	111	8 ⎱	284	14
Child behaviour/family relationships/etc.	151	19	17	3	168	12	296	15
Delinquency	27	3	2	—	29	2		
Financial/material/housing/etc.	41	5	14	2	55	4	554	27
Mental illness/emotional disturbance	40	5	13	2	53	4 ⎱	152	8
Mental handicap	18	2	23	4	41	3		
Other	62	8	47	8	109	8	119	6
Totals	804	100	620	100	1,424	100	2,019	100

* Main problem tackled during the most recent review in the study year.
† Main problem given at first referral in the study year.

of help received by clients in the different problem groups, whether typical patterns of service delivery emerge for different client groups, and how these relate to the organisation of the agency, the use of social work skills, and the reasons for closure. We shall use the statistical information derived from the case review form as well as the descriptive material from our intensive study of the sample cases.

It will also be remembered that we had quarterly feedback meetings with the long-term teams in which their work was discussed from many aspects. These discussions afforded us some insight into different team members' attitudes and ways of working which formed a valuable back-cloth to the interpretation of the case review data.

NOTE

1   The number of transferred cases is so small that we shall refer to the closed and transferred cases as 'closed'.

Chapter 10

LONG-TERM SOCIAL WORK WITH THE ELDERLY AND DISABLED

THE FRAIL AND PHYSICALLY DISABLED ELDERLY

As Table 9.2 shows, the social workers had dealt with problems of physical disability and frailty among the elderly in roughly 500 cases. But only 124 (24%) of these were on individual social workers' caseloads, and the rest – 384 – received occasional surveillance as agency review cases. Altogether the 508 physically frail elderly clients constituted some 36 per cent of all the long-term clientele. Three-fifths were over the age of 75, and about half lived alone.

By far the most common situations among the allocated cases were those where the client, usually living alone, could barely manage to live independently despite a full complement of services which often included warden-supervised housing, and where it was likely that some form of residential care would be required before long. Among those disabled elderly clients who lived with their families social work help was as much concerned with easing the strain on the relatives as with providing physical and social comforts for the elderly themselves.

The elderly assigned to agency review usually lived alone or with an elderly spouse. As a rule they had no outstanding problems apart from their frailty and limited mobility.

As one would expect, the allocated cases received more intensive and varied help than those on agency review (Table 10.1): the contact rate was almost three times as high (3·5) as that for agency review cases (1·2).

In general, the social work response to the problem situations just described was along the lines of surveillance and co-ordination of services, alert to changes in the old person's circumstances. Accordingly, check-up/review visiting was the predominant social worker activity, occurring in over three-quarters of these cases (Table 10.1): it was considered to be the most important activity in 51 per cent of the allocated and 63 per cent of the agency review cases. Mobilising resources such as domiciliary services, medical attention or residential care was reported in 30 per cent of the allocated cases and in 20 per cent of the agency review cases. This is in sharp contrast to the intake phase where practical

Table 10.1 Summary of Help Given, Workers Involved, Future Plans and Reasons for Closure for the Physically Disabled (65+ years) and Elderly

All cases

Social workers' activities	Allocated %	Agency Review %	Total %
Review visiting	77	79	78
Mobilising resources	30	20	23
Exploration/assessment	19	20	20
Information/advice	23	15	17
Problem solving	15	5	8
Sustaining/nurturing	20	4	8
Advocacy	13	2	5
Practical help			
Aids/adaptations	15	17	17
Help with applications	15	8	10
Part III: long-term	10	2	4
Part III: short-term	10	1	4
None	50	62	59

Cases open at the most recent review

Major change areas	Allocated %	Agency Review %	Total %
No change intended	69	75	73
Social/personal environment	17	21	20
Major environmental	12	3	6
Behaviour/attitude	1	1	1
Social role	—	—	—
Estimated time before closure			
Up to one year	17	5	9
Up to three years	30	28	28
More than three years	53	67	63

Base (= 100%) 304

(No. allocated = 81; no. agency review = 223)

Outside agencies	Allocated %	Agency Review %	Total %
GPs	33	14	19
Hospitals	25	8	12
Health visitors/nurses	14	8	9
Housing Department	12	5	7
None	40	69	62
Types of workers			
Qualified social worker	69	23	35
Social work assistant	14	23	21
Unqualified social worker	11	12	12
Occupational therapist	8	9	9
Volunteer	—	9	7
None	2	30	23
Average no. contacts per quarter	3·5	1·2	1·8

Base (= 100%) 508
(No. allocated = 124; no. agency review = 384)

Cases closed at the most recent review

Reasons for closure	Allocated %	Agency Review %	Total %
Department withdraws	37	60	55
Aims achieved	21	12	14
Client died	23	10	13
Client withdraws	2	12	10
Change in circumstances	7	2	3
Referral to other facilities	2	1	1
Other	7	2	3

Base (= 100%) 211
(No. allocated = 43; no. agency review = 168)

Explanatory notes to Tables 10.1–13.2.

(1) The data presented are taken from the most recent review on each case in the study year.

(2) Where there are less than 30 cases numbers rather than percentages are shown.

(3) In the first three categories (i.e. social workers' activities, practical help, and outside agencies) items are usually included if recorded for at least 10% of the cases in the problem group. The exception to this occurs in Table 10.1 in which items are included if recorded for at least 10% of either the allocated or agency review cases.

(4) It may be noted that the total of closures plus cases remaining open may differ from the total of all cases. There are two reasons for this: some cases were transferred to other area offices within the same authority; in other cases the problems present, which form the base for future plans, may differ from the problems tackled during the review period.

services of all kinds were provided for over two-thirds of these clients, while review visits were paid to just over a quarter. This makes sense. Basic practical services will usually be arranged as a response to a request for help and therefore the long-term concern will be to monitor their appropriateness in relation to the needs of the client.

In 20 per cent of the allocated cases admission to a welfare home had been arranged, but half of them were on a short-term basis, sometimes to provide a recuperative holiday after a hospital episode or to give over-burdened relatives a break. Twenty per cent may seem a high figure, but it needs to be remembered that most of the clients on the margin of residential care were on individual caseloads, while the less precarious cases were on agency review and of these only 3 per cent were admitted to residential care during the review period. Table 10.1 shows that altogether only 8 per cent of these 508 very elderly and frail clients had received care in a welfare home during the last review period, half of them on a short-term basis.

The study of our intensive sample showed vividly how hard some clients struggled, supported by the social workers and a variety of aids and services, to continue an independent existence if at all possible. Usually admission to a welfare home was only considered after all the domiciliary resources were exhausted. 'Casework', that is helping old people to unburden themselves and discuss their difficulties in an endeavour to resolve problems, was only reported in 39 of the 508 elderly physically disabled clients. This reticence to deal with attitudes, behaviour and feelings among the elderly is also reflected in the aims pursued. In only 4 cases did the social workers record that they were aiming at changes in role, attitudes or behaviour.

Contacts with outside agencies which were reported in 84 per cent of the recently referred clients were only made on behalf of half that proportion among the long-term elderly (38%), though these contacts were more frequent for the 124 old people allocated to individual social workers (60%). As in the intake phase, the agencies concerned were mainly the health services – the GP topping the list followed by hospitals and out-patient clinics.

It may come as a surprise that qualified social workers were involved in over two-thirds (69%) of the allocated cases, since other studies show that the care of the elderly is usually assigned to social work assistants (Holme and Maizels, 1978; Stevenson and Parsloe, 1978). Most of these cases were carried by two ex-welfare officers with a special interest in the elderly. None of the other more recently qualified social workers, except one senior, carried more than one or two physically frail elderly clients on their caseloads. The bulk of the agency reviews was undertaken by the seniors, often by post or telephone, and by unqualified staff. Latterly, one of the seniors used a small group of volunteers for occasional review visits.

What aims did the social workers pursue? In just under three-quarters of all the cases that were to remain open the preservation of the *status quo* was all the social workers hoped for. Yet is not the purpose of providing additional services (as happened for two-fifths of the cases) the greater well-being of the old people and improvement, however small, in the quality of their lives, and not merely the prevention of deterioration? These more positive aims were only recorded for a fifth of the cases. As we have already pointed out, behavioural, attitudinal or role changes were hardly ever contemplated. Does this convey a stoic acceptance by social workers of the *status quo* among the elderly, or a failure to appreciate how much the appropriate kind of emotional or practical support at the right time can contribute to a more easeful life of the very old? (Goldberg, Mortimer and Williams, 1970; Glampson and Goldberg, 1976; Challis, 1978).

Outcome

On the last review recorded during the study year, two-fifths of the cases were closed: of the rest, almost two-thirds were estimated to remain open for more than three years, the majority of them as agency review cases. Calculations based on comparing estimates with actual closures suggest that the social workers almost certainly over-estimated the length of time cases would remain open in this frail very elderly group, where death, hospitalisation or other changes in circumstances frequently lead to closure.

Looking at the reasons for closure, we see a sharp contrast between these long-term cases and the referrals dealt with on a short-term basis: while in over half the intake cases the social workers considered that their aims had been achieved, this only applied to 14 per cent of the long-term cases. On the other hand, in over half of the long-term cases the reason for closure was 'department withdraws', in contrast to 13 per cent of the short-term closures. How can these differences be explained? Our study of cases, and the discussions with the social workers, suggested that the category 'department withdraws' had a very different meaning in long-term situations than it had during the intake phase. Among the former, this entry often signified that the social workers considered that they had done all that was possible and that the situation had stabilised although certain problems still remained. In a number of these cases an early-warning system was in operation, since home helps were still going in or meals-on-wheels were being delivered. On the other hand, during the intake phase the very provision of these services had been the main aim. Hence, the social workers in the intake team would tick 'aims achieved' in circumstances very similar to those in which a long-term case was closed as 'department withdraws'.

When comparing social work plans with aims achieved, it appeared that in over two-thirds of the cases for whom a continuance of domiciliary services and occasional surveillance were prescribed, unanticipated events outside the control of the social workers intervened before the next review. Such events could be illness necessitating admission to hospital, increasing frailty leading to a crisis and sometimes resulting in admission to a welfare home, or death. These observations raise the question of how useful the occasional social work type of contact is in the social care and surveillance of the very frail and elderly, and whether much closer neighbourhood contact and support or other early-warning systems would not prove more effective means of 'keeping in touch'.

THE PHYSICALLY DISABLED UNDER 65

The 151 physically disabled clients under the age of 65 carried by the long-term teams during the study year form a distinct group. Almost two-thirds were in the 45 to 64 age range and 16 per cent were children. In contrast to the elderly disabled, practically all of them lived with their families. Most of them were very severely disabled. The middle-aged suffered mainly from progressive neurological diseases such as multiple sclerosis, and there were a number of severely disabled stroke cases and some clients with arthritic conditions which made them practically immobile; the children usually had very severe handicaps such as spina bifida or cerebral palsy.

Most of these clients, of whom nearly three-quarters were on agency review for occasional surveillance, had long client careers. Two-thirds had been known to the department for over two years, and nearly all cases (93%) left open at the latest review were estimated to remain so for more than three years (Table 10.2). In contrast to the frail elderly, four-fifths of the forty handicapped clients allocated to individual social workers received some practical help, mainly in the form of aids and adaptations, though this only applied to two-fifths of the agency review cases. Review visiting was not as prominent as in the elderly group, but information and advice and the mobilising of resources was recorded more often, and indicates the more active nature of the support given to this younger group of disabled clients.

But perhaps the most interesting feature of the work with this client group is the difference in emphasis between the work of the occupational therapist who was involved in over half of the allocated cases and that of her social work colleagues. The occupational therapist considered it essential to reassess needs for aids and adaptations regularly, since functional impairments fluctuated among the adults and the needs of growing children changed over the years. Hence exploration and assessment figured more prominently in her work than in that of her colleagues. Whilst her practical help was mainly concentrated on aids and adaptations, the social workers provided other kinds of services as well. The occupational therapist was in contact with an outside agency on behalf of all her allocated clients. These were mainly medical agencies on behalf of the adults and schools on behalf of the children. The social workers' contacts with GPs, hospitals, and schools were less frequent.

Table 10.2 *Summary of Help Given, Workers Involved, Future Plans and Reasons for Closure for the Physically Disabled Under 65*

All cases		Cases open at the most recent review	
Social workers' activities	%	Major change areas	%
Review visiting	62	No change intended	62
Information/advice	40	Social/personal	
Mobilising resources	36	environment	33
Exploration/assessment	31	Major environmental	4
		Behaviour/attitude	1
		Social role	—
Practical help	%		
Aids/adaptations	31	Estimated time before	
Help with applications	19	closure	%
None	48	Up to one year	5
		Up to three years	2
		More than three years	93
Outside agencies	%		
GPs	19	Base (= 100%) 101	
Hospitals	17		
None	53		
Types of workers	%	Cases closed at the most recent review	
Occupational therapist	25		
Qualified social worker	24		
Social work assistant	21		
Unqualified social worker	13	Reasons for closure	%
Volunteer	5	Department withdraws	61
Social worker with		Client withdraws	14
specialised knowledge	1	Aims achieved	10
None	20	Client died	6
		Referral to other facilities	4
Average no. contacts		Change in circumstances	—
per quarter	1·4	Other	4
Base (= 100%) 151		Base (= 100%) 49	

For explanatory notes see Table 10.1.

Although the occupational therapist saw her role as strictly instrumental, periodically reassessing for aids and closely collaborating with other caregivers, she was well aware of the emotional and social problems associated with physical disability. For example, she was involved in a training scheme for student counsellors who were going to provide much-needed intellectual and social stimuli for isolated homebound patients suffering from multiple sclerosis. She, as well as the social workers, was also familiar with the defensive manœuvre of denial which occasionally imposed severe restraints on their ability to help. An example quoted was a grossly incontinent multiple sclerosis patient who denied her difficulties and refused any form of help with them, her husband silently colluding and carrying the burden. Feelings of depression and isolation in reasonably ambulant patients were mainly tackled by the provision of day care and stimulation of interests rather than by any kind of casework approach.

Some of these differences in the frequency of reassessment and contacts with other caregivers between the occupational therapist and the social workers may be explained by the fact that the occupational therapist had proportionately more children in her caseload (47%) than the social workers (14%). Possibly also some of her clients were more severely disabled, although a careful study of the sample cases did not reveal such differences. It may well be that the occupational therapist's specialist training as a member of a medical team enabled her to collaborate more closely with her medical colleagues and to detect more possibilities for specialised help.

Outcome is difficult to judge in these chronic conditions. As Table 10.2 shows, forty-nine cases – about a third of those reviewed in the study year – were closed. In 61 per cent of these closures the workers considered that the situation was sufficiently stable and well supported by the family or other caregivers for the department to withdraw.

THE VISUALLY HANDICAPPED

This client group – 80 per cent of them over the age of 65 – formed 14 per cent of the long-term client population while they only contributed 1 per cent to the referrals during the study year. The explanation of this ratio of one to fourteen between incidence and prevalence is simple: three-quarters of these clients had been known to the department for more than two years and were kept under surveillance more or less for the rest of their lives. Of the 199 current cases, 20 were closed during the year on their deaths, 1 left the area, and 1 further client was referred to another agency (Table 10.3). All but 6 of the remaining 169 cases were estimated to remain open for more than three years.

able 10.3 *Summary of Help Given, Workers Involved, Future Plans and Reasons for Closure for the Visually Handicapped*

All cases		Cases open at the most recent review	
ocial workers' activities	%	Major change areas	%
Review visiting	75	Social/personal	
Information/advice	68	environment	57
Mobilising resources	51	No change intended	34
Sustaining/nurturing	36	Major environmental	7
Problem solving	18	Social role	1
Exploration/assessment	16	Behaviour/attitude	1
		Estimated time before	
ractical help	%	closure	%
Day centres/clubs/outings	67	Up to one year	2
Financial	53	Up to three years	2
Material help	41	More than three years	96
Help with applications	33		
Aids/adaptations	23	Base (= 100%) 169	
Home help	13		
None	7		
)utside agencies	%		
Health visitors/nurses	24	*Cases closed at the most recent review*	
GPs	22		
Hospitals	16		
None	43	Reasons for closure	No.
		Client died	20
ypes of workers	%	Referral to other facilities	1
Home teacher for the		Aims achieved	—
blind	72	Change in circumstances	—
Other with specialised		Client withdraws	—
knowledge	28	Department withdraws	—
Qualified social worker	1	Other	1
average no. contacts			
per quarter	4·1		
Base (= 100%) 199		Total = 22 cases	

For explanatory notes see Table 10.1.

roblem situations

[wo home teachers for the blind dealt exclusively with this client group. [hey did not make use of the agency review system for occasional :heck-up visiting by less specialised workers, since they held the view that all visually handicapped people – whatever their circumstances – need support from a skilled specialist. For example, a partially-sighted m living with his wife and daughter, who until recently had been able to r his grocery business quite successfully (which he had to close down f reasons unconnected with his handicap) wanted to take up other inte ests. The social worker saw it as her task to put him in touch with the ma varied leisure activities that are available to the visually handicapped the area, and to continue the contact indefinitely. Similarly, a soc worker intended to keep in touch with a couple where a somewh backward partially-sighted girl had recently married a much older sim larly handicapped man, who seemed to adopt a protective and father attitude towards her. They were both attending the social centre once week and had the services of a home help. Their life together and the relationship seemed to satisfy their mutual needs.

Social work
Apart from review contacts for three-quarters of the clients, which oft took place at the social centre for the blind, much information and advi (68% of cases) was given on the many facilities available for the visua handicapped in the area. In contrast to the other elderly client grou where most of the practical help was arranged during the intake pha the mobilisation of resources on behalf of the blind continued on long-term basis. Different kinds of outings and holidays were offer according to the physical capacity and preferences of the clients, spec Christmas gifts, both in kind and money, were available for all t registered clients, and a host of other aids were provided, such as talki books, talking newspapers, special knitting needles etc. Hence the lar proportion of entries in relation to day centres, clubs and outings (67% financial help (53%) and material help (41%). Indeed, all but 7 per ce of the visually handicapped received some practical help during the stu period. The average number of services per client was 2·8, the highest f any of the three disabled client groups. Since most of these clients we elderly the workers did not engage in braille teaching. Comparative little casework was reported (18%) in contrast to the intake phase (47% This is readily understandable, since sensitive casework is most need during the initial crisis when a newly blind person will have to come terms with a changed life situation. Similarly, the need to contact outsi agencies, mainly in connection with assessment and registration, was at i peak when the blind person first came into contact with the Departmen Thus contacts with GPs and hospitals were much more frequent durir the intake phase (53% and 76% of cases) than during the relative quiescent surveillance period, when GPs were contacted on behalf of 2 per cent and hospitals on behalf of 16 per cent of this client group.
Some change was aimed for in two-thirds of the cases – the highe

roportion of any problem group. This change was largely related to the any practical services provided, which were intended to enrich the blind erson's social life. The question arises, however, whether these varied rvices, such as Christmas gifts, gadgets, outings, holidays, and so on, to hich all the registered visually handicapped were entitled in this area, ıd to be provided and monitored by skilled specialists on a permanent ısis.

Chapter 11

---◆---

LONG-TERM SOCIAL WORK WITH CHILD
AND FAMILY PROBLEMS

PROBLEMS ARISING FROM LONG-TERM FOSTER AND
RESIDENTIAL CARE

While it seemed appropriate in the intake analysis to amalgamate all th
cases in which family disruption and children's behaviour were the mai
problems, since they usually presented different facets of a family crisi
this did not prove to be adequate in the long-term situations.

One group of cases which clearly formed a separate entity were those i
which problems arising from residential or foster care were considered t
be most outstanding. These children – some 50 per cent of those in car
during the study year – were as a rule well settled in their foster o
residential home, and were expected to remain there until the discharg
of the care order; a small number were in the process of being adopted b
their foster parents, and a few were being rehabilitated to their ow
parents. Most of these children had been in care from infancy and ha
come from very severely disrupted family backgrounds, but almost b
definition the crises and traumatic events of their early childhood ha
receded into the background. In most cases contacts with their natura
parents were minimal or non-existent.

This group comprised 8 per cent of all the long-term cases and 13 pe
cent of the allocated caseloads. Only 9 of these 111 children were o
agency review, although we estimate that some 20 per cent were actuall
being supervised by another authority or by a voluntary agency on behal
of this local authority's social services department.

This group of 111 children contained similar proportions of boys an
girls under the age of 17. Fifty-one per cent were in foster homes and 4
per cent in different kinds of residential homes. As all these children an
adolescents were in long-term care, it is readily understandable that th
large majority – nearly three-quarters of them – had been in contact wit
the Department for more than five years, and that 72 per cent wer
expected to be open for more than three years after the last review (Tabl
11.1).

Review visiting was carried out in 81 per cent of the cases – the highes
proportion of any problem group – and it was the most important socia

worker activity in 40 per cent of the cases. This is to be expected, since by definition there were few current crises in this group. When problems did occur they were often those associated with the business of growing up in a foster or residential home, such as a change of school, starting work, or learning more about one's origins. Possibly the social workers underestimated the foster parents' need for active support and encouragement, since in our consumer survey (described in Chapter 3) foster parents stood out as the most complaining consumers, mentioning the infrequency of visiting and the youth and inexperience of social workers.

Table 11.1 *Summary of Help Given, Workers Involved, Future Plans and Reasons for Closure for Cases Involving Problems Arising from Care*

All cases		Cases open at the most recent review	
Social workers' activities	%	Major change areas	%
Review visiting	81	No change intended	47
Problem solving	35	Behaviour/attitude	24
Information/advice	30	Major environmental	18
Exploration/assessment	29	Social/personal	
Sustaining/nurturing	29	environment	6
Mobilising resources	22	Social role	4
Practical help	%	Estimated time before closure	%
Financial	26	Up to one year	13
Change in living group	12	Up to three years	15
None	53	More than three years	72
Outside agencies	%	Base (= 100%) 114	
Educational	40		
Community homes	14		
Other social services depts	14	*Cases closed at the most recent review*	
Voluntary agencies	13		
None	32	Reasons for closure	No.
		Aims achieved	5
Types of workers	%	Change in circumstances	3
Qualified social worker	72	Client died	—
Unqualified social worker	20	Client withdraws	—
Social worker with		Department withdraws	—
specialised knowledge	10	Referral to other facilities	—
		Other	—
Average no. contacts			
per quarter	3·0		
Base (= 100%) 111		Total = 8 cases	

For explanatory notes see Table 10.1.

Recently a club for foster parents has been established in the area which may meet their needs more adequately than occasional support.

The most frequently mentioned practical service was financial help (26%) which mostly took the form of supplementing the boarding-out allowances by grants for holidays, special lessons such as music or swimming, or for the purchase of school uniforms. Schools topped the list of the outside agencies contacted, partly because school reports have to be obtained by statute for the six-monthly child care reviews.

Problem solving was mentioned in over a third of the cases. For example, it was sometimes necessary to help children work through the rejections they experienced from their natural families, and to sort out the bewildering relationships between themselves, their siblings who might live with their natural families or foster parents in other parts of the country, their half-siblings (possibly by different fathers), and step-siblings who could appear and disappear from their homes along with 'uncles' and 'aunts'. Reading the records of repeated rejections, removals and other vicissitudes some of these children had survived, one is struck by their resilience and tempted to ask how and why some children appear to be able to ride out these storms and others succumb however much help is being offered (Clarke and Clarke, 1976).

One example of a 'survivor' was a boy whose mother left him at the mother and baby home, offered him to several people for adoption, and then disappeared with him. Soon after, she placed him with someone whose husband later deserted the family. At the age of 2½ he was back once more with his mother, who refused to collect him when he was discharged after a spell in hospital. He was then taken into care and placed with foster parents who later wanted to adopt him, but his mother refused to sign the appropriate forms. Eventually he had to leave this foster home where he was happily settled for some technical reason, and was admitted to a children's home where he was said to be 'dead unhappy'. However, while there he attached himself to a cleaning lady who was prepared to look after him and who was duly approved as a foster parent. Now 11 years of age, he is doing very well in this self-selected foster home.

Another example was a boy of 13 belonging to a family of mixed race with several sets of half-siblings, whose father suddenly turned up from the West Indies after eight years' absence. Both the psychiatrist at his community home and the social worker tried to help him to work through the maze of family relationships and to understand the reasons for him being pushed out of the nest. His mother was still living in the same town, and he was visiting her and his half-siblings at weekends. One weekend his mother sent him away, saying that there was not enough food to go round; he hurried back to his community home and returned with a food parcel, only to be upbraided by his siblings and his mother for being so 'disloyal' as to divulge their affairs to his house-parents. Undeterred, he kept up contact with the parental home.

In a few cases the social workers had struggled in vain to contain very precarious family relationships, reinforced by family aides, but eventually had to admit defeat and place the children away from their homes. In discussing such cases and piecing together the case review forms over a period, some workers suggested that the goal-oriented review questions made them realise that they had avoided painful decisions, prolonging well-intentioned support in face of a reality that pointed to the hopelessness of their endeavour. They felt that they would make more rational decisions sooner in future.

Most of the work with this group of children was undertaken by qualified social workers (72%), although a considerable proportion of these situations were very stable and possibly well within the capacity of a mature welfare assistant.

Looking at the aims of the social work endeavour, we find that in half the on-going cases no particular change was intended since these children were well settled and progressing satisfactorily. In twenty-one cases (18%) a major environmental change was intended; most of these changes involved rehabilitation and a few were related to employment, such as joining the navy. In nearly a quarter of the cases – considerably more than in the disabled or elderly groups – the aim was to bring about a change in attitudes and behaviour mainly associated with the problems of rejection and identity already discussed.

Since most of these cases were long-term statutory placements with little hope of rehabilitation, only eight of them were closed. Five had a positive outcome: children either completed their care order in good shape, were adopted by their foster parents, or were rehabilitated to their parents. 'Change in circumstances' made up the rest. For example, a planned adoption order did not go through because the natural parents had married and were now anxious to take over the care of the child. Thus on the whole outcomes were favourable in this settled group of children in congenial foster or community homes.

PROBLEMS OF CHILD BEHAVIOUR AND FAMILY RELATIONSHIPS

In about 200 cases (14 per cent of the long-term clientele), the social workers reported that the most outstanding problem tackled during the period under review was related to a child's or young person's behaviour, including 'official' delinquency or to difficulties in family relationships. In a minority of cases this was the only problem. Most of these families were experiencing a multiplicity of troubles, the average number of problems coded per case being three (ranging from one to seven). In practically all instances where a child's behaviour difficulties were the subject of attention, family relationships were also ticked as problem areas. In the chronic problem families, difficulties related to home management and lack of money usually accompanied the behavioural and relationship problems.

There were more boys than girls in this problem group – 44 per cent as against 33 per cent; 10 per cent were young people over the age of 17, and in 10 per cent of the cases the family was designated as the client. The majority of the children and young persons were living with their own families, but most of them had been in care at some time and some 20 per cent were under supervision orders. Twenty-eight per cent of the boys and girls were receiving some form of residential care during the period under review, ranging from boarding schools through community homes to Borstals.

Problem situations
Although far more children lived at home with at least one natural parent than in the settled long-term care group, the problems were by no means early or transient ones. By no stretch of the imagination could the work involved be described as 'preventive', by which we mean getting hold of a problem early on in the hope of preventing severe or chronic disorder. The families were characterised by chronic emotional and material stress; in only a tiny minority of cases did the children live with both their natural parents. Delinquent fathers in and out of prison, alcoholism, deserting mothers, gross emotional instability, were common occurrences. Some children experienced several spells of care while mothers had to go into hospital, disappeared, or just could not cope under the stress of their emotional and material living conditions. In many families several children showed signs of disturbance, and in discussing families with the workers concerned one soon learnt not to concentrate on the designated client only, since as a rule other siblings had at some time been the subject of the Department's caring functions, or soon would be.

The social workers who dealt with these families were often caught up in a vicious circle: a crisis would erupt, they would react by sorting out the most urgent problems such as debts, threats of eviction, parents running off or being in such a state that they might harm the child, only to be overtaken by the next crisis. There appeared to be little scope for a consistent treatment plan. Decisions to separate children from their parents were not taken lighly, despite the chaotic circumstances in which some of these families lived. There was a detectable tendency for the younger siblings to be removed more readily from environments which had proved harmful to their older siblings. In several instances these youngest children were said to be doing well in either foster or residential care.

Since most of these children were not in long-term care, the contacts with the Department did not reach as far back as those with the children settled in long-term placements nor did the social workers estimate that they were likely to stay open as long (Table 11.2). Earlier closure was also related to the fact that this was an older group and that a higher proportion were nearing the age of 18, when from a statutory point of view they were expected to be responsible for their own lives. Several clients in this age group were already living with a sexual partner in their own establishment, and one social worker in particular felt that care orders extending to the age of 18 ignored the earlier maturity of young people in the second half of this century.

The large majority of the cases in this problem group – 178 – were on individual social workers' caseloads, and only 19 – some 10 per cent – were on agency review. Almost two-thirds were handled by qualified social workers, some with long experience in the child care field, and a quarter by unqualified staff. Thus slightly fewer received attention from qualified staff than in the long-term care group. Yet many of these cases seemed more complex, requiring more skill and judgement than some of the children well settled in long-term care. The intensive sample contained several difficult and chronic problem situations in which an unqualified social worker consistently suggests in his reviews that a qualified social worker should handle the case. An example is a family in which a very much older hemiplegic man was married to an incompetent and unstable girl; there were three children, all of them reacting in disturbed ways to the home situation. One entry reads: 'incompetent mother, disabled father, financial problems, poor home, unlucky children', and under changes to be aimed at, the social work assistant writes: 'visit weekly, hassle DHSS, get volunteer, review in six months, try to change above situation (ho ho)', and the next entry reads: 'present situation a complete shambles' (seven problem areas were ticked, with child behaviour as the most outstanding problem).

Social work
This client group received more intensive social work than any of the groups so far discussed. The average number of contacts per client per quarter was 5.4. Outside agencies were involved in 87 per cent of the cases. Contacts with schools were made on behalf of half the cases in this problem group. Courts and solicitors were involved in a third of the cases, the police in 20 per cent, and the probation service in 16 per cent. The health and psychiatric services also played an important role in these disturbed families, as Table 11.2 shows. All this is in sharp contrast to the routine contacts recorded in the comparatively stable group of children in long-term residential or foster homes.

Some form of problem solving was attempted in half these cases, and was considered the most important activity in over a quarter – higher

Table 11.2 *Summary of Help Given, Workers Involved, Future Plans and Reasons for Closure for Cases Involving Problems of Child Behaviour/Family Relationships/etc.*

All cases		*Cases open at the most recent review*	
Social workers' activities	%	Major change areas	%
Review visiting	61	No change intended	40
Problem solving	52	Behaviour/attitude	35
Exploration/assessment	40	Major environmental	14
Information/advice	37	Social/personal	
Mobilising resources	35	environment	10
Sustaining/nurturing	31	Social role	1
Advocacy	19		
Practical help	%	Estimated time before closure	%
Change in living group	21	Up to one year	21
Change in legal		Up to three years	21
responsibility	17	More than three years	58
Financial	13		
Holidays	12		
None	36		
Outside agencies	%	Base (= 100%) 125	
Educational	51		
Courts/solicitors	32		
Police	20		
Community homes	18		
GPs	16		
Probation	16		
Health visitors/nurses	14		
Child Guidance Clinic	13		
DHSS	13		
Voluntary agencies	11		
Housing Department	10		
None	13	*Cases closed at the most recent review*	
Types of workers	%	Reasons for closure	%
Qualified social worker	64	Department withdraws	32
Unqualified social worker	25	Aims achieved	25
Social worker with		Change in circumstances	14
specialised knowledge	9	Referral to other facilities	11
Social work assistant	3	Client died	4
Other with specialised		Client withdraws	—
knowledge	2	Other	14
Volunteer	1		
None	1		
Average no. contacts			
per quarter	5·4		
Base (= 100%) 197		Base (= 100%) 56	

For explanatory notes see Table 10.1.

proportions than in any other problem group. Although review visiting still tops the list in three-fifths of the cases, it was recorded as the most important activity in only 29 per cent of the cases. Very few, some 16 per cent of the families, received review visits only. Since these families produced many unexpected crises, renewed exploration and assessment was often necessary to take crucial decisions: for example, whether to take a child into care. Practical resources – financial help, holidays, reception into care – were mobilised on behalf of 35 per cent of the children and families. Advocacy with the Housing Department, the Supplementary Benefits Commission and other bodies was undertaken in a fifth of the cases. The frequent moves of these children can be deduced from the entry 'change in living group' in 21 per cent of the cases, and 'change in legal responsibility' in 17 per cent. Such moves included at one extreme a return home to parents, and at the other departures to Borstal.

When it comes to aims, this is probably the most difficult client group for whom and with whom to plan realistically either on a short- or long-term basis. Although no change was intended in two-fifths of the cases, this does not mean that the social workers felt satisfied with the *status quo*. It often indicated a resignation on the social worker's and possibly also on the client's part to life as it was. When trying to compare social work aims with achievement in the intensive sample of cases, we found that although plans were at times quite specific, for example to improve a girl's school attendance or to help a boy get a job, such plans were upset by unexpected events such as the boy committing further delinquencies and being committed to residential treatment, or the girl proving to be deeply disturbed by a sexual assault. In other instances there was some kind of token aim such as 'general support'. Since most of the target problems were related to behaviour, attitudes and relationships, the major change area where contemplated at all, was that of behaviour and attitudes (35%) – far above the proportion for all client groups (10%).

Whether these aims were realistic in these grossly disturbed and deprived families is doubtful. Outcomes were rarely positive. As Table 11.2 shows, fifty-six cases – just over a quarter – were closed during the review period, and in only fourteen (25%) did the social workers think that their aims had been achieved. These included some children who had returned home and seemed to be weathering the storms of their difficult environment, and also a few matrimonial supervision orders in which the social worker had been able to help the divorced parent to sort out his or her problems. The entry 'department withdraws' in this group (32%) often meant that a crisis had passed in a relatively unchangeable family situation, and that the case was to be closed until the next crisis broke. One group that stood out as largely unsuccessful were adolescents whose most outstanding problem was delinquency. Of the five delinquents in the intensive sample, three landed in Borstal, one was transferred to the probation service on getting into further trouble, and the fifth, although he had just reappeared in court on an assault charge, was allowed by the magistrates to join the merchant navy. These outcomes raise the issue of specialisation, but also possibly indicate that supervision orders within the context of severely disorganised family situations are almost bound to fail.

In general, this group of chronic family problems raises many questions about the residual functions of the social services department which cannot refuse to take on cases at risk, however impervious they may be to social work intervention. These issues will be taken up in the concluding discussion.

Chapter 12

ENVIRONMENTAL PROBLEMS

The group in which financial, material or housing problems were reported to be the most outstanding ones was the smallest, making up 4 per cent (fifty-five cases) of the long-term population. As we have already seen, other problem groups also experienced financial, housing and employment difficulties but the social workers did not consider them to be the most outstanding problems.

PROBLEM SITUATIONS

Three social groups made up most of this problem category. Twenty were family-type cases, a much higher proportion than in any other problem constellation: they consisted of single-parent families facing debts, families split by divorce, and so-called 'problem families' struggling with money problems and difficulties in home management.

The second-largest group (seventeen cases) were children and young people whose discharge from care depended on the creation of reasonable environmental conditions to which they could return.

Thirdly, there were ten elderly people who largely as a result of their mild confusion and eccentricity seemed unable to manage their financial and home affairs effectively. One old lady, for example, would spend all her pension in the pub and on the fruit machines unless the social worker appeared regularly once a week to take care of her rent and other basic bills. Another old man had neglected his personal hygiene and home to such an extent that his house had to be cleaned by the Salvation Army, but again it proved possible, through regular home help and supervision of his financial affairs, to keep him going in the community.

There were also a few elderly people in private residential homes who had run out of funds and had to be transferred to local authority welfare homes. Lastly, a few old people living alone needed rehousing in warden-supervised flats to continue a reasonably independent life.

SOCIAL WORK

This problem group had a comparatively short client career, received a great deal of practical help, and outcomes were reasonably favourable.

The activities of the social workers, the kind of practical help provided, and the outside agencies involved, differed markedly from the other problem groups. Although review visiting was again the most frequently recorded activity, it was considered the most important in only 27 per cent of the cases (Table 12.1). Information and advice, and mobilising resources, were mentioned in over half the cases; only the visually impaired received a similar amount of such help. Casework and advocacy were mentioned in a third of the cases. This high proportion of advocacy indicates the amount of negotiation and pleading needed to further the rehousing, to sort out the fuel debts, and to disentangle the income-maintenance problems of this group of clients.

These active forms of intervention were very different from those adopted at intake with clients facing similar problems. At that stage, information and advice was the preferred strategy, offered to three-quarters of these clients, fewer resources were mobilised on their behalf, and advocacy and casework were also much less in evidence.

All but one of the allocated cases, and just under two-thirds of the agency review cases, received some practical help – again in contrast to the short-term cases where less than half received this kind of help. Financial help, directly or indirectly through liaison and advocacy with varous agencies, or advice on budgeting, was provided for 42 per cent of all these cases. Help with applications also ranked fairly high – many forms had to be filled in for the DHSS, the housing authorities, the fuel boards, and so on. This is the only group in which help with employment was recorded for more than 10 per cent of cases.

The social workers were involved with an outside agency on behalf of forty-nine of the fifty-five cases – the Housing Department in 44 per cent of the cases and the DHSS in 40 per cent. The variety of agencies contacted is only surpassed by the child and family problem group, and suggests that problems other than material ones were also causing concern. The contact rate with clients was also very high – an average of 5·3 contacts per quarter.

The active nature of the social work is also reflected in its goal orientation. Some change was planned for three-fifths of the cases that were to remain open. The improvement of the social and personal environment mainly through material aid was the aim in nine of the thirty-two open cases. The major environmental changes were mostly plans for rehousing, while changes in behaviour and attitudes were often aimed at better home management. Plans and achievement correlated most highly in this problem group in which aims were well defined and of a concrete nature, and there was hardly any evidence of outside events upsetting the plans made.

Table 12.1 *Summary of Help Given, Workers Involved, Future Plans and Reasons for Closure for Cases Involving Financial, Material or Housing Problems*

All cases		*Cases open at the most recent review*	
Social workers' activities	%	Major change areas	%
Review visiting	65	No change intended	38
Information/advice	56	Social/personal	
Mobilising resources	51	environment	28
Problem solving	36	Major environmental	17
Advocacy	33	Behaviour/attitude	17
Exploration/assessment	27	Social role	—
Sustaining/nurturing	22		
Practical help	%	Estimated time before closure	%
Financial	42	Up to one year	16
Help with applications	33	Up to three years	25
Material help	18	More than three years	59
Rehousing	13		
Change in living group	11		
Help with employment	11		
None	11		
Outside agencies	%	Base (= 100%) 32	
Housing Department	44		
DHSS	40		
Educational	27		
Voluntary agencies	16		
Courts/solicitors	15		
GPs	13		
Health visitors/nurses	13		
Hospitals	11		
Other	18		
None	11	*Cases closed at the most recent review*	
Types of workers	%	Reasons for closure	No.
Qualified social worker	56	Aims achieved	10
Unqualified social worker	26	Department withdraws	5
Social worker with		Change in circumstances	3
specialised knowledge	7	Client withdraws	2
Social work assistant	6	Client died	1
Volunteer	2	Referral to other facilities	—
Other with specialised		Other	1
knowledge	2		
None	4		
Average no. contacts			
per quarter	5·3		
Base (= 100%) 55		Total = 22 cases	

For explanatory notes see Table 10.1.

The relatively specific aims probably also contributed to the high proportion – ten out of twenty-two closures – in which the social workers considered that they had achieved their aims.

The general picture emerging in this group of environmental problems is of purposive activity in collaboration with a large variety of other agencies in situations which, whilst not as complex as those associated with family and child care problems, contained similar features of disruption and emotional stress. The relative success of this work raises the question whether this line of attack would repay work with families in which relationship problems were the main target of attention, and whose material problems received comparatively little attention.

Chapter 13

PROBLEMS OF MENTAL AND EMOTIONAL DISORDER

The long-term cases in which mental or emotional disorders were considered to be the most outstanding problem comprised 7 per cent of the total caseload, a similar proportion as among the referrals.[1] This category contained problem situations related to mental handicap, diagnosed mental illness, and emotional disturbances ranging from recognisable depression and anxiety to deep-seated personality disorders. While the comparatively crude information available at intake obliged us to combine all these categories in our analysis of short-term work at the intake stage, this did not apply to the long-term cases. The demographic characteristics and problem situations of the mentally ill and the emotionally disturbed differed from those of the mentally handicapped. Hence, we shall discuss these two categories separately.

MENTAL ILLNESS AND EMOTIONAL DISTURBANCE

This group comprised fifty-three cases, the largest groups being children and families (34%), the elderly (29%) and the middle-aged (25%).

Where children were involved it was usually the emotional disturbance or mental illness of the mother which was the cause of the social worker's concern. Sometimes the parent's illness necessitated receiving children into short- or long-term care. If the mother returned home after a stay in hospital, the social work consisted in helping the parent to cope with home and family. In cases of chronic mental illness when children remained in long-term care, the social worker's concern was to maintain contact between parents and children. The most demanding situations were those in which the parent's emotional disturbance was not amenable to any specific 'treatment' but had very harmful effects on the family's functioning. Examples are the very depressed mother cooped up on the thirteenth floor of a tower block who was neglecting her small son; the unsettled, delinquent single mother continually on the verge of homelessness, accumulating debts but unable to accept any reasonable plans for a more settled life, and paying little attention to the needs of her children; the highly destructive marital tensions of two disturbed partners which threatened the mental health of their children.

The problems of the middle-aged were quite different. Almost all were people in their 50s living on their own, who had been in-patients in psychiatric hospitals. The sample illustrated the intractable problems of a chronic depressive alcoholic who after several readmissions to hospital and many endeavours by community nurses and social workers to support him in the community was eventually admitted to a welfare home at the age of sixty-four as the only feasible solution. But there were also instances of middle-aged patients who after a long period as in-patients were able to settle down to life on their own with sheltered employment or regular attendance at the industrial therapy unit of the psychiatric hospital.

The elderly had a variety of problems and needs. Practically all lived alone and were very vulnerable on account of both their serious mental disturbance and their physical frailty. Most of them were on the verge of residential care. Some were suffering from senile dementia, barely able to look after themselves, in constant need of alert surveillance and practical support. There were also those who were depressed and lonely, forever complaining, and who had proved difficult to help and support.

Social work
Three-quarters of these cases were allocated to social workers, of whom over two-thirds were qualified, though none in psychiatric social work. The contact rate of eight per quarter per case was the highest among any problem group. This is largely explained by the regular weekly visits to some of the confused elderly, and the crisis situations surrounding those clients who had to be readmitted to hospital. As in all the other long-term cases, check-up review visiting (66%) was recorded for the majority of the cases (Table 13.1). 'Sustaining and nurturing' was reported in over two-fifths of the allocated cases. The mentally disturbed elderly clients, in particular, received this type of support, as they were often cut off and isolated from the outside world. This kind of activity was also mentioned in some family cases: as one social worker put it, 'I am acting as a sponge to absorb their problems.' The hope was that if such parents could pour out their unhappiness and discontent to the social worker, they might refrain from taking their frustrations out on their children. Since the problems of this group were largely of a psychological and inter-personal nature, mobilising resources was only reported for 25 per cent of the cases. Such practical help involved arranging day care (12%), in- or out-patient treatment (12%), and receiving children of mentally ill parents into short- or long-term care (10%). It also sometimes involved sorting out the financial tangles of confused elderly people, and the debts of unsettled and unstable parents threatened by homelessness in an attempt to prevent the children's reception into care. Contact with outside agencies in 77 per cent of the cases was among the highest for any

problem group. These contacts were mainly with health agencies – GPs, health visitors, psychiatric and other hospitals – but strangely no contacts with child guidance clinics were mentioned.

A relatively high proportion (38%) of the fifty-three cases in this group were closed on the last review in the study year. In nearly half of these the reason for closure was given as 'department withdraws'. Once more this category is ambiguous and covers a variety of situations, including a favourable outcome. For example, in two after-care cases in which a few check-up visits had been paid during the study year, the situation at closure was described as 'appears to be well, doing voluntary work for neighbour' and 'no problem – closed'. Since there had been no specific plan except surveillance, the workers clearly hesitated to tick 'aims achieved'.

On the whole, the impression was gained that the social workers were holding a watching brief, unless a crisis forced them to arrange for the care of children or the admission to hospital of adult clients. How far this somewhat passive support was due to comparative lack of knowledge and skill in the field of emotional disorder, and how much to the fact that the specialist team was looking after the younger and possibly more hopeful psychiatric clients, is difficult to determine from the data available.

THE MENTALLY HANDICAPPED

The forty-one mentally handicapped clients – the majority of them severely handicapped – were either children (25%) or adults between the ages of 20 and 60 (75%).

In contrast to the mentally ill, a high proportion (56%) of the mentally handicapped were on agency review. These were mainly clients who had stabilised either at home, in a hostel or a group home, were attending an industrial training centre, and only needed occasional surveillance and reassessment. A much higher proportion of the mentally handicapped were looked after by unqualified workers (46%) than in the mentally ill group (29%) or in any other problem group (Table 13.2).

The social work with the few children allocated to individual workers shows determined efforts to intregrate them with children of normal intelligence wherever possible. The case review forms of a boy of 9 who was also in care illustrated this point. When the case started in 1966 he was in hospital. The social worker first found foster parents for holidays and occasional weekends. The next step was to place him in a small hostel for mentally handicapped children. At the end of the study year the social worker was trying to find a place for this boy in an ordinary children's home. Placement in a special boarding school with holidays at home was achieved in another case of severe mental handicap. In the case of an adolescent, on the other hand, diligent attempts to get him into

Table 13.1   *Summary of Help Given, Workers Involved, Future Plans and Reasons for Closure for Cases Involving Mental Illness or Emotional Disturbance*

All cases		*Cases open at the most recent review*	
Social workers' activities	%	Major change areas	%
Review visiting	66	No change intended	57
Sustaining/nurturing	36	Behaviour/attitude	23
Exploration/assessment	34	Major environmental	13
Information/advice	34	Social/personal	
Problem solving	30	environment	3
Mobilising resources	25	Social role	3
Advocacy	13		
Practical help	%	Estimated time before closure	%
Help with applications	23	Up to one year	23
Financial	15	Up to three years	13
Change in living group	13	More than three years	63
Day centres/clubs/outings	12		
Referral to hospital/clinic	12		
Reception into care	10		
Discharge from Part III/			
care	10	Base (= 100%) 30	
None	33		
Outside agencies	%		
Psychiatric hospitals	32		
GPs	26		
Health visitors/nurses	25		
Educational	15		
Voluntary agencies	15		
Other	13		
None	23	*Cases closed at the most recent review*	
Types of workers	%	Reasons for closure	No.
Qualified social worker	69	Department withdraws	9
Unqualified social worker	19	Aims achieved	4
Social work assistant	10	Client died	3
Other with specialised		Referral to other facilities	2
knowledge	2	Client withdraws	1
None	6	Change in circumstances	—
		Other	1
Average no. contacts			
per quarter	8·1		
Base (= 100%) 53		Total = 20 cases	

For explanatory notes see Table 10.1.

sheltered employment and eventually into open employment finally failed.

The thirty-one young and middle-aged adults lived either with their families, often in stressful circumstances, or in hostels or group homes. Where family relationships were precarious or the handicapped client prone to disturbed behaviour, support was planned for an indefinite

Table 13.2 *Summary of Help Given, Workers Involved, Future Plans and Reasons for Closure for the Mentally Handicapped*

All cases		Cases open at the most recent review	
Social workers' activities	%	Major change areas	No.
Review visiting	54	No change intended	18
Mobilising resources	34	Major environmental	4
Information/advice	29	Social/personal	
Exploration/assessment	24	environment	3
Problem solving	15	Behaviour/attitude	2
		Social role	—
Practical help	%	Estimated time before closure	%
Holidays	20	Up to one year	—
Day centres/clubs/outings	15	Up to three years	2
Help with applications	15	More than three years	25
None	49		
		Total = 27 cases	
Outside agencies	%		
GPs	15		
Psychiatric hospitals	15		
Educational	15		
Health visitors/nurses	10		
Other social services depts	10		
Other	22	*Cases closed at the most recent review*	
None	37		
Types of workers	%	Reasons for closure	No.
Qualified social worker	49	Department withdraws	7
Unqualified social worker	24	Aims achieved	4
Social work assistant	22	Change in circumstances	1
None	13	Client died	—
		Client withdraws	—
Average no. contacts		Referral to other facilities	—
per quarter	2·1	Other	—
Base (= 100%) 41		Total = 12 cases	

For explanatory notes see Table 10.1.

period. Occasionally a spell of residential treatment was needed to relieve the strain on the family. The cases of clients who were reasonably settled at home or in a hostel, either attending the local industrial training centre or doing simple outside work, tended to be closed after a period on agency review. However, if the client made obvious strides in social skills the social worker would not be content to leave him in a protective environment, but would help him towards an independent existence in the community in lodgings or a flat.

Social workers provided much practical help for the eighteen allocated cases, which included arrangements for holidays, help with employment, or alternative accommodation. Information and advice was given to half of these clients. An outside agency was contacted on behalf of fifteen of the eighteen clients, health and psychiatric services topping the list for the adults and the educational services for the children. Seven of the eighteen allocated cases were closed on the last review since they seemed to manage reasonably well on their own.

It is difficult to draw any general conclusions from work with this very small group of handicapped clients. Considerable effort appears to have gone into enabling the younger people in particular to lead as full and as normal a life in the community as possible. But the nagging doubt remains whether the area office was aware of all the severely mentally handicapped people living in their area, since they and their families are as a rule the most hidden client group, making few if any demands on the social services (Tizard and Grad, 1961; Bayley, 1973).

SOME ISSUES AND QUESTIONS

This scrutiny of long-term social work in an area office has raised some important issues and questions. One of the outstanding features was the concentration on surveillance and review visiting, which was recorded for nearly three-quarters of all cases and was considered to be the most important social worker activity in two-fifths of them. In over half of these long-term situations no change was expected, and nearly three-quarters of the cases were to remain open indefinitely. If this picture is at all typical, then one of the issues emerging is how to delineate more precisely the care needs of these long-term clients, and how best to deploy the limited statutory and voluntary resources available to meet these ends.

For example, work with the very frail elderly brought into sharp focus the question of how to ensure continuous support and surveillance for them, since the occasional social work visit did not seem to be the appropriate means of support or early warning system of approaching crises.

The care of the younger physically disabled highlighted the contribution of the occupational therapist, and raised the question of collaboration between social and medical personnel.

We noted that the emotional needs of the frail elderly and of the younger disabled and those of their families were rarely the target of social work intervention. On the other hand, we questioned the necessity for specialised workers to give so much permanent practical and emotional support to the visually handicapped, almost irrespective of their actual needs.

The chronically disorganised and disturbed families presented the greatest challenge to social work skills. We observed that they took up an inordinate amount of social work resources, sometimes over many years with few visible results. Hence one might question the wisdom of closing within the intake phase as 'low priority' those family cases whose problems are not as yet very severe. One might also question in this connection the sharp division into intake/short-term/long-term teams which tends to obscure the overall view of these problems.

In contrast to the families where child behaviour and problems in relationships were considered to be the most important ones, we observed the relatively favourable outcomes of work with families where material problems were tackled. We speculated whether a more task-centred approach to the chronically disturbed families would similarly lead to more positive outcomes.

The issues of the possible need for more specialised skills at field level arose in relation to adolescent delinquents and among clients and families where mental disorder was a central concern.

In our concluding chapter we shall try to pursue these and other issues identified in our examination of intake procedures and short-term work a little further, and to consider some possible answers.

NOTE

1 A good deal of the social work with the mentally ill and their families was carried out by a specialist team, closely associated with the psychiatric services, housed in different premises, and covering the whole of the city.

Chapter 14

◆

THE SOCIAL WORKER'S EVALUATION OF THE CASE REVIEW SYSTEM

How did the area staff react to this new monitoring tool, and how did it affect their attitudes and practices? It is difficult to judge the impact of the introduction of the CRS on the area's work for several reasons: the researchers' own involvement in the change processes they tried to assess casts some doubt on the objectivity of their judgements. Innovatory practices, especially when they require extra effort and come on top of many other changing demands and reorganisational measures, are bound to meet some resistance. Other developments in the area office – also influenced by the presence of the research team – such as the establishment of an intake team brought about considerable changes in practice and reduced the pressure of bombardment and emergency referrals on the other teams. This development may have been a countervailing influence in that it enabled some members of the 'long-term' teams to adhere to their long-ingrained social work habits of routine surveillance for vulnerable groups and of long-term, unfocused 'support'. Other writers on intake teams have made similar observations (Boucher, 1976; Gostick, 1976). Finally, some of the concepts of planned, goal-oriented social work embodied in the CRS may not have been in tune with the teaching and socialisation experienced by the majority of fieldworkers and supervisors.

Although we were aware of all these possible sources of bias we tried to obtain the area social workers' views on the CRS by issuing a brief questionnaire at the end of the study year. Everybody answered anonymously and in a very frank manner. The participatory spirit had taken so much root that one respondent devoted one paragraph to a critique of the questionnaire, pointing to the overlapping of questions and calling the whole thing 'bitty'!

After inquiring whether the respondent had participated in the development of the CRS, we asked how much it had contributed to his work with clients, to caseload management, to professional development and to the awareness of the relationship between his work and the area as a whole, and whether it had facilitated consultation and supervision. We inquired about the usefulness of the feedback information, whether the

CRS had contributed to the organisation of the area office, whether the respondent thought that its potentialities had been fully exploited, whether it should be extended to other area offices, and finally, whether it had been worth the effort.

Since numbers are necessarily very small (there were twenty-seven effective replies, since several workers had only joined the area office so recently that they could not commit themselves to firm opinions) we shall only report the main trends of the replies. The answers relating to three of the four questions on the influence of the CRS on their own work showed a fairly uniform distribution. Roughly between a quarter and a third of the social workers felt that it had made no difference to their practice, their caseload management and their professional development and a similar proportion said that the CRS had contributed considerably or greatly, and the rest hovered in the middle. In contrast only 12 per cent felt that the CRS had made no contribution at all to the awareness of the relationship of their work to the area as a whole. We reported in an earlier chapter that over four-fifths (82%) thought that the feedback information and its discussion had been quite or very useful and that a similar proportion thought that the system should be extended (Chapter 5). An even greater majority (88%) thought that the CRS had contributed to the way in which the area office was organised, mentioning in particular the setting up of the intake team and the development of the agency review concept. More reservations could be detected in the answers to the question whether the CRS had been worth the effort they put into it. Three-fifths answered enthusiastically 'yes certainly', 27 per cent said 'possibly', and 12 per cent 'hardly'. Nobody admitted that it had not been worth their effort at all.

In general then the replies convey a partial commitment to the CRS as an aid to individual practice but a much wider acceptance of it as a monitoring and planning tool which enabled them to compare their own contributions with those of their colleagues and with the work of the area office as a whole. There is one other interesting finding: those who had participated in the working parties which developed the system expressed a greater enthusiasm for it than those who had not done so.

The most instructive part of the questionnaire was the comments for which we left a good deal of room and the majority of respondents took advantage of this opportunity. The positive aspects mentioned in relation to the use of the CRS in individual practice were the help in setting goals and becoming more explicit about aims, in clarifying priorities, and in defining limits, including time limits. One social worker said that the CRS had given 'shape to our activities which previously were flabby and rather woolly'. On the negative side one or two people only saw additional paper chores in the introduction of the case review form and several others felt that its value was more to management than to individual casework practice. Some claimed that they had always planned their work and that the only possible interest lay in the insight the CRS gave them into other people's work! One person complained that the form did not give an expression to the consumers' feelings and opinions. (In principle there is no reason why such a form should not be filled in with the client.) Most of the respondents felt that the kind of case evaluation represented by the CRS could be useful in the supervisory sessions but that it had not as yet been applied in any systematic way for this purpose. 'Maybe people are too disorganised and can't change', one worker remarked. But another said, 'it gives an aid to structuring discussion – a clear list of possibilities, rather than a hazy ill-defined area, but still leaves room for new lines of approach'. For others, the form was too structured and they preferred a more wide-ranging style of conversation in their supervisory sessions.

As already indicated, the potentiality of the CRS as a general information and planning tool was recognised by almost everyone. Many different comments showed that it had been an eye-opener from this point of view; it was said that it enabled them to see individual needs in relation to the client group as a whole; that it threw light on the distribution of resources; that it had helped them to become aware of the different services to the clients in the area; that it showed them how much time and effort had been spent on different types of cases; and that it gave them an understanding of the commitment entered into by the area as a whole. Some social workers had become interested in the possibilities of comparing different social workers' caseloads and ways of working. One person thought that the CRS was encouraging greater uniformity in case recording and in methods of working.

Most thought that the potentialities of the CRS had not been fully exploited as yet: more avenues could have been explored, more questions could have been asked of the data; its maximum potential could only be realised if it was extended to the whole authority so that comparisons could be made as to how resources were distributed in relation to needs of different areas. At the other end of the spectrum it also needed to be integrated more fully into the individual's system of work and used more consistently in evaluating casework in relation to aims pursued. Some expressed the view that a fuller and more thoughtful use of the CRS could only be achieved if the amount of other paperwork were to be reduced.

There was general consensus that the system and the presence of the research team had generated new thinking, new ideas and enthusiasm, and had contributed to the generally good morale of the area and to a sense of purpose, but the problem now was how to keep the interest going. It was suggested that the intake team would have been set up in any case but it would not have been so thorough-going and rigorous in its policies. The accountability element was also acknowledged: 'The area is in a strong position to be held accountable for our decisions about what work is done and what work is not done. People may disagree with our reasons, but we can account for what is happening and that is important.'

The two most serious general reservations about the system were its cost and whether the resultant benefit justified the social workers' efforts. Linked to this was the question whether simpler and cheaper means could achieve similar results. Secondly, it was felt that the CRS had not attracted sufficient attention and encouragement from top management and that the research team had failed to appreciate the influence upon social workers of higher managerial factors and statutory constraints.

Perhaps the following comment best sums up the social workers' evaluation of the introduction of the system: '*The act* of creating the system plus the presence of the research team has been both a personal stimulus and a stimulus to the area itself. We have yet to realise and demonstrate the value of the *fact* of having the system. The potential is definitely there, subject no doubt to continuing modification and development.'

What is the researchers' response to this cautious summing up? The perceptive comment quoted above points at the ever-present dilemma of action research, how to convert the interactive change-producing educational experience into a more permanent, systematic increment in knowledge and practice. The comment also raises the following question. What would the take up be if such an evaluative instrument was to be introduced 'cold', as it were, into an area office? Would it be dismissed as an irrelevant statistical exercise for the benefit of 'them' (management)? The answer in the long run will be that if the kind of evaluative thinking embodied in the CRS is to become an essential ingredient of social work practice, the need for which we argued in the first chapter, it will have to become part and parcel of basic social work training.

Chapter 15

CONCLUSIONS AND REFLECTIONS

What can we learn from this intensive exploration in one southern English town of clients' and social workers' perspectives and from the systematic monitoring of one year's field social work?

In the following discussion we have abandoned excessive caution which seeks to qualify every single finding and on occasions have generalised beyond the safe boundaries of the data which refer to one area office only. Our justification for doing this is that we had opportunities of presenting the material contained in this book to a number of social workers in different parts of Britain as well as to administrators at local and national level. These discussions suggested that the facts and issues uncovered in this study are not atypical and have relevance for the organisation and practice of field social work in the personal social services generally. Secondly, results of other studies are becoming available which enable us to place our findings into a broader context. Thirdly, comparable data are now being assembled in area offices in other parts of the country. The picture emerging so far is broadly similar to the findings in Seatown.

EXPECTATIONS AND SATISFACTIONS OF CONSUMERS AND SOCIAL WORKERS

Our consumer study in Seatown indicated that the majority of the consumers were reasonably satisfied with the services they received, partly because they expected in the main practical help and advice. The two client groups who received this type of help in large measure – the elderly and those with predominantly material problems – turned out to be the most satisfied. Social workers, on the other hand, often felt frustrated that they were only able to offer practical services and advice and were aware of the functions they were not able to fulfil: those of the caseworker attending to the emotional problems of their clients. Accordingly they expected their clients to be equally dissatisfied and to voice more complaints than they actually did.

Curiously, in the very group in which the social workers reported most casework activity, namely among those experiencing family and child care problems, dissatisfaction was greater and complaints more numerous than among the elderly and among those with material problems. The clients' comments in the consumer interviews, impressions from our observations and discussions in the area office, and a small pilot study of short-term clients in which we interviewed clients and social workers on individual cases, threw some light on the reasons for the divergencies in perceptions between some clients and their social workers. These reasons did not seem so much related to social class and cultural gaps or to the psychodynamic preconceptions of the social workers as to lack of experience, and of specialised knowledge and skills, and to time pressures. In some instances the consumers' stories suggested that the social workers had not got hold of the problems that really bothered them or those within their immediate social networks. Hence, the subsequent social work activity had not been experienced as relevant or helpful. An accurate assessment which arrives at the problem which the client experiences as most troublesome is probably one of the most important keys to successful social work intervention. One is tempted to speculate that in the pressured atmosphere of an intake team concerned with continuous screening, 'one-off' advice and the delivery of a wide variety of practical services, careful exploration and assessment may be in danger of atrophy.

In the following reflections on intake functions and longer-term social work we shall consider whether a redeployment of professional skills would enable social workers to use and develop their expertise where it is really needed.

GATEKEEPING FUNCTIONS

The intake data showed that the large majority of incoming cases received short-term help. Four-fifths of these cases had been closed by the end of three months and only 6 per cent remained open by the end of the study year.

The social workers in the intake team spent a great deal of their time:

(1) in screening incoming demands, many of them for simple advice and straightforward practical services;
(2) providing practical help and services of many kinds for the disabled and elderly;
(3) acting as a kind of citizens advice bureau for a great variety of material and inter-personal problems; and
(4) as a go-between with other statutory and voluntary bodies, the most important among them being the DHSS and the Housing Department.

Casework, usually held to be the main activity of social workers, in the sense of helping people to clarify and solve problems in a calm atmosphere, was only recorded in 20 per cent of the cases in both intake and long-term teams.

At the same time, our consumer studies pointed to a growing tendency for clients to rely on the social services department as an information centre and referral point to more specialised agencies.

The question was raised whether the current training of social workers equipped them to act as information-givers, advisers and service-providers on such a broad front. We are aware that social workers specialising in intake have opportunities for developing these skills, but, as some investigations have shown, it is doubtful whether social workers can master all the intricacies of welfare rights (Hill and Laing, 1978), or keep abreast of the many new developments in neighbourhood care or be knowledgeable about the latest aids to daily living for the elderly and the disabled. One member of our research team spent much time and thought on helping the area teams to design and compile an effective resource index, but the vital problem of how to keep such an essential tool updated was never solved.

Thus, the organisation of effective gatekeeping functions emerges as a vital issue. A variety of solutions can be visualised and some are already being tried out in various parts of the country. For example, an area team in Wakefield has been experimenting with a highly decentralised method of intake and service provision for some time (Cooper, 1978) and an independent evaluative study is now in progress. In an Inner London area office volunteers play an important part in initial screening procedures. Whatever type of organisation or model is chosen, using whatever mix of disciplines and levels of training, three vital needs will have to be met: one is an effective information and advice service. This could take the form of a special information and advice section manned by information officers with specialised training, or it could involve joint arrangements with voluntary bodies such as citizens advice bureaux or neighbour-hood centres which have developed a formidable body of expertise in this field.

Secondly, since we can expect a large increase in the population aged 75 and over within the next ten years assessment procedures in response to requests for domiciliary and related services for the elderly will have to be overhauled. It is unrealistic to imagine that it is possible or even desirable for trained social workers to carry out such assessments. The initial screening can and is being carried out by a variety of personnel – home help organisers, social service officers or occupational therapists. Much thought and further study will have to be devoted to the establish-ment of criteria for allocating service resources – criteria tailored to individual needs, but to needs seen in the context of the overall policy aims of keeping elderly people 'active and independent' in their own homes (DHSS, 1978). In the development of such criteria, consideration would have to be given to personal capacity (both physical and psychological), to social circumstances and to help already available.

Thirdly, it will be necessary to allocate resources to in-service training of frontline personnel in order to equip them to carry out initial assessments for domiciliary and other services reliably and sensitively, and above all to spot those clients who appear to need help beyond the specific service requested. Only at that point might a trained social worker enter the case, possibly as a consultant and adviser in the first place.

Inherent in these suggestions is the concept of delineating clearer tasks in response to specific needs within the context of a social services team containing a variety of skills and abandoning the idea of the intake worker as a Jack of all trades. Such a redeployment of skills would free trained social workers to devote time and thought to the assessment of complex situations where environmental factors, inter-personal and personality factors intermingle and pose formidable obstacles to a reasonably clear problem definition and to the determination of feasible objectives.

Service responses geared towards specific tasks in relation to specific demands may enable social workers to undertake short-term work with incipient psycho-social problems which are at present closed as 'low priority'.

LONG-TERM PERSPECTIVES

We saw that some 10 per cent of the 2,000 incoming cases were passed on for more extended help to the long-term teams. These were mainly children who had been received into care or who were in need of surveillance and protection for other reasons, and the very vulnerable elderly and disabled persons. Lastly, this long-term caseload contained all the visually handicapped, almost irrespective of their specific needs for social work or surveillance.

Our examination of long-term work has highlighted the need to think afresh about a strategy of care for those client groups 'who cannot care for themselves and must be cared for' (Morris, 1977). We saw that a good deal of manpower was concentrated on surveillance and review visiting which was recorded for nearly three-quarters of all the 1,400 long-term cases and was considered to be the most important social worker activity in two-fifths of them. No change was expected in over half these long-term situations and nearly three-quarters of the cases were to remain open indefinitely.

Another outstanding feature was the somewhat uneven distribution of social work resources among the different problem groups. Although the physically disabled group outnumbered the child and family problems by two to one, they only made up 20 per cent of the allocated cases, while almost all the child and family problems were allocated to individual workers, accounting for 35 per cent of all individual caseloads.

On the other hand, the disabled and elderly received far more domiciliary services and aids than other problem groups.

The scrutiny of long-term social work has also raised questions about the appropriateness of methods of intervention and the deployment of social work skills, particularly in relation to the elderly and to families under chronic stress. Last but not least this exploration led us to question how helpful to both clients and social workers the division into intake and long-term teams proves to be.

THE ELDERLY

Among the elderly our monitoring exercise as well as other research (Goldberg, Mortimer and Williams, 1970) has indicated the importance of distinguishing between those who can manage on their own with the help of domiciliary or other practical services, those who need to be in close touch with a supportive helping network, and those who in addition require skilled social work help. These distinctions were not always clearly made; hence, planning for long-term care was often haphazard. Only the very frail or confused elderly clients whose ability to lead an independent life in the community was seriously impaired received some form of long-term surveillance. But the case review records showed clearly that the occasional routine check-up visits were rarely the appropriate means of support or of anticipating approaching crises.

There is fairly general agreement now that the local authority personal social services can only hope to provide basic services for the majority of the growing number of very elderly clients. This would include information and advice (though this could also be supplied through the voluntary channels of citizens advice bureaux or neighbourhood advice centres); domiciliary services and aids to daily living; and the major part of day and short- or long-term residential care. With a rational deployment of manpower resources, skilled social work for those elderly and their supporters who face particularly difficult situations should also be available. Relief of isolation and loneliness, friendly surveillance of vulnerable, frail old people living alone or with aged spouses, help with small chores, emotional and practical support to informal carers will need to be provided by volunteers or 'good neighbours' either under the sponsorship of the statutory or voluntary sector.

Many neighbourhood care schemes of different kinds and other volunteer efforts are springing up all over the country, and a few are being monitored and evaluated by independent researchers (Hare, 1977; Abrams, 1978; Power, 1978; Kent Community Care Project, 1979). One of the challenges within the next years will be to develop flexible mechanisms which ensure collaboration and complementarity between the statutory and voluntary services so that together they form a continuum of care, rather than parallel and possibly even conflicting systems.

The Wolfenden Report (1977) has urged clearer and more positive policies on the part of local authorities towards the ways in which voluntary organisations can contribute to the welfare of the community. Research projects are now in progress with a special remit of exploring the patterns of relationship between local authorities and voluntary organisations, and it is hoped that possible models of collaboration will evolve from these researches.

The increasing momentum towards localised voluntary or semi-voluntary community care support for the elderly and other chronically disabled people will affect the roles of social workers and other statutory care givers, including GPs, health visitors and district nurses. Some social workers will become quasi community workers acting as initiators, enablers, co-ordinators and advisers to neighbourhood schemes. Social workers may also find themselves in advisory roles *vis-à-vis* home helps, who, as they take on more personal tasks for the frail and confused elderly, may turn increasingly to social workers for consultation rather than to home help organisers. One could visualise a team concerned with the needs of the elderly and disabled consisting of a social worker, an occupational therapist, social service officers, home helps, volunteers and a community worker.

FAMILIES UNDER CHRONIC STRESS

We have been impressed, as have been other investigators (Sainsbury and Nixon, 1978; Stevenson and Parsloe, 1978;) by the amount of social work time (as well as other resources such as day and residential care) taken up by a comparatively small number of chronically disorganised and disturbed families. The families appear to be in an almost constant state of crisis. Thus, social workers have argued on occasions when discussing the planning functions of the CRS that social work plans tended to be disrupted by crises which demanded immediate attention. It seems that a thoroughgoing study of 'crises', how they are defined, how they arise and are dealt with is overdue. We also observed (as did Stevenson and her colleagues) among social workers involved with family problems and children at risk, a fairly constant anxiety arising from the Maria Colwell Inquiry and its numerous sequelae to 'cover themselves' in case they should be held responsible for some catastrophic mishap. Another feature of this insurance policy against any possible disaster was to allocate the large majority of child-care/family cases to trained social workers, including those children who were well settled in long-established foster homes. This left very little trained manpower for the complex social, emotional and family problems which often accompany disability, both among younger and older people, and possibly also limited the development of expertise and interest in the problems related to mental illness and mental handicap. It may be timely to question the growing societal pressures on social services departments to become a kind of permanent protective police force ready and able to stem the tide of violence erupting in certain families and generally to regulate people's behaviour. The stimulation of more informed public discussion may help to highlight the complexity of the issues involved and thus reduce the unreasonable expectations of the protective functions of the social services. Whether the boundaries of personal accountability and responsibility could be defined more clearly is another question worth exploring. If such clarification proved feasible in this sensitive and fluid area it might help to lessen the burden of individual responsibility some social workers feel for events which few experts can either predict of prevent.

The conclusions we draw from our monitoring exercise point in the opposite direction of constant availability to families in a permanent state of disequilibrium. It may prove more helpful to these families in the long run to limit the resources at present expended on long-term and often aimless casework and surveillance and instead to invest some resources in experimenting with other methods, including those developing within the framework of task-centred casework (Reid and Epstein, 1972 and 1977). These suggestions are reinforced by a study of long-term social work in a social services department as well as in other settings, recently completed by Sainsbury and Nixon (1978). They found that the preferred style of casework practice with families in the social services setting was ventilation of feelings, and that although much advocacy was undertaken, relatively little use was made of techniques intended to help clients to manage their own material affairs more efficiently. Sainsbury and Nixon also comment on how little use was made of voluntary helpers to undertake befriending functions. 'The tradition of the encapsulated individual caseload appears to preclude the full use of auxiliary help.' The authors mention the *ad hoc* nature of the contacts which decline over time and report the expressed wish of some third of the clients for social workers to be firmer and more purposeful. These observations accord well with findings on task-centred casework which indicate that clients gain a considerable sense of achievement from learning how to tackle and resolve small problems, one at a time (Goldberg, Walker and Robinson, 1977; Goldberg and Stanley, 1979). We have observed the growth in confidence, self-worth and competence among a number of very deprived clients who after many years of dependence on a social worker have achieved small objectives agreed between them and a social worker within an encouraging and yet time-limited and task-centred relationship.

Another action study dealing with marital problems of materially and emotionally very deprived families coming to social services departments also concludes that intermittent long-term support, punctuated by hectic activity in times of crisis, rarely results in any change of behaviour or in personal growth. The authors suggest that a sustained but time-limited relationship within which clients feel safe enough to confront their emotional problems can lead to a less crisis-ridden existence and in some cases to behaviour changes (Mattinson and Sinclair, 1979).

Thus concentration on more intensive time-limited methods with some objective in mind – possibly in conjunction with some voluntary neighbourhood support – may prove more effective than the policy of long-term 'containment'.

In contrast, some voluntary organisations such as the Family Service Units and the NSPCC are providing more long-term nurturing experiences to multi-problem families, including those who neglect or injure their children. Social workers offer continuous support as well as behavioural teaching, apparently with encouraging outcomes (Baher *et al.*, 1976).

The tentative results of these exploratory action studies employing different methods and time perspectives now call for the setting up of controlled experiments to assess the relative effectiveness of these different methods in the treatment of families chronically beset by a multiplicity of problems. But in doing so investigators should heed Helen Perlman's observation, when discussing the negative results of an experiment in casework with multi-problem families in the USA, that you can't expect people to pull themselves up by their boot straps if they have no boots.

ALTERNATIVE APPROACHES TO INTERVENTION

So far our conclusions have forced us to recognise that demographic trends, particularly in relation to the aged and their widespread social needs, and the intractability of many of the human problems landing on the doorstep of the social services departments, call into question the ability of the statutory services to provide comprehensive help from the cradle to the grave. We have referred to the growing importance of the voluntary sector in filling the gaps and in pioneering new approaches. But of even greater importance will be the investment of some resources in preventive activities. Rutter (1978) suggested recently that demographic trends related to the family such as growth in illegitimacy, divorce and separation and other trends such as the rising employment rates of young mothers and the increase of multiple admissions of children to hospital, call for new preventive programmes so that 'experiences which are going to happen to children anyway will do good and not harm' (p. 112). Brown and Harris's findings (1978) that certain material and environmental factors as well as psycho-social lacks such as a warm and supportive relationship with a companion are associated with the widespread phenomenon of depression in young mothers also point to the need for more preventive community programmes. Group work and mutual help opportunities for lone parents at strategic points in the local community, day-care facilities of various kinds for young children, development of part-time employment opportunities for women are all possible growth points.

In addition, more widespread outposting of social service personnel, for example in primary health care teams and schools, may prove a fertile means of secondary prevention. There is some evidence (Goldberg and Neill, 1972; Corney and Briscoe, 1977) to show that clients referred to social workers in primary health care settings differ significantly in the problems they present from those referred to social services departments: fewer clients were referred to social workers in general practice for predominantly material needs, such as financial or accommodation problems. In contrast, difficulties in family relationships, personality problems, and problems related to emotional and mental illness amounted to about half the referrals to the social workers attached to general practices whilst they comprised less than a quarter of the social services referrals. These differences may be due to differences in perception of social worker roles in the two settings, but it is also likely that the primary health care team spots and selects earlier manifestations of social and psychiatric morbidity for referral to their social worker. These findings possibly also indicate that certain manifestations of emotional disorders and disturbed relationships may be more amenable to social work intervention within the confines of general practice than in an area office of a social services department. For example, early counselling and support to parents who have produced a handicapped child; help in terminal care and bereavement; marital casework; work with people who have attempted suicide; social after-care of some schizophrenic patients who may find it easier to accept help within the familiar context of general practice. A realignment of social work activities along such lines seems particularly worth exploring in view of our findings that the more benign situations in which short-term casework might bring about some changes tend to be crowded out in the social services departments by those situations which have to be taken on because of statutory obligations or because they entail serious risk to those who cannot defend themselves.

However, in many problem situations confronting an area office, casework or 'visiting' combined with practical services may not be appropriate remedies. The so-called unitary approach to social work (Pincus and Minahan, 1973; Specht and Vickery, 1977) which provides a wider, more flexible framework for viewing and tackling social problems than the older, individually oriented theories of social work may show the way to more appropriate solutions. This model helps to distinguish more sharply those problem situations in which only a structural or organisational change can offer any solution, those in which a group or community response may yield possible solutions and those in which individual guidance, counselling or casework seems the appropriate answer. At the same time this approach focuses our attention on who is to be the target of intervention – the client, his informal network, other caregivers already involved or formal organisations such as the DHSS or the Housing Department.

A new housing development in our study area which accommodates both the young and the old provides a good example of how a group or community approach, rather than the occasional social work visit and a routine meals-on-wheels delivery, might be a more appropriate form of intervention for some frail and lonely elderly people. Observation and case discussions suggested that some of these old people stimulated by social workers, home helps, or voluntary helpers might have been able to prepare their own meals. One also observed that the community facilities in these sheltered flats were empty while the old people ate their meals in isolated silence in their little flats. One Inner London borough now increasingly locates their luncheon clubs in the community facilities of new housing estates and encourages and financially supports the tenants' associations in running the meals service.

Another example was the similarity of problems in home management, budgeting and child care experienced by many young families on certain housing estates. Once more it seemed that a group approach, which enabled them to learn together how to make more appropriate use of the welfare system or how to draw on their own potential skills and ability, may have been more rewarding than hurried advice and referral to the DHSS. Information supplied by the CRS on the concentration, characteristics and problems of one-parent families in one of the particularly deprived neighbourhoods in our study area (cluster 8) has helped to further plans for group work with these families (Warburton and Willmott, 1976). We have already referred to the development of group activities for foster parents which might prove more stimulating than routine follow-up visits.

At this point it is worth recalling that a third of our consumer sample of Seatown's Social Services showed positive interest in some form of participation. Several consumers came forward with specific suggestions as to how they might contribute to the development of the social services. Unfortunately, despite extensive discussion of these findings little progress was made in initiating a dialogue between consumers and social service providers.

SPECIALISATION

How do the findings emerging from this monitoring exercise of intake, short-term and long-term social work in an area office affect the issue of specialisation?

A broader community and neighbourhood-based approach to a variety of family difficulties and to problems related to ageing and disability would accentuate the roles of group and community workers. Such developments would make the role of casework more specific. Caseworkers would devote themselves to the more complex material and non-material problems of the elderly and disabled and their supporters, to problems of family disturbance and child care, and the inter-personal and social repercussions of mental illness and handicap. We have suggested that some of this work may fit better into the setting of primary health care. Caseworkers would not undertake routine screening activities, straightforward service delivery and surveillance or review visiting.

We have further argued that there appears to be much room for specialisation in gatekeeping functions, especially in relation to information and advice, advocacy and appropriate assessment and delivery of practical services.

The broad scope of our inquiry makes it difficult to speculate how much specialisation is required at field level in relation to specific client groups. We have sketched a possible role for a team of workers with different skills dealing with the disabled and elderly. It is also likely that some members of an area team will need to acquire more specialised knowledge in the field of mental and emotional disorder. What emerged clearly from our study was the need for easily accessible specialist consultation very near field level, as Stevenson also found in her studies (Stevenson and Parsloe, 1978). At present, specialist advisers operate at a great distance from the fieldworkers and are rarely used for case consultation. Some advisers prefer to deal with policy issues and abrogate responsibilities related to practice. In our experience, the occupational therapist was the only specialist in the social services department who is readily appreciated and consulted, partly no doubt because her skills are so obviously useful, but also one suspects because she is easily accessible as a colleague at field level.

Our examination of both short- and long-term work in an area office, particularly that with disturbed families, throws doubt on the one type of specialisation which is fairly common, the division into intake and long-term work. The long-term struggle to 'contain' chronically disorganised families can be very disheartening to social workers, and, as already indicated, foster undue dependence in the families who may lose all belief in their own ability to solve problems. It prevents some social workers from experiencing positive outcomes in work with early manifestations of family tensions and breakdown. It may reinforce a tendency to aimless 'visiting' and support well beyond the point of positive benefit to the clients. It prevents the intake workers from observing, living with and learning from the outcome of their original decisions, and it can hinder cross-fertilisation from short- to long-term work and vice versa. Finally, however, we question the usefulness and effectiveness, except in rare cases, of the model of one long-term social worker attached to a case over a period of years. We visualise the use of other resources – such as home helps, neighbourhood care groups, individual volunteers, self-help groups – for long-term support while the social worker, possibly acting as a resource person to these helpers, might only intervene directly at certain critical points; for instance, when difficulties prove too severe for the customary support system, at a period of transition when a foster child is about to leave school, when someone faces serious loss or bereavement, and so on. In other words, the model of the social worker, either in the image of a passive therapist who follows his client on a long journey of self-exploration, or as a universal aunt or 'nanny' forever hovering around, ready to support, prop up and 'speak for' her clients, is being superseded by more specific social work roles, both direct and indirect, linked to the network of other caregivers, both statutory and voluntary.

WHERE DO WE GO FROM HERE?

The CRS, which asks some basic questions about the aims and methods of field social work, as well as the more subjective views of social workers and clients, has presented us with a broad picture of social work and social service activities during one year in one area office in England. A majority of clients said that they got what they had hoped for from the social services, and that the help received made a difference to their lives. This is a very important finding that should not be ignored in the prevailing pessimism about social work and its outcome. But some of the outcomes in conjunction with emerging demographic and social trends made us question the deployment of social work resources and the appropriateness of the methods used in tackling some of the tasks facing an area office. We have considered how skills might be redeployed and tasks defined more realistically, and how statutory work could mesh into voluntary and semi-voluntary efforts which we hoped might eventually include the clients themselves. Experimentation with new ways of deploying social work and social service resources is taking place in several areas and more rigorous evaluative studies testing the effectiveness of certain innovations are also in progress. But in addition we need more epidemiological evidence using similar monitoring tools to the CRS about the nature of current demands on services and how they are met in different geographic areas with different demographic features and differing internal administrative arrangements, together with some broad indicators of outcome. However, this need for information on the distribution of needs, demands and patterns of service delivery should not obscure the purpose of case review as a monitoring tool to make social work practice more explicit, more responsive to clients' problems and more goal-oriented.

REFERENCES

Abrams, P. (1978a). 'Community care: some research problems and priorities', in J. Barnes and N. Connelly (eds), *Social Care Research* (Bedford Square Press).

Abrams, P. (1978b). 'Patterns of neighbourhood care: a preliminary report on a national survey' (unpublished conference paper, University of Durham).

Amos, F. J. C. (1971). *Social Malaise in Liverpool: Interim Report on Social Problems and Their Distribution* (Liverpool Corporation).

Baher, E., Hyman, C., Jones, C., Jones, R., Keu, A. and Mitchell, R. (1976). *At Risk: An Account of the Work of the Battered Child Research Department* (Routledge & Kegan Paul).

BASW (1977). *The Social Work Task* (BASW Publications).

Bayley, M. (1973). *Mental Handicap and Community Care* (Routledge & Kegan Paul).

Boucher, R. (1976). 'The first 12 months of an intake team', *Social Work Today*, vol. 8, no. 10.

Bradshaw, J. (1972). 'Taxonomy of social need', in G. McLachlan (ed.), *Problems and Progress in Medical Care* (OUP).

Brown, G. E. (ed.) (1968). *The Multi-Problem Dilemma: A Social Research Demonstration with Multi-Problem Families* (Metuchen, NJ: Scarecrow Press).

Brown, G. W. and Harris, T. (1978). *Social Origins of Depression. A Study of Psychiatric Disorder in Women* (Tavistock Publications).

Butler, J., Bow, I. and Gibbons, J. S. (1978). 'Task-centred casework in marital problems', *British Journal of Social Work*, vol. 8, no. 4.

Camden Social Services Department: Planning Unit (1975). 'Referrals to the Department – Area Summaries' (Background Notes).

Central Statistical Office (1976). *National Income and Expenditure 1965–75* (HMSO).

Challis, D. J. (1978). 'The measurement of outcome in social care of the elderly' (unpublished conference paper, University of Kent at Canterbury, Personal Social Services Research Unit).

Cherns, A. (1971). 'Social research and its diffusion', in F. D. Caro (ed.). *Readings in Evaluation Research* (New York: Russell Sage).

Clarke, A. M. and Clarke, A. D. B. (1976). *Early Experience: Myth and Evidence* (Open Books).

Colwell Report (1974). *Report of the Committee of Inquiry into the Care and Supervision Provided in Relation to Maria Colwell* (DHSS).

Cooper, M. (1978). 'Normanton area office "patch system"', in G. Darvill, 'Area teams and the volunteer community: three projects', *Social Work Service*, no. 18.

Corney, R. H. and Briscoe, M. E. (1977). 'Social workers and their clients: a comparison between primary health care and local authority settings', *Journal of the Royal College of General Practitioners*, vol. 27 (May).

Corrie, E. (1976). 'Intake: friend or foe?', *Social Work Today*, vol. 6, no. 23.

Curtis Report (1946). *Report of the Care of Children Committee*, Cmd 6922 (HMSO).

Davies, B. (1978). 'The role of volunteers and the changing balance of social service demands and resources' (unpublished conference paper, University of Kent at Canterbury, PSSRU).

Davies, M. (1969). *Probationers in Their Social Environment* (HMSO, Home Office Research Studies no. 2).

DHSS (1977). *Health and Personal Social Services Statistics* (HMSO).

DHSS (1978). *A Happier Old Age* (HMSO).

DHSS Management Services Branch and London Borough of Islington Personnel Department: O and M Section, Joint Assignment Report (1978). *Relations between the Social Services Department and Local Offices (Supplementary Benefits)* (DHSS/LBI, February).

DHSS Social Work Development Group (1977). *Records in Social Services Departments* (HMSO).

Devon County Council Social Services Department (1977). *Referrals and Caseloads – '77* (December).

Duncan, T. M. (1973). 'Intake in an integrated team', *Health and Social Service Journal* (10 February).

Eysenck, H. J. (1957). *The Dynamics of Anxiety and Hysteria* (Routledge & Kegan Paul).

Fischer, J. (1973). 'Is casework effective? A review', *Social Work*, vol. 18, no. 1.

Folkard, M. S., Smith, D. E. and Smith, D. D. (1976). *IMPACT Intensive Matched Probation and After-care Treatment. Vol. II – The Results of the Experiment* (HMSO, Home Office Research Studies no. 36).

Gibbons, J. S., Elliot, J., Urwin, P. and Gibbons, J. L. (1978). 'The urban environment and deliberate self-poisoning', *Social Psychiatry*, vol. 13.

Glampson, Ann and Goldberg, E. M. (1976). 'Post Seebohm social services: (2) the consumer's viewpoint', *Social Work Today*, vol. 8, no. 6.

Goldberg, E. M. and Fruin, D. J. (1976). 'Towards accountability in social work: a Case Review System for social workers', *British Journal of Social Work*, vol. 6, no. 1.

Goldberg, E. M., Mortimer, Ann and Williams, B. T. (1970). *Helping the Aged: A Field Experiment in Social Work* (Allen & Unwin).

Goldberg, E. M. and Neill, June E. (1972). *Social Work in General Practice*, National Institute Social Services Library no. 24 (Allen & Unwin).

Goldberg, E. M. and Stanley, J. S. (1979). 'A task-centred approach to probation', in Joan King (ed.), *Pressures and Changes in the Probation Service* (Institute of Criminology, Cambridge).

Goldberg, E. M., Walker, D. and Robinson, J. (1977). 'Exploring the task-centred casework method', *Social Work Today*, vol. 9, no. 2.

Goldberg, E. M., Warburton, R. W., Lyons, L. J. and Willmott, R. R. (1978). 'Towards accountability in social work: long term social work in an area office', *British Journal of Social Work*, vol. 8, no. 3.

Goldberg, E. M., Warburton, R. W., McGuinness, B. and Rowlands, J. H. (1977). 'Towards accountability in social work: one year's intake to an area office', *British Journal of Social Work*, vol. 7, no. 3.

Gostick, C. (1976). 'The intake phenomenon', *Social Work Today,* vol. 8, no 10.

Hare, E. J. (1977). *Three Score Years and Then? A Study of Practical Alternatives to Residential Care,* Seebohm House, 2/4 Queen Street, Norwich NR2 4TB.

Harris, Amelia I. (1971). *Handicapped and Impaired in Great Britain, Part 1* (HMSO).

Heraud, B. J. (1973). 'Professionalism, Radicalism and Social Change', in *Professionalisation and Social Change,* Sociological Review Monograph no. 20 (University of Keele).

Hill, M. and Laing, P. (1978). *Money Payments, Social Work and Supplementary Benefits. A Study of Section One of the 1963 Children and Young Persons Act* (University of Bristol School for Advanced Urban Studies).

Hirsch, F. (1977). *Social Limits to Growth* (Routledge & Kegan Paul).

HM Treasury (1978). *The Government's Expenditure Plans, 1978–79 to 1981–82,* Cmnd 7049 (HMSO).

Holme, Anthea and Maizels, Joan (1978). *Social Workers and Volunteers* (Allen & Unwin).

Imber, Valerie (1977). *Classification of the English Personal Social Services Authorities* (HMSO, DHSS Statistical and Research Report Series no. 16).

Jones, J. W. (1974). 'The intake group as an alternative service delivery structure', *Health and Social Service Journal* (23 March).

Keller, S. I. (1968). *The Urban Neighbourhood* (New York: Random House).

Kent Community Care Project (1979). 'The Kent Community Care Project: an interim report' (Project Paper No. 30/1).

Kingston upon Thames Social Services Department: Development Section (1976). 'Referral statistics' (unpublished).

Klein, R. (1973). *Complaints against Doctors: A Study in Professional Accountability* (Charles Knight).

Leonard, P. (1975). 'Towards a paradigm for radical practice', in R. Bailey and M. Brake (eds), *Radical Social Work* (Edward Arnold).

London Borough of Hillingdon, Social Services Research (1976). 'Referrals to area teams, 1975' (unpublished).

Lowenstein, C. (1974). 'An intake team in action in a social services department', *British Journal of Social Work,* vol. 4, no. 2.

Mattinson, J. and Sinclair, I. A. C. (1979). *Mate and Stalemate. Working with Marital Problems in a Social Services Department* (Blackwell).

Mayer, J. E. and Timms, N. (1970). *The Client Speaks* (Routledge & Kegan Paul).

McKay, A., Goldberg, E. M. and Fruin, D. J. (1973). 'Consumers and a social services department', *Social Work Today,* vol. 4, no. 16.

Meyer, H. J., Borgatta, E. E. and Jones, W. C. (1965). *Girls at Vocational High: An Experimental Study in Social Work Intervention* (New York: Russell Sage).

Morris, J. N. (1975). *Uses of Epidemiology* (Churchill Livingstone).

Morris, R. (1977). 'Caring for vs. caring about people', *Social Work,* vol. 22, no 5.

Mullen, E. J. (1969). 'Differences in worker style in casework', *Social Casework,* vol. 50 (June).

Mullen, E. J., Chazin, R. M. and Feldstein, D. H. (1970). *Preventing Chronic Dependency* (New York: Community Service Society).

National Institute for Social Work Research Unit (1973). 'The Containment of Schizophrenic Patients Within Their Families' (unpublished).

Neill, June E. (1974). *Study of Referrals*, National Institute for Social Work Research Unit, internal publication.

Neill, June E., Fruin, D. J., Goldberg, E. M. and Warburton, R. W. (1973). 'Reactions to integration', *Social Work Today*, vol. 4, no. 15.

Neill, June E., Warburton, R. W. and McGuinness, B. (1976). 'Post Seebohm social services: (1) The social worker's viewpoint', *Social Work Today*, vol. 8, no. 5.

O'Loughlin, G. and Birkhead, B. (1975). 'How intake works in Wallasey', *Health and Social Service Journal* (13 September).

Pincus, A. and Minahan, A. (1973). *Social Work Practice: Model and Method* (Peacock).

Power, Michael (1978). 'The Home Care of the Very Old' (unpublished report, University of Bristol).

Rees, S. (1974). 'No more than contact: an outcome of social work', *British Journal of Social Work*, vol. 4, no. 3.

Reid, W. J. (1967). 'Characteristics of casework intervention', *Welfare in Review*, vol. 5, no. 8.

Reid, W. J. and Shyne, A. W. (1969). *Brief and Extended Casework* (New York: Columbia University Press).

Reid, W. J. and Epstein, L. (1972). *Task-Centred Casework* (New York: Columbia University Press).

Reid, W. J. (1974). 'Developments in the use of organized data', *Social Work*, vol. 19, no. 5.

Reid, W. J. and Epstein, L. (eds) (1977). *Task-Centred Practice* (New York: Columbia University Press).

Rutter, M. L. (1978). 'Research into prevention of psychosocial disorders in childhood', in J. Barnes and N. Connelly (eds), *Social Care Research* (Bedford Square Press).

Sainsbury, E. and Nixon, S. (1978). *Organisational Influences on Perceptions of Social Work* (unpublished).

Seebohm Report (1968). *Report of the Committee on Local Authority and Allied Personal Social Services*, Cmnd 3703 (HMSO).

Shaw, Margaret (1974). *Social Work in Prison* (HMSO, Home Office Research Studies no. 22).

Sinclair, I. A. C. (1971). *Hostels for Probationers* (HMSO, Home Office Research Studies no. 6).

Sinclair, I. A. C., Shaw, M. J. and Troop, J. (1974). 'The relationship between introversion and response to casework in a prison setting', *British Journal of Social and Clinical Psychology*, vol. 13, no. 1.

Smith, S. M., Hanson, R. and Noble, S. (1974). 'Social aspects of the battered baby syndrome' *British Journal of Psychiatry*, vol. 125 (December).

Specht, H., and Vickery, A. (1977). *Integrating Social Work Methods* (Allen & Unwin).

Steiner, C. (1974). 'Principles in radical psychiatry', in Radical Therapist/Rough Times Collective (eds), *The Radical Therapist* (Pelican).

Stevenson, O. (1978). 'Seebohm – seven years on', *New Society* (2 February).

Stevenson, O. and Parsloe, P. (Directors, DHSS Social Work Research Project) (1978). *Social Service Teams: The Practitioner's View* (HMSO).

Titcomb, B. (1974). 'Setting up an intake team', *Community Care* (28 August).

Tizard, J. and Grad, J. C. (1961). *The Mentally Handicapped and their Families* (Oxford University Press).

Town, S. W. (1964). 'Action research and social policy', *Sociological Review*, vol. 12, no. 4.

Townsend, P. (1957). *The Family Life of Old People: An Inquiry in East London* (Routledge & Kegan Paul; Penguin, 1970).

Warburton, R. W. and Willmott, R. (1976). 'Referrals of Single Parent Families to an Area Office', National Institute for Social Work (unpublished).

Webber, R. J. (1975). *Liverpool Social Area Study, 1971 Data: Final Report* (Centre for Environmental Studies, PRAG Technical Paper, TP14).

Wedge, P. and Prosser, H. (1973). *Born to Fail?* (Arrow Books).

Wetton, Kate (1976). 'The Cheltenham intake team: an evaluation', in *Clearing House for Local Authority Social Services Research*, no. 2 (University of Birmingham).

Wolfenden Report (1977). *The Future of Voluntary Organisations* (Croom Helm).

Wootton, Barbara (1959). *Social Science and Social Pathology* (Allen & Unwin).

Young, Michael and Willmott, Peter (1962). *Family and Kinship in East London* (Penguin).

Appendix I

CASE REVIEW SYSTEM

Case Review Form Coding Instructions

When to fill in a Case Review Form

1 On any new case for which an Action Note has been completed and which has been added to your caseload.
2 Whenever a case on your caseload is due for a scheduled review.
3 When for any reason you wish to review a case before the scheduled date.
4 When any member of the Intake Team passes on a case to colleagues in the Long-Term Teams.
5 When you close or transfer a case to another social worker in your authority.
6 In the Intake Team for all cases which are closed.

Dates

Whenever a date is asked for and you cannot be sure of the actual day please give month and year.

How to fill in a Case Review Form

Case Surnames: Please fill in from the left-hand side the surname first, one letter in each box. Insert a comma after the surname and then put the initials, one in each box.

Last Review on: Please enter the approximate date to the best of your knowledge. All dates are entered in a similar way: for example 27 March 1975 becomes 27 03 75.

Last Reviewed by: Please enter the initials of the last social worker to review this case in the first three boxes, and the letter identifying the team in the fourth box. If there are only two initials in the name, please leave the first box blank.

This Review due: Please enter the approximate date in the standard manner.

Since last Review/Before next Review

N.B. The date you fix for the next Case Review will clearly affect your plans. On the left-hand side of the form you will find two columns for:

Practical services/tangible changes
Outside agencies in contact with social worker
Types of workers
Social worker activities

If the review is a first review please consider the first column as if it were headed 'Since Referral' or 'Since Allocation'.

If you are reviewing a case for the second time or thereafter we would like you to put in the first column what actually happened since you last reviewed it, i.e. what services the client was receiving, what agencies you were in contact with, what type of worker was looking after the case, what social work activities you engaged in. Under the second column 'Before next Review' tick what services or changes you are planning for, what outside agencies you plan to contact and what social work activities you intend to engage in. But for type of workers please indicate who would *ideally* be needed to look after the case.

If the review is your last review on closure then you would not need to fill in the column 'Before next Review'.

Practical services/tangible changes
Please tick only those services you have arranged or changes that have occurred since the last review or which you are planning.

01 *None* – Ticking this negative category is as important as ticking the positive categories.
02–06 Self-explanatory
07 *Material improvements* – e.g. furniture or other improvements in house decoration, better amenities, or money intended for specific material improvements.
08 *Financial* – any help related to income maintenance or connected with raising grants, etc.
09 *Volunteer referral* – enlistment of any kind of voluntary helper in the care of the client or his family.
10 *Assistance with Applications* – help given with filling in forms or in making requests to formal organisations.
11 *Changes in Living Group* – e.g. a move from a community home to a foster home, or to lodgings or from a marital household to parents, etc.
12 *Help with employment* – any help given in relation to finding work, either directly or indirectly, easing problems at work, etc.
13 *Temporary accommodation* i.e. homelessness – self-explanatory.
14 *Permanent accommodation* i.e. rehousing – self-explanatory.
15 *Admission/referral for assessment/treatment* – e.g. referrals to a child guidance clinic, arrangements to see a specialist or to see a G.P., etc.
16–19 Self-explanatory
20 *Change of legal responsibility to client* – refers to change in care or supervision order, guardian ad litem, etc.

Outside agencies in contact with social worker
01 *None* – as with practical services and tangible changes, the appropriate

ticking of this negative category is as important as the ticking of the positive categories.

02–18   Self-explanatory

19   *Other* (specify) – write in, if necessary, the name(s) of agencies not covered in the above list.

Types of Workers

This category refers to social worker(s) and other staff based in the social services department and volunteers in touch with them.

Tick in the first column the type of worker who dealt with the case since last review. In the second column please assess as objectively as possible what type of worker is needed in the future, taking into consideration any changes that may have occurred in the case. If you think that two or more kinds of worker are ideally required, for example a qualified social worker and a volunteer, you can tick two boxes.

01   *None* – e.g. a case may have had services and then been put on agency review or you may plan for agency reviews.

02   *Qualified Social Worker* – a social worker who has either a professional social work qualification or, by virtue of long experience, is deemed to be qualified.

03   *Unqualified Social Worker* – someone who is graded as a social worker but who has not had a social work training or substantial social work experience.

04   *Social Work Assistant* – graded as Social Work Assistant.

05   *Volunteer* – an unpaid voluntary helper.

06   *Others with specialised knowledge* – someone who is not a social worker but has specialised knowledge and skills needed in this particular case, i.e. the OT.

07   *Social Worker plus specialised knowledge* – qualified social worker who in addition to his basic skills can bring specialised knowledge to bear on a case, for instance in child care, intermediate treatment or mental disorder, etc.

Social Worker Activities

These categories attempt to describe the content of social work. Again you are asked to tick what happened in the preceding period in the first column and what you intend to do in the future in the second column.

01   *None* – no one may have been engaged in or intend to be engaged in any of the following activities.

02   *Exploratory/(re)assessment activity* – largely concerned with exploration of current and past situations in order to gain an understanding of the present issues and to re-assess possibilities and constraints of future work.

03   *Information/advice* – self-explanatory

04   *Mobilising resources* – activities mainly concerned with arranging practical help, such as aids, meals-on-wheels, holidays, clubs, grants, work possibilities, voluntary help, etc.

05   *Advocacy* – activities in which social workers plead their clients' cases with formal organisations, such as Housing Departments DHSS, Electricity Boards and with other professionals of various kinds.

06 *Education in social skills* – examples would be helping families with budgeting, home management, practical child care or teaching the disabled how to use aids or other environmental supports to daily living.

07 *Check up/review visiting* – short 'popping in' visits to ensure that everything is OK.

08 *Facilitating problem solving/decision making* – various ways of counselling or casework, e.g. helping clients to ventilate their feelings, to discuss, sort out and try to solve problems, make choices, become aware of their behaviour and its effect on others, and so on.

09 *Sustaining/nurturing* – mainly friendly encouragement and 'caring' rather than activities directed towards problem solving or change.

10 *Group activities* – engaging in group work with clients either as a group leader or as an active member of the group.

Most Important Activity – always code the most important activity, even if you have or intend to engage in one activity only.

Estimate no. of contacts – again, consider past and future and make approximate estimates.

Problems

In the first column please tick the major problems you have tackled since the last review.

In the second column please tick the major problems present at this review. Also the second column should be considered when closing a case since problems may still be present.

01 *Physical disability/illness* – in this category are included all kinds of disability, such as blindness, deafness, physical handicap, chronic sickness, frailty and disability in old age, etc.

02 *Elderly* – those pensioners who by virtue mainly of age are at risk.

03 *Mental illness* – refers to overt and usually diagnosed mental illness.

04 *Mental handicap* – signifies subnormality, ranging from slight to severe.

05 *Emotional disturbance in adults* – includes disturbances of emotion and behaviour not amounting to overt mental disorder, e.g. anxiety, grief, drinking problems, gambling, psychopathy, mental confusion in old people, etc.

06 *Social isolation and/or loneliness* – refers on the one hand to the objective state of people being isolated in the community or from their families; loneliness refers to the subjective feeling of loneliness which can occur in situations in which people are not necessarily seriously isolated.

07 *Child behaviour problems* – include such items as school refusal, bed wetting, etc.

08 *Delinquency* – agency reported criminal behaviour in any age group.

09 *Family relations problems* – include any kind of family difficulties, parent/child, marital, sibling rivalry, etc.

10 *Family break-up* – includes death, separation, desertion and long-term absences, such as parent in prison.

11 *Child neglect* – self-explanatory

12 *Problems in home management* – refers to young families who find it difficult to cope because of various problems and inadequacies, as well as the old who may neglect themselves or their home.
13 *Financial difficulties* – self-explanatory
14 *Housing problems* – this may include overcrowding, homelessness, but also difficulties, such as lack of facilities, e.g. an outside lavatory for an old lady or steps that cannot be negotiated.
15 *Employment difficulties* – self-explanatory
16 *Problems arising from residential or foster care* – includes support to parents, or where an elderly person has difficulty settling in residential accommodation.
17 *Transport difficulties* – self-explanatory
18 *Other* – specify – if none of the above categories applies then please name the problem with which you are at present coping.

Most Outstanding Problem tackled since last Review – indicate the most outstanding problem which was the focus of your social work intervention.
Most Outstanding Problem being tackled now – indicate the most outstanding problem which is the focus of your social work intervention even if you have only ticked one problem.

Child in care of LA – self-explanatory

Present situation/reason for closure – self-explanatory

Case Status
1 *A current case* – is one which is receiving social work service
2 *A dormant case* – is one which is not at present receiving social work service but is likely to do so within the next year.
3 *A closed case* – is one which is unlikely to receive social work service in Social Services Department in your authority in the forseeable future.
4 *A transferred case* – is one which is to be transferred to another Social Services Department area office in your authority.

OPEN CASES: FUTURE
What changes are you aiming for? Here we would like you to give a very short description of the actual changes you wish to bring about, e.g. in a child care case you may aim to change the child's foster home within the next period or in the case of an old person your aim may be to relieve isolation and loneliness and so on.

Major Change Area
1 *No change intended* – this category often applies to dormant or agency review cases where no change is anticipated. In some cases where a stable equilibrium has been achieved (e.g. a stable, happy foster home placement), the aims may be to preserve the status quo.
2 *Major environmental changes* – denotes a complete change of the physical environment, e.g. rehousing, move to a foster home, admission to a residential home, etc.

3   *Changes in social/personal environment* – denotes changes in the immediate environment brought about by a variety of services (e.g. home help, aids, grants, holidays, clubs), which are intended to enable clients to lead fuller and more satisfying lives.

4   *Changes in social role* – here the aim of social work is to help people in their transition and adjustment to role changes, for example adjustment to widowhood, to disablement, to giving up one's home, to starting work again and so on.

5   *Changes in behaviour/attitudes/relationships* – the aim of intervention may be to help clients towards a better marital or parent/child relationship, to help a mentally ill person to become more active socially or a child to become less anti-social, etc.

Time before a case likely to be closed – self-explanatory

CLOSED CASES: Reason for Closure

1   *Aim achieved* – e.g. client or family able to cope, Part III successfully arranged, foster parents approved, supervision period successfully completed, etc.

2   *Change in circumstances* – events occurring outside control of social worker, e.g. deregistration due to successful operation, statutory obligation ended when a youngster reaches his 18th birthday.

3   *Client died* – self-explanatory

4   *Client withdrew* – e.g. client requests service to be discontinued, client refuses help or resources offered, prospective foster parents withdraw, etc.

5   *Client left area* – client moves out of area without being referred to another agency.

6   *Contact not achieved* – social worker unsuccessfully attempts to make contact with client by home visits, letters and phone calls.

7   *Social Worker/Dept. withdraws* – case closed because of low priority, lack of co-operation, lack of suitable resources, etc.

8   *Referral to other facilities* – e.g. case referred to probation, housing etc., but NOT a transfer to another Social Services Department area office in your authority.

9   *Other* – specify

Date of last social work contact: Please try to be as accurate as you can be, but do not spend a long time chasing through your records. If you have not recorded the date make the best guess possible.

Today's date: self-explanatory

Date of next Case Review: Please decide in the light of the present situation when the case should come up for review. We suggest that the next review date should not be scheduled for less than a month (because this would indicate that the case was under constant review) nor should the date be more than one year away because this would hardly indicate any active social work.

Appendix II

HOW THE SYSTEM WORKS

An important part of the project was to design a system to handle the large number of referral forms and reviews that were filled in, to remind workers which cases were due for review, and to provide speedy feedback.

It was crucial that the system did not make onerous demands on the social workers or team clerks. Since the case review project was developmental and was additional to the routines of the office, a full-time clerical assistant was initially employed to ensure the system ran smoothly and to spot difficulties as they arose. When the Social Services Department took over the day-to-day running of the CRS they were able to make this post half-time. If in other authorities case review forms are integrated more fully into existing procedures it is possible that little or no extra clerical support would be needed once initial teething troubles have been resolved.

Yet if case review is to run smoothly it is essential that it is not grafted on to a poor administrative system in which, for example, it is difficult to identify whether or not clients have been, or are, in contact with the area office, or where existing numbering systems are inadequate, and so on. The CRS will not solve these difficulties, but merely highlight them.

The system designed for Seatown is best described by following a case from referral through to closure or allocation.

(1)   An inquiry by letter or telephone or made by a person calling at the office is identified as a referral. In this area office, apart from automatic notifications for delinquency from the police, a referral was defined as 'any incoming case requiring some social work input and which is neither currently on an allocated nor the agency review caseload'. The definition of a 'referral' is likely to vary between area offices – even in the same authority!

(2)   Existing records are then checked to see if the client is already known to the department. The client's name and address, details of how the referral was made, plus information on the dates of, and reasons for, past contacts, are entered on to the referral form. If an area clerk has received the referral she then passes the form on to a social worker who completes information on the problem presented by the referrer, the referrer's request and details on the client's household. Otherwise the duty officer taking the referral enters all the information. Sometimes in Seatown it was not possible to get all the information, if the referral was made in a letter or over the telephone. In these cases, additional information was collected when further contact with the client or referrer was made.

(3)   The referral form used during the project was adapted from the Social Services Department's form, and like the case review form, is produced as a

no-carbon-required document. On completion the top sheet is torn off and handed to the project's clerical assistant. The bottom copy is retained in the case file.

(4) If the case can be closed shortly after referral then a review form, detailing problems tackled, work done, and reasons for closure, is completed. If the case is allocated for further work, either within the intake team or to one of the long-term teams a review form, giving details of work done since referral and plans for the immediate future, is completed.

(5) As with the referral form, the top sheet of the no-carbon-required review form is handed to the clerical assistant while the bottom copy is inserted into the case file.

(6) On receipt of the referral and review forms the clerical assistant checks them to make sure that the information has been entered correctly, that those parts of the form that cross-reference are consistent and that all categories have been filled in. Each week, when on average 50 or so referrals and 50 reviews of intake cases and between 30 and 40 reviews of on-going long-term cases are completed, all the forms are sent off for keypunching on computer punch cards. (The form in Seatown was laid out with keypunching in mind. For instance, the information is set out in an unambiguous way and numbers are provided along most of the boxes to help the keypunch operators keep track of where they are when punching the data. If other systems of aggregating the data are planned then the form should be laid out to facilitate this.)

(7) After keypunching the punch cards are fed through a series of computer checks resulting in a print-out of cases with inconsistency errors or omissions.

(8) If errors are detected on the cards, then the corresponding forms are returned to the clerical assistant in the area office. She then takes them back to the social workers for correction. The corrected forms are subsequently sent off again for re-keypunching with the next weekly batch of referral and review forms.

During our handling of the computer side of the CRS certain types of errors occurred more frequently than others. If a certain worker or groups of workers continually made the same mistakes an effort was made to point this out to them. The most frequent errors occurred when:

– Workers indicated that some practical help had been provided or some outside agency contacted whilst at the same time ticks were recorded in the 'none' box for these categories. Possibly after completing the form, workers would remember some service they had arranged or somebody they had contacted and tick the appropriate boxes without altering what they had first recorded.

– The problem indicated as the most outstanding was not one of the problems ticked as tackled since the last review. This possibly happened either because the CRS instructions were not clear – or had not been read – or because the form's layout made it a little difficult to see which code was the right one for the most outstanding problem.

– Plans for the future were completed when a case had been closed or a reason for closure was recorded when a case was still to be on-going. Again, perhaps the instructions were not explicit enough or the design of the form led to these errors.

– The review number of the current review did not tally with the number on the previous review. This type of error was usually made when a worker completed a review before the scheduled date and did not consult his records thoroughly enough to see which was his last review on the case.

– The dates on the form, such as dates of last social work contact or the next review, did not make sense. For instance, it was quite common for the next review date to pre-date the day on which the current review was filled in.

If other area offices think of trying case review it would be worthwhile to note the above errors, and, perhaps by more precise instructions and modifications in layout, to try to avoid them.

(9)　Each week new referrals and reviews for on-going cases were added to a computer file. The data were arranged in such a way on the computer file (Figure 1) that for any one case information was retained on the three most recent referrals, the three most recent reviews plus the first-ever review.

Figure 1

Case No. & Name;　Present address
Most recent referral (m)　information;　Referral　(m − 1);　Referral (m − 2)
Most recent review (n)　information:　e.g.　services, problems, etc.
Review (n − 1)
Review (n − 2)
First-ever review 01

This format can of course be changed and more reviews stored in the computer file to suit social workers' and managements' requirements. However, there is a danger of collecting so much data that most of it is neither used nor useful.

(10)　Each month cases due for review are printed out by the computer. The listing of cases provides enough information to enable the clerical assistant to fill out the 'administrative' part of the case review form giving case number, case name(s), who reviewed last time and on what date, the scheduled date for the current review and its number. These partially filled-out reviews are then handed to the social workers for completion.

Occasionally, workers would either fail to complete reviews within three months of the review date. Cases for whom reviews are overdue by more than three months are also listed by the computer and special efforts are made to ensure that these reviews eventually get done.

Of course workers do not have to wait until the scheduled review date in order to review a case. The case review form is a tool for practice and can be used when events dictate that it should. For instance, cases may be reviewed if a crisis calls for a reassessment, if the case is closed due to changes of circumstances occurring before the review date, if a worker transfers a case to a colleague within the area team, and so on.

The above model is capable of refinement and simplification. Authorities without computers may feel disadvantaged but there are other ways of filing and aggregating data. The chosen method of documentation and filing will depend on the uses to which area offices wish to put their case review data.

Yet local authorities willing to allocate some of their computer time to case review will be in a strong position. With a computer, edit checks are quickly and accurately carried out; a computer can handle large amounts of information, and store information on client careers; but most important of all a computer is capable of providing aggregated information quickly and efficiently.

INDEX